ANNOTATED LEADING CASES OF

INTERNATIONAL CRIMINAL TRIBUNALS

VOLUME XXXVI:

THE INTERNATIONAL CRIMINAL TRIBUNAL
FOR RWANDA 2009

ANNOTATED LEADING CASES OF

INTERNATIONAL CRIMINAL TRIBUNALS

VOLUME XXXVI:

THE INTERNATIONAL CRIMINAL TRIBUNAL
FOR RWANDA 2009

André KLIP and Göran SLUITER (eds.)

Cambridge – Antwerp – Portland

Intersentia Publishing Ltd.
Trinity House | Cambridge Business Park | Cowley Road
Cambridge | CB4 0WZ | United Kingdom
Tel.: +44 1223 393 753 | Email: mail@intersentia.co.uk

Distribution for the UK:
Hart Publishing Ltd.
16C Worcester Place
Oxford OX1 2JW
UK
Tel.: +44 1865 517 530
Email: mail@hartpub.co.uk

Distribution for the USA and Canada:
International Specialized Book Services
920 NE 58th Ave. Suite 300
Portland, OR 97213
USA
Tel.: +1 800 944 6190 (toll free)
Email: info@isbs.com

Distribution for Austria:
Neuer Wissenschaftlicher Verlag
Argentinierstraße 42/6
1040 Wien
Austria
Tel.: +43 1 535 61 03 24
Email: office@nwv.at

Distribution for other countries:
Intersentia Publishing nv
Groenstraat 31
2640 Mortsel
Belgium
Tel.: +32 3 680 15 50
Email: mail@intersentia.be

Please cite as: Decision on "Joseph Nzirorera's Appeal from refusal to investigate [a] prosecution witness for false testimony" and on Motion for Oral Arguments, *Prosecutor v. Karemera, Ngirumpatse and Nzirorera*, Case No. ICTR-98-44-AR.91, A. Ch., 22 January 2009, Klip/ Sluiter, ALC-XXXVI-9.

Annotated Leading Cases of International Criminal Tribunals
André Klip and Göran Sluiter (eds.)
Cover illustration: Annelies Der Kinderen

© 2013 Intersentia
Cambridge – Antwerp – Portland
www.intersentia.com | www.intersentia.co.uk

ISBN 978-1-78068-034-7
D/2013/7849/5
NUR 828

British Library Cataloguing in Publication Data. A catalogue record for this book is available from the British Library.

No part of this book may be reproduced in any form, by print, photoprint, microfilm or any other means, without written permission from the publisher.

TABLE OF CONTENTS

Table of Contents 5

Preface 7

Part 1 / Procedural Matters

1. Standards for investigation of false testimony

Decision on "Joseph Nzirorera's Appeal from refusal to investigate [a] prosecution witness for false testimony" and on Motion for Oral Arguments, *Prosecutor v. Karemera, Ngirumpatse and Nzirorera*, Case No. ICTR-98-44-AR.91, A. Ch., 22 January 2009 9

Commentary *Marjolein Cupido* 16

2. Fair trial

Decision on Continuation of Trial (Articles 19 and 20 of the Statute and Rule 82(B) of the Rules of Procedure and Evidence), *Prosecutor v. Karemera, Ngirumpatse and Nzirorera*, Case No. ICTR-98-44-T, T. Ch. III, 3 March 2009 25

Decision on Trial Date, *Prosecutor v. Ngirabatware*, Case No. ICTR-99-54-T, T. Ch. II, 12 June 2009 37

Decision on Appeal Concerning the Severance of Matthieu Ngirumpatse, *Karemera, Ngirumpatse and Nzirorera v. Prosecutor*, Case No. ICTR-98-44-AR73.16, A. Ch., 19 June 2009 49

Decision on Édouard Karamera's Motion relating to his right to be tried without undue delay (Article 21 (4) (d) of the Statute), *Prosecutor v. Karemera, Ngirumpatse and Nzirorera*, Case No. ICTR-98-44-T, T. Ch. III, 23 June 2009 57

Commentary *Caroline Fournet* 62

3. Review/Evidence

Decision on the Prosecutor's Appeal Concerning the scope of Evidence to be Adduced in the Retrial, *Prosecutor v. Muvunyi*, Case No. ICTR-2000-55A-AR73, A. Ch., 24 March 2009 69

Joint Dissenting Opinion of Judges Shahabuddeen and Meron 75

Decision on Motion requesting Preliminary Conference with Former Legal Team for the Preparation of a Request for the Assignment of Counsel for the Purpose of a Review, *Musema-Uwimana v. Prosecutor*, Case No. ICTR-96-13-R, A. Ch., 18 June 2009 77

Decision on Jean-Bosco Barayagwiza's Motion for Review and/ or Reconsideration of the Appeal Judgement of 28 November 2007, *Barayagwiza v. Prosecutor*, Case No. ICTR-99-52A-R, A. Ch., 22 June 2009 81

Decision on Motion for Legal Assistance, *Kamuhanda v. Prosecutor*, Case No. ICTR-99-54A-R, A. Ch., 21 July 2009 91

Commentary *Cristina Fernandez-Pacheco Estrada* 97

4. Provisional release

Decision on Matthieu Ngirumpatse's Appeal against Decision on Remand on Provisional Release, *Karemera, Ngirumpatse and Nzirorera v. Prosecutor*, Case No. ICTR-98-44-AR65, A. Ch., 8 December 2009 105

Dissenting Opinion Judge Liu Daqun 112

Commentary *Mariam Pathan* 114

Part 2 / Judgements and Sentencing

5. Judgements

Judgement, *Karera v. Prosecutor*, Case No. ICTR-01-74-A, A. Ch., 2 February 2009 121

Commentary *Sandhiya Singh* 205

Judgement, *Proseuctor v. Rukundo*, Case No. ICTR-2001-70-T, T. Ch. II, 27 February 2009 213

Commentary *Michele Panzavolta* 341

Judgement, *Prosecutor v. Kalimanzira*, Case No. ICTR-05-88-T, T. Ch. III, 22 June 2009 359

Commentary *Pedro Caeiro and Miguel Ângelo Lemos* 496

Judgement, *Prosecutor v. Nshogoza*, Case No. ICTR-07-91-T, T. Ch. III, 7 July 2009 509

Commentary *Joachim Renzikowski* 574

Judgement and Sentence, *Prosecutor v. Renzaho*, Case No. ICTR-97-31-T, T. Ch. I, 14 July 2009 .. 583

Commentary *Hilde Farthofer* 772

Judgement, *Zigiranyirazo v. Prosecutor*, Case No. ICTR-01-73-A, A. Ch., 16 November 2009 777

Commentary *Ward Ferdinandusse* 803

Sentencing Judgement, *Prosecutor v. Bagaragaza*, Case No. ICTR-05-86-S, T. Ch. III, 17 November 2009 811

Commentary *David Taylor* 823

Index 831

Contributors and Editors 833

PREFACE

This is the thirty-sixth volume in the series 'Annotated Leading Cases of International Criminal Tribunals' and contains the most important decisions of the International Criminal Tribunal for Rwanda (ICTR) of the whole year of 2009. It is the twelfth volume in the series containing decisions of the ICTR. A further volume on ICTR case law will be selected soon and will cover decisions up to the fall of 2010.

In its approach and structure, the present volume is similar to previous volumes. Thus, the book contains the full text of all the decisions and judgements, including separate, concurring and dissenting opinions, as well as annexes to the decisions. As with previous volumes, the editors have ensured that the decisions are fully identical to the *written* original text, as issued by the ICTR Press and Information Office, which bears the signatures of the judges. We are aware that almost all decisions are available on the internet. However, only the written decisions bearing the signatures of the judges can be considered as authoritative versions. In the course of our editorial work on this and previous volumes, we have occasionally discovered inconsistencies between the written original version of the decision and the internet version, if the latter is available at all. Much of our editorial efforts consist in making the texts in this series identical to the written original version.

We could only include the full text of the decisions in this volume by reducing their original format. Still, we wanted the reader to be able to identify the page number of the original text, which is throughout the text put in brackets. We are again very happy that a number of distinguished scholars in the field of international criminal law were prepared to write interesting and stimulating commentaries regarding the decisions.

A few words regarding the selection of decisions may give the user insight into our working method. In principle, we select all final judgements. In addition, we publish decisions taken at any stage of the procedure that are important for other reasons: because they deal with a specific legal question, because they are representative of a specific type of decision, or because they enter new legal waters. Of course, we cannot publish all decisions. As a result, we may not publish decisions in which issues have been decided in a way similar or identical to a decision that has already been selected.

The decisions are presented in different parts and under different headings.

Part 1, 'Procedural matters', deals with a decision on false testimony, some decisions on the length of the proceedings, some on the scope of evidence during the retrial, as well as a decision concerning provisional release.

Part 2, 'Judgement and Sentencing', contains seven judgements and covers by far the largest part of this volume. As mentioned above, judgements are by definition included in this series, because of their importance, both from a factual and legal perspective.

We owe acknowledgements to many persons without whom we could not have completed this thirty-second volume. These include Registrar Adama Dieng of the ICTR and his staff, who offered generous assistance in obtaining all the hard copies of decisions. Our publisher Intersentia, in particular Hans Kluwer, Tom Scheirs and Isabelle van Dongen, facilitated our work. We also acknowledge the work of our student assistants, Mariam Pathan and Anzinga Low (Maastricht), and Jeroen Gunning (Amsterdam), who assisted with the corrections of the text and without whom we would not be able to publish this series. The Netherlands School of Human Rights Research stimulated our work. Anzinga Low, the student-assistant at Maastricht University, offered tremendous help by correcting our English. Last but not least, we wish to thank the distinguished authors for their commentaries on the decisions.

We owe many thanks to Mariam Pathan, who was our student-assistant in Maastricht. Mariam has assisted us since volume XXI on the decisions of the Special Court for Sierra Leone. Over the years she has been a most reliable linchpin between contributors, editors and the publisher. We wish her all the best in her future endeavours.

On 26 March 2010, our dear colleague Peter Bal passed away in a hospital on the island of Bali, Indonesia. Peter contributed to volume XVI on the East Timorese case law on one of his favorite topics: the fitness to stand trial. It was an excellent contribution in which he was able to draw many comparisons with US law. We remember Peter as a high-spirited and dedicated colleague. His competent and energetic teaching style was very well appreciated by his students. Among his colleagues, Peter was known to be a qualified, passionate and charming scholar. In memory of him, his friends wrote a book that was dedicated to him.[1] We will sadly miss him.

We hope that this volume will contribute to the further dissemination of the important work of the ICTR and that it will provide access to its decisions to practitioners, academics and students.

André Klip and Göran Sluiter

Maastricht/ Amsterdam, August 2012

---

[1] Frans Koenraadt and Ria Wolleswinkel (eds.), Homo ludens en humaan strafrecht, funderen – vergelijken – onderwijzen, Gedenkbundel Peter Bal, Pompe Reeks 67, Boom Lemma uitgevers Den Haag 2011 (362 p.).

International Criminal Tribunal for Rwanda
Tribunal pénal international pour le Rwanda

IN THE APPEALS CHAMBER

Before: Judge Liu Daqun, Presiding
Judge Carmel Agius
Judge Mohamed Shahabuddeen
Judge Fausto Pocar
Judge Theodor Meron

Registrar: Mr. Adama Dieng

Date: 22 January 2009

THE PROSECUTOR

v.

Édouard KAREMERA
Mathieu NGIRUMPATSE
Joseph NZIRORERA

Case No. ICTR-98-44-AR.91

DECISION ON "JOSEPH NZIRORERA'S APPEAL FROM REFUSAL TO INVESTIGATE [A] PROSECUTION WITNESS FOR FALSE TESTIMONY" AND ON MOTION FOR ORAL ARGUMENTS

Counsel for the Appellant:

Mr. Peter Robinson and Mr. Patrick Nimy Mayidika Ngimbi

Counsel for Co-Accused:

Ms. Dior Diagne Mbaye and Mr. Félix Sow for Édouard Karemera
Ms. Chantal Hounkpatin and Mr. Frédéric Weyl for Mathieu Ngirumpatse

Counsel for the Prosecution:

Mr. Hassan Bubacar Jallow
Mr. Don Webster
Ms. Alayne Frankson-Wallace
Mr. Iain Morley

Mr. Saidou N'Dow
Ms. Gerda Visser
Ms. Sunkarie Ballah-Conteh
Mr. Takeh Sendze

[page 2]1. The Appeals Chamber of the International Criminal Tribunal for the Prosecution of Persons Responsible for Genocide and Other Serious Violations of International Humanitarian Law Committed in the Territory of Rwanda and Rwandan Citizens Responsible for Genocide and Other Such Violations Committed in the Territory of Neighbouring States between 1 January 1994 and 31 December 1994 ("Appeals Chamber" and "Tribunal", respectively) is seized of:

(1) "Joseph Nzirorera's Appeal from Refusal to Investigate [a] Prosecution Witness for False Testimony" filed on 24 November 2008 ("Appeal" and "Appellant", respectively); and

(2) "Motion for Oral Argument: Joseph Nzirorera's Appeal from Refusal to Investigate [a] Prosecution Witness for False Testimony" filed on 23 December 2008 ("Motion for Oral Arguments").

2. On 1 December 2008, the Prosecution filed its Response, opposing the Appeal,[1] and the Appellant filed his Reply on 3 December 2008.[2] The Prosecution filed its Response opposing the Motion for Oral Arguments on 29 December 2008.[3]

A. Background

3. The trial in the Appellant's case commenced on 19 September 2005 before Trial Chamber III ("Trial Chamber").[4] On 14 October 2005, the Appellant made an oral motion for an order directing an *amicus curiae* to investigate whether there were sufficient grounds for initiating proceedings for false testimony against Prosecution Witness Ahmed Mbonyunkiza ("Mbonyunkiza"),[5] which was denied.[6] On 29 May 2006, the Appellant filed a motion requesting, once again, an order directing that an *amicus curiae* be appointed to investigate Mbonyunkiza for false testimony,[7] which was also denied.[8] On 10 September 2008, the Appellant filed a motion in which he *inter alia* requested reconsideration of the Decision of 14 October 2005 and the Decision of 29 December 2006.[9] In its "Decision on Joseph Nzirorera's Omnibus Motion on the Testimony [page 3] of Ahmed Mbonyunkiza, Notice of 15th Violation of Rule 72(E), and Motion to Strike the Prosecution's Response" of 19 November 2008 ("Impugned Decision"), the Trial Chamber *inter alia* denied this request and also denied Counsel's fees in relation to the Motion of 10 September 2008.[10] The Appellant now appeals against the Impugned Decision, submitting that the Trial Chamber erred: (1) by imposing "too high a burden of establishing intent"; (2) by finding that conflicting testimony does not suffice to demonstrate that a contradicted witness has given false testimony; and (3) by imposing sanctions on Counsel.[11] He also requests that a hearing be held on 2 February 2009 to present oral arguments.[12]

B. Submissions

4. The Appellant contends that the Appeal is admissible and draws similarities with a decision issued by the Appeals Chamber of the International Criminal Tribunal for the Former Yugoslavia ("ICTY") in the

---

[1] Prosecution's Response to Joseph Nzirorera's Appeal from Refusal to Investigate Prosecution Witness for False Testimony, 1 December 2008 ("Response").
[2] Reply Brief: Joseph Nzirorera's Appeal from Refusal to Investigate Prosecution Witness for False Testimony, 3 December 2008 ("Reply").
[3] Prosecutor's Response to "Joseph Nzirorera's Motion for Oral Argument: Joseph Nzirorera's Appeal from Refusal to Investigate Prosecution Witness for False Testimony, 29 December 2008 ("Response to the Motion for Oral Arguments").
[4] Decision on Defence Motion for Investigation of Prosecution Witness Ahmed Mbonyunkiza for False Testimony, 29 December 2006 ("Decision of 29 December 2006"), para. 1.
[5] T. 14 October 2005 pp. 19, 20.
[6] T. 14 October 2005 p. 21 ("Decision of 14 October 2005").
[7] *See* Motion for Investigation of Witness Ahmed Mbonyunkiza for False Testimony, 29 May 2006.
[8] Decision of 29 December 2006, p. 5.
[9] Joseph Nzirorera's Omnibus Motion on the Testimony of Ahmed Mbonyunkiza, 10 September 2008 ("Motion of 10 September 2008").
[10] Impugned Decision, paras. 10-14, p. 5.
[11] Appeal, para. 26.
[12] Motion for Oral Arguments, para. 3.

Decision on refusal to investigate false testimony

Šešelj case,[13] in this regard.[14] He states that in the Šešelj Decision, it was held that an appeal against the refusal to initiate an investigation for contempt proceedings, pursuant to Rule 77 of the ICTY Rules of Procedure and Evidence ("ICTY Rules"), was admissible.[15] In this regard, he argues that the provisions of Rule 77 of the ICTY Rules are identical to those of Rule 91 of the Tribunal's Rules of Procedure and Evidence ("Rules"), and that, therefore, the Appeal filed under Rule 91 is admissible.[16]

5. The Appellant submits that the Trial Chamber applied an incorrect legal standard by requiring a high standard of proof of intent to mislead the Trial Chamber and to cause harm.[17] In this regard, he refers to the Šešelj Decision and asserts that the ICTY Appeals Chamber in the Šešelj case held that the "sufficient grounds" standard envisaged in Rule 77(D) of the ICTY Rules requires the Trial Chamber only to establish whether the evidence before it gives rise to a *prima facie* case of contempt of the Tribunal.[18] He claims that the Trial Chamber committed a similar error to the Trial Chamber in the Šešelj case by requiring evidence beyond that which is necessary to establish a **[page 4]** *prima facie* case.[19] The Appellant argues that had the Trial Chamber applied the correct standard in his case, it would have concluded that a *prima facie* case for false testimony had been made out.[20]

6. The Appellant further contends that the Trial Chamber erred when it excluded contradictory evidence as a source of proof of false testimony.[21] He argues that it is not logical to conclude that the testimonies of five witnesses are insufficient to constitute strong grounds for believing that Mbonyunkiza's testimony was false, since it is contradictory evidence which has been the basis for many of the Trial Chamber's decisions on the credibility of witnesses.[22] The Appellant also asserts that this approach goes against public interest because it allows for prosecution only of those who confess to have given false testimony.[23] He argues that it encourages those who lied to remain steadfast in their denials, while deterring those who are ready to tell the truth.[24]

7. The Appellant claims that the Trial Chamber erred in finding that his motion for reconsideration was frivolous and consequently erred in sanctioning his Counsel. He argues that should the Appeals Chamber find merit in the Appeal, it is only fair that in reversing the decision of the Trial Chamber it reverses the imposition of the sanction against his Counsel.[25]

8. The Appellant argues that the Appeals Chamber should hear oral arguments before deciding the Appeal because the issue of false testimony is of general importance to the jurisprudence of the *ad hoc* Tribunals and the decision on the Appeal will set valuable precedent.[26] The Appellant asserts that given that the legal issues on appeal are substantial and novel, it is the first opportunity for the Appeals Chamber to interpret Rule 91 of the Rules.[27] He further asserts that the hearing of oral arguments will not cause any inconvenience to the Appeal Chamber, as it will sit in Arusha in February 2009 to deliver judgement in another case.[28] The Appellant also claims that there will be no additional travel expenses, as his Counsel, as well as the Prosecution, will already be in Arusha,[29] and that the Tribunal and the East African Community will benefit from observing what would be the first ever interlocutory appeal hearing in Arusha.[30] The

---

[13] *Prosecutor v. Vojislav Šešelj*, Case No. IT-03-67-AR77.2, Decision on the Prosecution's Appeal Against the Trial Chamber's Decision of 10 June 2008, 25 July 2008 ("Šešelj Decision" and "Šešelj case", collectively).
[14] Appeal, paras. 21-25.
[15] Appeal, para. 22.
[16] Appeal, paras. 23, 24.
[17] Appeal, paras. 28-32.
[18] Appeal, para. 28.
[19] Appeal, paras. 28, 29.
[20] Appeal, para. 29.
[21] Appeal, para. 35.
[22] Appeal, paras. 33, 34
[23] Appeal, para. 34.
[24] Appeal, para. 35
[25] Appeal, para. 37.
[26] Motion for Oral Arguments, paras. 3, 5.
[27] Motion for Oral Arguments, para. 6.
[28] Motion for Oral Arguments, para. 7.
[29] Motion for Oral Arguments, para. 9.
[30] Motion for Oral Arguments, para. 10.

Appellant submits that the "Presiding Judge of the Appeals Chamber in the instant case is a trial judge of the ICTY", who has never participated as a member of the Appeals Chamber, and hearing oral arguments will allow him **[page 5]** to observe the Tribunal first hand and to take into account the differences in cultures and operations between the Tribunal and the ICTY, "which partially accounts for the high incidence of perjury at the [Tribunal]."[31]

9. In response, the Prosecution contends that the Appellant is in error as to the scope and application of the *Šešelj* Decision.[32] It argues that the facts and the applicable law which gave rise to the *Šešelj* Decision are clearly distinguishable from those in the present case.[33] According to the Prosecution, the Trial Chamber did not require production of conclusive proof of evidence,[34] and the Trial Chamber's conclusion that it did not have strong reasons for believing that Mbonyunkiza had knowingly and wilfully given false testimony bears upon the fact that the Appellant had failed to make a *prima facie* case of false testimony.[35]

10. The Prosecution submits that, while there may be similarities between Rule 77(D) of the ICTY Rules and Rule 91(B) of the Rules, a strict comparison between these rules cannot be made because: they apply to different issues; to different stages of the proceedings; and they encompass a different legal threshold.[36] It argues that Rule 91(B) of the Rules requires the existence of "strong grounds" for believing that a witness has knowingly and wilfully given false testimony, which must be seen as an even higher requirement than the "sufficient grounds" threshold encompassed in Rule 77(D) of the ICTY Rules.[37]

11. The Prosecution contends that the Appellant has failed to identify any discernible error of the Trial Chamber, and merely repeats arguments already considered and diligently ruled upon by the Trial Chamber.[38] It asserts that the Appellant's contention is that once there are inconsistencies in a witness's testimony, or inconsistencies between witnesses, these witnesses are guilty of giving false testimony.[39] According to the Prosecution, this is an incorrect statement of the principles relevant to the offence of false testimony.[40]

12. The Prosecution submits that good cause for hearing oral arguments has not been demonstrated.[41] It contends that the arguments advanced by the Appellant in support of his request for the hearing of oral arguments, can be made for most issues that are addressed in interlocutory **[page 6]** appeals, and that the Appeals Chamber should not be persuaded by them.[42] The Prosecution argues that the issue is whether the Trial Chamber correctly exercised its discretion and not whether the Impugned Decision was correct, in the sense that the Appeals Chamber would agree with it.[43] It asserts that this issue is not so complex as to warrant oral arguments, and that the written submissions will suffice.[44] Finally, the Prosecution argues that the Appeals Chamber's presence in Arusha cannot be advanced as an argument to depart from the general practice of considering interlocutory appeals on written submissions.[45]

C. Standard of Review

13. The Impugned Decision concerns the alleged false testimony of a witness and relates to the general conduct of trial proceedings in the Appellant's case. Decisions relating to the general conduct of trial proceedings fall within the discretion of a Trial Chamber, to which the Appeals Chamber must accord

---

[31] Motion for Oral Arguments, para. 8.
[32] Response, paras. 9-13.
[33] Response, para. 10.
[34] Response, para. 11.
[35] Response, para. 11.
[36] Response, para. 12
[37] Response, para. 12.
[38] Response, paras. 14, 15.
[39] Response, para. 16.
[40] Response, para. 16.
[41] Response to the Motion for Oral Arguments, para. 4.
[42] Response to the Motion for Oral Arguments, para. 5.
[43] Response to the Motion for Oral Arguments, para. 5.
[44] Response to the Motion for Oral Arguments, para. 5.
[45] Response to the Motion for Oral Arguments, para. 6.

deference.[46] As such, the Impugned Decision is a discretionary decision. Where an appeal is filed against a discretionary decision of a Trial Chamber, the issue on appeal is not whether the decision was correct, in the sense that the Appeals Chamber agrees with it, but rather whether the Trial Chamber has correctly exercised its discretion in rendering the decision.[47] Consequently, the Trial Chamber's exercise of discretion will only be reversed where it is demonstrated that the Trial Chamber committed a discernible error in rendering the Impugned Decision, based on an incorrect interpretation of the governing law, a patently incorrect conclusion of fact, or where the Impugned Decision was so unfair or unreasonable as to constitute an abuse of the Trial Chamber's discretion.[48]

D. Discussion

14. The Appeals Chamber notes, in relation to the Motion for Oral Arguments, that interlocutory appeals are generally considered on arguments made in briefs without a hearing. A **[page 7]** party requesting leave to make oral arguments must demonstrate that the issues on appeal cannot be effectively addressed through written arguments.[49] In the present case, the Appellant has failed to show that the Appeal cannot be effectively addressed through written arguments and that oral arguments are, therefore, warranted. Consequently, the Appeals Chamber will proceed to consider the Appeal solely on the basis of the written briefs filed by the Parties.

15. On the issue of the admissibility of the Appeal, the Appeals Chamber notes that Rule 91(I) of the Rules provides that any decision rendered by a Trial Chamber under Rule 91 of the Rules shall be subject to appeal, and that such appeal must be filed within fifteen days from the filing of the impugned decision. In the present case, the Impugned Decision ruled on a request for reconsideration of the Decision of 14 October 2005 and the Decision of 29 December 2006, both of which were issued pursuant to Rule 91(A) and (B) of the Rules. Since both of these decisions could have been the subject of an appeal, a decision issued in their reconsideration, as the Impugned Decision, may also be appealed under Rule 91(I) of the Rules. Consequently, the Appeal, which was filed within the prescribed time-limit, is admissible.

16. The Appellant contends that the Trial Chamber ought to have concluded that a *prima facie* case for false testimony had been made out, but that it instead applied an incorrect legal standard by requiring a higher standard of proof.[50] The Appeals Chamber notes that in the Decision of 29 December 2006, the Trial Chamber stated:

> In determining whether "strong grounds" exist that the witness gave false testimony, a Chamber must therefore find, on a case-by-case basis in the particular circumstances of each case, evidence of an intention to commit this offence. Contradictory evidence between witness' testimony is insufficient evidence to demonstrate that a witness intended to mislead the Chamber and to cause harm. Instead, contradictory evidence is used when determining the probative value of the evidence presented by the parties during trial.[51]

17. In the Motion of 10 September 2008, the Appellant requested the Trial Chamber to reconsider the aforementioned reasoning, in view of the findings in the *Šešelj* Decision, which he submitted was new law.[52]

---

[46] *The Prosecutor v. Édouard Karemera et al.*, Case No. ICTR-98-44-AR73.11, Decision on the Prosecution's Interlocutory Appeal Concerning Disclosure Obligations, 23 January 2008 ("*Karemera et al.* Decision of 23 January 2008"), para. 7, referring to *The Prosecutor v. Édouard Karemera et al.*, Case No. ICTR-98-44-AR73.10, Decision on Nzirorera's Interlocutory Appeal Concerning his Right to be Present at Trial, 5 October 2007, para. 7 ("*Karemera et al.* Decision of 5 October 2007"); *The Prosecutor v. Élie Ndayambaje et al.*, Case No. ICTR-98-42-AR73, Decision on Joseph Kanyabashi's Appeals against the Decision of Trial Chamber II of 21 March 2007 concerning the Dismissal of Motions to Vary his Witness List, 21 August 2007 ("*Ndayambaje et al.* Decision of 21 August 2007").

[47] *The Prosecutor v. Édouard Karemera et al.*, Case No. ICTR-98-44-AR73.13, Decision on "Joseph Nzirorera's Appeal from Decision on Tenth Rule 68 Motion", 14 May 2008, para. 6, referring to *The Prosecutor v. Vojislav Šešelj*, Case No. IT-03-67-AR73.5, Decision on Vojislav Šešelj's Interlocutory Appeal Against the Trial Chamber's Decision on Form of Disclosure, 17 April 2007, para. 14.

[48] *Karemera et al.* Decision of 23 January 2008, para. 7 referring to *Karemera et al.* Decision of 5 October 2007, para. 7; *Ndayambaje et al.* Decision of 21 August 2007, para. 10.

[49] *Prosecutor v. Momčilo Krajišnik*, Case No. IT-00-39-AR31.1, Decision on Interlocutory Appeal of Decision on Second Defence Motion for Adjournment, 25 April 2005, para. 4.

[50] Appeal, paras. 28-32.

[51] Decision of 29 December 2006, para. 7 (internal citations omitted).

[52] Motion of 10 September 2008, paras. 25-35.

The *Šešelj* Decision held "that the 'sufficient grounds' standard under Rule 77(D) of the [ICTY] Rules requires the Trial Chamber only to establish whether the evidence before it gives rise to a *prima facie* case of contempt of the Tribunal and not to make a final finding [page 8] on whether contempt has been committed".[53] The Trial Chamber denied the Appellant's request and reasoned that

> [t]he new law brought to the Chamber's attention does not concern Rule 91(B). The *Šešelj* Decision, which clarifies the standard for instigating contempt proceedings in the context of the disclosure of confidential information, confines itself to Rule 77(D), and does not mention or shed any new light on Rule 91(B).[54]

18. The Appeals Chamber agrees. Rule 91(B) of the Rules which concerns false testimony states that where there are "strong grounds" for believing that a witness has knowingly and wilfully given false testimony, a Chamber may direct the Prosecutor to investigate the matter with a view to submitting an indictment against the witness, or it may direct the Registrar to appoint an *amicus curiae* to investigate the matter as to whether there are sufficient grounds for initiating proceedings for false testimony against the witness. This provision is materially different from Rule 77(C) of the ICTY Rules and the analogous provision in Rule 77(C) of the Rules, which concern contempt of the Tribunal and provide for an investigation when a Chamber has "reason to believe" that a person may be in contempt. On completion of the process envisaged in Rule 91(B) of the Rules, the Chamber will then consider whether there are "sufficient grounds" to proceed against a witness for false testimony.[55] This provision is similar to that of Rule 77(D) of the ICTY Rules, and Rule 77(D) of the Rules, in that it also envisages a "sufficient grounds" standard.

19. The Appeals Chamber notes that in the *Šešelj* Decision, which forms the basis of the Appellant's arguments, the ICTY Appeals Chamber held that the "sufficient grounds" standard under Rule 77(D) of the ICTY Rules requires the Trial Chamber only to establish whether the evidence before it gives rise to a *prima facie* case of contempt of the Tribunal and not to make a final finding on whether contempt has been committed.[56] Putting this decision in context, it is worth noting that following an earlier appointment of an *amicus curiae*, the Trial Chamber in the *Šešelj* case took into account a report prepared by her to ascertain whether sufficient grounds existed to prosecute the persons concerned.[57] Since a *prima facie* case must be established to confirm an indictment,[58] it is therefore logical for a Chamber to employ this standard when ordering the prosecution of an individual. However, in the Appellant's case, the Trial Chamber was not required to make a determination on whether to prosecute Mbonyunkiza, pursuant to Rule 91(C) of the Rules, but to consider whether to direct the Registrar to refer the matter to an *amicus curiae* for [page 9] investigation, pursuant to Rule 91(B) of the Rules. Hence, the "sufficient grounds" standard and the requisite finding of a *prima facie* case are not applicable in the circumstances of the present case.

20. The Appeals Chamber recalls that in the *Kamuhanda* case it applied the "strong grounds" standard as prescribed in Rule 91(B) of the Rules and directed the Prosecutor to undertake a general investigation *inter alia* with a view to preparing and submitting an indictment for false testimony.[59] In this regard, the Appeals Chamber took into account significant discrepancies in testimonies given by witnesses, as well as evidence of allegations against two Tribunal employees in relation to the influence of a witness, and it had reason to believe that there may have been attempts to pervert the course of justice with the solicitation of false testimony.[60] The nature of these factors is materially different from that of the present case where the Appellant merely alleges discrepancies among testimonies of Prosecution witnesses in an ongoing trial.

21. The Appeals Chamber reiterates that a decision to initiate this type of proceedings falls within a Trial Chamber's discretion, as evidenced by the wording of Rule 91(B) of the Rules ("If a Chamber has strong

---

[53] *Šešelj* Decision, para. 16.
[54] Impugned Decision, para. 13 (internal citation omitted).
[55] See Rule 91(C) of the Rules.
[56] *Šešelj* Decision, para. 16.
[57] *Prosecutor v. Vojislav Šešelj*, Case No. IT-03-67-T, Decision on Motions by the Prosecution and the Accused to Investigate Contempt against Ms. Dahl (from the Office of the Prosecutor) and Mr. Vučić (Associate of the Accused), 10 June 2008, paras. 7, 12.
[58] Article 18 of the Statute of the Tribunal and Article 19 of the Statute of the ICTY provide that an indictment shall be confirmed where a *prima facie* case has been established.
[59] *Jean de Dieu Kamuhanda v. The Prosecutor*, Case No. ICTR-99-54A-A, Oral Decision (Rule 115 and Contempt of False Testimony), 19 May 2005 ("*Kamuhanda* Decision"), pp. 2, 3.
[60] *Kamuhanda* Decision, p. 2.

ground ... it may...").[61] In exercising this discretion, a Trial Chamber will take into account certain factors, such as (i) indicia as to the *mens rea* of the witness, including his intent to mislead and cause harm; (ii) the relationship between the statement in question and a material matter in the case; (iii) the possible bearing of the statement in question on the Chamber's final decision.[62] In other words, a Chamber will have to consider carefully if these proceedings are the most effective and efficient way to ensure compliance with obligations flowing from the Statute or the Rules in the specific circumstances of the case.

22. On the basis of the foregoing, the Appeals Chamber finds that the Appellant has failed to show that the Trial Chamber committed a discernible error in rendering the Impugned Decision. On the issue of the sanctions imposed on Counsel, the Appeals Chamber will not consider the request because there is no right of appeal in this regard.[63] **[page 10]**

E. Disposition

23. For the aforementioned reasons, the Appeals Chamber:

DENIES the Motion for Oral Arguments; and

DENIES the Appeal.

Done in English and French, the English text being authoritative.

Dated this the 22nd day of January 2009,

at The Hague, Judge Liu Daqun,
The Netherlands. Presiding

[Seal of the Tribunal]

---

[61] Emphasis Added. *Cf.* Rule 77(A) and (D) of the Rules.
[62] *See e.g. The Prosecutor v. Jean-Paul Akayesu*, Case No. ICTR-96-4-T, Decision on Defence Motions to Direct the Prosecutor to Investigate the Matter of False Testimony by Witness "R", 9 March 1998 (signed on 24 March 1998), referred to in the Impugned Decision, para. 11.
[63] *Joseph Nzirorera v. The Prosecutor,* Case No. ICTR-98-44-AR73(F), Decision on Counsel's Appeal from Rule 73(F) Decisions, 9 June 2004, p. 3.

Commentary

I. Introduction

The orchestrators of atrocities tried before the modern international criminal courts and tribunals have generally left few written records. The vast majority of evidence presented before these court and tribunals therefore consists of eyewitness testimony.[1] Legal scholars have increasingly expressed their concerns about the accuracy of these testimonies.[2] In particular, Nancy Combs' transcript study thoroughly addresses the difficulties of witnesses to accurately describe past events. Defects in eyewitness testimony are caused by 'innocent' factors, such as educational deficiencies, cultural divergences and translation errors, but also result from perjury.[3] According to Combs, in particular at the International Criminal Tribunal for Rwanda (ICTR), 'a great deal of lying is taking place'.[4]

The ICTR exercises an inherent power to punish perjury.[5] It has defined perjury as a false statement made in Court under oath or solemn declaration.[6] The crime encompasses four elements: the witness has made a solemn declaration; the false statement is contrary to the solemn declaration; the witness believed the statement was false at the time it was made; and there is a relevant relationship between the statement and a material matter in the case.[7]

To effectively respond to acts of perjury, Rule 91(B) of the Rules of Procedure and Evidence (RPE) grants the ICTR a discretionary power to order an investigation into alleged perjury if a Chamber has *strong grounds for believing* that a witness has knowingly and wilfully given false testimony. The ICTR has, in this respect, consistently held that the onus is on the party pleading a case of false testimony to *convince* the Chamber that there exist such strong grounds by means of *proving* the elements of perjury.[8] By so reasoning, the Tribunal imposes a strict standard that is difficult to meet in practice. Most requests for an investigation

---

[1] For example, R. Cryer, Witness evidence before international criminal tribunals, 3 The Law and Practice of International Criminal Courts and Tribunals 2003, p. 411; N.A. Combs, Fact-finding without facts: The uncertain evidentiary foundations of international criminal convictions, Cambridge University Press, Cambridge 2010, p. 12; A. Zahar, Witness memory and the manufacture of evidence at the international criminal tribunals in C. Stahn & L. van den Herik (eds.), Future perspectives on international criminal justice, TMC Asser Press, Den Haag 2010, p. 601.

[2] Combs, *supra* note 1, p. 14–62; Zahar, *supra* note 1, p. 600–610; A. Zahar, Klip/ Sluiter, ALC-XXV-620, p. 509–522.

[3] Cryer, *supra* note 1, p. 420–438; Combs, *supra* note 1, p. 63–105; and 122–129.

[4] Combs, *supra* note 1, p. 130.

[5] For critical reflections on the inherent powers doctrine see: A. Klip, Witnesses before the International Tribunal for the Former Yugoslavia, 67 Revue Internationale de Droit Pénal 1996, p. 277–278; A. Klip, Klip/ Sluiter ALC-I-214, p. 214; M. Bohlander, International criminal tribunals and their power to punish contempt and false testimony, 12 Criminal Law Forum 2001, p. 91–118; G. Sluiter, The ICTY and offences against the administration of justice, 2 Journal of International Criminal Justice 2004, p. 632–635.

[6] ICTR, Decision on the Defence motion to direct the Prosecutor to investigate the matter of false testimony by witness "R", *Prosecutor v. Akayesu*, Case no. ICTR-96-4-T, T. Ch. I, 9 March 1998 (hereinafter Akayesu decision.).

[7] For example, Akayesu decision; ICTR, Decision on defence motion to direct the Prosecutor to investigate the false testimony by witness "E", *Prosecutor v. Rutaganda*, Case no. ICTR-96-3-T, T. Ch. I, 10 March 1998 (hereinafter Rutaganda witness E decision); ICTR, Decision on the Defence motion to direct the Prosecutor to investigate the matter of false testimony by witness "C", *Prosecutor v. Rutaganda*, Case No. ICTR-96-3-T, T. Ch. I, 10 March 1998 (hereinafter Rutaganda witness C decision); ICTR, Decision on the request of the Defence for the Chamber to direct the Prosecutor to investigate a matter with a view to the preparation and submission of an indictment for false testimony, *Prosecutor v. Bagilishema*, Case No. ICTR-95-1A-T, T. Ch. I, 11 July 2000 (hereinafter Bagilishema decision), par. 4; ICTR, Decision on Defence request for an investigation into alleged false testimony of witness DO, *Prosecutor v. Bagosora et al.*, Case No. ICTR-98-41-T, T. Ch. I, 3 October 2003 (hereinafter Bagosora et al. decision), par. 8; ICTR, Decision on the Defence motion seeking the appointment of *amicus curiae* to investigate possible false testimony by witnesses GFA, GAP, GKB, *Prosecutor v. Bizimungu et al.*, Case No. ICTR-99-50-T, T. Ch. II, 23 July 2008 (hereinafter Bizimungu et al. decision), par. 5; ICTR, Decision on Ntahobali's motion for an investigation relative to false testimony and contempt of court, *Prosecutor v. Ntahobali*, Case No. ICTR-97-21-T, T. Ch. II, 7 November 2008 (hereinafter Ntahobali decision), par. 20; ICTR, Decision on Ntahobali's motion for an investigation into false testimony and Kanyabashi's motion for an investigation into contempt of court relative to Prosecution witnesses QY and SJ, *Prosecutor v. Nyiramasuhuko et al.*, Joint Case No. ICTR-98-42-T, T. Ch. II, 19 March 2009 (hereinafter Nyiramasuhuko et al. decision), par. 11.

[8] For example, Akayesu decision; Rutaganda witness E decision; Rutaganda witness C decision; Bagilishema decision, par. 5; Bizimungu et al. decision, par. 6; Bagosora et al. decision, par. 9. Also see ICTR, Decision on the Defence motion to direct the Prosecutor to investigate the matter of false testimony by witness "AEN" in terms of Rule 91(B), *Prosecutor v. Nahimana*, Case No. ICTR-96-11-1, T. Ch. I, 27 February 2001 (hereinafter Nahimana decision); ICTR, Decision on the third request for review, *Prosecutor v. Niyitegeka*, Case No. ICTR-96-14-R, T. Ch. III, 23 January 2008 (hereinafter Niyitegeka decision), par. 32.

into alleged perjury are rejected and, when investigations are ordered they hardly ever result in prosecutions. So far only one person has been convicted for giving false testimony before the ICTR.[9]

Alexander Zahar in his commentary to the Rwamakuba Trial Chamber judgment in this series critiques the ICTR's reluctance to prosecute perjury. He convincingly argues that the Tribunal's strict requirement of *proof* of the *actus reus* and *mens rea* of perjury imposes a misleading and inaccurate standard on the parties.

> [P]roof" is something to be pursued not by the party raising the suspicion, but upon an indictment by an amicus investigator/ prosecutor before a different bench of judges; it has nothing to do with the original Trial Chamber's determination or the burden of the party initiating the action.[10]

The clause 'strong grounds for believing' rather indicates that the requesting party satisfies the Chamber that 'there exists a sufficient suspicion of perjury to warrant a formal investigation'.[11] The ICTR's interpretation and application of the 'strong grounds for believing' criterion was recently addressed and re-evaluated by the Appeals Chamber in the Karemera et al. case.

The Karemera et al. case concerns the accused Matthieu Ngirumpatse and Édouard Karemera.[12] They were the President and Vice-President, respectively, of the *Mouvement républicain national pour la démocratie et le développement* (MRND), the ruling political party during the Rwandan genocide. On 2 February 2012, the Trial Chamber convicted Karemera and Ngirumpatse for their participation in an (extended) joint criminal enterprise to commit genocide and crimes against humanity. According to the Trial Chamber, the accused actively and passively instigated and encouraged the killings committed by the *Interahamwe* by means *inter alia* of speeches and the adoption of a Civil Defence Plan.

Thus, they contributed to the common purpose to destroy the Tutsi population of Rwanda and had *dolus eventualis* in respect of the various forms of sexual violence that were the foreseeable result of this purpose. Furthermore, the accused were held responsible on the basis of superior responsibility for the failure to prevent and punish their subordinates once they were informed of the crimes these subordinates had committed. Both accused were sentenced to life imprisonment.

The convictions of Karemera and Ngirumpatse are largely based on eyewitnesses testimony. The defence raised concerns about the credibility of several of these witnesses. Arguing that there were *strong grounds for believing* that a witness knowingly and wilfully gave false testimony, they requested the Tribunal to order an investigation of alleged perjury on the basis of Rule 91(B).[13]

This commentary evaluates the Karemera Appeals Chamber's interpretation and application of the 'strong grounds for believing' criterion in its decision on the defence request to start an investigation of false testimony in relation to witness Mbonyunkiza.[14] The commentary formulates two objections in this respect.

---

[9] ICTR, Judgement, *Prosecutor v. GAA*, Case No. ICTR-07-90-R77-I, T. Ch. III, 4 December 2007 (hereinafter GAA judgement). Legal scholars have even qualified the rules on perjury as 'symbolic' or 'legislation without teeth'; See Bohlander, *supra* note 5, p.118; Sluiter, *supra* note 5, p. 640.

[10] Zahar, *supra* note 1, p. 513–514.

[11] Zahar *supra* note 1, p. 512.

[12] Originally, the case encompassed a third accused, Joseph Nzirorera. The case against him, however, terminated prematurely due to his sudden death on 1 July 2010 following complications of a long illness. ICTR, Decision relating to Registrar's submission notifying the demise of accused Joseph Nzirorera, *Prosecutor v. Karemera et al.*, Case No. ICTR-98-44-T, T. Ch. III, 12 August 2010.

[13] ICTR, Decision on defence motion for investigation of prosecution witness Ahmed Mbonyunkiza for false testimony, *Prosecutor v. Karemera et al.*, Case No. ICTR-98-44-T, T. Ch. III, 29 December 2006 (hereinafter Karemera initial Trial Chamber decision); ICTR, Decision on defence motion for appointment of *amicus curiae*, *Prosecutor v. Karemera et al.*, Case No. ICTR-98-44-T, T. Ch. III, 26 September 2007 (hereinafter Karemera *amicus curiae* decision); ICTR, Decision on Prosecutor's confidential motion to investigate BTH for false testimony, *Prosecutor v. Karemera et al.*, Case No. ICTR-98-44-T, T. Ch. III, 14 May 2008 (hereinafter Karemera witness BTH decision); ICTR, Decision on Joseph Nzirirera's omnibus motion on the testimony of Ahmed Mbonyunkiza, Notice of 5th violation of Rule 72(E), and motion to strike the Prosecutor's response, *Prosecutor v. Karemera et al.*, Case No. ICTR-98-44-T, T. Ch. III, 19 November 2008 (hereinafter Karemera second Trial Chamber decision); ICTR, Decision on "Joseph Nzirorera's appeal from refusal to investigate [a] prosecution witness for false testimony" and a motion for oral arguments, *Prosecutor v. Karemera et al.*, Case No. ICTR-98-44-AR.91, A. Ch., 22 January 2009, in this volume, p. 9 (hereinafter Karemera Appeals Chamber decision); ICTR, Decision on Joseph Nzirorera's motion to appoint an *amicus curiae* to investigate GAP for false testimony and to appoint an *amicus curiae* to investigate Prosecution witness BDW for false testimony, *Prosecutor v. Karemera et al.*, Case No. ICTR-98-44-T, T. Ch. III, 6 April 2010 (hereinafter Karemera witness GAP and BDW decision).

[14] Karemera Appeals Chamber decision.

First, it is argued that the Karemera Appeals Chamber rejects the defence motion on the basis of unconvincing legal arguments. Secondly, regarding the application Rule 91(B), the commentary contends that the flexible character of the criterion formulated by the Karemera Appeals Chamber is insufficiently expressed in the ICTR's continuously restrictive application of this criterion. This is because of the Tribunal's neglect to properly adopt a casuistic methodology.

II. Interpreting Rule 91(B)

In its decision of 29 December 2006, the Karemera Trial Chamber rejected the defence motion for an investigation of false testimony in relation to the witness Mbonyunkiza on the basis of the established interpretation of the 'strong ground for believing' criterion that the onus is on the parties to provide proof of the elements of perjury.[15] The defence draws on the Šešelj Appeals Chamber decision to challenge this interpretation. In that decision, the ICTY with regard to Rule 77(D) considered that:

> in finding that it did not have sufficient elements "to determine" whether Vučič committed contempt of the Tribunal, based on the conclusions of the *amicus curiae* that the mental element of contempt had not been "establish[ed]" and that it would have to be "proven" that Vučič had effective knowledge that [redacted] was a protected witness, the Trial Chamber required a final finding of contempt. The Appeals Chamber recalls, however, that the "sufficient grounds" standard under Rule 77(D) of the Rules required the Trial Chamber only to establish whether the evidence before it gives rise to a *prima facie* case of contempt of the Tribunal and not to make a final finding on whether contempt has been committed. The Appeals Chamber accordingly finds that the Trial Chamber applied an incorrect legal standard (…).[16]

The defence draws similarities between Rule 91(B) of the ICTR RPE and Rule 77(D) of the ICTY and ICTR RPE, and accordingly argues that the Karemera Trial Chamber applied an overly strict legal standard by 'requiring evidence beyond that which is necessary to establish a *prima facie* case'.[17] The Karemara Appeals Chamber, however, rejects this alleged analogy. According to the Chamber, '[t]he Šešelj Decision confines itself to Rule 77(D) and does not mention or shed any new light on Rule 91(B)'.[18] The former Rule relates to contempt of Court, whereas the latter concerns the crime of perjury. Furthermore, the 'strong grounds for believing' criterion of Rule 91(B) formulates the standard for the initiation of an investigation into alleged false testimony. Rule 77(D), conversely, applies where such an investigation into alleged contempt of Court has already taken place and the Court subsequently needs to decide whether there are 'sufficient grounds to proceed' by means of ordering the prosecution of the crime of contempt.

The differences that the Appeals Chamber observes are indeed accurate. They do, however, not justify the Chamber's complete rejection of the analogy with the Šešelj decision, nor do they legitimize a continuation of the Tribunal's restrictive interpretation of the 'strong grounds for believing' criterion. Within the system of the *ad hoc* Tribunals, perjury and contempt of Court are regulated by an analogous procedure, whereby the order of a prosecution follows the order of an investigation. Although the criteria to order an investigation differ – Rule 91(B) formulates the 'strong grounds for believing' criterion, whereas Rule 77(C) formulates the less stringent 'reason to believe' criterion – Rule 91(C) and Rule 77(D) concerning the decision to prosecute both formulate a 'sufficient grounds to proceed' criterion. This criterion has been interpreted as requiring the finding of a *prima facie* case.

Because the order to prosecute has more drastic effects than the initiation of an investigation, the former is logically governed by stricter limitations than the latter. Even when recognizing that the 'strong grounds for believing' criterion of Rule 91(B) is stricter than the 'reason to believe' criterion of Rule 77(C), the Tribunal's authority to order an investigation for false testimony should on this view be governed by a test that is at least less stringent than the '*prima facie* case' standard of the 'sufficient grounds to proceed' criterion as laid down in Rule 91(C). Terms such as 'prove', 'determine', 'convince' and 'establish', which have so far been used by the ICTR to describe the 'strong grounds for believing' criterion, express an unjustly restrictive interpretation of that criterion.

---

[15] Karemera initial Trial Chamber decision, par. 6.
[16] ICTY, Decision on the Prosecution's appeal against the Trial Chamber's decision of June 2008, *Prosecutor v. Šešelj*, Case No. IT-03-67-AR77.2, A. Ch., 25 July 2008.
[17] Karemera Appeals Chamber decision, par. 5.
[18] Karemera Appeals Chamber decision, par. 18.

Furthermore, it should be observed that the different standards to evaluate the motions for an investigation into the crimes of false testimony and contempt of Court are the result of a choice that is typical for the *ad hoc* Tribunals. Article 70 of the Rome Statute of the International Criminal Court (ICC), for example, qualifies both crimes as offences against the administration of justice. Motions for an investigation into false testimony or contempt of Court are consequently subject to the same standard of review. Naturally, this assembling of offences against the administration of justice in the Rome Statute does not require the *ad hoc* Tribunals to similarly evaluate these crimes on the basis of a uniform legal standard. (note: no new paragraph) The different approach the ICC takes towards the investigation of offences against the administration of justice does, however, illustrate that the adoption of differentiated standards for the investigation of perjury and contempt of Court does not logically follow from any alleged material difference between these crimes. Reliance upon this finding in combination with the previous systemic point of critique, the adoption of a more lenient *prima facie* case standard would have been feasible.

Significantly, while rejecting the defence arguments for the adoption of the *prima facie* case standard, the Chamber does formulate a new interpretation of the 'strong grounds for believing' criterion. Instead of requiring proof of the *actus reus* and *mens rea* of perjury, the Chamber holds that

> [i]n exercising this discretion [to order an investigation into false testimony] a Trial Chamber will take into account certain *factors, such as* (i) indicia as to the *mens rea* of the witness, including his intent to mislead and cause harm; (ii) the relationship between the statement in question and a material matter in the case; (iii) the possible bearing of the statement in question on the Chamber's final decision.[19]

The terms 'factors' and 'such as' in this interpretation imply that, on the one hand, strong grounds for believing that a witness falsely testified may also be accepted without proof of all four elements of the crime of perjury while, on the other hand, other relevant circumstances could determine the Tribunal's decision to order an investigation. By so reasoning, the Appeals Chamber apparently adopts a flexible understanding of the 'strong ground for believing' criterion, which enables the ICTR to address the concerns raised by legal scholars and defence counsel in relation to the Tribunal's strict requirement of proof of the elements of perjury.

It is, however, unclear whether the Karemera Appeals Chamber decision will indeed have such a fundamental effect. Contrary to the practice of the *ad hoc* Tribunals to follow previous Appeals Chamber decisions,[20] the Karemera Appeals Chamber's interpretation of the 'strong grounds for believing' criterion has not been systematically adopted by the Trial Chambers in the few subsequent decisions concerning Rule 91(B).[21] Consequently, it cannot yet be conclusively determined that the Appeals Chamber's change of terminology marks the beginning of a new understanding of the 'strong grounds for believing' criterion.

Furthermore, the Tribunal's different interpretation of the 'strong grounds for believing' criterion, does not appear to result in a different application of the criterion in practice. The analysis in the following sector illustrates that, thus far, the ICTR has not applied Rule 91(B) to a more extensive range of circumstances. This continuous restrictive application may, at least partly, be explained by the ICTR's reluctance to properly express the flexible character of the newly formulated 'strong grounds for believing' criterion through the adoption of a casuistic methodology.

---

[19] Karemera Appeals Chamber decision, par. 21. The Karemera Appeals Chamber allegedly derives from the Akayesu decision. The Akayesu Trial Chamber, however, observes these factors as 'constituent elements'. The only previous decision in which terms similar to the Karemera Appeals Chamber decision were used, is the Karemera second Trial Chamber decision.

[20] The Aleksovski Appeals Chamber judgment in this respect held that 'a proper construction of the Statute requires that the *ratio decidendi* of its decisions is binding on Trial Chambers (…)'. The Appeals Chamber itself is only free to depart from previous decision in exceptional cases 'for cogent reasons in the interests of justice'; that is in cases where the previous decision has been decided on the basis of a wrong legal principle or cases where a previous decision has been wrongly decided, usually because the judge or judges were ill-informed about the applicable law. Furthermore, deviation from previous Appeals Chamber decision is only permissible 'after the most careful consideration has been given to it, both as to the law, including the authorities cited, and the facts'; ICTY, Judgement, *Prosecutor v. Aleksovski*, Case No. ICTY-9-14/1-A, A. Ch., 24 March 2000, par. 92–113. For a scholarly review of the doctrine of precedent before the *ad hoc* Tribunals, see C. Harris, Precedent in the practice of the ICTY in R. May et al. (eds.), Essays on ICTY procedure and evidence in honour of Gabrielle Kirk McDonald, Kluwer Law International, Den Haag 2001, p. 344–356.

[21] In the Karemera witness GAP and BDW decision, the Trial Chamber initially adopts a similar terminology, but later recalls that the 'moving party bears the burden of proving the predicate elements of false testimony' (par. 10). The reasoning of the Trial Chamber in the Nyiramasuhuko et al. decision is rather restrictive. No reference is made to the elements of perjury as either requirements that have to be proven or as factors the establishment of which may be relevant for the finding of 'strong grounds for believing' that a witness gave false testimony.

III. Applying Rule 91(B)

The defence motion to start an investigation of false testimony in relation to witness Mbonyunkiza is primarily based on the fact that parts of the witness's statements 'have been contradicted by the testimony of other Prosecution witnesses and will be contradicted by Defence witnesses in the future'.[22] According to the Karemara Trial Chamber, this circumstance is insufficient to find strong grounds for believing that Mbonyunkiza has knowingly and wilfully given false testimony.

> The Defence does not provide any details as to the content of the evidence of these potential Defence witnesses, and mostly does not adduce evidence of any harmful intent of Witness Mbonyunkiza to make a false testimony. As already recalled, mere contradictions or discrepancies between the testimonies of different witnesses do not, as such, constitute sufficient ground for believing that a witness has knowingly and willfully given false testimony. Also the Defence has not shown that the requirements set forth by the Rule for ordering an investigation for false testimony have been met.[23]

This finding was later affirmed by the Trial Chamber in a decision regarding a second Defence request[24] and by the Appeals Chamber.[25] The Chambers' argumentation and conclusion conform to the ICTR's consistent finding that the mere presentation of inconsistencies and contradictions within a witness testimony or between a witness testimony and other evidence does not meet the 'strong grounds for believing' standard.[26] Instead, inconsistencies are considered to merely raise doubts as to the credibility of the witness which will be evaluated upon the final determination of the probative value of the evidence presented at trial. The Karemera Trial Chamber did accordingly not rely on the inconsistent testimony of witness Mbonyunkiza as far as his crucial, but uncorroborated testimony concerned the accused's calls for the elimination of the Tutsi's.[27]

An analysis of the ICTR case law indicates a whole range of additional circumstances and situations that are considered insufficient to meet the threshold of the 'strong grounds for believing' criterion.[28] In fact, an order to investigate alleged false testimony has only been issued in two rather specific situations. First, when inconsistent or contradictory evidence is accompanied by a witness's confession that he gave false testimony.[29] The Tribunal in this respect takes a conditional approach. The witness's confession of false testimony should be directly related to the case of the accused. A confession in another case does not give rise to strong grounds for believing that a witness also falsely testified in the case against the accused.[30]

---

[22] Karemera initial Trial Chamber decision, par. 2.
[23] Karemera initial Trial Chamber decision, par. 9.
[24] Karemera second Trial Chamber, par. 12–14. In fact, the Trial Chamber even finds the Defense motion 'so lacking in legal and logical support both as to the relief requested and the arguments made in support thereof, that it must be deemed frivolous, and all fees related to it should be denied'.
[25] Karemera Appeals Chamber decision, par. 20. It should in this respect be noted that the Appeals Chamber's standard of review is marginal. '[t]he issue on appeal is not whether the decision was correct, in the sense that the Appeals Chamber agrees with it, but rather whether the Trial Chamber has correctly exercised its discretion in rendering the decision. Consequently, the Trial Chamber's exercise of discretion will only be reversed where it is demonstrated that the Trial Chamber committed a discernible error in rendering the Impugned Decision, based on an incorrect interpretation of governing law, a patently incorrect conclusion of fact, or where the Impugned Decision was so unfair or unreasonable as to constitute an abuse of the Trial Chamber's discretion' (par. 13). Thus it may only be concluded from the Appeals Chamber's rejection of the Defense motion that the Trial Chamber interpreted Rule 91(B) correctly and applied it reasonably.
[26] For example, Akayesu decision; Rutaganda witness C decision; Bagilishema decision, par. 6–7; Karemera witness GAP and BDW decision; Bizimungu et al. decision, par. 7. Also see ICTR, Decision on Arsène Shalom Ntahobali's motion to have perjury committed by Prosecution witness QY investigated, *Prosecutor v. Nyiramasuhuko and Ntahobali*, Case No. ICTR-97-21-T, T. Ch. II, 23 September 2005 (hereinafter Nyiramasuhuko and Ntahobali decision), par. 11–12.
[27] ICTR, Judgement, *Prosecutor v. Karemera et al.*, Case No. ICTR-98-44-T, T. Ch. III, 2 February 2012, par. 203.
[28] Insufficient circumstances are *inter alia* the fact that the witness, upon confrontation with discrepancies in his testimony, denied ever making the statement, refused to answer the questions, or gave implausible answers (Bagosora et al. decision, par. 11; Nyiramasuhuko and Ntahobali decision, par. 5 and 12); the fact that a witness testified in relation to evidence that was found to be forged (Karemera *amicus curiae* decision, par. 9; Karemera witness GAP and BDW decision, par.13); and the fact that the witness acknowledged the inaccuracy of his own statement immediately after it was made and without being confronted with irrefutable proof that the statement was wrong (Bagosora et al. decision, par. 13).
[29] Karemera witness BTH decision; Bizimungu et al. decision.
[30] Bizimungu et al. decision, par. 27.

Similarly, the confession of false testimony only has consequences in relation to the person confessing. Allegations by one witness that another witness is lying do not meet the 'strong grounds for believing' threshold.[31] Furthermore, the Tribunal requires that the alleged false statements relate to a material matter of the case, or have a bearing on the ultimate disposition of the case,[32] and that the statement was revoked before an independent party or, when revoked before an interested party, is corroborated by independent evidence.[33]

Secondly, the 'strong grounds for believing' standard is met when inconsistencies in the witness's testimony or confession of false testimony are accompanied by reliable allegations that the witness has been induced to falsely testify.[34] In these situations, the false testimony results from the threatening, intimidation or bribery of the witness and thus concurs with the crime of contempt of Court. According to the ICTR, such situations obviate an investigation, in particular when the staff of the Tribunal may have been involved.[35]

It is currently still unclear whether the Karemera Appeals Chamber's novel interpretation of the 'strong grounds for believing' criterion will lead to the recognition of additional situations and circumstances that meet the threshold of this criterion. Neither the Karemera Appeals Chamber decision itself, nor the subsequent decisions in relation to Rule 91(B), support such a development. In these decisions the ICTR still finds that mere inconsistencies do not give rise to sufficient grounds for believing that a witness falsely testified.[36] Furthermore, the Tribunal continuously takes a conditional approach towards confessions of false testimony,[37] and requires that the testimony relates to a material matter of the case.[38] This unremitting restrictive application of the 'strong grounds for believing' criterion may, at least partly, be explained by the ICTR's reluctance to properly express the flexible character of the newly formulated 'strong grounds for believing' criterion through the adoption of a casuistic methodology.

By using terms such as 'factors' and 'case-by-case evaluation; the Chamber expresses a casuistic understanding of the 'strong grounds for believing' criterion. 'Casuistry' entails a holistic assessment of the relevant circumstances of a case. In other words, the circumstances of the case are to be observed and evaluated as a whole and in relation to each other.[39] The Tribunal, however, fails to give effect to this casuistic methodology. Instead, an individualistic assessment of relevant factual circumstances persistently determines the Tribunal's application of Rule 91(B). That is, the Tribunal generally assesses per circumstance whether the 'strong grounds for believing' standard was met.[40] The parties should therefore bring forward factual circumstances that in themselves give rise to strong grounds for believing that a witness falsely testified.

Recent Rule 91(B) decisions invalidly preserve this restrictive assessment of the relevant factual circumstances.[41] The Karemera Trial Chamber, for example, rejected a defence motion for an investigation of false testimony, by evaluating per argument presented whether this individually meets the threshold of the 'strong grounds for believing' standard. Consequently, despite the Karemera Appeals Chamber's formulation of a novel flexible interpretation of the 'strong grounds for believing' criterion, the criterion continues to imply a strict standard that is difficult to meet in practice.

---

[31] Karemera *amicus curiae* decision, par. 10; Niyitegeka decision, par.32; Bizimungu et al. decision, par. 27. Also see ICTR, Decision on Ntahobali's motion for an investigation relative to false testimony and contempt of court, *Prosecutor v. Ntahobali*, Case No. ICTR-97-21-T, T. Ch. II, 7 November 2000 (hereinafter Ntahobali decision), par. 25.
[32] Karemera witness BTH decision, par. 6; Bizimungu et al. decision, par. 15. It follows from the Karemera witness GAP and BDW decision that a matter becomes material to the case when it concerns facts that are laid down in the indictment (par. 7).
[33] Karemera witness GAP and BDW decision, par. 11.
[34] Ntahobali decision; Nyiramasuhuko et al. decision; GAA judgement. Also see ICTR, Oral decision (Rule 115 and contempt of false testimony), *Prosecutor v. Kamuhanda*, Case No. ICTR-99-54A-A, A. Ch., 19 May 2005.
[35] Nyiramasuhuko et al. decision, par. 11.
[36] Karemera Appeals Chamber decision, par. 22; Karemera witness GAP and BDW decision, par. 10.
[37] Karemera witness GAP and BDW decision, par. 12.
[38] Karemera witness GAP and BDW decision, par. 7.
[39] M. Cupido, The policy underlying crimes against humanity: Practical reflections on a theoretical debate, 22 Criminal Law Forum 2011, p. 307; K. van Willigenburg, Casuïstiek en scherpe normen in het materiële strafrecht, 27 Delikt en Delinkwent 2011, p. 371–372. Van Willigenburg in this respect derives from J. Dancy, Ethics without Principles, Oxford University Press, Oxford 2004.
[40] For example, Bizimungu et al. decision, par. 18–21; Karemera witness GAP and BDW decision, par. 9–13.
[41] See particularly Karemera witness GAP and BDW decision, par. 10–13.

Thus, the ICTR's current attempt to secure the restrictive interpretation and application of Rule 91(B) should be rejected for two reasons: the presentation of unconvincing legal arguments and the adoption of an overly individualistic methodology. Instead, the Tribunal's understanding of the 'strong grounds for believing' criterion should be modelled and evaluated on the basis of its conception of the rationale underlying the criminalization of perjury.

IV. Rationale underlying Rule 91(B)

The ICTR primarily links the investigation, prosecution and punishment of perjury to the reliability of evidence, the truth-seeking objective of the Tribunal, the fairness of trial against the accused and the possibility for miscarriages of justice. In this regard, the Tribunal, for example consistently holds that lying under oath can only be qualified as perjury when a false testimony relates to a material matter of the case and has a bearing on the decision.[42] This relation between the ancillary punishment of perjury and the implications of a false testimony for the primary prosecution of international crimes does not, however, imply that the finding of a false testimony necessarily 'contaminates' the entire proceedings and renders them unjust.

The reliability of evidence and the accuracy of proceedings can be ensured even when it is established that a witness falsely testified. For that purpose, the Tribunal does not necessarily need to investigate and prosecute alleged perjury more actively. Like in many national criminal justice systems,[43] it may prefer to safeguard the reliability of the evidence and the accuracy of the proceedings through the evaluation of the credibility of witnesses and by means of excluding testimonies from the evidence insofar as doubts concerning their truthfulness have risen.[44] The proper evaluation of the credibility of eyewitness testimony thus becomes a fundamental condition for the just and accurate functioning of the international criminal justice system.

Legal scholars have, in this respect, extensively criticized the Tribunal for being indifferent to vagueness and inconsistencies. According to Combs:

> the Trial Chambers rarely even mention the vagueness of a particular witness's testimony or an inability to answer date, distance, and place questions, and in the uncommon instances in which they do acknowledge such testimonial deficiencies, they do not consider them to impair the reliability or the usefulness of the testimony.[45]

Furthermore,

> the Trial Chambers do pay some attention to inconsistencies and will conclude that a witness lacks credibility when the inconsistencies are especially numerous or severe, but they also overlook or explain away a great number of inconsistencies that would be severe enough to shred a witness's credibility in a domestic courtroom.[46]

Acknowledging Comb's critique, it should be emphasized that, generally, inconsistencies and vagueness do not necessarily make a witness statement erroneous.[47] Cognitive psychological research into the relation between accuracy and consistency in eyewitness memory illustrates that a witness's failure to remember facts brought forward in a previous statement, or his introduction of new facts that were not remembered beforehand, do not make a witness by definition unreliable.[48]

---

[42] Akayesu decision; Rutaganda witness E decision; Rutaganda witness C decision; Bagilishema decision, par. 4; Bagosora et al. decision, par. 8; Bizimungu et al. decision, par. 5; Ntahobali decision, par. 20; Nyiramasuhuko et al. decision, par. 11.

[43] Bohlander, *supra* note 5, p. 115. In the Netherlands the convictions for perjury have dropped significantly over the last three years from 71 in 2009 to 27 in 2011 (WODC statistics).

[44] For a different view see for example, A. Klip, Klip/ Sluiter ALC-I-214, p. 214; Sluiter, *supra* note 5, p. 640; Zahar, *supra* note 1, p. 519.

[45] Combs, *supra* note 1, p. 192.

[46] Combs, *supra* note 1, p. 195. Also see Zahar, *supra* note 1, p. 605; Zahar, *supra* note 1, p. 518–519.

[47] Although this research does not take account of the specificities of the system and context of international criminal law, it may nevertheless nuance the previously expressed critiques and concerns.

[48] See for example, N. Brewer et al., Beliefs and data on the relationship between consistency and accuracy of eyewitness testimony, 13 Applied Cognitive Psychology 1999, p. 297–313; R.P. Fisher & B.L. Cutler, The relation between consistency and accuracy of eyewitness testimony in G. Davies et al. (eds.), Psychology, law and criminal justice: International developments in research and practice, De Gruyter, Berlin 1995, p. 21–28; G. Odinot, Eyewitness confidence: The relation between the accuracy and confidence in episodic memory, Doctoral Thesis, University of Leiden, 2008 (https://openaccess.leidenuniv.nl/handle/1887/13360); T. Smeets et al., Accuracy, completeness, and consistency of emotional memories, 117 American Journal of Psychology 2004, p. 595–609.

Although this is obviously true for contradictory inconsistencies, it is not true for inconsistencies due to incomplete statements. Witnesses should not be judged as unreliable when previously given information is omitted in later statements or when in later statements additional information is provided.[49]

It thus follows that a generally permissive attitude towards incomplete witness statements does not negatively affect the reliability of the evidence and the accuracy of the proceedings. Conversely, in relation to contradictory witness statements, a stricter approach is required to assure the accuracy of criminal proceedings. For that purpose, the ICTR, should conduct a more thorough and sound evaluation of the credibility of eyewitness testimony, and exclude testimonies from the evidence when doubts concerning their truthfulness have risen.

V. Concluding remarks

The ICTR's interpretation and application of the 'strong grounds for believing' criterion illustrate the Tribunal's paradoxical relationship with eyewitnesses. On the one hand, the successful prosecution of international crimes committed during the Rwandan genocide is impossible without eyewitness testimonies. As was acknowledged by the ICTY

> [T]he success of trials held before the Tribunal depends greatly on the willingness of witnesses to come to the Tribunal to testify. Witnesses help to establish the facts of crimes with which the accused are charged, thus contributing to the process which establishes the responsibility of the accused and creates a historical record (…).[50]

On the other hand, eyewitnesses seriously complicate the fact-finding process. As a consequence of more and less innocent causes, eyewitness testimonies regularly entail serious defects that detract from their evidentiary value.

In view of this paradoxical relation, the ICTR, with respect to the investigation and prosecution of perjury, emphasizes the importance of eyewitness testimony for the Tribunal and the negative practical consequences of perjury prosecutions for the Tribunal's ability to adjudicate international crimes. The Tribunal seems reluctant to let the prosecution of international crimes be unnecessarily 'disturbed' by the ancillary prosecution of perjury. Perjury investigations and prosecution require scarce time, money and personnel, and risk the willingness of witnesses to testify before the ICTR.[51] They should therefore be observed as an *ultimum remedium*. The Karemera Appeals Chamber decision expresses this thought when considering that, in evaluating the 'strong grounds for believing' criterion:

> a Chamber will have to consider carefully whether the investigation and prosecution of false testimony are 'the most effective and efficient way to ensure compliance with obligations following from the Statute or the Rules in the specific circumstances of the case.[52]

Naturally, these practical considerations cannot justify the Tribunal's use of unconvincing legal arguments and its neglect to properly adopt a casuistic methodology in order to preserve a restrictive interpretation and application of Rule 91(B). They do, however, put the observed practice in perspective and explain the Tribunal's stringent approach towards the 'strong grounds for believing' criterion.[53] This approach was once more affirmed in the Karemera Appeals Chamber decision. Even though the Chamber formulated a flexible interpretation of the 'strong grounds for believing' criterion, it apparently remains inclined to a restrictive application of this criterion in legal practice.

While raising objections in relation to the Appeals Chamber's legal arguments and methodology, the ICTR's restrictive approach towards perjury prosecutions is in itself consistent with the rationale underlying the criminalization of perjury. The Tribunal's limited use of its power to investigate, prosecute and punish perjury

---

[49] Odinot, *supra* note 48, p. 51–52.
[50] Www.icty.org/sid/158.
[51] Combs, *supra* note 1, p. 282; Sluiter, *supra* note 5, p. 638; Zahar, *supra* note 1, p. 519. Also see W.A. Shabas, The International Criminal Court, a commentary on the Rome Statute, Oxford University Press, Oxford 2010, p. 853.
[52] Karemera Appeals Chamber decision, par. 21.
[53] For a more critical view, see Zahar, *supra* note 1, p. 519. According to Zahar, practical difficulties cannot be valid and sufficient reasons to adopt a restrictive approach towards the prosecution of perjury, because this would 'trivialize what is self-evidently serious'.

is not necessarily detrimental to the truth-seeking objective, or the fairness of a trial against the accused. A thorough and sound evaluation of the credibility of testimonies is, for that purpose, however, essential.

Marjolein Cupido

International Criminal Tribunal for Rwanda
Tribunal pénal international pour le Rwanda

OR: ENG

TRIAL CHAMBER III

Before Judges: Dennis C. M. Byron, Presiding
Gberdao Gustave Kam
Vagn Joensen

Registrar: Adama Dieng

Date: 3 March 2009[1]

THE PROSECUTION
v.
Édouard KAREMERA
Matthieu NGIRUMPATSE
Joseph NZIRORERA

Case No. ICTR-98-44-T

DECISION ON CONTINUATION OF TRIAL
Articles 19 and 20 of the Statute and Rule 82(B) of the Rules of Procedure and Evidence

Office of the Prosecution:
Don Webster
Iain Morley
Saidou N'Dow
Gerda Visser
Sunkarie Ballah-Conteh
Takeh Sendze

Defence Counsel for Édouard Karemera
Dior Diagne Mbaye and Félix Sow

Defence Counsel for Matthieu Ngirumpatse
Chantal Hounkpatin and Frédéric Weyl

Defence Counsel for Joseph Nzirorera
Peter Robinson and Patrick Nimy Mayidika Ngimbi

---

*   Editor's note: the editors have incorporated in this decision the corrigendum of 16 March 2009 (Corrigendum to Decision on Urgent Request for Precision or Alternatively Correction of the Decision of 3 March 2009 on Continuation of Trial, Prosecutor v. Karemera, Nziirorera, and Ngirumpatse, Case No. ICTR-98-44-T and Case No. ICTR-98-44E-T, T. Ch. III. 16 March 2009)

[page 2] INTRODUCTION

1. This trial started on 19 September 2005. After 169 trial days, on 4 December 2007, the Prosecution closed its case.[1] The Defence case started on 7 April 2008. In August 2008, during Édouard Karemera's presentation of his case, Matthieu Ngirumpatse became ill and the ICTR Chief Medical Officer, Dr. Épée Hernandez, estimated that Ngirumpatse would be unfit to attend trial for one month. The Chamber ordered a stay of proceedings accordingly.

2. On 28 October 2008, the Chamber held a status conference in the absence of Matthieu Ngirumpatse, who was still unfit to attend, but in the presence of his counsel. On that occasion, Dr. Épée Hernandez stated that Ngirumpatse would need treatment for at least six months before it was possible to assess whether and when he would again be fit to attend trial. However, Counsel for Ngirumpatse indicated that Ngirumpatse had agreed on an exceptional basis that four witnesses could be heard in his absence before the next session.

3. On 6 November 2008, in view of the submissions of Matthieu Ngirumpatse's counsel, the Chamber decided not to consider severance at that time but ordered a stay of proceedings until February 2009 for the trial to continue in his absence with his consent.[2]

4. On 9 February 2009, the Chamber held a status conference, again in the absence of Matthieu Ngirumpatse who was unfit to attend, but in the presence of his counsel. Dr. Épée Hernandez stated that Ngirumpatse would need further treatment for three months before an assessment could be made as to whether or when he would be fit to attend trial. The Chamber then invited the Parties to make submissions on the continuation of the trial.

5. On 10 February 2009, the Prosecution filed a motion to sever Matthieu Ngirumpatse from the trial pursuant to Rule 82(B) of the Rules of Procedure and Evidence ("Rules").[3] Following an order of the Chamber,[4] the three Accused filed written submissions.[5] The Parties made further submissions in a hearing on 16 February 2009. The Registry also made **[page 3]** submissions during the oral hearing, followed by written filings on the same issues.[6]

6. All Parties have objected to the trial proceedings being continued in the absence of Matthieu Ngirumpatse without his consent and all three Accused have objected to Ngirumpatse being severed from the trial. Counsel for Ngirumpatse, supported by Counsel for the Co-Accused, has in the alternative moved for the proceedings to be stayed for a further three months to allow for an update on Ngirumpatse's condition. If his condition has improved sufficiently by then to enable him to participate in his defence from his place of treatment, Ngirumpatse consents to the trial then continuing in his absence.[7]

7. The Chamber will, therefore, after assessing the information available regarding Ngirumpatse's health condition, address whether the trial can, after a further stay of proceedings, continue in Ngirumpatse's absence, whether the trial should be stayed indeterminately until he might be fit to attend again or whether Ngirumpatse should be severed from the trial.

---

[1] The Prosecution case was closed save for the cross-examination of Witness BDW who completed his examination during the following trial session.
[2] T. 6 November 2008, p. 3.
[3] Prosecutor's Motion to Sever Mathieu Ngirumpatse Pursuant to Rule 82(B), filed on 10 February 2009 ("Motion for Severance"). In its Motion for Severance, the Prosecution indicated that "[w]hile the prosecution may still wish to address this matter orally on 12 February 2009, as this Chamber had anticipated, the Prosecution file[d] nonetheless this [...] written submission in order to narrow the issues and to clarify its position well in advance.", para. 6.
[4] *Karemera et al.*, Case No. ICTR-98-44-T, Scheduling Order (TC), 11 February 2009.
[5] Joseph Nzirorera's Opposition to Prosecution Motion for Severance, filed 13 on February 2009 ("Nzirorera's Submissions"); Soumission de Édouard Karemera sur le maintien du process joint, filed on 13 February 2009 ("Karemera's submissions"); Opposition de M. Ngirumpatse à la disjonction d'instances demandées par le Procureur ("Ngirumpatse's Submissions"), filed on 13 February 2009.
[6] The Registrar's Submission on Mission Requests filed by the Ngirumpatse's Defence Team, filed on 16 February 2009
[7] Ngirumpatse's Submissions, para. 17-18; T. 16 February 2009, p. 29; Karemera's Submissions, pp. 4 and 7.

Decision on Continuation of Trial

DELIBERATIONS

The Information Available regarding Ngirumpatse's Condition

8. Matthieu Ngirumpatse has declined to waive his right to medical confidentiality and consequently opposes the disclosure of information on the nature of his illness to other persons, including the Chamber and the other Parties, save other doctors.[8]

9. Information regarding his medical condition has been provided to the Chamber and the Parties either in written form or during oral hearings from Dr. Épée Hernandez, the Registrar and Matthieu Ngirumpatse's counsel.[9]

10. On 18 August 2008, the Chamber was informed that Matthieu Ngirumpatse was ill, would not be fit to attend trial for one week and that he would be transferred to the Hospital in Moshi.[10] On 25 August 2008, Dr. Épée Hernandez reported that Ngirumpatse would not be **[page 4]** fit for a minimum of one more month.[11] The Chamber and the Parties were later informed on 5 September 2008, that Ngirumpatse had been brought back to Arusha and that on 8 October 2008, he had been transferred to Nairobi to undergo further tests.[12] Ngirumpatse has been in Nairobi since then, receiving care in a fully equipped medical facility capable of treating his pathology.[13]

11. At the status conference on 28 October 2008, Dr. Épée Hernandez reported as follows: Matthieu Ngirumpatse was suffering from a longstanding condition which according to himself had begun in 1976, but was only recently discovered by the UN Medical Clinic; his prognosis was "reserved"; there was a possibility that his present condition could improve as "medicine can do miracles" but he would not be fit to attend trial for a further six months.[14] Moreover, his treatment was provoking significant side effects. He was generally quite weak, had to stay in bed and was awake for one or two hours only.[15] The treatment he was receiving was the same treatment he would receive anywhere else for the condition in question, including in Europe.[16] His treatment required that he stay in Nairobi for six months while being treated. Dr. Épée Hernandez's opinion that he would be incapacitated for 6 months or even one year was confirmed by a panel of doctors in Nairobi.[17] However, after three months of treatment, it would be possible to do a provisional evaluation of his condition.[18]

12. As of 3 November 2008, Counsel for Matthieu Ngirumpatse indicated that Ngirumpatse had been unable to read anything whatsoever.[19]

13. At the status conference on 9 February 2009, Dr. Épée Hernandez stated that Matthieu Ngirumpatse's clinical condition was improving remarkably. His medication would continue for three more months at which point the doctors would be able to provide a more comprehensive report. However, this did not reflect on his ability to be present in the courtroom.[20]

---

[8] T. 16 February 2009, p. 10.
[9] *See* Interoffice Memoranda from Dr. Épée, dated 19 August 2008, 21 August 2008, 1 September 2008, 5 December 2008, 26 January 2009, 27 February 2009; Observations du Greffier suite à l'Ordonnance de la Chambre du 29 septembre 2008 relative à la situation médicale de M. Ngirumpatse, filed on 1 October 2008; Oral hearings of 28 October 2008, 9 February 2009, 16 February 2009.
[10] T. 18 August 2008, pp. 2-3, 10.
[11] T. 25August 2008, pp. 3, 9.
[12] T. 28 October 2008, pp. 7-8.
[13] *See* Observations du Greffier suite à l'Ordonnance de la Chambre du 29 Septembre 2008 relative à la situation médicale de M. Ngirumpatse, filed on 1 October 2008.
[14] T. 28 October 2008, p. 8-10.
[15] T. 28 October 2008, p. 10.
[16] T. 28 October 2008, p. 10.
[17] T. 28 October 2008, pp. 11, 14, 15.
[18] T. 28 October 2008, p. 14.
[19] T. 3 November 2008, p. 5.
[20] T. 9 February 2009, p. 17.

14. At the oral hearing on 16 February 2009, Dr. Épée Hernandez stated that Matthieu Ngirumpatse would not be fit to attend trial for a further nine months, but this was **[page 5]** nonetheless only a speculative projection.[21] His health condition cannot be completely cured, but can be stabilised.[22] His condition is within her field of expertise and her assessments have been made in consultation and in agreement with Ngirumpatse's attending physician and two professors with the relevant expertise from the hospital where he is being treated.[23]

15. In a report of 27 February 2009, Dr. Épée Hernandez stated that Ngirumpatse is currently clinically stable, and is continuing with his specific treatment. Although laboratory results have not shown response to the treatment, the medical team has decided to give Ngirumpatse six more months of treatment, after which he will be reassessed.[24]

Continuation of the Trial in Ngirumpatse's Absence

16. At the status conference on 6 November 2008, Counsel for Matthieu Ngirumpatse indicated that if the proceedings were further stayed until the beginning of 2009, Ngirumpatse would consent to the proceedings being continued in his absence provided that adequate facilities were put in place for him to follow the proceedings from his place of treatment and that he had by then recovered sufficiently for him to participate in his defence.[25]

17. As a consequence, the Chamber granted the requested stay of proceedings. The Chamber also changed the order for the presentation of the defence cases so that Ngirumpatse would be the last to present his case, scheduled the trial to recommence with sittings only three days a week to allow Ngirumpatse to familiarise himself with the proceedings and consult with his Counsel on a weekly basis before the commencement of the next week's session.[26]

18. Furthermore, on the Chamber's orders, the Registry arranged for a weekly delivery of hardcopies of transcripts, documents used during trial, and motions and other written submissions, DVDs containing the same material plus the video recordings of the trial and provided Ngirumpatse with a laptop to view the DVDs.[27] **[page 6]**

19. In an interim medical report of 26 January 2009, Dr. Épée Hernandez reported that Matthieu Ngirumpatse's treatment has side effects which make him weak. The duration of the weakness varies between one and two days involving some few hours during which he is unfit. Otherwise, Ngirumpatse is clinically well controlled, oriented in time, people and place and capable to achieve intellectual exercise. Other than when suffering from side effects, Ngirumpatse is able to have two hours of concentrated reading in the morning and afternoon at his own pace. He can also watch DVDs and provide comments on them.[28] Dr. Épée Hernandez later clarified that two hours in the morning and afternoon meant one hour in the morning and one hour in the afternoon.[29]

20. At the status conference on 9 February 2009 and in his written submissions, Counsel for Matthieu Ngirumpatse indicated that the conditions for Ngirumpatse's consent to the trial proceeding in his absence were not met.[30] All Parties objected to the proceedings continuing in Ngirumpatse's absence should he not consent.[31]

---

[21] T. 16 February 2009, pp. 8, 19.
[22] T. 16 February 2009, p. 9.
[23] T. 16 February 2009, pp. 8, 14.
[24] Interoffice Memorandum, Progress Medical report for Mathieu Ngirumpatse, From Dr. Épée Hernandez, 27 February 2009.
[25] T. 6 November 2008, pp. 3.
[26] *Karemera et al.*, Décision sur les diverses requêtes relatives à l'état de santé de Mathieu Ngirumpatse (TC), 6 February 2009 (« Decision of 6 February 2009 »).
[27] Registry's Submission Under Rule 33(B) of the Rules on the Efforts Made by the Registry to Provide Facilities to Mathieu Ngirumpatse Since his Admission into Hospital, filed on 16 February 2009 ("Registry's Submissions on facilities provided to Ngirumpatse"); T. 16 February 2009, pp. 5-6.
[28] Interoffice Memorandum, Interim Medical Report for Mr. Mathieu Ngirumpatse, from Dr. Épée Hernadez, 26 January 2009.
[29] T. 16 February 2009, pp. 19-20.
[30] Ngirumpatse's Submissions, para. 6-10.
[31] T. 9 and 16 February 2009.

21. The presence of an accused at his trial is considered a fundamental right pursuant to Article 20(4)(d) of the Statute of the Tribunal ("Statute").[32] Any restriction on a fundamental right, such as the right to be present during the proceedings, must be the least intrusive instrument amongst those which might achieve the desired result.[33] The Chamber considers, along with the Parties, that there are other available options, less intrusive on the rights of the Accused, than continuing the proceedings in Ngirumpatse's absence without his consent.

22. Counsel for Matthieu Ngirumpatse, supported by the Co-Accused seeks a three-month stay on the basis that, in light of Dr. Épée Hernandez's report to the Chamber on 9 February 2009, one can reasonably think that Ngirumpatse's medical condition will have sufficiently improved so that he will be able to contribute to his defence from his hospital bed.[34] The Prosecution opposes a further stay of proceedings.[35]

[page 7]

23. The Chamber relies on the assessment of Matthieu Ngirumpatse's ability to attend trial that has been made by the Tribunal's Chief Medical Officer, Dr. Épée Hernandez, in consultation and agreement with Ngirumpatse's attending physician and specialists with the relevant expertise.

24. It follows from these assessments that, in three months, the doctors will have a better foundation for assessing when, if ever, Matthieu Ngirumpatse will be able to attend trial, but that, in any event, he will not be able to do so before nine months.

25. For the proceedings to continue in Matthieu Ngirumpatse's absence would, in the Chamber's opinion, require that Ngirumpatse be able to familiarise himself with the proceedings reasonably contemporaneously, that is on a weekly basis. The familiarisation process would include a viewing of the videotapes of the proceedings and/or a reading of the transcripts together with the documents used during trial as well the motions and other written submission which are extraordinarily numerous in this case. Ngirumpatse's present condition would only allow him to concentrate on this material about 6 hours a week before consulting with his Counsel, which in the Chamber's opinion, is by far insufficient for the trial to continue with the required minimum of expeditiousness.

26. The Chamber considers that Counsel for Matthieu Ngirumpatse's suggestion that Ngirumpatse may be in a significantly better condition in three months is highly speculative since the treatment which affects his ability to follow the proceedings will be continued for further six months and since he has so far not responded to it.

27. Taking into account that the proceedings – apart from the exceptional examination of four witnesses – have now been stayed for more than six months, and that the updated assessment to be made in three months would, in the best case, support a prognosis that Matthieu Ngirumpatse will be fit to attend trial in nine months, the Chamber finds that the delay of the trial has reached a proportion that makes it imperative for the Chamber to now address whether Ngirumpatse should be severed from the trial or whether the proceedings be stayed until it is determined either that Ngirumpatse is fit to participate or that he is unable to do so for the foreseeable future.

Stay of Proceedings

28. Whether to sever Matthieu Ngirumpatse from this trial or to stay the proceedings until he becomes fit to attend trial or it be ascertained that he will not be fit to attend trial in the [page 8] foreseeable future, if ever, involves a balancing of several legal principles. The primary concern is that the decision must not violate the fundamental right of all three Accused to a fair trial pursuant to Article 20(2) of the Statute or

---

[32] *See also Strugar*, Case No. IT-01-42-T, Decision re the Defence Motion to Terminate Proceedings (TC), 26 May 2004, para. 32; *Zigiranyirazo*, Case No. ICTR-2001-73-AR73, Decision on interlocutory Appeal (AC), 30 October 2006, para. 12; S/25704, Report of the Secretary General Pursuant to Paragraph 2 of Security Council Resolution 808, 3 May 1993, para. 101.

[33] *Stanišić and Simatović*, Case IT-03-69-AR73.2, Decision on Defence Appeal of the Decision on Future Course of the Proceedings (AC), para. 16.

[34] Ngirumpatse's Submissions, para. 19, 59.

[35] Motion for Severance, para 7.

unfairly violate the right of the Co-Accused, Édouard Karemera and Joseph Nzirorera, to be tried without undue delay pursuant to Article 20(4)(c) of the Statute.

29. In the *Bizimungu et al.* case, the Trial Chamber stated that the "Accused's right to be tried without undue delay should be balanced with the need to ascertain the truth about the serious crimes with which the Accused is charged."[36] In the same case, the Appeals Chamber stated that the fundamental purpose of the Tribunal must not be taken into account as a factor when determining whether there has been undue delay.[37]

30. A finding of undue delay depends on the circumstances of each case.[38] A joint trial might last longer than that of a single accused case without necessarily infringing upon the right to be tried without undue delay. According to the Appeals Chamber in *Bizimungu et al.*, the determination of whether an accused person's right to be tried without undue delay has been violated must necessarily include a consideration of, *inter alia*: the length of the delay; the complexity of the proceedings such as the number of charges, the number of accused, the number of witnesses, the volume of evidence, and the complexity of facts and law; the conduct of the parties; the conduct of the relevant authorities; and the prejudice to the accused, if any.[39]

31. In the *Bizimungu et al.* case, the Trial Chamber held that when making a determination as to whether there has been undue delay, a chamber will only consider delay that has already occurred and will not speculate on whether an accused's right to trial without undue delay **[page 9]** might be violated at a future date.[40] Further, the reasonableness of a period of delay cannot be translated into a fixed length of time and is dependant on consideration of a number of factors.[41] A full inquiry into the role of the parties in the alleged undue delay should also be undertaken.[42]

32. However, the delays at issue in *Bizimungu et al.* were the general pace of the trial and not delays caused by the inability of an accused to attend trial for a lengthy period. In the present case, the Chamber finds it relevant to also take into consideration that a stay of proceedings for Matthieu Ngirumpatse to be fit to attend trial again, will, according to the doctor's assessment, in the best case result in a further delay of nine months in addition to the current delay of six months.

33. Matthieu Ngirumpatse, in support of his request for a further stay of proceedings, refers extensively to the *Stanišić* case. He argues that in the *Stanišić* case the Appeals Chamber held that, with respect to the fundamental rights of the accused, a three-month stay of proceedings was the best solution.[43] Following this holding, the Trial Chamber decided to order a further three-month stay, which amounted to a ten-month stay, as a result of Stanišić's health situation.[44]

---

[36] *Mugenzi*, Case No. ICTR-99-50-I, Decision on Justin Mugenzi's Motion for Stay of Proceedings or in the Alternative Provisional Release (Rule 65) and in Addition Severance (Rule 82(B)), dated 8 November 2002 but filed on 11 November 2002, para. 32.

[37] Decision on Prosper Mugiraneza's Interlocutory Appeal from Trial Chamber II Decision of 2 October 2003 denying the Motion to Dismiss the indictment, Demand Speedy trial and for Appropriate relief (AC), 27 February 2004, p. 3.

[38] *Mugenzi*, Case No. ICTR-99-50-I, Decision on Justin Mugenzi's Motion for Stay of Proceedings or in the Alternative Provisional Release (Rule 65) and in Addition Severance (Rule 82(B)) (TC), dated 8 November 2002 but filed on 11 November 2002, para. 33.

[39] *Bizimungu et al.*, Case No. ICTR-99-50, Decision on Justin Mugenzi's Motion Alleging Undue Delay and Seeking Severance (TC), 14 June 2007, para. 11; Decision on Prosper Mugiraneza's Interlocutory Appeal from Trial Chamber II Decision of 2 October 2003 denying the Motion to Dismiss the indictment, Demand Spee dy trial and for Appropriate relief (AC), 27 February 2004, p. 3; *Ngirumpatse et al.*, Case No. ICTR-98-44, Decision on Prosecutor's Motion for Joinder of Accused and on the Prosecutor's Motion for Severance of the Accused (TC), 29 June 2000, para. 38; *Bagosora et al.*, Case No. ICTR-98-41, Decision on the Prosecutor's Request for Leave to Amend the Indictment (TC), 23 October 1999.

[40] *Bizimungu et al.*, Decision on Justin Mugenzi's Motion Alleging Undue Delay and Seeking Severance (TC), 14 June 2007, para. 14.

[41] *Bizimungu et al.*, Decision on Justin Mugenzi's Motion Alleging Undue Delay and Seeking Severance (TC), 14 June 2007, para. 14; *Kanyabashi*, Decision on the Defence Extremely Urgent Motion on Habeas Corpus and for Stoppage of the proceedings (TC), 23 May 2000, para. 68; *Kanyabashi*, Case No. ICTR-98-42, Decision on the Defence Motion for the Provisional Release of the Accused (TC), 21 February 2001, para. 11; *Bizimungu et al.*, Decision on Prosper Mugiraneza's Second Motion to Dismiss for Deprivation of His Right to Trial Without Undue Delay (TC), 29 May 2007, para. 27.

[42] Decision on Prosper Mugiraneza's Interlocutory Appeal from Trial Chamber II Decision of 2 October 2003 denying the Motion to Dismiss the indictment, Demand Speedy trial and for Appropriate relief (AC), 27 February 2004, p. 3.

[43] Ngirumpatse's Submissions, para.46-47.

[44] Ngirumpatse's Submissions, para.

Decision on Continuation of Trial

34. The Chamber has undertaken a careful review of the current proceedings and considers that the reasons that led the Chamber to order further stay of proceedings in the *Stanišić* case do not apply to the present instance. The Chamber notes that in the *Stanišić* case, the trial commenced on 28 April 2008 and was adjourned on 16 May 2008. At that time, only one Prosecution witness had been heard by the Trial Chamber which considered that the case would have to recommence and that consequently the case was still at pre-trial stage.[45] The **[page 10]** Accused had not participated at all in the trial proceedings.[46] Both Accused were provisionally released until the commencement of the trial.

35. In contrast, in the present case, the three Accused have been in detention since 1998 and in trial since November 2003. The current trial started on 19 September 2005 and is at a much more advanced stage than in *Stanišić*. The Prosecution finished presenting its case at the end of 2007 and the first Accused has started to present his evidence. Thus a further stay of proceedings will complicate matters significantly, and cause significant prejudice to the accused.

36. Édouard Karemera and Joseph Nzirorera submit that they do not mind waiting for Matthieu Ngirumpatse's health to improve and will not suffer any prejudice from this delay. The Chamber, however, does not accept the Accused's submission that there is no prejudice from such a delay. While the Chamber accepts that the Parties' positions regarding prejudice resulting from delays are extremely important factors to take into account in a determination of this nature, they are not the sole or decisive factors. Parties may allege prejudice where a Chamber finds that there is none; equally, a party may submit that it suffers no prejudice and it is open to a Chamber to find that this is indeed the case.

37. The suspension of the proceedings has resulted in considerable difficulties for the Parties. Some of Édouard Karemera's witnesses have come to Arusha several times without being able to testify, or only after prolonged delay. For example, two of Karemera's witnesses came to Arusha on two occasions and stayed for a total of almost two months. The witnesses did not take the stand on the first occasion but did testify on the second occasion, one for less than a day and the other for two days. Others witnesses have remained in Arusha for approximately one month, only to testify for less than a day and a half. The cross-examination of one defence witness has been pending since 16 July 2008.

38. In short, the case of one accused has been brought to a halt mid-way through and the others are at a standstill. Such a situation must be assessed in light of the presumption of innocence. The Chamber finds that, given how far the trial has proceeded, and that the defence cases are prepared to proceed imminently and expected to finish within the year, it has become seriously prejudicial to simply let the accused sit in detention while Matthieu Ngirumpatse's health problems are addressed. In the circumstances, the Chamber finds that **[page 11]** the delay in the proceedings, to this point, has become such that the rights of the accused to be tried without undue delay have been violated.

Severance

39. Pursuant to Rule 82(B), a Trial Chamber may order separate trials of persons jointly charged if (i) it considers it necessary in order to avoid a conflict of interests that might cause serious prejudice to an accused, or (ii) to protect the interests of justice. It is clear from the use of the conjunctive word 'or' that either condition, if satisfied, will be sufficient to enable the Trial Chamber to make an order of severance.[47] The provisions of Sub-Rule 82(B) gives discretion to the Trial Chamber in the determination of whether an accused jointly charged should be granted separate trial.[48]

---

[45] *Stanišić and Simatović*, Case IT-03-69-PT, Decision on Provisional Release (TC), 26 May 2008, para. 62-63.
[46] *Stanišić and Simatović*, Case IT-03-69-AR73.2, Decision on Defence Appeal of the Decision on Future Course of the Proceedings (AC), para. 3.
[47] *Delalić et al.*, Case no. IT-96-21, Decision on the Motion by Defendant Delalić Requesting Procedures for Final Termination of the Charges Against Him (TC), 1 July 1998, para. 34.
[48] *Simić et al.* Decision on Defence Motion to Sever Defendants and Counts (TC), 15 March 1999; *Brdjanin and Talić*, Decision on request to Appeal (TC), 16 May 2000; *Brdjanin and Talić*, Decision on Prosecution's Oral Request for the Separation of Trials, 20 September 2002, para. 19. *Delalić et al.*, Decision on the Motion by Defendant Delalić Requesting Procedures for Final Determination of the Charges Against Him (TC), 1 July 1998, para. 35; *Ntahobali*, Case No. ICTR-97-21-T, Decision on Ntahobali's Motion for Separate Trial (TC), 2 February 2005, para. 32. *Nyiramasuhuko and Ntahobali*, Case No. ICTR-97-21-T, Joint Case No. ICTR-98-42-T, Decision on Nyiramasuhuko's Motion for Separate Proceedings, a New Trial, and a Stay of Proceedings (TC),

40.   The Trial Chamber in the *Delalić et al.* case stated that both the preconditions of causing serious prejudice to the accused, and the protection of the interest of justice, involve the exercise of judicial discretion.[49] The same Trial Chamber considered that it was obvious from the formulations of the reasons for granting separate trials pursuant to Rule 82(B) that the overriding principle is the interest of justice.[50] The jurisprudence states that judicial economy and expediency of trials are two of the essential pre-conditions to be borne in mind when a Trial Chamber considers a case under Rule 82(B).[51]

41.   An order for severance may be made after a trial has begun as the prejudice of a joint trial may only become apparent as the trial unfolds.[52] In the *Bagosora et al.* case, the Trial Chamber stated that "[a] factor militating against severance, however, is that the prejudice **[page 12]** was apparent or discoverable before trial and that the case has proceeded for significant period."[53]

42.   Matthieu Ngirumpatse submits that the Tribunal's completion strategy cannot play any role in the determination of the interests of justice[54] The Chamber agrees and is mindful that, in the event of a conflict between the principles involved, judicial economy and expeditiousness are secondary to the right of the Accused to a fair trial.

43.   The Defence submits that there is no conflict of interests between the three Accused that would justify severance. They want to continue in a joint trial.[55] Although there may not be any conflict of interests between the Accused resulting from an antagonistic defence,[56] the Chamber considers that the prejudice sustained by Édouard Karemera and Joseph Nzirorera from the further delay, if the proceedings were to be stayed until Ngirumpatse might become fit to attend trial again, constitutes a conflict of interest.

44.   All three Accused submit that they will be prejudiced in the event of a severance of Ngirumpatse from the case, and that severance will not serve judicial economy. The charges against them, including the charge of being members of the same joint criminal enterprise, are closely interlinked.

45.   They argue that they have divided the issues between them, in accordance with the Chamber's orders. If severance is granted, Joseph Nzirorera and Édouard Karemera will have to call a number of the witnesses on Matthieu Ngirumpatse's witness list and would need a considerable delay of proceedings to prepare this part of their defence. Similarly, in his separate trial, Ngirumpatse would have to call a number of witnesses from Nzirorera's and Karemera's witness lists.

46.   The Accused further submit that witnesses who have agreed to testify in the defence of one of the Accused may not be willing to testify if called by another Accused. Each Accused may not be willing to testify if called by another Accused. Witnesses will be put under considerable hardship and suffer additional security risks if they have to come to Arusha more than once to testify and may refuse to do so. Thus severance would only benefit the **[page 13]** Prosecution and prejudice the Defence as a whole and have damageable and irreversible consequences.[57]

---

7 April 2006, para. 64; *Ntabakuze*, Decision (Appeal of the Trial Chamber I "Decision on Motions by Ntabakuze for severance and to establish a reasonable schedule for the presentation of prosecution witnesses" of 9 September 2003 (AC), 28 Octobre 2003, p. 5.
[49]   *Delalić et al.*, Decision on the Motion by Defendant Delalić Requesting Procedures for Final Determination of the Charges Against Him (TC), 1 July 1998, para. 35.
[50]   *Delalić et al.*, Decision on the Motion by Defendant Delalić Requesting Procedures for Final Determination of the Charges Against Him (TC), 1 July 1998, para. 36.
[51]   *Brđjanin and Talić*, Decision on Motion by Momir Talić and for a separate Trial and fot Leave to File Reply, 9 March 2000, para. 26.
[52]   See *Brđjanin and Talić* case; *Bagosora et al.*, Decision on Motions by Ntabakuze for Severance and to Establish Reasonable Schedule for the Presentation of Prosecution Witnesses (TC), 9 September 2003, para. 20.
[53]   *Bagosora et al.*, Decision on Motions by Ntabakuze for Severance and to Establish Reasonable Schedule for the Presentation of Prosecution Witnesses (TC), 9 September 2003, para. 28.
[54]   Ngirumpatse's Submissions, para. 57.
[55]   Ngirumpatse's Submissions, para. 34.
[56]   Though the jurisprudence is clear that the possibility of "mutually antagonistic defences" does not constitute a conflict of interests capable of causing serious prejudice. See *Simić et al.*, Case No. IT-95-9-PT, Decision on Defence Motion to Sever Defendants and Counts, 15 March 1999; *Brđjanin and Talić*, Case No. IT-99-36, Decision on Prosecution's Oral Request for the Separation of Trials, 20 September 2002, para. 21.
[57]   Ngirumpatse's Submissions, para. 39-42.

47. The Chamber does not agree that severance will induce a partial presentation of facts and evidence. On the contrary, because the Prosecution has finished the presentation of its case, each and every accused, has a clear knowledge of the case against him. Each of them will also have the opportunity to present evidence against the case presented against him by the Prosecution.

48. Joseph Nzirorera further argues that, considering that his request at the pre-trial stage for severance was denied, it would be the height of unfairness if the Trial Chamber were to allow only the Prosecution to develop a full picture of this case while depriving the Defence of developing the full picture during the Defence evidence.[58] The Chamber reminds Joseph Nzirorera that the reasons that lead it to deny him his request for severance in 2000 were very different from the situation this trial is facing at the moment.

49. The Chamber recalls that the reasons that lead it to deny Joseph Nzirorera's request for severance in 2000 were very different from the situation this trial is facing at the moment. The Chamber moreover recalls that in June 2007, Counsel for Nzirorera indicated that instead of proceeding in the absence of an accused, the Chamber should consider the alternative solution of severing the case.[59]. Then in July 2007, when Nzirorera appealed the Trial Chamber's Decision to proceed in his absence, he indicated that "[i]nstead, if [the Chamber] were concerned with the expeditiousness of the trial in face of illness of the accused which was likely to re-occur, the Trial Chamber should have considered other alternatives, such as severance of Mr. Nzirorera's case from that of his co-accused, as suggested by Mr. Nzirorera."[60]

50. The Chamber notes that some single accused persons before this Tribunal have been accused of conspiracy to commit genocide. In light of those proceedings, it is evident that ordering severance of this case will not prevent Matthieu Ngirumpatse or the two other Accused from defending themselves against the charge of conspiracy to commit genocide.[61] The Chamber considers that the same conclusion applies to the allegation of participation in a **[page 14]** joint criminal enterprise.[62] Consequently, severance would not cause any prejudice with respect to the charges and modes of participation in crimes set out in the Indictment.

51. The Trial Chamber of this Tribunal is composed of professional judges and is able to assess the evidence in a case involving conflicting defence and prosecution evidence in a fair and just manner without prejudice to any of the accused.[63] Furthermore, the Chamber considers that there is no objective reasons for it to believe that severance would result in any lack of coherence.

52. The Chamber considers that by ordering severance Matthieu Ngirumpatse will have his right to be present and defend himself safeguarded while retaining his right to an expeditious trial when he is fit again to participate in his trial.

53. The Chamber also considers that severance would not in average create more hardship on witnesses than a further lengthy stay of proceedings. Indeed, as stated above, several witnesses have come to Arusha without being able to testify. Some of them have been anticipated to testify for many months in this case but their testimony has been delayed on many occasions because of the cancellation of proceedings due to Matthieu Ngirumpatse's health condition. A significant number of the witnesses on the witness lists of the Accused, including the Accused themselves, have previously testified on several occasions in different cases before this Tribunal and thus there is no evidence that the added burden of testifying in more cases will prevent these witnesses from testifying again. In any event, a further lengthy stay of proceedings might also result in witnesses no longer able or willing to testify.

54. Considering that Matthieu Ngirumpatse, according to the doctor's assessment, will undergo the same treatment that currently affects his ability to concentrate for another six months and will, in the best case, not be fit to attend trial before nine months, the Chamber finds that the severance of Ngirumpatse is the least

---

[58] Nzirorera's Submissions, para. 35.
[59] T. 27 June 2007, p. 12.
[60] Joseph Nzirorera's Appeal from Decision to Proceed in the Absence of the Accused, filed 16 July 2007, para. 30.
[61] See e.g. Zigiranyirazo, Kambanda, Kajelijeli, Rugambarara cases where single accused where charged with conspiracy to commit genocide.
[62] See e.g. Mpambara, Bikindi, Zigiranyirazo cases.
[63] See Brdjanin and Talić, Decision on Motion by Momir Talić and for a separate Trial and for Leave to File Reply, 9 March 2000, para. 32.

intrusive solution. This conclusion is bolstered by a consideration of the right of each accused to a fair trial and to be tried without undue delay, as well as the similar interests of victims and the international community that trials concerning serious crimes be completed without unnecessary delays. As a secondary concern, the Chamber also finds that severance significantly serves judicial economy. Thus, it is in the interest of justice to sever Ngirumpatse from this case. **[page 15]**

Consequences of Severance

55. The Prosecution submits that if the Chamber were to order severance it would oppose any motion for a new trial or to exclude evidence. It does not intend to amend the Indictment or to modify its case in any manner. It has proven its case against each Accused individually and therefore each of the Accused must defend himself against the entirety of the Prosecution case.[64]

56. Édouard Karemera submits that in the event of a severance, the Indictment must be amended, the Prosecution's evidence must be assessed with regards to the principle that in criminal law responsibility is individual,[65] and the Prosecution must abandon the charge of joint criminal enterprise.[66] He further submits that the Defence must be allowed to make submissions on a new amended indictment, be allowed to call new witnesses[67] and the proceedings must be stayed until June 2009 to allow the Defence to prepare its cases.[68] Matthieu Ngirumpatse submits in the event of a severance, new separate Indictments must be filed.[69]

57. The Chamber notes that the Prosecution has presented its case-in-chief against all three Accused and produced *prima facie* evidence for the charges. There is therefore no basis for the Chamber to order the Prosecutor to make substantial amendments to the Indictment.

58. Whether or not Matthieu Ngirumpatse will be entitled to a trial *de novo* may depend upon whether the same bench will be in a position to continue his case, if and when he becomes fit to attend trial.

59. The Chamber is mindful that as a result of the severance Karemera and Nzirorera will have to lead evidence to rebut the charges that the Defence had organised for Ngirumpatse to lead and will grant them the necessary leave for them to vary their witness lists and the appropriate time for additional preparation of their defence cases.

Certification to Appeal

60. Joseph Nzirorera requests that certification to appeal be granted should the Chamber **[page 16]** order severance of Matthieu Ngirumpatse's case.[70]

61. The Chamber finds that ordering the severance of Matthieu Ngirumpatse from this trial could significantly affect the outcome of the trial, and that an immediate resolution of this issue would materially advance the proceedings. Consequently the Trial Chamber grants certification to appeal the entirety of this decision.

62. An appeal does not entail a stay of proceedings, and the Chamber finds no reason to order a stay of proceedings during the appeal, considering the delay that has already occurred, and the fact that some witnesses have been waiting to testify for a long time. Furthermore, if the appeal is granted, the likely remedy would be the hearing *de novo* of witnesses who have testified since the order of severance. Édouard Karemera must therefore resume his defence case on 23 March 2009.

63. Consequently, the Witness and Victims Support Section of the Tribunal shall immediately take steps to bring Édouard Karemera's witnesses to Arusha for the next trial session.

---

[64] Prosecution's submissions, para. 17-19; *see also* T. 16 February 2009, p. 34.
[65] Karemera's Submissions, p. 5.
[66] Karemera's Submissions, p. 7.
[67] Karemera's Submissions, p. 8.
[68] Karemera's Submissions, p. 8.
[69] Ngirumpatse's Submissions, para. 55.
[70] Nzirorera's Submissions, para. 61-63.

FOR THE FOREGOING REASONS, THE CHAMBER

DENIES Matthieu Ngirumpatse's request for further stay of proceedings;

ORDERS that Matthieu Ngirumpatse be severed from this trial; and

ORDERS that the trial of Édouard Karemera and Joseph Nzirorera shall resume with the hearing of Karemera's next witness on 23 March 2009.

Arusha, 3 March 2009, done in English.

Dennis C. M. Byron
Presiding Judge

Gberdao Gustave Kam
Judge

Vagn Joensen
Judge
(absent during signature)

[Seal of the Tribunal]

International Criminal Tribunal for Rwanda
Tribunal pénal international pour le Rwanda

OR: ENG

TRIAL CHAMBER II

Before Judges: Judge William H. Sekule, Presiding
Judge Solomy Balungi Bossa
Judge Mparany Rajohnson

Registrar: Mr. Adama Dieng

Date: 12 June 2009

The PROSECUTOR

v.

Augustin NGIRABATWARE

Case No. ICTR-99-54-T

DECISION ON TRIAL DATE

Office of the Prosecutor
Mr. Wallace Kapaya
Mr. Patrick Gabaake
Mr. Brian Wallace
Mr. Iskandar Ismail

Defence Counsel
Mr. David C. Thomas
Ms. Mylene Dimitri

[page 1] THE INTERNATIONAL CRIMINAL TRIBUNAL FOR RWANDA (the "Tribunal"),

SITTING as Trial Chamber II composed of Judges William H. Sekule, Presiding, Solomy Balungi Bossa, and Mparany Rajohnson (the "Trial Chamber");

RECALLING the "Decision on Augustin Ngirabatware's Appeal of Decisions Denying Motions to Vary Trial Date" of 12 May 2009 (the "Appeals Chamber Decision"), which "remands the determination of a trial date consistent with this decision to the Trial Chamber";[1]

RECALLING the "Decision on Defence Motion to Vacate Trial Date of 4 May 2009" of 25 February 2009 and the "Decision on Defence Motion to Vary Trial Date" of 25 March 2009 denying variation of the Trial date (the "Impugned Decisions");

RECALLING the "Scheduling Order" of 12 May 2009;[2]

BEING SEIZED OF:

a) "Dr. Ngirabatware's Submission Regarding an Appropriate Trial Date Pursuant to the Trial Chamber Scheduling Order", filed on 18 May 2009 (the "Defence Submission");

b) The "*Observations du Procureur sur* 'Dr. Ngirabatware's Submission Regarding an Appropriate Trial Date Pursuant to the Trial Chamber's Scheduling Order dated 12 May 2009'", filed on 19 May 2009 (the "Response"); and

c) The "Defence Reply to the Prosecutor's Observations on Dr. Ngirabatware's Submission Regarding an Appropriate Trial Date", filed on 25 May 2009 (the "Reply");

CONSIDERING the Statute of the Tribunal (the "Statute") and the Rules of Procedure and Evidence (the "Rules");

NOW DECIDES pursuant to Rule 73 of the Rules:

INTRODUCTION

1. On 25 February 2009, the Chamber rendered the Decision on Defence Motion to Vacate Trial Date of 4 May 2009, denied the Motion, and ordered that the trial shall commence on 18 May 2009.

2. On 25 March 2009, the Chamber issued its Decision on Defence Motion to Vary Trial Date, in which it denied the Motion and ordered the trial to commence on 18 May 2009. **[page 2]**

3. On 15 April 2009, in its Decision on Defence Motion for Certification to Appeal the Trial Chamber's Decision of 25 March 2009 on Defence Motion to Vary Trial Date, the Chamber granted the Motion and stayed the commencement of trial, pending a determination of the appeal.

4. On 12 May 2009, the Appeals Chamber granted Ngirabatware's Appeal of the Chamber's Decisions denying the motions to vary trial date of 18 May 2009 and remanded the determination of a trial date to the Trial Chamber, consistent with the Appeals Chamber Decision.[3]

5. On 13 May 2009, the Trial Chamber issued a Scheduling Order instructing the Parties to file written submissions addressing the issues raised in the Appeals Chamber Decision, to propose an appropriate date for the commencement of trial, and to specify the reasons for proposing this date.

---

[1] Appeals Chamber Decision, para. 33.
[2] Scheduling Order, 12 May 2009.
[3] The complete procedural history prior to the Appeals Chamber Decision is set out in the Appeals Chamber Decision at paragraphs 2-7.

SUBMISSIONS OF THE PARTIES

Defence Submission

6. The Defence submits that this case is very complex because the Amended Indictment[4] adds numerous new allegations; refers to numerous events which allegedly took place between January and July 1994; refers to sites located throughout Rwanda, all of which need to be visited; and refers to the participation of 51 alleged accomplices, all of whom need to be investigated.[5] The Defence also submits that the complexity of the case is increased by the charge of diversion of funds, which is a "technical and complex matter, involving many documents and witnesses".[6]

7. The Defence emphasises that each crime with which the Accused is charged "carries a life sentence" and is of the gravest nature. It further underlines that the Prosecution alleges every mode of responsibility provided for in the Statute and many different incidents.[7]

8. According to the Defence, its ability to conduct investigations is seriously hindered by the Prosecution's failure to comply with its disclosure obligations. It submits that the following documents should be disclosed, pursuant, to Rule 66 :

- The statement of Witness ANAB; **[page 3]**
- All of the documents referred to in Witness ANAC's statement because Annexes I, II and III of the 15 May 2009 disclosure are "confusing tables" and do not provide any information regarding the contents of the tables;
- The documents supporting the Report by Witnesses ANAB and ANAC and the documents produced by the "SAP Follow-up Committee" mentioned in ANAC's statement;
- The full identifying information of Witnesses ANAB, ANAC and ANAP;
- The French translation of Witness ANAL's second statement, disclosed on 8 May 2009;
- The previous statements of Witnesses ANAA, ANAI, and ANAN;
- The names of the "foreigners" who were working in the Ministry of Planning and who were alleged accomplices in the diversion of funds.[8]

9. Further, the Defence contends that it should receive the criminal histories of all the Prosecution witnesses, including their *Gacaca* records, pursuant, to Rule 68.[9]

10. The Defence reiterates the submissions in its Motion in objection to the Prosecutor's Pre-Trial Brief with respect to the alleged flaws contained in the Prosecution Pre-Trial Brief and in the attached list of witnesses.[10]

11. The Defence contends it has not yet received the list of exhibits with the required information, or the exhibits themselves.

12. The Defence submits that a lengthy and complex statement by Witness ANAN was disclosed for the first time on 8 May 2009, which it requires additional time to analyse because it contains numerous new allegations.[11]

---

[4] Amended Indictment, filed on 14 April 2009 ("Amended Indictment").
[5] Defence Submission, paras. 4-5.
[6] Defence Submission, para. 6.
[7] Defence Submission, paras. 7-9.
[8] Defence Submission, para. 10.
[9] Defence Submission, para. 11.
[10] Defence Submission, para. 12.
[11] Defence Submission, para. 14.

13. In the 15 May 2009 disclosure many documents are provided only in French or only in Kinyarwanda; the Defence requests their translation.[12]

14. Regarding the status of its investigation, the Defence submits that witness investigation and analysis of documents will involve at least five to six months of work.[13] It further submits that it started its investigation in mid-February and was burdened by the filing of an Amended Indictment on 13 April 2009, which added more witnesses to the case.[14] The Defence further submits that its investigative work is also hindered by the erroneous connection of Prosecution witnesses to paragraphs of the Amended Indictment **[page 4]** and the vague and imprecise nature of the dates and locations contained in the Amended Indictment.[15]

15. The Defence reiterates that the charge of diversion of funds is complex and involves the analysis of substantial documentary evidence, including more than 150 documents received.[16]

16. The Defence submits that its witnesses are located all over the world and it has only conducted initial interviews of about one fourth of its potential witnesses. In addition, it has not yet been able to undertake a mission to Rwanda to interview potential witnesses there, nor has it interviewed potential witnesses in the United States or Canada.[17]

17. Regarding staffing matters, the Defence informs the Trial Chamber that it is now fully staffed with two investigators and two legal assistants.[18]

18. Lastly, the Defence submits that the estimated length of the trial is short and that the more time the Defence is provided for preparation, the more focused and brief its case will be. The Accused is in custody and therefore has no interest in delaying the trial unnecessarily. The Defence states that setting a trial date only a few months from now would not be consistent with the Appeals Chamber Decision and that the Accused could probably be ready by December 2009. The Defence suggests January 2010 for the start of the trial.[19]

Prosecution Response

19. The Prosecution submits that the Defence Submission should be dismissed as unfounded.[20] It argues that the allegations of the case have been reduced to the minimum and clearly set out. Its Pre-Trial Brief was filed on 30 March 2009 and it intends to call less than 20 witnesses. Therefore, the Prosecution rejects the argument of the complexity of the case made by the Defence in support of its Submission.[21]

20. Regarding disclosure issues, the Prosecution contends that it has fully discharged its obligations pursuant to Rule 66 (A) (i) and (ii):

- The statement of Witness ANAB was disclosed on 13 March 2009;

- The annexes to the Report are unambiguous and were disclosed on 15 May 2009; **[page 5]**

- The Prosecutor does not have "the document" in its possession;

- The full identities of Witnesses ANAB, ANAC and ANAP were disclosed on 22 April and 15 May 2009;

- The Prosecution has discharged its duty by disclosing the Witness ANAL's statement in English on 8 May 2009;

---

[12] Defence Submission, paras. 15, 23.
[13] Defence Submission, para. 24.
[14] Defence Submission, para. 16, 17.
[15] Defence Submission, paras. 20, 19, referring to the Defence Objections to the Prosecutor's Pre-Trial Brief, 16 April 2009, paras. 37-49 and Defence Reply to the Prosecutor's Response to the Defence Objections to the Prosecutor's Pre-Trial Brief, 27 April 2009.
[16] Defence Submission, para. 18.
[17] Defence Submission, paras. 21-22.
[18] Defence Submission, paras. 25-26.
[19] Defence Submission, paras. 27-33.
[20] Response, para. 10.
[21] Response, para. 3.

- The statements of Witnesses ANAA, ANAI and ANAN were disclosed on 13 March 2009;
- The Prosecution has never mentioned any foreigners working at the Ministry of Planning at the time who were accomplices to the diversion of funds charge and requests the Defence to clarify this matter.[22]

21. The Prosecution submits it has disclosed the report of Witnesses ANAB and ANAC on 13 March 2009, as well as sketches and photographs of locations on 15 May 2009.[23]

22. The Prosecution further submits that the statement of Witness ANAN disclosed on 8 May 2009 does not contain new allegations.[24]

23. The Prosecution claims that it has disclosed the documents referred to in paragraph 15 of the Defence Submission as "the new batch of disclosure sent to the Defence on May 15". Some were in French, which is an official language of the Tribunal, and some were in Kinyarwanda, which is the language of the Accused, and the Kinyarwanda documents have been sent for translation.[25]

24. Furthermore, the Prosecution avers that the Amended Indictment does not add new witnesses.[26]

25. Regarding the connection of witnesses to paragraphs of the Amended Indictment, the Prosecution submits that this was amended and revised and that, in any case, this is a matter pertaining to evidence to be discussed at trial.[27]

26. With regard to Rule 68, the Prosecution underlines that the disclosure obligation is ongoing and is limited to documents it has in its possession. The Prosecution states that not all its witnesses are convicted criminals and that the criminal records of Witnesses ANAA, ANAD, ANAI and the *Gacaca* documents of Witnesses ANAO and ANAH were disclosed on 15 May 2009. The Prosecution avers that it will continue to discharge its Rule 68 disclosure obligations.[28] **[page 6]**

27. The Prosecution submits that the large amount of documents disclosed before January 2009 should have enabled the Defence to start its investigations at that time.[29] According to the Prosecution, the Defence does not need more than 90 days to complete its investigations. However, should the Defence need more time, additional investigations could be conducted at the end of the Prosecution's case.[30] The Prosecution states that it is ready to start the trial at any time but that should the Chamber estimate that more time is needed for the Defence, July 2009 is an appropriate time. It strongly opposes the Defence's proposed date of January 2010.[31]

Defence Reply

28. The Defence notes that the Prosecution failed to show that it would be prejudiced by the trial date proposed by the Defence, and that there is, therefore, no reason not to set the trial date in accordance with the Defence Submission. The Defence reiterates that the Accused, who is in custody, has no interest in causing undue delay to his trial.[32]

29. Further, the Defence notes that the Prosecution does not make any observations regarding the number of counts and charges and their gravity. It also notes that the Prosecution contests the description of the case as a complex one, though it asserts that the description has been endorsed by the Appeals Chamber. The Defence provides as an example that the Prosecution fails to address the fact that diversion of funds is a

---

[22] Response, para. 4 a).
[23] Response, para. 4 b).
[24] Response, para. 4 c).
[25] Response, para. 4 d).
[26] Response, para. 4 e).
[27] Response, para. 4 f).
[28] Response, para. 5.
[29] Response, para. 6.
[30] Response, para. 7.
[31] Response, paras. 8-10.
[32] Reply, paras. 5-7.

technical charge involving many documents and witnesses, and the Prosecution does not contest that there are over 51 alleged accomplices named in the Amended Indictment and/or in the Pre-Trial Brief.[33]

30. With regard to disclosure, the Defence submits that it has not yet received the CD-ROMs disclosed on 15 May 2009, and notes that although the Prosecutor has continually represented that he has complied with his disclosure obligations additional disclosures have been made on an almost daily basis.[34] It therefore concludes that had the trial started on 18 May 2009 this voluminous disclosure would have been received during the trial. The Defence deems the Prosecution's representations regarding his disclosure compliance as simply not credible.[35]

31. The Defence submits that the Prosecution's disclosure has been consistently tardy and deficient, and many issues remain to be resolved.[36] It lists the outstanding disclosure as follows: **[page 7]**

- The identification material for Witnesses ANAB and ANAC do not comply with the general requirements regarding identifying data for the Prosecution witnesses and do not enable the Defence to know essential confidential data concerning those witnesses. Witness ANAP's identifying information was disclosed on 18 May 2009, after the Defence Submission.[37]

- The document disclosed by the Prosecution on 13 March 2009 is a report, not a statement. Witness ANAB's statement needs to be disclosed as was done for Witness ANAC.[38]

- The Defence refers the Prosecution to Witness ANAC's statement dated 27 February 2008 in which an office for a "foreigner" at the Ministry of Planning is mentioned. It reasserts that these "foreigners" mentioned appear to be accomplices in the diversion of funds and that their names must be disclosed to the Defence.[39]

- The Defence contends that the Prosecution has failed to address its submission regarding the annexes to the Report and has made no indication regarding the origin, author, date or source of such documents, and that furthermore these materials bear no indicia of reliability.[40] Additionally, it asserts that it is the Prosecution's duty to find the documents which allegedly directly support the information contained in the Report and that, without them, the Report bears no indicia of reliability or authenticity.[41]

- The Defence reaffirms that the statement of Witness ANAN disclosed on 8 May 2009 contains numerous allegations, which are not contained in either the Amended Indictment or the Pre-Trial Brief.[42]

- The Defence reiterates that it has not received the French translation of Witness ANAL's statement.[43]

- According to Witness ANAA's statements disclosed on 13 March 2009 and 15 May 2009, ANAA met with the Prosecutor several previous times and made statements in other cases before the Tribunal. The Defence requests to be served with those other statements.[44]

32. With regard to the status of its investigations, the Defence repeats its arguments made in its 18 May 2009 Submission. It further submits that the 14 April 2009 Amended **[page 8]** Indictment modified

---

[33] Reply, paras. 8-12.
[34] Reply, paras. 13-14. The Defence states that it received disclosures on 13, 15, 18 and 21 May 2009 and that the 18 May 2009 disclosure consists of 88 pages, while the 21 May 2009 disclosure consists of 86 pages.
[35] Reply, para. 14.
[36] Reply, para. 16.
[37] Reply, para. 15 a).
[38] Reply, para. 15 b).
[39] Reply, para. 15 c).
[40] Reply, para. 15 d).
[41] Reply, paras. 15 d) and e).
[42] Reply, para. 15 f).
[43] Reply, para. 15 g).
[44] Reply, para. 15 h).

paragraphs 37 and 60 of the Indictment and added many names of new alleged accomplices, which requires substantial additional investigation time.[45]

33. The Defence adds that it appears that one Prosecution investigator, whose *curriculum vitae* has been disclosed, is now going to testify regarding sketches and pictures taken in Gisenyi though the Prosecutor may not add new witnesses without having sought leave to vary his witness list, which he failed to do.[46]

34. The Defence contends that the Prosecution wrongly submits that the erroneous connection of Prosecution witnesses to the paragraphs of the Amended Indictment has been addressed. The Defence submits that it is the right of an accused to know with precision, as soon as the witness statements are disclosed, to what paragraph of the indictment the factual allegations refer. The Defence claims it is compelled to speculate on the links between each allegation, the Indictment, and the Pre-Trial Brief, due to numerous flaws that remain.[47]

35. According to the Defence, the Prosecution has no knowledge with respect to the nature and scope of the Defence investigation and no factual basis for asserting that the Defence needs no more than 90 days to be trial ready.[48] The Defence claims it must undertake investigative missions to Rwanda to verify the accuracy of the sketches and photographs recently disclosed in order to be able to ascertain their authenticity. The Defence still has about 50 potential witnesses to contact to determine whether or not they will be called, following which a second round of interviews should be conducted in order to prepare the witnesses to testify. This process should require at least five to six months.[49] The Defence contends that the Prosecution is seeking to place the Accused at a disadvantage by suggesting a trial date of July 2009.[50]

DELIBERATIONS

36. The Chamber recalls the Appeals Chamber Decision, granting Ngirabatware's Appeal to vary the trial date and remanding the determination of a new trial date to the Trial Chamber, consistent with the Appeals Chamber Decision. The Chamber further recalls the Appeals Chamber finding that the Trial Chamber failed to address the factors relevant to its making a fully informed and reasoned decision on the trial date, in light of the Accused's right to a fair trial, in particular his right to have adequate time to prepare his defence.[51] The Appeals Chamber referred to, among others, six factors a Chamber must consider in determining whether an accused has adequate time to prepare a defence: the complexity of the case, the number of counts and charges, the gravity of the crimes **[page 9]** charged, the individual circumstances of the accused, the status and scale of the Prosecution's disclosure, and the staffing of the Defence team.[52]

37. More specifically, the Appeals Chamber noted that Lead Counsel for the Defence was assigned on 2 December 2008,[53] while a legal assistant and investigator were assigned in January and February 2009 respectively, and that no co-counsel had yet been assigned on 5 May 2009. It further noted that the Indictment was amended significantly on 5 February 2009, and further amended on 14 April 2009; that the amendments added "a considerable number of new allegations"; that the Accused is charged with six different counts relating to six different offences and a large number of different incidents; that the Accused is charged under two different sections of the Statute, Articles 6 (1) and 6 (3); and that pre-trial matters were still pending at the time of decision.[54] The Appeals Chamber concluded that, while none of these factors would individually

---

[45] Reply, para. 17.
[46] Reply, para. 18, referring to disclosure of the CV on 15 May 2009 and the Order of Appearance of witnesses, disclosed on 22 May 2009.
[47] Reply, para. 19.
[48] Reply, para. 20.
[49] Reply, para.22.
[50] Reply, paras. 23-24.
[51] Appeals Chamber Decision, para. 27.
[52] Appeal Decision, para. 28 recalling *The Prosecutor v. Slobodan Milošević*, Case No. IT-02-54-AR-73.6, Decision on the Interlocutory Appeal by the *Amici Curiae* Against the Trial Chamber Order Concerning the Presentation and Preparation of the Defence Case, 20 January 2004 ("*Milošević* Decision"), paras. 8-19.
[53] The letter of appointment of Lead Counsel, dated 25 November 2008, was sent to Mr. Thomas on 1 December 2008 by fax and the Statement of Availability received from Mr. Thomas was transmitted to the Tribunal by fax on 2 December 2008.
[54] Appeal Decision, para. 29.

have justified intrusion in the Chamber's discretion in the determination of the appropriate date for the commencement of trial, considered together, the factors led the Appeals Chamber to conclude, in light of the particular circumstances of this case, that the Defence was not allowed enough time to prepare for trial.[55]

38. The Chamber recalls its Scheduling Order of 13 May 2009, in which it instructed the Parties to file written submissions regarding the commencement of the trial, addressing the issues raised in the Appeals Chamber Decision. The Chamber notes that the Defence has submitted additional issues which had not been raised in the Appeals Chamber Decision.[56] The Chamber will consider the matters raised in the motions leading to the Impugned Decisions, the Parties' submissions before the Appeals Chamber,[57] as well as any additional submissions which may be relevant to the determination of an appropriate trial date.

Staffing of the Defence Team

39. Regarding the staffing of the Defence team, the Chamber recalls that Lead Counsel was appointed on 2nd December 2008, a legal assistant was appointed 15 January 2009, an investigator was appointed on 6 February 2009, a second legal assistant was appointed on 15 February 2009,[58] a second investigator was appointed on 2 May 2009, and a Co-Counsel was appointed on 1 June 2009, which makes the Defence team fully staffed as of **[page 10]** this date.[59] The Chamber recalls that the issue of the staffing of the Defence team was first addressed by the Chamber on 9 February 2009 during a status conference. In March, the Defence was reminded of the issue in the Decision on Defence Motion to Vary Trial Date.[60] On 4 May 2009, the Chamber observed that "intervention by Lead Counsel was necessary before a Co-Counsel could be appointed" and it expected "that the staffing position of the Defence team will be addressed and completed in a timely manner."[61] On 19 May 2009, the Chamber instructed the Registrar to make submissions regarding the issue of appointment of Co-Counsel pursuant to Rule 33(B) of the Rules.[62] On 20 May 2009, the Registrar submitted that Lead Counsel had presented requests for assignments of Co-Counsel who could not be appointed as they were already assigned to other cases.[63] The Chamber notes that even if the Defence team was not fully staffed at the time of the Impugned Decisions, the investigation should have started from the appointment of the Defence investigator on 6 February 2009. Indeed, the Defence submits that its investigation started mid-February 2009.[64] Consequently, the Chamber considers that the Defence investigation has now been ongoing for about four months.

Amendment of the Indictment and Other Submissions Related to the Nature of the Case[65]

40. With respect to the fact that the Accused is charged with six different counts relating to six different offences and a large number of different incidents, under Articles 6 (1) and 6 (3) of the Statute,[66] the Chamber notes that the present case is a single accused case, that the number of Prosecution witnesses may be limited to 16, and that the Prosecution has indicated that it would need ten days to complete its case in chief.[67] The Chamber considers that the timing of the Amended Indictment and the nature of the charges against the Accused may be relevant considerations in the scheduling of the appropriate trial date.

---

[55] Appeal Decision, para. 30.
[56] Particular issues of disclosure and specific points relating to the state of the Defence investigation were not raised in the Parties submissions before the Appeals Chamber.
[57] See Appeals Chamber Decision, para. 14.
[58] Defence Motion to Continue 18 May 2009 Trial Date, paras. 1, 3, 9 and 11.
[59] See letter from the Chief Defence Counsel and Detention Management Section to Mrs. Mylene Dimitri, titled "Your Assignment as Co-counsel to Represent the Accused Augustin Ngirabatware", dated 28 May 2009.
[60] Decision on Defence Motion to Vary Trial Date, 25 March 2009.
[61] Decision on Defence Motion to Vacate Trial Date of 4 May 2009, para. 11, *citing* Status Conference, Daily Case Minutes, 9 February 2009, para. 1 (d).
[62] Status Conference, T. 19 May 2009, p. 13.
[63] Registrar's Submissions under Rule 33 (B) of the Rules of Procedure and Evidence Regarding the Status of the Composition of the Defence Team and the Assignment of Co-Counsel to the Accused Ngirabatware of 20 May 2009.
[64] Defence Submission, para. 16.
[65] *See supra*, para. 36, (i) the complexity of the case, (ii) the number of counts and charges, and (iii) the nature of the charges.
[66] Appeals Chamber Decision, para. 29.
[67] Order of Appearance of witnesses, disclosed on 22 May 2009.

41. The Chamber notes the Appeals Chamber observation that the indictment was amended significantly on 5 February 2009, and further amended on 14 April 2009 and that the amendments added "a considerable number of new allegations. The Chamber recalls the Decision on Prosecution Motion for Leave to Amend the Indictment of 29 January 2009, which granted amendments on the grounds that they would "narrow down the indictment, [...] increase the fairness and efficiency of the proceedings, [...] **[page 11]** contribute to the specificity and accuracy of the indictment," as well as "result in a more expeditious trial," "thus protecting the accused person's rights to a fair trial."[68] It further held that "while most of the proposed amendments contain new factual allegations, they concretise broad and vague allegations made in the original indictment in support of the Counts by listing particular acts or omissions by the Accused" and held that "these additional factual allegations are described with sufficient specificity to permit focused investigations by the Defence."[69] The Chamber further notes that the 14 April 2009 Amended Indictment did not render the case more complex but rather clarified it after the Chamber partially granted a Defence Preliminary Motion.[70] More specifically, the Defence alleged that paragraphs 37 and 60 of the 14 April 2009 Amended Indictment added many names of new alleged accomplices. The Chamber notes that the modifications of these two paragraphs provided the names of *Interahamwe* militia members from Gisenyi prefecture and thus should, as a result, have facilitated the Defence investigation. Otherwise, the Chamber considers that the nature of the case against the Accused has been substantially known since 5 February 2009, when the Amended Indictment was issued, more than four months ago and more than three months before the initial trial date of 18 May 2009.

Pre-Trial Matters

42. With respect to the issue of pending motions which had been raised by the Parties prior to the Impugned Decisions, the Chamber notes that there are only two pending motions at this stage of the proceedings. The first one, filed on 10 June 2009, objects to certain aspects of the Prosecution Revised Pre-Trial Brief.[71] The other concerns the transfer of detained witnesses. The latter motion is contingent upon the setting of a trial date.[72] These two motions have no impact on the scheduling of the trial date.

43. The Chamber notes that disclosure issues were not discussed in as much detail in the Parties' submissions prior to the Appeals Chamber Decision.[73] However, Rule 66 (A) disclosures will be considered by the Chamber, as they may be relevant to the scheduling of the trial. With respect to disclosure under Rule 66 (B), the Chamber reminds the Parties that requests for inspection differ from disclosure obligations under Rule 66 (A) (i) and (ii), insofar as inspection under this Rule is triggered by a request from the Defence. It could be an ongoing process which may not necessarily impact on the scheduling of the trial date. **[page 12]**

44. Having considered the Parties' submissions regarding the alleged lack of a statement by Witness ANAB, who is now expected to testify as a factual witness, the Chamber takes note of the Prosecution's submission that the Report prepared by Witnesses ANAB and ANAC also constitutes the statement of Witness ANAB.[74] The Defence asserts that a Report cannot constitute a statement, but does not substantiate this assertion. Thus, the Chamber denies this submission.

---

[68] Decision on Prosecution Motion for Leave to Amend the Indictment, 29 January 2009, paras. 24-25.
[69] Decision on Prosecution Motion for Leave to Amend the Indictment, 29 January 2009, para. 27.
[70] *See* Decision on Defence Motion to Dismiss Based upon Defects in the Amended Indictment, 8 April 2009, para. 37 in which the Chamber stated "[h]owever, the Chamber considers that the general reference to information "referred to herein above" appears vague. The Chamber directs the Prosecution to specify the paragraphs of the Amended Indictment the Prosecution is referring to when using this formulation."
[71] Defence Objections to the Prosecution's Revised Pre-Trial Brief, 10 June 2009.
[72] Prosecution Request for an Order Transferring Detained Witnesses Pursuant to Rule 90*bis* of the Rules of Procedure and Evidence, 28 April 2009.
[73] *See* "Dr. Ngirabatware's Consolidated Reply to Prosecutor's Responses Filed on March 13, 2009", para. 4 (j) and (k), The Defence had argued that Rule 66 (A) disclosures were not complete and that the latest disclosures made on 13 March 2009 at the time, did not affect the Defence submission that it needed time to investigate Defence and Prosecution witnesses, as well as gather documentary evidence.
[74] Prosecutor's Response to the Defence Motion for Disclosure Pursuant to Rule 66(A)(ii) of the Rules of Procedure and Evidence, 13 March 2009, para. 3 a).

45. Concerning the Defence request for previous statements by Witness ANAA,[75] the Chamber considers that this issue pertains to Rule 66 (A) (ii) disclosure, and notes that Witness ANAA's statements appear to have mentioned three previous meetings with the Prosecution in two separate statements.[76] The Chamber notes that the Prosecution has not responded to this specific submission, whether or not statements were made from these alleged meetings, and it instructs the Prosecution to clarify its position. If additional statements were taken from Witness ANAA, the Chamber instructs the Prosecution to disclose them within five days.

46. The remaining disclosure issues raised by the Parties following the Chamber's 13 May 2009 Scheduling Order were not considered by the Appeals Chamber and are therefore outside the scope of its Decision. However, since the status and scale of the Prosecution's disclosure are relevant to the determination of the trial date, the Chamber will consider them.

47. With regard to the Defence request for the documents which Witness ANAC stated were used to establish the Report drafted jointly by Witnesses ANAB and ANAC, the Chamber considers that this is a matter for inspection under Rule 66(B), according to which the Defence should request for inspection of the alleged documents from the Prosecution. Moreover, as already noted, Rule 66(B) may not impact as such the scheduling of the Trial.

48. Concerning the identifying information for Witnesses ANAB, ANAC and ANAP, which the Defence claims does not comply with the general requirements regarding identifying data for Prosecution witnesses,[77] the Chamber recalls that Rule 69 (C) only provides for disclosure of the identity of the victim or witness. The Chamber notes that the Prosecution's 15 May 2009 disclosure contains a *curriculum vitae* of Witness ANAP, as well as biographical information on Witnesses ANAB and ANAC: full names, dates and places of birth, previous and current occupations, contact details, organisation membership for Witness ANAC and current occupation, and organisation membership, publications, and interviews for Witness ANAB.[78] The Prosecution's 22 April 2009 disclosure further contains identifying information for all three witnesses, *i.e.* full names **[page 13]** and contact details.[79] The Defence has not substantiated its allegation that this information is insufficient. Accordingly, this submission is denied.

49. With respect to Witness ANAC's alleged reference to the presence of "foreigners" at the Ministry of Planning in his statement, and to the allegation that Witness ANAN's statement contains new allegations, the Chamber considers that these matters are best left for the cross-examination of Witness ANAC.

50. Regarding the Defence submission that it has not received the CD-ROMs disclosed on 15 May 2009 by the Prosecution, the Chamber notes that the Defence has since been given a copy of the CD-ROMs by the Registry.[80]

51. With respect to the exhibits and the exhibit list, the Chamber notes that after the filing of the Reply, and upon the Chamber's instructions of 18 May 2009[81] and 2 June 2009,[82] the Prosecution filed an exhibit list and exhibits in Annex II to its revised Pre-Trial Brief,[83] as well as clarifications,[84] and considers that this issue is now moot.

---

[75] The Defence initially asked for Witnesses ANAA, ANAI and ANAN's statements, the Defence limited its request to Witness ANAA's previous statements in its Reply.
[76] *See* statement dated 12 September 2003, disclosed on 15 May 2009, and statement dated 16 April 2003, disclosed on 13 March 2009, in which the witness says that he has met with the Prosecution before and given "testimonies."
[77] Reply, para. 15 a).
[78] Interoffice Memorandum, "More Disclosure to Ngirabatware, Augustin", 15 May 2009.
[79] Confidential Annex C for Prosecutor's Response to the Defence Objections, Pursuant to Rule 73 *bis*, to the Prosecution's Pre-Trial Brief, 22 April 2009.
[80] *See* Proof of Service signed by Lead Counsel David Thomas, 2 June 2009.
[81] Chamber's Inter-office Memorandum to the Parties, dated 18 May 2009.
[82] Decision on Defence Motion Objection to Prosecution's Pre-Trial Brief, 2 June 2009.
[83] The Prosecutor's Revised Pre-Trial Brief, 25May 2009 with annexes I to III, respectively the List of Intended Prosecution witnesses, the List of Exhibits and Exhibits, the Notice to Admit Facts; *See also* Decision on Defence Motion Objecting to the Prosecution's Pre-Trial Brief, 2 June 2009, para. 29.
[84] Prosecution's Clarifications to Revised Pre-Trial Brief Made Pursuant to Court Order Dated 2 June 2009 and Rule [73 *bis* (B)] of the Rules of Procedure and Evidence, 8 June 2009.

Decision on Trial Date

52. As to the missing French translation of Witness ANAL's statement, the Chamber notes that Witness ANAL's statement was filed in English on 8 May 2009. With respect to the documents disclosed on 15 May 2009 and submitted either in French or in Kinyarwanda, the Chamber notes that the Prosecution indicated that the Kinyarwanda documents are being translated. The Chamber recalls Article 31 of the Statute and Rule 3 (A) of the Rules providing that the working languages of the Tribunal are English and French. Thus, the Chamber considers that the Defence should be able to carry out its investigations on the basis of documents filed in one of the working languages of the Tribunal as it is composed of a bilingual team and that members of its team are also able to understand Kinyarwanda. However, the Chamber urges the Registry to complete translations of the documents requested as soon as possible.

53. Concerning Rule 68 disclosure obligation, the Chamber notes that this obligation is continuous on the part of the Prosecution and may also be triggered when the Defence makes a *prima facie* showing that the Prosecution possesses exculpatory material.[85] The Chamber reminds the Prosecution to continue to fulfil this obligation as and when such documents are discovered.

54. Regarding the Defence submission on the alleged deficiencies in the Prosecution witness list, the Chamber recalls that it rejected this submission as general, and lacking **[page 14]** specificity, in its decision of 2 June 2009.[86] The issue remains unsubstantiated and the submission is rejected.

55. Lastly, with respect to the Defence allegation that the Prosecution added a witness to its proposed witness list without seeking leave to vary its witness list, the Chamber reminds the Defence that Rule 73 *bis* (E) requires the Prosecutor to seek leave to amend its witness list from the Chamber after the start of trial, not before.

56. The Chamber has fully considered the totality of the issues raised in the Parties' submissions, including submissions made before the Impugned Decisions were rendered and before the Appeals Chamber. The Chamber has borne in mind the balance between a fair and speedy trial, and the rights of the accused person to prepare for trial, and considers that none of the reasons advanced by the Defence would justify delaying the start of trial until December 2009, as the Defence requests. The Chamber notes that besides translation issues that should not prevent the conduct of investigations only the disclosure of any additional statements by Witness ANAA, if they exist, and the Defence's newly filed Objections to the Prosecution's Pre-Trial Brief are pending issues. The Chamber does not consider that the current pending pre-trial matters are of such a nature as to delay the start of the case for an additional six months. The Chamber also recalls that in certifying the Decision to appeal, it underscored "that pre-trial matters should continue to be addressed pending the outcome of the appeal in order to have the case ready for trial."[87] The Chamber further notes that, according to the Defence, its investigations started mid-February,[88] almost four months ago, and that the Defence team was fully constituted on 1 June 2009. In addition, the Chamber reminds the Defence that the investigations regarding the Defence case need not be fully completed by the start of trial. Moreover, it will allow for a break not exceeding two months between the Prosecution case and the Defence case, during which the Defence investigations may continue.

57. Taking into account all of the above, the Chamber has considered and determined that the date of 3 August 2009 will afford the Defence objectively adequate time to prepare for the presentation of the Prosecution's case in a manner consistent with the rights of the Accused. Two months and two weeks will have been added to the initial scheduled date of 18 May 2009, and the Defence will have had between five and six months from the start of its investigation to investigate and prepare for trial.[89]

---

[85] *See* Decision on Ngirabatware's Motion for Disclosure Pursuant to Rule 68, 25 March 2009, para. 4.
[86] Decision on Defence Motion Objecting to the Prosecution's Pre-Trial Brief, 2 June 2009, para. 74.
[87] Decision on Defence Motion for Certification to Appeal the Trial Chamber's Decision of 25 March 2009 on Defence Motion to Vary Trial Date, 15 April 2009, para. 21.
[88] Defence Submission, para. 16.
[89] *See* Defence Submission, paras. 16, 17.

FOR THE ABOVE REASONS, THE TRIBUNAL

ORDERS the trial to start on 3 August 2009;

Arusha, 12 June 2009

William H. Sekule	Solomy Balungi Bossa	Mparany Rajohnson
Presiding Judge	Judge	Judge

[Seal of the Tribunal]

Tribunal pénal international pour le Rwanda
International Criminal Tribunal for Rwanda

IN THE APPEALS CHAMBER

Before:	Judge Patrick Robinson, Presiding
	Judge Fausto Pocar
	Judge Liu Daqun
	Judge Theodor Meron
	Judge Iain Bonomy

Registrar:	Mr. Adama Dieng

Date:	19 June 2009

ÉDOUARD KAREMERA
MATTHIEU NGIRUMPATSE
JOSEPH NZIRORERA

v.

THE PROSECUTOR

Case No. ICTR-98-44-AR73.16

DECISION ON APPEAL CONCERNING THE SEVERANCE OF
MATTHIEU NGIRUMPATSE

Counsel for the Appellants:
Ms. Dior Diagne Mbaye and Mr. Félix Sow for Édouard Karemera
Ms. Chantal Hounkpatin and Mr. Frédéric Weyl for Matthieu Ngirumpatse
Mr. Peter Robinson and Mr. Patrick Nimy Mayidika Ngimbi for Joseph Nzirorera

The Office of the Prosecutor:
Mr. Hassan Bubacar Jallow
Mr. Don Webster
Mr. Saidou N'Dow
Mr. Arif Virani
Ms. Sunkarie Ballah-Conteh
Ms. Takeh Sendeze

[page 1] 1. The Appeals Chamber of the International Criminal Tribunal for the Prosecution of Persons Responsible for Genocide and Other Serious Violations of International Humanitarian Law Committed in the Territory of Rwanda and Rwandan Citizens Responsible for Genocide and Other Such Violations Committed in the Territory of Neighbouring States, between 1 January and 31 December 1994 ("Appeals Chamber" and "Tribunal", respectively) is seized of three appeals from Mr. Édouard Karemera, Mr. Matthieu Ngirumpatse, and Mr. Joseph Nzirorera ("Appellants"), filed on 2 April 2009,[1] against the decision of Trial Chamber III to deny a stay of the joint proceedings and to sever Mr. Ngirumpatse from the *Karemera et al.* case.[2] The Prosecution filed a consolidated response on 9 April 2009.[3] Mr. Ngirumpatse and Mr. Nzirorera filed their replies on 11 May 2009.[4] Mr. Karemera did not file a reply.

INTRODUCTION

2. The Appellants have been in detention since 1998, and their trial originally commenced in November 2003.[5] After successfully challenging the composition of the bench, their trial was restarted before the present bench on 19 September 2005.[6] The Prosecution closed its case on 4 December 2007, and Mr. Karemera's defence started on 7 April 2008.[7] Although each Appellant intends to present his own case, they have also, at the Trial Chamber's urging, divided some of the common issues among themselves and intend to call certain mutually beneficial witnesses on key areas.[8]

3. On 18 August 2008, the Trial Chamber learned that Mr. Ngirumpatse was ill and could not attend trial.[9] Accordingly, the Trial Chamber stayed the proceedings. Estimates for his recovery **[page 2]** were initially one week and then one month.[10] Instead of returning to trial, on 8 October 2008, Mr. Ngirumpatse was transferred to Nairobi for further medical tests where he has remained for treatment.[11] Neither the parties nor the Chamber are aware of the full nature of his illness.[12]

4. On 28 October 2008, the Trial Chamber held a status conference. Dr. Épée Hernandez, the Tribunal's Chief Medical Officer, estimated that Mr. Ngirumpatse would need treatment for at least six months, but that she could provide a provisional evaluation of his condition in three months.[13] Mr. Ngirumpatse, through his counsel, indicated that four defence witnesses could be heard in his absence.[14] His counsel further indicated that, if proceedings were stayed until early 2009, Mr. Ngirumpatse would consent to proceedings being continued in his absence provided that adequate facilities were put in place for him to follow the case from his place of treatment.[15] The Trial Chamber made arrangements to provide Mr. Ngirumpatse with the video

---

[1] *Mémoire d'Appel suite à la décision du 3 Mars 2009 relative à la continuation du procès*, 2 April 2009 ("Karemera Appeal"); *Appel de Matthieu Ngirumpatse contre « Decision on Continuation of Trial » du 3 Mars 2009*, 2 April 2009 ("Ngirumpatse Appeal"); Joseph Nzirorera's Appeal from Decision to Sever Case of Mathieu (*sic*) Ngirumpatse, 2 April 2009 ("Nzirorera Appeal").
[2] *The Prosecutor v. Édouard Karemera et al.*, Case No. ICTR-98-44-T, Decision on Continuation of Trial, 3 March 2009 ("Impugned Decision").
[3] Prosecutor's Consolidated Response to "Joseph Nzirorera's Appeal From Decision to Sever Case of Mathieu (*sic*) Ngirumpatse", *"Appel de Matthieu Ngirumpatse contre « Decision on Continuation of Trial » du 3 Mars 2009"* and Édouard Karemera's *"Mémoire d'Appel suite à la décision du 3 Mars 2009 relative à la continuation du procès"*, 9 April 2009 ("Prosecution Response").
[4] *Réplique de Matthieu Ngirumpatse à la réponse consolidée du procureur sur l'appel de la "Decision on Continuation of Trial" due 3 mars 2009*, 11 May 2009 ("Ngirumpatse Reply"); Reply Brief: Joseph Nzierorera's Appeal from Decision to Sever Case of Mathieu (*sic*) Ngirumpatse, 11 May 2009 ("Nzirorera Reply"). Mr. Ngirumpatse also filed an intermediate reply on 23 April 2009 highlighting his intention to reply to the Prosecution Response and his urgent need for a translation. *See Mémoire en réplique intérimaire de M Ngirumpatse sur l'appel de la décision de continuation du procès en date du 3 mars 2009*, 23 April 2009.
[5] Impugned Decision, para. 35.
[6] Impugned Decision, para. 1.
[7] Impugned Decision, para. 1.
[8] Impugned Decision, para. 45.
[9] Impugned Decision, para. 10.
[10] Impugned Decision, para. 10.
[11] Impugned Decision, para. 10.
[12] Impugned Decision, para. 8. The Tribunal's Chief Medical Officer, Dr. Épée Hernandez has provided periodic oral and written updates after consulting with his treating physicians on his general condition and prognosis for recovery. *See* Impugned Decision, paras. 9, 14.
[13] Impugned Decision, para. 11.
[14] Impugned Decision, para. 2.
[15] Impugned Decision, para. 16.

Appeal Concerning the Severance of Ngirumpatse

recordings and written material connected with the proceedings.[16] After hearing these witnesses, the proceedings were adjourned until February 2009.[17]

5. On 9 February 2009, Dr. Hernandez provisionally noted that Mr. Ngirumpatse's condition had improved "remarkably", but that a comprehensive report would only be available in three months.[18] This encouraging assessment – coupled with complaints about the timely receipt of trial related materials and his access to counsel – prompted Mr. Ngirumpatse to withdraw his consent to be tried in his absence.[19] Joined by his co-accused, Mr. Ngirumpatse sought a three-month stay of proceedings to allow for his condition to improve and for a full assessment of his prognosis.[20]

6. This request was opposed by the Prosecution, which filed a competing motion to sever Mr. Ngirumpatse on 10 February 2009.[21] A subsequent assessment by Dr. Hernandez provided less encouraging information about Mr. Ngirumpatse's prospects for a quick return to trial. She **[page 3]** explained at a status conference on 16 February 2009 and in a report filed on 27 February 2009 that Mr. Ngirumpatse would not be fit to attend trial for at least nine months and that he was not responding to treatment.[22] She added that his attending physicians decided to continue his treatment for a further six months, which she had previously noted weakened Mr. Ngirumpatse and impacted his ability to concentrate for more than two hours a day.[23]

7. On 3 March 2009, the Trial Chamber denied the request to stay the joint proceedings and granted the Prosecution motion to sever Mr. Ngirumpatse from the case.[24] It further ordered the trial of Mr. Karemera and Mr. Nzirorera to resume on 23 March 2009 with the hearing of Mr. Karemera's next witness.[25] Finally, the Trial Chamber granted certification to appeal the entirety of its decision.[26] After Mr. Ngirumpatse waived his right to be present while the appeal was pending, the Trial Chamber stayed the execution of the severance order and continued the presentation of the defence case of Mr. Karemera pending the outcome of the appeal.[27]

8. In denying the Appellants' requests to stay the proceedings, the Trial Chamber reasoned that any further delay in the proceedings would constitute a violation of Mr. Karemera's and Mr. Nzirorera's right to be tried without undue delay, in particular in view of their already lengthy pre-trial detention, the advanced stage of the proceedings, and the fact that the "defence cases are prepared to proceed imminently and expected to finish within the year".[28] The Trial Chamber further pointed to several difficulties which had already resulted from the suspension of the proceedings. For example, some of Mr. Karemera's witnesses were brought to Arusha several times without being able to testify or doing so only after a considerable delay.[29]

9. The Trial Chamber further determined that "the prejudice sustained by Édouard Karemera and Joseph Nzirorera from the further delay, if the proceedings were to be stayed until Ngirumpatse might become fit to attend trial again, constitutes a conflict of interest" and primarily for that reason severed Mr. Ngirumpatse

---

[16] Impugned Decision, para. 18.
[17] Impugned Decision, para. 3.
[18] Impugned Decision, para. 13. *See also* T. 9 February 2009 p. 17 ("[Mr. Ngirumpatse's] clinical state of health is improving remarkably. His medication will continue for three more months, when we will be able to provide a more comprehensive report."). At the status conference of 16 February 2009, Dr. Hernandez suggested that she did not say this and instead only indicated that his condition had stabilized. *See* T. 16 February 2009 pp. 17, 18.
[19] Impugned Decision, para. 20. *See also* T. 9 February 2009 pp. 22-25, 27, 28; Ngirumpatse Appeal, paras. 22-30; Ngirumpatse Reply, para. 46.
[20] Impugned Decision, paras. 6, 20. *See also* T. 9 February 2009 pp. 25, 27, 28; Ngirumpatse Appeal, paras. 29, 30.
[21] Impugned Decision, paras. 5, 22.
[22] Impugned Decision, paras. 14, 15.
[23] Impugned Decision, paras. 11, 15, 19.
[24] Impugned Decision, p. 16.
[25] Impugned Decision, p. 16.
[26] Impugned Decision, para. 61. On 12 March 2009, the Trial Chamber clarified that its decision granted certification to all parties. *See also The Prosecutor v. Édouard Karemera et al.*, Case Nos. ICTR-98-44-T and ICTR-98-44E-T, Decision on Urgent Request for Precision or Alternatively Correction of the Decision of 3 March 2009 on Continuation of Trial, 12 March 2009, para. 3.
[27] T. 23 March 2009 p. 23.
[28] Impugned Decision, para. 38.
[29] Impugned Decision, para. 37.

from the case.[30] The Trial Chamber rejected claims that the accused would suffer prejudice from the severance. In particular, it noted that there was no evidence that [page 4] witnesses for one accused would not also appear for the others.[31] The Trial Chamber further emphasized that the assessment of Mr. Ngirumpatse's condition suggested that he may not be fit to attend trial for at least another nine months.[32] It determined therefore that his severance was "the least intrusive solution", bearing in mind "the right of each accused to a fair trial and to be tried without undue delay, as well as the similar interests of victims and the international community that trials concerning serious crimes be completed without unnecessary delays".[33] As a secondary concern, it held that Mr. Ngirumpatse's severance served judicial economy and thus was in the interests of justice.[34]

SUBMISSIONS OF THE PARTIES

10. Several main themes emerge in the Appellants' submissions challenging the Impugned Decision. The Appellants submit that the Trial Chamber relied on incorrect, inconsistent, or inadequate information, in particular related to Mr. Ngirumpatse's health and prognosis for recovery, when assessing the possible prejudice resulting from a further stay of proceedings.[35] The Appellants challenge the Trial Chamber's reliance on the Tribunal's Chief Medical Officer's assessment as well as the Trial Chamber's refusal to allow an independent medical expert to assess Mr. Ngirumpatse's condition.[36] Mr. Nzirorera claims that the Chief Medical Officer provided inconsistent reports to the Trial Chamber, first offering a positive prognosis on 9 February 2009, when it appeared that Mr. Ngirumpatse would continue to waive his right to be present, followed by a more pessimistic outlook after he requested a stay of proceedings.[37] Finally, Mr. Nzirorera submits that, in relying solely on information provided by the Chief Medical Officer, the Trial Chamber deviated from the practice at the Tribunal and the International Criminal Tribunal for the former Yugoslavia ("ICTY") in similar matters.[38]

11. Mr. Ngirumpatse also contests the Trial Chamber's characterization of his ability to follow and participate in trial proceedings through counsel while receiving treatment.[39] He emphasizes that [page 5] his mental faculties remain intact, and thus he disputes the Trial Chamber's conclusion that they are insufficient to allow the trial to proceed expeditiously.[40] In this respect, he highlights that he receives regular reports from his counsel who are capable of defending his interests and discerning the limits of their representation without seeking his opinion.[41] Mr. Ngirumpatse further challenges the Trial Chamber's statement in the Impugned Decision that his counsel stated that, since 3 November 2008, he could no longer read,[42] whereas, he submits, his counsel simply highlighted that he no longer regularly received documents related to his case.[43]

12. The Appellants further contend that the Trial Chamber erred in concluding that a stay would unduly delay the proceedings concerning Mr. Karemera and Mr. Nzirorera, which necessitated the severance of Mr. Ngirumpatse.[44] They submit that the Trial Chamber erred in finding a conflict of interest among them and

---

[30] Impugned Decision, paras. 43, 54.
[31] Impugned Decision, para. 53.
[32] Impugned Decision, para. 54.
[33] Impugned Decision, para. 54.
[34] Impugned Decision, para. 54.
[35] Ngirumpatse Appeal, paras. 76-81; Ngirumpatse Reply, paras. 43-49; Karemera Appeal, paras. 9-20, 48-53; Nzirorera Appeal, paras. 41-77; Nzirorera Reply, paras. 4, 6-15.
[36] Ngirumpatse Appeal, paras. 36, 76-81; Karemera Appeal, paras. 48-53; Nzirorera Appeal, paras. 41-77; Nzirorera Reply, paras. 4, 6-15.
[37] Nzirorera Appeal, paras. 68; Nzirorera Reply, paras. 9, 10. Furthermore, Mr. Nzirorera submits that the Chief Medical Officer's report of 27 February 2009, which suggests that Mr. Ngirumpatse was not responding to treatment, is contradicted by laboratory results submitted by Mr. Ngirumpatse reflecting "a decrease in bad cells from 35% to 5%". Nzirorera Appeal, para. 69. *See also* Nzirorera Reply, para. 10.
[38] Nzirorera Appeal, paras. 71-76; Nzirorera Reply, paras. 8, 13.
[39] Ngirumpatse Appeal, paras. 77-80.
[40] Ngirumpatse Appeal, paras. 77, 78.
[41] Ngirumpatse Appeal, para. 79.
[42] Ngirumpatse Appeal, para. 80.
[43] Ngirumpatse Appeal, para. 80.
[44] Ngirumpatse Appeal, paras. 53-75; Karemera Appeal, paras. 36-40; Nzirorera Appeal, paras. 84-90.

that severance served judicial economy.[45] They note that Mr. Karemera and Mr. Nzirorera supported the stay of proceedings and waived their right to trial without undue delay insofar as it involved delay arising from Mr. Ngirumpatse's medical condition.[46]

13. Finally, the Appellants argue that the Trial Chamber failed to properly consider the prejudice to their cases that would result from the severance, notably in view of the joint nature of their defence strategy.[47] They highlight the potential harm they will suffer from the severance by noting that some of the witnesses they intend to call may not be willing to testify in cases of the other Appellants.[48]

14. The Prosecution responds that the Trial Chamber did not err in refusing a further stay of the proceedings and ordering the severance of Mr. Ngirumpatse.[49] The Prosecution acknowledges that the Trial Chamber did not rely on the extent of medical expertise comparable to that procured by Chambers in the ICTY.[50] However, according to the Prosecution, the Trial Chamber had an adequate basis for assessing Mr. Ngirumpatse's medical prognosis and fitness for trial as it relied on **[page 6]** regular updates from three medical professionals charged with treating him, which were conveyed through the Chief Medical Officer.[51]

15. The Prosecution further submits that the Trial Chamber properly held that the fair trial rights of the Appellants favored severance.[52] In particular, it submits that, given Mr. Ngirumpatse's condition and unwillingness to waive his right to be present, severance was the only option.[53] With respect to Mr. Nzirorera and Mr. Karemera, the Prosecution emphasizes that the Trial Chamber granted them leave to expand their witness lists to take account of the loss of Mr. Ngirumpatse's witnesses.[54] It also describes as speculation their inability to obtain the attendance of witnesses.[55] Finally, it argues that ensuring that their trials are expedient is consistent with their fair trial rights.[56] It further submits that the Trial Chamber properly considered judicial economy and the public interests of victims and the international community in expedient trials as a secondary consideration.[57] In this respect, the Trial Chamber's "decision to trump the waiver of the two co-accused was symbolic of the inherent jurisdiction of the Chamber to control its own process and ensure the promotion of the public interest and the protection of fair trial rights".[58]

DISCUSSION

16. Decisions related to the general conduct of trial are matters within the discretion of the Trial Chamber.[59] The Appeals Chamber will only overturn a Trial Chamber's discretionary decision where it is found to be: (i) based on an incorrect interpretation of governing law; (ii) based on a patently incorrect conclusion of fact; or (iii) so unfair or unreasonable as to constitute an abuse of the Trial Chamber's discretion.[60]

---

[45] Ngirumpatse Appeal, paras. 53-75, 82-95; Karemera Appeal, paras. 30-47; Nzirorera Appeal, paras. 84-106; Nzirorera Reply, paras. 22-31.
[46] Ngirumpatse Appeal, para. 60; Karemera Appeal, para. 39; Nzirorera Appeal, paras. 85-88.
[47] Ngirumpatse Appeal, paras. 82-95; Ngirumpatse Reply, paras. 25-42; Karemera Appeal, paras. 30-35, 41-47; Nzirorera Appeal, paras. 91-106; Nzirorera Reply, paras. 19-21.
[48] Ngirumpatse Appeal, paras. 86, 87; Karemera Appeal, para. 24; Nzirorera Appeal, paras. 91-102.
[49] Prosecution Response, para. 2.
[50] Prosecution Response, para. 46.
[51] Prosecution Response, paras. 3, 43-48.
[52] Prosecution Response, paras. 23-30.
[53] Prosecution Response, para. 24.
[54] Prosecution Response, para. 25.
[55] Prosecution Response, para. 29.
[56] Prosecution Response, para. 30.
[57] Prosecution Response, paras. 17-22, 31-35.
[58] Prosecution Response, para. 40.
[59] Decision on Nzirorera's Interlocutory Appeal Concerning His Right to Be Present at Trial, 5 October 2007, para. 7; *Prosecutor v. Jovica Stanišić and Franko Simatović*, Case No. IT-03-69-AR73.2, Decision on Defence Appeal of the Decision on Future Course of Proceedings, 16 May 2008, para. 4 ("*Stanišić and Simatović* Appeal Decision"); *Prosecutor v. Zdravko Tolimir et al.*, Case No. IT-04-80-AR73.1, Decision on Radivoje Miletić's Interlocutory Appeal Against the Trial Chamber's Decision on Joinder of Accused, 27 January 2006, para. 5 ("*Tolimir et al.* Appeal Decision").
[60] *See, e.g.*, Decision on Matthieu Ngirumpatse's Appeal from the Trial Chamber Decision of 17 September 2008, 30 January 2009, para. 18; Decision on Interlocutory Appeal Regarding Witness Proofing, 11 May 2007, para. 3. *See also Stanišić and Simatović* Appeal Decision, para. 5; *Tolimir et al.* Appeal Decision, para. 6.

17. The state of Mr. Ngirumpatse's health and his prognosis for recovery lie at the core of the Trial Chamber's decision to deny the request for a further stay of proceedings and instead to sever **[page 7]** him from the case. In refusing to order a further stay, the Trial Chamber dismissed as "highly speculative" Mr. Ngirumpatse's claim that his health might sufficiently improve within three months to allow him to more actively participate in his defence from his hospital bed.[61] In this respect, it pointed to the Chief Medical Officer's assessment that Mr. Ngirumpatse required six more months of treatment, which impaired his ability to concentrate; that he has so far not responded to the treatment; and that he would not be fit to attend trial for at least nine months.[62] The Trial Chamber considered that the impact on the proceedings resulting from such a scenario, coupled with the earlier delay, would result in serious prejudice to Mr. Karemera and Mr. Ngirumpatse.[63]

18. Rule 82(B) of the Rules provides that a "Trial Chamber may order that persons accused jointly under Rule 48 be tried separately if it considers it necessary in order to avoid a conflict of interests that might cause serious prejudice to an accused, or to protect the interests of justice." In severing Mr. Ngirumpatse, the Trial Chamber concluded principally that there was a conflict of interests among the Appellants as a result of the prejudice Mr. Karemera and Mr. Nzirorera would suffer if the proceedings were stayed until Mr. Ngirumpatse became fit to attend trial.[64] The Trial Chamber noted that, "according to the doctor's assessment", Mr. Ngirumpatse "will, in the best case, not be fit to attend trial before nine months."[65] The Trial Chamber also considered the interests of justice, namely, the interests of the victims and the international community that trials concerning serious crimes be completed without unnecessary delays.[66] It also noted that severance "significantly serves judicial economy".[67]

19. The Appeals Chamber notes that, in practice, Trial Chambers generally consider various professional opinions before taking an important procedural decision arising from an accused's medical condition which may impact the course of a trial.[68] In this respect, Rule 74*bis* of the **[page 8]** Tribunal's Rules of Procedure and Evidence ("Rules") expressly provides that "a Trial Chamber may, *proprio motu* or at the request of a party, order a medical [...] examination of the accused."

20. In the present case, the Trial Chamber relied exclusively on the assessment of the Tribunal's Chief Medical Officer.[69] As a preliminary matter, the Appeals Chamber finds no merit in Mr. Nzirorera's submission that the Trial Chamber erred in not requiring the Chief Medical Officer to take the oath prescribed for witnesses in Rule 90(B) of the Rules.[70] The Chief Medical Officer did not appear as a witness, rather, her

---

[61] Impugned Decision, paras. 25, 26.
[62] Impugned Decision, paras. 26, 27.
[63] Impugned Decision, paras. 38, 54.
[64] Impugned Decision, para. 43.
[65] Impugned Decision, para. 54.
[66] Impugned Decision, para. 54.
[67] Impugned Decision, para. 54.
[68] *See, e.g., Prosecutor v. Jovica Stanišić and Franko Simatović*, Case No. IT-03-69-PT, Decision on Prosecution Motion for Re-Assessment of Jovica Stanišić's Health and Re-Commencement of Trial and Decision on Prosecution Motion to Order Further Medical Reports on Jovica Stanišić's Health, 17 December 2008, para. 6 ("*Stanišić and Simatović* Trial Decision")(in assessing whether to further adjourn proceedings based on the chronic health problems of Jovica Stanišić, the Trial Chamber considered at least 11 medical reports from numerous experts); *The Prosecutor v. Théoneste Bagosora et al.*, Case No. ICTR-98-41-T, Decision on Nsengiyumva's Motions to Call Doctors and to Recall Eight Witnesses, 19 April 2007, paras. 4-6, 13 (considering several detailed medical reports on the Accused's fitness to stand trial submitted by the Tribunal's Chief Medical Officer, surgical consultants, and the Accused's personal physician); *Slobodan Milosević v. Prosecutor*, Case No. IT-02-AR73.7, Decision on Interlocutory Appeal of the Trial Chamber's Decision on the Assignment of Defence Counsel, 1 November 2004, para. 6 (in assigning Slobodan Milosević court appointed counsel based on "mounting health problems", the Trial Chamber ordered two separate medical examinations by his treating physician and an independent cardiologist with no prior involvement in the case); *Prosecutor v. Radoslav Brđanin and Momir Talić*, Case No. IT-99-36-T, Decision on Prosecution's Oral Request for the Separation of Trials, 20 September 2002, paras. 5-10 (in severing Momir Talić based on health consideration, the Trial Chamber considered reports from the Medical Officer at the detention unit, which it confirmed after appointing two medical experts and holding an evidentiary hearing).
[69] Impugned Decision, para. 23. The Trial Chamber noted that the Chief Medical Officer's assessment was made "in consultation and agreement" with Mr. Ngirumpatse's treating physicians. The Trial Chamber did not consult directly with the attending doctors.
[70] Nzirorera Appeal, paras. 41-49.

assessment, like other information submitted by the witness protection or defence counsel management section, is akin to a submission under Rule 33(B) of the Rules.

21. A review of the Chief Medical Officer's various assessments from when Mr. Ngirumpatse first became unable to attend trial in August 2008 reveals a significant fluctuation and uncertainty in his prospects for recovery.[71] Moreover, in February 2009, the Chief Medical Officer emphasized the provisional nature of her assessment and the need for additional time for making a comprehensive prognosis.[72] While the Trial Chamber dismissed as speculative Mr. Ngirumpatse's suggestion in February 2009 that he could be in a position to attend trial or at least more effectively participate in the proceedings from his hospital bed in three months,[73] the Trial Chamber also described as "speculative" the Chief Medical Officer's projection that he might only be fit to attend trial in nine months.[74] **[page 9]**

22. It is appropriate to take proper account of an assessment made by the Chief Medical Officer and, in some cases, to rely exclusively on it. However, the Appeals Chamber considers that particular care is warranted where, as here, the assessment is provisional and lacking in detail, is disputed by the parties, and plays a significant role in the Trial Chamber's assessment of prejudice. The Appeals Chamber also observes that the Trial Chamber had no specific information concerning the nature of Mr. Ngirumpatse's medical problem. While a Trial Chamber may adopt reasonable measures to protect the privacy interests of an accused, these measures cannot serve to deprive it of information essential to reaching an informed decision. In view of the foregoing, the Appeals Chamber finds that, in this instance, the Trial Chamber reached its conclusions on prejudice without having assessed all relevant factors. It therefore committed a discernible error in the exercise of its discretion. Accordingly, the Appeals Chamber need not consider the other arguments on appeal.

23. In their replies, Mr. Ngirumpatse and Mr. Nzirorera also point to the significant improvement in Mr. Ngirumpatse's condition since the Impugned Decision was taken. In particular, Mr. Nzirorera refers to a report submitted by the Registry indicating that Mr. Ngirumpatse is scheduled to return to Arusha where he may soon be able to attend trial.[75] The Appeals Chamber has not taken this into account in assessing the nature of the information available to the Trial Chamber at the time of the Impugned Decision. Any developments subsequent to the Impugned Decision should be first properly considered by the Trial Chamber.

24. The three-month period which the Chief Medical Officer indicated would be necessary before a more comprehensive report could be filed has elapsed. Consequently, the Appeals Chamber considers it particularly appropriate to remand this matter back to the Trial Chamber for further evaluation based on the present circumstances of Mr. Ngirumpatse's condition.

DISPOSITION

25. For the foregoing reasons, the Appeals Chamber **REVERSES** the Impugned Decision and **REMANDS** the matter to the Trial Chamber for further consideration consistent with this opinion.

---

[71] Impugned Decision, para. 10 ("On 18 August 2008, the Chamber was informed that Matthieu Ngirumpatse [...] would not be fit to attend trial for one week [...] On 25 August, Dr. Épée Hernandez reported that Ngirumpatse would not be fit for a minimum of one more month."); T. 9 February 2009 p. 17 ("Dr. Épée Hernandez: [...] [Mr. Ngirumpatse's] clinical state of health is improving remarkably."); T. 16 February 2009 p. 9 ("Given the current state of Mr. Ngirumpatse, clinically and biologically, he is not in a position to be present within three months, six months and even in nine months. And that is still hypothetical.").

[72] Impugned Decision, para. 11. *See also* T. 9 February 2009 p. 17 ("His medication will continue for three more months, when we will be able to provide a more comprehensive report [...] after three months we would be able to make a report that will be more reflective of the reality. We are in an intermediary phase at this point in time, and we cannot come up with any specific conclusion. [...] I said that the initial treatment was for a period of six months. It's still six months. We are in an intermediary period that after three months we can say something. But last time I said it would take six months.").

[73] Impugned Decision, para. 26.

[74] Impugned Decision, para. 14.

[75] *See* Ngirumpatse Reply, para. 7; Nzirorera Reply, para 11 (citing *Observations supplémentaire du greffier, en vertu de l'article 33(B) du règlement de procédure et de preuve a la suite de dépôt du rapport du médecin chef du TPIR en date du 27 Avril 2009*, 4 May 2009).

Done in English and French, the English version being authoritative.

Done this 19th day of June 2009,

At The Hague,
The Netherlands.

Judge Patrick Robinson **[page 10]**
Presiding

[Seal of the Tribunal]

International Criminal Tribunal for Rwanda
Tribunal pénal international pour le Rwanda

OR: ENG

TRIAL CHAMBER III

Before Judges:	Dennis C. M. Byron, Presiding
	Gberdao Gustave Kam
	Vagn Joensen
Registrar:	Adama Dieng
Date:	23 June 2009

THE PROSECUTOR

v.

Édouard KAREMERA
Matthieu NGIRUMPATSE
Joseph NZIRORERA

Case No. ICTR-98-44-T

DECISION ON ÉDOUARD KAREMERA'S MOTION RELATING TO HIS RIGHT TO BE TRIED WITHOUT UNDUE DELAY
Article 21(4)(d) of the Statute

Office of the Prosecution:	**Defence Counsel for Édouard Karemera**
Don Webster	Dior Diagne Mbaye and Félix Sow
Saidou N'Dow	
Arif Virani	**Defence Counsel for Matthieu Ngirumpatse**
Sunkarie Ballah-Conteh	Chantal Hounkpatin and Frédéric Weyl
Takeh Sendze	
	Defence Counsel for Joseph Nzirorera
	Peter Robinson and Patrick Nimy Mayidika Ngimbi

[page 2] INTRODUCTION

1. In its Decision on Continuation of Trial of 3 March 2009, the Trial Chamber held that "the delay in the proceedings, to this point, has become such that the rights of the accused to be tried without undue delay have been violated."[1] In a motion filed on 18 May 2009, Édouard Karemera moves the Trial Chamber to remedy the violation of his right to be tried without undue delay by revoking the Indictment against him, bringing an immediate end to the proceedings in his case and ordering his immediate release.[2] The Prosecution opposes Karemera's Motion.[3]

DELIBERATIONS

2. Article 21(4)(d) of the Statute of the International Tribunal, reflecting international human rights standards,[4] provides for the right to be tried without undue delay. This was specified by the Appeals Chamber in the *Kvočka et al.* case: "The right to an expeditious trial is an inseparable and constituent element of the right to a fair trial."[5]

3. Édouard Karemera interprets the Chamber's holding regarding his right to be tried without undue delay as referring to the six-year period since the start of his first trial in 2003.[6] However, as is clear from the Decision on Continuation of Trial, the delay to which the Chamber was referring in its holding actually ran from August 2008, when Ngirumpaste became ill, to March 2009, when Ngirumpaste was severed from the trial.[7] Accordingly, the [page 3] question before the Chamber is whether the relief sought by Karemera is an appropriate remedy for the violation of his right to be tried without undue delay over a period of eight months as a result of the inability of one of his co-Accused to participate in the trial due to illness.

4. The Appeals Chamber has held that "any violation, even if it entails a relative degree of prejudice, requires a proportionate remedy."[8] A remedy for a human rights violation is to be granted on a case-by-case basis, taking into account the subject matter as well as the nature of the right allegedly violated.[9] In particular, the nature and form of the remedy should be proportional to the gravity of harm that is suffered.[10]

5. Édouard Karemera submits that the appropriate remedy in the present case is the withdrawal of the Indictment against him, the termination of the proceedings in his case and his immediate release.[11]

---

[1] *The Prosecutor v. Édouard Karemera, Mathieu Ngirumpatse, Joseph Nzirorera*, Case No. ICTR-98-44-T ("*Karemera et al.*"), Decision on Continuation of Trial, 3 March 2009, para. 38 ("*Karemera* Decision on Continuation"). The Chamber notes that while the remedy of severance ordered by the Chamber in this decision has been overturned on appeal, the Appeals Chamber's findings do not affect the particular ruling at issue in this decision: *Karemera et al.*, Decision on Appeal concerning the Severance of Matthieu Ngirumpatse, 19 June 2009.

[2] Requête relative à la violation du droit à être jugé sans retard excessif, filed on 18 May 2009 ("Karemera's Motion").

[3] Prosecutor's Response to Édouard Karemera's "Requête relative à la violation du droit à être jugé sans retard excessif," filed on 25 May 2009 ("Prosecutor's Response").

[4] See, *e.g.*, Article 14(3)(c) of the International Covenant on Civil and Political Rights of 16 December 1966, 999 U.N.T.S. 171; Article 6(1) of the European Convention for the Protection of Human Rights and Fundamental Freedoms of 4 November 1950, CETS 005.

[5] *The Prosecutor v. Miroslav Kvočka et al.*, Case No. IT-98-30/1-AR73.5, Decision on Interlocutory Appeal by the Accused Zoran Žigić Against the Decision of Trial Chamber I Dated 5 December 2000, 25 May 2001, para. 20.

[6] *Ibid.*, paras 6-10, referring to The *Prosecutor v. Jean Bosco Barayagwiza*, Case No. ICTR-97-19-AR72, Decision, 3 November 1999 ("*Barayagwiza* Decision").

[7] *Karemera* Decision on Continuation, para. 38. The full paragraph reads as follows: "In short, the case of one accused has been brought to a halt mid-way through and the others are at a standstill. Such a situation must be assessed in light of the presumption of innocence. The Chamber finds that, given how far the trial has proceeded, and that the defence cases are prepared to proceed imminently and expected to finish within the year, it has become seriously prejudicial to simply let the accused sit in detention while Matthieu Ngirumpatse's health problems are addressed. In the circumstances, the Chamber finds that the delay in the proceedings, to this point, has become such that the rights of the accused to be tried without undue delay have been violated."

[8] *Laurent Semanza v. The Prosecutor*, Case No. ICTR-97-20-A, Decision, 31 May 2000, para. 125 ("*Semanza* Appeal Decision").

[9] *The Prosecutor v. André Rwamakuba.*, Case No. ICTR-98-44-T ("*Rwamakuba*"), Decision on Appropriate Remedy, 31 January 2007, para. 68 ("*Rwamakuba* Decision on Remedy").

[10] *Rwamakuba*, Decision on Appeal against Decision on Appropriate Remedy, 13 September 2007, para. 27 ("*Rwamakuba* Appeal Decision on Remedy"); *Semanza* Appeal Decision, para. 125.

[11] Karemera's Motion.

6. In the jurisprudence of the *ad hoc* tribunals, the remedy of the termination in the proceedings has been found to be an extraordinary remedy applicable in exceptional circumstances. The Appeals Chamber has held that while a Trial Chamber may use its discretion, in light of the circumstances of a case, to decline to exercise jurisdiction, it should only do so "where to exercise that jurisdiction in light of serious and egregious violations of the accused's rights would prove detrimental to the court's integrity."[12] The Appeals Chamber has held such circumstances to include those "where an accused is very seriously mistreated, maybe even subject to inhuman, cruel or degrading treatment, or torture, before being handed over to the Tribunal, this may constitute a legal impediment."[13] Outside of such exceptional circumstances, the Appeals Chamber has held that the remedy of the termination of the proceedings would "be disproportionate."[14]
[page 4]

7. The remedy of the termination of the proceedings is also an exceptional remedy in other international jurisdictions. In the *Lubanga* case, at the International Criminal Court, the Appeals Chamber described the threshold for the imposition of a stay in the proceedings as follows:

> Where the breaches of the rights of the accused are such as to make it impossible for him/her to make his/her defence within the framework of his rights, no fair trial can take place and the proceedings can be stayed. [...] Unfairness in the treatment of the suspect or the accused may rupture the process to an extent making it impossible to piece together the constituent elements of a fair trial. In those circumstances, the interest of the world community to put persons accused of the most heinous crimes against humanity on trial, great as it is, is outweighed by the need to sustain the efficacy of the judicial process as a potent agent of justice.[15]

The threshold for the application of the remedy of the termination of the proceedings is similarly elevated in the decisions of the Human Rights Committee[16] and the European Court of Human Rights,[17] where it has only been ordered in cases involving egregious violations, such as a 13 year delay in the delivery of a written appeals court decision.[18]

8. In the present case, while the Chamber gives due weight to the violation of Édouard Karemera's right to be tried without undue delay, it does not find that this violation rises to a level of egregiousness justifying the exceptional remedy of the withdrawal of the indictment, the termination of the proceedings and his immediate release.

9. First, Édouard Karemera's case does not fall within the exceptional category of cases where the termination of the proceedings is warranted. Karemera relies on the Appeals Chamber's decision of November 1999 in which it ordered the immediate release of Jean-Bosco Barayagwiza.[19] In *Barayagwiza*, the Appeals Chamber found that a number of the **[page 5]** accused's human rights had been violated and that

---

[12] *Barayagwiza*, Decision, para. 74.
[13] *The Prosecutor v. Dragan Nikolić*, Case No. T-94-2-PT ("*Nikolić*"), Decision on Defence Motion Challenging the Exercise of Jurisdiction by the Tribunal, para. 114; *Nikolić*, Decision on Interlocutory Appeal Concerning Legality of Arrest, paras. 28, 30; *The Prosecutor v. Juvénal Kajelijeli*, Case No. IT98-44A, Appeal Judgement, 23 May 2005, para. 206.
[14] *Nikolić*, Decision on Interlocutory Appeal Concerning Legality of Arrest, para. 30; *Kajelijeli* Appeal Judgement, para. 206
[15] *The Prosecutor v. Thomas Lubanga Dyilo*, ICC-01/04-01/06-772, Judgement on the Appeal of Mr. Thomas Lubanga Dyilo against the Decision on the Defence Challenge to the Jurisdiction of the Court pursuant to article 19 (2) (a) of the Statute of 3 October 2006, 14 December 2006, para. 39.
[16] See, *e.g.*, *Currie v. Jamaica*, CCPR/C/50/D/377/1989 (31 March 1994) (granting release to a defendant unable to appeal death sentence to Constitutional Court of Jamaica due to lower appeals court's failure to issue written opinion 13 years after judgment); *Pratt and Morgan v. Jamaica*, CCPR 210/1986 and 225/1987 (6 April 1989) *Pratt and Morgan v. Jamaica*, CCPR 210/1986 and 225/1987 (6 April 1989) (commuting the sentence of two death row inmates on account of a 3 year, 9 month delay in the delivery of a written appeal decision and an Art. 7 violation in not informing defendants of a stay of execution granted the day before until 45 minutes prior to the scheduled execution).
[17] See, *e.g.*, *Majaric v. Slovenia*, ECHR Application no. 28400/95 (8 February 2000) (finding a delay of 4 years, 5 months to be a violation and imputing it to the domestic court and the government's failure to properly organize the court system, but granting a remedy of only 300,000 Slovenian Tolars*); Krejcír v. the Czech Republic*, ECHR Application no. 39298/04, 8723/05 (26 March 2009) (finding a violation of Arts 5(3) and 5(4), but holding that the finding of the violation constituted just satisfaction); *Yankov v. Bulgaria*, ECHR Application no. 39084/97 (11 December 2003) (finding a violation of Arts. 3, 5(3), 5(4), 5(5), 6(1), 10 and 13, and awarding a total of 12,000 Euros); *Eckle v. German*, Application no. 8130/78 (15 July 1982) (finding a delay of 17 years to be a violation of Art. 6(1), but a finding of violation was considered just satisfaction in addition to sentence mitigation).
[18] See *Currie v. Jamaica*, CCPR/C/50/D/377/1989 (31 March 1994).
[19] Karemera's Motion, para. 6.

this was the result of the Prosecutor's negligent and egregious failure to prosecute his case.[20] The Appeals Chamber thus found that "to proceed with Barayagwiza's trial when such violations have been committed, would cause irreparable damage to the integrity of the judicial process" and that an immediate release was "the only effective remedy for the cumulative breaches of the accused's rights."[21] On the other hand, the delay in Karemera's proceedings was the result of the illness of a co-Accused, not of prosecutorial misconduct, and it was not accompanied by other violations of Karemera's rights. As such, the facts in the *Barayagwiza* decision are clearly distinguishable from those in Karemera's case and his reliance on the *Barayagwiza* decision is misplaced.

10. Second, the Chamber finds that the prejudice suffered by Édouard Karemera as a result of the violation of his right to be tried without undue delay is not so material as to warrant the termination of the proceedings against him. The Chamber notes that it has sought to expedite the proceedings in a number of ways and thus minimize the difficulties caused by the stay in the proceedings, including by severing Matthieu Ngirumpatse's case from Karemera's[22] (a decision which Karemera has successfully appealed),[23] limiting the number of witnesses and court time to what is necessary for the fair and proper conduct of the proceedings,[24] changing the order of appearance of witnesses to save time,[25] and proactively dealing with delays caused by translation issues.[26] In addition, the Chamber also notes that Karemera himself has in previous submissions before the Chamber as well as in submissions before the Appeals Chamber denied suffering any prejudice and has in fact consented to further delays in his case.[27] **[page 6]**

11. Third, the Chamber recalls that the Appeals Chamber has held that the *ad hoc* tribunals must maintain the correct balance between "the fundamental rights of the accused and the essential interests of the international community in the prosecution of persons charged with serious violations of international humanitarian law."[28] In the circumstances of this case, including the nature and extent of the violation of Édouard Karemera's right to be tried without undue delay and the advanced stage of the proceedings, the Chamber finds that it is in the interests of justice for his trial to continue.

12. The Prosecution argues that the Chamber has already provided Édouard Karemera with a remedy for the violation of his right to a trial without undue delay by severing Mathieu Ngirumpatse from this trial.[29] To the extent that the Chamber's order of severance has been reversed, this argument is now moot.[30] The Chamber nonetheless points out that while severance is indeed a measure that can avoid further prejudicing an accused's right to be tried without undue delay,[31] it cannot retroactively provide a remedy for the past violation of this right. As such, regardless of whether the Chamber decides to once again sever Ngirumpatse from this trial, it will remain open to Karemera to invoke, at the close of this case, the issue of the violation of his right to be tried without undue delay between August 2008 and March 2009 as a result of delays caused by Ngirumpatse's illness in order to seek an appropriate remedy.

---

[20] *Barayagwiza* Decision, paras 106. See also *ibid.*, para. 109. The Appeals Chamber found that Barayagwiza's rights to challenge the legality of his detention, to be promptly charged, to be informed of the charges against him, to an initial appearance without delay and to be tried without undue delay had been violated.

[21] *Ibid.*, para. 108. The Appeals Chamber's decision of March 2000, in which it reconsidered its earlier decision, also makes it clear that the remedies of the dismissal of charges and the immediate release of the accused were remedies that were justified by the "role played by the failings of the Prosecutor as well as the intensity of the violation of the rights of the Appellant.": *Barayagwiza*, Decision (Prosecutor's Request for Review or Reconsideration), 31 March 2000, para. 71.

[22] *Karemera et al.*, Decision on Continuation of Trial, 3 March 2009.

[23] *Karemera et al.*, Decision on Appeal concerning the Severance of Matthieu Ngirumpatse, 19 June 2009.

[24] See, *e.g.*, *Karemera et al.*, Order to Joseph Nzirorera to Reduce his Witness List, 24 October 2008.

[25] See, *e.g.*, *Karemera et al.*, Scheduling Order, 8 May 2009.

[26] See, *e.g.*, *Karemera et al.*, Order Directing the Parties to File Submissions Regarding the Translation of Trial Exhibits, 22 June 2009.

[27] Soumission de Édouard Karemera sur le maintient du process joint, filed on 13 February 2009, p. 4; Mémoire d'Appel suite à la Décision du 03 Mars 2009 relative à la Continuation du Procès, filed on 2 April 2009, paras 14-16, 39, 55.

[28] Dragan Nikolić, Decision on Interlocutory Appeal Concerning Legality of Arrest, para. 30; Kajelijeli Appeal Judgement, para. 206

[29] Prosecutor's Response, para. 19, referring to *Karemera* Decision on Continuation.

[30] *Karemera et al.*, Decision on Appeal concerning the Severance of Matthieu Ngirumpatse, 19 June 2009.

[31] *Karemera* Decision on Continuation, para. 38.

FOR THESE REASONS, the Chamber

DENIES Karemera's Motion in its entirety.

Arusha, 23 June 2009, done in English.

Dennis C. M. Byron	Gberdao Gustave Kam	Vagn Joensen
Presiding Judge	Judge	Judge

[Seal of the Tribunal]

Commentary

1. Introduction

These four decisions[1] issued by the International Criminal Tribunal for Rwanda (ICTR) address fundamental issues in international criminal procedural law, all related to the effective functioning of international criminal justice and its respect for the fairness of proceedings. These matters appear to be recurring themes before international bodies, and ones that consistently generate scrupulous judicial scrutiny. The reason behind such close monitoring is probably to be found in the history of international criminal justice itself. It is worth recalling that one of the harshest criticisms expressed against the Nuremberg Charter and trial, and which led to fierce and fervent debates, was precisely the alleged unfairness of the proceedings. Even if such criticism may now be easily dismissed the fact remains that such accusations of unfairness have somehow stained international criminal justice.

In this context therefore, it does not seem too emphatic to assert that the question of fairness before international criminal courts and tribunals is one that – if overlooked – could lethally harm the credibility of the whole system and ultimately put its very existence into jeopardy.

The four decisions analysed in the present commentary deal with different aspects of the right to a fair trial and, as it will be shown, in all these decisions the ICTR has proved meticulous in its assessment of the different situations, mindful of the rights of all the parties to the proceedings and respectful of human rights law norms.

2. Right to a fair trial

The right to a fair trial is one of the fundamental rights protected by all human rights instruments. One of the authoritative definitions of this right is enshrined in article 14 of the International Covenant on Civil and Political Rights (ICCPR),[2] which contains an authoritative definition of this right, putting the emphasis on equality before the law and detailing the sub-elements of the right to a fair trial and notably the right to be tried without undue delay (article 14 (c), ICCPR) and the right of the accused to be tried in his presence (article 14 (d), ICCPR). Such guarantees offered by article 14 of the ICCPR and other human rights law instruments[3] are reproduced *verbatim* in international criminal procedural law.[4]

Without aiming at establishing a hierarchy of rights, the right to a fair trial is one of the most important human rights, insofar as it contains within itself the seeds of democracy: without the guarantees of a fair trial, any human rights instrument is bound to remain a purely theoretical declaration of rights and good intentions, and thus dead letter. Unsurprisingly therefore, the importance of this right is reflected quantitatively as one which has arguably triggered the most case law before human rights judicial bodies.

A glance at the case law of the European Court of Human Rights reveals the huge amount of decisions involving article 6 of the European Convention on Human Rights (ECHR), which protects the right to a fair trial. As reported by White and Ovey, "Article 6 is the provision of the Convention most frequently invoked by applicants to Strasbourg",[5] a statement confirmed in the latest available Annual Report of the European Court of Human Rights, which explicitly notes that "[t]he Convention provision which gave rise to the greatest number of violations was Article 6, firstly with regard to the right to a hearing within a reasonable

---

[1] ICTR, Decision on Continuation of Trial, *Prosecutor v. Karemera, Ngirumpatse and Nzirorera*, Case No. ICTR-98-44-T, T. Ch. III, 3 March 2009 + Corrigendum 16 March 2009, in this volume, p. 25; ICTR, Decision on Trial Date, *Prosecutor v. Ngirabatware*, Case No. ICTR-99-54-T, T. Ch. II, 12 June 2009, in this volume, p. 37; ICTR, Decision on Appeal Concerning the Severance of Matthieu Ngirumpatse, *Prosecutor v. Karemera, Ngirumpatse and Nzirorera*, Case No. ICTR-98-44-T, A. Ch., 19 June 2009, in this volume, p. 49; ICTR, Decision on Édouard Karamera's Motion relating to his right to be tried without undue delay, *Prosecutor v. Karemera, Ngirumpatse and Nzirorera*, Case No. ICTR-98-44-T, T. Ch. III, 23 June 2009, in this volume, p. 57.
[2] International Covenant on Civil and Political Rights, Adopted and opened for signature, ratification and accession by General Assembly resolution 2200A (XXI) of 16 December 1966; entry into force 23 March 1976, in accordance with Article 49.
[3] See e.g. Article 6 of the European Convention on the Protection of Human Rights and Fundamental Freedoms (ECHR), 1950.
[4] See in particular Article 21 of the Statute of the International Criminal Tribunal for the Former Yugoslavia (ICTY); Article 20 of the ICTR Statute; and Article 67 of the Rome Statute of the International Criminal Court (ICC).
[5] R.C.A. Jacobs, White and Ovey, The European Convention on Human Rights, Fifth Edition, Oxford University Press., Oxford 2010, p. 242.

time, then with regard to the right to a fair trial".[6] Indeed, from 1959 to 2010, out of 11,438 judgments 3,461 concerned the right to a fair trial and 4,469 concerned the length of proceedings.[7]

The importance of such a right is two-fold: not only does it reflect the dedication of human rights instruments and bodies to the rule of law and to the democratic system in which violations of the law are justiciable, it also illustrates the idea that human rights must not simply be declared and defined, they also need to be protected, an idea famously expressed and reiterated by the Strasbourg Court in the following terms: "The Court does not regard this possibility, of itself, as conclusive of the matter. The Convention is intended to guarantee not rights that are theoretical or illusory but *rights that are practical and effective*."[8]

3. Impartiality

Interestingly for the purpose of the present analysis, not only does article 20 of the ICTR Statute mirror article 6 of the ECHR, the ICTR also seems to have adopted the same method of legal reasoning as the Strasbourg Court, proceeding in each instance with a case-by-case assessment of the particular situation brought before it. The Karemera *et al.* case having raised a series of different procedural questions – if not challenges – it provided the ICTR with a great opportunity to rule on different aspects of the very functioning of international criminal justice and the right to a fair trial.

One of the issues the ICTR had to address relates to the exigency of impartiality on the part of the judges, as a fundamental ingredient of the right to a fair trial. In April 2004, accusations of impartiality were indeed raised against the Presiding Judge Adresia Vaz. As recalled by the Appeals Chamber:

> The trial in the present case commenced on 27 November 2003 before a section of Trial Chamber III composed of Judge Vaz, presiding, and *ad litem* Judges Lattanzi and Arrey. On 27 April 2004 Nzirorera requested disqualification of Judge Vaz on the basis of her alleged association with a Prosecution counsel taking part in the case. The Trial Chamber dismissed this request. Thereafter, Nzirorera and Rwamakuba moved for Judge Vaz's disqualification from the case before the Bureau of the Tribunal. Prior to the Bureau's ruling on these motions, Judge Vaz withdrew from the case on 14 May 2004. On 17 May 2004 the Bureau declared moot the motions for disqualification of Judge Vaz.[9]

Pursuant to Rule 15*bis* (D) of the ICTR's Rules of Procedure and Evidence,[10] the two remaining judges decided to continue the proceedings, a decision subsequently reversed by the Appeals Chamber, which found that "the remaining Judges erred in the exercise of their discretion in reaching the Impugned Decision".[11] Nearly a month later, the Appeals Chamber provided the reasons for this decision,[12] thereby carefully reviewing and detailing the judicial role and power under Rule *15bis* (D):

> Rule 15*bis*(D) of the Rules explicitly prescribes that the 'remaining Judges' may decide to continue the proceedings. The Appeals Chamber noted this in the *Butare* case: 'The new Rule 15*bis*(D) gives judicial power to *the two remaining judges*, namely, the power to decide whether or not it is in the interests of justice to continue a part-heard case with a substitute judge.' The fact that the remaining Judges have *ad litem* rather than permanent status does not change anything under Rule 15*bis*(D). Article 12*quater* of the Statute unequivocally provides that *ad litem* Judges enjoy the same powers as the permanent Judges of the Tribunal, except in expressly delimited circumstances which do not include the power to decide to continue the

---

[6] European Court of Human Rights, Annual Report 2010, Strasbourg: Council of Europe Publishing, 2010, p. 79.
[7] *Ibid.*, p. 157.
[8] European Court of Human Rights, *Airey v. Ireland*, 9 October 1979, Application No. 6289/73, par. 24. Emphasis added.
[9] ICTR, Decision on interlocutory appeals regarding the continuation of proceedings with a substitute Judge and on Nzirorera's motion for leave to consider new material, *Prosecutor v. Karemera, Ngirumpatse, Nzirorera and Rwamakuba*, Case No. ICTR-98-44-AR15*bis*.2, A. Ch., 28 September 2004, par. 2. Footnotes omitted.
[10] Rule 15*bis* (D) reads: "If, in the circumstances mentioned in the last sentence of paragraph (C), the accused withholds his consent, the remaining Judges may nonetheless decide to continue the proceedings before a Trial Chamber with a substitute Judge if, taking all the circumstances into account, they determine unanimously that doing so would serve the interests of justice. This decision is subject to appeal directly to a full bench of the Appeals Chamber by either party. If no appeal is taken or the Appeals Chamber affirms the decision of the Trial Chamber, the President shall assign to the existing bench a Judge, who, however, can join the bench only after he or she has certified that he or she has familiarised himself or herself with the record of the proceedings. Only one substitution under this paragraph may be made".
[11] Prosecutor v. Karemera *et. al, supra,* note 9, par. 8.
[12] ICTR, Decision on interlocutory appeals regarding the continuation of proceedings with a substitute Judge and on Nzirorera's motion for leave to consider new material, *Prosecutor v. Karemera, Ngirumpatse, Nzirorera and Rwamakuba*, Case No. ICTR-98-44-AR15*bis*.2, A. Ch., 22 October 2004, Klip/ Sluiter, ALC-XVIII-213.

proceedings under Rule 15*bis*(D). Accordingly, on 21 June 2004, the Appeals Chamber directed the remaining Judges in the case to re-consider their decision to continue the proceedings with a substitute Judge after giving the parties an opportunity to be heard and taking account of their submissions.[13]

Putting the emphasis on the interests of justice, the Appeals Chamber further added that:

> The issue under Rule 15*bis*(D) is whether taking all the circumstances into account, the Judges find that continuing the trial would serve the interests of justice. In answering this question, the Judges are to assess the totality of the circumstances rather than whether a party has demonstrated that continuing or re-starting the trial would better serve the interests of justice.[14]

Most interestingly, the Appeals Chamber also meticulously considered the two-fold issue of bias and appearance of bias noting that:

> [t]he allegations of appearance of bias are supported by Judge Vaz's admission of association and cohabitation with a Prosecution counsel who was one of the trial attorneys appearing in the present case. The question remains whether these circumstances gave rise to an appearance of bias.[15]

Directly quoting its Yugoslav counterpart in the Furundžija case, the ICTR Appeals Chamber recalled that

> [t]here is a general rule that a Judge should not only be subjectively free from bias, but also that there should be nothing in the surrounding circumstances which objectively gives rise to an appearance of bias.[16]

Probably mindful of not upsetting the sensitivity of the judges, the Appeals Chamber thus clearly distinguished between actual bias and the appearance of bias, emphasising that "this is not a finding of actual bias on the part of Judge Vaz, but rather a finding, made in the interests of justice, that the circumstances of the case gave rise to an appearance of bias."[17] This careful approach notwithstanding, the Appeals Chamber nonetheless proved very strict in its appreciation of impartiality and ultimately ruled that "this appearance [of bias] also extended to Judges Lattanzi and Arrey because, although aware of the circumstances of Judge Vaz's association with the Prosecution counsel, they acquiesced in rejecting Nzirorera's motion and, therefore, in continuing the trial with Judge Vaz on the Bench."[18]

As a result of the Appeals Chamber's ruling, the trial restarted afresh before a newly constituted Trial Chamber on 19 September 2005. The 'judicial ballet' in this case was not to stop there and, in January 2007, one of the new judges had to withdraw from the case for health reasons, thereby prompting the appointment of a substitute judge in May 2007.

4. Trials *in absentia*

Not only did the Karemera *et al.* case thus raise a series of questions regarding presence on the bench, it also addressed the right of the accused to be present at his trial. As a matter of principle, trials *in absentia* are not permitted on the international criminal justice scene. As expressed by the United Nations Secretary-General in his Report pursuant to paragraph 2 of Security Council Resolution 808:

> A trial should not commence until the accused is physically present before the International Tribunal. There is a widespread perception that trials in absentia should not be provided for in the statute as this would not be consistent with article 14 of the International Covenant on Civil and Political Rights, which provides that the accused shall be entitled to be tried in his presence.[19]

This Report notwithstanding, the different statutes of the various international courts and tribunals – including that of the ICTR – have remained silent on the matter. Unsurprisingly perhaps, the ICTY Appeals Chamber was however faced with the issue and, in its Blaškić judgment refrained from excluding the possibility of trials *in absentia* in absolute terms. Rather, it found that:

---

[13] *Ibid.*, par. 49. Footnotes omitted.
[14] *Ibid.*, par. 54.
[15] *Ibid.*, par. 66.
[16] Prosecutor v. Karemera *et al., supra,* note 12, par. 66. Footnotes omitted.
[17] *Ibid.*, par. 67.
[18] *Ibid.*, par. 69.
[19] Report of the Secretary-General Pursuant to Paragraph 2 of Security Council Resolution 808 (1993), UN doc. S/25704, 3 May 1993, par. 101. Footnote omitted.

[g]enerally *speaking*, it would not be appropriate to hold *in absentia* proceedings against persons falling under the primary jurisdiction of the International Tribunal (i.e., persons accused of crimes provided for in Articles 2-5 of the Statute). Indeed, even when the accused has clearly waived his right to be tried in his presence (Article 21, paragraph 4 (d), of the Statute), it would prove extremely difficult or even impossible for an international criminal court to determine the innocence or guilt of that accused. By contrast, *in absentia* proceedings may be exceptionally warranted in cases involving contempt of the International Tribunal, where the person charged fails to appear in court, thus obstructing the administration of justice. These cases fall within the ancillary or incidental jurisdiction of the International Tribunal.[20]

Conscious that it was here addressing a crucial human rights law matter, the Appeals Chamber did not hesitate to explicitly refer – and admittedly defer - to the position of the Strasbourg Court on the compatibility of *in absentia* proceedings with human rights law standards:

If such *in absentia* proceedings were to be instituted, all the fundamental rights pertaining to a fair trial would need to be safeguarded. Among other things, although the individual's absence would have to be regarded, under certain conditions, as a waiver of his «right to be tried in his presence», he should be offered the choice of counsel. The Appeals Chamber holds the view that, in addition, *other guarantees provided for in the context of the European Convention on Human Rights should also be respected.*[21]

In the Karemera *et al.* case, one of the accused – Matthieu Ngirumpatse – was medically found unfit to attend the proceedings, a situation which prompted the Trial Chamber to give due consideration to the right of an accused to be present during the proceedings, a fundamental right to which any restriction "must be the least intrusive instrument amongst those which might achieve the desired result"[22] and here found that there are less intrusive options available. Yet, the Chamber also carefully explained that "the delay of the trial has reached a proportion that makes it imperative for the Chamber to now address whether Ngirumpatse should be severed from the trial or whether the proceedings be stayed until it is determined either that Ngirumpatse is fit to participate or that he is unable to do so for the foreseeable future."[23]

Prior to consider severance however, the Trial Chamber temporarily ordered a stay of proceedings, pending an evolution of the accused's health. Conscious of the potential repercussions of severance on the fairness of the proceedings and of any possible criticism, the Trial Chamber here interestingly explained its reasoning and methodology, specifying that it will

[a]fter assessing the information available regarding Ngirumpatse's health condition, address whether the trial can, after a further stay of proceedings, continue in Ngirumpatse's absence, whether the trial should be stayed indeterminately until he might be fit to attend again or whether Ngirumpatse should be severed from the trial.[24]

In reaching its decision, the Trial Chamber proved extremely conscious of the length of the proceedings and was undoubtedly mindful of the rights of all the accused, recognising that

[w]hether to sever Matthieu Ngirumpatse from this trial or to stay the proceedings until he becomes fit to attend trial or it be ascertained that he will not be fit to attend trial in the foreseeable future, if ever, involves a balancing of several legal principles. *The primary concern* is that the decision must not violate the fundamental right of all three Accused to a fair trial pursuant to Article 20 (2) of the Statute or unfairly violate the right of the Co-Accused, Édouard Karemera and Joseph Nzirorera, to be tried without undue delay pursuant to Article 20 (4) (d) of the Statute.[25]

Mirroring the Strasbourg position regarding the reasonableness of the delay, the Trial Chamber was able to find that "the reasonableness of a period of delay cannot be translated into a fixed length of time and is dependant on consideration of a number of factors"[26] and that "a finding of undue delay depends on the

---

[20] ICTY, Judgement on the request of the Republic of Croatia for Review of the Decision of Trial Chamber II of 18 July 1997, *Prosecutor v. Blaškić*, Case No. IT-95-14-AR108*bis*, A. Ch., 29 October 1997, par. 59. Emphasis added.
[21] *Ibid*. Footnote omitted. Emphasis added.
[22] ICTR, Decision on Continuation of Trial, *Prosecutor v. Karemera, Ngirumpatse and Nzirorera*, Case No. ICTR-98-44-T, T. Ch. III, 3 March 2009, par. 21, referring to ICTY, Decision on Defence Appeal of the Decision on Future Course of the Proceedings, *Prosecutor v. Stanišić and Simatović*, Case No. IT-03-69-AR73.2, A. Ch., par. 16.
[23] Decision on Continuation of Trial, *supra*, note 22, par. 27.
[24] *Ibid*.,, par. 7.
[25] Decision on Continuation of Trial, *supra*, note 22, par. 28. Emphasis added.
[26] *Ibid*.,par. 31.

circumstances of each case".[27] Considering that "[t]he suspension of the proceedings has resulted in considerable difficulties for the Parties",[28] the Chamber assessed the situation in light of the presumption of innocence and stated that "it has become seriously prejudicial to simply let the accused sit in detention while Matthieu Ngirumpatse's health problems are addressed"[29] and that "the delay in the proceedings, to this point, has become such that the rights of the accused to be tried without undue delay have been violated".[30]

Taking into account all the circumstances of the case, the chamber found that ordering the severance of Matthieu Ngirumpatse would be in the interest of justice insofar as it will enable him to "have his right to be present and defend himself safeguarded while retaining his right to an expeditious trial when he is fit again to participate in his trial."[31] The Appeals Chamber subsequently ruled on the appeal lodged against this decision only three months later, and, reviewing the evolution of Ngirumpatse's state of health, remanded the matter back to the Trial Chamber "for further evaluation based on the present circumstances of Mr. Ngirumpatse's condition."[32]

Simultaneously, and following the Trial Chamber's decision on continuation of trial, Karemera attempted to use at his own advantage the above-mentioned finding that "the delay in the proceedings, to this point, has become such that the rights of the accused to be tried without undue delay have been violated".[33] He indeed filed a motion on 18 May 2009, arguing that his right to be tried within a reasonable time had been violated and that this breach should be remedied by the revocation of the indictment against him, the termination of the proceedings in his case and his immediate release. Ruling on this motion one month later, the Trial Chamber reasonably came to the conclusion that, while it gives

> [d]ue weight to the violation of Édouard Karemera's right to be tried without undue delay, it does not find that this violation rises to a level of egregiousness justifying the exceptional remedy of the withdrawal of the indictment, the termination of the proceedings and his immediate release.[34]

5. Conclusion

The decision of the Trial Chamber in response to Karemera's motion is obviously to be welcomed. Karemera and his co-accused indeed stand trial for extremely serious crimes, having been charged with conspiracy to commit genocide, direct and public incitement to genocide, genocide or alternatively complicity in genocide, rape and extermination as crimes against humanity as well as murder and causing violence to health and physical or mental well-being as serious violations of Article 3 Common to the Geneva Conventions and Additional Protocol II.[35] All of them held senior positions within the *Mouvement Républicain National pour la Démocratie et le Développement* (MRND), Rwanda's ruling political party in 1994 and are thus suspected of having played a decisive role in the orchestration and organisation of the 1994 genocide. While there is no doubt that this case has suffered heavy delays, one can only concur with the chamber's finding that these should not justify such exceptional leniency. The gravity of the crimes perpetrated should take precedence over procedural defects and it is undoubtedly in the interests of justice that they should be tried.

Yet, it would seem an understatement to assert that this case has been extremely lengthy. While the trial started on 27 November 2003 before Trial Chamber III, the first Trial Chamber decisions date back to 2000.[36]

---

[27] *Ibid.*, par. 30.
[28] *Ibid.*, par. 37.
[29] *Ibid.*, par. 38.
[30] *Ibid.*, par. 38.
[31] *Ibid.*, par. 52.
[32] ICTR, Decision on Appeal concerning the severance of Matthieu Ngirumpatse, *Prosecutor v. Karemera, Ngirumpatse and Nzirorera*, Case No. ICTR-98-44-AR73.16, A. Ch., 19 June 2009, par. 24.
[33] Decision on Continuation of Trial, *supra*, note 22, par. 38.
[34] ICTR, Decision on Édouard Karemera's Motion relating to his right to be tried without undue delay, *Prosecutor v. Karemera, Ngirumpatse and Nzirorera*, Case No. ICTR-98-44-T, T. Ch. III, 23 June 2009, par. 8.
[35] ICTR, Amended Indictment of 24 August 2005, *Prosecutor v. Karemera, Ngirumpatse and Nzirorera*, Case No. ICTR-98-44-I.
[36] See ICTR, Corrigendum to the decision on the Defence motion for the restitution of documents and other personal or family belongings seized (Rule 40 (c) of the Rules of Procedure and Evidence, and the exclusion of such evidence which may be used by the Prosecutor in preparing an Indictment against the Applicant, *Prosecutor v. Karemera*, Case No. ICTR-98-44-I, T. Ch. II, 13 April 2000 and ICTR, Decision on the Prosecutor's Motion for joinder of Accused and on the Prosecutor's Motion for severance of the Accused, *Prosecutor v. Ngirumpatse, Nzirorera and Kajelijeli*, Case No. ICTR-98-44-I, T. Ch. II, 29 June 2000.

Ironically perhaps, the main reason behind such delay is probably to be found in the ICTR's considerations for fairness of the proceedings, which paradoxically impeded the trial from progressing smoothly. So as to ensure respect for the rights of the defence, the ICTR had to do so at the expenses of another component of the right to a fair trial namely, the right to be tried without undue delay. The decisions commented here overwhelmingly demonstrate the judicial meticulousness attached to all the procedural issues potentially harmful to the rights of the defence to the point that the Trial Chamber felt at some point compelled to recall that it was "composed of professional judges" and "able to assess the evidence in a case involving conflicting defence and prosecution evidence in a fair and just manner without prejudice to any of the accused."[37]

Perhaps more probing of the ICTR's concerns is the length of the decisions analysed here, which undoubtedly reveal the care with which the tribunal deals with procedural matters and its awareness of the potential impact of such matters on the right to a fair trial. In this respect, the Trial Chamber's decision on a trial date in the *Ngirabatware* case is arguably symptomatic of the willingness of the tribunal to preserve itself from criticism. By its length, detail and judicial motivation, this decision leaves indeed little doubt that both the Appeals Chamber and the Trial Chamber have taken the motion filed by the defence to vary trial date very seriously.[38] Yet, and while such procedural care is of course to be celebrated, it remains regretful that international criminal trials can suffer such delays. As of October 2011, the Ngirabatware, Karemera and Ngirumpatse cases are still in progress. – Nzirorera's death in the course of the proceedings having impeded his conviction,[39] thereby reinforcing the idea that justice delayed can indeed amount to justice denied.

Caroline Fournet

---

[37] ICTR, Decision on Continuation of Trial, *Prosecutor v. Karemera, Ngirumpatse and Nzirorera*, Case No. ICTR-98-44-T, T. Ch. III, 3 March 2009, para. 51. Footnote omitted.
[38] ICTR, Decision on Trial Date, *Prosecutor v. Ngirabatware*, Case No. ICTR-99-54-T, T. Ch. III, 12 June 2009, in this volume, p. 37.
[39] It is to be noted that, originally, the trial was joined with that of André Rwamakuba, who was subsequently severed at the prosecution's request and later acquitted. ICTR, Judgment, *Prosecutor v. Rwamakuba*, Case No. ICTR-98-44-C-T, T. Ch. III, 20 September 2006, Klip/ Sluiter, ALC-XXV-439.

Tribunal pénal international pour le Rwanda
International Criminal Tribunal for Rwanda

IN THE APPEALS CHAMBER

Before:
    Judge Fausto Pocar, Presiding
    Judge Mohamed Shahabuddeen
    Judge Liu Daqun
    Judge Theodor Meron
    Judge Carmel Agius

Registrar: **Adama Dieng**

Date: 24 March 2009

THE PROSECUTOR

v.

THARCISSE MUVUNYI

Case No. ICTR-2000-55A-AR73

DECISION ON THE PROSECUTOR'S APPEAL CONCERNING THE SCOPE OF EVIDENCE TO BE ADDUCED IN THE RETRIAL

The Office of the Prosecutor:

Hassan Bubacar Jallow
Charles Adeogun-Phillips
Ibukunolu Alao Babajide
Thembile M. Segoete

Counsel for Tharcisse Muvunyi:

William E. Taylor III
Abbe Jolles
Dorian Cotlar

[page 1] 1.	The Appeals Chamber of the International Criminal Tribunal for the Prosecution of Persons Responsible for Genocide and Other Serious Violations of International Humanitarian Law Committed in the Territory of Rwanda and Rwandan Citizens Responsible for Genocide and Other Such Violations Committed in the Territory of Neighbouring States, between 1 January and 31 December 1994 ("Appeals Chamber" and "Tribunal", respectively) is seized of an appeal, filed on 5 February 2009 by the Prosecution,[1] against a decision of Trial Chamber III concerning the scope of evidence it is permitted to adduce during the retrial of Tharcisse Muvunyi.[2] Mr. Muvunyi filed his response on 13 February 2009,[3] and the Prosecution filed its reply on 17 February 2009.[4]

BACKGROUND

2.	On 12 September 2006, Trial Chamber II convicted Mr. Muvunyi of three counts of genocide, direct and public incitement to commit genocide, and other inhumane acts as crimes against humanity, and sentenced him to 25 years' imprisonment.[5] The Appeals Chamber reversed these convictions on 29 August 2008 and ordered a retrial limited to the allegation under Count 3 of the Indictment that Mr. Muvunyi is responsible for direct and public incitement to commit genocide based on a speech he purportedly gave at the Gikore Trade Center.[6]

3.	Three witnesses testified on this event at trial: Prosecution Witnesses YAI and CCP and Defence Witness MO78.[7] The Appeals Chamber stated that: "From the discussion of the evidence in the Trial Judgement, [it] cannot conclude whether a reasonable trier of fact could have relied on the testimony of Witnesses YAI and CCP to convict [Mr.] Muvunyi for this event."[8] The Appeals Chamber also considered that the Trial Chamber did not provide sufficient reasons for preferring the evidence of the two Prosecution witnesses over that of the Defence and found that the Trial [page 2] Chamber failed to provide a reasoned opinion on this point.[9] In particular, it noted that the Trial Chamber did not point to any inconsistencies in Witness MO78's account of the meeting or any other reasons for doubting his credibility whereas it did expressly recognize the need to treat the evidence of the two Prosecution witnesses with caution.[10] Given the aggregate errors in addressing the apparent inconsistencies between the accounts of the witnesses, the Appeals Chamber was not in a position to determine whether the Trial Chamber exhaustively and properly assessed the entire evidence on this point.[11] Accordingly, the Appeals Chamber quashed the conviction and "order[ed] a retrial"[12] on this issue "to allow the trier of fact the opportunity to fully assess the entirety of the relevant evidence and provide a reasoned opinion."[13] It further concluded that, if a new Trial Chamber were to enter a conviction on this charge after retrial, any sentence could not exceed the 25 years of imprisonment imposed by the first Trial Chamber.[14]

---

[1]	Prosecutor's Appeal of the Decision of Trial Chamber III Limiting the Scope of the Evidence the Prosecutor Is Entitled to Adduce in a Retrial Pursuant to Rule 118(C), 5 February 2009 ("Appeal").
[2]	*The Prosecutor v. Tharcisse Muvunyi*, Case No. ICTR-2000-55A-PT, Oral Decision, T. 14 January 2009 p. 3 ("Impugned Decision"). Certification to appeal was granted on 29 January 2009. *See The Prosecutor v. Tharcisse Muvunyi*, Case No. ICTR-2000-55A-R73(B), Decision on Prosecution Motion for Certification to Appeal the Limitation of the Scope of the Retrial (Rule 73(B) of the Rules of Procedure and Evidence), 29 January 2009, p. 2.
[3]	Accused Tharcisse Muvunyi's Response to Prosecutor's Appeal of the Decision of the [*sic*] Trial Chamber III Limiting the Scope of the Evidence the Prosecutor Is Entitled to Adduce in a Retrial Pursuant to Rule 118(C), 13 February 2009 ("Response").
[4]	Prosecutor's Reply to Tharcisse Muvunyi's Response to Prosecutor's Appeal of the Decision of Trial Chamber III Limiting the Scope of the Retrial Pursuant to Rule 118(C), 17 February 2009 ("Reply").
[5]	*Prosecutor v. Tharcisse Muvunyi*, Case No. ICTR-2000-55A-T, Judgement and Sentence, 18 September 2006, paras. 531, 545 ("*Muvunyi* Trial Judgement"). The Trial Judgement was pronounced on 12 September 2006, and the written judgement was filed with the Registry on 18 September 2006.
[6]	*Tharcisse Muvunyi v. The Prosecutor*, Case No. ICTR-2000-55A-A, Judgement, 29 August 2008, paras. 148, 171 ("*Muvunyi* Appeal Judgement").
[7]	*Muvunyi* Appeal Judgement, paras. 142-148; *Muvunyi* Trial Judgement, paras. 191-211. The Trial Chamber also referred to Defence Witness MO30 in its recitation of the relevant evidence, but did not discuss his evidence in its deliberations.
[8]	*Muvunyi* Appeal Judgement, para. 144.
[9]	*Muvunyi* Appeal Judgement, para. 147.
[10]	*Muvunyi* Appeal Judgement, para. 147.
[11]	*Muvunyi* Appeal Judgement, para. 148.
[12]	*Muvunyi* Appeal Judgement, para. 171 (emphasis omitted).
[13]	*Muvunyi* Appeal Judgement, para. 148.
[14]	*Muvunyi* Appeal Judgement, para. 170.

4. At a status conference on 28 November 2008, the Prosecution expressed that the scope of evidence to be presented during the retrial should not be limited to the witnesses who testified in the original trial.[15] In its Pre-Trial Brief, filed on 4 December 2008, the Prosecution listed five factual witnesses as well as the expert witness heard during the original trial to be called during the retrial.[16] With respect to the event at Gikore Trade Center, the factual witnesses include only one of the two witnesses who testified on the event in the initial proceedings, namely Witness CCP, and three other witnesses who were not previously heard (Witnesses FBX, AMJ, and CCS), but whose statements the Prosecution had disclosed to the Defence during the original trial.[17]

5. During a status conference on 14 January 2009, Judge Byron of Trial Chamber III orally issued the Impugned Decision. He held that the scope of the retrial was limited to the evidence adduced during the initial proceedings as the Appeals Chamber found that the Trial Chamber had not provided sufficient reasons in its assessment of the evidence. He decided that the retrial was limited to correcting the Trial Chamber's failure and that the Prosecution could therefore not call new witnesses, namely Witnesses FBX, AMJ, and CCS.[18] **[page 3]**

SUBMISSIONS OF THE PARTIES

6. In its Appeal, the Prosecution submits that the Trial Chamber erred in law by equating retrial, as provided for in Rule 118(C) of the Rules of Procedure and Evidence of the Tribunal ("Rules"), with a remittance to consider a narrow issue and requests the Appeals Chamber to reverse the Impugned Decision limiting the scope of evidence it may adduce in the retrial.[19] In its view, the retrial in the instant case is a trial *de novo,* giving the Prosecution the right to expand or reduce the scope of the evidence to be presented to the extent that it does not cause material prejudice to the accused.[20] In this respect, it relies on the definition of retrial in Black's Law Dictionary and the Criminal Procedure Code of Malaysia which indicate that a retrial is to be conducted as if there had been no trial in the first instance.[21] Similarly, the Prosecution also refers to the interpretation of the term "rehearing" made by Trial Chamber III in the *Karemera et al.* case, in which the Chamber decided that prior orders and decisions related to the evidence in that case no longer had any effect once proceedings had restarted.[22]

7. The Prosecution also contends that narrowing the scope of the retrial runs contrary to the language of the Appeals Chamber's express intention "to allow the trier of fact the opportunity to fully assess the entirety of the relevant evidence and to provide a reasoned opinion."[23] It submits that, as it is impossible to empanel the original Bench, the Appeals Chamber's order cannot be construed solely as a corrective measure to remedy the deficiencies in the Trial Chamber's reasoning.[24] According to the Prosecution, even if the Trial Chamber were composed of the same Judges, restricting the Prosecution to calling the same witnesses who appeared in the initial trial would frustrate the purposes of retrial in the event that they were no longer available.[25] **[page 4]**

---

[15] T. 28 November 2008 pp. 2, 3. *See also* Appeal, paras. 13, 14, 17.
[16] *The Prosecutor v. Tharcisse Muvunyi*, Case No. ICTR-2000-55A-PT, The Prosecutor's Pre-Trial Brief, 4 December 2008, Annex 1 ("Pre-Trial Brief"). *See also* Impugned Decision, p. 3; Appeal, para. 16; Response, para. 3.
[17] Appeal, para. 16; Response, para. 7; Pre-Trial Brief, Annex 3 (disclosure chart). The Prosecution also intends to call Witness NN, who appeared in the initial trial, as a factual witness in order to provide a contextual overview of the prevailing situation in Butare prefecture at the time. *See* Pre-Trial Brief, para. 12, Annex 1.
[18] Impugned Decision, p. 3.
[19] Appeal, paras. 2-10, 23-36; Reply, para. 6. The Prosecution also refers to paragraph 15 of the partial dissenting opinion of Judge Wald in *Prosecutor v. Goran Jelisić*, Case No. IT-95-10-A, Judgement, 5 July 2001 in which she distinguishes between retrial and remittance.
[20] Appeal, paras. 6-8; Reply, paras. 5, 7-14.
[21] Appeal, para. 33, citing Black's Law Dictionary (7th Edition 1990), p. 1317; Criminal Procedure Code (Act 593)(revised – 1999) §316 (reprinted in the Annotated Statutes of Malaysia, Volume 5, Part (2)1, (Malayan L. J. Sdn. Bhd. 2001)).
[22] Appeal, paras. 34-36, citing *The Prosecutor v. Édouard Karemera et al.*, Case No. ICTR-98-44-PT, Decision on Severance of André Rwamakuba and Amendments of the Indictment, 7 December 2004, para. 14.
[23] Appeal, para. 39, quoting *Muvunyi* Appeal Judgement, para. 148. *See also* Appeal, paras. 8, 26, 37-48; Reply, para. 15.
[24] Appeal, paras. 46-48.
[25] Appeal, para. 47.

8. Finally, the Prosecution argues that the inclusion of new witnesses in the Prosecution witness list could cause no possible prejudice to Mr. Muvunyi, since the proposed evidence is drawn from materials disclosed to the Defence during the initial trial.[26]

9. Mr. Muvunyi responds that the Impugned Decision properly determined that the scope of the retrial ordered by the Appeals Chamber is limited to the witnesses heard during the original proceedings in order to correct the initial Trial Chamber's failure to issue a reasoned opinion.[27] He observes that, contrary to what is suggested by the Prosecution, the inclusion of new witnesses would result in allowing the Prosecution "to correct its mistakes – to the extreme detriment of the Accused".[28]

10. Mr. Muvunyi submits that trying an accused for the same charges constitutes an inadmissible violation of the *non bis in idem* principle and that allowing the Prosecution to present new evidence would place him in double jeopardy.[29] As a corollary, he submits that the Prosecution should be bound by the initial list of witnesses offered at the first trial.[30] Furthermore, he appears to observe that, pursuant to Rule 73*bis*(E) of the Rules, the Prosecution may vary its witness list if it demonstrates that such a variation is "in the interest of justice".[31] He submits that, in the present case, the Prosecution failed to provide such a demonstration, considering that the addition of new witnesses would not be the consequence of newly discovered evidence nor a mechanism to expedite the proceedings.[32]

11. Finally, Mr. Muvunyi argues that there is no logic in the Prosecution's argument that, because the Trial Chamber is no longer composed of the same Judges, the Prosecution is to be allowed to present new evidence.[33] He submits that "[t]here is no impediment in the law to having another Trial Chamber hear the evidence considered by the initial Trial Chamber and making a proper analysis".[34] **[page 5]**

DISCUSSION

12. Rule 118(C) of the Rules provides that "[i]n appropriate circumstances the Appeals Chamber may order that the accused be re[-]tried before the Trial Chamber." This rule does not specify the scope of any retrial that the Appeals Chamber may order; indeed, that scope is given by the Appeals Chamber in a particular instance. Furthermore, the Appeals Chamber has the inherent power to remit limited issues to either the original or to a new Trial Chamber.[35]

13. The Appeals Chamber considers that a retrial pursuant to Rule 118(C) of the Rules inherently includes the possibility of hearing evidence that was not presented during the initial proceedings.[36] Neither the Rules nor the Tribunal's jurisprudence prohibit a Trial Chamber from hearing the testimony of new witnesses when a retrial is ordered. Whether new evidence should be allowed at the retrial is a determination to be made within the Trial Chamber's discretion which is guided by the same criteria governing the admission of evidence at trial. In contrast, a remittance to consider limited issues is not a new trial on the remitted questions; as such, it does not allow for the possibility of new evidence in the absence of express

---

[26] Appeal, para. 6.
[27] Response, paras. 5, 6, 8-25.
[28] Response, para. 6.
[29] Response, para. 15.
[30] Response, para. 15.
[31] Response, para. 21. Mr. Muvunyi incorrectly refers to Rule 78*bis*(E) of the Rules, which does not exist. He appears to mean Rule 73*bis*(E) of the Rules.
[32] Response, para. 21.
[33] Response, para. 23.
[34] Response, para. 23.
[35] *Prosecutor v. Zdravko Mucić et al.*, Case No. IT-96-21-A*bis*, Judgement on Sentence Appeal, 8 April 2003, paras. 9, 10, 16, 19 (*Mucić et al.* Appeal Judgement").
[36] *See, e.g., Patterson v. Haskins*, 470 F.3d 645, 669 (6th Cir. 2006)("[A]n appellate court's reversal of a conviction for trial error, unless specifically stated, does not oblige the government on remand to present a virtually identical version of the evidence and arguments that led to the initial reversal. In light of this court's statement in *Davis,* and because the type of limitation sought by Patterson is not ordinarily imposed, we conclude that our prior opinion did not intend to impose restrictions on the amount or type of evidence that the state could present during his retrial.").

authorization.[37] The Appeals Chamber considers that its inherent power to remit limited issues to a Trial Chamber also allows it to impose restrictions on the scope of a retrial under Rule 118(C) of the Rules, including the admission of new evidence. However, such restrictions must be explicit.

14. In the present case, in quashing Mr. Muvunyi's conviction under Count 3 of the Indictment, the Appeals Chamber expressly found that the circumstances were appropriate for retrial pursuant to Rule 118(C) of the Rules on the allegation related to the Gikore Trade Center. If the Appeals Chamber had wished to further narrow the scope of subsequent proceedings in this case, it would have acted instead under its discretionary power to remit the original Trial Chamber's assessment of the evidence for additional consideration or explicitly limited the retrial to the original evidence. There is nothing in the Appeals Chamber's disposition of the *Muvunyi* Appeal Judgement or its **[page 6]** conclusion of the ground of appeal related to the Gikore Trade Center event which suggests that the retrial should be limited to the original evidence.

15. To the contrary, the operative paragraph of the *Muvunyi* Appeal Judgement reflects that the purpose of the retrial was to allow the trier of fact "the opportunity to fully assess *the entirety of the relevant evidence* and to provide a reasoned opinion."[38] This broad formulation does not limit consideration of evidence to the witnesses heard during the initial proceedings, but rather implies that the Trial Chamber is to take into consideration all of the admissible and relevant evidence proposed by the parties, in order to provide a reasoned opinion on Count 3. It would be unreasonable to hold that, by ordering the exceptional measure of a retrial, the Appeals Chamber wanted to pursue the same goal that it could have reached by simply remitting the question to the Trial Chamber for a further assessment of the available evidence.

16. In addition, the Appeals Chamber finds no merit in Mr. Muvunyi's argument that allowing the Prosecution to present new evidence at the retrial stage would constitute a violation of the *non bis in idem* principle. The *non bis in idem* principle aims to protect a person who has been finally convicted or acquitted from being tried for the same offence again.[39] The Appeals Chamber quashed Mr. Muvunyi's conviction related to his alleged conduct at the Gikore Trade Center and ordered a retrial on Count 3 of the Indictment for that event, in accordance with the Rules. As such, there is no final judgement with respect to that allegation.

17. Furthermore, Rule 73*bis*(E) of the Rules, which delimits the Prosecution's ability to amend its witness list, is not relevant in the present context. The considerations under that rule apply "after [a] commencement of Trial" and not to the filing of an initial witness list in a retrial. However, the Appeals Chamber draws to the attention of the Prosecution that, in the circumstances of this case, it shall present all the evidence produced in the trial on Count 3, apart from any additional evidence it might want to adduce.

18. Finally, the Appeals Chamber considers that, contrary to Mr. Muvunyi's submissions, allowing the Prosecution to present new evidence in the retrial would not prejudice him. The fact that the Prosecution has changed its trial strategy in the subsequent proceedings is not a factor for consideration in the interpretation of the order for the retrial in the *Muvunyi* Appeal Judgement. All fair trial principles governing trial also apply to the retrial proceedings. The Prosecution proposes to call only six witnesses, which suggests that the duration of the proceedings will not be significantly **[page 7]** longer than if it were limited to those called to testify on this point in the initial trial. Mr. Muvunyi has also been in possession for several years of the statements of the three witnesses who did not appear in his original trial but whom the Prosecution proposes to call during the retrial. He has made no submissions that the addition of these witnesses will require

---

[37] *Mucić et al.* Appeal Judgement, para. 17 ("Once the Appeals Chamber exercised its inherent power to remit those limited issues to the Trial Chamber to be determined, the Trial Chamber had no power to go beyond determining the limited issues remitted to it. The Trial Chamber was not conducting a new trial on the issue of sentence, and – just as the situation would have been had the Appeals Chamber determined those limited issues itself – Rule 101(B) did not require the Trial Chamber to have regard to further evidence from the parties when determining those issues. The Trial Chamber's ruling, effectively that further evidence was inadmissible in the circumstances of this case, was correct. The argument that the Trial Chamber was obliged to receive further evidence in accordance with Rule 101(B) is rejected.").
[38] *Muvunyi* Appeal Judgement, para. 148 (emphasis added).
[39] *See* International Covenant on Civil and Political Rights, Article 14(7) ("No one shall be liable to be tried or punished again for an offence for which he has already been finally convicted or acquitted in accordance with the law and penal procedure of each country.").

significantly more investigations on his part. Moreover, as a further safeguard, the Appeals Chamber limited any possible sentence to be imposed in the new trial to no more than the 25 years' imprisonment ordered in the initial proceedings.[40] Therefore, Mr. Muvunyi is not prejudiced by the limited expansion of the Prosecution's witness list during the retrial.

19. In light of the above considerations, the Appeals Chamber finds that the Impugned Decision erred in law in interpreting the *Muvunyi* Appeal Judgement as imposing restrictions on the scope of evidence to be considered at the retrial.[41]

DISPOSITION

20. For the foregoing reasons, the Appeals Chamber **GRANTS**, Judges Shahabuddeen and Meron dissenting, the Appeal.

Done in English and French, the English version being authoritative.

Done this 24th day of March 2009,
At The Hague,
The Netherlands.

Judge Fausto Pocar
Presiding

[Seal of the Tribunal] [page 8]

---

[40] *Muvunyi* Appeal Judgement, para. 170.
[41] This does not mean that the Trial Chamber cannot exercise its discretion under Rule 73*bis*(D) of the Rules to order the Prosecution to reduce the number of its witnesses if it considers that an excessive number of witnesses are being called to prove the same facts.

JOINT DISSENTING OPINION OF JUDGES SHAHABUDDEEN AND MERON

A. The Scope of the Trial Chamber's Order that Muvunyi be Retried

1.   The core issue facing the Appeals Chamber is the scope of limitation on Muvunyi's retrial. On this question, Presiding Judge Byron of the Trial Chamber found that the Appeals Chamber's order for retrial was limited "to the allegation . . . [that Muvunyiğ made a speech at the Gikore trade centre . . . [and to] assessment of the evidence adduced before the first Trial Chamber."[1] There is no disagreement that the retrial was limited "to the allegation under Count 3 of the Indictment that Mr. Muvunyi is responsible for direct and public incitement to commit genocide based on a speech he purportedly gave at the Gikore Trade Center."[2] We disagree with the majority's broad interpretation of what evidence may be introduced in the retrial.

2.   The majority quotes the *Muvunyi* Appeal Judgement's statement that the retrial should serve as an "'opportunity to fully assess *the entirety of the relevant evidence* and to provide a reasoned opinion.'"[3] On the basis of this language, it concludes that the *Muvunyi* Appeal Judgement's "broad formulation does not limit consideration of evidence to the witnesses heard during the initial proceedings, but rather implies that the Trial Chamber is to take into consideration all of the admissible and relevant evidence proposed by the parties, in order to provide a reasoned opinion on Count 3."[4]

3.   The majority's logic hinges on the phrase "the entirety of the relevant evidence." Its focus on one sentence of the Appeals Judgement does not, however, appropriately take into account the context of the decision to order retrial. The Appeals Chamber explained that its quashing of Muvunyi's conviction under Count 3 was based on the Trial Chamber's "aggregate errors in addressing the apparently inconsistent testimony of Witnesses YAI, CCP, and MO78."[5] In particular, these errors included the "utter lack of any discussion [...] in the Trial Judgement" of the "numerous inconsistencies" in the testimonies of Prosecution witnesses YAI and CCP.[6] The Appeals Chamber also noted that the Trial Chamber "failed to provide a reasoned opinion" **[page 9]** explaining its preference for "the testimony of Witnesses YAI and CCP over that of [Defence] Witness MO78."[7]

4.   Once the broader discussion of the order that Muvunyi be retried is considered, the parameters of the Appeals Chamber's concerns are patent, and thus the appropriate scope of retrial is also clear. The relevant evidence is the testimonies of Witnesses YAI, CCP and MO78, which the Trial Chamber "failed to provide a reasoned opinion on"[8] when assessing. The purpose of the ordered retrial was to correct this significant flaw in the initial Trial Judgement, allowing the Trial Chamber an additional opportunity to assess the testimony of the original witnesses at trial and provide a reasoned explanation for choosing which account of Muvunyi's speech it believed. In this sense, the Appeals Chamber's order reflected the fact that "it is not, as a general rule, in the best position to assess the reliability and credibility of [. . .] evidence."[9]

5.   The majority's singular focus on one fragment of the *Muvunyi* Appeals Judgement disregards the surrounding discussion. While the language quoted by the majority might well stand for a full retrial in isolation, in context it can only be understood as authorizing retrial on the concerns identified by the Appeals Chamber – in this case, the lack of explanation for choosing one set of witness accounts over another.

B. The Impact of the Prosecution's Proposed Trial Strategy

6.   We note also that the new, expansive trial strategy proposed by the Prosecution is troubling. The Prosecution proposes to drop one of the two witnesses whose inconsistent testimony was identified by the

---

[1]   Impugned Decision, p.3.
[2]   *See* Appeals Chamber Decision, para. 3.
[3]   *Ibid.*, para. 15 (quoting *Muvunyi* Appeal Judgement, para. 148 (emphasis added by the Appeals Chamber)).
[4]   *Ibid.*, para. 15.
[5]   *Muvunyi* Appeal Judgement, para. 148.
[6]   *Ibid.*, para. 144.
[7]   *Ibid.*, para. 147.
[8]   *Ibid.*
[9]   *See, e.g., Prosecutor v. Mom~ilo Krajišnik* Case No. IT-00-39-A, Judgement, 17 March 2009, para. 798.

Appeals Chamber as a major concern, and add the testimony of three additional witnesses.[10] The Prosecution's proposed strategy underscores the problematic nature of retrial, where the Prosecution is effectively given a second chance to make its case. It may also have the effect of obscuring rather than explaining discrepancies in its witnesses' testimony. When retrial is ordered, it is particularly important to safeguard defendants' rights through means such as limitations on which evidence the Prosecution may adduce; we believe the *Muvunyi* Appeals Judgement intended just that. **[page 10]**

Done in English and French, the English version being authoritative.

Done this 24th day of March 2009,
At The Hague,
The Netherlands.

Judge Mohamed Shahabuddeen   Judge Thedor Meron

[Seal of the Tribunal]

---

[10]   *See* Appeals Chamber Decision, para. 4.

**Tribunal pénal international pour le Rwanda
International Criminal Tribunal for Rwanda**

IN THE APPEALS CHAMBER

Before: Judge Patrick Robinson, Presiding
                Judge Mehmet Güney
                Judge Fausto Pocar
                Judge Liu Daqun
                Judge Andrésia Vaz

Registrar: Mr. Adama Dieng

Date: 18 June 2009

Alfred MUSEMA-UWIMANA

v.

THE PROSECUTOR

Case No. ICTR-96-13-R

DECISION ON MOTION REQUESTING PRELIMINARY CONFERENCE WITH FORMER LEGAL TEAM FOR THE PREPARATION OF A REQUEST FOR THE ASSIGNMENT OF COUNSEL FOR THE PURPOSE OF A REVIEW

The Applicant

Mr. Alfred Musema-Uwimana, *pro se*

Office of the Prosecutor

Mr. Hassan Bubacar Jallow
Mr. Alex Obote-Odora
Mr. George W. Mugwanya
Ms. Inneke Onsea

[page 2] **THE APPEALS CHAMBER** of the International Criminal Tribunal for the Prosecution of Persons Responsible for Genocide and Other Serious Violations of International Humanitarian Law Committed in the Territory of Rwanda and Rwandan Citizens Responsible for Genocide and Other Such Violations Committed in the Territory of Neighbouring States between 1 January and 31 December 1994 ("Appeals Chamber" and "Tribunal", respectively),

BEING SEIZED OF the "Motion Requesting Preliminary Conference With Former Legal Team for the Preparation of a Request for the Assignment of Counsel for the Purpose of a Review", filed confidentially on 1 May 2009 ("Motion") by Mr. Alfred Musema-Uwimana ("Applicant"), in which he requests the Appeals Chamber to use its inherent jurisdiction to facilitate a "preliminary stage pre-review conference" with his former legal team in The Hague, The Netherlands, for a period of 14 days in order to receive legal advice on potential grounds of review and the assignment of counsel if sufficient grounds exist to apply for review;[1]

NOTING that the Prosecution opposes the Motion on the grounds that (i) the Appeals Chamber has consistently held that, "as a matter of principle, it is not for the Tribunal to assist a convicted person whose case has reached finality with any new investigation he would like to conduct or any new motion he may wish to bring by assigning him legal assistance at the Tribunal's expense and that it is only in exceptional circumstances that a convicted person will be granted legal assistance by the Tribunal after a final judgement has been rendered against him";[2] and (ii) the information provided by the Applicant as to the potential grounds of review and the assignment of counsel does not justify the Applicant's request;[3]

NOTING the Appeal Judgement of 16 November 2001 affirming the sentence of life imprisonment imposed on the Applicant who was convicted by Trial Chamber I on 27 January 2000;[4]

NOTING the transfer of the Applicant to the Republic of Mali for the enforcement of his sentence;[5]

NOTING the Agreement between the Government of the Republic of Mali and the United Nations on the Enforcement of Sentences of the International Criminal Tribunal for Rwanda signed on 12 February 1999 ("Agreement"); [page 3]

RECALLING that the Applicant may be assisted by a counsel in connection with a request for review at his own expense, at the expense of a third party, or on a *pro bono* basis, provided that the counsel files a power of attorney with the Registrar and satisfies the requirements to appear before the Tribunal;[6]

CONSIDERING that a counsel representing a convicted person on such a basis would be able to obtain access to the trial and appellate record from the Registry or his client and would also be able to meet with his client at his place of detention at his own expense;

CONSIDERING that nothing in the Statute, Rules of Procedure and Evidence, or practice of the Tribunal provides for the transfer of a convicted person to another State for purposes of meeting with a counsel;

CONSIDERING that, pursuant to Article 4 of the Agreement, the transfer of a person whose sentence is being enforced in the Republic of Mali is envisioned only in the event that the Tribunal orders that the person appear as a witness before it;

NOTING that the Motion contains no information requiring confidential status;

---

[1] Motion, paras. 1, 24.
[2] Prosecutor's Response to Applicant's Request for Preliminary Conference with Former Legal Counsel in The Hague, 7 May 2009 ("Response"), para. 2.
[3] Response, para. 3.
[4] *The Prosecutor v. Alfred Musema*, Case No. ICTR-96-13-T, Judgement and Sentence, 27 January 2000, p. 285; *Alfred Musema v. The Prosecutor*, Case No. ICTR-96-13-A, Judgement, 16 November 2001, p. 130.
[5] Motion, para. 4.
[6] Decision on Motion for Reconsideration of Decision on Request for Assignment of Counsel of 27 February 2009, 23 April 2009, p. 6; *see Jean-Bosco Barayagwiza v. The Prosecutor*, Case No. ICTR-99-52A-R, Decision on Jean-Bosco Barayagwiza's Motion of 6 March 2008, 11 April 2008, p. 4.

CONSIDERING that all submissions filed before the Appeals Chamber shall be public unless there are exceptional reasons for keeping them confidential;[7]

FOR THE FOREGOING REASONS,

DISMISSES the Motion and **DIRECTS** the Registrar to remove its confidential status.

Done this 18th day of June 2009,
at The Hague,
The Netherlands.

                                              Patrick Robinson
                                              Presiding Judge

[Seal of the Tribunal]

---

[7]   *Cf.* Rules 78 and 107 of the Rules of Procedure and Evidence of the Tribunal; *see also Sylvestre Gacumbitsi v. The Prosecutor*, Case No. ICTR-01-64-A, Decision on the Appellant's Rule 115 Motion and Related Motion by the Prosecution, 21 October 2005, para. 5.

Tribunal pénal international pour le Rwanda
International Criminal Tribunal for Rwanda

IN THE APPEALS CHAMBER

Before: Judge Fausto Pocar, Presiding
Judge Mehmet Güney
Judge Liu Daqun
Judge Andrésia Vaz
Judge Theodor Meron

Registrar: Mr. Adama Dieng

Date: 22 June 2009

JEAN-BOSCO BARAYAGWIZA

v.

THE PROSECUTOR

Case No. ICTR-99-52A-R

DECISION ON JEAN-BOSCO BARAYAGWIZA'S MOTION FOR REVIEW AND/OR RECONSIDERATION OF THE APPEAL JUDGEMENT OF 28 NOVEMBER 2007

The Applicant:

Mr. Jean-Bosco Barayagwiza, *pro se*

Office of the Prosecutor:

Mr. Hassan Bubacar Jallow
Mr. Alex Obote-Odora
Ms. Christine Graham
Ms. Linda Bianchi
Ms. Béatrice Chapaux

[page 1] 1. The Appeals Chamber of the International Criminal Tribunal for the Prosecution of Persons Responsible for Genocide and Other Serious Violations of International Humanitarian Law Committed in the Territory of Rwanda and Rwandan Citizens Responsible for Genocide and Other Such Violations Committed in the Territory of Neighbouring States, between 1 January 1994 and 31 December 1994 ("Appeals Chamber" and "Tribunal", respectively) is seized of a motion filed by Jean-Bosco Barayagwiza ("Applicant") on 10 December 2008[1] for review and/or reconsideration of the Appeal Judgement rendered on 28 November 2007 in the case of *Ferdinand Nahimana, Jean-Bosco Barayagwiza and Hassan Ngeze v. The Prosecutor*.[2]

I. BACKGROUND

2. On 3 December 2003, Trial Chamber I ("Trial Chamber") convicted the Applicant of conspiracy to commit genocide, genocide, direct and public incitement to commit genocide, and persecution and extermination as crimes against humanity,[3] and acquitted him of complicity in genocide, murder as a crime against humanity, and serious violations of Article 3 Common to the Geneva Conventions and of Additional Protocol II.[4] The Applicant was sentenced to thirty-five years' imprisonment.[5]

3. On 28 November 2007, the Appeals Chamber reversed the Applicant's convictions based on Article 6(1) of the Statute of the Tribunal ("Statute") for the crimes of direct and public incitement to commit genocide for his acts within the *Coalition pour la défense de la République* party ("CDR") and conspiracy to commit genocide, as well as his convictions based on Article 6(3) of the Statute with respect to his acts within *Radio télévision libre des mille collines S.A.* ("RTLM") and the CDR for the crimes of genocide, direct and public incitement to commit genocide, and extermination and persecution as crimes against humanity.[6] The Appeals Chamber affirmed the Applicant's convictions based on Article 6(1) of the Statute for genocide, under the mode of responsibility of instigation; extermination as a crime against humanity, under the mode of responsibility of ordering or instigating and planning; and persecution as a crime against humanity, [page 2] under the mode of responsibility of instigation.[7] As it reversed some of the Applicant's convictions, the Appeals Chamber also reduced his sentence to thirty-two years' imprisonment.[8]

4. Since the delivery of the Appeal Judgement on 28 November 2007, the Applicant has made several requests for assignment of counsel and access to documents to prepare a request for review and/or reconsideration.[9] On 11 April 2008, the Appeals Chamber filed a decision denying the Applicant's request for assignment of counsel at the Tribunal's expense to assist him in the preparation of a motion for review and/or reconsideration of the Appeal Judgement.[10] The Applicant's request to reconsider this decision was denied on 9 September 2008.[11]

---

[1] *Mémoire du requérant en vue de la révision et/ou reconsidération de l'arrêt du 28 novembre 2007*, filed on 10 December 2008 ("Motion").
[2] *Ferdinand Nahimana et al. v. The Prosecutor*, Case No. ICTR-99-52-A, Judgement, 28 November 2007 ("Appeal Judgement").
[3] *The Prosecutor v. Ferdinand Nahimana et al.*, Case No. ICTR-99-52-T, Judgement, 3 December 2003 ("Trial Judgement and Sentence"), para. 1093.
[4] *Ibid.*
[5] Trial Judgement, para. 1107.
[6] Appeal Judgement, para. 1096.
[7] *Ibid.*
[8] *Ibid*, para. 1097.
[9] *Recours très urgent de Jean-Bosco Barayagwiza contre le refus du Greffier de répondre à la demande d'assistance juridique en vue de la révision et/ou examen de l'Arrêt du 28 novembre 2007*, filed on 6 March 2008; *Jean-Bosco Barayagwiza v. The Prosecutor*, Case No. ICTR-99-52-A ("*Barayagwiza*"), *Requête aux fins de reconsidération de la décision du 11 avril 2008 et de protection des droits fondamentaux du requérant Jean-Bosco Barayagwiza*, filed on 2 May 2008; *Barayagwiza, Demande de clarifications en relation avec la Décision du 9 septembre 2008 à propos de la Requête de Jean-Bosco Barayagwiza du 2 mai 2008*, filed on 15 September 2008.
[10] *Barayagwiza*, Case No. ICTR-99-52-A-R, Decision on Jean-Bosco Barayagwiza's Motion of 6 March 2008, 11 April 2008 ("11 April 2008 Decision"), p. 4.
[11] *Barayagwiza*, Decision on Jean-Bosco Barayagwiza's Motion of 2 May 2008, 9 September 2008 ("9 September 2008 Decision"), p. 4.

5. On 2 October 2008 and 16 December 2008, the Appeals Chamber directed the Registrar to provide an exhaustive response to the Applicant's requests for documents.[12] The Registrar responded by delivering additional documents to the Applicant on 3 November 2008[13] and 16 December 2008.[14]

6. The Applicant filed his Motion on 10 December 2008, and moved for a scheduling order for the submissions related to the Motion on 11 December 2008.[15] On 6 January 2009, after the Registrar filed his submission, the Applicant requested an extension of time and authorization to file a supplement to the Motion.[16] On 28 January 2009, the Appeals Chamber dismissed the request for a scheduling order, partially granted the request for an extension of time, and instructed the **[page 3]** Applicant to file his supplement within 20 days of the filing of the decision.[17] The Appeals Chamber also ordered that the time limit for the Prosecution's response start to run from the filing of the Applicant's supplement to the Motion.[18]

7. The Applicant filed a supplementary brief to the Motion on 13 February 2009.[19] The Applicant then filed a corrigendum to both the Motion and the Supplementary Brief on 17 February 2009, which addressed several grammatical and typographical errors in the Motion.[20] The Prosecution responded on 25 March 2009,[21] and the Applicant replied on 9 April 2009.[22]

II. OVERVIEW OF SUBMISSIONS

8. As a preliminary issue, the Applicant contends that the Tribunal placed him in a position of inequality of arms *vis-à-vis* the Prosecution by denying his repeated requests for assignment of counsel and by denying him the facilities to gather documentation necessary for preparing his Motion.[23] He requests that the Appeals Chamber make findings on this specific aspect before it considers the merits of the Motion.[24]

9. The Applicant submits that he recently discovered new facts relating to his "trial *in absentia*" and the competence of his counsel, which are "capable of correcting the conspicuous injustice done to him had they been presented before the Trial Judges for adversarial argument".[25] The Applicant requests that the Appeals Chamber reconsider and/or review its findings in the Appeal Judgement that his "trial *in absentia*" was legal[26] and that he did not receive an unfair trial due to lack of effective and adequate representation.[27] The

---

[12] *Barayagwiza*, Decision on Barayagwiza's Motion of 15 September 2008, 2 October 2008 ("2 October 2008 Decision"); *Barayagwiza*, Order Regarding Communication of Documents, 16 December 2008. *See also Barayagwiza*, The Registrar's Submission in Regard to the Appeals Chamber's "Decision on Jean-Bosco Barayagwiza's Motion of 15 September 2008", filed confidentially on 3 November 2008 ("Registrar's Submission of 3 November 2008"). *Réponse au mémoire du Greffier du 3 novembre 2008 intitulé* The Registrar's Submission in Regard to the Appeals Chamber's Decision on Jean-Bosco Barayagwiza's Motion of 15 September 2008, filed on 10 November 2008.
[13] Registrar's Submission of 3 November 2008.
[14] *Barayagwiza*, Submission by the Registrar under Rule 33(B) of the Rules of Procedure and Evidence on the "Order Regarding Communication of Documents" dated 16 December 2008, 23 December 2008.
[15] *Barayagwiza, Rêquete pour une ordonnance définissant le calendrier et les délais de dépôt des écritures relativement à la demande de révision de l'arrêt du 28 novembre 2007*, filed on 11 December 2008.
[16] *Barayagwiza, Rêquete demandant la prolongation du délai de dépôt de la réponse au mémoire du Greffier intitulé* «Submission by the Registrar under rule 33(B) of the Rules of Procedure and Evidence on the «Order Regarding Communication of Documents» dated 16 December 2008», *et sollicitant l'autorisation de déposer un complément au mémoire en révision et/ou reconsidération déposé le 11 décembre 2008*, filed on 6 January 2009.
[17] *Barayagwiza*, Decision on Jean-Bosco Barayagwiza's Motions of 11 December 2008 and 6 January 2009, 28 January 2009, p. 6.
[18] *Ibid*.
[19] *Mémoire complémentaire au «Mémoire du requérant en vue de la révision et/ou reconsidération de l'arrêt du 28 novembre 2007»*, filed on 13 February 2009 ("Supplementary Brief").
[20] *Corrigendum au «Mémoire du requérant en vue de la révision et/ou reconsidération de l'arrêt du 28 novembre 2007» du 11 decembre 2008 et au «Mémoire complémentaire» date du 11 fevrier 2009*, filed on 17 February 2009 ("Corrigendum").
[21] Prosecutor's Response to Barayagwiza's "Mémoire du requérant en vue de la révision et/ou reconsidération de l'arrêt du 28 Novembre 2007", 25 March 2009 ("Prosecutor's Response").
[22] *Mémoire en réplique à la réponse du procureur au mémoire du requérant en vue de la révision et/ou réconsidération de l'arrêt du 28 Novembre 2007*, filed on 9 April 2009 ("Reply").
[23] Motion, paras. 2-4, *referring to* 11 April 2008 Decision; 9 September 2008 Decision; 2 October 2008 Decision.
[24] *Ibid*. para. 4.
[25] *Ibid*. para. 1.
[26] *Ibid*. para. 217; *see ibid*. paras. 21-91.
[27] *Ibid*. para. 217; *see ibid*. paras. 92-217.

Applicant further seeks the review of an Appeals Chamber decision of 31 March 2000 concerning the legality of his arrest and detention and the related findings in the Appeal Judgement.[28] Finally, alleging disproportion between the convictions retained on appeal and the sentence, the Applicant seeks the reconsideration of his **[page 4]** sentence.[29] The Applicant bases his request on the Appeal Chamber's inherent discretionary power to reconsider its previous decisions[30] and its power of review pursuant to Article 25 of the Statute and Rule 120 of the Rules of Procedure and Evidence of the Tribunal ("Rules").[31] Finally, the Applicant requests that the submissions of the parties in relation to his Motion be heard orally.[32]

10. In his Supplementary Brief, the Applicant submits that additional evidence, which he received from the Registrar on 29 December 2008, further supports his argument that Counsel Caldarera and Pognon were "incompetent".[33]

11. The Prosecution responds that the Motion should be dismissed in its entirety.[34]

12. In his Reply, the Applicant argues that details of the documents, which he uses to support his contention that his "trial *in absentia*" was illegal, were not discoverable by him through the exercise of due diligence.[35] He further contends that details of these documents would have been decisive factors for the Appeals Chamber to consider regarding his "trial *in absentia*".[36] The Applicant also claims that new facts show that his counsel did not investigate factual allegations made by the Prosecution,[37] and that the interests of justice require that the Appeals Chamber take all of his alleged new facts into account.[38]

III. DISCUSSION

A. Preliminary Issue: Allegation of Inequality of Arms in the Review and Reconsideration Proceedings

13. The Applicant argues that the Tribunal placed him "in a position of inequality of arms *vis-à-vis* the Prosecution" because it denied his request for assignment of counsel to assist him in preparing the Motion.[39] The Applicant contends that it was unjust for the Tribunal to force him to prepare the Motion without legal assistance while the Prosecution was endowed with "sufficient **[page 5]** human and material resources".[40] The Applicant claims that he has "suffered unacceptable injustice due to the [Appeals Chamber's] refusal to assign him Counsel for the review proceedings",[41] and requests the Appeals Chamber to order the Registrar to assign him a "Defence team" to "help him finalize the Review proceedings initiated".[42]

14. The Appeals Chamber considers that the Applicant is in fact requesting the reconsideration of the 11 April 2008, 9 September 2008, and 2 October 2008 Decisions denying him the assignment of counsel for the preparation of a request for review. The Appeals Chamber recalls that it may reconsider a previous non-final decision pursuant to its inherent discretionary power if a clear error of reasoning has been demonstrated or if it is necessary to prevent an injustice.[43]

---

[28] *See ibid*. paras. 218-225, *referring to Barayagwiza*, Case No. ICTR-97-19-AR72, Decision (Prosecutor's Request for Review or Reconsideration), 31 March 2000.
[29] *Ibid*. paras. 226, 227.
[30] *Ibid*. paras. 5-13.
[31] *Ibid*. paras. 14-20.
[32] *Ibid*. para. 228.
[33] Supplementary Brief, paras. 6-27.
[34] Prosecutor's Response, para. 4.
[35] Reply, para. 17.
[36] *Ibid*. para. 18.
[37] *Ibid*. paras. 31-37.
[38] *Ibid*. para. 46.
[39] Motion, paras. 2-4, *referring to* 11 April 2008 Decision; 9 September 2008 Decision; 2 October 2008 Decision; *see also* Reply, para. 5.
[40] Motion, para. 3.
[41] Reply, para. 5.
[42] *Ibid*. para. 49.
[43] 9 September 2008 Decision, p. 3; *The Prosecutor v. Tharcisse Muvunyi*, Case No. ICTR-00-55A-A, Decision on Motion for Reconsideration of the Decision on Request to Admit Additional Evidence, 16 November 2007, p. 2; *The Prosecutor v. Édouard*

15. The arguments set forth by the Applicant do not establish a clear error of reasoning in the 11 April 2008, 9 September 2008, and 2 October 2008 Decisions, nor that reconsideration is necessary to prevent an injustice. The Applicant merely submits that the Appeals Chamber placed him "in a position of inequality of arms *vis-à-vis* the Prosecutor" when it denied his requests for assignment of counsel, and that this forced him to research and prepare the Motion alone, without proper resources or expertise.[44] In doing so, the Applicant is simply repeating part of the argument that he set forth in his original motion for assignment of counsel,[45] which the Appeals Chamber has already denied three times.[46]

16. In addition, the Appeals Chamber recalls "that review is an exceptional remedy and that an applicant is only entitled to assigned counsel, at the Tribunal's expense, if the Appeals Chamber authorizes the review".[47] "Nonetheless, counsel may be assigned at the preliminary examination stage, normally for a very limited duration, if it is necessary to ensure the fairness of the proceedings".[48] The Appeals Chamber notes that the Applicant's submissions in support of his request for review are extensive and detailed, and that the Applicant does not express the need to file additional submissions prior to the examination of his Motion. The Appeals Chamber therefore **[page 6]** reiterates its findings that the assignment of counsel under the auspices of the Tribunal's legal aid system is not warranted in this case.

17. Accordingly, the Appeals Chamber denies the Applicant's request for reconsideration of the 11 April 2008, 9 September 2008, and 2 October 2008 Decisions.

B. Request for Reconsideration of the Appeal Judgement

18. The Applicant argues that he is entitled to a reconsideration of the Appeal Judgement because the Appeals Chamber has an inherent power to reconsider its decisions.[49] While he acknowledges that the Appeals Chamber has held that "there is no power to reconsider a final judgement",[50] the Applicant contends that a final judgement may still be reconsidered because a decision of the International Criminal Tribunal for the Former Yugoslavia ("ICTY") Appeals Chamber states that the Tribunal may reconsider its decisions, which cannot be subject to review proceedings.[51] The Prosecution responds that the jurisprudence of the Appeals Chamber is such that reconsideration of a final judgement is not possible, and that there is no legal basis for the Appeals Chamber to depart from this established jurisprudence and in the interests of justice reconsider the issues raised by the Applicant.[52]

19. In the Reply, the Applicant reiterates his argument that a final judgement may be reconsidered and also argues that the Appeals Chamber should reconsider the Appeal Judgement because "in certain specific cases, the Appeals Chamber has power to reconsider its previous decision, in the interests of justice".[53]

20. The Appeals Chamber does not have an inherent power to reconsider final judgements.[54] As stated in the *Žigić* Decision, to which the Applicant refers:

Karemera et al., Case No. ICTR-98-44-AR73.10, Decision on Ngirumpatse's Motion for Reconsideration, 5 October 2007, p. 3.
[44] Motion, paras. 2-4.
[45] *See* 9 September 2008 Decision, p. 3.
[46] *See* 11 April 2008 Decision; 9 September 2008 Decision; and 2 October 2008 Decision.
[47] *Georges Anderson Nderubumwe Rutaganda v. The Prosecutor*, Case No. ICTR-96-03-R, Decision on Requests for Reconsideration, Review, Assignment of Counsel, Disclosure, and Clarification, 8 December 2006 ("*Rutaganda* Review Decision"), para. 41. *See also* Decision on Niyitegeka's Urgent Request for Legal Assistance, 20 June 2005("*Niyitigeka* Decision of 20 June 2005"), p. 4.
[48] *Rutaganda* Review Decision, para. 41. *See also Niyitegeka* Decision of 20 June 2005, p. 4.
[49] Motion, paras. 5-13.
[50] *Ibid.* para. 9, *quoting Prosecutor v. Zoran Žigić a/k/a "Ziga"*, Case No. IT-98-30/1-A, Decision on Zoran Žigić's "Motion for Reconsideration of Appeals Chamber Judgement IT-98-30/1-A Delivered on 28 February 2005", 26 June 2006 ("*Žigić* Decision"), para. 9 (emphasis added).
[51] *Ibid.*
[52] Prosecutor's Response, para. 21.
[53] Reply, paras. 7, 8.
[54] *Žigić* Decision, para. 9.

To allow a person whose conviction has been confirmed on appeal the right to further contest the original findings against them on the basis of mere assertions of errors of fact or law is not in the interests of justice to the victims of the crimes or the convicted person, who are both entitled to certainty and finality of legal judgements.[55] **[page 7]**

The Appeals Chamber has upheld and maintained that the mechanism of reconsideration is not applicable and cannot be used in respect of a final judgement.[56]

21. The jurisprudence cited by the Applicant in support of his contention that the Appeals Chamber may reconsider the Appeal Judgement refers exclusively to the Appeals Chamber's inherent power to reconsider *non-final* decisions, not final judgements.[57] As a consequence, the Appeals Chamber finds no merit in the Applicant's contention.

C. Request for Review of the Appeal Judgement

1. Standard of Review

22. The Appeals Chamber recalls that review proceedings are governed by Article 25 of the Statute and Rules 120 and 121 of the Rules. The Appeals Chamber emphasizes that review of a final judgement is an exceptional procedure and not an additional opportunity for a party to re-litigate arguments that failed at trial or on appeal.[58] In order for review to be granted, the moving party must show that: (1) there is a new fact; (2) the new fact was not known to the moving party at the time of the original proceedings; (3) the lack of discovery of that new fact was not the result of a lack of due diligence by the moving party; and (4) the new fact could have been a decisive factor in reaching the original decision.[59] In wholly exceptional circumstances, the Appeals Chamber may grant review even where the new fact was known to the moving party at the time of the original proceedings, or the lack of discovery of the fact was the result of a lack of due diligence by the moving party, if ignoring the new fact would result in a miscarriage of justice.[60]

23. The Appeals Chamber further recalls that the term "new fact" refers to new evidentiary information supporting a fact that was not in issue during the trial or appeal proceedings.[61] The requirement that the fact was not in issue during the proceedings means that "it must not have been among the factors that the deciding body could have taken into account in reaching its **[page 8]** verdict."[62] Essentially, the moving party must show that the Chamber did not know about the fact in reaching its decision.[63]

2. Alleged New Facts

24. In accordance with the standard applicable in review proceedings, the Appeals Chamber will not address the Applicant's allegations of errors in the Appeal Judgement unless they are related to alleged new facts. Accordingly, the following contentions of errors are dismissed without further consideration: (1) that the Applicant lacked effective and adequate representation between 23 October 2000 and 6 February 2001;[64] (2) that he suffered prejudice due to the continuation of his trial without any legal representation between 6

---

[55] *Ibid.*
[56] *See, e.g., Hassan Ngeze v. The Prosecutor*, Case No. ICTR-99-52-R, Decision on Hassan Ngeze's Motions and Requests Related to Reconsideration, 31 January 2008, p. 3; *Ferdinand Nahimana v. The Prosecutor*, Case No. ICTR99-52B-R, Decision on Ferdinand Nahimana's "Notice of Application for Reconsideration of Appeal Decision Due to Factual Errors Apparent on the Record", 21April 2008, p. 2.
[57] Motion, para. 9, *citing Žigić* Decision, para. 9.
[58] *Eliézer Niyitegeka v. The Prosecutor*, Case No. ICTR-96-14-R, Decision on Fourth Request for Review (Public Redacted Version), 12 March 2009 ("*Niyitigeka* Fourth Review Decision"), para. 21; *Rutaganda* Review Decision, para. 8.
[59] *Niyitigeka* Fourth Review Decision, para. 21; *Rutaganda* Review Decision, para. 8; *The Prosecutor v. Aloys Simba*, Case No. ICTR-01-76-A, Decision on Aloys Simba's Requests for Suspension of Appeal Proceedings and Review, 9 January 2007, para. 8. *See also Prosecutor v. Tihomir Blaškić*, Case No. IT-95-14-R, Decision on Prosecutor's Request for Review or Reconsideration, 23 November 2006 ("*Blaškić* Review Decision"), para. 7.
[60] *Niyitigeka* Fourth Review Decision, para. 21; *Rutaganda* Review Decision, para. 8; *Blaškić* Review Decision, para. 8.
[61] *Niyitigeka* Fourth Review Decision, para. 22; *Rutaganda* Review Decision, para. 9; *Blaškić* Review Decision, paras. 14, 15.
[62] *Ibid.*
[63] *Niyitigeka* Fourth Review Decision, para. 22; *Rutaganda* Review Decision, para. 9; *Blaškić* Review Decision, para. 14.
[64] Motion, paras. 92-100; Reply, para. 19; Appeal Judgement, paras. 123-125.

and 12 February 2001;[65] (3) that the Trial Chamber "knew the limits of Counsel's competence and skill to ensure adequate and effective defence";[66] (4) that the repeated absences and lateness of his counsel during hearings should have been sanctioned;[67] (5) that his refusal to cooperate could not absolve his counsel from their duty to adequately defend him with due diligence;[68] (6) that his motions of 28 July 2000 and 26 September 2005 remain to be considered on their merits;[69] and (7) that his sentence is unjust, on the ground that it was not sufficiently reduced in view of the convictions that were set aside by the Appeals Chamber.[70] The Appeals Chamber will now turn to the Applicant's arguments which are supported by alleged new facts. The Applicant alleges that there are new facts supporting his contentions that:

(1) the Trial chamber erred in trying him "in *absentia*";[71] and (2) his trial was unfair due to the lack of effective and adequate representation.[72]

(a) Alleged New Facts Related to the "Trial *in Absentia*"

25. The Applicant argues that he has discovered new facts concerning the alleged illegality of his "trial *in absentia*", which his Defence Counsel failed to produce before the Trial Chamber.[73] According to the Applicant, those facts are contained in documents,[74] which concern opinions and **[page 9]** proposals set forth by various entities and individuals during the preparatory work for the establishment of the International Criminal Court ("ICC").[75]

26. According to the Applicant, these documents demonstrate the extreme divergence of positions regarding the possibility of a trial in the absence of an accused, which led to the exclusion of trial *in absentia* from the Statute and Rules of the ICTY and the Tribunal, and the Statute of the ICC.[76] The Applicant further argues that the only permissible exception to the rule against trial *in absentia* is "where the accused has to be removed from court because of continued disruption of the trial."[77] The Applicant asserts that these are new facts, which establish that the Trial Chamber had no legal basis for trying him in his absence and, consequently, that the Appeals Chamber should have quashed the Trial Judgement.[78]

27. The Prosecution responds that the *travaux préparatoires* presented by the Applicant do not constitute new facts for the purpose of review because the Appeals Chamber already took them into account when determining whether the Trial Chamber correctly proceeded with a trial against the Applicant in his absence.[79] Additionally, the Prosecution contends that these alleged new facts were known, or must have been known to the Applicant through the exercise of due diligence. Finally, it submits that even if these facts could be characterized as "new", they could not have been decisive factors for the Appeals Chamber in reaching its original decision.[80]

---

[65] Motion, paras. 101, 102; Reply, paras. 20, 21; Appeal Judgement, paras. 170-179.
[66] Motion, paras. 178-182; Appeal Judgement, paras. 136-138.
[67] Motion, paras. 183-191; Appeal Judgement, paras. 139-157.
[68] Motion, paras. 192-194; Appeal Judgement, para. 138.
[69] Motion, paras. 218-225; Reply, para. 47.
[70] Motion, paras. 226, 227; Reply, para. 48.
[71] Motion, paras. 1, 21-91.
[72] *Ibid.* paras. 1, 92-191.
[73] *Ibid.* para. 22.
[74] The documents that the Applicant refers to are: "(1) Report of the International Law Commission on the work of its forty-fifth session, 3 May-July 1993, Official Records of the General Assembly, Forty-eighth session, Supplement No. 10. (2) Proposals of States and Organizations for the Statute and Rules of Procedure and Evidence of the International Tribunal in relation to the Question of Trials in absentia. (3) Proposals of States and Organizations for the Rules of Procedure and Evidence of the International Tribunal in relation to the question of Trials in absentia. (4) Statement by the President of the Tribunal for the Former Yugoslavia. (5) Reports relating to *travaux préparatoires* of the Rome Treaty on the establishment of the ICC. the Statute of the ICC..(6) Statement by the ICTR Prosecutor, Abubakar Jallow, at the 5904th Session of the Security Counsel, held in New York on 4 June 2008". Motion, para. 23.
[75] *Ibid.* paras. 23, 24.
[76] *Ibid.* para. 25.
[77] *Ibid.* para. 72.
[78] *Ibid.* para. 79.
[79] Prosecutor's Response, para. 30.
[80] *Ibid.*

28. The Appeals Chamber notes that, on appeal, the Applicant contended that neither the Statute nor the Rules permitted the Trial Chamber to try him *in absentia*.[81] In support of this argument, the Applicant invoked the *travaux préparatoires* of the Statute of the ICTY, and emphasized the fact that the Statute of the ICC does not provide for a trial *in absentia*.[82] Having considered these submissions, the Appeals Chamber stated that it could not "determine any error in the finding reached by the Trial Chamber in regard to the Appellant's refusal to attend trial".[83] Therefore, the documents the Applicant sets forth in the Motion regarding trial *in absentia* do not constitute "evidentiary information supporting a fact that was not in issue during the trial or appeal **[page 10]** proceedings".[84] Accordingly, they are not new facts that would justify review of the Appeal Judgement by the Appeals Chamber.

(b)   Alleged New Facts Related to the "Incompetence" of Counsel and Inadequate Representation

29. The Applicant further submits that new evidence[85] received from the Registrar confirms that he did not receive adequate and effective representation before the Trial Chamber because Counsel Caldarera and Pognon were "incompetent".[86] The Applicant contends that the new evidence proves that the counsel were "incompetent" because it shows that: (1) they did not conduct a field investigation in Rwanda;[87] (2) they did not attempt to retain Investigator Maniragena after his contract was terminated by the Tribunal;[88] (3) Counsel Pognon withdrew prematurely from the Applicant's defence;[89] and (4) they were not competent to adequately represent the Applicant and demonstrated a manifest lack of diligence.[90]

30. Based on jurisprudence from national jurisdictions, which he had not previously cited at trial or on appeal,[91] and a letter he recently received from the Registry,[92] the Applicant contends that

Counsel Caldarera and Pognon were "incompetent" and demonstrated a manifest lack of diligence when they represented him at trial. The Applicant claims that the "incompetence" and lack of diligence of Counsel Caldarera and Pognon are demonstrated by the fact that they: (1) "were not familiar with the adversarial system at the time of their assignment";[93] (2) "did not conduct investigations required to prepare an adequate and effective defence before delving into the substance of the case";[94] and (3) "conducted inappropriate cross-examination".[95]

31. Based on work programs that he recently received from the Registry, the Applicant argues that Counsel Caldarera and Pognon never conducted a field investigation in Rwanda.[96] The **[page 11]** Applicant claims that during the period of 8 February 2001 to 1 October 2002, most of the activities of Counsel Caldarera and his legal assistant took place in Arusha, Tanzania, or at his law firm in Catane, Italy, and that Counsel Caldarera never went to any African country on a working mission.[97] The Applicant also contends

---

[81]   Appeal Judgement, para. 94.
[82]   *Ibid.*
[83]   Appeal Judgement, paras. 99, 115, 116.
[84]   *Niyitigeka* Decision, para. 14; *Rutaganda* Review Decision, para. 9; *Blaškić* Review Decision, paras. 14, 15 (internal quotations omitted).
[85]   The new evidence, which the Applicant received from the Registrar, consists of various documents such as correspondence between Counsel Caldarera and Pognon and the Registry; time sheets, work programs, and other employment forms for Counsel Caldarera and Pognon; and other miscellaneous documents such as faxes, notes, and written requests. *See* Motion, para. 104; Supplementary Brief, para. 5. The Applicant received one batch of documents from the Registry in response to the 2 October 2008 Decision. *See Barayagwiza*, Registrar's Submission of 3 November 2008. The Applicant received a second batch of documents from the Registry on 29 December 2008. *See* Supplementary Brief, para. 5.
[86]   Motion, paras. 104-117.
[87]   *Ibid.* paras. 118-120.
[88]   *Ibid.* paras. 121-129.
[89]   *Ibid.* paras. 130-143.
[90]   *Ibid.* paras. 143-191.
[91]   *Ibid.* paras. 143-191.
[92]   *See, e.g., Ibid.* para. 168, Fn. 241.
[93]   *Ibid.* p. 53, paras. 150-156.
[94]   *Ibid.* paras. 157-167.
[95]   *Ibid.* p. 56, paras. 168-177.
[96]   *Ibid.* paras. 118-120.
[97]   *Ibid.* para. 118.

that during the period of 5 March 2001 to 6 October 2002, the activities of Counsel Pognon and his legal assistant were carried out solely at his law firm in Benin and in Arusha, and that Counsel Pognon never went to any African country on a working mission.[98]

32. Based on recently received correspondence between Counsel Caldarera and the Registry, the Applicant argues that Counsel Caldarera committed gross professional misconduct by "not using all the means available to him to maintain the services of Investigator Théophile Maniragena".[99] According to the Applicant, Counsel Caldarera never intervened to prevent the termination of Maniragena's contract once the Registry informed him that they had suspended it.[100] The Applicant claims that the Registry finalized the termination of Maniragena's contract once it realized that Counsel Caldarera had not objected to it.[101]

33. Based on recently received correspondence between Counsel Caldarera and Pognon and the Registry, the Applicant argues that Counsel Pognon withdrew prematurely from his case without demonstrating the required "exceptional circumstances" for his withdrawal.[102] The Applicant also states that Counsel Pognon withdrew simply "to renege on the undertaking he had made, with full knowledge of the facts"[103] so that he could "be assigned to the defence of Father Athanase Seromba".[104]

34. The Applicant argues that the new evidence regarding Counsel Caldarera and Pognon demonstrates that he did not benefit from a truly adversarial trial or equality of arms during trial,[105] and that it was therefore impossible to adequately establish his guilt.[106] The Applicant also argues that gross injustice resulted from the "inadequate representation in a trial conducted in his absence".[107] **[page 12]**

35. The Prosecution responds that the competence of the Applicant's trial counsel was raised and comprehensively dealt with during the appeal proceeding and, therefore, that none of the arguments related to this issue concerns a new fact that would justify review of the Appeal Judgement.[108]

36. The Appeals Chamber recalls that, on appeal, the Applicant claimed that his trial counsel were "incompetent" and that he had lacked effective representation at trial. The Appeal Judgement addressed the following allegations made by the Applicant: (1) that Counsel Caldarera did not allow enough time to familiarize himself with the case;[109] (2) that his counsel were frequently late or absent from the proceedings;[110] (3) that there was a conflict of interest between the Applicant and his counsel;[111] (4) that the Applicant was not granted assistance from a Kinyarwanda speaker;[112] (5) that his counsel failed to investigate and to ask crucial questions, and relied improperly on information from third parties;[113] (6) that his counsel failed to recall Prosecution witnesses heard between 23 October 2000 and 6 February 2001;[114] (7) that his counsel failed to cross-examine certain witnesses;[115] and (8) that his counsel made a bad decision to call an expert witness.[116]

37. It is therefore clear that the alleged "incompetence" of Counsel Caldarera and Pognon was in issue during the appeal proceedings. Thus, the facts the Applicant sets forth in the Motion regarding the "incompetence" of Counsel Caldarera and Pognon do not constitute "evidentiary information supporting a

---

[98] *Ibid.* p. 71.
[99] *Ibid.* paras. 121-125.
[100] *Ibid.* p.ara. 122.
[101] *Ibid.* para. 123.
[102] *Ibid.* para. 136.
[103] *Ibid.* para. 138.
[104] *Ibid.* para. 139.
[105] *Ibid.* paras. 195-204.
[106] *Ibid.* paras. 205-214.
[107] *Ibid.* paras. 215-217.
[108] Prosecutor's Response, para. 44.
[109] Appeal Judgement, paras. 136-138.
[110] *Ibid.* paras. 139-157.
[111] *Ibid.* paras. 158-160.
[112] *Ibid.* paras. 161-163.
[113] *Ibid.* para. 164.
[114] *Ibid.* para. 165.
[115] *Ibid.* paras. 166-168.
[116] *Ibid.* para. 169.

fact that was not in issue during the trial or appeal proceedings".[117] Accordingly, they are not new facts that would justify a review of the Appeal Judgement by the Appeals Chamber.

38. Regarding the Applicant's claims that he was not offered a truly adversarial trial, and that inequality of arms and gross injustice resulted from "inadequate representation in a trial conducted in his absence",[118] the Appeals Chamber notes that these arguments are premised on the facts set forth by the Applicant concerning the alleged incompetence of Counsel Caldarera and Pognon and the alleged illegality of his "trial *in absentia*". Having already determined that the facts set forth by the Applicant concerning the alleged incompetence of Counsel Caldarera and Pognon and the **[page 13]** legality of the Applicant's "trial *in absentia*" are not new facts, which merit a review of the Appeal Judgement, the Appeals Chamber declines to address the Applicant's arguments that he did not receive a truly adversarial trial and that he suffered from inequality of arms and gross injustice during trial.

3. Conclusion

39. The Appeals Chamber reiterates that review is an exceptional remedy. In the instant case, the Applicant has failed to demonstrate that such a remedy is warranted.

IV. DISPOSITION

40. For the foregoing reasons, the Appeals Chamber:

DENIES the Motion in its entirety.

Done in English and French, the English version being authoritative.

Done this 22nd day of June 2009,
at The Hague,
The Netherlands.

Judge Fausto Pocar
Presiding

[Seal of the Tribunal]

---

[117] *Niyitigeka* Fourth Review Decision, para. 14; *Rutaganda* Review Decision, para. 9; *Blaškić* Review Decision, paras. 14, 15.
[118] Motion, paras. 215-217.

Tribunal pénal international pour le Rwanda
International Criminal Tribunal for Rwanda

IN THE APPEALS CHAMBER

Before: Judge Patrick Robinson, Presiding
Judge Liu Daqun
Judge Andrésia Vaz
Judge Theodor Meron
Judge Carmel Agius

Registrar: Mr. Adama Dieng

Date: 21 July 2009

JEAN DE DIEU KAMUHANDA

v.

THE PROSECUTOR

Case No. ICTR-99-54A-R

DECISION ON MOTION FOR LEGAL ASSISTANCE

The Applicant

Mr. Jean de Dieu Kamuhanda, *pro se*

Office of the Prosecutor

Mr. Hassan Bubacar Jallow
Mr. Alex Obote-Odora
Mr. George W. Mugwanya
Ms. Evelyn Kamau

[page 2] 1. The Appeals Chamber of the International Criminal Tribunal for the Prosecution of Persons Responsible for Genocide and Other Serious Violations of International Humanitarian Law Committed in the Territory of Rwanda and Rwandan Citizens Responsible for Genocide and Other Serious Violations Committed in the Territory of Neighbouring States, between 1 January and 31 December 1994 ("Appeals Chamber" and "Tribunal", respectively) is seized of the "Motion for Legal Assistance for Preliminary Proceedings Relating to the Review of the Judgement Delivered by the Appeals Chamber on 19 September 2005", filed by Jean de Dieu Kamuhanda ("Kamuhanda") on 15 May 2009 ("Motion").[1]

A. Procedural Background

2. On 22 January 2004, Trial Chamber II of the Tribunal ("Trial Chamber") convicted Kamuhanda for genocide and extermination as a crime against humanity pursuant to Article 6(1) of the Statute of the Tribunal ("Statute") on the basis of his involvement in a massacre at Gikomero Parish Compound on 12 April 1994 and sentenced him to imprisonment for the remainder of his life.[2] Kamuhanda lodged an appeal against the Trial Judgement.

3. During the appellate proceedings, the Appeals Chamber granted in part a motion filed by Kamuhanda for admission of additional evidence, admitting new statements from Witnesses GAA and GEX and ordering that these witnesses be heard.[3] On 18 May 2005, Witnesses GAA and GEX were heard together with two witnesses called by the Prosecution in rebuttal.[4] During the evidentiary hearing, Witness GAA testified that he had lied during trial when he stated that he had been at the Gikomero Parish Compound and that he had seen Kamuhanda there.[5] Witness GEX testified before the Appeals Chamber that, contrary to her earlier statement given to the Prosecution,[6] she had not seen Kamuhanda at Gikomero, nor had she heard his name spoken there.[7]

4. In an oral decision rendered at the close of the evidentiary hearing on 19 May 2005, the Appeals Chamber directed the Prosecutor, pursuant to Rules 77(C)(i) and 91(B) of the Rules of Procedure and Evidence of the Tribunal ("Rules"), to investigate allegations of attempted interference with a witness who had given evidence in proceedings before the Tribunal and [page 3] discrepancies arising from testimony given during the hearing of the merits of the appeal and the consequent possibility of false testimony.[8] As a result, the Prosecutor appointed a Special Counsel to conduct the investigation ("Special Counsel").[9]

5. In its Judgement of 19 September 2005, the Appeals Chamber found Witness GAA's recantation during the evidentiary hearing of May 2005 not credible and Witness GEX's testimony before the Appeals Chamber unreliable.[10] While vacating the convictions for instigating and aiding and abetting genocide and extermination, the Appeals Chamber affirmed the convictions for ordering genocide and extermination as a crime against humanity, as well as the sentences imposed by the Trial Chamber.[11]

---

[1] Originally filed in French, English version filed on 22 June 2009.
[2] *The Prosecutor v. Jean de Dieu Kamuhanda*, Case No. ICTR-99-54A-T, Judgement and Sentence, 22 January 2004 ("Trial Judgement"), paras. 651, 652, 700, 702, 750, 770.
[3] *Jean de Dieu Kamuhanda v. The Prosecutor*, Case No. ICTR-99-54A-A, Judgement, 19 September 2005 ("Appeal Judgement"), para. 442.
[4] Appeal Judgement, para. 442.
[5] Appeal Judgement, para. 213.
[6] Witness GEX provided a statement to the Prosecution prior to the trial phase, which was disclosed to the Defence. Witness GEX was not called to testify at trial. Appeal Judgement, para. 222.
[7] Appeal Judgement, para. 223.
[8] *See Jean de Dieu Kamuhanda v. The Prosecutor*, Case No. ICTR-99-54A-A, Oral Decision (Rule 115 and Contempt of False Testimony), 19 May 2005.
[9] *The Prosecutor v. Jean de Dieu Kamuhanda*, Case No. ICTR-01-54A-A, Prosecutor's Reply by Way of Clarification in Relation to Jean de Dieu Kamuhanda's Response to the "Prosecutor's Disclosure Pursuant to Rule 75(F) of the Rules, of the Confidential Transcript of the Testimony of Defence Witness 7/14, in *Prosecutor v. Rwamakuba*", 20 March 2006, para. 10.
[10] Appeal Judgement, paras. 221, 226.
[11] Appeal Judgement, para. 365.

6. On 7 April 2006, the Appeals Chamber dismissed Kamuhanda's motion filed on 13 March 2006 in which he, *inter alia*, asked to be provided with a copy of the investigation report produced by the Special Counsel.[12]

7. On 11 June 2007, an indictment charging Witness GAA with false testimony, contempt, and attempts to commit contempt was issued.[13] Witness GAA concluded a plea agreement with the Prosecution in which he acknowledged having knowingly and willfully given false testimony during the evidentiary hearing before the Appeals Chamber on 18 May 2005 by testifying *inter alia* that he was not present at Gikomero Parish on 12 April 1994.[14] He also stated that his false testimony was induced by Léonidas Nshogoza ("Nshogoza"), a former investigator in Kamuhanda's Defence team who gave him money and offered him a reward for giving false testimony.[15] On 4 December 2007, Trial Chamber III found Witness GAA guilty of giving false testimony under solemn declaration and contempt of the Tribunal and sentenced him to nine months of imprisonment.[16] **[page 4]**

8. Subsequently, Nshogoza was indicted and prosecuted for contempt of the Tribunal and attempt to commit acts punishable as contempt of the Tribunal.[17]

9. Kamuhanda filed his Motion on 15 May 2009 and the Prosecution responded on 18 May 2009.[18] Kamuhanda did not file a reply.

10. Following the filing of the Motion, the Prosecution disclosed to Kamuhanda, on 28 May 2009, witness statements and trial transcripts from the *Nshogoza* case,[19] including statements of Witness GAA made before the Special Counsel.[20]

11. On 7 July 2009, Trial Chamber III convicted Nshogoza of committing contempt of the Tribunal by repeatedly meeting with and disclosing protected information of Witnesses GAA and A7/GEX, in knowing violation of, or with reckless indifference to, the protective measures ordered by the *Kamuhanda* Trial Chamber on 7 July 2000 and sentenced him to 10 months of imprisonment.[21]

B. Submissions

12. In his Motion, Kamuhanda requests the assignment of a legal assistant at the expense of the Tribunal to assist him and his former counsel in the preparation of a motion for review of the Appeal Judgement that he intends to file pursuant to Article 25 of the Statute and Rules 120 and 121 of the Rules.[22] Kamuhanda submits that his former counsel, Ms. Aïcha Condé, would be willing to assist him *pro bono* in the preparation and drafting of a motion for review but that, due to the workload in her practice, she would need the support of a legal assistant paid by the Tribunal.[23]

---

[12] *The Prosecutor v. Jean de Dieu Kamuhanda,* Case No. ICTR-99-54A-A, Decision on Jean de Dieu Kamuhanda's Request Related to Prosecution Disclosure and Special Investigation, 7 April 2006 ("Decision of 7 April 2006"), paras. 6, 8.
[13] *The Prosecutor v. GAA,* Case No. ICTR-07-90-R77-I, Judgement and Sentence, 4 December 2007 ("GAA Trial Judgement"), para. 1.
[14] GAA Trial Judgement, para. 5.
[15] GAA Trial Judgement, para. 5.
[16] GAA Trial Judgement, Disposition, p. 6.
[17] *The Prosecutor v. Léonidas Nshogoza,* Case No. ICTR-07-91-I, Indictment, 7 January 2008.
[18] Prosecution's Response to Kamuhanda's "*Requête aux fins de demande d'une assistance juridique pour la procédure préliminaire de révision de l'Arrêt rendu par la Chambre d'Appel le 19 septembre 2005*", 18 May 2009 ("Response").
[19] *The Prosecutor v. Léonidas Nshogoza,* Case No. ICTR-07-91-T.
[20] *See* Memorandum from Abdoulaye Seye, Appeals Counsel for the Office of the Prosecutor entitled "Disclosure to Mr. Jean de Dieu Kamuhanda of Witness Statements and trial Transcripts from the Case *The Prosecutor v. Léonidas Nshogoza*", confidential, 28 May 2009.
[21] *The Prosecutor v. Léonidas Nshogoza,* Case No. ICTR-07-91-T, Judgement, 7 July 2009, paras. 188, 189, 233.
[22] Motion, paras. 1, 5, 83.
[23] Motion, paras. 78, 79. Kamuhanda emphasizes that the following tasks would *inter alia* have to be undertaken: assess the evidence which he intends to rely on; carry out research on the case-law; search on the Tribunal's database and on EDS; file motions to obtain confidential or unavailable documents. *See* Motion, para. 79.

13. Kamuhanda submits that he has obtained evidence which was not available during the trial and appeal proceedings and which "clearly shows that there has been a miscarriage of justice in [his] case".[24] He also contends that he has been informed of the existence of other relevant evidence **[page 5]** in the possession of the Prosecution.[25] Kamuhanda specifically refers to the following: (1) the investigation report on false testimony and contempt, and the statements of the persons the Special Counsel interviewed, including Witness GAA;[26] (2) the evidence gathered during the trial of Léonidas Nshogoza regarding Kamuhanda's presence at Gikomero Parish on 12 April 1994;[27] (3) the evidence from André Rwamakuba's trial, including the testimony of Witness 7/14, the statements of Witnesses 9/31, 3/11, 3/1, 3/22, 7/3, as well as the Judgement delivered in André Rwamakuba's case;[28] and (4) other new material consisting of the record of the Gikomero *Gacaca* trial, a list of accused persons drawn up by the *Gacaca* Tribunal of Mutokerezwa *cellule*, and an affidavit by two Judges of Gikomero *Gacaca* Tribunal.[29]

14. Kamuhanda further alleges that the Prosecution violated its obligations under Rule 68 of the Rules by failing to disclose to him the report containing the conclusions of the Special Counsel's investigation and the written statements of the persons the Special Counsel interviewed, which, in his view, constitute exculpatory material.[30] He adds that the Prosecution should have disclosed the said material not only to him and his counsel but also to the Appeals Chamber for its consideration during the deliberations.[31]

15. Kamuhanda submits that his lack of knowledge of law and English, the need to request disclosure from the Prosecution, and the absence of Registry services in the prison of Koulikoro, Mali where he is serving his sentence warrant that he receives the legal assistance sought.[32] More specifically, he argues that, because of his lack of technical legal knowledge, he is not able to make use of the materials and evidence, to expose how they justify a review of the Appeal Judgement, and to explain how the Prosecution failed to meet its obligations under Rule 68 of the Rules.[33]

16. The Prosecution responds that the Motion is without merit and should be dismissed in its entirety.[34] It submits that despite the justifications provided by Kamuhanda, the latter was able to prepare a detailed and extensive briefing "in one of the official languages of the Tribunal, have it transmitted from his place of incarceration to the seat of the Tribunal, and to have it presented to the **[page 6]** Prosecution and Appeals Chamber".[35] According to the Prosecution, the issues at stake are sufficiently briefed in the Motion to be considered by the Appeals Chamber without further elaboration.[36]

C. Discussion

17. The Appeals Chamber recalls that as a matter of principle it is not for the Tribunal to assist a convicted person whose case has reached finality. It is only in exceptional circumstances that a convicted person will be granted legal assistance at the expense of the Tribunal after a final judgement has been rendered against him.[37] This type of legal assistance may take different forms, such as the assignment of a counsel or a legal assistant, where the convicted person is indigent. At the preliminary examination stage of a request for review, such assistance will be granted only if the Appeals Chamber deems it "necessary to ensure the

---

[24] Motion, para. 4.
[25] Motion, para. 4.
[26] Motion, paras. 7-37.
[27] Motion, paras. 38-40.
[28] Motion, paras. 41-52.
[29] Motion, paras. 53-57.
[30] Motion, paras. 15, 16, 33, 34, 36. Kamuhanda submits that his former Counsel asked without success to obtain the investigative report from the Prosecution. He specifies that on 26 March 2007 the Prosecution appeals section responded that the said report would be made available at the appropriate time. Motion, paras. 7-9.
[31] Motion, paras. 24, 34, 36.
[32] Motion, paras. 59-76.
[33] Motion, paras. 60, 61, 65.
[34] Response, paras. 2, 6.
[35] Response, para. 5.
[36] Response, para. 4.
[37] *Eliézer Niyitegeka v. The Prosecutor*, Case No. ICTR-96-14-R, Decision on Fourth Request for Review, Public Redacted Version, signed on 12 March 2009 and filed on 21 April 2009 ("*Niyitegeka* Fourth Review Decision"), para. 52.

fairness of the proceedings".[38] This necessity is, to a great extent, assessed in light of the potential grounds for review put forward by the applicant.[39]

18. The Appeals Chamber cannot rule on Kamuhanda's potential grounds for review as currently presented; the Motion is neither fully articulated in this respect nor is it intended to be a request for review *per se*, and Kamuhanda has yet to consider the material disclosed to him by the Prosecution in May 2009. Nevertheless, unlike other requests for legal assistance for review proceedings brought before the Appeals Chamber, Kamuhanda's Motion provides information on the materials he considers to be "new facts" and explains how they could have been a decisive factor in reaching the original decision. Having carefully considered Kamuhanda's arguments, as well as the material recently disclosed by the Prosecution, the Appeals Chamber is not in a position to exclude that Kamuhanda's potential grounds of review may have a chance of success.[40]

19. The Appeals Chamber observes that Kamuhanda was able to file a detailed and coherent request despite his asserted lack of technical legal skills. However, in the exceptional circumstances of this particularly complex case, involving false testimony and subsequent contempt proceedings, the Appeals Chamber is of the view that Kamuhanda lacks the necessary legal expertise to properly **[page 7]** assess and weigh the material now in his possession to determine whether a request for review is warranted and, if need be, to prepare such a request.

20. Accordingly, the Appeals Chamber finds that Kamuhanda has shown that it is necessary in order to ensure the fairness of the proceedings at the preliminary examination stage that he be afforded limited legal assistance under the auspices of the Tribunal's legal aid system. In light of Ms. Condé's reported willingness to assist Kamuhanda *pro bono*, the Appeals Chamber considers that this legal assistance should take the form of the assignment of a legal assistant for a period of three months. The Appeals Chamber emphasizes that, pursuant to Rule 44(A) of the Rules, it is incumbent on Ms. Condé to file her power of attorney with the Registrar at the earliest opportunity.

21. Finally, the Appeals Chamber considers that the Prosecution should clarify whether it was provided with a report containing the conclusions of the Special Counsel's investigation. The Appeals Chamber notes that counsel for the Office of the Prosecutor declared in the *Nshogoza* case that no such report existed.[41] However, the Prosecution has failed to inform Kamuhanda whether this report which he has been requesting actually exists. **[page 8]**

D. Disposition

22. For the foregoing reasons, the Appeals Chamber

GRANTS the Motion;

DIRECTS the Registrar, after consulting with Ms. Aïcha Condé, to assign a legal assistant for a period of three months, starting when, and provided that, Ms. Aïcha Condé files her power of attorney with the Registrar to represent Kamuhanda *pro bono*, for the purpose of assisting Kamuhanda at this preliminary stage of potential review proceedings; and

ORDERS the Prosecution to clarify whether it was provided with a report containing the conclusions of the Special Counsel's investigation within one week of the date of this Decision.

---

[38] *Niyitegeka* Fourth Review Decision, para. 52.
[39] *Ibid.*
[40] This determination is without prejudice to the evaluation of the grounds of review that the Appeals Chamber would undertake if a motion for review were to be filed.
[41] *The Prosecutor v. Léonidas Nshogoza*, Case No. ICTR-07-91-PT, T. 30 October 2008 pp. 10, 11. *See also The Prosecutor v. Léonidas Nshogoza*, Case No. ICTR-07-91-T, Decision on Defence Motion for Certification of the Trial Chamber's "Decision on the Defence's Urgent Motion for a Subpoena to Ms. Loretta Lynch", 19 February 2009, para. 10.

Done in English and French, the English version being authoritative.

Done this twenty-first day of July 2009,
At The Hague,
The Netherlands.

Judge Patrick Robinson
Presiding

[Seal of the Tribunal]

Commentary

1. Introduction: reconsideration, review and retrial

The decisions under review[1] deal with post-conviction requests addressed to the Appeals Chamber and entail a comprehensive revision of a decision or a judgement, whether final or not. Revision proceedings such as reconsideration or retrial are envisaged as extraordinary remedies for unfair situations. Although the possibility of modifying final decisions or judgements puts legal principles under threat, taking into consideration the magnitude of international criminal cases – dealing with large amounts of evidence, numerous witnesses and long lists of charges for different episodes – the possibility of finding new facts or discovering errors cannot be entirely ruled out.

The importance of these issues is self-explanatory. A wide interpretation of the grounds upon which a review can be granted could jeopardize the tribunal's work and transform an extraordinary mechanism like revision into a new form of appeal. Moreover, the risk of a flood of applications in such cases cannot be overseen, since review and reconsideration are the only way for prisoners seeking a reduction of their long sentences or an early release.[2]

The decisions under review deal with three different mechanisms: reconsideration, review and retrial and therefore belong to very different stages in the procedure. Two were raised on a preliminary stage and requested legal aid at the tribunal's expense;[3] another one included a request for review;[4] and the last one dealt with retrial matters.[5] The comparative analysis of the decisions enables us to fully grasp the revision possibilities existing in every stage and the different requirements needed in each proceeding.

2. Reconsideration proceedings

Reconsideration proceedings are neither regulated in the Statute nor in the Rules of Procedure and Evidence. Rather, the power to reconsider is based on precedents,[6] but has been limited to exceptional circumstances "if a clear error of reasoning has been demonstrated or if it is necessary to prevent an injustice".[7]

While it is uncontroversial that decisions can be reconsidered,[8] it is contested whether judgements can be subjected to this procedure. The Čelebići case asserted that the tribunal has the power to reconsider a final

---

[1] ICTR, Decision on the Prosecutor's Appeal concerning the scope of evidence to be adduced in the retrial, *Prosecutor v. Muvunyi*, Case No. ICTR-00-55A-AR73, A. Ch., 24 March 2009, in this volume, p. 69; ICTR, Decision on Motion requesting preliminary Conference with former legal Team for the Preparation of a Request for the Assignment of Counsel for the Purpose of a Review, *Musema-Uwimana v. Prosecutor*, Case No. ICTR-96-13-R, A. Ch., 18 June 2009, in this volume, p. 77; ICTR, Decision on Jean-Bosco Barayagwiza's Motion for Review and/or Reconsideration of the Appeal Judgement of 28 November 2007, *Barayagwiza v. Prosecutor*, Case No. ICTR-99-52A-R, A. Ch., 22 June 2009, in this volume, p. 81; ICTR, Decision on Motion for Legal Assistance, *Kamuhanda v. Prosecutor*, Case No. ICTR-99-54A-R, A. Ch., 21 July 2009, in this volume, p. 91.

[2] For example, Niyitegeka has requested review four times; Žigić has filed three motions on this regard; Barayagwiza has repeatedly requested assignment of counsel to prepare a review.

[3] ICTR, Decision on Motion requesting preliminary Conference with former legal Team for the Preparation of a Request for the Assignment of Counsel for the Purpose of a Review, *Musema-Uwimana v. Prosecutor*, Case No. ICTR-96-13-R, A. Ch., 18 June 2009; ICTR, Decision on Motion for Legal Assistance, *Kamuhanda v. Prosecutor*, Case No. ICTR-99-54A-R, A. Ch., 21 July 2009.

[4] ICTR, Decision on Jean-Bosco Barayagwiza's Motion for Review and/or Reconsideration of the Appeal Judgement of 28 November 2007, *Barayagwiza v. Prosecutor*, Case No. ICTR-99-52A-R, A. Ch., 22 June 2009.

[5] ICTR, Decision on the Prosecutor's Appeal concerning the scope of evidence to be adduced in the retrial, *Prosecutor v. Muvunyi*, Case No. ICTR-00-55A-AR73, A. Ch., 24 March 2009.

[6] Among others, ICTY, Decision on Zoran Žigić's Motion for Reconsideration of Appeals Chamber Judgement IT-98-30/1-A delivered on 28 february 2005, *Prosecutor v. Zoran Žigić a/k/a Ziga*, Case No. IT-98-30-1-A, 26 June 2006, par. 5; ICTR, Decision on Prosecutor's Request for Review or Reconsideration, *Prosecutor v. Jean-Bosco Barayagwiza*, Case No. ICTR-97-19-AR72, 31 March 2000, Klip/ Sluiter, ALC-VI-223, par. 18; Decision on Interlocutory Appeal from Refusal to reconsider Decisions relating to Protective Measures and Application for a Declaration of Lack of Jurisdiction, *Prosecutor v. Bagosora*, Case No. ICTR-98-41-A, A. Ch., 2 May 2002, par. 6 and 10; Decision on Defence's Request for Reconsideration, *Prosecutor v. Galić*, Case No. IT-98-29-A, A. Ch., 16 July 2004, par. 2.

[7] ICTR, Decision on Jean-Bosco Barayagwiza's Motion for Review and/or Reconsideration of the Appeal Judgement of 28 November 2007, *Prosecutor v. Barayagwiza*, Case No. ICTR-99-52A-R, A. Ch., 22 June 2009, par. 14.

[8] In fact, what is said is that "[w]hether or not a Chamber does reconsider its decision is itself a discretionary decision", ICTR, Decision on Interlocutory Appeal from Refusal to Reconsider Decisions Relating to Protective Measures and Application for a Declaration of "Lack of Jurisdiction", *Prosecutor v Bagosora et al*, Case NO. ICTR-98-41-A, 2 May 2002, par. 10; ICTY, Judgement on Sentence Appeal, *Prosecutor v. Mucić, Delić and Landžo*, Case No. IT-96-21-Abis, A. Ch., 8 April 2003, Klip/ Sluiter, ALC-XIV-847, par. 49.

judgement when "a clear error of reasoning in the previous judgement has been demonstrated by, for example, a subsequent decision of the Appeals Chamber itself, the International Court of Justice, the European Court of Human Rights or a senior appellate court within a domestic jurisdiction, or that the previous judgement was given *per incuriam*"; and when "the judgement of the Appeals Chamber sought to be reconsidered has led to an injustice".[9] However, this position has been challenged, with some dissent, reaching the opposite conclusion, i.e., that only decisions can be reconsidered while judgements can only be reviewed.[10]

This discussion is examined in some detail in the Decision on Jean-Bosco Barayagwiza's motion for Review and/or Reconsideration of the Appeal Judgement of 28 November 2007,[11] in which the applicant requested reconsideration of three decisions that denied him legal aid at the tribunal's expense[12] and reconsideration and/ or review of the appeal judgement, which convicted Barayagwiza to thirty-two years' imprisonment.[13]

As to the reconsideration of the decisions, the Appeals Chamber found that the applicant failed to establish a clear error of reasoning and merely repeated part of the arguments he had already set forth in the previous proceedings.[14] As a result, the applicant's request to be granted financed legal aid was denied.[15] The Appeals Chamber welcomed the opportunity to reiterate that the assignment of counsel can only be provided if the Appeals Chamber authorizes the review and only extraordinarily can this kind of legal support be provided at the preliminary examination stage; however, assistance is only allowed for a limited time because, "(…) it is necessary to ensure the fairness of the proceedings".[16]

Regarding the request for reconsideration of the appeal judgement, the chamber maintained that final judgements cannot be reconsidered, because such reconsideration would not be in the interest of justice to the victims of the crimes or the convicted person, it would infringe the right to certainty and finality of legal judgements.[17] Therefore, the applicant's request on this regard was also denied.[18]

Although the issue of the object of the reconsideration was sufficiently commented in other volumes, it is interesting to corroborate the strengthening of the position, according to which final judgements cannot be reconsidered, as opposed to what was held in the Čelebići Judgement on Sentence Appeal.[19] This means that decisions can be revised – either through review or reconsideration – whenever new facts are found but also when there was a clear error of reasoning; conversely, judgements can only be revised if new facts – not to be interpreted as legal grounds – are found. Therefore, if a clear error of reasoning is found, reconsideration of a judgement is not possible.

As already pointed out, reconsideration is neither envisaged by the Statute nor by the Rules of Procedure and Evidence, so these restrictions are more or less artificially imposed by the chambers. Provided that the

---

[9] ICTY, Judgement on Sentence Appeal, *Prosecutor v. Mucić, Delić and Landžo*, Case No. IT-96-21-Abis, A. Ch., 8 April 2003, Klip/ Sluiter, ALC-XIV-847, par. 49.
[10] ICTY, Decision on Zoran Žigić's Motion for reconsideration of Appeals Chamber Judgement IT-98-30/1-A delivered on 28 February 2005, *Prosecutor v. Žigić*, Case No. IT-98-30/1-A, 26 June 2006, par. 9. See also, the accompanying Declaration of Judge Shahabuddeen.
[11] ICTR, Decision on Jean-Bosco Barayagwiza's Motion for Review and/or Reconsideration of the Appeal Judgement of 28 November 2007, *Barayagwiza v. Prosecutor*, Case No. ICTR-99-52A-R, A. Ch., 22 June 2009.
[12] ICTR, Decision on Jean-Bosco Barayagwiza's Motion of 6 March 2008, *Prosecutor v. Barayagwiza*, Case No. ICTR-99-52A-R, 11 April 2008; ICTR, Decision on Jean-Bosco Barayagwiza's Motion of 2 May 2008, *Prosecutor v. Barayagwiza*, Case No. ICTR-99-52A-R, 9 September 2008; ICTR, Decision on Jean-Bosco Barayagwiza's Motion of 15 September 2008, *Prosecutor v. Barayagwiza*, Case No. ICTR-99-52A-R, 2 October 2008.
[13] ICTR, Decision on Jean-Bosco Barayagwiza's Motion for Review and/or Reconsideration of the Appeal Judgement of 28 November 2007, *Prosecutor v. Barayagwiza*, Case No. ICTR-99-52A-R, A. Ch., 22 June 2009, par. 14.
[14] *Ibid.*, par. 15.
[15] *Ibid.*, par. 15.
[16] *Ibid.*, par. 16.
[17] *Ibid.*, par. 20, citing ICTY, Decision on Zoran Žigic''s motion for reconsideration of Appeals Chamber Judgement IT-98-30/1-A delivered on 28 February 2005, *Prosecutor v. Zoran Žigić a/k/a Ziga*, Case No. IT-98-30-1-A, 26 June 2006, par. 9.
[18] ICTR, Decision on Jean-Bosco Barayagwiza's Motion for Review and/or Reconsideration of the Appeal Judgement of 28 November 2007, *Barayagwiza v. Prosecutor*, Case No. ICTR-99-52A-R, A. Ch., 22 June 2009, par. 21.
[19] ICTY, Judgement on Sentence Appeal, *Prosecutor v. Mucić, Delić and Landžo*, Case No. IT-96-21-Abis, A. Ch., 8 April 2003, Klip/ Sluiter, ALC-VI-223, par. 49.

final goal of all review mechanisms is to avoid injustice, the conclusion reached by the Appeals Chamber would be contradictory, since the judgements affect the accused's rights in a much more direct way than decisions.

Ultimately, the risk of a flood of applications for reconsideration could have also played an important role in this limitation; but as pointed out by Judge Shahabuddeen in Declaration to the Žigić Decision on Reconsideration, in the years that followed the Čelebići Judgement on Sentence Appeal, such a cascade of applications did not happen.[20]

3. Review proceedings

As set out in the Decision on Jean-Bosco Barayagwiza's motion for review and/ or reconsideration of the Appeal Judgement of 28 November 2007[21], reconsideration and review are different mechanisms. Review proceedings are regulated in article 25 of the ICTR Statute and Rules 120 to 123 of the Rules of Procedure and Evidence. According to these provisions, judgements can only be reviewed if "a new fact has been discovered".[22] If the Chamber finds that the new fact could have been decisive in reaching the decision, review may result in a new judgement after hearing both parties.[23]

In contrast to the persistent doubts regarding reconsideration of judgements, it is uncontested that judgements can be reviewed, whether delivered by the Trial Chamber or by the Appeals, even when they are final.[24] The effect of this provision is appalling: a final judgement can be revised and the sentence can therefore be modified. Due to the extraordinary nature of the provision, the circumstances upon which a judgement can be reviewed are very limited.

According to article 25 of the ICTR Statute "[w]here a new fact has been discovered which was not known at the time of the proceedings before the Trial Chamber or the Appeals Chamber and which could have been a decisive factor in reaching the decision, the convicted person or the Prosecutor may submit to the International Tribunal for Rwanda an application for review of the judgement." Therefore, review is only possible when:
    a. There is a new fact.
    b. The new fact was not known at the time of the proceedings by the moving party.
    c. The new fact could have been decisive in reaching the decision.

Rule 120 adds another requirement, that the new fact "could not have been discovered through the exercise of due diligence". However, jurisprudence has lowered the standards of review in this regard stating that "[i]n wholly exceptional circumstances" a review may be granted, even where the new fact was known to the moving party, at the time of the original proceedings or the lack was the result of a lack of diligence, if ignoring the new fact would result in a miscarriage of justice.[25] Such an extensive interpretation is hardly justifiable, since it departs substantially from the provision, being the legality principle at stake.

The chambers have repeatedly confirmed the nature of this proceeding: "the review of a final judgement is an exceptional procedure and not an additional opportunity for a party to re-litigate arguments that failed at trial or on appeal".[26] It is basically relying on this criterion that the applicant's submissions have been examined in the decisions under review.

---

[20]   ICTY, Decision on Zoran Žigić's motion for reconsideration of Appeals Chamber Judgement IT-98-30/1-A delivered on 28 February 2005, *Prosecutor v. Zoran Žigić a/k/a Ziga*, Case No. IT-98-30-1-A, 26 June 2006, Declaration of Judge Shahabuddeen, par. 7.
[21]   ICTR, Decision on Jean-Bosco Barayagwiza's Motion for Review and/or Reconsideration of the Appeal Judgement of 28 November 2007, *Barayagwiza v. Prosecutor,* Case No. ICTR-99-52A-R, A. Ch., 22 June 2009.
[22]   Article 25, Statute of the International Criminal Tribunal for Rwanda.
[23]   Rule 121, Rule of Procedure and Evidence.
[24]   See Rule 120 of the Rules of Procedure and Evidence.
[25]   ICTR, Decision on Jean-Bosco Barayagwiza's Motion for Review and/or Reconsideration of the Appeal Judgement of 28 November 2007, *Barayagwiza v. Prosecutor,* Case No. ICTR-99-52A-R, A. Ch., 22 June 2009, par. 22, citing previous ICTR and ICTY decisions.
[26]   *Ibid.,* par. 22.

In the Decision on Jean-Bosco Barayagwiza's motion for Review and/ or Reconsideration of the Appeal Judgement of 28 November 2007[27], the accused requested review of the appeal judgement on the basis of numerous alleged new facts, most of which were dismissed without further considerations.[28] Two were examined in some detail: the findings related to trials *in absentia*[29] and the alleged incompetence of his counsel.[30]

First, the applicant argued that he had discovered new facts concerning the illegality of trials *in absentia*. These alleged new facts were contained in documents, such as the *travaux preparatoires* for the establishment of the International Criminal Court.[31] As correctly pointed out by the Appeals Chamber, this could hardly be considered new facts and, as a result, the review was not possible.[32]

In my opinion, it is essential to consider that Barayagwiza's absence in the trial was due to his unwillingness to participate in the hearings; therefore, this situation should not be considered as a trial *in absentia* (not envisaged by the ICTR), but rather as a trial in the absence of the accused (envisaged in Rule 82 bis). In this regard, it would have been worth noticing the discussion of this issue in the appeals judgement.[33]

The second argument set forth by the applicant was the alleged incompetence of his counsel, which was based on new information granted to the applicant by the registrar.[34] The main ground to dismiss this request for review was that the facts were not new, but had in fact been duly addressed on appeal.[35]

Decisions dealing with review typically include preliminary requests regarding financing of legal aid. As a general rule, the tribunal has been very clear regarding the funding of legal assistance, noting that "it is not for the Tribunal to assist a convicted person whose case has reached finality"[36] and only in exceptional circumstances will the convicted person be granted legal assistance at the expense of the tribunal after a final judgement has been rendered against him.[37] This assistance may take different forms such as the assignment of counsel or legal assistance, where the convicted person is indigent.[38] However, as recalled in one of the decisions under review, even if funding is denied that does not mean that the request for review is impossible, but rather that it will need to be done at the applicant's own expense, at the expense of a third party or on *pro bono* basis.[39]

In the decisions under review, in order to determine when this legal assistance is required, the Appeals Chamber generally focuses on whether exceptional circumstances are present and whether legal assistance is needed to ensure the fairness of the proceedings.[40] Such an assessment includes examining the potential

---

[27] ICTR, Decision on Jean-Bosco Barayagwiza's Motion for Review and/or Reconsideration of the Appeal Judgement of 28 November 2007, *Barayagwiza v. Prosecutor,* Case No. ICTR-99-52A-R, A. Ch., 22 June 2009.
[28] *Ibid.,* par. 24.
[29] *Ibid.,* par. 25–28.
[30] *Ibid.,* par. 29–38.
[31] The documents referred are cited in ICTR, Decision on Jean-Bosco Barayagwiza's Motion for Review and/or Reconsideration of the Appeal Judgement of 28 November 2007, *Barayagwiza v. Prosecutor,* Case No. ICTR-99-52A-R, A. Ch., 22 June 2009, fn. 74.
[32] *Ibid.,* par. 28.
[33] ICTR, Judgement, *Nahimana, Barayagwiza and Ngeze v. Prosecutor*, Case No. ICTR-99-52-A, A. Ch., 28 November 2007, Klip/ Sluiter, ALC-XXXI-257, par. 94–116.
[34] ICTR, Decision on Jean-Bosco Barayagwiza's Motion for Review and/or Reconsideration of the Appeal Judgement of 28 November 2007, *Barayagwiza v. Prosecutor,* Case No. ICTR-99-52A-R, A. Ch., 22 June 2009, par. 29.
[35] ICTR, Judgement, *Nahimana, Barayagwiza, and Ngeze v. Prosecutor*, Case No. ICTR-99-52-A, 28 November 2007, Klip/Sluiter, ALC-XXXI-257, par. 136–169.
[36] ICTR, Decision on Motion for Legal Assistance, *Kamuhanda v. Prosecutor*, Case No. ICTR-99-54A-R, A. Ch., 21 July 2009, par. 17.
[37] *Ibid.* par. 17; ICTR, Decision on fourth Request for Review, *Prosecutor v. Niyitegeka,* Case No. ICTR-96-14-R, A. Ch., 12 March 2009, par. 52.
[38] ICTR, Decision on Motion for Legal Assistance, *Kamuhanda v. Prosecutor*, Case No. ICTR-99-54A-R, A. Ch., 21 July 2009, par. 17.
[39] ICTR, Decision on Motion requesting preliminary Conference with former legal Team for the Preparation of a Request for the Assignment of Counsel for the Purpose of a Review, *Musema-Uwimana v. Prosecutor,* Case No. ICTR-96-13-R, A. Ch., 18 June 2009, p. 3.
[40] ICTR, Decision on Motion for Legal Assistance, *Kamuhanda v. Prosecutor*, Case No. ICTR-99-54A-R, A. Ch., 21 July 2009, par. 17; ICTR, Decision on fourth Request for Review, *Prosecutor v. Niyitegeka,* Case No. ICTR-96-14-R, A. Ch., 12 March 2009, par. 52.

grounds for review as pointed out by the applicant,[41] which seems reasonable, as it is necessary to determine if the request is well-founded.

In the Decision on Motion requesting preliminary Conference with former Legal Team for the Preparation of a Request for the Assignment of Counsel for the Purpose of a Review, Musema approached the Appeals Chamber with a request to facilitate a preliminary conference in The Hague with his former legal team at the tribunal's expense, in order to receive legal advice on potential grounds of review.[42] The motion was dismissed based on different grounds. First, the applicant may be assisted by counsel to examine his requests but it should be done "at his own expense, at the expense of a third party, or on a pro bono basis".[43] The requested transfer of the applicant to The Hague could hardly be justified: nothing in the Statute, Rules of Procedure and Evidence or jurisprudence provides for such a transfer. Furthermore, transfer is envisioned for those whose sentence is being enforced in the Republic of Mali only to appear as a witness before the tribunal.[44] Consequently, the request was correctly dismissed.

Another aspect to consider in these preliminary requests regarding financing of legal aid seems to be the evaluation of whether the applicant would be capable of doing it alone. As an example, Kamuhanda asserted he lacked technical legal skills; the Court found he was able to file a detailed and coherent request but also concluded that the complexity of the case and the exceptional circumstances spoke in favour of his request for legal assistance.

The circumstances were indeed exceptional, as they involved false testimony and contempt. Moreover, Kamuhanda requested different pieces of evidence presented in other trials (from the trials of Léonidas Nshogoza, Rwamakuba and Gikomero Gacaca).[45] Two further subsidiary aspects may explain this exceptional granting of legal assistance. First, the accused did not request legal counsel *stricto sensu*, but legal assistance for a short period of time to support the work of his counsel, who worked on a *pro bono* basis.

Second, it was unclear if all documents had been properly disclosed to the defence and, in this regard, the Appeals Chamber asked for clarification regarding one specific piece of evidence because "the Prosecution has failed to inform Kamuhanda whether this report which he has been requesting actually exists".[46] In fact, subsequent decisions confirmed an infringement of Rule 68 by the prosecution.[47]

In my view, legal assistance is required not only for review but also for reconsideration purposes. Finding errors of law overseen by the chambers by an accused who doesn't have a legal background is rather unlikely; but discovering new facts from a prison in a third country is even more unlikely. Provided it is required to successfully request review or reconsideration to give concrete information – whether factual or legal – of the grounds for the revision, some kind of assistance would generally be needed. Of course, the tribunal does not necessarily need to provide this support; however, the economic capacity of an accused to fund legal aid is doubtful because of long term imprisonment and self-representation before the international tribunals has proved to be even more problematic. In any case, the strict interpretation of the requirements to grant this kind of support is fully understandable, in order to avoid funding frivolous motions of review or reconsideration.

4. Retrial

The last decision under review deals with a different mechanism that was raised at the final stage of the proceedings: retrial. In particular, the aspect discussed thoroughly in the decision is the scope of the evidence that is permitted to be adduced on retrial in the case against Tharcisse Muvunyi. However, what is ultimately

---

[41] ICTR, Decision on Motion requesting preliminary Conference with former legal Team for the Preparation of a Request for the Assignment of Counsel for the Purpose of a Review, *Musema-Uwimana v. Prosecutor,* Case No. ICTR-96-13-R, A. Ch., 18 June 2009, p. 3.
[42] *Ibid.*, p. 2.
[43] *Ibid.*, p. 3.
[44] *Ibid.*, p. 3.
[45] ICTR, Decision on Motion for Legal Assistance, *Kamuhanda v. Prosecutor,* Case No. ICTR-99-54A-R, A. Ch., 21 July 2009, par. 7–57.
[46] *Ibid.*, par. 21–22.
[47] ICTR, Decision on Motion for Disclosure, *Prosecutor v. Kamuhanda,* Case No. ICTR-99-54A-R68, A. Ch., 4 March 2010, par. 45.

discussed is the very nature of the retrial as such, and specifically whether it amounts to a new trial or is a mere reconsideration.

On first instance Muvunyi was convicted of three counts of genocide – direct and public incitement to commit genocide, among others – and sentenced to 25 years' imprisonment.[48] The appeal reversed the conviction and ordered a retrial limited to count number 3, which regarded direct and public incitement to commit genocide allegedly perpetrated at the Gikore Trade Centre.[49] The ground for this retrial was the Trial Chamber's defective argumentation on the credibility of two witnesses, which was especially controversial as the conviction on public incitement relied on their statements.[50] Consequently, the Appeals Chamber quashed the conviction and ordered a retrial on this issue.[51]

For the purpose of the retrial, the prosecution listed four witnesses to testify about the events that occurred at Gikore Trade Centre. One of the witnesses had also testified in the initial proceedings; however, three other witnesses had not been heard before, although their statements had been disclosed to the defence.[52] Trial Chamber III decided that, in view of the Appeals Chamber Judgement and in order to correct the Trial Chambers failure regarding the assessment of evidence, the retrial should be limited to the same evidence. As a result, new witnesses could not be called.[53]

Prosecution appealed the decision, in the belief that retrial should be understood as a trial *de novo*; therefore, allowing to modify the scope of the evidence.[54] For the defence such an expansion would prejudice the accused, violating the *non bis in idem* principle.[55]

The only reference in the legal documents is Rule 118(C), which enables the Appeal Chamber to order a retrial, but does not point out how it should be carried out.[56] Therefore, the jurisprudence must clarify the limits of retrial. Following US jurisprudence, the Appeals Chamber stated that "a retrial pursuant to Rule 118(C) of the Rules inherently includes the possibility of hearing evidence that was not presented during the initial proceedings"[57] since "[n]either the Rules nor the Tribunal's jurisprudence prohibit a Trial Chamber from hearing the testimony of new witnesses when a retrial is ordered".[58] This would be the general rule regarding retrial. However, when the issue at stake is "a remittance to consider limited issues", new evidence should be expressly authorised.[59]

In the case of Muvunyi, the Appeals Chamber found that "the circumstances were appropriate for retrial pursuant to Rule 118(C) of the Rules on the allegation related to the Gikore Trade Center" and that on this regard no restriction of the scope was made.[60] Furthermore, the Appeals Chamber reiterated that the goal of the retrial was to provide "the opportunity to fully assess the entirety of the relevant evidence and to provide a reasoned opinion".[61] Therefore, the Trial Chamber was "to take into consideration all of the admissible and relevant evidence proposed by the parties, in order to provide a reasoned opinion on Count 3".[62] As a result,

---

[48] ICTR, Judgement, *Prosecutor v. Muvunyi*, Case No. ICTR-00-55A-T, T. Ch. III, 11 February 2010, par. 531.
[49] ICTR, Judgement, *Prosecutor v. Muvunyi*, Case No. ICTR-2000-55A-A, A. Ch., 29 August 2008, par. 148.
[50] ICTR, Judgement, *Prosecutor v. Muvunyi*, Case No. ICTR-00-55A-T, T. Ch. III, 11 February 2010, par. 144.
[51] ICTR, Judgement, *Prosecutor v. Muvunyi*, Case No. ICTR-2000-55A-A, A. Ch., 29 August 2008, par. 171.
[52] ICTR, Decision on the Prosecutor's Appeal concerning the scope of evidence to be adduced in the retrial, *Prosecutor v. Muvunyi*, Case No. ICTR-00-55A-AR73, A. Ch., 24 March 2009, par. 4.
[53] *Ibid.*, par. 5, citing the Impugned Decision issued at the Status Conference on 14 January 2009.
[54] *Ibid.*, par. 6, citing the Prosecution's Appeal to the Impugned Decision.
[55] *Ibid.*, par. 9–11, citing the Response to the Impugned Decision.
[56] Rule 118 (C) RPE: "In appropriate circumstances the Appeals Chamber may order that the accused be retried before the Trial Chamber".
[57] ICTR, Decision on the Prosecutor's Appeal concerning the scope of evidence to be adduced in the retrial, *Prosecutor v. Muvunyi*, Case No. ICTR-00-55A-AR73, A. Ch., 24 March 2009, par. 13, citing *Patterson v. Haskins*, 470 F.3d 645, 669 (6th Cir. 2006).
[58] *Ibid.*, par. 13.
[59] *Ibid.*
[60] *Ibid.*, par. 14.
[61] ICTR, Judgement, *Prosecutor v. Muvunyi*, Case No. ICTR-2000-55A-A, A. Ch., 29 August 2008, par. 148.
[62] ICTR, Decision on the Prosecutor's Appeal concerning the scope of evidence to be adduced in the retrial, *Prosecutor v. Muvunyi*, Case No. ICTR-00-55A-AR73, A. Ch., 24 March 2009, par. 15.

the Appeals Chamber found that the Trial Chamber erred in limiting the scope of evidence and granted the prosecution's appeal.[63]

As for the alleged prejudice caused to the accused by the admission of new evidence, the arguments opposed by the defence were further examined concluding that there had been no violation of the *non bis is idem* principle, because the conviction related to this count had been quashed.[64] Moreover, the Appeals Chamber considered that this new evidence would not prejudice the accused, even if this allowed for the prosecution to change strategy, because the fair trial principles also apply on retrial.[65] To reach this conclusion, the Appeals Chamber relied upon the fact that the statements of the three new witnesses were already disclosed to the defence and that the possible sentence to be imposed in the new trial would not exceed the 25 years ordered in the initial proceedings.[66] However, if, as pointed out by the Appeals Chamber, the retrial amounts to a trial *de* novo, then these last arguments would be unnecessary.

As pointed out in the Joint Dissenting Opinion of Judges Shahabuddeen and Meron, a retrial in these terms would certainly have an effect on the safeguard of the defendant's rights, which is particularly important due to the problematic nature of retrial.[67] Although the phrase referring to "the entirety of the relevant evidence" could be interpreted as the absence of any limitations to the scope of evidence and taking into account the whole context of the decision, it is clear that "[t]he purpose of the ordered retrial was to correct this significant flaw in the initial Trial Judgement, allowing the Trial Chamber an additional opportunity to assess the testimony of the original witnesses at trial and provide a reasoned explanation for choosing which account of Muvunyi's speech it believed".[68]

Nevertheless, if the goal was only to let the trial judgement re-examine the issue at stake, the appropriate mechanism would have probably been reconsideration; when the Appeals Chamber orders a retrial, it should be understood as something different than a mere reconsideration; therefore, it seems logical that it involves new witnesses.

On the other hand, it is through no fault of the accused that the Trial Chamber erred in its legal ruling. In this sense, the retrial and extension of the scope of the evidence was clearly prejudicial to the accused's interests. In fact, after this second opportunity the judgement issued in 2011 confirmed the conviction for incitement to commit genocide in Gikoro Trade Center. If, as stated by the appeals judgement, the problem was the Trial Chambers defective assessment of evidence and that a reasonable trier of fact could not be concluded, maybe the most reasonable conclusion would have been to acquit the accused of this count, rather than giving the Trial Chamber a new opportunity to address the issue.

5. Conclusions

Revision mechanisms can be seen as a threat to legal principles, since they challenge the finality of the judgement, but may be needed on an exceptional basis to remedy unfair situations. However, in order to make them compatible with the tribunals standards, the requirements and effects should be extremely clear, so that revision is restricted only to the strictly necessary cases; an abuse of these proceedings would entail an "eternal recurrence" that would turn them into a new opportunity for an accused to seek the reduction of his sentence and would therefore distort the nature of these mechanisms and endanger the tribunal's work.

It is particularly regrettable that neither the Statute nor the Rules of Procedure and Evidence regulate these important mechanisms in detail. For instance, from a continental law perspective, it is hardly acceptable that reconsideration is not envisaged in the Tribunal's legal documents. As for those that are envisaged, interpretation of the provisions should be restrictive, avoiding extensive and analogical ones. For example review should not be possible when the alleged new fact was indeed known or when it was not known due to a lack of diligence, because it directly contradicts Rule 120.

---

[63] *Ibid.*, par. 19–20.
[64] *Ibid.*, par. 16.
[65] *Ibid.*, par. 18.
[66] *Ibid.*
[67] ICTR, Decision on the Prosecutor's Appeal concerning the scope of evidence to be adduced in the retrial, *Prosecutor v. Muvunyi*, Case No. ICTR-00-55A-AR73, A. Ch., 24 March 2009, Joint Dissenting Opinion of Judges Shahabuddeen and Meron, par. 6.
[68] *Ibid.*, par. 4.

More than a decade after the establishment of the tribunals, essential questions – such as, whether judgements can be reconsidered or the nature of retrial – do not have a clear answer and the interpretation of the requirements or the scope of each of these proceedings remain, to a certain extent, unclear. Therefore, it could be asserted that dealing in depth with revision mechanisms is a partially unresolved matter in the tribunal's legacy.

Cristina Fernandez-Pacheco Estrada

Tribunal pénal international pour le Rwanda
International Criminal Tribunal for Rwanda

IN THE APPEALS CHAMBER

Before: Judge Patrick Robinson, Presiding
         Judge Fausto Pocar
         Judge Liu Daqun
         Judge Theodor Meron
         Judge Carmel Agius

Registrar: Mr. Adama Dieng

Date: 8 December 2009

ÉDOUARD KAREMERA
MATTHIEU NGIRUMPATSE
JOSEPH NZIRORERA

v.

THE PROSECUTOR

Case No. ICTR-98-44-AR65

DECISION ON MATTHIEU NGIRUMPATSE'S APPEAL AGAINST DECISION ON REMAND ON PROVISIONAL RELEASE

Office of the Prosecutor:
Mr. Hassan Bubacar Jallow
Mr. Don Webster
Mr. Saidou N'Dow
Mr. Arif Virani
Mr. Eric Husketh
Ms. Sunkarie Ballah-Conteh
Mr. Takeh Sendze

Counsel for the Defence:
Ms. Dior Diagne Mbaye and Mr. Félix Sow for Mr. Édouard Karemera
Ms. Chantal Hounkpatin and Mr. Frédéric Weyl for Mr. Matthieu Ngirumpatse
Mr. Peter Robinson and Mr. Patrick Nimy Mayidika Ngimbi for Mr. Joseph Nzirorera

[page 1] 1.   The Appeals Chamber of the International Criminal Tribunal for the Prosecution of Persons Responsible for Genocide and Other Serious Violations of International Humanitarian Law Committed in the Territory of Rwanda and Rwandan Citizens Responsible for Genocide and Other Such Violations Committed in the Territory of Neighbouring States, between 1 January and 31 December 1994 ("Appeals Chamber" and "Tribunal", respectively), is seized of an appeal filed by Matthieu Ngirumpatse ("Ngirumpatse") on 25 September 2009,[1] against the "Decision on Remand in Respect of Matthieu Ngirumpatse's Motion for Provisional Release", issued on 10 September 2009.[2] The Prosecution responded on 5 October 2009.[3] No reply was filed.

A. Background

2.   On 6 February 2009, Trial Chamber III of the Tribunal ("Trial Chamber") rejected Ngirumpatse's request for provisional release.[4] Ngirumpatse appealed this decision on 13 February 2009.[5] On 7 April 2009, the Appeals Chamber quashed the Decision on Provisional Release and remanded the matter to the Trial Chamber for reconsideration.[6] Ngirumpatse's medical condition also gave rise to the issue of the continuation of the *Karemera et al.* trial and on 3 March 2009, the Trial Chamber severed Ngirumpatse from the *Karemera et al.* case.[7] However, on 19 June 2009, the Appeals Chamber reversed the Decision on Continuation of Trial and remanded the matter to the Trial Chamber for further consideration.[8]

3.   On 14 April 2009, Ngirumpatse filed a new motion before the Trial Chamber requesting provisional release.[9] On 29 May 2009, the President of the Tribunal issued an order varying [page 2] Ngirumpatse's conditions of detention, as a result of which Ngirumpatse was transferred from his place of hospitalization to Arusha.[10] Subsequently, the Trial Chamber ordered an expert medical examination of Ngirumpatse to assess both his ability to participate in the proceedings and whether his treatment required transferring him

---

[1]   *Mémoire d'Appel de M. Ngirumpatse contre la Décision en renvoi sur la Requête de Matthieu Ngirumpatse en demande de mise en liberté provisoire*, 25 September 2009 ("Appeal"). See also Decision on Matthieu Ngirumpatse's Motion for Extension of Time to File Appeal Submissions Against Trial Chamber's Decisions of 10 September 2009, 17 September 2009.

[2]   *The Prosecutor v. Édouard Karemera et al.*, Case No. ICTR-98-44-T, Decision on Remand in Respect of Matthieu Ngirumpatse's Motion for Provisional Release, filed in French on 10 September 2009, English version filed on 22 October 2009 ("Impugned Decision").

[3]   Prosecutor's Brief: Response to Matthieu Ngirumpatse's Appeal against *Decision en renvoi ... en demande de mise en liberté provisoire*, 5 October 2009 ("Response").

[4]   *The Prosecutor v. Édouard Karemera et al.*, Case No. ICTR-98-44-T, Decision on the Various Motions Relating to Matthieu Ngirumpatse's Health, filed in French on 6 February 2009, English version filed on 11 March 2009 ("Decision on Provisional Release"), paras. 14-23, p. 10.

[5]   *The Prosecutor v. Édouard Karemera et al.*, Case No. ICTR-98-44-AR65, Ngirumpatse's Appeal from the Decision on Various Motions on Matthieu Ngirumpatse's Health Rendered on 6 February 2009, 13 February 2009.

[6]   *The Prosecutor v. Édouard Karemera et al.*, Case No. ICTR-98-44-AR65, Decision on Matthieu Ngirumpatse's Appeal Against Trial Chamber's Decision Denying Provisional Release, 7 April 2009 ("Appeal Decision on Provisional Release"), para. 17.

[7]   *The Prosecutor v. Édouard Karemera et al.*, Case No. ICTR-98-44-T, Decision on Continuation of Trial, 3 March 2009 ("Decision on Continuation of Trial"), p. 16.

[8]   *The Prosecutor v. Édouard Karemera et al.*, Case No. ICTR-98-44-AR73.16, Decision on Appeal Concerning the Severance of Matthieu Ngirumpatse, 19 June 2009, para. 25.

[9]   *The Prosecutor v. Édouard Karemera et al.*, Case No. ICTR-98-44-T, *Mémoire en extrême urgence pour Matthieu Ngirumpatse suite à la décision de la Chambre d'Appel du 7 avril 2009 sur la demande de mise en liberté provisoire*, 14 April 2009 ("Motion"). See also *The Prosecutor v. Édouard Karemera et al.*, Case No. ICTR-98-44-T, *Mémoire complémentaire en extrême urgence pour Matthieu Ngirumpatse suite à la décision de la Chambre d'appel du 7 avril 2009 sur la demande de mise en liberté provisoire*, 16 April 2009; *The Prosecutor v. Édouard Karemera et al.*, Case No. ICTR-98-44-T, *Observations du Greffier en vertu de l'article 33 (B) du Règlement de procédure et de preuve au sujet du Mémoire en extrême urgence pour M. Matthieu Ngirumpatse suite à la décision de la Chambre d'appel du 7 avril 2009 sur la demande de mise en liberté provisoire*, 20 April 2009; *The Prosecutor v. Édouard Karemera et al.*, Case No. ICTR-98-44-T, Prosecutor's Response to Matthieu Ngirumpatse's Supplemental Submission for Provisional Release in Light of the Appeal[s] Chamber Decision of 7 April 2009, 20 April 2009; *The Prosecutor v. Édouard Karemera et al.*, Case No. ICTR-98-44-T, *Réplique pour Matthieu Ngirumpatse aux réponses du Greffier et du Procureur à son mémoire consécutif à la décision de la Chambre d'appel du 7 avril 2009 sur la demande de mise en liberté provisoire*, 22 April 2009; *The Prosecutor v. Édouard Karemera et al.*, Case No. ICTR-98-44-T, *Mémoire additionnel pour Matthieu Ngirumpatse consécutif à la décision de la Chambre d'appel du 7 avril 2009 sur la demande de mise en liberté provisoire*, 28 April 2009; *The Prosecutor v. Édouard Karemera et al.*, Case No. ICTR-98-44-T, *Demande de mesures urgentes pour Matthieu Ngirumpatse*, 28 April 2009.

[10]   *The Prosecutor v. Édouard Karemera et al.*, Case No. ICTR-98-44-T, Decision Varying Matthieu Ngirumpatse's Conditions of Detention, filed confidentially on 29 May 2009.

to other facilities.[11] The independent medical expert designated by the Trial Chamber ("Independent Medical Expert") submitted his confidential and *exparte* report on 11 August 2009.[12] The Independent Medical Expert's Report was disclosed to the parties in redacted form on 24 August 2009[13] and in unredacted form on 28 August 2009.[14]

4. On 10 September 2009, the Trial Chamber issued its decision on remand regarding the continuation of the trial.[15] On the basis of the report of the Tribunal's Chief Medical Officer and the Independent Medical Expert's Report, it found that there was no basis at this time to sever Ngirumpatse from the proceedings and accordingly vacated its initial Decision on Continuation of Trial.[16] The Trial Chamber ordered that the trial proceedings recommence on 19 October 2009 and requested the Tribunal's Chief Medical Officer to provide the Trial Chamber and the parties with updated reports on the state of Ngirumpatse's health.[17] On the same day, the Trial Chamber issued the Impugned Decision rejecting his application for provisional release. It found that based on the information of Ngirumpatse's medical condition provided by the Independent Medical Expert, and **[page 3]** considering the scheduled resumption of the trial, there were no grounds for his provisional release.[18] The trial recommenced on 19 October 2009 as scheduled.

B. Standard of Review

5. A decision on provisional release by a Trial Chamber under Rule 65 of the Rules of Procedure and Evidence ("Rules") is discretionary. Accordingly, the relevant inquiry is whether the Trial Chamber correctly exercised its discretion in reaching that decision, not whether the Appeals Chamber agrees with it. The Appeals Chamber will only overturn a Trial Chamber's decision on provisional release where it is found to be: (i) based on an incorrect interpretation of governing law; (ii) based on a patently incorrect conclusion of fact; or (iii) so unfair or unreasonable as to constitute an abuse of the Trial Chamber's discretion.[19] The Appeals Chamber will also consider whether the Trial Chamber has given weight to extraneous or irrelevant considerations or has failed to give weight or sufficient weight to relevant considerations in reaching its decision.[20]

C. Applicable Law

6. Under Rule 65(B) of the Rules, a Trial Chamber may order provisional release only if it is satisfied that, if released, the accused will appear for trial and will not pose a danger to any victim, witness or other

---

[11] *The Prosecutor v. Édouard Karemera et al.*, Case No. ICTR-98-44-T, Order Concerning Medical Examination of Matthieu Ngirumpatse, 23 June 2009, p. 4; *The Prosecutor v. Édouard Karemera et al.*, Case No. ICTR-98-44-T, *Ordonnance concernant la désignation d'un expert médical*, 3 July 2009, p. 4.
[12] See *The Prosecutor v. Édouard Karemera et al.*, Case No. ICTR-98-44-T, Decision on Motion for Disclosure of Medical Information and for Extension of Time, 28 August 2009, Confidential and *Ex-Parte* Annex B ("Independent Medical Expert's Report").
[13] *The Prosecutor v. Édouard Karemera et al.*, Case No. ICTR-98-44-T, *Ordonnance concernant la reprise du procès*, 24 August 2009.
[14] *The Prosecutor v. Édouard Karemera et al.*, Case No. ICTR-98-44-T, Decision on Motion for Disclosure of Medical Information and for Extension of Time, 28 August 2009.
[15] *The Prosecutor v. Édouard Karemera et al.*, Case No. ICTR-98-44-T, Decision on Remand Regarding Continuation of Trial, 10 September 2009 ("Decision on Remand on Continuation of Trial").
[16] Decision on Remand on Continuation of Trial, para. 19, p. 7.
[17] Decision on Remand on Continuation of Trial, para. 19, pp. 7, 8. Ngirumpatse sought certification to appeal the Decision on Remand on Continuation of Trial; however, certification was denied: *The Prosecutor v. Édouard Karemera et al.*, Case No. ICTR-98-44-T, *Décision sur la demande de certification en appel contre la* « Decision on Remand Regarding Continuation of Trial », 16 October 2009.
[18] Impugned Decision, para. 13, p. 6.
[19] See, e.g., *The Prosecutor v. Tharcisse Muvunyi*, Case No. ICTR-2000-55A-AR65, Decision on Appeal Concerning Provisional Release, 20 May 2009 ("*Muvunyi* Appeal Decision"), para. 6; Appeal Decision on Provisional Release, para. 4; *Prosecutor v. Jadranko Prlić et al.*, Case No. IT-04-74-AR65.11, Decision on Praljak's Appeal of the Trial Chamber's 2 December 2008 Decision on Provisional Release, 16 December 2008 ("*Prlić et al.* Appeal Decision of 16 December 2008"), para. 4.
[20] See, e.g., *Prosecutor v. Vujadin Popović et al.*, Case No. IT-05-88-AR65.10, Decision on Radivoje Miletić's Appeal Against Decision on Miletić's Motion for Provisional Release, 19 November 2009, para. 5; *Prosecutor v. Jadranko Prlić et al.*, Case No. IT-04-74-AR65.17, Decision on Prosecution's Appeal Against Decision on Prlić's Motion for Provisional Release, 23 July 2009 ("*Prlić et al.* Appeal Decision of 23 July 2009"), para. 4; *Prosecutor v. Vujadin Popović et al.*, Case No. IT05-08-AR65.7, Decision on Vujadin Popović's Interlocutory Appeal Against the Trial Chamber's Decision Denying his Provisional Release, 1 July 2008, para. 6.

person and after giving the host State and the State to which the accused seeks to be released the opportunity to be heard.

7. In deciding whether the requirements of Rule 65(B) of the Rules have been met, a Trial Chamber must consider all relevant factors which a reasonable Trial Chamber would have been expected to take into account before coming to a decision.[21] It must then provide a reasoned opinion **[page 4]** indicating its view on those relevant factors.[22] What these relevant factors are, as well as the weight to be accorded to them, depends upon the particular circumstances of each case; decisions on motions for provisional release are fact-intensive and cases are considered on an individual basis in light of the particular circumstances of the individual accused.[23] The Trial Chamber is required to assess these circumstances not only as they exist at the time when it reaches its decision on provisional release but also, as much as can be foreseen, at the time the accused is expected to return to the Tribunal.[24] If the Trial Chamber is satisfied that the requirements of Rule 65(B) of the Rules have been met, it has the discretion to grant provisional release to an accused.[25] Finally, an application for provisional release brought at a late stage of proceedings, and in particular after the close of the Prosecution case, should only be granted when sufficiently compelling humanitarian reasons exist, Judge Liu dissenting.[26]

D. Submissions

8. Ngirumpatse asks the Appeals Chamber to reverse the Impugned Decision, order consultation with proposed host States, request their cooperation, and order his provisional release.[27] Alternatively, he asks that his request for provisional release be considered and ruled upon by a different Chamber, which would take into account all the relevant factors before reaching its decision.[28]

9. As a preliminary matter, Ngirumpatse submits that the Trial Chamber did not render the Impugned Decision in a timely manner and that the process was not fair and impartial.[29] In this respect, he claims that the Trial Chamber was seized with the matter since 7 April 2009 and that it could not have properly considered the medical reports, as they were provided in French and the **[page 5]** Trial Chamber is primarily English speaking.[30] Further, he questions the impartiality of the Judges given their differential treatment of the application for provisional release and the continuation of trial.[31] In this regard, he argues that the Trial Chamber failed to request submissions from the parties on the medical reports in relation to provisional release whereas it did so in respect of the continuation of trial.[32]

---

[21] See, e.g., *Prosecutor v. Ante Gotovina et al.*, Case No. IT-06-90-AR65.3, Decision on Ivan Čermak's Appeal Against Decision on his Motion for Provisional Release, filed confidentially on 3 August 2009, public redacted version filed on 4 August 2009 ("*Gotovina et al.* Appeal Decision"), para. 6; Appeal Decision on Provisional Release, para. 13; *Prlić et al.* Appeal Decision, para. 7; *Prosecutor v. Ramush Haradinaj et al.*, Case No. IT-04-84-AR65.2, Decision on Lahi Brahimaj's Interlocutory Appeal Against the Trial Chamber's Decision Denying His Provisional Release, 9 March 2006, para. 10.

[22] See, e.g., *Gotovina et al.* Appeal Decision, para. 6; *Prosecutor v. Jadranko Prlić et al.*, Case No. IT-04-74-AR65.8, Decision on Prosecution's Appeal Against Decision on Gvero's Motion for Provisional Release, 20 July 2009 ("*Prlić et al.* Appeal Decision on Gvero's Motion for Provisional Release of 20 July 2009"), para. 6; *Prlić et al.* Appeal Decision of 16 December 2008, para. 7.

[23] *Gotovina et al.* Appeal Decision, para. 6; *Prlić et al.* Appeal Decision of 16 December 2008, para. 7; *Prosecutor v. Ljube Boškoski and Johan Tarčulovski*, Case No. IT-04-82-AR65.1, Decision on Johan Tarčulovski's Interlocutory Appeal on Provisional Release, 4 October 2005, para. 7.

[24] *Gotovina et al.* Appeal Decision, para. 6; *Prlić et al.* Appeal Decision of 16 December 2008, para. 7.

[25] *Gotovina et al.* Appeal Decision, para. 6; *Prlić et al.* Appeal Decision of 23 July 2009, para. 6; *Prosecutor v. Jadranko Prlić et al.*, Case No. IT-04-74-AR65.16, Decision on Prosecution's Appeal Against Decision on Pušić's Motion for Provisional Release, 20 July 2009, para. 6; *Prlić et al.* Appeal Decision on Gvero's Motion for Provisional Release of 20 July 2009, para. 6.

[26] *Gotovina et al.* Appeal Decision, para. 6; *Prlić et al.* Appeal Decision of 16 December 2008, paras. 7, 15; *Prosecutor v. Jadranko Prlić et al.*, Case No. IT-04-74-AR65.7, Decision on "Prosecution's Appeal from *Décision relative à la demande de mise en liberté provisoire de l'accusé Petković* Dated 31 March 2008", 21 April 2008, paras. 15, 17. See also *Muvunyi* Appeal Decision, para. 8, fn. 28.

[27] Appeal, para. 77.
[28] Appeal, para. 77.
[29] Appeal, paras. 35-43.
[30] Appeal, para. 38.
[31] Appeal, para. 39.
[32] Appeal, para. 40.

10.   With respect to the merits of the Impugned Decision, Ngirumpatse submits that the Trial Chamber erred in relying on the fact that none of the States to which he seeks to be released had agreed to host him. He claims that this factor is irrelevant as it is for the Registrar, not the accused, to coordinate with potential host States.[33] In addition, he argues that the Trial Chamber erred in relying on the medical reports of the Chief Medical Officer of the Tribunal and the Independent Medical Expert.[34] In this respect, he asserts that the Chief Medical Officer of the Tribunal had a conflict of interest and the Independent Medical Expert's opinion was based upon a review of an incomplete dossier and was therefore speculative.[35] He further asserts that the Independent Medical Expert's Report did not effectively or professionally answer the questions posed, particularly with regard to the issue of provisional release as his mandate was first and foremost to report on Ngirumpatse's ability to participate in his trial.[36] He points to an independent medical opinion solicited by his Counsel, dated 10 September 2009, which finds that the Independent Medical Expert's Report underestimated the gravity of his actual health.[37] He submits that there are compelling humanitarian reasons for allowing his provisional release.[38] He recalls that he is a 70 year old man who has been in detention for 11 years, during one year of which he was gravely ill.[39] He further contends that he only became so ill because his condition had not been treated since 2003.[40] Finally, he submits that the fact that the trial is set to recommence on 19 October 2009 should not be a reason to refuse his provisional release.[41]

11.   The Prosecution responds that the Appeal is without merit and should be dismissed in its entirety.[42] It argues that Ngirumpatse has failed to meet the standard of appellate review as he has failed to identify any discernible error in the Trial Chamber's exercise of its discretion warranting **[page 6]** the Appeals Chamber's intervention.[43] The Prosecution submits that Ngirumpatse failed to articulate an error with respect to the production of a host State guarantee.[44] It also asserts that the Trial Chamber sufficiently considered the humanitarian and medical grounds and other relevant factors in reaching its decision.[45] Finally, it asserts that Ngirumpatse's attempt to challenge the credibility of the Independent Medical Expert's Report and the Tribunal's Chief Medical Officer is "misplaced".[46] It contends that the medical reports Ngirumpatse filed before the Appeals Chamber should be disregarded because they were not part of the record before the Trial Chamber and Ngirumpatse failed to seek to have them admitted as additional evidence on appeal pursuant to Rule 115 of the Rules.[47]

E. Discussion

12.   At the outset, the Appeals Chamber rejects Ngirumpatse's argument that the Impugned Decision was not rendered in a timely manner. The Appeals Chamber is not convinced that there was an undue delay in the rendering of the Impugned Decision. While the Motion was filed before the Trial Chamber on 14 April 2009, the Independent Medical Expert's Report was not made available to the Trial Chamber until 11 August 2009.[48] In this circumstance, and considering that the information contained in the Independent Medical Expert's Report was a relevant factor for the Trial Chamber to consider,[49] the Appeals Chamber is not persuaded that the Impugned Decision was untimely.

---

[33]   Appeal, paras. 44-46.
[34]   Appeal, paras. 47-60.
[35]   Appeal, paras. 48-57. *See also ibid.*, paras. 72-74.
[36]   Appeal, para. 42.
[37]   Appeal, paras. 58, 59, *citing* letter of opinion of Dr. Pierre Cornier on the Independent Medical Expert's Report, 10 September 2009, annexed to the Appeal.
[38]   Appeal, paras. 61-74.
[39]   Appeal, para. 62.
[40]   Appeal, paras. 64-71.
[41]   Appeal, para. 75.
[42]   Response, paras. 2, 4, 12.
[43]   Response, paras. 4, 6, 11.
[44]   Response, para. 8.
[45]   Response, paras. 9, 10.
[46]   Response, para. 12.
[47]   Response, para. 12.
[48]   Impugned Decision para. 3, *citing* Independent Medical Expert's Report.
[49]   Appeal Decision on Provisional Release, para. 14. The Appeals Chamber specifically found that the Trial Chamber should have considered the medical and humanitarian grounds advanced by Ngirumpatse in deciding on his request for provisional release.

13. The Appeals Chamber is also not persuaded that Ngirumpatse has established his claim that the decision-making process was not fair and impartial. The Appeals Chamber recalls that the official languages of the Tribunal are English and French[50] and it can be assumed that the Trial Chamber is able to work in both languages, especially as the Impugned Decision was written in French. Thus, the Appeals Chamber considers that Ngirumpatse's argument that the Trial Chamber could not have properly considered the Independent Medical Expert's Report because it was filed in French is speculative and without merit. In relation to Ngirumpatse's argument that the Independent Medical Expert's Report did not properly address the issue of provisional release, the Appeals Chamber observes that the Independent Medical Expert's Report explicitly concluded that **[page 7]** Ngirumpatse's detention was not impeding his recovery and that it was not necessary to transfer him.[51] Ngirumpatse's contention that he was not given the opportunity to make submissions on the Independent Medical Expert's Report in relation to his request for provisional release is also unfounded given that the Trial Chamber explicitly invited the parties to do so in its order of 26 June 2009.[52] Additionally, Ngirumpatse made submissions on the Independent Medical Expert's Report in relation to the continuation of trial on 26 August 2009,[53] and the Appeals Chamber considers that he could also have addressed the Independent Medical Expert's Report in relation to his request for provisional release at that time.

14. Turning to the merits of the Impugned Decision, the Appeals Chamber observes that, in considering whether the requirements for granting provisional release pursuant to Rule 65(B) of the Rules had been met, the Trial Chamber first noted that Ngirumpatse had appended to his Motion correspondence with the governments of states to which he sought to be released.[54] Having considered this material, the Trial Chamber concluded that the first requirement of Rule 65(B) of the Rules, that the state to which the accused seeks to be released have the opportunity to be heard, had been fulfilled.[55] Accordingly, the Appeals Chamber finds no merit in Ngirumpatse's submission that the Trial Chamber erred in relying on the fact that no state had agreed to host him to dismiss his request.[56]

15. Having recalled that a request for provisional release brought at a late stage of proceedings should only be granted when sufficiently compelling humanitarian reasons exist,[57] the Trial Chamber next turned to consider Ngirumpatse's medical condition.[58] In this respect, it noted the reports of the Tribunal's Chief Medical Officer and the Independent Medical Expert.[59] It considered the Independent Medical Expert's conclusions that Ngirumpatse's treatment was having an effect on his illness, that the quality of medical care he was receiving conformed to the most exacting standards of care, that no negative consequences on Ngirumpatse's illness resulting from his detention were observed, and that there was no reason to transfer him to another facility as the risk **[page 8]** of a complication arising from his current mode of detention was not significantly higher than in the regular population.[60] In light of this, it concluded that there was no justification for the provisional release of Ngirumpatse.[61]

16. Ngirumpatse advances a number of challenges to the Trial Chamber's conclusions regarding his medical condition and its reliance on the reports of the Tribunal's Chief Medical Officer and the Independent Medical Expert. However, the Appeals Chamber considers that Ngirumpatse has failed to demonstrate that the Trial Chamber abused its discretion in relying on the Independent Medical Expert's Report in rendering its decision. While Ngirumpatse argues that the Independent Medical Expert relied on an incomplete medical record, the Independent Medical Expert undertook a physical examination of Ngirumpatse, relied on up-to-

---

[50] Article 31 of the Statute of the International Criminal Tribunal for Rwanda.
[51] Independent Medical Expert's Report, pp. 7, 8.
[52] *The Prosecutor v. Édouard Karemera et al.*, Case No. ICTR-98-44-T, *Ordonnance concernant certaines requêtes pendantes*, 26 June 2009 ("Order of 26 June 2009"), p. 5 ("***ORDONNE*** *à Matthieu Ngirumpatse, au Procureur et au Greffier de présenter à la Chambre leurs arguments ou observations concernant la demande de mise en liberté provisoire de Ngriumpatse à la suite du dépôt des versions caviardées des rapports médicaux concernant l'état de sa santé.*").
[53] *The Prosecutor v. Édouard Karemera et al.*, Case No. ICTR-98-44-T, *Mémoire pour Matthieu Ngirumpatse suite à l'ordonnance du 24 août 2008 concernant la reprise du procès*, 26 August 2009.
[54] Impugned Decision, para. 9.
[55] Impugned Decision, para. 9.
[56] Appeal, paras. 45, 46.
[57] Impugned Decision, para. 7.
[58] Impugned Decision, para. 10.
[59] Impugned Decision, para. 10.
[60] Impugned Decision, para. 10.
[61] Impugned Decision, para. 13.

date laboratory tests dated 20 and 31 July 2009, and was clearly familiar with Ngirumpatse's medical history.[62] In addition, Ngirumpatse did not challenge the Independent Medical Expert's Report prior to the rendering of the Impugned Decision, despite having been invited to submit his views on it in the Order of 26 June 2009.[63] In view of these factors, the Appeals Chamber finds that it was not unreasonable for the Trial Chamber to have relied on the Independent Medical Expert's Report in reaching its conclusion. Furthermore, the Appeals Chamber dismisses Ngirumpatse's argument that the Tribunal's Medical Officer has a "manifest conflict of interest" as Ngirumpatse has failed to substantiate this claim in any way.[64]

17. The Appeals Chamber observes that Ngirumpatse appended to his Appeal a medical report of his own, from Dr. Pierre Cornier, commenting on the Independent Medical Expert's Report, as well as medical records going back a number of years.[65] However, this material was not before the Trial Chamber and Ngirumpatse did not seek to have it admitted as additional evidence on appeal pursuant to Rule 115 of the Rules. Consequently, this material is not part of the record and the Appeals Chamber will not consider it.[66]

18. The Appeals Chamber further finds that, given the medical information before it, it was not unreasonable of the Trial Chamber to have concluded that Ngirumpatse's medical condition did not constitute compelling humanitarian reasons to grant provisional release. In relation to Ngirumpatse's age, length of detention, and the fact that his condition was undiagnosed for a period of time, the Appeals Chamber notes that the Independent Medical Expert was clearly aware of these **[page 9]** elements in his consideration of whether Ngirumpatse's detention was detrimental to his health condition.[67] As such, although the Trial Chamber did not consider these factors independently, given that the Trial Chamber accepted the findings of the Independent Medical Expert and they were factors taken into account by the Independent Medical Expert, the Appeals Chamber considers that they formed part of the basis for the Impugned Decision. Furthermore, Ngirumpatse has failed to demonstrate that the Trial Chamber erred in taking into account the fact that trial was set to resume.[68]

19. Consequently, the Appeals Chamber finds that Ngirumpatse has failed to demonstrate that the Trial Chamber erred in the exercise of its discretion in denying his request for provisional release.

F. Disposition

20. For the foregoing reasons, the Appeals Chamber **DISMISSES** the Appeal in its entirety, Judge Liu dissenting.

Done in English and French, the English text being authoritative.

Done this eighth day of December 2009,
at The Hague,
The Netherlands.

Judge Patrick Robinson
Presiding

[Seal of the Tribunal]

---

[62] Independent Medical Expert's Report, pp. 4, 5.
[63] Order of 26 June 2009, p. 5.
[64] Appeal, para. 48.
[65] Appeal, paras. 58, 59, Annex.
[66] *Prosecutor v. Jovica Stanišić and Franco Simatović*, Case No. IT-03-69-AR65.1, IT-03-69-AR65.2, Decision on Prosecution's Application Under Rule 115 to Present Additional Evidence in Its Appeal Against Provisional Release, 11 November 2004, para. 7.
[67] Independent Medical Expert's Report, pp. 1, 2, 4, 7, 8.
[68] *Cf. Prosecution v. Vujadin Popović et al.*, Case No. IT-05-88-AR65.2, Decision on Defence's Interlocutory Appeal of Trial Chamber's Decision Denying Ljubomir Borovčanin Provisional Release, 30 June 2006, para. 46 ("The Appeals Chamber finds that the Defence has failed to demonstrate that the Trial Chamber erred in taking into consideration the trial start date in reaching its decision on provisional release.").

[page 1] DISSENTING OPINION OF JUDGE LIU DAQUN

1. I respectfully disagree that any application for provisional release made after the close of the Prosecution case "should only be granted when sufficiently compelling humanitarian reasons exist".[1] In my view, the Majority decision to impose an additional requirement of "sufficiently compelling humanitarian reasons" to the criteria listed under Rule 65(B) of the Rules[2] undermines the continuing presumption of innocence and represents an *ultra vires* extension of the Rules.[3]

2. In accordance with Rule 65(B) of the Rules, a Trial Chamber may grant provisional release "only if it is satisfied that the accused will return for trial and, if released, will not pose a danger to any victim, witness or other person". When satisfied that these two requirements are met, a Trial Chamber may exercise its discretion to grant provisional release. In so doing, it must consider all relevant factors,[4] including the existence of humanitarian reasons. Thus, humanitarian reasons *may* be a salient factor in assessing whether provisional release should be granted but should be considered in the context of the two requirements of Rule 65(B) of the Rules.[5] The "weight attached to [humanitarian reasons] as justification for provisional release will differ from one defendant to another depending upon all of the circumstances of a particular case".[6]
[page 2]

3. Because there is no requirement for humanitarian reasons, much less "sufficiently compelling" humanitarian reasons, under Rule 65(B) of the Rules, I consider that the Majority's decision represents an *ultra vires* extension of the Rules. The above requirement amounts to reinstating, for post-Rule 98*bis* proceedings, the criterion of "exceptional circumstances" which was previously required by the Rules for the provisional release of an accused pending trial, and which was abrogated by the amendment of 27 May 2003.[7] Such a requirement undermines the important distinctions between convicted persons[8] and those who still enjoy the presumption of innocence under Article 20(3) of the Statute, and I cannot subscribe to it.

---

[1] Majority Decision, para. 7. This approach follows the interpretation of Rule 65(B) of the Rules in *Prosecutor v. Vujadin Popović et al.*, Case No. IT-05-88-AR65.10, Decision on Radivoje Miletić's Appeal Against Decision on Miletić's Motion for Provisional Release, 19 November 2009 ("*Miletić* Decision"), para. 7. *See also Prosecutor v. Ante Gotovina et al.*, Case No. IT-06-90-AR65.3, Decision on Ivan ^ermak's Appeal Against Decision on his Motion for Provisional Release, 3 August 2009 ("*^ermak* Decision"), para. 6; *Prosecutor v. Jadranko Prlić et al.*, Case No. IT-0474-AR65.15, Decision on Prosecution's Appeal Against the Trial Chamber's Decision on Slobodan Praljak's Motion for Provisional Release, 8 July 2009, para. 7; *Prosecutor v. Jadranko Prlić et al.*, Case No. IT-04-74-AR65.14, Decision on Jadranko Prlić's Appeal Against the *Décision relative à la démande de mise en liberté provisoire de l'Accusé Prlić*, 9 April 2009, 5 June 2009 ("*Prlić* Decision"), para. 8; *Prosecutor v. Jadranko Prlić et al.*, Case No. IT04-74-AR65.11, Decision on Praljak's Appeal of the Trial Chamber's 2 December 2008 Decision on Provisional Release, 17 December 2008, para. 7.

[2] Rules of Procedure and Evidence, as amended on 14 March 2008.

[3] This dissenting opinion is consistent with those expressed in previous decisions relating to Rule 65(B) of the Rules. See *Miletić* Decision, Joint Dissenting Opinion of Judges Güney and Liu; *Čermak* Decision, Partly Dissenting Opinion of Judges Güney and Liu; *Prosecutor v. Jadranko Prlić et al.*, Case No. IT-04-74-AR65.16, Decision on Prosecution's Appeal Against Decision on Pušić's Motion for Provisional Release, 20 July 2009, Dissenting Opinion of Judge Güney; *Prosecutor v. Vujadin Popović et al.*, Case No. IT-05-88-AR65.8, Decision on Prosecution's Appeal Against Decision on Gvero's Motion for Provisional Release, 20 July 2009, Dissenting Opinion of Judge Güney; *Prlić* Decision, Partly Dissenting Opinion of Judge Güney; *Prosecutor v. Vujadin Popović et al.*, Case Nos IT-05-88-AR65.4, IT-05-88AR65.5, IT-05-88-AR65.6, Decision on Consolidated Appeal Against Decision on Borovčanin's Motion for a Custodial Visit and Decisions on Gvero's and Miletić's Motions for Provisional Release During the Break in the Proceedings, 15 May 2008 ("*Popović* Decision"), Partly Dissenting Opinions of Judge Güney and Judge Liu; *Prosecutor v. Jadranko Prlić et al.*, Case No. IT-04-74-AR65.7, Decision on "Prosecution's Appeal from *Décision relative à la demande de mise en liberté provisoire de l'Accusé Petković* dated 31 March 2008", 21 April 2008, Partly Dissenting Opinion of Judge Güney.

[4] *See* Majority Decision, paras 6-7.

[5] *Prosecutor v. Ljube Boškoski and Johan Tarčulovski*, Case No. IT-04-82-AR65.4, Decision on Johan Tarčulovski's Interlocutory Appeal on Provisional Release, 27 July 2007, para. 14.

[6] *See Popović* Decision, Partly Dissenting Opinion of Judge Güney, para. 4, *citing Prosecutor v. Vujadin Popović et al.*, Case No. IT-05-88-AR65.3, Decision on Interlocutory Appeal of Trial Chamber's Decision Denying Ljubomir Borovčanin Provisional Release, 1 March 2007, para. 20.

[7] Prior to this amendment, Rule 65(B) of the Rules stated: "Provisional release may be ordered by a Trial Chamber *only in exceptional circumstances*, after hearing the host country and only if it is satisfied that the accused will appear for trial and, if released, will not pose a danger to any victim, witness or other person." (Emphasis added.)

[8] Pursuant to Rule 65(I)(iii) of the Rules, a convicted person is required to demonstrate that special circumstances exist to warrant provisional release.

4. In the present instance, the Trial Chamber failed to consider the criteria of Rule 65(B) of the Rules beyond noting that the host country and the country to which the accused seeks to be released have been given the opportunity to be heard.[9] By focusing exclusively on the existence of "compelling humanitarian reasons" the Trial Chamber dispensed with the formal requirements set out in Rule 65(B) of the Rules and, consequently, committed a discernable error. In these circumstances, I believe that this matter should be remanded to the Trial Chamber to determine in accordance with Rule 65(B) of the Rules.

Done in English and French, the English text being authoritative.

Dated this eighth day of December 2009
At The Hague,
The Netherlands

Judge Liu Daqun

[Seal of the Tribunal]

---

[9] Impugned Decision, para. 9.

Commentary

1. Introduction

Mathieu Ngirumpatse is over 70 years old and awaiting his judgment for approximately 13 years. In 1998, he was arrested in Mali and in 2005 his trial commenced. The ICTR has scheduled closing arguments for the end of September 2011.[1]

He has been charged with conspiracy to commit genocide, direct and public incitement to commit genocide and genocide or alternatively complicity in genocide; rape and extermination as crimes against humanity; as well as murder and violence to health and physical or mental well-being as serious violations of Common article 3 of the Geneva Conventions and Additional Protocol II.[2]

During the time that is covered in the indictment, Ngirumpatse was the president of the MRND[3] and a member of its steering committee. In this capacity, he had authority over the *Interhamwe*, the MRND's youth wing.[4] Before that he held several high political and judicial positions. Ngirumpatse is tried jointly with his co-accused Édouard Karemera and Joseph Nzirorera, both of whom held high positions in the MRND as well.[5]

2. Previous considerations of Ngirumpatse's provisional release

Ngirumpatse's requests for provisional release have occupied the chambers of the ICTR several times.[6] The Trial Chamber first ruled on the matter in February 2009. He had not been able to attend his trial since August 2008 due to health reasons until the decision in February 2009.[7]

Ngirumpatse wanted to be treated in a specialized hospital in Europe and blamed his deteriorating health on the conditions of detention and medical care provided to him.[8] He claimed his age, the length of his detention and the condition of his health as reasons for releasing him. Ngirumpatse assured the chamber of his limited flight risk due to the nature of the treatment he sought. His good behavior and personality were to warrant that he would not pose any danger to witnesses. Furthermore, he asked the chamber to facilitate his transfer by negotiating with the respective states and the host state Tanzania.[9]

The chamber concluded that the care provided was appropriate for his condition. According to the chief medical officer of the tribunal, Ngirumpatse received a treatment that is similar to the one he would receive in Europe.[10] The chamber denied the request to hire an independent medical expert.[11] The Court held that negotiating his transfer with the respective states fell outside of the chambers' tasks; furthermore, the chamber required that a state guarantee his attendance at the trial. Based on the aforementioned, the Trial Chamber held that the requirements for provisional release had not been met.[12]

---

[1] Hirondelle News Agency, 14.07.11, ICTR/CASES, ICTR Six Months Achievements, www.hirondellenews.com/content/view/14577/26/.
[2] ICTR, Amended Indictment, *Prosecutor v. Karemera, Ngirumpatse and Nzirorera*, Case No. ICTR-98-44-I, 24 August 2005.
[3] Mouvement Révolutionnaire Nationale pour le Développement later renamed to Mouvement Révolutionnaire Nationale pour la Démocratie le Développement.
[4] ICTR, Redacted Indictment, *Prosecutor v. Karemera, Ngirumpatse and Nzirorera*, Case No. ICTR-98-44-I, 22 August 1998.
[5] Amended Indictment, *Prosecutor v. Karemera, Ngirumpatse and Nzirorera*, supra note 2, p. 2.
[6] ICTR, Decision on the various motions relating to Matthieu Ngirumpatse's health, *Prosecutor v. Karemera, Ngirumpatse and Nzirorera*, Case No. ICTR-98-44-T, T. Ch. III, 6 February 2009; ICTR, Decision on Matthieu Ngirumpatse's appeal against Trial Chamber's decision denying provisional release, *Prosecutor v. Karemera, Ngirumpatse and Nzirorera*, Case No. ICTR-98-44-AR65, A. Ch., 7 April 2009; ICTR, Decision on remand in respect of Matthieu Ngirumpatse's motion for provisional release, *Prosecutor v. Karemera, Ngirumpatse and Nzirorera*, Case No. ICTR-98-44-T, T. Ch. III, 10 September 2009 and ICTR, Decision on Matthieu Ngirumpatse's Appeal against Decision on Remand on Provisional Release, *Prosecutor v. Karemera, Ngirumpatse and Nzirorera*, Case No. ICTR-98-44-AR65, A. Ch., 8 December 2009, in this volume, p. 105.
[7] ICTR, Decision on the various motions relating to Matthieu Ngirumpatse's health, *Prosecutor v. Karemera, Ngirumpatse and Nzirorera*, Case No. ICTR-98-44-T, T. Ch. III, 6 February 2009, par. 1.
[8] *Ibid.*, par. 7.
[9] *Ibid.*, par. 17, 18 and 19.
[10] *Ibid.*, par. 22.
[11] *Ibid.*, par. 25.
[12] *Ibid.*, par. 21 and 23.

On appeal, this decision was quashed.[13] The provision of a state guarantee cannot become a decisive requirement for provisional release.[14] Although the Trial Chamber may impose such a condition, it may not become the "threshold for consideration".[15] The decision to deny provisional release ought to have been based on a reasoned opinion which takes into account all relevant factors. Particularly, Ngirumpatse's argument that his medical condition limits his flight risk, should have been considered.[16] The matter was referred back for reconsideration. In the meantime, Ngirumpatse reapplied for provisional release on 14 April 2009.

In a parallel decision on the continuation of the trial, Ngirumpatse was severed from the Karemera *et al.* trial by the Trial Chamber. This decision was reversed by the Appeals Chamber as well.[17] Ngirumpatse's case was joined with the Karemera *et al* trial again in September, because the Trial Chamber did not see a reason to sever him from the trial according to the independent medical expert's opinion.[18]

As Ngirumpatse's health deteriorated in late spring of 2009, he was transferred to a hospital. Upon those events, the Trial Chamber decided to hire an independent medical expert to assess Ngirumpatse's state of health,[19] even though it had denied this in the earlier decision.

On 10 September 2009, the Trial Chamber denied Ngirumpatse's provisional release again.[20] In the mean time the prosecution closed its case, which, according to the Trial Chamber allows for a revaluation of the accused's guarantee that he will appear for trial. In this stage of the proceedings, provisional release can only be granted if, in addition to the usual requirements, there are sufficiently compelling humanitarian reasons for release. One example of a compelling humanitarian reason for release is that the accused suffers from a terminal illness in the final stages. This reasoning is based on a decision of the ICTY Appeals Chamber on the impact of a ruling on motions for a judgment of acquittal after the prosecution closed its case. According to this decision, a ruling on a 98*bis* motion moves the proceedings to a new stage, which allows for revaluation of the requirements or release.[21]

Ngirumpatse tried to obtain a state guarantee which would support his application, but none of the states that he contacted were willing to receive him. The requirement of giving states an opportunity to be heard was hereby fulfilled.[22] The independent medical expert did not find a necessity for Ngirumpatse to be treated in a specialized hospital and concluded that he was treated appropriately under the care of the tribunal.[23] Also based on the decision not to sever Ngirumpatse from the trial, the chamber ruled that there was no justification for releasing him. It was considered consistent not to release him, given the fact that his trial was not separated from the Karemera *et al* trial which was about to continue.[24]

---

[13] ICTR, Decision on Matthieu Ngirumpatse's appeal against Trial Chamber's decision denying provisional release, *Prosecutor v. Karemera, Ngirumpatse and Nzirorera*, Case No. ICTR-98-44-AR65, A. Ch., 7 April 2009.
[14] *Ibid.*, par. 12.
[15] *Ibid.*, par. 13.
[16] *Ibid.*, par. 14.
[17] ICTR, Decision on Continuation of Trial, *Prosecutor v. Karemera, Ngirumpatse and Nzirorera*, Case No. ICTR-98-44-T, T. Ch. III, 3 March 2009, par. 16; ICTR, Decision on Appeal Concerning the Severance of Matthieu Ngirumpatse, Case No. ICTR-98-44-AR73, 19 June 2009, par. 25.
[18] ICTR, Decision on Remand Regarding Continuation of Trial, *Prosecutor v. Karemera, Ngirumpatse and Nzirorera*, Case No. ICTR-98-44-T, T. Ch. III, 10 September 2009.
[19] ICTR, Decision Varying Matthieu Ngirumpatse's Conditions of Detention, *Prosecutor v. Karemera, Ngirumpatse and Nzirorera*, Case No. ICTR-98-44-T, T. Ch. III, 29 May 2009.
[20] ICTR, Decision on remand in respect of Matthieu Ngirumpatse's motion for provisional release, *Prosecutor v. Karemera, Ngirumpatse and Nzirorera*, Case No. ICTR-98-44-T, T. Ch. III, 10 September 2009.
[21] ICTY, Decision on prosecution's consolidated appeal against decisions to provisionally release the accused Prlić, Stojić, Praljak, Petkovic and Ćorić, *Prosecutor v. Prlić, Stojić, Praljak, Petković, Corić and Pušić*, Case No. IT-04-74-AR65.5, A. Ch., 11 March 2008.
[22] Decision on remand in respect of Matthieu Ngirumpatse's motion for provisional release, *Prosecutor v. Karemera, Ngirumpatse and Nzirorera*, T. Ch. III, *supra* note 6, par. 9.
[23] *Ibid.*, par. 10.
[24] *Ibid.*, par. 13.

The Appeals Chamber took a final decision on this matter in December 2009.[25] The chamber emphasized again that the decision of the Trial Chamber is discretional. Hence, the standard of review is whether the Trial Chamber used its discretion correctly.[26]

Ngirumpatse challenged the timeliness, fairness and impartiality of the decision and the quality of the independent medical expert's report. He also asked the registry to negotiate with states, as the Trial Chamber erred in finding that no state wanted to host him. Furthermore, he stressed again the length of his detention.[27] Additionally, he submitted that the approaching recommencement of the trial is no reason to deny his request.

The Appeals Chamber did not consider the proceedings untimely or unfair.[28] As to the expert's report, it ruled that the report addresses all relevant matters and that he had the opportunity to address the report earlier.[29] A report by Ngirumpatse's doctor attached to the appeal is rejected as evidence on procedural grounds.[30] The Appeals Chamber agrees with the finding of the Trial Chamber as to the willingness of states to accept Ngirumpatse in their territory.[31] It holds that the Trial Chamber considered all of Ngirumpatse's challenges through the independent medical expert's report sufficiently.[32] Dealing with each challenge individually, was not required. In conclusion, the Appeals Chamber holds that Ngirumpatse did not demonstrate that the Trial Chamber used its discretion erroneously.[33]

Judge Liu dissents to the need for sufficiently compelling humanitarian reasons for provisional release at this stage of the proceedings.[34] Humanitarian reasons can be taken into account when assessing the flight risk of the accused,[35] but to introduce such a requirement in general would violate the presumption of innocence.[36] Therefore, the dissent recommends referring the decision to the Trial Chamber for reconsideration.[37]

3. Additional requirement for provisional release?

The outcome of the decision is in line with the ICTR's history of consequently denying provisional release.[38] This has not changed despite the 2003 amendment of Rule 65,[39] which waived the requirement of exceptional circumstances. The requirement of exceptional circumstances that warrant release had to be proven by the defence. In order to show that exceptional circumstances existed, the defence typically described the personal hardship that the accused suffered from continued detention. The chamber would decide whether this requirement was fulfilled based on "reasonable suspicion that he committed the crime or crimes as charged, his alleged role in the said crime or crimes, and the length of the accused's detention".[40]

---

[25] Decision on Matthieu Ngirumpatse's Appeal against Decision on Remand on Provisional Release, *Prosecutor v. Karemera, Ngirumpatse and Nzirorera*, A. Ch., 8 December 2009, *supra* note 6.
[26] *Ibid.*, par. 5.
[27] *Ibid.*, par. 9 and 10.
[28] *Ibid.*, par. 13.
[29] *Ibid.*, par. 13, 15 and 18.
[30] *Ibid.*, par. 18.
[31] *Ibid.*, par. 14.
[32] *Ibid.*, par. 18.
[33] *Ibid.*, par. 19.
[34] ICTR, Decision on Matthieu Ngirumpatse's Appeal against Decision on Remand on Provisional Release, Dissenting Opinion by Judge Liu, *Prosecutor v. Karemera, Ngirumpatse and Nzirorera*, A. Ch., in this volume, p. 112, par. 1.
[35] *Ibid.*, par. 2.
[36] *Ibid.*, par. 3.
[37] *Ibid.*, par. 5.
[38] For example ICTR, Decision on Augustin Ndindiliyimana's Emergency Motion for Temporary Provisional Release, *Prosecutor v. Bizimungu, Ndindiliyimana, Nzuwonemeye and Sagahutu*, Case No. ICTR-00-56-T, T. Ch. II, 11 November 2003, par. 18; ICTR, Decision on Defence Motion to Fax a Date for the Commencement of the Trial of Father Emmanuel Rukundo or, in the Alternative, to Request his Provisional Release, *Prosecutor v. Rukundo*, Case No. ICTR-2001-70-T, T. Ch. III, 18 August 2003, par. 22; ICTR, Decision on Defence Motion for His Provisional Release, *Prosecutor v.Rukundo*, Case No. ICTR-2001-70-I, T. Ch. III, 18 March 2004.
[39] See ICTR, Decision on motion to set a date for trial of the accused or for provisional release, *Prosecutor v. Ndindabahizi*, Case No. ICTR-2001-71-T, T. Ch. I, 30 June 2003; Decision on Defence Motion to Fax a Date for the Commencement of the Trial of Father Emmanuel Rukundo or, in the Alternative, to Request his Provisional Release, *Prosecutor v. Rukundo*, T. Ch. III, *supra* note 38. According to data on the ICTR website no accused has been provisionally released yet, Status of Detainees, www.unictr.org/Cases/tabid/202/Default.aspx.
[40] ICTY, Decision on Motion for Provisional Release Filed By the Accused Zejnil Delalic, *Prosecutor v. Delalić*, Case No. IT-96-21-T, T. Ch. II, 25 September 1996, par. 13 *et seq.*

Rule 65 of the Rules of Procedure and Evidence of the ICTR (RPE)[41] provides the regime for provisional release. Release can only take place upon order of a Trial Chamber.[42] The requirements for release give the states involved the opportunity to be heard. The chamber needs to be assured that the accused will appear for trial and will not pose a danger to anyone.[43] Additional conditions may be imposed on the accused,[44] as for example the provision of a state guarantee[45] or the obligation to report daily to a local police station during release.[46]

In 2003, the requirement of proving exceptional circumstances for release in Rule 65(B) was removed.[47] Nevertheless, this requirement still exists for provisional release of convicted persons.[48] Provisional release is possible in all stages of the proceedings; however, different requirements apply for example while an appeal is pending.[49] If there was a ruling on a motion for a judgment of acquittal after the prosecution closed its case,[50] the Trial Chamber may reassess the flight risk of the accused.[51]

The requirements in Rule 65(B) are cumulative,[52] which explains the practice of the ICTR not to test the other requirements, if one requirement has not been fulfilled.[53] In Ngirumpatse's case only the requirement of giving the states involved the opportunity to be heard was fulfilled, according to the chambers.[54] The chamber noted that none of the requested states wanted to receive Ngirumpatse in their territory, which emphasizes the fact that Ngirumpatse's provisional release does not only depend on the decision of the Trial Chamber, but also on the willingness of the host state and any recipient state. Both chambers made it clear that it was not the chamber's task to lead these negotiations for the accused. The prosecutor also submitted that there is no duty for states to assist the accused.[55] According to the ICTR's practice, an application for provisional release could be denied based on the lack of consent of the relevant states.[56]

Ngirumpatse's flight risk was not assessed in detail in any decision. However, it was mentioned that a state guarantee would be the only means to assure the chamber that Ngirumpatse would not flee.[57] The Appeals Chamber made clear that this could not be the only consideration, but in the follow up decision Ngirumpatse's flight risk was not mentioned anymore. The potential danger to witnesses, victims or other persons that Ngirumpatse could cause while released was not analyzed either.

---

[41] Rules of Procedure and Evidence of the International Criminal Tribunal for Rwanda, 9 February 2010.
[42] Rule 65 (A) RPE.
[43] Rule 65 (B) RPE.
[44] Rule 65 (C) RPE.
[45] Decision on Matthieu Ngirumpatse's appeal against Trial Chamber's decision denying provisional release, *Prosecutor v. Karemera, Ngirumpatse and Nzirorera*, A. Ch., *supra* note 6.
[46] ICTY, Decision on Simo Zarić's Application for Provisional Release, *Prosecutor v. Simić, Simić, Tadić, Todorović and Zarić*, Case No. IT 95 9 PT, T. Ch. III, 4 April 2000, Klip/ Sluiter, ALC-IV-81 and G. Mols, Commentary, Klip/ Sluiter ALC-III-182.
[47] Amendments Adopted: at Thirteenth Plenary Session, 26–27 May 2003.
[48] Rule 65 (I) iii RPE.
[49] W. Schomburg, The Role of International Criminal Tribunals in Promoting Respect for Fair Trial Rights, 8 Northwestern Journal of International Human Rights 2009, p. 25 and 28 and Rule 65 (I) iii.
[50] Rule 98*bis* RPE.
[51] W. Schomburg The Role of International Criminal Tribunals in Promoting Respect for Fair Trial Rights, *supra* note 48, p. 26 and Decision on prosecution's consolidated appeal against decisions to provisionally release the accused Prlić, Stojić, Praljak, Petkovic and Ćorić, *Prosecutor v. Prlić, Stojić, Praljak, Petković, Corić and Pušić*, A. Ch., *supra* note 21, par. 19 *et seq*.
[52] ICTR, Decision on the defence motion for the setting of a date for commencement of trial and Provisional Release, *Prosecutor v. Nzabririnda*, Case No. ICTR-01-77-T, T. Ch. II, 13 October 2006, par. 13; See also ICTY, Decision on Motion for Provisional Release filed by the Accused Zejnil Delalić, *Prosecutor v. Delalić, Mucić, Delić and Landžo*, Case No. IT-96-21-T, T. Ch. II, 25 September 1996, par. 1.
[53] H. Friman, Commentary, ALC-IX-348.
[54] Decision on remand in respect of Matthieu Ngirumpatse's motion for provisional release, *Prosecutor v. Karemera, Ngirumpatse and Nzirorera*, T. Ch. III, *supra* note 6, par. 9.
[55] ICTR, Prosecutor's Response to Matthieu Ngirumpatse's Motion for Provisional Release, *Prosecutor v. Karemera, Ngirumpatse and Nzirorera*, Case No. ICTR-98-44-T, T. Ch. III, par. 6.
[56] H. Friman, Commentary, ALC-IX-353 and for example Decision on Augustin Ndindiliyimana's Emergency Motion for Temporary Provisional Release, *Prosecutor v. Bizimungu, Ndindiliyimana, Nzuwonemeye and Sagahutu*, T. Ch. II, par. 18, *supra* note 38; Decision on Defence Motion to Fax a Date for the Commencement of the Trial of Father Emmanuel Rukundo or, in the Alternative, to Request his Provisional Release, *Prosecutor v. Rukondo*, T. Ch. III, *supra* note 38, par. 22; Decision on Defence Motion for His Provisional Release, *Prosecutor v. Rukondo*, T. Ch. III, *supra* note 38.
[57] Decision on the various motions relating to Matthieu Ngirumpatse's health, *Prosecutor v. Karemera, Ngirumpatse and Nzirorera*, T. Ch. III, *supra* note 6, par. 21.

In taking the discretional decision to deny provisional release, the chamber has to consider all relevant factors and determine their weight case by case. According to the standard procedure, humanitarian reasons are a factor which is taken into account after testing the requirements of Rule 65(B).[58]

Still, the requirements were not tested entirely in Ngirumpatse's case. Instead, compelling humanitarian reasons are considered after the first requirement,[59] which indicates that the factor of compelling humanitarian reasons is elevated to a mandatory requirement for the decision on provisional release. Since the Appeals Chamber reiterated this reasoning, this factor was now promoted to become a requirement at this stage of the proceedings.[60] Compelling humanitarian reasons are a factor similar to proportionality which can always be taken into account in discretionary decisions.[61] It is, therefore, not entirely new to the considerations on provisional release.

Factors like the length of Ngirumpatse's detention or his age were considered only indirectly in the sense that the independent medical expert was aware of them.[62] The lack of compelling humanitarian reasons which was determined mainly on the basis of the independent medical expert's report was the sole substantive basis for the decision not to grant release. The requirement for states to be heard is procedural.

By introducing the requirement of compelling humanitarian reasons to the jurisprudence of the ICTR, both chambers in Ngirumpatse's case applied a precedent of the ICTY's Appeals Chamber in the Prlić case without discussing the reasoning independently.[63] This is an interesting move since the ICTR chambers have repeatedly emphasized their independence from the ICTY in the context of provisional release.[64] The ICTR maintained the requirement of exceptional circumstances long after the ICTY and the Appeals Chamber justified this by stating that the ICTR is a "separate sovereign body"[65] and that Rules of Procedure and Evidence could only be amended by the chambers of the ICTR.[66]

Judge Liu notes in the dissenting opinion that an additional requirement of sufficiently compelling humanitarian reasons reintroduces the requirement of extraordinary circumstances.[67] In fact serious health conditions have been qualified as extraordinary conditions in the earlier case law of the ICTY[68] and such health conditions are now qualified as compelling humanitarian reasons. The threshold that the accused has to meet appears to be similar under the old requirement of extraordinary circumstances.

This eliminates the difference between convicted persons who have to show extraordinary circumstances for release[69] and accused who have not been proven guilty beyond a reasonable doubt.[70]

---

[58] See the chamber's own wording on the procedure of taking a decision, Decision on remand in respect of Matthieu Ngirumpatse's motion for provisional release, *Prosecutor v. Karemera, Ngirumpatse and Nzirorera*, T. Ch. III, *supra* note 6, par. 7.

[59] Decision on remand in respect of Matthieu Ngirumpatse's motion for provisional release, *Prosecutor v. Karemera, Ngirumpatse and Nzirorera*, T. Ch. III, *supra* note 20, par. 10.

[60] Decision on Matthieu Ngirumpatse's Appeal against Decision on Remand on Provisional Release, *Prosecutor v. Karemera, Ngirumpatse and Nzirorera*, A. Ch., *supra* note 6, par. 15 and 18.

[61] H. Friman, Commentary, ALC-IX-345.

[62] Decision on Matthieu Ngirumpatse's Appeal against Decision on Remand on Provisional Release, *Prosecutor v. Karemera, Ngirumpatse and Nzirorera*, A. Ch., *supra* note 6, par. 10 and 18.

[63] Decision on prosecution's consolidated appeal against decisions to provisionally release the accused Prlić, Stojić, Praljak, Petkovic and Ćorić, *Prosecutor v. Prlić, Stojić, Praljak, Petković, Ćorić and Pušić*, A. Ch., *supra* note 21, par. 6 as mentioned in Decision on remand in respect of Matthieu Ngirumpatse's motion for provisional release, *Prosecutor v. Karemera, Ngirumpatse and Nzirorera*, T. Ch. III, *supra* note 6, par. 7 and Decision on Matthieu Ngirumpatse's Appeal against Decision on Remand on Provisional Release, *Prosecutor v. Karemera, Ngirumpatse and Nzirorera*, A. Ch., *supra* note 6, par. 7.

[64] ICTR, Decision on the defence motion for the provisional release of the accused, *Prosecutor v. Kanyabashi*, Case No. ICTR-96-15-T, T. Ch. II, 21 February 2001, par. 4, 5, and 6; J. O'Dowd, Commentary, Klip/ Sluiter ALC-VII-96.

[65] *Ibid.*, par. 4.

[66] *Ibid.*

[67] Decision on Matthieu Ngirumpatse's Appeal against Decision on Remand on Provisional Release, Dissenting opinion by Judge Liu, *Prosecutor v. Karemera, Ngirumpatse and Nzirorera*, A. Ch., *supra* note 34, par. 3.

[68] A. Zahar, G. Sluiter, International Criminal Law, Oxford University Press, Oxford 2008, p. 341.

[69] Rule 65 (C) iii.

[70] Decision on Matthieu Ngirumpatse's Appeal against Decision on Remand on Provisional Release, Dissenting opinion by Judge Liu, *Prosecutor v. Karemera, Ngirumpatse and Nzirorera*, A. Ch., *supra* note 34, par. 3.

3. Concluding remarks

It has been stated repeatedly that, at the *ad hoc* tribunals, detention is the rule and release the exception.[71] This situation would be unacceptable in domestic criminal proceedings where the legality of detention is constantly scrutinized. However, International criminal tribunals are facing a different reality than national systems. The ICTY and the ICTR have acknowledged this situation and identified the causes for extensive detention: the gravity of the crimes charged, the complexity of the cases and the lack of an independent enforcement authority. Nevertheless, the accused has the right to challenge detention. This right is meaningless if decisions denying release are not taken in a transparent manner considering all relevant factors for each individual case. Due to the discretionary nature of the decision to deny release, a thoroughly reasoned opinion underlying that decision will prevent the impression that provisional release is never an option. It will also allow for full consideration of the individual circumstances of an accused. Nevertheless, the requirement of compelling humanitarian reasons at a late stage in the proceedings will probably not change the practice of denying provisional release at the ICTR. The ability of the ICTR Trial Chambers to grant provisional release depends to a large extent on the political will of states to ensure return of the accused for trial. Absences of provisional releases can only be evaluated in the light of the surrounding political realities, which arguably have a larger impact on the proceedings than the specific wording of the requirements for release.

No continuous check of the legality of detention is required at the international tribunals, which is a shortcoming of international criminal justice.[72] However, the presumption of innocence is also an underlying principle in international criminal proceedings. Ngirumpatse should still be considered innocent, as he has not been proven guilty beyond reasonable doubt. He has been waiting for his judgment in the first instance for 13 years now. Except for the discussion in the dissent, this factor has not been considered in the entire provisional release proceedings of Mathieu Ngirumpatse.

Mariam Pathan

---

[71] ICTY, Decision on Momčilo Krajišnik's Notice of Motion for Provisional Release, *Prosecutor v. Krajišnik and Plavsić,* Case No. IT-00-39 & 40-PT, T. Ch. III, 8 October 2001, Klip/ Sluiter, ALC-VIII-45, par. 12.
[72] W. Schomburg, The Role of International Criminal Tribunals in Promoting Respect for Fair Trial Rights, *supra* note 48, p. 23.

Tribunal pénal international pour le Rwanda
International Criminal Tribunal for Rwanda

IN THE APPEALS CHAMBER

Before: Judge Fausto Pocar, Presiding
         Judge Mohamed Shahabuddeen
         Judge Mehmet Güney
         Judge Liu Daqun
         Judge Theodor Meron

Registrar: Mr. Adama Dieng

Date: 2 February 2009

FRANÇOIS KARERA

v.

THE PROSECUTOR

Case No. ICTR-01-74-A

JUDGEMENT

Counsel for the Appellant

Ms. Carmelle Marchessault
Mr. Alexandre Bergevin
Mr. Christian Deslauriers, Assistant

Office of the Prosecutor

Mr. Hassan Bubacar Jallow
Mr. Alex Obote-Odora
Ms. Dior Sow Fall
Mr. Abdoulaye Seye
Mr. François-Xavier Nsanzuwera
Mr. Alfred Orono Orono
Ms. Florida Kabasinga
Ms. Béatrice Chapaux

[page i] CONTENTS

I. INTRODUCTION 1
    A. BACKGROUND 1
    B. THE APPEAL 2

II. STANDARDS OF APPELLATE REVIEW 3

III. ALLEGED GENERAL ERRORS IN THE ASSESSMENT OF THE EVIDENCE (GROUND OF APPEAL 2, IN PART) 5
    A. ALLEGED GENERAL ERRORS IN THE ASSESSMENT OF THE APPELLANT'S TESTIMONY 5
        1. Rules Applicable to the Assessment of an Accused's Testimony and Provision of a Reasoned Opinion 5
        2. Alleged Error concerning Inferences that the Trial Chamber Should Have Drawn from the Prosecution's Absence of Cross-Examination of the Appellant 8
    B. ALLEGED ERRORS IN THE ASSESSMENT OF CIRCUMSTANTIAL EVIDENCE 11
    C. ALLEGED ERRORS IN THE ASSESSMENT OF HEARSAY EVIDENCE 12
    D. ALLEGED ERRORS IN THE ASSESSMENT OF UNCORROBORATED EVIDENCE 14
    E. ALLEGED ERRORS RELATING TO THE OBSERVATIONS MADE DURING THE SITE VISIT 15
    F. CONCLUSION 16

IV. ALLEGED ERRORS RELATING TO THE FINDING THAT THE APPELLANT ACTED AS PREFECT *DE FACTO* IN "KIGALI-RURAL" BEFORE 17 APRIL 1994 (GROUND OF APPEAL 3) 17
    A. ALLEGED ERROR RELATING TO THE OFFICIAL DESIGNATION OF KIGALI PREFECTURE IN 1994 17
    B. ALLEGED ERROR IN FINDING THAT FORMER PREFECT CÔME BIZIMUNGU WAS EMPOWERED TO APPOINT THE APPELLANT PREFECT *AD INTERIM* 18
    C. ALLEGED ERRORS IN FINDING THAT THE APPELLANT ACTED AS *DE FACTO* PREFECT BEFORE 17 APRIL 1994 19
        1. Alleged Error relating to the Letters Signed by the Appellant "for the Prefect" 20
        2. Alleged Error in Relying on Circumstantial Evidence 21
        3. Alleged Errors in Assessing the Evidence and in Failing to Provide a Reasoned Opinion ... 21
        4. Allegation that No Evidence was Adduced that the Appellant had Exercised Powers of the Prefect after 14 January 1994 23
    D. CONCLUSION 23

V. ALLEGED ERRORS RELATING TO THE APPELLANT'S INVOLVEMENT IN THE MRND AND HIS AUTHORITY OVER THE *INTERAHAMWE* (GROUND OF APPEAL 4) 24

VI. ALLEGED ERRORS RELATING TO THE FINDING THAT THE APPELLANT WAS INVOLVED IN A CAMPAIGN TO KILL TUTSIS IN NYAMIRAMBO SECTOR, NYARUGENGE COMMUNE (GROUND OF APPEAL 5) 28
    A. ALLEGED ERRORS RELATING TO THE APPELLANT'S AUTHORITY OVER COMMUNE POLICEMEN 29
        1. Alleged Error in Failing to Provide a Reasoned Opinion 29
        2. Alleged Error in Relying on Prosecution Evidence 30
        3. Alleged Error in Failing to Give Proper Weight to Defence Evidence 38
    B. ALLEGED ERRORS RELATING TO THE APPELLANT'S ORDERS TO KILL KABUGUZA'S FAMILY 40
    C. ALLEGED ERRORS RELATING TO THE FINDING THAT THE APPELLANT ORDERED THE KILLING OF TUTSIS AND DESTRUCTION OF THEIR HOMES IN NYAMIRAMBO 42
        1. Alleged Error in Making a Finding of Fact on a General and Redundant Allegation 42
        2. Alleged Error in the Assessment of Prosecution and Defence Evidence .... 43 **[page ii]**

   3. Conclusion 47
D. ALLEGED ERRORS RELATING TO THE FINDING THAT THE APPELLANT ORDERED THAT CERTAIN HOUSES OF TUTSIS BE SPARED 47
E. ALLEGED ERRORS RELATING TO THE FINDING THAT KAHABAYE WAS KILLED ON THE APPELLANT'S ORDERS 49
F. ALLEGED ERRORS RELATING TO THE FINDING THAT THE APPELLANT ORDERED POLICEMAN KALIMBA TO KILL MUREKEZI 52
G. ALLEGED ERRORS RELATING TO THE FINDING THAT THE APPELLANT WAS INVOLVED IN THE MURDER OF NDINGUTSE 54
H. ALLEGED ERRORS RELATING TO THE KILLING OF NYAGATARE ON THE APPELLANT'S ORDERS 56
I. CONCLUSION 58

VII. ALLEGED ERRORS RELATING TO THE KILLING OF TUTSIS IN NTARAMA (GROUND OF APPEAL 6) 59

A. ALLEGED ERRORS IN THE ASSESSMENT OF PROSECUTION EVIDENCE 59
   1. Alleged Error in Relying on Prosecution Witnesses Who Lied 60
   2. Alleged Collusion by Prosecution Witnesses 63
   3. Alleged Inconsistencies in the Prosecution Evidence 65
B. ALLEGED ERRORS IN THE ASSESSMENT OF DEFENCE EVIDENCE 70
C. CONCLUSION 73

VIII. ALLEGED ERRORS RELATING TO THE KILLING OF TUTSIS IN RUSHASHI COMMUNE (GROUNDS OF APPEAL 1 AND 7 AND GROUND OF APPEAL 2, IN PART) 74

A. ALLEGED ERRORS RELATING TO ROADBLOCKS 74
B. ALLEGED ERRORS RELATING TO MEETINGS HELD IN RUSHASHI BETWEEN APRIL AND JUNE 1994 76
   1. Alleged Errors relating to a Meeting Held at Rwankuba Secondary School in April 1994 76
   2. Alleged Errors relating to a Meeting Held at Rushashi Sub-Prefecture Office in June 1994 78
   3. Conclusion 79
C. ALLEGED ERRORS RELATING TO "PACIFICATION MEETINGS" 79
D. ALLEGED ERRORS RELATING TO THE DISTRIBUTION OF WEAPONS 83
E. ALLEGED ERRORS RELATING TO THE MURDER OF GAKURU, *CONSEILLER* OF KIMISANGE SECTOR 85
   1. Alleged Inconsistencies between the Testimonies of Witnesses BMR, BMO, BMN and BMM 86
   2. Alleged Failure to Provide Reasons for Rejecting the Appellant's Testimony 89
   3. Alleged Failure to Determine the Place, Date, and Identity of the Perpetrators 89
F. CONCLUSION 92

IX. ALLEGED ERRORS RELATING TO THE ALIBI (GROUND OF APPEAL 8) 93

A. ALLEGED ERRORS IN THE APPLICATION OF THE BURDEN OF PROOF 93
B. ALLEGED ERRORS RELATING TO THE POSSIBILITY OF TRAVELLING FROM RUHENGERI 97
C. ALLEGED ERRORS IN THE ASSESSMENT OF THE EVIDENCE ON ALIBI 100
D. CONCLUSION 102

X. ALLEGED ERRORS RELATING TO THE TRIAL CHAMBER'S LEGAL FINDINGS (GROUND OF APPEAL 10) 103

XI. ALLEGED ERROR IN HEARING THE CASE OF THARCISSE RENZAHO WHILE PARTICIPATING IN DELIBERATIONS ON THE APPELLANT'S CASE (GROUND OF APPEAL 11) .... 107 [page iii]

XII. ALLEGED ERRORS RELATING TO SENTENCING (GROUND OF APPEAL 12) 110

XIII. DISPOSITION **114**

XIV. ANNEX A: PROCEDURAL BACKGROUND **116**
    A. Notice of Appeal And Briefs 116
    B. Assignment of Judges..116
    C. Motion Related to the Admission of Additional Evidence 117
    D. Hearing of the Appeal 117

XV. ANNEX B: CITED MATERIALS AND DEFINED TERMS... **118**
    A. Jurisprudence 118
        1. ICTR 118
        2. ICTY 120
    B. Defined Terms and Abbreviations 122

[page 1] 1.   The Appeals Chamber of the International Criminal Tribunal for the Prosecution of Persons Responsible for Genocide and Other Serious Violations of International Humanitarian Law Committed in the Territory of Rwanda and Rwandan Citizens Responsible for Genocide and Other Such Violations Committed in the Territory of Neighbouring States between 1 January 1994 and 31 December 1994 ("Appeals Chamber" and "Tribunal", respectively) is seized of an appeal by François Karera ("Appellant") against the Judgement rendered on 7 December 2007 in the case of *The Prosecutor v. François Karera* ("Trial Judgement") by Trial Chamber I of the Tribunal ("Trial Chamber").

I. INTRODUCTION

A. Background

2.   The Appellant was born in 1938, in Huro sector, Musasa commune, Kigali prefecture.[1] For fifteen years he was the *bourgmestre* of Nyarugenge commune, in Kigali-Ville prefecture.[2] On 9 November 1990, the Appellant was appointed sub-prefect in Kigali prefecture and on or around 17 April 1994, he was appointed by the Interim Government as prefect of Kigali prefecture.[3]

3.   The Appellant was tried on the basis of an amended indictment dated 19 December 2005 ("Amended Indictment"), which charged him with individual criminal responsibility under four counts: genocide (Count 1); complicity in genocide (Count 2); extermination as a crime against humanity (Count 3); and murder as a crime against humanity (Count 4). He was additionally charged with superior responsibility under Counts 1, 3 and 4. These counts related to attacks against and the murder of Tutsis in Nyamirambo sector (Nyarugenge commune, Kigali-Ville prefecture); in Kigali prefecture and at the Ntarama Church (Ntarama sector, Kakenze commune, Kigali prefecture).

4.   The Trial Chamber found the Appellant guilty, under Article 6(1) of the Statute of the Tribunal ("Statute"), of genocide (Count 1)[4] and extermination and murder as crimes against humanity (Counts 3 and 4, respectively).[5] The Trial Chamber acquitted the Appellant of the alternative charge of complicity in genocide (Count 2) in light of his conviction for genocide.[6] While the Trial Chamber also found that the Appellant was responsible as a superior pursuant to [page 2] Article 6(3) of the Statute, it did not enter a separate conviction on that basis but considered the Appellant's "superior position as an aggravating factor in sentencing".[7] It imposed a single sentence of imprisonment for the remainder of the Appellant's life.[8]

B. The Appeal

5.   The Appellant presents twelve grounds of appeal challenging his convictions and his sentence. He requests the Appeals Chamber to overturn his convictions and to order his release.[9] In the alternative, he requests the Appeals Chamber to order a retrial or, as a further alternative, to quash his life sentence and substitute it with an appropriate sentence.[10] In his Appellant's Brief, the Appellant dropped his Ninth Ground of Appeal[11] and as a consequence, the Appeals Chamber will not address this ground of appeal.

---

[1] Trial Judgement, para. 21. The Appeals Chamber notes that the Trial Chamber erred in designating the prefecture "Kigali-Rural" as in 1994 it was officially named Kigali prefecture. *See infra* paras. 55-58. *See also* Exhibit P14: *Loi 29/90 du 28 mai 1990, modifiant et complétant la loi du 15 avril 1963 sur l'organisation territoriale de la République (Journal Officiel, 1/08 /1990)*.
[2] Trial Judgement, para. 23.
[3] Trial Judgement, para. 24.
[4] Trial Judgement, paras. 540, 544, 548.
[5] Trial Judgement, paras. 557, 560, 561.
[6] Trial Judgement, para. 549.
[7] Trial Judgement, paras. 566, 577.
[8] Trial Judgement, para. 585.
[9] Notice of Appeal, p. 28; Appellant's Brief, p. 61.
[10] Notice of Appeal, p. 28; Appellant's Brief, p. 61.
[11] The Appellant acknowledges that "the [Trial] Chamber's erroneous finding of fact did not occasion a miscarriage of justice for the Appellant". Appellant's Brief, para. 310.

6. The Appeals Chamber heard oral arguments regarding this appeal on 28 August 2008. Having considered the written and oral submissions of the parties, the Appeals Chamber hereby renders its Judgement.[12] **[page 3]**

II. STANDARDS OF APPELLATE REVIEW

7. The Appeals Chamber recalls the applicable standards of appellate review pursuant to Article 24 of the Statute. The Appeals Chamber reviews only errors of law which invalidate the decision of the Trial Chamber and errors of fact which have occasioned a miscarriage of justice.[13]

8. As regards errors of law, the Appeals Chamber has stated:

> Where a party alleges that there is an error of law, that party must advance arguments in support of the submission and explain how the error invalidates the decision. However, if the appellant's arguments do not support the contention, that party does not automatically lose its point since the Appeals Chamber may step in and, for other reasons, find in favour of the contention that there is an error of law.[14]

9. Where the Appeals Chamber finds an error of law in the trial judgement arising from the application of an incorrect legal standard, the Appeals Chamber will articulate the correct legal interpretation and review the relevant factual findings of the Trial Chamber accordingly. In so doing, the Appeals Chamber not only corrects the legal error, but, when necessary, applies the correct legal standard to the evidence contained in the trial record and determines whether it is itself convinced beyond reasonable doubt as to the factual finding challenged by the appellant before that finding may be confirmed on appeal.[15]

10. As regards errors of fact, it is well established that the Appeals Chamber will not lightly overturn findings of fact made by a Trial Chamber:

> Where the Defence alleges an erroneous finding of fact, the Appeals Chamber must give deference to the Trial Chamber that received the evidence at trial, and it will only interfere in those findings where no reasonable trier of fact could have reached the same finding or where the finding is wholly erroneous. Furthermore, the erroneous finding will be revoked or revised only if the error occasioned a miscarriage of justice.[16]

11. A party cannot merely repeat on appeal arguments that did not succeed at trial, unless it can demonstrate that the Trial Chamber's rejection of those arguments constituted an error warranting the intervention of the Appeals Chamber.[17] Arguments which do not have the potential to cause the impugned decision to be reversed or revised may be immediately dismissed by the Appeals Chamber and need not be considered on the merits.[18] **[page 4]**

12. In order for the Appeals Chamber to assess arguments on appeal, the appealing party must provide precise references to relevant transcript pages or paragraphs in the decision or judgement to which the challenge is made.[19] Further, the Appeals Chamber cannot be expected to consider a party's submissions in detail if they are obscure, contradictory, vague, or suffer from other formal and obvious insufficiencies. Finally, the Appeals Chamber has inherent discretion in selecting which submissions merit a detailed reasoned opinion in writing and will dismiss arguments which are evidently unfounded without providing detailed reasoning.[20] **[page 5]**

---

[12] The Appeals Chamber points out that some aspects of the Appellant's grounds of appeal are inextricably intertwined. Therefore, for ease of analysis, Ground of Appeal 1 and part of Ground of Appeal 2 will be addressed under Ground of Appeal 7.
[13] See *Muvunyi* Appeal Judgement, para. 8. See also *Martić* Appeal Judgement, para. 8.
[14] See *Muvunyi* Appeal Judgement, para. 9 citing *Ntakirutimana* Appeal Judgement, para. 11 (citations omitted).
[15] See *Martiü* Appeal Judgement, para. 10.
[16] *Muvunyi* Appeal Judgement, para. 10 citing *Krstić* Appeal Judgement, para. 40 (citations omitted).
[17] See *Muvunyi* Appeal Judgement, para. 11. See also *Martić* Appeal Judgement, para. 14.
[18] See *Muvunyi* Appeal Judgement, para. 11. See also *Oriü* Appeal Judgement, para. 13.
[19] Practice Direction on Formal Requirements for Appeals from Judgement, para. 4(b). See *Muvunyi* Appeal Judgement, para. 12.
[20] See *Muvunyi* Appeal Judgement, para. 12. See also *Martiü* Appeal Judgement, para. 14.

III. ALLEGED GENERAL ERRORS IN THE ASSESSMENT OF THE EVIDENCE (GROUND OF APPEAL 2, IN PART)

13. In his Second Ground of Appeal,[21] the Appellant submits that in its assessment of the evidence, the Trial Chamber committed "numerous errors of law" that invalidate the Trial Judgement and made erroneous factual findings occasioning a miscarriage of justice.[22] Specifically, he contends that the Trial Chamber erred by applying incorrect standards of law in its assessment of his testimony and in considering conflicting, hearsay, circumstantial, and uncorroborated evidence.[23] He further alleges several errors related to the Trial Chamber's conduct of a site visit.[24]

14. The Appeals Chamber will address the Appellant's arguments in turn.[25]

A. Alleged General Errors in the Assessment of the Appellant's Testimony

15. The Appellant contends (i) that special rules should apply to the assessment of an accused's testimony and that the Trial Judgement did not provide a reasoned opinion in this respect; and (ii) that the Trial Chamber erred in law by failing to conclude that the portions of his testimony on which the Prosecution did not cross-examine him were established.

1. Rules Applicable to the Assessment of an Accused's Testimony and Provision of a Reasoned Opinion

16. Relying on Canadian case law, the Appellant first avers that "special rules for the assessment of evidence that flow from the presumption of innocence apply when an accused chooses to testify in his own trial".[26] In such a situation, Judges should first evaluate the accused's credibility, then state whether they believe him, and, if applicable, explain why they are satisfied beyond reasonable doubt of his guilt despite contradictory evidence.[27] In the Appellant's view, such **[page 6]** a procedure prevents the Judges from unduly shifting the burden of proof to the accused and from erroneously examining whether the accused's testimony raises a reasonable doubt regarding the charges against him.[28] He emphasizes that such an approach is supported by the Appeals Chamber's holding in *Muhimana* to the effect that "[a]n accused does not need to prove at trial that a crime 'could not have occurred' or 'preclude the possibility that it could occur'".[29]

17. The Appellant next submits that in order for a convicted person to understand the reasons supporting his conviction, the Trial Judgement should set out clearly why the Trial Chamber accepted or rejected certain allegations and the accused's explanations about them.[30] He states that "the main criticism against the Trial Chamber is not only that it failed to provide adequate reasons for its findings, but also that it failed to explain

---

[21] Notice of Appeal, paras. 16-45; Appellant's Brief, paras. 6-46.
[22] Notice of Appeal, para. 17.
[23] The Appellant also gives notice that he intends to detail under each ground of appeal the factual and legal errors in the Trial Judgement (Appellant's Brief, para. 46). In the Appellant's Brief (paras. 7, 15, 30) and in the Brief in Reply (paras. 9, 11, 12, 14, 17, 87), the Appellant additionally alleges general errors in the assessment of his defence of alibi. The Appeals Chamber notes that in his Notice of Appeal, the Appellant does not allege such errors under the Second Ground of Appeal, but under the Eighth Ground of Appeal (Notice of Appeal, paras. 221-239). The Appeals Chamber will therefore consider all the Appellant's arguments related to the alibi below under Chapter IX.
[24] Appellant's Brief, paras. 41-46.
[25] The following two arguments will be addressed below in Chapter VIII: (i) The allegation that the Trial Chamber erred in law by failing to consider that its finding that the Appellant held pacification meetings was incompatible with the Prosecution's allegations relating to his participation in meetings encouraging crimes in Rushashi and those relating to murders or incitement to commit murder. Appellant's Brief, para. 27, referring to Trial Judgement, paras. 417, 316-456. Appellant's Brief, para. 29. *See also* Brief in Reply, paras. 77, 78; and (ii) the Appellant's contention that the Trial Chamber's reasons for rejecting his testimony, at paragraph 406 of the Trial Judgement, are inadequate and constitute an error of law. Appellant's Brief, para. 21.
[26] Appellant's Brief, para. 14; Notice of Appeal, para. 29.
[27] Notice of Appeal, para. 29; Appellant's Brief, paras. 14, 15, 18, 19; Brief in Reply, para. 84.
[28] Appellant's Brief, paras. 16-18; Brief in Reply, paras. 86, 87.
[29] Appellant's Brief, para. 17, citing *Muhimana* Appeal Judgement, para. 18.
[30] Appellant's Brief, paras. 7, 8.

why it did not believe Karera's evidence on practically all the facts alleged against him".[31] Relying again on Canadian case law, he contends that such a failure constitutes an error of law.[32]

18. The Prosecution responds that the Appellant's submissions are presented "in very general terms" and that they do not establish that the Trial Chamber disregarded its obligation to provide a reasoned opinion or committed an error capable of affecting the Trial Judgement.[33] It submits that a proper reading of the Trial Judgement shows that the Trial Chamber considered and evaluated the Appellant's testimony together with the evidence called by both the Prosecution and the Defence.[34] The Prosecution further contends that the Trial Chamber provided clear, reasoned findings of fact as to each element of each crime charged, as required by the Tribunal's jurisprudence.[35]

19. Regarding the Appellant's contention that special rules should apply when assessing an accused's testimony, the Appeals Chamber recalls that the Tribunal's Chambers are not bound by national rules of evidence or national case law.[36] While "[t]here is a fundamental difference between being an accused, who might testify as a witness if he so chooses, and a witness",[37] this does not imply that the rules applied to assess the testimony of an accused are different from those applied with respect to the testimony of an "ordinary witness". A trier of fact shall decide which witness's testimony to prefer, without necessarily articulating every step of its reasoning in reaching **[page 7]** this decision.[38] In so doing, as for any witness, a trier of fact is required to determine the overall credibility of an accused testifying at his own trial[39] and then assess the probative value of the accused's evidence in the context of the totality of the evidence.[40] There is no requirement in the Tribunal's jurisprudence that the accused's credibility be assessed first and in isolation from the rest of the evidence in the case.

20. Furthermore, it is settled jurisprudence that every accused has the right to a reasoned opinion under Article 22 of the Statute and Rule 88(C) of the Rules.[41] A reasoned opinion ensures that the accused can exercise his right of appeal and that the Appeals Chamber can carry out its statutory duty under Article 24 of the Statute.[42] However, the reasoned opinion requirement relates to the Trial Judgement as a whole rather than to each submission made at trial.[43] Indeed,

> the Trial Chamber is not under the obligation to justify its findings in relation to every submission made during the trial. The Appeals Chamber recalls that it is in the discretion of the Trial Chamber as to which legal arguments to address. With regard to the factual findings, the Trial Chamber is required only to make findings of those facts which are essential to the determination of guilt on a particular count. It is not necessary to refer to the testimony of every witness or every piece of evidence on the trial record. It is to be presumed that the Trial Chamber evaluated all the evidence presented to it, as long as there is no indication that the Trial Chamber completely disregarded any particular piece of evidence. There may be an indication of disregard when evidence which is clearly relevant to the findings is not addressed by the Trial Chamber's reasoning, but not every inconsistency which the Trial Chamber failed to discuss renders its opinion defective. […] If the Trial Chamber did not refer to the evidence given by a witness, even if it is in contradiction to the Trial Chamber's finding, it is to be presumed that the Trial Chamber assessed and weighed the evidence, but found that the evidence did not prevent it from arriving at its actual findings.[44]

---

[31] Appellant's Brief, para. 22.
[32] Appellant's Brief, paras. 22-24; Notice of Appeal, para. 31.
[33] Respondent's Brief, para. 58.
[34] Respondent's Brief, paras. 60-62, 69.
[35] Respondent's Brief, para. 59.
[36] Rule 89(A) of the Rules of Procedure and Evidence of the Tribunal ("Rules"); *The Prosecutor v. Édouard Karemera et al.*, Case No. ICTR-98-44-AR73.8, Decision on Interlocutory Appeal Regarding Witness Proofing, 11 May 2007, paras. 7, 11.
[37] *Galiü* Appeal Judgement, para. 17; *Kvopka* Appeal Judgement, para. 125; *Prliü et al.* Decision of 5 September 2008, para. 11.
[38] *Kupreškiü et al.* Appeal Judgement, para. 32.
[39] *Ntakirutimana* Appeal Judgement, para. 391, citing *Musema* Appeal Judgement, para. 50.
[40] See *Musema* Appeal Judgement, para. 50 (regarding the assessment of documentary evidence tendered by an accused in support of his alibi); *Muhimana* Appeal Judgement, para. 19.
[41] *Muvunyi* Appeal Judgement, para. 144, citing *Simba* Appeal Judgement, para. 152; *Kamuhanda* Appeal Judgement, para. 32; *Kajelijeli* Appeal Judgement, para. 59; *Semanza* Appeal Judgement, paras. 130, 149.
[42] See, e.g., *Limaj et al.* Appeal Judgement, para. 81.
[43] *Limaj et al.* Appeal Judgement, para. 81; *Kvo~ka et al.* Appeal Judgement, para. 23.
[44] *Kvo~ka et al.* Appeal Judgement, para. 23 (citations omitted); *Simba* Appeal Judgement, para. 152; *Ntagerura et al.* Appeal Judgement, para. 206; *Niyitegeka* Appeal Judgement, para. 124; *Kajelijeli* Appeal Judgement, para. 60; *Musema* Appeal Judgement, paras. 18-20; *Limaj et al.* Appeal Judgement, para. 81; *Naletilić and Martinović* Appeal Judgement, para. 603.

Additionally, a Trial Chamber does not need to set out in detail why it accepted or rejected a particular testimony.[45] This is equally applicable to all evidence, including that tendered by the accused person.

21. A review of the Trial Judgement reveals that the Trial Chamber did consider the Appellant's testimony and made assessments of the probative value of that evidence.[46] It was not obliged to **[page 8]** systematically justify why it rejected each part of that evidence. The Appellant's claim that the Trial Chamber erred by failing to explain why it did not believe him is therefore dismissed.

2. Alleged Error concerning Inferences that the Trial Chamber Should Have Drawn from the Prosecution's Absence of Cross-Examination of the Appellant

22. The Appellant submits that the Trial Chamber erred in law in failing to conclude that those portions of his testimony that the Prosecution did not cross-examine were established.[47] Referring to Rule 90(G)(ii) of the Rules, the *Rutaganda* Appeal Judgement,[48] and Canadian jurisprudence, he submits that the "failure to cross-examine a witness on an aspect of his testimony implies a tacit acceptance of the truth of the witness's evidence on the matter".[49] The Appellant also contends that the Trial Chamber's failure to provide a reasoned opinion on this question constitutes an error of law, since he cannot ascertain the Trial Chamber's reasons for disbelieving him.[50]

23. The Prosecution responds that it was open to the Trial Chamber not to draw a negative inference from the Prosecution's decision not to cross-examine the Appellant on certain details of his testimony where he repeated his denial of the allegations against him.[51] In this respect, the Prosecution recalls that the Trial Chamber already heard the parties' arguments on this issue and ruled that "the Prosecution is under no obligation to cross-examine the Accused on all aspects of its case".[52]

24. The Appeals Chamber finds that Rule 90(G)(ii) of the Rules does not support the Appellant's contention. The rule merely states that "[i]n the cross-examination of a witness who is able to give evidence relevant to the case for the cross-examining party, counsel shall put to that witness the nature of the case of the party for whom that counsel appears which is in contradiction of the evidence given by the witness." The ICTY Appeals Chamber has previously stated, regarding the similarly worded Rule 90(H)(ii) of the ICTY Rules, that it:

> seeks to facilitate the fair and efficient presentation of evidence whilst affording the witness being cross-examined the possibility of explaining himself on those aspects of his testimony contradicted by the opposing party's evidence, so saving the witness from having to reappear needlessly in **[page 9]** order to do so and enabling the Trial Chamber to evaluate the credibility of his testimony more accurately owing to the explanation of the witness or his counsel.[53]

25. The central purpose of this rule is to "promote the fairness of the proceedings by enabling the witness [...] to appreciate the context of the cross-examining party's questions, and to comment on the contradictory version of the events in question".[54]

---

[45] *Muhimana* Appeal Judgement, para. 99; *Simba* Appeal Judgement, para. 152; *Musema* Appeal Judgement, paras. 18-20.
[46] See, *inter alia,* Trial Judgement, paras. 30, 34, 48, 49, 64, 65, 72, 73, 104, 133, 275-278, 309, 342-345, 373, 390-394, 402, 406, 415, 430, 448, 463-466, 479-481, 515, 516.
[47] Notice of Appeal, para. 25. The authoritative French version of this paragraph reads: "*La Chambre de première instance a erré en droit en [ne] concluant pas que les portions du témoignage de l'appelant sur lesquelles il n'avait pas été contre-interrogé devraient être tenues pour avérées.*" The English translation inaccurately reads: "The Trial Chamber erred in law in finding that those portions of the Appellant's testimony on which he was not cross-examined were to be considered established", while it should read: "The Trial Chamber erred in law in **not** finding that those portions of the Appellant's testimony on which he was not cross-examined were to be considered established". Appellant's Brief, paras. 25, 26.
[48] *Rutaganda* Appeal Judgement, para. 310.
[49] Appellant's Brief, para. 26 (citation omitted); Notice of Appeal, para. 26.
[50] Appellant's Brief, para. 26.
[51] Respondent's Brief, para. 67.
[52] Respondent's Brief, para. 67, quoting Trial Judgement, para. 191, and fn. 250.
[53] *Prosecutor v. Radoslav Brÿanin and Momir Taliü*, Case No. IT-99-36-AR73.7, Decision on the Interlocutory Appeal against a Decision of the Trial Chamber, as of Right, 6 June 2002, p. 4.
[54] On this issue, the Appeals Chamber approves of the language used by the Trial Chamber in *Prosecutor v. Vujadin Popoviü et al.,* Case No. IT-05-88-T, Order Setting Forth Guidelines for the Procedure Under Rule 90(H)(ii), 6 March 2007 ("*Popoviü* Order"), para. 1.

26. For the requirements of this rule to be fulfilled, there is no need for the cross-examining party to explain every detail of the contradictory evidence. Furthermore, the rule allows for some flexibility depending on the circumstances at trial.[55] This therefore implies that if it is obvious in the circumstances of the case that the version of the witness is being challenged, there is no need for the cross-examining party to waste time putting its case to the witness.[56]

27. The Appeals Chamber notes that the term "witness" under Rule 90 of the Rules does not always equate to an accused who chooses to testify. There is a fundamental difference between the accused, who might testify as a witness if he so chooses, and a witness. The Tribunal "does not reflexively apply rules governing any other witness to an accused who decides to testify in his own case".[57] When an accused testifies in his own defence, he is well aware of the context of the Prosecution's questions and of the Prosecution's case, insofar as he has received sufficient notice of the charges and the material facts supporting them.[58] Furthermore, the accused's version of the events is for the most part challenged by the Prosecution, while his testimony is aimed at responding to Prosecution's evidence and allegations. In these circumstances, it would serve no useful purpose to put the nature of the Prosecution's case to the accused in cross-examination. The Appeals Chamber therefore does not find that Rule 90(G)(ii) of the Rules was intended to apply to an accused testifying as a witness in his own case. The Appeals Chamber notes that, in any event, **[page 10]** Rule 90(G)(ii) of the Rules is silent on any inferences that may be drawn by a Trial Chamber from a witness's testimony that is not subject to cross-examination.

28. The Appeals Chamber further notes that the relevant holding of the Appeals Chamber in *Rutaganda* reads:

> La Chambre d'appel estime que, d'une manière générale, une partie qui ne contre-interroge pas un témoin sur une déclaration donnée admet tacitement la véracité de la déposition dudit témoin sur ce point. La Chambre de première instance n'aurait donc pas commis une erreur de droit en l'espèce, en induisant du fait que l'Appelant n'avait pas contre-interrogé le témoin Q sur la distribution d'armes, que celui-ci ne contestait pas la véracité de la déposition dudit témoin sur ce point. Ceci étant dit, il ne ressort pas clairement du Jugement que la Chambre de première instance est effectivement parvenue à une telle conclusion. Il semble plutôt qu'elle se soit limitée à noter que l'Appelant n'avait pas contre-interrogé le témoin Q sur la question visée, sans toutefois en tirer quelques conséquences que ce soit dans ses conclusions factuelles. De l'avis de la Chambre d'appel, cet argument est dépourvu de fondement.59

---

[55] On this issue, the Appeals Chamber approves of the language used by the Trial Chamber in *Prosecutor v. Radoslav Brÿanin and Momir Taliü*, Case No. IT-99-36-T, Decision on "Motion to Declare Rule 90(H)(ii) Void to the Extent It Is in Violation of Article 21 of the Statute of the International Tribunal" by the Accused Radoslav Brÿanin and on "Rule 90(H)(ii) Submissions" by the Accused Momir Taliü, 22 March 2002 ("*Brÿanin* Decision"), paras. 13, 14; *Prosecutor v. Naser Oriü*, Case No. IT-03-68-T, Decision on Partly Confidential Defence Motion Regarding the Consequences of a Party Failing to Put its Case to Witnesses Pursuant to Rule 90(H)(ii), 17 January 2006, pp. 1-2; *Popoviü* Order, para. 2.

[56] The Appeals Chamber notes that the case of *Browne v. Dunn* (on which the *Brÿanin* Decision, confirmed by the Appeals Chamber, relies) states that the requirement to put the case to the witness does not apply when it is "otherwise perfectly clear that he has had full notice beforehand that there is an intention to impeach the credibility of the story which he is telling. Of course I do not deny for a moment that there are cases in which that notice has been so distinctly and unmistakably given, and the point upon which he is impeached, and is to be impeached, is so manifest, that it is not necessary to waste time in putting questions to him upon it". *Browne v. Dunn* (1893) 6 R. 67 (H.L.).

[57] *Prliü et al*, Decision of 5 September 2008, para. 11.

[58] The question of the lack of notice will be treated separately by the Appeals Chamber, see below Chapter VIII(D) and Chapter X.

[59] *Rutaganda* Appeal Judgement, para. 310 (footnote omitted). The Appeals Chamber notes that the English version does not accurately reflect the French authoritative version. The English version reads: "The Appeals Chamber considers that a party who fails to cross-examine a witness upon a particular statement tacitly accepts the truth of the witness's evidence on the matter. Therefore the Trial Chamber did not commit an error of law in the case at bar, in inferring that the Appellant's failure to cross-examine Witness Q on the weapons distribution meant that he did not challenge the truth of the witness's evidence on the matter. That being said, it is unclear from the Trial Judgement whether the Trial Chamber drew inferences from this failure. Rather, it appears that it only noted that the Appellant failed to cross-examine Witness Q regarding the specific statement, without making any inferences in its factual conclusions. It is the opinion of the Appeals Chamber that this argument is without foundation." In order to fully reflect the nuances introduced by the Appeals Chamber in its finding, the English translation of the first two sentences of this paragraph should read: "The Appeals Chamber considers that, **[in general]**, a party who fails to cross-examine a witness upon a particular statement tacitly accepts the truth of the witness's evidence on the matter. Therefore the Trial Chamber **[would have]** not commit**[ted]** an error of law in the case at bar, in inferring that the Appellant's failure to cross-examine Witness Q on the weapons distribution meant that he did not challenge the truth of the witness's evidence on the matter."

29. The Appeals Chamber recalls that in *Kamuhanda,* the Appeals Chamber stated that this holding in *Rutaganda* "does not stand for the proposition that a trier of fact *must* infer that statements not challenged during cross-examination are true," and that it is within the discretion of a Trial Chamber to decline to make such an inference.[60] Thus, the Appeals Chamber emphasizes that a Trial Chamber has the discretion to infer (or not) as true statements unchallenged during cross-examination, and to take into account the absence of cross-examination of a particular witness when assessing his credibility.[61]

30. The Appeals Chamber notes that in this instance, the Appellant, who testified at the end of the case, had consistently denied the allegations against him throughout the proceedings and claimed that he did not know anything about the crimes alleged.[62] The Prosecution cross-examined the Appellant on a number of issues.[63] Under this sub-ground of appeal, the Appellant has failed to point to any finding allegedly affected by the lack of cross-examination by the Prosecution but **[page 11]** merely makes a general reference to his oral arguments at trial.[64] In these circumstances, the Appellant has not demonstrated that the Trial Chamber committed an error of law in not considering as established those portions of his testimony on which the Prosecution did not cross-examine him.[65]

31. The Appeals Chamber further declines to consider the unsubstantiated assertion made by the Appellant with respect to the lack of a reasoned opinion on this point.

32. For the foregoing reasons, this sub-ground of appeal is dismissed.

B. Alleged Errors in the Assessment of Circumstantial Evidence

33. The Appellant submits that the Trial Chamber committed "many errors of law in its assessment of circumstantial evidence".[66] He argues that "[w]hen the [Prosecution] relies on circumstantial evidence to prove an allegation, the guilt of the accused must be the only possible inference to be drawn from that evidence."[67] He contends that the Trial Chamber "disregarded many cultural and social factors which could have shed a different light on the evidence, and based on which it could have made different findings."[68] He also contends that a "quick analysis of the evidence [...] in relation to all the Trial Chamber's findings shows that a reasonable trier of fact could never have drawn the factual conclusions that the Trial Chamber drew".[69]

34. It is well established that a conclusion of guilt can be inferred from circumstantial evidence only if it is the only reasonable conclusion available from the evidence.[70] Whether a Trial Chamber infers the existence of a particular fact upon which the guilt of the accused depends from direct or circumstantial evidence, it must reach such a conclusion beyond reasonable doubt. If there is another conclusion which is also reasonably open from that evidence, and which is consistent with the non-existence of that fact, the conclusion of guilt beyond reasonable doubt cannot be drawn.[71] **[page 12]**

---

[60] *Kamuhanda* Appeal Judgement, para. 204.
[61] *Kajelijeli* Appeal Judgement, para. 26; *Nahimana et al.* Appeal Judgement, paras. 820, 824 and fn. 1893.
[62] T. 21 August 2006; T. 22 August 2006; T. 23 August 2006.
[63] T. 22 August 2006 pp. 31-61; T. 23 August 2006 pp. 1-44.
[64] *See* Notice of Appeal, paras. 24-26; Appellant's Brief, paras. 25, 26.
[65] Any specific arguments raised by the Appellant in relation to this allegation will be dealt with below in the respective Chapters.
[66] Notice of Appeal, para. 33.
[67] Appellant's Brief, para. 32, referring to *Nahimana* Appeal Judgement, para. 524, *Ntagerura et al.* Appeal Judgement, paras. 306, 399, and *Mpambara* Trial Judgement, para. 163; Notice of Appeal, para. 34.
[68] Notice of Appeal, para. 35.
[69] Notice of Appeal, para. 36.
[70] *Ntagerura et al.* Appeal Judgement, para. 306. *See also Seromba* Appeal Judgement, para. 221; *Nahimana et al.* Appeal Judgement, paras. 524, 906; *Ýelebiüi* Appeal Judgement, para. 458; *Stakiü* Appeal Judgement, para. 219; *Vasiljeviü* Appeal Judgement, para. 120; *Krstiü* Appeal Judgement, para. 41; *Kvopka et al.* Appeal Judgement, para. 237.
[71] *Ntagerura et al.* Appeal Judgement, para. 306. *See also ýelebiüi* Appeal Judgement, para. 458; *Stakiü* Appeal Judgement, para. 219.

35. Under this sub-ground of appeal, however, the Appellant merely makes general allegations regarding the Trial Chamber's assessment of circumstantial evidence without substantiating them or providing any reference to the Trial Judgement. Therefore this sub-ground of appeal is dismissed.[72]

C. Alleged Errors in the Assessment of Hearsay Evidence

36. The Appellant submits that the Trial Chamber systematically erred in giving hearsay evidence weight or probative value contrary to the standard developed by the ICTY in the *Aleksovski* Decision, according to which "the weight or probative value to be afforded to that evidence will usually be less than that given to the testimony of a witness who has given it under a form of oath and who has been cross-examined, although even this will depend upon the infinitely variable circumstances which surround hearsay evidence".[73] He argues, in this respect, that the Trial Chamber erred in fact by giving weight to evidence that a reasonable trier of fact could simply not have considered,[74] and by disregarding "a good deal of evidence" favourable to him which it should have accepted.[75] He further argues that the Trial Chamber erred in law in failing to justify, in many instances, why it preferred hearsay evidence to the Appellant's uncontradicted testimony.[76]

37. The Prosecution disputes the Appellant's allegations that the Trial Chamber did not assess hearsay evidence properly, and notes that the Appellant did not point to any specific example or show how the Trial Chamber erred.[77] It contends that in such circumstances, it is sufficient to note that the Trial Chamber cautiously assessed hearsay evidence in accordance with the Tribunal's jurisprudence.[78]

38. The Appellant replies that with respect to the allegations concerning events in Nyamirambo, the Trial Chamber erred in preferring second or third-degree hearsay evidence to the Appellant's corroborated and un-contradicted testimony.[79] He also submits that neither the Trial Chamber nor the Prosecution provided justification for this preference.[80] [page 13]

39. It is well established that, as a matter of law, it is permissible to base a conviction on hearsay evidence.[81] A Trial Chamber has the discretion to cautiously consider hearsay evidence[82] and has the discretion to rely on it.[83] While the weight and probative value to be afforded to that evidence will usually be less than that accorded to the evidence of a witness who has given it under oath and who has been cross-examined, it will depend upon "the infinitely variable circumstances which surround hearsay evidence".[84] Thus, the fact that the evidence regarding a specific event is hearsay evidence does not in itself suffice to render it not credible or unreliable.[85] The source of information,[86] the precise character of the information,[87] and the fact that other evidence corroborates the hearsay evidence[88] are relevant criteria in assessing the weight or probative value

---

[72] The Appeals Chamber will address separately the Appellant's arguments related to the assessment of circumstantial evidence that have been raised with greater specificity under other grounds. *See* below Chapter IV.
[73] Notice of Appeal, paras. 38-40; Appellant's Brief, paras. 33, 34, citing *Aleksovski* Decision, para. 15 (citation omitted); Brief in Reply, paras. 33, 34, also citing *Aleksovski* Decision, para. 15 (citation omitted).
[74] Notice of Appeal, para. 40.
[75] Notice of Appeal, para. 39; Appellant's Brief, paras. 33, 34.
[76] Appellant's Brief, para. 35.
[77] Respondent's Brief, para. 63.
[78] Respondent's Brief, para. 63.
[79] Brief in Reply, para. 33.
[80] Brief in Reply, paras. 33, 35.
[81] *Muvunyi* Appeal Judgement, para. 70; *Muhimana* Appeal Judgement, para. 49; *Gacumbitsi* Appeal Judgement, para. 115.
[82] *Rutaganda* Appeal Judgement, para. 34; *Ndindabahizi* Appeal Judgement, para. 115; *Akayesu* Appeal Judgement, paras. 288, 289, 292.
[83] *Nahimana et al.* Appeal Judgement, para. 831; *Akayesu* Appeal Judgement, para. 292; *Naletilić and Martinović* Appeal Judgement, para. 217.
[84] *Aleksovski* Decision, para. 15.
[85] *See, e.g., Nahimana et al.* Appeal Judgement, paras. 215, 473.
[86] *Nahimana et al.* Appeal Judgement, para. 831; *Ndindabahizi* Appeal Judgement, para. 115 (about "unverifiable hearsay" evidence); *Semanza* Appeal Judgement, para. 159; *Rutaganda* Appeal Judgement, paras. 154, 156, 159.
[87] *Ndindabahizi* Appeal Judgement, para. 115.
[88] *Nahimana et al.* Appeal Judgement, para. 473 (for an illustration of hearsay testimonies corroborating each other); *Gacumbitsi* Appeal Judgement, para. 115.

of hearsay evidence. In any event, it is for the appealing party to demonstrate that no reasonable trier of fact could have relied upon hearsay evidence in reaching a specific finding.[89]

40. The Appeals Chamber rejects the unsubstantiated and vague contentions made under this sub-ground of appeal that the Trial Chamber systematically erred in its assessment of hearsay evidence, that it failed to provide a reasoned opinion in relation to its assessment of hearsay evidence, and that it also failed to explain why it relied upon that evidence and disregarded evidence favourable to the Appellant.

41. Furthermore, the Appeals Chamber finds no merit in the Appellant's contention that the Trial Chamber erred in preferring hearsay testimony to the Appellant's uncontradicted testimony. Contrary to the Appellant's assertion,[90] his testimony denying his participation in all of the crimes was challenged by Prosecution evidence and was thus contradicted.[91] As noted above, the fact that the evidence regarding a specific event is hearsay evidence does not in itself suffice to render it not credible or unreliable.[92] Such an assessment will depend upon the particular circumstances of each case. **[page 14]**

42. For the foregoing reasons, this sub-ground of appeal is dismissed.

D. Alleged Errors in the Assessment of Uncorroborated Evidence

43. The Appellant submits that the Trial Chamber erred in law by applying the Tribunal's jurisprudence on corroboration erratically and by failing to provide a reasoned opinion in relation to the corroboration of evidence.[93] He contends that "the allegations of many witnesses should have been discounted" on this ground.[94] The Appellant argues that the possibility of collusion between witnesses could constitute a situation where corroboration is required.[95] In this respect, he alleges that the Trial Chamber erred by not requiring corroboration of the allegations made by four Prosecution witnesses concerning the events in Ntarama despite its observation of the possibility of collusion among them.[96] He also submits that a lack of reasoned opinion in the Trial Judgement makes it impossible to know the basis to believe, or not, uncorroborated evidence, "the level of corroboration required […] and what is considered as corroborating evidence."[97]

44. The Prosecution responds that the Trial Chamber consistently indicated where the evidence was corroborated, and where corroboration was required in relation to the Appellant's presence at the crime scene and his participation in the crimes alleged.[98]

45. The Appeals Chamber recalls that a Trial Chamber has the discretion to decide, in the circumstances of each case, whether corroboration of evidence is necessary[99] and to rely on uncorroborated, but otherwise credible, witness testimony.[100] Therefore, a Trial Chamber may, depending on its assessment, rely on a single witness's testimony for the proof of a material fact.[101] It may thus convict an accused on the basis of evidence

---

[89] *Nahimana et al.* Appeal Judgement, para. 509 (concerning second-degree hearsay evidence); *Semanza* Appeal Judgement, para. 159; *Naletilić and Martinović* Appeal Judgement, paras. 217, 218.
[90] Appellant's Brief, para. 35; Brief in Reply, paras. 33, 35.
[91] *See, e.g.,* Trial Judgement, paras. 110-122, 401-417, 431-438, 499-510.
[92] *See supra* para. 39.
[93] Appellant's Brief, paras. 36, 39.
[94] Notice of Appeal, para. 42.
[95] Appellant's Brief, paras. 37, 38.
[96] Appellant's Brief, para. 40.
[97] Appellant's Brief, para. 39.
[98] Respondent's Brief, para. 65, referring to Trial Judgement, paras. 174, 215, 219, 366, 552-561. The Appeals Chamber observes that the reference to paragraphs 552-561 is obviously incorrect.
[99] *Muhimana* Appeal Judgement, para. 49; *Kajelijeli* Appeal Judgement, para. 170, citing *Niyitegeka* Appeal Judgement, para. 92; *Rutaganda* Appeal Judgement, para. 29.
[100] *Muvunyi* Appeal Judgement, para. 128; *Muhimana* Appeal Judgement, paras. 101, 120, 159, 207; *Nahimana et al.* Appeal Judgement, paras. 547, 633, 810.
[101] *Kajelijeli* Appeal Judgement, para. 170, citing *Niyitegeka* Appeal Judgement, para. 92; *Semanza* Appeal Judgement, para. 153. *See also Kordić and Ćerkez* Appeal Judgement, para. 274, citing *Kupreškić et al.* Appeal Judgement, para. 33.

from a single witness, although such evidence must be assessed with appropriate caution.[102] Any appeal based on the absence of **[page 15]** corroboration must therefore necessarily be against the weight attached by the Trial Chamber to the evidence in question.[103]

46. The Appeals Chamber dismisses the assertions made by the Appellant under this sub-ground of appeal as general and unsubstantiated. The Appellant's submission relating to possible collusion between the four Prosecution witnesses testifying about the events in Ntarama[104] will be addressed below.[105]

47. For the foregoing reasons, this sub-ground of appeal is dismissed.

E. Alleged Errors relating to the Observations Made during the Site Visit

48. The Appellant submits that the Trial Chamber erred in law by failing to provide the factual findings arising from the site visit, thus denying him the opportunity to present a full defence, as well as the right to an intelligible judgement.[106] The Appellant further submits that the Trial Chamber erred in fact by making factual findings which are contrary to the observations it made during its site visit in Rwanda from 1 to 3 November 2006.[107] He argues that observations made during the site visit brought to light certain details about the Ntarama area that are not revealed in the Trial Judgement.[108] He argues that, absent a *procès-verbal*, pictures or admissions, it is now impossible to use the observations made during the site visit to challenge the credibility of unreliable witnesses and to demonstrate the Trial Chamber's errors in this respect.[109] He also contends that this prevents the Appeals Chamber from assessing the accuracy of the evidence collected during the site visit.[110]

49. The Prosecution responds that the Appellant makes only vague assertions, without establishing how the Trial Chamber erred by disregarding or omitting to consider any specific fact or observation, such as to make appellate intervention necessary.[111] It avers that the Appellant failed to show any error of law or fact in the Trial Chamber's assessment of witnesses' testimonies and the parties' submissions on the observations made during the site visit.[112] The Prosecution further **[page 16]** asserts that the Appellant does not establish that the failure to produce a separate report amounts to an error that could have any impact on the verdict.[113]

50. Turning to the Appellant's contention that the Trial Chamber erred in law by failing to keep records from the site visit, the Appeals Chamber first notes that at no time during the trial proceedings did the Appellant object to the absence of such materials.[114] Moreover, the Appeals Chamber notes that the Trial Chamber considered the parties' submissions on the observations made during the site visit in reaching its

---

[102] *Kordiü and ýerkez* Appeal Judgement, para. 274. In *Kordiü and ýerkez*, the Appeals Chamber also held that "care must be taken to guard against the exercise of an underlying motive on the part of the witness." *Kordiü and ýerkez* Appeal Judgement, para. 274. *See also Ntagerura et al.* Appeal Judgement, para. 203. In *Ntagerura et al.*, the Appeals Chamber confirmed that "considering that accomplice witnesses may have motives or incentives to implicate the accused person before the Tribunal, a Chamber, when weighing the probative value of such evidence, is bound to *carefully* consider the totality of the circumstances in which it was tendered." *Ntagerura et al.* Appeal Judgement, para. 204 (citation omitted).
[103] *Kordiü and ýerkez* Appeal Judgement, para. 274.
[104] Trial Judgement, paras. 250, 308, 313.
[105] *See infra* paras. 231-235.
[106] Appellant's Brief, para. 44.
[107] Notice of Appeal, paras. 43, 44.
[108] Appellant's Brief, para. 43. *See also* Appellant's Brief, para. 207; AT. 28 August 2008 p. 54.
[109] Appellant's Brief, para. 45; AT. 28 August 2008 pp. 12, 13. The Appellant submits that he was not obliged to request that minutes be taken during the site visit and that it was the obligation of the Trial Chamber to ensure that a report of the site visit be produced. AT. 28 August 2008 p. 13.
[110] Appellant's Brief, para. 42; AT. 28 August 2008 p. 55.
[111] Respondent's Brief, para. 73.
[112] Respondent's Brief, para. 76.
[113] Respondent's Brief, para. 76; AT. 28 August 2008 pp. 41, 42.
[114] The Appeals Chamber observes that the Appellant consented without reservation to the site visit. *See The Prosecutor v. François Karera*, Case No. ICTR-2001-74-T, Defence Response to the Prosecutor's Motion for a View (Locus in Quo) (Rules 4, 54, and 89 of the Rules of Procedure and Evidence), 12 May 2006.

findings,[115] and explained how its observations affected the assessment of the evidence.[116] Therefore, the Appeals Chamber does not agree that, in relying on its observations, the Trial Chamber denied the Appellant the right to present a full defence and to be provided with a reasoned opinion. The Appeals Chamber emphasizes that detailed records of Trial Chamber's site visits should normally be kept. The purpose of a site visit is to assist a Trial Chamber in its determination of the issues and therefore it is incumbent upon the Trial Chamber to ensure that the parties are able to effectively review any findings made by the Trial Chamber in reliance on observations made during the site visit.[117] The Appeals Chamber however finds that in this case the Appellant has not demonstrated that he was prejudiced by his inability to challenge the Trial Chamber's observations and that the parties had the opportunity to make arguments based on their observations of the site visit in their closing arguments and closing briefs to which the Trial Chamber referred in its Judgement.[118]

F. Conclusion

51. Accordingly, the Second Ground of Appeal is dismissed in part. The remaining arguments presented in the Second Ground of Appeal will be considered below under Chapter VII. **[page 17]**

IV. ALLEGED ERRORS RELATING TO THE FINDING THAT THE APPELLANT ACTED AS PREFECT *DE FACTO* IN "KIGALI-RURAL" BEFORE 17 APRIL 1994 (GROUND OF APPEAL 3)

52. The Trial Chamber found that, before his formal appointment as prefect of Kigali prefecture on 17 April 1994, the Appellant exercised at least some of the authority which would normally have been exercised by the prefect.[119] It rejected the submission that he only exercised authority as subprefect responsible for economic and technical affairs.[120]

53. Under this ground of appeal, the Appellant submits that the Trial Chamber erred in finding: (i) that the prefecture where he exercised authority was named "Kigali-Rural"; (ii) that, under Rwandan law, the former prefect, Côme Bizimungu ("Bizimungu"), was empowered to appoint him prefect *ad interim*; and (iii) that he acted as prefect *de facto* of "Kigali-Rural" before his official appointment to this post on 17 April 1994.[121]

54. The Appeals Chamber will consider the Appellant's arguments in turn.

A. Alleged Error relating to the Official Designation of Kigali Prefecture in 1994

55. The Appellant submits that the Trial Chamber erred in designating "Kigali-Rural" the prefecture where he successively exercised functions as sub-prefect and prefect, while in 1994, its official name was Kigali prefecture.[122] He contends that this error shows the superficial nature of the Trial Chamber's assessment of the evidence.[123]

56. The Prosecution responds that this claim is groundless.[124]

---

[115] Trial Judgement, paras. 133, 159 (and fn. 217), 160 (and fn. 218), 161, 305. *See also* Prosecution Closing Brief, paras. 20, 24, 389, 418, 452, and fn. 414; Defence Closing Brief, paras. 93, 111, 184, 235, fns 255-256, 451; T. 23 November 2006 pp. 7, 35, 38, 40, 41, 53.
[116] Trial Judgement, paras. 133, 159, 160, 161, 305.
[117] Such records may take different forms and it will depend on the circumstances of the specific case to deternine which form will be most appropriate.
[118] *See* Trial Judgement, paras. 133, 159, 161.
[119] Trial Judgement, paras. 77, 247.
[120] Trial Judgement, para. 120.
[121] Notice of Appeal, paras. 46-74; Appellant's Brief, paras. 47, 48, 51, referring to Exhibit D49, Rwandan Official Gazette, 15 October 1993.
[122] Notice of Appeal, paras. 48, 49; Appellant's Brief, para. 48.
[123] Notice of Appeal, paras. 50, 51.
[124] Respondent's Brief, para. 79.

57. The Appeals Chamber agrees with the Appellant that the Trial Chamber erred in designating the prefecture "Kigali Rural" as it was officially named Kigali prefecture in 1994.[125] However, the Appellant has not shown that this error adversely impacted the Trial Chamber's findings.

58. Accordingly, this sub-ground of appeal is dismissed. **[page 18]**

B. Alleged Error in Finding that Former Prefect Côme Bizimungu was Empowered to Appoint the Appellant Prefect *Ad Interim*

59. The Appellant submits that the Trial Chamber erred in finding that he exercised *de jure* powers of the prefect subsequent to his "appointment" to this position by the former prefect Bizimungu on 24 August 1993.[126] He claims that the Trial Chamber erred in finding that Article 12 of Legislative Decree No. 10/75 of 11 March 1975 ("Legislative Decree No. 10/75") allowed Prefect Bizimungu to appoint a successor. He contends that, pursuant to Legislative Decree No. 10/75, only the President of the Republic could appoint a prefect.[127] He argues that, in any event, since Bizimungu's position as prefect had been terminated on 4 August 1993, Bizimungu could not exercise any power after that date and consequently could not have appointed him prefect *ad interim*.[128]

60. The Prosecution responds that the Appellant exercised functions *de jure* as prefect *ad interim*.[129] It recalls the Trial Chamber's finding to the effect that, pursuant to Article 12 of Legislative Decree No. 10/75, Bizimungu was entitled to delegate some of his powers as prefect after his appointment to a new position.[130] It further points to Defence Witness MZR's testimony that a prefect was entitled to assign a sub-prefect for the coordination of the prefecture's activities.[131]

61. In a letter dated 24 August 1993, Bizimungu informed the Appellant that he was "hereby designated prefect *ad interim* of Kigali prefecture to continue to act as [he] did during [Bizimungu's] leave which expires today".[132] The Appellant does not challenge the existence or authenticity of this letter. Rather, he denies having accepted this appointment and claims that Bizimungu was not legally empowered to appoint him.[133] No evidence has been presented to show that the Appellant formally accepted the appointment.

62. The Trial Chamber rejected the Appellant's submissions and evidence that no one was appointed to replace Bizimungu before 17 April 1994 and that only the President had the power to designate a prefect *ad interim* or an acting prefect.[134] In so doing, it reasoned that "the Rwandan legislation did not prevent Bizimungu from delegating certain official powers to [the Appellant] in **[page 19]** August 1993" and that Articles 17 and 19 of Legislative Decree No. 10/75 did not reserve the competence to designate "a sub-prefect as an 'interim' or 'acting' prefect" exclusively to the President.[135] The Trial Chamber therefore implicitly found that Bizimungu was legally entitled to delegate his powers or to appoint a prefect *ad interim* even after the termination of his appointment as prefect on 4 August 1993.

63. The Appeals Chamber considers that nothing in Legislative Decree No. 10/75 suggests that Bizimungu was entitled to delegate prefectoral powers or to appoint a successor, even temporarily, after the termination

---

[125] Exhibit P14.
[126] Appellant's Brief, paras. 49-52.
[127] Notice of Appeal, paras. 53-56; Appellant's Brief, paras. 49-51; AT. 28 August 2008 p. 5.
[128] Notice of Appeal, paras. 57, 58; Appellant's Brief, paras. 53, 62, 63; AT. 28 August 2008 p. 5.
[129] Respondent's Brief, para. 80.
[130] Respondent's Brief, para. 80.
[131] Respondent's Brief, para. 80.
[132] Exhibit P15, p. 10.
[133] Appellant's Brief, paras. 51, 63; AT. 28 August 2008 pp. 5-7.
[134] Trial Judgement, paras. 75, 76.
[135] Trial Judgement, paras. 75, 76. The Trial Chamber's finding at paragraph 75 of the Trial Judgement refers to "August 1993". It is clear however that the question at stake was whether Bizimungu could delegate his powers or appoint the Appellant as prefect *ad interim* after 4 August 1993.

of his appointment.[136] However, the Trial Chamber's interpretation of Legislative Decree No. 10/75 could not have adversely impacted its assessment of the Appellant's power, since it did not find that the Appellant, before his official appointment as prefect on 17 April 1994, exercised functions of a prefect *de jure*. Instead the Trial Chamber merely concluded that he "exercised at least some of the authority which would normally have fallen under the [prefect]", which is a finding of a *de facto* exercise of power.[137]

64. In light of the foregoing, this sub-ground of appeal is dismissed.

C. Alleged Errors in Finding that the Appellant Acted as De Facto Prefect before 17 April 1994

65. Under this sub-ground, the Appellant argues that in finding that he had acted as *de facto* prefect before 17 April 1994, the Trial Chamber erred: (i) in relying on letters signed by the Appellant "for the prefect"; (ii) in relying on circumstantial evidence; and (iii) in the assessment of the evidence and by failing to provide a reasoned opinion.[138] The Appellant also asserts that no evidence was adduced to prove that he had exercised powers of the prefect after 14 January 1994 and before his appointment as prefect on 17 April 1994.[139] The Appeals Chamber addresses these arguments in turn. **[page 20]**

1. Alleged Error relating to the Letters Signed by the Appellant "for the Prefect"

66. The Appellant submits that the Trial Chamber erred in relying on letters signed by the Appellant "for the prefect between late August 1993 and 14 January 1994" to find that he had exercised *de facto* powers of the prefect.[140] He argues that "these letters are only a minute portion of the official correspondence from Kigali prefecture" in that period and submits that other subprefects at the Kigali prefecture also signed correspondence or presided over meetings after the termination of Bizimungu's appointment on 4 August 1993.[141] He asserts that the letters of 22 September, 21 October, and 25 October 1993, which the Trial Chamber considered crucial as they related to security matters in the prefecture, do not support the Trial Chamber's factual conclusions that the Appellant exercised *de facto* powers of the prefect of Kigali prefecture. According to the Appellant, the letters of 22 September and 25 October 1993 are merely invitations to a meeting of the Security Council of the Kigali prefecture, while the security measures described in the letter of 21 October 1993 were taken for the end of the year and New Year festivities and did not continue until April 1994.[142] The Appellant also claims that the Trial Chamber erred in finding that these three letters "[coincided] with evidence relating to the killings which took place in Nyamirambo, Rushashi and Ntarama, in which [the Appellant] was allegedly involved".[143]

67. The Prosecution responds that it was reasonable for the Trial Chamber to conclude on the basis of all the evidence, and in particular, these three letters, that the Appellant had acted as prefect before his official appointment to that post.[144]

68. The Appeals Chamber finds that the Appellant's argument is insufficient to demonstrate that no reasonable trier of fact could have found, as the Trial Chamber did, on the basis of the letters of 22 September, 21 October, and 25 October 1993, that the Appellant had exercised, prior to April 1994, powers beyond the

---

[136] Article 17 of Legislative Decree No. 10/75 suggests that no legal delegation of powers could occur unless the prefect was on duty and Legislative Decree No. 10/75 is silent as to the *interim* exercise of powers in case of vacancy of a prefectoral position. It states *inter alia* that "the sub-prefects are hierarchically subordinate to the prefect" and that a sub-prefect in charge of a subprefecture "represents the prefect in all its function" but "under the responsibility and authority of the prefect". (Exhibit P14, Exhibit D68). *See also* Exhibit D49, Rwandan Official Gazette, 15 October 1993; Trial Judgement, para. 75.
[137] Trial Judgement, para. 77.
[138] Notice of Appeal, paras. 59-70; Appellant's Brief, paras. 54-69.
[139] Appellant's Brief, paras. 58-61.
[140] Notice of Appeal, paras. 59, 70; AT. 28 August 2008 p. 9.
[141] Notice of Appeal, para. 60; Appellant's Brief, paras. 56-60, 64; AT. 28 August 2008 p. 8. The Appellant states that there were four sub-prefects of the prefecture responsible for a given department in the Kigali prefecture and the three sub-prefects of the prefecture, whose responsibilities covered a distinct territory of the prefecture. Notice of Appeal, para. 60; Appellant's Brief, para. 56.
[142] Appellant's Brief, para. 58; AT. 28 August 2008 p. 8.
[143] Appellant's Brief, paras. 59, 60.
[144] Respondent's Brief, para. 83.

capacity of a sub-prefect for economic and technical affairs. Contrary to the Appellant's claim, it was open to the Trial Chamber to make this finding by reference to the evidence contained in the three letters. By signing "for the prefect" letters relating to matters falling **[page 21]** outside his normal duties as sub-prefect in charge of economic and technical affairs,[145] at a time when no prefect was on duty, the Appellant effectively exercised some of the powers of the prefect.

69. The possibility, suggested by the Appellant, that other sub-prefects may have also signed other letters "for the [prefect]" is merely speculative. In any case, the Trial Chamber took that possibility into account in concluding that "[e]ven assuming, as stated by [the Appellant] that other sub-prefects may have signed letters on behalf of the prefect, the correspondence shows that [the Appellant] exercised at least some of the authority which would normally have fallen under the [prefect]".[146]

2. Alleged Error in Relying on Circumstantial Evidence

70. The Appellant submits that the Trial Chamber erred in law by reaching its conclusion that he had acted *de facto* as prefect on the basis of circumstantial evidence, "whereas this evidence could also be interpreted otherwise"[147] and by failing to consider "uncontradicted [Defence] witnesses" explaining "in a coherent manner the situation that existed before the appointment of [the Appellant as prefect on 17 April 1994]".[148]

71. The Appeals Chamber does not agree. As recalled above, in finding that the Appellant had exercised "at least some of the authority" of a prefect, the Trial Chamber relied on letters he had signed in that capacity. These letters were direct rather than circumstantial evidence of his *de facto* authority as prefect prior to his formal appointment to that position.

3. Alleged Errors in Assessing the Evidence and in Failing to Provide a Reasoned Opinion

72. The Appellant claims that the Trial Chamber's finding that he exercised prefectoral powers was based on a "completely erroneous" assessment of the evidence and amounts to a miscarriage of justice.[149] He argues that the Trial Chamber failed to provide a reasoned opinion for rejecting the evidence of Defence witnesses who coherently explained the situation that existed before the Appellant's appointment as prefect and demonstrated that there was a reasonable possibility that the allegation that he had acted *de facto* as prefect prior to his appointment was false.[150] Further, the Appellant submits that the Trial Chamber failed to take into account that the Rwandan Patriotic Front (RPF) and the Rwandan Armed Forces (FAR) were fighting in certain areas of Kigali **[page 22]** prefecture and that, on 17 April 1994, the date of his appointment as prefect, only three out of the sixteen communes of Kigali prefecture were under government control.[151]

73. The Prosecution responds that the Appellant's reiteration of Defence evidence falls short of demonstrating that the Trial Chamber erred in the assessment of the evidence.[152] It asserts that the Trial Chamber took into account the Appellant's testimony and that of Defence Witness MZR and validly rejected their assertion that no one had exercised the duties of the prefect of Kigali prefecture for about eight months, from August 1993 to 17 April 1994.[153] The Prosecution recalls that the Trial Chamber found credible the evidence of Witnesses BMJ and BMK to the effect that, at a meeting in Ntarama on 14 April 1994, the Appellant had presented himself as prefect.[154]

---

[145] Exhibit P15, pp. 11-23. These three letters were filed only in Kinyarwanda. Upon request by the Appeals Chamber, the Registry has provided their translation into French and English.
[146] Trial Judgement, para. 77.
[147] Appellant's Brief, para. 68.
[148] Appellant's Brief, para. 69; AT. 28 August 2008 p. 9.
[149] Appellant's Brief, para. 66.
[150] Appellant's Brief, paras. 68, 69; AT. 28 August 2008 p. 9.
[151] Appellant's Brief, para. 60. The Appellant affirms that this fact – arising from his testimony – was not contested by the Prosecution and mentions the communes of Musasa, Rushashi, and Tare, all located in the Rushashi sub-prefecture.
[152] Respondent's Brief, para. 84.
[153] Respondent's Brief, para. 82.
[154] Respondent's Brief, para. 82.

74. Contrary to the Appellant's assertion, the Trial Chamber took into account the evidence presented by the Defence, addressed its submissions, and provided a reasoned opinion.[155] The Trial Chamber was not compelled to accept the Appellant's general denial that he assumed a law-enforcement role over and above his responsibilities as sub-prefect, especially in view of the fact that he acknowledged that he had signed letters in the capacity of prefect relating to security matters.[156] The Trial Chamber noted and addressed the Appellant's assertion that other sub-prefects may have signed similar letters on behalf of the prefect.[157] With regard to Witness MZR, although he testified that between 4 August 1993 and 17 April 1994[158] there was no prefect or acting prefect in Kigali prefecture, and that he never witnessed the Appellant introducing himself in such a capacity during that period, he nonetheless conceded that during the absence of the prefect, a subprefect could have signed invitations to meetings and could have chaired a meeting.[159]

75. The Appeals Chamber finds that the Appellant has failed to explain how the assertion concerning fighting in certain areas of Kigali prefecture, as well as the assertion that on 17 April 1994, only three out of the sixteen communes of the Kigali prefecture were under government control contradicts the Trial Chamber's finding regarding his exercise of "some authority" of the prefect in Kigali prefecture prior to that date. Therefore, the Appellant has not demonstrated that no reasonable trier of fact could have concluded that he exercised some authority of a prefect prior to his appointment to that post on 17 April 1994. **[page 23]**

76. Finally, the Appellant submits that the Trial Chamber erred in law by failing to apply the standard "beyond reasonable doubt" when assessing the evidence.[160] He argues that the Trial Chamber should have found that in view of Defence evidence, there was a reasonable possibility that the Prosecution's allegations were false.[161] The Appeals Chamber considers that this argument is not sufficiently substantiated to demonstrate any error on the part of the Trial Chamber.

4. Allegation that No Evidence was Adduced that the Appellant had Exercised Powers of the Prefect after 14 January 1994

77. The Appellant contends that no evidence was adduced that he had exercised powers of the prefect after 14 January 1994.[162]

78. This assertion falls short of demonstrating any error on the part of the Trial Chamber. The Trial Chamber did not find that the Appellant continuously exercised the authority of the prefect from August 1993 to April 1994, but rather made a finding that he had exercised some of the authority of a prefect.[163] Contrary to the Appellant's contention, the Trial Chamber accepted evidence that the Appellant acted on some occasions as prefect between 14 January and 17 April 1994. Specifically, based on the testimonies of Witnesses BMJ and BMK, the Trial Chamber found that the Appellant had called himself prefect before the latter date[164] and that, at a meeting at Ntarama sector office on 14 April 1994, he had promised Tutsi refugees that he would provide them with security, thus acting within the ambit of the prefect.[165]

79. In light of the foregoing, this sub-ground of appeal is dismissed.

D. Conclusion

80. For the foregoing reasons, the Appellant's Third Ground of Appeal is dismissed in its entirety. **[page 24]**

---

[155] Trial Judgement, paras. 60-77.
[156] Trial Judgement, paras. 72, 73.
[157] Trial Judgement, paras. 72, 73, 77.
[158] T. 16 May 2006 p. 34. The witness mentioned 17 April 1993. However, it is obvious from the context that he meant 17 April 1994.
[159] T. 15 May 2006 p. 29; T. 16 May 2006 pp. 33, 34.
[160] Appellant's Brief, para. 69.
[161] Appellant's Brief, para. 69.
[162] Notice of Appeal, paras. 61-65; Appellant's Brief, para. 58; AT. 28 August 2008 p. 9.
[163] Trial Judgement, para. 77.
[164] Trial Judgement, paras. 234, 238, 247.
[165] Trial Judgement, para. 254.

V. ALLEGED ERRORS RELATING TO THE APPELLANT'S INVOLVEMENT IN THE MRND AND HIS AUTHORITY OVER THE *INTERAHAMWE* (GROUND OF APPEAL 4)

81. The Trial Chamber found that the Appellant exercised authority over the *Interahamwe* in 1994.[166] The Trial Chamber convicted the Appellant, pursuant to Article 6(1) of the Statute, for ordering, instigating, and aiding and abetting genocide, and murder and extermination as crimes against humanity, based in part on the involvement of the *Interahamwe* in the killings of Tutsis in Nyamirambo, Ntarama, and Rushashi.[167]

82. The Trial Chamber found that the Appellant's position as President of the MRND in Nyarugenge commune after April 1992 had not been established beyond reasonable doubt,[168] but that this in itself did not exclude the fact that he exercised authority over the *Interahamwe* in 1994.[169] The Trial Chamber based this finding on his previous presidency and continuing membership in the MRND, combined with his importance as the former *bourgmestre* of Nyarugenge commune and subsequent functions as sub-prefect and prefect of Kigali prefecture.[170]

The Trial Chamber found that the evidence specific to this question, in particular the testimonies of Witnesses BMA and BLX, in conjunction with the evidence relating to the events in Nyamirambo, Ntarama, and Rushashi, was sufficient to find that the Appellant exercised authority over the *Interahamwe* in 1994.[171]

83. The Appellant submits that the Trial Chamber erred in its assessment of the evidence of Witnesses BMA and BLX relating to his alleged involvement in the MRND in Nyarugenge after 1992 and in concluding that he exercised authority over the *Interahamwe* in 1994.[172]

84. The Appellant contends that the Trial Chamber erred in law by accepting parts of Witness BLX's testimony despite certain factors that cast doubt on his evidence.[173] He recalls that the Trial Chamber itself decided to consider Witness BLX's evidence with caution because of the witness's involvement in proceedings before Rwandan courts.[174] Further, the Appellant contends that Witness **[page 25]** BLX contradicted himself when he asserted before the Trial Chamber that the Appellant held the position of President of the MRND in April 1994, while he had testified in the *Karemera et al.* case that it was Hamadi Nshimiyimana who held this position at that time.[175] He claims that the Trial Chamber's conclusion that there was no contradiction in the witness's testimony on this point was "completely erroneous."[176] In his view, Witness BLX's testimony in the *Karemera et al.* case corroborated the Appellant's testimony that following his resignation, in April or May 1992, Hamadi Nshimiyimana replaced him as MRND President in Nyarugenge commune.[177]

85. The Prosecution responds that the Trial Chamber correctly found that the Appellant's authority over the *Interahamwe* in 1994 was based on his previous presidency and continuing membership in the MRND, his importance as a former *bourgmestre*, as well as his subsequent functions as sub-prefect and prefect.[178] It submits that this ground of appeal is unfounded and should be dismissed in its entirety.[179]

86. The Appeals Chamber finds no merit in the Appellant's submissions challenging the Trial Chamber's assessment of Witness BLX. The Trial Chamber addressed in detail the alleged discrepancy between

---

[166] Trial Judgement, para. 56. The Trial Chamber found that it had not been established that his authority over the *Interahamwe* in Nyamirambo, Rushashi or Ntarama extended beyond his personal influence. Trial Judgement, para. 567.
[167] Trial Judgement, paras. 535-548, 552-561.
[168] Trial Judgement, para. 55.
[169] Trial Judgement, para. 56.
[170] Trial Judgement, para. 56.
[171] Trial Judgement, para. 56.
[172] Notice of Appeal, paras. 75, 76; Appellant's Brief, paras. 70-82.
[173] Appellant's Brief, para. 77.
[174] Notice of Appeal, para. 76; Appellant's Brief, paras. 72, 74, referring to Trial Judgement, para. 52.
[175] Appellant's Brief, para. 75, referring to Trial Judgement, para. 54.
[176] Appellant's Brief, para. 75.
[177] Appellant's Brief, para. 76. *See also* Appellant's Brief, para. 71.
[178] Respondent's Brief, paras. 86-88.
[179] Respondent's Brief, para. 89.

Witness BLX's testimony in the present case and his previous testimony in the *Karemera et al.* case before the Tribunal.[180] It noted that during his testimony in the *Karemera et al.* case, the witness mentioned Hamadi Nshimiyimana twice, first stating that Hamadi Nshimiyimana held the position of Vice-President of the MRND in Nyarugenge and subsequently stating that he was President of the MRND in that commune in 1994.[181] The Trial Chamber found that there was "no clear discrepancy" between his testimonies in the two cases because the witness had stated in both cases that Hamadi Nshimiyimana held the position of Vice-President of the MRND in April 1994.[182] On appeal, the Appellant merely repeats the argument he raised at trial. The Appeals Chamber is not a second trier of fact, and a party cannot simply repeat arguments on appeal that did not succeed at trial in the hope that the Appeals Chamber will consider them afresh.[183] The Appellant does not demonstrate that the Trial Chamber's finding was erroneous. Accordingly, the Appellant's appeal on this point is dismissed. **[page 26]**

87. The Appellant also challenges the testimony of Witness BMA, asserting that the witness "lied outright" and that the Trial Chamber erred by failing to reject his testimony in its entirety.[184] The Appellant notes the following discrepancies: while Witness BMA told the Rwandan authorities that he had not seen the Appellant during the war, he testified before the Trial Chamber that he had seen the Appellant after 6 April 1994 on at least three occasions in the office of the Kigali prefecture.[185] During cross-examination, the witness claimed that he might have been talking about "a different Karera", while he had stated at the beginning of his testimony that he only knew one person bearing this name.[186] Furthermore, in his testimony before the Trial Chamber, the witness testified to the Appellant's position within the MRND and his resulting authority over the *Interahamwe*, whereas in pre-trial statements to the Tribunal's investigators, the witness had never implicated the Appellant as a high-ranking member of the MRND.[187]

88. The Appeals Chamber finds no merit in the Appellant's submissions challenging the Trial Chamber's assessment of Witness BMA. The Appellant solely contests that part of the witness's testimony which the Trial Chamber found inconsistent and which it therefore rejected.[188] The Appeals Chamber recalls that a Trial Chamber may accept some parts of a witness's testimony while rejecting others.[189] In the instant case, the Trial Chamber found credible and relied on the witness's testimony concerning the Appellant's support to the *Interahamwe* in 1991 and 1992.[190] The Appellant has not demonstrated an error on the part of the Trial Chamber in this regard. Accordingly, the Appellant's argument on this point is dismissed.

89. Finally, the Appellant submits that the Trial Chamber's holding that it had not been established beyond reasonable doubt that he continued to be President of the MRND in Nyarugenge after April 1992 meant that Witnesses BMA and BLX who had testified to this effect[191] had lied.[192] The Appellant thus concludes that the Trial Chamber erred in law by accepting, without explanation, other parts of the witnesses' testimonies to find that the Appellant supported the *Interahamwe* in 1991 and 1992 and exercised authority over them in 1994.[193]

90. The Appeals Chamber rejects the Appellant's contention on this point. As noted above, a Trial Chamber may accept some parts of a witness's testimony while rejecting others. The Appeals **[page 27]** Chamber further recalls that a Trial Chamber has the obligation to provide a reasoned opinion, but is not

---

[180] Trial Judgement, para. 54.
[181] Trial Judgement, para. 54, fn. 81 referring to *Karemera et al.*, T. 10 March 2006 p. 18. The Trial Chamber observed that Hamadi Nshimiyimana's position was not at issue in that case.
[182] Trial Judgement, para. 54.
[183] *Semanza* Appeal Judgement, para. 9.
[184] Appellant's Brief, para. 79, referring to Trial Judgement, para. 53.
[185] Appellant's Brief, para. 80, referring to Exhibit D7A, p. 29, and D7B, p. 20; T. 19 January 2006 pp. 28-30.
[186] Appellant's Brief, para. 81, referring to T. 19 January 2006 pp. 41-46.
[187] Appellant's Brief, para. 81, referring to Exhibit D10A.
[188] Trial Judgement, para. 53.
[189] *See Seromba* Appeal Judgement, para. 110, citing *Simba* Appeal Judgement, para. 212; *Kamuhanda* Appeal Judgement, para. 248, citing *Kupreškiŭ et al.* Appeal Judgement, para. 333.
[190] Trial Judgement, para. 56.
[191] Trial Judgement, paras. 38, 42.
[192] Appellant's Brief, para. 82.
[193] Appellant's Brief, para. 82.

required to articulate every step of its reasoning in detail.[194] In the present case, the Trial Chamber explicitly stated that it found the witnesses' testimonies concerning the Appellant's support to the *Interahamwe* in 1991 and 1992 credible.[195] The Appellant has not demonstrated an error in this finding. The Appellant's argument that the witnesses lied is speculative and does not require further consideration.

91. The Appeals Chamber observes that, in any event, the Trial Chamber made no finding on the Appellant's authority based on the evidence of Witnesses BMA and BLX alone. The Trial Chamber's reliance on Witnesses BMA and BLX is limited to a general illustration of the Appellant's authority over the *Interahamwe* without any link to particular events. The Trial Chamber merely noted that the evidence of Witnesses BMA and BLX regarding the Appellant's support to the *Interahamwe* in 1991 and 1992 was credible and supported the fact that the Appellant exercised authority over the *Interahamwe*.[196] In addition, it held that the evidence adduced in relation to the specific events in Nyamirambo, Ntarama, and Rushashi also showed that the Appellant exercised authority over the *Interahamwe*.[197]

92. For the foregoing reasons, the Appeals Chamber rejects the Appellant's submissions that the Trial Chamber erred in the assessment of the evidence of Witnesses BMA and BLX relating to his involvement in the MRND in Nyarugenge after 1992 and in finding that he exercised authority over the *Interahamwe* in 1994. Accordingly, this ground of appeal is dismissed. **[page 28]**

VI. ALLEGED ERRORS RELATING TO THE FINDING THAT THE APPELLANT WAS INVOLVED IN A CAMPAIGN TO KILL TUTSIS IN NYAMIRAMBO SECTOR, NYARUGENGE COMMUNE (GROUND OF APPEAL 5)

93. The Trial Chamber found that in April 1994 three policemen, Kalimba, Habimana, and Kabarate, who "were stationed in [the Appellant's] house in Nyamirambo [...] committed crimes together with the *Interahamwe* operating in that area".[198] Specifically, the Trial Chamber found that:

– Between 8 and 10 April [1994], the *Interahamwe* followed after Kabahaye, a Tutsi, and killed him in Butamwa, not far away from Nyamirambo. They then reported to the policemen that he had been killed [...];

– Between 8 and 10 April 1994, policeman Kalimba forced a man to kill Murekezi, a Tutsi, at the roadblock near Karera's house [...];

– On 10 April 1994, Ndingutse, a Tutsi, was arrested and killed by the policemen and *Interahamwe* not far away from Karera's house [...];

– On 24 April 1994, Palatin Nyagatare, a Tutsi, was killed at a roadblock about three plots from his house by policeman Kalimba [...].[199]

94. The Trial Chamber further found that the perpetrators were aware that the victims were Tutsis and that they killed them pursuant to the Appellant's order to kill Tutsis.[200] Based on these findings, the Trial Chamber convicted the Appellant, pursuant to Article 6(1) of the Statute, for ordering genocide and extermination and murder as crimes against humanity.[201]

95. The Appellant submits that the Trial Chamber erred in its factual findings in relation to his involvement in a campaign to kill Tutsis in Nyamirambo sector, Nyarugenge commune.[202] He argues that the Trial Chamber erred in finding that: (i) he exercised authority over the three policemen involved in the killings; (ii) he ordered, by telephone, the killing of Kabuguza's family members between 7 and 10 April 1994; (iii) he gave orders to kill Tutsis and to demolish their houses in Nyamirambo between 7 and 15 April 1994; (iv) he gave orders to spare certain Tutsis and their houses between 7 and 15 April 1994; (v) a man called Kahabaye was killed in April 1994 as a consequence of the orders given by him; (vi) he ordered policeman

---

[194] See *Simba* Appeal Judgement, para. 152.
[195] Trial Judgement, para. 56.
[196] Trial Judgement, para. 56.
[197] Trial Judgement, para. 56, referring to Trial Judgement, Sections II.4-6.
[198] Trial Judgement, para. 535.
[199] Trial Judgement, para. 535.
[200] Trial Judgement, para. 536.
[201] Trial Judgement, paras. 540, 557, 560, 561.
[202] Notice of Appeal, paras. 77-140; Appellant's Brief, paras. 83-184; AT. 28 August 2008 pp. 24, 25.

Judgement

Kalimba to kill a Tutsi called **[page 29]** Murekezi between 8 and 10 April 1994; (vii) he was involved in the killing of Jean Bosco Ndingutse on 10 April 1994; and (viii) a man called Palatin Nyagatare was killed following his orders to kill Tutsis at Nyamirambo.[203] The Appeals Chamber will consider these arguments in turn.

A. Alleged Errors relating to the Appellant's Authority over Commune Policemen

96. The Trial Chamber found that the Appellant had authority over the three policemen who guarded his house in Nyamirambo and manned a roadblock near his house.[204] The Trial Chamber further found that the three policemen committed crimes in the area of Nyamirambo.[205]

97. In this section, the Appeals Chamber considers the following allegations of errors related to the finding that the Appellant had authority over the policemen: (i) alleged failure to provide a reasoned opinion; (ii) alleged error in assessing Prosecution evidence; and (iii) alleged failure to give proper weight to Defence evidence.

1. Alleged Error in Failing to Provide a Reasoned Opinion

98. The Appellant submits that the Trial Chamber erred in law in failing to identify the evidence showing the Appellant's alleged *de jure* or *de facto* authority over the communal policemen Kalimba, Habimana, and Kabarate allegedly posted at his house in Nyamirambo and in omitting to explain how he could have exercised any authority over policemen who were outside the administrative territory in which he worked.[206]

99. The Prosecution primarily responds that the Trial Chamber duly considered the evidence of several witnesses to establish that the three policemen took orders from the Appellant and committed criminal acts.[207]

100. A review of the Trial Judgement reveals that, contrary to the Appellant's contention, the Trial Chamber provided a reasoned opinion for the impugned findings and identified the underlying evidence.[208] The Trial Chamber relied on the evidence of Witnesses BMF, BMH, BLX, BMU, BMA, BMG, and BME to find that the policemen Kalimba, Habimana, and Kabarate were "communal policemen" under the Appellant's authority, rather than under the authority of the prefect of Kigali-Ville prefecture.[209] The Trial Chamber's conclusion that the Appellant exercised authority over these policemen is not based on the premise that he had *de jure* authority over them, **[page 30]** even though the Trial Chamber recalled that in a state of emergency a prefect can requisition communal police.[210] Instead, the Trial Chamber's conclusion is supported by the evidence of several Prosecution witnesses who testified that the policemen were guarding the Appellant's house and manning a roadblock in front of it, that these policemen claimed to be the Appellant's subordinates, that the Appellant ordered them to kill Tutsis and destroy their houses, and that people said that they obeyed the Appellant's orders.[211]

101. This argument is therefore dismissed.

2. Alleged Error in Relying on Prosecution Evidence

102. The Appellant submits that the Trial Chamber erred in finding that throughout the month of April 1994 he exercised authority over certain commune policemen since the evidence does not permit this inference.[212] He contends that this error of fact occasioned a miscarriage of justice.[213]

---

[203] Appellant's Brief, paras. 183, 184.
[204] Trial Judgement, paras. 122, 537.
[205] Trial Judgement, paras. 168, 192, 196, 203, 535.
[206] Notice of Appeal, paras. 82-84; AT. 28 August 2008 p. 14.
[207] Respondent's Brief, paras. 91-96, sp. para. 95.
[208] Trial Judgement, paras. 110-122.
[209] Trial Judgement, para. 122.
[210] Trial Judgement, paras. 120-122.
[211] Trial Judgement, paras. 112-118, 121, 122.
[212] Appellant's Brief, para. 89.
[213] Appellant's Brief, para. 89, referring to Trial Judgement, para. 537.

103. The Appellant asserts that since there was no legal basis for the allegation that he had authority over the policemen, the Prosecution had to support its allegation by providing evidence that he continuously and effectively exercised *de facto* authority over the policemen during April 1994.[214] He submits that this allegation was "bizarre" considering the Trial Chamber's findings that the Appellant left Kigali on 7 April 1994 and remained in Ruhengeri between 7 and 19 April 1994.[215]

104. The Appellant argues that the Trial Chamber failed to take into account existing "compelling reasons for discounting" the evidence provided by Prosecution witnesses[216] and ignored evidence contradicting the Prosecution allegation or "render[ing] it less plausible".[217] More specifically, he asserts that the Trial Chamber erred in relying on the testimony of Prosecution Witnesses BMU, BLX, BMA, BMG, BMF, BMH, and BME.[218]

105. The Appeals Chamber will consider the Appellant's arguments in turn. **[page 31]**

(a) Witness BMU

106. Witness BMU, an official from Nyamirambo, testified that around 10 April 1994, three commune policemen, Safari, Kalimba, and Thomas, manned a roadblock in front of the Appellant's house and were engaged in killings.[219] According to the witness, on 10 April 1994, the policemen told him that they reported to the Appellant and not to Tharcisse Renzaho, the prefect of Kigali-Ville prefecture.[220]

107. The Appellant asserts that Witness BMU lied and made contradictory statements. He argues that Witness BMU's testimony established too tenuous a link between the Appellant and the policemen manning a roadblock in front of his house to support the finding made by the Trial Chamber.[221]

108. The Prosecution responds that the Appellant simply reiterates his submissions at trial on the credibility of Prosecution witnesses, including Witness BMU, while failing to show that the Trial Chamber acted unreasonably in relying on this evidence.[222]

109. In assessing Witness BMU's evidence, the Trial Chamber observed that, as an official in Nyarugenge in 1994 and someone who knew the Appellant personally, the witness was in a good position to observe the events.[223] However, the Trial Chamber decided to consider his evidence with caution, since it found that the witness "may have been influenced by a wish to positively affect the criminal proceedings against [him] in Rwanda."[224]

110. The Trial Chamber then observed that Witness BMU's prior statements of 1998 and 2002 ("1998 Statement" and "2002 Statement", respectively) do not mention policemen at a roadblock in front of the Appellant's house and that "[h]e explained that he was not asked about them and added that in his 1998 statement he only described what people told him, and not what he saw."[225] While the Trial Chamber considered that this was "not quite consistent with his testimony that he had heard from a subordinate about the policemen's position at the roadblock," it nevertheless found that this inconsistency did not affect the witness's credibility.[226] The Trial Chamber accepted Witness BMU's explanations for the discrepancies between his testimony and prior statements regarding the number of roadblocks in Nyamirambo and his

---

[214] Appellant's Brief, para. 87. The Appellant recalls that Nyamirambo was located in Kigali-Ville prefecture, and not in Kigali prefecture, of which he was a sub-prefect.
[215] Appellant's Brief, para. 88, referring to Trial Judgement, paras. 478, 500.
[216] Notice of Appeal, paras. 85, 86.
[217] Appellant's Brief, para. 90.
[218] Appellant's Brief, paras. 91-113.
[219] The Trial Chamber "consider[ed] it likely that Safari and Thomas were the first names of Kabarata and Habimana". Trial Judgement, para. 111.
[220] Trial Judgement, para. 89.
[221] Appellant's Brief, paras. 92-96.
[222] Respondent's Brief, paras. 96-98.
[223] Trial Judgement, para. 113.
[224] Trial Judgement, para. 113.
[225] Trial Judgement, para. 115.
[226] Trial Judgement, para. 115.

knowledge of the roadblocks when he **[page 32]** left his house on 10 April 1994.[227] The Trial Chamber also accepted Witness BMU's evidence about the policemen and their crimes at the roadblock in front of the Appellant's house in April 1994, including that they claimed to be subordinates of the Appellant and not of the prefect of Kigali-Ville.[228]

111. The Appellant asserts without more detail that the Trial Chamber erred in considering Witness BMU's evidence because he lied.[229] A review of the Trial Judgement reveals that the Trial Chamber accepted the witness's evidence only after a careful consideration of the various factors relevant to the assessment of his credibility.[230] In this respect, the Appellant has failed to establish that the Trial Chamber erred in accepting the evidence of Witness BMU.

112. The Appellant further argues that contrary to Witness BMU's explanation in cross-examination that in the 1998 and 2002 Statements he only recounted what people had told him, those statements in fact included details of what he saw in the sector after 6 April 1994 and even mentioned the specific persons who manned the roadblocks and those who were killed at such roadblocks.[231] In addition, the Appellant asserts that Witness BMU should have mentioned the names of the policemen in his statements since he stated that he learned their names from a report he received from someone else.[232] Finally, he argues that Witness BMU provided a different explanation in court by stating that he had omitted mentioning the role of the Appellant and the policemen "because he was not asked any question [sic] about them".[233]

113. In the 1998 Statement, Witness BMU recounted in general terms the events in Rwanda and in his sector from the beginning of the war in October 1990 to the end in 1994.[234] The focus was not on specific situations arising in the area of Nyamirambo but rather on broader events. The witness mentioned in general the setting up of roadblocks where Tutsis were killed and the failure of competent authorities to stop these killings, but gave no description of a particular roadblock or killing. In addition, the Appeals Chamber notes that, as with the 2002 Statement, the 1998 Statement focussed on the role of Tharcisse Renzaho in the genocide. In these circumstances, it is understandable that Witness BMU did not mention the presence of three particular policemen at a roadblock and the crimes they committed under the Appellant's alleged authority. In addition, Witness BMU was not only recounting what he witnessed personally, but also referred to what he had heard from others. The Appeals Chamber therefore considers that Witness BMU's explanations **[page 33]** were not at odds with the content of the 1998 Statement. Turning to the 2002 Statement, it is clear that the focus again was Renzaho's role during the genocide. While in this statement, the witness recounted the existence and functioning of roadblocks in general, he did not describe specific events at roadblocks.

114. Witness BMU explained in his testimony that he did not, in these previous statements, mention the setting up of a roadblock in front of the Appellant's house and the commission of crimes by policemen under the Appellant's control because he was not asked any questions about them. This explanation is consistent with the subject-matter of these statements.[235] The Appellant has not demonstrated that no reasonable trier of fact could have found that these omissions did not affect Witness BMU's credibility.

115. Pointing to the alleged contradiction between Witness BMU's testimony and the 2002 Statement regarding the number of roadblocks in Nyamirambo, the Appellant claims that the "inflated number of roadblocks clearly shows Witness BMU's desire to aggravate the charges against Karera".[236] The Appeals Chamber recalls that the Trial Chamber addressed this alleged inconsistency and accepted the explanation provided by the witness that in the 2002 Statement he was asked only about the number of roadblocks on the

---

[227] Trial Judgement, paras. 115, 116.
[228] Trial Judgement, para. 115.
[229] Appellant's Brief, para. 96.
[230] Trial Judgement, paras. 113, 115, 116.
[231] Appellant's Brief, para. 92.
[232] Appellant's Brief, para. 92.
[233] Appellant's Brief, para. 93.
[234] 1998 Statement, pp. 3-5.
[235] Trial Judgement, paras. 115, 116.
[236] Appellant's Brief, para. 95. In addition, the Appellant points to the Trial Chamber's observation at paragraph 116 of the Trial Judgement that Witness BMU stated in his 1998 Statement that he was astonished to notice the roadblocks some time after 10 April 1994, whereas at trial he testified that he had previously received reports about the roadblocks. Appellant's Brief, para. 95. However, the Appellant does not claim that the Trial Chamber erred in accepting Witness BMU's explanation for that apparent discrepancy.

main road from the regional stadium to the centre of town, and not about the entire sector.[237] The Appellant has not shown that the Trial Chamber erred in reaching this conclusion. Witness BMU's explanation is consistent with the fact that in the 2002 Statement, the number of roadblocks was mentioned in relation to his own role in distributing weapons at roadblocks in the sector.[238] In addition, the Appeals Chamber notes that the Appellant's assertion that the witness inflated the number of roadblocks to aggravate the charges against him is mere speculation.

116. The Appellant further contends that, of the three witnesses who testified to the presence of policemen at a roadblock in front of the Appellant's house, only Witness BMU established a link between the policemen and the Appellant, and that this link was too tenuous to support a finding that the Appellant exercised any authority over the policemen.[239] The Appellant asserts that "[a]ll **[page 34]** what [sic] Witness BMU said on this point is that the policemen boasted that they reported to Karera rather than to Renzaho, the *préfet* of Kigali-*Ville*".[240]

117. The Appeals Chamber disagrees. The link established by Witness BMU between the three policemen and the Appellant was not tenuous. According to Witness BMU, the policemen, who were aware of the witness's official position, told him that they were obeying instructions of the Appellant and were working for him, not for Renzaho, the prefect of Kigali-Ville prefecture.[241] In addition, the Trial Chamber's finding on the Appellant's position of authority over the policemen does not stand on Witness BMU's testimony alone. This aspect of his testimony was corroborated by the testimonies of Witnesses BMF, BMH, BMG, and BME.[242]

118. The Appellant's contention that the Trial Chamber erred in the assessment of Witness BMU's evidence is therefore dismissed.

(b) Witnesses BMA and BLX

119. The Appellant submits that he cannot "comprehend how Witnesses BMA and BLX could have been believed on the issue of commune policemen, whereas the [Trial] Chamber rejected their testimonies in relation to [other allegations against the Appellant and] also rejected Witness BLX's testimony as to the distribution of weapons in Nyamirambo".[243]

120. The Appeals Chamber recalls that it is not unreasonable for a Trial Chamber to accept some parts of a witness's testimony while rejecting others.[244] The Appellant has not shown how the Trial Chamber erred in accepting only portions of the evidence of these witnesses. The Appellant's contention is therefore dismissed.

(c) Witnesses BMF and BMH

121. The Trial Chamber found that "[t]he testimonies of [...] Witnesses BMF and BMH, are generally consistent about the police officers. They said that Karera left Nyamirambo but continued to visit there, that policemen remained at his house, regarded Karera as their superior and communicated with him by phone, that they committed crimes, distributed machetes, and ordered others to commit crimes."[245] **[page 35]**

122. With regard to Witness BMF, the Appellant claims that she provided many details regarding the presence of commune policemen in front of the Appellant's house, but that nothing in her testimony shows

---

[237] Trial Judgement, para. 116.
[238] 2002 Statement, pp. 4, 5.
[239] Appellant's Brief, para. 98.
[240] Appellant's Brief, para. 98.
[241] T. 23 January 2006 p. 24. *See also* T. 24 January 2006 pp. 3, 6, 7.
[242] *See* Trial Judgement, paras. 112, 117, 118.
[243] Appellant's Brief, para. 97.
[244] *See supra* Chapter IV Alleged Errors Relating to the Appellant's Involvement in the MRND and his Authority over the *Interahamwe* (Ground of Appeal 4). para. 87.
[245] Trial Judgement, para. 112.

that a superior-subordinate relationship existed between him and the policemen.[246] 123. The Appeals Chamber finds that contrary to the Appellant's contention, Witness BMF's testimony supports the finding that the Appellant exercised authority over the three policemen. Indeed, the witness testified that she knew the policemen and that they had been guarding the Appellant's house before April 1994.[247] She also testified that in the second half of May 1994, she heard policeman Kalimba tell his colleague Habimana that the Appellant had instructed him by telephone to spare some Tutsi families.[248] The Trial Chamber was therefore entitled to take these aspects of Witness BMF's testimony into account in assessing whether the Appellant exercised authority over the policemen.

124. The Appellant submits that Witness BMH lied with regard to the relationship between the Appellant and the policemen and that the Trial Chamber erred in assessing the evidence on this point.[249] The Appellant argues that Witness BMH could not have witnessed the Appellant ordering the policemen to destroy houses of Tutsi between 10 and 15 April 1994, since she was not present in the area during that period, as evidenced by her 1998 Statement where she said that prior to 22 May 1994, she had spent one and a half months in a place other than her house.[250] He further submits that when confronted with this discrepancy, she provided an explanation that even the Prosecution did not believe and which, therefore, should not have been accepted by the Trial Chamber. The Appellant asserts that Witness BMH's explanation to the effect that she had informed the Prosecution that there was an error in her 1998 Statement one year prior to her testimony contradicts the Prosecution's assertion that this information had been made available to it only twenty-four hours before her testimony.[251]

125. These arguments were already addressed and dismissed by the Trial Chamber.[252] The Appellant has not shown how the Trial Chamber erred in accepting Witness BMH's explanations as to the discrepancies between her trial testimony and prior statements. This contention is therefore dismissed. **[page 36]**

126. The Appellant further contends that the testimonies of Witnesses BMF and BMH were not accepted by the Trial Chamber in several respects, namely with regard to the Appellant's presence during an attack on 8 April 1994, the order to kill Kabuguza, and the circumstances of his death.[253] He argues that Witness BMF's testimony regarding the killing of her younger brother and twenty Tutsis was also not admitted.[254] He further submits that the Trial Chamber did not find these witnesses credible with regard to the events of 8 April 1994 and should have rejected these testimonies in their entirety.[255]

127. With regard to the attack of 8 April 1994, the Trial Chamber found that Witnesses BMH and BMF were generally credible and concluded based on their testimony that the attack had taken place.[256] However, it did not find established beyond reasonable doubt that the Appellant observed the attack and that members of his family were also present, despite the evidence provided by both witnesses to this effect. The Appellant claims that since the Trial Chamber's findings suggested that Witnesses BMF and BMH had falsely attempted to implicate him, the Trial Chamber erred in law "in believing the rest of their testimonies."[257] The Appeals Chamber recalls that the Trial Chamber had the discretion to accept only part of the witnesses' evidence. The Trial Chamber reached its conclusion on the evidence of these witnesses after having carefully considered the credibility challenges made by the Defence, including the allegation of collusion.[258] It did not find that these witnesses had attempted to falsely implicate the Appellant, but merely refrained from entering a finding on the presence of the Appellant at the attack because it was not persuaded beyond reasonable doubt

---

[246] Appellant's Brief, para. 101.
[247] Trial Judgement, para. 97.
[248] Trial Judgement, paras. 137, 171.
[249] Appellant's Brief, para. 102.
[250] Appellant's Brief, para. 103. The Appellant's Brief refers to a statement of 19 August 2006. It is apparent from the context as well as the exhibit number that the Appellant meant to refer to the Statement of 19 August 1998.
[251] Appellant's Brief, paras. 104-106.
[252] Trial Judgement, paras. 163, 164.
[253] Appellant's Brief, para. 100, referring to Trial Judgement, paras. 133, 139, 140, 145.
[254] Appellant's Brief, para. 100, referring to Trial Judgement, para. 199.
[255] Trial Judgement, paras. 107, 108.
[256] Trial Judgement, para. 135.
[257] Appellant's Brief, para. 108.
[258] Trial Judgement, paras. 130-135.

with respect to the part of their evidence that directly implicated the Appellant.[259] The Trial Chamber expressed doubt as to whether it would have been possible for the witnesses to recognize someone from their vantage points, given the circumstances of the attack.[260] The Trial Chamber's reasoning shows that it did not disbelieve the witnesses' accounts of the attack but that it applied additional caution to their identification of the Appellant and declined to enter a conviction on the basis of their evidence. The Appellant has not shown how the Trial Chamber erred in failing to disregard the testimonies of these witnesses in their entirety.

(d) Witness BME

128. The Trial Chamber found credible Witness BME's evidence regarding a meeting held on the morning of 15 April 1994 at the Appellant's house where the Appellant ordered a large crowd to **[page 37]** destroy houses of Tutsis.[261] It noted that the witness testified that the policemen who stayed at the Appellant's house participated in the meeting and concluded that her testimony corroborated the evidence given by other witnesses regarding the Appellant and the policemen.[262]

129. The Appellant claims that the testimony of Witness BME at best permits a finding that he gave orders to the commune policemen on the morning of 15 April 1994, but does not support any inference that he exercised authority over them during the entire month of April 1994.[263]

130. The Appeals Chamber agrees that the evidence of Witness BME alone could not support a finding of the Appellant's authority over the policemen through April 1994. However, the Trial Chamber only considered this evidence as corroborative of other evidence regarding the relationship between the Appellant and the policemen. From a review of the relevant portion of the Trial Judgement, it is evident that the Trial Chamber considered that Witness BME's evidence corroborated the testimonies of Witnesses BMF, BMH, BLX, BMA, BMU, and BMG in relation to the presence and role of the policemen at the Appellant's house and the nature of their relationship with the Appellant.[264] Witness BME's testimony was not only corroborative of these other testimonies, but also supported a finding that, on 15 April 1994, the Appellant was in a position to give orders to the policemen.

131. The Appellant further contends that the testimony of Witness BME could not be believed.[265] He avers that, if believed, this testimony would conflict with the Prosecution's allegation that the Appellant was in Ntarama on the same day.[266] He further claims that Witness BME's evidence that the Appellant ordered a crowd to kill Tutsis and destroy houses belonging to Tutsis on 15 April 1994 also contradicts the Trial Chamber's findings that the killings resulting from these orders had been committed prior to that date.[267] These submissions will be considered below under Section C.

(e) Witness BMG

132. With regard to Witness BMG, the Appellant merely states that the Trial Chamber did not believe him regarding the killing of Félix Dix and Kabuguza and recites his testimony that the Appellant's house was guarded by commune policemen, namely Kalimba, Habimana, and **[page 38]** Kabarate.[268] The Appellant acknowledges that Witness BMG gave details of the links which existed between these policemen and the Appellant and points out that the witness clearly explained that he did not see the Appellant committing or ordering any crime.[269]

---

[259] Trial Judgement, para. 135.
[260] Trial Judgement, paras. 133,134.
[261] Trial Judgement, paras. 103, 118.
[262] Trial Judgement, para. 118.
[263] Appellant's Brief, paras. 109, 110.
[264] Trial Judgement, para. 118.
[265] Appellant's Brief, para. 111.
[266] Appellant's Brief, para. 111.
[267] Appellant's Brief, para. 111, referring to other sub-sections of the Appellant's Brief dealing with the killings of Kabuguza, Kahabaye, Murekezi, and Ndingutse.
[268] Appellant's Brief, para. 112.
[269] Appellant's Brief, para. 112.

133. The Appellant does not attempt to show an error on the part of the Trial Chamber in assessing this witness's evidence. Accordingly, the Appeals Chamber rejects the Appellant's vague and unclear assertions in relation to Witness BMG.

3. Alleged Error in Failing to Give Proper Weight to Defence Evidence

134. At the outset of its assessment of the Defence evidence related to the Appellant's authority over the policemen, the Trial Chamber recalled its findings under a previous section of the Trial Judgement that it accorded "limited weight" to the evidence of the Appellant's relatives, Witnesses ATA, KD, and BBK.[270] The Trial Chamber then proceeded to consider the testimonies of Defence Witnesses KBG, KNK, and ZBM, but accorded them limited or no weight. In so doing, it reasoned that "Witness KBG, who did not notice anything peculiar, only passed by Karera's house in Nyamirambo about three times in April [1994]".[271] It noted that "[a]lthough he did not personally see crimes being committed, he confirmed that the people who manned the roadblock in Nyarugenge committed crimes against civilians."[272] With regard to Witness KNK, the Trial Chamber noted that her evidence that "there was no roadblock near Karera's house was based on her visits in the area between January and 6 April 1994, whereas the roadblocks were set up later".[273] The Trial Chamber found that Witness ZBM "lacked first-hand knowledge about the events," and that "[h]is testimony that he was not told about the involvement of Karera or the policemen in the killings in Cyivugiza in 1994 carries limited weight compared to direct and consistent evidence from other witnesses implicating them in the killings."[274]

135. The Appellant submits that the Trial Chamber erred by "unreasonably dismiss[ing] the testimonies of Witnesses ATA, KD, BBK, KBG, KNK and ZBM, without providing satisfactory explanations for such a decision."[275]

136. The Appeals Chamber notes that eight Defence witnesses, namely, the Appellant, three witnesses related to him (Witnesses ATA, KD, and BBK), and Witnesses KBG, KNK, ZBM, and **[page 39]** BMP, testified in relation to the Prosecution's allegation that the Appellant was present in Nyamirambo in April 1994 and that he gave orders to the policemen under his authority.[276]

137. In the course of its assessment of the relevant Defence evidence, the Trial Chamber stated that it accorded limited weight to the evidence of witnesses who were related to the Appellant on the ground that "[w]hile these relationships do not, in themselves, discredit the witnesses, they may account for the witnesses' inclination to resolve any lapse in their recollections in a manner favourable to Karera."[277] These observations merely demonstrate that the Trial Chamber viewed the evidence from Defence witnesses who had close relationships with the Appellant or his family members with caution and does not demonstrate *per se* that the Trial Chamber erred in law in its assessment of this evidence.

138. The Appeals Chamber notes that Witnesses ATA, KD, and BBK were away from the Appellant's house in Nyamirambo after 7 April 1994.[278] Therefore, the evidence of these three witnesses was not significant with regard to the presence and role of the three policemen at the Appellant's house after 7 April 1994. In these circumstances, the Appeals Chamber sees no error in the Trial Chamber according limited weight to the evidence of these witnesses on this point.

139. With regard to Witnesses KBG, KNK, and ZBM, the Trial Chamber considered their testimonies but it is apparent from the Trial Judgement that it did not find their evidence relevant or significant regarding the

---

[270] Trial Judgement, para. 119.
[271] Trial Judgement, para. 119.
[272] Trial Judgement, para. 119.
[273] Trial Judgement, para. 119.
[274] Trial Judgement, para. 119.
[275] Appellant's Brief, para. 114, referring to Trial Judgement, para. 119.
[276] Trial Judgement, paras. 104-109.
[277] Trial Judgement, para. 499.
[278] *See* Trial Judgement, para. 105 for the summary of the witnesses' testimonies.

Appellant's authority over the three policemen and their role in the commission of crimes in Nyamirambo.[279] The Appellant has not shown any error in this approach.

140. The Appeals Chamber recalls that the the task of weighing and assessing evidence lies, in the first place, with the Trial Chamber. The Trial Chamber had therefore the discretion to assess the relevance and weight of evidence given by both Prosecution and Defence witnesses when reaching a decision as to the Appellant's authority.[280] The Appellant has not demonstrated how the Trial Chamber abused its discretion in this respect. Accordingly, the Appeals Chamber dismisses this sub-ground of appeal. **[page 40]**

B. Alleged Errors relating to the Appellant's Orders to Kill Kabuguza's Family

141. The Trial Chamber found that between 7 and 10 April 1994, the Appellant gave, via telephone, an order to kill Kabuguza.[281] At the same time, the Trial Chamber held that it could not conclude beyond reasonable doubt that Kabuguza was killed by the policemen stationed at the Appellant's house, since the time and place of the killing were unclear, no one observed the alleged killing, and no one heard anyone assume responsibility for it.[282]

142. The Appellant submits that the Trial Chamber erred in law by making this finding based on contradictory and implausible evidence.[283] Since the Trial Chamber based its finding on the testimonies of Witnesses BMH, BMU, and BMF, the Appellant first reiterates his previous submissions that the testimonies of these three witnesses should be rejected in their entirety.[284] Next, the Appellant recalls that the Trial Chamber listed the various contradictions and inconsistencies in the testimonies of Witnesses BMF and BMH and claims that there were additional inconsistencies that the Trial Chamber did not note.[285] However, he points to only one example: the fact that Witness BMF testified that the Appellant ordered that Kabuguza's entire family be killed, while Witness BMH stated that the Appellant instructed that the other members of Kabuguza's family be spared.[286] The Appellant contends that Witnesses BMF, BMH, and BMU lied in their testimonies.[287] He argues that the Trial Chamber "speculated in order to make up for the shortcomings of the Prosecutor's case," thus ignoring the "reasonable possibility that Karera had nothing to do with the killing."[288] The Appellant asserts that this finding has impacted on the Trial Chamber's conclusion that the Appellant exercised authority over the policemen in Nyamirambo.[289]

143. The Prosecution responds that this sub-ground of appeal is unfounded.[290] It submits that the Trial Chamber duly examined the witnesses' evidence, considered the contradictions, and provided a reasoned explanation for accepting the testimonies.[291] It claims that the Appellant has failed to show how the Trial Chamber's explanation was unreasonable or unfounded.[292] Moreover, the Prosecution notes that even though the Trial Chamber found that the Appellant ordered Kabuguza **[page 41]** to be killed, a "reading of the Trial Chamber's legal findings shows that it did not hold the Appellant responsible for this murder."[293] The Prosecution concludes that the Appellant has not demonstrated the impact that a possible error as to his role in Kabuguza's killing could have had on the verdict and that this sub-ground of appeal should accordingly be dismissed.[294]

---

[279] Trial Judgement, para. 119.
[280] *Musema* Appeal Judgement, para. 18; *Rutaganda* Appeal Judgement, para. 392; *Kupreškiü et al.* Appeal Judgement, para. 31.
[281] Trial Judgement, para. 145.
[282] Trial Judgement, para. 145.
[283] Notice of Appeal, paras. 94, 95; Appellant's Brief, para. 127; AT. 28 August 2008 pp. 14, 42, 43.
[284] Appellant's Brief, paras. 92-96, 120.
[285] Appellant's Brief, para. 125, citing Trial Judgement, paras. 140-144.
[286] Appellant's Brief, para. 125.
[287] Appellant's Brief, para. 126.
[288] Appellant's Brief, paras. 127, 128.
[289] AT. 28 August 2008 p. 14.
[290] Respondent's Brief, para. 101.
[291] Respondent's Brief, para. 99.
[292] Respondent's Brief, para. 99.
[293] Respondent's Brief, para. 100, citing Trial Judgement, paras. 538, 559.
[294] Respondent's Brief, para. 101; AT. 28 August 2008 pp. 42, 43.

144. The Trial Chamber's impugned finding stands on the evidence of Witnesses BMU, BMF, and BMH. The Trial Chamber found that "Witnesses BMF and BMH gave a generally consistent account about overhearing a policeman talk on the telephone in Karera's house about killing Kabuguza".[295] However, it noted a number of problematic elements in the evidence related to the Appellant's alleged order to kill Kabuguza and to his alleged murder. Specifically, Witness BMU stated that the killing of Kabuguza occurred between 7 and 10 April 1994, Witness BMH did not provide a date for the phone conversation, but implicitly situated it in April 1994, and Witness BMF said that both the phone conversation and the killing of Kabuguza took place in May 1994. In addition, Witness BMH's testimony indicated that several days separated the phone conversation and the killing of Kabuguza while Witness BMF testified that the killing took place on the morning after the conversation. Furthermore, Witness BMF testified that Kabuguza's entire family was killed, information corroborated by Witness BMU, while Witness BMH stated that the Appellant had decided that Kabuguza's wife and children could live.[296] On the basis of these inconsistencies, the Trial Chamber considered that the circumstances, the location, and the time of the killing remained unclear and as a consequence, refrained from concluding "beyond reasonable doubt that Kabuguza was actually killed by the police officers stationed at Karera's house".[297]

145. The Appeals Chamber finds, however, that the Trial Chamber should have adopted a more cautious approach in its assessment of the Prosecution evidence regarding the person who ordered the killing. The testimonies of Witnesses BMF and BMH were not corroborative as to the period of the Appellant's purported order to kill Kabuguza. The evidence provided by Witness BMH is speculative as to the identity of the person who ordered the killing.[298] Furthermore, no clarity exists as to whether the scope of the order was to kill the entire family of Kabuguza or to spare his wife and children. The Appeals Chamber therefore finds that the Trial Chamber erred in finding that, between 7 and 10 April 1994, the Appellant ordered the murder of Kabuguza.

146. Nevertheless, this error could not lead to a miscarriage of justice since no conviction was entered on the basis of the alleged order to murder Kabuguza. The Trial Chamber's assessment of **[page 42]** the Appellant's authority over the policemen is primarily based on the evidence that in 1994, they lived in and guarded his house, that they received orders from him, that they referred to him as "boss" and that they manned a roadblock near his house.[299] Accordingly, the Appeals Chamber dismisses this sub-ground of appeal.

C. Alleged Errors relating to the Finding that the Appellant Ordered the Killing of Tutsis and Destruction of their Homes in Nyamirambo

147. The Trial Chamber found that between 7 and 15 April 1994, the Appellant gave orders to kill Tutsis and destroy their houses in Nyamirambo at locations near his house.[300] It further found that between 8 and 10 April 1994 or around these dates, the policemen who guarded the Appellant's house destroyed the houses of Kahabaye and Félix Dix with the assistance of the *Interahamwe*.[301] In finding that these events took place pursuant to the Appellant's orders, it relied on the evidence provided by Witnesses BME, BMG, BMH, BMF, BMU, and BLX.[302]

148. The Appellant submits that the Trial Chamber erred in law and fact in finding that he had ordered the killing of Tutsis and the destruction of their property in Nyamirambo.[303]

149. The Appeals Chamber will consider the Appellant's arguments in turn.[304]

---

[295] Trial Judgement, para. 139.
[296] Trial Judgement, paras. 139-144.
[297] Trial Judgement, para. 145.
[298] *See* Trial Judgement, para. 136.
[299] Trial Judgement, paras. 110-122, 139-145, 162-168, 173, 182, 192, 195-196, 203.
[300] Trial Judgement, para. 168.
[301] Trial Judgement, para. 168, cross-referring Section II.4.7 of the Trial Judgement where these killings are discussed.
[302] Trial Judgement, paras. 159-166.
[303] Notice of Appeal, para. 99; Appellant's Brief, paras. 129-145.
[304] The Appellant's arguments in relation to his alibi (Appellant's Brief, para. 130) are considered below under Chapter IX.

1. Alleged Error in Making a Finding of Fact on a General and Redundant Allegation

150. The Appellant first contends that the Prosecution's underlying allegation itself was "general and redundant" and that the Trial Chamber erred by making a finding of fact from evidence in support of such an allegation.[305] This argument is summarily dismissed as the Appellant only raised it in the Notice of Appeal and did not develop it sufficiently to enable the Appeals Chamber to assess the alleged error. **[page 43]**

2. Alleged Error in the Assessment of Prosecution and Defence Evidence

151. The Appellant next contends that the Trial Chamber committed a number of errors, which are detailed below, in the assessment of Prosecution and Defence evidence related to this allegation.[306]

(a) Alleged Inconsistencies in Dates and Times Provided by Prosecution Witnesses

152. The Appellant lists and highlights alleged inconsistencies in the dates and times provided by Prosecution witnesses in relation to the alleged orders.[307] He contends that "[i]t is absolutely unbelievable that the Chamber found, on the basis of this evidence, that Karera gave orders, **between 7 and 15 April 1994**, to kill the Tutsi and destroy their houses in Nyamirambo and that, consequently, **between 8 and 10 April 1994**, the policemen who were guarding [his] house destroyed the houses of Kahabaye and Félix Dix, with the assistance of the *Interahamwe*".[308] He suggests that "[t]he evidence must have been examined in an offhand manner to make the finding that an impossible fact has been proven beyond a reasonable doubt".[309]

153. The Appellant argues that the testimonies of the Prosecution witnesses who testified about the alleged order to kill Tutsis were "so contradictory" that the Trial Chamber "ought to admit" that they were probably speaking of different events.[310] He further submits that the Trial Chamber erred in concluding that there were several stages of destruction resulting from more than one order given by the Appellant, despite the fact that all the witnesses who testified about the destruction of the houses of Tutsis stated that it occurred immediately after the order had been given.[311]

154. The Prosecution responds that the Appellant simply lists inconsistencies in the Prosecution witnesses' evidence "without demonstrating specifically and in a well argued manner how the Trial Chamber failed to make good use of its power to assess the evidence."[312] It submits that the Trial Chamber duly considered the testimonies of all the witnesses, including Defence witnesses, and recalls that it is within a Trial Chamber's discretion to assess the contradictions in light of the entire evidence and determine a witness's credibility.[313]

155. The Appeals Chamber recalls that the task of weighing and assessing evidence lies, in the first place, with the Trial Chamber and that it is within the Trial Chamber's discretion to assess any **[page 44]** inconsistencies in the testimony of witnesses and to determine whether, in light of the overall evidence, the witnesses are nonetheless reliable and credible.[314]

156. The Appeals Chamber notes that, under Section 4.7 of the Trial Judgement,[315] the Trial Chamber found that "the *Interahamwe* in Nyamirambo followed after Kahabaye, killed him in [the neighbouring *commune* of] Butamwa between 8 and 10 April [1994], and reported to Karera's policemen that the killing

---

[305] Notice of Appeal, paras. 96, 99.
[306] Appellant's Brief, paras. 131-144.
[307] Appellant's Brief, paras. 131-136, summarizing the testimonies of Witnesses BMU, BMG, BMF, BMH and BME.
[308] Appellant's Brief, para. 137 (emphasis in original), referring to Trial Judgement, para. 168.
[309] Appellant's Brief, para. 137 (emphasis in original).
[310] Appellant's Brief, para. 138.
[311] Appellant's Brief, para. 139, referring to Trial Judgement, para. 166.
[312] Respondent's Brief, para. 103.
[313] Respondent's Brief, para. 104.
[314] *See Bagileshema* Appeal Judgement, para. 78.
[315] Trial Judgement, Section 4.7 (Killings of Joseph Kahabaye and Félix Dix).

had taken place" and that "[t]he killing was a consequence of Karera's order".[316] As to the killing of Félix Dix, the Trial Chamber found that "it must have occurred between 8 and 15 April [1994], when the Tutsi houses were destroyed" but declined to enter a conviction on that basis, reasoning that there was not "sufficient evidence to find beyond reasonable doubt that the three policemen were responsible of killing Félix Dix [sic]."[317]

157. There is no doubt that the Trial Chamber's mention of the destruction of houses of Tutsis in this section of the Trial Judgement is a reference to its prior findings in Section 4.5 of the Trial Judgement.[318] There the Trial Chamber held that "between 8 and 10 April 1994 or around these days, the policemen who guarded Karera's house destroyed the houses of Kahabaye and Dix, with the assistance of the *Interahamwe*".[319]

158. It is apparent that in making this finding, the Trial Chamber relied chiefly on Witness BMU's testimony.[320] The Trial Chamber also considered the testimonies of Witnesses BMG, BMF, BMH, BLX, and BME, and it appears to have found them corroborative of Witness BMU's testimony on this point.[321] The Trial Chamber considered the differences in these testimonies as to the date of the events and did not find that these differences amounted to a conflict in the evidence.[322] The Appeals Chamber notes that the range of dates provided by Witnesses BMG, BMF, BME, and BMH included the shorter time-frame given by Witness BMU. The Trial Chamber specifically concluded that "Witness BMH's testimony that Karera gave the order to destroy houses between 10 and 15 April [1994] does not contradict Witness BMU's evidence that Kahabaye's and Dix's houses had been demolished by 10 April [1994]" and that the "evidence suggests that there was more than one order and several stages of destruction".[323] The Appellant has not demonstrated **[page 45]** that no reasonable trier of fact could have concluded that the evidence of Witnesses BMG, BMF, BMH, BLX, and BME was consistent as to the date of the events.

159. The Trial Chamber found Witness BME's testimony credible and accepted that her testimony that the events in question occurred on 15 April 1994 was given honestly.[324] It however concluded that "it [was] likely that Witness BME erred regarding the precise date of the event, in view of her traumatic situation" and the circumstances.[325] The Trial Chamber considered whether her testimony contradicted Witness BMU's evidence that Kahabaye's and Dix's houses had been destroyed between 7 and 10 April 1994.[326] It concluded that Witness BME's evidence that the order to destroy houses took place on 15 April 1994 did "not exclude that Kahabaye's and Dix's houses had already been demolished".[327] The Appeals Chamber finds that the Appellant has not demonstrated that the Trial Chamber erred in making such a finding.

160. The Appeals Chamber finds no error in the Trial Chamber's finding that "between 7 and 15 April 1994, Karera gave orders to kill Tutsi and destroy their houses in Nyamirambo, at locations near his house."[328] This finding is supported by the evidence given by Witnesses BMU, BMG, BMF, BMH, BLX, and BME, which the Appellant has not successfully challenged. The Appeals Chamber will address below, under Sections E, F, G, and H, the Appellant's arguments related to the link between the alleged killings and these orders.

(b) <u>Allegation of a Reasonable Possibility that the Houses Had Been Destroyed before the Appellant Allegedly Ordered their Destruction</u>

161. The Appellant claims that the Trial Chamber's holding leaves open the "reasonable possibility that the houses were destroyed before [he] gave the order to destroy them."[329]

---

[316] Trial Judgement, paras. 182, 183.
[317] Trial Judgement, paras. 184, 185.
[318] Trial Judgement, Section 4.5 (Order to Kill Tutsi and Destroy their Houses).
[319] Trial Judgement, para. 168.
[320] Trial Judgement, paras. 152, 166, 167.
[321] Trial Judgement, paras. 159-166.
[322] Trial Judgement, para. 166.
[323] Trial Judgement, para. 166.
[324] Trial Judgement, paras. 159-161, 162, 166.
[325] Trial Judgement, para. 160.
[326] Trial Judgement, para. 166.
[327] Trial Judgement, para. 166.
[328] Trial Judgement, para. 168.
[329] Appellant's Brief, para. 140.

162. The Appeals Chamber notes that in its reasoning leading to the conclusion that the Appellant committed genocide based on the killing of Kabahaye, Murekezi, Ndingutse, and Nyagatare the Trial Chamber found that they "were killed pursuant to Karera's orders to the policemen and *Interahamwe* to kill Tutsi[s] and destroy their homes, which were given between 7 and 15 April [1994]"[330] and that the Appellant's order to destroy the houses of Kahabaye and Felix Dix also demonstrate his genocidal intent.[331] The Trial Chamber considered the alleged **[page 46]** inconsistency between the time-frames identified by some witnesses of the order and the timing of the houses' destruction. While one witness stated that the Appellant ordered the destruction of houses on 10 April 1994, another witness testified that the order was given on 15 April 1994, and two other witnesses testified that similar orders were made on or after 8 April 1994. The Trial Chamber reasoned that "[t]he evidence suggests that there was more than one order and several stages of destruction"[332] and accepted the possibility that Kahabaye's and Dix's houses had already been destroyed on 10 April 1994. The Appeals Chamber sees no error in this reasoning and finds therefore that the Appellant has not shown that no reasonable trier of fact could have reached the conclusion that the Appellant ordered the destruction of the houses on the basis of the evidence. Furthermore, the Appellant has not shown that no reasonable trier of fact could have reached the conclusion that his order to destroy houses of Tutsis as well as the destruction of the houses of Kahabaye and Felix Dix illustrate his genocidal intent.

(c) Alleged Differential Treatment of Defence and Prosecution Witnesses

163. The Appellant further alleges, without elaboration, differential treatment of Defence and Prosecution witnesses by the Trial Chamber and claims that the Trial Chamber failed to explain why it did not believe the Defence evidence.[333]

164. A review of the Trial Judgement reveals that the Trial Chamber took into account the totality of the evidence and discussed in detail the evidence given by both Prosecution and Defence witnesses.[334] Contrary to the Appellant's claim, the Trial Chamber explained why the evidence given by Defence witnesses "did not weaken the evidence adduced by Prosecution witnesses":[335]

> Witness KGB confirmed that, generally, those who manned the roadblocks attacked and looted civilians. Witness ATA's testimony confirms that Kahabaye's house had been destroyed between 7 April 1994 and 1997. Witness KD, who said that it was demolished in late June 1994, did not observe its destruction and her account was based on information from others and is not in conformity with evidence from other witnesses.[336]

165. The Appellant has not demonstrated how the Trial Chamber erred in making this finding. His appeal on this point is therefore dismissed. **[page 47]**

(d) Alleged Shifting of the Burden of Proof

166. The Appellant alleges that the Trial Chamber's statement that the Defence witnesses did not weaken the Prosecution evidence illustrates that it erroneously shifted the burden of proof.[337]

167. The Prosecution responds that the Trial Chamber did not reverse the burden of proof and that "[h]aving seen and heard the witnesses testify, the Trial Chamber could very well prefer the testimonies [of the] Prosecution witnesses […] to the extent that these witnesses gave reliable and credible descriptions of what they observed in person, although with minor contradictions."[338]

168. The Appellant has not shown how the statement in question demonstrates that the Trial Chamber shifted the burden of proof.

---

[330] Trial Judgement, para. 538.
[331] Trial Judgement, para. 539.
[332] Trial Judgement, para. 166.
[333] Appellant's Brief, paras. 142, 143, 145.
[334] Trial Judgement, paras. 146-167.
[335] Trial Judgement, para. 167.
[336] Trial Judgement, para. 167.
[337] Appellant's Brief, para. 144, citing Trial Judgement, para. 167.
[338] Respondent's Brief, para. 107 (citations omitted), citing Trial Judgement, paras. 159, 162, 165.

3. Conclusion

169. For the foregoing reasons, this sub-ground of appeal is dismissed.

D. Alleged Errors relating to the Finding that the Appellant Ordered that Certain Houses of Tutsis be Spared

170. The Trial Chamber concluded that in the period between 7 and 15 April 1994, the Appellant ordered that certain houses of Tutsis should not be destroyed.[339] In making this finding, the Trial Chamber relied mainly on the testimony of Witnesses BMF and BMH[340] and also considered that Witness BMG's evidence corroborated that of Witness BMF about sparing the life of a Tutsi man named Callixte Kalisa.[341]

171. The Appellant submits that the Trial Chamber's assessment of the evidence of these witnesses and its finding that certain houses of Tutsis were spared on the Appellant's orders are erroneous.[342] The Prosecution responds that the Trial Chamber properly assessed the evidence concerning the order that certain houses of Tutsis be spared.[343]

172. The Appellant first contends that Prosecution Witnesses BMG, BMF, and BMH do not corroborate each other since none of them "gave the same reasons advanced by [the Appellant] or **[page 48]** by those persons who were quoting him, as to why the lives and houses of some Tutsi had to be spared."[344]

173. The Appeals Chamber recalls its holding in the *Nahimana et al.* Appeal Judgement that:

> two testimonies corroborate one another when one *prima facie* credible testimony is compatible with the other *prima facie* credible testimony regarding the same fact or a sequence of linked facts. It is not necessary that both testimonies be identical in all aspects or describe the same fact in the same way. Every witness presents what he has seen from his own point of view at the time of the events, or according to how he understood the events recounted by others. It follows that corroboration may exist even when some details differ between testimonies, provided that no credible testimony describes the facts in question in a way which is not compatible with the description given in another credible testimony.[345]

174. The Appeals Chamber further recalls that minor inconsistencies commonly occur in witness testimony without rendering it unreliable and that it is within the discretion of the Trial Chamber to evaluate such inconsistencies and to consider whether the evidence as a whole is credible, without explaining its decision in every detail.[346]

175. While the Trial Chamber did not explicitly address this matter, the Appeals Chamber finds that the alleged inconsistency is minor and that it is not relevant to the material facts underlying the conviction. Accordingly, the Trial Chamber's failure to address this issue does not render its reliance on the witnesses erroneous.

176. The Appellant next alleges that Witness BMG's testimony is "very confusing" and contradicts Witness BMF as to the time period of the orders allegedly given by the Appellant.[347] 177. The Appeals Chamber notes that the Trial Chamber chiefly relied on Witness BMF's testimony, not Witness BMG's, in making the finding on the Appellant's order to spare the lives of certain Tutsis.[348] While Witness BMG's testimony suggests that the order to spare Callixte's life was given sometime before 15 April 1994, Witness BMF testified that the order was given in the second half of May 1994.[349] In reaching its conclusion that the

---

[339] Trial Judgement, para. 173.
[340] Trial Judgement, paras. 173, 174.
[341] Trial Judgement, para. 174.
[342] Notice of Appeal, para. 102; Appellant's Brief, para. 149.
[343] Respondent's Brief, paras. 110, 111.
[344] Appellant's Brief, para. 148.
[345] *Nahimana et al.* Appeal Judgement, para. 428.
[346] *Kvočka et al.* Appeal Judgement, para. 23.
[347] Appellant's Brief, para. 148.
[348] Trial Judgement, para. 174.
[349] Trial Judgement, paras. 137, 171.

evidence of Witness BMG corroborated that of Witness BMF "about the sparing of Callixte",[350] the Trial Chamber reasoned that it was not clear from Witness BMG's testimony whether he personally heard the Appellant make the order, or learned about it from others[351] without addressing the apparent discrepancy between the dates identified by the two witnesses as to when the Appellant ordered that the life and **[page 49]** house of Callixte Kalisa be spared. While it would have been preferable for the Trial Chamber to address such an apparent discrepancy, the Appeals Chamber does not find that this omission amounts to an error since the testimonies are not incompatible.

178. The Appellant finally submits that Witness BMH's evidence must be dismissed since it was "obtained from other persons and does not tally with the evidence of the two other witnesses [BMF and BMG]."[352] This unsubstantiated submission is dismissed since the Appellant has not explained what differences exist between the testimony of Witness BMH and Witnesses BMF and BMG. To the extent that the Appellant is challenging the hearsay nature of Witness BMH's testimony, the Appeals Chamber recalls that "hearsay evidence is admissible as long as it is of probative value," and that a Trial Chamber has the discretion to cautiously consider hearsay evidence and to rely on it.[353]

179. The Appeals Chamber finds that the Appellant has not shown that the Trial Chamber erred in relying on Witnesses BMF, BMH, and BMG in reaching its finding on this point.

180. This sub-ground of appeal is therefore dismissed.

E. Alleged Errors relating to the Finding that Kahabaye was Killed on the Appellant's Orders

181. The Trial Chamber found that, pursuant to the Appellant's order to kill Tutsis, *Interahamwe* in Nyamirambo followed Joseph Kahabaye and killed him in Butamwa between 8 and 10 April 1994.[354] The *Interahamwe* then reported the killing to the Appellant's policemen.[355] Partly on the basis of these findings, the Trial Chamber found the Appellant guilty of ordering genocide and extermination and murder as crimes against humanity.[356]

182. The Appellant submits that the Trial Chamber erred in finding that Kahabaye was killed on his orders[357] and contends that the Trial Chamber erred in the assessment of the evidence.[358] The **[page 50]** Appellant contends that all three Prosecution witnesses, upon whom the Trial Chamber relied in making the above finding, Witnesses BMU, BMF, and BMG, gave hearsay evidence and provided no direct evidence implicating the Appellant in Kahabaye's murder.[359] He claims that the Trial Chamber relied on the "incomplete accounts" of witnesses and particularly opposes the Trial Chamber's acceptance of the testimony of Witness BMU in light of its prior assessment of this witness.[360] He further alleges that no causal link was established between the order and Kahabaye's killing.[361] The Appellant claims that the Trial Chamber failed to examine the factual contradictions in the witnesses' testimonies and erroneously made its

---

[350] Trial Judgement, para. 174.
[351] Trial Judgement, para. 174.
[352] Appellant's Brief, para. 148. *See also* Notice of Appeal, para. 101.
[353] *See supra* para. 39.
[354] Trial Judgement, paras. 182, 536.
[355] Trial Judgement, para. 182.
[356] Trial Judgement, paras. 540, 555, 557, 559, 560.
[357] Notice of Appeal, paras. 103-115; Appellant's Brief, paras. 150-165.
[358] Appellant's Brief, paras. 151-165. The Appellant cites paragraphs 108-113 of the Trial Judgement to demonstrate that the Trial Chamber was wary of Witness BMU and "noted all the same that he was lying." The Appeals Chamber notes that the Trial Chamber held that Witness BMU's testimony should be considered with caution (since he may have been influenced by a wish to positively affect the criminal proceedings against him in Rwanda) but, contrary to the statement in the Appellant's Brief, the Trial Chamber did not conclude that the witness was lying. Trial Judgement, para. 113. Therefore, the Appeals Chamber need not address the unsubstantiated argument that this fact was never pleaded in the Amended Indictment. Notice of Appeal, para. 112.
[359] Appellant's Brief, para. 163. *See also* Brief in Reply, para. 33.
[360] Appellant's Brief, para. 152.
[361] Appellant's Brief, para. 159.

finding even though "it has not been proved beyond a reasonable doubt that Kahabaye was killed on Karera's orders."[362]

183. The Prosecution responds that the Trial Chamber correctly found that Kahabaye was killed on the Appellant's orders.[363] It submits that the Trial Chamber relied on the testimonies it deemed credible and found that the Appellant had given orders to the *Interahamwe* and policemen.[364] Further, the Prosecution points to the Trial Chamber's previous finding that the Appellant exercised authority over the *Interahamwe* and the three policemen guarding his house.[365] Thus, the Prosecution concludes that "the death of Kahabaye was undoubtedly the direct consequence of the Appellant's orders, and the Trial Chamber did not commit any error in this regard."[366]

184. The Appeals Chamber notes that the Trial Chamber relied on the testimonies of Witnesses BMU, BMG, and BMF in making its finding on this point.[367] Witness BMG stated that he heard that Kahabaye had been killed in Butamwa, a location outside Nyamirambo, but did not know by whom.[368] Witness BMF observed the Appellant telling Kalimba that he no longer wanted to see the "filth" of houses of Tutsis in front of his house, pointing to the houses nearby, such as those of Joseph Kahabaye, Felix, and Vianney Hitimana.[369] He testified that Kahabaye was arrested and killed by *Interahamwe* in April 1994.[370] As summarized by the Trial Chamber, Witness BMF also testified that *Interahamwe* boasted "to the policemen about having killed [Kahabaye]".[371] Witness **[page 51]** BMU received a telephone report from a subordinate that "the policemen at Karera's roadblock had killed Joseph Kahabaye and Félix Dix and their families õand that] they also destroyed their houses, accompanied by *Interahamwe*".[372] He further testified that on the same day he personally saw the ruins of the houses and noticed that "Joseph Kahabaye's folks" had been killed.[373]

185. The Appeals Chamber notes that no direct evidence supports the Trial Chamber's conclusion that the "*Interahamwe* in Nyamirambo followed after Kahabaye, killed him in Butamwa between 8 and 10 April [1994], and reported to Karera's policemen that the killing had taken place".[374] The Trial Judgement is insufficiently clear as to how the Trial Chamber reached this conclusion. Furthermore, in finding that "the killing was a consequence of Karera's order"[375] the Trial Chamber omitted to specify which order it referred to and did not reveal how it established a link between the murder of Kahabaye and any order given by the Appellant.

186. Based on the Trial Chamber's factual findings, the Appeals Chamber finds that no reasonable trier of fact could have concluded beyond reasonable doubt that Kahabaye's murder was a consequence of an order to kill Tutsis given by the Appellant. The evidence regarding the location of the crime and the identity of the perpetrators accepted by the Trial Chamber was not corroborated and, in fact, remained conflicting. Witness BMG testified that the murder occurred in Butamwa, while Witness BMU seemed to place it in Nyamirambo. Witness BMF testified that the murder had been perpetrated by *Interahamwe* while, according to Witness

---

[362] Appellant's Brief, para. 159.
[363] Respondent's Brief, para. 112.
[364] Respondent's Brief, para. 114.
[365] Respondent's Brief, para. 114, citing Trial Judgement, paras. 563, 567.
[366] Respondent's Brief, para. 115.
[367] Trial Judgement, paras. 175-180, 182.
[368] Trial Judgement, paras. 177, 182.
[369] Trial Judgement, para. 178.
[370] Trial Judgement, paras. 178, 182.
[371] Trial Judgement, para. 178. No specific information is given as to the identity of the said policemen. It seems that the Trial Chamber inferred from the context that the people involved here were the policemen guarding the Appellant's house. Witness BMF testified that he was not present when Kahabaye was killed but that "[t]his information [...] was related to [him]." He further stated that "*Interahamwes [sic]* were boasting about what they had done, and so they had no reason to lie". He specified that he did "not remember exactly the name of the person from whom [he] got that information, but [that] there were many *Interahamwes [sic]* passing by this location, and they came to brief the policemen regarding the people that they had killed". Finally, he stated that he "heard this from the *Interahamwes [sic]* themselves because they were reporting to the policemen. They were not telling me about the incident. They were talking to the policemen." T. 18 January 2006 p. 7.
[372] Trial Judgement, paras. 177, 182.
[373] Trial Judgement, para. 179.
[374] Trial Judgement, para. 182.
[375] Trial Judgement, para. 182.

BMU, the perpetrators were the policemen under the Appellant's authority. The Trial Chamber itself recognized that there was "limited information concerning the specific circumstances of his death [and that] no witness observed the killing"[376] but entered a finding that "the killing [of Kahabaye] was the consequence of Karera's order",[377] without explaining how it reached this conclusion.

187. In sum, the Appeals Chamber finds that the Trial Chamber erred in finding that Joseph Kahabaye's killing was "a consequence of Karera's order". Accordingly, the Appeals Chamber grants this sub-ground of appeal and reverses the Appellant's convictions for genocide and extermination and murder as crimes against humanity based on this event. **[page 52]**

F. Alleged Errors relating to the Finding that the Appellant Ordered Policeman Kalimba to Kill Murekezi

188. The Trial Chamber found that between 8 and 10 April 1994, policeman Kalimba forced a man to kill Murekezi, a Tutsi, at the roadblock near the Appellant's house and later boasted that he had carried out the killing following the Appellant's order.[378] It found that the testimonies of Witnesses BMU and BMG corroborated each other and were reliable despite their hearsay nature.[379] Partly on this basis, the Trial Chamber found the Appellant guilty of ordering genocide and extermination and murder as crimes against humanity.[380]

189. The Appellant submits that the Trial Chamber erred in finding that he had ordered Kalimba to kill Murekezi.[381] The Appellant claims that the Trial Chamber based its finding on "purely circumstantial evidence" and that this finding "amounts to speculation and is, therefore, erroneous."[382]

190. The Appellant claims that the testimonies of Witnesses BMG and BMU, on the basis of which the Trial Chamber made this finding, are inconsistent and fail to provide a sufficient link between him and the murder.[383] The Appellant highlights that the Trial Chamber "never mentioned or explained how it could be satisfied that conflicting evidence which it treated with caution proves a contested fact beyond reasonable doubt."[384]

191. The Prosecution responds that the Trial Chamber did not err in making this finding.[385]

192. The Trial Chamber relied primarily on the testimony of Witness BMG in making the impugned finding.[386] It also found that Witness BMU's evidence corroborated Witness BMG's evidence.[387] The Appeals Chamber has recalled above that two testimonies corroborate one another when one *prima facie* credible testimony is compatible with the other *prima facie* credible testimony regarding the same fact or a sequence of linked facts and that it is not necessary that both testimonies be identical in all aspects or describe the same fact in the same way.[388] It follows that corroboration may exist even when the testimonies differ on some details, provided that no credible **[page 53]** testimony describes the facts in question in a way which is incompatible with the description given in another credible testimony.[389]

193. Contrary to the Appellant's contention, the evidence of Witnesses BMG and BMU is not inconsistent or conflicting. The witnesses corroborate each other as to the fact that Murekezi was killed and as to the location of his killing. Witness BMG saw policeman Kalimba force a young man to kill Murekezi at the

---

[376] Trial Judgement, para. 182.
[377] Trial Judgement, para. 182.
[378] Trial Judgement, para. 192.
[379] Trial Judgement, para. 189.
[380] Trial Judgement, paras. 540, 557, 560.
[381] Notice of Appeal, paras. 116-127; Appellant's Brief, paras. 166-173; Brief in Reply, para. 34.
[382] Notice of Appeal, para. 125.
[383] Notice of Appeal, paras. 118, 119, 121; Appellant's Brief, para. 169; Brief in Reply, para. 34.
[384] Brief in Reply, para. 34.
[385] Respondent's Brief, paras. 116-119.
[386] Trial Judgement, paras. 186, 188-190.
[387] Trial Judgement, para. 189.
[388] See *supra* para.173.
[389] See *supra* para. 173.

roadblock in front of the Appellant's house between 8 and 15 April 1994.[390] Subsequently, Kalimba boasted that the Appellant had ordered him "to go and get Murekezi and his wife", but that he did not find the wife.[391] Witness BMU testified that between 7 and 10 April 1994 a subordinate reported to him over the phone that the *Interahamwe* and the policemen who guarded the Appellant's house had killed Murekezi and his two sons at the roadblock in front of the Appellant's house.[392] The time-frames provided by the two witnesses are consistent. The Appellant has not shown how the Trial Chamber erred in finding these testimonies corroborative.

194. The Appellant submits that the Trial Chamber relied on evidence containing "three hearsays" and favoured Witness BMG without providing an explanation for why it found his evidence reliable.[393]

195. The Appeals Chamber dismisses the Appellant's contention. The Trial Chamber chiefly relied on the testimony of Witness BMG who saw policeman Kalimba force a man to kill Murekezi. Witness BMG was therefore an eyewitness to the killing. He was also a direct witness to Kalimba boasting that he had carried out the Appellant's order "to go and get Murekezi and his wife."[394]

196. In any case, the Appeals Chamber has already recalled that it is for the appealing party to demonstrate that no reasonable trier of fact could have taken into account hearsay evidence in **[page 54]** reaching a specific finding.[395] The Appellant has not done so in this instance and therefore his contention that the Trial Chamber erred in relying on hearsay testimony is dismissed.

197. Finally, the Appellant reiterates his argument made at trial that he was not cross-examined about his denial of the incident and submits that the Trial Chamber erred in law by not considering that such unchallenged denial constitutes tacit acceptance of his account.[396]

198. The Appeals Chamber recalls that a Trial Chamber has the discretion as to whether or not to infer that statements which have not been challenged during cross-examination are true.[397] It has already rejected the general contention that the Trial Chamber erred in not making such an inference from the fact that the Prosecution did not cross-examine the Appellant.[398] Contrary to the Appellant's assertion, the absence of cross-examination does not imply that the Prosecution accepted the Appellant's denial of this incident. The Appellant's argument is dismissed.

199. This sub-ground of appeal is therefore dismissed.

G. Alleged Errors relating to the Finding that the Appellant was Involved in the Murder of Ndingutse

200. The Trial Chamber found that on 10 April 1994, Jean Bosco Ndingutse, a Tutsi, was arrested and killed not far away from the Appellant's house by *Interahamwe* and the policemen who were guarding the

---

[390] Trial Judgement, para. 186.
[391] Trial Judgement, para. 186.
[392] Trial Judgement, para. 187.
[393] Appellant's Brief, para. 170.
[394] Trial Judgement, para. 186. Witness BMG stated that: "[h]e was brought there by *Interahamwes* who were accompanied by a policeman who was guarding [the Appellant's] house, and when they got next to [the Appellant's] house, the policeman led Murekezi and compelled him to lie down, and then he ordered a young man to kill him, but the young man refused to do that. I no longer remember the name of that young man. So when the young man refused to do so, the policeman loaded his rifle and – in order to fire – to shoot at the young man. So when the young man saw that, he just took his machete and killed Murekezi. That was the circumstance of Murekezi's death. He had been taken from a place which was further away from there, and he was brought to the roadblock in order to be killed. And I would also like to add that the policeman's name was Kalimba. Later on, he boasted that it was [the Appellant] who ordered him to go and get Murekezi and Helen, that is Murekezi's wife, but the policeman did not find Murekezi's wife. He provided this information later, but I was there when he brought Murekezi there at the roadblock." T. 9 January 2006 p. 21.
[395] *See supra* para. 39.
[396] Appellant's Brief, para. 171.
[397] *See supra* para. 29.
[398] *See supra* para. 30.

Appellant's house.[399] The Trial Chamber found that this killing was one of the killings perpetrated pursuant to the Appellant's orders given to the policemen and *Interahamwe* between 7 and 15 April 1994 to kill Tutsi members of the population.[400] In making this finding, the Trial Chamber primarily relied on Witness BMU who testified that he saw Ndingutse being arrested by the policemen during the afternoon of 10 April 1994, about 300 metres from the Appellant's house.[401] Later that day, one of Witness BMU's subordinates reported to him that Ndingutse had been killed by the policemen and *Interahamwe*.[402] Partly on this basis, the Trial Chamber found the Appellant guilty of ordering genocide and extermination and murder as crimes against humanity.[403] **[page 55]**

201. The Appellant submits that the Trial Chamber made an erroneous finding since the evidence did not show that he ordered the murder of Ndingutse.[404] He contends that the Trial Chamber relied solely on the hearsay testimony of Witness BMU, which did not provide any direct evidence of the Appellant's involvement in the incident leading to Ndingutse's murder.[405]

202. The Prosecution responds that the Trial Chamber properly assessed the evidence concerning the murder of Ndingutse.[406] It submits that the Trial Chamber was within its discretion in finding Witness BMU credible and relying solely on his testimony.[407]

203. The Appeals Chamber finds that the Trial Chamber erred in finding that Ndingutse had been killed pursuant to the Appellant's orders given between 7 and 15 April 1994 to the policemen and *Interahamwe* to kill Tutsi. The Trial Chamber found that the killing occurred shortly after the Appellant had given an order to kill Tutsis and destroy their houses and in a place near the location where the order was given. However, Witness BMU was the only witness who testified about this event and the Trial Chamber decided to consider his testimony with caution,[408] since he might "have been influenced by a wish to positively affect the criminal proceedings against [him] in Rwanda".[409]

204. Witness BMU testified that he saw the policemen guarding the Appellant's house arrest Ndingutse and that later they "took two vehicles [belonging to Ndingutse], a minibus and a Peugeot 504" to the Appellant's compound.[410] He also testified that he was told by a subordinate that Ndingutse was killed by "Karera's policemen" and *Interahamwe.411* The Appeals Chamber finds that no reasonable trier of fact could have accepted this witness's uncorroborated hearsay testimony that the policemen who killed Ndingutse were the policemen who guarded the Appellant's house. Furthermore, no reasonable trier of fact could have concluded on the basis of that circumstantial evidence that the only reasonable inference was that Ndingutse had been killed pursuant to the Appellant's orders to kill Tutsis.

205. In sum, the Appeals Chamber finds that the Trial Chamber erred in fact in finding that Ndingutse had been killed pursuant to the Appellant's order. Accordingly, the Appeals Chamber grants this sub-ground of appeal and reverses the Appellant's convictions for genocide and extermination and murder as crimes against humanity based on this event. **[page 56]**

---

[399] While the Trial Chamber did not specify which policemen perpetrated the crime, it is clear from the context that it meant to refer to the policemen who, under the authority of the Appellant, guarded his house in Nyamirambo. *See* Trial Judgement, paras. 193, 196, 535.
[400] Trial Judgement, paras. 535, 536, 538.
[401] Trial Judgement, paras. 193-195.
[402] Trial Judgement, para. 193.
[403] Trial Judgement, paras. 540, 557, 560.
[404] Notice of Appeal, para. 131; Appellant's Brief, para. 179.
[405] Brief in Reply, para. 34; Appellant's Brief, para. 176.
[406] Respondent's Brief, para. 120.
[407] Respondent's Brief, para. 122, citing *Niyitegeka* Appeal Judgement, para. 171. *See also Muhimana* Appeal Judgement, para. 101; *Niyitegeka* Appeal Judgement, para. 92; *Gacumbitsi* Appeal Judgement, para. 72.
[408] Trial Judgement, para. 113.
[409] Trial Judgement, para. 113.
[410] T. 23 January 2006 pp. 17, 24.
[411] Trial Judgement, para. 193.

Judgement

H. Alleged Errors relating to the Killing of Nyagatare on the Appellant's Orders

206. The Trial Chamber found that a Tutsi man named Palatin Nyagatare was killed at a roadblock by policeman Kalimba on 24 April 1994 and that this followed the Appellant's orders to kill Tutsis in Nyamirambo.[412] Partly on this basis, the Trial Chamber found the Appellant guilty for ordering genocide and extermination and murder as crimes against humanity.[413]

207. The Appellant submits that the Trial Chamber erred in fact in finding that he was responsible for the killing of Palatin Nyagatare.[414] He contends that even assuming that he gave the order to kill Tutsis in Nyamirambo, the Trial Chamber committed a factual error in finding that this order resulted in Nyagatare's killing.[415] The Appellant recalls that the witnesses who claimed that he gave such an order pointed to the time period between 7 and 15 April 1994, whereas Nyagatare was killed on 24 April 1994.[416] This, the Appellant contends, coupled with the fact that the Prosecution was unable to prove that the Appellant gave a specific order to kill Nyagatare, illustrates that there is no evidence that Nyagatare's murder was the result of his alleged order.[417] He further claims that the Trial Chamber failed to meet its obligation to provide a reasoned opinion on this finding.[418]

208. The Prosecution responds that the Trial Chamber properly found that the Appellant's order resulted in the killing of Nyagatare.[419] First, it submits that Witnesses BMH and BMF corroborated each other on the facts of the killing.[420] Second, the Prosecution argues that the Appellant's contention relating to the ten day difference between the date of the alleged order and the killing is "without merit" since "the period of ten days is not too far removed" and the Trial Chamber found beyond reasonable doubt that policeman Kalimba killed Nyagatare on the Appellant's orders.[421]

209. In making the impugned finding, the Trial Chamber relied on the circumstantial hearsay evidence of Witnesses BMF and BMH. Both witnesses stated that Nyagatare was killed on 24 April 1994 and mentioned the involvement of Kalimba, one of the policemen who were guarding the Appellant's house, in the killing of Nyagatare.[422] Witness BMF testified that Kalimba confirmed to **[page 57]** her that he (Kalimba) had ordered Nyagatare's execution.[423] Witness BMH stated that Nyagatare was killed by a group which included *Interahamwe* and the Appellant's policemen.[424] Witness BMH further testified that Kalimba subsequently told the assailants at Nyagatare's house to spare his children, stating "we have just killed their father".[425]

210. In assessing the testimonies of Witnesses BMF and BMH on this point, the Trial Chamber noted:

> The testimony of the two relatives was consistent in relation to the time, location and perpetrators. They both testified that Palatin [Nyagatare] was killed on 24 April and heard Kalimba admitting to being involved in the killing. The Chamber recalls that the witnesses were personally acquainted with Kalimba, and that Witness BMF enjoyed his protection […]. It is also clear that Palatin was killed at a roadblock in the area […].[426]

211. The Appeals Chamber recalls that a person in a position of authority may incur responsibility for ordering another person to commit an offence[427] if the person who received the order subsequently commits the offence. Responsibility is also incurred when an individual in a position of authority orders an act or

---

[412] Trial Judgement, para. 203.
[413] Trial Judgement, paras. 540, 557, 560.
[414] Notice of Appeal, para. 140; Appellant's Brief, para. 181; Brief in Reply, para. 33.
[415] Notice of Appeal, para. 135; Appellant's Brief, para. 181.
[416] Notice of Appeal, paras. 136, 137; Appellant's Brief, para. 181.
[417] Appellant's Brief, para. 181.
[418] Appellant's Brief, para. 183.
[419] Respondent's Brief, paras. 123, 124.
[420] Respondent's Brief, para. 123.
[421] Respondent's Brief, para. 123.
[422] Trial Judgement, paras. 200, 201.
[423] T. 18 January 2006 p. 31; Trial Judgement, para. 200.
[424] Trial Judgement, para. 201.
[425] Trial Judgement, para. 201.
[426] Trial Judgement, para. 202.
[427] *Nahimana et al.* Appeal Judgement, para. 481. *See also Galiü* Appeal Judgement, para. 176; *Ntagerura et al.* Appeal Judgement, para. 365; *Kordiü and Ýerkez* Appeal Judgement, paras. 28, 29.

omission with the awareness of the substantial likelihood that a crime will be committed in the execution of that order, and if that crime is committed by the person who received the order.[428] No formal superior-subordinate relationship between the accused and the perpetrator is required; it is sufficient that there is proof of some position of authority on the part of the accused that would compel the perpetrator to commit a crime pursuant to the accused's order.[429]

212. The Appeals Chamber notes that, contrary to the Appellant's contention, the Prosecution was not compelled to prove that the Appellant gave the specific order to kill Nyagatare. However, the Appeals Chamber is not satisfied, in the circumstances of the case, that the elements of the mode of responsibility of ordering were established beyond reasonable doubt. While the evidence demonstrates that Kalimba was involved in the murder of Nyagatare, a relatively long time lapsed between the Appellant's general order to kill Tutsis and the killing of Nyagatare, and no clear link has been established between the order and the evidence relating to the murder. The Appeals Chamber finds therefore that no reasonable trier of fact could have found that the only reasonable conclusion available from the circumstantial hearsay evidence of Witnesses BMF and BMH was that Nyagatare was killed as a result of the Appellant's general order to kill Tutsis in Nyamirambo. [page 58]

213. Accordingly, this sub-ground of appeal is granted.

I. Conclusion

214. The Appeals Chamber grants the Fifth Ground of Appeal in part and reverses the Appellant's convictions for ordering genocide and extermination and murder as crimes against humanity, based on the alleged murders of Kahabaye, Ndingutse, and Nyagatare. [page 59]

VII. ALLEGED ERRORS RELATING TO THE KILLING OF TUTSIS IN NTARAMA (GROUND OF APPEAL 6)

215. The Trial Chamber found that at a meeting at Ntarama sector office on 14 April 1994, the Appellant promised to provide security by bringing soldiers to protect the refugees.[430] It further found that on 15 April 1994, the Appellant encouraged a group of *Interahamwe* and soldiers to attack the refugees at the Ntarama Church instead of providing the security he had promised.[431] Several hundred Tutsis were killed during the attack.[432] Based on these findings, the Trial Chamber found that the Appellant "substantially contributed" to the attack and thus instigated genocide.[433] Additionally, the Trial Chamber found that the Appellant was present during the attack and that he participated in it by shooting, thus committing genocide.[434] Based on these findings, the Trial Chamber also found that the Appellant instigated and committed extermination as a crime against humanity,[435] and instigated murder as a crime against humanity.[436]

216. The Appellant challenges these findings and contends that the Trial Chamber committed errors of fact and law in reaching them.[437] He submits that the Trial Chamber erred in its assessment of the evidence and that it should have found that the allegation that he was present and participated in the attack at the Ntarama Church was "pure fabrication".[438] The Appellant claims that the Trial Chamber's findings are "unreasonable"[439] and that, at the very least, there is reasonable doubt as to his participation in this attack.[440] The Prosecution

---

[428] *Nahimana et al.* Appeal Judgement, para. 481. *See also Galiü* Appeal Judgement, paras. 152, 157; *Kordiü and yerkez* Appeal Judgement, para. 30; *Blaškić* Appeal Judgement, para. 42.
[429] *Semanza* Appeal Judgement, para. 361.
[430] Trial Judgement, paras. 246-254.
[431] Trial Judgement, paras. 292-315.
[432] Trial Judgement, para. 315.
[433] Trial Judgement, paras. 541-544.
[434] Trial Judgement, para. 543.
[435] Trial Judgement, paras. 554, 557.
[436] Trial Judgement, para. 560.
[437] Notice of Appeal, paras. 141-179; Appellant's Brief, paras. 185-225.
[438] Appellant's Brief, paras. 188-225, sp. para. 211.
[439] Appellant's Brief, para. 191.
[440] Appellant's Brief, para. 211.

responds that this ground of appeal has no merit and should be summarily dismissed.[441] The Appeals Chamber will consider the Appellant's specific contentions in turn.[442]

A. Alleged Errors in the Assessment of Prosecution Evidence

217. The Appellant submits that the Trial Chamber erred in relying on witnesses who lied.[443] He also submits that the Trial Chamber erred by admitting testimonies of Prosecution witnesses who **[page 60]** colluded among themselves to implicate him,[444] and that the inconsistencies in the evidence of the Prosecution witnesses raise reasonable doubt as to his involvement in the attack on the Ntarama Church on 15 April 1994.[445]

1. Alleged Error in Relying on Prosecution Witnesses Who Lied

218. The Appellant argues that Prosecution Witnesses BMI and BMK lied and that the Trial Chamber erred in explaining or accepting inconsistencies in their testimonies.[446]

(a) Witness BMI

219. Witness BMI testified that on 15 April 1994, the Appellant, in the company of soldiers, *gendarmes*, and *Interahamwe*, attacked the Ntarama Church.[447] The witness described the Appellant as a "commander" who directed the attackers.[448] The Trial Chamber accepted Witness BMI's evidence as to the Appellant's involvement in the attack on the Ntarama Church.[449] The Trial Chamber considered that there were similarities between Witness BMI's account of the events and the accounts of the three other Prosecution Witnesses BMJ, BML, and BMK who testified about this attack.[450]

220. The Appellant contends that Witness BMI lied[451] and claims that the Trial Chamber provided an explanation for Witness BMI's "lies" without any basis in the evidence.[452]

221. The Prosecution responds that even if the Trial Chamber did find that it had not been proved beyond reasonable doubt that, as testified by Witness BMI, the Appellant issued, on 9 April 1994, an order to kill Tutsis and loot their property, the Trial Chamber had discretion to accept other aspects of the witness's evidence.[453]

222. The Appellant argues that the Trial Chamber did not believe Witness BMI when he testified that, at a meeting in Gatoro *cellule* on 9 April 1994, the Appellant ordered the killing of Tutsis and the looting of their property.[454] In this regard, the Trial Chamber stated that "Witness BMI was not clear" in that he testified not only to the alleged meeting in April 1994 but also to an event in 1992 **[page 61]** and that his "testimony also raised other issues".[455] The Trial Chamber stated that even if some of the discrepancies in his testimony could be ascribed to the fact that he was not accustomed to court proceedings and that he had communication problems,[456] the witness's seeming confusion of two different meetings remained a matter of concern.[457] The

---

[441] Respondent's Brief, para. 127.
[442] The Appellant's contention that his alibi raised a reasonable doubt will be considered below in Chapter IX.
[443] Appellant's Brief, para. 191.
[444] Appellant's Brief, paras. 200-205.
[445] Appellant's Brief, para. 209; AT. 28 August 2008 pp. 25, 26. The Appellant asserts that the Trial Chamber examined these inconsistencies at paragraphs 293 to 303 of the Trial Judgement. Appellant's Brief, para. 209.
[446] Appellant's Brief, paras. 188, 196-199.
[447] Trial Judgement, paras. 269-274, summarizing Witness BMI's testimony.
[448] Trial Judgement, para. 272.
[449] Trial Judgement, para. 303.
[450] Trial Judgement, para. 294.
[451] Appellant's Brief, para. 196.
[452] Appellant's Brief, para. 198, referring to Trial Judgement, para. 229.
[453] Respondent's Brief, para. 129.
[454] Appellant's Brief, para. 196; Corrigendum to the Appellant's Brief, para. 2.
[455] Trial Judgement, para. 228.
[456] Trial Judgement, para. 229.
[457] Trial Judgement, para. 229.

Trial Chamber took into account the lack of corroborating evidence and concluded that the allegation relating to the meeting in Gatoro *cellule* had not been proved beyond reasonable doubt.[458]

223. The Trial Chamber's reasoning does not suggest that it found Witness BMI to be dishonest or to otherwise lack credibility. Rather, it suggests that the Trial Chamber considered that the substance of the witness's evidence, particularly since he was the only witness to testify about the alleged meeting in Gatoro *cellule*, did not support a finding beyond reasonable doubt in relation to this allegation. This finding did not preclude the Trial Chamber from considering and relying on Witness BMI's evidence in relation to other allegations. As already recalled, it is not unreasonable for a Trial Chamber to accept some parts of a witness's testimony while rejecting others.[459] Consequently, the Appellant's argument is rejected.

224. The Appellant further argues that there is a discrepancy between Witness BMI's prior statement of 4 May 2001[460] and his testimony at trial in relation to the burning down of his house.[461] The Appeals Chamber notes that the evidence at trial was that the witness discovered that his house was burned down on 14 April 1994.[462] The witness's prior statement of 4 May 2001 indicates that his house was burned down on 8 April 1994.[463] The Appellant also argues that Witness BMI denied meeting a member of the Prosecution team after 18 January 2006, yet the Prosecution's will-say statements indicate that the witness informed the Prosecution on 23 January 2006 and 26 January 2006 that there were errors in his written statement.[464] A review of the transcripts indicates that, under cross-examination, the witness testified that he arrived in Arusha on 16 January 2006 and met the Prosecution on 18 January 2006 and that he did not meet with the Prosecution on 23 or 26 January 2006.[465]

225. Having observed Witness BMI in court, the Trial Chamber considered that the witness was not accustomed to court proceedings and had problems communicating, and that some **[page 62]** inconsistencies could be attributed to this.[466] The Trial Chamber expressly noted the inconsistencies relating to the date Witness BMI's house was burned down and the date when he met with the Prosecution prior to his testimony.[467] The Appeals Chamber recalls that it falls within the Trial Chamber's discretion to determine whether an inconsistency is sufficient to cast doubt on a witness's credibility.[468] The Appellant's arguments fail to show that the Trial Chamber erred in assessing Witness BMI's credibility and in relying on his evidence.

(b) Witness BMK

226. Witness BMK testified that, on 14 April 1994, he attended a meeting chaired by the Appellant at the Ntarama sector office.[469] He stated that the Appellant opened the meeting by announcing the death of the President.[470] The witness also stated that the Appellant addressed the Tutsis at the meeting and claimed that they were the ones who killed the President and that they were "going to pay for that".[471] Witness BMK further testified that, on 15 April 1994, the Appellant, in the company of *Interahamwe* and soldiers, arrived in Ntarama sector on board one of six buses.[472] He stated that the attackers, including the Appellant, emerged

---

[458] Trial Judgement, paras. 229, 230.
[459] *See supra* para. 88.
[460] Appellant's Brief, para. 197, referring to Exhibit D19 containing Witness BMI's statement of 4 May 2001.
[461] Appellant's Brief, para. 197.
[462] Trial Judgement, paras. 227, 241.
[463] Exhibit D19A.
[464] *See* Exhibits D20, D21.
[465] T. 31 January 2006 p. 9.
[466] Trial Judgement, para. 229.
[467] Trial Judgement, para. 229, fn. 288.
[468] *Seromba* Appeal Judgement, para. 116, referring to *Rutaganda* Appeal Judgement, para. 443; *Musema* Appeal Judgement, para. 89; *Čelebići* Appeal Judgement, para. 497; *Kupreškić et al.* Appeal Judgement, para. 156.
[469] Trial Judgement, para. 237.
[470] Trial Judgement, para. 238.
[471] Trial Judgement, para. 238.
[472] Trial Judgement, para. 262.

from the buses and started to shoot at the refugees[473] who were in the vicinity of the Ntarama Church, the sector office, and the school.[474]

227. The Trial Chamber found that it had not been established beyond reasonable doubt that the Appellant threatened Tutsi refugees in a meeting at the Ntarama sector office on 14 April 1994.[475] It reasoned that a threat of this nature "would be of a dramatic character and not easy to forget" and that it was "significant" that only one of the three Prosecution witnesses who testified about this meeting, Witness BMK,[476] mentioned this threat.[477] The Trial Chamber found, nevertheless, no basis to conclude that Witness BMK lied.[478]

228. The Appellant contends that Witness BMK lied and "tried to implicate [him] falsely" in the events at the Ntarama Church.[479] In this regard, he claims that the witness also falsely testified **[page 63]** that the Appellant "threatened thousands of Tutsis" at a meeting the day before the attack on the Ntarama Church.[480]

229. The Prosecution responds that even if the Trial Chamber found that it had not been proven beyond reasonable doubt that the Appellant threatened Tutsi refugees, it did not conclude that Witness BMK's entire evidence was not credible.[481]

230. The Appeals Chamber considers that the fact that the Trial Chamber did not rely on this witness's testimony about the Appellant threatening Tutsis at this meeting does not mean that his testimony about the Appellant's involvement in the attack at the Ntarama Church on 15 April 1994 lacked credibility. As stated above, it is not unreasonable for a Trial Chamber to accept some parts of a witness's testimony while rejecting others.[482] Consequently, the Appellant has failed to show that the Trial Chamber erred in relying in part on Witness BMK's evidence.

2. Alleged Collusion by Prosecution Witnesses

231. The Appellant submits that the Trial Chamber erred in law by admitting, without corroboration, the testimonies of Prosecution Witnesses BML, BMJ, BMK, and BMI, despite having found implicitly that it was likely that there was collusion among them.[483] He asserts that these witnesses colluded to implicate him.[484] The Appellant argues that there were details in the witnesses' testimonies that they would not have remembered without discussing them with each other, particularly since they testified to an event which had occurred twelve years earlier.[485] The Appellant states that all four witnesses testified that, on 15 April 1994, buses with soldiers and *Interahamwe* arrived in Ntarama and that the Appellant alighted from the second bus carrying a long rifle and wearing a long coat.[486] He submits that Witnesses BML and BMJ were interviewed on the same day and at the same location, and that on another occasion Witnesses BMI and BMK were also interviewed on the same day and at the same location.[487] The Appellant also claims that Witnesses BMJ and BML made similar "corrections" to their statements, as well as similar "mistakes",[488] and that there were striking similarities in the descriptions they provided.[489] He argues that the discrepancy in the testimonies of the four witnesses with regard to their "mutual **[page 64]** acquaintances" is "suspicious" and asserts that Witness BMI admitted that they all stayed in the same witness protection house while in Arusha and even

---

[473] Trial Judgement, para. 263.
[474] Trial Judgement, para. 262.
[475] Trial Judgement, para. 253.
[476] *See* Trial Judgement, para. 253.
[477] Trial Judgement, para. 253.
[478] Trial Judgement, para. 307.
[479] Appellant's Brief, para. 199.
[480] Appellant's Brief, para. 199; AT. 28 August 2008 p. 26.
[481] Respondent's Brief, para. 129.
[482] *See supra* para. 88.
[483] Appellant's Brief, paras. 200, 224.
[484] Appellant's Brief, paras. 204, 205.
[485] Appellant's Brief, para. 202.
[486] Appellant's Brief, para. 202.
[487] Appellant's Brief, para. 195.
[488] Appellant's Brief, para. 201. The Appellant claims that both witnesses initially stated that Bizimana was a school director and later changed their statements to say that he was a prison director.
[489] Appellant's Brief, para. 205.

shared their meals.[490] The Appellant submits that the only rational conclusion that could be drawn from this is that the witnesses had discussed the events and that their attempt to deny this fact should have urged the Trial Chamber to dismiss their testimonies in their entirety.[491]

232. The Appellant also submits that paragraphs 250 and 307 of the Trial Judgement contain contradictory findings.[492] He argues that in paragraph 250 of the Trial Judgement, the Trial Chamber did not exclude that there might have been collusion, while in paragraph 307 of the Trial Judgement, the Trial Chamber found no basis for the Defence contention that the witnesses discussed the events before testifying.[493]

233. The Prosecution responds that the Trial Chamber properly dismissed, as "unfounded", the Appellant's allegation of collusion.[494] It submits that the Appellant's arguments do not show an error on the part of the Trial Chamber[495] and argues that the fact that there were similarities in the descriptions of the events by Witnesses BMK, BMJ, BML, and BMI does not in itself amount to collusion.[496]

234. The Appeals Chamber notes that collusion can be defined as an agreement, usually secret, between two or more persons for a fraudulent, unlawful, or deceitful purpose.[497] If an agreement between witnesses for the purpose of untruthfully incriminating an accused were indeed established, their evidence would have to be excluded pursuant to Rule 95 of the Rules.[498] In the present instance, the Trial Chamber rejected the possibility of collusion between the four **[page 65]** Prosecution witnesses testifying about the events in Ntarama.[499] The Trial Chamber held that it could not "exclude that the witnesses may have discussed the events of 1994, in spite of [their] general denials of having done so".[500] It took into account that two of the witnesses gave their respective statements to investigators on the same day at the same place and that the other two gave their statements on another day at the same location.[501] It also considered that all four witnesses lived in the same area, travelled together to Arusha in connection with the trial, and had their meals together in the safe house.[502] However, the Trial Chamber reasoned that the differences in the testimonies of the four witnesses did not support the allegation of collusion[503] and concluded that there was no basis to find that they colluded to untruthfully implicate the Appellant.[504] The Appellant has failed to show that the Trial Chamber erred in reaching this conclusion.

235. Furthermore, the Appeals Chamber is not convinced by the Appellant's claim that the Trial Chamber contradicted itself at paragraphs 250 and 307 of the Trial Judgement. The Trial Chamber consistently stated in both paragraphs that it did not exclude the possibility that the witnesses may have jointly discussed the

---

[490] Appellant's Brief, para. 203.
[491] Appellant's Brief, para. 204.
[492] Notice of Appeal, paras. 169, 170.
[493] Notice of Appeal, paras. 169, 170.
[494] Respondent's Brief, paras. 132-137.
[495] Respondent's Brief, para. 132.
[496] Respondent's Brief, para. 133.
[497] The Appeals Chamber notes that Black's Law Dictionary, 6th Edition defines collusion as "[a]n agreement between two or more persons to defraud a person of his rights by the forms of law, or to obtain an object forbidden by law. It implies the existence of fraud of some kind, the employment of fraudulent means, or of unlawful means for the accomplishment of an unlawful purpose".
[498] Rule 95 of the Rules states: "No evidence shall be admissible if obtained by methods which cast substantial doubt on its reliability or if its admission is antithetical to, and would seriously damage, the integrity of the proceedings." *See, also, mutatis mutandis, Nahimana et al.* where the Appeals Chamber dismissed the testimony of a witness insofar as it was not corroborated by other credible evidence, having found that even if the evidence was "insufficient to establish with certainty that [this witness] was paid for his testimony against [the accused], it [was] nonetheless difficult to ignore this possibility, which undeniably casts doubt on the credibility of this witness." It also ruled that "if the Trial Chamber had been aware of the fact that the Prosecutor's investigator questioned the witness' moral character, suspecting him of having been involved in the subornation of other witnesses and of being prepared to testify in return for money – the Trial Chamber would have been bound to find that these matters cast serious doubt on [this witness's] credibility. Hence, like any reasonable trier of fact, it would have disregarded his testimony, or at least would have required that it be corroborated by other credible evidence." *Nahimana et al.* Appeal Judgement, para. 545.
[499] Trial Judgement, paras. 250, 308, 313.
[500] Trial Judgement, para. 250. *See also* Trial Judgement, para. 308 ("[a]s observed previously, it cannot be excluded that the witnesses may have discussed the events of 1994, either previously or in connection with travelling to Arusha or taking their meals together.").
[501] Trial Judgement, para. 250.
[502] Trial Judgement, para. 250.
[503] Trial Judgement, para. 250.
[504] Trial Judgement, para. 308.

events of 1994 but that there was insufficient basis to conclude that they colluded amongst themselves in order to untruthfully implicate the Appellant. Consequently, the Appellant's argument is rejected.

3. Alleged Inconsistencies in the Prosecution Evidence

236. The Appellant contends that the inconsistencies in the evidence of Witnesses BMK, BML, BMI, and BMJ raise a reasonable doubt as to his alleged involvement in the attack on the Ntarama Church on 15 April 1994[505] and that the Trial Chamber down-played these inconsistencies by finding explanations for them.[506] He also suggests that the forensic report[507] tendered by the Prosecution as well as the Trial Chamber's observations during its site visit are inconsistent with the evidence of the Prosecution witnesses.[508] Also in this regard, he claims that Prosecution Witness BME testified that the Appellant was not present in Ntarama in the morning of 15 April 1994, but rather that he was in Nyamirambo.[509] He also contends that the site visit showed, with respect to **[page 66]** Ntarama, "that it was impossible to see the school from the Church [and] that the rear of the Church was more damaged than the front".[510] The Appellant submits that this "could mean that the attackers came from the hill rather than from the road".[511] The Appellant further contends that since "the doors of ONATRACOM buses opened to the right and not to the left, as asserted by the witnesses suspected of collusion" if the buses were coming from Kigali, the Prosecution witnesses who testified on the circumstances of the attack could not have seen the people who were alighting from them.[512]

237. The Prosecution responds that the differences and variations in the testimonies of these witnesses can be reasonably explained.[513] It submits that the Appellant has not demonstrated that there are no reasonable explanations to justify these discrepancies and variations.[514]

238. The Appeals Chamber recalls that a Trial Chamber, as the primary trier of fact, has the responsibility to consider inconsistencies that may arise among the testimonies of witnesses.[515] In undertaking this responsibility, the Trial Chamber is required to consider any explanations offered for these inconsistencies when weighing the probative value of the evidence.[516] In the present case, the Appellant does not specify any of the alleged inconsistencies, but refers generally to paragraphs 293 to 303 of the Trial Judgement where, he notes, the Trial Chamber examined the inconsistencies.[517] The Trial Chamber held that the four Prosecution witnesses described the attack similarly in terms of location, time, attackers, mode of transport, and the Appellant's presence.[518] It considered that there were variations in the evidence in relation to the Appellant allegedly addressing the attackers, but held that these variations did not affect the credibility of the witnesses.[519] The Trial Chamber reasoned that these witnesses may not have heard some parts of the Appellant's "alleged statement because their positions were different" and also because "their memories may vary, due to the lapse of time since the event".[520] The Appeals Chamber accepts that different people may see and hear things differently from different vantage points.[521] Consequently, the Appeals Chamber is not satisfied that the Appellant has demonstrated that the Trial Chamber's finding is unreasonable. **[page 67]**

239. With regard to the Appellant's contention that it was impossible to see the Ntarama school from the Ntarama Church, the Appeals Chamber notes that the Appellant is merely reiterating an argument which he

---

[505] Appellant's Brief, para. 209. The Appellant asserts that the Trial Chamber examined these inconsistencies at paragraphs 293 to 303 of the Trial Judgement.
[506] Notice of Appeal, paras. 150, 167.
[507] Exhibit P30.
[508] Appellant's Brief, paras. 43, 207.
[509] Appellant's Brief, para. 210.
[510] Appellant's Brief, para. 43.
[511] Appellant's Brief, para. 43.
[512] Appellant's Brief, para. 43.
[513] Respondent's Brief, para. 135.
[514] Respondent's Brief, para. 135.
[515] *Simba* Appeal Judgement, para. 103.
[516] *Muhimana* Appeal Judgement, para. 58; *Niyitegeka* Appeal Judgement, para. 96.
[517] Appellant's Brief, para. 209.
[518] Trial Judgement, para. 294.
[519] Trial Judgement, para. 295.
[520] Trial Judgement, para. 295.
[521] *See Gacumbitsi* Appeal Judgement, para. 80, referring to *Niyitegeka* Appeal Judgement, para. 142.

already presented at trial and which was fully addressed in the Trial Judgement. The Defence challenged Witness BMK's testimony, who stated that, from his vantage point, somewhere in the valley, below the Ntarama school, he saw the Appellant attacking the Ntarama Church on the morning of 15 April 1994.[522] The Trial Chamber, in assessing the credibility of Witness BMK, considered the evidence of Defence Witnesses ZAC and NKZ to the effect that it was impossible to see the school from the church because eucalyptus trees and banana plantations were blocking the view.[523] The Trial Chamber concluded that Witness BMK was credible on this point. In reaching this conclusion, the Trial Chamber took into account the following elements: Witness ZAC was not in a position to assess the visibility conditions; Witness BMK, who "was at a considerable distance from the school, towards the church", stated that while there was an eucalyptus forest nearby, at his location the land was free of vegetation.[524] The Appeals Chamber finds that the Appellant has failed to show how the Trial Chamber erred in its assessment of Witness BMK's testimony on this point. The Appeals Chamber defers to the finding of the Trial Chamber and notes that it legitimately exercised its discretion in determining which version of the events relating to the attack on the Ntarama Church was credible.[525]

240. With respect to his argument that the forensic report tendered as a Prosecution exhibit is inconsistent with other Prosecution evidence in relation to the attack on the Ntarama Church,[526] the Appellant asserts that the forensic report indicates that the weapons found at the site were a machete, a knife, several clubs, one lance, and one broken arrow; that the assault took place through holes made below the Church windows with the massacre taking place in the middle of the Church; and that most of the victims were killed with machetes or blows to the head.[527] The Appellant also states that it is evident from the site visit and the photographs in the forensic report that the attackers entered the Church through the front, which faced the hill.[528] He claims that this scenario is in conformity with the Defence evidence that the attack commenced on Kinkwi Hill and that the Tutsis were chased to the Ntarama Church, and that it is inconsistent with the Prosecution's evidence that the attackers arrived at the Church in buses.[529] **[page 68]**

241. The Prosecution responds that the forensic report is not conclusive regarding the weapons that were used by the attackers.[530]

242. The Trial Chamber is primarily responsible for assessing and weighing evidence presented at trial and it is incumbent on the Trial Chamber to take an approach it considers most appropriate in this regard.[531] In the present case, the Trial Chamber had the discretion to consider the forensic report in its assessment of the totality of the evidence. While the Trial Chamber acknowledged the existence of the forensic report,[532] it only referred to it in relation to its finding that, at Ntarama, a large number of refugees were killed.[533] Although certain evidence may not have been referred to by a Trial Chamber, in the particular circumstances of a given case it may nevertheless be reasonable to assume that the Trial Chamber took it into account.[534]

243. The Appeals Chamber agrees with the Prosecution's submission that the forensic report is not conclusive regarding the weapons that were used by the attackers, and that the forensic doctors identified the causes of death only from the skulls they had analyzed.[535] The Appeals Chamber further notes that the forensic report does not *per se* contradict the Trial Chamber's findings, based on Prosecution evidence, that the attackers of Ntarama Church used guns, traditional weapons and grenades.[536] Indeed, the forensic report

---

[522] Trial Judgement para. 305; T. 17 August 2006 p. 15.
[523] Trial Judgement, para. 305.
[524] Trial Judgement, para. 305.
[525] *See supra* para. 10.
[526] Appellant's Brief, paras. 192-194, 207, 208.
[527] Appellant's Brief, para. 194.
[528] Appellant's Brief, para. 207.
[529] Appellant's Brief, para. 207.
[530] Respondent's Brief, para. 140.
[531] *Rutaganda* Appeal Judgement, para. 188.
[532] Trial Judgement, paras. 256, 292, fn. 354.
[533] Trial Judgement, paras. 257-315, sp. 292, fn. 354.
[534] *Simba* Appeal Judgement, para. 152, referring to *Musema* Appeal Judgement, para. 19.
[535] Respondent's Brief, para. 140.
[536] Trial Judgement, para. 292; Forensic Report, p. 15.

acknowledges that the number of bodies examined is appreciably less than the number of people killed.[537] The forensic report also notes the existence of the impact of shrapnel "on the corner of the building".[538] In these circumstances, the Appeals Chamber considers that the Appellant has failed to demonstrate that the Trial Chamber erroneously failed to consider any inconsistency in the Prosecution's evidence arising from the forensic report.

244. With regard to the claim that the site visit and the photographs in the forensic report show that the attack commenced on Kinkwi Hill and that the Tutsis were chased to the Ntarama Church is inconsistent with the Prosecution's evidence that the attackers arrived at the church in buses, the Appeals Chamber observes that the Trial Chamber concluded that several hundred attackers participated in the attack against Ntarama Church which started at 10.00 a.m. on 15 April 1994 and that several hundred Tutsis were killed during the attack.[539] The Appeals Chamber notes that contrary to the Appellant's contention, the forensic report does not necessarily show that the attack started on Kinkwi Hill. Furthermore, the fact that the attackers might have come from a surrounding **[page 69]** hill does not necessarily contradict the Trial Chamber's findings that the Appellant and other assailants came in buses and that the Appellant "encouraged a group of *Interahamwe* and soldiers to hurry up and attack the refugees" assembled in the church.[540] Finally, the Appeals Chamber finds that since the question at stake is related to the chronology of the attack the Appellant could not have been prejudiced by the absence of a record of the site visit on this point.

245. The Appellant claims that Witness BME testified that the Appellant was not in Ntarama but rather in Nyamirambo on the morning of 15 April 1994.[541] He further contends that in finding that the Appellant was at Ntarama on 15 July 1994, the Trial Chamber failed "to address the conflicting evidence by Witness BME, who allege[d] that on 15 April 1994, between 9 a.m. and 10 a.m., Karera was instead in Nyamirambo".[542] The Appellant avers that, if believed, this testimony conflicts with the Prosecution's allegation that he was in Ntarama on the same day.[543]

246. The Appellant merely reiterates an argument that he presented at trial and that the Trial Chamber addressed and dismissed.[544] He does not show how the Trial Chamber erred in doing so. The Appeals Chamber notes that Witness BME's testimony that the Appellant was at Nyamirambo between 9.00 a.m. and 10.00 a.m.[545] might conflict with the testimonies of Prosecution Witnesses BMK and BMI placing the Appellant at the Ntarama Church on the same day at or around 10.00 a.m.[546] However, while the Trial Chamber found Witness BME credible with regard to her testimony that she saw the Appellant instructing a large crowd to kill Tutsis and destroy their houses,[547] it found it "likely that Witness BME erred regarding the precise date of the event, in view of her traumatic situation"[548] and thus refrained from entering any specific finding as to the date and time of that event based on her testimony. In these circumstances, it was within the discretion of the Trial Chamber to consider that Witness BME's testimony that the Appellant was in Nyamirambo on 15 April 1994 did not raise any reasonable doubt as to his presence in Ntarama on the same day. The Appellant has therefore failed to show how the Trial Chamber erred in not considering that Witness BME's evidence raised a reasonable doubt as to his involvement in the attack on the Ntarama Church on 15 April 1994.

247. Accordingly, the Appeals Chamber dismisses this sub-ground of appeal. **[page 70]**

---

[537] Respondent's Brief, para. 140.
[538] Exhibit P30.
[539] Trial Judgement, paras. 292, 315.
[540] Trial Judgement, para. 315.
[541] Appellant's Brief, para. 210.
[542] Brief in Reply, para. 54.
[543] Appellant's Brief, para. 111.
[544] *See* Trial Judgement, para. 160, referring to Defence Closing Brief, para. 229.
[545] *See* Trial Judgement, para. 147.
[546] *See* Trial Judgement, paras. 262, 269.
[547] Trial Judgement, paras. 147, 159.
[548] Trial Judgement, para. 160.

B. Alleged Errors in the Assessment of Defence Evidence

248. The Appellant contends that the evidence presented by the Defence, through Witnesses NKZ, ZIH, ZAC, MZN, and DSM, renders the Trial Chamber's findings unreasonable.[549] He provides his account of the testimonies of these five witnesses,[550] but only makes specific arguments in relation to Witnesses NKZ, ZIH, and ZAC.[551] The Appellant argues that the Trial Chamber erred in law by failing to consider "a reasonable probability" offered by his alibi that he was not present at the attack at the Ntarama Church[552] and by failing to accept the corroborating testimonies of the Defence witnesses who testified that he did not participate in this attack.[553] He asserts that this evidence raises a reasonable doubt in the Prosecution's case[554] and that the Trial Chamber erred in finding that he participated in the attack in view of the inconsistencies in the testimonies of the Prosecution witnesses when weighed against the probative value of the Defence evidence.[555]

249. The Prosecution responds that the Appellant's submissions should fail as they are insufficient to call into question the Trial Chamber's approach in assessing the Defence evidence or the reasonableness of the impugned findings.[556]

250. Witnesses NKZ and ZIH both testified that they participated in the attack and did not see the Appellant.[557] The Appellant challenges the Trial Chamber's observation that it was possible for him to be present without Witnesses NKZ and ZIH seeing him.[558] The Appeals Chamber notes that in assessing the evidence of Witness NKZ, the Trial Chamber took into account that the witness was not certain about the date of the attack but learned about it from others, that he had seen the Appellant only once before, when the Appellant was *bourgmestre* of Nyarugenge commune, and that it was not clear when in this period (from 1975 to 1990) the witness had seen him.[559] The Trial **[page 71]** Chamber also took into account that the witness was not present when the attack commenced and would not therefore have observed the Appellant's arrival.[560] Furthermore, the witness did not observe any buses, which contradicts the consistent evidence of four Prosecution witnesses.[561] The Trial Chamber concluded that Witness NKZ's evidence had "limited weight".[562]562

251. In relation to Witness ZIH, the Trial Chamber took into account that a friend had pointed out the Appellant to the witness when the Appellant was *bourgmestre* and that between 1978 and 1994 the witness had seen the Appellant on only three occasions.[563] The Trial Chamber considered that under these circumstances, the witness's ability to recognize the Appellant in the midst of "a high number of persons running helter-skelter" would be limited and that the witness's assumption that Thaddée Sebuhindo, who by

---

[549] Appellant's Brief, paras. 212-219.
[550] Appellant's Brief, paras. 213-219. The Appellant asserts *inter alia* that Witness NKZ, who participated in the attack, testified that he did not see the Appellant and that the Appellant was not mentioned in the *Gacaca* hearings in relation to the attack; Witness ZIH, who participated in the attack, did not see the Appellant and also did not hear that the Appellant was involved in the attack when he attended the *Gacaca* hearings; Witness ZAC, who participated in a "committee similar to that of the *Gacaca* Courts" (italics added) as well as in the *Gacaca* hearings and who heard twenty prisoners testify about the Ntarama attacks, including confessions of Witnesses NKZ and ZIH, did not hear the Appellant's name mentioned in relation to this attack until recently when four persons returning from Arusha testified to his involvement; Witness MZN, a soldier who was acquitted of genocide, testified that he did not hear that the Appellant was involved in the attack; and Witness DSM, a police office, did not hear of the Appellant being involved in the attack.
[551] Appellant's Brief, paras. 212-219.
[552] The Appellant's submissions concerning alibi will be addressed below in Chapter IX.
[553] Appellant's Brief, para. 223.
[554] Appellant's Brief, para. 223.
[555] Notice of Appeal, para. 177.
[556] Respondent's Brief, para. 148.
[557] Trial Judgement, paras. 279, 282, 283, 286.
[558] Appellant's Brief, para. 221, referring to Trial Judgement, para. 309.
[559] Trial Judgement, para. 309.
[560] Trial Judgement, para. 309.
[561] Trial Judgement, para. 309.
[562] Trial Judgement, para. 309.
[563] Trial Judgement, para. 310.

the witness's account led the attack,[564] would have pointed out the Appellant to the witness was speculative.[565] The Trial Chamber concluded that the witness's evidence had limited reliability.[566]

252. It is within a Trial Chamber's discretion to accept or reject a witness's testimony after seeing the witness testify and observing him or her under cross-examination.[567] The Appellant has failed to show that the Trial Chamber erred in assigning limited weight to the evidence of Witnesses NKZ and ZIH.

253. In relation to Witness ZAC, the Appellant argues that the Trial Chamber's assessment of this witness's evidence demonstrated its "biased manner" when it reasoned that the evidence was of limited significance because it was hearsay.[568] Witness ZAC testified that he was a prisoner who chaired the "Urumali committee" and listened to the confessions made by Witnesses NKZ and ZIH and three other prisoners relating to the Ntarama attacks.[569] In addition, the witness listened to approximately twenty civilian prisoners describe the Ntarama attacks at the *Gacaca* proceedings and, according to him, none of them mentioned the Appellant.[570] The witness asserted that it was only in the *Gacaca* proceedings in 2006, and after having testified before the Tribunal, that four survivors indicated that the Appellant was present at the attacks in Ntarama.[571] The Trial Chamber **[page 72]** assessed the evidence of Witness ZAC and concluded that it had "limited significance" because it was "hearsay" evidence.[572]

254. The Appeals Chamber notes the Appellant's argument concerning bias on behalf of the Trial Chamber Judges. As stated in previous judgements of the Appeals Chambers of this Tribunal and the ICTY, it is for the appealing party alleging bias to rebut the presumption of impartiality enjoyed by Judges of the Tribunals.[573] In this respect, the Appeals Chamber consistently held that there is "a high threshold to reach in order to rebut the presumption of impartiality" that attaches to a Judge or a Tribunal.[574]

255. In support of his contention that the Trial Chamber was biased, the Appellant argues that the Trial Chamber did not hesitate to convict him "solely on questionable hearsay evidence, and sometimes by triple hearsay, but was not swayed by the honest and consistent testimony of an individual like Witness ZAC".[575] The Appellant refers to paragraphs 162, 167, 168,[576] and 192 to 194 of the Trial Judgement in support of his argument.[577]

256. Hearsay evidence is admissible if it has probative value, and the Trial Chamber has the discretion to consider this evidence.[578] In paragraph 162 of the Trial Judgement, the Trial Chamber expressed its satisfaction that Prosecution Witnesses BMG, BMF, and BMH gave truthful accounts of what they had observed. Witnesses BMG, BMF, and BMH testified to what they had heard the Appellant say, but their testimonies must be distinguished from Witness ZAC's testimony, which was based on what he heard from third parties. These three witnesses also provided their respective observations of what the Appellant was doing and whom he was addressing. In these circumstances, it was reasonable for the Trial Chamber to prefer the direct evidence of Witnesses BMG, BMF, and BMH to the hearsay evidence of Witness ZAC.

257. In view of the above, the Appeals Chamber finds that the Appellant has failed to demonstrate bias on the part of the Trial Chamber as a result of its assessment of Witness ZAC's evidence. The Appellant has also not shown that a reasonable trier of fact would have found that the evidence of Defence witnesses raised

---

[564] Trial Judgement, para. 283.
[565] Trial Judgement, para. 310.
[566] Trial Judgement, para. 310.
[567] *Seromba* Appeal Judgement, para. 116, referring to *Akayesu* Appeal Judgement, para. 147.
[568] Appellant's Brief, para. 222.
[569] Trial Judgement, para. 287.
[570] Trial Judgement, para. 287.
[571] Trial Judgement, para. 288.
[572] Trial Judgement, para. 312.
[573] See e.g. *Niyitegeka* Appeal Judgement, para. 45; *Rutaganda* Appeal Judgement, paras. 39-125.
[574] *Nahimana et al.* Appeal Judgement, paras. 47-90. See also *Furundžija* Appeal Judgement, para. 197.
[575] Appellant's Brief, para. 222.
[576] In paragraph 168 of the Trial Judgement, the Trial Chamber found that the Appellant had ordered the killing of Tutsis and the destruction of their houses and that the policemen guarding the Appellant's house had destroyed the houses of Kahabaye and Dix. This finding has no direct significance to the Appellant's argument.
[577] Appellant's Brief, para. 222.
[578] See *supra* para. 39.

reasonable doubt about the Appellant's participation in the attack at the Ntarama Church and that the Trial Chamber's finding is unreasonable. The Appeals Chamber therefore dismisses this sub-ground of appeal. **[page 73]**

C. Conclusion

258. The Appeals Chamber finds that the Appellant has failed to demonstrate any error in the Trial Chamber's findings in relation to his participation in the meeting at the Ntarama sector office on 14 April 1994 and his participation in an attack at the Ntarama Church on 15 April 1994. Accordingly, this ground of appeal is dismissed in its entirety. **[page 74]**

VIII. ALLEGED ERRORS RELATING TO THE KILLING OF TUTSIS IN RUSHASHI COMMUNE (GROUNDS OF APPEAL 1 AND 7 AND GROUND OF APPEAL 2, IN PART)

259. The Trial Chamber found that many Tutsis were killed in Rushashi commune starting on 7 April 1994.[579] The Trial Chamber found that the Appellant was aware that, from that date, roadblocks had been set up in Rushashi commune where Tutsis were killed.[580] The Trial Chamber also found that between April and June 1994, the Appellant held meetings in Rushashi commune, where he raised money for weapons, encouraged youths to join the *Interahamwe*, and urged the commission of crimes against Tutsis.[581] The Trial Chamber found that in April or May 1994, the Appellant brought more than twenty guns to the Rushashi commune office, which were subsequently used to kill Tutsis at roadblocks.[582] Based on these findings, the Trial Chamber convicted the Appellant, pursuant to Article 6(1) of the Statute, for instigating and aiding and abetting genocide and extermination as a crime against humanity.[583]

260. The Trial Chamber also found that in April or May 1994, at a roadblock in Rushashi commune, the Appellant instigated the killing of Théoneste Gakuru.[584] Based on this finding, the Trial Chamber convicted the Appellant, pursuant to Article 6(1) of the Statute, for instigating and aiding and abetting murder as a crime against humanity.[585]

261. The Appellant raises several challenges to the Trial Chamber's findings which the Appeals Chamber addresses in turn.

A. Alleged Errors relating to Roadblocks

262. The Trial Chamber found that

> several roadblocks, at least four, were established in Rushashi commune following the President's death on or about 7 April 1994. Civilians, including *Interahamwe*, were amongst those who manned them. Tutsis were targeted at the roadblocks. The Chamber is satisfied that Karera visited Rushashi briefly between 7 and 10 April and that he was fully aware that roadblocks existed there and that Tutsi were being killed at them from April onwards.[586]
> **[page 75]**

In making this finding, the Trial Chamber relied on Prosecution Witnesses BMR, BMM, BMO, and BMB.[587] While the Trial Chamber did not rely solely on the aforementioned finding to enter a conviction against the Appellant, it considered this finding in holding that the Appellant's conduct during the meetings held in Rushashi between April and June 1994 amounted to instigating genocide and extermination as a crime

---

[579] Trial Judgement, para. 545, referring to the factual findings in Section II.6 of the Trial Judgement.
[580] Trial Judgement, para. 546, referring to the factual findings in Section II.6.3 of the Trial Judgement.
[581] Trial Judgement, para. 546, referring to the factual findings in Section II.6.4 of the Trial Judgement.
[582] Trial Judgement, para. 547, referring to the factual findings in Section II.6.5 of the Trial Judgement.
[583] Trial Judgement, paras. 548, 557.
[584] Trial Judgement, para. 559, referring to the factual findings in Section II.6.6 of the Trial Judgement.
[585] Trial Judgement, para. 560.
[586] Trial Judgement, para. 376. *See also* Trial Judgement, para. 546.
[587] Trial Judgement, paras. 363-376.

against humanity.[588] Similarly, the Trial Chamber's finding is relevant to its finding that he brought guns to the Rushashi commune office "which were aimed for the use at the roadblocks."[589]

263. The Appellant's main contention is that the Trial Chamber erred in preferring Prosecution evidence to Defence evidence in order to find that the Appellant was present in Rushashi before 19 April 1994 and was aware that there were roadblocks and that Tutsis were being killed at them from April onwards.[590] The Appeals Chamber will address this submission below.[591]

264. The Appellant further submits that the Trial Chamber's finding that the decision to erect roadblocks could not have been taken without consultation with senior officials at the prefecture office did not support the Trial Chamber's finding that he was aware of the existence of roadblocks before 19 April 1994.[592] The Appellant argues that he could not have been one of those "senior officials" because he had exercised no authority in Rushashi commune prior to his appointment as prefect of Kigali prefecture on 17 April 1994, and he did not have a direct link with the commune authorities.[593]

265. The Appellant also submits that the Prosecution[594] and Defence witnesses[595] presented the Trial Chamber with "two diametrically opposed versions of testimonies" regarding the killings at roadblocks.[596] According to the Prosecution witnesses, the Appellant "was indifferent to the killings at roadblocks", whereas Defence witnesses testified that he "did his best, and not without success, [page 76] to pacify the region where he was stationed".[597] The Appellant finally submits that the Trial Chamber "presumed his liability" and "accorded weight only to the evidence which supports a finding of the Appellant's liability".[598]

266. A review of the Trial Judgement reveals, however, that the Trial Chamber did not "presume his liability" or rely on its implicit finding that he was a senior official at the prefecture office to conclude that the Appellant knew about the erection of roadblocks in Rushashi prior to 19 April 1994. Instead it relied on the evidence of Prosecution Witnesses BMM, BMR, and BMO, who saw him at roadblocks.[599]

267. Accordingly, this sub-ground of appeal is dismissed.

B. Alleged Errors relating to Meetings Held in Rushashi between April and June 1994

268. The Trial Chamber found that between April and June 1994, the Appellant held several meetings in Rushashi commune, where he raised money for weapons, encouraged youths to join the *Interahamwe*, and urged the commission of crimes against Tutsis.[600] The Trial Chamber found that "[t]hese statements instigated the commission of crimes against Tutsis", that "[a]s an authority figure, Karera's encouragement would have a substantial effect in the killings which followed" and that "[h]is threats against those who did not participate in anti-Tutsi acts would be taken seriously."[601] The Trial Chamber relied on these factual

---

[588] Trial Judgement, para. 546, referring to the factual findings in Section II.6.3 of the Trial Judgement (*see* Trial Judgement, para. 376); Trial Judgement, paras. 555-557.
[589] Trial Judgement, para. 547.
[590] Notice of Appeal, paras. 188-190; Appellant's Brief, paras. 240-243. The title of this sub-ground of appeal (Notice of Appeal, p. 20, title of Section 7.1: "The Trial Chamber erred in finding that Karera was involved in setting up roadblocks at Rushashi"; Appellant's Brief, p. 42, title of Section 7.1: "The Trial Chamber erred by finding that Karera was involved in the erection of roadblocks in Rushashi") is misleading. While the title refers to alleged errors in finding that the Appellant was involved in setting up roadblocks in Rushashi, the Appellant has not developed this argument in his Appellant's Brief and, in fact, has acknowledged that the Trial Chamber made no finding to this effect. Appellant's Brief, para. 239, referring to Trial Judgement, para. 367.
[591] *See infra* Sections (B) and (C) and Chapter IX.
[592] Notice of Appeal, paras. 192, 193.
[593] Notice of Appeal, para. 192. In this regard, he recalls Witness BMR's account that the commune authorities had organized the erection of the roadblocks. Notice of Appeal, para. 192, referring to Trial Judgement, para. 327.
[594] The Appellant refers to the testimony of Prosecution Witnesses BMR, BMM, BMB, BMO, and BMN. Appellant's Brief, paras. 226-231.
[595] The Appellant refers to his own testimony as well as the testimony of Defence Witnesses YNZ, YCZ, YAH, and MZR. Appellant's Brief, paras. 232-238.
[596] Appellant's Brief, para. 240.
[597] Appellant's Brief, para. 240.
[598] Notice of Appeal, paras. 189, 190.
[599] Trial Judgement, paras. 368-370.
[600] Trial Judgement, paras. 417, 546.
[601] Trial Judgement, para. 546.

findings in convicting the Appellant for instigating genocide and extermination as a crime against humanity.[602]

269. The Appellant submits that the Trial Chamber committed errors of law and fact in making these findings.[603] The Appeals Chamber will consider each of these alleged errors in turn.

1. Alleged Errors relating to a Meeting Held at Rwankuba Secondary School in April 1994

270. The Trial Chamber found that "[a]t the Rwankuba secondary school in April 1994, Karera spoke in favour of establishing and reinforcing roadblocks and encouraged the youth to co-operate with the army."[604] It found that "[t]his was done in a period when Tutsis were being targeted at **[page 77]** roadblocks by *Interahamwe*."[605] In making this finding, the Trial Chamber relied on the evidence of Witness BMB.[606] The Trial Chamber also considered the Appellant's testimony "that he held a pacification meeting at the school on 22 or 23 April" and did not find it convincing "[t]o the extent this is alleged to have been the same meeting as the one referred to by Witness BMB."[607] The Trial Chamber further found that "[h]is evidence that it was decided to remove roadblocks from certain places [in Rushashi] [was] unclear, and not corroborated by other evidence".[608]

271. The Appellant submits that the Trial Chamber erred in law and in fact when it rejected his account concerning the alleged meeting in Rwankuba in April 1994.[609] He contends that, contrary to the Trial Chamber's finding, his testimony was corroborated by Witness YAH.[610] The Appellant further submits that the Trial Chamber erred in law in relying on the uncorroborated evidence of Witness BMB while requesting corroboration for the Appellant's testimony.[611] The Prosecution responds that the Appellant has not demonstrated that the Trial Chamber abused its discretion.[612] 272. The Appellant's contention that the Trial Chamber erred in fact in failing to find that his testimony was corroborated by Witness YAH is unfounded. While the Appellant testified about a meeting held at Rwankuba secondary school on 22 or 23 April 1994,[613] Witness YAH testified about a meeting held in the second week of May 1994 in Rushashi commune,[614] without describing more specifically the location where the meeting was held or the persons who allegedly attended it.[615] Thus the fact that the Trial Chamber did not make a finding to the effect that Witness YAH referred to the same meeting as the Appellant and therefore corroborated the latter's account reveals no error.

273. Turning to the Appellant's contention that the Trial Chamber erred in accepting Witness BMB's uncorroborated testimony, the Appeals Chamber recalls that it is well established that a Trial Chamber has the discretion to decide in the circumstances of each case whether corroboration of evidence is necessary.[616] The Trial Chamber observed that Witness BMB was about sixteen metres away from the Appellant when listening to his speech and was satisfied that the witness **[page 78]** "must have heard what he said".[617] The Appellant challenges the Trial Chamber's reliance on Witness BMB's testimony on the sole basis that it lacked corroboration without advancing any reason why Witness BMB's testimony would have required corroboration. As noted above, acceptance of and reliance on uncorroborated evidence, *per se*, does not constitute an error in law.

---

[602] Trial Judgement, paras. 546, 548, 555 (referring to Trial Judgement, Section II.6 and to the legal findings on genocide), 557.
[603] Notice of Appeal, paras. 198, 201, 204; Appellant's Brief, paras. 245-258.
[604] Trial Judgement, para. 417. *See also* Trial Judgement, para. 406.
[605] Trial Judgement, para. 417.
[606] Trial Judgement, para. 406.
[607] Trial Judgement, paras. 392, 406.
[608] Trial Judgement, para. 406, referring to Trial Judgement, Section II.6.3.
[609] Appellant's Brief, para. 252.
[610] Appellant's Brief, para. 252, referring to Trial Judgement, para. 399.
[611] Notice of Appeal, paras. 200, 201. Appellant's Brief, paras. 251, 252.
[612] Respondent's Brief, para. 158.
[613] Trial Judgement, para. 392.
[614] T. 11 May 2006 pp. 67-70; T. 12 May 2006 p. 2.
[615] T. 11 May 2006 pp. 67-70; T. 12 May 2006 p. 2.
[616] *See supra* para. 45.
[617] Trial Judgement, para. 406.

274. The Trial Chamber rejected the Appellant's testimony in relation to this incident noting that it was unclear and not corroborated by other evidence.[618] In light of Witness BMB's account, which the Trial Chamber found credible, and in light of its observations about the Appellant's testimony in relation to this incident, the Appeals Chamber does not find that the Trial Chamber acted unreasonably in rejecting the Appellant's uncorroborated testimony. Accordingly, this sub-ground of appeal is dismissed.

2. Alleged Errors relating to a Meeting Held at Rushashi Sub-Prefecture Office in June 1994

275. The Trial Chamber found that "[a]t the Rushashi [sub-prefecture] office in June 1994, Karera asked whether the 'work' had been done, which in that context meant the killing of Tutsis, and asked why Vincent Mundyandamutsa [sic], a moderate Hutu belonging to the MDR party, had not been killed."[619] In making this finding, the Trial Chamber relied on the account of Witness BMB which it found credible, noting that it was generally in conformity with the witness's prior statement to investigators.[620]

276. The Appellant submits that the Trial Chamber erred in fact and in law in making this finding.[621] The Appellant contends that, according to Defence Witnesses YCZ and YAH, he had in fact protected Vincent Munyandamutsa.[622] In his view, the Appellant erred in law by failing to find that their testimonies on this point shed reasonable doubt on the Prosecution's evidence.[623] The Appellant also submits that the Trial Chamber committed an error of fact in its assessment of the credibility of Witnesses YCZ and YAH.[624] He argues that the Trial Chamber's approach shows bias.[625] The Prosecution responds that the Trial Chamber correctly rejected the evidence given by Witnesses YCZ and YAH that the Appellant had protected Vincent Munyandamutsa.[626] **[page 79]**

277. A review of the Trial Judgement reveals that the Trial Chamber explicitly considered that "Witnesses YCS [sic][627] and YAH testified that Vincent Munyandamutsa, a Tutsi, was protected by Karera", but rejected their testimony.[628] The Trial Chamber assessed the evidence given by these witnesses as follows:

> Witness YAH testified about a meeting held by Karera in May 1994, saying that the commune had become calm. However, he also stated that his wife continued to be threatened by bandits. This contradiction weakens his credibility. Furthermore, the witness said that the meeting in the third week of May in Musasa was co-chaired by Karera and a civil defence officer, who was responsible for recruiting youths to reinforce the military. Witness YCZ also said that Karera and a military officer were the key speakers at an outdoor meeting in Musasa in June 1994. It is surprising that meetings chaired by military and civil defence leaders were aimed at contributing to reconciliation and pacification, rather than encouraging youths to join the battle. The Chamber has some doubts about these two testimonies.[629]

278. The Appeals Chamber sees no error in the Trial Chamber's assessment of the evidence of Witnesses YAH and YCZ. The Appellant has not submitted any argument to demonstrate that it was unreasonable for the Trial Chamber to prefer the Prosecution evidence on this point. Furthermore, the Appellant has failed to advance any argument in support of his submission that the Trial Chamber's reasoning shows bias.

3. Conclusion

279. For the foregoing reasons, this sub-ground of appeal is dismissed.

---

[618] Trial Judgement, para. 406.
[619] Trial Judgement, para. 417.
[620] Trial Judgement, para. 408.
[621] Appellant's Brief, para. 253.
[622] Appellant's Brief, para. 253, referring to Trial Judgement, paras. 357, 360.
[623] Appellant's Brief, paras. 253, 254, referring to Trial Judgement, para. 374. The Appellant also submits that he and Witnesses YNZ and MZR testified that he had held several meetings for the restoration of peace in Rushashi commune. Notice of Appeal, para. 202.
[624] Appellant's Brief, paras. 255, 256, referring to Trial Judgement, para. 416.
[625] Appellant's Brief, para. 258.
[626] Respondent's Brief, paras. 159, 160.
[627] It is apparent from the context of this paragraph that the Trial Chamber was referring to Witness YCZ.
[628] Trial Judgement, para. 374, referring to Trial Judgement, Section II.6.4.
[629] Trial Judgement, para. 416.

C. Alleged Errors relating to "Pacification Meetings"

280. The Appellant submits that the Trial Chamber was faced with two conflicting versions of events regarding meetings held in Rushashi between April and June 1994.[630] Based on the evidence given by the Prosecution witnesses, the Appellant notes, the Trial Chamber found that between April and June 1994, he participated in six meetings in Rushashi during which he incited the looting and killing of Tutsis.[631] On the other hand, he notes that the Trial Chamber deduced from his testimony and the evidence given by Defence witnesses that he might have participated in "pacification meetings" in Rushashi and Musasa.[632] The Appellant contends that the Trial Chamber erred in law by failing to address the conflicting evidence in respect of the meetings, and by failing **[page 80]** to conclude that it cast a reasonable doubt on the Prosecution evidence.[633] In particular, the Appellant challenges the Trial Chamber's statement that it would "focus on the meetings at which Karera, according to the Prosecution Witnesses, allegedly was present".[634] He submits that this statement reveals that the Trial Chamber incorrectly assessed the evidence and "might have even shifted the burden of proof" to him, raising the issue of bias.[635]

281. The Appellant argues that the Trial Chamber in the *Mpambara* case was faced with a similar situation where the witnesses gave two different versions of events, one in which the accused encouraged killings and the other in which he discouraged attacks.[636] The Appellant notes that in that case the Trial Chamber gave the accused the benefit of the doubt in light of the conflicting evidence, and contends that the Trial Chamber in his case should have at least articulated its reasons for not relying on the conflicting evidence it had previously accepted.[637]

282. The Prosecution responds that the Appellant's arguments are premised on a misinterpretation of the facts and of the Trial Chamber's finding.[638] It submits that the Appellant merely summarizes the evidence of Prosecution and Defence witnesses as recounted in the Trial Judgement and suggests "another way to assess the evidence" without establishing any error on the part of the Trial Chamber.[639] It argues that the fact that Prosecution and Defence witnesses gave contradictory accounts of the events does not in itself imply a reasonable doubt.[640]

283. The Trial Chamber assessed the Defence evidence relating to the "pacification meetings" in detail.[641] While it found that these meetings, except for one,[642] did not relate to any of the meetings alleged by the Prosecution,[643] it noted that the evidence could "arguably throw some light" on what the Appellant may have said at other meetings.[644] When reaching its findings about the incriminating meetings held in Rushashi, the Trial Chamber explicitly stated that it did not "exclude that [the] so-called pacification meetings were held" and that it "assessed the totality of the evidence" on this point.[645] **[page 81]**

---

[630] Appellant's Brief, para. 247.
[631] Appellant's Brief, paras. 245 (referring to Trial Judgement, paras. 379-389), 247 (referring to Trial Judgement, paras. 401-417).
[632] Appellant's Brief, paras. 246 (referring to Trial Judgement, paras. 390, 400), 247 (referring to Trial Judgement, paras. 402, 403).
[633] Notice of Appeal, para. 198; Appellant's Brief, paras. 27-29, 249, 250; Brief in Reply, paras. 77, 78. The Appellant contends that the only reasonable inference the Trial Chamber could have made from the evidence was one similar to the inference made by the Trial Chamber in *Mpambara*.
[634] Appellant's Brief, para. 248, citing Trial Judgement, paras. 404, 415.
[635] Appellant's Brief, para. 248.
[636] Appellant's Brief, para. 243, pointing to *Mpambara* Trial Judgement, paras. 64-68, 70.
[637] Appellant's Brief, paras. 27, 28, referring to *Mpambara* Trial Judgement, paras. 70, 144, 146.
[638] Respondent's Brief, para. 151.
[639] Respondent's Brief, paras. 152, 153.
[640] Respondent's Brief, para. 153.
[641] Trial Judgement, paras. 402, 403, 415, 416.
[642] Trial Judgement, para. 406. *See infra* Sub-section 2, discussing alleged errors relating to this meeting.
[643] Trial Judgement, paras. 415, 416.
[644] Trial Judgement, para. 404.
[645] Trial Judgement, para. 417.

284. In accepting that "pacification meetings" had taken place,[646] the Trial Chamber observed that the evidence was "not clear as to whether such pacification meetings were aimed at preventing crimes being committed between the Hutus (for instance by the *Abaseso* from Ruhengeri against the *Abambogo*), preventing infiltration by unknown persons, achieving reconciliation between extreme and moderate Hutus, or mitigating animosity between Hutu and Tutsi."[647] However, the sole fact that the Trial Chamber made no determinative conclusion regarding the purpose of these meetings does not constitute an error. In the instant case, the remaining doubt about the purpose of these meetings was to the benefit of the Appellant, because the Trial Chamber made its findings based on the presumption that such meetings had taken place.[648] It is implicit from the Trial Judgement that the Trial Chamber considered the fact that the Appellant held these "so-called pacification meetings" was not irreconcilable with the fact that he participated in other meetings in Rushashi.[649] It is well established that a Trial Chamber does not have to articulate every step of its reasoning.[650] Taking into account that the aim of the "so-called pacification meetings" was unclear, the Appeals Chamber finds no merit in the Appellant's contention that the Trial Chamber failed to provide a reasoned opinion with regard to the alleged conflict between the evidence regarding the "pacification meetings" and the evidence in relation to the Appellant's participation in meetings encouraging crimes in Rushashi.

285. A review of the Trial Judgement further reveals that the Appellant cited the Trial Chamber's statement that it would focus on the meetings alleged by the Prosecution out of context. The Appeals Chamber finds that this statement[651] simply reflects the Trial Chamber's approach to first consider the evidence related to the meetings alleged by the Prosecution, and to subsequently assess whether the Defence evidence cast reasonable doubt on it. As noted above, the Trial Chamber explicitly recognized that statements the Appellant made at meetings which did not form part of the Prosecution's case might have some relevance as to "what he [was] likely to have stated elsewhere in the same period" and it thus explicitly considered the Defence evidence in this regard.[652] The Appellant has not demonstrated that the Trial Chamber's approach shows bias or that it shifted the burden of proof. Accordingly, this submission is dismissed. **[page 82]**

286. The Appeals Chamber finds that the Appellant has not substantiated his allegation that the evidence that he participated in "pacification meetings" is incompatible with evidence that he was involved in the killings in Rushashi and Nyamirambo. Although the Trial Chamber did not make a specific finding on how the Appellant could have been involved in the killings in Rushashi and Nyamirambo while he participated in "so-called pacification meetings", this omission does not amount to an error. The Trial Chamber legitimately exercised its discretion in determining which version of events was more credible and the Appeals Chamber defers to this finding.

287. Accordingly, the Appeals Chamber dismisses this sub-ground of appeal.

D. Alleged Errors relating to the Distribution of Weapons

288. The Trial Chamber found that during April and May 1994, the Appellant transported weapons to the Rushashi commune office and that these weapons were given to the *conseillers* and subsequently reached the *Interahamwe* at the roadblocks, where they were used to kill Tutsis.[653] The Trial Chamber held that "[b]y bringing guns" the Appellant assisted in the killing of Tutsis and convicted him pursuant to Article 6(1) of the Statute for aiding and abetting genocide and extermination as a crime against humanity.[654]

---

[646] Trial Judgement, para. 375.
[647] Trial Judgement, para. 375.
[648] Trial Judgement, paras. 375, 417.
[649] Trial Judgment, para. 417. *See, inter alia,* the Trial Chamber's findings that (i) at the sector office in Rushashi, the Appellant publicly ordered the looting and the killing of Tutsis; (ii) outside the commune office, he sought contributions for weapons in order to fight the *Inkotanyi*, their accomplices and the MRND opponents; and (iii) outside the commune office, he sought contributions and encouraged hundreds of administrative, intellectual and business leaders to fight the *Inkotanyi* saying that there should be no survivors at the roadblocks.
[650] *Simba* Appeal Judgement, para. 152.
[651] Trial Judgement, para. 404.
[652] Trial Judgement, paras. 404, 415, 416.
[653] Trial Judgement, para. 438.
[654] Trial Judgement, paras. 547, 548, 555, 557.

289. Under his First Ground of Appeal, the Appellant submits that the Trial Chamber erred in law in entering his conviction for aiding and abetting genocide and extermination as a crime against humanity based on this event.[655] The Appellant primarily contends that he did not have adequate notice of these charges since the allegation of weapons distribution in Rushashi was not pleaded in the Amended Indictment.[656] He also argues that the Trial Chamber erred in its assessment of the evidence.[657] The Appellant finally submits, under his Seventh Ground of Appeal, that the Prosecution failed to establish a nexus between the Appellant and the events at the roadblocks.[658]

290. With respect to the lack of adequate notice, the Appellant submits that the allegation that he distributed weapons in Rushashi did not feature in the Amended Indictment and that, as a matter of law, the omission of this allegation could not have been cured through timely, clear, and consistent **[page 83]** information.[659] He claims that this omission could have been cured only through an amendment of the Amended Indictment,[660] which the Prosecution failed to request.[661]

291. The Prosecution responds that the Trial Chamber correctly found that the Appellant had received sufficient notice of the allegation of weapons distribution in Rushashi and that any defect in the Amended Indictment had been cured by subsequent timely, clear, and consistent information provided to the Appellant.[662] The Prosecution submits that the distribution of weapons in Rushashi was not a new charge but rather a material fact underpinning the charges of genocide and extermination and murder as crimes against humanity.[663]

292. The charges against an accused and the material facts supporting those charges must be pleaded with sufficient precision in an indictment so as to provide notice to an accused.[664] Whether a fact is "material" depends on the nature of the Prosecution's case.[665] The Appeals Chamber has previously held that where it is alleged that the accused planned, instigated, ordered, or aided and abetted in the planning, preparation, or execution of the alleged crimes, the Prosecution is required to identify the "particular acts" or "the particular course of conduct" on the part of the accused which forms the basis for the charges in question.[666]

293. An indictment which fails to set forth the specific material facts underpinning the charges against the accused is defective.[667] The defect may be cured if the Prosecution provides the accused with timely, clear, and consistent information detailing the factual basis underpinning the charge.[668] However, a clear distinction has to be drawn between vagueness in an indictment and an indictment omitting certain charges altogether.[669] While it is possible, as stated above, to remedy the vagueness **[page 84]** of an indictment, omitted charges can be incorporated into the indictment only by a formal amendment pursuant to Rule 50 of the Rules.[670]

---

[655] Notice of Appeal, paras. 9-15, 205-210; Appellant's Brief, paras. 5, 259-280.
[656] Notice of Appeal, paras. 9-15, 205; Appellant's Brief, paras. 259-274.
[657] Notice of Appeal, paras. 9-15, 206-210; Appellant's Brief, paras. 275-286.
[658] Notice of Appeal, para. 191; Appellant's Brief, para. 244.
[659] Notice of Appeal, paras. 9-15, 205; Appellant's Brief, paras. 265, 267.
[660] Appellant's Brief, para. 267; AT. 28 August 2008 pp. 52, 53.
[661] Appellant's Brief, para. 259; AT. 28 August 2008 p. 52.
[662] Respondent's Brief, paras. 28, 38.
[663] Respondent's Brief, paras. 36, 37; AT. 28 August 2008 p. 34.
[664] *Muvunyi* Appeal Judgement, para. 18; *Seromba* Appeal Judgement, paras. 27, 100. *See also Simba* Appeal Judgement, para. 63, referring to *Muhimana* Appeal Judgement, paras. 76, 167, 195; *Gacumbitsi* Appeal Judgement, para. 49.
[665] *Nahimana et al.* Appeal Judgement, para. 322; *Ndindabahizi* Appeal Judgement, para. 16; *Ntagerura et al.* Appeal Judgement, para. 23.
[666] *Seromba* Appeal Judgement, para. 27, citing *Ntagerura et al.* Appeal Judgement, para. 25.
[667] *Ntagerura et al.* Appeal Judgement, para. 22; *Niyitegeka* Appeal Judgement, para. 195; *Kupreškić et al.* Appeal Judgement, para. 114.
[668] *Muvunyi* Appeal Judgement, para. 20, referring to *Seromba* Appeal Judgement, para. 100; *Simba* Appeal Judgement, para. 64; *Muhimana* Appeal Judgement, paras. 76, 195, 217; *Gacumbitsi* Appeal Judgement, para. 49. *See also Ntagerura et al.* Appeal Judgement, paras. 28, 65.
[669] *Ntagerura et al.* Appeal Judgement, para. 32. *See also Muvunyi* Appeal Judgement, para. 20, citing *Bagosora et al.*, Decision on Aloys Ntabakuze's Interlocutory Appeal on Questions of Law Raised by the 29 June 2006 Trial Chamber I Decision on Motion for Exclusion of Evidence, para. 30.
[670] *Ntagerura et al.* Appeal Judgement, para. 32. *See also Muvunyi* Appeal Judgement, para. 20, citing *Bagosora et al.*, Decision on Aloys Ntabakuze's Interlocutory Appeal on Questions of Law Raised by the 29 June 2006 Trial Chamber I Decision on Motion for Exclusion of Evidence, para. 30.

Judgement

294. The Trial Chamber found that the distribution of weapons in Rushashi did not form part of the Amended Indictment and that, as a material fact underpinning the counts relating to genocide and extermination as a crime against humanity, it should have been pleaded therein.[671] However, the Trial Chamber further found that the Appellant received sufficient notice of this allegation through the Prosecution Pre-Trial Brief and the summaries of the anticipated testimonies of Witnesses BMA, BLY, BMM, and BMN, which were annexed to the Prosecution Pre-Trial Brief, as well as the Prosecution Opening Statement.[672] The Trial Chamber found that since the Defence had "at no time during the trial"[673] objected to the admission of evidence concerning the distribution of weapons in Rushashi, the burden of proof had shifted to it to "demonstrate that lack of notice prejudiced Karera."[674] The Trial Chamber held that the Defence failed to meet this burden.[675]

295. None of the paragraphs in the Amended Indictment makes an allegation of weapons distribution in Rushashi. The Amended Indictment includes two allegations of weapons distribution. Paragraphs 9 and 10 allege that the Appellant distributed weapons to commune police or civilian militias in Nyamirambo and that as a direct consequence of his conduct, many Tutsi civilians were killed by commune police or civilian militias and local residents in Nyamirambo in April and May 1994.[676] Paragraphs 25, 26, and 27 of the Amended Indictment allege that from 7 April 1994, the Appellant organized and ordered a campaign of extermination against Tutsi civilians in the commune of Nyarugenge, which included, *inter alia*, the distribution of firearms to commune police.[677] These paragraphs are not vague, but specifically describe the circumstances of two particular incidents of weapons distribution in locations other than Rushashi.[678]

296. Therefore, in alleging the distribution of weapons in Rushashi, the Prosecution Pre-Trial Brief, the annexed witness summaries, and the Prosecution's Opening Statement did not simply add **[page 85]** greater detail to a more general allegation already pleaded in the Amended Indictment. Rather, these submissions expanded the charges specifically pleaded in the Amended Indictment by charging an additional incident of weapons distribution at a new location. This is an impermissible, *de facto* amendment of the Amended Indictment.

297. For the foregoing reasons, the Appeals Chamber finds that the Trial Chamber erred in finding that, as a matter of law, the Prosecution's post-indictment communications could cure the failure to include the allegation of the Rushashi weapons distribution in the Amended Indictment and that they in fact did so. The Appeals Chamber therefore need not address the Appellant's remaining arguments under the First and Seventh Grounds of Appeal in relation to the Rushashi weapons distribution. The Appeals Chamber grants the First Ground of Appeal and reverses in part the Appellant's convictions for aiding and abetting genocide and extermination as a crime against humanity in so far as they are based on the Rushashi weapons distribution.

E. Alleged Errors relating to the Murder of Gakuru, *Conseiller* of Kimisange Sector

298. Relying on Witnesses BMR, BMO, BMN, and BMM,[679] the Trial Chamber found that

> in April or May 1994, Karera said to the *Interahamwe* at the Kinyari centre roadblock that Gakuru, the *conseiller* of Kimisange sector, was an *Inkotanyi* or *Inyenzi* and ordered that he be arrested. By doing so, Karera left him in the hands of *Interahamwe*. Under the prevailing circumstances, he must have understood that Gakuru would be killed.[680]

---

[671] Trial Judgement, paras. 418, 419.
[672] Trial Judgement, paras. 420, 421.
[673] The Trial Chamber noted that "[o]nly [the Defence] Closing Brief contained an objection." Trial Judgement, para. 421.
[674] Trial Judgement, para. 421.
[675] Trial Judgement, para. 421.
[676] Amended Indictment, paras. 9, 10.
[677] Amended Indictment, paras. 25-27.
[678] The Appeals Chamber notes that the Trial Chamber addressed in two different sections of the Trial Judgement the allegation in paragraphs 9 and 10 of the Amended Indictment. *See* Trial Judgement, Section 4.14, addressing the allegation of weapons distribution in Nyamirambo; and Trial Judgement, Section 6.5, addressing the allegation of weapons distribution in Rushashi.
[679] Trial Judgement, paras. 449-456.
[680] Trial Judgement, para. 456.

299. The Trial Chamber concluded from the Appellant's conduct at several locations, including the incident at the Kinyari centre roadblock, that "the principal perpetrators as well as Karera had the intention to kill prior to the act of killing."[681] It found that by these acts, the Appellant "intended to bring about the death of these persons or at the very least was aware of the substantial likelihood that murder would be committed as a result of his conduct."[682] Based on this event, the Trial Chamber convicted the Appellant for instigating and aiding and abetting murder as a crime against humanity.[683]

300. The Appellant submits that the Trial Chamber erred in law in entering this conviction.[684] In this section, the Appeals Chamber considers three principal questions arising from the Appellant's contentions discussed below: (i) whether the Trial Chamber erred in relying on Prosecution Witnesses BMR, BMO, BMN, and BMM despite contradictions between their testimonies; (ii) **[page 86]** whether the Trial Chamber erred in rejecting the Appellant's testimony without providing adequate reasons; and (iii) whether the Trial Chamber erred in holding him responsible for instigating and aiding and abetting Gakuru's murder when it was unable to determine the place, the date, and the perpetrators thereof.

1. Alleged Inconsistencies between the Testimonies of Witnesses BMR, BMO, BMN and BMM

301. The Appellant submits that the Trial Chamber erred in assessing the evidence by finding that he was involved in the killing of Gakuru.[685] He contends that the Trial Chamber "mainly relied on the testimonies of [Witnesses] BMR and BMO to construct the narrative of this event" and alleges a number of contradictions between the testimonies.[686] He submits that the Trial Chamber erred in law in failing to address these contradictions.[687] The Appellant submits that in light of the differences between the various accounts given by the witnesses, the Trial Chamber erred in finding that the allegation was proven beyond reasonable doubt.[688]

302. The Appellant, in particular, highlights the following inconsistencies:

- Witness BMR testified that the event occurred at the end of May 1994 while Witness BMO testified that it was sometime in April 1994;[689]

- Witness BMR testified to having seen Gakuru arrive in a Toyota Corolla while Witness BMO claimed he saw a Peugeot 505.[690] The Appellant submits that the Trial Chamber relied on the evidence of Witnesses BMR and BMO who allegedly had seen the Appellant using Gakuru's vehicle after he had been killed. In his view, this finding "is of little relevance" in light of the contradictory accounts regarding the vehicle driven by Gakuru, as well as the fact that the Appellant owned a car similar to the car described by Witness BMO.[691]

- Witness BMR testified that the *conseiller*, his wife, and a driver were inside the car while Witness BMO testified that he saw the *conseiller*, his wife, and their two children.[692]

303. The Prosecution responds that the Appellant has not advanced any argument establishing that the passage of time, referred to by the Trial Chamber, was not a reasonable explanation for justifying the discrepancy in the testimony regarding the precise date and time relevant to the events **[page 87]** that led to the killing of Gakuru.[693] It submits that the Appellant has failed to challenge the common features of the

---

[681] Trial Judgement, para. 560.
[682] Trial Judgement, para. 560.
[683] Trial Judgement, paras. 560, 561.
[684] Notice of Appeal, paras. 211-220; Appellant's Brief, paras. 281-290.
[685] Appellant's Brief, para. 290.
[686] Appellant's Brief, para. 284.
[687] Appellant's Brief, para. 289.
[688] Notice of Appeal, para. 219.
[689] Notice of Appeal, para. 216.
[690] Notice of Appeal, para. 216; Appellant's Brief, para. 284.
[691] Notice of Appeal, para. 217; Appellant's Brief, paras. 284, 286.
[692] Notice of Appeal, para. 216; Appellant's Brief, para. 284.
[693] Respondent's Brief, para. 169.

witnesses' accounts accepted by the Trial Chamber. In its view, the Trial Chamber duly assessed the evidence before it, including the Appellant's arguments and the alleged discrepancies.[694]

304. As a preliminary matter, the Appeals Chamber considers that the alleged inconsistencies should be viewed against the backdrop of the numerous similarities found by the Trial Chamber in Witnesses BMR's and BMO's accounts which are not challenged on appeal:

> Both testified that the *conseiller* arrived at the Kinyari centre roadblock in a white sedan car with others, that Karera and a man called Vianney Simparikubwabo were there, that Karera was asked to confirm the *conseiller's* identity, that he ordered his arrest and detention, and that the *conseiller* was later killed. These two witnesses, as well as Witness BMM, also said that Karera had the power to save the *conseiller*. It is noted that they both saw Karera use Gakuru's car after he was killed.[695]

Moreover, contrary to the Appellant's contention, the Trial Chamber explicitly addressed the alleged inconsistencies and noted that "[i]n light of the important similarities outlined above, the Chamber does not consider these discrepancies significant."[696] It further explained that "[c]onsiderable time has passed since the event, and the witnesses may have recalled the date and perceived the vehicle differently."[697]

305. It is within a Trial Chamber's discretion to assess any inconsistencies in the testimony of witnesses, and to determine whether, in the light of the overall evidence, the witnesses were nonetheless reliable and credible.[698] The Appellant has not advanced any reason to demonstrate that the Trial Chamber's explanation was unreasonable.

306. The Appellant further submits that Witness BMR testified that the Appellant had stated that the passengers at the roadblock were Tutsis whereas, according to Witness BMO, the Appellant did not mention their ethnicity.[699] He contends that this contradiction is particularly significant because it is central to the allegation that he told the *Interahamwe* at the roadblock that Gakuru was a Tutsi.[700] **[page 88]**

307. The Trial Chamber explicitly addressed this difference and considered it insignificant.[701] It explained that "[b]oth witnesses conveyed that Karera created an impression that the *conseiller* or his companions were Tutsi or accomplices."[702] The Appellant has not explained why this explanation by the Trial Chamber was unreasonable.

308. The Appellant submits that Witnesses BMR, BMO, BMM, and BMN also differed in their testimonies as to the date and time when they had learnt about Gakuru's murder.[703] He submits that Witness BMR learned at 3 p.m. from people who "seemed" to have been eyewitnesses to these killings that the detainees had been killed.[704] According to the Appellant, Witness BMO heard "later" when he returned to the area that the *conseiller* and his wife had been killed.[705] Witness BMM[706] had seen after 6 p.m., on a date he could not specify, four individuals killed at the commune office following an order from the Appellant.[707] Witness BMN testified that she saw Gakuru at the commune office at 1 p.m., that he was led away, and that she saw him again at the prison. Witness BMN further testified that she later heard some *Interahamwe* boasting that they had killed Gakuru.[708]

309. The Appeals Chamber fails to see how the fact that the witnesses learned about the murder of Gakuru at different times and occasions presents a contradiction in their accounts. Moreover, the Trial Chamber

---

[694] Respondent's Brief, para. 170.
[695] Trial Judgement, para. 450.
[696] Trial Judgement, paras. 451, 452.
[697] Trial Judgement, para. 452.
[698] *See supra* para. 155.
[699] Notice of Appeal, para. 216; Appellant's Brief, para. 284.
[700] Appellant's Brief, para. 285.
[701] Trial Judgement, para. 451.
[702] Trial Judgement, para. 451.
[703] Appellant's Brief, para. 286.
[704] Notice of Appeal, para. 218; Appellant's Brief, para. 286, citing Trial Judgement, para. 442.
[705] Notice of Appeal, para. 218.
[706] The Appellant erroneously refers to Witness BMN. However, the context reveals that he intended to refer to Witness BMM.
[707] Notice of Appeal, para. 218; Appellant's Brief, para. 286.
[708] Notice of Appeal, para. 218; Appellant's Brief, para. 287.

addressed the alleged contradiction between Witnesses BMR's, BMO's, and BMM's testimonies on this point in the Trial Judgement and stated that "[t]he fact that one of the witnesses may have given an incorrect time estimate, thirteen years after the event, does not affect his overall credibility."[709] The Appellant has not challenged the Trial Chamber's reasoning. This sub-ground of appeal is accordingly dismissed.

310. Finally, the Appeals Chamber notes the Appellant's contention that Witness BMR testified that he and his colleagues sent someone to look for the Appellant in a bar whereas Witness BMO testified that the Appellant was at the roadblock when the *conseiller* requested to speak to him.[710] **[page 89]**

311. The Trial Chamber did not explicitly address this matter. The Appeals Chamber recalls that minor inconsistencies commonly occur in witness testimony without rendering it unreliable and that it is within the discretion of a Trial Chamber to evaluate the testimony and to consider whether the evidence as a whole is credible, without explaining its decision in every detail.[711] In light of the Trial Chamber's detailed analysis of both similarities and differences in the witnesses' accounts, the Appeals Chamber finds that the alleged inconsistency is minor. The Trial Chamber's failure to address this issue does not render its reliance on the witnesses erroneous.

312. Accordingly, the Appellant's appeal on this point is dismissed.

2. Alleged Failure to Provide Reasons for Rejecting the Appellant's Testimony

313. The Appellant recalls that he testified at trial that he knew Gakuru but that he had never heard that Gakuru was present or that he was killed in Rushashi. [712]He submits that the Trial Chamber erred in law in failing to justify its decision to reject his testimony on this point.[713]

314. The Appeals Chamber has previously held that if a "Trial Chamber did not refer to the evidence given by a witness, even if it is in contradiction to the Trial Chamber's finding, it is to be presumed that the Trial Chamber assessed and weighed the evidence, but found that the evidence did not prevent it from arriving at its actual findings."[714] The Trial Chamber explicitly noted that it based its finding on the totality of the evidence before it, including the Appellant's testimony.[715]The Appellant has not shown that the Trial Chamber acted unreasonably by not explicitly discussing his evidence, particularly in light of the fact that the testimony was limited to denying the allegation against him.[716] Accordingly this appeal is dismissed.

3. Alleged Failure to Determine the Place, Date, and Identity of the Perpetrators

315. The Appellant submits that the Trial Chamber erred in law in finding that it had been proven beyond reasonable doubt that he had instigated and aided and abetted Gakuru's murder when in fact it was unable to determine the place, the date, and the perpetrators of that crime.[717] The Appellant submits that the elements of the modes of responsibility for which he was held responsible were not established.[718] He contends that the evidence does not reflect that those persons who received his **[page 90]** "contribution" committed any crime.[719] In his view, it was impossible to establish the elements of aiding and abetting since it was unknown who eventually killed Gakuru on whose orders, and where he was killed.[720] He submits that according to the

---

[709] Trial Judgement, para. 454.
[710] Notice of Appeal, para. 216; Appellant's Brief, para. 284. He also submits that Witness BMN testified that the Appellant was at the commune office while Witness BMM stated that he was at Kinyari centre. Appellant's Brief, para. 284.
[711] *See supra* para. 20.
[712] Appellant's Brief, para. 283.
[713] Appellant's Brief, para. 289.
[714] *See supra* para. 20.
[715] Trial Judgement, para. 456.
[716] Trial Judgement, para. 448.
[717] Notice of Appeal, para. 220; Appellant's Brief, paras. 288, 289; AT. 28 August 2008 pp. 27, 59.
[718] AT. 28 August 2008 p. 27. The French original version of the transcripts reflects that Counsel for the Appellant makes reference to the Trial Judgement in *Oriü. See* AT. 28 August 2008 p. 35 of the French transcripts.
[719] AT. 28 August 2008 p. 27.
[720] AT. 28 August 2008 p. 27.

Prosecution evidence he never asked that Gakuru be killed, but merely instructed that he be taken away and detained.[721]

316. The Prosecution responds that the Appellant prompted the *Interahamwe* to commit the offence, and that he at least knew that Gakuru was likely to be killed.[722] It submits that the Appellant did not merely facilitate the killing of Gakuru, and that Gakuru had hoped that the Appellant would save his life.[723] When the Appellant was asked to confirm Gakuru's identity, the Appellant said that Gakuru was an "*Inyenzi*". In the Prosecution's view this statement indicated to the *Interahamwe* that they had to kill Gakuru.[724] The Prosecution also refers to Witness BMR's testimony, which the Trial Chamber found credible: according to that witness, "these people would be taken to a place where everything was taken away from them, their clothes, shoes, watches and so on, and then they were killed."[725]

317. The *actus reus* of "instigating" implies prompting another person to commit an offence.[726] It is not necessary to prove that the crime would not have been perpetrated without the involvement of the accused; it is sufficient to demonstrate that the instigation was a factor substantially contributing to the conduct of another person committing the crime.[727]

318. Contrary to the Appellant's contention, the specific identification of the perpetrators, who were identified in the Trial Judgement as *Interahamwe*, was not required for a finding that the Appellant instigated the killing of Gakuru. In any event, the Trial Chamber did identify the perpetrators. It is implicit, but certain, in the Trial Judgement that the Trial Chamber found that Gakuru was killed by the *Interahamwe* who were informed by the Appellant that Gakuru was an "*Inyenzi*" and who received his order to arrest him. The Trial Chamber found that "[b]y doing so, Karera left him [Gakuru] in the hands of *Interahamwe*" and that "[u]nder the prevailing circumstances, he must have understood that Gakuru would be killed".[728] That the Trial Chamber **[page 91]** made such a finding is implicit in its recollection of the evidence of Witnesses BMO and BMN.[729] While it would have been preferable for the Trial Chamber to explicitly state that it identified the perpetrators of Gakuru's murder as being the *Interahamwe* to whom the Appellant indicated that Gakuru was an "*Inyenzi*" and who received the order to arrest him, this omission does not amount to an error.

319. However, based on the Trial Chamber's factual findings, the Trial Chamber could not have reasonably concluded that the Appellant prompted the perpetrators to kill Gakuru. The Trial Chamber made no factual findings supporting such a conclusion. It merely concluded that the Appellant had informed the *Interahamwe* who later killed Gakuru that he was an "*Inyenzi*" and ordered them to arrest him. The Trial Chamber should have further explained how, on the basis of these factual findings, it inferred that the Appellant had prompted the *Interahamwe* to kill Gakuru. In the absence of such an explanation, the Appeals Chamber finds that the Trial Chamber erred in convicting the Appellant for instigating Gakuru's murder.

320. The Appeals Chamber now turns to the Appellant's submission that the Trial Chamber erred in entering a conviction for aiding and abetting murder as a crime against humanity.

321. The *actus reus* of aiding and abetting is constituted by acts or omissions that assist, further, or lend moral support to the perpetration of a specific crime, and which substantially contribute to the perpetration of the crime.[730] The *mens rea* for aiding and abetting is knowledge that acts performed by the aider and abettor assist in the commission of the crime by the principal.[731] It is well established that it is not necessary for an accused to know the precise crime which was intended and which in the event was committed, but he

---

[721] AT. 28 August 2008 p. 27.
[722] AT. 28 August 2008 p. 40.
[723] AT. 28 August 2008 p. 40.
[724] AT. 28 August 2008 p. 40.
[725] AT. 28 August 2008 p. 40, citing T. 1 February 2006 p. 24.
[726] *Nahimana et al.* Appeal Judgement, para. 480; *Ndindabahizi* Appeal Judgement, para. 117; *Kordiü and ýerkez* Appeal Judgement, para. 27.
[727] *Nahimana et al.* Appeal Judgement, para. 480; *Gacumbitsi* Appeal Judgement, para. 129; *Kordiü and ýerkez* Appeal Judgement, para. 27.
[728] Trial Judgement, para. 456.
[729] *See* Trial Judgement, paras. 445, 447.
[730] *Nahimana et al.* Appeal Judgement, para. 482.
[731] *Nahimana et al.* Appeal Judgement, para. 482.

must be aware of its essential elements.[732] If an accused is aware that one of a number of crimes will probably be committed, and one of those crimes is in fact committed, he has intended to facilitate the commission of that crime.[733]

322. The Trial Chamber found that the Appellant told the *Interahamwe* that Gakuru was an "*Inyenzi*" and that he ordered his arrest by the *Interahamwe*, which he must have understood would result in his murder.[734] On the basis of these findings, it was reasonable for the Trial Chamber to conclude that the Appellant aided and abetted the murder of Gakuru.[735] By instructing the *Interahamwe* to arrest Gakuru and telling them that Gakuru was an "*Inyenzi*", it was reasonable to conclude that the Appellant substantially contributed to the commission of his murder through **[page 92]** specifically assisting and providing moral support to the principal perpetrators. Furthermore, in light of the evidence adduced, the Appeals Chamber finds no error in the Trial Chamber's finding that the Appellant had the requisite *mens rea*.

323. For the foregoing reasons, the Appeals Chamber grants this sub-ground of appeal in part and reverses the Appellant's conviction for instigating murder as a crime against humanity based on this event. The Appellant's conviction for aiding and abetting murder as a crime against humanity based on the killing of Gakuru is upheld.

F. Conclusion

324. The Appeals Chamber grants the Appellant's First Ground of Appeal and reverses the Appellant's conviction for aiding and abetting genocide and extermination as a crime against humanity, based on the alleged weapons distribution in Rushashi commune.

325. The Appeals Chamber further grants the Seventh Ground of Appeal, in part, and reverses the Appellant's conviction for instigating murder as a crime against humanity based on the killing of Gakuru. **[page 93]**

IX. ALLEGED ERRORS RELATING TO THE ALIBI (GROUND OF APPEAL 8)

326. At trial, the Appellant raised an alibi in his defence.[736] He submitted that on 7 April 1994, he left his house in Nyamirambo for his son Ignace's house at the Nyakinama campus of the Rwanda National University in Ruhengeri prefecture.[737] The Appellant stated that he arrived at the campus on that day and did not leave until 19 April 1994, when he moved to Rushashi to assume the post of prefect of Kigali prefecture.[738] The Trial Chamber found that the Appellant and his relatives travelled from Nyamirambo to his son's house in Nyakinama on 7 April 1994[739] and that he stayed there until 19 April 1994.[740] However, the Trial Chamber concluded that the Appellant did not remain "consistently and exclusively" in Ruhengeri prefecture and stated that it had no doubt that he was present in Nyamirambo and Ntarama sectors and Rushashi commune when the crimes were committed.[741]

327. The Appellant contends that the Trial Chamber erred in law and in fact in not finding that he remained in Ruhengeri during the period from 7 to 19 April 1994.[742] He submits that the Trial Chamber erred in its

---

[732] *Nahimana et al.* Appeal Judgement, para. 482.
[733] *See Stakić* Appeal Judgement, para. 50; *Nahimana et al.* Appeal Judgement, para. 482.
[734] Trial Judgement, para. 456.
[735] Trial Judgement, para. 560.
[736] Notice of alibi pursuant to Rule 67 (A)(ii) of the Rules served on the Prosecution on 9 January 2006 (unredacted version) annexed to the Prosecution's Motion for Further and Better Alibi's Particulars, filed on 23 January 2006 and the Corrigendum filed on 26 January 2006 ("Notice of Alibi"). *See also* Decision on Motion for Further Alibi Particulars, 7 March 2006 (TC); Trial Judgement, paras. 457-510.
[737] Trial Judgement, para. 459.
[738] Trial Judgement, para. 459.
[739] Trial Judgement, para. 478.
[740] Trial Judgement, para. 510.
[741] Trial Judgement, para. 510.
[742] Notice of Appeal, paras. 221-239; Appellant's Brief, paras. 291-309.

application of the burden of proof, in its assessment of the possibility of travelling from Ruhengeri during the period covered by his alibi, and in its assessment of the Defence evidence relating to the alibi.[743]

A. Alleged Errors in the Application of the Burden of Proof

328. The Appellant contends that the Trial Chamber incorrectly applied the burden of proof in relation to his alibi.[744] He submits that the Trial Chamber's consideration of his alibi at the very end of the evidence constitutes an "important indication that the [Trial] Chamber shifted the burden of proof".[745] He argues that the Trial Chamber erroneously assessed the "plausibility" of his alibi on the basis of whether the evidence of the Prosecution witnesses eliminated the reasonable possibility that he remained consistently in Nyakinama,[746] and assessed this issue in the context of the "number **[page 94]** of times" he was seen in Nyakinama, the possibility of travelling by road from Ruhengeri at that time, and the credibility and reliability of Prosecution evidence.[747] He also argues that according to the Trial Chamber's reasoning, he was required to prove beyond reasonable doubt that he did not at any time between 7 and 19 April 1994 leave Nyakinama, if his alibi were to be accepted.[748] He claims that the Trial Chamber erred in its analysis of the evidence by simply comparing the credibility of Prosecution and Defence evidence,[749] as well as in its finding that the Defence witnesses who testified to the alibi had credibility problems.[750]

329. The Prosecution responds that the Trial Chamber committed no error in its statement of the applicable law[751] and that there is no merit in the Appellant's argument that the Trial Chamber misdirected itself in the application of the legal standards and evidential burden when considering the alibi.[752] It argues that the approach adopted by the Trial Chamber is consistent with the established jurisprudence of the Appeals Chamber, and that the Appellant has not demonstrated that the Trial Chamber reversed the burden of proof in relation to his alibi.[753] The Prosecution asserts that the Trial Chamber committed no error in considering the credibility and reliability of the witnesses and correctly placed the burden of proof on the Prosecution.[754]

330. The Appeals Chamber recalls that where an alibi is pleaded, an accused denies that he was in a position to commit the crime for which he is charged because at the time of its commission, he was not at the scene of the crime, but elsewhere.[755] It is settled jurisprudence of the two *ad hoc* Tribunals that in putting forward an alibi, an accused need only produce evidence likely to raise a reasonable doubt in the Prosecution's case.[756] The onus remains on the Prosecution to prove beyond reasonable doubt the facts underpinning the crimes charged.[757] Indeed, it is incumbent on the Prosecution to establish beyond reasonable doubt that, despite the alibi, the facts alleged are nevertheless true.[758] **[page 95]**

331. In the present case, the Appeals Chamber is satisfied that the Trial Chamber correctly enunciated the law applicable in relation to the burden and standard of proof concerning an alibi[759] by stating that

---

[743] Notice of Appeal, paras. 221-239; Appellant's Brief, paras. 291-309.
[744] Appellant's Brief, para. 291; AT. 28 August 2008 p. 15.
[745] Appellant's Brief, para. 30; Brief in Reply, paras. 9, 87.
[746] Appellant's Brief, para. 295; AT. 28 August 2008 p. 16.
[747] Appellant's Brief, para. 296.
[748] Appellant's Brief, para. 303.
[749] Appellant's Brief, para. 304.
[750] Appellant's Brief, para. 306.
[751] Respondent's Brief, para. 185.
[752] Respondent's Brief, paras. 72, 186. The Prosecution also submits that the Trial Chamber's placing of the factual findings in relation to the alibi evidence towards the end of the Trial Judgement "cannot be construed as indicia of the reversal of the burden of proof and an error of law by the Trial Chamber". Respondent's Brief, para. 60 (citation omitted).
[753] Respondent's Brief, para. 186.
[754] Respondent's Brief, para. 208.
[755] *Kajelijeli* Appeal Judgement, para. 42, citing *Niyitegeka* Appeal Judgement, para. 60, citing *Kayishema and Ruzindana* Appeal Judgement, para. 106.
[756] *Niyitegeka* Appeal Judgement, para. 60, referring to *Kayishema and Ruzindana* Appeal Judgement, para. 113.
[757] *Niyitegeka* Appeal Judgement, para. 60.
[758] *Niyitegeka* Appeal Judgement, para. 60, referring to *Musema* Appeal Judgement, para. 202.
[759] See e.g. *Nahimana et al.* Appeal Judgement, para. 414; *Musema* Appeal Judgement, paras. 205, 206.

an accused need only produce evidence likely to raise a reasonable doubt in the Prosecution case. The alibi does not carry a separate burden. The burden of proving beyond reasonable doubt that, despite the alibi, the facts alleged are nevertheless true remains squarely on the shoulders of the Prosecution.[760]

332. With regard to the Appellant's contention that the Trial Chamber erred by failing to consider his testimony and alibi first, the Appeals Chamber notes that at the beginning of the section on alibi in the Trial Judgement, the Trial Chamber stated that "[n]otwithstanding [the] structure [of the Trial Judgement], in making its factual findings, [it] has assessed the Prosecution and Defence evidence in its totality"[761] and went on to analyze in detail the Appellant's testimony and alibi.[762] The Appeals Chamber therefore finds that the discussion of the Appellant's alibi towards the end of the Trial Judgement does not indicate that it shifted the burden to the Appellant.

333. The Appellant argues that the Trial Chamber erred when it considered the issue to be, and accordingly assessed, whether the Prosecution witnesses eliminated the reasonable possibility that he remained consistently at Nyakinama between 7 and 19 April 1994.[763] The Appellant contends that the Trial Chamber erred in its assessment of his alibi by first considering the Prosecution's evidence tendered to discredit it.[764] In this regard, the Appellant argues that this approach imposed a burden of proof on him, as he was required to produce "more convincing alibi evidence" than the Prosecution's evidence tendered to discredit the alibi.[765]

334. The Appeals Chamber notes that the Trial Chamber articulated the issue to be whether the evidence of Prosecution witnesses who testified to seeing the Appellant in Nyamirambo sector, Ntarama sector, and Rushashi commune eliminates the reasonable possibility that the Appellant "remained consistently in Nyakinama in Ruhengeri prefecture".[766] The Trial Chamber further explained that in its view "this depends on how frequently [Karera] was observed in Nyakinama, whether he could use the roads to the other areas, and the reliability and credibility of the **[page 96]** Prosecution's evidence placing him in Nyamirambo and Ntarama sectors and Rushashi commune".[767]

335. The Trial Chamber found that the reasonable possibility that the Appellant remained "consistently and exclusively" in Ruhengeri prefecture is eliminated by the "credibility issues raised in connection with Defence evidence", as well as the "reliable and credible evidence" which placed the Appellant in Nyamirambo sector, Ntarama sector, and Rushashi commune during this period.[768] Consequently, the Trial Chamber concluded that there was no doubt that the Appellant was present in Nyamirambo and Ntarama sectors and Rushashi commune when the crimes were committed.[769] The Trial Chamber's approach is consistent with the legal standards discussed above. Therefore, the Appeals Chamber finds that the Appellant has failed to demonstrate any error on the part of the Trial Chamber in this regard.

336. The Appellant finally argues that the Trial Chamber's reasoning erroneously suggests that for his alibi to be accepted he had to prove beyond reasonable doubt that he did not leave Nyakinama between 7 and 19 April 1994.[770] In this regard, the Appeals Chamber notes the Trial Chamber's finding that the "credibility issues" in relation to the alibi evidence, coupled with the "reliable and credible" Prosecution evidence placing the Appellant in Nyamirambo, Ntarama, and Rushashi, together eliminated the reasonable possibility that the Appellant remained consistently and exclusively in Ruhengeri prefecture.[771] The Trial Chamber's

---

[760] Trial Judgement, para. 462.
[761] Trial Judgement, para. 457.
[762] In the introductory paragraphs of the chapters addressing the events in Nyamirambo and Ntarama, the Trial Chamber specified that the Appellant presented an alibi and summarized his defence. Trial Judgement, paras. 81, 222. For each factual finding, and when appropriate, the Trial Chamber systematically summarized both the Prosecution and Defence evidence, and discussed them. It also specifically considered the Appellant's testimony (*see* Trial Judgement, paras. 30, 34, 48, 49, 64, 65, 72, 73, 104, 133, 275-278, 309, 342-345, 373, 390-394, 402, 406, 415, 430, 448), and his alibi (*see* Trial Judgement, paras. 4, 26, 81, 123, 222, 275) throughout the Trial Judgement.
[763] Appellant's Brief, para. 295; Brief in Reply, para. 11; AT. 28 August 2008 p. 16.
[764] Appellant's Brief, para. 303.
[765] Appellant's Brief, para. 303; AT. 28 August 2008 p. 16.
[766] Trial Judgement, para. 500.
[767] Trial Judgement, para. 500.
[768] Trial Judgement, para. 510.
[769] Trial Judgement, para. 510.
[770] Appellant's Brief, para. 303; AT. 28 August 2008 p. 15.
[771] Trial Judgement, para. 510.

reasoning does not indicate the imposition of any obligation on the Appellant to prove beyond reasonable doubt that he stayed permanently in Nyakinama between 7 and 19 April 1994.

337. Contrary to the Appellant's contention, the Trial Chamber did not conclude that the Appellant returned every day to Nyakinama. Instead, it found that the Appellant could travel on the morning and return "on some days".[772] The Trial Chamber found that there were significant gaps in the alibi evidence allowing for his presence on some days at the crime sites.[773] There is no indication that the Trial Chamber considered that the Appellant must necessarily have undertaken the journeys from Nyakinama to the crime sites and back on the same day, between the morning and the afternoon.[774] The Trial Chamber's assessment of the Defence evidence about accessibility of the roads does not contradict this interpretation. The Trial Chamber focused on whether it was **[page 97]** possible to travel at that period between Nyakinama and the crime sites and not whether it was feasible on the same day. Consequently, the Appeals Chamber finds no merit in the Appellant's argument.

338. This sub-ground of appeal is accordingly dismissed.

B. Alleged Errors relating to the Possibility of Travelling from Ruhengeri

339. The Appellant submits that the Trial Chamber erroneously assessed the Prosecution's evidence in relation to the possibility of travelling from Ruhengeri prefecture after 6 April 1994.[775] The Appellant argues that the Trial Chamber determined, in error, that Defence Witness KNK corroborated the evidence of Defence Witnesses BBA and KBG that the main road between Ruhengeri and Kigali was blocked but that an alternative road was available passing through Gitarama.[776] The Appellant also contends that speculating on the possibility of travelling from Ruhengeri to Kigali, without evidence that such a journey was actually undertaken, does not impair the reasonable possibility that he remained in Ruhengeri.[777] He further argues that the Trial Chamber's finding that he moved around without difficulty because of his position and the fact that he could use an official vehicle is not supported by evidence.[778] In addition, he asserts that the Trial Chamber erred in finding that he was at the Ntarama Church on the morning of 15 April 1994 while accepting his alibi that he was in Ruhengeri every day in the morning and after 4 p.m.[779] The Appellant argues that the evidence demonstrated that it was impossible and unrealistic for him to undertake in such a time-frame the 410 kilometre return journey from Ruhengeri to the Ntarama Church through the itinerary accepted by the Trial Chamber which would have meant passing through Gitarama town, Kigoma commune, and Ngenda commune, as it was the only possible route.[780]

340. In response, the Prosecution submits that the Trial Chamber correctly found that Witness KNK's evidence corroborated the evidence of Witnesses BBA and KBG on the point of the accessibility of the Ruhengeri-Kigali road.[781] It further submits that the Appellant adduced no tangible evidence to demonstrate that it was impossible to travel during the period in question, and the evidence adduced by both parties was that although travel was difficult, it was possible through **[page 98]** secondary roads.[782] The Prosecution argues that the Appellant's submission in relation to the Trial Chamber's finding that the Appellant moved around without difficulty is false.[783]

341. In relation to the Appellant's argument that the Trial Chamber erred in finding that Witness KNK corroborated the testimonies of Witnesses BBA and KBG, the Appeals Chamber notes that the Trial

---

[772] Trial Judgement, para. 505.
[773] *See* Trial Judgement, para. 505.
[774] The Appeals Chamber notes the following statement "It is important that [Witness YMK] did not see Karera every day, as he testified that he occasionally missed the program." (footnote omitted). Trial Judgement, para. 505.
[775] Appellant's Brief, paras. 298-302; AT. 28 August 2008 p. 22.
[776] Appellant's Brief, para. 299.
[777] Appellant's Brief, para. 300.
[778] Appellant's Brief, paras. 301, 302.
[779] Brief in Reply, paras. 50-52.
[780] Brief in Reply, paras. 50-52.
[781] Respondent's Brief, paras. 196-198.
[782] Respondent's Brief, para. 201.
[783] Respondent's Brief, paras. 203, 204.

Chamber concluded that it was possible to travel from Nyakinama to Nyamirambo, through Gitarama, without using the main Ruhengeri-Kigali road, based on the following assessment:

> Witness BBA testified that travel was possible from Nyakinama to Gitarama without using the main Ruhengeri-Kigali road, and Witness KBG said that the road from Gitarama to Nyamirambo was open for travel between April and July 1994. Their evidence is corroborated by Witness KNK, who testified that she travelled from Ruhengeri via Gitarama to Kigali on 16 April 1994.[784]

342. During cross-examination, Witness BBA testified that there was an unpaved road leading from Ruhengeri to Gitarama, through Nyakinama, without passing through Kigali. However, he could not testify on whether the road was accessible by a motor vehicle.[785]

343. The Appeals Chamber also notes that Witness KBG testified that in April 1994, after the killing of President Habyarimana, and in May 1994,[786] the only road accessible by a motor vehicle from Kigali to Gitarama passed through the Nyamirambo road, Mt. Kigali, and Nyabarongo.[787] Witness KBG specified that he followed that road because it was the only safe road and that the other roads were blocked.[788]

344. Witness KNK also indicated that the "usual road" from Kigali to Ruhengeri was "blocked" but that it was possible to travel by an alternate route through Gitarama, which was safe.[789]

345. Therefore, according to the testimony of Witness KNK, corroborated by the evidence of Witnesses BBA and KBG, it was possible to travel from Nyakinama to Nyamirambo, through Gitarama, without using the main Ruhengeri-Kigali road. The Appellant has not shown any error in the Trial Chamber's finding that Witness KNK corroborated the evidence of Witnesses BBA and KBG.

346. The Appellant argues that even if it was possible to travel between Ruhengeri and the Kigali region, the reasonable possibility that he remained in Ruhengeri cannot be questioned without **[page 99]** evidence that he actually took such a journey.[790] The Appeals Chamber disagrees. The Trial Chamber excluded the reasonable possibility that the Appellant remained "consistently and exclusively" in Ruhengeri.[791] In reaching these findings, the Trial Chamber considered the evidence of a number of witnesses and reasoned that "it was possible to travel from Nyakinama to Nyamirambo, through Gitarama, without using the main Ruhengeri-Kigali road";[792] that "Karera could have travelled from Nyakinama to Ntarama between April and July 1994"[793] using an official vehicle; and that since he had an influential government position and was well known he would have passed roadblocks without major problems.[794]

347. The Trial Chamber also considered the credibility of the Defence evidence in relation to the Appellant being in Nyakinama and the reliability and credibility of the Prosecution's evidence which placed him at Nyamirambo and Ntarama sectors and Rushashi commune, the locations of the crimes.[795] The Appeals Chamber therefore finds that the Appellant has failed to show that the Trial Chamber committed an error in reaching this conclusion.

348. The Appellant finally contends that the Trial Chamber's finding that he moved around without difficulty by virtue of his position and the fact that he could use an official vehicle is not supported by evidence and is therefore erroneous.[796] Having considered this finding,[797] the Appeals Chamber notes that

---

[784] Trial Judgement, para. 506.
[785] T. 15 August 2006 p. 48.
[786] T. 9 May 2006 p. 3.
[787] T. 9 May 2006 p. 11.
[788] T. 9 May 2006 p. 37.
[789] T. 9 May 2006 p. 39.
[790] Appellant's Brief, para. 300.
[791] Trial Judgement, para. 510.
[792] Trial Judgement, para. 506.
[793] Trial Judgement, para. 507.
[794] Trial Judgement, para. 508.
[795] Trial Judgement, paras. 500-510.
[796] Appellant's Brief, paras. 301, 302.
[797] Trial Judgement, para. 508 which reads: "[…] However, as Karera had an influential governmental position and was well known, the Chamber considers that he would have passed roadblocks controlled by *Interahamwe, gendarmes*, soldiers or civilians, without major problems. The use of an official vehicle, which Karera said that he had while in Ruhengeri, would facilitate his travel."

while the Trial Chamber did not cite any evidence in relation to it, there was relevant evidence on the record supporting this conclusion. The Appeals Chamber notes, for instance, that when the Appellant testified, he stated that on the morning of 7 April 1994 he was recognized as an authority by one of the "gendarmes" manning a roadblock and could continue his travel after his vehicle had been checked.[798] The Appellant also testified that on 7 April 1994, he travelled through "three roadblocks and one military check-point".[799] Therefore, the Appeals Chamber finds no merit in the Appellant's argument.

349. The Appeals Chamber notes that the Trial Chamber generally did not embark on an assessment of the time needed to travel from Nyakinama to the crime scenes.[800] However, the **[page 100]** Appeals Chamber finds that the Trial Chamber did not necessarily conclude that the Appellant had to travel from Nyakinama to the crimes sites in Nyamirambo or Ntarama on the same day. Rather, its finding that "Karera could have lived in Ruhengeri, but travelled during the daytime to Nyamirambo or Ntarama sectors, returning on some days to the Nyakinama campus by 4.00 p.m"[801] does not preclude an interpretation that although on some days he returned to Nyakinama by 4.00 p.m., on other days he travelled from Nyakinama to a crime site and returned on another day.

C. Alleged Errors in the Assessment of the Evidence on Alibi

350. The Appellant contends that the Trial Chamber erroneously found that the Defence witnesses who testified to his alibi had credibility problems.[802] He states that the contradictions relating to Defence Witnesses ATA and KD are trivial when compared to the problems of credibility affecting the Prosecution witnesses.[803] He also argues that the Trial Chamber did not provide good reasons for doubting the alibi evidence.[804]

351. The Prosecution responds that the Trial Chamber has unfettered discretion in assessing the evidence presented by the parties, and that the Appellant has failed to demonstrate in what way the Trial Chamber abused that discretion.[805]

352. Witness ATA testified that she enrolled in school a week after her arrival in Ruhengeri and that the Appellant was at home when she left for school at 7.00 a.m. and when she returned at 3.00 or 4.00 p.m.[806] The witness stated that in mid-April 1994, the Appellant was appointed prefect and began travelling to Rushashi.[807] The Trial Chamber found that the witness's testimony could only relate to a few days since she started school around 14 April 1994 and the Appellant was appointed **[page 101]** prefect on 17 April 1994. The Trial Chamber further noted that the witness was less specific about the period before 14 April 1994 stating that the Appellant stayed at home all the time.[808]

---

[798] T. 23 August 2006 p. 18.
[799] T. 23 August 2006 p. 17.
[800] *See* Trial Judgement, paras. 506, 507.
[801] Trial Judgement, para. 505.
[802] Appellant's Brief, para. 306.
[803] Appellant's Brief, para. 306.
[804] Appellant's Brief, para. 307.
[805] Respondent's Brief, para. 210.
[806] Trial Judgement, para. 482. During her testimony Witness ATA stated that when she was going to school she would leave her home at about 7 a.m. and would return home every evening after school. She specified that classes started at 8 a.m. and that the distance between her home and the school was quite long. The classes ended at about 2 p.m., and she "was able to get back home between 3 p.m. and 4 p.m." When returning from school she found the Appellant at home. She further testified that from 7 April 1994, the Appellant had no specific work because he stayed at home, in Ruhengeri and that, before the period when she was going to school, the Appellant "was with us because he had no other work to do, so he didn't go anywhere" T. 5 May 2006 p. 6.
[807] Trial Judgement, para. 482. *See*: T. 5 May 2006 p. 6 [Q. As for your father, in April 1994, to the best of your recollection, did he leave Ruhengeri? ATA. (…) I remember that in the middle of April, he informed us that he had been appointed *préfet* of Kigali-rural and that he intended to go to Rushashi, which was one of the *commune*s in Kigali-rural *préfecture*. Q. Do you remember whether he, indeed, went to Rushashi? A. I remember that he went there because during that period I no longer saw him at home, but during the weekends -- that is, on Saturday or Sunday, he came back to see us. Q. And when did he leave again? A. I said that he would arrive on Saturday and return to Rushashi on Monday morning. Q. (…) For how long did your father, François Karera, travel from Ruhengeri to Rushashi and from Rushashi back to Ruhengeri? A. As I have already pointed out, he went to Rushashi in mid-April and returned to Ruhengeri in early July.].
[808] Trial Judgement, para. 501.

353. Witness KD testified that between 7 April 1994 and mid-April 1994, the Appellant occasionally left his son's house at the Nyakinama campus of the Rwanda National University to watch television at the university campus or to visit professors, but he never left the campus and did not visit the sub-prefecture office in Rushashi.[809] The witness stated that after mid-April, she started a business and that the Appellant was at home when she left for work in the morning and when she returned home for lunch and from work.[810] The Trial Chamber took into account that the witness stated that the Appellant did occasionally leave the house[811] and that during the period of 7 to 15 April 1994, she had not yet started her business.[812]

354. The Appeals Chamber recalls that it is within a Trial Chamber's discretion to accept or reject a witness's testimony, after seeing the witness, hearing the testimony, and observing him or her under cross-examination.[813] In the present case, the Appeals Chamber finds that the Appellant has failed to demonstrate that the Trial Chamber erred in the assessment of the testimonies of Witnesses ATA and KD.

355. The Appellant further argues that the Trial Chamber did not advance any reason for doubting the evidence adduced in support of the alibi.[814] The Appeals Chamber disagrees. In its assessment of the relevant Defence witnesses, the Trial Chamber articulated that there were "credibility issues".[815] In relation to Witness KD, the Trial Chamber was of the view that inconsistencies in her testimony affected her credibility.[816] The Trial Chamber was also of the view that Witnesses KD and ATA sought to exaggerate the Appellant's presence in Ruhengeri.[817] In relation to Defence Witnesses BBA and YMK, the Trial Chamber considered that their evidence **[page 102]** did not reliably indicate that the Appellant remained consistently in Ruhengeri.[818] The Appellant has not shown how the Trial Chamber abused its discretion in making these findings.

356. Therefore, this sub-ground of appeal is dismissed.

D. Conclusion

357. The Appeals Chamber finds that the Appellant has failed to demonstrate any error in the Trial Chamber's reasoning and findings in relation to the Appellant's alibi. Therefore, this ground of appeal is dismissed in its entirety. **[page 103]**

X. ALLEGED ERRORS RELATING TO THE TRIAL CHAMBER'S LEGAL FINDINGS (GROUND OF APPEAL 10)

358. Under this ground of appeal, the Appellant submits that the Trial Chamber's legal findings are erroneous and "must obviously be revisited in the light of admissible evidence".[819]

359. The Appeals Chamber observes that all of the arguments advanced under this ground of appeal challenge the Trial Chamber's factual findings. The Appeals Chamber has already addressed these arguments in the respective sections of this Judgement.[820] Since no additional arguments are presented under this ground of appeal, no further discussion is warranted.

---

[809] Trial Judgement, para. 483. The Appellant testified that the sub-prefect office was in Rushashi. Trial Judgement, para. 342. *See* testimony of Witness KD: T. 8 May 2006 p. 27. Q. [...] So is it your testimony that from the 7th of April to the 15th of April, which is the middle of April, during those approximately eight days, he did not go to the sub-*préfecture* office? A. He did not go there. During that period, I, myself, had not yet started my commercial activities. From the 7th up until he left for Ruhashya, he did not leave the compound.).
[810] Trial Judgement, para. 483. *See* testimony of Witness KD: T. 5 May 2006 p. 45. (Q. From what time to what time were you involved in this small business? A. It depended on whether we had gone to purchase other foodstuffs in the market or not, but we started at 10 a.m. and we closed at 5 p.m. or 5:30 p.m. [...] Q. When you left your brother [...]'s home in the mornings, was your father there? A. Yes, I left after breakfast and my father was there. [...] Q. Was your father home when you returned? A. Yes, I found my father at home.).
[811] Trial Judgement, para. 502.
[812] Trial Judgement, para. 502.
[813] *Seromba* Appeal Judgement, para. 116, referring to *Akayesu* Appeal Judgement, para. 147.
[814] Appellant's Brief, para. 307; AT. 28 August 2008 p. 24.
[815] Trial Judgement, para. 510.
[816] Trial Judgement, para. 502.
[817] Trial Judgement, para. 503.
[818] Trial Judgement, paras. 504, 505.
[819] Notice of Appeal, para. 243.
[820] *See supra* Chapters V to IX.

360. However, the Appeals Chamber, *proprio motu*, has considered the question of whether the Trial Chamber erred in using its findings that the Appellant was responsible for the killings of Joseph Kahabaye, Murekezi, Jean Bosco Ndingutse, and Palatin Nyagatare in support of the convictions it entered under Count 1 of the Amended Indictment for genocide and under Count 3 for extermination as a crime against humanity.[821] The Appeals Chamber invited the parties to address this issue at the appeal hearing.

361. The Appellant did not directly address this issue.[822] The Prosecution submits that it was permissible for the Trial Chamber to use its finding on the killings of these four individuals in support of the Appellant's conviction for genocide and extermination since the Appellant had received timely, clear, and sufficient notice that these killings were to be used in support of these charges.[823] In this respect, the Prosecution contends that the Amended Indictment has to be read as a whole,[824] and that the Prosecution Pre-Trial Brief discussed the factual allegations by location, including Nyamirambo, rather than with respect to each count. According to the Prosecution, the Appellant was therefore given proper notice that these four individuals were among the victims of his genocidal and extermination campaign at that location.[825]

362. The Appeals Chamber has already quashed the Trial Chamber's findings in relation to the killings of Joseph Kahabaye, Jean Bosco Ndingutse, and Palatin Nyagatare for other reasons.[826] Therefore, it need only consider whether it was permissible for the Trial Chamber to convict the **[page 104]** Appellant for genocide and extermination as a crime against humanity based on the murder of Murekezi.

363. The Appeals Chamber notes that the allegation of the murder of Murekezi is only made at paragraph 33 of the Amended Indictment in support of Count 4 for murder as a crime against humanity. The Appeals Chamber further notes that, at trial, the Defence objected that "several allegations relating to events in Nyamirambo and Rushashi are too vague or not mentioned in the Indictment, or relate only to Count 4 (murder) [and that the] [e]vidence in support of these allegations should therefore be excluded or considered only with respect to the murder charge".[827] The Trial Chamber rejected the Defence objection on the grounds that:

> [...] the Defence did not object to any of this evidence at the time it was admitted or at the close of the Prosecution case. Nor did it make a general pre-trial objection. Rather, the Defence makes these exclusion requests for the first time in its closing submissions. It offers no explanation for failing to object to this evidence at the time it was admitted or at a later point during the trial proceedings. The Chamber finds that there is no reasonable explanation for the Defence's lack of objections at an earlier stage in the trial. In the exercise of its discretion, it holds that the burden of proof has shifted to the Defence to demonstrate that the lack of notice prejudiced the Accused in the preparation of his defence.[828]

364. Subsequently, the Trial Chamber considered the Defence objection in connection with the allegation of killings at Nyamirambo on 7 April 1994.[829] The Trial Chamber found "it clear that Counts 1, 2 and 3 include events that occurred on 7 April [1994]".[830] When considering the alleged killings of Joseph Kahabaye, Félix Dix, Murekezi, Jean Bosco Ndingutse, and Palatin Nyagatare,[831] the Trial Chamber discussed whether paragraph 33 of the Amended Indictment pleaded these events with sufficient specificity.[832] However, the Trial Chamber did not consider whether the allegations contained in this paragraph, under Count 4 (murder) could also support the charges of genocide and extermination as a crime against humanity.

---

[821] Order for Preparation of the Appeal Hearing, p. 2.
[822] The Defence addressed the issue of the defects in the Amended Indictment without making direct reference to the sufficiency of notice relating to the killings of the four individuals which were charged under Count 4 of the Amended Indictment for murder as a crime against humanity. AT. 28 August 2008 pp. 52-54.
[823] AT. 28 August 2008 p. 37.
[824] AT. 28 August 2008 p. 37.
[825] AT. 28 August 2008 p. 38.
[826] *See supra* Chapter VI, sp. para. 214.
[827] Defence Closing Brief, paras. 193-197, 318-319; Defence closing arguments (T. 24 November 2006 pp. 12-14). The Defence stated that the allegations of killing made under Count 4 (murder) could "only be taken into consideration [under that Count]". Defence Closing Brief, para. 197. *See also* Trial Judgement, paras. 18, 85.
[828] Trial Judgement, para. 19.
[829] Trial Judgement, para. 85.
[830] Trial Judgement, para. 86.
[831] *See* Trial Judgement, Sections 4.7, 4.8, 4.9, 4.11.
[832] *See* Trial Judgement, paras. 183, 184, 196, 202.

365. In *Muvunyi*, the Appeals Chamber observed that "the Prosecution's failure to expressly state that a paragraph in the Indictment supports a particular count in the Indictment is indicative that the allegation is not charged as a crime".[833] The Appeals Chamber considers that the same may be said where a particular allegation is charged under a particular count only. In the present case, the Amended Indictment put the Appellant on notice that the Prosecution was charging him for the **[page 105]** murder of Murekezi only under Count 4. In view of this, there is some basis for argument that by reading the Amended Indictment alone, the Appellant would not have understood that he was also charged for the same fact under Counts 1 and 3. In regard to the Amended Indictment, the Prosecution knew the identity of a finite number of victims and was able, when it sought to amend the Indictment, to specify the circumstances of their murder. It chose not to list Murekezi's killing in the statements of facts pertaining to counts alleging genocide and extermination as a crime against humanity. The Appeals Chamber has previously held that "[e]ven in cases where a high degree of specificity is 'impractical [...] since the identity of the victim is information that is valuable to the preparation of the defence case, if the Prosecution is in a position to name the victims, it should do so.'"[834]

366. Turning to the Prosecution's submission that the Amended Indictment has to be read as a whole, the Appeals Chamber notes that while the statement of facts supporting Count 4 incorporates the statements of facts supporting Counts 1 and 3, the reverse is not true. The statements of facts supporting Counts 1 and 3 do not incorporate the statement of facts supporting Count 4. This lack of reciprocity might have added to the impression that Murekezi's murder was not incorporated in Counts 1 and 3 of the Amended Indictment.

367. The Appeals Chamber further notes that the process of amending the initial Indictment might have laid the groundwork for confusion on this issue. Originally, Murekezi's killing was listed in a statement of facts pertaining to both Counts 3 and 4. However, this statement of facts was eventually severed, and Murekezi's killing was subsequently mentioned only in the statement of facts applicable to Count 4. While the rationale for the severing of the original, combined statement of facts did not centre on Murekezi, the amendment may have given the message that Murekezi's killing related only to Count 4 of the Indictment, rather than serving as a key basis for the gravest of the charges involved.[835] The Prosecution's decision not to refer to Murekezi at all in Counts 1 and 3 of the Amended Indictment, especially in the context of the Indictment amendment process, **[page 106]** resulted in vagueness with potentially serious consequences for the preparation of the Appellant's defence. In these circumstances, the Appeals Chamber considers that reversal of the affected convictions is appropriate.[836]

368. The Appeals Chamber further notes that the Amended Indictment was issued on 19 December 2005, seven days *after* the filing of the Prosecution Pre-Trial Brief.[837] As a result, while the Prosecution Pre-Trial Brief included a summary of anticipated witness testimony, the text of the Prosecution Pre-Trial Brief and the summaries referred to either the Indictment or the draft amended indictment annexed to the Prosecution Motion to Amend the Indictment,[838] but not to the Amended Indictment itself. Turning to the Prosecution's contention that the Prosecution Pre-Trial Brief presented "the factual allegations by location, including

---

[833] *Muvunyi* Appeal Judgement, para. 156.

[834] *Ntakirutimana* Appeal Judgement, para. 25 (quoting *Kupreškić et al.* Appeal Judgement, para. 90)

[835] More specifically, on 25 November 2005, the Prosecution filed a request for leave to amend the Indictment. The Prosecution, *inter alia*,, requested authorization to present Counts 3 (extermination as a crime against humanity) and 4 (murder as a crime against humanity) cumulatively instead of alternatively. *See* Prosecution's Motion for Leave to Amend the Indictment, paras. 1.2, 3.5-3.7. The Trial Chamber granted the Prosecution's request in part, allowing the cumulative pleading of Counts 3 and 4, the deletion of some paragraphs, sections and words, and the insertion of names of victims in one paragraph. The Trial Chamber also instructed the Prosecution to specify "the location, time and manner of the death of Theoneste Gakuru" and "clarify the facts which are *intended to support the charge of murder as a crime against humanity, as opposed to extermination as a crime against humanity*" (emphasis added). It specified that "such clarification should include the names of the victims, the location, time and manner of the alleged murders". *See* Decision on the Prosecutor's Request for Leave to Amend the Indictment, Rule 50 of the Rules of Procedure and Evidence, 12 December 2005 p. 5. The Amended Indictment, incorporating the Trial Chamber's instructions, was filed on 19 December 2005. *See The Prosecutor v. François Karera*, Amended Indictment, 19 December 2005. The concise statement of facts supporting Counts 3 and 4 was severed and the murder of Murekezi was no longer mentioned under Count 3, only being pleaded under Count 4. *Compare* Amended Indictment pp. 5, 6, *with* Amended Indictment, p. 7.

[836] *See Ntakirutimana* Appeal Judgement, para. 27.

[837] *Compare The Prosecutor v. François Karera*, Amended Indictment, 19 December 2005, *with* Prosecution Pre-Trial Brief, 12 December 2005.

[838] The Prosecution Pre-Trial Brief, which was filed after the Prosecution Motion to Amend the Indictment, merely refers to "the indictment" without specifying whether it points to the Initial Indictment or the draft amended indictment.

Nyamirambo, rather than with respect to each count", the Appeals Chamber does not see how this argument is capable of demonstrating that any defect in the Amended Indictment relating to the facts underlying Counts 1 and 3 was cured by the Prosecution Pre-Trial Brief.

369. In a world of limited legal resources, the Appellant's counsel might have focused more attention on Murekezi's killing had this key material fact been more specifically linked to a larger number of counts concerning crimes such as genocide and extermination as a crime against humanity, which on their face appear even more serious than murder. Instead, the Amended Indictment may have given the opposite impression. This error and the confusion it might have generated justify reversal of the Appellant's convictions under Counts 1 and 3, insofar as they rely on the murder of Murekezi.

370. Accordingly, these convictions are quashed. **[page 107]**

XI. ALLEGED ERROR IN HEARING THE CASE OF THARCISSE RENZAHO WHILE PARTICIPATING IN DELIBERATIONS ON THE APPELLANT'S CASE (GROUND OF APPEAL 11)

371. The Appellant submits that the Trial Chamber erred in law by hearing the case of Tharcisse Renzaho,[839] the former prefect of Kigali,[840] while it was deliberating on the Appellant's case.[841] The Appellant alleges an appearance of bias on the part of the Trial Judges.[842] He submits that a reasonable observer would have concluded "that the deliberations of the Trial Chamber [in the present case] were tainted by its hearing of the *Renzaho* case".[843]

372. In his Appellant's Brief, the Appellant states that "[f]or now" he "formally declines to raise this ground of appeal".[844] Instead, the Appellant makes several "observations" in relation to the Prosecution's obligation to disclose potentially exculpatory material pursuant to Rule 68 of the Rules.[845] He submits that it is impossible for him to know whether protected witnesses who testified in his trial will subsequently return to testify in other cases[846] since they will testify under different pseudonyms.[847] The Appellant contends that he therefore has to rely on the Prosecution's compliance with its disclosure obligations pursuant to Rule 68 of the Rules.[848] In this regard, he submits that the Prosecution has failed to disclose potentially exculpatory witness statements and testimonies of three protected witnesses who testified in the *Renzaho* trial and who had previously testified in his trial.[849] The Appellant also alleges a violation of his right to be tried without undue delay.[850]

373. The Prosecution provides no argument in response, noting that the Appellant abandoned this ground of appeal.[851] **[page 108]**

374. The Appeals Chamber notes that the Appellant's submissions relating to the Prosecution's failure to discharge its disclosure obligations and the Trial Chamber's violation of his right to a trial without undue delay were raised for the first time in the Appeal Brief and the Brief in Reply.[852] In light of the fact that the Appellant failed to "indicate the substance of the alleged errors" in his Notice of Appeal, as required by Rule

---

[839] *The Prosecutor v. Tharcisse Renzaho*, Case No. ICTR-97-31-T. The trial in that case started on 8 January 2007.
[840] Notice of Appeal, paras. 245-248; Appellant's Brief, para. 320; Brief in Reply, para. 63.
[841] Notice of Appeal, para. 245.
[842] Notice of Appeal, paras. 246-248.
[843] Notice of Appeal, para. 248.
[844] Appellant's Brief, para. 319.
[845] Brief in Reply, paras. 63-68.
[846] Brief in Reply, paras. 65, 67.
[847] Brief in Reply, paras. 65, 67.
[848] Brief in Reply, para. 68.
[849] Brief in Reply, para. 64. He also submits that the testimony of Witness AIA, a protected witness in the *Renzaho* case, could be relevant to a determination whether the Appellant had authority over the policemen in the region, since Witness AIA stated that he was a policeman in Nyarugenge. The Appellant submits that the witness gave the remaining part of his testimony in closed session, and that, as such, it was not accessible to the Appellant. Brief in Reply, para. 66.
[850] Appellant's Brief, para. 320.
[851] Respondent's Brief, para. 7.
[852] Appellant's Brief, para. 320; Brief in Reply, paras. 59-68.

108 of the Rules, the Appeals Chamber finds that the Appellant's arguments do not warrant any consideration to ensure the fairness of the proceedings and the Appeals Chamber declines to consider them.

375. The Appeals Chamber now turns to the arguments raised in the Notice of Appeal under this ground to the effect that the Trial Chamber was tainted by the evidence it heard in the *Renzaho* case while deliberating on the present case. The Appeals Chamber notes that, at the appeal hearing and in response to a question raised by the Appeals Chamber, the Appellant declared that he had not abandoned this ground of appeal.[853] The Appeals Chamber finds that the explanations given by the Appellant for reinstating this ground of appeal which it had "formally dropped" in the Appellant's Brief are unclear.[854] However, in light of the particular circumstances of this case and absent an objection by the Prosecution, the Appeals Chamber will address the Appellant's argument concerning the alleged lack of independence and impartiality.

376. The Appellant argues that in light of the positions respectively held by Tharcisse Renzaho and the Appellant in April 1994, respectively, and the locations where they allegedly committed crimes, the facts of both cases are linked.[855] The Appellant submits that the Trial Judges heard witnesses in the *Renzaho* case who had previously testified in his trial and that by doing so they lost the appearance of independence and impartiality.[856] The Appellant alleges that, when hearing the same witnesses in different cases, the Trial Judges would eventually be incapable of distinguishing the witnesses' testimonies.[857]

377. In *Nahimana et al.*, the Appeals Chamber recalled that

> [t]he right of an accused to be tried before an independent tribunal is an integral component of his right to a fair trial as provided in Articles 19 and 20 of the Statute. [...] [T]he independence of the Judges of the Tribunal is guaranteed by the standards for their selection, the method of their appointment, their conditions of service and the immunity they enjoy. The Appeals Chamber further notes that the independence of the Tribunal as a judicial organ was affirmed by the Secretary-General at the time when the Tribunal was created, and the Chamber reaffirms that this institutional independence means that the Tribunal is entirely independent of the organs of the United Nations and of any State or group of States. Accordingly, the Appeals Chamber considers **[page 109]** that there is a strong presumption that the Judges of the Tribunal take their decisions in full independence, and it is for the Appellant to rebut this presumption.[858]

378. The Appeals Chamber notes that Judges of this Tribunal are sometimes involved in trials which, by their very nature, cover overlapping issues.[859] In this regard, the Appeals Chamber previously held that

> [i]t is assumed, in the absence of evidence to the contrary, that, by virtue of their training and experience, the Judges will rule fairly on the issues before them, relying solely and exclusively on the evidence adduced in the particular case. The Appeals Chamber agrees with the ICTY Bureau that "a judge is not disqualified from hearing two or more criminal trials arising out of the same series of events, where he is exposed to evidence relating to these events in both cases".[860]

Accordingly, the fact that the Trial Judges heard the *Renzaho* case while, at the same time, they participated in deliberations on the Appellant's case does not in itself demonstrate an appearance of bias on the part of the Trial Judges.

379. For the foregoing reasons, this ground of appeal is dismissed. **[page 110]**

XII. ALLEGED ERRORS RELATING TO SENTENCING (GROUND OF APPEAL 12)

380. The Trial Chamber sentenced the Appellant to life imprisonment for the crimes of genocide and extermination and murder as crimes against humanity.[861]381. The Appellant submits that the Trial Chamber

---

[853] AT. 28 August 2008 p. 57.
[854] AT. 28 August 2008 pp. 56, 57.
[855] Appellant's Brief, para. 320; Brief in Reply, para. 67.
[856] Notice of Appeal, paras. 245-248.
[857] AT. 28 August 2008 p. 57.
[858] *Nahimana et al.* Appeal Judgement, para. 28 (citations omitted).
[859] *Nahimana et al.* Appeal Judgement, para. 78.
[860] *Nahimana et al.* Appeal Judgement, para. 78 (citations omitted).
[861] Trial Judgement, para. 585.

committed an error of law in sentencing him to imprisonment for the remainder of his life.[862] The Appellant claims that "[t]he numerous errors of law and fact that affect the [Trial] Chamber's findings are such that the [Trial] Chamber should have acquitted the Appellant, and a sentence should never have been imposed on him."[863] He posits an alternate factual conclusion that, in his view, the Trial Chamber should have reached,[864] claiming that "[t]his version of [the] factual finding is also as plausible as that made by the [Trial] Chamber."[865] In the alternative, the Appellant argues that the Trial Chamber should have imposed a reduced sentence[866] and pleads for the Appeals Chamber to substitute the current sentence with an "appropriate sentence".[867]

382. The Appellant further submits that the Trial Chamber did not take into account the factors it should have considered in determining the sentence.[868] To this end, the Appellant points to factors that according to him should have mitigated his sentence but were not considered by the Trial Chamber: the "pacification meetings" which he held in Rushashi;[869] his efforts to ensure the safety of Vincent Munyandamutsa, a well-known RPF supporter;[870] the time (thirteen months) spent in detention awaiting judgement during the Trial Chamber's deliberations;[871] and the fact that being sentenced for the remainder of his life, the Appellant is not in a position to benefit from the reduction of the sentence granted by the Presiding Judge during the delivery of the Trial Judgement.[872] **[page 111]**

383. The Prosecution responds that this ground of appeal should be summarily dismissed because the Appellant advances no argument to demonstrate that the Trial Chamber failed to exercise its discretion adequately or that it committed a manifest error in determining the sentence.[873]

384. The Appeals Chamber will first address the merits of the Appellant's arguments against the Trial Chamber's determination of the sentence and then will consider how its findings on the Appellant's convictions impact upon the sentence.

385. Article 24 of the Statute allows the Appeals Chamber to "affirm, reverse or revise" a sentence imposed by a Trial Chamber. However, the Appeals Chamber recalls that Trial Chambers are vested with a broad discretion in determining the appropriate sentence. This stems from their obligation to tailor the sentence according to the individual circumstances of the accused and the gravity of the crime.[874] Generally, the Appeals Chamber will not substitute its own sentence for that imposed by the Trial Chamber unless it has been shown that the latter committed a discernible error in exercising its discretion, or failed to follow the applicable law.[875]386. The Appellant claims that the Trial Chamber failed to consider mitigating factors in sentencing him.

387. In addressing the mitigating circumstances, the Trial Chamber stated that:

> [it] does not consider that there are any significant mitigating circumstances. Since 1958, Karera was a teacher and later became a director of primary education. He helped build schools and establish a soccer team for Kigali city [...]. Prior contributions to community development have been considered by both Tribunals as a mitigating factor

---

[862] Notice of Appeal, paras. 249-255; Appellant's Brief, paras. 323-326.
[863] Notice of Appeal, para. 250.
[864] Appellant's Brief, para. 324.
[865] Appellant's Brief, para. 326.
[866] Notice of Appeal, para. 253.
[867] Appellant's Brief, para. 326.
[868] Notice of Appeal, para. 251.
[869] Notice of Appeal, para. 252; Appellant's Brief, para. 325.
[870] Appellant's Brief, para. 325 (where the Appellant challenges the Trial Chamber's factual findings).
[871] Notice of Appeal, para. 254; Appellant's Brief, para. 326.
[872] Notice of Appeal, paras. 254, 255. At paragraph 254, the Appellant submits that "[t]he Trial Chamber did not take into account [...] the fact that the Presiding Judge of the [Trial] Chamber had stated, during delivery of the Judgement on 7 December 2007, that the Appellant had to be given credit for the period he spent in detention since his arrest in Kenya, that is, 4 years and 16 days."
[873] Respondent's Brief, para. 244.
[874] *Nahamina et al.* Appeal Judgement, para. 1037; *Ntagerura et al.* Appeal Judgement, para. 429; *Naletiliü and Martinoviü* Appeal Judgement, para. 593; *Kajelijeli* Appeal Judgement, para. 291; *Semanza* Appeal Judgement, para. 312; *ýelebiüi* Appeal Judgement, para. 717.
[875] *Nahamina et al.* Appeal Judgement, para. 1037; *Ntagerura et al.* Appeal Judgement, para. 429; *Naletiliü and Martinoviü* Appeal Judgement, para. 593; *Jokiü* Appeal Judgement, para. 8; *Kajelijeli* Appeal Judgement, para. 291; *Semanza* Appeal Judgement, para. 312; *Musema* Appeal Judgement, para. 379; *Tadiü* Judgement on Sentencing Appeal, para. 22.

and the Chamber accords this some weight. There is no evidence that Karera discriminated against Tutsis before April 1994, and this is also accorded some weight by the Chamber. The Defence claims that Karera saved Tutsi civilians during the genocide, but the Chamber did not find the evidence regarding these rescues credible. Karera showed no remorse and did not cooperate with the Prosecution. The Chamber is of the view that the aggravating circumstances outweigh the mitigating circumstances.[876]

388. The Appellant made no sentencing submissions during closing arguments. In such circumstances, the Trial Chamber was not under an obligation to seek out information that counsel did not see fit to put before it at the appropriate time.[877] Rule 86(C) of the Rules clearly indicates that sentencing submissions shall be addressed during closing arguments, and it was therefore the **[page 112]** Appellant's prerogative to identify any mitigating circumstances instead of directing the Trial Chamber's attention to the record in general.

389. The Appeals Chamber further finds that in pointing to the "pacification meetings" in Rushashi and to his alleged efforts to ensure the safety of Vincent Munyandamutsa, the Appellant merely presents factual assertions without showing how the mitigating circumstances were undervalued by the Trial Chamber. Therefore, the Appellant has not demonstrated that the Trial Chamber committed a discernible error in its assessment of the individual mitigating circumstances. This sub-ground of appeal is accordingly dismissed.

390. The Appeals Chamber considers that, in sentencing, the Trial Chamber correctly took into account the gravity of the offences and the degree of liability of the convicted person,[878] the individual circumstances of the Appellant, and his role in the crimes, including any mitigating circumstances,[879] as well as the sentencing practices of the Tribunal and in Rwanda.[880] It found it appropriate to impose the maximum sentence.[881] The Appellant makes no submission suggesting that the crimes for which he was convicted are not grave. The Appeals Chamber recalls that even where mitigating circumstances exist, a Trial Chamber "is not precluded from imposing a sentence of life imprisonment, where the gravity of the offence requires the imposition of the maximum sentence provided for."[882] Mindful of the gravity of the Appellant's crimes, the Appeals Chamber does not find any discernible error in sentencing.

391. Turning to the Appellant's claims that the Trial Chamber erred in sentencing him to life imprisonment, when the charges against him were not proven beyond reasonable doubt, the Appeals Chamber recalls that it has upheld a number of the Appellant's grounds of appeal and has reversed several of the Appellant's convictions, namely: for aiding and abetting genocide and extermination as a crime against humanity, based on the alleged weapons distribution in Rushashi commune; for ordering genocide and extermination and murder as crimes against humanity, based on the alleged murders of Joseph Kahabaye, Jean Bosco Ndingutse, and Palatin Nyagatare; and for instigating murder as a crime against humanity, based on the murder of Gakuru. In addition, the Appeals Chamber, *proprio motu*, has reversed the Appellant's convictions for ordering genocide and extermination as a crime against humanity, based on the killing of Murekezi.

392. Therefore the question before the Appeals Chamber is whether it should revise the sentence imposed by the Trial Chamber in view of the findings made in this Judgement. **[page 113]**

393. The Appeals Chamber considers that the crimes for which the Appellant remains convicted on appeal are extremely grave: they include genocide and extermination and murder as crimes against humanity, and resulted in the death of a large number of civilians.[883] Considering that the Trial Chamber exercised its discretion to impose a single sentence reflecting the totality of the criminal conduct of the Appellant instead of imposing concurrent sentences,[884] and in light of the seriousness of the outstanding convictions, the Appeals Chamber finds that the reversals do not warrant a reduction of the sentence imposed by the Trial Chamber.

---

[876] Trial Judgement, para. 582 (footnotes omitted).
[877] *Kupreškić et al.* Appeal Judgement, para. 414.
[878] Trial Judgement, paras. 574, 575.
[879] Trial Judgement, paras. 576-582.
[880] Trial Judgement, paras. 583, 584.
[881] Trial Judgement, para. 585.
[882] *Niyitegeka* Appeal Judgement, para. 267, quoting *Musema* Appeal Judgement, para. 396.
[883] *See* Trial Judgement, paras. 192, 315, 376, 456.
[884] Trial Judgement, para. 585.

394. The Appeals Chamber has considered the mitigating and aggravating factors discussed by the Trial Chamber, and concurs with the Trial Chamber that the aggravating factors outweigh the mitigating factors.[885]

395. The Appellant's unsubstantiated contention that in assessing the sentence, the time spent in detention during the Trial Chamber's deliberations should have been taken into account is also dismissed. The Appellant has not demonstrated how the deliberations period in this case calls for a reduction of sentence.

396. Accordingly, the Appeals Chamber affirms the Appellant's sentence of imprisonment for the remainder of his life.

397. The Appeals Chamber finally dismisses the Appellant's claim that the sentence deprived him of the benefit of any credit based on the period already spent in detention. Rule 101(C) of the Rules states that "[c]redit shall be given to the convicted person for the period, if any, during which the convicted person was detained in cutody pending his surrender to the Tribunal or pending trial or appeal". This provision does not affect the ability of a Chamber to impose the maximum sentence, as provided by Rule 101(A) of the Rules. **[page 114]**

XIII. DISPOSITION

398. For the foregoing reasons, **THE APPEALS CHAMBER**,

PURSUANT to Article 24 of the Statute and Rule 118 of the Rules;

NOTING the written submissions of the parties and their oral arguments presented at the hearing on 28 August 2008;

SITTING in open session;

ALLOWS the Appellant's First Ground of Appeal and **REVERSES** the Appellant's convictions for aiding and abetting genocide and extermination as a crime against humanity, based on the alleged weapons distribution in Rushashi commune;

ALLOWS, in part, the Appellant's Fifth Ground of Appeal and **REVERSES** the Appellant's convictions for ordering genocide and extermination and murder as crimes against humanity, based on the alleged murders of Joseph Kahabaye, Jean Bosco Ndingutse, and Palatin Nyagatare;

PROPRIO MOTU, **REVERSES** the Appellant's convictions for ordering genocide and extermination as a crime against humanity, based on the killing of Murekezi;

ALLOWS, in part, the Appellant's Seventh Ground of Appeal and **REVERSES** the Appellant's conviction for instigating murder as a crime against humanity, based on the murder of Gakuru;

DISMISSES the Appellant's appeal in all other respects;

AFFIRMS the Appellant's conviction for instigating and committing genocide during the attack against Tutsi refugees at Ntarama Church on 15 April 1994; **AFFIRMS** the Appellant's convictions for instigating and committing extermination and murder as crimes against humanity through the killings of Tutsi refugees at Ntarama Church on 15 April 1994; **AFFIRMS** the Appellant's conviction for ordering murder as a crime against humanity based on the killing of Murekezi; **AFFIRMS** the Appellant's conviction for aiding and abetting murder as a crime against humanity based on the killing of Gakuru; **AFFIRMS** the Appellant's convictions for instigating genocide and extermination as a crime against humanity, based on his alleged conduct at meetings held in Rushashi commune between April and June 1994.

AFFIRMS the Appellant's sentence of imprisonment for the remainder of his life, subject to credit being given under Rules 101(D) and 107 of the Rules for the period in which the Appellant was deprived of his liberty for the purposes of this case, that is from 20 October 2001; **[page 115]**

RULES that this Judgement shall be enforced immediately pursuant to Rule 119 of the Rules; and

---

[885] Trial Judgement, para. 582.

ORDERS, in accordance with Rules 103(B) and 107 of the Rules, that the Appellant is to remain in the custody of the Tribunal pending his transfer to the State in which his sentence will be served.

Done in English and French, the English text being authoritative.

Fausto Pocar	Mohamed Shahabuddeen	Mehmet Güney
Presiding Judge	Judge	Judge

Liu Daqun	Theodor Meron
Judge	Judge

Done this 2nd day of February 2009,

at Arusha,

Tanzania.

[Seal of the Tribunal] [page 116]

XIV. ANNEX A: PROCEDURAL BACKGROUND

1. The main aspects of the appeal proceedings are summarized below.

A. Notice of Appeal and Briefs

2. The Trial Chamber pronounced the Trial Judgement in this case on 7 December 2007 and rendered it in writing on 14 December 2007.

3. On 21 December 2007, the Pre-Appeal Judge denied the Appellant's request that the time limit for filing his notice of appeal accrue from the date on which the Trial Judgement was served on him and on his Lead Counsel in French, but granted *proprio motu* an extension of time of seven days.[1] On 9 January 2008, the Pre-Appeal Judge denied the Appellant's request for reconsideration of the 21 December 2007 Decision and for a further extension of time.[2]

4. The Appellant filed his Notice of Appeal on 14 January 2008[3] and his Appellant's Brief on 7 April 2008.[4] On 16 May 2008, the Prosecution filed its Respondent's Brief.[5] The Appellant filed his Brief in Reply on 2 June 2008.[6]

B. Assignment of Judges

5. On 14 December 2007, the following Judges were assigned to hear the appeal: Judge Fausto Pocar, Presiding; Judge Mehmet Güney; Judge Liu Daqun; Judge Theodor Meron; and Judge Wolfgang Schomburg.[7] Judge Fausto Pocar issued an order designating himself as the Pre-Appeal Judge in this case.[8] Subsequently, on 19 June 2008, Judge Mohamed Shahabuddeen was assigned to replace Judge Wolfgang Schomburg, with immediate effect.[9] **[page 117]**

C. Motion related to the Admission of Additional Evidence

6. On 28 August 2008, the Appellant filed a Motion for Additional Evidence.[10] The Prosecution opposed this motion and requested its dismissal.[11] On 6 October 2008, the Appellant filed a reply.[12] On 29 October 2008, the Appeals Chamber dismissed the Appellant's motion.[13]

---

[1] Decision on François Karera's Motion for Extension of Time for Filing the Notice of Appeal, issued on 21 December 2007 and filed on 31 December 2007 ("21 December 2007 Decision"). The French translation of the Trial Judgement was filed on 19 May 2008.

[2] Decision on Requests for Extension of Time for Filing the Notice of Appeal and/or for Reconsideration, 9 January 2008 ("9 January 2008 Decision").

[3] Defence Notice of Appeal, filed in French (*Avis d'Appel*) on 14 January 2008.

[4] Appellant's Brief, filed in French (*Mémoire d'appel (Article 24 du Statut, Règle 111 du Règlement de Procédure et de Preuve*) on 7 April 2008. The Appellant initially submitted an Appellant's Brief on 28 March 2008 that exceeded the word limit imposed by the Tribunal's Practice Direction on the Length of Briefs and Motions on Appeal by approximately 7,000 words. The Appellant did not seek advance authorization to exceed the word limit but submitted a motion regarding this issue on the day of filing his Appellant's Brief. The Pre-Appeal Judge dismissed this motion and declared that the Appellant must file an amended motion complying with the word limit by 7 April 2008. *See* Decision on Motion for Leave to Exceed the Word Limit, 3 April 2008.

[5] Respondent's Brief, filed on 16 May 2008.

[6] Brief in Reply, filed in French (*Réplique au Mémoire de l'Intimé*) on 2 June 2008.

[7] Order Assigning Judges to a Case before the Appeals Chamber, 14 December 2007.

[8] Order Designating a Pre-Appeal Judge, 18 December 2007.

[9] Order Replacing a Judge in a Case before the Appeals Chamber, 19 June 2008.

[10] Extremely Urgent Defence Motion To Present Additional Evidence, Filed in French (*Requête extrêmement urgente de la Défense aux fins de présenter des éléments de preuve supplémentaires*) on 28 August 2008.

[11] Prosecutor's Response to Appellant *Karera's 'Requête extrêmement urgente de la Défense aux fins de présenter des éléments de preuve supplémentaires'*, filed on 16 September 2008.

[12] Reply to the Prosecutor's Response to Appellant *Karera's 'Requête extrêmement urgente de la Défense aux fins de présenter des éléments de preuve supplémentaires'*, filed in French (*Réplique à la réponse du Procureur à la Requête extrêmement urgente de la Défense aux fins de présenter des éléments de preuve supplémentaires*) on 6 October 2008.

[13] Decision on the Appellant's Request to Admit Additional Evidence Pursuant to Rule 115 of the Rules of Procedure and Evidence, 29 October 2008.

D. Hearing of the Appeal

7. Pursuant to a Scheduling Order of 1 July 2008,[14] the Appeals Chamber heard the parties' oral arguments on 28 August 2008 in Arusha, Tanzania. On 22 September 2008, the Appeals Chamber granted an oral motion submitted by the Defence at the appeal hearing[15] requesting the Appeals Chamber to recognize as validly filed the Appellant's Appeal Book and Book of Authorities, submitted to the Registry on 4 August 2008.[16] **[page 118]**

XV. ANNEX B: CITED MATERIALS AND DEFINED TERMS

A. Jurisprudence

1. ICTR

Akayesu

The Prosecutor v. Jean-Paul Akayesu, Case No. ICTR-96-4-A, Judgement, 1 June 2001 (*"Akayesu* Appeal Judgement")

Bagosora et al.

The Prosecutor v. Bagosora et al., Case No. ICTR-98-41-AR73, Decision on Aloys Ntabakuze's Interlocutory Appeal on Questions of Law Raised by the 29 June 2006 Trial Chamber I Decision on Motion for Exclusion of Evidence, 18 September 2006

Gacumbitsi

Sylvestre Gacumbitsi v. The Prosecutor, Case No. ICTR-2001-64-A, Judgement, 7 July 2006 (*"Gacumbitsi* Appeal Judgement")

Kajelijeli

Juvénal Kajelijeli v. The Prosecutor, Case No. ICTR-98-44A-A, Judgement, 23 May 2005 (*"Kajelijeli* Appeal Judgement")

Kamuhanda

Jean de Dieu Kamuhanda v. The Prosecutor, Case No. ICTR-95-54A-A, Judgement, 19 September 2005 (*"Kamuhanda* Appeal Judgement")

Karemera et al.

The Prosecutor v. Édouard Karemera et al., Case No. ICTR-98-44-AR73.8, Decision on Interlocutory Appeal Regarding Witness Proofing, 11 May 2007

Kayishema and Ruzindana

The Prosecutor v. Clément Kayishema and Obed Ruzindana, Case No. ICTR-95-1-A, Judgement (Reasons), 1 June 2001 (*"Kayishema and Ruzindana* Appeal Judgement") **[page 119]**

Mpambara

The Prosecutor v. Jean Mpambara, Case No. ICTR-01-65-T, Judgement, 11 September 2006 (*"Mpambara* Trial Judgement")

---

[14] Scheduling Order, 1 July 2008. *See also*: Order for Preparation of Appeal Hearing, 20 August 2008.
[15] AT. 28 August 2008 pp. 29-31.
[16] Decision on the Appellant's Oral Motion to Declare his Appeal Book and Book of Authorities Validly Filed, 22 September 2008.

Muhimana

Mikaeli Muhimana v. The Prosecutor, Case No. ICTR-95-1B-A, Judgement, 21 May 2007 (*"Muhimana* Appeal Judgement")

Musema

Alfred Musema v. The Prosecutor, Case No. ICTR-96-13-A, Judgement, 16 November 2001 (*"Musema* Appeal Judgement")

Muvunyi

Tharcisse Muvunyi v. The Prosecutor, Case No. ICTR-00-55A-A, Judgement, 29 August 2008 (*"Muvunyi* Appeal Judgement")

Nahimana *et al.*

Ferdinand Nahimana, Jean-Bosco Barayagwiza and Hassan Ngeze v. The Prosecutor, Case No. ICTR-99-52-A, Judgement, 28 November 2007 (*"Nahimana et al.* Appeal Judgement")

Ndindabahizi

Emmanuel Ndindabahizi v. The Prosecutor, Case No. ICTR-01-71-A, Judgement, 16 January 2007 (*"Ndindabahizi* Appeal Judgement")

Niyitegeka

Eliézer Niyitegeka v. The Prosecutor, Case No. ICTR-96-14-A, Judgement, 9 July 2004 (*"Niyitegeka* Appeal Judgement")

Ntagerura *et al.*

The Prosecutor v. André Ntagerura, Emmanuel Bagambiki, and Samuel Imanishimwe, Case No. ICTR-99-46-A, Judgement, 7 July 2006 (*"Ntagerura et al.* Appeal Judgement") **[page 120]**

Ntakirutimana

The Prosecutor v. Elizaphan Ntakirutimana and Gérard Ntakirutimana, Cases Nos. ICTR-96-10-A and ICTR-96-17-A, Judgement, 13 December 2004 (*"Ntakirutimana* Appeal Judgement")

Rutaganda

Georges Anderson Nderubumwe Rutaganda v. The Prosecutor, Case No. ICTR-96-3-A, Judgement, 26 May 2003 (*"Rutaganda* Appeal Judgement")

Semanza

Laurent Semanza v. The Prosecutor, Case No. ICTR-97-20-A, Judgement, 20 May 2005 (*"Semanza* Appeal Judgement")

Seromba

The Prosecutor v. Athanase Seromba, Case No. ICTR-2001-66-A, Judgement, 12 March 2008 (*"Seromba* Appeal Judgement")

Simba

Aloys Simba v. The Prosecutor, Case No. ICTR-01-76-A, Judgement, 27 November 2007 (*"Simba* Appeal Judgement")

2. ICTY

Aleksovski

Prosecutor v. Zlatko Aleksovski, Case No. IT-95-14/1-AR73, Decision on Prosecutor's Appeal on Admissibility of Evidence, 16 February 1999 (*"Aleksovski* Decision")

Blagojević and Jokić

Prosecutor v. Vidoje Blagojević and Dragan Jokić, Case No. IT-02-60-A, Judgement, 9 May 2007 ("*Blagojević and Jokić* Appeal Judgement")

Blaškić

Prosecutor v. Tihomir Blaškić, Case No. IT-95-14-A, Judgement, 29 July 2004 ("*Blaškić* Appeal Judgement") **[page 121]**

Čelebići

Prosecutor v. Zejnil Delalić et al., Case No. IT-96-21-A, Judgement, 20 February 2001 ("*Čelebići* Appeal Judgement")

Furundžija

Prosecutor v. Anto Furundžija, Case No. IT-95-17/1-A, Judgement, 21 July 2000 ("*Furundžija* Appeal Judgement")

Galić

Prosecutor v. Stanislav Galić, Case No. IT-98-29-A, Judgement, 30 November 2006 ("*Galić* Appeal Judgement")

Kordić and Čerkez

Prosecutor v. Dario Kordić and Mario Čerkez, Case No. IT-95-14/2, Judgement, 17 December 2004 ("*Kordiü and Čerkez* Appeal Judgement")

Krstić

Prosecutor v. Radislav Krstić, Case No. IT-98-33-A, Judgement, 19 April 2004 ("*Krstić* Appeal Judgement")

Kupreškić et al.

Prosecutor v. Zoran Kupreškić et al, Case No. IT-95-16-A, Judgement, 23 October 2001 ("*Kupreškić et al.* Appeal Judgement")

Kvočka et al.

Prosecutor v. Miroslav Kvočka et al., Case No. IT-98-30/1-A, Judgement, 28 February 2005 ("*Kvočka et al.* Appeal Judgement")

Limaj et al.

Prosecutor v. Fatmir Limaj et al., Case No. IT-03-66-A, Judgement, 27 September 2007 ("*Limaj et al.* Appeal Judgement") **[page 122]**

Martić

Prosecutor v. Milan Martić, Case No. IT-95-11-A, Judgement, 8 October 2008 ("*Martić* Appeal Judgement")

Naletilić and Martinović

Prosecutor v. Mladen Naletilić and Vinko Martinović, Case No. IT-98-34-A, Judgement, 3 May 2006 ("*Naletilić and Martinović* Appeal Judgement")

Orić

Prosecutor v. Naser Orić, Case No. IT-03-68-A, Judgement, 3 July 2008 ("*Orić* Appeal Judgement")

Prlić et al.

Prosecutor v. Jadranko Prlić et al., Case No IT-04-74, Decision on Prosecution's Appeal against Trial Chamber's Order on Contact between the Accused and Counsel during an Accused's Testimony Pursuant to Rule 85(C), 5 September 2008 ("*Prlić et al.,* Decision of 5 September 2008").

Annex B

Stakić

Prosecutor v. Milomir Stakić, Case No. IT-97-24-T, Judgement, 31 July 2003 ("*Stakić* Trial Judgement")

Prosecutor v. Milomir Stakić, Case No. IT-97-24-A, Judgement, 22 March 2006 ("*Stakić* Appeal Judgement")

Vasiljević

Prosecutor v. Mitar Vasiljević, Case No. IT-98-32-A, Judgement, 25 February 2004 ("*Vasiljević* Appeal Judgement")

B. Defined Terms and Abbreviations

Amended Indictment	*The Prosecutor v. François Karera*, Case No. ICTR-01-74-I, Amended Indictment, dated 19 December 2005
Appellant	François Karera **[page 123]**
Appellant's Brief	*The Prosecutor v. François Karera*, Case No. ICTR-01-74-A, Appellant's Brief, filed in French on 7 April 2008 (*Mémoire d'Appel de François Karera*)
AT.	Transcript page from Appeal hearings held on 28 August 2008 in *François Karera v. The Prosecutor*, Case No. ICTR-01-74-A. All references are to the official English transcript, unless otherwise indicated
Brief in Reply	*The Prosecutor v. François Karera*, Case No. ICTR-01-74-A, Reply to the Respondent's Brief, filed in French (*Réplique au Mémoire de l'Intimé*) on 2 June 2008
cf.	[Latin: *confer*] (Compare)
Defence	Appellant, and/or the Appellant's counsel
Exhibit D/Exhibit P	Defence Exhibit/Prosecution Exhibit
FAR	Rwandan Armed Forces
fn.	footnote
ICTY	International Tribunal for the Prosecution of Persons Responsible for Serious Violations of International Humanitarian Law Committed in the Territory of the Former Yugoslavia since 1991
Indictment	*The Prosecutor v. François Karera*, Case No. ICTR-01-74-I, Indictment, dated 2 August 2001
Karera Final Trial Brief	*The Prosecutor v. François Karera*, Case No. ICTR-01-74-T, Defense Closing Arguments, filed confidentially on 10 November 2006
Kigali prefecture	Préfecture de Kigali
Kigali-Ville prefecture	Préfecture de la Ville de Kigali
MRND	*Mouvement révolutionnaire national pour le développement* [before July 1991]
	Mouvement républicain national pour la démocratie et le développement [after July 1991]
Notice of Appeal	*The Prosecutor v. François Karera*, Case No. ICTR-01-74-A, Defence Notice of Appeal, filed in French on 14 January 2008 (*Avis d'Appel de la Défense*)
para. (paras.)	paragraph (paragraphs)

Prosecution	Office the Prosecutor
Prosecution Final Trial Brief	*The Prosecutor v. François Karera*, Case No. ICTR-01-74-T, The Prosecutor's Closing Brief, filed confidentially on 10 November 2006 **[page 124]**
Prosecution Pre-Trial Brief	*The Prosecutor v. François Karera*, Case No. ICTR-01-74-I, The Prosecutor's Pre-Trial Brief, filed on 12 December 2005
Respondent's Brief	*The Prosecutor v. François Karera*, Case No. ICTR-01-74-A, Respondent's Brief, filed on 16 May 2008
Rules	Rules of Procedure and Evidence of the ICTR
RPF	Rwandan Patriotic Front
Statute	Statute of the International Tribunal for Rwanda established by Security Council Resolution 955 (1994)
T.	Trial Transcript page from hearings in *Prosecutor v. François Karera*, Case No. ICTR-01-74. All references are to the official English transcript, unless otherwise indicated
Trial Judgement	*The Prosecutor v. François Karera*, Case No. ICTR-01-74-T, Judgement and Sentence, 7 December 2007
Tribunal or ICTR	International Criminal Tribunal for the Prosecution of Persons Responsible for Genocide and Other Serious Violations of International Humanitarian Law Committed in the Territory of Rwanda and Rwandan Citizens responsible for genocide and other such violations committed in the territory of neighbouring States, between 1 January 1994 and 31 December 1994
UN	United Nations

Commentary

1. Introduction

This commentary analyses the ICTR's Appeal Chamber judgment in the case of *Karera v. Prosecutor*.[1] The focus will be on selected issues that were raised as grounds of appeal and not merely those that were granted. In addition, the Appeals Chamber's decision to consider certain aspects of the trial chamber's judgment *proprio motu* and the effect thereof on the outcome of the appeal will also be considered.

2. Background

Karera was the *Bourgmestre* of Nyarugenge Urban Commune for more than 15 years (from 1975 to 1990). Subsequently, in 1990, he served as *sous-prefet* of Kigali- Rural Prefecture. In 1991, he was appointed president of the MRND (*Mouvement Révolutionaire National pour le Développement*) in Nyarugenge Commune. Finally, on or around 17 April 1994, he was appointed as prefect of Kigali Prefecture.

The charges brought against Karera at the ICTR were: genocide (count 1); alternatively, complicity in genocide (count 2); extermination as a crime against humanity (count 3); and murder as a crime against humanity (count 4). The indictment charges him with all these crimes in terms of his individual criminal responsibility under Article 6, paragraph 1 of the ICTR Statute and his superior responsibility under Article 6, paragraph 2 of the Statute. As required by Rule 47 (c) of the ICTR Rules of Procedure and Evidence (RPE), each count was supported by a statement of facts.

3. Selected issues and principles

The appellant appealed the Trial Chamber's decision on twelve grounds. In assessing these grounds, the Appeals Chamber deemed it appropriate to group some of the grounds, and in some instances the sub-grounds.

The following aspects of the judgment are of particular interest either for firmly setting out the obligations of tribunals such as the ICTR or because they constitute a re-statement and, in some instances, a clarification of rules and/or principles.

3.1 Site visits

The substance of the defence's allegation in relation to site visits was that the Trial Chamber erred in failing to keep records of a site visit to Rwanda from 1 to 3 November 2006 and, in so doing, "denied the Appellant the right to present a full defence and to be provided with a reasoned opinion."[2]

The Appeals Chamber noted that the appellant had consented to the site visit.[3] Although this sub-ground of appeal was dismissed, the Appeals Chamber in no uncertain terms indicated its displeasure at the Trial Chamber's failure to keep such records.

The Appeals Chamber emphasised that:

> [D]etailed records of (the) Trial Chamber's site visits should normally be kept. The purpose of a site visit is to assist a Trial Chamber in its determination of the issues and therefore it is incumbent upon the Trial Chamber to ensure that the parties are able to effectively review any findings made by the Trial Chamber in reliance on observations made during the site visit.[4]

However, because the appellant had failed to show that he was prejudiced by this failure, this sub-ground of appeal was dismissed. The ICTR's Rules of Procedure and Evidence[5] (RPE) do not expressly refer to site visits. However, there are at least three rules which, when read together, may permit site visits and require that records of such a visit be maintained by the tribunal. Rule 4, provides that "a Chamber or a Judge may exercise their functions away from the Seat of the Tribunal, if so authorized by the President in the interests of justice."

---

[1] ICTR, Judgement, *Karera v. Prosecutor*, ICTR-01-74-A, A. Ch., 2 February 2009, in this volume, p. 121.
[2] Appeal Judgment, *supra*, note 1, par. 50.
[3] *Ibid.*, par.114.
[4] *Ibid.*
[5] Adopted on 29 June 1995, as amended.

Rule 54 provides that "at the request of either party or *proprio motu*, a Judge or a Trial Chamber may issue such orders, summonses, subpoenas, warrants and transfer orders as may be necessary for the purposes of an investigation or for the preparation or conduct of the trial." Rule 81 states that "the Registrar shall cause to be made and preserve a full and accurate record of all proceedings, including audio recordings, transcripts and, when deemed necessary by the Trial Chamber, video recordings (…) The Registrar shall retain and preserve all physical evidence offered during the Proceedings" and "photography, video-recording or audio-recording of the trial, otherwise than by the Registry, may be authorised at the discretion of the Trial Chamber."

Where a site visit will be instrumental in the discovery of the truth, the motion for a site visit should be granted.[6] In this regard, the ICTR will look at:

> [W]hether disputed issues at trial relate to physical attributes of various sites relevant to the case. A site visit may assist a chamber in its assessment of issues of visibility, layout of building, distances between locations and correlative proximity of places.[7]

Like the Appeals Chamber in Karera, the Trial Chamber in Gatete, which post-dates the Karera appeal, concluded that "a detailed record of a Chamber's visit should be made."[8] The Gatete Trial Chamber acknowledged its responsibilities by stating that it was "mindful of its obligations to respect the rights of the accused, as well as the need to maintain a detailed record of the site visit."[9] This finding was made taking into account the Practice Direction on Site Visits[10] that was issued only after the Karera Appeals Chamber decision. No similar practice direction has ever been issued in the ICTY. It would seem that in as much as it may have triggered the president of the ICTR to issue the 2010 Practice Direction, the Karera Appeal decision also informed the Gatete decision.

Karera had argued that "observations made during the site visit brought to light certain details about the Ntarama area that (were) not revealed in the Trial judgment."[11] He further argued that, "absent a *proces-verbal*, pictures or admissions, it (was) impossible to use the observations made during the site visit to challenge the credibility of unreliable witnesses and to demonstrate the Trial Chamber's errors in this respect."[12] This, according to the defence, would prevent "the Appeals Chamber from assessing the accuracy of the evidence collected during the site visit."[13] Laetitia Husson, in apparent agreement, notes that "absent a record of the exchanges between the parties during the visit, and, most often, absent the admission of supporting material in the form of pictures taken on the sites, Chambers have no evidence on which they can rely for their findings concerning what they saw in Rwanda."[14]

In Karera, the appellant had consented to the site visit and "at no time during the trial proceedings did (he) object to the absence of (records)."[15] The Appeals Chamber considered that the Trial Chamber had explained how its observation affected the assessment of the evidence.[16]

The Appeals Chamber noted that the "detailed records of the Trial Chamber's site visits"[17] and that site visits "may take different forms and it will depend on the circumstances of the specific case to determine which form will be most appropriate."[18]

---

[6] SCSL, Decision on the Prosecution Motion for a Locus in Quo Visit to Karina, Bombali District, The Republic of Sierra Leone, *Prosecutor v. Brima and Others*, Case No. SCSL-04-16 -T, T. Ch. II, 25 October 2005.

[7] ICTR, Decision on Site Visit to Rwanda, *Prosecutor v. Gatete*, ICTR-2000-61-T, T. Ch. III, 17 June 2010, par. 4; (Referring to ICTR, Decision on Defence Motion for a View Locus in Quo, *Prosecutor v. Rwamakuba*, Case No. ICTR-98-44C-T, T. Ch. III, 16 December 2005, par. 8.).

[8] Gatete Decision, *supra*, note 7, par. 4.

[9] *Ibid.*, par. 10.

[10] Practice Direction on Site Visits, 3 May 2010.

[11] Appeal Judgment, *supra*, note 1, par. 48.

[12] *Ibid.*

[13] *Ibid.*

[14] L. Husson, 'The Karera Appeal Judgment: Some Observations, The Hague Justice Portal. Available at www.haguejusticeportal.net.

[15] Appeal Judgement, *supra*, note 1, par 50.

[16] *Ibid.*

[17] *Ibid.*

[18] *Ibid.*, footnote 117.

Returning to the main question then, did the Trial Chamber's failure to maintain a record of the site visit effectively deny "the Appellant the right to present a full defence and to be provided with a reasoned opinion?"[19]

Although the Appeals Chamber answered in the negative, it chastised the Trial Chamber for failing to maintain records of the site visit. The Appeals Chamber's attitude gives the impression that, under different circumstances, it may well have found that such failure prejudiced the appellant in his preparation to challenge the Trial Chamber's observations. It would seem as if the Appeals Chamber's ultimate conclusion that this ground of appeal be dismissed, would have been different if the appellant had not consented to the site visit or if he had objected to the absence of a record and used these factors as a basis for establishing prejudice. Additionally, the appellant had the opportunity, during closing arguments and closing briefs, to raise arguments regarding observations made during the site visit – the fact that he did not do so also weighed heavily against him.[20]

Ultimately, establishing prejudice appears to be crucial when attempting to challenge the Chamber's findings on site visits. The 2010 Practice Direction provides certainty about what is expected. Trial Chambers should be mindful of how their failure to maintain site visit records may detract from the duty to ensure a fair trial.

3.2 Corroboration, hearsay and circumstantial evidence

The appellant challenged the truthfulness of a witness who, he claimed, "had lied outright"[21] and whose testimony, he said, ought to have been rejected by the Trial Chamber "in its entirety."[22]

The witness in question, witness BMA, changed his version of events including the fact of whether he had seen the appellant in a specific location on a particular day. He went so far as to say, at the beginning of the trial, that he knew only one Karera but later, under cross-examination, claimed that he might have been talking about another Karera. As in other cases, the Appeals Chamber stated that "a Trial Chamber may accept some parts of a witness's testimony while rejecting others."[23]

The tribunals established by the United Nations have adopted the flexible approach of civil law systems in so far as hearsay is concerned. In Tadić, the Appeals Chamber stated that "the mere fact that particular testimony was in the nature of hearsay did not operate to exclude it from the category of admissible evidence."[24] In that case, the "hearsay testimony was admitted into evidence and assessed in the usual way for its probative value pursuant to Rule 89."[25]

Rule 89 (c) provides that "a Chamber may admit any relevant evidence which it deems to have probative value." This provision was held in the Kordić case,[26] to confer upon the Trial Chamber "a broad discretion (…) to admit relevant hearsay evidence." It was also held in the Kordić decision[27] that "this discretion is however not unlimited and on the contrary it has been found that 'the reliability of a statement is relevant to its admissibility, and not just to its weight. A piece of evidence may be so lacking in terms of the *indicia* of reliability that it is not 'probative' and is therefore inadmissible.'" For this reason, the applicable test for admissibility is set quite high.[28]

The need to fully understand the ICTR's discretion with regard to hearsay goes to the heart of the Appeal's Chamber finding that uncorroborated hearsay evidence with respect to the murder of one the deceased, in

---

[19] *Ibid.*, par. 50.
[20] *Ibid.*
[21] Appeal Judgment, *supra*, note 1, par. 87.
[22] *Ibid.*
[23] *Ibid.*, par. 87.
[24] ICTY, Opinion and Judgement, *Prosecutor v. Tadić*, IT-94-1-T, T. Ch. II, 7 May 1997, Klip/ Sluiter, ALC-I-287, par. 555, citing ICTY, Decision on the Defence Motion on Hearsay, *Prosecutor v. Tadić*, IT-94-1-T, T. Ch. II, 5 August 1996, Klip/ Sluiter, ALC-I-193.
[25] *Ibid.*, par. 556.
[26] ICTY, Decision on Appeal Regarding the Admission Into Evidence of Seven Affidavits and one Formal Statement, *Prosecutor v. Kordić and Čerkez*, Case No. IT-95-14/2-AR73.6, A. Ch., 18 September 2000, Klip/ Sluiter, ALC-V-165, par. 24.
[27] ICTY, Decision on Appeal Regarding Statement of a Deceased Witness, *Prosecutor v. Kordić and Čerkez*, Case No. IT-95-14/2-AR73.5, A. Ch., 21 July 2000, Klip/ Sluiter, ALC-V-157, par. 24.
[28] *Ibid.*

particular Ndingutse, was unfounded. This resulted in the convictions for extermination and murder as a crime against humanity and genocide, in so far as they related to the deceased, being reversed. The Chamber held that:

> [N]o reasonable trier of fact could have accepted (the) witness's uncorroborated hearsay testimony that the policemen who killed Ndingutse were the policemen who guarded the Appellant's house. Furthermore, no reasonable trier of fact could have concluded on the basis of that circumstantial evidence that the only reasonable inference was that Ndingutse had been killed pursuant to the Appellant's orders to kill Tutsis.[29]

Before the Karera Trial Chamber decision and certainly before the Appeals chamber decision, the ICTY expressed the following sentiments on whether corroboration was necessary:

> Quite apart from the effect of the Rules, it is not correct to say that in present day civil law systems corroboration remains a general requirement. The determinative powers of a civil law judge are best described by reference to the principle of free evaluation of the evidence: in short, the power inherent in the judge as a finder of fact to decide solely on the basis of his or her personal intimate conviction. This wide discretionary power is subject to a limited number of restrictions. However, the principle reflected in the Latin maxim *unus testis, nullis testis*,[30] which requires testimonial corroboration of a single witness's evidence as to a fact in issue, is in almost all modern continental legal systems no longer a feature.[31]

According to Tadić,[32] corroboration is not part of customary international law and should not be required by the ICTY. Why was uncorroborated hearsay insufficient? Simply because it was not reliable evidence and has very little or no probative value. While neither hearsay nor uncorroborated evidence is always inadmissible, together, they create too many possibilities that would make it difficult for a tribunal to reach a definitive conclusion that a particular act did or did not happen.

With respect to the murder of Nyagatare, the Appeals Chamber held that drawing the conclusion that Nyagatare was killed as a result of the appellant's general order to kill Tutsis was based on circumstantial hearsay and the conclusion reached by the Trial Chamber was not the only reasonable conclusion that could be drawn.

With respect to the murder of Kahabaye, the Appeals Chamber held that there was no causal connection between the appellant's orders and the deceased's death. The Appeals Chamber concluded that:

> [N]o reasonable trier of fact could have concluded beyond a reasonable doubt that Kahabaye's murder was a consequence of an order to kill Tutsis given by the Appellant. The evidence regarding the location of the crime and the identity of the perpetrators accepted by the Trial Chamber was not corroborated and, in fact, remained conflicting.[33]

With respect to the death of one Murekezi, the Appeals Chamber upheld the Trial Chamber's decision that that Kalimba, a policeman, forced someone else to kill Murekezi.

3.3 Vagueness of the amended indictment and court's *proprio motu* consideration of aspects not raised on appeal by the appellant

What makes the Karera Appeal Chamber judgment particularly interesting is the fact that the Chamber's findings with respect to Kahabaye, Ndingutse, Nyagatare and Murekezi led the Appeals Chamber to *proprio motu* consider whether the Trial Chamber had erred in using its findings that the appellant was responsible for killing them. In other words, was the Trial Chamber permitted to convict the appellant for genocide and extermination as a crime against humanity based on Murekezi's murder?

The allegation of Murekezi's murder is made in support of count 4 for murder as a crime against humanity.[34] This had the effect of putting the appellant on notice that the prosecutor was charging him for the murder of Murekezi only under count 4. Originally, Murekezi's murder was included in the statement of facts pertaining

---

[29] Appeal Judgement, *supra*, note 1, par. 204.
[30] One witness is no witness.
[31] ICTY, Opinion and Judgment, *Prosecutor v. Tadić*, Case No. IT-94-1-T, T. Ch. II, 7 May 1997, Klip/ Sluiter, ALC-I-287, par. 537.
[32] *Ibid.*, par. 539.
[33] Appeal Judgement, *supra*, note 1, par. 186.
[34] Amended Indictment, par. 33.

to counts 1 and 3 as well. But it seems that in the process of amending the indictment, Murekezi was completely omitted from the statement of facts supporting those counts.

As the amended indictment stood, the statement of facts supporting count 4 incorporated the statements of facts supporting counts 1 and 3, but the reverse was not true. The statements of facts supporting counts 1 and 3 did not incorporate the statement of facts supporting count 4. The difficulty here was that the overall result was twofold: the possibility that the amended indictment was defective due to vagueness and that such vagueness was so serious as to negatively impact the defence's preparation for trial, to the extent that it resulted in an unfair trial. Clearly, if the latter was true, the Appeals Chamber would have to reverse the affected convictions.

In Kupreškić,[35] the Appeals Chamber of the ICTY explained the two-pronged test to determine whether the vagueness of an indictment justified an acquittal on the impugned charge, namely:
1. Did the Trial Chamber return convictions on the basis of material facts not pleaded in the amended indictment?
2. If the Appeals Chamber finds that the Trial Chamber did rely on such facts, whether the trial was rendered unfair.[36]

4. Did the Trial Chamber return convictions on the basis of material facts not pleaded in the Amended Indictment?

The Appeals Chamber pointed out that "the goal of expediency should never be allowed to over-ride the fundamental rights of the accused to a fair trial"[37] which would require that "the accused... be informed of the material facts of the specific allegation that the Prosecution is making against him so as to prepare his defence adequately."[38]

The Appeals Chamber concluded that the "Trial Chamber erred in entering convictions on the persecution Count because these convictions depended upon material facts that were not properly pleaded in the Amended Indictment."[39] The indictment as the "primary accusatory instrument must plead with sufficient detail the essential aspects of the Prosecution case,[40] otherwise it will be materially defective."[41] It is sometimes possible that "a defective indictment can be cured if the Prosecution provides the accused with timely, clear and consistent information detailing the factual basis underpinning the charges against him."[42] However, the Kupreškić appeal judgment made it clear that the nature of the crimes within the jurisdiction of tribunals such as the ICTY and ICTR, which are filled with "factual and legal complexities"[43] meant that there are "a limited number of cases that fell within the category of cases where defective indictments could be so cured."[44]

To counter this potential problem, the prosecution in the Karera Appeal argued that its pre-trial brief presented the factual allegations by location rather than with respect to each count. The Appeals Chamber held that this did not cure any defect in the amended indictment relating to counts 1 and 3, ultimately finding that the amended indictment was vague to the extent that it prejudiced the appellant in his preparation for trial. Consequently, it ordered that the convictions for Murekezi's murder under counts 1 and 3 be reversed.

4.1 Did the defects in the amended indictment render the trial unfair?

With respect to the second leg of the test, the vagueness of the amended indictment must have constituted "neither a minor defect nor a technical imperfection[45](...) goes to the heart of the substantial safeguards that

---

[35] ICTY, Appeal Judgement, *Prosecutor v. Kupreškić et al.*, Case No. IT-95-16-A, A. Ch., 23 October 2001, Klip/ Sluiter, ALC-VIII-429, par. 87.
[36] *Ibid.*
[37] *Ibid.*, par. 100.
[38] *Ibid.*, par. 105.
[39] *Ibid.*, par. 113.
[40] *Ibid.*, par. 114.
[41] *Ibid.*
[42] *Ibid.*
[43] *Ibid.*, par.114.
[44] *Ibid.*
[45] Kupreškić Appeal Judgment, *supra*, note 35, par. 122.

an indictment is intended to furnish the accused, namely to inform him of the case he has to meet."[46] If the ability of the accused to prepare his defence is materially impaired, the trial would, according to the Appeals Chamber, be rendered unfair.[47]

4.2 Campaign to kill Tutsis in Nyamirambo and Nyarugenge

Due to the reversal (on appeal) of the appellant's convictions for the murders of Kahabaye, Ndingutse and Nyagatare committed in Nyamirambo, it followed that the Appeal's Chamber had to reverse the appellant's convictions for ordering genocide and extermination as a crime against humanity.

4.3 Weapons distribution in Rushashi Commune – *de facto* amendment of indictment.

In terms of Rule 50 (A) (i) stipulates:

> The Prosecutor may amend an indictment, without prior leave, at any time before its confirmation, but thereafter, until the initial appearance of the accused before a Trial Chamber pursuant to Rule 62, only with leave of the Judge who confirmed it but, in exceptional circumstances, by leave of a Judge assigned by the President. At or after such initial appearance, an amendment of an indictment may only be made by leave granted by that Trial Chamber pursuant to Rule 73. If leave to amend is granted, Rule 47 (G) and Rule 53 bis apply mutatis mutandis to the amended indictment.

Subsection (ii) of Rule 50, further states:

> In deciding whether to grant leave to amend the indictment, the Trial Chamber or, where applicable, a Judge shall, mutatis mutandis, follow the procedures and apply the standards set out in Sub-Rules 47 (E) and (F) in addition to considering any other relevant factors.

Pursuant to Rule 50 (B):

> If the amended indictment includes new charges and the accused has already appeared before a Trial Chamber in accordance with Rule 62, a further appearance shall be held as soon as practicable to enable the accused to enter a plea on the new charges.

Rule 50 dictates a formal procedure to be followed in order to amend an indictment. The rule does not accommodate *de facto* amendments. One of the issues that the Appeal Chamber had to deal with was whether the prosecution's post-indictment communications, which referred to weapons distribution specifically in Rushashi, in effect expanded the charges contained in the amended indictment, by adding a new incident of weapons distribution in a new location.[48]

The amended indictment had referred to two incidents of weapons distribution elsewhere, but not in Rushashi. The Appeals Chamber's view was that the post indictment communication amounted to a *de facto* amendment of the amended indictment, which was impermissible. Having had to deal with the issue of vagueness in the indictment in the earlier stages of the judgment, the Appeals Chamber emphasised that omission of the Rushashi incident in the amended indictment was not a question of vagueness of the latter. It acknowledged that vagueness is capable of being cured, but felt that "a clear distinction (had) to be drawn between vagueness in an indictment and an indictment omitting certain charges altogether,"[49] with the latter requiring a formal amendment to include new charges.

Consequently, the Appeals Chamber held that the Trial Chamber erred in holding that, as a matter of law, the prosecution's post indictment communications could cure the failure to include the allegation of the Rushashi weapons distribution in the amended indictment and they in fact did so.

The Appeals Chamber focused more on the issue of post-indictment communications and less on Rule 50. One would have expected that the Appeals Chamber's criticism to be based largely on the fact that allowing the inclusion of the Rushashi weapons distribution was procedurally incorrect. It is suggested that the Appeals Chamber's weak criticism does not send out a strong enough message to prosecutors and Trials Chambers to be mindful of such procedural irregularities.

---

[46] *Ibid.*
[47] *Ibid.*
[48] Appeal Judgement, *supra*, note 1, par 296.
[49] *Ibid.*

5. Conclusion

This commentary has attempted to illustrate some of the serious issues raised in the Karera Appeal. The Appeals Chamber's firm stance on maintaining records of site visits is most welcome for creating a standard by which other Trial Chambers can measure the correctness of their approaches.

On the issue of vagueness of the indictment, tribunals may now be more cautious in convicting where no material facts have been pleaded in support of a charge. Prosecution teams have made the mistake of vagueness once too often and now hopefully the unnecessary errors that seem to be the product of carelessness will not be made. Closely linked, but separate from the question of vagueness, is the *de facto* amendment of the indictment. The Appeals Chamber quite rightly drew a distinction between the two, by concluding that while the former is sometimes curable, the latter is fatal. *De facto* amendments are avoidable and seem to be the product of not paying close enough attention to the actual charges and who the victims are. What is clear is that *de facto* amendments and vagueness of charges have the potential to prejudice the accused and to, thereby, render the trial unfair.

Hearsay evidence has been acceptable in some legal systems under specific circumstances, so too has uncorroborated evidence of a single witness. However when hearsay evidence is uncorroborated there is a great danger that the truth will not be arrived at if such evidence becomes admissible. For that reason the Appeals Chamber's view that such evidence was unacceptable is welcomed. It is hoped that the restatement of some of the principles mentioned in Karera and the clarification of some rules therein leads to a better understanding of the Appeals Chamber's expectations of the prosecution and the Trial Chamber.

Sandhiya Singh

International Criminal Tribunal for Rwanda
Tribunal pénal international pour le Rwanda

OR: ENG

TRIAL CHAMBER II

Before: Judge Asoka de Silva, Presiding
Judge Taghrid Hikmet
Judge Seon Ki Park

Registrar: Mr. Adama Dieng

Date: 27 February 2009

THE PROSECUTOR

v.

Emmanuel RUKUNDO

Case No. ICTR-2001-70-T

JUDGEMENT

Office of the Prosecutor:
William T. Egbe
Sulaiman Khan
Veronic Wright
Patrick Gabaake
Thembile Segoete
Amina Ibrahim

Counsel for the Defence:
Aïcha Condé
Alison Turner

[page i] **Contents**

I. CHAPTER I: INTRODUCTION 1
   A. THE TRIBUNAL AND ITS JURISDICTION... 1
   B. THE ACCUSED 1
   C. INDICTMENT 2
   D. SUMMARY OF PROCEDURAL HISTORY 2
   E. OVERVIEW OF THE CASE 2

II. Chapter II: PRELIMINARY ISSUES 4
   A. ISSUES RELATING TO THE INDICTMENT 4
      1. Facts not Pleaded in the Indictment 4
      2. The Pleading of Joint Criminal Enterprise 6
         (a) Notice 6
         (b) The Indictment 7
         (c) Has the Defect in the Indictment Been Cured? 8
            (i) The Pre-Trial Brief 8
            (ii) Post-Indictment Disclosures 9
            (iii) Conclusion 10
   B. EVIDENTIARY MATTERS 10
   C. DECISION ON DEFENCE MOTION FOR ACQUITTAL 11
   D. JUDICIAL NOTICE 12

III. CHAPTER III: FACTUAL FINDINGS 15
   1. EVIDENCE RELATING TO PRE-1994 EVENTS 15
      (a) Indictment 15
      (b) Evidence and Deliberations 15
         (i) Expulsion from the St. Léon Minor Seminary in 1973 15
         (ii) Ngarukiragihugu (Salvation Committee), Solidarity March, Fund-Raising and
            Alleged Change of Attitude 15
   2. ALLEGATION OF MOBILIZATION OF HUTU AGAINST TUTSI IN FEBRUARY 1994 18
   3. EVENTS AT THE *IMPRIMERIE DE KABGAYI* ROADBLOCK 19
      (a) Indictment 19
      (b) Evidence 19
      (c) Deliberations 26
   4. EVENTS AT ST. JOSEPH'S COLLEGE 30
      (a) Indictment 30
      (b) Evidence 30
      (c) Deliberations 41
      (d) Findings 50
   5. EVENTS AT THE NYABIKENKE COMMUNAL OFFICE 53
      (a) Indictment 53
      (b) Evidence 53
      (c) Deliberations 64
   6. EVENTS AT THE KABGAYI BISHOPRIC 67
      (a) Indictment 67
      (b) Evidence 67
      (c) Deliberations 73

7. EVENTS RELATING TO THE ST. LÉON MINOR SEMINARY	80
(a) Indictment	80
(b) Evidence	80 **[page ii]**
(c) Deliberations	99
(i) Preliminary Issue: Pleadings in the Indictment	99
a. Paragraphs 12 and 13 are vague	99
b. Allegation of incitement to Hutu refugees not to collect water is not pleaded in the Indictment	99
(ii) Allegation: Beating of Refugees	100
(iii) Allegation: Abduction and Killing of Refugees	101
(iv) Allegation: Sexual Assault on a Young Tutsi Woman at the St. Léon Minor Seminary	110
a. Evidence	110
b. Deliberations	113
i. Was the Act of a Sexual Nature?	115
ii. Were there coercive circumstances?	116
iii. Did Witness CCH suffer serious mental harm?	117
8. EVENTS AT THE CND	119
(a) Indictment	119
(b) Evidence	119
(c) Deliberations	132
9. EVENTS AT THE KABGAYI MAJOR SEMINARY	137
(a) Indictment	137
(b) Evidence: Causing Serious Mental Harm to Tutsi Priests at the Kabgayi Major Seminary	137
(c) Deliberations	145
(d) Evidence: Abduction and Killing of Tutsi Clergy from the Kabgayi Major Seminary	148
(e) Deliberations on the Abduction and Killing of Tutsi Clergy	163
(i) Preliminary Issue: Alibi	163
(ii) Merits of the Allegation	163
IV. CHAPTER IV: LEGAL FINDINGS	**167**
A. INTRODUCTION	167
B. GENOCIDE	167
(a) Applicable Law	167
(b) Deliberations	168
(i) Attack on St. Joseph's College: Killing of Madame Rudahunga, Beating of Two of her Children and Two Other Tutsi Civilians	169
(ii) Abductions and Killings at the St. Léon Minor Seminary	171
(iii) Sexual Assault at the St. Léon Minor Seminary	172
C. CRIMES AGAINST HUMANITY (MURDER)	172
(a) Applicable Law	172
(b) Deliberations	173
(i) Attack on St. Joseph's College: Killing of Madame Rudahunga	173

D. CRIMES AGAINST HUMANITY (EXTERMINATION) 174
   (a) Applicable Law 174
   (b) Deliberations 174
      (i) Attack on St. Joseph's College: Killing of Madame Rudahunga; Beating of her Children
      and Two Tutsi Civilians 175
      (ii) Abductions and Killings at the St. Léon Minor Seminary 175

V. CHAPTER V: VERDICT 176

VI. CHAPTER VI: SENTENCING 177

   (a) Applicable Law 177
   (b) Determination of the Sentence 177
      (i) Gravity of the Offence 178
      (ii) Aggravating Circumstances 178
      (iii) Mitigating Circumstances .... 179 **[page iii]**
   (c) Sentencing Practice 179
   (d) Credit for Time Served 181
   (e) Conclusion 181

VII. Dissenting opinion of Judge Park 183

ANNEX A: PROCEDURAL HISTORY i

   (a) Pre-Trial Phase i
   (b) The Indictment iii
   (c) Trial Phase iv
   (d) Further Proceedings viii

Annex B – Glossary i

   A. LIST OF DEFINED TERMS, ACRONYMS AND ABBREVIATIONS I
   B. JURISPRUDENCE II
      1. ICTR ii
      2. ICTY vii
   C. OTHER MATERIAL IX

[page 1] I. **CHAPTER I: INTRODUCTION**

A. **THE TRIBUNAL AND ITS JURISDICTION**

1. The Judgement in the case of *Prosecutor v. Emmanuel Rukundo* is issued by Trial Chamber II (the "Chamber") of the International Criminal Tribunal for Rwanda (the "Tribunal"), composed of Judges Asoka de Silva, presiding, Taghrid Hikmet, and Seon Ki Park.

2. The Tribunal is governed by the Statute annexed to United Nations Security Council Resolution 955 (the "Statute") and by the Rules of Procedure and Evidence (the "Rules").[1]

3. The Tribunal has the authority to prosecute persons responsible for serious violations of international humanitarian law committed in the Republic of Rwanda, and Rwandan citizens responsible for such violations committed in the territory of neighbouring states.[2] Its jurisdiction is limited to acts of genocide, crimes against humanity, and serious violations of Article 3 common to the Geneva conventions and of Additional Protocol II thereto, committed between 1 January 1994 and 31 December 1994.[3]

B. **THE ACCUSED**

4. Emmanuel Rukundo was born on 1 December 1959, at Mukingi *commune*, Nyagakambe *cellule*, Rugogwe *secteur*, Gitarama *préfecture* in Rwanda.[4] Rukundo studied at the Nyakibanda Major Seminary from 1985 until 1991.[5] After being ordained as a priest on 28 July 1991 he served as a parish priest in Kanyanza Parish in Gitarama *préfecture*.[6] In February 1993, Rukundo was appointed military chaplain for the Rwandan Armed Forces ("RAF"). Following this appointment, he was posted to the Ruhengeri and Gisenyi military sectors in May 1993, and then transferred to Kigali in May 1994.[7] He left Rwanda after the defeat of the RAF by the Rwandan Patriotic Front ("RPF") in September 1994, and went into exile in Burundi and then later in Europe.[8] [page 2]

C. **INDICTMENT**

5. In the amended Indictment of 6 October 2006 ("Indictment"), the Prosecution charged Emmanuel Rukundo ("Accused") with three counts pursuant to Articles 2 and 3 of the Statute: genocide and murder and extermination as crimes against humanity. According to the Indictment, the Accused bears individual criminal responsibility for these crimes pursuant to Article 6(1) of the Statute.

D. **SUMMARY OF PROCEDURAL HISTORY**

6. On 5 July 2001, Judge Pavel Dolenc issued a Warrant of Arrest and an Order for Transfer and Detention and for Search and Seizure.[9] On 12 July 2001, Emmanuel Rukundo was arrested in Geneva, Switzerland and was transferred on 20 September 2001 to the UN Detention Facility in Arusha. On 26 September 2001 the Accused made his initial appearance before Judge Erik Møse and entered a plea of not guilty to all of the counts in the Indictment.[10]

---

[1] The Statute and the Rules are available at the Tribunal's website: http://www.ictr.org.
[2] Articles 1 and 5 of the Statute.
[3] Article 1 of the Statute.
[4] Amended Indictment of 6 October 2006 ("Indictment"), para. II A; T. 5 October 2007, p. 1; Prosecution Closing Brief, para. 13.
[5] T. 5 October 2007, pp. 12-13; Prosecution Closing Brief, para. 13.
[6] Indictment, para. II B(i); T. 8 October 2007, pp. 13, 15, 18.
[7] Indictment, para. II B(ii); Prosecution Closing Brief, para. 14; T. 8 October 2007, pp. 23, 38; T. 9 October 2007, pp. 13-15; T. 4 September 2007, p. 18.
[8] T. 9 October 2007, pp. 60-61; T. 10 October 2007, pp. 23, 26; Para. 21 of the Indictment states that Emmanuel Rukundo left Rwanda after the defeat of the Rwanda army by the RPF in July 1994, and went into exile in Switzerland. The Chamber notes this discrepancy between the Indictment and the testimony of the Accused.
[9] Warrant of Arrest and Orders for Transfer and Detention and for Search and Seizure, 5 July 2001.
[10] T. 26 September 2001, pp. 38-41.

7. On 14 September 2006, the case was formally transferred from Trial Chamber III to Trial Chamber II. On 28 September 2006, Judge Asoka de Silva, granted in part the Prosecution's Motion to Amend the Indictment.[11] The Prosecution filed an Amended Indictment on 6 October 2006.

8. The trial commenced on 15 November 2006 and closed on 20 February 2008. The Prosecution presented a total of 18 witnesses over the course of 25 trial days. The Defence case started on 2 July 2007. During 41 trial days, the Defence called a total of 32 witnesses. The procedural history of this Trial is set out in full in Annex A to this Judgement.

E. OVERVIEW OF THE CASE

9. During the course of 1994, particularly between 6 April and 17 July 1994, there were widespread and systematic attacks against the Tutsi throughout Rwanda including Gitarama *préfecture*.[12] As a result, many Tutsi from this *préfecture* fled their homes and sought refuge in various places in Kabgayi, including the premises under the control of the Kabgayi diocese such as **[page 3]** the St. Léon Minor Seminary, St. Joseph's College, the Kabgayi Major Seminary, the Gitarama Parish and TRAFIPRO otherwise known as the CND.[13]

10. According to the Prosecution, Emmanuel Rukundo was known to be a Hutu extremist. In 1973, he was allegedly expelled from the St. Léon Minor Seminary in Kabgayi because of his extremist attitudes and actions. The Prosecution alleges that Emmanuel Rukundo promoted anti-Tutsi extremism while he was a student at the Nyakibanda Major Seminary. The Prosecution further claims that Emmanuel Rukundo's extremism towards Tutsi was evidenced by the campaigns he led in opposition to the Arusha Accords in February 1994.

11. The Prosecution alleges that the Accused relied on his authority as a priest and a military chaplain in the RAF to order, instigate, or aid and abet soldiers, *Interahamwe* and armed civilians in various places in Gitarama *préfecture* to commit the crimes set out in the Indictment, notably at the Nyabikenke communal office, the Kabgayi Bishopric, the St. Léon Minor Seminary, the CND, St. Joseph's College, the Kabgayi Major Seminary, two primary schools in Kabgayi and in other locations in Kabgayi where Tutsi refugees had sought protection between April and June 1994. The Indictment further states that Emmanuel Rukundo ordered, instigated, or aided and abetted *gendarmes* to perpetrate the killing of a Tutsi priest in Cyangugu *préfecture*.[14]

12. The Defence submits that Emmanuel Rukundo was not an extremist and that his relationship with Tutsi members of the clergy was friendly and cordial. The Defence further contends that Emmanuel Rukundo was not involved in any of the crimes in either Gitarama or Cyangugu *préfectures* as charged in the Indictment.[15] **[page 4]**

---

[11] Decision on the Prosecutor's Request to File an Amended Indictment, 28 September 2006.
[12] Indictment, para. 10. The Appeals Chamber of the ICTR held that the existence of systematic and widespread attacks against a civilian population based on Tutsi ethnic identification between April and June 1994 is a fact of common knowledge and therefore not amenable to reasonable dispute. See *Karemera et al.*, Decision on Prosecutor's Interlocutory Appeal of Decision on Judicial Notice (AC), 16 June 2006, para. 33.
[13] Indictment, para. 10.
[14] Indictment, para. 17.
[15] Defence Closing Brief, paras. 86, 1796.

II. CHAPTER II: PRELIMINARY ISSUES

A. ISSUES RELATING TO THE INDICTMENT

1. Facts not Pleaded in the Indictment

13.   The Defence alleges that the Prosecution adduced evidence in respect of several allegations which were not pleaded in the Indictment.[16] The Defence argues that since it did not have sufficient notice of this evidence to be able to defend against it, the evidence should be excluded.[17] It also argues that the testimonies of several Prosecution witnesses are inconsistent with the Indictment.[18] The Defence further contends that the Indictment is vague in respect of several allegations.[19]

14.   Article 20(4)(a) of the Statute guarantees an accused the fundamental right "to be informed promptly and in detail in a language which he or she understands of the nature and cause of the charges against him or her." The Appeals Chamber has interpreted this provision as placing an obligation on the Prosecution "to state the material facts underpinning the charges in the indictment, but not the evidence by which such material facts are to be proven".[20]

15.   The Appeals Chamber has further noted that charges against an accused and the material facts supporting those charges must be pleaded with sufficient precision in an indictment so as to provide notice to the accused.[21] The Prosecution is expected to know its case before proceeding to trial and cannot mould the case against the accused in the course of the trial depending on how the evidence unfolds.[22] However, defects in an indictment may come to light during the proceedings because the evidence turns out differently than expected. This calls for the Trial Chamber to consider whether a fair trial requires an amendment of the indictment, an adjournment of proceedings or the exclusion of evidence outside the scope of the indictment.[23]

16.   The Appeals Chamber has also held that criminal acts that were physically committed by the accused must be set forth in the indictment specifically, including where feasible "the identity of the **[page 5]** victim, the time and place of the events and the means by which the acts were committed."[24] In certain circumstances, the sheer scale of the alleged crimes makes it impracticable to require a high degree of specificity in matters such as the identity of the victims and the dates of the commission of the crimes.[25]

17.   An indictment lacking the requisite precision is defective. However, the defect may be cured if the Prosecution provides the accused with timely, clear, and consistent information detailing the factual basis underpinning the charge.[26] Such information includes a Pre-Trial Brief and annexed witness summaries, the opening statement and motions to vary witness lists. Yet, the principle that a defect in an indictment may be cured is not without limits. In this respect, the Appeals Chamber has emphasized:

---

[16]   This includes, *inter alia*: 1) Parts of Witness BLJ's testimony regarding the allegation of the attack at St. Joseph's College; 2) A part of Witness CSE's testimony regarding the allegation concerning the roadblock near the Kabgayi printing press; and 3) A part of Witness BLC's testimony concerning the allegation at the St. Léon Minor Seminary.
[17]   Defence Closing Brief, paras. 162-231.
[18]   See for example Prosecution Witnesses AMA, BUW, BLP, CSH, BLC, CCN.
[19]   Defence Closing Brief, paras. 841-848, 1304-1313.
[20]   *Kupreškić et al.*, Judgement (AC), para. 88; *Karera*, Judgement (TC), para. 12.
[21]   *Seromba,* Judgement (AC), paras. 27, 100; *Simba*, Judgement (AC) para. 63; *Muhimana*, Judgement (AC), paras. 76, 167, 195; *Gacumbitsi*, Judgement (AC), para. 49; *Ndindabahizi*, Judgement (AC), para. 16.
[22]   *Ntagerura et al.*, Judgement (AC), para. 27. See also *Kvočka et al.*, Judgement (AC), para. 30; *Niyitigeka,* Judgement (AC), para. 194; *Kupreškić et al.,* Judgement (AC), para. 92.
[23]   *Ntagerura et al.*, Judgement (AC), para. 27. See also *Kvočka et al.*, Judgement (AC), para. 31; *Niyitigeka*, Judgement (AC), para. 194; *Kupreškić et al.*, Judgement (AC), para. 92.
[24]   *Seromba*, Judgement (AC), para. 27; *Muhimana,* Judgement (AC), para. 76; *Ndindabahizi,* Judgement (AC), para. 16; *Gacumbitsi*, Judgement (AC), para. 49; *Ntakirutimana,* Judgement (AC), para. 32, quoting *Kupreškić et al.*, Judgement (AC), para. 89; *Muvunyi*, Judgement (AC), para. 120.
[25]   *Muvunyi*, Judgement (AC), para. 94; *Muhimana,* Judgement (AC), para. 79; *Gacumbitsi*, Judgement (AC), para. 50; *Kupreškić et al.,* Judgement (AC), para. 89.
[26]   *Seromba*, Judgement (AC), para 100; *Simba*, Judgement (AC), para. 64; *Muhimana*, Judgement (AC), paras. 76, 195, 217; *Gacumbitsi*, Judgement (AC), para. 49. See also *Ntagerura et al.*, Judgement (AC), paras. 28, 65; *Muvunyi,* Judgement (AC), para. 20.

[T]he "new material facts" should not lead to a "radical transformation" of the Prosecution's case against the accused. The Trial Chamber should always take into account the risk that the expansion of charges by the addition of new material facts may lead to unfairness and prejudice to the accused. Further, if the new material facts are such that they could, on their own, support separate charges, the Prosecution should seek leave from the Trial Chamber to amend the indictment and the Trial Chamber should only grant leave if it is satisfied that it would not lead to unfairness or prejudice to the Defence.[27]

18. The Chamber also recalls that it is to be assumed that "an Accused will prepare his defence on the basis of material facts contained in the Indictment, not on the basis of all the material disclosed to him that may support any number of additional charges, or expand the scope of existing charges."[28] The Appeals Chamber in *Karera* recently emphasized the clear distinction between vagueness in an indictment and omission in an indictment of certain charges altogether, which can be incorporated into the indictment only by a formal amendment.[29] The Chamber also recalls that **[page 6]** the Appeals Chamber in the *Muvunyi* case held that a Trial Chamber can convict an accused only of crimes that are charged in the indictment.[30]

19. The Chamber will now address the Defence submissions concerning the exclusion of the pleading of joint criminal enterprise.

20. The Defence request to exclude specific factual evidence and contentions regarding inconsistencies and vagueness in the Indictment will be addressed in the Chamber's analysis of the corresponding sections in Factual Findings below.

2. The Pleading of Joint Criminal Enterprise

21. The Defence contends that the Prosecution's pleading is ambiguous and therefore defective in respect of the Accused's alleged criminal liability under the theory of joint criminal enterprise ("JCE"). As a consequence, the Defence submits, Emmanuel Rukundo was not in a position to understand the charge against him.[31] During the Closing Arguments, the Prosecution submitted that it relies on JCE as a mode of commission, as well as other forms of liability under Article 6(1) including ordering, instigating and aiding and abetting.[32] The Prosecution's Closing Brief, however, does not make any reference to JCE.

22. Under Article 6(1) of the Statute any person who planned, instigated, ordered, committed or otherwise aided and abetted in the planning, preparation or execution of a crime referred to in Articles 2 to 4 of the Statute shall be individually responsible for the crime. Article 6(1) does not make explicit reference to "joint criminal enterprise". However, the Appeals Chamber has held that participation in a JCE is considered as a form of "commission" under Article 6(1).[33]

23. There are three categories of joint criminal enterprise which have the status of customary international law: basic, systemic and extended.[34]

(a) Notice

24. When the accused is charged with "committing" pursuant to Article 6(1) of the Statute, the indictment must specify whether the term is to be understood as physical commission, and/or as **[page 7]** participation

---

[27] *Bagosora et al.*, Decision on Aloys Ntabakuze's Interlocutory Appeal on Questions of Law Raised by the 29 June 2006 Trial Chamber I Decision on Motion for Exclusion of Evidence (AC), 18 September 2006, para. 30 (internal citations omitted); also cited in *Muvunyi*, Judgement (AC), para. 20.
[28] *Muvunyi*, Decision on the Prosecution Interlocutory Appeal against Trial Chamber II Decision of 23 Februar 2005, 12 May 2005, para 22; *Muvunyi*, Judgement (AC), para. 100.
[29] *Karera*, Judgement (AC), para. 293.
[30] *Muvunyi*, Judgement (AC), para.18; *Nahimana et al.*, Judgement (AC), para. 326; *Ntagerura et al.*, Judgement (AC), para. 28; *Kvočka et al.*, Judgement (AC), para. 33.
[31] Defence Closing Brief, paras. 237-266.
[32] Prosecution Closing Argument, T. 20 February 2008, p. 6.
[33] *Ntakirutimana*, Judgement (AC), citing *Tadić*, Judgement (AC), paras. 188 and 226.
[34] *Tadić*, Judgement (AC), paras. 195-226; *Ntakirutimana*, Judgement (AC), paras. 463-465; *Vasiljević*, Judgement (AC), paras. 96-99; *Krnojelać*, Judgement (AC), paras. 83-84.

Judgement

in a JCE.[35] Furthermore, if the Prosecution relies on a theory of JCE, then the purpose of the enterprise, the identity of the participants and the nature of the accused's participation in the enterprise must all be pleaded in the indictment.[36] Finally, the indictment should clearly indicate which form of JCE is being alleged.[37] Failure to plead these elements will result in a defective indictment. As explained above, a defect can only be cured in exceptional circumstances.[38]

(b) The Indictment

25. The Indictment states the following under the title of "individual criminal responsibility" in the *chapeau* of the concise statement of facts for Counts 1 and 2:

> Pursuant to Article 6(1) of the Statute, the accused, Emmanuel Rukundo, is individually responsible for the crime of [Genocide/Murder as a Crime Against Humanity] because he planned, instigated, ordered, committed, or otherwise aided and abetted in the planning, preparation or execution of this crime, with the object, purpose and foreseeable outcome being the commission of [genocide/crimes against humanity] against the Tutsi racial or ethnic group, and persons identified as Tutsis, in Gitarama and Cyangugu Prefectures, Rwanda. With respect to the commission of this crime, **Emmanuel RUKUNDO**, relying on the authority due to his position as a priest and military chaplain in the RAF, ordered, instigated, or aided and abetted soldiers, armed civilians and the *Interahamwe* militia, for at least the period of 6 April through 17 July 1994, to do the acts described below in this indictment. The particulars that give rise to his individual criminal responsibility are set forth in paragraphs 3 through 22 below.

26. The paragraph makes a general reference to JCE. It states the purpose of the JCE (the commission of genocide/crimes against humanity against the Tutsi), the timeframe of the JCE (6 April to 17 July 1994), the nature of the Accused's participation and the co-participants (although this is a vague reference to general categories of persons including "soldiers", "armed civilians" and the "*Interahamwe* militia"). However, the words "joint criminal enterprise" are neither mentioned in the paragraphs on individual criminal responsibility, nor is there any specific form of JCE pleaded. The Chamber recalls that it is possible that other phrasings, other than a specific reference to "joint criminal enterprise" might effectively convey the same concept.[39] The question is not whether particular words have been used, but whether an accused has been meaningfully "informed of the nature of the charges" so as to be able to prepare an effective defence.[40]

[page 8]

27. Apart from the two paragraphs relating to individual criminal responsibility discussed above and the *chapeau* to the concise statement of facts for Count 3 (extermination as a crime against humanity) which states only that Rukundo "…committed or otherwise aided and abetted…", none of the other paragraphs in the Indictment refer to Rukundo's participation in a JCE. Indeed, the majority of the paragraphs set out specific factual allegations and state only that Rukundo "ordered, instigated or aided and abetted" the killing of Tutsi.[41] The reference to "commission" in the two paragraphs relating to individual criminal responsibility is particularly ambiguous when read in light of the particulars allegedly giving rise to individual criminal responsibility which refer only to the Accused's mode of participation as "ordering, instigating or aiding and abetting".

28. The Chamber therefore finds that the pleading of JCE in the Indictment does not provide adequate notice to the Accused of his alleged involvement in a JCE and is defective.[42]

---

[35] *Krnojelać*, Judgement (AC), para. 138; *Ntakirutimana*, Judgement (AC), para. 475.
[36] *Kvočka et al.*, Judgement (AC), para. 28. See also *Ntagerura et al.*, Judgement (AC), para. 24; *Krnojelać*, Judgement (AC), paras. 138-139; *Gacumbitsi*, Judgement (AC), para. 162; *Simba*, Judgement (AC), para. 63; *Simić*, Judgement (AC), para. 22.
[37] *Simba*, Judgement (AC), para. 63; *Simić*, Judgement (AC), para. 22; *Ntagerura et al.*, Judgement (AC), para. 24.
[38] See Section II.A.1.
[39] *Gacumbitsi*, Judgement (AC), para. 165; *Ntakirutimana*, Judgement (AC), footnote 783.
[40] *Gacumbitsi*, Judgement (AC), para. 165 quoting *Ntakirutimana*, Judgement (AC), para. 470. The Appeals Chamber notes, however, that because ICTY and ICTR cases now routinely employ the phrase "joint criminal enterprise", the phrase should, for the sake of maximum clarity, preferably be included in future indictments where JCE is being charged.
[41] See *Nchamihigo*, Judgement (TC), para. 328.
[42] In its Decision on the Prosecutor's Request for Leave to file an Amended Indictment (TC) dated 28 September 2006, para. 12, the Chamber evaluated the pleading of JCE in the Amended Indictment of 6 October 2006 and determined the Indictment's ambiguity in respect of paragraph 15.

(c) Has the Defect in the Indictment Been Cured?

(i) The Pre-Trial Brief

29. The Chamber notes that the Pre-Trial Brief refers extensively to JCE and states that Emmanuel Rukundo's participation in a JCE is pleaded in "various paragraphs of the [I]ndictment including 3, 10, 11, 12, 14, 15, 16, 18, 22, 33, 35, 36, and 40."[43] However, the paragraph references appear to refer to an old Indictment dated 27 March 2003.[44] The Chamber will therefore not consider the Prosecution's submission in this regard.

30. The Chamber further notes that the Pre-Trial Brief does not indicate the specific form of JCE in which Rukundo is alleged to have participated. Paragraph 78 of the Pre-Trial Brief states that "the Prosecutor will adduce evidence that speaks to all the categories of joint criminal enterprise enumerated above." The Chamber notes that no such categories of JCE were actually "enumerated above". Although the Prosecution set out the legal definition of the three categories of JCE, at no point did it specify the category of JCE upon which it intends to rely. The Chamber considers that the Prosecution was clearly in a position to determine the category of **[page 9]** JCE upon which it would rely.[45]

31. The Chamber has found the reference to "commission" in the Indictment particularly ambiguous, when read in light of the paragraphs on individual criminal responsibility describing the Accused's mode of participation as "ordering, instigating or aiding and abetting".[46] In the Pre-Trial Brief, the Prosecution submits that "in furtherance of the common criminal purpose of eliminating Tutsis, Emmanuel RUKUNDO participated... in planning or organizing the massacres in diverse locations, in ordering and publicly instigating militiamen, local authorities, soldiers, gendarmerie and the Hutu population to eliminate Tutsis, and in planning, instigating, ordering aiding and abetting the massacres, he supported all."[47] The Chamber notes that the Pre-Trial Brief does not provide any clarification on the ambiguity surrounding the Accused's mode of participation in the alleged crimes.

32. In addition, the Pre-Trial Brief makes only general statements in respect of the allegation of JCE. Paragraph 98 is an example of such a vague submission:

> "Between 6 April and 17 July 1994, Emmanuel RUKUNDO participated in the formulation and/or supported the adoption and implementation of various directives, decisions, policies, orders etc, to further the common criminal purpose of eliminating Tutsis. Local authorities, including *prefets, bourgmestres, conseillers and responsables de cellule*, Interahamwe, the civil defence, FAR, *gendarmerie* and the Hutu population were mobilized to carry out the common criminal purpose of killing Tutsis."[48]

33. In light of the aforementioned, the Chamber finds that the Pre-Trial Brief does not provide clear, consistent and timely notice to the Defence to defend a charge of JCE. The references to JCE in the Pre-Trial Brief therefore do not cure the Indictment's defective pleading.

(ii) Post-Indictment Disclosures

34. In its opening statement, the Prosecution provided no additional detail about the alleged JCE. The Prosecution argued only that Rukundo's role was subtle, "involving instigation, aiding and abetting the soldiers, *Interahamwe* and armed civilians who physically committed the crimes that are charged in this

---

[43] Prosecutor's Pre-Trial Brief, footnote 51.
[44] The Amended Indictment dated 6 October 2006 only has a total of 30 paragraphs while the former Indictment dated 27 March 2003 has 41 paragraphs. In respect of the Indictment dated 27 March 2003, none of the 13 paragraph numbers listed in the Pre-Trial Brief refer to "joint criminal enterprise" nor do they stipulate which specific category of JCE is pleaded. Furthermore none of the 13 paragraphs make reference to how Rukundo "committed" such crimes. Only 3 of the 13 paragraphs refer to how Rukundo "planned, instigated, ordered or aided" respective crimes, whilst the other 10 paragraphs do not refer to the Accused's specific mode of participation.
[45] For instance, the Prosecution cannot reasonably argue that it intends to rely on the second category of JCE in a case where it does not even allege the existence of a system of ill treatment (*Bikindi*, Judgement (TC), para. 400).
[46] See Section II.A.2.b.
[47] Prosecutor's Pre-Trial Brief para. 99.
[48] Prosecutor's Pre-Trial Brief para. 98.

Indictment."[49] Furthermore at no point in post-indictment disclosures or **[page 10]** during the trial did the Prosecution mention Rukundo's alleged involvement in a JCE or in a common criminal plan or purpose.

(iii) Conclusion

35. The Chamber has already found that the Indictment is defective in respect of the pleading of JCE. The Chamber further finds that neither the Pre-Trial Brief nor other post-indictment disclosures provide clear, consistent and timely notice to the Defence of the Prosecution's intention to demonstrate the Accused's responsibility under the theory of JCE. Therefore the Chamber will not consider any charge that Emmanuel Rukundo participated in a JCE.

B. EVIDENTIARY MATTERS

36. Article 20(3) of the Statute guarantees the presumption of innocence of each accused person. The burden of proving the guilt of the accused beyond reasonable doubt rests solely on the Prosecution and never shifts to the Defence. The Chamber must be satisfied beyond reasonable doubt that the accused is guilty before a verdict may be entered against him or her.[50]

37. While the Defence does not have to adduce rebuttal evidence to the Prosecution case, the Prosecution will fail to discharge its burden of proof if the Defence presents evidence that raises a reasonable doubt regarding the Prosecution case.[51] An accused person must be acquitted if there is any reasonable explanation for the evidence other than his or her guilt.[52] Refusal to believe or rely upon Defence evidence does not automatically amount to a guilty verdict. The Chamber must still determine whether the evidence it does accept establishes the accused's guilt beyond reasonable doubt.[53]

38. The general principle enshrined in Rule 90(A) of the Rules is that witnesses should be heard directly by the Trial Chamber.[54] However, there are well established exceptions to the Chamber's preference for direct, live, in-court testimony, including the taking of witness testimony by deposition,[55] and the admission of written statements, in lieu of oral testimony, which do not go to proof of the alleged conduct of the accused as charged in the indictment.[56] **[page 11]**

39. While direct evidence is preferred, hearsay evidence is not *per se* inadmissible before the Trial Chamber.[57] The Trial Chamber has the discretion to treat such hearsay evidence with caution, depending on the circumstances of the case.[58] In certain circumstances, hearsay evidence may require other credible or reliable evidence adduced by the Prosecution in order to support a finding of fact beyond reasonable doubt.

40. In general, a Chamber can make a finding of fact based on the evidence of a single witness if it finds such evidence to be relevant and credible.[59] Corroboration of a witness's testimony is not a requirement in the practice of the Tribunal.[60] Similarly, even if the Trial Chamber finds that a witness's testimony is inconsistent or otherwise problematic, it may still choose to accept the evidence because it is corroborated by other evidence.[61]

---

[49] T. 15 November 2006, p. 3.
[50] See also Rule 87(A) of the Rules: "[…] A finding of guilty may be reached only when a majority of the Trial Chamber is satisfied that guilt has been proved beyond reasonable doubt."
[51] *Kayishema,* Judgement (AC), para. 117; *Niyitegeka,* Judgement (AC), paras. 60-61.
[52] *Čelebići,* Judgement (AC), para. 458.
[53] *Nchamihigo,* Judgement (TC), para. 13.
[54] *Simba,* Judgement (AC), para. 19.
[55] Rule 71 of the Rules.
[56] Rule 92*bis* of the Rules.
[57] *Muvunyi,* Judgement (TC), para. 12; *Rutaganda,* Judgement (AC), para. 34.
[58] Rule 89 of the Rules; *Rutaganda,* Judgement (AC), para. 34; *Aleksovski,* Decision on Prosecutor's Appeal On Admissibility Of Evidence (AC), 16 February 1999, para. 15.
[59] *Karera,* Judgement (AC), para. 45; *Musema,* Judgement (AC), paras. 37-38.
[60] *Karera,* Judgement (AC), para. 45; *Musema,* Judgement (AC), para. 36; *Ntakirutimana,* Judgement (AC), para. 132.
[61] *Ntakirutimana,* Judgement (AC), para. 132.

41. The Chamber further notes that the evidence of accomplices and detained witnesses is admissible. However, when necessary, the Chamber will approach such evidence with caution in order to ensure a fair trial and to avoid prejudice to the accused.[62]

42. When assessing the evidence, a Trial Chamber has broad discretion to determine the weight to be given to the discrepancies between a witness's testimony and his prior statements.[63] It is for the Chamber to decide if an alleged inconsistency is sufficient to cast doubt on a witness's evidence, and the Chamber may accept such evidence, notwithstanding the discrepancies.

C. DECISION ON DEFENCE MOTION FOR ACQUITTAL

43. In its Decision on the Defence Motion for Acquittal ("Judgement of Acquittal"), following the close of the Prosecution case, the Chamber found that the evidence, even if believed, could not support a finding beyond reasonable doubt that Rukundo was responsible for the murder of Father **[page 12]** Mbuguje. Accordingly, the Chamber acquitted the Accused of the murder of Father Mbuguje under Count 2 (murder as a crime against humanity).[64]

44. The Chamber notes that the murder of Father Mbuguje has also been pleaded in the Indictment in support of the charge of genocide under Count 1.[65] The Chamber, however, notes that the Prosecution in its Closing Brief no longer relies on this allegation in support of the count of genocide. The Chamber will therefore not consider the evidence of the murder of Father Mbuguje in its analysis of the count of genocide against the Accused.

45. Furthermore, in its Judgement of Acquittal, the Chamber noted the Prosecution's concession that it had not led evidence on paragraphs 10(i) and 25(i) of the Indictment, and granted its request to withdraw these paragraphs.[66] The Chamber also granted the Prosecution's request to withdraw paragraph 16 from the Indictment, since it had not led any evidence on it.[67]

D. JUDICIAL NOTICE

46. Rule 94(A) provides that the Trial Chamber shall not require proof of facts of common knowledge, but shall take judicial notice thereof. The Appeals Chamber has held that the following are all facts of common knowledge, not subject to reasonable dispute, and therefore qualify for judicial notice under Rule 94(A): (1) between 6 April 1994 and 17 July 1994, there was a genocide in Rwanda against the Tutsi ethnic group; (2) between 6 April 1994 and 17 July 1994, there were widespread or systematic attacks throughout Rwanda

---

[62] *Ntagerura et al.*, Judgement (AC), paras. 203-205; *Niyitigeka*, Judgement (AC), para. 98; *Muvunyi*, Judgement (TC), para. 13. In *Simba*, the Trial Chamber viewed the testimonies of Witnesses YH and KXX, the alleged accomplices of the Accused, with appropriate caution. The Chamber also treated the testimony of Witness YC with appropriate caution since he was a detained witness who had pleaded guilty to acts of genocide in the relevant area. See *Simba*, Judgement (TC), paras. 164, 288.
[63] *Gacumbitsi*, Judgement (AC), para. 74; *Kajelijeli*, Judgement (AC), para. 96.
[64] Decision on Defence Motion for Judgement of Acquittal Pursuant to Rule 98*bis* (TC), 22 May 2007 ("98*bis* Decision"), para. 16. Para. 23 of the Indictment states: On or about 14 May 1994, **Emmanuel RUKUNDO** spoke to the Bernadine Sisters, in Nyarugenge secteur and commune in Kigali-Ville Prefecture, describing Father Alphonse MBUGUJE, as an *Inkotanyi* and saying that his whereabouts were known and indicating that Father Alphonse MBUGUJE would be killed. Father Alphonse MBUGUJE was killed on 30 May 1994 by *gendarmes* in Cyangugu Prefecture. As noted in paragraph 7 above, **Emmanuel RUKUNDO** denounced this victim as an *Inkotanyi* to the authorities, and this denunciation contributed substantially to the killing of the victim. **Emmanuel RUKUNDO** thus instigated or aided and abetted the killing of Father Alphonse MBUGUJE
[65] Paras. 7, 17 of the Indictment.
[66] 98*bis* Decision, paras. 7-8 and disposition. Paras. 10(i) and 25(i) of the Indictment both read as follows: In April 1994, **Emmanuel RUKUNDO** moved around in Gitarama, dressed in military uniform, armed with a pistol and an R4 rifle, and escorted by four or five soldiers. Sometime in this month, **Emmanuel RUKUNDO** went to Gitarama Parish hunting for the parish priest Father Juvenal BAMBONEYEHO, accusing him of hiding Tutsis in his parish and threatening that their days were numbered, meaning that Tutsis were all soon to be killed.
[67] 98*bis* Decision, paras. 7-8 and disposition. Para. 16 of the Indictment reads as follows: On a date sometime in the period between about 7 April and the end of May 1994, **Emmanuel RUKUNDO** led a group of armed soldiers to Gitarama Parish, Diocese of Kabgayi, Gitarama Prefecture, in search of Tutsi refugees to kill. When **Emmanuel RUKUNDO** did not find the parish priest whom he accused of being an accomplice of the *Inkotanyi*, he threatened a Tutsi man whom he met, saying that the days of the "*Inkotanyi*" (meaning all Tutsis) were numbered. By so doing, **Emmanuel RUKUNDO** caused this Tutsi man serious mental harm.

against a civilian population based on Tutsi **[page 13]** ethnic identification; and (3) between 1 January 1994 and 17 July 1994 in Rwanda, there was an armed conflict not of an international character.[68]

47. In its Decision of 29 November 2006, the Trial Chamber took judicial notice of the following facts of common knowledge, pursuant to Rule 94(A):[69]

   (i)   Between 6 April 1994 and 17 July 1994, genocide against the Tutsi ethnic group occurred in Rwanda;

   (ii) Between 1 January 1994 and 17 July 1994, the Twa, Tutsi and Hutu existed in Rwanda as protected groups falling under the Genocide Convention;

   (iii) Between 6 April 1994 and 17 July 1994, throughout Rwanda, there were widespread or systematic attacks against a civilian population based on Tutsi ethnic identification. During the attacks, some Rwandan citizens killed or caused serious bodily or mental harm to persons perceived as Tutsi. As a result of the attacks, there were a large number of deaths of persons of Tutsi ethnic identity;

   (iv) Between 6 April 1994 and 17 July 1994, there was an armed conflict in Rwanda that was not of an international character;

   (v)   Between 1 January 1994 and 17 July 1994, Rwanda was a State party to the Convention on the Prevention and Punishment of the Crime of Genocide (1948), having acceded to it on 16 April 1975; and

   (vi) Between 1 January 1994 and 17 July 1994, Rwanda was a State Party to the Geneva Conventions of 12 August 1949 and their Additional Protocol II of 8 June 1977, having acceded to the Geneva Convention of 12 August 1949 on 5 May 1964, and having acceded to Protocols Additional thereto of 1977 on 19 November 1984.

48. Taking judicial notice of the above facts does not relieve the Prosecution of its burden to lead evidence to prove beyond reasonable doubt that the Accused's conduct and mental state **[page 14]** rendered him individually responsible for genocide and crimes against humanity as charged in the Indictment.[70] **[page 15]**

III. CHAPTER III: FACTUAL FINDINGS

1. EVIDENCE RELATING TO PRE-1994 EVENTS

(a) Indictment

   (3) Emmanuel Rukundo was known as an extremist. He hated the Tutsi. Since about 1973, he fought against his Tutsi colleagues at the Saint Léon Minor Seminary in Kabgayi. He was expelled from this seminary in 1973, because of his racist tendencies and was known to be sectarian at the Nyakibanda Major Seminary, in Butare, by several clergy.

   (4) After the attack by the RPF, in Rwanda, in October 1990, Emmanuel Rukundo, while at the Nyakibanda Major Seminary, created and led a group of extremists called *Ngarukiragihugu* to collect money to purchase ammunition and compose songs with extremist passions to support the RAF in fighting the RPF. At that time he swore that he would take to the bush if the RPF won the war.

   (5) In spite of his attitude, he was ordained a priest in July 1991, by Monsignor Thadée Nsengiyumva, and was appointed as priest of Kanyanza Parish in Gitarama.

   (6) From 1990 through 1994, Emmanuel Rukundo showed hatred for Tutsi priests and systematically denounced them as accomplices of the *Inkotanyi*, saying that the Nyakibanda Major Seminary was a bastion of the Tutsi, and that it was difficult to live in such a milieu as a Hutu, and as one who would become a priest.

---

[68] *Karemera et al.*, Decision on Interlocutory Appeal of Decision on Judicial Notice (AC), 16 June 2006.
[69] Decision on Prosecutor's Motion for the Trial Chamber to take Judicial Notice of Facts of Common Knowledge Pursuant to Rule 94(A) (TC), 29 November 2006.
[70] *Semanza*, Judgement (AC), para. 192; *Karemera et al.*, Decision on Prosecutor's Interlocutory Appeal of Decision on Judicial Notice (AC), 16 June 2006, para. 30.

(b) Evidence and Deliberations

(i) Expulsion from the St. Léon Minor Seminary in 1973[71]

49. The Prosecution concedes in its Closing Brief that it did not adduce any evidence in support of this charge.[72] The Chamber therefore considers this allegation withdrawn.

(ii) Ngarukiragihugu (Salvation Committee), Solidarity March, Fund-Raising and Alleged Change of Attitude[73]

50. The Chamber recalls that at the pre-trial phase of this case, the Prosecution submitted before Trial Chamber III that it would rely on paragraphs 1-6 of the Indictment of 17 September 2001 (which are almost identical to paragraphs 3-6 of the current Indictment) as contextual material. In its Decision on Defence Preliminary Motions, the Trial Chamber held that it is permissible for an indictment to plead facts that fall outside the temporal jurisdiction of the Tribunal for the purpose of providing context or clarifying the events in the indictment. The Chamber found, however, **[page 16]** that such pre-1994 facts cannot constitute elements of the crimes charged.[74] On appeal, the Appeals Chamber confirmed that an Indictment may refer to facts or criminal conduct that occurred before 1994 provided that such facts or conduct do not constitute independent charges, but are introduced as evidence to support the commission of crimes in 1994.[75]

51. In its Closing Brief, the Prosecution submits that it led evidence of Rukundo's conduct in 1990 and 1991 to demonstrate that "Rukundo had the requisite *mens rea* to commit the offences charged."[76] It is unclear from this statement whether the Prosecution still relies on the evidence of Rukundo's pre-1994 conduct as contextual material.

52. The Chamber notes that the primary requirement for the admission of evidence before the Tribunal is that it must be relevant and have probative value.[77] Although the temporal jurisdiction of the Tribunal is from 1 January to 31 December 1994, it is permissible, under certain circumstances, to adduce evidence on events prior to this time where such evidence satisfies the criteria of relevance and probative value and there is no compelling reason to exclude it. As examples, the Appeals Chamber states that the Trial Chamber could admit and subsequently rely on evidence of acts which took place prior to 1994 when 1) it clarifies a given context, 2) it establishes by inference the elements of criminal conduct occurring in 1994, or 3) demonstrating a deliberate pattern of conduct.[78]

53. The Appeals Chamber, however, stated that an accused person can only be convicted for a crime committed in 1994. The *actus reus* must have occurred in 1994, and at the time of such acts or omissions, the accused must have had the requisite intent (*mens rea*) to carry out that crime.[79]

54. In this case, the Prosecution submits that the pre-1994 evidence should be used generally to support the crime of genocide because it shows that Rukundo was a Hutu extremist even before the start of the genocide.[80] The Prosecution, however, has made no link between the pre-1994 evidence of Rukundo's alleged extremist behaviour, and the specific factual allegations in the Indictment. It has also not shown how the evidence clarifies any particular context. Taken at its best, the mere fact that Rukundo might have been a Hutu extremist prior to the genocide in the context of his schooling is not sufficient to prove that he had the specific intent required for the particular criminal acts as **[page 17]** alleged in the Indictment. The Chamber

---

[71] Para. 3 of the Indictment.
[72] Prosecution Closing Brief, para. 107.
[73] Paras. 4 and 6 of the Indictment.
[74] Decision on Defence Preliminary Motion (TC), 26 February 2003, para 12.
[75] Décision (*Acte D'Appel relative à la Décision du 26 Février 2003 relative aux exceptions préjudicielles*) (AC), 17 October 2003, p. 5.
[76] Prosecution Closing Brief, para. 111.
[77] *Simba*, Decision on Interlocutory Appeal Regarding Temporal Jurisdiction (AC), 29 July 2004, p. 4.
[78] *Nahimana et al.*, Judgement (AC), 28 November 2007, para. 315.
[79] *Nahimana et al.*, Judgement (AC), paras. 313-314, 317.
[80] Prosecution Closing Brief, paras. 103-111.

Judgement

will therefore not consider the evidence relating to Rukundo's acts prior to 1994 at the Nyakibanda Major Semimary. **[page 18]**

2. ALLEGATION OF MOBILIZATION OF HUTU AGAINST TUTSI IN FEBRUARY 1994

55. The Chamber notes that the Prosecution has not led any evidence on paragraphs 9 and 24 of the Indictment. The Chamber therefore dismisses this allegation. **[page 19]**

3. EVENTS AT THE IMPRIMERIE DE KABGAYI ROADBLOCK

(a) Indictment

56. Paragraphs 10(ii) and 25(ii) of the Indictment read as follows:

> Between 12 and 15 April 1994, **Emmanuel RUKUNDO,** dressed in military uniform, armed and accompanied by soldiers, stopped at a roadblock around *Imprimerie de Kabgayi,* near the St. Léon Minor Seminary, to talk to and observe the activities of soldiers who were checking the identity cards of persons who passed through the roadblock. Several Tutsis were arrested by soldiers and *Interahamwe* at this roadblock and killed nearby. **Emmanuel RUKUNDO's** presence at this roadblock provided encouragement to these soldiers and *Interahamwe* to carry on with the killing of Tutsis at this location. **Emmanuel RUKUNDO** thus instigated or aided and abetted the killing of Tutsis at the *Imprimerie de Kabgayi* roadblock.

(b) Evidence

Prosecution Witness BLP

57. Prosecution Witness BLP, a Hutu who worked at St. Joseph's College in 1994, knew the Accused Rukundo as a priest and saw him at religious celebrations in Kabgayi. The witness saw the Accused in mid-April, a few days after the shooting down of the presidential plane. On that occasion, Witness BLP had left church and was on his way to St. Joseph's College when he was stopped by soldiers manning a roadblock close to the Kabayi printing press and asked to show his identity card. Rukundo, dressed in military uniform, was at the roadblock. The witness recalled that Rukundo wore a black beret (the type worn by the RAF), military boots, camouflage trousers, a camouflage shirt with a cross on his epaulette and had a pistol in his belt.[81]

58. According to Witness BLP, Rukundo arrived at the roadblock in a white Suzuki Samurai jeep with a military registration. Rukundo was accompanied by a driver wearing a camouflage shirt and a black beret, and another soldier who was in the back of his vehicle. Rukundo's vehicle stopped about four meters from where Witness BLP stood, and when Rukundo alighted from the vehicle to greet the soldiers, he was about one metre away from Witness BLP.[82]

59. Rukundo spoke with two of the soldiers who were checking the identification cards of people detained at the roadblock. Witness BLP observed that Rukundo knew the soldiers manning the roadblock because of the way they laughed together. The soldiers greeted Rukundo, saying "Good morning, Father". Witness BLP testified that he did not stay long at the roadblock. He also **[page 20]** noted, as he left, that there were people sitting on the ground next to the roadblock, who, he believed, did not have identity cards. He further noted that the task of those manning the roadblock was to identify the people going through the roadblock. Witness BLP stated that certain people were allowed to go through, whilst others were retained because they were Tutsi or because they did not have identity cards. According to Witness BLP, Tutsi were sought out because they were considered to be the enemy. Witness BLP also said that when Tutsi were found, they were often killed.[83]

---

[81] T. 15 November 2006, pp. 11-14, 27; T. 16 November 2006, pp. 10, 13.
[82] T. 15 November 2006, pp. 13-14; T. 16 November 2006, p. 23.
[83] T. 15 November 2006, pp. 13-14; T. 16 November 2007, pp. 22-23.

60. Witness BLP was informed by a man whom he had met at the roadblock that the people who were retained there were later taken to a wooded area about 40 metres downhill and killed.[84] In cross-examination, Witness BLP attested that he did not know the man who gave him this information, but knew that he was a refugee in Kabgayi.[85] Witness BLP said that he passed the roadblock on his way to work and the amount of time he would spend there varied. Some days he would remain there for a long time and on other days he would go through quickly. On one particular day, he was retained for 20 minutes and was asked to sit on the ground.[86]

61. Witness BLP estimated that the roadblock close to the Kabgayi printing press was erected about four days after the downing of President Habyarimana's plane and that it was removed on the morning of 6 June 1994 when the *Inkotanyi* arrived in Kabgayi and the soldiers abandoned the roadblock. According to Witness BLP, there were several roadblocks in Kabgayi and the surrounding area.[87]

Prosecution Witness CSE

62. Witness CSE, a Tutsi from Gitarama *préfecture*, sought refuge in Kabgayi after the death of President Habyarimana on 6 April and remained there until 2 June 1994. Witness CSE testified that he saw Rukundo in Kabgayi in March 1993 and again in Kabgayi, at a roadblock between the church and the printing press store in St. Andre, sometime in April 1994. Rukundo and Witness CSE were about five to six metres apart from each other. According to the witness, Rukundo was wearing camouflage trousers and a shirt, usually referred to as *tash-tash*. Witness CSE testified that at the roadblock he saw soldiers, who were the authorities' escorts, beating a person with the butts of their guns. Rukundo was standing approximately five to six metres away from the soldiers, **[page 21]** facing them and talking to other people. Witness CSE testified that the beating went on for a long time. Other people also saw the soldiers beating this person and commented that they were surprised that Rukundo as a priest did not intervene. In cross-examination, Witness CSE stated that when he saw Rukundo at the roadblock, he was travelling to Gahando to seek assistance after hearing shots the previous night. However, when the witness saw the person being beaten at the roadblock, he turned around and sought shelter in the church, where he remained until the danger subsided.[88]

The Accused

63. Rukundo recalled seeing a roadblock outside the Kabgayi printing press on either 21 April or 7 May 1994. He stated that he was "under the impression" that on 15 April 1994, there was no roadblock at that location. When Rukundo arrived at the roadblock on 15 April 1994 he, like everybody else, was checked by those manning the roadblock. He was allowed to drive through and then went on to the Bishopric. Rukundo said that he went through those roadblocks two or three times during the course of his visits to Kabgayi and that he never saw anyone being beaten there. He also never saw any incident take place at the roadblock or noticed any person being mistreated. Rukundo testified that he would not have allowed such attacks to continue and, with the assistance of his escort, would have done his best to stop such violence. Rukundo did not know the people manning the roadblock. They simply asked him to show the necessary papers, which he did, and then they would open the roadblock and he would drive through.[89]

64. In cross-examination, Rukundo testified that, on one occasion, he saw three soldiers at the roadblock who were checking civilians passing through. Rukundo testified that there was a small wooded area on the other side of the main road leading to Butare, but he could not see into that area and did not know if there were dead bodies there. Rukundo attested that he did not see anyone killed or abused at the roadblock near the printing press or at any other roadblock in 1994.[90]

---

[84] T. 15 November 2006, p. 14.
[85] T. 16 November 2006, p. 24.
[86] T. 16 November 2006, p. 22.
[87] T. 16 November 2006, pp. 21- 22.
[88] T. 17 November 2006, pp. 2-6, 13-14, 18-20, 21-23. A photograph where the witness indicated the various positions at the roadblock was admitted as Exhibit D. 5 (T. 17 November 2006, pp. 26, 34-35).
[89] T. 9 October 2007, pp. 48-49; T. 10 October 2007, pp. 53-54.
[90] T. 10 October 2007, pp. 53-54.

Judgement

65. Rukundo denied that he drove a Suzuki Samurai with military license plates. The official vehicle of the military chaplaincy was the Mazda from the Episcopal Council. As a military chaplain, Rukundo stated that he never drove a military jeep, although other priests sometimes used **[page 22]** such vehicles to access certain areas. He added that Witness BLP may have referred to a jeep to concoct his story.[91]

66. Rukundo testified that on both his first and second visits from Ruhengeri to Kabgayi via Gitarama and Rango on 15 and 21 April 1994, he came across several roadblocks. As a precaution he had asked the commander of Camp Mukamira, Laurent Bizabarimana, to provde him with official travel authorisation indicating that he was on a mission to Gitarama.[92]

Defence Witness SJC

67. Witness SJC knew Rukundo when the latter was studying at the St. Léon Minor Seminary. Witness SJC also attended Rukundo's ordination as a priest.[93] On 6 April 1994, Witness SJC was at his father's house in Kabgayi. After President Habyarimana's plane was shot down, the authorities announced that people should stay at home. Witness SJC stayed at home for two weeks after 6 April 1994.[94] On or about 20 April 1994, he received information that his cousin was injured and had been admitted to the Kabgayi hospital. He visited his cousin at the hospital and stayed there from 20 April to 1 May 1994.[95]

68. Witness SJC testified that he saw a roadblock in Kabgayi, near the printing press and St. Joseph's College, manned by people wearing soldiers' uniforms. There was one soldier on each side of the roadblock. Witness SJC did not know when the roadblock was erected, but it was removed when the *Inkotanyi* arrived on 2 June 1994. Witness SJC said that every time he passed the roadblock he was required to show his identity card. All Rwandan citizens could pass freely through the roadblock if they presented their identification documents. Witness SJC never saw anyone being stopped at the roadblock and said that both Hutu and Tutsi could travel freely through the roadblock. He recalled that on some days there was a queue of people waiting to be allowed through the roadblock. Witness SJC acknowledged that there was a small wooded area on the other side of the road near the roadblock. He said that he never saw or heard of people being killed there, but he did not deny that such incidents may have happened without his knowledge.[96]

69. Witness SJC stated that there was no roadblock at the Kabgayi Major Seminary, although there was only one permanent gate at the entrance guarded by soldiers. The soldiers did not ask **[page 23]** Witness SJC for his identity card, but they may have asked other people. According to the witness, the soldiers were stationed at the gate to protect the refugees from the RPF militia. Witness SJC testified that soldiers were posted at the CND, as well as at the St. Léon Minor Seminary, St. Joseph's College, St. Andre Primary School and Kabgayi hospital to protect the refugees. He acknowledged that the majority of refugees at these locations were Tutsi.[97]

Defence Witness EVA

70. Witness EVA was employed at the Kabgayi Bishopric in 1994.[98] Witness EVA knew Rukundo, having seen him on more than 20 occasions when she worked at the Bishopric.[99]

71. Witness EVA said that two roadblocks were erected in Kabgayi between April and June 1994. One roadblock was on the road between her home and the Kabgayi Bishopric buildings; the other was further down on the road to Butare. Witness EVA had to pass through the roadblock between the printing press and St. Joseph's College, which was manned by two soldiers, every day on her way to work. Different soldiers manned the roadblock in the morning and in the afternoon, and the witness at times had difficulties crossing

---

[91] T. 9 October 2007, p. 49; T. 10 October 2007, pp. 44-45.
[92] T. 9 October 2007, p. 9; T. 11 October 2007, p. 10.
[93] T. 3 September 2007, p. 16.
[94] T. 3 September 2007, pp. 14-15.
[95] T. 3 September 2007, pp. 40-41.
[96] T. 3 September 2007, pp. 52-56.
[97] T. 3 September 2007, pp. 56-59.
[98] T. 19 July 2007, pp. 5, 12-13, 15.
[99] T. 19 July 2007, p. 23.

the roadblock. People without identity papers, were made to sit down close to the roadblock. Occasionally Witness EVA saw individuals sitting at the roadblock however when she returned after lunch they were always gone. Witness EVA said that she did not see anyone being mistreated at the roadblock. Witness EVA explained that the purpose of the roadblocks was to prevent people from gathering at the refugee camps, and the purpose of showing identification was to ensure security. Without identification, a person could be a suspect.[100] Witness EVA did not normally have trouble passing through the roadblock. She did, however, have problems passing through on two occasions when she had forgotten her identification papers at home. The soldiers detained her for about 20 minutes until the Chancellor, Bernadin, went to her house and retrieved her papers. After the second incident, Chancellor Bernadin drove her to and from work twice each day until after 2 June 1994. Witness EVA acknowledged that she was afraid to pass through the roadblocks because she thought that she would be killed. She said that she would no longer go to work unless she was driven.[101] **[page 24]**

72. Witness EVA testified that she saw Rukundo in Kabgayi around 14 or 15 April 1994.[102]

Defence Witness GSA

73. Witness GSA was employed at the Kabgayi Major Seminary in April 1994 and knew the Accused as a theology student.[103]

74. Witness GSA provided an account of the killing of a young man at a roadblock in Kabgayi. Witness GSA had given a young man, whose brother he knew well, a ride. When the witness's vehicle was stopped at a roadblock between the Kabgayi printing press and St. Joseph's College, the young man was taken from the car. According to Witness GSA, two priests arrived while he was attempting to negotiate the young man's release. The priests, who carried out the negotiations, due to the possible danger facing the witness, told the witness to leave. When the young man saw Witness GSA departing, he became afraid and ran towards him, only to be shot in the back. The two priests informed Witness GSA that, if he travelled through the roadblock again, he would be in danger.

75. Witness GSA stated that, on this particular day when the young man was shot, the roadblock had been moved closer to the Gitarama highway. However, it was relocated to its former position after the incident. Witness GSA did not know who shot the young man at the roadblock. Witness GSA thought that the incident at the roadblock had occurred in May 1994, around Ascension, which is celebrated 40 days after Easter.[104]

76. Witness GSA testified that Brother Martin and Brother Fidele from St. Joseph's College and Sister Bénigne travelled through that roadblock (between the Kabgayi printing press and the Josephite Brothers' house) on their way to their offices from the Kabgayi Major Seminary, where they had sought refuge. Witness GSA added that nothing "untoward" happened to them at the roadblock.[105]

Defence Witness SAE

77. Witness SAE, a superior officer in the Gitarama Military Camp, testified that he was informed by his subordinates about incidents at different military positions in the area. Witness SAE testified that Rukundo could not have spoken to soldiers and encouraged acts of violence **[page 25]** without informing his immediate commander. Witness SAE explained that it was not within the ambit of Rukundo's duties to speak to the soldiers as if he were their commander. He explained that military chaplains were attached to a command office in order to advise on religious services and morality. In principle, a military chaplain did not receive orders from a military commander.[106]

---

[100] T. 19 July 2007, pp. 19-22, 53-58; Documents marked by Witness EVA showing the location of the roadblock were admitted as Exhibit D. 33 (T. 19 July 2007, p. 38).
[101] T. 19 July 2007, pp. 21-22, 54, 56.
[102] T. 19 July 2007, pp. 25-27, 44-46.
[103] T. 1 October 2007, p. 61; T. 2 October 2007, p. 1.
[104] T. 1 October 2007, pp. 61, 75-76; T. 2 October 2007 pp. 38-39, 48-49.
[105] T. 1 October 2007 pp. 67-69; T. 2 October 2007, p. 39.
[106] T. 24 September 2007, pp. 60-61.

78. Witness SAE denied ever hearing that Rukundo had participated in any criminal activity at Kabgayi. Witness SAE explained that if Rukundo had taken part in such acts, information would have been provided to him by the soldiers stationed in Kabgayi.[107]

79. Witness SAE testified that he was not aware that killings of members of the population had taken place in his area. Witness SAE refuted that the reason why he did not know about the killings was because his soldiers had not reported such incidents to him. Witness SAE testified that no soldier single-handedly manned a roadblock. According to the witness, each soldier belonged to a team, which was part of a section, and a section was part of a platoon. As the soldiers' superior, Witness SAE was expected to know about all of their activities.[108]

Defence Witness ATT

80. Witness ATT testified that there was a "heap of stones" near St. Andre and the Kabgayi printing press, which was manned by "bandits." He stated that it was a "mobile roadblock," not a "real roadblock," and that on certain days, when he passed by he did not see anyone around the "heap of stones".[109] Witness ATT pleaded guilty to having participated in attacks against Tutsi refugees in Kabgayi in 1994. He was convicted and served eleven years in prison in Rwanda.[110]

Defence Witness EVC

81. In April 1994, Defence Witness EVC was a priest in Kabgayi. Witness EVC knew Emmanuel Rukundo. During April and May 1994, Witness EVC might have seen Rukundo once in Kabgayi and shared a beer with him. Witness EVC denied that there were soldiers throughout Kabgayi between April and June of 1994. However, he affirmed that there were soldiers at the roadblocks on the main roads. He stated that the military presence at the time could possibly be explained by the fact that the transitional government had provisionally relocated to Gitarama, in the nearby *préfecture*. Witness EVC could not confirm that soldiers were amongst the killers in and **[page 26]** around Kabgayi. Although the witness had been informed that people had been killed in the area, he did not know any details about the killings. In examination-in-chief, Witness EVC testified that between April and May 1994 he saw Rukundo once in Kabgayi when they may have shared a beer. However, in cross-examination, Witness EVC denied hearing anyone mention that Rukundo was in Kabgayi during this period of time.[111]

(c) Deliberations

82. The Indictment states that between 12 and 15 April 1994, Rukundo was present when Tutsi were arrested at the printing press- *Imprimerie de Kabgayi*- roadblock and killed nearby and that his presence instigated[112] or aided and abetted[113] these killings. The Chamber also heard evidence from Prosecution Witness CSE that sometime in April 1994, a person was beaten at that roadblock when Rukundo was present. The Defence submits that the evidence presented by Witness CSE is different from that which is pleaded in paragraphs 10(ii) and 25(ii) of the Indictment.[114] The Chamber notes that in the Prosecution's Closing Brief, the Prosecution misquoted the Indictment by stating that the soldiers "killed or harmed" Tutsi, whereas the Indictment only refers to killing.[115] It appears, however, that the Prosecution is not relying on the alleged

---

[107] T. 24 September 2007, pp. 61-62.
[108] T. 25 September 2007, pp. 2-6.
[109] T. 18 July 2007, pp. 59-60.
[110] T. 18 July 2007, pp. 3-4, 8.
[111] T. 11 September 2007, pp. 36, 52-54.
[112] "Instigating" requires that the Accused encouraged, urged, or otherwise prompted another person to commit an offence under the Statute. See for example, *Kordić and Čerkez*, Judgement (AC), para. 27; *Ndindabahizi*, Judgement (AC), para. 117; *Muvunyi*, Judgement (TC), para. 478.
[113] "Aiding and abetting" is a form of accessory liability. It refers to any act of assistance or support in the commission of the crime by another person". See for example, Akayesu, Judgement (TC), para. 484; Bagilishema, Judgement (TC), paras. 33, 186; Nzabirinda, Judgement (TC), para 16.
[114] Defence Closing Brief, para. 208.
[115] Prosecution Closing Brief, para. 214.

beatings to establish an allegation of serious bodily or mental harm.[116] Therefore, the Chamber will only rely on Witness CSE's evidence to the extent that it supports the allegation of killing as pleaded in the Indictment.

83. Both Witness BLP and Witness CSE testified that they saw Rukundo at a roadblock near the Kabgayi printing press. Witness BLP placed Rukundo, wearing a military uniform, there in mid-April 1994, a few days after the presidential plane crash.[117] Witness CSE saw Rukundo, in a military uniform and accompanied by soldiers, sometime after 7 April 1994 between the church and the printing press store.[118] Rukundo also testified that he was in Kabgayi on 15 April 1994.[119] **[page 27]**

84. The existence of the roadblock was not contested by any Defence witness.[120] However, there are inconsistencies regarding the date when the roadblock was established. Witness BLP stated that the roadblock was erected about four days after President Habyarimana's death.[121] According to Witness CSE, the roadblock, where he saw Rukundo, was erected sometime in April 1994.[122] Witness EVA stated that this roadblock was established at the end of April or the beginning of May.[123] Witness GSA referred to an incident that took place at the roadblock in May 1994, but stated that it had not been the first time that he had passed through this roadblock.[124] Rukundo testified that he saw a roadblock outside the Kabgayi printing press on either 21 April or 7 May 1994. However, he did not remember a roadblock situated at that location on 15 April 1994.[125]

85. Witness BLP and Witness CSE testified that the roadblock was manned by soldiers, as confirmed by Defence Witnesses EVA,[126] SJC,[127] EVC[128] and by Rukundo.[129]

86. Based on the above evidence, the Chamber finds that a roadblock manned by soldiers was established near the Kabgayi printing press sometime after the death of President Habyarimana on 6 April 1994.

87. Prosecution Witness BLP testified that, on the day when he saw Rukundo, there were people standing at the roadblock, waiting for their identification cards to be examined, whilst others were seated at the side of the roadblock. Witness BLP explained that the people retained at the roadblock were Tutsi and people who carried no identification. Witness BLP stated that, when Tutsi were found, they were often killed. According to Witness BLP, a man whom he had met at the roadblock told him that, on the same day in mid-April, individuals retained at the roadblock were taken downhill to a wooded area, about 40 metres away and killed.[130] Witness BLP did not know this man but said that he was a refugee in Kabgayi.[131] Prosecution Witness CSE testified that he saw Rukundo, in military uniform, at the roadblock watching a person being beaten by soldiers with **[page 28]** their gun butts. Witness CSE said that people were surprised that as a priest, Rukundo did not intervene.[132]

88. The testimonies of Prosecution Witnesses BLP and CSE were contradicted by the evidence presented by Defence Witness EVA who stated that she travelled through the roadblock each day and never saw anyone

---

[116] Prosecution Closing Brief, para. 217 (reference to a Tutsi youth who was being "severely beaten") and para. 220 ("His presence, chat and camaraderie with the soldiers amounted to encouragement for the soldiers to continue to *kill* Tutsi" (emphasis added)).
[117] T. 15 November 2006, p. 12.
[118] T. 17 November 2006, pp. 4-6.
[119] T. 9 October 2007, pp. 48-49; T. 10 October 2007, p. 53.
[120] T. 3 September 2007, p. 52 (Witness SJC); T. 2 October 2007, pp. 38-39 (Witness GSA); T. 18 July 2007, p. 60 (According to Witness ATT the roadblock consisted of a "heap of stones").
[121] T. 16 November 2006, pp. 21- 22.
[122] T. 17 November 2006, pp. 3-6, 13-14, 18-20, 22-23, 26, 34-35.
[123] T. 19 July 2007, pp. 20-21.
[124] T. 1 October 2007, pp. 75-76; T. 2 October 2007 pp. 48-49.
[125] T. 9 October 2007, p. 48; T. 10 October 2007, p. 53.
[126] T. 19 July 2007, p. 20.
[127] T. 3 September 2007, p. 52.
[128] "But I must say that there were soldiers at roadblocks on the main roads. Yes, there were roadblocks manned by soldiers" (T. 11 September 2007, pp. 52-53).
[129] T. 10 October 2007, p. 53.
[130] T. 15 November 2006, pp. 13-14; T. 16 November 2006, p. 23.
[131] T. 15 November 2006, p. 14; T. 16 November 2006, p. 24.
[132] T. 17 November 2006, pp. 5-6.

being mistreated there. However, Witness EVA also stated that, after two frightening experiences, she rode in a vehicle through the roadblock to and from her work, as she was afraid that she would be killed, if she were to travel through on foot.[133]

89. The Chamber treats Witness BLP's testimony with caution.[134] The Chamber notes that Witness BLP's evidence regarding the alleged killing of the Tutsi arrested at the roadblock near the Kabgayi printing press is hearsay evidence. However, the fact that this evidence is hearsay does not in itself suffice to render it not credible or reliable.[135] Indeed the Chamber recalls that it has been well established that it is permissible to base a conviction on hearsay evidence.[136] In the instant case, however, the Chamber notes that the identification of Witness BLP's source of information is not clear. Furthermore, it is not clear whether the evidence is firsthand or secondhand hearsay, as the Prosecution has not established whether the refugee from whom Witness BLP got his information was himself an eyewitness to the killing or was subsequently informed by another person.

90. The Chamber notes that the circumstances under which Witness CSE allegedly met Rukundo for the first time in Kabgayi in 1993 and the exact date of the meeting have not been established. Further, the Chamber notes that the witness could not indicate on what date he fled to Kabgayi or when he allegedly met Rukundo at the roadblock. The Chamber finds that these issues can be explained by the passage of time between the events in Rwanda in 1994 and the witness's testimony 12 years later before the Chamber, and is satisfied that the issues do not affect Witness CSE's overall credibility.

91. Regarding the evidence given by Witness CSE, namely the beating of a person by soldiers, the Chamber notes that Witness CSE did not give any information as to the person's ethnicity. Furthermore, no evidence was adduced to establish, assuming that the person was indeed Tutsi, the severity of the injury, if any, which resulted from the beating. More importantly, however, the **[page 29]** Chamber notes that the testimonies of Witnesses BLP and CSE appear to relate to two different incidents. Indeed, no evidence has been adduced to suggest that the two incidents happened on the same date or were part of the same criminal transaction. Therefore, Witness BLP's hearsay account is the only evidence of the killing of Tutsi at the roadblock as alleged in the Indictment.

92. As mentioned above, Witness BLP's source of information has not been clearly established, and his hearsay evidence has not been corroborated.

93. In light of the aforementioned, the Chamber finds that the Prosecution has not proved beyond reasonable doubt that Rukundo instigated or aided and abetted the killing of Tutsi at the *Imprimerie de Kabgayi* Roadblock as alleged in paragraph 10(ii) of the Indictment. **[page 30]**

4. EVENTS AT ST. JOSEPH'S COLLEGE

(a) Indictment

94. Paragraphs 10(iii) and 22 of the Indictment read as follows:

> 10(iii): Between 12 and 15 April 1994, **Emmanuel RUKUNDO** brought soldiers to St. Joseph's College, Kabgayi, and ordered or instigated a search of Tutsi refugees purportedly having links with the *Inkotanyi*. During this period, the soldiers killed refugees, including Madame RUDAHUNGA, who was killed at her home. The soldiers also took away Tutsi refugees, including two of Madame RUDAHUNGA's children; a young man named Justin; and a young woman named Jeanne, all Tutsis, to the home of the RUDAHUNGAs, where they had killed Madame RUDAHUNGA, and grievously beat the two children, Justin and Jeanne with machetes and left them for dead. **Emmanuel RUKUNDO**, who was at the location at all material times, ordered, instigated or aided and abetted the killing of Madame RUDAHUNGA and the causing of grievous bodily harm to her two children, and to Justin and Jeanne.

---

[133] T. 19 July 2007, p. 56.
[134] See Section III.4.c.
[135] *Karera*, Judgement (AC), para. 39.
[136] *Karera*, Judgement (AC), para. 39; *Muvunyi*, Judgement (AC), para. 70.

22: Between 12 and 15 April 1994, Emmanuel RUKUNDO brought soldiers to St. Joseph's College, Kabgayi and ordered or instigated a search of Tutsi refugees purportedly having links with the INKOTANYI. The soldiers took away Madame RUDAHUNGA and shot and killed her at her home. Emmanuel RUKUNDO, who was at the location at all material times, ordered, instigated, or aided and abetted the killing of Madame RUDAHUNGA, a Tutsi.

(b) Evidence

Prosecution Witness BLP

95. The Chamber has already considered Witness BLP's evidence in relation to the alleged incident at the *Imprimerie de Kabgayi* roadblock.

96. Witness BLP testified that after having seen Rukundo at the *Imprimerie de Kabgayi* roadblock, he saw Rukundo again very close to the main entrance of St. Joseph's College sometime between 12 and 15 April 1994, at about 8.00 a.m.[137] However, in cross-examination, Witness BLP appears to place the Rudahunga incident sometime around late April 1994.[138] At that time, Rukundo was accompanied by some soldiers. Witness BLP also saw three vehicles parked outside St. Joseph's College – a blue Hiace taxi, a khaki-coloured Toyota pick-up Hilux and a white Suzuki Samurai vehicle with a military registration number.[139] When Witness BLP arrived at St. Joseph's College the soldiers ordered him to remain there and not to move. At around 10.00 a.m. he saw **[page 31]** some soldiers coming out of St. Joseph's College. They were armed with rifles and carrying documents taken from St. Joseph's College which they showed to Rukundo.[140]

97. The soldiers also brought Louis Rudahunga's wife out of St. Joseph's College. They asked her to take them to her house and show them the weapons hidden there. The soldiers got Madame Rudahunga to climb aboard their vehicle and drove off. Rukundo followed them in his white Suzuki Samurai vehicle.[141]

98. Twenty minutes after taking Madame Rudahunga to her house, the same soldiers returned to St. Joseph's College and picked up two of Madame Rudahunga's children, a young woman called Jeanne[142] and a young man called Justin, who was a teacher in Kabgayi. When the soldiers returned, Witness BLP was working inside the premises of St. Joseph's College. From his vantage point, he observed the blue Hiace mini bus and saw the soldiers taking these people away.[143] Later that day, Witness BLP saw Jeanne again at St. Joseph's College. She was seriously wounded and bleeding a lot. Jeanne did not speak to Witness BLP directly, but she spoke to other refugees at St. Joseph's College. Witness BLP subsequently heard from the other refugees that Jeanne told them that when she arrived at Madame Rudahunga's house, she discovered

---

[137] T. 15 November 2006, p. 14.
[138] Witness BLP testified that the incident which occured at the Major Seminary (See Section III.9.d) took place towards the end of May 1994, *about a month after* (emphasis added) the incident involving the Rudahunga family. (T. 16 November 2006, p. 30).
[139] T. 15 November 2006, pp. 13-14; T. 16 November 2006, p. 50.
[140] T. 15 November 2006, pp. 14-15. Witness BLP testified as follows: "After a while I saw soldiers coming out of the Saint-Joseph's College, and who were carrying things they had found in the college. These were mainly documents, and they were carrying rifles. They showed the papers and the other objects that they had found in Saint-Joseph's College to Father Rukundo around 10:00H."
[141] T. 15 November 2006, pp. 13-16.
[142] Sometimes this person is referred to in the evidence as Jeannine or Jannine.
[143] T. 15 November 2006, pp. 15-16. During examination-in-chief, BLP testified as follows:
"Q. Now, you also said that about 20 minutes later, the soldiers came back. Am I right?
A. Yes, you are right.
Q. And were those the same soldiers who took the two children, Jeannine and Justine?
A. Yes.
Q. And did they come back in those same vehicles?
A. I was already at work, and I saw the Hiace minibus *blowing colour,* but from where I was located I cannot say if those were the same vehicles that went to the woman's house."
In the French language transcript however, it appears that the Witness spoke about a Blue Toyota vehicle:
« Q. Est-ce qu'ils sont revenus à bord du même véhicule ?
R. J'étais déjà à mon service, j'ai vu le minibus de marque (inaudible) **de couleur bleue** ; mais à l'endroit où je me trouvais, je ne pouvais pas bien voir si c'étaient exactement les mêmes véhicules qui étaient déjà partis au domicile de cette dame.» (T. 15 November 2006, p. 19 (French)).

that Madame Rudahunga had been killed. Jeanne also said that those who were with her had been wounded but that the Rudahunga's children and Justin were still alive.[144]

Prosecution Witness BLJ

99. Prosecution Witness BLJ, a Tutsi, testified that in the evening of 7 April 1994 her father received a telephone call from a friend in Kigali. The caller indicated that Tutsi were being killed in **[page 32]** Kigali. Furthermore, during cross-examination, Witness BLJ stated that her father's name was announced on RTLM radio as a targeted person in Kabgayi. As a result of that information, Witness BLJ's father told Witness BLJ, her younger brother, her cousin, and a domestic worker to leave the house and go into hiding.[145] On the same day, *i.e.* 7 April 1994, they sought refuge at St. Joseph's College in Kabgayi, where they stayed for approximately one week before returning home early one morning. That evening, their parents sent them back to St. Joseph's College. When they returned to St. Joseph's College, they noticed that the number of Tutsi refugees had increased. A few days later, Madame Rudahunga also sought refuge at St. Joseph's College. She occupied the same room as Witness BLJ. Witness BLJ stayed at St. Joseph's College until 27 April 1994 and has not returned there since.[146]

100. Witness BLJ testified that around 20 April 1994, a soldier in military uniform accompanied by another man in civilian clothes, asked to speak to Madame Rudahunga. The two men took Madame Rudahunga away for 20-30 minutes and then brought her back. Upon her return, Madame Rudahunga did not tell Witness BLJ where she had been taken by the soldiers, nor did she say what transpired between her and the soldiers. However, Witness BLJ noticed that Madame Rudahunga was unhappy after meeting the soldiers.[147]

101. Witness BLJ testified that on 27 April 1994, at about 6.00 a.m. four soldiers knocked on the door of Witness BLJ's room which she shared with Madame Rudahunga at St. Joseph's College. The soldiers threatened to break down the door if it was not opened. When the soldiers entered, they asked for "Rudahunga's wife." Madame Rudahunga identified herself and was asked to produce an identity card. The soldiers led Madame Rudahunga away.[148] Witness BLJ told the Chamber that Madame Rudahunga never returned to St. Joseph's College.[149]

102. Witness BLJ testified that about 30 minutes after Madame Rudahunga was taken away, the same four soldiers returned to St. Joseph's College. This time they took away Witness BLJ and the three other Tutsi civilians who were with her at St. Joseph's College. They were transported in a blue Toyota pick-up vehicle which was parked outside the College. The soldiers took Witness BLJ to the Rudahunga's house. Witness BLJ discovered that the house had been totally destroyed. When **[page 33]** she entered the living room, she saw Madame Rudahunga's dead body. Madame Rudahunga had been shot in the head. The soldiers then attacked Witness BLJ and her brother, beating them with the backs of their guns "so as not to waste their bullets". One soldier hit Witness BLJ on the head and she fell on her face. Another soldier stabbed her in the hip with a knife.[150]

103. Witness BLJ testified that after the soldiers' departure, she was bleeding heavily from her injuries and "fell asleep". When she woke up about an hour later, she found that her brother and cousin were still alive. Witness BLJ left the house to look for help and saw a neighbour who agreed to assist her and her family. The neighbour advised her to seek shelter in a neighbouring house and to be careful because "the car, that same car that brought you here, is still around." A short while later, her neighbour returned with Father Alfred Kayibanda. Witness BLJ told Father Kayibanda what had happened to her and informed him that other injured people were inside the Rudahunga's house. Father Kayibanda told Witness BLJ that he could take

---

[144] T. 15 November 2007, pp. 16-17.
[145] T. 9 March 2007, pp. 3-4, 24.
[146] T. 9 March 2007, pp. 5-8.
[147] T. 9 March 2007, pp. 6, 12, 28.
[148] T. 9 March 2007, p. 12. Witness BLJ described their encounter with the soldiers as follows: "And then when they came in, they asked [Madame Rudahunga] … 'Are you Rudahunga's wife? Madame. Rudahunga'? She said, 'Yes'. And they asked her for a piece of ID. She gave them her employment card. Then they were, like, 'You have to come with us.' And she had to go."
[149] T. 9 March 2007, p. 13.
[150] T. 9 March 2007, p. 13.

them to the hospital, but he could only take them one at a time. Father Kayibanda also told Witness BLJ to lie down in the back seat of his car so that people would not see him taking her to the hospital, and added that "Father Emmanuel's car was still around".[151] According to Witness BLJ, Father Kayibanda's remarks about "Father Emmanuel's car" initially did not make sense to her. However, at the time those remarks were made, she noticed the same blue Toyota pick-up that she had previously seen at St. Joseph's College that morning with soldiers on board when they came to get Madame Rudahunga and then was used to take her and the three other Tutsi civilians to the Rudahunga's house. Later, however, Witness BLJ was able to make a connection between the soldiers, the pick-up and Rukundo.[152]

104. After Father Kayibanda had taken them to the Kabgayi hospital, she and her brother received treatment for their wounds.[153]

105. Witness BLJ stayed at the hospital from 27 April to 2 June 1994, when the RPF forces took over Kabgayi. Witness BLJ testified that during her stay at the hospital, she saw Rukundo on two occasions. Witness BLJ testified that about one week after she was admitted to the Kabgayi hospital, in the morning sometime in early May 1994, she saw the Accused in military uniform at the Kabgayi hospital accompanied by two of the four soldiers "that came to get us from Saint Joseph [C]ollege." Witness BLP testified that they were all wearing military uniform and would walk around the hall and hold up a "human arm" or "human head" and intimidate the patients **[page 34]** by saying "this is you next".[154] According to Witness BLJ, Rukundo and the two soldiers took the list and files of the patients in order to select certain patients to take away from the hospital. The patients who they removed from the hospital never returned. On the second occasion, Rukundo was in civilian clothes and was accompanied by Bishop Thaddée Nsengiyumva and other priests. Witness BLJ testified that the group walked around the hospital ward and left. According to Witness BLJ, Rukundo did not see her or her brother at the hospital because they hid under the bed covers.[155]

Prosecution Witness BLC

106. Witness BLC, a Tutsi, was a student at the St. Léon Minor Seminary in 1994.[156] He testified that when President Habyarimana died on 6 April 1994, he was at his village. The situation in his village changed after the President's death; neighbours started killing cattle, torching houses and decimating banana plantations. About one week after 6 April 1994, Witness BLC and his family decided to seek shelter in Kabgayi and moved to the St. Léon Minor Seminary.[157] Witness BLC testified that before 1994, he knew Rukundo by name as a priest, but got to know him more closely in 1994. Witness BLC stated that when he saw Rukundo in 1994, the Accused was of average height and athletic build with fairly large eyes and wore glasses. Witness BLC identified Rukundo in court. Witness BLC testified that Rukundo "frequently" visited the St. Léon Minor Seminary during that year and was usually accompanied by soldiers. Witness BLC estimated that Rukundo normally came to the St. Léon Minor Seminary with two to three soldiers, but on one occasion, he came with about 15 soldiers.[158] This happened around 1.00 p.m. on a day when it was raining; the soldiers wore overalls and their vehicle, a pick-up truck, was covered in mud. On this occasion, Witness BLC heard Rukundo, who had come from the Rudahunga's house, say to Emmanuel Uwimana, the Rector of the St. Léon Minor Seminary, that "We entered in Rudahunga's Inyenzi's house, we killed the wife and the children, but the idiot managed to get away from us."[159] Witness BLC explained that Rukundo spoke in a loud voice and anyone who was around him could have heard what he said. Witness BLC testified that he did not know the circumstances surrounding Madame Rudahunga's death. All he knew was that she was killed in 1994. However, Witness BLC knew Bernard Rudahunga, one of the Rudahunga's children as they were both

---

[151] T. 9 March 2007, pp. 13-14.
[152] Witness BLJ concluded that "putting two pieces together, somehow there was something common [...] between the soldiers, the car, and Father Emmanuel." T. 9 March 2007, pp. 14, 19; T. 12 March 2007, p. 11.
[153] T. 9 March 2007, pp. 14-15.
[154] T. 9 March 2007, p. 16.
[155] T. 9 March 2007, pp. 16-17; T. 12 March 2007, pp. 12-14, 30-32.
[156] T. 4 December 2006, p. 8; Exhibit P. 13.
[157] T. 4 December 2006, pp. 10-11.
[158] T. 4 December 2006, pp. 14-16.
[159] T. 4 December 2006, pp. 21-22.

students at the St. **[page 35]** Léon Minor Seminary. Sometime in 1994, Witness BLC heard that Bernard had been killed in Kigali in the same year.[160]

Prosecution Witness CCH

107. Witness CCH first knew Rukundo in 1991 when the Accused was ordained as a priest. Witness CCH also attended his ordination ceremony.[161]

108. Witness CCH testified that on 8 April 1994 many people arrived in her town explaining that their houses were being set on fire. Witness CCH decided that there were too many people in her town and so decided to seek refuge at her grandmother's house. After members of the public started being killed, Witness CCH went to seek refuge at the St. Léon Minor Seminary in Kabgyi. Witness CCH stayed at the St. Léon Minor Seminary from mid-May 1994 until 3 June 1994.[162]

19. Witness CCH testified that she was a neighbour of the Rudahunga family. She knew that Louis Rudahunga worked at the printing press and that he was arrested and detained in 1990 for being an RPF accomplice. Witness CCH was in the same class at school as the Rudahunga's children.[163] Sometime in May 1994, Witness CCH met Rukundo at the St. Léon Minor Seminary. Rukundo told her that they had found documents at Louis Rudahunga's place which included names of people who made financial contributions to the *Inkotanyi*. Rukundo told Witness CCH that Louis Rudahunga had to be killed.[164] Rukundo also told Witness CCH that her relative's name was on the list found at the Rudahunga's home and that "the names of people on that list were the names of people who gave money to the *Inkotanyi*".[165]

The Accused

110. Emmanuel Rukundo testified that he knew Louis Rudahunga very well and that he had worked as an accountant at the Kabgayi printing press since Rukundo was at the Seminary in Kabgayi. Rukundo also stated that he knew Madame Rudahunga as she was a nurse at the Kabgayi **[page 36]** hospital as well as the Rudahunga's eldest daughter called Alice. However, Rukundo did not know the names of the Rudahunga's three other children because they were too young.[166]

111. Rukundo testified that he never went to St. Joseph's College during the events of 1994. In particular, he denied that between 12 and 15 April 1994, he was present at St. Joseph's College and was accompanied by soldiers. Rukundo stated that he did not know that members of the Rudahunga family had been abducted from St. Joseph's College. He further stated that at the time he only knew that Louis Rudahunga had been killed. Rukundo explained that he did not drive a blue pick-up truck except for a pick-up he drove which was lent to him by nuns from the Rwaza school.[167]

112. Rukundo told the Chamber that he had never had any problems with Louis Rudahunga or any other members of his family.[168] He added that he did not even know that Madame Rudahunga and her children had sought refuge at St. Joseph's College or that she had been killed.[169] Rukundo stated that he did not learn about Madame Rudahunga's death until he came to this Tribunal. However he subsequently admitted that he had

---

[160] T. 4 December 2006, pp. 21, 23.
[161] T. 13 February 2007, pp. 55, 60, 62-63; T. 14 February 2007, p. 5.
[162] T. 13 February 2007, pp. 56, 62.
[163] T. 13 February 2007, p. 68.
[164] T. 13 February 2007, p. 58. Witness CCH described her discussion with Rukundo in the following terms:
"I said hello to him, I introduced myself, and I told him that [...] was a relative of mine, and then I asked him for protection, I asked him to hide me. And he answered as follows: 'If [...] is your relative, then you all have to die, because [...] was assisting *Inyenzi*. He was my friend, but when he started helping the *Inyenzi*, he is no longer my friend. We do not even talk to each other. He's no longer my friend.' He went on to say that they had found some documents at Louis Rudahunga's place and who had to be killed, and that this document included a list of people who were making financial contributions to the *Inkotanyi*."
[165] T. 14 February 2007, p. 9.
[166] T. 9 October 2007, p. 45.
[167] T. 9 October 2007, pp. 53-54; T. 10 October 2007, pp. 42-45.
[168] T. 9 October 2007, p. 46.
[169] T. 9 October 2007, pp. 53-54.

Prosecutor v. Rukundo

learnt about her death earlier from information he had read in a "Goliath publication" and wrote an article defending himself against the allegation that he was responsible for her killing.[170]

113. Contrary to Prosecution Witness BLC's evidence, Rukundo denied that he said "We are returning from the house of Louis Rudahunga, the *Inyenzi*. We have already killed his wife and children but he escaped from us." Rukundo maintained that such remarks could never be made by a priest especially in the presence of his colleagues.[171] Rukundo only heard of Louis Rudahunga's death on 21 May 1994 during a visit to Kabgayi. Rukundo also denied Prosecution Counsel's suggestion that he met Father Kayibanda at the Kabgayi Bishopric on 7 May 1994.[172]

Defence Witness SJD

114. Witness SJD was a teacher at St. Joseph's College in 1994. He knew the Rudahunga family and their children.[173] He testified that the Rudahunga's house was located less than one kilometre **[page 37]** away from St. Joseph's College.[174] Witness SJD did not know Rukundo in April 1994. However, in August or September 1994, he heard that there was a military chaplain present with soldiers when Tutsi refugees were abducted from St. Joseph's College in the morning of 26 April 1994. Witness SJD did not know the name of the military chaplain, and could not recall the person who gave him that information. Witness SJD did not recall specifically seeing Rukundo at St. Joseph's College on 26 April 1994.[175]

115. Witness SJD testified that the Rudahunga family arrived at St. Joseph's College between 10 and 20 April 1994. On 26 April 1994, at about 4.30 or 5.00 a.m., Witness SJD heard someone knocking on his door. He opened it and a soldier walked in and searched the room. The soldier asked to see Witness SJD's identity card, which he inspected and then left. Witness SJD testified that all the buildings were searched. Witness SJD estimated that, at that time, there were between 15 and 20 soldiers inside the premises of St. Joseph's College.[176]

116. On his way to mass on the morning of 26 April 1994, Witness SJD met a group of soldiers at the main gate of St. Joseph's College. He also saw a Toyota pick-up vehicle outside the gate and recognised four people who were sitting in the vehicle, two of whom were the Rudahunga's children.[177] There was also a teacher from the Kabgayi Technical School and a young lady called Jeanne. Witness SJD asked the soldiers where they were taking the children. One of them answered that they were taking them back to their home. Another soldier told Witness SJD "Now, if you want to know where we are taking them, then please join us." Witness SJD told the Chamber that at the time, he already knew that the Rudahunga's home had been destroyed and therefore thought that it would be dangerous to go there. Witness SJD continued on his way to mass at the Kabgayi Basilica.[178]

117. Witness SJD spent about one hour at mass and then returned to St. Joseph's College where he went to the refectory to eat breakfast. Whilst at the refectory, one of his colleagues walked in with Jeanne who was one of the people taken away by soldiers along with members of the Rudahunga family earlier that morning. Jeanne told Witness SJD that the people who the soldiers **[page 38]** had taken away with her had been grievously injured and that Madame Rudahunga had been killed. Witness SJD could see that Jeanne was seriously injured as her scalp had been cut open.[179]

---

[170] T. 10 October 2007, pp. 42-44.
[171] T. 9 October 2007, p. 46.
[172] T. 10 October 2007, pp. 42-44.
[173] T. 28 September 2007, pp. 4-6.
[174] T. 28 September 2007, p. 11.
[175] T. 28 September 2007, p. 21.
[176] T. 28 September 2007, pp. 6, 8, 10, 22.
[177] T. 28 September 2007, pp. 9-10. Defence Witness SJD testified that "that morning I saw two vehicles. One was blue; that is certain. But I did not see the blue vehicle around our institutions, but in the vicinity of the Rudahungas. But the other vehicle was a Toyota, whose colour could be red, or it could be some other colour. But it was a Toyota-styled. Of that I am certain." (T. 28 September 2007, p. 10).
[178] T. 28 September 2007, p. 9.
[179] T. 28 September 2007, p. 13.

118. Witness SJD and his colleague decided to seek help for the Rudahunga family from a doctor in Kabgayi. The doctor told Witness SJD to take the patients to the Kabgayi hospital and explained that he would treat them there. Witness SJD, accompanied by Father Kayibanda and Jeanne, then went to the Rudahunga's house to pick up the injured members of that family. On their way, Witness SJD saw a blue Toyota Stout vehicle similar to the one he had seen at St. Joseph's College earlier that morning. The vehicle was located about 20 or 30 meters from the junction leading to the Rudahunga's home and was occupied by soldiers. Witness SJD told the people in the car "There they are again" because he realised that these were the same soldiers who had taken members of the Rudahunga family away from St. Joseph's College that morning.[180]

119. Witness SJD testified that he avoided the soldiers and went to a house that was near the Rudahunga's home where he found Witness BLJ. Witness BLJ was covered in blood, but still conscious and able to speak. Witness BLJ told Witness SJD that Madame Rudahunga had been killed and that her brother had been grievously injured. Witness SJD put Witness BLJ in the vehicle and drove to the Kabgayi hospital. Witness SJD drove the vehicle, Father Kayibanda sat in the front passenger seat and the two girls, Jeanne and Witness BLJ, sat in the back seat. Witness SJD and Father Kayibanda handed the two girls to a nurse at the emergency unit of the hospital. Later that afternoon, Father Kayibanda borrowed Witness SJD's car in order to take Justin to the hospital. Father Kayibanda informed Witness SJD that he had received a message from Justin that he had been seriously injured.[181]

Defence Witness SLA

120. In April 1994 Defence Witness SLA worked at the St. Léon Minor Seminary. He testified that he knew Emmanuel Rukundo. During the events of 1994, Witness SLA saw Rukundo twice at the St. Léon Minor Seminary sometime in mid-April and mid-May 1994. On both occasions, Rukundo arrived in a beige or white-coloured private vehicle wearing military uniform and accompanied by a soldier. Witness SLA never saw nor heard that Rukundo drove a pick-up vehicle. Witness SLA testified that the only purpose of Rukundo's visits "was to see us, greet us, and to discuss the prevailing developments on the national scene." Witness SLA explained that on his first **[page 39]** visit, Rukundo told him that he had fired his gun in the air to save certain Tutsi at Nyabikenke Parish from being attacked. On the second visit, Rukundo told the seminarians that he had been transferred from Ruhengeri to Kigali.[182]

121. Witness SLA testified that he never saw Rukundo speaking to Father Daniel Nahimana at the St. Léon Minor Seminary. He also confirmed that he had known Louis Rudahunga, but had never heard Rukundo mention Rudahunga's name.[183]

Defence Witness SJC

122. The Chamber has already considered Witness SJC's evidence in relation to the alleged incident at the *Imprimerie de Kabgayi* roadblock.

123. Witness SJC testified that on or about 20 April 1994, he received information that his cousin was injured and had been admitted to the Kabgayi hospital. He visited his cousin at the hospital and stayed there from 20 April to 1 May 1994. During the first nine days of his stay (*i.e.* until 29 April 1994), Witness SJC spent the night at the hospital. After that date, he would leave at 3.00 or 4.00 p.m. and return the next day at 7.30 a.m.[184]

124. Witness SJC told the Chamber that in addition to his cousin, he also helped other patients, including the Rudahunga's two children. He knew the Rudahunga family and at some point worked with Louis Rudahunga.[185]

---

[180] T. 28 September 2007, pp. 13, 15.
[181] T. 28 September 2007, pp. 15-17.
[182] T. 1 October 2007, pp. 12, 22-23.
[183] T. 1 October 2007, pp. 22-23, 25.
[184] T. 3 September 2007, pp. 15, 40-41.
[185] T. 3 September 2007, pp. 25-26.

125. Witness SJC told the Chamber that he never saw Rukundo whilst he was at the Kabgayi hospital and in Kabgayi town in 1994.[186] Witness SJC added that he did not see any government or religious authorities visiting the hospital. In addition, he could not recall any incident when the *Interahamwe* or soldiers threatened patients at the hospital or carried body parts.[187]

Defence Witness EVC

126. The Chamber has previously considered Witness EVC's testimony in relation to the *Imprimerie de Kabgayi* roadblock. **[page 40]**

127. Witness EVC testified that one day, Father Alfred Kayibanda told him that Rudahunga and his entire family had been killed. According to Witness EVC, Father Kayibanda explained that "he was present, that he had seen the dead bodies of that family, but that he had saved the children from that place of killing." However, Father Kayibanda did not say who the attackers were who killed the Rudahunga family. Witness EVC testified that when Father Kayibanda talked about the incident he did not mention Rukundo's name. Witness EVC stated that had Father Kayibanda known that Rukundo was involved in the attack on members of the Rudahunga family he would not have withheld such information and would have informed the diocese.[188]

Defence Witness SJA

128. Witness SJA, who lived at St. Joseph's College in Kabgayi from 1983 to June 1994, knew Emmanuel Rukundo from the time Rukundo was at the Nyakibanda Major Seminary. Witness SJA attended Rukundo's ordination in 1991. Witness SJA knew about Rukundo's appointment as a military chaplain and that he was posted to Kigali and subsequently to Ruhengeri.[189]

129. Witness SJA also knew Louis Rudahunga, Madame Rudahunga and all of their children. At some point, he worked in the same office with Louis Rudahunga. In April 1994, Witness SJA lived in a residential block at St. Joseph's College with eight other people. From his window, he could see part of the compound and the gate of St. Joseph's College.[190]

130. Witness SJA testified that refugees started arriving at St. Joseph's College from about 6 April 1994. He said that at the peak of the crisis, there were about 4,000 refugees at St. Joseph's College. Witness SJA saw members of the Rudahunga family at St. Joseph's College for the first time between 10 and 12 April and again around 20 April 1994 when they were being "driven" out of St. Joseph's College by soldiers to Gahogo. Witness SJA explained that at about 5.20 a.m. on 20 April 1994, two soldiers knocked on his door and when he opened it, they said they were searching for weapons and *Inyenzi*. Witness SJA testified that they were still searching the establishment at about 10.00 a.m.[191]

131. Witness SJA testified that later that day, soldiers took away Madame Rudahunga, her two children, as well as a girl called Jeanne who had been staying with the Rudahunga family, from St. Joseph's College. Witness SJA was on the veranda of his block, outside his room, when he saw **[page 41]** the group pass by. Witness SJA testified that he saw the group from the back and was about 40 to 50 metres away from the soldiers and the Rudahunga family. Witness SJA was told by the refugees who were in the same block as the Rudahunga family that the soldiers said that they wanted to take members of the Rudahunga family to search their house. He subsequently heard that the Rudahunga's family home had been demolished. Witness SJA testified that later on, Jeanne returned with a bleeding wound on her head and reported that Madame Rudahunga had been killed and that the children "were still in a state of agony." According to Witness SJA, Father Kayibanda, who was in charge of security at St. Joseph's College, went with another person to take the children to the hospital.[192]

---

[186] T. 3 September 2007, pp. 26, 46-47.
[187] T. 3 September 2007, pp. 23-24.
[188] T. 11 September 2007, pp. 36-38.
[189] T. 22 October 2007, pp. 3-4, 6.
[190] T. 22 October 2007, pp. 4-5.
[191] T. 22 October 2007, pp. 6-8, 10.
[192] T. 22 October 2007, pp. 10-14.

(c) Deliberations

132. The Indictment alleges that, between 12 and 15 April 1994, Emmanuel Rukundo brought soldiers to St. Joseph's College, in Kabgayi, and ordered[193] or instigated a search of Tutsi refugees purportedly having links with the *Inkotanyi*. During this period, the soldiers killed refugees, including Madame Rudahunga, who was killed at her home. The soldiers also took away Tutsi refugees, including two of Madame Rudahunga's children, and a young man named Justin, and a young woman named Jeanne, all Tutsi, to the Rudahunga's home, where they had killed Madame Rudahunga, and grievously beat the Rudahunga's two children, and Justin and Jeanne with machetes and left them for dead. Emmanuel Rukundo, who was at the location at all material times, ordered, instigated or aided and abetted the killing of Madame Rudahunga and the causing of grievous bodily harm to her two children and to Justin and Jeanne.

133. In support of this allegation, the Prosecution relies on the evidence of Witnesses BLP, BLC, BLJ and CCH. To challenge the Prosecution evidence, the Defence relies on the evidence of Witnesses SJD, SLA, SJC, EVC, SJA and the Accused himself.

134. The Chamber notes that, although the Prosecution alleges that other Tutsi refugees were killed, no evidence was led on this issue. The Chamber therefore dismisses the allegation in respect of the killing of other Tutsi refugees. [page 42]

135. There is no dispute that Madame Rudahunga was abducted from St. Joseph's College and killed and that her two children and two other Tutsi civilians, Justin and Jeanne, were abducted from that location and seriously injured sometime in April 1994.[194]

136. Three eye witnesses, Witnesses BLP, SJD and BLP, testified that the abductions and the subsequent crimes committed at the Rudahunga's home occurred around 27 April 1994.[195] The Chamber notes that this date is about two weeks after the approximate dates set out in the Indictment, 12-15 April 1994. Nevertheless, the Chamber finds that the allegation has been clearly specified in the Indictment, and that the difference in dates between the Indictment and the testimonies of Witnesses BLJ, SJD and BLP has not impaired the ability of the Defence to prepare its case in respect of the allegation.

137. The only question remaining for the Chamber is to determine the Accused's involvement, if any, in the abduction and killing of Madame Rudahunga and the abduction and causing of serious bodily harm[196] to the Rudahunga's two children and to the two Tutsi civilians, Justin and Jeanne.

138. Witness BLP purports to be an eye witness to the abductions of Madame Rudahunga and her two children and two other Tutsi civilians from St. Joseph's College.[197] He stated that he saw some soldiers coming out of St. Joseph's College, bringing Louis Rudahunga's wife and carrying documents taken from St. Joseph's College which they showed to Rukundo.[198] Then he saw the soldiers put Madame Rudahunga in their vehicle and drive away, followed by Rukundo in his white Suzuki Samurai vehicle.[199] Twenty minutes after taking Madame Rudahunga to her house, Witness BLP saw the same soldiers return to St. Joseph's College and abduct two of Madame Rudahunga's children and two other Tutsi civilians.[200] Later that day,

---

[193] "Ordering" presupposes that a person in a position of authority orders another person to commit an offence. This position of authority is used to convince another person to commit a crime punishable under the Statute. See for example, *Bagilishema*, Judgement (TC), para. 30; *Muvunyi*, Judgement (TC) para. 481; *Stakić*, Judgement (TC) para. 444.
[194] See in particular Prosecution Witnesses BLP and BLJ and Defence Witnesses SJD and SJA.
[195] Witness BLP, T. 16 November 2006, p. 30; Witness BLJ, T. 9 March 2007, p. 12; Witness SJD, T. 28 September 2007, pp. 13, 20-21.
[196] The quintessential examples of serious bodily harm are torture, rape, and non-fatal physical violence that causes disfigurement or serious injury to the external or internal organs (*Semanza*, Judgement (TC), para. 320, referring to *Kayishema and Ruzindana*, Judgement (TC), para. 109; *Ntagerura et al.*, Judgement (TC), para. 664); see also Sections III.6, III.7.c.iv, iii.9.b which deal with serious mental and bodily harm.
[197] T. 15 November 2006, pp. 14-15.
[198] T. 15 November 2006, pp. 14-15. Witness BLP testified as follows: "After a while I saw soldiers coming out of the Saint-Joseph's College, and who were carrying things they had found in the college. These were mainly documents, and they were carrying rifles. They showed the papers and the other objects that they had found in Saint-Joseph's College to Father Rukundo around 10:00H."
[199] T. 15 November 2006, pp. 13-16.
[200] T. 15 November 2006, p. 15.

Witness BLP saw one of the civilians, Jeanne, again at St. Joseph's College. She was seriously wounded and bleeding a lot. **[page 43]**

139. The Chamber notes that there are some credibility issues involving Witness BLP. Witness BLP testified before the Chamber on 15 and 16 November 2006. On 8 March 2007, the Defence filed a confidential motion to recall Witness BLP based on a letter dated 8 February 2007 given to the Defence investigator, Leonidas Nshogoza, in which Witness BLP allegedly admitted to having given false testimony before the Chamber.[201] Following these submissions, Witness BLP was recalled.[202] On 2 July 2007,[203] Witness BLP appeared again before the Chamber and testified that he did not wish to vary any of his earlier testimony given in November 2006.[204]

140. Following Witness BLP's second appearance, the Chamber ordered an independent investigation, pursuant to Rules 54 and 91 of the Rules, into Witness BLP's alleged false testimony and related issues, including the circumstances surrounding Witness BLP's meetings with the Defence investigator and the possible violation of protective measures.[205] On 11 October 2007, Mr. Jean Haguma, a Defence Attorney based in Kigali, who was appointed by the Registrar as an independent investigator, appeared in Court to present the findings of his investigation.[206]

141. The Haguma Report[207] concluded that, after having testified before this Tribunal, Witness BLP was influenced by Father Ndagijimana, a detainee at Gitarama Prison, to contact Leonidas Nshogoza, in order to "exculpate Father Rukundo."[208] As a result, Witness BLP met Mr. Nshogoza on several occasions between 30 December 2006 and 8 February 2007 "always for the same issue".[209] Mr. Nshogoza gave Witness BLP a letter dated 10 January 2007, which Witness BLP agreed to copy "in order to protect himself." It appears that Witness BLP was also given a second letter dated 8 February 2007 which was addressed to Father Rukundo. The Haguma Report concluded that since the letter of 10 January 2007 was the only one that Witness BLP agreed "to copy … the other statements must be considered as void."[210] **[page 44]**

142. The Chamber accepts the Haguma Report and finds that it establishes that Witness BLP's alleged recantation of his testimony given on 15 and 16 November 2006, was due to pressure exerted upon him by the Defence investigator and Father Ndagijimana. Consequently, the Chamber does not believe that Witness BLP intended to recant his testimony before the Chamber. Based on the Haguma Report, the Chamber also finds that Mr. Nshogoza initiated contact with Witness BLP through Father Ndagijimana and continued to remain in contact with Witness BLP over a considerable period of time in violation of the Chamber's protective measures. The Chamber also finds that the Defence investigator prepared two letters dated 10 January 2007 and 8 February 2007 for Witness BLP to copy and sought to influence Witness BLP to change his testimony before the Chamber.

143. The Chamber, however, notes that there are some other issues that might affect Witness BLP's credibility. The Chamber recalls that during his testimony on 15 November 2006, Witness BLP gave a description of the Accused as he knew him in 1994, and stated that the Accused "used to wear plain glasses." However, when asked by Prosecution Counsel to identify the Accused from amongst the people in the

---

[201] *Requête Ex Parte en Extrême Urgence et Confidentielle aux Fins de Rappeler le Témoin du Procureur BLP aux Fins d'Etre Réentendu au Vu des Eléments Nouveaux*, filed on 8 March 2007.
[202] Decision on Defence Motion to Recall Prosecution Witness BLP (TC), 30 April 2007, paras. 2, 4, 6.
[203] Scheduling Order Following the Pre-Defence Conference (TC), 7 May 2007, para. IV.
[204] T. 2 July 2007, p. 42.
[205] T. 2 July 2007, p. 43; Decision on the Motions Relating to the Scheduled Appearances of Witness BLP and the Defence Investigator (TC), 4 July 2007, disposition.
[206] T. 11 October 2007, pp. 36-51.
[207] Chamber Exhibit X. 1: Investigative Report by Mr. Haguma of 11 October 2007 and Annexes, admitted on 11 October 2007 ("Haguma Report").
[208] Haguma Report, p. 2 (English version).
[209] The Haguma Report specificies that Mr. Nshogoza met with Witness BLP on 30 December 2006 at the church; on 6 January 2007 at the church; on 10 January 2007 at Clecam; on 7 Feberuary 2007 at Mupagasi Bar; and several times at the office. See the Haguma Report, p. 3 (English version) and T. 11 October 2007, pp. 36-51.
[210] Haguma Report, p. 4 (English version).

courtroom, Witness BLP pointed to another individual wearing glasses.[211] On the next day, and with the Chamber's permission, Witness BLP correctly identified the Accused.[212]

144. The Chamber also notes that, during cross-examination, Witness BLP admitted that in his testimony before the Rwandan Gacaca courts, he never mentioned Rukundo's presence or participation in the attack on St. Joseph's College.[213] The Chamber further notes that Witness BLP and 19 other prisoners detained at Gitarama prison contributed to a joint statement, dated 27 April 2005, in which they described events in Kabgayi in April and May 1994, including the attacks on St. Joseph's College. They gave names of some of the attackers and victims, and provided various dates on which the attacks took place. The statement makes no mention of Rukundo. Witness BLP explained that the Accused was omitted from the document for security reasons because, at the time that the statement was prepared, he and the other prisoners did not reveal the role of any surviving priest or clergy in the Kabgayi killings.[214] **[page 45]**

145. Most importantly, however, the Chamber notes that at the time of his testimony Witness BLP was on provisional release in Rwanda, after having given a written confession to the Rwandan authorities.[215] During cross-examination, Witness BLP admitted that he participated in the attacks on Tutsi refugees at St. Joseph's College in April 1994, the very location he is alleging Rukundo's participation in crimes against members of the Rudahunga family and other Tutsi.[216] The Chamber notes that the evidence of an accomplice is not *per se* unreliable, especially where the accomplice is thoroughly cross-examined.[217] However, the Chamber also notes that accomplice witnesses may have motives or incentives to implicate an accused person before the Tribunal. Thus the Chamber, in weighing the probative value of such evidence, is bound to carefully consider the totality of the circumstances in which it was tendered.[218]

146. In light of the aforementioned, the Chamber will treat Witness BLP's evidence with caution and will rely on it only if it is corroborated by, or itself corroborates, other reliable evidence.

147. Witness BLJ was one of the victims who was abducted from St. Joseph's College. She testified that around 20 April 1994, Madame Rudahunga was taken away for questioning for 20 to 30 minutes by a soldier in military uniform, accompanied by another man in civilian clothes.[219] On 27 April 1994, at about 6.00 a.m., four soldiers abducted Madame Rudahunga from St. Joseph's College.[220] About 30 minutes later, the same four soldiers returned to St. Joseph's College and took Witness BLJ and three other Tutsi civilians who were with her at St. Joseph's College to the Rudahunga's home, where Madame Rudahunga had been shot in the head and was dead. The soldiers then attacked Witness BLJ and another person.[221] Witness BLJ fell to the ground and "fell asleep." When she woke up, she went to search for help. A neighbour advised Witness BLJ to be careful because "the car, that same car that brought you here, is still around."[222] A short while later, her neighbour returned with Father Alfred Kayibanda. Father Alfred Kayibanda warned the witness that "Father Emmanuel's car was still around," before driving her to the hospital.[223] This warning initially did not make sense to her. Later, however, based on that remark, Witness BLJ was able to **[page 46]** make a link between

---

[211] T. 15 November 2006, p. 12.
[212] The Chamber however recalls that in-court identification of the Accused has little probative value, and must be treated cautiously. Such identification is only one element to be considered when evaluating the witness's evidence. See *Kunarac et al.,* Judgement (AC), para. 320; *Kamuhanda,* Judgement (AC), paras. 243-244.
[213] T. 16 November 2006, p. 62.
[214] T. 16 November 2006, pp. 57-62. "The people who provided this information in this document did so but maybe they did not include other information in this document for security reasons. They actually accused – they did not accuse themselves but they wanted to make sure that when they gave any information, such information would not jeopardise their security, and that is why the name of Father Rukundo is not included in the document because we were afraid that his fellow members of the clergy would not (sic) harm us but the reason I decided to give all of the information I have before this Court is that I know that everything that I say here would be confidential" (T. 16 November 2006, p. 62).
[215] T. 16 November 2006, p. 63.
[216] T. 16 November 2007, p. 53.
[217] . *Ntagerura et al.*, Judgement (AC), para. 204; *Niyitegeka,* Judgement (AC), para. 98.
[218] *Ntagerura et al.*, Judgement (AC), paras. 204, 206.
[219] T. 9 March 2007, pp. 6, 12, 28.
[220] T. 9 March 2007, p. 12.
[221] T. 9 March 2007, p. 13.
[222] T. 9 March 2007, pp. 13-14.
[223] T. 9 March 2007, p. 14.

Prosecutor v. Rukundo

the blue Toyota pick-up that she saw close to her house and the one that was used in the two abductions, and the soldiers and the Accused.[224]

148. About one week after she was admitted to Kabgayi hospital, one morning in early May 1994, Witness BLJ saw the Accused in military uniform at the Kabgayi hospital accompanied by two of the four soldiers who had removed members of the Rudahunga family from St. Joseph's College. Rukundo and the two soldiers walked through the hall which was mostly full of Tutsi patients. They picked up a human arm or a head and intimidated those at the hospital by threatening "this is you next." According to Witness BLJ, Rukundo and the two soldiers took the list and files of the patients in order to select certain patients to abduct from the hospital. The patients whom they removed from the hospital never returned.[225]

149. The Defence submits that Witness BLJ's testimony in respect of Father Kayibanda's comment about the presence of Father Emmanuel's car at the scene of the crime is a material fact which establishes a link between the Accused and the attack on the refugees and therefore should have been pleaded in the Indictment. The Defence requests the Chamber to exclude this part of Witness BLJ's testimony.[226]

150. The Chamber is not convinced by the Defence submissions. The Chamber notes that the charge against the Accused is that, between 12 and 15 April 1994, he brought soldiers to St. Joseph's College to search for Tutsi refugees, purportedly having links with the *Inkontanyi* and then participated in the killing of Madame Rudahunga at her house and in the abduction and causing of serious bodily harm to two of the Rudahunga's children and two other Tutsi civilians at the home of Madame Rudahunga. The Indictment further alleges that Rukundo "was at the location at all material times." The Chamber finds that Witness BLJ's testimony is evidence given in support of an existing charge pleaded in the Indictment.[227] The Chamber will therefore not exclude Witness BLJ's testimony about the presence of the Accused's car near the home of the Rudahunga family. **[page 47]**

151. The Defence also seeks to exclude Witness BLJ's testimony regarding the Accused's alleged first visit to the Kabgayi hospital in May 1994.[228] The Defence submits that the Accused's visit to the Kabgayi hospital, as described by Witness BLJ, constitutes a material fact which should have been specifically pleaded in the Indictment. The Defence submits that the allegation that the Accused waved human limbs whilst threatening the Tutsi patients at the hospital introduces a new charge of causing serious bodily and mental harm to the patients. The Defence further submits that the allegation that the Accused looked at the patients' files is extremely prejudicial since it implies that the Accused's selection of victims was premeditated.[229]

152. The Chamber notes that the Indictment does not plead the Accused's actions in Kabgayi hospital, as described by Witness BLJ. The Chamber finds that Witness BLJ's testimony regarding the intimidation of Tutsi patients at the hospital, and the abduction of some of these patients, indeed constitutes a new allegation of criminal conduct on the part of the Accused, which the Prosecution did not specifically plead in the Indictment.[230] The Chamber therefore excludes Witness BLJ's evidence in respect of the Accused's alleged actions (the intimidation of Tutsi patients at the hospital and the abduction of some of the Tutsi patients) during his first visit to the Kabgayi hospital.

153. The Chamber notes that in her statement given to the Office of the Prosecutor on 20 and 21 December 2003, Witness BLJ did not mention that Father Kayibanda told her that "Father Emmanuel's car was still around." The Chamber, however, finds that this omission does not change Witness BLJ's overall account of

---

[224] T. 9 March 2007, pp. 14, 19; T. 12 March 2007, p. 11. Witness BLJ states "At that time it did not make sense to me, because he say that Father Emmanuel's car -- but, then again, when we were taken in that car, it was --to me it was a soldier's car. And then, it's after that I saw this -- the two soldiers -- two of the four soldiers that took us -- that took [Madame Rudahunga] to go kill her and then come back for us that I made a connection to what the -- what Father Kayibanda said about the car and the -- the affiliation of the car and Emmanuel. Because the soldiers were in that car, and -- and the car -- and those same soldiers were with Father Rukundo. So that's how I made the connection of -- that's why it made sense to me that that's what he meant; he means by the car being Emmanuel's" (T. 9 March 2007, p. 19).
[225] T. 9 March 2007, pp. 16-17; T. 12 March 2007, pp. 12-14, 30-32.
[226] Defence Closing Brief, paras. 178, 184, 188.
[227] See Section II, A.1.
[228] Defence Closing Brief, paras. 201, 204.
[229] Defence Closing Brief, paras. 192-193.
[230] See Section II, A.1.

the events which took place. The Chamber accepts that, nine years after this traumatic incident, when she spoke to representatives of the Office of the Prosecutor, she may have forgotten some details but could have later remembered them as she re-lived and recounted the experience before the Chamber. The Chamber finds Witness BLJ to be a credible witness and believes her evidence.

154. Witness BLC testified that, whilst he was at the St. Léon Minor Seminary, he saw Rukundo with about 15 soldiers. On this occasion, Witness BLC heard Rukundo, who had come from the Rudahunga's home, say to Emmanuel Uwimana "We entered in Rudahunga's *Inyenzi*'s house, we killed the wife and the children, but the idiot [Louis Rudahunga] managed to get away from us."[231] **[page 48]**

155. During cross-examination, the Defence challenged Witness BLC's credibility on the grounds that he bore a grudge against the Rwandan Catholic Church for dismissing him from the Kabgayi Minor Seminary, and that implicating Rukundo in the events of 1994 was the witness's way of defaming the Church.[232] The Chamber notes that Witness BLC stated that, after his dismissal, he subsequently completed his studies. Therefore, the fact that Witness BLC was earlier dismissed from the Kabgayi Minor Seminary does not provide a sufficient reason to infer that he bore a grudge against the Church and that he wrongly implicated Rukundo in the crimes.

156. The Chamber has also considered the Defence submission that Witness BLC is not credible because his evidence about Rukundo's involvement in the killing of Madame Rudahunga is inconsistent with the contents of his *mémoire* (statement) written in 1997.[233] The Defence maintains, and Witness BLC admits, that in this *mémoire*, he indicated a series of events involving the Accused: that Rukundo went to the Rudahunga's home escorted by soldiers, killed Madame Rudahunga and her children and ordered inhabitants in the vicinity to destroy the Rudahunga's home. He also stated that Rukundo then went to the St. Léon Minor Seminary sometime between 12.00 and 1.00 p.m. and boasted about the killings.[234] According to the Defence, there is a material inconsistency between this account and Witness BLC's testimony that, whilst at the St. Léon Minor Seminary, he heard Rukundo talking about his role in the killing of Madame Rudahunga.

157. The Chamber notes Witness BLC's explanation that his *mémoire* was a personal recollection of events during the 1994 genocide, and was not intended to give the impression that he was present at the Rudahunga's home when Rukundo allegedly ordered the local community to destroy it.[235] The Chamber also notes that the *mémoire* was written in 1997, before Rukundo had been charged with any crimes and that it is not a witness statement in the sense of a record generated following an interview with the Office of the Prosecutor.[236] The Chamber finds that the alleged inconsistency is minor and does not affect Witness BLC's general credibility.

158. Witness CCH testified that in May 1994, whilst at the St. Léon Minor Seminary, she introduced herself to Rukundo as a relative of one of his friends, and asked him to protect her.[237] Rukundo told her, amongst other things, that they had found documents at Louis Rudahunga's place **[page 49]** which included names of people who made financial contributions to the *Inkotanyi*.[238] Rukundo also told Witness CCH that her relative's name was on the list found at the Rudahunga's home and that "the names of people on that list were the names of people who gave money to the *Inkotanyi*." Rukundo also told her that Louis Rudahunga had to be killed.[239]

---

[231] T. 4 December 2006, pp. 15, 21-22.
[232] T. 8 December 2006, pp. 11-12.
[233] T. 8 December 2006, pp. 2-4. Witness BLC noted that the year is not legible on the document, but clarified that the statement formed part of his *mémoire* which he started writing in 1997 but did not complete. He added that he communicated the document to the Office of the Prosecutor in 1998 (T. 8 December 2006, p. 2).
[234] T. 8 December 2006, Exhibits D. 9 (French) and D. 9A (English).
[235] T. 8 December 2008, pp. 3-4.
[236] See *Niyitegeka*, Judgement (AC), paras. 31-34 on the requirements of a witness statement or a record of interview.
[237] T. 13 February 2007, pp. 56, 58, 64; T. 14 February 2007, p. 7.
[238] T. 13 February 2007, p. 58. Witness CCH described her discussion with Rukundo in the following terms: "I said hello to him, I introduced myself, and I told him that [...] was a relative of mine, and then I asked him for protection, I asked him to hide me. And he answered as follows: 'If [...] is your relative, then you all have to die, because [...] was assisting *Inyenzi*. He was my friend, but when he started helping the *Inyenzi*, he is no longer my friend. We do not even talk to each other. He's no longer my friend.' He went on to say that they had found some documents at Louis Rudahunga's place and who had to be killed, and that this document included a list of people who were making financial contributions to the *Inkotanyi*."
[239] T. 14 February 2007, p. 9.

159. The Chamber finds Witness CCH to be credible and believes her evidence.[240]

160. Defence Witness SJD testified that, on the morning of 26 April 1994, he saw a group of soldiers at the main gate of St. Joseph's College and four people who were sitting in a Toyota pick-up vehicle outside the gate. He identified the four people as two children from the Rudahunga family, a teacher from the Kabgayi Technical School and a young lady called Jeanne.[241] Witness SJD did not recall specifically seeing Rukundo at St. Joseph's College on this date.[242]

161. On the same day, Witness SJD saw Jeanne again at the refectory. She told him that she and the other three individuals who had been taken away in the morning had been seriously injured and that Madame Rudahunga had been killed. Witness SJD could see that Jeanne's scalp had been cut open.[243] Witness SJD, Father Kayibanda and Jeanne went to the Rudahunga family's home to assist the injured victims. In the vicinity of the home, Witness SJD saw soldiers in another blue Toyota Stout vehicle. He realised that the soldiers in the blue Toyota were the same soldiers whom he had seen in the morning in front of St. Joseph's College with two members of the Rudahunga family and two other Tutsi civilians.[244] In August or September 1994, Witness SJD heard that a military chaplain was involved in the abduction of Tutsi refugees from St. Joseph's College on 26 April 1994.[245] **[page 50]**

162. Defence Witness SLA saw Rukundo twice at the St. Léon Minor Seminary, sometime in mid-April and mid-May 1994.[246] On both occasions, Rukundo arrived in a beige or white-coloured private vehicle. Witness SLA neither saw nor heard that Rukundo drove a pick-up vehicle.[247] Witness SLA confirmed that he knew Louis Rudahunga, but said that he never heard Rukundo mention Rudahunga's name.[248]

163. Defence Witness EVC heard from Father Alfred Kayibanda that Rudahunga and his entire family had been killed. According to Witness EVC, Father Kayibanda did not mention who had killed the Rudahunga family.[249] In particular, he did not mention Rukundo in relation to the incident. According to Witness EVC, if Father Kayibanda had known that Rukundo was involved in the attack on members of the Rudahunga family, he would have informed the diocese.[250]

164. Witness SJA testified that he was outside on the veranda of his residence in St. Joseph's College, when the Rudahunga family was abducted. Witness SJA said that, from a distance of approximately 40 to 50 metres, he saw the backs of the soldiers and the victims.[251] Witness SJA testified that later that day, Jeanne returned with a bleeding wound on her head. She said that Madame Rudahunga had been killed and that the children "were still in a state of agony".[252]

(l) Findings

165. The Chamber notes that all four Prosecution witnesses connect the Accused to the killing of Madame Rudahunga and the causing of grievous bodily harm to her two children and the two Tutsi civilians, Jeanne and Justin. Prosecution Witness BLP testified that he saw the Accused at the scene of the abduction. He saw the soldiers put Madame Rudahunga aboard their vehicle and drive away,[253] saw Rukundo following them in

---

[240] See Witness CCH's credibility assessment, Section III.7.c.iv.
[241] T. 28 September 2007, pp. 9-10. When asked to describe the colour of the vehicle outside St. Joseph's College, Witness SJD replied "That morning I saw two vehicles. One was blue; that is certain. But I did not see the blue vehicle around our institutions, but in the vicinity of the Rudahungas. But the other vehicle was a Toyota, whose colour could be red, or it could be some other colour."
[242] T. 28 September 2007, p. 21.
[243] T. 28 September 2007, p. 13.
[244] T. 28 September 2007, pp. 13, 15.
[245] T. 28 September 2007, p. 21.
[246] T. 1 October 2007, pp. 12, 22.
[247] T. 1 October 2007, p. 23.
[248] T. 1 October 2007, p. 25.
[249] T. 11 September 2007, pp. 36-37.
[250] T. 11 September 2007, pp. 37-38.
[251] T. 22 October 2007, p. 13.
[252] T. 22 October 2007, pp. 10-11.
[253] T. 15 November 2006, pp. 14-15.

Judgement

his white Suzuki Samurai vehicle,[254] and saw the same soldiers, approximately 20 minutes later, return to St. Joseph's College and abduct two of the Rudahunga's children and two other Tutsi civilians.

166. Witness BLJ, one of the victims of the second abduction, corroborates Witness BLP's account that the same group of soldiers, who took away Madame Rudahunga, returned about 20 minutes later to St. Joseph's College for her, her brother and two other Tutsi civilians. Most **[page 51]** importantly, Witness BLJ corroborates Witness BLP's evidence that Rukundo acted together with the soldiers. After having been admitted to the hospital after the incident, the witness saw Rukundo again, in the presence of two of the four soldiers who had abducted Madame Rudahunga and then her, her brother and two other Tutsi civilians. When she saw these two soldiers she made the link between Father Kayibanda's comment about "Father Emmanuel's car", the pick-up truck that she saw close to her house after the attack and the same pick-up that was used in both abductions, and the soldiers and the Accused.[255]

167. Prosecution Witness BLC provides a further connection between Rukundo and the abductions, the killing and the beatings. He attested to hearing Rukundo boast at the St. Léon Minor Seminary, "We entered in Rudahunga's Inyenzi's house, we killed the wife and the children, but the idiot managed to get away from us."[256] Witness BLC testified that, when boasting about the killing, Rukundo had just come from the Rudahunga's home in the company of soldiers. The Chamber notes that Witness BLC's testimony is consistent with the evidence of Witnesses BLP and BLJ.

168. Finally, Witness CCH's evidence also connects Rukundo to the crimes. According to the witness, sometime in May 1994, at the St. Léon Minor Seminary, Rukundo told her that Louis Rudahunga had to be killed. According to the evidence, Witness CCH arrived at the St. Léon Minor Seminary in mid-May, after the death of Madame Rudahunga. Witness CCH's testimony regarding Rukundo's statement that Louis Rudahunga had to be killed is therefore consistent with Witness BLC's account of hearing Rukundo say that they killed Madame Rudahunga and her children but the "idiot" (Louis Rudahunga) managed to get away from them. Furthermore, Witness CCH's evidence that Rukundo told her that they had found documents at Louis Rudahunga's home is consistent with that of Witness BLC, who stated that when Rukundo boasted about the killing of Madame Rudahunga and her two children, Rukundo had just come from the Rudahunga's home.

169. In addition to the aforementioned, the Chamber has considered the short lapse of time between the abduction of Madame Rudahunga by a group of soldiers and the return of the same soldiers to St. Joseph's College to abduct two of her children and two other Tutsi civilians. The Chamber has also considered the short distance between St. Joseph's College and the Rudahunga's home, estimated by Witness SJD to be about one kilometre. In view of the close proximity, it is plausible that soldiers could drive from St. Joseph's College to the home, shoot Madame Rudahunga, and return to the College within a space of 20 to 30 minutes. **[page 52]**

170. The Chamber has assessed the totality of the evidence presented and considers that the evidence presented by the Defence does not discredit the Prosecution evidence. In particular, the Chamber notes that neither Defence Witnesses SLA nor EVC were present at St. Joseph's College when the abductions occurred. Concerning Witness SJD, the Chamber notes that he did not know Rukundo in 1994; therefore, his evidence that he did not see Rukundo at St. Joseph's College in April 1994 carries little weight. Finally, the Chamber notes that Defence Witness SJA, who testified not to have seen the Accused at the scene of the abduction, only saw the backs of the people who were abducted from St. Joseph's College. It is not even clear whether Witness SJA, who was on his veranda, could actually have seen the Accused.

171. In light of the foregoing, the Chamber finds that the Prosecution has proved beyond reasonable doubt that, sometime in April 1994, Madame Rudahunga, a Tutsi woman, was abducted from St. Joseph's College in Kagbayi by Emmanuel Rukundo, acting together with unknown soldiers, and was taken to her home located near St. Joseph's College, where she was shot and killed. The Chamber also finds that the same group of soldiers returned to St. Joseph's College about twenty minutes after abducting Madame Rudahunga and

---

[254] T. 15 November 2006, pp. 13, 14, 16.
[255] T. 9 March 2007, p. 19.
[256] T. 4 December 2006, p. 21.

took away two of the Rudahunga's children and two other Tutsi civilians, Justin and Jeanne. All four victims were severely beaten and injured by the soldiers and left for dead. Having considered the totality of the evidence, and, in particular the short interval between the first and second abduction, the evidence of both abductions carried out by the same soldiers driving a vehicle identified as belonging to the Accused, the evidence that Rukundo followed the abductors in another vehicle and the evidence that Rukundo boasted about having killed Madame Rudahunga and her two children, the Chamber finds that the Accused participated in a series of actions, which all form part of the same criminal transaction.

172. The Chamber further finds that Rukundo participated in the entire criminal transaction from the beginning, when the soldiers showed Rukundo documents taken from St. Joseph's College, before abducting Madame Rudahunga, until its completion, when Witness BLC heard Rukundo boasting, "We entered in Rudahunga's *Inyenzi*'s house, we killed the wife and the children, but the idiot managed to get away from us."[257] **[page 53]**

5. EVENTS AT THE NYABIKENKE COMMUNAL OFFICE

(a) Indictment

173. Paragraphs 10(iv) and 25(iv) of the Indictment read as follows:

> On or about 15 April 1994, **Emmanuel RUKUNDO** went to the Nyabikenke Commune office in Gitarama where several Tutsis had taken refuge and ordered or instigated policemen to shoot at Tutsi refugees at that location resulting in several deaths. By so doing, **Emmanuel RUKUNDO** ordered, instigated, or aided and abetted the killing of Tutsis at the Nyabikenke Commune office.

(b) Evidence

Prosecution Witness BUW

174. Prosecution Witness BUW, a Tutsi teacher, sought refuge at the Nyabikenke communal office on 11 April 1994, after the killing of Tutsi had begun in his commune. Witness BUW testified that he knew Rukundo from when the Accused was a deacon in 1989 and 1990.[258]

175. According to Witness BUW, the refugees at the communal office were attacked by Hutu for the first time on the night of 14 April 1994. The Hutu attackers threw grenades into the facilities. The refugees were also attacked with machetes and clubs. Witness BUW added that some of the refugees died during that night and that there was another attack on the following day which resulted in the death of many refugees.[259]

176. Witness BUW further stated he saw the Accused at the Nyabikenke communal office on 15 April 1994 between 2.00 p.m. and 3.00 p.m.[260] Rukundo arrived in a dark green military truck; he was armed with a pistol and a rifle and accompanied by about ten soldiers, carrying firearms.[261] Rukundo was wearing military colours, a "whitish" helmet and military boots.[262] At the time of his arrival, the attackers were throwing stones (and grenades) at the refugees. When Rukundo arrived, they stopped throwing stones[263] and withdrew a short distance.[264] According to Witness BUW, the attackers waited to see the reaction from the soldiers who had just arrived.[265] Rukundo then came **[page 54]** directly over to the refugees in the courtyard of the communal office.[266] Witness BUW greeted the Accused and showed him the refugees in the inner courtyard,

---
[257] T. 4 December 2006, p. 21.
[258] T. 19 February 2007, pp. 2-3, 9.
[259] T. 19 February 2007, pp. 3, 50-51.
[260] T. 19 February 2007, pp. 10, 35.
[261] T. 19 February 2007, pp. 3, 28-29.
[262] T. 19 February 2007, pp. 29-30.
[263] T. 19 February 2007, p. 4.
[264] T. 19 February 2007, p. 52.
[265] T. 19 February 2007, pp. 20-21, 30.
[266] T. 19 February 2007, p. 3.

including the dead and the injured. Witness BUW requested Rukundo to assist with asking the attackers to leave the premises. Witness BUW thought that as Rukundo was a priest and military chaplain, he would have some moral authority over the soldiers accompanying him and could therefore order them to chase away the attackers.[267] The Accused, however, replied that he had not come to provide assistance or to fight at the communal office, as it was none of his business. Rukundo added that he was going to Butaro *commune* in Ruhengeri to fight against the *Inyenzi* and *Inkotanyi*, and that they did not have sufficient weapons to save the refugees. He further stated that he did not know why the Hutu and Tutsi were fighting each other.[268]

177. Rukundo then left the inside courtyard and spent about five minutes talking to the 30 to 50 attackers. Witness BUW stated that he was approximately 300 to 400 metres away at that time and could not hear what Rukundo was saying to the attackers.[269] Witness BUW later corrected himself and stated that the distance between himself and the Accused was 40 metres.[270] The Accused then got into his vehicle and left the communal office. The attacks against the refugees resumed and intensified after Rukundo's departure. Witness BUW further testified that he did not know whether or not Rukundo had any authority over the attackers. However Witness BUW did not think that Rukundo had asked the attackers to stop attacking the refugees but he had the impression that the attackers would have respected Rukundo if he would have asked them to stop. Witness BUW stated that as a priest, Rukundo had a certain degree of authority and could have ordered the attackers to stop their attack.[271]

178. At the time that the Accused was at the Nyabikenke communal office on 15 April 1994, there were four communal policemen on duty. According to Witness BUW, Laurent Habumurenyi, the communal police brigadier, sat next to the fence everyday with a firearm, in an attempt to frighten away the refugees. He did nothing to protect the refugees, although the refugees may have thought that they were being protected by him. Another policeman, Gérard Munyabarenzi, helped the attackers advance towards the refugees by pushing back the Tutsi and firing in the air to **[page 55]** intimidate them.[272] The third policeman, Janvier Habinshuti, was in front of the communal office and observed the Accused's truck arrive. Witness BUW added that only the policemen carried arms, while the attackers only had grenades. Witness BUW did not notice any particular reaction from the communal policemen when the Accused arrived.[273]

179. Witness BUW stated that Father André Lerusse also visited the communal office on 15 April 1994, once in the morning and then again at about 4.30 p.m., after the Accused had left. During his afternoon visit, Witness BUW heard Father Lerusse instruct the communal policemen to repel the attackers, so that the refugees could escape via the backyard of the communal office. According to Witness BUW, two policemen remained at the communal office while two others accompanied the refugees and Father Lerusse. Witness BUW testified that those refugees who remained in the multi-purpose hall were locked in by brigadier Laurent Habumurenyi and they were killed. Witness BUW explained that when he asked the brigadier to open the door to the hall, the brigadier responded that if he (Witness BUW) had the authority then he should open the door. Witness BUW then left the communal office in the company of Father Lerusse. Witness BUW stated that all of this occurred after Rukundo had left the communal office.[274]

Prosecution Witness CCJ

180. Prosecution Witness CCJ is from the Accused's region and had known the Accused since 1977.[275]

181. In 1996 or 1998, Father Lerusse told Witness CCJ that Rukundo had visited the Nyabikenke communal office "during the genocide". Witness CCJ further testified that according to Father Lerusse, Rukundo talked

---

[267] T. 19 February 2007, pp. 4-5.
[268] T. 19 February 2007, pp. 4, 33.
[269] T. 19 February 2007, pp. 5, 41.
[270] T. 19 February 2007, p. 39.
[271] T. 19 February 2007, pp. 6, 32-33.
[272] T. 19 February 2007, pp. 15-16, 18-19. In his testimony, Witness BUW clarified that it was Munyabarenzi who was firing shots in the air to intimidate the refugees, and not the brigadier Habumurenyi. See T. 19 February 2007, p. 51.
[273] T. 19 February 2007, pp. 20, 30-32, 34.
[274] T. 19 February 2007, pp. 35-37, 41-42.
[275] T. 14 February 2007, pp. 8, 28.

to the policemen who were guarding the refugees and after their conversation, the policemen fired at the refugees. According to Witness CCJ, Father Lerusse did not know what Rukundo told the policemen. Witness CCJ further testified that according to Father Lerusse, this happened in the evening and the refugees fled, running throughout the night until they reached Kabgayi. Witness CCJ also testified that Father Lerusse was not a direct witness, but had heard about the events from a source unknown to the witness. Witness CCJ stated that he did not know when the incident took place.[276] **[page 56]**

The Accused

182. In his testimony, Rukundo confirmed that he went to the Nyabikenke communal office on one occasion on 15 April 1994.[277] He stated that on 15 April 1994, whilst staying at Mukamira Camp, he escorted Jean-Marie Vianney and his family, who were Tutsi, to Gitarama and Ruhango. He borrowed a Toyota pick-up and was accompanied by two soldiers. On 15 April 1994, he left Mukamira Camp between 9.30 and 10.00 a.m. and arrived in Ruhango around 11.30 a.m., where he dropped off the Vianney family behind the buildings of the Ruhango trading centre. On his trip back to Ruhengeri, Rukundo stopped at the Kabgayi Bishopric to greet the Bishop and then went to the St. Léon Minor Seminary in Kabgayi around 1.30 or 2.00 p.m., where he spent 30 minutes drinking a beer.[278]

183. The Accused stated that on his return to Ruhengeri from Kabgayi, he went via Nyabikenke and Vunga and made several stops along the way. He first stopped at the Remera trading centre in Nyabikenke *commune*, two and a half to three kilometers from Kanyanza Parish, where there was tension between residents of the trading centre and a group of attackers from a neighbouring hill. Rukundo asked his soldiers to fire warning shots in order to ward off the attackers. When they fired three or four shots into the air, the attackers dispersed. Rukundo further confirmed that he alighted from his vehicle with his soldiers in order to greet people and to drink a glass of beer, which was offered to him. After visiting the Remera trading centre, Rukundo stopped at the Kanyanza Parish with the intention of greeting Father André Lerusse. Rukundo was then informed that Father Lerusse had gone to the Nyabikenke communal office, where an incident similar to the one at the Remera trading centre had occurred.[279]

184. The Accused arrived at the Nyabikenke communal office around 4.00 p.m. When he got to the level of the communal office, Rukundo noticed that there was a crowd of people along the road armed with machetes and clubs. As Rukundo approached the communal office, he saw Father Lerusse, the communal policemen in their positions in front of the communal office and a crowd that had gathered in front of the communal office. The attackers began to step back when they saw the soldiers at the back of the Accused's vehicle. According to Rukundo, Lerusse asked for his assistantce.[280] **[page 57]**

185. In response, Rukundo immediately approached the attackers. Some of the attackers had already moved backwards, and those who were still at the front retreated to a distance of 100 metres as Rukundo approached them. This was because some of the attackers recognised him, as they had been his parishioners. He testified that, at that time, he only carried a pistol and did not ask the soldiers to accompany him. When they were at a "reasonable" distance from the communal office, Rukundo talked to the attackers and tried to dissuade them, whilst also trying to avoid any direct confrontation with them. The attackers listened to Rukundo and started moving away. Rukundo also told the five to ten attackers who had stayed behind that if "they continued to insist on their points of view, then he was going to ask the policemen to neutralise them." Rukundo then asked the remaining attackers to drop their machetes, following which three of them did. Rukundo collected the machetes and put them in the vehicle.[281] He further clarified that he did not ask his soldiers to fire warning shots in the air at the Nyabikenke communal office as he did at the Remera trading centre because there were a greater number of attackers who were much closer to the communal office.[282]

---

[276] T. 14 February 2007, pp. 39-40; T. 15 February 2007, p. 4.
[277] T. 9 October 2007, p. 5.
[278] T. 8 October 2007, pp. 53-55.
[279] T. 8 October 2007, pp. 55-57; T. 10 October 2007, pp. 57-58.
[280] T. 8 October 2007, p. 57.
[281] T. 8 October 2007, pp. 57-58; T. 9 October 2007, p. 3.
[282] T. 10 October 2007, p. 58.

186. After his conversation with the attackers, Rukundo approached the communal office and noticed that people had begun to move out of the buildings. According to Rukundo, Father Lerusse took advantage of the fact that Rukundo had warded off the attackers, to move some of the refugees from the communal office. As Rukundo felt that there was no more impending danger, he got back into his vehicle and left the communal office.[283]

187. Rukundo testified that he spent between 15 and 30 minutes at the Nyabikenke communal office on that day. The only people he spoke with were Father Lerusse, the policeman in front of the communal office whom he greeted, and the assailants. Rukundo stated that he did not go anywhere near the refugees in the courtyard of the communal office whilst he was there, and he did not know if any of them were his parishioners. According to Rukundo, the refugees were inside the premises of the communal office up until the time he arrived, and he only saw them when he went back to retrieve his vehicle after having reprimanded the attackers. He did not speak to the refugees. Rukundo claimed that, whilst he was at the communal office, there were no gunshots or attacks because by that time the bulk of the attackers had left. Rukundo confirmed that there was nothing in his attitude which could have led to suspicions that he was conniving with the assailants.[284] **[page 58]**

188. Rukundo knew Prosecution Witness BUW well because he was one of his parishioners in 1991-1992, and they had also attended meetings together. He claimed, however, that he did not know until recently that Witness BUW was one of the refugees at the Nyabikenke communal office. He further stated that, contrary to Witness BUW's testimony, he never saw him at that location.[285] Rukundo, however, admitted that Witness BUW could not have been mistaken about his presence at the communal office.[286]

Defence Witness André Lerusse

189. Witness André Lerusse is a Belgian priest who spent time in Rwanda in 1972 and between 1982 and 1998. He knew Rukundo from around 1986–1988, when Rukundo came to Karambi to help build one of his colleague's houses. Witness Lerusse also worked with Rukundo at Kanyanza, after Rukundo was posted there as a priest following his ordination in July 1991.[287]

190. Witness Lerusse testified that he held a number of meetings with the authorities at the Nyabikenke communal office after 6 April 1994, in order to assist the refugees. He thought that the policemen at the communal office were defending the refugees and did not observe any hostile attitude on their part towards the refugees.[288]

191. Witness Lerusse testified that he visited the Nyabikenke communal office on 15 April 1994 at about 10.00 or 11.00 a.m. He saw that there were attackers who had surrounded the communal office, and that no refugee could leave that location. He heard the refugees say that they would be killed that evening and he subsequently left to look for assistance in Kabgayi. Witness Lerusse returned to the communal office around 4:00 or 4.30 p.m., at which time there was a large group of attackers with weapons waiting to attack. Two of the communal policemen, wearing yellow berets, were lying down with their guns held in shooting position, in an attempt to stop the attackers from coming in through the road. Soon afterwards, the attackers advanced and started throwing stones.[289]

192. According to Witness Lerusse, Rukundo then arrived at the communal office, about ten or 20 minutes after he had arrived. The Accused arrived with soldiers in two military jeeps and placed his gun in the vehicle after alighting. At this point, the attack on the communal office had stopped. Witness Lerusse requested the Accused to assist him during a brief three minute conversation, following which Rukundo walked towards the attackers and uttered some calming words in **[page 59]** Kinyarwanda.[290] Witness

---

[283] T. 8 October 2007, pp. 57-58.
[284] T. 9 October 2007, pp. 3-5; T. 10 October 2007, pp. 59-60.
[285] T. 9 October 2007, p. 4.
[286] T. 10 October 2007, pp. 59-60.
[287] T. 12 September 2007, pp. 29-30.
[288] T. 12 September 2007, pp. 36, 41.
[289] T. 12 September 2007, pp. 42-47, 52; T. 13 September 2007, p. 24.
[290] T. 12 September 2007, pp. 47, 51-52, 62.

Lerusse admitted that he did not recall the exact words used by the Accused, since he did not have a sufficient level of Kinyarwanda. Witness Lerusse did not hear more than the first few words uttered by the Accused.[291]

193. Witness Lerusse was helped by one of the soldiers accompanying Rukundo to get to the courtyard of the communal office. He opened the doors of the communal office and told the refugees to leave. When he turned around he saw that Rukundo and the soldiers had left the premises, but no shots had been fired and no one had been attacked. Witness Lerusse and the refugees then left the communal office with the help of a policeman. According to Father Lerusse, Rukundo could not have entered the building or the inner courtyard where the refugees were located because he did not have the time to do so.[292] Witness Lerusse did not know what exactly transpired between the Accused and the attackers, but he observed that the refugees were not attacked as they were taken out of the building.[293] Witness Lerusse testified that when he helped the refugees out of the communal office, he was accosted by some *Interahamwe* in two pick-ups and later by two other men with machetes, but neither Witness Lerusse nor the refugees were harmed.[294] Witness Lerusse did not know how many refugees were left behind at the communal office[295] or whether the refugees left behind were attacked after he had left.[296]

194. Witness Lerusse stated that two hours later he recounted what had happened to Father Jean-Marie Dussart at Cyeza. Witness Lerusse added that Rukundo's intervention at the Nyabikenke communal office was providential since he had come at the right time to enable Witness Lerusse to move the refugees. Witness Lerusse also confirmed that he met Witness CCJ a few years later, but he could not recall if they discussed the events at the communal office.[297]

195. Witness Lerusse stated that he knew Witness BUW as a friend and that he trusted him. He further stated that Witness BUW was at the communal office on 15 April 1994 and that Witness BUW was one of the last persons to leave the communal office.[298] **[page 60]**

Defence Witness BCB

196. Witness BCB testified that Tutsi refugees started arriving at the communal office from 11 April 1994.[299] Witness BCB knew Witness BUW, who was one of the first refugees to arrive at the communal office.[300]

197. Witness BCB further testified that on 15 April 1994, attackers arrived at the communal office around 10.00 a.m. They threw stones at the refugees, wounding some people.[301] He estimated the number of attackers to be in the "thousands".[302] The communal policemen tried to repel the assailants and prevent killings at the communal office, but they were constrained by the lack of resources and reinforcement.[303] Father Lerusse arrived at the communal office at noon and came back again at 4.00 p.m. Prior to Father Lerusse's first visit to the communal office, the policemen had fired some shots in the air to keep the attackers away.[304]

198. Witness BCB testified that on his second visit to the communal office, Father Lerusse stated that he wanted to take the refugees away to a safe location. Witness BCB said that the policemen assisted Lerusse to move the refugees.[305] Shortly after Father Lerusse's arrival, Rukundo arrived at the communal office

---

[291] T. 13 September 2007, p. 10.
[292] T. 12 September 2007, pp. 47-48, 52.
[293] T. 13 September 2007, pp. 10-11.
[294] T. 12 September 2007, pp. 48-49.
[295] T. 13 September 2007, pp. 12-13, 24.
[296] T. 13 September 2007, p. 5.
[297] T. 12 September 2007, pp. 53, 65.
[298] T. 12 September 2007, pp. 59, 61-63.
[299] T. 18 September 2007, pp. 5-6.
[300] T. 18 September 2007, pp. 10-11.
[301] T. 18 September 2007, p. 12.
[302] T. 19 September 2007, pp. 3, 31.
[303] T. 18 September 2007, pp. 12-13; T. 19 September 2007, pp. 19-20.
[304] T. 18 September 2007, p. 14.
[305] T. 18 September 2007, pp. 14-15.

wearing military uniform, with approximately five soldiers in a Hilux vehicle.[306] Witness BCB stated that he and his colleagues greeted the Accused when he arrived at the communal office and pointed out the attackers. Witness BCB could not say if Lerusse and Rukundo had a short conversation, because they arrived at approximately the same time.[307]

199. According to Witness BCB, the attackers looked discouraged and began stepping back upon Rukundo's arrival.[308] The refugees and the attackers stopped throwing stones when Rukundo arrived and the attackers continued to maintain some distance.[309] Witness BCB first testified that Rukundo confiscated the attackers' traditional weapons and threw them into his vehicle.[310] However, he subsequently stated that because Rukundo did not stay for very long he was only able to **[page 61]** disarm those who had machetes.[311] Witness BCB later clarified that he did not personally witness Rukundo confiscate the weapons, but was told that machetes were seen in the Accused's vehicle.[312] Witness BCB further stated that, because he was approximately 200 metres away on the veranda of the communal office, he did not hear the conversation between the Accused and the attackers.[313] The Accused then left the communal office in the direction of Ruhengeri and did not return.[314] According to Witness BCB, Rukundo never entered the buildings of the communal office.[315]

200. Witness BCB testified that Father Lerusse was involved in taking the refugees out of the buildings of the communal office through the backyard. At this point, the attackers had moved further away and were no longer close to the communal office. Three policemen left with Father Lerusse to escort the refugees, whilst two policemen stayed behind at the communal office. After Father Lerusse left with the majority of the refugees, Witness BCB estimated that there were about 50 refugees, including five who were wounded, left in the communal office. Contrary to Witness BUW, Witness BCB stated that after the Accused's arrival at the communal office on 15 April 1994, there had been no attempts to lock up or shoot the refugees. Witness BCB stated that in the morning of the following day, he and others spoke to the small group of refugees left at the communal office and insisted that they leave for safety reasons. Whilst some of the refugees left, approximately 18 refugees stayed at the communal office. Attackers subsequently killed those who stayed at the communal office that day.[316]

Defence Witness RUE

201. In April 1994, Defence Witness RUE was a soldier in Camp Mukamira in Ruhengeri. Witness RUE knew the Accused as a chaplain of the Ruhengeri operational *secteur* between August 1993 and May 1994.[317]

202. During cross-examination, Witness RUE stated that on 15 April 1994 he was assigned to escort Rukundo to Ruhango in order to take the Tutsi refugees, Jean-Marie Vianney and his wife and child to the house of Vianney's parents-in-law.[318] Witness RUE further testified that seven **[page 62]** people (including Rukundo) left for Ruhango at 9.00 a.m. in a pick-up truck and dropped Vianney and his family off around 1.00 p.m. On the return journey to Camp Mukamira, Rukundo and those remaining in the vehicle stopped briefly to greet the Bishop at Kabgayi. Witness RUE stated that when they got to the Remera centre in Nyabikenke, they chased away some possible *Interahamwe* attackers who were looting. The attackers then

---

[306] T. 18 September 2007, pp. 15-16, 18; T. 19 September 2007, p. 8. Witness BCB later insisted that *gendarmes* and not soldiers accompanied Rukundo (T. 19 September 2007, pp. 8-9).
[307] T. 19 September 2007, p. 17-19.
[308] T. 18 September 2007, p. 16.
[309] T. 19 September 2007, p. 15.
[310] T. 18 September 2007, pp. 15-16. The witness first stated that the refugees were asked to gather the traditional weapons of the attackers and put them in the vehicle. However, the witness later testified that the Accused took away the traditional weapons and threw them into the vehicle. (See T. 18 September 2007, p. 15).
[311] T. 19 September 2007, p. 12.
[312] T. 19 September 2007, p. 31.
[313] T. 19 September 2007, pp. 13-14, 31.
[314] T. 18 September 2007, p. 16; T. 19 September 2007, pp. 10-12.
[315] T. 19 September 2007, p. 14.
[316] T. 18 September 2007, pp. 17-20; T. 19 September 2007, pp. 10, 15-16, 20.
[317] T. 21 September 2007, pp. 8-10, 17; T. 24 September 2007, p. 7.
[318] T. 21 September 2007, pp. 18, 22-23; T. 24 September 2007, p. 19.

tried to attack them and called them *Inyenzi*. When they arrived at the Nyabikenke communal office they saw *Interahamwe* threatening refugees. Witness RUE testified that they disbursed the attackers. Later on, he said that a person, whom he did not identify, alighted from the vehicle and spoke to the attackers, sending them away. Witness RUE estimated that they spent 15 minutes at the Nyabikenke communal office before leaving for Camp Mukamira. He testified that they were back in Ruhengeri at 5.30 p.m.[319]

Defence Witness Jean-Marie Dussart (GSB)

203. Witness Jean-Marie Dussart was Rukundo's colleague in the Kabgayi diocese when Rukundo was posted to Kanyanza parish to work with Father André Lerusse and Father Felix Ntaganira in September 1991.[320]

204. Witness Dussart testified about an incident told to him by Father Lerusse. Witness Dussart stated that on 15 April 1994, he was in Cyeza with Father Michel. Witness Dussart further testified that, at about 8.00 p.m. on 16 April 1994, Father Lerusse arrived at that location, stating that he had "escaped from the lion's mouth." According to Witness Dussart, Lerusse explained that while he was in Kanyanza, he discovered that hundreds of refugees at the Nyabikenke communal buildings had been attacked. He then took his motorbike and went to the *commune* to assist the refugees. The communal policeman, Laurent, was on guard before the attack and fired a gun to try to deter the attackers.[321] According to Witness Dussart, Lerusse said that he was surprised to find Rukundo passing by the Nyabikenke communal office with his usual escort. Father Lerusse further informed Witness Dussart that the Accused helped to repel the attackers. Witness Dussart testified that Lerusse described Rukundo's arrival at the location as "providential", because Rukundo pushed back the attackers and enabled Lerusse to convince the refugees to come out of the communal office buildings. Witness Dussart admitted, however, that Lerusse did not inform him of the exact chronology of the events at the Nyabikenke communal office.[322] **[page 63]**

Defence Witness EVB

205. Witness EVB, a priest and teacher, testified that he first got to know Rukundo when they were both students at the St. Léon Minor Seminary in Kabgayi in 1972. Witness EVB also saw Rukundo during meetings at the Kabgayi diocese.[323] Witness EVB gave hearsay testimony that Rukundo had a very good reputation in the Kanyanza region because he had stopped attacks in the Remera market square in Nyabikenke *commune* and at the Nyabikenke communal office.[324]

206. Witness EVB also heard that attackers from across the Nyabarongo River in Ruhengeri and Ndusu and Musasa in Kigali were terrorising refugees in the Nyabikenke communal office, who were being guarded by the communal policemen. He was told that Father André Lerusse was not able to solve the situation. The Accused Rukundo then arrived at the location and was able to reason with the attackers and convince them not to harm the refugees.[325] It was only then that Father Lerusse was able to help the refugees leave the communal office and go into the nearby banana plantation before returning to Kabgayi. Witness EVB admitted, however, that his version of these events was based on what certain witnesses had told him and that it was possible that there may be other versions of the event, as it took place many years ago.[326] When Witness EVB was confronted with his earlier statement of 2001,[327] he explained that he had narrated the events as they had been recounted to him by the Accused, Father Lerusse and a witness of the parish staff.[328]

---

[319] T. 24 September 2007, pp. 22-25.
[320] T. 10 September 2007, pp. 3-5.
[321] T. 10 September 2007, pp. 12-13, 17-18.
[322] T. 10 September 2007, pp. 17-18, 54-55.
[323] T. 20 July 2007, pp. 4, 7.
[324] T. 20 July 2007, p. 29.
[325] T. 20 July 2007, p. 29; T. 23 July 2007, p. 25.
[326] T. 23 July 2007, pp. 25-26.
[327] Exhibit P. 46A.
[328] T. 23 July 2007, p. 31.

Defence Witness BCD

207. Witness BCD testified that Rukundo saved some Tutsi at the Remera trading centre between 10 and 15 April 1994.

208. Witness BCD lived in Remera *cellule* in Nyabikenke *commune*, approximately 100 metres from the Remera trading centre in April 1994. He testified that when he saw the Accused in the trading centre between 10 and 15 April 1994, the Tutsi refugees in the trading centre were attacked by a group of 60 to 100 attackers from a neighbouring hill.[329] Rukundo was accompanied by between eight to 12 soldiers.[330] Witness BCD and another man told Rukundo about the attack and asked him to help them. Rukundo agreed and went to see the attackers and ordered his escort to fire **[page 64]** shots in the air to drive the attackers away. When the soldier fired three shots in the air, the people scattered and returned to their homes. Witness BCD fled to Kabgayi after learning that his name was on a list of persons to be killed.[331]

(c) Deliberations

209. The Indictment alleges that on or about 15 April 1994, Emmanuel Rukundo went to the Nyabikenke communal office in Gitarama and ordered or instigated policemen to shoot at Tutsi refugees hiding at that location, resulting in several deaths. The Prosecution alleges that by so doing, Rukundo ordered, instigated, or aided and abetted the killing of Tutsi at the Nyabikenke communal office.[332]

210. There is no dispute that Tutsi refugees, who had sought refuge at the Nyabikenke communal office, were attacked by a group of Hutu attackers on 15 April 1994. Further, there is no dispute that Rukundo visited the Nyabikenke communal office on 15 April 1994. The only remaining issue for the Chamber is to determine the role the Accused played in the events at the communal office on that day.

211. The Defence submits that the Prosecution evidence presented by Witness BUW does not match paragraphs 10(iv) and 25(iv) of the Indictment.[333] The Indictment alleges that the Accused ordered or instigated policemen to shoot at Tutsi refugees who had sought shelter at the Naybikenke communal office. Witness BUW testified that the Accused failed to order a group of Hutu civilian attackers who had surrounded the communal office to cease their attack on the Tutsi refugees and that after the Accused had left the communal office, the attacks against the Tutsi refugees intensified.[334]

212. The Chamber does not need to make a finding on that Defence contention because the Prosecution evidence, in any case, does not establish any criminal conduct on the part of the Accused.

213. The Prosecution has presented the evidence of Witness BUW in support of this alleged event. According to Witness BUW's firsthand account, Rukundo arrived at the Nyabikenke communal office in the company of about ten soldiers, during an attack on the refugees who had **[page 65]** sought shelter there. Witness BUW testified that shortly thereafter, the attackers ceased throwing stones and hurling grenades and withdrew, waiting for the reaction of the soldiers who had just arrived. Rukundo walked to the courtyard of the communal office and spoke to the refugees. Then he went to speak with the assailants, who were about 40 metres away. Witness BUW attested that he was unable to hear what Rukundo said to them. The Accused then boarded his vehicle and left the communal office, following which, the attack against the refugees resumed and intensified.

214. Witness BUW expressed the opinion that Rukundo, as a priest, wielded significant moral authority over the attackers, and, that if Rukundo had told the assailants to cease their attack, they would have done so.

---

[329] T. 20 September 2007, pp. 3, 5-6.
[330] T. 20 September 2007, pp. 13-14.
[331] T. 20 September 2007, pp. 6-8.
[332] Paras. 10(iv) and 25(iv) of the Indictment. The Chamber notes that in its Closing Brief (para. 224), the Prosecution appears to rely only on the modes of ordering and instigating the killing of Tutsi at the communal office.
[333] Defence Closing Brief, paras. 1140-1144.
[334] T. 19 February 2007, pp. 3-6, 28-29, 30, 32-33, 41, 52-53.

215. In respect of the Prosecution's charge of ordering or instigating, the Chamber notes that Witness BUW presented no evidence that Rukundo gave any orders to the attackers or that he saw Rukundo instigate the assailants to attack the Tutsi refugees. Witness BUW testified that he did not hear what Rukundo said to the assailants.

216. In respect of the Prosecution's charge that Rukundo aided and abetted the attackers, the Chamber observes that, according to the evidence of Witness BUW the attack ceased while Rukundo was present at the communal office only to resume after he had left. This is consistent with the testimony of Defence Witness André Lerusse.[335]

217. Witness BUW also testified that after the Accused had left the communal office on 15 April 1994, Laurent Habumurenyi, the communal Brigadier, locked the remaining refugees inside the multi-purpose hall at the Nyabikenke communal office, and that they were eventually killed.[336]

218. The Chamber notes that no causal link between Rukundo's presence at the communal office on 15 April 1994 and the policemen's subsequent actions has been established by the evidence. There is no indication as to when the brigadier locked the refugees in the hall. Furthermore, there is no evidence to suggest that the policemen's actions were based on Rukundo's orders or instigation or that Rukundo aided and abetted the brigadier or the policemen. In fact, Witness BUW does not mention whether Rukundo talked to the policemen at all. The only reference Witness BUW makes to Rukundo and the policemen is that he did not notice any particular reaction from the policemen when Rukundo arrived at the communal office. The only other Prosecution witness to testify about this allegation, Witness CCJ, provides uncorroborated hearsay evidence that following a **[page 66]** conversation with the Accused, the communal policemen fired at the refugees, causing them to escape and seek refuge in Kabgayi.[337]

219. Consequently, the Chamber finds that the Prosecution has not established beyond reasonable doubt that Rukundo ordered, instigated or aided and abetted policemen to shoot at the Tutsi refugees gathered at Nyabikenke communal office on 15 April 1994 as alleged in paragraphs 10(iv) and 25(iv) of the Indictment. **[page 67]**

6. EVENTS AT THE KABGAYI BISHOPRIC

(a) Indictment

220. Paragraphs 10(v) and 25(v) of the Indictment read as follows:

> On or about 16 of April 1994, **Emmanuel RUKUNDO**, dressed in military uniform, armed, and escorted by armed soldiers, moved about the Bishop's house at Kabgayi, yelling and asking if any Tutsi or "*Inkotanyi*" were hiding there. As a result, Tutsi priests, fearing for their lives, went into hiding. By so doing, **Emmanuel RUKUNDO** caused Tutsi who had taken refuge at the Bishop's house at Kabgayi serious mental harm.

(b) Evidence

Prosecution Witness CCJ

221. The Chamber has previously considered Witness CCJ's evidence in relation to the events at the Nyabikenke communal office.

222. Witness CCJ attested to seeing the Accused, accompanied by two soldiers, enter the Kabgayi Bishopric before noon on 15 or 16 April 1994. The Accused was armed with two guns. One of the weapons was slung over his shoulder and the other was attached to his waistband. Witness CCJ first testified that he was in the Vicar General's office when he saw the Accused enter the Bishopric. Later in his testimony, the witness stated that he was in the Bishop's office when he saw Rukundo arrive.

---

[335] T. 12 September 2007, pp. 47, 52; T. 13 September 2007, pp. 10-11.
[336] T. 19 February 2007, pp. 36, 37, 42.
[337] T. 14 February 2007, p. 39.

223. Witness CCJ stated that, from a distance of about "two metres," he watched the Accused and heard him ask in a loud voice, "Are there no *Inkontanyis* here?" Following this outburst, the Vicar General spoke with Rukundo outside his office. The Vicar later urged the witness to hide from Rukundo, who seemed to be "demented." Witness CCJ, after hiding behind a door, retired to his room once Rukundo left the Bishopric. The witness left his room at midday to have lunch at the refectory of the Bishopric, before leaving for Burundi.[338]

224. Witness CCJ testified that he was so terrified that he had goose bumps after hearing Rukundo's question, "Are there no *Inkotanyis* here?" The witness understood, from Rukundo's words, that he was not safe at the Bishopric. His concern for his security was heightened by the fact that there were a number of soldiers moving around Kabgayi hunting for Tutsi, or *Inkotanyi*. Witness CCJ testified that he was certain that, if Rukundo had seen him at the Kabgayi Bishopric, **[page 68]** Rukundo would have killed him or would have identified him to others who would have killed him.[339]

225. Witness CCJ could not recall whether the incident involving Rukundo prompted a discussion among the clerics who gathered at the refectory for lunch. He explained that, because he sat to the side of the clerics, he did not hear their conversation. He further testified that the Bishop asked him to raise the volume of a radio next to his table. For these reasons, he could not remember whether the clerics who had gathered at the refectory discussed the incident involving Rukundo.[340]

226. Prosecution Witness CCJ did not recall whether Rukundo or Defence Witness EVB had lunch at the refectory on this day.[341]

Prosecution Witness BPA

227. Prosecution Witness BPA was born in Uganda to Rwandan immigrants. He testified that he was unacquainted with any ethnic issues in Rwanda. He further testified that, when he was a child, "this whole business of ethnic origin did not exist. And when the war broke out, my parents died, so I do not know my ethnic origin." The witness did not recall his date of birth.[342]

228. Witness BPA testified that, as an intern at the Kabgayi diocese in 1989, before being ordained as a priest, he met the Accused Rukundo.[343]

229. Witness BPA testified, in examination-in-chief, that whilst Rukundo was a student at the Nyakibanda Major Seminary, he was an ethnic extremist and referred to Tutsi colleagues as *Inyenzi*.[344] However, in cross-examination, Witness BPA admitted that he had not studied with Rukundo at the Seminary but had heard from other seminarians, during the Christmas holidays in 1990, about Rukundo's alleged anti-Tutsi attitude and conduct.[345]

230. Witness BPA attested that, before 11 or 12 April 1994, he saw Rukundo in the corridor of the Bishopric, whilst the witness was waiting to see the Bishop. Witness BPA stated that Rukundo, accompanied by one or two soldiers, was wearing a camouflage military uniform and was carrying an SMG firearm and a cartridge holder.[346] The witness heard Rukundo talking to himself as he **[page 69]** strode through the hallway and recalled that he said, "The time had come ... to kill the *Inyenzi*." The witness, who was alone in the corridor, was afraid, even though Rukundo did not address him personally and his threat was not directed to anyone in particular. Witness BPA said that, to his knowledge, Rukundo neither carried out his threats nor killed anyone.

231. Witness BPA stated that, as a Ugandan, he had good reason to be frightened by Rukundo's threatening words, because at the time it was said that people from Uganda were comparable to Tutsi, and were

---

[338] T. 14 February 2007, p. 38; T. 15 February 2007, p. 2.
[339] T. 14 February 2007, p. 38.
[340] T. 15 February 2007, p. 3.
[341] T. 15 February 2007, pp. 3-4.
[342] T. 7 March 2007, pp. 39, 43, 45.
[343] T. 7 March 2007, pp. 4, 10-11.
[344] T. 7 March 2007, pp. 4-7.
[345] T. 7 March 2007, pp. 5-6, 10-12.
[346] T. 7 March 2007, pp. 7-8, 32-34.

accomplices of the *Inyenzi*.[347] According to Witness BPA, this was the first time that he had seen an armed military chaplain, and he was fearful, after meeting "Father Rukundo with a rifle." However, on further examination, Witness BPA admitted that he had seen the Accused quite frequently before the war, and that the Accused, after his appointment as a military chaplain, had told him "he had to fight against the *Inyenzi."*[348]

Prosecution Witness CCN

232. Prosecution Witness CCN recalled meeting Emmanuel Rukundo in either 1992 or 1993 at a garage in Nyabisundu in Gitarama. Rukundo told the witness that if the *Inkotanyi* were ever to arrive in Kigali, "we will exterminate you."[349] Witness CCN responded that "we shall see whether we are the ones who are going to exterminate you or you are the ones that are going to exterminate us." Witness CCN stated that he understood Rukundo's statement at the garage to mean that if the RPF army moved into Kigali, the Tutsi would be exterminated. Witness CCN further testified that Rukundo's use of the term *"Inkotanyi"* was a reference to the RPF army.[350]

233. Witness CCN met Rukundo as he was leaving the Bishop's house on 12 or 13 April 1994. Both the witness and the Accused were alone. According to Witness CCN, Rukundo was dressed in military uniform and carried a weapon tucked into his belt and another weapon strapped on his shoulder. Witness CCN testified that he greeted Rukundo, who was in a hurry and looked angry. The witness recalled that Rukundo responded to his greeting, "You will see, you will see, you will get it from us." Witness CCN testified that this encounter frightened him, and he left the Bishopric, as he believed that Rukundo could "either kill me or get me killed".[351]

234. Witness CCN attested that he was fearful of Rukundo because of his past experiences with him. The witness explained that, prior to 1994, they had lived together in Nyakibanda, where **[page 70]** Rukundo had called him an *Inyenzi* or an *Inkotanyi* accomplice. The witness also recalled Rukundo's threatening words spoken at the garage in Gitarama, as set out above.[352]

235. Witness CCN visited the Bishopric the following day, a Friday, to inform the Bishop about his decision to go into exile.[353]

The Accused

236. Rukundo testified that, on 15 April 1994, he visited the Bishop of Kabgayi at the Bisphoric, accompanied by three soldiers, all who remained with his vehicle.[354] He sated that he walked alone to the refectory and to the Bishop's home.[355]

237. Rukundo testified that, on 15 April 1994, he did not ask or attempt to discover whether there were any *Inkotanyi* at the Bishopric. Rukundo explained that he knew all the individuals at the Bishopric and could not possibly suspect any of them of being an *Inkotanyi*. He added that it would have been totally inappropriate to ask about Inkotanyi in the presence of his hierarchical superiors and that "one really has to be a mad person to do so." Rukundo dismissed Witness CCJ's allegation, that he saw Rukundo gesticulating and screaming about *Inkotanyi* at the Bishopric, as a "fabrication of lies."[356]

238. Rukundo testified that he did not see Witness CCN at the Bishopric on 15 April 1994 and consequently could not have threatened him. Rukundo dismissed Witness CCN's allegation as "fabrication designed to incriminate" him. He also denied meeting Witness CCN at a garage in Gitarama in 1993. He added that the

---

[347] T. 7 March 2007, pp. 7-9, 32, 37.
[348] T. 7 March 2007, pp. 6, 35-36.
[349] T. 23 February 2007, p. 15; T. 26 February 2007, p. 17.
[350] T. 26 February 2007, pp. 17-20.
[351] T. 23 February 2007, pp. 15, 17.
[352] T. 23 February 2007, pp. 15, 17.
[353] T. 26 February 2007, pp. 39-40.
[354] T. 8 October 2007, pp. 54-55.
[355] T. 9 October 2007, pp. 18, 25.
[356] T. 9 October 2007, pp. 21-22; T. 10 October 2007, p. 36.

priests had their own garage where their vehicles were repaired and refuelled and that there was no reason for him to visit another garage.[357]

239. Rukundo also denied having met Prosecution Witness BPA at the Kabgayi Bishopric on 15 April 1994 or having threatened Witness BPA on 12 April at the Kabgayi Bishopric. According to Rukundo, Witness BPA's allegation of threatening words was "simply a story designed to accuse someone."[358] **[page 71]**

240. Rukundo testified that he had lunch at the refectory of the Bishopric on 15 April 1994. He stated that the lunch was attended by a number of people, some of whom were permanently based at the Bishopric and others who were not. Amongst those who were not permanently based at the Bishopric were Vincent Nsengiyumva, Joseph Ruzindana, Father Stanislas Mubiligi, Father Denis Mutabazi and Prosecution Witness CCJ.[359]

241. Rukundo testified that he saw Prosecution Witness CCJ for the first time on 15 April 1994 at the Bishopric in the refectory. Rukundo affirmed that he spoke with Witness CCJ whilst having lunch, but attested that they did not have a private discussion.[360]

Defence Witness EVA

242. The Chamber has previously considered Witness EVA's evidence in relation to the events at the *Imprimerie de Kabgayi* roadblock.

243. Witness EVA recalled seeing Rukundo at the Kabgayi Bishopric on the afternoon of 14 or 15 April 1994, after she had distributed travel documents to three priests – Prosecution Witnesses CCJ, BPA, and CCN – who departed that day for Burundi. According to the witness, Rukundo, accompanied by two bodyguards, was dressed in military uniform and had a pistol tucked into his waistband. Witness EVA did not hear anyone yelling, screaming or threatening anyone on that day.[361]

244. Witness EVA testified that she had never heard Rukundo utter anti-Tutsi statements nor was she informed that he made such statements or played any role in the events in Rwanda between 7 April and 2 June 1994.[362]

Defence Witness EVB

245. The Chamber has previously considered Witness EVB's evidence in relation to the events at the Nyabikenke communal office.

246. Witness EVB knew Prosecution Witness CCJ. According to Witness EVB, Witness CCJ arrived at the Kabgayi Bishopric on a Sunday, after 6 April 1994, and remained there for about a week before departing for Burundi. Witness EVB recalled that, prior to Witness CCJ's departure, he requested Witness EVB to collect his personal belongings from his parish. Witness EVB placed **[page 72]** Witness CCJ's departure for Burundi around 15 April 1994. According to Witness EVB, Witness CCJ left for Burundi in the company of Prosecution Witnesses BPA and CCN.[363]

247. Defence Witness EVB testified that he saw Rukundo at the Kabgayi Bishopric on the morning of 15 April 1994. On this date, he did not hear Rukundo shout or gesticulate as he entered the premises of the Kabgayi Bishopric or when he left the Bishop's office and walked to the refectory.[364]

248. Witness EVB spoke with Prosecution Witness CCJ about general issues prior to having lunch at the refectory of the Bishopric on or about 15 April 1994. Witness EVB testified that he never heard Prosecution Witness CCJ make any mention of meeting Rukundo that morning.[365]

---

[357] T. 9 October 2007, pp. 22, 24.
[358] T. 9 October 2007, pp. 24-25.
[359] T. 9 October 2007, pp. 20, 25; T. 10 October 2007, p. 35.
[360] T. 9 October 2007, p. 21.
[361] T. 19 July 2007, pp. 23, 26-27.
[362] T. 19 July 2007, pp. 35-36.
[363] T. 20 July 2007, pp. 13-14.
[364] T. 20 July 2007, pp. 21, 23-24.
[365] T. 20 July 2007, p. 24.

249. Witness EVB testified that he shared a meal at the refectory of the Bishopric with Rukundo, the Bishop and other priests who resided at the Bishopric. He testified that Prosecution Witness CCJ shared a table with Rukundo and the Bishop during the lunch. According to Witness EVB, Rukundo was at ease during the lunch.[366]

250. Witness EVB attested that he did not ever hear Rukundo ask, "Are there any *Inkontanyis* in the Bishopric?" or, shout, "The time has come to kill the *Inyenzi*". He added that it would have been completely inappropriate for Rukundo to utter such statements in the company of the three Bishops who were then residing at the Kabgayi Bishopric.[367]

Defence Witness EVD

251. Defence Witness EVD testified that he attended the Nyakibanda Major Seminary with Rukundo.[368]

252. Witness EVD attested to seeing Rukundo at the Bishopric on 15 or 16 April 1994.[369] According to Witness EVD, Rukundo was dressed in military uniform and had a pistol on his waistbelt.[370] **[page 73]**

253. Witness EVD recalled that, on this date in mid-April, he had lunch at the refectory of the Bishopric. He testified that amongst the other people who were present at the lunch were the three Bishops, Defence Witness EVB, Prosecution Witness CCJ and Rukundo. He estimated that the lunch did not last longer than 30 to 40 minutes. According to Witness EVD, the atmosphere during the lunch was calm, friendly and respectful given the presence of the important people. Witness EVD testified that Rukundo's conduct during lunch was normal and calm. Witness EVD did not observe anything unusual in respect of Prosecution Witness CCJ.[371]

254. Defence Witness EVD testified that he heard of no threats made against Tutsi on that day and had no recollection of Vicar General Rwabalinda telling him anything about Emmanuel Rukundo.[372]

(c) Deliberations

255. The Indictment alleges that on or about 16 April 1994 Emmanuel Rukundo, armed and dressed in military uniform and accompanied by armed soldiers, moved about the Bishop's house at Kabgayi, yelling and asking if any Tutsi or *Inkotanyi* were hiding there. As a result of Rukundo's alleged conduct, Tutsi priests, fearing for their lives, went into hiding.[373] The Indictment further alleges that, by this conduct, the Accused caused serious mental harm to Tutsi who had taken refuge at the Bishopric in April 1994.[374] In support of this allegation, the Prosecution relies on the evidence of Witnesses CCJ, BPA and CCN. The Defence presented the evidence of Witnesses EVA, EVD, EVB and the Accused to challenge the Prosecution's allegation.

256. The Chamber notes that the Prosecution's evidence appears to refer to three separate incidents at the Bishopric. The evidence of Prosecution Witnesses CCJ, BPA and CCN differs with regard to the Accused's alleged words during each of these incidents. The Prosecution's evidence also differs with respect to the dates on which the incidents at the Bishopric are alleged to have taken place. Prosecution Witnesses CCJ, BPA and CCN placed their respective encounters with the Accused at the Bishopric on different dates ranging between 11 and 15 April 1994. The Chamber notes, however, that the Indictment refers to a timeframe of "on or about 16 April." The Chamber considers that the dates between 11 and 15 April 1994 fall within the

---

[366] T. 20 July 2007, pp. 24-25.
[367] T. 20 July 2007, pp. 25-26; T. 23 July 2007, p. 54.
[368] T. 3 October 2007, p. 7.
[369] Witness EVD stated that Rukundo arrived "three or four days" after 12 April 1994. The witness recalled the date of 12 April, as a reference, because on this day the religious committee first met to plan assistance for the refugees, and the telephones at the Bishopric were disconnected.
[370] T. 3 October 2007, pp. 39-40; T. 4 October 2007, p. 25.
[371] T. 3 October 2007, p. 42.
[372] T. 3 March 2007, pp. 42-43.
[373] See paragraphs 10(v) and 25(v) of the Indictment.
[374] *Ibid.*

timeframe specified in the Indictment. The Chamber therefore finds that there is no significant difference between the **[page 74]** Prosecution's evidence and the Indictment in respect of the timeframe within which the events were alleged to have taken place. Since the evidence of the Prosecution witnesses appears to refer to three separate incidents, the Chamber will address the evidence of each Prosecution witness in turn.

257. Prosecution Witness CCJ testified that he arrived at the Kabgayi Bishopric on Monday, 12 April 1994, and that he left the Bishopric on the following Friday, 16 April 1994. Witness CCJ claimed to have seen Rukundo at the Bishopric before noon on 15 or 16 April 1994. Witness CCJ stated that he was in the Vicar General's office when he saw Rukundo enter the premises of the Bishopric. Later in his testimony, however, he attested to being in the Bishop's office, located near the entrance to the Bishopric. Witness CCJ claimed to have heard Rukundo ask in a loud voice, "Are there no *Inkotanyis* here," as a result of which Witness CCJ was frightened. Witness CCJ testified that he was certain that, had Rukundo seen him at the Kabgayi Bishopric, Rukundo would have killed him or would have identified him to others who would have killed him. Witness CCJ could not recall whether either the Accused or Defence Witness EVB was present at the lunch served at the refectory of the Bishopric after the alleged incident.

258. The Chamber has doubts about Witness CCJ's credibility, given that after the alleged threat by Rukundo, Witness CCJ could not recall whether Rukundo was present at the refectory a short while later. The Chamber notes that Rukundo's presence at the refectory is a fact established by Defence Witness EVB and the Accused.[375] In the Chamber's opinion, it is surprising that Witness CCJ should fail to remember whether the Accused was present in the refectory, in view of the witness's detailed recollection of the prior incident the same morning involving the Accused.

259. The Indictment alleges that Rukundo, through his yelling and threatening words, caused serious mental harm to Tutsi who had taken refuge at the Bishop's house. Whilst the term "serious bodily and mental harm" is not defined in the Statute, the Chamber notes that the ICTR and ICTY have developed a considerable body of jurisprudence on serious mental harm as a constituent element of the crime of genocide. In *Rutaganda*, Trial Chamber I stated that,

> "[f]or the purposes of interpreting Article 2(2)(b) of the Statute, the Chamber understands the words 'serious bodily or mental harm' to include acts of bodily or mental torture, inhumane or degrading treatment, rape, sexual violence, and persecution. The Chamber is of the opinion that 'serious harm' need not entail permanent or irremediable harm."[376]

260. According to this jurisprudence, serious mental harm should be "more than minor or temporary impairment of mental faculties such as the infliction of strong fear or terror, intimidation **[page 75]** or threat."[377] In order to support a finding of serious mental harm as a constituent element of genocide, the mental harm inflicted on a member of one of the identified protected groups must be of such a serious nature as to threaten its destruction in whole or in part.[378]

261. Whether an act is considered to amount to serious mental harm must be assessed on a case-by-case basis.[379] The Chamber notes that even if it were to believe Witness CCJ's testimony, the Accused's words and conduct would not constitute a sufficient basis to find serious mental harm, in accordance with the established jurisprudence. The Chamber notes that, apart from Witness CCJ's assertion that he was frightened, no further evidence was led to prove that Witness CCJ suffered more than minor or temporary impairment of his mental faculties as a result of Rukundo's alleged conduct at the Bishopric.

262. The Chamber further notes that information on the immediate circumstances surrounding the alleged incident, although not a condition for a finding of serious mental harm, is valuable in determining whether an act is considered to amount to serious mental harm. In *Seromba*, the Appeals Chamber noted that "nearly all convictions for the causing of serious bodily or mental harm involve rapes or killings."[380] The Chamber

---

[375] See Rukundo (T. 9 October 2007, pp. 20, 25) and Defence Witness EVB (T. 20 July 2007, p. 24).
[376] *Rutaganda*, Judgement (TC), para. 50. See also *Brđanin*, Judgement (TC), para. 690.
[377] *Seromba*, Judgement (AC), para. 46, citing *Kajelijeli*, Judgement (TC), para. 815, referring to *Kayishema and Ruzindana*, Judgement (TC), para. 110; *Semanza*, Judgement (TC), para. 321.
[378] *Seromba*, Judgement (AC), para. 46.
[379] *Blagojević and Jokić*, Judgement (TC), para. 646; *Kamuhanda*, Judgement (TC), para. 634.
[380] *Seromba*, Judgement (AC), para. 46.

notes that no evidence was adduced by the Prosecution to suggest that the immediate context surrounding the incident in question involved any of the crimes alluded to above. In fact, the Prosecution's evidence does not refer to the immediate context surrounding Rukundo's conduct at the Bishopric. In the Chamber's view, such information could have clarified the danger that Rukundo's threatening words posed in the immediate context and indicated whether there was an immediate possibility of killing or infliction of suffering by torture or other degrading treatment.

263. For these reasons, the Chamber finds that the Prosecution has not proved beyond reasonable doubt that Rukundo inflicted serious mental harm on Witness CCJ as a result of his alleged threats to Witness CCJ at the Kabgayi Bishopric on 15 April 1994.

264. Witness BPA testified that he met Rukundo in Kabgayi around 11 or 12 April 1994 whilst he was waiting to see the Bishop. Witness BPA saw Emmanuel Rukundo striding down the corridor of the Bishopric frightening people and heard him say that "the time had come for them to kill the *Inyenzi*." Witness BPA attested that Rukundo's threats were not addressed to anyone in particular **[page 76]** and that Rukundo did not directly address Witness BPA or call his name when he made the alleged threats against Tutsi. Witness BPA testified that Rukundo was speaking to himself in the corridor. Witness BPA was alone in the corridor leading to the Bishop's office when he heard Rukundo make the threatening remarks. Witness BPA testified that he was afraid when he heard Rukundo make such remarks because people like himself who came from Uganda were considered comparable to Tutsi who were accomplices of the *Inyenzi*. Witness BPA stated that he was afraid, after seeing "Father Rukundo with a rifle" and that this was the first time he had seen a military chaplain.

265. The Chamber notes that the Accused's alleged threatening words heard by Witness BPA ("The time had come for [us] to kill the *Inyenzi*") differ slightly from the phrasing in the Indictment. The Chamber, however, finds that alleged statement, as recalled by the witness, conveys the same meaning as the wording in the Indictment – "the threatening of Tutsi priests" – and that there is therefore no material difference between Witness BPA's evidence and the Indictment.

266. The Chamber notes that Witness BPA testified that he had seen Rukundo quite frequently before the war. The witness also stated that he saw Rukundo dressed in military uniform in Kabgayi after the war had broken out. According to Witness BPA, after Rukundo's appointment as military chaplain, he met Witness BPA and said that "he had to fight against the *Inyenzi*."[381] The Chamber is therefore not satisfied that Witness BPA's meeting with Rukundo at the Kabgayi Bishopric was the first occasion that the witness saw him, after his appointment as a military chaplain. Consequently, the Chamber is not convinced by Witness BPA's claim that that he was afraid after seeing "Father Rukundo with a rifle" and that this was the first time that he had seen a military chaplain.

267. The Chamber notes that throughout the examination-in-chief, Witness BPA provided what appeared to be a firsthand account of Rukundo's alleged extremist activities at the Nyakibanda Major Seminary.[382] The Chamber, however, notes that, during cross-examination, Witness BPA denied being a student at the Nyakibanda Major Seminary and explained that his information about Rukundo's anti-Tutsi behaviour at the Nyakibanda Major Seminary had been conveyed to him by seminarians from the Seminary during the Christmas holidays in 1990.[383] The Chamber also notes that Witness BPA gave the impression, in examination-in-chief, that he had studied at the Nyakibanda Major Seminary with the Accused and had therefore witnessed Rukundo's alleged extremism. **[page 77]**

268. Furthermore, Witness BPA's demeanour did not inspire confidence in his credibility. For instance, the Chamber notes that Witness BPA was evasive when asked to state his ethnic background and to indicate whether his parents fled from Rwanda to Uganda in 1959. Witness BPA explained that he could not answer such questions because his parents had passed away before the outbreak of the war and he was not acquainted with the history of ethnic problems in Rwanda. The Chamber notes that Witness BPA is an educated man who should have had no difficulties answering questions about his background and family. The Chamber

---

[381] T. 7 March 2007, pp. 6, 35-36.
[382] T. 7 March 2007, pp. 4-7.
[383] T. 7 March 2007, pp. 10-12.

Judgement

finds Witness BPA's explanation of his inability to answer such questions to be implausible. For the foregoing reasons, the Chamber does not find Witness BPA to be credible.

269. The Chamber finds that, even if it were to believe Witness BPA's testimony, it is not satisfied that Rukundo's threatening words are sufficient to support a finding of serious mental harm. The Chamber notes that Witness BPA admitted in the course of his testimony that Rukundo did not address him directly or did not refer to his name when he stated that the time had come for them to kill the *Inyenzi*. Witness BPA further admitted that Rukundo did not personally threaten him and appeared to be speaking only to himself as he uttered his threats. In fact, the Chamber notes that, according to Witness BPA's testimony, Rukundo was not even aware that Witness BPA was physically close to him or that he was within earshot when Rukundo uttered such remarks. The Chamber further notes that, apart from Witness BPA's statement that he feared for his life as a result of hearing Rukundo's remarks at the Bishopric, the Prosecution did not adduce further evidence to prove that Witness BPA suffered more than a minor or temporary damage as a result of Rukundo's alleged threats. Furthermore, the Chamber notes that Witness BPA's evidence does not refer to the immediate circumstances surrounding Rukundo's conduct at the Bishopric. As mentioned above, the Chamber notes that such information could have been valuable in determining the likely impact of Rukundo's remarks on Witness BPA's mental state. For the foregoing reasons, the Chamber finds that it has not been established that Witness BPA suffered serious mental harm as a result of Rukundo's alleged conduct at the Bishopric.

270. Witness CCN testified that he saw Rukundo in the compound of the Bishopric on 12 or 13 April 1994. The witness stated that he greeted Rukundo, but that Rukundo did not return his greeting. Rather, Rukundo intimidated him, with the following threat: "You will see, you will see, you will get it from us."[384] Witness CCN stated that, on the basis of his past experience with Rukundo, these threatening words frightened him, and he left the Bishophric. **[page 78]**

271. The Defence submits that the threatening words that Prosecution Witness CCN attributed to Rukundo differ from the phrasing in the Indictment. The Defence argues that, according to Witness CCN, Rukundo did not use the words "*Inkotanyi*" or "Tutsi." According to Witness CCN, Rukundo said only, "You will see, you will see, you will get it from us."[385] The Defence argues that the difference between Witness CCN's evidence and the Indictment in respect of what the Accused is alleged to have said could constitute an additional allegation against the Accused. The Defence therefore requests the Chamber to exclude Witness CCN's evidence.[386]

272. The Chamber is not persuaded that there is a significant difference between Witness CCN's evidence and the phrasing in the Indictment, such that the witness's evidence could be deemed to constitute an additional allegation. According to Witness CCN, the Accused did not expressly refer to "*Inkontanyi*" or "Tutsi" when addressing him at the Bishopric. The Chamber, however, notes that Rukundo addressed his words to Witness CNN, who is a Tutsi priest. The Chamber further notes that the words that Rukundo is alleged to have spoken were of a threatening nature. The Chamber finds that the Accused's conduct corresponds with the conduct pleaded in the Indictment: that he threatened Tutsi at the Bishopric. Therefore the Chamber finds that Witness CCN's evidence does not fall outside the scope of the Indictment.

273. The Chamber finds Witness CCN to be credible and believes the evidence which he presented. The Chamber therefore finds that it has been established that, on 12 or 13 April 1994, Rukundo spoke the words "You will see, you will see, you will get it from us."[387] The Chamber further finds that the fact that Defence Witnesses EVA, EVB and EVD never heard or were informed that Rukundo issued anti-Tutsi statements does not cast a reasonable doubt upon this finding.

274. The Chamber, however, finds that the Prosecution has not established that Witness CCN suffered serious mental harm as a result of Rukundo's words. The Chamber notes that, apart from Witness CCN's claim that he feared for his life as a result of Rukundo's threats against him at the Bishopric, the Prosecution did not adduce further evidence to prove that Witness CCN suffered more than minor or temporary damage

---

[384] T. 23 February 2007, p. 15; see also T. 23 February 2007, p. 16 (French) "Vous allez voir…Vous allez nous voir".
[385] T. 23 February 2007, p. 15; see also T. 23 February 2007, p. 16 (French) "Vous allez voir…Vous allez nous voir".
[386] Defence Closing briefs, paras. 572, 577, 578.
[387] T. 23 February 2007, p. 15; see also T. 23 February 2007, p.16 (French) "Vous allez voir…Vous allez nous voir".

as a result of Rukundo's threats. Furthermore, like the evidence of Witnesses CCJ and BPA, Witness CCN's testimony does not refer to the immediate circumstances surrounding Rukundo's conduct at the Bishopric. Given the lack of evidence about Witness CCN's mental state after the incident and about the immediate circumstances surrounding **[page 79]** the incident, the Chamber does not find that Witness CCN suffered serious mental harm as a result of Rukundo's conduct at the Bishopric.

275. Accordingly, the Chamber finds that the Prosecution has not proved beyond reasonable doubt that Rukundo's alleged conduct, as set out in paragraphs 10(v) and 25(v) of the Indictment, caused serious mental harm to the Tutsi who sought refuge at the Bishopric in April 1994. **[page 80]**

7. EVENTS RELATING TO THE ST. LÉON MINOR SEMINARY

(a) Indictment

276. Paragraphs 12 to 14 of the Indictment state as follows:

12. During the months of April and May 1994, **Emmanuel RUKUNDO** visited the Saint Léon Minor Seminary, and identified Tutsi refugees, who were then taken away by soldiers and killed, and on one such occasion he had a list of names of Tutsi refugees to be killed, which list was used by soldiers and *Interahamwe* who had accompanied him, to remove and kill the victims. By so doing, **Emmanuel RUKUNDO** ordered, instigated, or aided and abetted the killing of Tutsis at this location.

13. On diverse dates during the months of April and May 1994, immediately following **Emmanuel RUKUNDO's** departure on several occasions from the Saint Léon Minor Seminary, soldiers and *Interahamwe* militiamen, as ordered, instigated, or aided and abetted by him, beat, kicked and whipped Tutsi refugees who had not been taken away to be killed. By subjecting these Tutsi refugees to such brutality, **Emmanuel RUKUNDO** ordered, instigated, or aided and abetted the causing of serious bodily and mental harm to these victims.

14. On one occasion on or about 15 May 1994, at the Saint Léon Minor Seminary, **Emmanuel RUKUNDO**, armed and escorted by an armed soldier, took a young Tutsi refugee woman into his room, locked the door, and sexually assaulted her. These acts of **Emmanuel RUKUNDO** caused her serious mental harm.

(b) Evidence

Prosecution Witness CSF

277. Prosecution Witness CSF testified that on 7 April 1994, following the death of President Habyarimana, conflict broke out between members of the population. Witness CSF testified that patrols commenced and roadblocks were mounted in his neighbourhood. It was said that the "enemy" was being chased away. On 11 April 1994, Witness CSF left on his own to seek refuge at the St. Léon Minor Seminary. He stayed there until 2 June 1994 when he and other refugees were set free by the *Inkotanyi*. Witness CSF testified that he was one of the first refugees to arrive at the St. Léon Minor Seminary. Witness CSF noted that a number of refugees had come from the regions bordering Gitarama *préfecture*. The number of refugees increased, because people believed that their security would be guaranteed at the St. Léon Minor Seminary. Witness CSF added that the mothers who had babies and the elderly sought refuge inside the Seminary building whilst the others remained outside.[388] **[page 81]**

278. Witness CSF told the Chamber that he did not know Rukundo before he saw him at the St. Léon Minor Seminary in 1994. Whilst at the St. Léon Minor Seminary, he learnt that some of the refugees knew Rukundo and had attended his ordination in 1991. According to Witness CSF, these refugees were surprised to see Rukundo at the St. Léon Minor Seminary in military uniform given that he was a priest. Witness CSF and some of the refugees wondered whether Rukundo was still a priest or whether he had become a soldier. When Witness CSF saw Rukundo at the St. Léon Minor Seminary on 20 or 21 April 1994, he was approximately 40 metres away from the Accused. Rukundo was wearing a military shirt and camouflage trousers, was

---

[388] T. 13 February 2007, pp. 2-3, 7, 9, 11.

carrying a pistol and held a piece of paper in his hand. Rukundo and the soldiers parked their cars outside the gate of the St. Léon Minor Seminary and walked into the premises.[389]

279. On 20 or 21 April 1994, whilst Witness CSF was in the courtyard of the St. Léon Minor Seminary, he saw Rukundo enter the premises accompanied by about six armed soldiers and *Interahamwe* militia. Witness CSF testified that from the time he arrived until the time he left, the refugees were in the courtyard of the St. Léon Minor Seminary. Witness CSF testified that it was difficult to distinguish between the *Interahamwe* and the soldiers because the *Interahamwe* were trained by the soldiers who passed on their old uniforms to the *Interahamwe*. The only difference between the soldiers and the *Interahamwe* were their shoes. On his first visit to the St. Léon Minor Seminary, Rukundo walked around the premises talking to soldiers and *Interahamwe*, but did not enter any of the buildings. Rukundo spoke to a number of refugees, then handed a piece of paper to one of the soldiers accompanying him and walked out of the premises.[390] Witness CSF estimated that Rukundo spent about 30 or 35 minutes at the St. Léon Minor Seminary. After Rukundo's departure, the soldiers read out the names on the list and a refugee, who was close to the soldier reading out the names, showed the soldier where the refugees were located. Witness CSF could not see what was written on the piece of paper but deduced that the names called out were the names that appeared on the list.[391] Witness CSF testified that those to whom Rukundo had given the piece of paper then started looking for the people whose names appeared on the list. Witness CSF attested to seeing this incident from inside the courtyard of the Seminary at a distance of about 40 metres from the Accused. Witness CSF explained that the refugees who were being taken out thought that they were being taken to a more secure place so they willingly identified themselves to the soldiers.[392] According to Witness CSF, the refugees did not know that they were going to be killed. Witness CSF testified that he walked 40 metres outside of the St. Léon Minor Seminary towards the **[page 82]** Kabgayi Cathedral and that the vehicle was parked less than 20 metres from the gate of the St. Léon Minor Seminary. He witnessed the refugees being taken out of the St. Léon Minor Seminary and loaded into a blue Toyota Stout pick-up truck, with a civilian licence plate, which was parked about 20 meters outside the entrance of the St. Léon Minor Seminary, near the tarmac road.[393] He also saw the pick-up truck depart towards the direction of Gitarama.[394] The refugees who were taken away on that day never returned to the St. Léon Minor Seminary.[395] Witness CSF added that he never saw Rukundo at the St. Léon Minor Seminary during the night and that the refugees were always abducted in broad daylight.[396]

280. Witness CSF saw Rukundo for the second time at the St. Léon Minor Seminary about four days after his first visit around 2.00 or 2.30 p.m. Rukundo was again accompanied by soldiers and *Interahamwe*. According to Witness CSF, Rukundo walked around the St. Léon Minor Seminary, gave a piece of paper to a soldier who was behind him and walked out of the premises. The soldier who had been given the list called out the names of the refugees. Many of the refugees who were called, refused to come out because they realised that they could be taken away and killed. The names of the refugees who did not voluntarily come out were read out again until they were found. Some of the refugees protested but they were taken away, forcibly loaded onto the vehicles and never returned to the St. Léon Minor Seminary. During cross-examination, Witness CSF stated he could not remember any of the names of the refugees who were taken away during Rukundo's second visit.[397]

281. Four days after the second visit, Rukundo returned for a third time to the St. Léon Minor Seminary accompanied by soldiers and *Interahamwe*. Rukundo walked around the premises accompanied by soldiers and *Interahamwe*. Rukundo gave a list to a soldier standing behind him and then left the premises. The soldier read out the refugees' names and other soldiers looked for the people who they had to take away. Witness CSF testified that there were names of people on the list who had not been found on the second visit.

---

[389] T. 13 February 2007, pp. 3-4, 16-18, 24.
[390] T. 13 February 2007, pp. 3, 7, 17, 19-24.
[391] T. 13 February 2007, pp. 23-26.
[392] T. 13 February 2007, pp. 4, 23.
[393] T. 13 February 2007, pp. 4, 11, 16-17, 26-27.
[394] T. 13 February 2007, p. 26.
[395] T. 13 February 2007, p. 4.
[396] T. 13 February 2007, p. 43.
[397] T. 13 February 2007, pp. 4-5, 27, 31.

The refugees whose names had been read out were subsequently loaded into vehicles parked nearby.[398] Witness CSF testified that the difference **[page 83]** between Rukundo's first, second and third visits to the St. Léon Minor Seminary was the number of people whose names were called out from the list.[399]

282. In mid-May 1994, Rukundo visited the St. Léon Minor Seminary for the fourth time, a few days before Kabgayi fell. He was again accompanied by *Interahamwe* and soldiers. According to Witness CSF, Rukundo's fourth visit was the worst. He explained that the government had moved towards Gitarama and the fighting continued. The *Interahamwe* and Rukundo had to do what they could to take away as many people as possible. Witness CSF explained that there were also soldiers who were not with Rukundo who were working on their own to take people out of the St. Léon Minor Seminary. On this occasion, Rukundo arrived with a very long list of names of refugees to be taken away. Rukundo gave the list to the soldiers who then took away people and loaded them onto buses. A large number of refugees were taken away on that day. During all of the visits, the soldiers specifically targeted intellectuals such as teachers, lecturers and magistrates. When the fourth abduction occurred, only a few boys, girls, and the elderly were left behind. Witness CSF recalled that a judge whose name he did not remember, and who worked at Nyambuye, was amongst the refugees being sought and that the *Interahmawe* said that they would not leave if they could not find him. When the *Interahamwe* found the judge, Witness CSF saw him being taken away. Soldiers also came and took away people and when the buses were full, they left the St. Léon Minor Seminary and then returned. Witness CSF testified that he did not know where the refuges were taken but he stated that they were killed by the *Interahamwe* and soldiers and none of them returned. According to Witness CSF, the *Interahamwe* returned to the St. Léon Minor Seminary singing songs and boasting about having killed the refugees.[400]

283. Witness CSF stated that the refugees at the St. Léon Minor Seminary were from various ethnic groups and that he did not know the ethnicity of the people who were taken away. Witness CSF explained that a large number of the people who were hiding after the first abduction were Tutsi. Witness CSF also stated that the victims in Rwanda were victims of their ethnicity and their political opinions.[401]

284. According to Witness CSF, Rukundo appeared to be the leader of the soldiers and *Interahamwe* during the attacks against the refugees at the St. Léon Minor Seminary. Witness CSF explained that the soldiers and the *Interahamwe* only seemed to be implementing and executing orders issued by Rukundo. Witness CSF added that sometimes soldiers and *Interahamwe* would **[page 84]** come to the St. Léon Minor Seminary without Rukundo. They would take people away and kill them in a wooded area not far from Kabgayi. The soldiers also demanded money from the refugees. Those who did not have money were either beaten or taken away into the woods.[402]

285. At some point during his stay at the St. Léon Minor Seminary, Witness CSF saw officials visit the St. Léon Minor Seminary, including Jean Kambanda. Kambanda was accompanied by soldiers and Father Alfred Kayibanda as well as many *gendarmes*. Kambanda and his entourage visited the refugees at the St. Léon Minor Seminary, but did not assist them. Witness CSF did not remember the date of Kambanda's visit.[403] Witness CSF never encountered any refugees from Nyacyonga.[404] Witness CSF also testified that they never saw anyone guarding the gate of the St. Léon Minor Seminary.[405]

Prosecution Witness CSG

286. Witness CSG lived in Gitarama in April 1994. She did not know Rukundo before 1994. After the attacks against Tutsi people began in her area, she sought refuge at the St. Léon Minor Seminary. She does not recall the date of her arrival at the St. Léon Minor Seminary because she was ill from beatings that she had received from two people at a roadblock in Rugano on her way to Kabgayi. According to Witness CSG,

---

[398] T. 13 February 2007, p. 5.
[399] T. 13 February 2007, pp. 25, 27.
[400] T. 13 February 2007 pp. 4-7, 29-31.
[401] T. 13 February 2007, pp. 7-8.
[402] T. 13 February 2007, pp. 7-8, 16.
[403] T. 13 February 2007, pp. 12, 30-31.
[404] T. 13 February 2007, p. 11.
[405] T. 13 February 2007, p. 43.

many Tutsi were being killed at roadblocks during that time. She later clarified that she arrived in Kabgayi two days after 20 April 1994. Witness CSG did not leave the premises of the St. Léon Minor Seminary until 6 June 1994, when the RPF took over Kabgayi and rescued the refugees. She had not been to the St. Léon Minor Seminary prior to seeking refuge there and has not returned since 6 June 1994.[406]

287. Witness CSG testified that she and others sought refuge at the St. Léon Minor Seminary because they thought they might be able survive there. However there was no food and attackers arrived in order to kill people. Witness CSG testified that Rukundo led the attack by the *Interahamwe* against Tutsi refugees at the St. Léon Minor Seminary.[407] She said that Rukundo came to the St. Léon Minor Seminary on "numerous occasions", sometimes twice a day.[408] On the first day that Witness CSG saw Rukundo at the St. Léon Minor Seminary, she was about six meters **[page 85]** away from the Accused.[409] Rukundo wore a military uniform comprising of a khaki shirt and camouflaged trousers with pockets on both sides. He carried a small gun attached to his belt. He was also escorted by a soldier who carried a sub-machine gun over his shoulder.[410]

288. Witness CSG testified that she came to know about Rukundo because each time the Accused came to the St. Léon Minor Seminary, the refugees would scream and say "You have to flee because Emmanuel Rukundo [is] coming." The first time that Witness CSG saw Rukundo she asked the refugees why they called him "Father Rukundo" because as far as she could see, he was a soldier. According to Witness CSG, the refugees fled whenever they heard Rukundo's name mentioned or saw him because they knew that the attackers would abduct and kill them. When Rukundo came to the St. Léon Minor Seminary, he carried a list of names and was followed by a lot of attackers.[411] Rukundo used the list to identify some Tutsi refugees. Witness CSG estimated that there were at least six metres between herself and Rukundo when she saw him on one occasion with a list. Witness CSG testified that Rukundo would walk amongst the refugees and consult his list before getting close to them, whilst the refugees tried to avoid him. Witness CSG explained that the refugees tried to avoid Rukundo but could not go that far and it was always possible for him to catch up with them. Each time Rukundo got close to one of the refugees and spoke to them, that refugee was abducted three to five minutes later on the same day. Rukundo would then walk back to the entrance of the St. Léon Minor Seminary with his escort and pass the *Interahamwe* at the entrance. The *Interahamwe* would then enter the St. Léon Minor Seminary with the same list to abduct those who appeared to be in good health or young. When there were a lot of refugees, the *Interahamwe* would guard the entrance to the St. Léon Minor Seminary to ensure that anyone who tried to leave would be intercepted and killed.[412]

289. Witness CSG testified that she thought that the *Interahamwe* were acting in collusion with Rukundo.[413] Witness CSG believed that the refugees who were identified by Rukundo were later taken away and killed by the *Interahamwe* because none of the refugees were ever seen again. When asked what time of day she saw someone who was pointed out to her as Rukundo, Witness CSG replied that it was impossible to distinguish between day and night.[414] Witness CSG added that some of the people who attacked the refugees at the St. Léon Minor Seminary wore military uniforms whilst others wore civilian clothes and were armed with machetes, clubs, and firearms. **[page 86]** Witness CSG stated that she saw soldiers at the entrance to the St. Léon Minor Seminary, but did not see any communal policemen. Witness CSF testified that the *Interahamwe* came to the St. Léon Minor Seminary aboard vehicles singing "We are coming. We are the *Interahamwe*".[415]

Prosecution Witness BLC

290. Witness BLC already gave evidence in relation to the allegations at St. Joseph's College.[416]

---

[406] T. 30 November 2006, pp. 3-4, 6-8, 13.
[407] T. 30 November 2006, pp. 4, 21.
[408] T. 30 November 2006, pp. 5, 21-22.
[409] T. 30 November 2006, p. 6.
[410] T. 30 November 2006, pp. 5, 13, 18-19, 24-25.
[411] T. 30 November 2006, pp. 6, 12-13, 18.
[412] T. 30 November 2006, pp. 4-6, 12-13, 18, 20-22, 24.
[413] T. 30 November 2006, pp. 6-7.
[414] T. 30 November 2006, p. 16.
[415] T. 30 November 2006, p. 21.
[416] See Section III.4.b.

291. In April and May 1994, Witness BLC was an 18 year old seminarian studying at the St. Léon Minor Seminary. After the death of President Habyarimana, Witness BLC and members of his extended family decided to flee their village. A Belgian parish priest called Jiji Michel advised Witness BLC not to seek refuge in the parish but to go to Kabgayi because he thought that they would be safer. On the way to Kabgayi, Witness BLC separated from his family because a priest who was a teacher at the St. Léon Minor Seminary gave him a lift on his motorbike to the St. Léon Minor Seminary. Two or three days after arriving at the St. Léon Minor Seminary, Witness BLC left to collect members of his immediate family and brought them to the premises. They arrived at the St. Léon Minor Seminary within the first week following the presidential plane crash and remained there until 2 June 1994.[417]

292. When Witness BLC first arrived at the entrance of the St. Léon Minor Seminary, he happened to meet Father Daniel Nahimana, a priest and lecturer at the Seminary. Witness BLC knew Father Nahimana because he was the godfather of one of Witness BLC's cousins. Witness BLC emotionally recounted to Nahimana how their houses had been destroyed and their cattle eaten. Nahimana told Witness BLC, "Well that is how it happens, so go and join the others, and I'm sorry about that". Witness BLC was shocked by Father Nahimana's response as it was not what he was expecting and was disillusioned by the way Father Nahimana had received him. Witness BLC observed that initially there were not many people at the St. Léon Minor Seminary, however the number of refugees soon increased. When he arrived at the St. Léon Minor Seminary, he saw that Tutsi refugees were already sheltering there. There was also a group of Hutu refugees from Byumba, who had fled the war between the Rwandan Army and the RPF forces. The latter were referred to as the refugees from Nyacyonga.[418] **[page 87]**

293. According to Witness BLC, the St. Léon Minor Seminary comprised of three sections: the classical seminary, the senior seminary, and the administrative buildings which were located at the entrance. The Nyacyonga refugees stayed in the "classical seminary", the women and children occupied "the senior seminary", and the men stayed in one or two classrooms. Towards the end of April 1994 this arrangement changed as the number of refugees increased. The St. Léon Minor Seminary no longer had enough space to provide living quarters for everyone and therefore many refugees had to settle where they could in the compound.[419]

294. In view of the security situation in Kabgayi, the refugees who were at the St. Léon Minor Seminary could not freely leave the premises. This was particularly true of Tutsi refugees who could not go out at all. Hutu refugees could only venture out of the St. Léon Minor Seminary if they were accompanied by policemen.[420]

295. Before 1994, Witness BLC had only heard of Rukundo but did not know him. He got to know Rukundo more closely whilst he was a refugee at the St. Léon Minor Seminary in 1994. According to Witness BLC, he frequently saw Rukundo at the St. Léon Minor Seminary during that time.[421]

296. Witness BLC testified that during these visits, Rukundo was dressed in military uniform which was a "deep khaki colour" with an insignia on the epaulette, carried weapons, and was normally escorted by two, three or four soldiers, apart from the one occasion when he arrived with between 10-15 soldiers, after coming from what Witness BLC presumed to be Rudahunga's house. As a young seminarian, Witness BLC was surprised to see Rukundo in military uniform at the St. Léon Minor Seminary. Witness BLC knew Rukundo as a priest who normally said mass while wearing his cassock. It was not until the end of the genocide that Witness BLC understood the nature of Rukundo's work as a military chaplain.[422]

297. According to Witness BLC, towards the end of April or the beginning of May 1994, Rukundo came to the St. Léon Minor Seminary with soldiers. Rukundo would either come with soldiers who took people away or he would come to see the priests, particularly Father Nahimana, and tell them about the military operations or he would come with soldiers, towards the end of May 1994, who would unload bottles of wine

---

[417] T. 4 December 2006, pp. 10-11, 19, 29.
[418] T. 4 December 2006, pp. 11-13; T. 7 December 2006, pp. 6-8.
[419] T. 4 December 2006, p. 14.
[420] T. 4 December 2006, p. 38.
[421] T. 4 December 2006, pp. 14-15.
[422] T. 4 December 2006, p. 15.

and take them to a store room. Witness BLC testified that Rukundo came in a pick-up which he parked between the palm tree and the church building or a **[page 88]** white Mazda which he parked in front of the administrative buildings. Witness BLC overheard some of the conversations at the St. Léon Minor Seminary when Rukundo spoke to other priests about what was going on in the country.[423] When briefing the priests, Witness BLC heard Rukundo call out names of people who were deemed to be RPF sympathizers and say that "something had to be done about such people".[424] According to Witness BLC, Rukundo also said, loudly so all around him could hear, that he had entered Rudahunga's house, that they "killed the wife and the children" but that Louis Rudahunga – "the idiot" – got away.[425] During the time that Rukundo spoke to his fellow priests, the soldiers accompanying him would walk around the crowd of refugees identifying those to be taken away that night.[426] Witness BLC spent a lot of time around the administrative building, which was used for the day-to-day management of the St. Léon Minor Seminary where one could not see the classrooms, dorms or senior seminary.[427]

298. Witness BLC said that on the days Rukundo came to the St. Léon Minor Seminary, people were abducted the same night. Witness BLC testified that the people who came in the day to identify the refugees were the same people who returned at night to abduct the refugees. Witness BLC testified that whenever the refugees saw Rukundo visit during the day they started to prepare themselves because they knew that at night people would be taken away and killed.[428] He stated that he heard the screams and crying sounds of the refugees as they were being abducted at night. Witness BLC explained that there were very few days when people were killed in the St. Léon Minor Seminary. The refugees were normally identified during the day and at night they were taken away to be killed outside the St. Léon Minor Seminary. There was one teacher who was tortured at his house in the courtyard of the St. Léon Minor Seminary, although he was taken outside the premises in order to be killed.[429]

299. Witness BLC gave two examples of abductions at the St. Léon Minor Seminary. The first one was the abduction at night of the occupants of the two rooms who were the parents of the seminarians. Witness BLC testified that people came and took all the refugees from one room in order to kill them and only one person survived, Witness BLC's father. The people were placed in **[page 89]** single file and then taken outside of the St. Léon Minor Seminary. Witness BLC's father, however, left the group and went and sat down in a ravine.[430] Witness BLC's father returned the same night and woke up Witness BLC. Witness BLC testified that during that night they heard screams for at least three hours. One of the communal policemen explained to Witness BLC's father that the parents of the seminarians were killed by knives which they used to stab them from one end of the rib to another.[431] Witness BLC testified that generally, when refugees were abducted, they were killed outside of the premises and Witness BLC only noticed their disappearance the following day.[432]

300. The second example was when Witness BLC recalled that soldiers had come to look for Merci, the lecturer, who was in a room with the other lecturers which was locked. The soldiers said to Witness BLC and others who were opposite that room, that if they did not open the locked door, they would break down all of the walls. Witness BLC testified that it was Sylver, a Seminarian who went to get the keys to open the door to the room where Merci was hiding.[433] According to Witness BLC, although Merci actually died outside the Minor Seminary, they started torturing him inside the St. Léon Minor Seminary.[434] Witness BLC testified that Merci died because he was on a list of people who contributed money to the RPF. He explained that there

---

[423] T. 4 December 2006, pp. 16-18, 20-21; T. 7 December 2006, p. 19.
[424] T. 4 December 2006, p. 21: "So he would give a briefing and he would say 'Such-and-such a person is helping the RPF, RPF infiltrators, I've seen that person's family members so we have to do something.' That's what he would say. So, you know, always active."
[425] T. 4 December 2006, p. 21.
[426] T. 4 December 2006, pp. 18-19.
[427] T. 4 December 2006, pp. 13-14, 34; T. 7 December 2006, pp. 18, 33; T. 8 December 2006, pp. 17-18.
[428] T. 4 December 2006, pp. 16-19: "And we reached a point when our parents, who were teachers who were known in the province, who were school inspectors, who were Tutsis that could have been identified, came to say, 'Well, he has come'."
[429] T. 4 December 2006, p. 19.
[430] T. 4 December 2006, pp. 18-20.
[431] T. 8 December 2006, p. 20.
[432] T. 4 December 2006, pp. 19-20; T. 7 December 2006, p. 15.
[433] T. 7 December 2006, p. 14.
[434] T. 4 December 2006, p. 19; T. 8 December 2006, p. 16.

Prosecutor v. Rukundo

was a campaign against these people to denounce and kill them. Witness BLC explained that he never saw Rukundo holding a list and he believed that although the people on the list were not killed by Rukundo, they were killed by soldiers whose actions were instigated by Rukundo.[435]

301. On the occasions that Witness BLC saw Rukundo at the St. Léon Minor Seminary, he formed the impression that Rukundo was a very determined soldier at war, rather than a priest. Rukundo would brief his colleagues and say "Such and such a person is helping the RPF infiltrators, I've seen that person's family members so we have to do something." Witness BLC testified that he heard screaming, crying and sounds of fighting at the time of the abductions.[436]

302. Witness BLC further testified that around mid-May 1994, there was a water shortage at the St. Léon Minor Seminary. He stated that Tutsi refugees could not go out of the St. Léon Minor Seminary to fetch water because they were afraid of being attacked. As a result, only the Hutu refugees went out to collect water to be used by all of the refugees at the St. Léon Minor Seminary. **[page 90]** Witness BLC testified that one day during mass, Father Daniel Nahimana preached about the Hutu of Burundi, who had been enslaved by the Tutsi for a number of years and how the process in Rwanda was to stop the advent of the Tutsi once again. Witness BLC referred to Nahimana as Rukundo's "special friend" because of how they behaved together and because, compared to the other priests, Rukundo would spend long periods of time at Nahimana's house.[437] Father Daniel Nahimana referred to the incident of fetching water by saying that, "Even at this time that we are engaged in this fight … you are serving them by going to fetch water for them to cook." The Hutu refugees from the Nyacyonga camp started hesitating and saying, "Well, we do not want to go and fetch water anymore." That evening, Rukundo and Father Daniel Nahimana went around the camp telling the Hutu refugees not to go and fetch water. The Hutu refugees refused to fetch the water and Rukundo later told them that those Tutsi who were not going to fetch water, "instead of […] being killed by machete they want to stay here, and you are going to die with them". Witness BLC added that in his view, by giving those instructions to the Hutu, Rukundo and Nahimana intended to force the Tutsi refugees to venture out of the Minor Seminary so that they could be attacked and killed.[438]

303. When Witness BLC arrived at the St. Léon Minor Seminary, he noticed that there were two communal policemen from Rutungo guarding the entrance. He explained that Tutsi could enter the St. Léon Minor Seminary but they could not go out. Hutu could leave, for example to fetch water, but they were given a coupon which allowed people to identify them and were normally accompanied by policemen.[439]

304. Witness BLC testified that around 29 May 1994, when Kambanda visited the St. Léon Minor Seminary, people were brought in on buses. Witness BLC explained that there were between five and six buses, one of which was blue as well as other vehicles. Only two or three people who were in Kambanda's buses survived due to some white journalists who Witness BLC informed "Look, they are taking people away to kill them." When the journalists started taking photographs two or three people were released. The rest of the buses left with most of the people on board.[440] **[page 91]**

Prosecution Witness CCH

305. The Chamber has previously considered Witness CCH's evidence in relation to the incident at St. Joseph's College.[441]

306. Witness CCH stayed at the St. Léon Minor Seminary between mid-May 1994 and 3 June 1994. Witness CCH's brothers and her mother were also with her at the St. Léon Minor Seminary. Sometime in the month of May 1994, one of Witness CCH's brothers was taken away in a vehicle and never returned. Witness

---

[435] T. 4 December 2006, p. 27.
[436] T. 4 December 2006, pp. 20-21; T. 8 December 2006, p. 19.
[437] T. 4 December 2006, p. 17.
[438] T. 4 December 2006, pp. 25-26; T. 7 December 2006, pp. 42-43; T. 8 December 2006, p. 16.
[439] T. 4 December 2006, p. 38.
[440] T. 4 December 2006, pp. 19-20; T. 7 December 2006, pp. 22-24.
[441] See Section III.4.c.

CCH did not know where he was killed. There were many other refugees at the St. Léon Minor Seminary when Witness CCH arrived.[442]

307. Witness CCH testified that there were both Tutsi and Hutu refugees at the St. Léon Minor Seminary. The Hutu refugees came from Nyacyonga after fleeing the fighting between Rwandan government troops and the *Inkotanyis*. Refugees from the two ethnic groups lived in separate parts of the St. Léon Minor Seminary. Witness CCH testified that she was amongst a group of Tutsi where the men and young people were in one room and the females and children were in another room. The refugees from Nyacyonga were stationed behind the classrooms. Witness CCH did not dare to go too close to the classrooms where the refugees from Nyacyonga were based. Witness CCH testified that sometimes the refugees from Nyacyonga set up roadblocks in front of the toilets so that the Tutsi could not go and relieve themselves. The refugees from Nyacyonga moved about during the night and sold firewood whilst the Tutsi refugees locked themselves in their rooms when it started to get dark around 4.00 p.m. Due to security reasons, only refugees with identity cards indicating that they were Hutu or people whose physical features did not resemble Tutsi, could leave the St. Léon Minor Seminary. Witness CCH testified that she did not leave the St. Léon Minor Seminary and stayed in the room that she occupied. It did not even occur to Witness CCH to approach the gate of the St. Léon Minor Seminary because it was guarded by people from Nyacyonga and Witness CCH was afraid that they could kill her.[443]

308. When Witness CCH arrived at the St. Léon Minor Seminary she did not see any policemen. Witness CCH, however, testified that there were people wearing communal police uniforms who came to the St. Léon Minor Seminary and took people away to be killed. Witness CCH recalled one **[page 92]** incident when the policemen came to take someone away from Taba. Apart from these policemen, Witness CCH did not see any *préfecture* authorities.[444]

309. Witness CCH saw Rukundo at the St. Léon Minor Seminary one week after she had arrived. The Accused arrived in a small white vehicle which he parked in the car park at the entrance to the classrooms. Rukundo was dressed in a green military uniform and carried a rifle. He was accompanied by a young soldier who was also carrying a weapon. Witness CCH was surprised to see Rukundo in military uniform because she knew that he was a priest. Witness CCH understood that Rukundo was hunting down the *Inkotanyi* because "he said that we had to die."[445]

Prosecution Witness CCG

310. Prosecution Witness CCG arrived as a refugee at the St. Léon Minor Seminary on 25 or 26 May 1994 where he joined his wife and children who were already there. After about one week, Witness CCG left the St. Léon Minor Seminary on 2 June 1994 once the area had fallen to the *Inkotanyis*. When Witness CCG arrived, he told the policeman who was on the gate that he wanted to see the Rector, whom he already knew. When the Rector arrived, he greeted Witness CCG and welcomed him to join the other refugees. Witness CCG clarified that he entered through the entrance close to the banana plantation as opposed to the main entrance of the St. Léon Minor Seminary. Witness CCG testified that the policemen who had come with the "war displaced" refugees from Nyacyonga were from Kigali. Witness CCG stated that there were two policemen at the entrance to the St. Léon Minor Seminary and that all of the policemen were wearing communal police uniforms. Witness CCG commented that when he arrived, there were many refugees, some of whom he knew.[446]

311. A few days after his arrival, Witness CCG was told by a family member that Rukundo said that another family member was an *Inyenzi* and that his name was on a list of people who had made contributions

---

[442] T. 13 February 2007, pp. 56, 62.
[443] T. 13 February 2007, pp. 64, 66-67.
[444] T. 13 February 2007, pp. 65-66.
[445] T. 13 February 2007, pp. 56, 64; T. 14 February 2007, pp. 6-7, 9. The rest of Witness CCH's evidence relates to the allegation of sexual assault, Section III.7.c.iv.
[446] T. 15 February 2007, pp. 19-20, 22, 31-32.

to the *Inkotanyi*. When Witness CCG heard this information he was frightened and tried to hide. At the end of May, early June 1994 Witness CCG discovered that this family member had been killed.[447] **[page 93]**

312. Witness CCG testified that there were many buildings in the St. Léon Minor Seminary and that whilst he was there, no one spent the night outside. Witness CCH heard that a teacher named Deogratias Merci, who had been at the St. Léon Minor Seminary, had been killed.[448]

313. Witness CCG knew Rukundo from the Major Seminary when the Accused studied alongside Witness CCG's brother. Rukundo and Witness CCG's brother were ordained on the same day. Witness CCG worked as a tailor and Rukundo was his customer. Witness CCG testified that he would greet Rukundo when they met and that their relationship could be described as a "good relationship".[449]

The Accused

314. Emmanuel Rukundo testified that he went to the St. Léon Minor Seminary on 15 April, 21 April and 21 May 1994 to visit his friends and colleagues with whom he had previously studied.[450] On his first visit (15 April 1994), Rukundo arrived at the St. Léon Minor Seminary in a white pick-up truck that was loaned to him by the Rwasa nuns around 2.00 p.m. He drove into the compound and parked his vehicle in front of the administrative buildings.[451] Upon his arrival, Rukundo greeted the priests coming out of the refectory and shared a drink with them in the refectory.[452] In his conversation with the other priests, Rukundo discussed the situation in the country and the purpose of his visit in Kabgayi on that day which was to evacuate the family of Jean-Marie Vianney.[453]

315. Emmanuel Rukundo told the Chamber that he was accompanied by three soldiers when he visited the St. Léon Minor Seminary on 15 April 1994. One of them was his regular escort, Jean-Paul Nshimiye. The other two were assigned to him by the commander of Mukamira military camp, in Ruhengeri. Rukundo stated that the three soldiers stayed near the vehicle throughout his visit. Rukundo spent about 30 to 40 minutes at the St. Léon Minor Seminary on this occasion and left together with all three soldiers in the same vehicle in which they arrived.[454]

316. On 21 April 1994, Rukundo arrived at the St. Léon Minor Seminary at approximately 2.00 p.m. He said that two policemen, who were guarding the entrance of the St. Léon Minor Seminary, opened the gate for him. Rukundo drank some beer with his colleagues and discussed the **[page 94]** prevailing situation in the country, information about some colleagues, and what he had done to save some nuns. Rukundo confirmed that on this occasion he was accompanied by three soldiers – two of whom were assigned to him by the *secteur* commander and his usual escort. During this time, the three soldiers remained close to the vehicle waiting for Rukundo. The soldiers left together with Rukundo in the same vehicle.[455]

317. Rukundo's third visit to the St. Léon Minor Seminary took place on 21 May 1994. Rukundo testified that this time he drove his usual vehicle, a Mazda 323, which had been given to him by the Bishop's Conference when he became a military chaplain. The purpose of this visit was to leave some of his personal belongings at the St. Léon Minor Seminary. Rukundo arrived in Kabgayi at about 12.00 p.m., accompanied by his usual escort, Jean-Paul. When he arrived at the St. Léon Minor Seminary, two policemen, who were at the entrance, opened the gate for Rukundo. Rukundo dropped off his personal belongings at the St. Léon Minor Seminary, had lunch with his colleagues, and thereafter proceeded to the Major Seminary to greet his colleagues, the nuns that he had helped on 21 April 1994 and the Bishop. According to Rukundo, the small room in which he stored his belongings was located next to the priests' kitchen and was locked. The bursar kept the keys to the room and unlocked and locked it again for Rukundo.[456]

---

[447] T. 15 February 2007, pp. 21-22.
[448] T. 15 February 2007, p. 33.
[449] T. 15 February 2007, pp. 22-23, 28.
[450] T. 9 October 2007, pp. 36-37.
[451] T. 8 October 2007, p. 55; T. 9 October 2007, pp. 17, 37.
[452] T. 9 October 2007, pp. 37-38.
[453] T. 8 October 2007, pp. 53-54; T. 9 October 2007, p. 38.
[454] T. 9 October 2007, pp. 38-39.
[455] T. 9 October 2007, pp. 38-40, 43.
[456] T. 9 October 2007, pp. 13-14, 40-41, 43.

Judgement

318. Rukundo testified that all three of his visits to the St. Léon Minor Seminary took place around lunchtime and that he never visited the premises twice on the same day. On 15 April 1994, Rukundo noticed that there were many people in the students' quarters of the Minor Seminary. During his visit to the Minor Seminary on 21 May 1994, he noticed that the number of people in the students' quarters had increased, and that there were many people in the inner courtyard. Rukundo told the Chamber that on all his visits to the Minor Seminary, he parked his vehicle in front of the administrative buildings, met with the priests and then left. He never had the opportunity to go to the place where the refugees were located, although he could see them moving around in the courtyard.[457] Rukundo told the Chamber that he did not notice any stir or particular emotion amongst the refugees when he entered the St. Léon Minor Seminary. Rukundo denied that he ever carried a list of people during his visits to the St. Léon Minor Seminary or that he moved around the refugees with a piece of paper. He reiterated that the soldiers who accompanied him on all three of **[page 95]** his visits to the St. Léon Minor Seminary remained near the parked vehicle close to the administration building.[458]

319. Rukundo denied that he had a real friendship with Father Daniel Nahimana and testified that their relationship was one of a former teacher and student.[459] Rukundo further testified that he never went to the St. Léon Minor Seminary in the company of 10 to 15 soldiers at the end of May 1994.[460]

Defence Witness SLA

320. The Chamber has previously considered Witness SLA's evidence in relation to the incidents at St. Joseph's College.

321. Throughout April and May 1994, Witness SLA lived at the St. Léon Minor Seminary. Witness SLA's main responsibility was to provide assistance to about 3,000 refugees at the primary school in Kabgayi. Witness SLA usually visited the primary school twice a day between 9.00 a.m. to 12.00 p.m., and between 3.30 to 5.00 p.m.[461]

322. Witness SLA explained that about one week after 6 April 1994, Hutu and Tutsi refugees started flocking into Kabgayi from other areas. The first group of refugees to arrive at the St. Léon Minor Seminary on 11 April 1994 were 20 students from Kigali. More refugees arrived the following week, including a group of Hutu from Nyacyonga who were accompanied by the *sous-préfet* of Rutongo, Alexis Mugambaz. Witness SLA estimated that there were a little less than 3,500 refugees at the St. Léon Minor Seminary at the height of the crisis. Witness SLA testified that there was a large and almost equal number of both Tutsi and Hutu refugees. Witness SLA explained that they separated the men from the women and put the women in a complex towards the St. Joseph Bishopric, whilst the men stayed in a complex occupied by "classical seminarians". The refugees were provided with food once a day.[462]

323. According to Witness SLA, policemen from Rutungo *commune* who had come with *sous-préfet* Mugambaz guarded the entrance to the St. Léon Minor Seminary. At no point were the gates of the St. Léon Minor Seminary ever guarded by the *Interahamwe* and no one was ever killed at the gates. Tutsi refugees could not move around freely because the security situation outside the Seminary was considered too dangerous for them due to the presence of soldiers, *gendarmes* and **[page 96]** *Interahamwe*. Witness SLA testified that they experienced massive kidnappings from the St. Léon Minor Seminary at an intense rate during the last days of the month of May 1994. There were five or six days of daily kidnappings. Witness SLA added that *sous-préfet* Misago was responsible for abducting the largest number of refugees although *gendarmes* and soldiers also came and took people away. Witness SLA explained that there had been no kidnappings before the ones that took place at the end of May 1994. Witness SLA remembered that Deogratias Merci was amongst those killed around 25 May 1994. Witness SLA described how a teacher called Zacharie was also abducted together with a group of about 20 refugees by *sous-préfet* Misago and taken away in a blue

---

[457] T. 9 October 2007, pp. 41-42; T. 11 October 2007, pp. 16-17.
[458] T. 9 October 2007, pp. 42-43.
[459] T. 9 October 2007, p. 43.
[460] T. 9 October 2007, p. 45.
[461] T. 1 October 2007, pp. 43-45.
[462] T. 1 October 2007, pp. 14-17; see also French transcript for clarification of location: T. 1 October 2007, p. 20.

Toyota Hiace minibus.[463] Misago came to the Seminary with a list of people allegedly wanted for questioning by the state prosecutor. Witness SLA confirmed that none of the refugees who were abducted were killed inside the St. Léon Minor Seminary.[464]

324. Defence Witness SLA saw Rukundo at the St. Léon Minor Seminary on at least two occasions between April and May 1994. At that time, Witness SLA said that Rukundo wore a military uniform and drove a private vehicle that was white or beige in colour. Witness SLA never saw Rukundo driving a pick-up truck. Rukundo was accompanied by a soldier on both visits. Witness SLA never saw Rukundo at the St. Léon Minor Seminary with ten soldiers. The purpose of Rukundo's visits to the St. Léon Minor Seminary was to greet the seminarians and discuss the prevailing situation in the country. During Rukundo's first visit, he told Witness SLA that he had fired in the air in order to save some Tutsi who had sought refuge at Nyabikenke Parish from being attacked by a group of Hutu. On his second visit, Rukundo spoke about his new appointment and transfer from Ruhengeri to Kigali. During this visit, Rukundo ate lunch together with the seminarians at about 1.00 p.m. and did not speak to the refugees. He spent about one hour altogether at the St. Léon Minor Seminary.[465]

325. Witness SLA told the Chamber that he never saw Rukundo with a list or sheet of paper in his hand, nor did he see the refugees in a state of panic upon Rukundo's arrival at the St. Léon Minor Seminary. In addition, Witness SLA never heard that soldiers returned to the St. Léon Minor Seminary to attack or abduct refugees after Rukundo's visit.[466] Witness SLA maintained that he was **[page 97]** based at the St. Léon Minor Seminary in April and May 1994, and therefore, it was unlikely that Rukundo could have visited the Minor Seminary without him knowing or hearing about it.[467]

326. Defence Witness SLA confirmed that Rukundo was allocated a small room at the Minor Seminary for the purpose of keeping his personal belongings. Witness SLA explained that Rukundo did not have direct access to the keys for the room, which were kept by the bursar. On the two occasions on which Witness SLA saw Rukundo at the St. Léon Minor Seminary, the Accused did not go into the room.[468]

327. Witness SLA also confirmed that from the end of April until June 1994, there were water problems at the St. Léon Minor Seminary. Witness SLA recalled that they asked Hutu staying at the St. Léon Minor Seminary to go and fetch water because the Tutsi were not safe outside the confines of the Seminary. Witness SLA did not recall that Father Daniel Nahimana incited the Hutu not to go out and fetch water.[469] Witness SLA never heard any reports that Jean Kambanda had come to visit the St. Léon Minor Seminary.[470] Witness SLA remembered meeting Witness BLC when he was on his motorbike. He testified that he did not give Witness BLC a ride on the bike and said that it would have been absurd to separate the boy from his family by giving him a ride.[471]

Defence Witness SLD

328. Witness SLD had known Emmanuel Rukundo since 1990-91 when Rukundo attended the Kabgayi Major Seminary. Witness SLD heard that Rukundo had sought refuge at the Bishopric in Kabgayi in 1994.[472] Whilst Witness SLD was at the St. Léon Minor Seminary, he never heard Rukundo's name mentioned in connection with any of the crimes which took place there. Witness SLD further testified that he never saw Rukundo at the St. Léon Minor Seminary nor did he hear from anyone that Rukundo had come to the St. Léon Minor Seminary.[473]

---

[463] T. 1 October 2007, pp. 19-22; T. 1 October 2007, p. 26 (French) (The colour of the minibus is unintelligible in the English transcript, but is clearly identified as blue in the French transcript).
[464] T. 1 October 2007, pp. 21-22, 40.
[465] T. 1 October 2007, pp. 21-24, 52.
[466] T. 1 October 2007, pp. 24-25.
[467] T. 1 October 2007, p. 27.
[468] T. 1 October 2007, pp. 32, 53.
[469] T. 1 October 2007, pp. 18-19.
[470] T. 1 October 2007, p. 22.
[471] T. 1 October 2007, pp. 27-29.
[472] T. 16 October 2007, pp. 6-7, 34.
[473] T. 16 October 2007, pp. 7-9.

Judgement

329. Witness SLD, a Tutsi, arrived as a refugee at the St. Léon Minor Seminary in Kabgayi between 23 and 25 April 1994 and left around 23 May 1994.[474] Witness SLD testified that there were more than 300 refugees at the St. Léon Minor Seminary and the number of refugees increased each day until at one point there were more than 700 refugees. Witness SLD noted that at some **[page 98]** point, there was a water shortage at the St. Léon Minor Seminary and some refugees attempted to go out and look for water. However, they could not go beyond the entrance to the St. Léon Minor Seminary. In general, Wtness SLD noted that for security reasons, refugees at the St. Léon Minor Seminary were not allowed to go out of the premises because there were killers waiting outside for the refugees to come out so that they could arrest them.[475]

330. A group of people referred to as the "Zulus" and others from Kamazuru, called *Igishwauru*, along with a person called Sylvain, abducted refugees from the St. Léon Minor Seminary. Sylvain had a list of names, which he gave to the attackers. The refugees screamed and fled whenever they saw Sylvain coming or heard him speaking.[476] Sometime between 15 and 20 May 1994, an attack was launched against the refugees at the St. Léon Minor Seminary and some of them were abducted. Witness SLD heard that some of the refugees who were abducted managed to escape and return to the St. Léon Minor Seminary. As a result of this attack, Witness SLD went into hiding in the banana plantations for about three days because he was afraid.[477]

331. Witness SLD testified that he started hiding in the banana plantations just outside the St. Léon Minor Seminary with about 30 other refugees who felt threatened in the day during the first few days of May 1994. Witness SLD explained that he hid in the banana plantations for more than three weeks but at times he would come back to the St. Léon Minor Seminary. Between 15 and 20 May 1994, Witness SLD spent three days in the banana plantations. Witness SLD admitted that because he went into hiding, he was not aware of what was happening at the St. Léon Minor Seminary.[478] Witness SLD confirmed that he spent the majority of his time at the St. Léon Minor Seminary in the banana plantation behind the St. Léon Minor Seminary, or close to the dormitories, or the toilet. Witness SLD never went to the inner courtyard or to the entrance of the St. Léon Minor Seminary.[479] **[page 99]**

(c) Deliberations

(i) Preliminary Issue: Pleadings in the Indictment

a. Paragraphs 12 and 13 are vague

332. The Defence alleges that paragraphs 12 and 13 of the Indictment are vague since they do not specify the identity of the victims and the specific dates on which the acts were alleged to have been committed by the Accused.[480] The Chamber does not agree with this proposition. The Chamber observes that the Indictment provides the Accused with a clear timeframe during which he is alleged to have visited the St. Léon Minor Seminary.[481] The Chamber notes that in respect of the victims' identity, paragraph 12 of the Indictment clearly states that once Rukundo had identified the refugees, soldiers and *Interahamwe* took away and killed Tutsi refugees from the St. Léon Minor Seminary. The Chamber further notes that paragraph 13 of the Indictment states that following Rukundo's departure on several occasions from the St. Léon Minor Seminary soldiers and *Interahamwe* militiamen beat, kicked and whipped Tutsi refugees who had not been taken away to be killed. The Chamber recalls that in cases where the Prosecution alleges specific criminal acts, such as the murder of a named individual, the indictment should set forth material facts such as "the identity of the victim, the time and place of the events and the means by which the acts were committed." However, such detail need not be pleaded where the sheer scale of the alleged crimes makes it impracticable

---

[474] T. 11 October 2007, p. 66; T. 16 October 2007, p. 11.
[475] T. 16 October 2007, pp. 2-4.
[476] T. 16 October 2007, pp. 4, 6.
[477] T. 16 October 2007, pp. 5-8, 33-34.
[478] T. 16 October 2007, pp. 2, 5, 32-33.
[479] T. 16 October 2007, pp. 33-34, 37.
[480] Defence Closing Brief, paras. 841-848.
[481] Para. 12 of the Indictment states "during the months of April and May 1994" and para. 13 of the Indictment states "on diverse dates during the months of April and May 1994".

to require the same degree of specificity.[482] The Chamber finds that the reference to "Tutsi refugees", certainly of a large number, is sufficiently specific in this instance. The Chamber is therefore satisfied that the Indictment provided the Accused with sufficient notice to enable him to adequately prepare his defence.

b. Allegation of incitement to Hutu refugees not to collect water is not pleaded in the Indictment

333. The Defence seeks to exclude Witness BLC's evidence where he discusses Rukundo's involvement in stopping the Hutu from fetching water for Tutsi refugees at the St. Léon Minor **[page 100]** Seminary during the genocide in 1994.[483] Witness BLC testified that at the St. Léon Minor Seminary, the Hutu had to leave the Seminary to fetch water because if the Tutsi went out, they would be killed. Witness BLC testified that Father Daniel Nahimana preached that the Hutu were being enslaved by the Tutsi and gave the example that the Hutu are forced to fetch water, instead of the Tutsi. Later that night in the Nyacyonga camp, Witness BLC stated that Father Nahimana and Rukundo went around ordering the Hutu refugees not to collect water, so as to force the Tutsi to leave the Seminary to fetch water knowing that they might ultimately be killed.[484] The Defence submits that this evidence introduces a new material fact and a new charge against the Accused which was not specifically pleaded in the Indictment.[485]

334. The Chamber notes that the Indictment does not contain any reference to Rukundo ordering Hutu refugees at the St. Léon Minor Seminary not to collect water. This evidence alleges a particular event and criminal conduct of the Accused against Tutsi refugees which was not pleaded in the Indictment. The Chamber notes that although the Indictment refers to three specific incidents at the St. Léon Minor Seminary,[486] Witness BLC's evidence constitutes a new allegation which falls outside the scope of the Indictment.[487] The Chamber therefore excludes Witness BLC's evidence in respect of the Accused's alleged instigation of Hutu refugees to stop collecting water outside of the St. Léon Minor Seminary in order to force the Tutsi to leave the premises.

(ii) Allegation: Beating of Refugees

335. The Indictment alleges in paragraph 13 that during the months of April and May 1994, soldiers and *Interahamwe* beat, kicked and whipped Tutsi refugees at the St. Léon Minor Seminary as a result of Rukundo's order, instigation or actions of aiding and abetting. The Chamber notes that Witness CSF was the only witness to testify to this particular allegation. She stated the following:

> "Whenever Rukundo left [the Minor Seminary], the soldiers would come and ask for money from the refugees. Those who could not find any money to give them were beaten. And … they would take some of them away with them to throw in the bushes."[488]

336. The Chamber notes that Witness CSF does not refer to any kicking or whipping as alleged in the Indictment, or anything beyond the above-stated passage, which refers generally to the soldiers beating refugees. More importantly, the witness does not link the Accused to the beatings. **[page 101]** The Chamber recalls that Witness CSF's evidence suggests that the beatings took place after Rukundo had left the Seminary and there is no other evidence adduced by the Prosecution to connect the Accused to the beatings of the refugees by the soldiers. Rather, from Witness CSF's testimony, when the refugees did not give money to the soldiers when they were asked, the refugees were beaten. Given the lack of any link between Rukundo and the beatings allegedly perpetrated by the soldiers, the Chamber finds that the Prosecution has not established beyond reasonable doubt that Rukundo ordered, instigated or aided and abetted the beating of Tutsi refugees at the St. Léon Minor Seminary.

---

[482] *Kupreskić*, Judgement (AC), para. 89; *Ntakirutimana*, Judgement (AC), para. 25.
[483] Defence Closing Brief, para. 229.
[484] T. 4 December 2006, pp. 25-26.
[485] Defence Closing Brief, paras. 225-226.
[486] See paras. 12, 13, 14 and 27 of the Indictment.
[487] See Section II.A.1.
[488] T. 13 February 2007, p. 8.

(iii) Allegation: Abduction and Killing of Refugees

337. Paragraph 12 of the Indictment alleges that during the months of April and May 1994, the Accused ordered, instigated, or aided and abetted soldiers and *Interahamwe* to kill Tutsi refugees at the St. Léon Minor Seminary by identifying specific refugees to be abducted, and that on one occasion, this was done using a list.

338. The main Prosecution witness on this allegation is Witness CSF. Prosecution Witnesses CSG and BLC provide additional testimony. Apart from Rukundo, the Defence presented Witnesses SLA and SLD to refute the Prosecution evidence. The Chamber notes that Rukundo does not deny that he visited the St. Léon Minor Seminary during the months of April and May 1994. In fact, he described in detail three visits that he made to the Seminary.[489]

339. Prosecution Witness CSF provided a firsthand and largely consistent account of four visits made by the Accused to the St. Léon Minor Seminary during the months of April and May 1994. According to Witness CSF, Rukundo was accompanied by soldiers and *Interahamwe* on all four occasions that he visited the Seminary. Witness CSF testified that on the first occasion, on 20 or 21 April 1994, Rukundo walked around for a while in the refugee camp and talked to a number of refugees. Then, Rukundo handed a piece of paper he held in his hand to one of the soldiers accompanying him and left. Witness CSF attested to seeing this incident from inside the courtyard of the Seminary at a distance of about 40 metres from the Accused.[490]

340. Witness CSF stated that following Rukundo's departure, soldiers then called out the names of individuals on the list and began searching for them. The refugees who were found boarded a blue truck parked near the tarred road and were taken away. Witness CSF testified that he followed **[page 102]** the soldiers and refugees who had been rounded up outside the St. Léon Minor Seminary and watched as they were loaded onto the truck. According to Witness CSF, these refugees never returned. He stated that this first abduction involved only a small number of refugees.[491]

341. Witness CSF testified that Rukundo returned to the St. Léon Minor Seminary approximately four days later around 2.00 or 2.30 p.m. This time, many refugees were taken away. Those whose names were called protested because they realised that they were going to be killed. However they were put on board the vehicles and driven away. These refugees did not return.[492]

342. Witness CSF stated that on the third visit, which again took place four days later, Rukundo had a list with names of people who had not been previously found. As before, Rukundo walked around the camp, then handed over the list to the same soldier and left. This soldier read out the names and other soldiers looked for the people they had to take away.[493]

343. According to Witness CSF, following Rukundo's fourth visit, which occurred a few days before Kabgayi fell,[494] many of the refugees were selected and driven away in buses.[495] These refugees, like the others who had been abducted from the St. Léon Minor Seminary, never returned. Witness CSF testified that when the *Interahamwe* returned to the Seminary they were singing songs and boasting of having killed the refugees.[496] According to Witness CSF, the soldiers had started taking away intellectuals such as teachers, lecturers, civil servants and particularly magistrates.[497] Only a few young girls and boys as well as elderly people were left when the fourth abduction occurred.[498]

---

[489] T. 9 October 2007, pp. 36-39.
[490] T. 13 February 2007, pp. 3, 4 15, 19-22.
[491] T. 13 February 2007, pp. 4, 11, 16-17, 25-26.
[492] T. 13 February 2007, pp. 4-5, 27.
[493] T. 13 February 2007, p. 21.
[494] Later on, the witness said it took place in mid-May 1994 (T. 13 February 2007, pp. 29-30).
[495] T. 13 February 2007, p. 6, line 1. Later (line 5), Witness CSF referred to "a bus".
[496] T. 13 February 2007, p. 6; T. 13 February 2007 (French), p. 7.
[497] T. 13 February 2007, p. 6.
[498] T. 13 February 2007, p. 6. Witness CSF also mentioned that a judge from the Nyambuye court, whom he knew, was being sought and the *Interahamwe* had said that they would not leave without that person. Finally, the judge was found and Witness CSF saw him being taken away (*Ibid*).

Prosecutor v. Rukundo

344. According to Witness CSF, all of the abductions he witnessed took place during the day.[499] Witness CSF was unable to positively identify the ethnicity of the refugees abducted from the St. Léon Minor Seminary. The Chamber, however, notes that Witness CSF explained that many of the refugees who were in hiding at the Seminary, particularly after the first abduction, were Tutsi.[500] **[page 103]**

345. The Defence submits that Witness CSF was not at the St. Léon Minor Seminary and that he did not see Rukundo, as described in his testimony.[501] The Chamber notes that Witness CSF provided the names of four people who, according to him, joined him at the St. Léon Minor Seminary in 1994.[502] The Chamber further notes that Witness CSF and Rukundo did not know each other before the events in Rwanda in 1994. Moreover, no evidence has been adduced to establish a motive for Witness CSF to provide false testimony against the Accused. On the contrary, the Chamber notes that the witness, throughout his testimony, could have further implicated Rukundo, but that he did not do so.[503] This is *indicia* of his credibility. The Chamber concludes that Witness CSF provided a generally clear and detailed description of incidents that he saw at the St. Léon Minor Seminary[504] and finds him to be a credible witness.

346. The Defence asserts that Witnesses CSF and CSG colluded to provide false testimony against Rukundo.[505] The Chamber is not convinced by the Defence submission. Even if the two **[page 104]** witnesses know each other, that, in itself, is not proof of collusion. Indeed, the differences in detail between the testimonies of Witness CSF and Witness CSG regarding the events at the St. Léon Minor Seminary do not support the allegation of collusion.

347. The Defence also submits that Witness CSG is not credible because she could not accurately describe the premises of the St. Léon Minor Seminary where she allegedly spent about six weeks and because her

---

[499] T. 13 February 2007, p. 43.
[500] T. 13 February 2007, pp. 7-8.
[501] T. 13 February 2007, p. 51.
[502] T. 13 February 2007, pp. 42-43.
[503] Q. They didn't come only to extort money from the refugees, because you also told the Prosecutor a short while ago that they also took away people and killed in the bushes. Is that correct?
A. Are you referring to the soldiers?
Q. That is what you told the Prosecutor.
A. Yes, *but when they did that, it was in the absence of Rukundo* (emphasis added; T. 13 February 2007, p. 16).
Yes, my question was generally -- general in nature. When you were inside Saint Léon could you see what was happening outside or did you have to go out?
A. I have told you that on the first occasion I was able to go out, I went away from the fence to be able to see what was happening to the refugees. On the other occasions, *I was not able to see how they were being loaded onto the vehicles* ... (emphasis added; T. 13 February 2007, p. 16).
[504] Q. At what distance -- if you can -- be able to estimate, at what distance were you from him when you saw him with a piece of paper?
A. There was a distance of *about 40 metres* between us, and I saw him hand over that piece of paper to that person (emphasis added; T. 13 February 2007, pp. 3-4).
Q. I would like you to tell this to the Court: This second time that you're telling the Court that they came again to take away refugees, after how long had it been since the first time?
A. He returned four days after he had come the first time, and it was in the afternoon, *around 2-2:30 p.m.* (emphasis added; T. 13 February 2007, p. 4).
Q. Mr. Witness, we have the impression that you are trying to distinguish between one soldier and the other people who were accompanying Mr. Rukundo. Am I understanding you correctly?
A. I am distinguishing between that soldier and the others who were accompanying Rukundo because it was to that soldier that Rukundo handed over a list of the people who had to be identified, and *this person was always the same* (emphasis added; T. 13 February 2007, p. 21).
Q. Mr. Witness, did Emmanuel Rukundo have the opportunity to address the refugees?
A. When he came there the first time, *the elderly women came forward* and greeted him like a priest (emphasis added; T. 13 February 2007, p. 22).
Q. Witness, you told us that you saw Emmanuel Rukundo arrive and that you also saw him leave, and we are talking about the first occasion here. Approximately how long did he stay between his arrival and his departure?
A. I am going to give you an approximation, but I would like to point out to you that that institution is very large. He moved around the premises. I would say that that took him *about 30 minutes*, then he stayed with the soldiers for *about five minutes*, then he left. So I can tell you that he was there about 35 minutes (emphasis added; T. 13 February 2007, p. 24).
[505] The Defence submits that Witness CSF claimed not to know Witness CSG but both witnesses gave the same person as their contact, they were both interviewed by the Office of the Prosecutor on the same day and at the same place, and they lived in the same village (Defence Closing Brief, paras. 969-970).

behaviour was "unruly" during her testimony. The Defence further asserts that the witness gave false testimony due to her membership in *Ibuka*, a genocide survivors' organization. The Defence finally submits that there were several unexplained inconsistencies in Witness CSG's testimony.[506]

348. The Chamber notes that Witness CSG had difficulties in providing details about the Seminary and provided only a general description of its buildings being constructed of "burnt bricks".[507] Furthermore, Witness CSG was unable to name one person who was with her at the St. Léon Minor Seminary and only vaguely referred to one woman with young children.[508] She further misidentified the St. Léon Minor Seminary as the Kabgayi Bishopric in a photograph.[509] The Chamber also observes that the witness did not know whether there were clergy at the St. Léon Minor Seminary, although other witnesses attested to their presence and assistance to the refugees.[510] At one point in her testimony, Witness CSG claimed to have hidden in a corner, inside one of Seminary's buildings,[511] but then later asserted that she remained outside in the Seminary's courtyard for the duration of her stay in the camp.[512] The witness attested that while at the St. Léon Minor Seminary, someone pointed out Rukundo to her. When asked what time of day this incident occurred, the witness testified that she did not know, as she could not tell the difference between day and night. The Chamber notes that Witness CSG was hesitant when answering certain questions.[513]

349. The Chamber finds that there are reasonable explanations for the above-mentioned issues, such as the effect of an injury when the witness arrived at the St. Léon Minor Seminary,[514] her **[page 105]** pregnancy at the time,[515] the prevailing desperate living conditions at the Seminary,[516] the passage of time since the occurrence of the events, and the fact that the witness has not returned to the St. Léon Minor Seminary since 1994. The Chamber also finds that no motive has been established to support a finding that Witness CSG provided false testimony to implicate Rukundo in the events at the St. Léon Minor Seminary. The mere fact that Witness CSG is a member of *Ibuka* is not a sufficient basis to raise doubts about her credibility. The Chamber also notes that Witness CSG did not know Rukundo before 1994.[517] The Chamber considers Witness CSG to be a witness who endeavoured to provide a truthful account of the incidents at the St. Léon Minor Seminary. Nevertheless, because of the above-mentioned issues, the Chamber will rely upon her evidence only if she corroborates other reliable evidence or if other reliable evidence corroborates her account of the events.

350. The Chamber finds that the testimony of Witness CSG corroborates material aspects of the evidence presented by Witness CSF. According to Witness CSG, Rukundo visited the St. Léon Minor Seminary on "numerous occasions", sometimes twice a day during April and May 1994.[518] While Witness CSF testified that he saw the Accused at the Seminary on only four occasions, other visits, attested to by Witness CSG, are not to be excluded. Witness CSG may have witnessed visits by Rukundo, which Witness CSF did not. Witness CSG also confirms that Rukundo visited the St. Léon Minor Seminary in the company of soldiers and *Interahamwe*. Witness CSG further corroborates Witness CSF's evidence that a list was used to identify the refugees. Witness CSG corroborates Witness CSF that Rukundo would walk around the camp before the refugees were abducted from the Seminary.[519] Witness CSG testified that Rukundo "always" came with an

---

[506] Defence Closing Brief, paras. 954-962.
[507] T. 30 November 2006, pp. 9, 27, 36.
[508] T. 30 November 2006, p. 37.
[509] T. 30 November 2006, pp. 26-27, 36; Exhibit D. 7.
[510] T. 30 November 2006, pp. 8, 11, 23; Witness BLC confirmed the presence of clergy (See for example T. 4 December 2006, p. 36; T. 7 December 2006, pp. 5, 36, 38); Witness CSF said that priests were abducted from St. Léon Minor Seminary (See for example T. 13 February 2007, p. 6); Witness CCH saw some priests at St. Léon Minor Seminary (See for example T. 13 February 2007, pp. 63-64).
[511] T. 30 November 2006, p. 9.
[512] T. 30 November 2007, pp. 11-12.
[513] T. 30 November 2007, pp. 9-11, 15-16.
[514] T. 30 November 2006, pp. 3, 6, 9.
[515] T. 30 November 2007, p. 15.
[516] T. 30 November 2006, pp. 4, 11, 17.
[517] T. 30 November 2006, pp. 12-13.
[518] T. 30 November 2006, pp. 5, 21-22.
[519] T. 30 November 2006, pp. 4-6.

escort,[520] which corresponds with Witness CSF's testimony that Rukundo handed over a list to a soldier escorting him. According to Witness CSG, Rukundo used a list to identify the refugees. Again, this slightly differs from Witness CSF's evidence, who said that Rukundo gave a list of refugees to a soldier on each visit before he left the Seminary, following which the soldier identified the refugees from the list. However, the Chamber does not find this perceived variation to be significant. Both witnesses confirm that Rukundo came with a list that was subsequently used to identify the refugees. Most importantly, the Chamber notes that Witness CSG corroborates Witness **[page 106]** CSF's evidence that, after identifying the refugees, Rukundo left the St. Léon Minor Seminary and shortly afterwards, the refugees were abducted.

351. According to Witness CSG, the abductions were carried out by *Interahamwe*, whereas Witness CSF testified that it was done by soldiers and *Interahamwe*. The Chamber accepts Witness CSF's explanation that it was difficult to distinguish between soldiers and *Interahamwe* because the *Interahamwe* wore old military uniforms and only their shoes were different.[521] On the basis of the totality of the evidence, the Chamber is satisfied that both soldiers and *Interahamwe* were involved in the abductions. Witness CSG also mentioned that when the *Interahamwe* came to the St. Léon Minor Seminary they were singing.[522] Furthermore, Witness CSG stated that when the Accused came to the St. Léon Minor Seminary, the refugees screamed "You have to flee because Emmanuel Rukundo [is] coming."[523]

352. The Defence submits that Witnesses CSF and CSG are the only witnesses to testify that there were no Hutu refugees from Nyacyonga at the St. Léon Minor Seminary, and that they did not see any communal policemen guarding the gate at the St. Léon Minor Seminary.[524] Concerning the Hutu refugees from Nyacyonga, the Chamber notes that several witnesses stated that Hutu refugees from Nyacyonga had also sought shelter at the Seminary.[525] A review of the transcript reveals that Witness CSF was asked by Counsel for Defence whether he had heard about the "displaced persons from Nyacyonga in upper Kigali." To this question, Witness CSF replied that he was not "aware" of those people. When then asked whether displaced persons from Nyacyonga had found refuge at the St. Léon Minor Seminary, the witness replied that he did not see any.[526] Contrary to the Defence submission, Witness CSF never claimed that there were no Hutu refugees at the St. Léon Minor Seminary; he merely said that he did not see them.

353. The Chamber notes that Hutu refugees from Nyacyonga were housed in one of the buildings belonging to the St. Léon Minor Seminary whereas the Tutsi refugees were located in a large open courtyard in the Seminary.[527] Given that Hutu and Tutsi refugees were allocated different locations within the St. Léon Minor Seminary, it is understandable that neither Witness CSF nor Witness CSG saw the Nyacyonga Hutu refugees.
[page 107]

354. The Defence further points out an inconsistency in the evidence of Witnesses CSF and CSG concerning the guards at the entrance to the Seminary.[528] Witness CSF claimed that the gate of the St. Léon Minor Seminary was not guarded, whilst Witness CSG testified that it was guarded by both soldiers and *Interahamwe*.[529] In the Chamber's view, this is a minor discrepancy that can be explained by an examination of the evidence presented by both witnesses.

355. Witness CSF attested to leaving the St. Léon Minor Seminary only on one occasion, when he followed the abducted refugees after Rukundo visited on 20 or 21 April 1994.[530] It was on this occasion when venturing outside of the Seminary that Witness CSF denied seeing any guards at the entrance to the St. Léon Minor Seminary.

---

[520] T. 30 November 2006, p. 5.
[521] T. 13 February 2007, p. 19.
[522] T. 30 November 2006, p. 21.
[523] T. 30 November 2007, pp. 4, 24.
[524] Defence Closing Brief, paras. 865, 970.
[525] Witnesses BLC and CCG confirmed the presence of Hutu refugees from Nyacyonga (T. 4 December 2006, pp. 12, 34-35 (BLC); T. 15 February 2007, p. 32 (CCG)).
[526] T. 13 February 2007, p. 11.
[527] Witness BLC (T. 4 December 2006, pp. 12-14, 36).
[528] Defence Closing Brief, para. 874. Witnesses BLC (T. 4 December 2006, p. 38) and CCG (T. 15 February 2007, pp. 31-32) saw two communal policemen guarding the Seminary entrance.
[529] T. 13 February 2007, p. 43 (CSF); T. 30 November, 2006, p. 21 (CSG).
[530] T. 13 February 2007, p. 11.

356. Witness CSG specified that *Interahamwe* were posted as guards at the entrance to the St. Léon Minor Seminary after the arrival of a large number of refugees. She further stated that the *Interahamwe* intercepted and killed anyone who attempted to leave the Seminary. To the extent that the *Interahamwe*, who gathered at the entrance to the St. Léon Minor Seminary, were involved in the abductions of refugees, it is understandable that Witness CSG would perceive them as "guarding" the gate. When asked whether she saw two communal policemen at the entrance to the Seminary, the witness stated that she only recalled seeing many soldiers, who rotated shifts.[531] In view of her background, as well as the tense situation of the refugees at the Seminary, it is understandable that Witness CSG did not distinguish between communal policemen, soldiers and *Interahamwe* wearing military uniforms.

357. Witness BLC, whom the Chamber has already found to be a credible witness in respect of the events alleged at St. Joseph's College,[532] testified that Rukundo, accompanied by soldiers, visited the St. Léon Minor Seminary "frequently" and that refugees were abducted on each occasion.[533] Although Witness BLC stated that the abductions occurred in the evening or at night, his evidence largely corroborates the pattern established by the evidence of Witnesses CSF and CSG: that abductions of refugees occurred after Rukundo's visits to the Seminary. Witness BLC specifically referred to the abduction and fatal stabbing of seminarians' parents at night, as well as the abduction of Merci, a lecturer at the Seminary, who was killed outside the St. Léon Minor **[page 108]** Seminary.[534] In this regard, the Chamber notes that Witness BLC stayed inside the Seminary buildings and near the administrative buildings during the day while Witnesses CSF and CSG were in the courtyard. Therefore, Witness BLC had a different vantage point. Witness BLC stated that the pattern of abductions became so regular that everyone knew that people would be taken away after Rukundo's visits to the Seminary. This is consistent with Witness CSF's testimony that the refugees resisted the abduction when Rukundo visited for the second time and with Witness CSG's testimony that the refugees were afraid when Rukundo came to the St. Léon Minor Seminary. Witness BLC confirmed that those abducted were Tutsi.

358. In addition to the aforementioned, the Chamber notes a similar pattern between the first abduction from the St. Léon Minor Seminary, as described by Witness CSF, and the abduction of Madame Rudahunga, two of her children and two other Tutsi civilians,[535] which occurred during the same time period in April 1994. In both abductions, the victims were specifically identified, sought after, brought to the entrances of the respective locations and loaded onto vehicles. On both occasions, a Toyota pick-up was used to transport the victims.

359. Defence Witness SLA, a priest, resided at the St. Léon Minor Seminary in April and May 1994. He confirmed that Rukundo visited the Seminary on at least two occasions during this period. However, he asserted that *sous-préfet* Misago was responsible for the fate of those Tutsi refugees. Witness SLA admitted that he was away from the St. Léon Minor Seminary for parts of each day, assisting refugees in another location in Kabgayi. The Chamber finds that, because of his frequent absences from the St. Léon Minor Seminary, when Rukundo was alleged to have participated in the abduction and subsequent killing of refugees, Witness SLA's testimony does not discredit the Prosecution's evidence about Rukundo's involvement in these crimes.

360. The Chamber has also considered the evidence of Witness SLD, who testified that he did not see Rukundo at the St. Léon Minor Seminary, where the witness had sought shelter for three weeks in April and May 1994. Witness SLD admitted that for the greater part of the three-week period, he hid in the banana plantations behind the St. Léon Minor Seminary and that he did not visit the courtyard or the entrance of the Seminary. The witness also stated that was not aware of what occurred at the St. Léon Minor Seminary during the day. The Chamber notes that the testimony of this witness in relation to Rukundo's involvement in the abduction and killing of Tutsi refugees is largely based on his assertion that he did not see the Accused. While the Chamber has no reason to disbelieve Witness SLD, it does not find that he has sufficient knowledge

---

[531] T. 30 November 2006, p. 21.
[532] See Section III.4.c.
[533] T. 4 December 2006, p. 15.
[534] T. 4 December 2006, pp. 18-20; T. 8 December 2006, pp. 16, 20.
[535] See Section III.4.c.

of the events **[page 109]** which occurred at the St. Léon Minor Seminary for the Chamber to make any findings concerning Rukundo's activities at the Seminary.

361. Based on Witness CSF's testimony, corroborated by the evidence of Witness CSG and Witness BLC, the Chamber finds that the Prosecution has established beyond reasonable doubt that, on at least four occasions during April and May 1994, Rukundo visited the St. Léon Minor Seminary, accompanied by soldiers and *Interahamwe*. At the Seminary, Rukundo identified Tutsi refugees with a list and then left the Seminary. Shortly after Rukundo's departure, those refugees who had been identified were abducted from the Seminary.

362. The Chamber is satisfied that the abductions from the St. Léon Minor Seminary resulted in the death of those who were abducted. The Appeals Chamber has held it to be a fact of common knowledge that widespread killings occurred against the Tutsi population in Rwanda in 1994.[536] In the present case, there is overwhelming evidence before the Chamber that Tutsi refugees were targeted and killed in Gitarama *préfecture* and in Kabgayi in April and May 1994.[537] Witnesses CSF, CSG and BLC all testified that those abducted from the St. Léon Minor Seminary were never seen again. Witness CSF testified that the *Interahamwe*, who had abducted the refugees, returned to the St. Léon Minor Seminary and sang songs in which they boasted about killing the refugees.[538] Witness BLC testified that the refugees abducted from the Seminary were usually killed outside the premises. He provided hearsay evidence of the abduction of the parents of seminarians. They were then killed by being stabbed through the ribs. He also described the abduction of Merci, a lecturer at the St. Léon Minor Seminary, who was killed outside the Seminary. Witness CCH testified that, sometime in the month of May 1994, her brother was taken away from the St. Léon Minor Seminary in a vehicle and never returned.[539] She also testified that she saw men wearing communal police uniforms, take and kill refugees from the Seminary.[540] Defence Witness SLA confirmed that refugees were abducted from the St. Léon Minor Seminary and killed.[541] Defence Witness SLD provided hearsay evidence about the abduction of Tutsi refugees from the St. Léon Minor Seminary by a group of people known as the "Zulus".[542] **[page 110]**

363. In light of the general context of systematic targeting and killing of Tutsi in Gitarama, the overwhelming evidence of abductions and killings of Tutsi from various places in Kabgayi, the observations by Witnesses CSF, CSG, BLC, CCH, SLA and SLD that the refugees were never seen again and the evidence that the *Interahamwe*, who abducted the refugees, returned to the Minor Seminary singing and boasting about the killing of the refugees, the Chamber finds that the only reasonable inference[543] to be drawn from this evidence is that those abducted from the St. Léon Minor Seminary were killed.

364. Based on the aforementioned, the Chamber finds that the Prosecution has established beyond reasonable doubt that, on at least four occasions during April and May 1994, Rukundo visited the St. Léon Minor Seminary, accompanied by soldiers and *Interahamwe*. At the Seminary, Rukundo identified Tutsi refugees with a list and then left the Seminary. Shortly after Rukundo's departure, those refugees who had been identified were taken from the Seminary by soldiers and *Interahamwe* to an unknown location, where they were killed.

---

[536] *Karemera et al.*, Decision on Prosecutor's Interlocutory Appeal of Decision on Judicial Notice (AC), para. 35.
[537] See Witnesses BLC, BLJ, BCD, BUW, CCH, CSF, SLA, SLD, AMA, CSE, CNB, CNC, CSH BLP, CSG, Emmanuel Rukundo. See also the events at the CND (Section III.8) and at the Kabgayi Major Seminary (Section III.9).
[538] T. 13 February 2007 p. 6.
[539] T. 13 February 2007, pp. 56, 62.
[540] T. 13 February 2007, pp. 65-66.
[541] T. 1 October 2007, pp. 20-22, 40.
[542] T. 16 October 2007, pp. 4-8.
[543] The Chamber can only rely on that fact for a finding of guilt if the inference drawn was the only reasonable one that could be drawn from the evidence presented (*Kayishema and Ruzindana*, Judgement (AC), para. 159; *Krstić*, Judgement (AC), para 34; *Stakić*, Judgement (AC), para. 219; *Čelebići*, Judgement (AC), para. 458).

(iv) Allegation: Sexual Assault on a Young Tutsi Woman at the St. Léon Minor Seminary

a. Evidence

Prosecution Witness CCH

365. The Chamber has previously considered Witness CCH's evidence in relation to the incident at St. Joseph's College and the abduction and killing of Tutsi refugees at the St. Léon Minor Seminary.[544] Witness CCH testified that she knew Rukundo from 1991 when she attended his ordination ceremony. Witness CCH, a Tutsi, further testified that she took refuge at the St. Léon Minor Seminary in Kabgayi in mid-May 1994 when she was 21 years old. About one week after her arrival, she saw the Accused arrive in a small white vehicle, dressed in military uniform and carrying a rifle, accompanied by an armed soldier.[545] Witness CCH greeted Rukundo, introduced herself and asked him if he could hide her. Rukundo responded that he could not help her because her entire family had to be killed, since her relative was an *Inyenzi*.[546] This conversation occurred [page 111] near Rukundo's vehicle.[547] Witness CCH thought that perhaps she could hide in Rukundo's vehicle because military vehicles never got stopped.[548]

366. Witness CCH testified that Rukundo removed a carton and a plastic bag from his vehicle, and Witness CCH assisted him to bring these things to a small room, which he opened with a key. Witness CCH explained that she had assisted Rukundo, in the hope that he would change his mind and save her by hiding her. In the room, there was a bed with a mattress and a small table near the bed. They both entered the room, and Rukundo opened a bottle of Primus beer, took a sip and then gave the bottle to Witness CCH. Rukundo then locked the door with the key. Witness CCH said that she became afraid after he locked the door, but tried not to show her fear. Rukundo asked her to sit down on the bed. She gave him the bottle of beer, which he put on the table, and then he began to caress her. She explained that she shared the beer with him because she thought this was his way of saying "thanks" to her for helping him. She also wished to show her appreciation and acknowledge his position of power and authority. Witness CCH said that Rukundo forced her to lie on the bed, opened the zipper of his trousers and lay on top of her. Witness CCH did not consent to lying on the bed. At some point, Witness CCH said that Rukundo put his pistol on the table next to the bed. He tried to force Witness CCH to remove her rose-coloured skirt. Although she resisted, he pulled it down. He caressed her hair without speaking, kissed her, but never actually touched her vagina. Witness CCH asked Rukundo what she should do if she became pregnant and did not die, and he responded that he was only asking her to allow them to make love.[549] She told Rukundo that she could not have sexual intercourse with him, and he told her that if she would, he would never forget her. Rukundo tried to spread her legs, but when she continued to resist, Rukundo gave up trying to have sexual intercourse. He lay on top of her, continued to rub himself against her body, squeezed her tightly in his arms until she felt him shake or shiver and then lose his erection. Rukundo told Witness CCH that he was very tired. She had the impression that he had spent the night at the front.[550] After this, Witness CCH testified that Rukundo let go of her, took the bottle of beer, sipped it, gave it to Witness CCH who sipped it, and then they left the room. Rukundo said goodbye to Witness CCH and told her that he might be back again another time.[551] Witness CCH knew that Rukundo was a Catholic priest at the time of the incident. She felt that ultimately, Rukundo took advantage of her position of weakness by trying to have sexual intercourse with her and by trying to [page 112] dishonour her. She said that she never consented to the sexual actions, or that she ever reacted in a way that might give him the impression of consent.[552]

---

[544] See Sections III.4.c and III.7.c.iii.
[545] T. 13 February 2007, pp. 55-56; T. 14 February 2007, pp. 5, 18.
[546] T. 13 February 2007, pp. 56-58.
[547] T. 14 February 2007, p. 7.
[548] T. 14 February 2007, pp. 9-10.
[549] T. 13 February 2007, pp. 59-61; T. 14 February 2007, pp. 11, 13-14.
[550] T. 13 February 2007, pp. 59-60; T. 14 February 2007, pp. 17-18.
[551] T. 13 February 2007, p. 60; T. 14 February 2007, pp. 14, 18.
[552] T. 13 February 2007, pp. 60-61; T. 14 February 2007, p. 22.

367. In cross-examination, Witness CCH further explained that she introduced herself to Rukundo, even though she had known him for a long time, because she was now grown up and was dirty after not having bathed for a long time. After entering the room with Rukundo, Witness CCH said that she could not have left, since he had just given her a beer and she had gone for a while without eating. Furthermore he had a gun and could easily have found her. She never realized that he could do something to her. Witness CCH stated that she became afraid of Rukundo only when he locked the door with the key. She further testified that she could not have escaped because he was on top of her and holding her down with his arms. She did not talk about the incident with her family or anyone else. She maintained that it was possible for a man to ejaculate simply by caressing a woman's head. Witness CCH stated that she was 21 years old at the time and was not yet sexually active. Witness CCH denied that she concocted the story of Rukundo's sexual assault because, according to some people, Rukundo was responsible for the death of her relative.[553]

The Accused

368. Rukundo admitted visiting the St. Léon Minor Seminary on 15 and 21 April and on 21 May 1994. Rukundo denied meeting Witness CCH at the St. Léon Minor Seminary on those days, although after the war, he heard that she and her family had taken refuge there. On 21 May 1994, he said that he stored his property in a store room for priests at the Minor Seminary, located next to the kitchen, and that the bursar held the key to the store room. He maintained that he had no access to any room at the Seminary since he was not a resident. If he wanted access to a room, he would have needed a key from the bursar.[554]

369. Rukundo testified that he knew Witness CCH before the war, but maintained that he never saw her between April and June 1994 or up until she came to testify. He was therefore not in a position to make any sexual advances upon her, contrary to her testimony. He added that perhaps Witness CCH came to testify to seek revenge for stories she might have read alleging Rukundo's involvement in the death of one of her relatives.[555] He denied that his counsel's questions to **[page 113]** Witness CCH regarding her consent to the sexual assault incident implied that the incident was true.[556]

Defence Witness SLA

370. The Chamber has previously considered Witness SLA's evidence in relation to the incident at St. Joseph's College and the abduction and killing of Tutsi refugees at the St. Léon Minor Seminary.

371. Witness SLA was a seminarian with Rukundo at the Nyakibanda Major Seminary.[557] He worked with the refugees at the St. Léon Minor Seminary starting in April 1994.[558] He saw Rukundo at the St. Léon Minor Seminary twice during the time between mid-April and mid-May 1994. Witness SLA confirmed that Rukundo was given a small room at the Minor Seminary, which was used as a store, to keep his belongings. The room was close to the refectory behind the hall where the community watched films. Witness SLA never opened the room and did not know what belongings were stored there. He confirmed that in April and May 1994 Rukundo never slept at the Minor Seminary and that he never saw Rukundo open the room where his belongings were kept when he saw him at the Minor Seminary.[559]

    b. Deliberations

372. The Indictment alleges that, on or about 15 May 1994, at the St. Léon Minor Seminary, Rukundo took a young Tutsi woman into his room, locked the door and sexually assaulted her, therefore causing her serious mental harm. Witness CCH, the alleged victim, is the only witness who testified in support of the Prosecution's case. Rukundo denied the allegation.

---

[553] T. 14 February 2007, pp. 6, 12-15, 18-21.
[554] T. 9 October 2007, pp. 36-37, 40, 47.
[555] T. 9 October 2007, pp. 47-48.
[556] T. 11 October 2007, pp. 26-28.
[557] T. 1 October 2007, p. 2.
[558] T. 1 October 2007, pp. 12, 14.
[559] T. 1 October 2007, p. 32.

373. Witness CCH's testimony is that, in the later part of May 1994, Rukundo came to the St. Léon Minor Seminary. Witness CCH greeted Rukundo, introduced herself and asked him if he could hide her. Rukundo responded that he could not help her. He said that her entire family had to be killed because her relative was an *Inyenzi*.[560] Nevertheless, Witness CCH assisted him in carrying some items to his room, in the hope that he would change his mind and hide her. While in the room, Rukundo locked the door, placed his pistol on the table next to the bed and began to caress the witness. He forced her onto the bed, opened the zipper on his trousers and lay on top of **[page 114]** her. He tried to spread her legs and have sexual intercourse, but she resisted. Following Witness CCH's continued resistance, Rukundo gave up trying to have intercourse, but rubbed himself against her until he ejaculated. Witness CCH said that she could not escape since he was on top of her, holding her down. He was also in a position of authority and had a gun.[561]

374. Rukundo admitted to visiting the St. Léon Minor Seminary on 21 May 1994, but maintained that he did not see Witness CCH. He further stated that he had no access to any room at the Seminary since he was not a resident. If he wanted access to a room, he would have needed to obtain a key from the bursar.[562]

375. The Defence argues that since Witness CCH is the only person to allege sexual assault by Rukundo, her story should not be believed. The Defence further claims that the witness has a motive to make false allegations against the Accused because she believes that Rukundo is responsible for the death of one of her relatives.[563] The Defence argues that Witness CCH's testimony is improbable and that, even if believed, the elements of the alleged crime have not been established.[564]

376. Witness CCH denied the proposition that she had made up the allegation of sexual assault to avenge the death of her relative. Witness CCH stated that she did not attribute her relative's death to Rukundo and she did not hear that Rukundo may have been responsible for the death, although she knew Rukundo wanted that relative dead. Witness CCH confirmed that she never told anyone of the incident because, as a young girl, one could not report an attempted rape, especially to a close relative.[565]

377. The Chamber finds Witness CCH to be a credible witness and believes her evidence. This conclusion is supported by her consistent and detailed evidence, by the Accused's admission that he visited the St. Léon Minor Seminary on 21 May 1994[566] and by Witness SLA's confirmation of the existence of a small room at the Seminary where Rukundo kept his belongings.[567]

378. Finally, the Chamber finds that the allegation that Witness CCH had a motive to give false testimony against the Accused in respect of the sexual assault is not tenable. The Chamber notes, in **[page 115]** particular, that the witness only testified that Rukundo attempted to have sexual intercourse with her, rubbed himself against her but did not touch her vagina. She could very well have testified that Rukundo had raped her, but she did not. She could have done so under the witness protection scheme, affording her a pseudonym and protection from public view. In light of the foregoing, the Chamber finds that Rukundo assaulted Witness CCH, as described in her testimony.

379. The Chamber recalls that rape and sexual violence "constitute genocide in the same way as any other act as long as they were committed with the specific intent to destroy, in whole or in part, a particular group, targeted as such."[568] Sexual violence was broadly defined in *Akayesu* as "…any act of a sexual nature which is committed on a person under circumstances which are coercive. Sexual violence is not limited to physical invasion of the human body and may include acts which do not involve penetration or even physical contact."[569] In order for the act of sexual violence to constitute genocide pursuant to Article 2(2)(b) of the Statute, it must have caused serious bodily or mental harm to members of the group.[570]

---

[560] T. 13 February 2007, pp. 56-58.
[561] T. 13 February 2007, pp. 59-61; T. 14 February 2007, pp. 10-11, 13-14, 18.
[562] T. 9 October 2007, p. 47.
[563] Defence Closing Brief, paras. 1014-1017, 1059-1062.
[564] Defence Closing Brief, paras. 1017, 1058.
[565] T. 14 February 2007, pp. 15, 21.
[566] T. 9 October 2007, p. 47.
[567] T. 1 October 2007, p. 32.
[568] *Akayesu*, Judgement (TC), para. 731.
[569] *Akayesu*, Judgement (TC), para. 688.
[570] *Akayesu*, Judgement (TC), paras. 688, 734.

380. From the evidence adduced in this case, the Chamber considers it proper to proceed as follows. First, the Chamber will determine whether the act in question was of a sexual nature. Second, the Chamber will determine whether there existed coercive circumstances. Third, the Chamber will determine whether the act, if sexual and committed under coercive circumstances, caused Witness CCH serious mental harm, as alleged by the Prosecution.

i. Was the Act of a Sexual Nature?

381. The actions in question were clearly of a sexual nature: Rukundo forced sexual contact with her by opening the zipper of his trousers, trying to remove her skirt, forcefully lying on top of her and caressing and rubbing himself against her until he ejaculated and lost his erection. Rukundo's actions and words, such as telling her that if she made love with him he would never forget her, support the Chamber's finding that his actions were of a sexual nature. **[page 116]**

ii. Were there coercive circumstances?

382. In *Akayesu*, the Trial Chamber stated that,

> "... coercive circumstances need not be evidenced by a show of physical force. Threats, intimidation, extortion and other forms of duress which prey on fear or desperation may constitute coercion, and coercion may be inherent in certain circumstances, such as armed conflict or the military presence of *Interahamwe* among refugee Tutsi women at the bureau communal."[571]

383. When it was put to Witness CCH in cross-examination that Rukundo did not use any threat or force to convince her to have sexual intercourse with him, she replied that "[y]ou don't need to use a gun to threaten somebody. He definitely did not point his gun at me. But, remember that he's the one who pushed me to the bed, and he took into account the weakness -- the weak point from which I was. That was also a disguised threat ..."[572] She further testified that she drank a beer with Rukundo to acknowledge his position of authority and that she ultimately thought he was taking advantage of his position.[573]

384. The Chamber notes that Witness CCH testified that the situation surrounding the Tutsi refugees at the St. Léon Minor Seminary from April until June 1994 was dangerous.[574] Other witnesses testified that many Tutsi refugees were regularly abducted from the St. Léon Minor Seminary and killed.[575] Witness CCH further testified that, fearing for her life, she implored the Accused to hide her. Rukundo compounded her fear by indicating that she and her family must be killed because her relative was an *Inyenzi*. At all material times, Rukundo was armed with a gun. After Witness CCH assisted Rukundo to bring some of his belongings to a small room, he locked her inside the room alone with him; and, placing a pistol on a nearby table, he proceeded to force himself upon her, while she struggled to free herself from his control. The Chamber finds that these events, taken together, clearly constitute coercive circumstances.

385. The Appeals Chamber has also stated that the element of non-consent in the crime of rape [or sexual violence] can be proved beyond reasonable doubt when the Prosecution demonstrates the existence of coercive circumstances under which meaningful consent is not possible. A Trial Chamber, however, is still entitled to admit evidence under certain special circumstances that the **[page 117]** victim specifically consented.[576] Although the Defence denied that Witness CCH's consent of sexual assault was in issue, in cross-examination, questions were put to her by Defence Counsel regarding the possible interpretation of her behaviour as consent.[577] After examining the evidence, the Chamber concludes that the coercive circumstances, as found above, indeed vitiated Witness CCH's ability to consent to the sexual assault in question.

---

[571] *Akayesu*, Judgement (TC), para. 688.
[572] T. 14 February 2007, p. 20.
[573] T. 13 February 2007, p. 61.
[574] T. 13 February 2007, pp. 66-67.
[575] See Witnesses CSF, CSG, BLC, SLA, SLD, *supra*.
[576] *Gacumbitsi*, Judgement (AC), paras. 155-157.
[577] T. 11 October 2007, pp. 26-28; T. 14 February 2007, pp. 17-20.

iii. Did Witness CCH suffer serious mental harm?

386. The Chamber has already expressed the general standard required to find serious mental harm with regards to the allegation at the Bishopric. Although the mental harm suffered must be more than a minor or temporary impairment of mental faculties, it need not be permanent or irremediable.[578] Additionally, the Trial Chamber in *Kamuhanda* stated that serious mental harm could be found when there is a non-mortal act, such as sexual assault, combined with the threat of death.[579] It has further been held that "rape and sexual violence certainly constitute infliction of serious bodily and mental harm on the victims and are even [...] one of the worst ways of inflicting harm on the victim as he or she suffers both bodily and mental harm."[580]

387. The evidence of Witness CCH, which the Chamber has accepted, describes a young Tutsi woman fearing for her life and seeking protection from a member of the clergy, known to her, who was in a position of authority. Instead of providing protection, Rukundo abused Witness CCH by sexually assaulting her under coercive circumstances.

388. The Chamber acknowledges that it has not had the benefit of any direct evidence on Witness CCH's mental state, following the sexual assault, apart from her testimony that she could not tell anyone about the incident. The Chamber, however, recalls that it may draw inferences from the evidence presented. The Chamber finds it necessary to look beyond the sexual act in question and finds it particularly important to consider the highly charged, oppressive and other circumstances surrounding the sexual assault on Witness CCH. The Chamber notes in particular the following circumstances:

   1) Members of her ethnic group were victims of mass killings; **[page 118]**

   2) She and her family, fearing death in this way, sought refuge in a religious institution;

   3) Upon seeing a familiar and trusted person of authority and of the church, *i.e.* the Accused, she requested protection for herself;

   4) When the Accused refused her the protection she had requested, he specifically threatened her – that her family was to be killed for its association with the "*Inyenzi*";

   5) Rukundo had a firearm;

   6) Still hoping to be protected, Witness CCH sought to ingratiate herself to Rukundo by assisting him to carry his effects into a nearby room;

   7) The Accused locked her in the room with him, put his firearm down nearby and proceeded to physically manhandle her in a sexual way; and

   8) At the time of the incident, Witness CCH was sexually inexperienced.

389. In light of the established jurisprudence and the totality of the evidence, in particular the surrounding circumstances of the sexual assault, the Chamber finds, Judge Park dissenting, that the only reasonable conclusion is that Witness CCH suffered serious mental harm as a consequence of Rukundo's actions. **[page 119]**

8. EVENTS AT THE CND

(a) Indictment

390. Paragraphs 11 and 15 of the Indictment read as follows:

> During the months of April and May 1994, **Emmanuel RUKUNDO** went regularly to the Saint Léon Minor Seminary at Kabgayi and to the place named TRAFIPRO, otherwise called CND, as he hunted for Tutsis to kill. **Emmanuel RUKUNDO** was dressed in military uniform, armed and had a military escort, and was often

---
[578] *Rutaganda*, Judgement (TC), para. 50; See also *Brđanin*, Judgement (TC), para. 690; *Seromba*, Judgement (AC), para. 46.
[579] *Kamuhanda*, Judgement (TC), para. 634.
[580] *Akayesu*, Judgement (TC), para. 731.

accompanied by other soldiers and the *Interahamwe* who committed killings of Tutsis at these two locations. His particular actions are described in paragraphs 12, 13, 14 and 15 below.

During the months of April and May 1994, **Emmanuel RUKUNDO** went several times to a place in Kabgayi named "TRAFIPRO", or otherwise called "CND", to kill Tutsis. On some of these occasions, he was seen in the company of authorities, including Prime Minister Jean KAMBANDA, Bishop Thaddée NSENGIYUMVA of Kabgayi, and others unknown to the Prosecutor. Very soon after each of these visits, soldiers and *Interahamwe* militiamen, as ordered, instigated, or aided and abetted by **Emmanuel RUKUNDO**, came back to the CND and killed several Tutsi refugees, and took away other Tutsi refugees and killed or inflicted serious bodily or mental harm upon them.

(b) Evidence

Prosecution Witness AMA

391. Witness AMA arrived in Kabgayi on 14 April 1994 and stayed there until 2 June 1994. In Kabgayi, Witness AMA sought refuge at the CND,[581] and also at Kagwa.[582]

392. Witness AMA stated that when he arrived in Kabgayi, he was sent to the CND by soldiers on patrol. Witness AMA estimated that there were about 17,000 refugees at the CND which covered an area about 200 meters long and 100 meters wide. On the other side of the CND building, there was a forest and a river in the valley down below the CND. The CND compound was surrounded by a fence constructed out of barbed wire and wooden planks about one and a half metres high.[583]

393. Witness AMA stated that he arrived at the CND with members of his family including his three older brothers, two younger brothers, five nephews, two sisters, and his father. Subsequently, other members of his family sought refuge at the CND. Witness AMA claimed to have been among the first group of refugees to arrive at the CND. His group arrived at night and they spent the night **[page 120]** outside. The following day, when his group attempted to settle inside the CND building, they discovered that other groups of refugees had arrived earlier and had already occupied the building. Witness AMA stated that it was impossible for everyone to be sheltered inside the building so only the women and children stayed inside while the men slept in the courtyard.[584]

394. Witness AMA fell sick on the third day after his arrival at the CND and remained ill for about ten days. Witness AMA later explained in cross-examination that he did not go to the hospital but was looked after by people at the CND who gave him medication. Over that ten day period, Witness AMA stayed in the courtyard of the CND. Witness AMA stated that around 20 May 1994, after he had recovered, he started sitting in the area close to the gate in the sun.[585]

395. Witness AMA testified that between 25 and 30 May 1994, Rukundo arrived at the CND in the company of six soldiers. Some soldiers were with him in a truck, while the other soldiers were in a blue minibus. A total of seven soldiers alighted from the vehicles. All of the soldiers, including Rukundo, wore greenish camouflage uniform. Four of the soldiers were carrying firearms, but Rukundo had left his firearm in the vehicle.[586]

396. Witness AMA stated that he had never seen Rukundo before 25 May 1994. However the refugees from Rukundo's native region, pointed him out to Witness AMA. They explained that he was wearing a camouflage uniform with a cross on the epaulette because he was a military chaplain. Witness AMA testified that Rukundo came towards the gate and told the refugees not to be afraid, saying, "I am Father Rukundo and I have come to bring you food supplies." He said that it was his duty to provide the refugees with food. Rukundo also told the refugees, "If anyone attacks you, you must defend yourself. You must scream and

---

[581] The CND is also known as TRAFIPRO. For the purposes of consistency, this judgement will only refer to that location as the CND.
[582] T. 27 February 2007, p. 2.
[583] T. 27 February 2007, pp. 2-3, 19-20.
[584] T. 27 February 2007, p. 20.
[585] T. 27 February 2007, pp. 3, 21-22.
[586] T. 27 February 2007, pp. 3, 5, 25-27.

shout in order to alert us." Witness AMA was less than one metre away from Rukundo at this time. Witness AMA added that Rukundo was outside the fence surrounding the CND compound, while he was inside the fence.[587]

397. According to Witness AMA, sometime between 1.00 and 4.00 p.m., Rukundo pulled out a list from a bag he was carrying, and called out names of people who he wanted to take to an unspecified location to assist him in bringing food provisions to the refugees at the CND. Witness AMA explained that he was close enough to where Rukundo stood to see that the list which he held was typewritten. A total of about 15 people, whose names Rukundo had called, went out of the fenced compound to where he stood. When the 15 refugees were outside, Rukundo asked them **[page 121]** where the other refugees were whose names he had read from the list. He was told that only these 15 refugees had been found. The 15 refugees were then asked to board the awaiting minibus which was driven by a soldier. A young boy called Floraine, a man called Jovith Rukaka, and another man from Witness AMA's native region were among the refugees who left the CND with Rukundo and the soldiers. Witness AMA explained that the people whose names Rukundo called out, voluntarily emerged from the compound and boarded the minibus accompanied by five soldiers. Witness AMA further testified that the 15 refugees who were taken were mostly Tutsi men. He stated that he saw everything that happened on that day despite the fact that Rukundo was on the other side of the fence. He added that the fence was made of barbed wire and he could therefore see through it.[588]

398. The minibus left with the 15 refugees aboard. Rukundo left in the truck together with the soldier who had arrived with him. According to Witness AMA, the two vehicles left, one after the other, in the direction of the church. When the minibus arrived at the gate in front of the football field, Floraine was thrown out of the car into a pit while the minibus continued. Floraine spent the night in the pit and returned to the CND the following morning smeared with blood and with a head injury. Floraine told them that he was thrown into a pit containing dead bodies, and that the remaining refugees were taken away. Witness AMA testified that apart from Floraine, none of the refugees who had earlier left in the minibus from the CND were ever seen again. From their disappearance, Witness AMA inferred that they had been killed.[589]

399. Witness AMA further stated that he only saw Rukundo at the CND during the incident involving the refugees. Witness AMA did not discount the possibility that Rukundo might have come to the CND while he was ill or far from the entrance. Witness AMA stated that soldiers, including the ones who accompanied Rukundo during his visit to the CND, came and abducted girls and spent the night with them. However, the girls would return the following day. Witness AMA never saw Bishop Nsengiyumva, Jean Kambanda or any other figure of authority at the CND, but it was possible that they could have visited the CND without him knowing.[590]

400. Witness AMA was not afraid when he first saw Rukundo and the soldiers who accompanied him disembark from the vehicles or when Rukundo called out the names of the people on his list. He recalled that up until that point in time, no refugees at the CND had been abducted. Witness AMA did not know if others were suspicious of Rukundo's motives. According to Witness AMA, the refugees were reassured by what they perceived as Rukundo's desire to help them. Rukundo **[page 122]** also advised them to protect themselves. It was only when they discovered that the refugees taken by Rukundo could not be accounted for, that they were concerned. At that point, Witness AMA also started to think that he might suffer the same fate.[591]

401. Witness AMA explained that when he left the CND, he joined the army up until 1996; then he moved to Kigali where he prepared skewered meat until 1999. Thereafter, he left Kigali and went back to his village where he became involved in farming until he was arrested in 2000.[592]

---

[587] T. 27 February 2007, pp. 4-5, 27.
[588] T. 27 February 2007, pp. 5-8, 23-24, 29, 38.
[589] T. 27 February 2007, pp. 6-8.
[590] T. 27 February 2007, pp. 8-9, 21.
[591] T. 27 February 2007, pp. 8, 25-28.
[592] T. 27 February 2007, p. 11.

Prosecution Witness CSE

402. The Chamber has already considered Witness CSE's testimony with regards to the allegation at the *Imprimerie de Kabgayi* roadblock.

403. Witness CSE stated that once he arrived at Kabgayi, he sought shelter in the building where catechism lessons were given and subsequently sought refuge at the CND. He testified that the CND building belonged to the Kabgayi diocese and that Emmanuel Rukundo was affiliated to the Kabgayi diocese. According to Witness CSE, the refugees at the CND were Tutsi who were fleeing massacres around the country.[593]

404. Witness CSE testified that he saw Rukundo at the CND while he was there. He was not certain about the number of times he had seen Rukundo at the CND but it was more than once. Witness CSE testified that Rukundo was dressed in the same military uniform as when he had previously seen him. Witness CSE testified that Rukundo was accompanied by Bishop Thaddée Nsengiyumva, Prime Minister Jean Kambanda, and other officials whose identity he did not know. According to Witness CSE, Rukundo and the officials did not do anything; they simply entered the building where the refugees were and then left the CND.[594]

405. Witness CSE testified that after each of Rukundo's visits to the CND, soldiers came to the CND and abducted refugees from the areas that Rukundo and his entourage had visited. Witness CSE stated that there was a period of two hours or less between Rukundo's visit to the CND and the subsequent abduction of the refugees by the soldiers. Witness CSE stated that the soldiers "knew what they were looking for" and they knew the place where they were supposed to abduct the refugees who had been earlier identified. Witness CSE explained that the soldiers who carried out the abduction were stationed in various locations in the Kabgayi diocese, including St. Kizito, the **[page 123]** hospital and the Bishop's house. In cross-examination, Witness CSE stated that the abduction of refugees was not a frequent occurrence.[595]

406. Witness CSE stated that the refugees who were abducted from the CND did not return to the CND, and thus he concluded that they had been killed. Witness CSE did not know where the refugees were killed.[596]

407. Witness CSE further testified that the soldiers who were behind the CND building would climb over the fence and shoot into the crowd of refugees, killing people on the spot. The shootings by the soldiers were not aimed at any particular refugee. Witness CSE further stated that the soldiers would also shoot at any refugee who attempted to leave the CND. According to Witness CSE, these shootings never occurred when Rukundo was at the CND. At times, these soldiers came into the compound to confirm whether the refugees they shot were dead, and to kill more refugees. Witness CSE added that their goal was to exterminate the refugees who had sought sanctuary at the CND. The bodies of the dead refugees were never removed and as a result, the CND premises were littered with human corpses. Witness CSE testified that given the abundance of dead bodies at the CND, it is almost certain that Rukundo and the other dignitaries must have seen the corpses during their visits to the CND.[597]

408. Witness CSE testified that neither the Kabgayi diocese nor Rukundo assisted the refugees or stopped their abductions from the CND. In cross-examination, however, Witness CSE stated that the Kabgayi diocese brought and distributed food to the refugees at the CND and the refugees had access to the food provisions stored in the CND building. Moreover, Witness CSE stated that vehicles belonging to the Kabgayi diocese were used to bring them food provisions. Witness CSE stated that he never heard Rukundo or any of the other dignitaries who had accompanied him to the CND, condemn the atrocities that had been committed against the refugees at the CND.[598]

The Accused

409. Rukundo testified that he never visited the CND buildings between April and May 1994. According to Rukundo, CND is a nickname that must have been given to the buildings after the events in 1994. Rukundo

---

[593] T. 17 November 2006, pp. 3, 6-7.
[594] T. 17 November 2006, pp. 7-8.
[595] T. 17 November 2006, pp. 8-9, 29-31.
[596] T. 17 November 2006, p. 12.
[597] T. 17 November 2006, pp. 10-12, 18, 29-31.
[598] T. 17 November 2006, pp. 10-13.

stated that he knew Jean Kambanda as Prime Minister of the interim government which was set up on 9 April 1994, but he never knew him personally. Contrary to the **[page 124]** testimony given by Witnesses AMA and CSE, Rukundo denied ever having been at the CND with Jean Kambanda. According to Rukundo, between April and June 1994, he never left the Bishopric in the company of Bishop Nsengiyumva to go to the CND or the hospital. Rukundo also denied having ever boarded a minibus at the CND.[599] In cross-examination, Rukundo conceded that there were people at the CND who knew him, since they were from Mushubati *commune*, but he could not say for sure if they were there since he never visited that location. The Bishop was known in the area while Kambanda was not well known. Rukundo added that he did not know Kambanda at all apart from the photographs he had seen of him.[600]

Defence Witness CNA

410. Defence Witness CNA stated that he is distantly related to Emmanuel Rukundo. Witness CNA testified that he knew that Rukundo was ordained as a priest and was also appointed as a military chaplain. Witness CNA stated, however, that he never saw Emmanuel Rukundo after his appointment as a military chaplain.[601] In cross-examination, Witness CNA stated that he had never seen Rukundo wearing a military uniform.[602] However, Witness CNA stated that he would have been able to recognize Rukundo if he had seen him wearing a military uniform.[603]

411. Witness CNA testified that he arrived at the CND on 23 April 1994 and stayed until 2 June 1994.[604] Witness CNA estimated that there were about 16,000 people at the CND on 23 April 1994 but added that this number increased over time. Witness CNA testified that during the period that he stayed at the CND, he was responsible for monitoring the distribution of food provisions to the refugees. Witness CNA mentioned that he kept his personal belongings in a tent, although he slept outside the tent since it was occupied by women and children.[605] During cross-examination, Witness CNA stated that his tent was in the courtyard on the opposite side to the main entrance. Witness CNA could not estimate the distance between his tent and the CND's main entrance but it was "not long" and from where he was one could easily see what was happening at the entrance.[606]

412. Witness CNA stated that he never left the CND despite the fact that the living conditions were very difficult. At some point Witness CNA saw Red Cross representatives providing food to **[page 125]** the refugees. He also saw nuns on one occasion, accompanied by some other people, giving biscuits to a few starving refugees and children who were suffering from diarrhoea. Witness CNA did not recall seeing any seminarians at the CND during the entire period that he spent there.[607]

413. Witness CNA testified that he only saw Jean Kambanda once at the CND in May 1994. According to Witness CNA, Kambanda was accompanied by *gendarmes*. Witness CNA stated that no one ever mentioned to him that Kambanda visited the CND apart from the one occasion when he saw him there.[608] Witness CNA stated that Kambanda was wearing a suit when he saw him at the CND. According to Witness CNA, Kambanda did not stay there for long; no more than 30 minutes. Witness CNA stated that the refugees at the CND applauded and shouted once they learnt that the Prime Minister had arrived at the CND. According to Witness CNA, Kambanda did not address the refugees when he visited the CND.[609] When Kambanda arrived, Witness CNA was on the other side of the CND near the plastic sheet shelters but he went to the main entrance when he heard about the Prime Minister's arrival.[610]

---

[599] T. 9 October 2007, pp. 52-53.
[600] T. 10 October 2007, pp. 40-42.
[601] T. 11 July 2007, pp. 38-39, 64-65; T. 12 July 2007, pp. 18, 39.
[602] T. 11 July 2007, p. 62.
[603] T. 12 July 2007, p. 16.
[604] T. 11 July 2007, pp. 43, 50; T. 12 July 2007, p. 9.
[605] T. 11 July 2007, pp. 44-45, 50.
[606] T. 12 July 2007, pp. 2, 10-12.
[607] T. 11 July 2007, p. 53.
[608] T. 11 July 2007, pp. 50-51, 54, 71.
[609] T. 11 July 2007, p. 54; 12 July 2007, p. 11.
[610] T. 12 July 2007, pp. 3-4.

414. Witness CNA testified that he witnessed two incidents where refugees were abducted from the CND. On the first occasion, a short man wearing a dark jacket and carrying a gun, came and abducted and killed Ruyenzi's children. Witness CNA testified that he did not know whether that person was a soldier or an *Interahamwe*, but he was accompanied by two other people, one of whom was also armed with a gun. On the second occasion, members of the *Interahamwe* abducted two women from Witness CNA's *commune*, Euphrasie and Hilaria, and two of their children. The two women and their children were taken to a place called Kamazuru, which was situated above the CND and were subsequently killed. Witness CNA testified that despite being a witness to this incident, he did not know the names of the *Interahamwe* who carried out the abduction. Witness CNA stated that Emmanuel Rukundo was not among the abductors, adding that since the abductions took place during the day, he could not have been mistaken about the fact that it was the *Interahamwe* rather than Rukundo who abducted the two women and their children.[611] Witness CNA testified that there were no other abductions or attacks of refugees from the CND apart from the two incidents that he recounted in his testimony.[612] **[page 126]**

415. Witness CNA testified that even though he knew of Bishop Nsengiyumva, he was not personally acquainted with him. Witness CNA testified that neither Bishop Nsengiyumva, any other Bishop, Rukundo, nor any other military chaplain ever visited the CND during the period he was there.[613] Witness CNA stated that Emmanuel Rukundo was not involved in the abduction of 15 refugees nor did he ever hear about the abduction of 15 refugees from the CND. Witness CNA never left the premises of the CND and therefore would have either seen or heard if Emmanuel Rukundo had visited the CND in a blue minibus and abducted 15 individuals from the CND.[614] Witness CNA added that during his stay at the CND he moved around inside the CND compound despite the fact that there were 16,000 refugees there and he maintained that he would have noticed had Rukundo or other figures of authority visited. Witness CNA testified that the distance between the back of the CND compound, where he was located, and the main entrance to the CND was on a raised level and not so large that he would not have been able to see if Rukundo had visited the CND.[615]

Defence Witness CNB

416. Witness CNB is a Tutsi who knew Rukundo's family. He arrived in Kabgayi together with his children on 26 April 1994 and took refuge at the CND. Witness CNB stayed there until 2 June 1994. Upon his arrival, Witness CNB was elected supervisor of the other refugees. Witness CNB described the CND as a place with buildings to the right and to the left, which was used for commercial purposes and surrounded by a fence. When Witness CNB was liberated from the CND by the RPF, there were 35,000 refugees in Kabgayi, with 20,000 refugees specifically at the CND.[616]

417. Witness CNB testified that women and children were accommodated inside the CND buildings while the men stayed outside the buildings in the rain. Later on, they were given tents by the Red Cross. According to Witness CNB, the distance between his tent and the main gate was about ten to 12 metres.[617]

418. Witness CNB testified that initially it was easy to leave the CND premises but later on it became difficult due to the insecurity caused by the *Interahamwe* who later killed people if they left the CND. Witness CNB stated that it was very difficult for him to remember the dates when he left **[page 127]** the CND. He remembered, however, that he went to a place known as Kamazuru in order to fetch something to drink. Later on, he clarified that Kamazuru was no more than ten metres away from the CND and he only stayed there for ten minutes.[618]

419. According to Witness CNB there was no large scale attack against the refugees while he was at the CND. Witness CNB stated, however, that almost everyday the *Interahamwe*, accompanied by a soldier,

---

[611] T. 11 July 2007, pp. 55-57.
[612] T. 12 July 2007, pp. 12-13.
[613] T. 11 July 2007, pp. 54-55, 59.
[614] T. 11 July 2007, p. 60.
[615] T. 12 July 2007, pp. 2-3, 10-12, 15.
[616] T. 9 July 2007, pp. 13, 17, 23-24, 32-33, 45-47, 51-52.
[617] T. 9 July 2007, pp. 15, 52-53.
[618] T. 9 July 2007, pp. 17, 39-40, 60.

came to the CND and selected people whom they abducted and subsequently killed. Witness CNB could not give an exact number of abductions, but testified that they happened often.[619] At first the refugees did not realize that those who were abducted would be killed. Witness CNB said that abductions at the CND took place in mid-May 1994 when the security situation deteriorated. According to Witness CNB, prior to that period the only problems that the refugees at the CND had to contend with were food shortages and exposure to the rain.[620] He stated that from his position inside the CND compound, he could clearly see the *Interahamwe* who were outside the CND compound.[621]

420. Witness CNB remembered that Ruyenzi's children were abducted and killed during one afternoon, but he could not remember the date. Witness CNB gave another example of an abduction from the CND when *Interahamwe*, working together with a soldier, abducted one of the refugees. Witness CNB explained that soldiers had the right to enter the complex whenever they thought it was necessary. On one occasion, a soldier entered the CND, accompanied by an *Interahamwe*, who indicated the person to be abducted. That person was then abducted and taken away. Witness CNB also remembered an incident when they came to get Mutijima who hid himself and survived.[622]

421. Witness CNB clarified that at times it was difficult to determine the identity of the abductors and whether or not they were *Interahamwe*. In their search for people to abduct, the abductors would enter the CND compound and pretend that they were visiting people they knew amongst the refugees. They were, however, using the visit as a pretext to enter the compound and abduct the refugees. Witness CNB noted that the abductors did not carry lists bearing the names of their victims and he therefore concluded that the abductors already knew their victims.[623]

422. Witness CNB testified that the refugees had been told by soldiers that if anybody turned up to abduct someone, they should try to protect themselves. On one occasion, Witness CNB said that **[page 128]** a man called Saddam, whom he knew, tried to attack them, but was killed within the CND complex. According to Witness CNB, this incident took place in May 1994 just before they were liberated by the RPF. Witness CNB could not give the names of the soldiers who told them to defend themselves but denied that it was Rukundo. Witness CNB added that some soldiers came to the CND and killed, while others came and gave them supportive advice.[624]

423. Witness CNB testified that Jean Kambanda came to the CND towards the end of May 1994, although he could not recall the exact date or the exact position held by Jean Kambanda at that time. According to Witness CNB, Kambanda was accompanied by three to four armed soldiers. Kambanda only visited the CND on one occasion. Witness CNB denied that anyone (soldiers or *Interahamwe*) came on that day or on the day following Kambanda's visit to abduct refugees. Witness CNB further testified that he knew Bishop Nsengiyumva but that the Bishop never came to the CND during the time that he was there. Furthermore, no one told Witness CNB that Jean Kambanda and Thaddée Nsengiyumva visited the CND together during that period.[625]

424. Witness CNB testified that he did not see any priests at the CND although he recalled seeing a seminarian from the Major Seminary called Bizimuremyi distributing blankets to the refugees. Witness CNB further testified that he did not see Emmanuel Rukundo at the CND; in fact, Witness CNB had not seen Rukundo before seeking refuge at the CND. He stated that amongst the refugees at the CND there were some who knew Rukundo and therefore had Rukundo or any other military chaplain visited the CND, they would have mentioned it to him. Finally, Witness CNB stated that he never saw Jean Kambanda in the company of Rukundo and the Bishop, insisting that it was only Kambanda who visited the CND.[626]

---

[619] T. 9 July 2007, pp. 18, 35-36, 54-55.
[620] T. 9 July 2007, p. 55.
[621] T. 9 July 2007, pp. 18-19.
[622] T. 9 July 2007, pp. 18-19.
[623] T. 9 July 2007, p. 55.
[624] T. 9 July 2007, pp. 19-20, 26.
[625] T. 9 July 2007, pp. 20-21, 25-27.
[626] T. 9 July 2007, pp. 25-26, 41-42.

425. Witness CNB stated that whoever said that Rukundo came to the CND in a pick-up and a blue minibus and abducted 15 refugees was telling lies. He also stated that he never heard or saw refugees at the CND board a blue minibus and a pick-up. Witness CNB stated that he saw every vehicle that came to the CND. When Jean Kambanda visited, for example, he came in a saloon car, although he did not know the make of the car. According to Witness CNB, it was possible to see the **[page 129]** vehicles from inside the camp.[627] Finally, Witness CNB also denied that soldiers and *Interahamwe* were stationed outside the CND and were shooting at the crowd.[628]

Defence Witness CNC

426. Witness CNC, a Tutsi, knew Rukundo as a priest and he also knew some members of Rukundo's family.[629]

427. Witness CNC testified that he and members of his family arrived in Kabgayi on 7 April 1994 and stayed there until 2 June 1994. Witness CNC sought refuge at the CND and met a number of refugees who came from his home area. According to Witness CNC, there were more than 2000 or 2500 refugees at the CND. Witness CNC could not recall how many people remained at the CND when it was liberated on 2 June 1994 because people had died and were abudcted, but confirmed that it was still quite a large number.[630]

428. Upon arrival, Witness CNC did not find shelter in the CND buildings and stayed in the courtyard where there were between 30 and 40 temporary accommodations made out of plastic sheets.[631] According to Witness CNC, many people were without shelter. Witness CNC testified that members of the Red Cross gave them food and blankets and a Non-Governmental Organization brought biscuits for children and elderly people. Nuns also came to the CND and distributed maize and biscuits to the children. Witness CNC could not recall if there were any seminarians at the CND.[632]

429. Witness CNC testified that he left the CND to go and see a friend in Gitarama on 18 and 30 April 1994, which took one hour to go and come back. Witness CNC also left the CND on 3 and 7 May to go to the Kabgayi hospital to visit his cousin's children who were sick.[633]

430. Witness CNC testified that he witnessed three incidents of abductions while he was at the CND. He stated that the CND compound was not surrounded with a fence and it was therefore possible to observe the abductions of the refugees as they occurred. According to Witness CNC, these abductions took place in May 1994; however, he could not recall the exact dates. According to Witness CNC, the first abduction involved two soldiers who abducted Ruyenzi's three children **[page 130]** during the day and later killed them. A member of the population who was a reservist in the army and Ruyenzi's neighbour, identified the children to the soldiers, but Witness CNC could not remember this person's name, only that he was about 55 years old.[634] Witness CNC testified that Rukundo was not involved in this abduction and since he knew Rukundo very well, he would have recognised him.[635] Witness CNC said that intellectuals and influential refugees were targeted as they were perceived to pose a threat should the RPF succeed in conquering the country; they did not look for refugees such as him.[636]

431. In respect of the second abduction which Witness CNC witnessed, he stated that a person called Gasirikare who worked as a cook for a brief period in the camp was gathering information about the refugees at the CND and relaying it to the *Interahamwe*. This man brought the *Interahamwe* into the camp when they abducted the refugees. Gasirikare was thrown out of the CND once people discovered that he was

---

[627] T. 9 July 2007, pp. 26, 39, 56-58.
[628] T. 9 July 2007, p. 27.
[629] T. 9 July 2007, pp. 64, 67-68.
[630] T. 9 July 2007, pp. 64-65, 69; T. 10 July 2007, pp. 6-9.
[631] T. 10 July 2007, pp. 7, 9-10.
[632] T. 9 July 2007, p. 69.
[633] T. 9 July 2007, pp. 65-66.
[634] T. 9 July 2007, pp. 70, 72-73.
[635] T. 10 July 2007, p. 36.
[636] T. 10 July 2007, p. 14.

collaborating with the *Interahamwe* in order to abduct refugees. Witness CNC clarified that Gasirikare arrived with a soldier, and they abducted three persons, including a man, a child and a young man.[637]

432. For the third abduction, Witness CNC stated that initially Gasirikare, and others tried to look for a person called Mutijima. When they could not find him, they put a mark on his tent and left without taking anyone.[638] They then returned in the night, shot at the tent and killed a lady.[639] Witness CNC further clarified that it was not Gasirikare who came to look for Mutijima, but another group of attackers. During cross-examination, Witness CNC clarified that in the third abduction Gasirikare abducted a woman, her child and a young man and that he was not accompanied by any soldiers.[640] Witness CNC said that the people who were abducted in the third abduction did not return because once they got outside the CND they were undressed, money was taken away from those who had any, and they were later killed. Witness CNC confirmed that Gasirikare was responsible for the abductions and that those who were abducted never returned.[641]

433. Witness CNC testified that there was no large scale attack against the refugees at the CND.[642] He added that there were no attacks during the four occasions when he left the CND to **[page 131]** attend to other matters. When he returned he never heard anyone talk about any attacks.[643] He did, however, state that a shell was thrown at the CND, but it did not explode.[644] Witness CNC explained that one person was killed by a reservist within the CND, but he did not know that person's identity. Witness CNC later stated that this person was killed by the refugees.[645] Witness CNC testified that he heard people talking about an attack that was alleged to have been carried out by Saddam, but he did not witness this attack. Witness CNC did not witness Saddam being killed.[646] He did not know Saddam and had never seen him.[647] Witness CNC had heard Saddam's name mentioned on many occasions and it was said that Saddam had killed many people. Witness CNC did not know what Saddam had done, but he was shown the place where Saddam had set up his roadblock, known as Kucyuzi Cyampanda.[648] Finally, Witness CNC described an attack that was launched on 2 June 1994 from the Gitarama stadium. The *Inkotanyi* arrived in Kabgayi on the same day around 10.00 a.m.[649]

434. Witness CNC stated that he never saw Emmanuel Rukundo at the CND. He had never heard anyone at the CND mention that Rukundo had visited the CND during the entire period when Witness CNC was in Kabgayi.[650] Witness CNC added that he knew Rukundo very well and would have been able to recognise him if he had come to the CND. Since Witness CNC did not sleep during the day and Rukundo did not come to the camp at night, he concluded that Rukundo did not come to the CND.[651] Witness CNC stated that the only soldiers which he saw at the CND were those who abducted and killed the refugees, and the RPF soldiers who arrived in June 1994 and freed them. Witness CNC disputed that Rukundo and the Bishop came to the CND together on several occasions, visited some part of the camp and when they left, "people" (soldiers) came and abducted refugees from the places that they had visited. Witness CNC also denied that Rukundo came to the CND with soldiers in vehicles and abducted 15 refugees.[652]

435. Witness CNC however stated that he saw a bus without doors that came to the camp at around 3.00 p.m. – apparently on the day that Jean Kambanda visited – with only the driver in the **[page 132]** bus. When

---

[637] T. 9 July 2007, p. 73; T. 10 July 2007, p. 10.
[638] T. 9 July 2007, p. 74. Sometimes also referred to as "Mutigima" (T. 10 July 2007, pp. 14-15).
[639] T. 9 July 2007, p. 74.
[640] T. 10 July 2007, pp. 11, 14.
[641] T. 9 July 2007, p. 74.
[642] T. 9 July 2007, p. 71; T. 10 July 2007, pp. 11-12, 34.
[643] T. 10 July 2007, p. 18.
[644] T. 9 July 2007, pp. 70-71.
[645] T. 10 July 2007, pp. 10, 12, 35-36.
[646] T. 10 July 2007, p. 12.
[647] T. 10 July 2007, p. 17.
[648] T. 10 July 2007, pp. 17, 36.
[649] T. 9 July 2007, p. 71.
[650] T. 9 July 2007, pp. 75-77; T 10 July 2007, pp. 18-20.
[651] T. 10 July 2007, pp. 17-18, 36.
[652] T. 9 July 2007, pp. 76-77.

the driver saw Jean Kambanda and the soldiers, he turned around and left. By the time that Kambanda and his soldiers left, the bus had already gone.[653]

436. Witness CNC explained that Jean Kambanda came to the CND sometime in May 1994, around 3.30 p.m., accompanied by three soldiers.[654] Kambanda arrived at the CND in a vehicle, he got out of the vehicle and walked into the CND compound. Witness CNC added that Kambanda's car, which was a military jeep with unusual doors, was parked outside the CND, near the nuns' convent. Witness CNC said it was very easy to see the vehicle, what people referred to as a *blindée* or armoured vehicle, from where he was located. Kambanda was wearing ordinary civilian clothes – a suit and a tie – and was escorted by three soldiers who were dressed in military clothing.[655] Witness CNC stated that a witness would be lying if he or she stated that the car that brought Kambanda to the CND was a saloon car since he never saw that type of vehicle when Kambanda visited.[656] Witness CNC testified that when Kambanda arrived, the refugees applauded since they thought he was coming to help them. Kambanda asked the refugees, "Why are you applauding? Am I a king?" Witness CNC further testified that Kambanda did not do or say anything to address the deplorable condition of the refugees at the CND. He turned around and walked out of the CND compound together with the soldiers.[657]

437. Witness CNC stated that he did not know Bishop Nsengiyumva, but he had heard of him. He never heard anyone mention that the Bishop had come to the CND.[658]

(c) Deliberations

438. The Indictment alleges that, during the months of April and May 1994, Emmanuel Rukundo went several times to the CND to kill Tutsi, that on some of these occasions, Rukundo was seen in the company of authorities, including Prime Minister Jean Kambanda and Bishop Thaddée Nsengiyumva, and that shortly after each visit, soldiers and *Interahamwe*, ordered, instigated, or aided and abetted by Emmanuel Rukundo, returned to the CND and killed several Tutsi refugees, and took away other Tutsi refugees and killed or inflicted serious bodily or mental harm upon them.

439. The Prosecution supported the above allegations with the testimonies of Witnesses CSE and AMA. The Defence called three witnesses, namely Witnesses CNA, CNB and CNC. **[page 133]**

440. As a preliminary matter, the Defence alleges that paragraph 15 of the Indictment is vague, since it does not specify the dates on which the acts were committed, the identities of the victims and the Accused's particular course of conduct.[659] The Chamber does not agree with this proposition. The Chamber notes that the Indictment provides the Accused with a clear timeframe, during which he is alleged to have visited the CND. The Indictment further specifies that the Accused visited the CND in the company of authorities, including Prime Minister Jean Kambanda and Bishop Thaddée Nsengiyumva. Additionally, the Indictment clearly states that soldiers and *Interahamwe* killed Tutsi at the CND or took Tutsi away to be killed shortly after the Accused's visits to the CND and that their actions were based on the orders, instigation or assistance of the Accused.

441. Concerning the identity of the victims, the Chamber recalls that in cases where the Prosecution alleges specific criminal acts, such as the murder of a named individual, the indictment should set forth material facts, such as "the identity of the victim, the time and place of the events and the means by which the acts were committed."[660] However, such detail need not be pleaded where the sheer scale of the alleged crimes makes it impracticable to require the same degree of specificity.[661] The Chamber finds that the reference to Tutsi refugees in the Indictment implies a large number, and therefore does not make it necessary

---

[653] T. 9 July 2007, pp. 76-77.
[654] T. 9 July 2007, pp. 74-75.
[655] T. 10 July 2007, pp. 15-16.
[656] T. 10 July 2007, p. 35.
[657] T. 9 July 2007, p. 74.
[658] T. 9 July 2007, p. 75.
[659] Defence Closing Brief, paras. 1304-1313.
[660] *Kupreskić*, Judgement (AC), para. 89; *Ntakirutimana*, Judgement (AC), para. 25.
[661] *Ibid.*

to be specific as to the identities of the victims. The Chamber is satisfied that the Indictment provided the Accused with sufficient notice to enable him to adequately prepare his defence.

442. The Defence also submits that the version of facts narrated by Witness AMA does not corroborate and is "totally inconsistent" with the Indictment. The Defence submits that Witness AMA did not testify about any of the essential elements of the Indictment.[662]

443. The Chamber notes that paragraphs 11 and 15 of the Indictment charge Rukundo with ordering, instigating or aiding and abetting the abduction, infliction of serious bodily harm or mental harm and killing of several Tutsi refugees on the basis that after Rukundo's visits to the CND, soldiers and *Interahamwe* returned to the CND and abducted, killed and caused serious bodily and mental harm to Tutsi refugees. The Chamber notes that Witness AMA testified about the abduction of about 15 Tutsi refugees at the CND at the end of May 1994. According to Witness AMA, Rukundo arrived, called out names from his list and instructed the refugees to follow him so **[page 134]** that they could be provided with food supplies. About 15 refugees were taken out of the fenced compound and into a minibus driven by a soldier. The refugees who boarded the bus were never seen again, apart from a young boy called Floraine, who, shortly after the bus left the CND, was hit on the head and thrown out of the bus into a ditch full of human corpses. Witness AMA testified that Floraine returned to the CND the following morning and told the other refugees what had happened to him.[663]

444. The Chamber finds that Witness AMA's evidence, if accepted, would expand the scope of the charge pleaded in paragraph 15 of the Indictment by accusing Rukundo of acts which are different from those set out in the Indictment.[664] Indeed, paragraph 15 of the Indictment specifically states that the abductions, killings and causing of serious bodily and mental harm took place after Rukundo had left the CND, whereas Witness AMA testified that the abduction occurred while Rukundo was present at the CND. The Chamber notes that consideration of Witness AMA's evidence would result in an impermissible *de facto* amendment of the Indictment. The Chamber finds that it could only consider Witness AMA's evidence if the Prosecution were to have amended paragraph 15 of the Indictment. The Chamber, therefore, will not consider Witness AMA's evidence in respect of the events which took place at the CND.

445. Prosecution Witness CSE testified that soldiers stationed at various locations in the Kabgayi diocese abducted refugees from within the CND.[665] The Chamber has already held that Witness CSE is a credible witness.[666]

446. In addition to Prosecution Witness CSE's testimony, all three Defence witnesses testified to abductions of refugees from within the CND. Defence Witness CNA stated that, during the time he spent at the CND, he witnessed two abductions. On one occasion, four or five *Interahamwe* came and abducted Ruyenzi's children. On the second occasion, the *Interahamwe* abducted two women and two of their children, taking them to Kamazuru, a place above the CND, where they were eventually killed.[667]

447. Witness CNB stated that the *Interahamwe*, accompanied by one soldier, came to the CND on several occasions to select people from amongst the refugees to be killed. Witness CNB stated that Ruyenzi's children were abducted and killed one afternoon. Witness CNB also remembered an **[page 135]** incident when abductors came to the CND in pursuit of a refugee called Mutijima who hid himself and survived.[668]

448. Finally, Witness CNC stated that he witnessed three abductions while he was at the CND in May 1994. On the first occasion, two soldiers arrived and abducted Ruyenzi's two sons and a daughter and later killed them.[669] Witness CNC also witnessed the abduction of three people by Gasirikare, who was

---

[662] Defence Closing Brief, paras. 1315-1316.
[663] T. 27 February 2007, pp. 5-8, 23-24, 29, 38.
[664] See *Karera,* Judgement (AC), para. 296.
[665] T. 17 November 2006, pp. 8-9, 30-31.
[666] See the evidence on the allegations at the Roadblock (Section III.3.c).
[667] T. 11 July 2007, pp. 55-57.
[668] T. 9 July 2007, pp. 18-19, 35-36, 54-55.
[669] T. 9 July 2007, p. 72.

accompanied by a soldier.[670] Witness CNC stated that, on the third occasion, Gasirikare abducted a woman, her child and a young man.[671]

449. Given that both Prosecution Witness CSE and the three Defence Witnesses concur that abductions took place, the Chamber therefore finds as a fact that, on several occasions in April and May 1994, soldiers and *Interahamwe* abducted refugees from inside the CND premises.

450. The Chamber will now determine what involvement, if any, Rukundo had with these abductions.

451. Witness CSE testified that Rukundo visited the CND on a number of occasions in the company of the Bishop of the Kabgayi diocese, Thaddée Nsengiyumva, and the then Prime Minister Jean Kambanda. According to Witness CSE, Rukundo and his entourage would visit certain parts of the CND, and "two hours or less than two hours" after each of these visits, soldiers would come and abduct refugees from the places that had been visited by Rukundo.[672] Witness CSE stated that the abducted refugees never returned to the CND and were never seen again. Therefore, Witness CSE presumed that they had been killed, even though he did not know the exact location where the refugees were killed.[673] All of the Defence Witnesses refuted Prosecution Witness CSE's testimony that Rukundo was present at the CND and was involved in the abductions of the refugees.[674]

452. The Chamber finds that Prosecution Witness CSE's evidence does not establish that Rukundo was involved in the abductions of refugees from inside the CND. The mere fact that Rukundo and his entourage visited the CND and that soldiers abducted refugees from the areas visited by Rukundo "two hours or less than two hours" afterwards is not sufficient to support a **[page 136]** finding of guilt beyond reasonable doubt. The Chamber notes that Witness CSE did not testify that Rukundo pointed out or otherwise identified prospective victims at the CND. On the contrary, Witness CSE stated that Rukundo and his entourage did "nothing" during these visits. It is unclear what happened between the visits by Rukundo and his entourage and the subsequent abductions. It has not been established if any order or instructions were given and, if so, by whom. The Chamber notes that, in general, Witness CSE's testimony concerning the events at the CND was rather vague. Witness CSE was not certain about the frequency of Rukundo's visits to the CND. He did not give any dates regarding the visits or indicate how long the visits lasted.

453. The Chamber therefore finds that the Prosecution has not proved beyond reasonable doubt that Emmanuel Rukundo ordered, instigated or aided and abetted soldiers and *Interahamwe* to kill Tutsi refugees at the CND or to abduct Tutsi refugees from the CND and kill them or inflict serious bodily or mental harm upon them, as alleged in paragraph 15 of the Indictment. **[page 137]**

9. EVENTS AT THE KABGAYI MAJOR SEMINARY

(a) Indictment

454. Paragraphs 18-20 and 28-30 read as follows:

> Paras. 18 and 28: During the month of May 1994, **Emmanuel RUKUNDO** went several times to the Kabgayi Major Seminary, and met the priests staying there, including some Tutsi priests, named Védaste NYIRIBAKWE, Célestin NIYONSHUTI, Tharcise GAKUBA, and one named Callixte MUSONERA. He publicly stated, within the hearing of the Tutsi priests, that the Major Seminary was full of *inyenzi* meaning Tutsis, and that they all must be killed. By his conduct, **Emmanuel RUKUNDO** inflicted serious mental harm on the priests, to whom he had spoken.
>
> Paras. 19 and 29: On or about 24 May 1994, a group of soldiers and *interahamwe,* led by **Emmanuel RUKUNDO,** launched an attack on the Kabgayi Major Seminary. The attackers, using a list, called out, removed and took away about twenty Tutsi clergy men and women and two Tutsi lay persons from the Kabgayi Major Seminary and then

---
[670] T. 9 July 2007, p. 73; T. 10 July 2007, p. 10.
[671] T. 10 July 2007, pp. 11, 14.
[672] T. 17 November 2006, pp. 7-9, 30.
[673] T. 17 November 2006, p. 12.
[674] T. 11 July 2007, pp. 57, 60 (CNA); T. 9 July 2007, pp. 26, 39 (CNB); T. 9 July 2007, pp. 76-77, T. 10 July 2007, p. 36 (CNC).

Judgement

killed them. By his conduct, **Emmanuel RUKUNDO** ordered, instigated, or aided and abetted the killing of these Tutsis.

Paras. 20 and 30: On a date sometime in the second half of May 1994, **Emmanuel RUKUNDO** went to the Bernadine sisters' convent in Nyarugenge secteur and commune in Kigali-Ville Prefecture, and told them that certain Tutsi clergy, including Father Felix NTAGANIRA, Father NIYONSHUTI Celestin, Father Tharcisse GAKUBA, Father Callixte MUSONERA, Father Martin, and Sister Bénigne, had been killed. (In fact, Father Felix NTAGANIRA had escaped death.)

(b) Evidence: Causing Serious Mental Harm to Tutsi Priests at the Kabgayi Major Seminary[675]

Prosecution Witness CSH

455. Prosecution Witness CSH knew the Accused Rukundo since 1981, when they attended the St. Léon Minor Seminary in Kabgayi. Witness CSH also studied with Rukundo for two years at the Major Seminary until the Accused was ordained as a priest. He attended the Accused's ordination ceremony at Byimana in Mukingi *commune* in July 1991. Witness CSH also met the Accused on several occasions during the genocide, when he was a refugee.[676]

456. In early April 1994, Witness CSH was on holiday with his family. He heard of President Habyarimana's death on the morning of 7 April 1994. His area was relatively calm until two weeks after the crash. On 16 April 1994, the Tutsi from Kibuye came to his neighbourhood to seek refuge. According to Witness CSH, a man responsible for MDR Power activities came to his area to incite people, following which the Hutu alerted the Tutsi by telling them that "[w]e have just been told **[page 138]** that we need to kill you." The Tutsi therefore moved to the parish for refuge, but were attacked there two days later by a group of *Interahamwe* led by the MDR Power man. Witness CSH then escaped with the other refugees and sought refuge at the Kabgayi Major Seminary around 20 or 21 April 1994, where he stayed until 2 June 1994.[677] Sometime between 21 and 24 April 1994, Witness CSH was able to go to the St. Léon Minor Seminary, but was later warned by Tutsi to hide. He had heard reports of people being killed outside the Seminary complex.[678]

457. Witness CSH testified that the refugees at the Kabgayi Major Seminary were a mix of both Tutsi and Hutu.[679] Amongst the people Witness CSH stayed with at the Major Seminary were the Josephite Brothers, who were always accused of segregationism, such as their former superior-general Martin Munyanshongore, who was allegedly pro-RPF. Also present amongst the refugees were Brother Fidele Murekezi, the headmaster of the Josephite School, Brother Rusezirangabo, Brother Gaspard Gatali, Brother Canisius Nyirinkindi, Brother Celestin Niwenshuti, Vedaste Nyiribakwe, Father Callixte Musonera, Father Tharcisse Gakuba, and Pierre Clavier Nkusi. There were also many nuns, including Sister Bénigne, Viateur Kalinda who was a journalist from Radio Rwanda, and some young seminarians.[680] Witness CSH also testified that the following people, who studied at the Nyakibanda Major Seminary, along with Rukundo and the witness, were present at the Kabgayi Major Seminary – Athanese Kagina, Jean-Bosco Munyangaba, Alexander Ngeze, Venuste Linjuyenea, and some Europeans such as Jean-Marie Dussart, Jean De La Croix and Abdoul Vedonc. During cross-examination, Witness CSH confirmed that there was a list of the refugees at the Kabgayi Major Seminary, but he only discovered that there was a list from Adalbert, a seminarian, after the events of 2 June 1994. He did not know, however, if the ethnic group of a person was specified on the list, since he did not see it himself.[681]

458. Witness CSH saw Rukundo once at the Kabgayi Major Seminary around the middle of May 1994, on either 12, 14, 15, or 16 May 1994. At around 2.00 p.m., Rukundo arrived with soldiers, wearing a military uniform and carrying a gun.[682] In cross-examination, Witness CSH said that Rukundo was on foot at that

---

[675] The Kabgayi Major Seminary is also known as the Philosophicum.
[676] T. 28 November 2006, pp. 19, 24-26.
[677] T. 28 November 2006, pp. 29-30; T. 29 November 2006, p. 2.
[678] T. 29 November 2006, p. 6.
[679] T. 29 November 2006, p. 3.
[680] T. 28 November 2006, pp. 30-31.
[681] T. 29 November 2006, pp. 4-6.
[682] T. 28 November 2006, p. 32; T. 29 November 2006, pp. 6-7.

time, and there was no vehicle near him. He further added that Rukundo was only accompanied by one soldier, who he thought was Rukundo's escort. While Witness CSH was walking around the compound after lunch, he saw Rukundo but he was not the **[page 139]** first to approach him. Witness CSH could not recall who was with him at that time.[683] Witness CSH and a group of nuns and priests approached Rukundo since they thought that he had come to bring them some comfort.[684] It was a mixed group of both Hutu and Tutsi that gathered around Rukundo, and most of the Tutsi in the group knew him.[685]

459. When they greeted him, Witness CSH was shocked to hear the Accused say the following in Kinyarwanda: "The Inyenzi must be exterminated. And for those who remain, those Inyenzi who are left over, we are going to set up a committee, a security committee which is going to seek them out." Witness CSH further explained that the term "security committee" referred to local gangs of killers like the *Interahamwe*. The group of people who had gathered around Rukundo withdrew, since they were shocked to hear this statement from a priest. Witness CSH himself said that, although, as a Tutsi, he was waiting for his death, and he knew Rukundo and his previous background from the Seminary in 1990, he was still frightened to hear Rukundo's words. He said it was "tragic" to hear a priest speak in those terms.[686] When Witness CSH was asked why he had expected words of comfort from Rukundo when he knew him to be an extremist, Witness CSH explained that, in the context of the genocide, "in the face of death, you expect salvation from whomever, from anybody." They also knew that he could not shoot at them in an open space and at a holy place such as the Seminary. According to Witness CSH, Rukundo remained there for about ten to 20 minutes. He did not see Rukundo after this occasion.[687]

460. Witness CSH agreed that he wrote a book regarding the testimonies of Kabgayi survivors. Witness CSH admitted that neither Rukundo's name nor that of any other army chaplain was mentioned in the book. However, he explained that he did not want to accuse someone in a book since it was not a judicial document and might have a wide readership. He did not incriminate the priests and Bishops, including Rukundo, and inserted nicknames for well-known politicians and *bourgmestres*. Witness CSH said that he had already given information about Rukundo to the Prosecution prior to the publication of the book.[688] Witness CSH denied that he was testifying against Rukundo because he had a personal grudge against him, and that he and Rukundo ever had any personal disagreements. He had even visited Rukundo's parents on several occasions. Witness CSH admitted that, after the genocide, in August 1994, he underwent para-military training with the RPF because he wanted to leave the clergy as a result of the revulsion he felt about the clergy's role **[page 140]** in the events in Rwanda in 1994. However, after training with the RPF, he returned to the Seminary in Nyakibanda, since he did not always agree with the RPF ideology.[689]

The Accused

461. Rukundo testified that, between April and June 1994, he went to Kabgayi on five occasions. The first visit was on 15 April 1994, the second was on 21 April 1994, the third time was on 7 May 1994, the fourth time was on 21 May 1994 and the last visit was on 2 June 1994. On 22 May 1994, he went through Kabgayi but did not stop.[690]

462. Rukundo testified that he helped to evacuate a nun named Félicité, who came from his parish, from Rwaza to Kabgayi on 7 May 1994. He also thought that he would take that opportunity to meet and bring food to members of his extended family who had already fled to Kigali. On that day, he left Camp Mukamira in his small Mazda vehicle, along with his escort Jean-Paul Nshimiye, and picked up Félicité. When he arrived in Kabgayi, Rukundo was told that many people had taken refuge at the Kabgayi Major Seminary, including the staff of the Episcopal Conference, and the nuns who worked at the Kigali Archbishopric. Sister Félicité asked to be dropped at the Major Seminary upon learning that another nun, who was a native of

---

[683] T. 29 November 2006, pp. 6-8.
[684] T. 28 November 2006, p. 32.
[685] T. 29 November 2006, p. 10.
[686] T. 28 November 2006, pp. 32-33.
[687] T. 29 November 2006, pp. 7-9, 11.
[688] T. 29 November 2006, pp. 39-43, 45, 47-48. The book was admitted as Exhibit D. 6.
[689] T. 29 November 2006, pp. 44, 49-50.
[690] T. 8 October 2007, pp. 52-53.

Byimana parish and her neighbour, was there. Rukundo said that he arrived at the Kabgayi Major Seminary around noon that day. Following this, he went to his home, then to Ruhango to see the Pallatine Sisters, and then to the Kabgayi Bishopric, before returning to Ruhengeri.[691]

463. Rukundo testified that, when they arrived at the Kabgayi Major Seminary between 11.30 a.m. and 12.00 p.m. (before lunch or prayers), Félicité registered at the reception. He parked his Mazda 323 vehicle at the bottom of the stairs leading to the small courtyard in front of the chapel. Rukundo went directly to meet his colleagues, who were in the small courtyard in front of the chapel. They stood near the bottom of the steps of the chapel. He had a brief discussion with them, after which they were joined by other priests, nuns and clerics, who all wanted information about the situation in the country. Rukundo was asked about the situation in Ruhengeri, and for information about certain priests, since they had heard that some priests in the Nyundo diocese had been killed. They also wanted to know about developments in the war and Rukundo's reasons for [page 144] visiting Kabgayi. Rukundo spent approximately 15 to 20 minutes there in discussion, but not more than 30 minutes.[692]

464. Rukundo stated that he remembered some of the people present in the group that day, including Jean-Marie Dussart, Monseigneur Kizito Bahumizihigo (the current Bishop), Father Claver Nkusi, Father Tharcisse Gakuba, Father Hildebrande Karangwa (who was a seminarian then, but now a priest) and Léonard Ntuyahaga (a seminarian who came from Kigali). Also present were Sister Dorothy, Brother Martin Munyanshongore, Fidèle Murekezi and Father Callixte Musonera. Most of the people in that group were Tutsi, but there were also a few Hutu, including Léonard Ntuyahaga.[693] In cross-examination, Rukundo confirmed that Hildebrande Karangwa was present on both his visits, as part of the group.[694] Rukundo testified that no one was surprised to see him in his military uniform, since most of them had already seen him dressed that way in 1993.[695]

465. Rukundo testified that, on 21 May 1994, he arrived in Kabgayi at around noon. After dropping off his personal effects at the St. Léon Minor Seminary and having lunch there, he went to greet his colleagues at the Kabgayi Major Seminary.[696] When Rukundo arrived at the Major Seminary on 21 May 1994, he saw some priests in the parking lot walk around (having just come out of the refectory), and then walk down the stairs to the courtyard in front of the chapel. A group of priests and nuns gathered around him, and they had a discussion for a few minutes. It was a mixed group of Hutu and Tutsi. Rukundo said that they discussed the same topics they had discussed on the previous visit, as well as the developments that had taken place in the last two weeks between the visits. Rukundo told them that he was moving from Ruhengeri to meet the head chaplain, and that he would not return to Ruhengeri due to security concerns.[697] He then visited the Bishop at the Bishopric, before taking the road to Kigali.[698]

466. Rukundo stated that he could not have made anti-Tutsi utterances especially in front of a group of people including Tutsi priests, since he is also a priest. According to Rukundo, Witness CSH was "inventing those words to find a reason for me to be convicted."[699] [page 142]

Defence Witness GSA

467. The Chamber has previously considered Witness GSA's evidence in relation to the alleged incidents at the *Imprimerie de Kabgayi* roadblock.

468. Witness GSA testified that he observed an influx of refugees from Kigali into Kabgayi a few days after 6 April 1994. At the beginning of the events, only priests on duty were present at the Kabgayi Major

---

[691] T. 9 October 2007, pp. 11-12.
[692] T. 9 October 2007, pp. 26-28; T. 10 October 2007, p. 46.
[693] T. 9 October 2007, p. 27.
[694] T. 10 October 2007, p. 46.
[695] T. 9 October 2007, p. 27.
[696] T. 9 October 2007, pp. 13-14, 26.
[697] T. 9 October 2007, p. 28; T. 10 October 2007, p. 46.
[698] T. 9 October 2007, p. 14.
[699] T. 9 October 2007, pp. 28-29.

Seminary, since the others were on vacation.[700] Witness GSA saw Rukundo at the Major Seminary on two occasions between April and May 1994: the first visit was in the first half of April, and the second one was during the beginning of May or the first half of May, sometime before 10 May 1994.[701] At the time of his visits, Rukundo was in military uniform[702] and carried a weapon, which Witness GSA thought was to help save civilians. Although Witness GSA believed that Rukundo was accompanied by a soldier who was his driver, he never saw the soldier. Witness GSA believed that Rukundo arrived at the Major Seminary aboard a vehicle.[703] In cross-examination, Witness GSA clarified that Rukundo had already arrived at the Seminary when he met him in the courtyard, but he believed that he had parked his vehicle near the entrance. However, he was not concerned with details of the vehicle, if Rukundo had one, at that time.[704]

469. As Rukundo arrived, a group of about five to ten people gathered around him to greet him and to hear news from outside the Seminary for several minutes. On these occasions, although he was not informed of the visit in advance, Witness GSA went to greet Rukundo and listened to him for a short time, never more than 10 or 15 minutes.[705] Rukundo remained in the compound talking to people, and did not stay for more than an hour. Witness GSA could not recall the people present during Rukundo's visit.[706] Witness GSA initially said that Rukundo was surrounded by a group of mixed persons, and no particular ethnic group stood out. The atmosphere in the group was congenial, since people were either curious to know what was happening or wanted to greet Rukundo.[707] **[page 143]**

470. Witness GSA testified that Rukundo spoke to the group about what he had seen along the road, and how the Tutsi were threatened and were in danger. He did not report anything that was new and not obvious to them. Witness GSA testified that he did not hear Rukundo make any anti-Tutsi statements. If Rukundo had made such statements, it would have created a scandal at the Major Seminary. Such statements, particularly if made by a priest, would have shocked not just the Tutsi, but also the priests and would have evoked a strong reaction, and they all would have known about it. Witness GSA admitted that he was absent from the Major Seminary from time to time when he visited the Bishopric; however, he did not spend much time outside the Major Seminary. Witness GSA emphasised that, whether he was physically present at the Seminary or not, if such a serious incident had occurred, news of it would have gone around the institution, and he would have been informed. In cross-examination, Witness GSA admitted that up until 2 June 1994, when Kabgayi was taken over by the RPF, he continued visiting the Archbishop and the diocesan bursary outside of the Major Seminary.[708]

Defence Witness Jean-Marie Dussart (formerly GSB)

471. The Chamber has previously considered Jean-Marie Dussart's evidence in relation to the events at the Nyabikenke communal office.

472. Witness Dussart sought refuge at the Kabgayi Major Seminary from 19 April 1994, until 2 June 1994. There were more than 100 clergymen and other members of the religious congregation present and there was a friendly atmosphere. However they were all afraid due to the insecurity caused by killings carried out by armed gangs. Staff members of the Major Seminary, including the Rector, Venuste Linguyeneza, Silas and other staff members welcomed the clergymen, but Witness Dussart did not know them all. He did not know the seminarians who were present, except for Hildebrand Karangwa. He had also heard Adalbert's name mentioned. Other clergymen included the Josephite Brother Martin Munyanshongore and his brother, and

---

[700] T. 1 October 2007, pp. 64-65.
[701] T. 2 October 2007, pp. 2-3, 29-30.
[702] T. 2 October 2007, p. 3, where the witness initially stated that Rukundo was a "Military chaplain of the *gendamerie*" and that he was wearing a "*gendamerie* uniform."
[703] T. 2 October 2007, pp. 3-4.
[704] T. 2 October 2007, p. 30.
[705] T. 2 October 2007, pp. 2-5, 30. Witness GSA marked the small courtyard, near the chapel and bell tower, in the Major Seminary, as the place where people had gathered around the Accused Rukundo. T. 2 October 2007, p. 25.
[706] T. 2 October 2007, pp. 4-5, 30.
[707] T. 2 October 2007, p. 6.
[708] T. 2 October 2007, pp. 5-7, 28-30, 73.

some Marist brothers, whom he met for the first time. The right wing of the Major Seminary was reserved for the families of officials, with whom he did not have much contact.[709]

473. Witness Dussart recounted that, on one occasion, Callixte Musonera had asked him for help to get out of the Major Seminary. Following this, Witness Dussart spoke to Bishop Nsengiyumva, who indicated that there may be such a possibility. On another occasion, Father Martin told him that he had been made to sit in an office, with an officer pointing a gun at his head. Both of these events **[page 144]** helped him to understand that the situation was serious. However, during the genocide, Witness Dussart only saw one person being killed, and only heard of the other atrocities after the genocide. He said that they were never attacked at the Major Seminary, even though there was never any physical barrier besides the administrative demarcation of Kabgayi-Gitarama.[710] In cross-examination, Dussart admitted that, while he was at the Kabgayi Major Seminary, he did not really have news of what was happening in Rwanda, apart from small snippets of news from the radio. He heard of attacks at the St. Léon Minor Seminary, and the murder of Louis [Rudahunga], who was the director of the Kabgayi printing press; other than this, he did not receive any information on killings.[711]

474. Witness Dussart said that on a date in May, sometime before 24 May 1994, Rukundo visited the Kabgayi Major Seminary. Witness Dussart was writing in his room when he learnt that Rukundo was around, and went to greet him. Witness Dussart was happy that Rukundo had come to greet them. When he asked him how things were, Rukundo replied "Well, I do nothing else but evacuate people from Ruhengeri towards the south, Gitarama and elsewhere." He further clarified that Rukundo had not said that he had "saved" people, but that he had "evacuated" them.[712] Witness Dussart only had a brief exchange with Rukundo, mostly in the context of a greeting. Their conversation lasted about two to three minutes, after which Dussart went back to his activities. Witness Dussart met Rukundo in the parking lot, about 10 to 15 metres from his room.[713] Rukundo was wearing the uniform of a military chaplain at the time. Witness Dussart was not sure if Rukundo was accompanied, or arrived in a vehicle.[714]

475. At the time of Rukundo's visit, there was a crowd of people around him. Witness Dussart could not, however, recall who was present. Witness Dussart did not see Rukundo leave the Major Seminary. He did not hear any additional information regarding what Rukundo may have said, after he had left. Further, he did not notice that any of his colleagues were shocked or offended by what Rukundo may have said.[715]

476. Witness Dussart stated that this was the last time that he saw Rukundo at the Major Seminary. He also did not hear of any subsequent visit by Rukundo to the Major Seminary. Witness **[page 145]** Dussart said that he was a "forced" resident of the Seminary in May 1994, and hardly ever left the location. He never heard Rukundo's name mentioned in a negative way.[716]

Defence Witness SJC

477. The Chamber has already considered Witness SJC's evidence in relation to the alleged incident at the *Imprimerie de Kabgayi* roadblock and in relation to the events at St. Joseph's College.

478. Witness SJC testified that he visited the Kabgayi Major Seminary every day between April and June 1994. Witness SJC said that the Seminary accommodated many people from all over Rwanda and that he knew many of the priests, seminarians and lay persons there. He helped staff by bringing them food, cigarettes and beer. He denied that he had ever heard Rukundo say that "the place was full of *Inkotanyi* and

---

[709] T. 10 September 2007, pp. 19-21.
[710] T. 10 September 2007, p. 21.
[711] T. 10 September 2007, pp. 50-52.
[712] T. 10 September 2007, pp. 26-28.
[713] T. 10 September 2007, pp. 27-28, 44. Witness Dussart identified the open area where he met Rukundo, on photographs of the Major Seminary shown to him. On photograph 394, he also identified the stairs used by Rukundo from the car park to the open area. T. 10 September 2007, pp. 37-38.
[714] T. 10 September 2007, p. 27.
[715] T. 10 September 2007, pp. 27-28.
[716] T. 10 September 2007, p. 28.

that they all had to be killed." Neither had he been told by anyone that Rukundo had done so. Witness SJC did not think that Rukundo could have made such a statement.[717]

(c) Deliberations

479. The Indictment alleges that, during the month of May 1994, Rukundo went to the Major Seminary several times, and met with priests. In public, and within the hearing of Tutsi priests, he allegedly stated that the Major Seminary was full of *Inyenzi*, meaning Tutsi, and that they must all be killed. By his conduct, Rukundo inflicted serious mental harm on the Tutsi priests who overheard his statement.

480. The Chamber notes that Witness CSH is the sole witness led by the Prosecution to support the allegation that the Accused directed anti-Tutsi statements towards a group of clergy at the Kabgayi Major Seminary. Witness CSH testified that he was a direct witness to Rukundo's visit to the Seminary around mid-May 1994, where he allegedly stated that the *Inyenzi* must be exterminated. He testified that when Rukundo arrived at the Seminary in the early afternoon, many members of the clergy surrounded him to receive comfort and news from the outside. Instead, to everyone's shock, the priest in military attire, carrying a gun and with a military escort, told the group consisting of both Hutu and Tutsi that the *Inyenzi* had to be killed and whoever was not killed would be "sought out by a local gang like the *Interahamwe*." Witness CSH testified that as a result of this statement, the group of people who had gathered around Rukundo withdrew, shocked to hear **[page 146]** Rukundo speak in this manner. Witness CSH thought that it was tragic for such a statement to come from a priest.[718]

481. Both Defence Witnesses GSA and Dussart testified that they saw the Accused when he visited the Major Seminary sometime in May 1994. According to their testimonies, Rukundo was surrounded by a crowd of people upon his arrival at the Seminary. Both witnesses further testified that Rukundo was dressed in military uniform, and had a military escort. Witness GSA confirmed that Rukundo carried a weapon.[719]

482. Rukundo admitted that he visited the Major Seminary in May 1994 and stated that Witness CSH was among the group of people he met during one of his visits to the Seminary.[720]

483. Based on the aforementioned, the Chamber finds it established that Rukundo, wearing military uniform, carrying a gun and in the company of soldiers, visited the Major Seminary sometime in May 1994. There is, however, some dispute as to the exact date of that visit. Witness CSH placed Rukundo's visit around 14, 15 or 16 May 1994.[721] Witness GSA saw Rukundo at the Major Seminary on a date in the first half of May,[722] while Witness Dussart stipulates that the visit was before 24 May 1994.[723]

484. The Chamber now turns to the question of whether or not the Accused uttered the anti-Tutsi statements that are the subject matter of paragraphs 18 and 28 of the Indictment.

485. The Defence submits that Witness CSH's evidence should not be believed because he wrote a book (Exhibit D. 6) in which he described the events in Kabgayi during the genocide but failed to mention Rukundo or link him to any criminal activity.[724] Witness CSH testified that his book was not a judicial document and that he did not wish to accuse any priests or other members of the clergy. Witness CSH added that he used pseudonyms for prominent political figures. Witness CSH further added that, by the time he published the book, he had already given a statement to the Prosecutor's investigators in which he described Rukundo's role in events at the Major Seminary.[725] The Chamber finds Witness CSH's explanations to be reasonable under the circumstances. **[page 147]**

---

[717] T. 3 September 2007, pp. 27-28.
[718] T. 28 November 2006, pp. 32-33; T. 29 November 2006, pp. 6-10.
[719] T. 2 October 2007, pp. 2-6, 29-30 (GSA); T. 10 September 2007, pp. 26-28, 44 (Dussart).
[720] T. 9 October 2007, p. 27.
[721] T. 28 November 2006, p. 32; T. 29 November 2006, p. 6.
[722] T. 2 October 2007, pp. 2-3, 29-30.
[723] T. 10 September 2007, pp. 26-27.
[724] Defence Closing Brief, paras. 728-734.
[725] T. 29 November 2006, pp. 39-43, 45, 47-48.

486. The Chamber does not believe that Witness CSH had any motive to lie about Rukundo or to wrongfully incriminate him before this Tribunal. The Chamber has also considered the fact that Witness CSH did not incriminate Rukundo with respect to the incident at the Kabgayi Major Seminary on 24 May 1994, on which the witness also testified. The Chamber is of the view that if Witness CSH had a motive to falsely incriminate Rukundo, he would have done so with respect to the more serious allegation relating to the abduction and killing of Tutsi from the Major Seminary on 24 May 1994. The Chamber therefore finds Witness CSH to be a credible witness and believes his evidence.

487. Defence Witnesses GSA and Dussart testified that they did not hear Rukundo make any offensive remarks. In addition, both Defence witnesses added that if such statements had been uttered by Rukundo, they would most likely have heard other people talk about them, which they did not.[726] The Chamber notes that Defence Witness GSA testified that he spent between 10 to 15 minutes listening to Rukundo address the crowd that had gathered around him.[727] Similarly, Witness Dussart testified that he spent between two to three minutes listening to Rukundo.[728] Defence Witness SJC, who was not at the Seminary on that day, visited the Major Seminary on several other occasions between April and June 1994 but never heard that Rukundo made offensive remarks against the Tutsi.[729] The Chamber finds that, since the Defence witnesses were not in Rukundo's presence for the duration of his visit, their evidence cannot discredit the firsthand evidence of Prosecution Witness CSH.

488. The Chamber therefore finds that the Prosecution has proved beyond reasonable doubt that, while at Kabgayi Major Seminary sometime in May 1994, the Accused said in the presence of several Tutsi clergymen that all *Inyenzi* had to be sought out and killed.

489. The Chamber, however, concludes that it has not been established that serious mental harm occurred as a result of Rukundo's conduct. The Chamber previously discussed the general legal standard required to prove serious mental harm in its discussion of the evidence at the Bishopric. The Chamber reiterates that the mental harm suffered must be more than a minor or temporary impairment of mental faculties although it need not be permanent or irremediable.[730] Further, according to the Appeals Chamber, nebulous invocations of "weakening" and "anxiety" do not **[page 148]** constitute serious mental harm for the purposes of a genocide conviction.[731] Witness CSH's evidence that he was "shocked" to hear this statement, and that it was "tragic" that it came from a priest, does not assist the Chamber in assessing how that statement occasioned more than a minor or temporary impairment of his mental faculties so as to constitute the serious mental harm envisioned by the Statute. Furthermore, Witness CSH's evidence neither suggests that Rukundo specifically described the Major Seminary as full of *Inyenzi* nor that the term *Inyenzi* was a reference to those from the Tutsi ethnic group. Rather, the Prosecution's evidence suggests that Rukundo uttered a general threat to "the *Inyenzi*" who "must be exterminated," and that a security committee would be set up to "seek out" such people. Finally, no evidence has been adduced as to the mental state of the Tutsi priests who were present or that an inference of mental harm could be made.

490. Accordingly, the Chamber finds that the Prosecution has not established beyond reasonable doubt that Rukundo's statement that the *Inyenzi* must be sought out and killed caused serious mental harm to the Tutsi priests.

(d) Evidence: Abduction and Killing of Tutsi Clergy from the Kabgayi Major Seminary

Prosecution Witness BLP

491. Witness BLP already testified in relation to the allegations at St. Joseph's College.[732] He testified that he met Rukundo at St. Joseph's College sometime towards the end of May 1994. Witness BLP was inside a

---

[726] T. 2 October 2007, pp. 5-7, 30, 73 (GSA); 10 September 2007, p. 28 (Dussart).
[727] T. 2 October 2007, pp. 4, 30.
[728] T. 10 October 2007, p. 28.
[729] T. 3 September 2007, pp. 27-28.
[730] *Rutaganda*, Judgement (TC), para. 50; See also *Brđanin*, Judgement (TC), para. 690; *Seromba*, Judgement (AC), para. 46.
[731] *Seromba*, Judgement (AC), para. 48.
[732] See Section III.4.b.

building at the College when a soldier asked him to join the refugees assembled outside, where there were other soldiers and civilians, and to identify himself. As Witness BLP came out of the building, he saw Rukundo near the vehicle parking lot. The soldiers, who were with Rukundo at the College, were looking for a priest called Fidele, whom they could not find, but who had sought refuge at the Kabgayi Major Seminary. When asked, Witness BLP told the soldiers that he knew where Fidele was. The soldiers asked him to take them to Fidele's location or be killed. Witness BLP explained that he had previously seen Fidele, who was a reverend brother of the Josephite congregation, at the Major Seminary. He explained that he boarded the soldiers' vehicle, and he told himself that since "they were with Father Rukundo, then they would wish only good for Fidele…" but he was also afraid for his safety if he did not go with the soldiers. Later in his testimony, Witness BLP explained that, prior to informing the soldiers of Fidele's location, they had been to several places, questioning and even torturing some people, in an effort to try and to locate Fidele. Witness BLP said that he told the soldiers this information because **[page 149]** he was scared of being harmed and did not want to be found out to have lied. Witness BLP saw Rukundo before he boarded the vehicle outside the College, since Rukundo had still not got into his vehicle. Witness BLP did not board the same vehicle as Rukundo, but they both arrived at the Kabgayi Major Seminary at the same time, around noon, in the same convoy.[733]

492. Upon arrival at the Kabgayi Major Seminary, the minibus which was in front of Witness BLP's vehicle, entered the compound, and one soldier alighted from it. Witness BLP was then told to sit down in the playground not far from the Major Seminary, while the soldiers proceeded to enter the Seminary. At this time, Rukundo remained standing near his vehicle in the parking lot not far from the Seminary. He was with Antoine Misago (a *sous-préfet*). Some soldiers went down to search the buildings on the lower side, while others remained at the entrance of the Major Seminary. Witness BLP stated that he saw the soldiers search almost all the buildings, before they stopped in front of the door of the chapel. They asked everyone inside the chapel to come out and show their identity cards. The soldiers allowed some people to return to the Major Seminary, while they asked others to go to the parking lot, where Rukundo and Misago were located.[734] According to Witness BLP, from where he was standing, he could clearly see the entrance to the chapel, where people were showing their identity papers, the bell tower of the chapel and the parking lot.[735]

493. Witness BLP said that Rukundo had a few sheets of paper, while the leader among the soldiers and the *sous-préfet* also had a piece of paper each. Witness BLP, however, did not know if the names of the people brought out of the chapel were on the list, since he could not read the list himself. Witness BLP recognised the following people who were made to board a vehicle at the Major Seminary – Brother Fidele, Nakanya Bénigne (a nun who lived in Kabgayi), Viateur Kalinda (a sports journalist with Radio Rwanda), a priest whose name he did not recall, some Josephite brothers living at St. Joseph's College and two members of the Marist order.[736] The vehicle then headed towards the tarmac road leading to Butare. Later, news spread in Kabgayi that the people in the vehicle had been killed in Byimana. Witness BLP said that he saw Rukundo leave with them, and he thought to himself that Rukundo was taking those people to safety. While it was difficult to **[page 150]** recognise the soldiers in the group, Witness BLP remembered one of the soldiers to be the one guarding General Bizimungu and the one who took Madame Rudahunga away.[737]

494. After the vehicle had left the Kabgayi Major Seminary, Witness BLP returned on foot to his place of work, which took him approximately five minutes.[738] He clarified in cross-examination that, contrary to what was stated in his pre-trial statement, he did not go to Byimana in the minibus.[739]

---

[733] T. 15 November 2006, pp. 17-18; T. 16 November 2006, pp. 30-32.
[734] T. 15 November 2006, p. 18; Misago's name is misspelled in this transcript as "Nsagwa".
[735] T. 15 November 2006, pp. 25-26; T. 16 November 2006, pp. 33-34. Exhibits P. 5, 5(A), 5(B), 5(C), 5(D), 5(E) and 5(F) were marked by Witness BLP as part of his identification of the locations in the Kabgayi Major Seminary; T. 16 November 2006, p. 9.
[736] T. 15 November 2006, pp. 18-19; T. 16 November 2006, p. 34.
[737] T. 15 November 2006, p. 19. On Exhibit P. 2, Witness BLP marked as "E" the Kabgayi Major Seminary, and also indicated the main road taken by the vehicle (T. 15 November 2006, p. 23).
[738] T. 15 November 2006, p. 19; T. 15 November 2006, pp. 28-29.
[739] T. 16 November 2006, p. 50

Judgement

Prosecution Witness CSH

495. Witness CSH was at the Kabgayi Major Seminary on 24 May 1994, which he described as "D-day". During the regular noon prayers at the Seminary, Witness CSH saw an armed group of soldiers and *Interahamwe* at the two entrances to the chapel. One seminarian, who was responsible for drawing up the list of refugees, asked them not to be afraid and announced that the armed group was only looking for four individuals. When Brother Martin Munyanshongore's name was called out several times by one of the armed men, he remained silent for a moment, but then went out with his prayer book. The soldiers called out other names including Father Callixte Musonera, Father Fidele Murekezi, and Father Celestin Niwenshuti, who were all Tutsi. Witness CSH testified that the rest of the refugees were ordered to form a queue and to show their identity cards. The Tutsi were made to go up the stairs, while the Hutu were told to go down the alley, leading to the building for the seminarians. Witness CSH saw about 10 to 15 Tutsi who were sitting or standing on the stairs, having already been arrested. The vehicle of the Seminary, a Toyota Hilux, and a blue minibus belonging to the *préfecture* were parked at the top of the stairs.[740]

496. When it was Witness CSH's turn in the queue, he told the soldiers that he had forgotten his identity card. He was asked to go and look for it, and so he returned to his room. Witness CSH then hid in the toilets of the building for a period of an hour and a half. When Witness CSH came out of hiding between 2.30 and 3.00 p.m., he was told that the armed group had left, and it was said that **[page 151]** those people were arrested on the orders of the Prosecutor and would be tried. Between midnight and 1.00 a.m., someone knocked on Witness CSH's door but left when it was not opened. The following day, at around 2.30 or 3.00 p.m., Witness CSH was told by someone whom he could not recall, that the people who had been abducted "had all been killed at Byimana in Gikomero, some eight kilometres from that place."[741] When asked, Witness CSH said that he did not know the people in the armed group, except for one man from Gitarama whose face was familiar but whose name was unknown. After the abduction, he heard people say that *sous-préfect* Misago was present, but he did not know that himself.[742]

497. Witness CSH testified that, on 2 June 1994, when he and the other refugees were liberated from the Kabgayi Major Seminary by the RPF, they were taken to a camp in Byimana where some peasants told them about the killings they had witnessed on 24 May 1994, which was a Thursday (a market day). The peasants explained that they had heard gunshots and Viateur Kalinda had tried to run away but was struck down by a machete. The others were shot. Witness CSH and the other refugees were shown the pile where the bodies were located; the blood was still fresh. At the end of 1994, Witness CSH participated in the exhumation of these bodies, which were re-buried in a tomb in Kabgayi. He recognized the bodies of Father Callixte, Father Celestin and a nun. They exhumed a total of 18 bodies.[743]

Prosecution Witness CCJ

498. The Chamber has already considered Witness CCJ's evidence in relation to the allegation at the Nyabikenke communal office. Witness CCJ was in Kanyanza at the beginning of the genocide, after which he fled to Kibuye. On 16 April 1994, after hearing that soldiers were inquiring about *Inkotanyi* at the Kabgayi Bishopric, he fled to Bujumbura in Burundi to seek refuge.[744] In cross-examination, Witness CCJ said that

---

[740] T. 28 November 2006, pp. 33-37; T. 29 November 2006, p. 14. Witness CSH identified a photograph admitted as Exhibit P. 9 as showing the Kabgayi Major Seminary, with the library, the housing for seminarians, the corridor where the Hutu gathered on 24 May 1994, and the area leading to the chapel. Witness CSH identified Exhibit P. 5D as a photo of the parking lot, the stairs where the Tutsi were held on 24 May 1994 in the Kabgayi Major Seminary, and the place the blue minibus that transported the people was parked. CSH said that Exhibit P. 5E was a photo of the tower and the prayer bell, the door to the chapel, and that Exhibit P. 5F was a photo of the building for seminarians, one of the two parking lots and the walkway to the parking lot. Witness CSH identified a photograph admitted as Exhibit P. 10 as showing the building which houses the seminarians, the first parking lot, a covered area going to the housing building, the multi-purpose hall, and the office of the director of the Kabgayi Major Seminary (T. 28 November 2006, pp. 38-42).
[741] T. 28 November 2006, pp. 34-35, 42.
[742] T. 28 November 2006, p. 37; T. 29 November 2006, p. 14.
[743] T. 28 November 2006, pp. 43-44. The photos identified as those of the final burial place were admitted as Exhibit P. 11 and Exhibit P. 11A.
[744] T. 14 February 2007, pp. 30-31.

without a calendar, he may have been mistaken about the date of his departure, but he was not wrong about the facts.[745] Witness CCJ explained that he fled Kabgayi because he was informed that his name and that of other priests were on a list of Tutsi priests who were wanted and targeted to be killed. On the day he escaped, Witness CCJ went to the **[page 152]** Kabgayi Major Seminary, which was full of people, and met some clergy, nuns and even foreigners who were going to Burundi.[746]

499. Witness CCJ said that, while in Burundi, he heard of the deaths of Callixte Musonera and Alphonse Mbuguje. He heard that Callixte was taken from the Kabgayi Major Seminary at the end of May, and then killed in Byimana with Father Celestin Nyonshuti, Father Tharcisse Gakuba, Father Védaste Nyiribakwe, Brother Martin and Sister Bénigne.[747] In cross-examination, Witness CCJ said that he had heard rumours that Callixte Musonera was an *Inkotanyi* accomplice, and that they were sometimes mistaken for each other.[748]

500. According to Witness CCJ, Rukundo had informed Marie Jose Mariboli at the Bernadine Sisters' Convent in Nyarugenge, Kigali, that he had been killed. Marie Jose Mariboli then told Rukundo that she knew that Witness CCJ was still alive and in Burundi.[749]

The Accused

501. Rukundo testified that, on 24 May 1994, he was in Kigali. He did not set foot in Kabgayi on that day.[750] Rukundo said that he did not know Witness BLP, and saw him for the first time when he testified before the Chamber. He also said that it was impossible to observe events at the Major Seminary from the football field as Witness BLP had claimed. Rukundo also stated that Witness CSH did not claim to have seen him at the location on that day, and that he was only able to identify the *sous-préfet* as one of the attackers.[751]

502. Rukundo said that he only heard of the death of the clergymen at the Major Seminary on 2 June 1994, when he went to Kabgayi with Father Kalibushi [now Bishop] to see the Bishop at the Bishopric. That was his fifth trip to Kabgayi during the period of April to June 1994. On that occasion, he arrived in Kabgayi at about 9.15 a.m. in a situation of great fear and mourning due to the events of 24 May 1994. Rukundo recalled that one of the priests at the Bishopric or the Bishop himself mentioned the news to him, although he did not remember who he specifically met that morning. Rukundo discussed the events of 24 May 1994 with the Bishop, but they did not spend too much time doing so since the Bishop himself was panicking at that time. Rukundo was told that the authorities were responsible for the abductions and killings, although he was not given any names. **[page 153]** These authorities had previously gone to the Bishopric with arrest warrants to ask for the clergymen.[752] In cross-examination, Rukundo confirmed that he had heard that the prefectural government authorities from Gitarama had come with arrest warrants to remove people from the Major Seminary. He did not know what offence they were being arrested for, under the warrants, although it could have been on suspicion of RPF complicity or for ethnic reasons. Those who were killed were Tutsi, and they were not tried in a court of law, but killed on the same day that they were abducted. Rukundo denied that he was one of the authorities responsible for the abductions and killings.[753]

503. In cross-examination, Rukundo testified that he knew the following people who were abducted from the Major Seminary and killed: Sister Benebikira (mother superior of the community in Kabgayi), Callixte Musonera, Tharcisse Gakuba, Célestin Niyonsote, Vedaste Nyilibakwe, Martin Munyansongore, Fidel Murekezi and Sister Bénigne. He also heard of a journalist Viateur Kalinda who was also killed on that day, although he did not know him. He did not know the precise number of people killed or all of those who were killed. Rukundo knew that Martin Munyansongore and Fidele Murekezi had been RPF supporters since

---

[745] T. 15 February 2007, p. 12.
[746] T. 14 February 2007, pp. 31, 60.
[747] T. 14 February 2007, pp. 33-34.
[748] T. 14 February 2007, pp. 59-60.
[749] T. 14 February 2007, p. 35; T. 15 February 2007, p. 7.
[750] T. 9 October 2007, p. 29; T. 10 October 2007, pp. 51-52.
[751] T. 9 October 2007, pp. 33-34.
[752] T. 9 October 2007, pp. 35-36.
[753] T. 10 October 2007, pp. 48-50, 52.

1990. He said that he had not been present at the presbyterium in the Kabgayi diocese in 1993, and did not know that they had openly declared themselves as RPF supporters. He said that it was only after he left Rwanda following the events of 1994 that he read in the *Document Soldaire Rwanda*, whilst he was in Rome, that Callixte Musonera was a member of the clandestine brigade of the RPF, but he did not see anything written about Felix Ntaganira. Although he had seen Callixte Musonera at the Major Seminary on both occasions, Callixte never told Rukundo that *gendarmes* had questioned him.[754]

504. When asked about Tharcisse Gakuba, Rukundo stated that he considered him as his brother and a friend. They both attended primary school, Catechist School and the Major Seminary together. Gakuba was ordained two years after Rukundo. Rukundo stated that he was saddened to have been accused of Gakuba's death. Rukundo knew Callixte Musonera from the Seminary for mature students when he arrived there in 1981. Musonera was one year ahead of Rukundo, and they attended the Major Seminary together. They became close friends, and Rukundo appreciated his jovial nature. Rukundo stated that Musonera was a good man and that he was greatly affected by his death.[755] **[page 154]**

505. Rukundo testified that he knew the Bernadine Sisters' Convent in Kigali and had a friendly relationship with many of the nuns there, including Mariboli, Specious Kamishago, Donate Kamurahiza and Isabelle Kanyahanga. While Rukundo was in Kigali between April and June 1994, he went to the Bernadine Sisters' Convent on probably two occasions. Rukundo's first visit to the Bernadine Sisters' Convent was on 23 May 1994. Father Laurent Kalibushi had expressed a concern that certain soldiers had proposed taking the nuns out of their community to an unspecified destination, and he was worried for the nuns since the sisters of the Remera Community were massacred in Kamomyi when they were evacuated. He therefore asked Rukundo to go and meet with the Bernadine Sisters. Rukundo personally dissuaded the Bernadine Sisters from going on a trip, and they all survived. On that first visit, Rukundo told Mariboli that her brother, Nkongoli, had been killed at a small trading centre close to his place, and had conveyed his condolences to her. He also told her that her mother was still alive. Rukundo said that at that point he already knew that Witness CCJ had gone to Burundi, and therefore had no reason to tell her that Witness CCJ was dead, contrary to Witness CCJ's testimony. Rukundo confirmed that Mariboli was present with the other sisters, during those two visits.[756]

506. Rukundo's second visit to the Bernadine Sisters' Convent was in June 1994 after he had heard of the death of clergy members in his diocese. Rukundo conveyed the news about the death of the clergymen, including Tharcisse Gakuba, Celestine Niyonteze, and Callixte Musonera. Rukundo thought that it was comforting for the Bernadine Sisters to be able to discuss the deaths.[757] In cross-examination, Rukundo denied that he went to the Convent on 2 June 1994. He stated that he heard of the death of the clergymen on 2 June 1994 when he was in Kabgayi with Father Laurent Kalibushi.[758] In cross-examination, Rukundo confirmed that the news of the killings was not broadcast on the radio, and that he did not hear about the killings at the Seminary until 2 June 1994.[759] He heard on 8 June 1994 about the killings of three Bishops, nine priests and a superior of the Josephite brothers on 5 June 1994. Rukundo only visited the Convent after that time.[760]

Defence Witness GSA

507. Witness GSA testified that Jean-Marie Dussart was one of the foreign priests who were at the Kabgayi Major Seminary from the beginning of the genocide. He stayed there until the RPF arrived in Kabgayi. Other foreign priests, including Father André Lerusse, went abroad for their **[page 155]** own security. Among the clergy present who were later killed were Brother Martin and Brother Fidele, who were Josephite Brothers, and Brother Canisius, Brother Gaspard and Brother Fabien, who were Marist Brothers, and Sister Bénigne.

---

[754] T. 10 October 2007, pp. 46-48.
[755] T. 9 October 2007, p. 29.
[756] T. 9 October 2007, pp. 55-57; T. 10 October 2007, pp. 37-38.
[757] T. 9 October 2007, p. 56.
[758] T. 10 October 2007, pp. 36-37.
[759] T. 10 October 2007, pp. 50-51.
[760] T. 10 October 2007, p. 36 (see also French transcript, T. 10 October 2007, p. 42).

The seminarians Adalbert, to whom Witness GSA gave the keys, and Gilda Brown were also present. Witness GSA met the members of the clergy who had sought refuge at the Major Seminary on several occasions.[761]

508. Witness GSA testified that the abduction of persons from the Major Seminary occurred on 24 May 1994, sometime between 12.00 and 2.00 p.m., when they had gathered in the chapel at prayer time after lunch. The attackers asked people to show their identity cards. Some people, after indicating that they had forgotten their identity cards, locked themselves in their rooms and did not return. The attackers went through the unlocked rooms to pull out people and ask them to display their identity cards. There were already people suspected of being RPF accomplices who were set aside "to be taken to the slaughter house." At some point, the attackers tried to locate a transmitter in the institution, and used that as a pretext to move around the institution for approximately two hours. Witness GSA said that the attackers asked Adalbert to locate the bursar in order to obtain spare keys for various rooms. Since the bursar was temporarily absent, the attackers threatened Witness GSA to give them access to the keys and asked for all of the doors to be opened.[762] At that time, Witness GSA was in his office; a soldier with a gun and two civilians came into the office and accompanied Adalbert to the rooms. The group of attackers scattered all over the Major Seminary searching, but did not force open any doors.[763] When asked in cross-examination if people were made to sit down on the back lawn during the searches, Witness GSA said that he did not see that situation himself, but it was possible.[764]

509. According to Witness GSA, the attackers presented themselves as officials – the *sous-préfet* Misago, the intelligence officers and the representatives of the Prosecutor's office. It was therefore a properly organized search operation with all of the necessary legal warrants. Some of the attackers wore military uniforms and carried weapons. Witness GSA did not see soldiers and civilians together all of the time, and estimated that there may have been four to five soldiers.[765] Witness GSA did not recognise any of the attackers, since the authorities in Gitarama had changed.[766] In cross-examination, Witness GSA clarified that, although he had heard that Misago was present, he **[page 156]** could not have identified him since he did not know him.[767] Witness GSA stated that Rukundo was not among the attackers. He added that, if Rukundo had been present, he would have recognised him, since he knew him well. Witness GSA further emphasised that he never heard anyone subsequently mention Rukundo's presence at the Major Seminary.[768]

510. Witness GSA said that, throughout the operation conducted by the attackers at the Major Seminary, he was able to move around and observe what was happening in various parts of the building.[769] Witness GSA clarified that he was not present when the initial attack took place, and arrived there 15-20 minutes afterwards. When the assailants arrived, he was on the other side of the building, along with the Archbishop of Kigali, Vincent Nsengiyumva. The first acts of the attack were therefore recounted to Witness GSA from people gathered in the chapel, since he did not witness them for himself.[770]

511. Witness GSA said that when he heard about the attack he went to the site of the event. He saw people in uniform, who had come with the attackers, standing near a blue Toyota eight-seater minibus close to the entrance where people were being taken away. He tried to intervene to help Brother Fidele, who had come to him. A soldier pointed his weapon at Witness GSA's throat and said that if he tried to intervene, Witness GSA would be considered one of Fidele's collaborators and killed.[771]

---

[761] T. 1 October 2007, pp. 67-68, 70.
[762] T. 2 October 2007, pp. 8-9, 21.
[763] T. 2 October 2007, pp. 62-63.
[764] T. 2 October 2007, p. 70.
[765] T. 2 October 2007, pp. 9-10, 54, 61.
[766] T. 2 October 2007, p. 14.
[767] T. 2 October 2007, p. 61.
[768] T. 2 October 2007, pp. 14, 72-73.
[769] T. 2 October 2007, pp. 10, 62.
[770] T. 2 October 2007, pp. 17-18, 20-21, 58-60, 62.
[771] T. 2 October 2007, pp. 18-20. Witness GSA marked the location of the vehicle when parked close to the entrance of the building, rooms, courtyard and chapel (T. 2 October 2007, p. 25).

Judgement

512. Witness GSA saw the people being loaded into the vehicle and knew that some of them would not return. The assailants brought the Seminary vehicle back in the evening.[772] Witness GSA testified that the same evening they heard that the people taken away had been killed, and they received confirmation of this information the following day. No one told them how they had been killed or where their bodies could be found.[773]

513. Witness GSA testified that there were four priests abducted that day from the Major Seminary: Célestin Winchuti, Védaste Nyibakwe, Callixte Musonera and Tharcisse. Two Josephite brothers (Martin and Fidele) and three Marist brothers (Brother Gaspard, Canisius and Fabien) were also abducted as well as Sister Bénigne of Benebikira, a journalist Kalinda and another lady whose name he did not know. Witness GSA confirmed that Martin, Fidele, Callixte, Célestin and the **[page 157]** journalist were specifically wanted for reasons apart from their ethnicity. A few weeks before the abduction, a list with the names of people purportedly from the RPF, their dates of birth, places of residence, places where they had infiltrated and war names was drawn up. Witness GSA confirmed that he had seen the list.[774] The names of Fidele and Callixte were on the list, along with those who constituted the nucleus of the Rwandan press, Philbert Muzima and Jean-Claude Nkubito.[775] In cross-examination, Witness GSA confirmed that there were 12 people in all who were abducted from the Major Seminary on 24 May 1994, and that they were the only ones to have been abducted, to the best of his knowledge.[776]

514. Witness GSA testified that he had never been accused of acting in concert with Rukundo and Misago in the abductions of 24 May 1994 from the Major Seminary. He had remained in the RPF zone until July, which according to him, would have been impossible if he had acted as an accomplice in the 24 May 1994 events.[777]

515. Witness GSA said that he saw information about Rukundo's arrest on the internet. He had known that Rukundo was accused of certain crimes, based on plays staged in Geneva and other places. Witness GSA was not surprised at Rukundo's arrest, since the church had been involved in some killings, and several priests were sought after to be arrested. However, he did not think that Rukundo was guilty.[778]

Defence Witness Jean-Marie Dussart (formerly GSB)

516. Witness Dussart testified that, at 11.00 a.m. on 24 May 1994, he went to Father Silas Ngerero's room. Around 12.00 or 12.30 p.m. (the time of noontime prayers in the chapel), as he headed towards the chapel, he saw a soldier. When Witness Dussart entered the chapel for prayers, someone in military uniform asked him for Father Martin's whereabouts. Witness Dussart said that he could be located after the prayers. Witness Dussart did not see the soldiers enter the chapel.[779] However, after prayers, and as the group that was in the chapel were going to lunch (approximately 30 to 40 of them), they were ordered to sit down on the lawn behind the buildings and were guarded by a soldier. They were only permitted to go to lunch at 3.00 p.m. From his location on the lawn, Witness Dussart could only see a group of two soldiers and one civilian inspecting the rooms. He **[page 158]** later heard that the civilian was the new *sous-préfet* from Kibungo, who was unknown in that area. Witness Dussart did not recall seeing any familiar faces among the people involved in that operation.[780] It was not physically possible to see the vehicles parked, if any, from his location, although he had a vague recollection of seeing some vehicles earlier in the parking lot. Witness Dussart could not see what was happening behind the tower at the entrance to the chapel, from his location on the lawn. He did not see the people being taken away or who was responsible for taking them away. Witness Dussart explained that those present at the Major Seminary on that day did not feel threatened at all; they did not feel that they were under "attack" because they "believed it was an operation carried out to

---

[772] T. 2 October 2007, pp. 22-23.
[773] T. 2 October 2007, p. 25.
[774] T. 2 October 2007, pp. 11-12, 29.
[775] T. 2 October 2007, pp. 13-14, 50-52.
[776] T. 2 October 2007, p. 28.
[777] T. 2 October 2007, pp. 70-71, 73.
[778] T. 2 October 2007, p. 26.
[779] T. 10 September 2007, pp. 29-30. Witness Dussart identified photograph 395 to show the entrance of the chapel, with the tower, and the flight of stairs that goes towards the Seminary buildings (T. 10 September 2007, p. 38).
[780] T. 10 September 2007, pp. 29-30.

check our identity and to find out whether we were safe and secure. So we weren't attacked or assailed, as such. It was peaceful. It was peaceful." In cross-examination, Witness Dussart could not recall the people with him on the lawn, since he did not know them. The Rector Venuste Linguyeneza was not present, although Witness Dussart later heard that when the Rector saw what was happening, he drove in his car to inform the Bishopric.[781]

517. Witness Dussart testified that on the morning of 25 May 1994, after mass and breakfast, he met Father Joseph from Byimana at the Bishopric, who informed him that the people taken away had been killed. Sylvestre at the St. Léon Minor Seminary then further confirmed this information. At this point, Witness Dussart became frightened and started writing down his observations in a bundle of seven diaries. In cross-examination, Witness Dussart clarified that it was only on the following morning that he was notified that a crime had been committed; until then he thought that the people had merely been taken away for a routine check.[782] He stated that the refugees previously felt safe at the Major Seminary, in contrast to the places of great insecurity where they had come from, and therefore felt that it was only a routine check. He admitted, however, that there was no other occasion when people had been brought back after having been taken from the Major Seminary for questioning.[783]

518. Witness Dussart remembered that Father Martin, Callixte Musonera, Father Pierre Celestin, Father Vedaste and Brother Fidele were among those abducted from the Major Seminary. Among the 17 people taken away, most were priests, although there was one journalist who was later killed. **[page 159]** Witness Dussart said that, although there was no roll call that evening, he noticed that some people were missing from the community.[784]

519. Witness Dussart testified that he never heard Rukundo's name or that of any other military chaplain mentioned in connection with the events of 24 May 1994.[785]

Defence Witness SJC

520. Witness SJC testified that one of his classmates, who had taken refuge at the Kabgayi Major Seminary at the time and who was a Tutsi survivor of the massacre, but is now deceased, told him that towards the end of May 1994, people were abducted from the Major Seminary. Witness SJC was told that the people were taken away in a minibus, and that attackers were sent by the prefectural authority.[786] Witness SJC admitted that he did not actually know who abducted the people from the Major Seminary[787] and disagreed that those from the prefectural authority could have been responsible for killings when they had the responsibility of protecting people.[788] Witness SJC heard that the people taken away had been killed when the Bishop of Kabgayi denounced the killers on Vatican radio the following day.[789] Some people who were abducted from the Kabgayi Major Seminary included Father Vedaste, Father Celestin, Father Tharcisse, Sister Bénigne, Father Callixte, and a journalist, Viateur Kalinda. They were killed in Mwanda, not far from Kabgayi.[790] Witness SJC stated that his source had mentioned names of those abducted and others that he could not recall. Witness SJC never found out how many people were abducted from the Seminary.[791]

521. Witness SJC said that during the time he spent in Kabgayi, from April 1994 until the time he left, he never saw Rukundo there nor heard of his presence.[792]

---

[781] T. 10 September 2007, pp. 29-30, 45.
[782] T. 10 September 2007, pp. 31, 45-47.
[783] T. 10 September 2007, pp. 52-53, 58.
[784] T. 10 September 2007, pp. 46-47.
[785] T. 10 September 2007, pp. 31-32.
[786] T. 3 September 2007, pp. 27-28, 47-50.
[787] T. 3 September 2007, pp. 49-50.
[788] T. 3 September 2007, pp. 62-63.
[789] T. 3 September 2007, pp. 28, 48.
[790] T. 3 September 2007, p. 32.
[791] T. 3 September 2007, pp. 48-49.
[792] T. 3 September 2007, pp. 46-47.

Defence Witness SJA

522. The Chamber has previously considered Witness SJA's evidence in relation to the incidents at St. Joseph's College. **[page 160]**

523. Witness SJA testified that he heard on the radio that Rukundo, who was in Switzerland at the time, had been accused of participating in a plot to abduct clergymen from the Major Seminary.[793]

524. At the outset of the genocide, Witness SJA testified that Fidele, a clergyman, was at St. Joseph's College and Martin, also a clergyman, remained in Gakurazo in Byimana. According to Witness SJA, Fidele and Martin arrived at the Major Seminary at the beginning of May 1994. Witness SJA had the opportunity to visit both Fidele and Martin at the Major Seminary on 24 May 1994, along with brother Celestin Munyankindi, who had a vehicle. That was the first time he visited the Seminary since the arrival of the refugees. He arrived at the Major Seminary around 8.00 a.m., after which he ran an errand for Fidele in Gitarama for 30 minutes. Upon his return, Witness SJA spent time talking to the Marist brothers, the Josephite brothers and some other refugees whom he knew. At about noon, when the bell for midday prayers rang, the clergy had to leave. Witness SJA then said goodbye to them and left to return to his home, along with Celestin.[794]

525. As they were leaving, Witness SJA noticed that many soldiers had taken up various positions at the Major Seminary. On their way to the vehicle, he saw Brother Fidele having a discussion with Venuste Linguyeneza. A soldier was standing next to them, telling them to hurry up. A little further to the right, some people were coming out of the chapel. A soldier, along with Brother Martin's driver, headed towards a green Hiace vehicle. Two people dressed in civilian attire were sitting down next to the Hiace vehicle, and one of them had documents in his hand. They forced Martin to enter the vehicle. Witness SJA later heard that one of them was Antoine Misago Rutegesha (the *sous-préfet* and the person heading the prefectoral committee on refugees), although he had never met him before. At that time, Sister Bénigne walked up behind him, reciting her rosary, as she was being led away by a soldier. After Martin went into the vehicle, Witness SJA left the Major Seminary in his own vehicle. Witness SJA saw Martin being taken away, but not Fidele or Sister Bénigne. He subsequently received information of the other abductions.[795]

526. Witness SJA did not know when the attackers arrived at the Major Seminary. He noticed that they were present at noon, when he left the people he had come to visit. He estimated that he spent 15 minutes between the time he left the people he visited and his own departure from the premises.[796] In cross-examination, Witness SJA admitted that he had remained at the location for **[page 161]** approximately 15 minutes, and was not in a position to comment on events after that time.[797] Witness SJA saw two soldiers near the door of the chapel, to whom the people leaving the chapel showed their identification papers. Other soldiers had taken positions next to the columns of the chapel. He estimated that there were about 10 soldiers at the Major Seminary that day; but he was not sure if there were more soldiers who he did not see.[798]

527. Witness SJA testified that he did not see Rukundo at the Major Seminary on 24 May 1994. He did not hear anyone mention Rukundo's name in connection with the abductions in his discussions with many people about the events of that day. Since Rukundo was well-known within the clergy, people would have known if he had come to the Major Seminary.[799]

528. Witness SJA was detained in Rwanda on 17 July 1997. He admitted that he had been convicted for complicity in certain events.[800] In cross-examination, Witness SJA stated that he knew Joseph Ndagijimana (a priest), Jean-Baptiste Gatsinzi (*sous-préfet*), and Emmanuel Ruzigana (*bourgmestre*), who were all

---

[793] T. 22 October 2007, pp. 15-16.
[794] T. 22 October 2007, pp. 16-18.
[795] T. 22 October 2007, pp. 18-21.
[796] T. 22 October 2007, p. 19.
[797] T. 22 October 2007, p. 33.
[798] T. 22 October 2007, p. 20.
[799] T. 22 October 2007, pp. 20, 36, 40.
[800] T. 22 October 2007, pp. 22-23.

detained with him in prison after being accused of genocide. Witness SJA denied that they had ever had a meeting regarding the allegations against Rukundo.[801]

Defence Witness SLD

529. The Chamber has previously considered Witness SLD's evidence in relation to the incidents at the St. Léon Minor Seminary.

530. Witness SLD testified that there was an information gathering exercise to determine those who were responsible for the crimes in Kabgayi in 1994, which became public in the Gacaca courts. Among the perpetrators were the major seminarian Sylvain, Brother Rwesero, *sous-préfet* Gatsinzi, the former *bourgmestre* Niyonteze, and a woman called Hakinesa, who was a major and was detained at Mulinsi. These were people who incited others to commit crimes and who participated in the crimes in Kabgayi.[802]

531. Witness SLD denied that Rukundo's name was mentioned in connection with the crimes in Kabgayi, and stated that, if this was the case, he would have heard since he knew Rukundo more **[page 162]** closely than those who were found responsible for the crimes.[803] He added that Rukundo was never spoken about in connection with the crimes in Kabgayi in 1994.[804]

Defence Witness EVD

532. The Chamber has previously considered Witness EVD's evidence in relation to the events at the Kabgayi Bishopric.

533. Witness EVD was not an eyewitness to the abductions and killings of priests and other civilians from the Kabgayi Major Seminary. The Vicar General, whom he accompanied to the Seminary to recover property belonging to the deceased priests to keep at the Bishopric, informed him about the incident. This task took place sometime between 20 and 25 May 1994. Although he did not spend much time at the Major Seminary, Witness EVD had the chance to speak to the sister of a priest who had been killed in the abductions. It was being said that the priests were abducted and killed by soldiers. Witness EVD denied hearing anyone mention Rukundo's presence during the abductions or his involvement in any other criminal activities in Kabgayi.[805]

Defence Witness EVA

534. The Chamber has previously considered Witness EVA's evidence in relation to the events at the *Imprimerie de Kabgayi* roadblock and the Kabgayi Bishopric.

535. Witness EVA testified that she learnt that the priests who were killed at the Kabgayi Major Seminary were abducted and killed on the basis of lists that had been found at the Rudahunga's home. She did not know who had handed over the lists to soldiers or whether soldiers had discovered those lists in the Rudahunga's home.[806]

Defence Witness EVB

536. The Chamber has previously considered Witness EVB's evidence in relation to the events at the Nyabikenke communal office and the Kabgayi Bishopric. **[page 163]**

537. Witness EVB stated that he heard that the soldiers who had come for the clergy at the Kabgayi Major Seminary had arrived with *sous-préfet* Misago.[807]

---

[801] T. 22 October 2007, pp. 33-35, 37.
[802] T. 16 October 2007, pp. 9-10
[803] T. 16 October 2007, p. 10.
[804] T. 16 October 2007, pp. 25-26.
[805] T. 4 October 2007, pp. 12-13, 24-25.
[806] T. 19 July 2007, pp. 66-67.
[807] T. 20 July 2007, pp. 17-19

Judgement

(c) Deliberations on the Abduction and Killing of Tutsi Clergy

(i) Preliminary Issue: Alibi

538. During his testimony, the Accused stated that he was not in Kabgayi on 24 May 1994, but rather he was in Kigali.[808] Before commencing cross-examination, the Prosecution objected to the Accused's assertion of this fact since it was not given prior notice of alibi, pursuant to Rule 67 of the Rules. The Defence responded that it could not have given such notice unless it was able to satisfy the requirements in the Rules and present a witness to support the alibi. Since it did not have any other witnesses in support of the alibi besides the Accused, the Defence did not think that this was required. The Defence argued that the Prosecution has many statements containing notice that Rukundo never purported to be in Kabgayi on that day.[809]

539. Rule 67 of the Rules states that the Defence must notify the Prosecution of its intent to enter the defence of alibi as soon as reasonably practicable. The Chamber finds that the Defence should have given this notice, even if it only relied on the Accused's evidence. The failure to provide such notice, however, does not limit the Accused from relying on this defence, but the Chamber may attach less weight to the alibi. In any event, the Chamber does not find that the Accused's assertion that he was in Kigali on 24 May 1994, in itself, raises reasonable doubt on the Prosecution case. Nevertheless, the Chamber still needs to be satisfied that the Prosecution has proved the allegations charged beyond reasonable doubt.

(ii) Merits of the Allegation

540. Paragraphs 19 and 29 of the Indictment allege that the Accused participated in the abduction and killing of Tutsi clergy and other persons from the Kabgayi Major Seminary on 24 May 1994.

541. Witness BLP testified that, towards the end of May 1994, he saw Rukundo with soldiers at St. Joseph's College looking for a priest called Fidele. Out of fear, Witness BLP told the soldiers [page 164] that Fidele was at the Kabgayi Major Seminary. He went with the soldiers to the Major Seminary in the same convoy as Rukundo.[810]

542. At the Kabgayi Major Seminary, Witness BLP saw Rukundo standing near his vehicle in the parking lot with *sous-préfet* Antoine Misago, while some soldiers searched the Seminary buildings. Witness BLP stated that he saw the soldiers search almost all the buildings, before they stopped in front of the chapel door. They asked everyone inside the chapel to come out and show their identity cards. The soldiers allowed some people to return to the Major Seminary, while they asked others to go to the place where Rukundo and Misago were located in the parking lot. Witness BLP said that Rukundo had a few sheets of paper, while the leader among the soldiers and the *sous-préfet* each had a piece of paper. Witness BLP recognised and named several people who were made to board a vehicle at the Major Seminary, which then left towards Butare. Witness BLP said that he saw Rukundo leave with them. Later, news spread in Kabgayi that the people in the vehicle had been killed in Byimana.[811]

543. On 24 May 1994, during the regular noon prayers at the Kabgayi Major Seminary, Witness CSH also saw an armed group of soldiers and *Interahamwe* at the two entrances to the chapel. They called out a list of names, and those people went outside along with others who showed their identity cards, and were found to be Tutsi. He saw the vehicle of the Seminary, a Toyota Hilux, and a blue minibus, belonging to the *préfecture*, at the top of the stairs and later heard that the group had left, that Misago had been there, and that the abducted persons were subsequently killed at Byimana.[812]

544. Defence Witnesses GSA and Dussart were also present at the Major Seminary on 24 May 1994, and confirmed before the Chamber that the abductions took place. Their testimonies corroborated the time of the

---

[808] T. 9 October 2007, p. 29; T. 10 October 2007, pp. 51-52.
[809] T. 10 October 2007, pp. 16-19.
[810] T. 15 November 2006, pp. 17-18; T. 16 November 2006, pp. 30-32.
[811] T. 15 November 2006, pp. 18-19; T. 16 November 2006, p. 34.
[812] T. 28 November 2006, pp. 33-43; T. 29 November 2006, p. 14.

abductions, the presence of soldiers, the showing of identity cards, Misago's presence, the minibus used to take people away and the identity of the individuals abducted.[813]

545. The Chamber therefore finds that many Tutsi clergy persons including Brother Martin Munyanshongore, Father Celestin Niwenshuti, Brother Fidele Murekezi, Sister Bénigne, Father Vedaste Nyilibakwe, Father Callixte Musonera, Father Tharcisse Gakuba, three Marist Brothers **[page 165]** (Canisius, Gaspard, Fabien) and at least one civilian, Viateur Kalinda, who was a journalist, were abducted from the Kabgayi Major Seminary on 24 May 1994, and then subsequently killed at Byimana.

546. The Chamber will now turn to the issue of the Accused's alleged involvement in these abductions and killings. Witness BLP testified that Rukundo was in the convoy from the St. Léon Minor Seminary to the Kabgayi Major Seminary on the day of the abductions and that he was with the soldiers who were looking for the priest, Fidele. The witness said that Rukundo was with *sous-préfet* Misago in the Seminary's parking lot while soldiers searched for people inside. Some people were ordered by the soldiers to go to the place where Rukundo was standing with Misago holding lists. Witness BLP testified that Rukundo left with those people, who were killed on that day.[814]

547. The Chamber notes that Witness BLP is the only witness who places the Accused at the scene of the abductions at the Major Seminary. The Chamber recalls that it can rely on the testimony of a single witness, if found credible.[815] However, with respect to Witness BLP, the Chamber reiterates its previous finding that it will only rely on this witness's testimony where it is corroborated by other reliable evidence, or itself corroborates such evidence.[816]

548. Prosecution Witnesses CSH and CCJ do not provide such corroboration.

549. Prosecution Witness CSH was an eyewitness to the abductions from the Major Seminary. However, he does not in any way connect Rukundo to the crimes committed against the Tutsi clergy at that location. The Chamber notes Witness CSH's admission that he went into hiding in one of the toilets of the building for one and half hours during the operation conducted by the soldiers.[817] This implies that he did not actually see all that transpired during the attack and might not have noticed everyone involved in that operation. The Chamber, however, considers that his failure to mention Rukundo's involvement is significant, especially in light of his earlier allegation that Rukundo had uttered anti-Tutsi statements to members of the clergy at the Major Seminary. In addition, the Chamber has considered the fact that Witness CSH told the Chamber that he subsequently heard that the abductions were attributed to *sous-préfet* Misago, rather than Rukundo.[818] This is consistent with the testimonies of Defence Witnesses GSA, SJA and EVB.[819] **[page 166]** The Chamber has already found Witness CSH to be credible[820] and is satisfied that, in relation to the above factors, if the witness had seen Rukundo during the attack on 24 May 1994, or subsequently heard of his involvement, he would have told the Chamber.

550. Prosecution Witness CCJ testified that, while in Burundi, he heard of the abduction and killing of clergymen and women from the Major Seminary.[821] However, like Witness CSH, this witness did not connect Rukundo to the incident at the Major Seminary.

551. After having considered the totality of the evidence, the Chamber finds that the Prosecution has not proved beyond reasonable doubt that Rukundo ordered, instigated or aided and abetted the abduction and killing of Tutsi from the Kabgayi Major Seminary, as alleged in paragraphs 19 and 29 of the Indictment.

---

[813] T. 1 October 2007, pp. 64-70; T. 2 October 2007, pp. 8-14, 18-23, 25-26, 28, 54, 61-63, 70-73 (GSA); 10 September 2007, pp. 29-32, 45-46 (Dussart).
[814] T. 15 November 2006, pp. 17-19; T. 16 November 2006, pp. 30-32.
[815] See Section II.B.
[816] See previous finding that Witness BLP's evidence must be corroborated in Section III.4.c.
[817] T. 28 November 2006, p. 34.
[818] T. 29 November 2006, p. 14.
[819] T. 2 October 2007, pp. 9, 61 (GSA); T. 22 October 2007, pp. 20-21 (SJA); T. 20 July 2007, pp. 17-19 (EVB).
[820] See previous finding of Witness CSH's credibility at Section III.9.c.
[821] T. 14 February 2007, pp. 33-34.

552. Having found that the Prosecution has failed to prove beyond reasonable doubt that Rukundo participated in the abduction and killing of Tutsi priests at the Kabgayi Major Seminary, the Chamber need not consider the allegation in paragraphs 20 and 30 of the Indictment that he subsequently reported the death of the priests to the Bernadine Sisters' Convent. **[page 167]**

IV. CHAPTER IV: LEGAL FINDINGS

A. INTRODUCTION

553. The Indictment charges Rukundo with genocide, as well as with murder and extermination as crimes against humanity. The crimes were allegedly committed in Gitarama *préfecture*, at the Gitarama communal office in Nyabikenke and at various locations in Kabgayi, including the Bishopric, the St. Léon Minor Seminary, the CND, the Kabgayi Major Seminary and St. Joseph's College.

554. Rukundo is charged with responsibility for these crimes, pursuant to Article 6(1) of the Statute, for having planned, instigated, ordered, committed[822] or otherwise aided and abetted the planning, preparation or execution of the crimes charged.[823] The Chamber will discuss these terms where relevant in its findings below.[824]

B. GENOCIDE

(a) Applicable Law

555. Count 1 of the Indictment charges Rukundo with genocide, pursuant to Article 2 of the ICTR Statute. Article 2(2) states:

> Genocide means any of the following acts committed with intent to destroy, in whole or in part, a national, ethnical, racial or religious group, as such:
>
> (a) Killing members of the group;
>
> (b) Causing serious bodily or mental harm to members of the group;
>
> ...

556. To find an accused guilty of the crime of genocide, it must be established that he committed any of the enumerated acts in Article 2(2) of the Statute with the specific intent to destroy, in whole or part, the members of a group, as such, defined by one of the protected categories of nationality, race, ethnicity, or religion.[825] The [specific] victims must be targeted because of their membership **[page 168]** in the protected group.[826] The actual destruction of a substantial part of the group is not a requirement of the offence, but may assist in determining whether the accused intended to bring about the result.[827]

557. In the absence of direct evidence demonstrating the perpetrator's specific intent to commit genocide, such intent may be inferred from his overt statements or other circumstantial evidence.[828] Factors that may enable a Trial Chamber to infer the perpetrator's genocidal intent include the general context, the perpetration

---

[822] The Chamber has found that joint criminal enterprise, which is one mode of commission under Article 6(1), was not pleaded with sufficient specificity in the Indictment, see Section II.A.1.
[823] *Chapeau* to paras. 3-21 of the Indictment.
[824] For a general explanation of these terms see *Mpambara*, Judgement (TC), paras. 6-8, 12, with references to established case law; *Zigiranyirazo,* Judgement (TC), paras. 381-382, 386. See also footnotes 112, 113, 193, *supra*.
[825] *Krstić*, Judgement (AC), para. 12 ("The intent requirement of genocide under Article 4 of the [ICTY] Statute is therefore satisfied where evidence shows that the alleged perpetrator intended to destroy at least a substantial part of the protected group"); *Ndindabahizi*, Judgement (TC), paras. 453-454; *Ntagerura et al.*, Judgement (TC), para. 662 ; *Niyitegeka*, Judgement (AC), para. 48.
[826] *Gacumbitsi,* Judgement (AC), para. 39; *Rutaganda,* Judgement (AC), paras. 524-525; *Jelisić*, Judgement (AC), para. 46; *Mpambara,* Judgement (TC), para. 8; *Simba,* Judgement (TC), para. 412.
[827] *Krstić*, Judgement (AC), para. 35.
[828] *Gacumbitsi*, Judgement (AC), paras. 40-41; *Semanza,* Judgement (AC), paras. 261-262; *Rutaganda*, Judgement (AC), paras. 525, 528; *Mpambara*, Judgement (TC), para. 8; *Simba,* Judgement (TC), paras. 413, 415; *Ndindabahizi*, Judgement (TC), para. 454.

of other culpable acts systematically directed against the same group, the scale of atrocities committed, the systematic targeting of victims on account of their membership in a particular group or the repetition of destructive and discriminatory acts.[829] The perpetrator need not be motivated solely by a genocidal intent, and having a personal motive will not preclude such a specific intent.[830]

(b) Deliberations

558. To establish Rukundo's criminal responsibility for genocide, the Prosecution relies on all of the allegations discussed in the Chamber's factual findings.[831]

559. The Chamber has found that the Prosecution has not established beyond reasonable doubt that Rukundo aided and abetted the killing of Tutsi at the *Imprimerie de Kabgayi* roadblock, as alleged in paragraph 10(ii) of the Indictment (Section III.3.c), that Rukundo ordered, instigated or aided and abetted policemen to shoot at the refugees gathered at the Nyabikenke communal office, as alleged in paragraph 10(iv) of the Indictment (Section III.5.c), that Rukundo's alleged conduct caused serious mental harm to the Tutsi priests who had taken refuge at the Bishopric in April 1994, as alleged in paragraph 10(v) of the Indictment (Section III.6.c), that Rukundo ordered, instigated or aided and abetted the beating of Tutsi refugees at the St. Léon Minor Seminary, as alleged in paragraph 13 of the Indictment (Section III.7.c.ii), that Emmanuel Rukundo ordered, instigated or aided and abetted soldiers and *Interahamwe* militiamen to kill Tutsi refugees at the CND or to **[page 169]** abduct them from that location and kill them or inflict serious bodily or mental harm upon them, as alleged in paragraph 15 of the Indictment (Section III.8.c), that Rukundo's statement that the *Inyenzi* must be sought out and killed caused serious mental harm to the Tutsi priests at the Kabgayi Major Seminary, as alleged in paragraph 18 of the Indictment (Section III.9.c), and that Rukundo ordered, instigated or aided and abetted the abduction and killing of Tutsi from the Kabgayi Major Seminary, as alleged in paragraph 19 of the Indictment (Section III.9.e.ii).

560. The Prosecution, however, has proved beyond reasonable doubt the following allegations:

(i) Attack on St. Joseph's College: Killing of Madame Rudahunga, Beating of Two of her Children and Two Other Tutsi Civilians

561. The Chamber has found that, in April 1994, Rukundo, with soldiers of the Rwandan army, abducted and killed Madame Rudahunga. Furthermore, the Chamber has held that Rukundo and the soldiers abducted and severely beat and injured two of the Rudahunga's children and two other Tutsi civilians, Jeanne and Justin.[832]

562. The Chamber recalls that "committing" is not limited to direct and physical perpetration and that other acts can constitute direct participation in the *actus reus* of the crime.[833] Therefore the question of whether an accused with his own hands committed a crime (for example killing people) is not the only relevant criterion.[834] In *Prosecutor v. Gacumbitsi*, Mr. Gacumbitsi was held to have committed genocide when he separated Tutsi from Hutu as part of a criminal act in which the concerned Tutsi were killed. In construing the criminal responsibility of Gacumbitsi in that case, the Appeals Chamber held that his actions were "as much an integral part of the genocide as were the killings which [they] enabled."[835]

563. On the basis of the totality of the evidence presented, the Chamber finds that the *Gacumbitsi* threshold has been met in the present case. Rukundo participated from the outset until the completion of the crime: from the time when the soldiers, acknowledging his authority, showed him documents taken from St.

---

[829] *Semanza,* Judgement (AC), paras. 261-262. See also *Rutaganda,* Judgement (AC), para. 525; *Ndindabahizi,* Judgement (TC), para. 454; *Ntagerura et al.,* Judgement (TC), para. 663.
[830] *Simba,* Judgement (AC), para. 269; *Ntakirutimana,* Judgement (AC), para. 304; *Niyitegeka,* Judgement (AC), para. 53; *Krnojelać,* Judgement (AC), para. 102; *Jelisić,* Judgement (AC), para. 49.
[831] Prosecution Closing Brief, paras. 107-112. See the Chamber's findings on pre-1994 evidence, Section III.1.
[832] See Section on St. Joseph's College, III.4.d.
[833] *Seromba,* Judgement (AC), para. 161; *Gacumbitsi,* Judgement (AC), para. 60; *Ndindabahizi,* Judgement (AC), para. 123.
[834] *Seromba,* Judgement (AC), para. 161.
[835] *Gacumbitsi,* Judgement (AC), para. 60; *Seromba,* Judgement (AC), para. 161.

Judgement

Joseph's College, before abducting Madame Rudahunga, and following the blue pick-up which carried Madame Rudahunga away from the College, until he boasted about killing Madame Rudahunga and her two children, therefore claiming ownership of the acts.[836] **[page 170]** Rukundo's acts were as much an integral part of the criminal act as were the killing and the causing of serious bodily harm which they enabled. His acts amount to "committing" under Article 6(1) of the Statute.

564. The Chamber further finds that Rukundo intended the killing of Madame Rudahunga and the serious bodily harm caused to her children and the two Tutsi civilians.

565. Whether by killing Madame Rudahunga and causing serious bodily harm to her children and the two Tutsi civilians Rukundo intended to destroy the Tutsi ethnic group, in whole or in substantial part, must be assessed within the context of ethnic killing in Rwanda in 1994. The Appeals Chamber has held that "during 1994, there was a campaign of mass killing intended to destroy, in whole or at least in very large part, Rwanda's Tutsi population".[837]

566. In addition to having taken judicial notice of this fact, the Chamber has heard overwhelming evidence that soon after 6 April 1994, Tutsi were targeted on the basis of their ethnicity in Gitarama *préfecture*. Indeed, several Prosecution and Defence witnesses testified that they had to flee because they were threatened or their houses were attacked and burned down.[838] Others testified that Tutsi were abused or mistreated at roadblocks.[839] Still many others testified to attacks at various places where the Tutsi had sought refuge in Kabgayi including St. Joseph's College, the St. Léon Minor Seminary, the Kabgayi Major Seminary, the CND and at the Nyabikenke communal office.[840]

567. Within this context, Rukundo led a group of soldiers who systematically searched for Tutsi refugees in St Joseph's College and checked identity cards to verify the refugees' Tutsi ethnicity.[841] The soldiers specifically asked Madame Rudahunga whether she was the wife of Louis Rudahunga, who was targeted as an RPF accomplice.[842] Shortly after the incident, Rukundo boasted about having entered Rudahunga's house and having killed his wife and two of his children, whom Rukundo referred to as *Inyenzi*.[843]

568. Considering the general context of mass ethnic killing in Gitarama *préfecture* and in Kabgayi, and, specifically, the systematic targeting of Tutsi at St. Joseph's College and the Accused's reference to the Rudahunga family as *Inyenzi*, the Chamber is satisfied that Madame **[page 171]** Rudahunga, her two children and the two other Tutsi civilians were targeted because they were Tutsi. Under these circumstances, the Chamber finds beyond reasonable doubt that Rukundo, when committing these crimes, possessed the intent to destroy, in whole or in part, the Tutsi ethnic group.

569. Accordingly, the Chamber finds Rukundo guilty on Count 1 of the Indictment, under Article 6(1) of the Statute, for committing genocide by killing Madame Rudahunga and causing serious bodily harm to two of her children and two other Tutsi civilians sometime in April 1994.

(ii) Abductions and Killings at the St. Léon Minor Seminary

570. The Chamber has found that, between mid-April and the end of May 1994, Rukundo participated, with soldiers and *Interahamwe*, on at least four occasions, in the abduction and subsequent killing of Tutsi refugees from the St. Léon Minor Seminary.[844]

---

[836] See Section III.4.d.
[837] *Karemera et al.*, Decision on Interlocutory Appeal of Decision on Judicial Notice (AC), 16 June 2006, para. 35.
[838] See Witnesses BLC, BLJ, BCD, BUW, CCH, CSF, SLA, SLD, AMA, CSE, CNB, CNC, CSH.
[839] See Witnesses BLP, CSG, CSF, CCH, Emmanuel Rukundo.
[840] See Section III.4.d, Sections III.7.c.iii, Section III.9.e.ii, Section III.8.c, Section III.5.c.
[841] T. 28 September 2007, pp. 8-10, 22; T. 9 March 2007, p. 12.
[842] Louis Rudahunga had been arrested and detained in 1990 on suspicion of being an RPF accomplice (T. 13 February 2007, p. 68).
[843] T. 4 December 2006, p. 21.
[844] See Section III.7.c.iii.

571. In light of its findings above,[845] the Chamber concludes that Rukundo's actions were as much an integral part of the crimes as the abductions of Tutsi refugees from the St. Léon Minor Seminary and the subsequent killing that they enabled. The Chamber therefore finds that Rukundo's conduct amounts to "committing," under Article 6(1) of the Statute.

572. Considering the general context of violence against the Tutsi in Gitarama *préfecture* and in Kabgayi, and, in particular, Rukundo's participation in the systematic abduction and killing of Tutsi refugees at the St. Léon Minor Seminary on the basis of lists, as well as his statement that "something had to be done" about RPF sympathizers, the Chamber finds beyond reasonable doubt that Rukundo, when committing these crimes, possessed the intent to destroy, in whole or in part, the Tutsi ethnic group.

573. Accordingly, the Chamber finds Rukundo guilty on Count 1 of the Indictment, under Article 6(1), for committing genocide through the abductions and the killing of Tutsi refugees from the St. Léon Minor Seminary between April 1994 and the end of May 1994. **[page 172]**

(iii) Sexual Assault at the St. Léon Minor Seminary

574. The Chamber has found that Rukundo sexually assaulted Witness CCH, a young Tutsi woman. The Chamber has further found, Judge Park dissenting, that Witness CCH suffered serious mental harm as a consequence of Rukundo's conduct.[846]

575. Considering the general context of mass violence against the Tutsi in Gitarama *préfecture* and in Kabgayi, and, specifically, Rukundo's words spoken prior to assaulting Witness CCH, that her entire family had to be killed for assisting the *Inyenzi*, the Chamber finds that Rukundo possessed the intent to destroy, in whole or in substantial part, the Tutsi ethnic group.

576. Accordingly, the Chamber finds, Judge Park dissenting, that Rukundo is guilty on Count 1 of the Indictment, under Article 6(1), for committing genocide, through his sexual assault of a young Tutsi woman at the St. Léon Minor Seminary in May 1994.

C. CRIMES AGAINST HUMANITY (MURDER)

(a) Applicable Law

577. In Counts 3 and 4 of the Indictment, the Prosecution charges Rukundo with crimes against humanity (murder and extermination), pursuant to Article 3 of the Statute. Article 3 states:

> [Crimes against humanity are] the following crimes when committed as part of a widespread or systematic attack against any civilian population on national, political, ethnic, racial or religious grounds:
>
> (a) Murder;
>
> (b) Extermination;
>
> …

578. For any of the enumerated crimes under Article 3 of the Statute to qualify as a crime against humanity, the Prosecution must prove that the act was committed as part of a widespread or systematic attack against a civilian population on national, political, ethnic, racial or religious grounds.[847] The general requirements for a crime against humanity are intended to be read as **[page 173]** disjunctive elements.[848] "Widespread" refers to the large scale of the attack,[849] whereas "systematic" describes its organized nature, as opposed to random or unrelated acts.[850] The perpetrator must have acted with knowledge of the broader context and

---

[845] See factual findings, paras. 361, 364.
[846] See Section III.7.c.iv.
[847] *Ntakirutimana*, Judgement (AC), para. 516; *Ntagerura et al.*, Judgement (TC), para. 697; *Simba*, Judgement (AC), para. 421.
[848] *Karera*, Judgement (TC), para. 551.
[849] *Simba*, Judgement (AC), para. 421; *Semanza*, Judgement (TC), paras. 328-329.
[850] *Ntakirutimana*, Judgement (AC), para. 516 and footnotes; *Kunarac et al.*, Judgement (AC), paras. 93-97.

knowledge that his acts formed part of the discriminatory attack.[851] However, he need not have shared the purpose or goals behind the broader attack, or have possessed a discriminatory intent.[852]

579. The crime of murder requires proof of the intentional killing of a person, or of the intentional infliction of grievous bodily harm with knowledge that such harm will likely cause the victim's death, or with recklessness as to whether death will result, without lawful justification or excuse.[853] Negligence or gross negligence is not sufficient for establishing murder as a crime against humanity.[854]

(b) Deliberations

580. To establish Rukundo's criminal responsibility for murder as a crime against humanity, the Prosecution relies on paragraph 22 of the Indictment.

(i) Attack on St. Joseph's College: Killing of Madame Rudahunga

581. Based on the totality of the evidence, the Chamber finds that a widespread or systematic attack against Tutsi civilians on ethnic grounds occurred in Gitarama *préfecture* and in Kabgayi between April and the end of May 1994.[855]

582. The Chamber further finds that Rukundo was aware of this widespread or systematic attack and that his actions formed part of the attack. By his own account, Rukundo knew that Tutsi were being targeted at roadblocks and elsewhere on the basis of their ethnicity.[856] Furthermore, the Chamber notes that Rukundo was at the Nyabikenke communal office when Tutsi, who had sought **[page 174]** refuge there, were attacked by *Interahamwe*. The Chamber also notes that Rukundo visited the various locations in Kabgayi, where thousands of Tutsi sought refuge and on several occasions participated, with soldiers and *Interahamwe*, in attacks against the Tutsi in two locations in Kabgayi.

583. The Chamber has already found that Rukundo intentionally participated in the killing of Madame Rudahunga and that his acts amounted to "committing."[857]

584. The Chamber notes its finding that the killing of Madame Rudahunga was established, beyond reasonable doubt, as a basis for Rukundo's conviction for genocide. The Chamber, however, recalls that cumulative convictions for genocide and crimes against humanity based on the same conduct are permitted, as each crime has a materially distinct element not contained within the other.[858]

585. Accordingly, the Chamber finds Rukundo guilty on Count 2 of the Indictment, under Article 6(1), for committing murder as a crime against humanity for the killing of Madame Rudahunga sometime in April 1994.

---

[851] *Gacumbitsi*, Judgement (AC), para. 86; *Kunarac et al.*, Judgement (AC), paras. 99-100; *Semanza*, Judgement (AC), paras. 268-269, quoting *Akayesu*, Judgement (AC), para. 467.
[852] *Gacumbitsi*, Judgement (AC), para. 86; *Kunarac et al.*, Judgement (AC), paras. 99-100; *Semanza*, Judgement (AC), paras. 268-269, quoting *Akayesu*, Judgement (AC), para. 467.
[853] *Ndindabahizi*, Judgment (TC), para. 487; *Muhimana*, Judgement (TC), para. 568; *Bagosora et al.*, 98*bis* Decision, para. 25. The Chamber notes that some Trial Chambers have held that murder requires an element of pre-meditation, not only intent. See *Bagilishema*, Judgement (TC), para. 86; *Ntagerura et al.*, Judgement (TC), para. 700; *Semanza*, Judgement (TC), para. 339.
[854] *Stakić*, Judgement (TC), para. 587; *Brđanin*, Judgement (TC), para. 386; *Martić*, Judgement (TC), para. 60.
[855] See Witnesses BLC, BLJ, BCD, BUW, CCH, CSF, CSG, SLA, SLD, AMA, CSE, CNB, CNC, CSH, BLP. See also *Semanza*, Judgement (AC), para. 192; *Karemera et al.*, Decision on Prosecutor's Interlocutory Appeal of Decision on Judicial Notice (AC), 16 June 2006, paras. 28-29.
[856] T. 8. October 2007, p. 53; T. 9 October 2007, pp. 6-7, 9; T. 10 October 2007, pp. 19-21.
[857] See Section IV.B.b.i.
[858] *Musema*, Judgement (AC), paras. 365-370; *Semanza*, Judgement (AC), para. 315. An element is materially distinct from another if it requires proof of a fact not required by the other element (*Krstić*, Judgement (AC), paras. 218-227).

D. CRIMES AGAINST HUMANITY (EXTERMINATION)

(a) Applicable Law

586. Extermination is distinguishable from murder because it is the act of killing on a large scale.[859] The expression "on a large scale," does not require a numerical minimum.[860] It requires proof that an accused participated in a widespread or systematic killing or in subjecting a widespread number of people to conditions of living that would inevitably lead to their deaths, and that by his acts or omissions, the accused intended this result.[861] The Prosecution is not required to name the victims.[862]

(b) Deliberations

587. To establish Rukundo's criminal responsibility for genocide, the Prosecution relies on the same allegations as for the crime of genocide. **[page 175]**

    (i) Attack on St. Joseph's College: Killing of Madame Rudahunga; Beating of her Children and Two Tutsi Civilians

588. The Chamber notes that there is no evidence that the murder of Madame Rudahunga and the serious bodily harm caused to two of the Rudahunga's children and the two Tutsi civilians were committed as part of killings on a large scale. The Chamber therefore finds that these crimes are insufficient to satisfy the charge of extermination.

    (ii) Abductions and Killings at the St. Léon Minor Seminary

589. Although no evidence was adduced before the Chamber regarding the specific number of deaths resulting from the abductions at the St. Léon Minor Seminary, the Chamber finds that, in light of the repetitive nature of the abductions and the fact that at least one bus was used to remove the identified refugees, the specific requirement for the crime of extermination, has been met in this case.

590. Accordingly, the Chamber finds Rukundo guilty on Count 3 of the Indictment, under Article 6(1), for extermination as a crime against humanity for abductions and killings of Tutsi refugees from the St. Léon Minor Seminary between April 1994 and the end of May 1994. **[page 176]**

V. CHAPTER V: VERDICT

591. For the reasons set out in this judgement, having considered all evidence and arguments, the Trial Chamber finds unanimously as follows in respect of Emmanuel Rukundo:

Count 1:   **GUILTY of Genocide**

Count 2:   **GUILTY of Murder as a Crime against Humanity**

Count 3:   **GUILTY of Extermination as a Crime against Humanity [page 177]**

---

[859] *Ntakirutimana*, Judgement (AC), paras. 516, 522.
[860] *Rugambarara*, Sentencing Judgement (TC), para. 23; *Ntakirutimana*, Judgement (AC), para. 516.
[861] *Ntakirutimana*, Judgement (AC), para. 522; See also *Gacumbitsi*, Judgement (AC), para. 86.
[862] *Ntakirutimana*, Judgement (AC), para. 521.

VI. CHAPTER VI: SENTENCING

(a) Applicable Law

592. The Chamber has found Emmanuel Rukundo guilty on Counts 1, 2 and 3 of the Indictment for genocide, and murder and extermination as crimes against humanity. The Chamber now determines the appropriate sentence.

593. A person convicted by the Tribunal may be sentenced to imprisonment for a fixed term or for the remainder of his life.[863] The penalty imposed should reflect the aims of retribution, deterrence and, to a lesser extent, rehabilitation.[864] Pursuant to Article 23 of the Statute and Rule 101 of the Rules, the Trial Chamber shall consider the general practice regarding prison sentences in Rwanda, the gravity of the offences (the gravity of the crimes for which the accused has been convicted and the form of responsibility for these crimes) as well as the individual circumstances of the convicted person, including aggravating and mitigating circumstances.[865] In addition, the Trial Chamber shall ensure that any penalty imposed by a court of any State on the accused for the same act has already been served,[866] and shall credit the accused for any time spent in detention pending his surrender to the Tribunal and during trial.[867]

(b) Determination of the Sentence

594. The Prosecution submits that the appropriate penalty is imprisonment for the remainder of the Accused's life.[868] The Prosecution seeks concurrent sentences for the remainder of the Accused's life for each count of the Indictment for which the Trial Chamber finds the Accused guilty.[869] The Defence submits that the Accused should be acquitted on all counts of the Indictment.[870]

595. All crimes under the Tribunal's Statute are serious violations of international humanitarian law. Trial Chambers are vested with a broad discretion in determining the appropriate sentence due **[page 178]** to their obligation to individualise the penalties to fit the circumstances of the convicted person and to reflect the gravity of the crime.[871]

(i) Gravity of the Offence

596. The Chamber has found Rukundo guilty of genocide: for committing the murder of Madame Rudahunga and causing serious bodily harm to two of the Rudahunga's children and two Tutsi civilians, Justin and Jeanne; his participation in the killing and abduction of Tutsi from the St. Léon Minor Seminary, and, Judge Park dissenting, sexually assaulting a young Tutsi woman. The Chamber has further found Rukundo guilty of murder, as a crime against humanity, for the murder of Madame Rudahunga. Finally, the Chamber has found Rukundo guilty of extermination, as a crime against humanity, for his participation in the abduction and killing of Tutsi refugees from the St. Léon Minor Seminary.

597. Genocide is, by definition, a crime of the most serious gravity which affects the very foundations of society and shocks the conscience of humanity. Crimes against humanity are also extremely serious offences because they are heinous in nature and shock the collective conscience of mankind.[872]

---

[863] Rule 101(A) of the Rules.
[864] See *Nahimana et al.*, Judgement (AC), para. 1057; *Stakić*, Judgement (AC), para. 402.
[865] *Bikindi*, Judgement (TC), para. 443.
[866] Articles 23(1) and 23(2) of the Statute and Rule 101(B) of the Rules.
[867] Rule 101(C) of the Rules.
[868] Prosecution Closing Brief, paras. 913, 928.
[869] Prosecution Closing Brief, paras. 953(2), 953(7).
[870] Defence Closing Brief, paras. 588, 718, 949, 1608, 1670.
[871] *Seromba*, Judgement (AC), para. 228; *Rugambarara*, Sentencing Judgement (TC), paras. 19-20.
[872] *Ruggiu*, Judgement (TC), para. 48; *Rugambarara*, Sentencing Judgement (TC), para. 19.

598. The Chamber has wide discretion in determining what constitutes mitigating and aggravating circumstances and the weight to be accorded thereto. Whilst aggravating circumstances need to be proved beyond reasonable doubt, mitigating circumstances need only be established on a "balance of probabilities."[873]

(ii) Aggravating Circumstances

599. The Prosecution submits that the aggravating factors against Rukundo include: his position and his breach of trust; his premeditation; his direct participation as a perpetrator; the violent and humiliating nature of his acts and the vulnerability of his victims; and the duration of the offences and suffering of his victims.[874] The Chamber notes that it is well established in the ICTR and ICTY's jurisprudence that the manner in which the accused exercised his command or the abuse of an accused's personal position in the community may be considered as an aggravating factor.[875] The **[page 179]** Chamber considers Rukundo's stature in Rwandan society to be an aggravating factor. As a military chaplain, Rukundo was a well-known priest within the community and in the Rwandan military. The Chamber considers it highly aggravating that Rukundo abused his moral authority and influence in order to promote the abduction and killing of Tutsi refugees and to sexually assault a Tutsi girl. The Chamber notes that Prosecution witnesses testified that because of Rukundo's position as a military chaplain, they trusted him and believed that he had a certain moral authority over the soldiers.[876]

600. The Chamber also considers the fact that the Accused is an educated person to be an aggravating factor. As an educated person, the Accused should have appreciated the dignity and value of human life and have been aware of the need for peaceful co-existence between communities.[877]

(iii) Mitigating Circumstances

601. Mitigating circumstances need not be directly related to the offence.[878] The Prosecution submits that there was no evidence of any mitigating circumstances.[879] The Defence claims that Rukundo did all that he could to evacuate people, including Jean-Marie Vianney's family, 13 Pallotine sisters, Félicité (one of the Rwaza nuns), a Tutsi woman called Florida and her son Eric, the priest Boniface Kagabo and a nun from the Benebikira congregation.[880] The Defence, however, does not specifically refer to Rukundo's efforts to save Tutsi as a mitigating factor.

602. The Chamber notes that, even if it were to believe this evidence,[881] the assistance provided by Rukundo to a selected number of Tutsi carries only limited, if any, weight as a mitigating factor.

(c) Sentencing Practice

603. The Chamber has considered that, under Rwandan law, genocide and crimes against humanity carry the possible penalties of life imprisonment, or life imprisonment with special **[page 180]** provisions, depending on the nature of the accused's participation.[882] In determining an appropriate sentence, the

---

[873] *Simba*, Judgement (AC), para. 328; *Nahimana et al.*, Judgement (AC), para. 1038; *Bikindi*, Judgement (TC), para. 449; *Rugambarara*, Sentencing Judgement (TC), para. 14.
[874] Prosecution Closing Brief, para. 931.
[875] *Seromba*, Judgement (AC), para. 230; *Aleksovski*, Judgement (AC), para. 183; *Kayishema and Ruzindana*, Judgement (AC), paras. 357-358; *Ntakirutimana*, Judgement (AC), para. 563; *Kamuhanda*, Judgement (AC), paras. 347-348; *Bisengimana*, Judgement (TC), para. 120; *Serugendo*, Judgement (TC), para. 48; *Ndindabahizi*, Judgement (AC), para. 136.
[876] T. 14 February 2007, p. 7; T. 19 February 2007, p. 4.
[877] *Nzabirinda*, Judgement (TC), paras. 59, 63; *Bisengimana*, Judgement (TC), para. 120.
[878] *Rugambarara*, Sentencing Judgement (TC), para. 30; *Nikolić*, Judgement (TC), para. 145; *Deronjić*, Judgement (TC), para. 155.
[879] Prosecution Closing Brief, para. 947.
[880] Defence Closing Brief, para. 1825.
[881] Witnesses RUC, RUE and RUA (Jean-Marie Vianney's family), Witnesses TMB and TMC (thirteen Pallotine sisters), Witness TMC (Félicité, one of the Rwaza nuns), Witness RUA (a Tutsi woman called Florida and her son Eric), Witness RUA (the priest Boniface Kagabo) and Witness MCC (a sister from the Benebikira congregation).
[882] Rwandan Organic Law No. 8/96, on the Organization of Prosecutions for Offences constituting Genocide or Crimes Against Humanity committed since 1 October 1990, published in the Gazette of the Republic of Rwanda, 35th year. No. 17, 1 September 1996, as amended by Organic Law No. 31/2007 of 25/07/2007 Relating to the Abolition of the Death Penalty.

Appeals Chamber has stated that, "sentences of like individuals in like cases should be comparable."[883] However, it has also noted the inherent limits to this approach because "any given case contains a multitude of variables, ranging from the number and type of crimes committed to the personal circumstances of the individual."[884]

604. The Chamber has taken into consideration the sentencing practice of the ICTR and the ICTY, and notes particularly that the penalty must first and foremost be commensurate to the gravity of the offence.

605. In the present case, the Chamber's sentencing needs to address the Accused's conviction for both genocide and crimes against humanity. From this Tribunal, principal perpetrators convicted of genocide and extermination as a crime against humanity have received sentences ranging from 25 years to imprisonment for the remainder of their lives, except in cases where the accused pleaded guilty or there existed other significant mitigating circumstances.[885] Senior authorities, in particular Ministers, have received the most severe sentences.[886] Life imprisonment has also been imposed on those at a lower level if they planned or ordered atrocities or if they participated in the crimes with particular zeal or sadism.[887] Secondary or indirect forms of participation have usually entailed a lower sentence.[888] As regards murder as a crime against humanity, the Chamber notes that on two occasions this Tribunal has given specific sentences for this crime: Nzabirinda, who pleaded guilty, was sentenced to seven years' imprisonment for his participation in aiding and abetting murder;[889] and Semanza was sentenced by the Appeals Chamber to ten years' imprisonment for instigating one murder and personally committing one murder, and **[page 181]** eight years' imprisonment for instigating the murder of six people.[890] The Chamber further recalls that the Appeals Chamber sentenced Tadić to 20 years' imprisonment for murder as a crime against humanity.[891] The Chamber, however, notes that it is more common for convictions for murder, as a crime against humanity, to form part of a single sentence of a fixed term or of life imprisonment for the totality of the conduct of the Accused.[892]

(d)   Credit for Time Served

606. Rukundo was originally arrested and detained on 12 July 2001 in Geneva, Switzerland. He was transferred to the Tribunal on 12 September 2001 and detained at the United Nations Detention Facility in Arusha, Tanzania. Pursuant to Rule 101(C) of the Rules, Rukundo is therefore entitled to credit for time served as of 12 July 2001.

---

[883]   *Kvocka et al.*, Judgement (AC), para. 681.
[884]   *Ibid.*
[885]   *Karera*, Judgement (TC), para. 583.
[886]   Life sentences have been imposed against senior government authorities in *Bagosora et al.*, Judgement (TC), paras. 2277-2279; *Kambanda*, Judgement (TC), paras. 44, 61-62 (Prime Minister); *Niyitegeka*, Judgement (TC), paras. 499, 502 (Minister of Information); *Ndindabahazi*, Judgement (TC), paras. 505, 508, 511 (Minister of Finance); *Kamuhanda*, Judgement (TC), paras. 6, 764, 770 (Minister of Higher Education and Scientific Research); *Kayishema and Ruzindana*, Judgement, (TC) para. 27 (prefect).
[887]   *Akayesu*, Judgement (TC), para. 12 (*bourgmestre*); *Rutaganda*, Judgement (TC), paras. 466-473 (second vice-president of *Interahamwe* at national level); *Musema*, Judgement (TC), paras. 999-1008 (influential director of a tea factory who exercised control over killers); *Musema*, Judgement (AC), para. 383; *Muhimana*, Judgement (TC), paras. 604-616 (*conseiller*); *Gacumbitsi*, Judgement, (AC), para. 207 (*bourgmestre*; increased by the Appeals Chamber from 30 years).
[888]   It is recalled that 45 years of imprisonment was the sentence in *Kajelijeli* (*bourgmestre*); 35 years in *Semanza* (*bourgmestre*); 25 years in *Ruzindana* (businessman) and *Gérard Ntakirutimana* (medical doctor).
[889]   *Nzabirinda*, Judgement (TC), paras. 57, 116.
[890]   *Semanza*, Judgement (AC), para. 311.
[891]   *Tadić*, Judgement (AC), para. 58. The sentence for murder as a crime against humanity was reduced by the Appeals Chamber from twenty-five years to twenty years.
[892]   The following cases are examples of where the accused was convicted of, *inter alia*, murder as a crime against humanity and was sentenced to a single sentence of a fixed term or life imprisonment for the totality of the conduct of the Accused: *Karera*, Judgement (TC), *Kambanda*, Judgement (TC), *Muhimana*, Judgement (TC), *Nahimana*, Judgement (TC), *Ndindabahizi*, Judgement (TC), *Niyitegeka*, Judgement (TC), *Ntakirutimana*, Judgement (TC), *Rutaganda*, Judgement (TC), *Serushago*, Judgement (TC), *Akayesu*, Judgement (TC).

Prosecutor v. Rukundo

(e) Conclusion

607. The Chamber has the discretion to impose a single sentence and notes that this practice is usually appropriate where the offences may be characterized as belonging to a single criminal transaction.[893]
[page 182]

608. Considering all the relevant circumstances discussed above and having ensured that the Accused is not being punished twice for the same offence, the Chamber sentences Emmanuel Rukundo for genocide and for murder and extermination as crimes against humanity to a single sentence of

TWENTY-FIVE (25) YEARS OF IMPRISONMENT

609. This sentence shall be enforced immediately and, pursuant to Rule 101(C) of the Rules, Emmanuel Rukundo shall receive credit for time served as of 12 July 2001.

610. In accordance with Rules 102(A) and 103 of the Rules, Rukundo shall remain in the custody of the Tribunal pending transfer to the State where he will serve his sentence.

Arusha, 27 February 2009

| Asoka de Silva | Taghrid Hikmet | Seon Ki Park |
| Presiding Judge | Judge | Judge |

Judge Park appends a Dissenting Opinion.

[Seal of the Tribunal] **[page 183]**

---

[893] *Karera*, Judgement (TC), para. 585; *Ndindabahizi*, Judgement (TC), para. 497.

VII. DISSENTING OPINION OF JUDGE PARK

1. With respect, I am unable to agree with the majority of the Trial Chamber in its conclusion that Witness CCH suffered serious mental harm as a result of the sexual assault carried out by Rukundo. I agree with the majority of the Trial Chamber that Witness CCH is a credible witness, that she was sexually assaulted as described in her testimony, and that there existed coercive circumstances at the time of the sexual assault. I do not, however, agree that the circumstances in this case, both independently, and as compared to other convictions for genocide by sexual assault at the *ad hoc* Tribunals, rise to the level of serious mental harm required for a conviction of genocide.

2. In my view, the majority's conclusion would make every incident of sexual assault committed with genocidal intent in the course of genocide, sufficient to convict its perpetrator of the crime of genocide. I support the strides made at this Tribunal and throughout international criminal jurisprudence in recognizing that rape and sexual assault can constitute genocide, crimes against humanity and war crimes. My intention is not to curb those strides, but rather to emphasize the serious nature of the crime of genocide. I recall that the Prosecution has charged the Accused only with genocide (Count 1) in relation to the alleged sexual assault against Witness CCH, and not as a crime against humanity or as a war crime.

3. I would like to reiterate that genocide is a crime of the most serious gravity which affects the very foundations of society and shocks the conscience of humanity.[894] To support a conviction for genocide, the bodily harm or the mental harm inflicted on members of a group must be of such a serious nature as to threaten its destruction in whole or in part.[895]

4. In making its finding that Witness CCH suffered serious mental harm, the majority notes that Witness CCH did not provide direct evidence about her mental state apart from the fact that she could not tell anyone about the incident. I further note that the Prosecution, in questioning the witness, did not even ask her how the incident has affected her life, her mental well-being, her subsequent sexual relationships, or put any other question to the witness which could assist the Chamber in making this finding. Consequently, the Chamber has reviewed the surrounding circumstances to determine whether, from those circumstances, the only reasonable conclusion is that Witness CCH suffered serious mental harm. The majority makes this inference from, *inter alia*, the existence of coercive circumstances, an ongoing genocide against the Tutsi, and the fact that [page 184] Witness CCH was a young Tutsi woman who feared for her life and sought help from a known clergyman in a position of authority, who then abused that authority and sexually assaulted her. The majority was further convinced by Witness CCH's explanation that she was sexually inexperienced at the time, and that the shame of the incident prevented her from telling anyone.

5. While I agree with the majority's review of the facts, I have doubts that these facts rise to the level of serious mental harm required for a conviction of genocide. Other factors in the surrounding circumstances assist me in this determination. First, I note that after Rukundo made a threatening remark to Witness CCH, she responded that he did not seem annoyed at the time and she thought he might change his mind to help her.[896] Second, the sexual assault took place in private, in a locked room at the St. Léon Minor Seminary.[897] Third, although Witness CCH testified that Rukundo had a gun which he placed on the table, there is no indication that his manner of removing the gun from his belt was anything more than to be able to unzip his trousers for the purposes of carrying out a sexual act.[898] Fourth, Witness CCH and Rukundo managed a dialogue during Witness CCH's resistance to Rukundo's sexual advances and touching, and, for whatever reason, Rukundo eventually gave up his attempt to have sexual intercourse with her and rubbed himself against her fully clothed body until he ejaculated.[899] Fifth, upon leaving Witness CCH after the incident,

---

[894] See for example *Zigiranyirazo*, Judgement (TC), para. 457; *Bikindi*, Judgement (TC), para. 448.
[895] *Seromba*, Judgement (AC), para. 46.
[896] T. 14 February 2007, p. 9.
[897] T. 13 February 2007, p. 59.
[898] T. 13 February 2007, pp. 59-60.
[899] T. 14 February 2007, p. 13: "But I was telling him, 'If it happened that I did not die and you made me pregnant now, what would I do?' You see, I was not going to shut my mouth. I was talking. But he was telling me that, '*I am simply asking you to allow us to make love*'"; T. 14 February 2007, pp. 17-18: "I told him that I could not have sex with him. He told me that if I accepted to have sex with him, *he would never forget me*, and I said that I could not do that." (emphasis added).

Rukundo said goodbye to her in a calm manner and stated that perhaps he would be back again.[900] I understand Rukundo's departing words as possibly an attempt to soothe the witness's fears, if only temporarily. I believe that all of these factors mitigate the seriousness of the incident such that it cannot be found to threaten the Tutsi group's destruction, in whole or in part.

6. Finally, I note that, in the *Akayesu* case, the Trial Chamber found that acts of sexual violence constituted genocide. In that case, in an incident where there was no sexual intercourse or rape, the Accused ordered the *Interahamwe* to undress a student and to force her to do gymnastics naked in the public courtyard of the *bureau communal*, in front of a crowd. The Trial Chamber referred to this act as the worst kind of public humiliation and that the sexual violence was an integral part of the process of destruction, specifically targeting Tutsi women and specifically **[page 185]** contributing to their destruction and to the destruction of the Tutsi group as a whole.[901] I agree with the Trial Chamber's finding in the *Akayesu* case, however, when comparing the severity of that incident and the one suffered by Witness CCH, I can only come to the conclusion that the circumstances in this case are much less severe and cannot be found to cause the kind of serious mental harm required for a conviction of the most heinous of crimes, genocide.

7. I would therefore conclude that the Prosecution has not proved beyond reasonable doubt that Witness CCH suffered serious mental harm, as alleged in the Indictment.

Arusha 27 February 2009

Seon Ki Park
Judge

[Seal of the Tribunal]

---

[900] T. 14 February 2007, p. 14.
[901] *Akayesu*, Judgement (TC), paras. 688, 731.

Annex A

[page i]ANNEX A: PROCEDURAL HISTORY

(a) <u>Pre-Trial Phase</u>

1. On 5 July 2001, a Warrant of Arrest and Order for Transfer and Detention and for Search and Seizure was issued by Judge Pavel Dolenc.[902] Emmanuel Rukundo was arrested on 12 July 2001 in Geneva, Switzerland and was transferred to the United Nations Detention Facility in Arusha, Tanzania on 20 September 2001.[903] The Accused made his initial appearance before Judge Erik Møse on 26 September 2001, and entered a plea of not guilty.

2. On 25 June 2001, the Prosecution filed an *ex parte* motion for non-disclosure of the names of witnesses and other identifying information in the Indictment, supporting materials and witness statements.[904] On 10 July 2001, Judge Pavel Dolenc granted in part the Prosecution's *ex parte* motion for non-disclosure of the names of witnesses and other identifying information in the Indictment, supporting materials and witness statements and ordered non-disclosure of the Indictment, including the act of confirmation and related orders, or any part thereof or any information pertaining to it until it is served on the Accused.[905]

3. On 11 December 2001, the Prosecution filed a motion requesting the Chamber to grant protective measures for victims and witnesses which it intended to call. Additional material in support of the Motion was filed on 21 May 2002, and an Addendum filed on 10 September 2002. On 24 October 2002, Trial Chamber III composed of Judge Lloyd G. Williams, presiding, Judge Yakov Ostrovsky and Judge Pavel Dolenc granted the requested protective measures to Prosecution witnesses and victims living in Rwanda and in neighbouring countries. However, the Chamber denied protective measures for witnesses not residing in Rwanda or neighbouring countries on the grounds that the Prosecution failed to provide evidence of the objective basis of the fear professed by those witnesses or to offer any explanation to justify their protection.[906] Futhermore, the Chamber denied the Prosecution's motion to order the registrar to provide photographs of the [page ii] Accused for the purposes of identification.[907] Similarly, the Chamber denied the Defence's motion for the return of documents and other seized personal items.[908]

4. On 18 August 2003, Judge Lloyd G. Williams, sitting as a single judge, dismissed in its entirety the Defence motion requesting to fix a date for the commencement of the trial or, in the alternative, to request Rukundo's provisional release.[909] The Defence appealed the Decision by Judge Williams dismissing its request for the provisional release of the Accused, and the Appeals Chamber found that by designating a single judge to adjudicate on an application for provisional release, Trial Chamber III had violated Rule 65 of the Rules.[910] The Appeals Chamber remanded the initial application for provisional release back to the Trial Chamber. On 18 March 2004, Trial Chamber III, composed of Judges Lloyd G. Williams, Andresia Vaz and Rashida Khan reiterated the reasoning adopted in the impugned decision of Judge Williams and denied the Defence motion for provisional release.[911]

5. On 22 March 2002, the Registrar assigned Phillipe Moriceau as Lead Counsel for the Accused, Emmanuel Rukundo. On 8 August 2005, the Accused wrote a letter to the Registrar requesting the withdrawal of assigned Counsel due to the fact that he had lost confidence in him. After various unsuccessful efforts to

---

[902] Warrant of Arrest and Orders for Transfer and Detention and for Search and Seizure, dated 5 July 2001.
[903] His arrest was made pursuant to the Request to the Government of Switzerland for Arrest, dated 12 July 2001.
[904] Prosecutor's *ex parte* Motion for Non-Disclosure of the Names of Witnesses and other Identifying Information in the Indictment, supporting Materials and Witness Statements, dated 25 June 2001.
[905] Order for Non-Disclosure (TC), dated 10 July 2001.
[906] Decision on the Prosecutor's Motion for Protective Measures for Victims and Witnesses (TC), dated 24 October 2002.
[907] Decision on the Prosecutor's Motion to Order the Registrar to Provide Photographs of the Accused for Purposes of Identification (TC), dated 25 October 2002.
[908] Decision on the Defence Motion for Return of Documents and Other Seized Personal Items (TC), dated 20 November 2002.
[909] Decision on Defence Motion to fix a Date for the Commencement of the Trial of Father Emmanuel Rukundo or, in the Alternative, to Request his Provisional release (TC), dated 18 August 2003.
[910] Decision on Leave to Appeal (Provisional Release)(AC), dated 18 December 2003. See also Decision on Appeal from the Decision of Trial Chamber III of 18 August 2003 denying Application for Provisional Release (AC), dated 8 March 2004 and Decision on the Motion for Provisional Release of Father Emmanuel Rukundo (Rule 65(B) of the Rules of Procedure and Evidence) (TC), dated 15 July 2004.
[911] Decision on Provisional Release (TC), dated 18 March 2004.

reconcile the Accused and Counsel Moriceau, the Registrar accepted the Accused's request and withdrew the assignment of Phillippe Moriceau as his lead counsel on 16 November 2005.[912]

6. On 5 March 2004, the Chamber partly granted the Defence's motion for translation into French of certain Prosecution and procedural documents.[913] The Defence later applied to fix the **[page iii]** opening date of the trial and transfer the matter to a national jurisdiction, however this request was denied in its entirety.[914]

(b) The Indictment

7. On 25 June 2001, the Prosecution filed an Indictment against Emmanuel Rukundo dated 22 June 2001 for review and confirmation by the Tribunal. On 5 July 2001, Judge Pavel Dolenc confirmed counts 1, 3 and 4 of the Indictment and ordered the Prosecution to amend parts of the Indictment within 15 days.[915]

8. The Prosecution filed an Amended Indictment dated 19 July 2001 for review and confirmation. On 12 September 2001, the proposed Amended Indictment against Emmanuel Rukundo was again partially confirmed by Judge Pavel Dolenc. The additional act of confirmation approved some of the proposed amendments, took note of the withdrawal of some of the charges, ordered the Prosecution to clarify one of the proposed amendments, and granted leave for further amendments.[916] On 21 September 2001, Judge Pavel Dolenc confirmed the Amended Indictment incorporating the amendments ordered by the Tribunal in its Order dated 12 September 2001. The Tribunal further decided that the second additional act of confirmation dated 21 September 2001 together with the additional act of confirmation of the Indictment of 19 July 2001 and confirmation of the original Indictment of 5 July 2001 shall be deemed to constitute a common act of confirmation of the Indictment against the Accused.[917]

9. On 26 February 2003, the Chamber decided on a number of preliminary issues related to the Indictment including ordering the Prosecution to amend the Indictment by adding certain specifications, and denying the Defence request for other specifications.[918] Leave to appeal this decision was granted and the Appeals Chamber changed its composition for this appeal several times.[919] On 17 October 2003, the Appeals Chamber rejected the appeal in its entirety.[920] **[page iv]**

10. Trial Chamber II composed of Judge Asoka de Silva, pursuant to Rule 73(A), granted in part the Prosecution's request for leave to file an Amended Indictment and ordered the Prosecution to file a further Amended Indictment in both French and English no later than 6 October 2006.[921] The Prosecution filed an Amended Indictment on 6 October 2006 in compliance with that Decision.[922]

11. The Amended Indictment charges the Accused with three counts: genocide, murder as a crime against humanity and extermination as a crime against humanity.

12. The Indictment alleges that these crimes were committed between 6 April and 31 May 1994 in various locations in Gitarama and Cyangugu *préfectures*, Rwanda. The Indictment alleges that at all material times referred to, there existed in Rwanda a minority ethnic or racial group known as Tutsi, officially identified as

---

[912] Decision of Withdrawal of Mr. Philippe Moriceau as Lead Counsel for the Accused Emmanuel Rukundo (TC), dated 16 November 2005.
[913] Decision on Defence Motion for Translation into French of Prosecution and Procedural Documents in the *Rukundo* case; Articles 20 and 31 of the Statute, and Rule 3 of the Rules of Procedure and Evidence (TC), dated 5 March 2004.
[914] "*Décision relative à la requête de la defense aux fins de fixation de la date d'ouverture du process ou, à défaut, du transfert de l'affaire devant une jurisdiction nationale; Articles 20 du Statut et 11bis du Règlement de procedure et de prevue*" (AC), dated 1 June 2005.
[915] Confirmation of the Indictment, dated 5 June 2001.
[916] Additional Act of Confirmation of the Indictment, dated 12 September 2001.
[917] Second Additional Act of Confirmation of the Indictment, dated 21 September 2001.
[918] Decision on Preliminary Motion (TC), dated 26 February 2003.
[919] Leave to Appeal was granted by the Appeals Chamber on 28 April 2003. See further Order of the President Assigning Judges (AC), dated 23 March 2003; Order of the Presiding Judge Assigning Judges (AC), dated 12 May 2003; The appellant was later ordered to file his reply to the Prosecution Response to its Appeal against this decision (see Decision on Motion for Extension of Time to File Reply (AC), dated 10 June 2003); Order of the Presiding Judge Replacing Judges in a Case Before the Appeals Chamber (AC), dated 1 October 2003.
[920] Décision (*Acte D'Appel relative à la Décision du 26 Février 2003 relative aux exceptions préjudicielles*) (AC), dated 17 October 2003.
[921] Decision on the Prosecutor's Request for Leave to File an Amended Indictment (TC), dated 28 September 2006.
[922] Amended Indictment, dated 6 October 2006.

such by the then government. The majority of the population was comprised of an ethnic or racial group known as Hutu, also officially identified as such by the government. According to the Indictment, during this period, there were widespread or systematic attacks against Tutsi civilians based on their ethnic affiliation. The Indictment further alleges that the Accused relied on his authority as a priest and military chaplain in the RAF to order, instigate, or aid and abet soldiers, *Interahamwe* and armed civilians to commit the crimes charged in the Indictment.

(c) Trial Phase

13. On 14 September 2006, the case against the Accused Emmanuel Rukundo was formally transferred from Trial Chamber III to Trial Chamber II. The Trial of the Accused commenced on 15 November 2006. The Prosecution called a total of 18 witnesses and the Defence called a total of 32 witnesses. The evidentiary phase of the trial concluded on 22 October 2007.

14. On 3 November 2006, the Prosecution's motion for the transfer of detained Witness AMA to the Arusha Detention Facility was approved on certain grounds.[923] This request was later amended and the period of temporary transfer was extended.[924] On 24 November 2006, the **[page v]** Chamber denied the Prosecution's motion for variation of protective measures for Witness CSH and directed the Prosecution to bring the matter to WVSS's attention for appropriate action.[925]

15. On 29 November 2006, the Chamber denied the Prosecution's Motion requesting protective measures for Witnesses CCF, CCJ, BLC, BLS and BLJ, who all live outside of Rwanda and its neighbouring countries, because no objective basis for the alleged fears expressed by those Prosecution witnesses was demonstrated.[926]

16. On 29 November 2006, following the Prosecution's motion, the Chamber, taking into account the jurisprudence of the Appeals Chamber, took judicial notice of the following facts: that between 6 April and 17 July 1994, there was a genocide against members of the Tutsi ethnic group; that between 6 April 1994 and 17 July 1994, that the Twa, Hutu and Tutsi ethnic groups existed in Rwanda as protected groups under the Genocide Convention; that between 6 April 1994 and 17 July 1994, throughout Rwanda, there were widespread or systematic attacks against a civilian population based on Tutsi ethnic identification and that during the attacks, some Rwandan citizens killed or caused serious bodily or mental harm to persons perceived to be Tutsi. As a result of the attacks, there were a large number of deaths of persons of Tutsi ethnic identity; that between 6 April 1994 and 17 July 1994, there was an armed conflict in Rwanda that was not of an international character, that between 1 January 1994 and 17 July 1994, Rwanda was a State Party to the Convention on the Prevention and Punishment of the Crime of Genocide (1948) having acceded to it on 16 April 1975 and that between 1 January 1994 and 17 July 1994, Rwanda was a State Party to the Geneva Conventions of 12 August 1949 and their Additional Protocol II of 8 June 1977, having acceded to the Geneva Convention of 12 August 1949 on 5 May 1965 and having acceded to the Additional Protocols of 1977 on 19 November 1984.[927]

17. On 14 February 2007, the Chamber granted two Prosecution motions to vary its witness list by adding Witness BUW and to give protective measures to Witnesses BUW, CCF, CCJ and BLJ. The Chamber also allowed the Prosecution to withdraw Witness BLS from its witness list.[928]

18. On 1 March 2007, the Chamber granted the Prosecution's motion to allow Witnesses BPA and BLR to testify via video-link, and ordered that their testimonies be heard from Kigali.[929] **[page vi]**

---

[923] Decision on the Prosecutor's Motion for the Transfer of Detained Witness AMA Pursuant to Rule 90*bis* of the Rules of Procedure and Evidence (TC), dated 3 November 2006.
[924] Decision on the Prosecutor's Extremely Urgent Motion to Extend the Period of Temporary Transfer of Detained Witness AMA Pursuant to Rule 90*bis*(F) and 73(A) of the Rules of Procedure and Evidence (TC), dated 14 February 2007.
[925] Decision on the Prosecution Motion for Variation of the Protective Measures for Witness CSH (TC), dated 24 November 2006.
[926] Decision on Prosecutor's Motion for Protective Measures for Witnesses CCF, CCJ, BLC, BLS and BLJ (TC), dated 29 November 2006.
[927] Decision on Prosecutor's Motion for the Trial Chamber to Take Judicial Notice of Facts of Common Knowledge Pursuant to Rule 94(A) (TC), dated 29 November 2006.
[928] Decision on the Prosecutor's Motions for Variation of Witness List and Protective Measures for Witnesses BUW, CCF, CCJ and BLJ (TC), dated 14 February 2007.
[929] Decision on the Prosecutor's Urgent Motion for Witnesses BPA, BLR and BLN to Give Testimony via Video-Link (TC), dated 14 February 2007.

Prosecutor v. Rukundo, Judgement

19. On 8 March 2007, the Defence filed a confidential motion to recall Witness BLP on the ground that new material relating to the witness had been discovered, or, in the alternative, to rescind Trial Chamber III's Decision on protective measures dated 24 October 2002 with respect to the Witness BLP and to allow the Defence to contact the witness.[930] On 30 April 2007, the Chamber denied the Defence motion to recall Witness BLP and issued a *proprio motu* order that Prosecution Witness BLP be called as a witness of the Trial Chamber and ordered his appearance on 15 June 2007. The Trial Chamber further ordered the appearance of the Defence investigator, Leonidas Nshogoza, in order to question him on the circumstances surrounding his meetings with Witness BLP.[931]

20. On 10 March 2007, Co-counsel for Rukundo, Ms. Annie Olivier, informed Lead Counsel of her intention to resign from her assignment as Co-counsel for the Accused due to the deterioration of her relationship with Lead Counsel. On 9 May 2007, the Registrar rejected Ms. Olivier's offer of resignation from her assignment as Co-counsel for Emmanuel Rukundo.[932] On 15 May 2007, the Defence filed a motion asking the Chamber to review the Registrar's decision of 9 May 2007. The Registrar, in accordance with Rule 33(b) of the Rules, and Ms. Olivier, presented their submissions. On 31 May 2007, the Chamber issued a Decision instructing the Registrar to replace Co-counsel for the Accused Rukundo as soon as reasonably practicable in view of the scheduled commencement of the Defence case on 2 July 2007.[933] On 1 June 2007, the Registrar withdrew the assignment of Ms. Olivier as Co-Counsel for the Accused.[934]

21. On 22 May 2007, following the Defence Motion for judgement of acquittal pursuant to Rule 98*bis* of the Rules, the Chamber granted the Accused partial acquittal on the charge of murder as a crime against humanity with respect to the killing of Father Alphonse Mbuguje, and the withdrawal of paragraphs 10(i), 16 and 25(i) from the Indictment. The Chamber, however, concluded that there **[page vii]** was sufficient evidence upon which a reasonable trier of fact could sustain a conviction in relation to the remainder of the counts charged in the Indictment.[935]

22. On 4 May 2007, the Chamber held a Pre-Defence conference to prepare for the commencement of the Defence case. On 7 May 2007, the Chamber ordered that the next Trial session, which was the start of the Defence case, should proceed from 2 July 2007 until 27 July 2007. The Chamber further ordered the Defence to file its Pre-Defence case submissions in compliance with Rule 73*ter* of the Rules and to disclose the identifying information of all Defence Witnesses to the Prosecution 21 days before the commencement of the Defence case. The Chamber also ordered that Witness BLP be heard before the commencement of the next Trial session on 2 July 2007, in variance of its prior order.[936]

23. On 16 May 2007, the Chamber granted the Defence request for protective measures for potential Defence witnesses.[937] On 27 June 2007, the Chamber issued a *proprio motu* order authorizing the transfer of detained Witness Nshogoza from Rwanda to the seat of the Tribunal in Arusha.[938] On 4 July 2007, the Chamber granted in part the Defence motion for a stay of proceedings and instructed the Registrar, pursuant to Rules 91 and 54 of the Rules, to conduct an investigation into the alleged false testimony of Witness BLP and other matters.[939] After issuing a warning to Lead Counsel for Rukundo pursuant to Rule 46(A) of the Rules, the Chamber instructed the Defence to immediately disclose the identities of all of its proposed

---

[930] *"Requête ex parte en extrême urgence et confidentielle aux fins de rappeler le témoin du Procureur BLP aux fins d'être réentendu au vu des Éléments nouveaux"*, dated 8 March 2007.
[931] Decision on Defence Motion to Recall Prosecution Witness BLP (TC), dated 30 April 2007.
[932] The Registrar's Decision Denying the Application for the Withdrawal of Ms. Annie Olivier, Co-counsel for the Accused, Mr. Emmanuel Rukundo, dated 9 May 2007.
[933] Decision on the Confidential and Extremely Urgent Defence Motion to Review the Registrar's Decision dated 9 May 2007 (TC), dated 31 May 2007.
[934] Registrar's Decision on Withdrawal of the Assignment of Ms. Annie Olivier Co-counsel for the Accused Emmanuel Rukundo, dated 1 June 2007.
[935] Decision on Defence Motion for Judgement of Acquittal Pursuant to Rule 98*bis* (TC), dated 22 May 2007.
[936] Scheduling Order following the Pre-Defence Status Conference (TC), dated 7 May 2007.
[937] Decision on the Defence Motion for Protective Measures for Defence Witnesses (TC), dated 16 May 2007.
[938] *Proprio Motu* Order for the Transfer of a Detained Witness (TC), dated 27 June 2007.
[939] Decision on the Motions Relating to the Scheduled Appearances of Witness BLP and the Defence Investigator (TC), dated 4 July 2007. The Defence's later request to appeal this decision was denied (Decision on the Defence Motion for Certification to Appeal the Chamber's decision of 4 July 2007 (TC), dated 25 July 2007).

witnesses.[940] Following a Status Conference, the Chamber ordered that the next Trial session should begin on 3 September 2007 and run until 5 October 2007.[941]

24. On 11 September 2007, the Chamber denied the Defence motion requesting the Swiss authorities to disclose the Accused's entire judicial dossier.[942] On the same day, the Chamber denied the Defence request for additional time to disclose the witnesses' identifying information, ordered that the remaining disclosure be done immediately, granted in part the Defence request to add Witnesses RUE, SLD, BCD, SJD, SAE and TMC and to delete Witnesses MCD, GSD, CNE, **[page viii]** SLC, SJB, BCC, NYE, RUB and TMF, from the witness list, and granted the Defence request to allow Witnesses SLA and GSA to testify via video-link.[943]

25. On 21 September 2007, the Chamber denied the Defence motion for subpoena and transfer of detained Witness SJA.[944] On 24 September 2007, the Chamber granted the Defence motion to subpoena Witness GSC.[945] On the same day, the Chamber granted the Defence's urgent and confidential motion requesting authorization for Witness SJD to testify via video-link.[946]

26. On 3 October 2007, the Chamber granted the Defence request to meet with the Accused during his examination-in-chief.[947] On the same day, the Chamber denied the Defence motion requesting authorization for Witness SLB to be heard via video-link.[948]

27. On 9 November 2007, in response to a Defence motion requesting additional time to file the closing briefs and the hearing of closing arguments than originally granted in an oral Decision, the Chamber instructed the parties to file their closing briefs by 14 January 2008 and scheduled the hearing of closing oral arguments in the week of 28 January to 1 February 2008.[949]

28. On 30 November 2008, the Chamber denied the Defence request to present additional witnesses and to file documentary evidence prior to the close of its case.[950] Leave for certification to appeal this Decision or, in the alternative, its reconsideration, was denied.[951] On 14 December 2007, in its Decision on the Haguma Report, the Chamber issued a warning to Lead Counsel pursuant to Rule 46 of the Rules for violating its Order for protective measures for witnesses by meeting with Witness BLP without its authorization.[952]

(d) Further Proceedings

29. Oral closing arguments were heard by the Chamber on 20 February 2008. **[page ix]**

30. The Chamber pronounced its unanimous Judgement in an oral summary on 27 February 2009. It found Emmanuel Rukundo guilty of the crimes of genocide, murder and extermination as crimes against humanity and sentenced him to 25 years' imprisonment. The Chamber filed the complete written Judgement on 13 March 2009. **[page ix]**

---

[940] Order on Disclosure of Identifying Information of Defence Witnesses (TC), dated 18 July 2007.
[941] Scheduling Order Following the Status Conference Held on 24 July 2007 (TC), dated 24 July 2007.
[942] Decision on Defence Motion Requesting Disclosure by Swiss Authorities of the Entire Judicial Dossier Relating to the Accused (TC), dated 11 September 2007.
[943] Decision on the Defence Motions for Additional to Disclose Witnesses' Identifying information, to Vary its Witness List and for Video-Link Testimony, and on the Prosecution's Motion for Sanctions (TC), dated 11 September 2007.
[944] Decision on Defence Motion for Subpoena and Transfer of Detained Witness SJA (TC), dated 21 Sepetmebr 2007.
[945] Decision on Defence Motion for Subpoena for Witness GSC (TC), dated 24 September 2007.
[946] Decision on the Defence Urgent and Confidential Motion Requesting Authorization for Witness SJD to Testify via Video-Link (TC), dated 24 September 2007.
[947] Decision on the Defence Request to Meet the Accused During his Examination-in-Chief (TC), dated 3 October 2007.
[948] Decision on Defence Motion for Video-Link Testimony for Witness SLB (TC), dated 3 October 2007.
[949] Decision on Defence Motion to Re-schedule the Filing of Closing Briefs and the Hearing of Closing Arguments (TC), dated 9 November 2007.
[950] Decision on Defence Motion to Present Additional Witnesses and to File Documentary Evidence Prior to the Close of its Case (TC), dated 30 November 2007.
[951] Decision on Defence Request for Certification to Appeal or in the Alternative, Reconsideration of the Chamber's Decision of 30 November 2007 (TC), dated 14 December 2007.
[952] Decision on the Haguma Report (TC), dated 14 December 2007.

[page i] ANNEX B – GLOSSARY

A. List of Defined Terms, Acronyms and Abbreviations

According to Rule 2(B), of the Rules of Procedure and Evidence, the masculine shall include the feminine and the singular the plural, and vice-versa.

Chamber (or **Trial Chamber**)	Trial Chamber II of the International Criminal Tribunal for Rwanda, composed of Judges Asoka de Silva, Presiding, Taghrid Hikmet and Seon Ki Park
Defence Closing Brief	The Prosecutor v. Emmanuel Rukundo, Case No. ICTR-2001-70-T, Defence Closing Brief, 4 March 2008
ICTY	International Criminal Tribunal for the Prosecution of Persons Responsible for Serious Violations of International Humanitarian Law Committed in the Territory of the Former Yugoslavia since 1991, established by Security Council resolution 927 of 25 May 1993
Indictment	The Prosecutor v. Emmanuel Rukundo, Case No. ICTR-2001-70-T, Amended Indictment Pursuant To the Decision of Trial Chamber II of 28 December (Decision on the Prosecutor's Request for Leave to file an Amended Indictment (TC)), 6 October 2006
JCE	Joint Criminal Enterprise
Judgement of Acquittal	The Prosecutor v. Emmanuel Rukundo Case No. ICTR-2001-70-T, Decision on Defence Motion for Judgement of Acquittal Pursuant to Rule 98*bis* (TC), 22 May 2007 ("98*bis* Decision")
MRND	*Mouvement révolutionnaire national pour le développement* (National Revolutionary Movement for Development)
Prosecution Closing Brief	The Prosecutor v. Emmanuel Rukundo, Case No. ICTR-2001-70-T, The Prosecutor's Final Trial Brief, 14 January 2008
Prosecution Pre-Trial Brief	The Prosecutor v. Emmanuel Rukundo, Case No. ICTR-2001-70-I, The Prosecutor's Pre-Trial Brief Pursuant To Article 73*bis* (B)(i) of the Rules of Procedure and Evidence, 16 August 2006
RAF	Rwandan Armed Forces
RPF	Rwandan Patriotic Front
Rules	Rules of Procedure and Evidence of the Tribunal, adopted pursuant to Article 14 of the Statute [page ii]
Statute	The Statute of the Tribunal adopted by Security Council Resolution 955 of 8 November 1994
T.	Transcript of the Trial Chamber hearings (English Version)
TRAFIPRO (or CND)	A place in Kabgayi

Annex B

Tribunal (or ICTR) — International Criminal Tribunal for the Prosecution of Persons Responsible for Genocide and Other Serious Violations of International Humanitarian Law Committed in the Territory of Rwanda and Rwandan Citizens Responsible for Genocide and Other such Violations Committed in the Territory of Neighboring States between 1 January 1994 and 31 December 1994, established by Security Council resolution 955 of 8 November 1994

B. Jurisprudence

1. ICTR

AKAYESU

The Prosecutor v. Jean-Paul Akayesu, Case No. ICTR-96-4-T, Judgement (TC), 2 September 1998 (*"Akayesu*, Judgement (TC)")

The Prosecutor v. Jean-Paul Akayesu, Case No. ICTR-96-4-A, Judgement (AC), 1 June 2001 (*"Akayesu*, Judgement (AC)")

BAGILISHEMA

The Prosecutor v. Ignace Bagilishema, Case No. ICTR-95-1A-T, Judgement (TC), 7 June 2001, (*"Bagilishema*, Judgement (TC)")

BAGOSORA ET AL.

The Prosecutor v. Théoneste Bagosora, Gratien Kabiligi, Aloys Ntabakuze, Anatole Nsengiyumva, Case No. ICTR-98-41-T, Decision on Motions for Judgement for Acquittal (TC), 25 February 2005 (*"Bagosora et al.*, 98 bis Decision")

The Prosecutor v. Théoneste Bagosora, Gratien Kabiligi, Aloys Ntabakuze, Anatole Nsengiyumva, Case No. ICTR-98-41-T, Judgement and Sentence (TC), 18 December 2008, (*"Bagosora*, Judgement (TC)")

The Prosecutor v. Théoneste Bagosora, Gratien Kabiligi, Aloys Ntabakuze, Anatole Nsengiyumva, Case No. ICTR-98-41-T, Decision on Aloys Ntabakuze's Interlocutory Appeal on Questions of Law Raised by the 29 June 2006 Trial Chamber I Decision on Motion for Exclusion of Evidence (AC), 18 September 2006 **[page iii]**

BIKINDI

The Prosecutor v. Simon Bikindi, Case No. ICTR-2001-72-T, Judgement (TC), 2 December 2008 (*"Bikindi*, Judgement (TC)")

BISENGIMANA

The Prosecutor v. Paul Bisengimana, Case No. ICTR-00-60-T, Judgement and Sentence (TC), 13 April 2006 (*"Bisengimana*, Judgement (TC)")

GACUMBITSI

The Prosecutor v. Sylvestre Gacumbitsi, Case No. ICTR-2001-64-T, Judgement (TC), 17 June 2004 (*"Gacumbitsi*, Judgement (TC)")

Sylvestre Gacumbitsi v. The Prosecutor, Case No. ICTR-2001-64-A, Judgement (AC), 7 July 2006 (*"Gacumbitsi*, Judgement (AC)")

KAJELIJELI

The Prosecutor v. Juvénal Kajelijeli, Case No. ICTR-98-44A-T, Judgment and Sentence (TC), 1 December 2003 ("*Kajelijeli*, Judgement (TC)")

Juvénal Kajelijeli v. The Prosecutor, Case No. ICTR-98-44A-A, Judgment (AC) 23 May 2005 ("*Kajelijeli*, Judgement (AC)")

KAMBANDA

The Prosecutor v. Jean Kambanda, Case No. ICTR- 97-23-S, Judgement (TC), 4 September 1998 ("*Kambanda*, Judgement (TC)")

KAMUHANDA

The Prosecutor v. Jean De Dieu Kamuhanda, Case No. ICTR-99-54A-T, Judgement (TC), 22 January 2004 ("*Kamuhanda*, Judgement (TC)")

Jean De Dieu Kamuhanda v. The Prosecutor, Case No. ICTR-99-54A-A, Judgement (AC), 19 September 2005 ("*Kamuhanda*, Judgement (AC)")

KARERA

The Prosecutor v. François Karera, Case No. ICTR-01-74-T, Judgement and Sentence (TC), 7 December 2007 ("*Karera*, Judgement (TC)")

KAREMERA ET AL.

The Prosecutor v. Édouard Karemera, André Rwamakuba, Mathieu Ngirumpatse, Joseph Nzirorera, Case No. ICTR-98-44-T, Decision on Prosecutor's Interlocutory Appeal of Decision on Judicial Notice (AC), 16 June 2006 **[page iv]**

KAYISHEMA AND RUZINDANA

The Prosecutor v. Clément Kayishema and Obed Ruzindana, Case No. ICTR-95-1-T, Judgement (TC), 21 May 1999 ("*Kayishema and Ruzindana*, Judgement (TC)")

The Prosecutor v. Clément Kayishema and Obed Ruzindana, Case No. ICTR-95-1-A, Judgement (Reasons) (AC), 1 June 2001 ("*Kayishema and Ruzindana*, Judgement (AC)")

MPAMBARA

The Prosecutor v. Jean Mpambara., Case No. ICTR-01-65-T, Judgement (TC), 11 September 2006 ("*Mpambara*, Judgement (TC)")

Muhimana

The Prosecutor v. Mikaeli Muhimana, Case No. ICTR-95-1B-T, Judgement (TC), 28 April 2005 ("*Muhimana*, Judgement (TC)")

Mikaeli Muhimana v. The Prosecutor, Case No. ICTR-95-1B-A, Judgement (AC), 21 May 2007 ("*Muhimana*, Judgement (AC)")

MUSEMA

The Prosecutor v. Alfred Musema, Case No. ICTR-96-13-A, Judgement (TC), 27 January 2000 ("*Musema*, Judgement (TC)")

Alfred Musema v. The Prosecutor, Case No. ICTR-96-13-A, Judgement (AC), 27 16 November 2001 ("*Musema*, Judgement (AC)")

MUVUNYI

The Prosecutor v. Tharcisse Muvunyi, Case No. ICTR-2000-55A-AR73, Decision on the Prosecution Interlocutory Appeal against Trial Chamber II Decision of 23 February 2005 (AC), 12 May 2005

Prosecutor v. Tharcisse Muvunyi, Case No.ICTR-2000-55A-T, Judgement and Sentence (TC), 12 September 2006 ("*Muvunyi,* Judgement (TC)")

Tharcisse Muvunyi v. The Prosecutor, Case No. ICTR-2000-55A-A, Judgement (AC), 29 August 2008 ("*Muvunyi,* Judgement (AC)")

NAHIMANA ET AL.

The Prosecutor v. Ferdinand Nahimana, Jean-Bosco Barayagwiza and Hassan Ngeze, Case No. ICTR-99-52-T, Judgement and Sentence (TC), 3 December 2003 ("*Nahimana et al.,* Judgement (TC)")

Ferdinand Nahimana, Jean-Bosco Barayagwiza and Hassan Ngeze v. The Prosecutor, Case No. ICTR-99-52-A, Judgement (AC), 28 November 2007 ("*Nahimana et al.,* Judgement (AC)")

NCHAMIHIGO

The Prosecutor v. Siméon Nchamihigo, Case No. ICTR-01-71-A, Judgement (TC), 12 November 2008 ("*Nchamihigo,* Judgement (TC)") **[page v]**

NDINDABAHIZI

The Prosecutor v. Emmanuel Ndindabahizi, Case No. ICTR-2001-71-I, Judgement (TC), 15 July 2004, ("*Ndindabahizi,* Judgement (TC)")

Emmanuel Ndindabahizi v. The Prosecutor, Case No. ICTR-01-63-T, Judgement (AC), 16 January 2007 ("*Ndindabahizi,* Judgement (AC)")

NIYITEGEKA

The Prosecutor v. Eliézer Niyitegeka, Case No. ICTR-96-14-T, Judgement and Sentence (TC), 16 May 2003 ("*Niyitegeka,* Judgement (TC)")

Eliézer Niyitegeka v. The Prosecutor, Case No. ICTR-96-14-A, Judgement (AC), 9 July 2004 ("*Niyitegeka,* Judgement (AC)")

NTAGERURA ET AL.

The Prosecutor v. André Ntagerura, Emmanuel Bagambiki and Samuel Imanishimwe, Case No. ICTR-99-46-T, Judgement (TC), 25 February 2004 ("*Ntagerura et al.,* Judgement (TC)")

The Prosecutor v. André Ntagerura, Emmanuel Bagambiki and Samuel Imanishimwe, Case No. ICTR-99-46-A, Judgement (AC), 7 July 2006 ("*Ntagerura et al.,* Judgement (AC)")

NTAKIRUTIMANA

The Prosecutor v. Élizaphan Ntakirutimana and Gérard Ntakirutimana, Case Nos. ICTR-96-10 and ICTR-96-17-T, Judgement (TC), 21 February 2003 ("*Ntakirutimana,* Judgement (TC)")

The Prosecutor v. Élizaphan Ntakirutimana and Gérard Ntakirutimana, Case Nos. ICTR-96-10-A and ICTR-96-17-A, Judgement (AC), 13 December 2004 ("*Ntakirutimana,* Judgement (AC)")

NZABIRINDA

The Prosecutor v. Joseph Nzabirinda Case No. ICTR-01-77-T, Judgement (TC), 23 February 2007 ("*Nzabirinda,* Judgement (TC)")

RUGAMBARARA

The Prosecutor v. Juvénal Rugambarara, Case No. ICTR-00-59-T, Sentencing Judgement (TC), 16 November 2007 ("*Rugambarara,* Judgement (TC)")

RUGGIU

The Prosecutor v. Georges Ruggiu, Case No. ICTR-97-32-I, Judgement and Sentence (TC), 1 June 2000 ("*Ruggiu,* Judgement (TC)")

RUKUNDO

The Prosecutor v. Emmanuel Rukundo, Case No. ICTR-2001-70-I, Warrant of Arrest and Orders for Transfer and Detention and for Search and Seizure (TC), 5 July 2001

The Prosecutor v. Emmanuel Rukundo, Case No. ICTR-2001-70-I, Decision on Preliminary Motion (TC), 26 February 2003 **[page vi]**

The Prosecutor v. Emmanuel Rukundo, Case No. ICTR-2001-70-I, Decision on the Prosecutor's Request to File an Amended Indictment (TC), 28 September 2006

The Prosecutor v. Emmanuel Rukundo, Case No. ICTR-2001-70-T, Decision on Prosecutor's Motion for the Trial Chamber to take Judicial Notice of Facts of Common Knowledge Pursuant to Rule 94(A) (TC), 29 November 2006

The Prosecutor v. Emmanuel Rukundo, Case No. ICTR-2001-70-T, Decision on Defence Motion to Recall Prosecution Witness BLP (TC), 30 April 2007

The Prosecutor v. Emmanuel Rukundo, Case No. ICTR-2001-70-T, Scheduling Order Following the Pre-Defence Conference (TC), 7 May 2007

The Prosecutor v. Emmanuel Rukundo, Case No. ICTR-2001-70-T, Decision on Defence Motion for Judgement of Acquittal Pursuant to Rule 98*bis* (TC), 22 May 2007 ("98*bis* Decision")

The Prosecutor v. Emmanuel Rukundo, Case No. ICTR-2001-70-T, Decision on the Motions Relating to the Scheduled Appearances of Witness BLP and the Defence Investigator (TC), 4 July 2007

Emmanuel Rukundo v. The Prosecutor, Décision (*Acte D'Appel relative à la Décision du 26 Février 2003 relative aux exceptions préjudicielles*) (AC), 17 October 2003

RUTAGANDA

The Prosecutor v. Georges Anderson Nderubumwe Rutaganda, Case No. ICTR-96-3, Judgement (TC), 6 December 1999 ("*Rutaganda*, Judgement (TC)")

Georges Anderson Nderubumwe Rutaganda v. The Prosecutor, Case No. ICTR-96-3-A, Judgement (AC), 26 May 2003 ("*Rutaganda*, Judgement (AC)")

SEMANZA

The Prosecutor v. Laurent Semanza, Case No. ICTR-97-20-T, Judgement (TC), 15 May 2003, ("*Semanza*, Judgement (TC)")

Laurent Semanza v. The Prosecutor, Case No. ICTR-97-20-A, Judgement (AC), 20 May 2005, ("*Semanza*, Judgement (AC)")

SEROMBA

The Prosecutor v. Athanase Seromba, Case No. ICTR-2001-66-A, Judgement (AC), 12 March 2008 ("*Seromba*, Judgement (AC)")

SERUGENDO

The Prosecutor v. Joseph Serugendo, Case No. ICTR-2005-84-I, Judgement (TC), 12 June 2006 ("*Serugendo*, Judgement (TC)")

SERUSHAGO

Prosecutor v. Omar Serushago, Case No. ICTR-98-39-S, Sentence (TC), 5 February 1999 ("*Serushago*, Judgement (TC)") **[page vii]**

SIMBA

The Prosecutor v. Aloys Simba, Case No ICTR-01-76-T, Judgement and Sentence, 13 December 2005 ("*Simba*, Judgement (TC)")

Aloys Simba v. The Prosecutor, Case No. ICTR-01-76-AR72.2, Decision on Interlocutory Appeal Regarding Temporal Jurisdiction (AC), 29 July 2004

Aloys Simba v. The Prosecutor, Case No. ICTR-01-76-A, Appeal Judgement (AC), 27 November 2007 (*"Simba,* Judgement (AC)")

ZIGIRANYIRAZO

The Prosecutor v. Protais Zigiranyirazo, Case No ICTR-01-76-T, Judgement (TC), 18 December 2008 (*"Zigiranyirazo,* Judgement (TC)")

2. ICTY

ALEKSOVSKI

The Prosecutor v. Zlatko Aleksovski, Case No. IT-95-14/1, Decision on Prosecutor's Appeal On Admissibility Of Evidence (AC), 16 February 1999

BLAGOJEVIĆ

The Prosecutor v. Vidoje Blagojević and Dragan Jokić, Case No. IT-02-60, Judgement (TC), 17 January 2005 (*"Blagojević,* Judgement (TC)")

BRĐANIN

The Prosecutor v. Radoslav Brđanin, Case No. IT-99-36, Judgement (TC), 1 September 2004 (*"Brđanin,* Judgement (TC)")

ČELEBIĆI

The Prosecutor v. Zejnil Delalić, Zdravko Mucić (aka "Pavo"), Hazim Delić and Esad Landžo (aka "Zenga"), Case No. IT-96-21-A, Judgement (AC), 20 February 2001 (*"Čelebići,* Judgement (AC)")

DERONIJIĆ

The Prosecutor v. Miroslav Deronjić, Case No. IT-02-61-S, Judgement (TC), 30 March 2004 (*"Deronjić* Judgement (AC)")

JELISIĆ

The Prosecutor v. Goran Jelisić, Case No. IT-95-10-A, Judgement (AC), 5 July 2001 (*"Jelisić,* Judgement (AC)")

KORDIĆ & ČERKEZ

The Prosecutor v. Dario Kordić and Mario Čerkez. Case No. IT-95-14/2-A, Judgement (AC), 17 December 2004 (*"Kordic and Cerkez* Judgement (AC)") **[page viii]**

KRSTIĆ

The Prosecutor v. Radislav Krstić, Case No. IT-98-33, Judgement (TC), 2 August 2001 (*"Krstić,* Judgement (TC)")

The Prosecutor v. Radislav Krstić, Case No. IT-98-33-A, Judgement (AC), 19 April 2004 (*"Krstić,* Judgement (AC)")

KUNARAC

The Prosecutor v. Dragoljub Kunarac, Radomir Kovac and Zoran Vukovic, Case No. IT-96-23, Judgement (TC), 14 January 2000 (*"Kunarac,* Judgement (TC)")

The Prosecutor v. Dragoljub Kunarac, Radomir Kovac and Zoran Vukovic, Case No. IT-96-23 & IT-96-23/1-A, Judgement (AC), 21 May 1999 (*"Kunarac,* Judgement (AC)")

KUPREŠKIĆ ET AL.

The Prosecutor v. Zoran Kupreškić, Mirjan Kupreškić, Vlatko Kupreškić, Drago Josipović, Vladimir Šantič, Case No. IT-95-16-A, Appeal Judgement (AC), 23 October 2001 (*"Kupreškić et al.,* Judgement (AC)")

KRNOJELAĆ

The Prosecutor v. Milorad Krnojelać, Case No. IT-97-25-A, Judgement (AC), 17 September 2003 (*"Krnojelac,* Judgement (AC)")

KRSTIĆ

The Prosecutor v. Radislav Krstić, Case No. IT-98-33-A, Judgement (AC), 19 April 2004 (*"Krstić,* Judgement (AC)")

KVOČKA ET AL.

The Prosecutor v. Miroslav Kvočka, Mlado Radić, Zoran Žigić and Dragoljub Prcać, Case No. IT-98-30/1-A, Judgement (AC), 28 February 2005 (*"Kvočka et al.,* Judgement (AC)")

MARTIČ

The Prosecutor v. Milan Martič, Case No. IT-95-11-T, Judgement (TC), 12 June 2007 (*"Martič,* Judgement (TC)")

NIKOLIĆ

The Prosecutor v. Dragan Nikolić, Case No. IT-94-2, Judgement (TC), 18 December 2003 (*"Nikolić,* Judgement (TC)")

SIKIRICA ET AL.

The Prosecutor v. Dusko Sikirica, Damir Dosen and Dragan Kolundzija, Case No. IT-95-8, Judgement (TC) 13 November 2001 (*"Sikirica,* Judgement (TC)") **[page ix]**

SIMIĆ

The Prosecutor v. Blagoje Simić, Case No. IT-95-9-A, Judgement (AC), 28 November 2006 (*"Simić,* Judgement (AC)")

STAKIĆ

The Prosecutor v. Milomir Stakić, Case No. IT-97-24-T, Judgement (TC), 31 July 2003 (*"Stakić,* Judgement (TC)")

The Prosecutor v. Milomir Stakić, Case No. IT-97-24-A, Judgement (AC), 22 March 2006 (*"Stakić,* Judgement (AC)")

TADIĆ

The Prosecutor v. Duško Tadić, Case No. IT-94-1-A, Judgement (AC), 15 July 1999 (*"Tadić,* Judgement (AC)")

VASILJEVIĆ

The Prosecutor v. Mitar Vasiljević, Case No. IT-98-32, Judgement (AC), 25 February 2004, (*"Vasiljević,* Judgement (AC)")

C. Other Material

United Nations Security Council Resolution 935, S/RES/955 (1994)

Rwandan Organic Law No. 8/96, on the Organization of Prosecutions for Offences constituting Genocide or Crimes against Humanity committed since 1 October 1990, published in the Gazette of the Republic of Rwanda, 35th year. No. 17, 1 September 1996, as amended by Organic Law No. 31/2007 of 25/07/2007 relating to the Abolition of the Death Penalty

Commentary

1. Introduction

The atrocities that took place in Rwanda in 1994 saw the involvement among others of religious authorities. In the present case Trial Chamber II of the tribunal has convicted the catholic priest Immanuel Rukundo for genocide, murder and extermination as crimes against humanity.

It is not the first conviction issued against a clergyman. Another catholic priest, Athanase Seromba, has been sentenced to life imprisonment by the Appeals Chamber.[1] A guilty verdict and a sentence of ten years' imprisonment were also entered against the pastor of the Seventh Day Adventist Church, Elizaphan Ntakirutimana.[2] The Catholic priest Hormisdas Nsengimana, who also had been charged with genocide, has instead been acquitted.[3]

The role of religious figures in the context of the 1994 atrocities raises challenging issues. In most cases religious authorities did not directly commit acts of violence amounting to genocide or crimes against humanity (which were perpetrated in large part by soldiers of the RAF or by members of the *Interahamwe*). Nonetheless they played an active role in the ethnically motivated brutalities of the period. Theirs is a hybrid role: formally, they did not direct any organization and had no authority over the direct perpetrators, yet they were vested with extremely high moral authority and could hence lend significant moral support to the acts that were being committed. This raises the issue of the proper mode of responsibility of religious figures in the genocidal events of Rwanda. Were they perpetrators, co-perpetrators, conspirators or mere accomplices of the crimes committed?

The theme of the mode of liability is the central matter in the judgement against Rukundo. However, it is not the only issue at stake of the decision. In the long judgement entered against Immanuel Rukundo the Trial Chamber also deals with the elements of genocide by sexual assault and, in particular, with the concept of serious harm and it discusses, albeit very briefly, multiple convictions based on the same set of facts and sentencing standards. Last but not least, the Trial Chamber faced several evidentiary issues throughout the trial mostly concerning the admissibility of evidence (accomplice and hearsay evidence in particular) and the credibility of witnesses. For the sake of brevity the present commentary will touch upon the two key issues in the logic of the decision. It will thus particularly focus on the following: 1) the proper mode of participation; 2) the concept of mental harm in genocide by sexual assault.

2. The facts attributed to Rukundo

Charged with several episodes amounting to genocide, murder as a crime against humanity and extermination as a crime against humanity, Rukundo is acquitted on most charges due to lack of evidence and is convicted for three allegations: i) having taken part to the abduction from a seminary and the subsequent killing of a Tutsi woman (Madame Rudahunga) and to a second abduction from the same seminary of four Tutsi civilians who were severely beaten and injured; ii) the abductions and killings of Tutsi refugees at another Seminary (St. Léon Minor Seminary) and iii) the sexual assault of a young Tutsi refugee at the same Seminary. With regard to the first set of facts, Rukundo is convicted for genocide and murder as a crime against humanity, with regard to the second he is found guilty of genocide, murder as a crime against humanity and extermination as a crime against humanity, with regard to the third he is found guilty of genocide by causing serious mental harm.

When the ethnic conflict ignited in Rwanda in the early spring of 1994, after the breakdown of the Presidential airplane, a large part of the population, especially Tutsi, sought refuge in church premises, seminars and other religious facilities. It is within this context that, according to the chamber, Rukundo's genocidal action develops. A catholic priest but also a military chaplain, Rukundo targeted Tutsi refugees with the support of

---

[1] ICTR, Judgement, *Prosecutor v. Seromba*, Case No. ICTR-2001-66-A, A. Ch., 12 March 2008, Klip/ Sluiter ALC-XXXI-757. The Appeals Chamber reversed the decision entered in first instance by the Trial Chamber (ICTR, Judgement, *Prosecutor v. Seromba*, Case No. ICTR-2001-66-T, T. Ch. III, 13 December 2006, Klip/ Sluiter ALC-XXV-523) and increased the amount of the sentence.
[2] ICTR, Judgement, *Prosecutor v. Elizaphan Ntakirutimana and Gérard Ntakirutimana*, Cases Nos. ICTR-96-10-A and 96-17-A, A. Ch., 13 December 2004, Klip/ Sluiter, ALC-XVIII-755.
[3] ICTR, Judgement, *Prosecutor v. Nsengimana*, Case No. ICTR-01-69-T, T. Ch. I, 17 November 2009.

the soldiers and of the *Interahamwe*. In detail, the Chamber considered to be proved beyond reasonable doubt the following facts alleged in the indictment:

1) (Events at St. Joseph's college) that in April 1994 a Tutsi woman (Madame Rudahunga) was abducted from St. Joseph's College in Kabgayi by Emmanuel Rukundo, acting together with unknown soldiers, and was taken to her home located near St. Joseph' College, where she was shot and killed by the soldiers. The same group of soldiers returned to St. Joseph's College, about twenty minutes after that first abduction and took away four civilians (among which two of the children of Madame Rudahunga). All four victims were severely beaten and injured by the soldiers and left for dead. The soldiers drove a vehicle identified as belonging to the accused, Rukundo was constantly present at the scene at all material times, following the abductors in another vehicle;[4]

2) (Events at the St. Léon Minor Seminary) between April and May 1994 Rukundo visited the St. Léon Minor Seminary, accompanied by soldiers and *Interahamwe*. There Rukundo identified Tutsi refugees with a list and then left the Seminary. Shortly after Rukundo's departure, the refugees who had been identified were abducted from the Seminary by soldiers and *Interahamwe* to an unknown location, where they were killed;[5]

3) In one occasion at the St. Léon Minor Seminary, Rukundo took a young Tutsi woman into his room, locked the door and sexually assaulted her causing her serious mental harm.[6]

3. The proper mode of participation between co-perpetration, complicity and joint criminal enterprise

Save for the latter allegation, concerning the sexual assault, Rukundo was not accused of having physically perpetrated the killings and the beatings. Nonetheless Rukundo is convicted on all three counts for having committed the offences. In the Court's view, "'committing' is not limited to direct and physical perpetration".[7] The Chamber followed the approach adopted in Gacumbitsi where a broad concept of commission was assessed.[8] By noting that "Rukundo participated from the outset until the completion of a crime", the Chamber concluded that "Rukundo's acts were as much an integral part of the criminal act as were the killing and the causing of serious bodily harm they enabled".[9] Following this line of reasoning Rukundo was hence convicted as a co-perpertrator of the crimes rather than an accomplice (aider or abettor).

Such a broad notion of commission does not go unchallenged in the case-law of the *ad-hoc* Tribunals. The majoritarian approach restricts the concept of commission to "physical perpetration". Commission means "first and foremost the physical perpetration [of a crime] by the offender himself or the culpable omission of an act that was mandated by a rule of criminal law.[10] Moving from this premise the *ad hoc* courts have mostly relied on the doctrine of joint criminal enterprise (JCE) to assess principal (primary) liability of defendants who did not physically commit the unlawful acts. If a defendant shared a common design (or

---

[4] ICTR, Judgement, *Rukundo v. Prosecutor*, Case No. ICTR-2001-70-T, T. Ch. II, 27 February 2009, in this volume, p. 213, par. 171.
[5] *Ibid.*, par. 364.
[6] *Ibid.*, par. 372–377.
[7] *Ibid.*, par. 562.
[8] ICTR, Judgement, *Gacumbitsi v. Prosecutor*, Case No. ICTR-2001-64-A, A. Ch., 7 July 2006, Klip/ Sluiter, ALC-XXIV-495, par. 60–61; ICTR, Judgement, *Prosecutor v. Seromba*, Case No. ICTR-2001-66-A, *supra* note 1, par. 161.
[9] ICTR, Judgement, *Prosecutor v. Rukundo*, *supra* note 4, par. 563 and 571.
[10] ICTY, Judgement, *Prosecutor v. Tadić*, Case No. IT-94-1-A, A Ch., 15 July 1999, Klip/ Sluiter, ALC-III-761, par. 188; ICTR, Judgement, *Prosecutor v. Gacumbitsi*, Case No. ICTR-2001-64-T, T. Ch. III, 17 June 2004, Klip/ Sluiter ALC-XVIII-481, par. 285; ICTR Judgement, *Prosecutor v. Kayishema and Ruzindana*, Case No. ICTR-95-1-A, A. Ch., 1 June 2001, Klip/ Sluiter, ALC-X-495, par. 187; ICTY Judgement, *Prosecutor v. Kunarac, Kovač and Vuković,*, Case No. IT-96-23-T and IT-96-23/ 1-T, 22 February 2001, Klip/ Sluiter ALC-V-617, par. 390. (Making clear that "there can be several perpetrators in relation to the same crime where the conduct of each one of them fulfills the requisite elements of the definition of the substantive offence"); ICTR, Judgement, *Prosecutor v. Semanza*, Case No. 97-20-T, T. Ch. III, 15 May 2003, Klip/ Sluiter ALC-XII-599, par. 383; ICTR, Judgement, *Prosecutor v. Kamuhanda*, Case No. ICTR-99-54A-T, T. Ch. II, 22 January 2003, Klip/ Sluiter, ALC-XVII-531, par. 595 ("To 'commit' a crime usually means to perpetrate or execute the crime by oneself or to omit to fulfill a legal obligation in a manner punishable by penal law. In this sense, there may be one or more perpetrators in relation to the same crime where the conduct of each perpetrator satisfies the requisite elements of the substantive offence"). For an express reference to indirect perpetration, ICTY *Prosecutor v. Simić, Tadić and Zarić*, Case No. IT-95-9-T, T. Ch. II, 17 October 2003, Klip/ Sluiter ALC-XV-141, par. 137 ("any finding of commission requires the personal or physical, direct or indirect, participation, of the accused in the relevant criminal act").

common plan, common purpose) with those who directly committed the criminal acts she is held liable as co-perpetrator (or joint principal) despite the fact that she did not physically participate to the commission of the crimes.[11] The doctrine of JCE has been shaped by the Tadić Appeals Chamber, which categorized three different forms of enterprise: basic, systemic (concentration camp cases) and extended.[12] Though much criticisms has been raised against the doctrine of JCE,[13] especially in its extended version,[14] it remains the tool to which the jurisprudence of *ad hoc* tribunals has mostly resorted for assessing co-perpetration beyond physical perpetration.[15]

3.1. Previous attempts to establish a doctrine of co-perpetration in alternative to JCE

The JCE doctrine is rooted in the restricted notion of commission of a crime. Consequently any extension of the notion delivers a blow to the doctrine itself. Attempts to substitute the doctrine of JCE with an extended notion of commission date back to the *Stakić* case,[16] there the Trial Chamber emphasised that: "[J]oint criminal enterprise is only one of several possible interpretations of the term 'commission' under Article 7(1) of the Statute and that other definitions of co-perpetration must equally be taken into account. Furthermore, a more direct reference to 'commission' in its traditional sense should be given priority before considering responsibility under the judicial term 'joint criminal enterprise'".[17] The Court went on to say that it preferred

> [T]o define 'committing' as meaning that the accused participated, physically or otherwise directly or indirectly, in the material elements of the crime charged through positive acts or, based on a duty to act, omissions, whether individually or jointly with others. The accused himself need not have participated in all aspects of the alleged criminal conduct. (...) For co-perpetration it suffices that there was an explicit agreement or silent consent to reach a common goal by coordinated co-operation and joint control over the criminal conduct. For this kind of co-perpetration it is typical, but not mandatory, that one perpetrator possesses skills or authority which the other perpetrator does not. These can be described as shared acts which when brought together achieve the shared goal based on the same degree of control over the execution of the common acts.[18]

The approach taken by the Trial Chamber was fiercely rejected by the Court of Appeals. The Court took on the issue of the proper mode of responsibility although no challenges had been raised by the parties on that point. The Appeals Chamber quashed the Tribunal's decision and restored the preference for the doctrine of joint criminal enterprise.[19] In the Court's words, "the Trial Chamber erred in conducting its analysis of the responsibility of the Appellant within the framework of 'co-perpetratorship'. This mode of liability, as defined and applied by the Trial Chamber, does not have support in customary international law or in the settled jurisprudence of this Tribunal, which is binding on the Trial Chambers".[20]

---

[11] As scholars put it, in the joint criminal enterprise or common purpose doctrine, "the essence of the wrong doing lies in the shared intent"; H. Olasolo, Joint Criminal Enterprise and its extended for: A Theory of Co-perpetration Giving Rise to Principal Liability, A Notion of Accessorial Liability, or A Form of Partenrship in Crime, 20 Criminal Law Forum 2009, p. 271.

[12] ICTY, Judgement, *Prosecutor v. Tadić*, Case No. IT-94-1-A, A Ch., 15 July 1999, Klip/ Sluiter, ALC-III-761.

[13] See among others; J.S. Martinez and A.M. Danner, Guilty Associations, Joint Criminal Enterprise, Command Responsibility, and the Development of International Criminal Law, 93 California Law Review 2005, p. 75: See also ICTY, Judgement, *Prosecutor v. Simić, Tadić and Zarić*, Separate Opinion of Judge Per-Johan Lindholm, *supra* note 10, par. 137: "The concept or 'doctrine' has caused confusion and a waste of time, and is in my opinion of no benefit to the work of the Tribunal or the development of international criminal law".

[14] K. Ambos, Joint Criminal Enterprise and Command Responsibility, 5 Journal of International Criminal Justice 2007, p. 167 (asserting that the JCE doctrine conflicts with the principle of culpability and proposing to substitute it with the theory of "control of the act by virtue of a hierarchical organization", the so called *Organisationherrschaft*); H. van der Wilt, Joint Criminal Enterprise. Possibilities and Limitations, 5 Journal of International Criminal Justice 2007, p. 101 (Wherein the proposal to substitute the doctrine of joint criminal enterprise with that of functional perpetration is argued).

[15] Some scholars have criticized the portrait of JCE as a form of perpetration, pointing out that it should instead be viewed as a form of criminal participation; Elies van Sliedregt, Joint Criminal Enterprise as a Pathway to Convicting Individuals for Genocide, 5 International Law Journal 2007, p. 184.

[16] ICTY Judgement, *Prosecutor v. Stakić*, Case No. IT-97-24-T, T. Ch. II, 31 July 2003, Klip/ Sluiter, ALC-XIV-545.

[17] *Ibid.*, par. 438.

[18] *Ibid.*, par. 439–440.

[19] ICTY, Judgement, *Prosecutor v. Stakić*, Case No. IT-97-24-A, A. Ch., 22 March 2006, Klip/ Sluiter, ALC-XXIX-213.

[20] *Ibid.*, par. 62.

In the Simić case a vibrant dissenting opinion by judge Johan Per-Johan Lindholm pleaded for the abandonment of the JCE doctrine in favor of a more classical concept of co-perpetration.[21] The majority of the court however endorsed the legitimacy of the JCE doctrine.[22] After the failure of these attempts it seemed that the doctrine of JCE had finally prevailed over any concurrent alternative approaches. However, in more recent years the extended notion of commission has been picked up at the ICTR, first in the Gacumbitsi case and then in the Seromba case, being in both occasions endorsed by the Appeals Chamber. Also the ruling in Ndindabahizi seems to support an extended notion of commission, albeit being specifically tailored to the crime of extermination.[23] The decision taken by the Trial Chamber in Rukundo strengthens this trend. Although the decision has been overturned in appeal, where Rukundo was found guilty of complicity, it must be noted that the appeal decision did not refute the logic at the basis of the decision. The appeal's reversal is in fact based on the fact that commission had not been properly pleaded in the indictment and hence Rukundo could have not been convicted for such mode of liability.[24]

3.2. Co-perpetration through an extended concept of commission: a feasible alternative to JCE?

The question now is whether assessing co-perpetration through the adoption of a broad notion of commission, as the Gacumbistsi, Seromba and Rukundo Chambers have done, can represent a proper instrument for the jurisdiction of the *ad hoc* tribunals and whether it will lead to the replacement of the JCE doctrine. Will these recent findings do away with the debated JCE doctrine? Is the extended notion of commission a better tool for facing the challenges of international criminal law than the JCE?

The answer seems to be in the negative. First, the extended concept of commission does not appear to have solid foundations yet. It is still strongly debated whether it finds support in customary international law: while the *Stakić* Appeal Chamber expressly denied that co-perpetration outside of a JCE has roots in customary international law,[25] the point is not explicitly addressed by the decision in Rukundo, nor by the previous recent ICTR judgements in the Gacumbitsi and Seromba case.

The extended concept of commission appears rather vague. The criteria for identifying commission in fact remain unknown.[26] In Rukundo, the chamber simply says, quoting Gacumbitsi, that the accused's actions constituted "an integral part" of the crime but such an explanation can in no way be considered satisfactory. The concept of integral part is nebulous to say the least. When does an action falling outside of the *actus reus* (other than the physical perpetration of the offence) constitute an integral part of the crime? When it is a causal contribution to the offence or just a substantial one?[27] It is not even clear whether there must have been an agreement between the co-perpetrators, or if it suffices that their actions combine to produce the harmful result without any form of mutual understanding.

In this respect one must observe that the recent ICTR interpretations stretching the concept of commission liability are far less refined than the original attempts made at the ICTY to introduce a new concept of co-perpetration. In the *Stakić* decision, just like in the dissenting opinion of Judge Lindholm, the notion of co-perpetration was defended by making express reference to the Roxin's theory of the control over the crime doctrine.

Second, the broad notion of commission inevitably overlaps with the area of complicity. Aiders and abettors do not commit the *actus reus* but offer a substantial contribution to the commission of the crime by giving

---

[21] ICTY, Judgement, *Prosecutor v. Simić, Tadić and Zarić*, Separate Opinion of Judge Per-Johan Lindholm, *supra* note 10.
[22] ICTY Judgement, *Prosecutor v. Simić, Tadić and Zarić*, Case No. IT-95-9-T, T. Ch. II, 17 October 2003, Klip/ Sluiter ALC-XV-141, par. 156–160.
[23] ICTR Judgement, *Prosecutor v. Ndindabahizi*, Case No. ICTR 2001-71-I, T. Ch. I, 15 July 2004, Klip/ Sluiter, ALC-XVIII-645,par. 479, 485. The ruling has been upheld on the point concerning the finding of "commission" by the Appeals Chamber: ICTR Judgement, *Ndindabahizi v. Prosecutor*, Case No. ICTR 2001-71-A, A. Ch, 16 January 2007, Klip/ Sluiter ALC-XXV-620, par. 121–123.
[24] ICTR, Judgement, *Rukundo v. Prosecutor*, Case No. ICTR-2001-70-A, A. Ch., 20 October 2010, par. 35–39.
[25] See *supra*, at note 14.
[26] ICTR, Judgement, *Prosecutor v. Seromba*, Dissenting opinion by Judge Liu, Case No. ICTR-2001-66-A, A. Ch., 12 March 2008, Klip/ Sluiter ALC-XXXI-813, par. 7 ("it is not clear what the criteria for this approach are, if any"); Kai Ambos and Katarzyna Geler, Commentary, Klip/ Sluiter, ALC-XXXI-828.
[27] It could not be anything less than a substantial contribution because a substantial contribution is needed for aiding and abetting, hence the conduct of "committing" could in no way be less significant than that required for complicity.

assistance (aiding), giving advice or facilitating the commission of the crime (abetting).[28] Instigators prompt another person to commit the crime.[29] No doubt that, just like the JCE doctrine, the extended concept of commission is also devised for holding liable as perpetrators those who would otherwise be considered accomplices. Rukundo's case is in this respect paradigmatic: the impression is that the Trial Chamber did not want Rukundo to walk away as an accomplice when in the chamber's eyes he bore a higher degree of moral culpability.

But what is then left of "instigating, ordering, aiding and abetting" when the notion of commission expands outside of its classic boundaries? Complicity almost pales into insignificance. Assuming that an extended notion of commission would cover all substantial contributions to the crime, the area of complicity ends up covering only marginal conducts, chiefly those substantial contributions given with knowledge of the crime but without sharing the perpetrators' intent. In other words, the distinction between principals and accomplices could be traced only at the level of the subjective element: while the former would have the intent to carry out the criminal action, the latter would only have the knowledge that a crime will occur.

Consequently, a narrow interpretation of the concept of commission seems to be imposed by the wording of Article 6, ICTR Statute (equivalent to Article 7, ICTY Statute). When the statute lists several forms of accomplice liability it inevitably requires to read commission in a restricted sense, as referred to those actions which more directly bring about the harmful result. It might be necessary in certain cases to expand the scope of primary liability beyond physical perpetration, because sometimes accomplices can be more culpable than direct physical perpetrators (principals). To assure the just desert to the mastermind of the criminal action, the perpetrator behind the perpetrator, one can then employ the joint criminal enterprise doctrine[30] or, alternatively, theories such as the control over the crime doctrine[31] or the doctrine of functional perpetration.[32]

Essentially, it does not seem that in the particular case of Rukundo the court wanted to assess the preference for an extended concept of commission over the doctrine of joint criminal enterprise. The chamber ruled out the possibility of a conviction for joint criminal enterprise not because it wanted to discard the doctrine but simply because joint criminal enterprise was not properly pleaded in the indictment.[33] Hence the chamber could not rely on the doctrine of joint criminal enterprise due to a defect in the indictment. In the court's own words, "the pleading of the JCE in the indictment does not provide adequate notice to the accused of his alleged involvement in a JCE and is defective".[34] Something similar happened both in the Gacumbitsi case and in the Seromba case: there too it was acknowledged that JCE had not been pleaded in the indictment.[35]

In light of the foregoing, the adoption of an extended notion of commission appears more as a way for circumventing a defective indictment in the pleading of a JCE than an attempt to introduce a new tool for a better evaluation of the criminal conducts in front of the international criminal tribunals. In sum, in the case

---

[28] ICTR Judgement, *Prosecutor v. Akayesu*, Case No. ICTR-96-4-T, T. Ch. I, 2 September 1998, Klip/ Sluiter, ALC-II-399, par. 484–485; ICTR, Judgement, *Prosecutor v. Gacumbitsi*, supra note 10, par. 286 ("Aiding means assisting or helping another to commit a crime. Abetting means facilitating advising or instigating the commission of a crime"); ICTR, Judgement, *Prosecutor v. Kamuhanda*, supra note 10, par. 596-597; ICTR, Judgement and Sentence, *Prosecutor v. Elizaphan Ntakirutimana and Gérard Ntakirutimana*, Cases No. ICTR-96-10 and ICTR-96-17-T, T. Ch. I, 21 February 2003, Klip/ Sluiter, ALC-XII-383, par. 787; ICTR, Judgement, *Prosecutor v. Alfred Musema*, Case No. ICTR-96-13-T, T Ch. I, 27 January 2000, Klip/ Sluiter ALC-VI-469, par. 176–183.

[29] ICTR Judgement, *Prosecutor v. Akayesu*, supra note 28, par. 482; ICTR Judgement, *Prosecutor v. Semanza*, supra note 10, par. 381; ICTR, Judgement, *Prosecutor v. Kamuhanda*, supra note 10, par. 593.

[30] Antonio Cassese, The Proper Limits of Individual Responsibility under the Doctrine of Joint Criminal Enterprise, 5 Journal of International Criminal Justice 2007, p. 109.

[31] K. Ambos, Joint Criminal Enterprise and Command Responsibility, supra note 13, p. 167. For a critical comparison of the theory of "control over with the crime" with the JCE doctrine, S. Manacorda and C. Meloni, Indirect Perpetration *versus* Joint Criminal Enterprise, 9 Journal of International Criminal Justice 2011, p. 159–178. For sharp criticisms of the "control over the crime" doctrine, see M. Osiel, Perpetration by Hierarchical Organization, Guest Lecture Series of the Office of the Prosecutor, 22 April 2009.

[32] H. van der Wilt, Joint Criminal Enterprise. Possibilities and Limitations, supra note 13, p. 101.

[33] ICTR, Judgement, *Prosecutor v. Rukundo*, supra note 4, par. 28.

[34] *Ibid.*, par. 28.

[35] ICTR, Judgement, *Prosecutor v. Gacumbitsi*, supra note 10, par. 289 ("The Prosecution seems to allege that the Accused participated in a joint criminal enterprise. However, the Chamber cannot make a finding on such allegation since it was not pleaded clearly enough to allow the Accused to defend himself adequately").

of Rukundo, just as in Gacumbitsi and in Seromba, stretching the notion of commission liability seems to be a way for avoiding that defendants are not just treated as mere aiders or abettors. The attribution of liability as a principal or as an accomplice bears direct consequences on the amount of the sentence to be imposed on the defendant. An aider deserves a milder, more lenient, treatment than a principal perpetrator.[36] Truly describing the role of religious figures like Rukundo and Seromba as mere aiders can sound improper. The moral authority of these figures was such that their role appears closer to that of leaders than of mere accomplices. Nonetheless, if the court was concerned with attributing the proper label to Rukundo's conduct, it could have at least attempted to frame it in the context of instigation which bears indeed a higher degree of culpability than mere aiding.[37] But in no way the attempt to attach the proper degree of moral culpability to each defendant can overcome the respect of the procedural rules on proper pleading and of the defendants' rights to prepare adequately the defence.

4. Mental harm

The indictment against Rukundo listed several other counts of genocide for having caused serious mental harm to Tutsi refugees. Most of these allegations pictured Rukundo threatening to kill Tutsi refugees on several occasions. The court acquitted Rukundo from these charges in that the accused's conduct had only brought about a minor or temporary impairment of mental faculties, in application of a criteria long acknowledged by the jurisprudence of the *ad hoc* tribunals.[38]

The Courts instead convicted Rukundo for genocide for causing serious mental harm in relation to the sexual assault of a young Tutsi woman. The decision was entered with a majority verdict, Judge Liu dissenting.

One day at the Seminary, Rukundo was approached by a young Tutsi girl who was seeking protection for herself. Despite Rukundo's denial of protection due to her Tutsi origin, the girl insisted and she followed the priest inside the premises of the seminary and into his room in the hope that he would change his mind. Once inside the small room, Rukundo offered the girl a beer and then locked the door of the room. He sat next to her in the bed and first started caressing her, then forced her to lie in the bed. At first the girl tried to resist until Rukundo pulled out his pistol and placed it over the table next to the bed. He opened the zipper of his trousers and laid on top of her. Despite the girl's opposition, Rukundo forcibly removed the skirt and even tried to spread her legs but as the girl continued to resist the priest gave up trying to have sexual intercourse but went on to rub himself against her until he ejaculated.

The court's reasoned that the act was indeed of a sexual nature.[39] The chamber also observed that, although no express intimidation had been made by Rukundo, the contextual scene was characterized by very clear coercive circumstances, the locking of the door and the presence of a gun above all. Such circumstances brought the chamber to rule out any possible form of consent on the part of the victim.

Last, the court evaluated whether the girl had suffered serious mental harm, once again applying the criteria for which "although mental harm suffered must be more than a minor or temporary impairment of mental faculties it need not be permanent or irremediable".[40]

On the basis of the witness' testimony and in the light of "the highly charged, oppressive and other circumstances surrounding the sexual assault"[41] the chamber concluded by majority that the victim had suffered serious mental harm. Judge Park entered a dissenting opinion on this point. In his view the chamber had adopted too lax of a standard in the assessment of the serious nature.

---

[36] ICTY, Judgement, *Prosecutor v. Vasiljević*, Case No. IT-98-32-A, A. Ch., 28 November 2006, par. 181–182; ICTY Judgement, *Prosecutor v. Krstić*, Case No. IT-98-33-A, A. Ch., 19 April 2004, Klip/ Sluiter, ALC-XIX-539, par. 268.

[37] F. Zorzi Giustiniani, Stretching the Boundaries of Commission Liability: The ICTR Appeal Judgment in *Seromba*, 6 Journal of International Criminal Justice 2008, p. 783–799.

[38] ICTR Judgement, *Prosecutor v. Akayesu, supra* note 26, par. 502; ICTR, Judgement, *Prosecutor v. Seromba*, ICTR-2001-66-A, *supra* note 1, par. 46, ICTR Judgement, *Prosecutor v. Kajelijeli*, Case No. ICTR-98-44A-T, T. Ch. II, 1 December 2003, Klip/ Sluiter ALC-XVII-27,par. 815; ICTR Judgement, *Prosecutor v. Semanza, supra* note 10, par. 321.

[39] ICTR, Judgement, *Prosecutor v. Rukundo, supra* note 4, par. 381.

[40] *Ibid.*, par. 386.

[41] *Ibid.*, par. 388.

Judge Park's dissent seems to be based on good reasons. It is true that the case-law repeatedly affirmed that mental harm need not result in a permanent or irremediable mental damage.[42] It must be pointed out however that the International Law Commission particularly insisted on the seriousness of the harm and it stressed that "to support a conviction for genocide, the bodily harm or the mental harm inflicted on members of a group must be of such a serious nature as to threaten its destruction in whole or in part;"[43] the statement can be found in the case-law as well.[44] There is no straightforward answer when assessing the mental harm suffered by a victim, but when looking at the episode of Rukundo's sexual assault it seems slightly more sensible to exclude that the victim suffered serious mental harm in that the conduct appears unable to threaten the destruction of the Tutsi group. But on top of all it seems that Rukundo lacked the proper *mens rea* for a genocide conviction on this count. In the sexual incident the accused did not show the special intention to destroy the ethnic group that is required for a genocide conviction to be entered.

Michele Panzavolta

---

[42] ICTR, Judgement, *Prosecutor v. Rukundo, supra* note 4.
[43] Report of the International Law Commission on the Work of its Forty-Eighth Session 6 May – 26 July 1996 (ILC Report 1996), UN GAOR International Law Commission, 51st Sess., Supp. No. 10, p. 91, UN Doc. A/51/10 (1996), 91.
[44] ICTR, Judgement, *Prosecutor v. Seromba*, ICTR-2001-66-A, *supra* note 1, par. 46; ICTR, Judgement, *Prosecutor v. Kamuhanda, supra* note 10, par. 633.

International Criminal Tribunal for Rwanda
Tribunal pénal international pour le Rwanda

OR: ENG

TRIAL CHAMBER III

Before Judges: Dennis C.M. Byron, Presiding
Geberdao Gustave Kam
Vagn Joensen

Registrar: Adama Dieng

Date: 22 June 2009

THE PROSECUTOR

v.

Callixte KALIMANZIRA

Case No. ICTR-05-88-T

JUDGEMENT

Office of the Prosecutor
Christine Graham
Veronic Wright
Ousman Jammeh

Defence Counsel
Arthur Vercken
Anta Guissé

[page i] TABLE OF CONTENTS

CHAPTER I – INTRODUCTION 1
    1. INDICTMENT 1
    2. PROCEDURAL SUMMARY 1
    3. OVERVIEW OF THE CASE 1

CHAPTER II – PRELIMINARY ISSUES 3
    1. INTRODUCTION 3
    2. DEFICIENT PLEADINGS 3
        2.1. Failure to Plead De Facto Authority 3
        2.2. Failure to Plead Superior Responsibility 4
        2.3. Incorrectly Pleaded Time Frames 6
        2.4. Withdrawal of Charges 6
    3. DEFECTIVE INDICTMENT 6
        3.1. Law 7
        3.2. Cumulative Effect of Defects in the Indictment 8
    4. DISCLOSURE VIOLATIONS 9
        4.1. Documents Used in Cross-Examination 9
        4.2. Gacaca Records 10
        4.3. Butare Trial Transcripts 11
    5. NOTICE OF ALIBI 14
    6. EVIDENTIARY ISSUES 15

CHAPTER III – FINDINGS 18
    1. PRELIMINARY FINDINGS 18
        1.1. The Accused 18
            1.1.1. Employment History 18
            1.1.2. Professional Position, 6 April – 25 May 1994 20
            1.1.3. Political Affiliations 21
            1.1.4. De Jure and De Facto Authority 22
        1.2. Alibi 23
            1.2.1. Evidence 23
            1.2.2. Deliberations 26
        1.3. Fabrication of Evidence 32
            1.3.1. Evidence 32
            1.3.2. Deliberations 35
    2. GENOCIDE 37
        2.1. Applicable Law 37
        2.2. "MRND Palace" Meeting, 19 April 38
            2.2.1. Evidence 38
            2.2.2. Deliberations 41
        2.3. Other Meetings and Visits to Butare, April to mid-July 42
            2.3.1. Notice 43
            2.3.2. Butare Prefectural Security Council Meetings 47
                2.3.2.1. Evidence 47
                2.3.2.2. Deliberations 48
            2.3.3. Muganza Commune Football Field Security Meeting 50
                2.3.3.1. Evidence 50
                2.3.3.2. Deliberations 52
            2.3.4. Cemetery Rally and Arboretum Search 52
                2.3.4.1. Evidence .... 52 **[page ii]**
                2.3.4.2. Deliberations 54

        2.3.5. Public Rally at Nyirakanywero 56
            2.3.5.1. Evidence 56
            2.3.5.2. Deliberations 58
        2.3.6. Inauguration of Élie Ndayambaje 59
            2.3.6.1. Evidence 60
            2.3.6.2. Deliberations 61
    2.4. Kabuye Hill, 23 April *63*
        2.4.1. Evidence 63
        2.4.2. Deliberations 75
    2.5. Sakindi Roadblock, early May *83*
        2.5.1. Evidence 83
        2.5.2. Deliberations 85
    2.6. Mugusa Commune, 5 June *86*
        2.6.1. Evidence 86
        2.6.2. Deliberations 89
    2.7. Erection and Supervision of Roadblocks, mid-April to late June *90*
        2.7.1. Notice 91
        2.7.2. Kabanga centre 93
            2.7.2.1. Evidence 93
            2.7.2.2. Deliberations 94
        2.7.3. Ndora commune office 94
            2.7.3.1. Evidence 94
            2.7.3.2. Deliberations 95
        2.7.4. Roadblock on Butare-Gisagara Road 96
            2.7.4.1. Evidence 97
            2.7.4.2. Deliberations 97
    2.8. Muganza Commune Football Field, May *100*
        2.8.1. Evidence 100
        2.8.2. Deliberations 102

3. COMPLICITY IN GENOCIDE 106

4. DIRECT AND PUBLIC INCITEMENT TO COMMIT GENOCIDE 107

    4.1. Applicable Law *107*
    4.2. Kanage Camp, 9 April *109*
        4.2.1. Evidence 109
        4.2.2. Deliberations 112
    4.3. Jaguar Roadblock, mid-April *113*
        4.3.1. Evidence 113
        4.3.2. Deliberations 115
    4.4. Kajyanama Roadblock, late April *119*
        4.4.1. Evidence 119
        4.4.2. Deliberations 121
    4.5. Nyabisagara Football Field, late May / early June *124*
        4.5.1. Evidence 124
        4.5.2. Deliberations 128
    4.6. Rwamiko Primary School, late May / early June *130*
        4.6.1. Evidence 130
        4.6.2. Deliberations 132
    4.7. Sakindi Roadblock, May *134*
        4.7.1. Evidence 134
        4.7.2. Deliberations 135
    4.8. Nyarusange Roadblock, May .... *135* **[page iii]**

        4.8.1. Evidence 135
        4.8.2. Deliberations 137
    4.9. Weapons Carrying, mid-April to June *140*
        4.9.1. Notice 140
        4.9.2. Roadblock at Nyarusange cellule 142
            4.9.2.1. Evidence 142
            4.9.2.2. Deliberations 143
        4.9.3. Road between Butare and Muganza 144
            4.9.3.1. Evidence 144
            4.9.3.2. Deliberations 145
        4.9.4. Kabuye Roadblock 146
            4.9.4.1. Evidence 146
            4.9.4.2. Deliberations 146
        4.9.5. Gisagara Marketplace 148
            4.9.5.1. Evidence 148
            4.9.5.2. Deliberations 149

5. GENOCIDAL INTENT 151

    5.1. Applicable Law *151*
    5.2. Deliberations *151*

CHAPTER IV – VERDICT 153

CHAPTER V – SENTENCE 154

    1. INTRODUCTION 154
    2. DETERMINATION OF THE SENTENCE 154
        2.1. Gravity of the Offences *154*
        2.2. Individual Circumstances *156*
            2.2.1. Aggravating Circumstances 156
            2.2.2. Mitigating Circumstances 156
        2.3. Credit for Time Served *157*
    3. CONCLUSION 158

ANNEX I – PROCEDURAL HISTORY 159

    1. PRE-TRIAL PHASE 159
    2. THE PROSECUTION CASE 160
    3. THE DEFENCE CASE 162

ANNEX II – CITED MATERIALS AND DEFINED TERMS 1

    1. JURISPRUDENCE 1
        1.1. International Criminal Tribunal for Rwanda *1*
        1.2. International Criminal Tribunal for the Former Yugoslavia *3*
    2. DEFINED TERMS AND ABBREVIATIONS 6

ANNEX III – INDICTMENT 9

[page 1] CHAPTER I – INTRODUCTION

1. INDICTMENT

1. On 21 July 2005, the Prosecution filed an indictment against Callixte Kalimanzira, which was confirmed the following day. The Prosecution charged Kalimanzira with three counts pursuant to Article 2 (3) of the Statute, namely Genocide, Complicity in Genocide, and Direct and Public Incitement to Commit Genocide. The Prosecution alleges Kalimanzira's individual criminal responsibility for each of these crimes under Article 6 (1) of the Statute.

2. The Indictment is set out in full in Annex III to this Judgement.

2. PROCEDURAL SUMMARY

3. On 1 September 2005, a warrant for Kalimanzira's arrest and transfer to the seat of the Tribunal was issued. On 8 November 2005, Kalimanzira surrendered in Nairobi, Kenya, to Tribunal officials, and arrived at the United Nations Detention Facility in Arusha the same day. At his initial appearance a few days later, Kalimanzira pleaded not guilty to all three counts in the Indictment.[1]

4. Kalimanzira's trial commenced on 5 May 2008. The Prosecution closed its case on 30 June 2008, after having called 24 witnesses over 16 trial days. The Defence case commenced on 17 November 2008 and was conducted over two trial sessions. The first session ended on 4 December 2008, and the second started on 26 January 2009 running until the last witness, Kalimanzira himself, completed his testimony, on 11 February 2009. Over 21 trial days, the Defence called 42 witnesses. The Prosecution tendered a total of 82 exhibits, and the Defence tendered 117. The Chamber rendered 19 interlocutory decisions and orders. Closing briefs were filed on 2 April 2009 and Closing Arguments were heard on 20 April 2009.

5. The procedural history of this case is set out in full in Annex I to this Judgement.

3. OVERVIEW OF THE CASE

6. The following state of affairs existed in Rwanda between 6 April 1994 and 17 July 1994. There was a non-international armed conflict. At the same time, genocide against the Tutsi ethnic group, as well as widespread or systematic attacks against a civilian population based on Tutsi ethnic identification, occurred. At that time, citizens native to Rwanda identified as Hutus, Tutsis and Twas were protected groups falling within the scope of the Genocide Convention.[2] During the attacks, some Rwandan citizens killed or caused serious bodily or mental harm to persons perceived to be Tutsi. As a result of the attacks, there were a large number of deaths of persons of Tutsi ethnic identity.[3]

7. Callixte Kalimanzira is a native of Butare *préfecture* and was born in 1953. The Prosecution alleges that, from 6 April to 25 May 1994, he acted, functionally, as the Minister of the Interior in Faustin Munyazesa's absence. He is also alleged to have been a high-ranking member of the MRND party and to have acted as the master of ceremonies at the MRND Palace meeting on 19 April 1994 aimed at triggering killings of Tutsis in Butare [page 2] *préfecture* to parallel those already underway throughout the rest of country. Kalimanzira, who was well-liked and highly respected by the local population, is accused of abusing his authority to instruct, encourage and prompt the population of Butare *préfecture* to kill their Tutsi neighbours.

8. The Defence contends that Kalimanzira was not a political man, but someone who worked to develop and empower his local community, Tutsi and Hutu alike, through the use of agriculture. He is presented as having discharged his duties as a civil servant with honour and integrity, without ever having harboured any

---

[1] T. 14 November 2005 p. 9 (Initial Appearance).
[2] Convention for the Prevention and Punishment of the Crime of Genocide. UN GA Resolution 260 A (III) of 9 December 1948.
[3] *The Prosecutor v. Callixte Kalimanzira*, Case No. ICTR-05-88-I, Decision on Judicial Facts of Common Knowledge, 22 February 2006.

anti-Tutsi sentiment in his life. Upon becoming *Directeur de Cabinet* in the Ministry of the Interior, Kalimanzira insists he was merely a technocrat, without any political authority. Apart from a few occasions, he claims to have remained in Gitarama *préfecture* throughout April and May 1994, thereby denying his presence at many of the incidents alleged by the Prosecution. Kalimanzira's alibi is discussed in full at III.1.2.

9. Having deliberated on the totality of evidence, the Chamber has convicted Kalimanzira under Count 1 (Genocide) and Count 3 (Direct and Public Incitement to Commit Genocide) of the Indictment. The Chamber has dismissed Count 2 (Complicity in Genocide), which was pleaded in the alternative to Count 1. The Chamber has sentenced him to a term of thirty (30) years' imprisonment, with credit for time served. In Chapter II, the Chamber will discuss some preliminary issues and address certain matters submitted by the Parties in their respective closing briefs. In Chapter III, the Chamber will then present its reasoned factual and legal findings on the events pleaded and crimes charged in the Indictment. The Chamber's verdict and sentence will be dealt with, respectively, in Chapters IV and V. **[page 3]**

CHAPTER II – PRELIMINARY ISSUES

1. INTRODUCTION

10. In its Closing Brief, the Defence raised several issues relating to the assessment of evidence, the Prosecution's disclosure obligations and the right to notice. The Prosecution responded to some of these submissions during Closing Arguments, and raised a few issues of its own in its Closing Brief relating to notice of alibi, incorrectly pleaded time frames in the Indictment, and the withdrawal of charges.

2. DEFICIENT PLEADINGS

2.1. Failure to Plead *De Facto* Authority

11. The Defence raises an issue as to whether Kalimanzira's alleged *de facto* authority has been properly pleaded. It is apparent that the English version of the Indictment invokes his *de facto* authority at paragraph 2, whereas the French version does not. Considering that the French version is the original, a faithful translation of it would have omitted *de facto* authority as a possible means by which Kalimanzira allegedly held influence or power over anyone in Butare *préfecture*.[4]

12. To resolve a similar issue which arose in respect of "commission" as a mode of liability under Count 3 (see III.4), which was included in the French original Indictment, but omitted from the English translation,[5] the Prosecution submitted that the translation error did not constitute a material defect and that the Defence suffered no material prejudice as a result because:

> "The working language of the Kalimanzira Defence is French. The Defence, therefore, would have used the French original version of the indictment to apprise themselves of the charges against their client, Callixte Kalimanzira. Similarly, during the initial appearance of the accused Kalimanzira on 14 November 2005, the Registry read out the indictment, including paragraph 18, to the accused Kalimanzira. The indictment was read as written in the original French version of the indictment."[6]

13. In this case, the opposite has occurred – a new allegation has curiously appeared solely in the English translation of the Indictment, which was filed two months after the French original. The Chamber notes that

---

[4] It is noteworthy that the first original Indictment against Kalimanzira, filed in French on 9 June 2005, included the term "de fait" in its articulation of Kalimanzira's authority at paragraph 2. The Indictment was confirmed in French on 21 July 2005 following modifications pursuant to Rule 47 of the Rules; this version omits the term "de fait" in what could have been a typographical error. Both versions were included in the Supporting Materials which Kalimanzira received with the confirmed Indictment.

[5] See T. 13 February 2009 pp. 19-21 (Status Conference) when the Chamber first raised the issue.

[6] Prosecution's Submissions on Paragraph 18 of the Indictment as Invited by the Trial Chamber on 13 February 2009, filed on 17 February 2009, para. 4.

a reading of the Indictment during his Initial Appearance,[7] the French version of the Corrected Indictment, and the Prosecution Pre-Trial Brief, do not mention Kalimanzira's alleged *de facto* control. In following with the Prosecution's own line of reasoning on the issue, the omission of *de facto* authority from paragraph 2 of the French original version of the Indictment would constitute a defect therein. **[page 4]**

14. The Defence suggests that any consideration of *de facto* authority should be ruled out because the defect has not been cured in any subsequent filings.[8] However, the Chamber notes that in its own Pre-Trial Brief, filed six and a half months before it raised the present issue, the Defence introduced the Prosecution's position on Kalimanzira's alleged control in Butare *préfecture* as including both *de jure* and *de facto* authority.[9] The Defence was clearly aware long ago that Kalimanzira's alleged *de facto* authority over the people of Butare was an issue in this trial and formed part of the Prosecution's case. The omission of "de fait" from the French version of the Indictment has not caused the Defence any prejudice or created any confusion. In fact, Kalimanzira's defence is premised on his high-standing and good reputation throughout Butare society. Kalimanzira's *de facto* authority is therefore not in serious contention (see also III.1.1.4); the question is whether he abused it to genocidal ends. The Defence's attempt to persuade the Chamber to dismiss a consideration of Kalimanzira's alleged *de facto* authority is therefore unfounded.

2.2. Failure to Plead Superior Responsibility

15. The Defence points out that Kalimanzira is only accused of individual criminal responsibility under Article 6 (1) of the Statute, and argues that because superior responsibility under Article 6 (3) has not been pleaded, Kalimanzira's alleged criminal responsibility may not be evaluated in light of any hierarchical powers he may have held. This contention stands to be rejected for the following reasons.

16. The language used in paragraph 2(vii) of the Indictment, *i.e.* that by virtue of the government positions Kalimanzira held, he exercised "*de jure* and *de facto* authority" over various Butare officials and civilians, "in that he could order these persons to commit or refrain from committing unlawful acts and discipline or punish them for their unlawful acts or omission," is similar to that used when pleading an accused's responsibility as a superior. However, crimes committed by virtue of an accused's abuse of his or her *de jure* or *de facto* powers are not limited to liability under Article 6 (3). Evidence of *de jure* or *de facto* authority can also assist in factually proving criminal liability under the modes of participation contained within Article 6 (1). In fact, at times it is more appropriate to convict under Article 6 (1) than 6 (3), even if an accused has *de jure* authority.[10]

17. The first portion of the underlined extract above refers to Kalimanzira's alleged ability to order others to commit crimes. Ordering is a mode of participation under Article 6 (1). With respect to ordering, a person in a position of authority[11] may incur responsibility for ordering another person to commit an offence,[12] if the person who received the order actually proceeds to commit the offence subsequently.[13] **[page 5]**

18. This is different from superior responsibility under Article 6 (3), which does not require proof that an order was given or that authority was exercised to instruct someone to commit a crime, and is aimed at

---

[7] During Kalimanzira's Initial Appearance on 14 November 2005, the courtroom representative of the Registry omitted to read out "Section II. The Accused", *i.e.* paragraphs 1 and 2 of the Indictment, to him. Kalimanzira did, however, confirm that he had received the Indictment and "other related documents" (see T. 14 November 2005 p. 3). Given that the Indictment was read to him as written in the original French version, it would not have included a reference to his alleged *de facto* authority.
[8] See Defence Closing Brief, fn 998.
[9] See Defence Closing Brief, para. 10.
[10] For instance, when, for the same count and the same set of facts, the accused's responsibility is pleaded pursuant to both Articles 6 (1) and 6 (3) and the accused could be found liable under both provisions, the Trial Chamber should rather enter a conviction on the basis of Article 6 (1) alone and consider the superior position of the accused as an aggravating circumstance. See *Nahimana et al.* Appeal Judgement, para. 487; *Kajelijeli* Appeal Judgement, para. 81; see also *Galić* Appeal Judgement, para. 186; *Jokić* Appeal Judgement, paras. 23-28; *Kordić and Čerkez* Appeal Judgement, paras. 34-35; *Blaškić* Appeal Judgement, para. 91.
[11] It is not necessary to demonstrate the existence of an official relationship of subordination between the accused and the perpetrator of the crime: *Galić* Appeal Judgement, para. 176; *Gacumbitsi* Appeal Judgement, para. 182; *Kamuhanda* Appeal Judgement, para. 75; *Semanza* Appeal Judgement, para. 361; *Kordić and Čerkez* Appeal Judgement, para. 28.
[12] *Galić* Appeal Judgement, para. 176; *Ntagerura et al.* Appeal Judgement, para. 365; *Kordić and Čerkez* Appeal Judgement, paras. 28-29.
[13] *Nahimana et al.* Appeal Judgement, para. 481.

criminalizing an omission to punish or prevent a crime from taking place. Therefore, the fact that superior responsibility under Article 6 (3) was not pleaded does not render Kalimanzira's alleged *de jure* and *de facto* authority irrelevant. Whether Kalimanzira had *de jure* and *de facto* authority, and to what extent, over the people and officials of Butare *préfecture* is factual element relevant to determining of whether he can be held individually criminally responsible for ordering others to commit genocide.

19. The remaining portion of the underlined extract above refers to Kalimanzira's ability to use his alleged *de jure* and *de facto* authority to prevent and punish others from committing crimes. An omission to do so is not only criminalized under Article 6 (3), but also under Article 6 (1), though under different circumstances. Because the Prosecution did not plead superior responsibility, it is unnecessary to pronounce the elements required to invoke Article 6 (3) here. All that is required is an illustration of how acts of omission may incur individual criminal responsibility under Article 6 (1) and how a position of authority may be relevant to this form of liability.

20. Omission proper may lead to individual criminal responsibility where there is a legal duty to act or to prevent a crime from being brought about, and failure to do so may constitute the *actus reus* of commission, instigation, or aiding and abetting under Article 6 (1). In some cases, the combination of a position of authority and physical presence at the crime scene may allow the inference that non-interference by the accused actually amounted to aiding and abetting by tacit approval and encouragement. In Kalimanzira's case, this is particularly relevant with regard to the allegations that he attended meetings aimed at inciting people to commit genocide and that his presence was enough to condone and encourage what was being said. There is, however, no special requirement that a position of superior authority be established before liability for aiding and abetting under Article 6 (1) can be recognized. An accused's position of authority constitutes one of many contextual factors that may go to proving the significance of his or her assistance in the commission of a crime.[14] Thus, whether Kalimanzira had *de jure* and *de facto* authority, and to what extent, over the people and officials of Butare *préfecture* is a contextual element in determining whether he can be held individually criminally responsible for omitting to prevent or punish people for committing genocide.

21. In conclusion, the issue raised by the Defence is unfounded. The Chamber will not consider superior responsibility under Article 6 (3) as a form of liability because it has not been pleaded. The Chamber will only consider whether Kalimanzira incurs individual criminal responsibility under Article 6 (1) for his alleged acts and omissions, and in doing so, will take into account his alleged *de jure* and *de facto* authority, wherever relevant. **[page 6]**

2.3. Incorrectly Pleaded Time Frames

22. In its Closing Brief, the Prosecution admits to two incorrectly pleaded time frames.[15]

The first is at paragraph 23, which alleges Direct and Public Incitement to Commit Genocide at the Nyabisagara football field. The second is at paragraph 24, which alleges Direct and Public Incitement to Commit Genocide at the Rwamiko Primary School. Rather than state that these events, which allegedly occurred just days apart, took place in late May or early June 1994, the Indictment states that they took place in late April or early May 1994.

23. The Prosecution points out that the evidence referred to in respect of these paragraphs in the Annotated Indictment, as well as the corresponding sections of the Pre-Trial Brief, and the Prosecution evidence led at trial, all rely on the late May or early June 1994 time period. The Prosecution submits the Defence has thereby received clear, consistent and timely notice as to the relevant time frame. It recalls that the Defence failed to raise an objection as to this time frame for either event and challenged the Prosecution evidence

---

[14] *Orić* Appeal Judgement, paras. 42-43; *Nahimana et al.* Appeal Judgement, para. 478; *Blagojević and Jokić* Appeal Judgement, para. 195; *Ntagerura et al.* Appeal Judgement, paras. 33, 370; *Orić* Trial Judgement, para. 273; *Kayishema and Ruzindana* Appeal Judgement, paras. 201-202. See also *Musema* Trial Judgement, para. 865, which states: "In relation to Article 6 (1), the nature of the authority wielded by an individual affects the assessment of that individual's role in planning, instigating, ordering, committing or otherwise aiding and abetting the planning, preparation or execution of a crime referred to in Articles 2 to 4 of the Statute. In particular, the presence of an authority figure at an event could amount to acquiescence in the event or support therefore, and, in the perception of the perpetrators, legitimize the said event."
[15] Prosecution Closing Brief, paras. 231 and 254.

accordingly. The Defence has raised no objection in its Closing Brief either, nor has it made mention of it during Closing Arguments. In the opinion of the Chamber, the error is not so significant as to have materially undermined the Defence's ability to prepare its case. The Chamber therefore accepts the relevant time frames for paragraphs 23 and 24 of the Indictment as being late May or early June 1994.

2.4. Withdrawal of Charges

24. At paragraph 11 of the Indictment, the Prosecution charges Kalimanzira with Genocide for ordering the killings of 100 Tutsi civilians at a roadblock near the Buzana River, and at Rango, a few kilometres away. He is accused of having personally beaten some of them to death.

25. At paragraph 16 of the Indictment, the Prosecution charges Kalimanzira with Genocide for distributing weapons to Bonaventure Nkundabakora in Kigembe *commune* two days after the death of President Habyarimana, and for periodically replenishing a stock of bladed weapons at the Muganza *commune* office. These weapons were allegedly distributed to the population under Kalimanzira's supervision and used to kill Tutsis.

26. At paragraph 19 of the Indictment, the Prosecution charges Kalimanzira with Direct and Public Incitement to Commit Genocide for inciting people to arm themselves and prepare to fight the "enemy" in late March 1994 at a meeting held at the Gisagara marketplace by local government officials. He is also accused of having encouraged people to manufacture traditional weapons and promised to supply them with firearms.

27. The Prosecution has withdrawn these allegations, having led no evidence on them at trial.[16] These charges are therefore dismissed.

3. DEFECTIVE INDICTMENT

28. In its Closing Brief, the Defence objects to the lack of precision in paragraph 15 of the Indictment, as well as to several events about which Prosecution witnesses testified, but which do not appear in the Indictment.[17] Where further particulars were provided in the **[page 7]** Prosecution Pre-Trial Brief, the Defence submits the new allegations nevertheless came too late, causing it significant prejudice.[18]

29. These objections are considered in the relevant section of the Chamber's deliberations. In some instances, the Chamber has *proprio motu* addressed questions of notice, even where no specific objection has been made by the Defence, based on the organisation and argumentation of the Prosecution Closing Brief, particularly in relation to paragraphs 8 and 27 of the Indictment. The Chamber recalls that a closing brief is not a relevant document in determining whether an accused had notice of the charges against him.[19] The Chamber has considered the challenges and issues in view of the pertinent principles, as recapitulated below.

3.1. Law

30. Articles 20 (4)(a) and 20 (4)(b) of the Statute, in conjunction with Articles 20 (2) and 17 (4) of the Statute and Rule 47 (C) of the Rules, express the Prosecution's obligation to plead the charges against an accused and the material facts supporting those charges with sufficient precision in an indictment so as to provide notice to the accused of the charges against him or her. Whether a fact is material depends upon the nature of the Prosecution's case. A decisive factor in determining the degree of specificity with which the Prosecution is required to particularize the facts of its case in the indictment is the nature of the alleged criminal conduct charged to the accused. For example, in a case where the Prosecution alleges that an accused personally committed the criminal acts, the material facts, such as the identity of the victim, the time and place of the events, and the means by which the acts were committed, have to be pleaded in detail. An indictment lacking this precision is defective; the prejudicial effects of a defective indictment can be

---

[16] Prosecution Closing Brief, para. 2.
[17] Defence Closing Brief, para. 1125.
[18] Defence Closing Brief, paras. 1139-1157.
[19] *Bagosora et al.* Trial Judgement, para. 122.

remedied or "cured", in exceptional cases only, if the Prosecution provided the accused with clear, timely and consistent information detailing the factual basis underpinning the charges against him or her, thus compensating for the failure of the indictment to give proper notice of the charges. The Appeals Chamber has held that a pre-trial brief in certain circumstances can provide such information.[20]

31. "Curing" is the process by which vague or general allegations in an indictment are given specificity and clarity through communications other than the indictment itself. Only material facts which can be reasonably related to existing charges may be communicated in such a manner. The mere service of witness statements or of potential exhibits by the Prosecution as part of its disclosure obligations is generally insufficient to inform the Defence of the material facts that the Prosecution intends to prove at trial. The presence of a material fact somewhere in the Prosecution's disclosures does not suffice to give reasonable notice to the accused; what is required is notice that the material fact will be relied upon as part of the Prosecution case, and how. An accused person can only be expected to prepare his or her defence on the basis of material facts contained in the indictment, not on the basis of all the material disclosed to him or her that may support any number of additional charges, or expand the scope of existing charges. In light of the volume of disclosure by the Prosecution in certain cases, a witness statement will not, without some other indication, adequately signal to the accused that the allegation is part of the Prosecution case. The essential question [page 8] is whether the Defence has had reasonable notice of, and a reasonable opportunity to investigate and confront, the Prosecution case.[21]

32. A clear distinction has to be drawn between vagueness in an indictment and an indictment omitting certain charges altogether. While it is possible, as stated above, to remedy the vagueness in an indictment, new or omitted charges can be incorporated into the indictment only by formal amendment pursuant to Rule 50 of the Rules. A count or charge is the legal characterization of the material facts which support that count or charge. In pleading an indictment, the Prosecution is required to specify the alleged legal prohibition infringed (*i.e.* the count or charge) and the acts or omissions of the accused that give rise to that allegation of infringement of a legal prohibition (*i.e.* the material facts). A "new charge" arises not only where there is a new count, but where new allegations could lead to liability on a factual basis that was not reflected in the indictment.[22]

33. Objections based on lack of notice should be specific and timely. The objection should be raised at the pre-trial stage, for instance in a motion challenging the indictment, or at the time the evidence of a new material fact is introduced. Although failing to object at the time the evidence is introduced does not prohibit the Defence from objecting at a later date, a Trial Chamber should determine whether the objection was so untimely that the burden of proof has shifted from the Prosecution to the Defence to demonstrate that the accused's ability to defend himself has been materially impaired. Relevant factors to consider include whether the Defence has provided a reasonable explanation for its failure to raise its objection at the time the evidence was introduced and whether the Defence has shown that the objection was raised as soon as possible thereafter.[23]

3.2. Cumulative Effect of Defects in the Indictment

34. In several sections of its deliberations, the Chamber has found that the Indictment was defective in a number of respects by failing to include pertinent material facts (see *e.g.* III.2.3.1, III.2.7.1 and III.4.9.1). The

---

[20] *Muvunyi* Appeal Judgement, para. 18; *Seromba* Appeal Judgement, paras. 27, 100; *Simba* Appeal Judgement paras. 63-64; *Muhimana* Appeal Judgement, paras. 76, 82, 167, 195, 217; *Gacumbitsi* Appeal Judgement, paras. 49, 57-58; *Ndindabahizi* Appeal Judgement, para. 16; *Ntagerura et al.* Appeal Judgement, paras. 27-28, 65; *Kamuhanda* Appeal Judgement, paras. 17, 24; *Ntakirutimana* Appeal Judgement, paras. 25, 27, 48; *Niyitegeka* Appeal Judgement, paras. 193-195. See also *Naletilić and Martinović* Appeal Judgement, para. 45; *Kupreškić et al.* Appeal Judgement, paras. 89-92, 114; *Kvočka et al.* Appeal Judgement, para. 34.

[21] *Muvunyi* Appeal Judgement, para. 166; *Simić* Appeal Judgement, para. 24; *Naletilić and Martinović* Appeal Judgement, para. 27; *Ntakirutimana* Appeal Judgement, para. 27; *Kupreškić et al.* Appeal Judgement, para. 323; see also *The Prosecutor v. Bagosora et al.*, Case No. ICTR-98-41-T, Decision on Kabiligi Motion for Exclusion of Evidence (TC), 4 September 2006, paras. 3 and 7.

[22] *Karera* Appeal Judgement, para. 293; *Ntagerura et al.* Appeal Judgement, para. 32. See also *Muvunyi* Appeal Judgement, para. 20, citing *Bagosora et al.* Interlocutory Appeal Decision, para. 29. See also *The Prosecutor v. Nchamihigo*, Case No. ICTR-01-63-I, Decision on Request for Leave to Amend the Indictment (TC), 14 July 2006, para. 20.

[23] *Bagosora et al.* Interlocutory Appeal Decision, paras. 45-46.

Chamber has also found many of those omissions to have been cured by the provision of timely, clear and consistent information on the basis of the Prosecution Pre-Trial Brief. The Appeals Chamber has held that, even if a Trial Chamber finds that the Prosecution has cured defects in the indictment through post-indictment submissions, it should consider whether the extent of those defects materially prejudiced the accused's right to a fair trial by hindering the preparation of a proper defence.[24]

35. The Indictment gave the Defence adequate notice of the essence of the Prosecution's case, namely that Kalimanzira played a key role in advancing and promoting the Rwandan genocide in Butare *préfecture*. The Chamber considers that, wherever defects are cured, the new material facts do not amount to a radical transformation of the Prosecution's case. In each instance, the material facts provided in the post-Indictment submissions relate to a general paragraph and serve to particularize the allegations contained therein, but do not change the substance of the allegations or add new elements to the case. The Defence's **[page 9]** ability to confront these new material facts is evidenced by its thorough cross-examination of the Prosecution's witnesses. In addition, the Defence was afforded four and a half months after the close of the Prosecution case before the commencement of its own case, giving it sufficient time to investigate and further rebut these new material facts. Notwithstanding the Prosecution's failure to plead a number of material facts in the Indictment, the Chamber finds that the Defence was not materially prejudiced, and that the trial was not rendered unfair, by the cumulative effect of the defects in the Indictment having been cured.

4. DISCLOSURE VIOLATIONS

36. In its Closing Brief, the Defence argues that Kalimanzira's rights to a fair trial have been compromised because of the Prosecution's repeated violations of Rule 68 (A) of the Rules, which requires the Prosecution to disclose to the Defence, as soon as practicable, any material which in the actual knowledge of the Prosecutor may suggest the innocence or mitigate the guilt of the accused or affect the credibility of Prosecution evidence.[25] The first complaint relates to documents that the Prosecution intended to use during cross-examination, the second relates to Prosecution witnesses' *Gacaca* records, and the third relates to transcripts and prior statements of witnesses who testified in the *Butare* trial. These three sets of alleged violations will be dealt with separately.

4.1. Documents Used in Cross-Examination

37. The Defence argues that the Prosecution violated its disclosure obligations under Rule 68 (A) of the Rules for repeatedly communicating the documents it intended to use in the cross-examination of Defence witnesses only after their cross-examination had already begun. The Defence submits that despite several warnings by the Chamber, the Prosecution persisted in this practice.[26]

38. While this Chamber has encouraged the cross-examining Party to provide the opposing Party with copies of the documents it intends to use *before* cross-examining a witness,[27] there is no binding rule to this effect; rather, this relates to the general conduct of trial proceedings, which is a matter falling within the discretion of the Trial Chamber.[28] The Defence's contention that this would constitute a violation of Rule 68 (A) is completely erroneous. Parties may choose to maintain a certain element of surprise. However, depending on the circumstances, a persistent defiance to respect the Chamber's instructions to provide such documents in advance could suggest a bad faith attempt to undermine the Defence.

39. In raising this argument, the Defence has not provided a single instance or reference to any occasion when such late communication by the Prosecution has occurred. The Chamber is not under any obligation, therefore, to even entertain this complaint. Nonetheless, in the interests of ensuring the integrity of the

---

[24] *Bagosora et al.* Interlocutory Appeal Decision, para. 26.
[25] Defence Closing Brief, paras. 1169-1196.
[26] Defence Closing Brief, paras. 1171 and 1177.
[27] See T. 12 May 2008 p. 47 (Witness BCF) when the Chamber first made the instruction in this case.
[28] *The Prosecutor v. Bagosora et al.*, Case No. ICTR-98-41-AR73, Decision on Interlocutory Appeal Relating to Disclosure Under Rule 66 (B) of the Tribunal's Rules of Procedure and Evidence (AC), 25 September 2006, para. 6.

proceedings and safeguarding the rights of the Accused, the Chamber finds that some consideration of the Defence's arguments is warranted here. **[page 10]**

40. A review of the record shows at least six occasions when the Prosecution distributed materials to the Defence after it had already begun cross-examining the Defence witness.[29] On five such occasions, the Chamber warned the Prosecution to observe its instruction to distribute the materials in advance,[30] and on the third warning, the Chamber admonished the Prosecution's failure to follow the Chamber's instruction.[31]

41. In each case, the Chamber considered whether the Defence might suffer any prejudice from late distribution and provided the appropriate remedy wherever necessary.[32] The Chamber concludes that there was no malice or bad faith on the Prosecution's part here, and that the Defence did not suffer any prejudice whatsoever. The Defence's contention that Kalimanzira's right to a fair trial has been violated in this respect is therefore unfounded.

4.2. *Gacaca* Records

42. The Defence further argues that the Prosecution violated its disclosure obligations under Rule 68 (A) of the Rules by failing to provide any *Gacaca* files for any of the Prosecution witnesses. The Defence suggests the Prosecution must have had the documents in its possession given that the Prosecution was able to produce the *Gacaca* files of certain Defence witnesses to challenge their credibility under cross-examination. The Defence further accuses the Prosecution of deliberately depriving the Defence of the records because on the rare occasion that its own best efforts resulted in the procurement of a Prosecution witness' *Gacaca* record, it proved decisive in challenging that witness' credibility.[33]

43. The determination of which materials are subject to disclosure under Rule 68 of the Rules is a fact-based inquiry made by the Prosecution. If an accused wishes to show that the Prosecution is in breach of its disclosure obligation, he or she must: (1) identify specifically the material sought; (2) show its *prima facie* probable exculpatory nature; and (3) show that the material requested is in the custody or under the control of the Prosecution. According to the Appeals Chamber, the obligation to disclose exculpatory material forms part of the Prosecution's duty to assist in the administration of justice, and is as important as the obligation to prosecute. The Prosecution is presumed to discharge its obligation in good faith. If the Chamber is satisfied that the Prosecution has failed to comply with its Rule 68 obligations, the Chamber will examine whether the accused has been prejudiced by a failure amounting to a violation of his right to a fair trial.[34] **[page 11]**

44. In this case, the Defence has specifically identified the materials sought, but the Prosecution disputes that the material is under its custody or control.[35] To show that the material requested is in the custody or under the control of the Prosecution, the Defence offers mere speculation that if the Prosecution had some Defence witnesses' *Gacaca* records, it must possess all of its own witnesses' *Gacaca* files; this does not fulfill the third prong of the test.

---

[29] See T. 17 November 2008 p. 32 (Witness MGR); T. 18 November 2008 p. 54 (Sylvestre Niyonsaba); T. 18 November 2008 pp. 75-76 (Jean Marie Vianney Harindintwali); T. 2 December 2008 p. 11 (Witness KXC); T. 27 January 2009 pp. 39-40 (Albert Barikwinshi); T. 2 February 2009 p. 16 (Witness ACB6).

[30] See T. 17 November 2008 p. 32 (Witness MGR); T. 18 November 2008 p. 54 (Sylvestre Niyonsaba); T. 18 November 2008 pp. 76-77 (Jean Marie Vianney Harindintwali); T. 27 January 2009 pp. 38-39 (Albert Barikwinshi); T. 2 February 2009 p. 16 (Witness ACB6).

[31] See T. 18 November 2008 pp. 76-77 (Jean Marie Vianney Harindintwali).

[32] See *e.g.* T. 17 November 2008 p. 33 (Witness MGR) and T. 27 January 2009 p. 40 (Albert Barikwinshi) where the Chamber considered whether it might be necessary to allow the Defence more time before reexamination to peruse the documents in question; see also T. 2 February 2009 p. 16 (Witness ACB6) where the Chamber considered the Defence had suffered no material prejudice.

[33] Defence Closing Brief, paras. 1172-1177.

[34] See *e.g. The Prosecutor v. Joseph Kanyabashi*, Case No. ICTR-96-15-T, Decision on Kanyabashi's Motion for Disclosure Pursuant to Rule 68 (TC), 25 February 2009, para. 22; *The Prosecutor v. Karemera et al.*, Case No. ICTR-98-44-AR73.13, Decision on "Joseph Nzirorera's Appeal from Decision on Tenth Rule 68 Motion" (AC), 14 May 2008, para. 12 ; *The Prosecutor v. Karemera et al.*, Case No. ICTR-98-44-AR73.7, Decision on Interlocutory Appeal Regarding the Role of the Prosecutor's Electronic Disclosure Suites in Discharging Disclosure Obligations (AC), 30 June 2006, paras. 8-9; *The Prosecutor v. Karemera et al.*, Case No. ICTR-98-44-AR73.6, Decision on Joseph Nzirorera's Interlocutory Appeal (AC), 28 April 2006, para. 16. See also *The Prosecutor v. Kordić and Čerkez*, Case No. IT-95-14/2-A, Decision on Motions to Extend Time for Filing Appellant's Briefs (AC), 11 May 2001, para. 14.

[35] T. 20 April 2009 p. 13 (Closing Arguments).

45. The Defence could have made a request under Rule 66 (B) of the Rules "to inspect any books, documents, photographs and tangible objects in [the Prosecution's] custody or control, which are material to the preparation of the defence". Such a request would have entailed a reciprocal obligation under Rule 67 (C) of the Rules. The Defence made no such request.

46. The Defence could also have sought assistance from the Chamber. Indeed, a practice has developed, subject to considerations of the interests of justice, of requiring the intervention of the Prosecution to obtain and disclose certain records, specifically Rwandan judicial records of Prosecution witnesses. In these situations, Trial Chambers have acted *proprio motu* under Rule 98 of the Rules to order the Prosecution to use its best efforts to obtain the relevant judicial dossier(s).[36] Under Rule 54 of the Rules, the Chamber may also issue orders as may be necessary for the conduct of the trial. Trial Chambers have resorted to these provisions, for instance, when the information could be considered as material to the preparation of the Defence case or to determine the credibility of Prosecution witnesses.[37]

47. In the present case, the issue of procuring *Gacaca* records arose early in the trial during the cross-examination of a Prosecution witness, and the Chamber offered to assist the Defence. The Defence indicated its intention to file a written motion to specify what documents it would request the Prosecution to disclose or seek assistance to obtain.[38]

However, no such motion was ever filed. Under the circumstances, the Defence's complaint of a disclosure violation in respect of Prosecution witnesses' *Gacaca* records is therefore unfounded.

4.3. *Butare* Trial Transcripts

48. The Defence further argues that the Prosecution violated its disclosure obligations under Rule 68 (A) of the Rules by failing to disclose the transcripts and prior statements of seven witnesses who testified in the *Butare* trial on the events at Kabuye hill.[39] This issue is **[page 12]** *res judicata* by virtue of a decision rendered on 13 February 2009;[40] the Defence now appears to be seeking reconsideration thereof.

49. A Trial Chamber may reconsider its own decision if a new fact is discovered that was not known to the Chamber at the time, if there is a material change in circumstances, or where there is reason to believe that a previous decision was erroneous and therefore prejudicial to either party.[41] In its Closing Brief and during Closing Arguments, the Defence simply reiterates its arguments in its previous motion, thereby showing discontent with the Chamber's 13 February 2009 Decision. The Chamber will now explain why it does not consider its decision to have been erroneous or prejudicial.

50. On 9 February 2009, the Defence for Kalimanzira filed a motion requesting to exclude the testimonies of Prosecution Witnesses BXG, BDK, BDC, BWO, BCF, BBO, and BXK; or, in the alternative, to recall these witnesses for further cross-examination.[42] The Prosecution responded orally to this motion on 13 February 2009, and the Defence replied orally to the Prosecution's response the same day.[43]

---

[36] It should be noted that Rule 98 does not give the parties any right to request additional evidence. It is for the Chamber to exercise its discretion.

[37] *The Prosecutor v. Karemera et al.*, Case No. ICTR-98-44-T, Decision on Defence Motion for Subpoenas to Prosecution Witnesses (TC), 10 May 2007, para. 15; *The Prosecutor v. Karemera et al.*, Case No. ICTR-98-44-T, Decision on Motions to Compel Inspection and Disclosure and to Direct Witnesses to bring Judicial and Immigration Records (TC), 14 September 2005, paras. 7-8; *The Prosecutor v. Karera*, Case No. ICTR-01-74-T, Decision on Defence Motion for Additional Disclosure (TC), 1 September 2006, paras. 5-7; *The Prosecutor v. Simba*, Case No. ICTR-01-76-T, Decision on Matters Related to Witness KDD's Judicial Dossier (TC), 1 November 2004, para. 11.

[38] See T. 20 May 2008 pp. 15 [closed], 16-19 (Witness BDC).

[39] Defence Closing Brief, paras. 1178-1196; see also T. 20 April 2009 pp. 29-30 (Closing Arguments).

[40] Oral Decision on Defence Motion to Exclude Evidence or Recall Witnesses Filed on 9 February (TC), 13 February 2009.

[41] See *e.g. The Prosecutor v. Karemera et al.*, Decision on Joseph Nzirorera's Motion for Reconsideration of 2 December 2008 Decision (TC), 27 February 2009, para. 2; *The Prosecutor v. Bagosora et al.*, ICTR-98-41-T, Decision on Bagosora Request for Certification or Reconsideration Concerning Admission of Correspondence, 8 May 2007, para. 5.

[42] *Requête en exclusion de preuve et à titre subsidiaire en rappel des témoins BXG, BDK, BDC, BWO, BCF, BBO et BXK*, filed on 9 February 2009.

[43] T. 13 February 2009 pp. 4-9 (Status Conference).

Prosecutor v. Kalimanzira

51. The Defence complained then as it does now that the Prosecution deliberately violated Rule 68 (A) of the Rules by failing to disclose "as soon as practicable" the transcripts of seven witnesses who testified in the *Butare* trial on the events at Kabuye hill. The Defence maintains that 16 July 2008 (*i.e.* 16 days after the close of the Prosecution case) is too late a date to disclose what, in its view, amounts to exculpatory evidence. The Defence argues it has suffered prejudice in having been denied the opportunity to cross-examine the *Kalimanzira* witnesses with these transcripts, as well as the opportunity to investigate the *Butare* witnesses to see if they had any useful information for Kalimanzira's defence.

52. The witnesses who testified in the *Butare* trial are not the same witnesses who testified in the *Kalimanzira* trial. The *Butare* witnesses gave similar evidence on Kabuye hill as the *Kalimanzira* witnesses, but never once did the *Butare* witnesses mention Kalimanzira's presence on Kabuye hill. This, the Defence submits, makes the evidence exculpatory. Moreover, the *Butare* witnesses testified four years prior to when the disclosure was made in the present case. The Defence argues that the Office of the Prosecutor is a single entity and that the Prosecution in *Kalimanzira* therefore had actual knowledge of these *Butare* transcripts long before making the disclosure. This, the Defence submits, indicates a deliberate decision on the Prosecution's part to withhold this evidence until it became useless to the Defence.

53. As remedial measures, the Defence sought the exclusion of the testimonies of Prosecution Witnesses BXG, BDK, BDC, BWO, BCF, BBO, and BXK. In the alternative, the Defence sought to recall these witnesses for further cross-examination. In addition, the Defence requested the Chamber to order the Prosecution to disclose the written statements of the seven *Butare* witnesses (EV, EP, RT, TW, QAQ, QBZ and FAU) made prior to their testimonies in the *Butare* trial. Finally, the Defence sought to admit into evidence the **[page 13]** transcripts of *Butare* Prosecution Witnesses EV, EP, RT, TW, QAQ, QBZ and FAU, as well as their prior written statements, pursuant to Rules 89 (C) and 92 *bis* (D) of the Rules.

54. The Defence submits that the subject heading of the Prosecution's correspondence by which it made its Rule 68 (A) disclosure[44] implies an admission by the Prosecution that it violated the letter and spirit of this Rule.[45] The Chamber does not agree. The Prosecution's correspondence suggests only that it considered the materials to be possibly relevant in the preparation of Kalimanzira's defence, and the Prosecution has clarified that, on that basis, it disclosed the materials as a courtesy.[46]

55. The materials disclosed were open session transcripts which are available on the internet at www.ictr.org through the Public Judicial Records Database. However, the public nature of the transcripts cannot, as such, replace the Prosecution's disclosure obligations under Rule 68 (A). The Prosecution must actively review the material in its possession for exculpatory material and, at the very least, inform the accused of its existence. The Prosecution's obligation to disclose exculpatory material is essential to a fair trial, and constitutes one of the Prosecution's most onerous responsibilities.

56. As previously mentioned, if an accused wishes to show that the Prosecution is in breach of its disclosure obligation under Rule 68 (A), he or she must: (1) identify specifically the material sought; (2) show its *prima facie* probable exculpatory nature; and (3) show that the material requested is in the custody or under the control of the Prosecution.

57. In this case, the Defence has specifically identified the materials sought, and has clearly shown that the materials were in the Prosecution's custody and control. The expression "actual knowledge" has been consistently interpreted as requiring that the material be in the possession of the Prosecution,[47] which must be understood as the Office of the Prosecutor as a whole. It is the duty of the Prosecution to disclose exculpatory material arising from related cases and this duty is a continuous obligation without distinction as to the public or confidential character of the evidence concerned.[48] It is, therefore, irrelevant whether the Prosecutor in charge of the case had actual knowledge of the material.

---

[44] "Disclosure: Notification of the existence of materials which may be of relevance to the Kalimanzira Defence".
[45] Defence Closing Brief, paras. 1184-1185; see also T. 20 April 2009 p. 30 (Closing Arguments).
[46] T. 13 February 2009 p. 5 (Status Conference).
[47] *Kajelijeli* Appeal Judgement, para. 262 ("Defence must first establish that the evidence was in the possession of the Prosecution).
[48] *Prosecutor v. Brđanin*, Case No. IT-99-36-A, Decision on Appellant's Motion for Disclosure Pursuant to Rule 68 and Motion for an Order to the Registrar to Disclose Certain Materials (AC), 7 December 2004, p. 4; *Blaškić* Appeal Judgement, para. 267.

58. With respect to the second prong of the test, a review of the transcripts in question reveals the absence of any mention of Kalimanzira. However, the witnesses did not assert that they did not see Kalimanzira there. Rather, no questions were asked regarding Kalimanzira, and therefore, he was simply not mentioned. Such evidence does not contradict the evidence adduced in the *Kalimanzira* trial. There is no indication whether the *Butare* witnesses knew Kalimanzira. Even if it could be shown that they knew him or knew of him, the mere omission to make mention of Kalimanzira's presence at Kabuye hill during the period at issue does not mean that Kalimanzira could not have been there. As such, the Defence has failed to make a *prima facie* showing of the exculpatory nature of evidence adduced by the seven *Butare* witnesses. **[page 14]**

59. In the absence of a violation of Rule 68 (A), the Defence requests for such remedial measures as the exclusion of evidence and the recall of witnesses were rejected. However, the Chamber admitted the transcripts of the *Butare* witnesses' testimonies into evidence pursuant to Rules 89 (C) and 92*bis* (D), as they are sufficiently relevant and probative (though not exculpatory) to the Kabuye hill allegations.[49] The Chamber specified that portions of the *Butare* transcripts which went to proof of Kalimanzira's acts and conduct would be excluded.[50]

60. It is noteworthy that the Defence's original motion came nearly seven months after the impugned Prosecution disclosure was made. As with many other late objections by the Defence, the Chamber has considered the Defence submissions in full and, in respect of the *Butare* evidence, twice now. Under the circumstances, the Chamber does not find that reconsideration is warranted. The Defence's repeated contentions of Rule 68 (A) disclosure violations in respect of the *Butare* evidence are therefore unfounded.

5. NOTICE OF ALIBI

61. In its Closing Brief, the Prosecution submits that the Defence failed to give adequate notice that it intended to use a defence of alibi, and that putting one forward in the last stages of the case diminishes the probative value of the alibi evidence.[51] On 4 February 2009, the third to last Defence witness, Marc Siniyobewe, testified to Kalimanzira's activities in Gitarama *préfecture* from mid-April to the end of May 1994, and placed Kalimanzira there on certain key dates when he was alleged to have been in Butare *préfecture*. The following day, Salomé Mukantwali (Kalimanzira's wife) testified that she was with her husband at certain relevant times in Kigali and Butare *ville*. Their evidence corroborates Kalimanzira's, who testified last.

62. Kalimanzira stated as early as his Initial Appearance in 2005 that he was working in Gitarama with the rest of the government until June 1994, when he left for Butare.[52] Part of his defence to the allegation that he was often in Butare is that he hardly left Gitarama from mid-April until the end of May 1994. This position is not new to the Prosecution.[53] However, specific information was limited and no notice was given that Marc Siniyobewe would provide evidence that he saw Kalimanzira on such key dates as 20 and 23 April 1994. This is clearly an alibi to the allegations at Kabuye hill. His wife also squarely places him at home with her from 6 to 11 April 1994, which is clearly an alibi to the allegation at Kanage Camp.

63. If the Defence intends to rely on an alibi defence, Rule 67 (A) (ii) (a) of the Rules requires it to notify the Prosecution as soon as reasonably practicable, before the commencement of the trial. Such notification must specify the place or places at which the accused claims to have been present at the time of the alleged crime and the names and addresses of witnesses and any other evidence upon which the accused intends to rely to establish the alibi. This provision is intended to allow the Prosecution adequate opportunity to prepare its case and meaningfully investigate the alibi. **[page 15]**

---

[49] Exhibits D82-D97.
[50] See *e.g.* Exhibit D92E (B) pp. 15-18 [T. 24 February 2004 pp. 26-29 [closed] (Witness QBZ)] where QBZ testified about Kalimanzira bringing weapons to the Muganza *commune* office.
[51] Prosecution Closing Brief, paras. 299 and 317.
[52] T. 14 November 2005 p. 9 (Initial Appearance).
[53] *Mémoire en réponse à la « Prosecution motion concerning Defence compliance with rule 73 ter and the Trial Chamber's orders »* datée du 22 octobre 2008, filed on 28 October 2008, paras. 17-25; see also Defence Pre-Trial Brief, para. 20 and annexed summaries of anticipated testimonies of witnesses ACB8, AK14 (Marc Siniyobewe), AX100, BB06, BB08, FG1, FG2, FG3, and MZ20.

64. The Defence never filed a notice of alibi before or during the trial. The Prosecution moved the Chamber to order the Defence to disclose all information pursuant to Rule 67 (A)(ii)(a) based on the inference from the Defence Pre-Trial Brief that it may intend to call certain alibi witnesses.[54] The Chamber considered that an inference of a possibility for the Defence to call alibi witnesses did not amount to notification of an alibi defence; it did not, therefore, issue the order sought.[55]

65. The Defence has long denied that it is relying on an alibi *stricto sensu,* contending that the time frames that the Prosecution attributes to the alleged crimes are so vague as to prevent it from providing one.[56] The Chamber, however, finds that the Defence has clearly adduced alibi evidence; it should therefore have filed a notice of alibi pursuant to Rule 67 (A)(ii)(a) of the Rules.

66. Rule 67 (B) of the Rules states that the "failure of the defence to provide such notice under this Rule shall not limit the right of the accused to rely on any of the above defences". This provision is consistent with the principle that the accused is presumed innocent until the Prosecution has proved his guilt beyond reasonable doubt. In the present case, in conformity with the practice of the Tribunal, the alibi defence will be considered.[57] However, lack of compliance with Rule 67 (A)(ii)(a) under the circumstances may suggest that the Defence has tailored the alibi evidence to fit the Prosecution's case; the Chamber will take this into consideration when assessing the extent to which it believes or relies on Kalimanzira's alibi.

67. Kalimanzira's alibi evidence is discussed in full at III.1.2.

6. EVIDENTIARY ISSUES

68. The Defence seeks a declaration of Kalimanzira's innocence, or in the alternative, a finding that the Prosecution has failed to prove all the charges against him beyond reasonable doubt. The Defence argues that in light of all the credibility issues with the Prosecution witnesses, and the various inconsistent and contradictory testimonies heard at trial, there is a clear and obvious doubt as to Kalimanzira's guilt. It submits that the accused has a right to benefit from even the slightest doubt, leading to an acquittal.[58]

69. Article 20 (3) of the Statute guarantees that each accused person is presumed innocent until proven guilty. Rule 87 (A) of the Rules provides that a majority of the Trial Chamber must be satisfied beyond reasonable doubt that the accused is guilty before a verdict may be entered against him or her. The burden of proving the guilt of the accused beyond reasonable doubt rests solely on the Prosecution and never shifts to the Defence. While the Defence does not have to adduce rebuttal evidence to the Prosecution case, the Prosecution will fail to discharge its burden of proof if the Defence presents evidence that raises a reasonable doubt regarding the Prosecution case. An accused person must be acquitted if there is any reasonable explanation for the evidence other than his or her guilt. Refusal to believe or rely upon Defence evidence does not automatically amount to a guilty verdict. The Chamber must **[page 16]** still determine whether the evidence it does accept establishes the accused's guilt beyond reasonable doubt.[59]

70. The Defence points to a number of Prosecution witnesses who are accomplices, or whose testimonies are uncorroborated, or both. The Defence argues that the recent *Rukundo* Trial Judgement has established that uncorroborated accomplice testimony is unreliable and must be dismissed, as exemplified in its treatment of Witness BLP. In the present case, the Defence seeks an intransigent application of the same, such that wherever an accomplice witness is uncorroborated, his or her testimony should automatically be dismissed.[60]

---

[54] Prosecution Motion Concerning Defence Compliance with Rule 73*ter* and the Trial Chamber's Orders, filed on 22 October 2008.
[55] Consolidated Decision on Prosecution Motion Concerning Defence Compliance with Rule 73*ter* and Defence Motions to Vary Witness List (TC), 13 November 2008, para. 7.
[56] See T. 20 April 2009 p. 47 (Closing Arguments); see also *Mémoire en réponse à la « Prosecution motion concerning Defence compliance with rule 73 ter and the Trial Chamber's orders »* datée du 22 octobre 2008, filed on 28 October 2008, paras. 17-25.
[57] *Rukundo* Trial Judgement, para. 539; *Nchamihigo* Trial Judgement, para 20.
[58] Defence Closing Brief, paras. 1224-1311.
[59] *Rukundo* Trial Judgement, paras. 36-37; *Nchamihigo* Trial Judgement, para. 13; *Kayishema* Appeal Judgement, para. 117; *Niyitegeka* Appeal Judgement, paras. 60-61.
[60] Defence Closing Brief, paras. 1197-1223.

71. Rule 89 (C) of the Rules gives the Trial Chamber discretion to admit any relevant evidence which it deems to have probative value. The Appeals Chamber has consistently held that a Trial Chamber is in the best position to evaluate the probative value of evidence and that it may, depending on its assessment, rely on a single witness's testimony for proof of a material fact. Accordingly, the Chamber does not necessarily require evidence to be corroborated in order to make a finding of fact on it. Though a Trial Chamber may prefer that a witness' testimony be corroborated, it is not a requirement or an obligation in the practice of this Tribunal.[61]

72. The jurisprudence of this Tribunal has also established that the evidence of accomplices and detained witnesses is not inadmissible, nor is it *per se* unreliable, especially where an accomplice is thoroughly cross-examined. However, considering that accomplice witnesses may have incentives to implicate the accused, a Chamber, when weighing the probative value of such evidence, is bound to carefully consider the totality of the circumstances in which it was tendered, and, when necessary, must approach such evidence with caution in order to ensure a fair trial and guard against the exercise of a possible underlying motive on the part of the witness. As a corollary, a Trial Chamber should at least briefly explain why it accepted the evidence of witnesses who may have had motives or incentives to implicate the accused.[62]

73. In addition, it may be necessary, depending on the circumstances of the case, to employ a critical approach towards witnesses who are merely charged with crimes of a similar nature. But in most cases, they will not have the same tangible motives for giving false evidence like a witness who was allegedly involved in the same criminal acts as the accused. Therefore, as long as no special circumstances have been identified, it is reasonable not to employ the same cautious approach towards the testimony of witnesses charged with similar crimes as to the testimony of accomplices in the ordinary sense of the word.[63]

74. Contrary to the Defence's arguments, lack of corroboration of accomplice testimony does not automatically render such testimony unreliable, and the law in this respect has not changed with the *Rukundo* Trial Judgement's treatment of Witness BLP's testimony.[64] In *Rukundo,* the Chamber viewed the testimony of BLP, an alleged accomplice of the Accused, **[page 17]** with appropriate caution. BLP was not only an accomplice witness, he was also on provisional release in Rwanda, his prior statements showed inconsistencies with his testimony on the stand, he failed to identify the Accused in the courtroom, and an issue arose as to whether he had given false testimony.[65] These are some of the reasons why the Chamber deemed it could only rely on his evidence if it was corroborated by, or itself corroborated, other reliable evidence. The level of caution to be exercised in respect of an uncorroborated accomplice witness' testimony is thus to be determined on a case-by-case basis.

75. While direct evidence is preferred, hearsay evidence is not *per se* inadmissible before the Trial Chamber. The Trial Chamber has the discretion to treat such hearsay evidence with caution, depending on the circumstances of the case. In certain circumstances, hearsay evidence may require other credible or reliable evidence adduced by the Prosecution in order to support a finding of fact beyond reasonable doubt.[66]

76. In determining witness credibility, the Trial Chamber has broad discretion to assess inconsistencies between a witness's pre-trial statements and his evidence in court and to determine the appropriate weight to be attached to such discrepancies. It is for the Chamber to decide if an alleged inconsistency is sufficient to cast doubt on a witness's evidence, and the Chamber may accept such evidence, notwithstanding the discrepancies.[67] **[page 18]**

---

[61] *Karera* Appeal Judgement, para. 45; *Niyitegeka* Appeal Judgement, para. 92; *Rutaganda* Appeal Judgment, para. 29; *Musema* Appeal Judgment, paras. 36-38; *Ntakirutimana* Appeal Judgement, para. 132; *Kayishema and Ruzindana* Appeal Judgement, paras. 154, 187, 320, 322; *Čelebići* Appeal Judgment, para. 506; *Aleksovski* Appeal Judgment, paras. 62-63; *Tadić* Appeal Judgment, para. 65; *Kupreškić et al.* Appeal Judgement, para. 33.
[62] *Niyitegeka* Appeal Judgement, para. 98; *Ntagerura et al.* Appeal Judgement, paras. 203-206; *Krajišnik* Appeal Judgement, para. 146.
[63] *Ntagurera et al.* Appeal Judgement, para. 234.
[64] Defence Closing Brief, paras. 1210-1212.
[65] *Rukundo* Trial Judgement, paras. 139-146.
[66] *Rukundo* Trial Judgement, para. 39; *Muvunyi* Trial Judgement, para. 13; *Rutaganda* Appeal Judgement, para. 34; see also Rule 89 of the Rules.
[67] *Rukundo* Trial Judgement, para. 42; *Muvunyi* Trial Judgement, para. 14; *Gacumbitsi* Appeal Judgement, para.
[74;] *Kajelijeli* Appeal Judgement, para. 96.

CHAPTER III – FINDINGS

77. Most Prosecution and Defence witnesses were granted protective measures in order to prevent public disclosure of their identities.[68] The Chamber seeks to set forth the basis of its reasoning as clearly as possible, whilst avoiding disclosure of any information that may reveal the identity of protected witnesses.

1. PRELIMINARY FINDINGS

1.1. The Accused

78. At paragraph 2 of the Indictment, the Prosecution outlines the various governmental positions that Kalimanzira allegedly held throughout his career, including his political allies and affiliations, to introduce the basis on which Kalimanzira had enough stature and authority in Butare *préfecture* to commit the crimes alleged. The evidence adduced at trial demonstrated that for the most part, Kalimanzira did not dispute the facts alleged. He disputes only that (i) between 6 April and 25 May 1994, he was acting Minister of the Interior, (ii) he was a prominent MRND member, and (iii) he had *de jure* and *de facto* authority over the people of Butare.

1.1.1. Employment History

79. The Prosecution alleges that Kalimanzira was a senior civil servant who held several positions; Kalimanzira does not deny this. Kalimanzira was born in Nyaguhuru *secteur* (Muganza *commune*, Butare *préfecture*) in 1953. He is married and has five children. His parents and five siblings were all farmers, and their education did not exceed the level of primary school. Kalimanzira was the only member of his family, and only one of three people of his generation from his area, to have pursued a university degree. After completing secondary school where he trained to become a teacher, Kalimanzira won a scholarship to attend the Rwandan National University. Rather than continuing to pursue a degree in education, he decided to study agronomy, in order to help improve the agriculture in, and sustainable development of, his native area.[69]

80. Upon graduating in 1981, Kalimanzira returned home as an agronomical engineer and began applying his acquired knowledge and techniques in his area, Kirarambogo. Malaria was rampant in the swampy Kirarambogo area, and malnutrition was a problem. To alleviate this, Kalimanzira trained the local inhabitants to develop the marshland by farming rice, fish and crops. He managed to secure financial assistance for his projects, including the establishment of cooperatives, from local benefactors and a non-governmental organization called INADES (*Institut africain pour le développement économique et social*).[70]

81. Kalimanzira worked with INADES in Gisenyi *préfecture* for five years, a position which required his secondment by Presidential Order. He explained that all university **[page 19]** graduates were automatically appointed to become civil servants, and that any request to work outside the civil service had to be approved by the government.[71]

82. In July 1986, Kalimanzira was appointed to be a *sous-préfet* of Butare. He testified that he did not seek the appointment and was not at all pleased with it, particularly as he was slated to replace the Director-General of INADES at that time, a position he says he would have preferred. He felt ill-equipped to perform administrative tasks, and did not appreciate the reduction in emoluments that the appointment implied.

---

[68] *The Prosecutor v. Callixte Kalimanzira*, Case No. ICTR-05-88-I, Decision on Prosecution Motion for Protective Measures, 8 November 2007; *The Prosecutor v. Callixte Kalimanzira*, Case No. ICTR-05-88-I, Decision on Defence Motion for Protective Measures, 14 December 2007.
[69] T. 10 February 2009 p. 2 (Callixte Kalimanzira); T. 5 February 2009 p. 4 (Salomé Mukantwali); see also Exhibits P13, P34, P35, P38 and P45.
[70] T. 10 February 2009 p. 3 (Callixte Kalimanzira); see also Exhibits P41 and P42.
[71] See Exhibits P28, P31, P32 and P37, which show that a representative for INADES made the request on 7 July 1981, and that the government at once appointed Kalimanzira to the Ministry of Agriculture and seconded him to INADES by Presidential Order on 30 December 1981.

However, he testified that it was impossible for him to refuse the governmental appointment; such an act would have entailed punishment. Therefore, Kalimanzira and his wife moved back to his native Butare, where he worked as *sous-préfet* until May 1987, and then acting *préfet* until November 1987.[72]

83. Kalimanzira was subsequently transferred to Byumba *préfecture* as *sous-préfet* of Ngarama *sous-préfecture*, bordering Uganda. He explained that he was even less pleased with this appointment, which he held until August 1989, and that he suffered clashes with local authorities engaged in the trafficking of livestock. Kalimanzira and Faustin Munyazesa, who was the *préfet* of Byumba at the time, tried to put a stop to the smuggling and reinstall peace in the area, but were met with resistance at high levels, including the Minister of Justice, resulting in their dismissal from the region and transfer to Gitarama *préfecture*.[73]

84. With the help of Faustin Munyazesa, who became *préfet* of Gitarama, Kalimanzira was appointed to the Ministry of Agriculture and Livestock in Ruhango *sous-préfecture* (Gitarama *préfecture*) in September 1989. In May 1990, Kalimanzira rose to the rank of Coordinator of Agricultural Services in Kigali *préfecture*, a position that he says pleased him because it entailed less administrative and more agriculture work. Then in April 1991, Kalimanzira was transferred to the Presidency, where he was appointed Director of Rural Development, much to his dismay because he lost all his benefits, including his vehicle, was given substandard housing, no longer had any subordinates, and disliked his new work environment.[74]

85. Kalimanzira remained at the Presidency from April to December 1991, during which time Faustin Munyazesa was appointed Minister of the Interior and Communal Development. Kalimanzira explained that his unstable employment history from 1986 to 1991 was partly due to his unwillingness to network his way to more favourable positions. He expressed aversion to having been appointed and repeatedly transferred to various government posts located in different parts of the country, which was often the result of regionalism or retaliation. Sympathetic to Kalimanzira's plight, Minister Munyazesa appointed Kalimanzira in January 1992 to become Secretary General of the Ministry of the Interior, and then *Directeur de Cabinet* in September 1992, a position he still maintained in April 1994.[75] **[page 20]**

1.1.2. Professional Position, 6 April – 25 May 1994

86. The Prosecution alleges that Kalimanzira acted as Minister of the Interior in Faustin Munyazesa's absence from 6 April to 25 May 1994;[76] Kalimanzira denies this. He insists he was merely a technocrat and while he may have signed documents on behalf of the Minister, he never took over the Minister's core duties, which always remained Munyazesa's. He maintained his position as *Directeur de Cabinet*, and spent most of his time in Gitarama where he continued to handle routine matters such as paying salaries of employees and implementing decisions taken by the government. He never attended any cabinet meeting or took any political or policy decision concerning the prevailing circumstances.[77]

87. According to the Rwandan Official Journal of 22 November 1992, the *Directeur de Cabinet* was the second most senior official within the Ministry of the Interior, replacing the Minister in his absence or incapacity in respect of day-to-day affairs.[78] During the period in question, Kalimanzira indeed signed documents on behalf of the absent Minister of the Interior, such as those suggesting the names of candidates for public office.[79]

88. The Chamber considers that the months of April and May 1994 were an extraordinary period during which the Ministry could not have functioned as it normally might have during peacetime. Kalimanzira's functions within the Ministry at that time, therefore, likely deviated somewhat from the terms of reference

---

[72] T. 10 February 2009 pp. 6-7 (Callixte Kalimanzira); see also Exhibits P26 and P27.
[73] T. 10 February 2009 pp. 7-10 (Callixte Kalimanzira); see also Exhibits P23 and P40.
[74] T. 10 February 2009 pp. 10-12 (Callixte Kalimanzira); see also Exhibits P15, P18, P19, P20, P21, P22 and P25.
[75] T. 10 February 2009 pp. 7-13 (Callixte Kalimanzira); see also Exhibits P14, P15, P16, P44 and P46.
[76] Paragraph 2(v) of the Indictment; Prosecution Pre-Trial Brief, para. 48; Prosecution Closing Brief, paras. 8-16.
[77] T. 10 February 2009 pp. 29, 45 and T. 11 February 2009 p. 44 (Callixte Kalimanzira); see also Defence Closing Brief, paras. 1099-1100.
[78] Exhibit D102 p. 1754.
[79] See *e.g.* Exhibits P47 & P53, P48.

outlined in the Rwandan Official Journal (Exhibit D102). In his sworn testimony, however, Kalimanzira was extremely evasive about his work and functions, minimizing them whenever necessary and wherever possible. Aside from signing payslips, ensuring cars had fuel, preparing the appointment of *préfets* and *bourgmestres*, and greeting refugees, the Chamber heard very little about what Kalimanzira specifically did during this time period.

89. The Chamber believes Kalimanzira's assertions that he was a civil servant, albeit one who also served as a political advisor to the Minister of the Interior. He was a talented, competent, and reliable professional who was highly appreciated by his employers and coworkers. Kalimanzira could have been chosen to officially replace Munyazesa, who was never sworn in as Minister after 9 April; instead, Kalimanzira remained *Directeur de Cabinet* while the position stayed unoccupied for nearly two months until Édouard Karemera's appointment.

90. At such a critical time, someone would have had to take necessary decisions beyond routine matters in Munyazesa's absence, and Kalimanzira could conceivably have been the one to do it. The Chamber does not consider, however, that the Prosecution has proven this allegation beyond reasonable doubt, and it is not for Kalimanzira to disprove it. Kalimanzira's *de jure* status does not necessarily reflect his *de facto* functions or the reality of the situation under the exceptional conditions of a genocide raging against a backdrop of civil war. Under such emergency circumstances, the Chamber deems that Kalimanzira might likely have exercised a more executive than initiative role in the Interim Government. Thus, while Kalimanzira was the most senior official in the Ministry of the Interior from 6 April to 25 May 1994, running its day-to-day affairs, it does not follow that he acted as Minister of **[page 21]** the Interior. Rather, the Chamber considers that the political powers of the Minister would have been exercised by persons in the political establishment of the Interim Government.

1.1.3. Political Affiliations

MRND Membership

91. The Prosecution alleges that Kalimanzira was a prominent long-term serving member and staunch supporter of the MRND;[80] Kalimanzira denies this. He explained that despite the advent of multiparty politics in Rwanda,[81] he did not join any political party. In fact, he testified that when all new political parties became operational, civil servants with administrative functions were specifically instructed to stay neutral and aloof of political parties so as to ensure equal assistance to everyone regardless of political leanings. He asserted that multiparty politics in Rwanda were wild, and that he preferred not to engage in political activities because they engendered tension, hostility, and ethnic conflict. He emphasized he was nothing more than a technocrat, completely unconcerned by politics and political activities.[82]

92. Yet, there is evidence on the record to suggest Kalimanzira was more politically inclined than he admits. For instance, Prosecution Witness AZC knew Kalimanzira to be a staunch supporter of the MRND.[83] In addition, Prosecution Witness BCA testified that he was nominated and appointed to his political office by virtue of the assistance and support he received from his fellow MRND members, which included Kalimanzira.[84] The fact that he became the political advisor to Minister Munyazesa, an MRND member, suggests that Kalimanzira's MRND membership not only pre-dates, but contributed to, his appointment to the Ministry of the Interior. Though he claims it was at the behest of his Minister, Kalimanzira even ran for and won an election on 31 May 1993 to join the MRND Butare Prefectural Committee, which included Théodore Sindikubwabo and Bernadette Mukarurangwa as members.[85]

---

[80] Paragraph 2(vi) of the Indictment; Prosecution Pre-Trial Brief, para. 47; Prosecution Closing Brief, paras. 23-24.
[81] The MRND was the sole political party in Rwanda until the advent of multiparty politics in 1991. Multipartyism had its effect on the local and national power structures from 1992 onwards. (See *e.g. Akayesu* Trial Judgement, para. 60).
[82] T. 10 February 2009 pp. 13-16, 25 (Callixte Kalimanzira).
[83] Exhibit D37; see also T. 25 June 2008 p. 41 (Witness AZC).
[84] T. 18 June 2008 p. 42 [closed] (Witness BCA).
[85] T. 10 February 2009 p. 14 and T. 11 February 2009 p. 35 (Callixte Kalimanzira); see also Exhibit P52.

93. Kalimanzira's prominence follows from his senior position in the Ministry of the Interior in combination with his reputation and high standing in society, particularly in Butare. Kalimanzira depicted himself as apolitical and uninterested in politics. However, his critical account of his unstable governmental employment history and his various complaints about having been a victim of corruption and regionalism indicate anything but indifference. The Chamber does not believe Kalimanzira to have been as politically passive and apathetic as he claims. Rather, the Chamber views Kalimanzira's harsh and unpleasant description of the Habyarimana regime as hypocritical in light of his willingness to run for MRND elections and accept incrementally favourable governmental positions. The MRND party was unpopular in Butare; for Kalimanzira to have joined it, let alone run for election to the MRND Butare Prefectural Committee, suggests an active and informed choice on his part, one which proved beneficial by enabling his promotion to *Directeur de Cabinet* of the Ministry of the Interior. While the Chamber does not find that this amounts to proving he was **[page 22]** a "staunch" MRND supporter, the Chamber does believe that Kalimanzira was an active and prominent MRND member.

Relationship with the President and Prime Minister

94. Paragraph 2 of the Indictment alleges that Kalimanzira shared a very close alliance with President Théodore Sindikubwabo and Prime Minister Jean Kambanda. In its Closing Brief, the Prosecution argues that the close political relationship between them is "[a] fact that is established by the evidence" beyond reasonable doubt, but offers little more than inference, primarily based on their common regional origin of Butare *préfecture*.[86] The only evidence placing the three men together is on 19 April 1994 at the MRND Palace meeting (see III.2.2), and even then the extent of Kalimanzira's alleged role does not exceed that of master of ceremonies, which hardly suggests any sort of alliance or relationship. Kalimanzira's allegiance was to his Minister, Faustin Munyazesa, who was most responsible for his rising career, and who was a native of Kigali. The Prosecution has failed to prove this allegation beyond reasonable doubt.

1.1.4. De Jure *and* De Facto *Authority*

95. The Prosecution alleges that Kalimanzira exercised *de jure* and *de facto* authority over various categories of people in Butare *préfecture*;[87] Kalimanzira denies this. The Prosecution submits that Kalimanzira's *de jure* authority over Butare prefectural, communal, and other local officials follows from his position as the second most senior official within the Ministry of the Interior (after the Minister himself). The Prosecution further submits that Kalimanzira's *de facto* authority derived from his general stature as a prominent member of Butare society, with his power and influence flowing from having served as *sous-préfet* and then acting *préfet* of Butare, as well as his position with the Ministry of the Interior.

96. The Rwandan Official Journal of 22 November 1992 lists the various offices within the Ministry of the Interior and Communal Development and their respective functions, and also contains an organisational chart depicting the Ministry's hierarchy and chain of command.[88] It follows from the chart that the Minister of the Interior was the direct superior in the chain of command over the *Directeur de Cabinet*. A detailed analysis of the list of offices within the Ministry of the Interior as well as the organisational chart reflects that the post of *Directeur de Cabinet* was the most senior one after that of the Minister. Among other things, the *Directeur de Cabinet* was in charge of coordinating and supervising the day-today work of the Ministry, and would replace the Minister in his absence.[89]

---

[86] Prosecution Closing Brief, paras. 17-22.
[87] Paragraph 2(vii) of the Indictment; Prosecution Closing Brief, paras. 25-28.
[88] Exhibit D102 pp. 1754 and 1759.
[89] The relevant portion of the journal (p. 1754) reads: *"Attributions propres au directeur de cabinet. – Direction, coordination, animation, orientation et contrôle des activités des Conseillers, de l'Attaché de Presse et des services d'appui relevant du Cabinet; – Distribution et suivi des affaires; – Elaboration de la politique générale du département et suivi de la mise en œuvre des options et décisions gouvernementales dans les domaines d'intervention du département; – Centralisation et vérification des dossiers et des actes à soumettre au visa ou à la signature du ministère; – Supervision, en étroite collaboration avec le Directeur général, de la programmation des activités du ministère à court et moyen termes et de l'élaboration du rapport annuel du ministère; – Animation du Conseil du ministère; – Coordination des activités de coopération intéressant le ministère; – Relations avec l'environnement socio-politique et les médias; – Remplacement du Ministre en cas d'absence ou d'empêchement de ce dernier pour ce qui concerne les affaires courantes; – Toute autre tâche confiée par le Ministre."*

97. The Ministry of the Interior had *de jure* authority over Rwanda's prefectural and communal administrative bodies, and whoever was in charge of the Ministry exercised that [page 23] authority. In April 1994 when Faustin Munyazesa, the Minister of the Interior, was on official mission in Tanzania, Kalimanzira replaced him. When Munyazesa did not return to Rwanda, Kalimanzira remained in charge of the Ministry until Édouard Karemera's appointment on 25 May 1994. However, Kalimanzira's *de jure* authority was restricted to the Ministry's daily business and routine matters.

98. Whether Kalimanzira exceeded the limits of his official functions is another matter. To the extent that he held some *de jure* authority over prefectural, communal, and other local officials while he was the officer in charge of the Ministry of the Interior, it follows that Kalimanzira would have also held a certain level of *de facto* power over them. In addition, to the extent that he was the officer in charge of the Ministry of the Interior for nearly two months, it follows that Kalimanzira maintained a certain level of influence and significance within the Interim Government for the duration of the events.

99. With respect to his influence in Butare *préfecture* in particular, it is not disputed that Kalimanzira was well-liked, even loved, and highly respected. Several witnesses, both Defence and Prosecution, affirmed this. He formed part of Butare's intelligentsia and his efforts at sustainable development in his time as an agronomist were much appreciated. His prior service as a *sous-préfet* was well-remembered and his rise to a senior national governmental position was known and admired. In a hierarchical society such as Rwanda's, Kalimanzira's high standing and good reputation, not to mention the incrementally important governmental positions he held throughout his career, would undeniably imply an increased level of reverence from and influence over the population of Butare *préfecture*.

1.2. Alibi

100. On 4 February 2009, the Chamber heard the third to last Defence witness, Marc Siniyobewe, provide Kalimanzira with an alibi for the 18 April to 30 May 1994 time period. His testimony was followed by Salomé Mukantwali's (Kalimanzira's wife) on 5 February 2009, who provided her husband with an alibi from 6 to 11 April and 31 May to 17 July 1994. Kalimanzira then testified in his own defence on 10 and 11 February 2009, to consolidate the evidence adduced in support of his alibi.

1.2.1. Evidence

101. When President Habyarimana's plane crashed on 6 April 1994, Kalimanzira and his wife were at home in Kigali. In the days that followed, Kalimanzira maintains that he and his family followed blanket instructions issued over the radio that everyone was to remain indoors until further notice. Kalimanzira says he did not leave his house before 11 April 1994 when he was summoned to a meeting at the *Hôtel des Diplomates*; this was also the first day he was able to regain access to a vehicle, with the help of a colleague.[90] His wife, Salomé, supported this by testifying that Kalimanzira's colleague, Aloys Ngendahimana, called to inform him that his presence was required at a meeting, and offered to drive him to the Kigali prefectural office so that he could regain access to his assigned vehicle (a red double-cabin Toyota Hilux pick-up) and driver, Issa Ngeze.[91] The Prosecution accepts Kalimanzira's assertion that he was in Kigali on 11 April 1994.[92] [page 24]

102. This is Kalimanzira's alibi in respect of the Prosecution's accusation at paragraph 20 of the Indictment that on 9 April 1994 he incited Burundian refugees in Kanage *cellule* (Kibayi *commune,* Butare *préfecture*) to commit genocide (see III.4.3).[93]

103. With gunfire and explosions continuing to rain over Kigali, on 12 April 1994 Kalimanzira sent his wife and children to Butare with his driver where he thought they would be safe. He decided to remain in Kigali to continue working and wait for his Minister, Faustin Munyazesa (Minister of the Interior), to return

---

[90] T. 10 February 2009 p. 23 (Callixte Kalimanzira); see also Exhibit D109.
[91] T. 5 February 2009 p. 6 (Salomé Mukantwali).
[92] Prosecution Closing Brief, para. 311.
[93] The Prosecution also accused Kalimanzira at paragraph 16 of distributing weapons in Kigembe *commune* two days after the plane crash, but led no evidence on this allegation at trial; this charge has therefore been dismissed (see II.2.2.4).

Judgement

from mission. Kalimanzira testified that when his driver, Issa Ngeze, returned the following evening, Ngeze informed him that various Ministers and other government officials had fled Kigali to set up office in Gitarama *préfecture*. Kalimanzira therefore arranged for a vehicle to take him there and on 14 April 1994, he left Kigali for Gitarama.[94]

104. After having travelled some 50 kilometres from Kigali, Kalimanzira arrived at 5:00 p.m. in Murambi (Gitarama *préfecture*), where the government had sought refuge and moved its seat. Upon his arrival, he observed that the spaces used for offices were grossly inadequate to accommodate the number of workers, who were "packed like bees", and that there was serious shortage of working equipment. He also learned that the others had arrived two days prior, on 12 April 1994. With no space for him to work or sleep in Murambi, Kalimanzira went to see the *préfet* of Gitarama on 16 April 1994 to request an office; the *préfet* offered him a space in the Gitarama prefectural office. Kalimanzira shared the space with the only four other employees of the Ministry of the Interior who came to Gitarama, including Defence Witness Marc Siniyobewe.[95]

105. Kalimanzira maintains that he stayed and worked in Gitarama for the next month and a half, until the end of May.[96] With the exception of a few dates on which he indicates he left Gitarama, this is Kalimanzira's alibi in respect of most of the Prosecution's allegations, discussed in full below. He admits to having attended the MRND Palace meeting in Butare *ville* on 19 April 1994, as alleged at paragraph 7 of the Indictment (see III.2.2). Kalimanzira's wife Salomé testified that he came to visit her and their children in Butare after the meeting that day, but could only stay ten minutes before returning to Gitarama. He testified in chief that apart from 19 April 1994, he did not go to Butare on any other occasion while he was in Gitarama.[97] He maintained this position under cross-examination until the Prosecution confronted him with a transcript of a radio broadcast placing him at a Prefectural Security Council meeting on 16 May 1994 in Butare; Kalimanzira claimed to have forgotten about it and admitted to having attended it.[98]

106. Kalimanzira testified he also left Gitarama on 21 April 1994 for Kibungo *préfecture* to install the newly appointed *préfet*, Anaclet Rudakubana. He, the driver, and *préfet* Rudakubana left Gitarama at 9:00 a.m., reaching Kibungo at 6:00 p.m after a long and arduous journey. After the 30-45 minute inauguration ceremony was over, Kalimanzira says he decided to spend the night in Kibungo, for fear of an imminent RPF attack. He reached Gitarama the next day at 6:00 p.m. exhausted from the trip and unable to resume work until **[page 25]** the day after, on 23 April 1994.[99] Siniyobewe confirmed this timeline, testifying that he did not see Kalimanzira in Gitarama on 21 or 22 April 1994, and that he had made the fuel and vehicle arrangements for Kalimanzira and the *préfet* to be taken to Kibungo.[100] The Prosecution accepts Kalimanzira's presence in Kibungo *préfecture* on 21 April 1994 to install the new *préfet*, which is confirmed by a radio transcript.[101]

107. Kalimanzira maintains that on the weekend of 23 and 24 April 1994, and for the next few days, he did not move from Gitarama. This is Kalimanzira's alibi in respect of the Prosecution's allegations at paragraphs 9 and 10 of the Indictment that he participated in and supervised the killings at Kabuye hill (see III.2.4). Kalimanzira admits to one other trip out of Gitarama on 3 May 1994 when he went to Ngororero in Gisenyi *préfecture* to help resettle an influx of newly displaced persons. Siniyobewe supports Kalimanzira's testimony by asserting that he and Kalimanzira worked in Gitarama together nearly every day from 23 April to 30 May 1994.[102]

108. On 30 May 1994, Gitarama came under attack causing everyone to flee the area in a panic and creating chaos. Kalimanzira left with a gendarme from Butare and took the road leading to Kibuye *préfecture*. As the Kigali-Butare road was already captured, they had to take a long detour to drive safer roads. They had to spend the night of 30 May in Gikongoro *préfecture* before reaching Butare on 31 May 1994, where

---

[94] T. 10 February 2009 pp. 23-25 (Callixte Kalimanzira); T. 5 February 2009 p. 6 (Salomé Mukantwali).
[95] T. 10 February 2009 pp. 25-27 (Callixte Kalimanzira).
[96] T. 10 February 2009 pp. 27 (Callixte Kalimanzira).
[97] T. 5 February 2009 p. 9 (Salomé Mukantwali).
[98] T. 11 February 2009 pp. 18-23 (Callixte Kalimanzira).
[99] T. 10 February 2009 pp. 39-42 (Callixte Kalimanzira).
[100] T. 4 February 2009 p. 24 (Marc Siniyobewe).
[101] See Exhibit D104 and Prosecution Closing Brief, para. 311.
[102] T. 4 February 2009 p. 25 (Marc Siniyobewe).

Kalimanzira immediately rejoined his family at the home they were renting out to their friend, Jean-Baptiste Sebalinda.[103]

109. Upon arriving to Butare, Kalimanzira says he stayed a few days with his wife and traumatized children to comfort them. Then sometime toward the end of the first week of June 1994, he and his driver went to visit his family in Kirarambogo. On the way there, Kalimanzira says he did not stop, though he did greet people. He took the road leaving Butare, going through Shyanda and Ndora *communes,* until Muganza *commune.* It was not until he travelled through Ndora *commune* and saw the extent of the destruction that he came to realize how disastrous and devastating the situation was.[104]

110. He remained in Butare with his wife and children until 30 June 1994. During the month of June, Kalimanzira says he ceased to work and did not follow the government when they set up new office in Gisenyi. He says for the most part he stayed home, save for a few occasions or events, such as the swearing-in ceremony of Butare's new *préfet,* Alphonse Nteziryayo, on 21 June 1994 at the Ngoma *commune* office, and the welcoming of the papal representative, Cardinal Etchegaray, on 24 June 1994.[105] This is Kalimanzira's alibi in respect several allegations placing him at various locations throughout Butare in the month of June, such as the Prosecution's allegations at paragraphs 12 and 14 of the Indictment that he incited the population to kill at the Gikonko *commune* office on 5 June 1994.

111. On 30 June 1994, Kalimanzira and his family fled Butare and went to the "Zone Turquoise" in Gikongoro *préfecture* where they remained for two weeks. On 16 July 1994, **[page 26]** they left for Cyangugu *préfecture,* where they spent the night before crossing over into Zaïre on 17 July 1994.[106]

1.2.2. Deliberations

112. It is well settled that, in assessing an alibi, an accused need only produce evidence likely to raise a reasonable doubt in the Prosecution's case. The alibi does not carry a separate burden. Refusal to believe or rely on an accused's alibi does not remove or shift the burden of proving the facts charged beyond reasonable doubt, which always remains squarely on the shoulders of the Prosecution.[107]

113. The Chamber recalls that Kalimanzira did not give notice that he intended to use the defence of alibi (see II.5). While this does not prevent him from relying on an alibi defence, it may diminish its probative value as it raises the question of whether the alibi was recently invented to fit the case against him.[108] In this case, the issue of recent fabrication had to be considered seriously. The main alibi witnesses were the last witnesses to be called by the Defence: Salomé Mukantwali (Kalimanzira's wife), Marc Siniyobewe (a close family friend), and Kalimanzira himself. The Defence therefore had access to them and their prospective testimony in time to give notice prior to the commencement of the Prosecution's case.

114. The Prosecution's allegations provide both very specific dates and more or less generalized dates. Kalimanzira's alibi defence was also partly specific and partly general. It can be divided into three main sections:
- From 6 to 14 April 1994, Kalimanzira was at his home in Kigali except on 11 April when he attended a meeting. On 12 April he sent his wife and children to Butare, and on 14 April he left for Gitarama;
- From 14 April to 30 May 1994, Kalimanzira stayed in Murambi/Gitarama where he worked with the Interim Government. He claims to have left only on a few specific occasions. Defence Witness Marc Siniyobewe confirms Kalimanzira's testimony and places him in Gitarama on 23 April 1994;
- From 30 May to July 1994, Kalimanzira went to Butare where he stayed at his home except on three occasions in June before moving to the "Zone Turquoise" and then fleeing to Zaïre.

---

[103] T. 10 February 2009 pp. 47-48 (Callixte Kalimanzira); T. 5 February 2009 p. 10 (Salomé Mukantwali); see also T. 4 February 2009 p. 26 (Marc Siniyobewe).
[104] T. 10 February 2009 p. 49 (Callixte Kalimanzira); T. 5 February 2009 p. 10 (Salomé Mukantwali).
[105] T. 10 February 2009 pp. 52-53 (Callixte Kalimanzira); T. 5 February 2009 pp. 10-11 (Salomé Mukantwali).
[106] T. 10 February 2009 pp. 53, 58-59 (Callixte Kalimanzira).
[107] *Bagosora et al.* Trial Judgement, para. 1943; *Simba* Appeal Judgement, para. 184, citing *Simba* Trial Judgement, para. 303.
[108] *Musema* Trial Judgement, para. 107.

6 – 14 April

115. There were several aspects of Kalimanzira and his wife's evidence which were unbelievable. On the issue of access to transport, his wife testified that he had an official vehicle and a driver who would typically park the vehicle in front of the Biryogo *secteur* office everyday after dropping Kalimanzira off at home.[109] They both testified that from 6 to 11 April, Kalimanzira had no access to his official vehicle or contact with his driver. Yet, the telephone lines were still working, as evidenced by the phone call Kalimanzira purportedly received from Aloys Ngendahimana (*Directeur Général* of the Ministry of the Interior) on 11 April, as well as from AX100's evidence that he used Kalimanzira's phone.[110] Moreover, for [page 27] Ngendahimana, a subordinate of Kalimanzira, to have access to vehicle while Kalimanzira did not, is unreasonable, as is the idea that high officials would not leave their homes to address an emergency situation. For Kalimanzira's driver not to have attended to him during such a tense period of heightened insecurity would have been a serious dereliction of duty. The particular responsibilities of the Ministry of the Interior made it all the more imperative that contact be made with the prefectural and communal administration authorities. The inference that Kalimanzira's driver came to seek him out to provide him with transport and that he undertook and performed administrative functions is inescapable.

116. On the issue of access to information, Kalimanzira and his wife testified that he was out of touch with ongoing governmental developments. On the stand, he was evasive about the purpose of the meeting to which he was summoned on 11 April, saying only that he learned about it through a radio announcement, whereas his wife claimed he had learned of it from Ngendahimana when he telephoned. Kalimanzira also purportedly learned from the announcement that the meeting was expected to be chaired by the Minister of the Interior, or, in the event of his absence, the Prime Minister.[111] The Chamber considers it unbelievable that Kalimanzira would have so inadvertently come to know of the 11 April meeting; he would most likely have been involved in the preparation of any meeting with all *préfets,* in particular one that was expected to be chaired by his Minister.

117. After moving his family to Butare on 12 April, Kalimanzira testified that he stayed behind in Kigali to continue his work, and then immediately contradicted himself by claiming that he had no work to do in the absence of his Minister, sitting idle while waiting for his return, and did not have a clue what was going on or what would happen.[112] The Chamber considers Kalimanzira to be feigning ignorance. In a time of such crisis, as *Directeur de Cabinet*, Kalimanzira would have had to be kept abreast of everything, particularly in the absence of his Minister. Even more unbelievable is Kalimanzira's account that he only came to learn of the government's transfer to Gitarama from his driver on the evening of 13 April. With the RPF quickly advancing on Kigali, the government moved to Gitarama on 12 April from the *Hôtel des Diplomates*, where just the day prior Kalimanzira had attended a meeting chaired by the Prime Minister. Kalimanzira testified that when he arrived in Murambi on 14 April, many government employees were already there,[113] having fled Kigali in a rush. Even if the Chamber were to accept his contention that the government's move to Gitarama was not planned but spontaneous and rushed,[114] Kalimanzira's intimation that he was one of the last persons to know about it is unconvincing.

14 April – 30 May

118. Kalimanzira's alibi defence for this period is supported by Defence Witness Marc Siniyobewe who testified that he was a staff member of the Ministry of the Interior and that after fleeing from Kigali to his home in Ruhengeri *préfecture,* he reported for duty in Murambi (Gitarama) on 18 April 1994. He said he met Kalimanzira that same day and every day thereafter until 30 May, except: (i) on 19 April when Kalimanzira went to Butare *préfecture*; and (ii) on 21 and 22 April when Kalimanzira went to Kibungo *préfecture*; (iii) sometime in May when Kalimanzira went to Gisenyi *préfecture*; and (iv) a few other days he might have

---

[109] T. 5 February 2009 pp. 6-7 (Salomé Mukantwali).
[110] T. 5 February 2009 p. 6 (Salomé Mukantwali); T. 29 January 2009 p. 36 (Witness AX100).
[111] T. 10 February 2009 p. 23 (Callixte Kalimanzira).
[112] T. 10 February 2009 p. 24 (Callixte Kalimanzira).
[113] T. 10 February 2009 p. 26 (Callixte Kalimanzira).
[114] T. 11 February 2009 p. 3 (Callixte Kalimanzira).

forgotten. He specified that he saw Kalimanzira on 23 April 1994 in the morning **[page 28]** and evening, but not during or just after lunch.[115] Siniyobewe is therefore Kalimanzira's chief alibi witness in respect of the Prosecution's allegation that he was at Kabuye hill on that day.

119. The Defence's sudden and belated introduction of such a specific alibi for what is the most important allegation against Kalimanzira strongly suggests rehearsal and tailoring to fit the Prosecution case. If he provided this alibi information to members of the Defence team in his earlier interviews, then the Defence should have disclosed it to the Prosecution; the failure to do so raises questions of when the idea to use Siniyobewe as an alibi witness was conceived and supports the inference of recent fabrication.

120. Siniyobewe came as a family friend of Kalimanzira, proclaiming his confirmation that Kalimanzira was innocent.[116] His evidence was unconvincing for several reasons. For instance, he testified that he never heard any ethnic stereotyping of, promoting contempt for, or calling for the extermination of Tutsis on the RTLM radio station.[117] At first he said that he could not recall ever having heard such incitement over the radio. However, when the Prosecution challenged him on how it could be possible to recall such specific dates 15 years after the fact but not radio broadcasts inciting hatred as early as October 1993,[118] he gave the unconvincing explanation that he could not possibly have been informed that hatred was being spewed over the radio because he did not take a radio to work or listen to it in his sleep. The Chamber notes that Siniyobewe was one of 42 persons to have founded the RTLM radio station in April 1993.[119] His feigned ignorance of the station's agenda and content therefore shows evasion and suggests bias.

121. Siniyobewe also had difficulty with dates in general, but was able to provide specific references to the dates of 19 to 23 April and the days immediately following when several witnesses testified that they saw Kalimanzira in the vicinity of Kabuye hill (see III.2.4). He professed to be able to recall the 23rd in particular because on that day, he noticed when he arrived to work as usual between 8:00-9:00 a.m. that Kalimanzira had already signed the lists for the payments of salaries that Siniyobewe had left in the office. He recalled not having seen Kalimanzira for lunch on that day, but saw him again in the evening.[120] Such precision in Siniyobewe's recollection of the events which unfolded on 23 April are unparalleled in his recollection of any other event, such as when Kalimanzira went on mission to Ngororero, which day Siniyobewe could not recall with any more precision than having been during the month of May, maybe even late April.[121]

122. This was also a feature of Kalimanzira's testimony as he testified that one of the major tasks he performed during the six-week period in Gitarama was supervising the preparation of those payment lists and signing them.[122] This aspect of both their testimonies was unconvincing. The evidence revealed that civil servants were paid by a completely different ministry and that their salaries were paid into bank accounts.[123] Kalimanzira testified at length and in detail about the administrative process by which civil servants and contract employees were paid, explaining that there existed a dual system whereby state employees under contract, such as daily workers and drivers, were paid from a separate **[page 29]** budget; he further indicated that this dual system prevented him from receiving his own salary.[124] His nearly exclusive fixation on describing the procedure for this insignificant task, requiring little more than his signature, highlights his evasion about his work and functions while in Gitarama. The idea that during a time of war Kalimanzira would be so preoccupied with ensuring that drivers, daily workers, and other "contract employees" were paid, while he did not receive his own salary, is unbelievable.

123. Kalimanzira's testimony about his stay and work in Gitarama was unreliable not only for its admissions but also for its omissions. For the most part, he only admitted to trips for which he had been provided with exhibits and transcripts of radio broadcasts establishing his presence somewhere. He asserted to being in

---

[115] T. 4 February 2009 pp. 17-25 (Marc Siniyobewe).
[116] T. 4 February 2009 pp. 54-55 (Marc Siniyobewe).
[117] T. 4 February 2009 pp. 49-52 (Marc Siniyobewe).
[118] Exhibit P78.
[119] T. 4 February 2009 pp. 50-52 (Marc Siniyobewe); Exhibit P77.
[120] T. 4 February 2009 p. 24 (Marc Siniyobewe).
[121] T. 4 February 2009 p. 25 (Marc Siniyobewe).
[122] T. 10 February 2009 pp. 32-33 (Callixte Kalimanzira).
[123] Exhibit P79.
[124] T. 10 February 2009 pp. 32-33 and T. 11 February 2009 pp. 12-15 (Callixte Kalimanzira).

Butare only one time in April and May 1994, namely at the MRND Palace Meeting, and vehemently denied Pauline Nyiramasuhuko's evidence in her own trial that Kalimanzira was present at a Prefectural Security Council meeting in Butare *ville* on 16 May 1994. However, when the Prosecution confronted him with a transcript of a radio broadcast undeniably placing him there, Kalimanzira confirmed that he attended the meeting and admitted the possibility that he may have forgotten about other events.[125]

124. Kalimanzira gave no information about his work in Gitarama with the government and Ministers and his evidence of how he spent his time there was evasive at best (see also III.1.1.2). He admitted that Édouard Karemera was appointed as the new Minister of the Interior on 25 May 1994 yet gave no information about any dealings with him. As *Directeur de Cabinet*, Kalimanzira would have either assumed those functions in relation to the new Minister or have been relieved of his duties. The absence of any explanation highlighted his evasion about his relationship with the political establishment.

125. Even more unsettling was Kalimanzira's feigned ignorance about the prevailing situation outside of Gitarama at the time. He gave an incredible story of having dispatched some aides on 24 April 1994 to go to neighbouring *communes* and investigate a rumour that a RPF *Inkotanyi* raid on Murambi was imminent. Upon their return that same evening, one of them informed Kalimanzira that some Tutsis had sought refuge in Mukingi *commune* and Kalimanzira immediately responded by working with the *préfet* to acquire buses and fuel in order to save to those refugees and bring them to Murambi.[126] This echoed Siniyobewe's testimony, albeit slightly different, that Kalimanzira was approached by the *bourgmestre* of Mukingi *commune* about Tutsi refugees on the brink of being killed, and that Kalimanzira responded immediately. Siniyobewe was tasked with providing the fuel but could not do so swiftly because he had "other tasks to attend to," which apparently angered Kalimanzira. When Siniyobewe could not provide the fuel in time, Kalimanzira scolded him for lack of diligence.[127] While attempting to depict Kalimanzira as a good samaritan, his perceived reasons for Kalimanzira's intervention to save those Tutsis seemed limited to the avoidance of liability for failure to act.[128]

126. The Chamber is disturbed with how this story trivializes the prevailing situation at the time, given the abundant evidence that over that same weekend thousands of Tutsis had been massacred at Kabuye hill and even more were being slaughtered in that same time period **[page 30]** throughout Butare and Rwanda, to Kalimanzira's purported total unawareness. His sole concern was fear of RPF infiltration, an obsession which he has demonstrated elsewhere, including his supposed reason for spending a sleepless night in Kibungo *préfecture* on 21 April and his reason for not stopping on the road when driving to his family's home in Kirarambogo in the first week of June.[129] The Chamber considers Kalimanzira's exhibited preoccupation lends support to the several Prosecution witnesses who have testified to his consistent calls on members of the population to erect roadblocks and to carry arms at all times (see *e.g.* III.2.7 and III.4.9).

127. With respect to his purported itinerary to and from Kibungo *préfecture,* evidence on the record shows that Kalimanzira was in Kibungo to commission the new *préfet* on 21 April 1994. However, he asserts that he did not return to Gitarama until the evening of the 22nd because he spent the night of the 21st in Kibungo, unable to sleep for fear of an imminent RPF raid on the town, but on guard and ready to flee in case they were attacked. Indeed, by Kalimanzira's own testimony, Kibungo fell to the RPF on 22 April, just hours after he purports to have left for Gitarama, and he considers himself lucky to have left the scene just in time.[130] Having been assigned two gendarmes to accompany him on this trip, it makes no sense that Kalimanzira would have waited until an already precarious situation became so dangerous that others started leaving before he or his protective escorts decided it was safe for him to leave. The Chamber does not believe that Kalimanzira spent the night of 21 April 1994 in Kibungo *préfecture*.

---

[125] T. 11 February 2009 pp. 20-24 (Callixte Kalimanzira).
[126] T. 10 February 2009 p. 43 (Callixte Kalimanzira).
[127] T. 4 February 2009 pp. 26-27, 55 (Marc Siniyobewe).
[128] See T. 4 February 2009 p. 55 (Marc Siniyobewe): "During that period, Kalimanzira acted with dispatch to get vehicles and he came to ask me to send buses to save those people so as to avoid anyone being killed at that place, because we would have difficulty explaining that."
[129] T. 10 February 2009 pp. 40-41, 49 (Callixte Kalimanzira).
[130] T. 10 February 2009 pp. 40-41 (Callixte Kalimanzira).

128. Kalimanzira testified that on 30 May 1994 the government fled Gitarama in a hurry and he was assigned the mission to manually fill all the authorities' cars with fuel equitably.[131] The Chamber considers this yet another manifestation of Kalimanzira's evasion about his role and functions while in Gitarama and a minimization of his status and authority. The Chamber does not accept that the *Directeur de Cabinet* of the Ministry of the Interior could be assigned such a task. Kalimanzira's depiction of himself as the humble and reliable servant leaves much to be desired in the absence of any further information about what other, more significant, tasks he must have been entrusted with during this critical period.

31 May – 17 July

129. Kalimanzira testified that he left Gitarama with his assigned vehicle and driver, Avit Mpabanyanga, having to take a detour through Gikongoro *préfecture* where they spent the night. Upon rejoining his family in Butare *ville* on 31 May 1994, Kalimanzira and his wife assert that except for three occasions, he did not leave his house or its immediate environs. His account of the first trip out in the first week of June to visit his family in Kirarambogo was strange. He took a road leaving Butare *ville* passing through Shyanda *commune*, Ndora *commune*, then Gisagara all the way to his home in Muganza *commune*. This was a road with which he was so familiar that he said he knew every family that lived on it. He testified that this trip marked the first time that he became aware of how much destruction and devastation had taken place, having by then heard killings had occurred in these *communes*. He said he continued on his journey without stopping for fear that he might be harmed and concerned about RPF infiltrations.[132] Bearing in mind this was his home area and that he admittedly knew all the local inhabitants, even greeting them as he drove by, the Chamber considers that the idea he would be afraid of them is not plausible. Kalimanzira's compulsive fears of RPF infiltration are particularly irrational in this context, which supports the Prosecution evidence **[page 31]** that he was aggressively preoccupied with ensuring that members of the population, in particular those manning roadblocks, be armed at all times.

130. Another peculiarity was Kalimanzira's mention of passing by to observe Charles Hategekimana's house, who he claimed to be a friend. He said he was saddened by Hategekimana's death, that people had accused him of the death and of destroying his house, whereas he knew nothing of it when passing by the house in June.[133] Upon reviewing this aspect of Kalimanzira's testimony, the Chamber sees no reason why he would go and look at that particular house at that time if he had not previously known about his killing. It seemed that the purpose of this testimony was to claim friendship and exhibit remorse over that particular killing, which witnesses have testified to in this case.[134]

131. Before visiting his family, Kalimanzira also said he stopped briefly in the Buseruka centre (Rwamiko *secteur*, Kibayi *commune*) to see the condition of his house there; this indirectly addresses certain allegations by other witnesses who testified to his presence and activities there at that time (see III.4.6.1 and III.4.8.1). He then went to Nyaguhuru *secteur* (Muganza *commune*) to find his mother, brothers and sisters were still alive, except his sister's Tutsi husband, who had been killed. Wanting to return back to his wife and children immediately in order to protect them from the imminent arrival of RPF troops, Kalimanzira stayed in Nyaguhuru only one hour, and drove back again without stopping, but waving at people along the way to say hello.[135]

132. Kalimanzira testified that in the weeks that followed, he left his house on only two more occasions. He said he had no contact with the government at this time, that he did not learn of their move to Gisenyi *préfecture* until mid-June, and that he only received information about how the war was unravelling from stepping out onto the road to ask passersby.[136] Once again, Kalimanzira's testimony of no contact with officialdom is unbelievable. He admittedly attended the swearing-in ceremony of Butare's new *préfet*,

---

[131] T. 10 February 2009 p. 47 (Callixte Kalimanzira).
[132] T. 10 February 2009 p. 49 (Callixte Kalimanzira).
[133] T. 10 February 2009 pp. 50-51 (Callixte Kalimanzira).
[134] See *e.g.* T. 24 June 2008 pp. 47-50 (Witness BCZ) and T. 24 November 2008 pp. 29-30 (Witness KXL); see also III.4.6.1.
[135] T. 10 February 2009 pp. 51-52 (Callixte Kalimanzira).
[136] T. 10 February 2009 p. 52 (Callixte Kalimanzira).

Judgement

Alphonse Nteziryayo, but neither he nor his wife gave any indication as to how he came to know about it.[137] Prosecution witnesses also placed him at the inauguration of Élie Ndayambaje as the new *bourgmestre* of Muganza *commune* (see III.2.3.6). Moreover, his appointment as Minister of Social Affairs and Refugees in the government in exile would have been unlikely if he simply fell off the radar for over a month.

133. Kalimanzira's wife supported his testimony on his activities in June. The Chamber finds her testimony has little probative value, not only because of her relationship with him, but because she was not always home as she testified that she was working at the Butare hospital where her services were required because all Tutsi doctors and nurses had been killed.[138]

Conclusion

134. The Chamber accepts that Kalimanzira was in Kigali in the days following the President's plane crash, that he relocated to Gitarama with the Interim Government, that he was at the MRND Palace meeting on 19 April, that he was in Kibungo *préfecture* on 21 **[page 32]** April, and that he went to Ngororero sometime in May. However, the Chamber does not accept that he was in Gitarama at all other times. Indeed, he was caught having lied about attending a Butare Prefectural Security Council meeting on 16 May 1994. He had access to vehicles and fuel. In particular, the Chamber considers his and Siniyobewe's account of his presence in Murambi on 23 April to be a recent fabrication. It therefore raises no reasonable doubt on the witnesses who testified to seeing him at Kabuye hill or elsewhere throughout Butare between April and May 1994.

135. The same finding applies for the period in which Kalimanzira says he stayed at his home in Butare *ville* save for three occasions. The Chamber accepts that Kalimanzira went home to see his family in Kirarambogo in the first week of June, that he attended Nteziryayo's swearing-in ceremony, and that he went to welcome Cardinal Etchegaray. However, the Chamber does not accept that he stayed at home at all other times. Indeed, after being shown a Radio Rwanda broadcast transcript, he could no longer deny having attended a civil defence and security meeting in Gikongoro *préfecture* on 3 June 1994.[139] He also admitted to the possibility that he may have forgotten about other occasions when he might have left his house during this period.[140]

136. For the above reasons, the Chamber does not believe Kalimanzira's alibi. The Chamber recalls that the Prosecution nevertheless retains the onus of having to prove its case beyond reasonable doubt.

1.3. Fabrication of Evidence

137. Part of the Defence case was premised on an alleged system and practice in Rwandan prisons of fabricating evidence. This was aimed at discrediting much of the Prosecution evidence in relation to certain events, in order to support the Defence theory that accusations against Kalimanzira are false.[141]

1.3.1. Evidence

Defence Witness Albert Barikwinshi

138. Barikwinshi is a former detainee of the Karubanda prison. He testified about an association called "*Ukuri*" (which means "truth" in Kinyarwanda), which has the primary goal of inducing detainees to confess to their crimes. This organization was well known to prison officials and other authorities, even occupying an office near the prison director's, and was well organised with a President, François Buhoyiki, and a Vice-

---

[137] T. 10 February 2009 p. 52 (Callixte Kalimanzira); T. 5 February 2009 p. 10 (Salomé Mukantwali).
[138] T. 5 February 2009 p. 11 (Salomé Mukantwali).
[139] T. 11 February 2009 p. 31 (Callixte Kalimanzira).
[140] T. 11 February 2009 p. 26 (Callixte Kalimanzira).
[141] See *e.g.* Defence Pre-Trial Brief, para. 17 and Defence Closing Brief, paras. 327, 349, 389, 425-426, 575, 604, 739, 838, 937, 974, 1086, 1220-1221, and 1286.

377

President, Nkuyubwatsi. The association would also be contacted by the Rwandan Prosecutor's Office whenever information was required.[142]

139. Barikwinshi was a member of the *Ukuri* association from 2000 to 2007, apart from periods when he was provisionally released or in camps. From 2000 to 2003 he was a "floor member" without special duties. In 2003 he was put in charge of convincing people from his native *commune*, Gishamvu, to confess. Barikwinshi asked President Buhoyiki for a position in the association because prisoners with jobs received better food rations. Barikwinshi would, with the approval of President Buhoyiki, to whom he reported, convene meetings of people from Gishamvu *commune* on the volleyball field inside the Rwandex block in the [page 33] Karubanda prison. Barikwinshi would contact people in prison and encourage them to confess. He would also identify those who were discouraging people from confessing.[143]

140. Barikwinshi named Lucien Simbayobewe, Ignace Yirirwahandi, Deo Nuwayo (a.k.a Kigango), Jérôme Singirankabo (a.k.a Rutwitsi), and Chrysologue Bimenyimana as officials of the *Ukuri* association who encouraged their fellow co-detainees to plead guilty and confess to their crimes, and assisted the Rwandan Prosecutor's Office with identifying prisoners charged with certain crimes committed in a given *commune* or *secteur*. With regards to guilty pleas, the *Ukuri* association also assisted the Prosecutor's Office by forwarding them the outcomes of any meetings and reports. The Rwandan Prosecutor's Office would then instruct President Buhoyiki on how to proceed, who in turn would pass this information onto the other *Ukuri* members. Detainees would write their confessions and the documents would be sent to the Rwandan Prosecutor's Office before being forwarded to the *Gacaca* courts.[144]

141. When attempting to elicit a confession, Barikwinshi would first contact and question a co-detainee. He would then explain the advantages of making a confession and when the detainee agreed to do so, the detainee would approach the *Ukuri* association to gain membership in it and receive assistance with drafting the confession. Sometimes there were authorities detained in the prison who did not confess, despite having instigated others to commit crimes. If the *Ukuri* association failed to persuade these authorities from confessing, a confession on their behalf would sometimes be fabricated and they would be indicted before the prison authorities. President Buhoyiki would then contact the Prosecutor's Office to advise on how to charge or indict the official. An *Ukuri* member from the official's *commune* would be identified to fabricate charges and testify against the official, claiming such things as the official had led an attack or organised a meeting.[145]

142. When fabricating charges, members of a particular *commune* would meet around a table and discuss their authorities before deciding how to implicate them. President Buhoyiki would then listen to the fabricated charges and, if unsatisfactory, would instruct them on what they should say instead. Barikwinshi attended such meetings. In May 2000, he overheard a conversation between Singirankabo and Simbayobewe discussing Muganza *commune* and Kalimanzira. Singirankabo proclaimed that he had to implicate Kalimanzira in order to lend credibility to his own confession so that it would be accepted. He then asked Simbayobewe how he was supposed to accuse Kalimanzira when he did not know him well and did not see him during the genocide. Simbayobewe advised Singirankabo to ask Yirirwahandi how he did it, implying that Yirirwahandi had fabricated charges against Kalimanzira.[146]

143. Aside from this conversation, Barikwinshi did not hear any other discussions about falsely accusing Kalimanzira. He recalled, however, that on one occasion at the end of a meeting, a woman from the Prosecutor's Office asked President Buhoyiki if he had witnesses ready to accuse Kalimanzira. President Buhoyiki replied that everything had been arranged and the witnesses were ready. However, Barikwinshi did not hear the woman say that the accusations against Kalimanzira were to be false.[147]

144. Barikwinshi indicated that President Buhoyiki advised him to testify against the authorities of his own *commune* if he wanted his guilty plea to be accepted. He also asked Barikwinshi to testify against

---

[142] T. 26 January 2009 pp. 60-61 (Albert Barikwinshi).
[143] T. 26 January 2009 pp. 60-61 and T. 27 January 2009 p. 3 (Albert Barikwinshi).
[144] T. 27 January 2009 p. 2 (Albert Barikwinshi).
[145] T. 27 January 2009 pp. 3-4 (Albert Barikwinshi).
[146] T. 27 January 2008 pp. 4-6 (Albert Barikwinshi).
[147] T. 27 January 2009 p. 7 (Albert Barikwinshi).

Joseph Kanyabashi, but Barikwinshi declined because he had **[page 34]** no accusations to make against him. President Buhoyiki then advised Barikwinshi to make false accusations against Kanyabashi, indicating that other detainees, including himself, had done so and that he must therefore accept it. Barikwinshi explained that there were three main advantages for people willing to fabricate testimony. Firstly, their confession would be accepted. Secondly, the *Ukuri* would have confidence in them and they would get a position within the association. Lastly, they might get to testify in Arusha where they would receive money and clothes. Barikwinshi does not know whether there was an advantage with regards to early release from detention.[148]

145. The *Ukuri* association distributed positions of responsibility within the prison, and Barikwinshi gave several examples of *Ukuri* members receiving coveted positions. Simbayobewe was in charge of security for the Rwandex block, making him second in command.[149] Nuwayo received a position leading detainees out of the prison on work duty, where they would often receive rice. Singirankabo had security duties and worked under the *commissaire*. Yirirwahandi was in charge of supplies, but then joined the Pentecostal Church and decided to leave the *Ukuri* after asking forgiveness from all those he had falsely accused. Bimenyimana was promoted to leader of the Rwandex block's kitchen. Barikwinshi heard that Bimenyimana has testified in Arusha and Barikwinshi believes that to be the reason behind Bimenyimana's promotion.[150]

Defence Witness Jean de Dieu Rutabana

146. Rutabana testified that he spent 11 years in prison in Rwanda before he escaped and fled to Burundi. He spent several years in the Karubanda prison and the Rwandex block. At one point, someone from the Prosecutor's Office approached Rutabana and others from his native *commune*, Mpare. Rutabana indicated that the deputy prosecutor in question gave the prisoners food and asked them to assist the Prosecutor's Office by testifying that Joseph Kanyabashi, also a native of Mpare *commune*, had come to their *commune* and asked the inhabitants to kill people and erect roadblocks. After the prisoners refused, indicating they had not seen Kanyabashi in Mpare during the events, the deputy prosecutor told them to think it over, that they could benefit from going to Arusha, and to go back to see him if they changed their minds about testifying against Kanyabashi. Rutabana was not questioned about any efforts to falsely accuse Kalimanzira.[151]

147. Rutabana testified that though he never joined the *Ukuri* assocation, he knew it consisted of a group of people who provided information to the *Gacaca* jurisdictions, which were organzised according to *communes*, through the Rwandan Prosecutor's Office. He indicated that the *Ukuri* association had its own office in the prison, which he never visited as it was not open for people to simply come in as they pleased.[152]

Defence Witness FJS

148. FJS testified that soon after she returned to Rwanda after having been in exile, she was arrested and "asked to go and accuse certain people". When she indicated that she could not provide the information sought, she was "beaten up and thrown into prison", where she was detained for six years before being released without having been charged or tried. FJS **[page 35]** was not examined further on this point; the Chamber infers that she was not asked to accuse Kalimanzira.[153]

Defence Witness Félicien Kajyibwami

149. Kajyibwami testified that he was encouraged to work with a commission investigating France's responsibility in the genocide by testifying to what he witnessed in July 1994 while staying at a camp in the French-guarded "Zone Turquoise". He was asked to accuse French soldiers of acts such as raping survivors, playing basketball on the remains of the dead, and giving food rations to Hutus but not to Tutsis. When

---

[148] T. 27 January 2009 pp. 7-8 (Albert Barikwinshi).
[149] Defence Witness Jean de Dieu Rutabana also testified that Lucien Simbayobewe was in charge of security in one of the blocks at Karubanda prison (see T. 3 February 2009 p. 11).
[150] T. 27 January 2009 pp. 8-11 (Albert Barikwinshi).
[151] T. 3 February 2009 pp. 11-14 (Jean de Dieu Rutabana).
[152] T. 3 February 2009 p. 11 (Jean de Dieu Rutabana).
[153] T. 28 January 2009 p. 43 [closed] (Witness FJS).

Kajyibwami refused, indicating he had not witnessed such acts, he was arrested and declared an enemy of the State. He managed to escape and fled to Malawi. He mentioned nothing about fabricating evidence against Kalimanzira.[154]

1.3.2. Deliberations

150. The Chamber notes that several Defence witnesses are or have been in detention in Rwanda.[155] Only four of them have testified about having been invited to falsely implicate others, with Barikwinshi the sole witness to testify about evidence fabrication against Kalimanzira.

151. Barikwinshi was in detention for many years, having been charged with participation in the genocide. On the one hand, he averred that he had done nothing wrong, but decided to confess in order to obtain early release and used the information he received from other detainees to fabricate his own confession. On the other hand, he testified about having participated in the search for Tutsis at the Arboretum near the Rwandan National University in Butare (see III.2.3.4.1). Barikwinshi asserts that he did not falsely accuse anyone, that he only lied about his own actions in order to get out of prison, but refuses to say he signed a judicial document that he knew was false for personal advantage.[156] Further, he testified that in order to obtain a privileged position in the prison, he had assisted other detainees in fabricating charges against others. Shortly after his release from prison, the *Gacaca* courts determined his confession to have been fabricated and he was re-arrested. Barikwinhi eventually managed to flee Rwanda. He remains a fugitive from justice.[157] The Chamber considers that this witness' demonstrably flexible attitude to telling the truth casts reasonable doubt on the credibility and reliability of his own testimony.

152. When asked for specific examples of other officials against whom charges were fabricated under the framework he described, Barikwinshi recounted two examples which amounted to little more than internal prison intrigues, whereby certain co-detainees were falsely accused of such things as trying to escape from jail so that these co-detainees could lose their coveted prison jobs.[158] Barikwinshi also alleged that he was approached to fabricate charges against Kanyabashi, but claims he declined because he had no allegations to make. His assertion does not fit with and contradicts the rest of his testimony. If he was willing to persuade co-detainees to fabricate charges against others, it does not follow that he would not be willing or persuaded to do so himself. In addition, if he obtained a privileged position in **[page 36]** prison by assuming the task of persuading others to fabricate charges, it does not follow that he could maintain that position after having refused to do so himself.

153. Barikwinshi's testimony about the method by which prisoners from the same *commune* of a certain official would be summoned to fabricate charges against that official does not explain why charges would be fabricated against Kalimanzira, a native of Muganza *commune*, by Singirankabo, Simbayobewe, or Yirirwahandi, none of whom come from Muganza *commune*. Though Kalimanzira resided in Kibayi *commune* for some time, only one of the three aforementioned prisoners was a native of Kibayi. None of the prisoners came from Gishamvu *commune* either, Barikwinshi's native *commune*, which raises the question as to why Barikwinshi came to attend the meeting where falsely accusing Kalimanzira was discussed. Barikwinshi did not adequately explain this discrepancy with his prior testimony about the way in which the *Ukuri* association functioned.

154. In addition, by Barikwinshi's own description, gathering evidence to be used in Arusha was not a primary concern of the *Ukuri* association.[159] The meeting allegedly took place in May 2000, which is over five years before Kalimanzira was indicted by this Tribunal. The Defence has tendered into evidence various lists of suspected *génocidaires* omitting Kalimanzira's name to support the contention that he was never

---

[154] T. 2 February 2009 pp. 26-28 (Félicien Kajyibwami).
[155] *E.g.* AK42, AM02, AM14, BTH, FJS, KBF, KUW, KXC, MAS, MVE, NDA, NGB, NJV, ABZ, Harindintwali, Kajyibwami, and Barikwinshi.
[156] T. 27 January 2009 p. 30 (Albert Barikwinshi).
[157] T. 26 January 2009 pp. 55-56 (Albert Barikwinshi).
[158] T. 27 January 2009 p. 5 (Albert Barikwinshi).
[159] T. 27 January 2009 p. 5 (Albert Barikwinshi).

Judgement

suspected or pursued in Rwanda either.[160] This raises the question as to why Kalimanzira would be discussed by the *Ukuri* at all, particularly nine years ago.

155. Barikwinshi's attempts to explain these discrepancies were unsatisfactory. He mentioned the meeting having been in the context of Muganza *commune*, but that the reason for discussing Kalimanzira was because Singirankabo was accused of crimes committed at Kabuye hill and was required to implicate Kalimanzira despite not having seen him at Kabuye hill. However, Kabuye hill is in Ndora *commune,* and neither Singirankabo, Simbayobewe, or Yirirwahandi, have testified before this Tribunal about Kalimanzira's involvement in the killings at Kabuye hill.

156. It does not follow from Barikwinshi's evidence that any Prosecution witnesses have made *false* accusations against Kalimanzira before this Tribunal. Whether or not any false accusations may have been doctored against Kalimanzira in Rwanda in the context of other *Gacaca* trials is irrelevant to the present case. It is noteworthy that the Defence never put any questions about the *Ukuri* association to any of the Prosecution witnesses during cross-examination, some of whom have been detained in the same Karubanda prison. The Chamber therefore considers that Barikwinshi's testimony does not affect the credibility of any of the Prosecution witnesses heard in this case. **[page 37]**

2. GENOCIDE

157. Under Count 1 of the Indictment, the Prosecution charges Kalimanzira with Genocide pursuant to Article 2 (3)(a) of the Statute, and with individual criminal responsibility under Article 6 (1). To establish Kalimanzira's criminal responsibility for Genocide, the Prosecution relies on paragraphs 1 to 17 of the Indictment.

2.1. Applicable Law

158. To find an accused guilty of the crime of genocide, it must be established that he committed any of the enumerated acts in Article 2 (2) with the specific intent to destroy, in whole or in part, a group, as such, that is defined by one of the protected categories of nationality, race, ethnicity, or religion ("genocidal intent"). Although there is no numeric threshold, the perpetrator must act with the intent to destroy at least a substantial part of the group. The perpetrator need not be solely motivated by a criminal intent to commit genocide, nor does the existence of personal motive preclude him from having the specific intent to commit genocide.[161] The law applicable to genocidal intent is discussed in full at III.5.1.

159. The Indictment charges Kalimanzira with killing and causing serious bodily or mental harm to members of the Tutsi group. It is firmly established that the Tutsi ethnicity is a protected group.[162] Killing members of the group requires a showing that the principal perpetrator intentionally killed one or more members of the group. The term "causing serious bodily harm" refers to acts of sexual violence, serious acts of physical violence falling short of killing that seriously injure the health, cause disfigurement, or cause any serious injury to the external or internal organs or senses. "Serious mental harm" refers to more than minor or temporary impairment of mental faculties. The serious bodily or mental harm, however, need not be an injury that is permanent or irremediable. This harm can include crimes of sexual violence, including rape.[163]

---

[160] See Exhibits D98, D99, and D100.
[161] *Bagosora et al.* Trial Judgement, para. 2115; *Nahimana et al.* Appeal Judgement, para. 492, 496, 522-523; *Niyitegeka* Appeal Judgement, paras. 48-54; *Gacumbitsi* Appeal Judgement, paras. 39, 44; *Brđanin* Trial Judgement, paras. 681, 695; *Seromba* Appeal Judgement, para. 175; *Simba* Trial Judgement, para. 412; *Semanza* Trial Judgement, para. 316; *Simba* Appeal Judgement, para. 269; *Ntakirutimana* Appeal Judgement, paras. 302-304; *Krnojelac* Appeal Judgement, para. 102, citing *Jelisić* Appeal Judgement, para. 49.
[162] *The Prosecutor v. Kalimanzira,* Decision on Judicial Notice of Facts of Common Knowledge (TC), 22 February 2008; *The Prosecutor v. Karemera et al.,* Decision on Prosecutor's Interlocutory Appeal of Decision on Judicial Notice (AC), 16 June 2006, para. 25.
[163] *Bagosora et al.* Trial Judgement, para. 2117; *Semanza* Appeal Judgement, para. 192; *Kayishema and Ruzindana* Appeal Judgement, paras. 110, 151; *Seromba* Appeal Judgement, paras. 46-49; *Ntagerura et al.* Trial Judgement, para. 664; *Kajelijeli* Trial Judgement para. 815; *Ntagerura et al.* Trial Judgement, para. 664; *Semanza* Trial Judgement, paras. 321-322; *Gacumbitsi* Trial Judgement, para. 292; *Akayesu* Trial Judgement, paras. 706-707.

160. In relation to Count 1, the Indictment recites all of the modes of participation prescribed at Article 6 (1) of the Statute, namely that Kalimanzira "planned, instigated, ordered, committed or otherwise aided and abetted in the planning, preparation or commission of the crimes." In addition, the Indictment alleges that Kalimanzira used his position of authority to incite and order persons under his authority to commit genocide.[164]

161. "Committing" implies, primarily, physically perpetrating a crime. "Planning" implies designing the preparation and execution of a crime. "Instigating" implies prompting or provoking another to commit a crime. With respect to ordering, a person in a position of authority may incur responsibility for ordering another person to commit an offence, if the person who received the order actually proceeds to commit the offence subsequently. "Aiding **[page 38]** and abetting" implies assisting, furthering or lending moral support to the perpetration of a crime. Thus, even if Kalimanzira has not "committed" genocide himself, his responsibility may be established under any one of the modes of liability provided for in Article 6 (1). The *mens rea* varies accordingly. Where an accused is charged with having planned, instigated, ordered or aided and abetted the commission of genocide pursuant to Article 6 (1), the Prosecution must establish that the accused's acts or omissions substantially contributed to the commission of acts of genocide. In addition, for liability of aiding and abetting to attach, the individual charged need only possess knowledge of the principal perpetrator's specific genocidal intent, whereas for planning, instigating and ordering, he must share that intent.[165]

2.2. "MRND Palace" Meeting, 19 April

162. At paragraph 7 of the Indictment, the Prosecution charges Kalimanzira with Genocide for his role as master of ceremonies at a meeting of Interim Government officials and local authorities held at the "MRND Palace" in Butare *ville* on 19 April 1994. Kalimanzira is accused of aiding and abetting genocide by showing no disapproval to inflammatory speeches delivered at this meeting, which triggered the subsequent massacre of thousands of Tutsi throughout Butare *préfecture*.

163. Kalimanzira admits to his presence at this meeting but denies playing the role alleged.

2.2.1. Evidence

Prosecution Witness AZM

164. AZM attended a meeting at the "MRND Palace" in Butare *ville* on 19 April 1994, the purpose of which was to replace the *préfet* of Butare, Jean-Baptiste Habyalimana (a Tutsi), with Sylvain Nsabimana (a Hutu). By virtue of his professional position, AZM was invited to the meeting by the public prosecutor, Mathias Bushishi. AZM arrived a little late to the meeting, which started at around 10:00 a.m. He recalled that the hall was almost full with around 300 people in attendance, including Butare's chiefs of services, leaders of political parties, religious leaders, *bourgmestres* of various *communes*, and military officers. Dignitaries present included the Prime Minister, Minister of Information, Minister of Justice, Minister of Finance, and Kalimanzira. Théodore Sindikubwabo (Interim President of Rwanda) made a surprise appearance towards the end of the ceremony at around 2:00 p.m. AZM explained that the Minister of the Interior was out of the country and therefore not in attendance.[166]

165. Those leading the meeting, including the Prime Minister and Kalimanzira, sat on the podium at the front of the hall. Kalimanzira was "in a way" the master of ceremonies and introduced each speaker to the audience before giving them the floor. The audience applauded between speakers, which included Eliézer Niyitegeka (Minister of Information). AZM recalled Jean Kambanda's (Prime Minister) speech, which emphasized that this was the last war, that victory was absolutely necessary, and that they needed to fight "to ensure the security of the country and avoid a situation where the country would be divided or taken over by

---

[164] See Indictment, paras. 2 and 6.
[165] *Nahimana et al.* Appeal Judgement, para. 478-483, 492; *Seromba* Appeal Judgement, para. 65; *Kordić and Čerkez* Appeal Judgement, para. 26; *Krstić* Appeal Judgement, para. 140.
[166] T. 17 June 2008 pp. 5-7 (Witness AZM).

the enemy". Prime Minister Kambanda also said that "there were people who were working against the security of the country", and that "those people should be sought and dealt with".[167] **[page 39]**

166. AZM recalled President Sindikubwabo spoke in a metaphorical manner that was very difficult to understand. He told the crowd that he had just returned from Gikongoro *préfecture* and noticed that, in comparison, many in Butare were indifferent to the current situation. He said that someone had "asked him if there were no men in Butare", to which he answered that there were none because those remaining were only looking out for their own interests, "their own stomachs". President Sindikubwabo stated that there were people receiving weapons training by the RPF in Kinihira and that they should be sought out and "handed over". He further indicated that the authorities who were unwilling to collaborate with him should be removed, and that only those who were ready to work should be put in their places. The President used the Kinyarwanda word "*gukora*" for work, which AZM eventually understood meant killing Tutsis, though that was not immediately clear to him at the time of the President's utterance.[168]

167. At no point during the meeting did he hear Kalimanzira object to what was being said. Kalimanzira did not address the meeting nor take the floor to approve or disapprove of what was being said. AZM recalled that the meeting ended at around 3:30 p.m., at which point he returned home. After the meeting, Hutus started killing Tutsis.[169]

Prosecution Witness BCA

168. BCA attended a meeting at the "MRND Palace" in Butare *ville* on 19 April 1994, to which he was invited by virtue of his professional position. The meeting, which started around 10:00 a.m. and ended around 3:00 p.m., was held in a hall which could hold about 1,000 people. There were over 100 people present, including President Sindikubwabo, Prime Minister Kambanda, "all the ministers, including Nyiramasuhuko, Niyitegeka, Nsabumukunzi", *bourgmestres,* Butare's chiefs of services, and Kalimanzira. BCA recalled those who spoke at the meeting included President Sindikubwabo, Prime Minister Kambanda, Minister Niyitegeka, and Joseph Kanyabashi (*bourgmestre* of Ngoma *commune*). Kalimanzira acted as the master of ceremonies.[170]

169. With respect to Prime Minister Kambanda's speech, BCA could recall only that he reminded the audience that the enemy of the Rwandan government was the RPF. BCA had a better memory of President Sindikubwabo's speech, in which he condemned the inhabitants of Butare for their indifference and apathy towards the war against the RPF. BCA also recalled the President mentioning some people undergoing weapons training in Kinihira, and the need to "get rid of those people".[171]

170. The Prosecution specifically asked whether the President used the word "*gukora*", to which BCA answered in the affirmative and explained its ordinary meaning to be that "one has work to do". BCA explained that at the time of the meeting, he did not understand the word to have any special significance; however, following the subsequent massacres he realised that it was a metaphor for killing the RPF and its accomplices. The accomplices were mainly Tutsis, but also included Hutu political opponents. The killings in Butare *préfecture* started on 20 April 1994; he personally witnessed people being killed at the junction right after the MRND Palace where the meeting took place the day prior.[172] **[page 40]**

Callixte Kalimanzira

171. Kalimanzira admits he attended the meeting at the "MRND Palace" in Butare *ville* on 19 April 1994, but denies having been the master of ceremonies. He testified that he travelled to the meeting in a convoy of ministers that left Murambi (Gitarama *préfecture*) at 9:00 a.m. and arrived at the MRND Palace at approximately 10:40 a.m. The meeting, which was to be Sylvain Nsabimana's swearing-in ceremony as the

---

[167] T. 17 June 2008 pp. 7-8 (Witness AZM).
[168] T. 17 June 2008 pp. 8-9 (Witness AZM).
[169] T. 17 June 2008 p. 10 (Witness AZM).
[170] T. 18 June 2008 pp. 46-47 (Witness BCA).
[171] T. 18 June 2008 p. 47 (Witness BCA).
[172] T. 18 June 2008 pp. 48-49 (Witness BCA).

new *préfet* of Butare, was not open to the public but to a certain political class. Those present included Butare's chiefs of services, *bourgmestres, conseillers*, religious authorities, schoolteachers, and ministers' entourages. He estimated that there were just over 100 persons in attendance.[173]

172. The meeting was impromptu; it was only announced over the radio on 18 April 1994, which did not leave the Butare prefectural authorities enough time to make necessary arrangements. His reason for attending the meeting was therefore to assist with organizing it and receiving guests. This was necessary for two reasons. Firstly, the Butare prefectural authorities were not familiar with all of the newly appointed Interim Government officials, including the new Prime Minister. Kalimanzira explained that it was customary in Butare for VIPs to be received by the prefectural authorities; since he was a native of Butare and also knew the officials coming from Murambi, he assisted. Secondly, because it was a time of war and there had already been attacks in Butare *ville*, security was an issue.[174]

173. The meeting was chaired by the Prime Minister. Guests arrived as early as 10:30 a.m., but the meeting did not start until midday because of the President's late arrival. Kalimanzira testified that in practical terms, his tasks were limited to those of a protocol and security officer. He assisted the ministers he knew with finding their seats on a podium facing the other dignitaries and the public. Then he returned to the hall's entrance to assist latecomers and those who wished to leave or go to the bathroom, and to prevent the entry of unknown civilians. Kalimanzira asserted that he did not speak, nor did he take a seat for the duration of the three-hour meeting. He insisted that he did not act as the master of ceremonies; rather, it was the Prime Minister who assumed the role of introducing and giving the floor to speakers.[175]

174. Kalimanzira heard Prime Minister Kambanda's and President Sindikubwabo's speeches, but could not follow them closely because he was preoccupied with incoming and outgoing guests. He could not remember who spoke first. He recalled that the Prime Minister spoke about the prevailing situation, describing how the current government was formed, talking about the war and different fighting zones in Kigali, and urging citizens to be cautious. He was already aware of much of this information. With respect to the President's speech, Kalimanzira recalled simply that he gave advice and instructions to the *préfets*, and gave the impression that he had not prepared his speech in advance.[176]

175. Kalimanzira said he did not interpret the speeches as a signal to trigger massacres in the Butare area. He recalled that after the meeting there was a reception at which the guests chatted. He explained that he did not consider the information conveyed at the meeting to be new, special, or unfamiliar, and he did not hear anyone incite anyone else to kill; rather, what he understood at the time was that the speeches were urging members of the population not to kill their neighbours and to stop massacres. However, some people may have believed that **[page 41]** other things were said given the prevailing situation. He returned to Murambi with the ministers he had arrived with, stopping briefly to visit his wife and children on the way.[177]

2.2.2. Deliberations

176. Both AZM and BCA are detainees in the same prison, awaiting their final judgements after having confessed to their participation in the genocidal acts that were allegedly triggered by the speeches given at this meeting. They may therefore have a motive to falsely accuse Kalimanzira. However, that does not *per se* make their testimony unreliable. The Chamber did not hear whether they have in fact accused Kalimanzira in their guilty confessions.

177. AZM's testimony concerning the MRND Palace meeting is confirmed by Kalimanzira's testimony on all uncontested points. On the contested point as to Kalimanzira's role at the meeting, AZM's testimony that Kalimanzira was "in a way" the master of ceremonies is not accusatory in nature: "He wasn't doing anything in particular, apart from indicating those people who had to take the floor. And whenever he indicated one

---

[173] T. 10 February 2009 pp. 34-35 (Callixte Kalimanzira).
[174] T. 10 February 2009 pp. 35-36 (Callixte Kalimanzira).
[175] T. 10 February 2009 pp. 36-37 and T. 11 February 2009 pp. 5-6 (Callixte Kalimanzira).
[176] T. 10 February 2009 pp. 37-38 and T. 11 February 2009 p. 5 (Callixte Kalimanzira).
[177] T. 10 February 2009 p. 38 and T. 11 February p. 7 (Callixte Kalimanzira).

person, he would give him the microphone".[178] BCA testified that Kalimanzira was the master of ceremonies, but was not examined further on this. His remaining testimony is moderate in nature with respect to Kalimanzira. BCA's testimony on other events, such as Kalimanzira's involvement in an archery training exercise in Muganza *commune* (see III.2.8), is equally moderate. Further, AZM's and BCA's participation in the meeting, whatever the role of Kalimanzira, is unlikely to give rise to criminal charges against them.

178. The Chamber therefore finds no indication that AZM or BCA had motives to falsely accuse Kalimanzira in respect of his role at the MRND Palace meeting.

179. Kalimanzira's testimony, on the other hand, was evasive on the contested points. As to his role at the meeting, he testified that a master of ceremonies is someone who gives the floor to speakers at weddings, not at meetings bringing together authorities.[179] However, under cross-examination, he stated that Prime Minister Kambanda was the one who gave the floor to the speakers and relies on documentary evidence to support his statement.[180] Prime Minister Kambanda's speech, which was admitted into evidence,[181] indicates that he introduced President Sindikubwabo and the cabinet Ministers, but does not indicate whether he had been given the floor by somebody else or consecutively gave the floor to others.

180. Further, Kalimanzira's claim that he could not have been the master of ceremonies and could not focus on what the speakers said because he was preoccupied with receiving dignitaries at the entrance and ensuring that no uninvited persons would enter the hall is unbelievable. He may have received dignitaries at the door, but that did not prevent him from giving an extensive account of Prime Minister Kambanda's speech, the possible inflammatory nature of which the Prosecution does not make an issue.[182] He claimed that he did not pay attention to President Sindikubwabo's allegedly inflammatory speech, although the President arrived late, when there would have been no more dignitaries to receive and to distract him from paying attention. As to checking whether unauthorized persons entered the hall, it is unlikely that the Butare prefectural staff would require Kalimanzira's assistance to identify local leaders. **[page 42]**

181. The Chamber finds that AZM's testimony, as supported by BCA, constitutes reliable evidence that Kalimanzira, without otherwise addressing the meeting, did announce the name of the next speaker and handed him the microphone. The evidence is in conformity with the submission of the Defence in its Pre-Trial Brief that the master of ceremonies "strictly performed protocol duties and exercised no censorship over the content of the speeches made."[183]

182. It is undisputed that in Kambanda's guilty plea, which was read onto the record,[184] the former Prime Minister accepted criminal responsibility for genocidal effects of President Sindikubwabo's speech at the MRND Palace meeting on 19 April 1994. However, the Chamber notes that in Kalimanzira's case, the evidence as a whole does not establish that he could have lent moral support or political credibility in any significant way to Sindikubwabo's speech in the particular circumstances of this meeting. As a civil servant, Kalimanzira was subordinate to the President and the Prime Minister; any authority or influence he may have possessed in the view of the audience paled in comparison to that of the President and the Prime Minister. The evidence concerning his limited participation in the meeting and the fact that he was not introduced by Prime Minister Kambanda, unlike President Sindikubwabo and the cabinet Ministers, also evinces the relative lack of significance of his political standing in this context. Although Kalimanzira was well-respected in Butare, the President and Prime Minister were also natives of Butare and thus would have gained little from Kalimanzira's endorsement or support in this regard.

183. For these reasons, Kalimanzira's presence during the speeches or his failure to object to any portions thereof could not have substantially contributed to the commission of any of the crimes alleged to have resulted from these speeches. The Chamber therefore finds that no criminal responsibility may attach to Kalimanzira for his role at the MRND Palace meeting on 19 April 1994.

---

[178] T. 17 June 2008 p. 7 (Witness AZM).
[179] T. 10 February 2009 p. 36 (Callixte Kalimanzira).
[180] T. 11 February 2009 p. 6 (Callixte Kalimanzira).
[181] See Exhibit D114.
[182] T. 20 April 2009 pp. 54-55 (Closing Arguments).
[183] Defence Pre-Trial Brief, para. 15.
[184] T. 11 February 2009 pp. 8-9 (Callixte Kalimanzira).

2.3. Other Meetings and Visits to Butare, April to mid-July

184. At paragraph 8 of the Indictment, the Prosecution charges Kalimanzira with Genocide for visiting Butare *préfecture* on several occasions between April and mid-July 1994, together with senior Interim Government dignitaries, including Théodore Sindikubwabo, Jean Kambanda, and Pauline Nyiramasuhuko, as well as senior local government officials such as Alphonse Nteziryayo, and high-ranking RAF officers such as Tharcisse Muvunyi. The purpose of these visits was to sensitize the population to the Government's policy and incite the population to kill Tutsis. Thousands of Tutsis were allegedly killed throughout Butare as a result of these visits.

185. In its Closing Brief, the Prosecution relies on the evidence of six witnesses who testified regarding five separate events to support this allegation, namely:

  i. AZM testified that Kalimanzira attended several meetings of the Butare Prefectural Security Council in April and May 1994, during which the massacres of Tutsis, the distribution of Tutsi property and the implementation of a civil defence programme were discussed. Kalimanzira also participated in a tour of Mugusa and Kibayi *communes* with the Security Council, in which he told the local population to destroy the houses of dead Tutsis; **[page 43]**

  ii. BWI testified regarding Kalimanzira's presence at a public security meeting at the football field close to the Muganza *commune* office at the end of April or early May 1994 where Kalimanzira instructed the crowd to kill Tutsis;

  iii. FAC testified about Kalimanzira's presence at a public rally next to the cemetery near the Rwandan National University in Butare in late May or June 1994 where Kalimanzira instructed the crowd to search for Tutsis in hiding and kill them;

  iv. AZT testified that Kalimanzira attended a public rally at Nyirakanywero in Nyabitare *secteur* (Muganza *commune*) at the beginning of June 1994 where Kalimanzira told the crowd to fight the accomplices;

  v. BCA and BBB testified about Kalimanzira's presence at the inauguration of Élie Ndayambaje on 21 or 22 June 1994 as *bourgmestre* of Muganza *commune*, where Ndayambaje instructed the crowd to kill remaining Tutsi survivors and Kalimanzira did not express disapproval of this instruction.[185]

186. The Defence denies these allegations. In addition, Kalimanzira relies on his alibi (see III.1.2).

2.3.1. Notice

187. In its Closing Brief, the Defence objected to the Prosecution's failure to plead the first, third and fifth events listed above in the Indictment.[186] The Defence has not, however, offered any explanation for its delay in raising these objections.

188. The Chamber recalls that on 6 June 2008, the Defence sought the exclusion of six Prosecution witnesses from testifying on the basis that their anticipated testimonies in the Prosecution Pre-Trial Brief were related to material facts not pleaded in the Indictment.[187]

The Chamber granted the motion in part; in respect of the parts of the motion that were denied, the Chamber found that the Defence had no case to answer after the close of the Prosecution case.[188] The Defence could have raised its current objections in its motion of 6 June 2008. The Chamber is under no obligation to address an argument that is raised for the first time in the Defence's closing brief. Nonetheless, failing to object at the

---

[185] Prosecution Closing Brief, paras. 43-75.
[186] Defence Closing Brief, para. 1140.
[187] See *Requête aux fins d'exclusion des témoins à charge BWM, BWN, BXB, BXC, BXD et BXL*, filed on 9 June 2008.
[188] Decision on Defence Motion to Exclude Prosecution Witnesses BWM, BWN, BXB, BXC, BXD and BXL (TC), 24 June 2008; Decision of No Case To Answer (TC), 3 September 2008.

time the evidence is introduced does not prohibit the Defence from objecting at a later date.[189] In the interests of ensuring the integrity of the proceedings and safeguarding the rights of the Accused, the Chamber finds that consideration of the Defence's arguments, as well as the omission of the second and fourth events listed above from the Indictment (to which the Defence did not specifically object) is warranted in this case.[190]

189. The Chamber will first consider whether the inclusion of the five events listed above constitute the introduction of new charges or new material facts to the Prosecution's case. The Chamber recalls that the count or charge is the legal characterisation of the material facts which support the charge. In pleading an indictment, the Prosecution is required to specify **[page 44]** the alleged legal prohibition infringed (the count or charge) and the acts or omissions of the accused that give rise to that allegation of infringement or a legal prohibition (material facts).[191]

190. Reading the Indictment as a whole, the Chamber notes that paragraph 6 of the Indictment indicates that the particulars of Counts 1 and 2 are set out in paragraph 7 to 17, which served to notify the Defence that paragraph 8 is a specific allegation against the accused. The Chamber finds that paragraph 8, although generally worded, contains a charge, namely, Kalimanzira's participation in several visits to Butare, the purpose of which was to sensitize the population to the Government's policy and instigate[192] the population to kill Tutsis. Paragraph 8 does not, however, provide detail regarding precisely when or where Kalimanzira engaged in this behaviour, or how. Save for one exception discussed below, the Chamber finds that the events, listed above, provide particulars underlying the charge contained in paragraph 8, and are therefore material facts.[193]

191. By failing to include these material facts in paragraph 8, the Indictment is defective. The Chamber must consider whether the Prosecution provided the Defence with clear, consistent and timely information detailing the facts underpinning the charge in paragraph 8 in order to cure this defect. The Chamber recalls that the timing of such communications, the importance of the information to the ability of the accused to prepare his defence, and the impact of the newly-disclosed material facts on the Prosecution's case are relevant to determining whether subsequent communications make up for the defect in the indictment.[194]

192. The Prosecution Pre-Trial brief discusses Kalimanzira's attendance in Butare from April to July 1994. The Prosecution specifically alleges that Kalimanzira was seen in Gisagara in Ndora *commune* encouraging and instructing the population to kill Tutsis; in Muganza *commune* where he attended public meetings during which attacks against Tutsis were discussed and encouraged; in Nkubi *secteur* (Ngoma *commune*) in the second half of April 1994 where he encouraged the population to defend themselves against the Tutsi enemy; in Sahera *secteur* (Ngoma *commune*) in April 1994 where he said that Tutsis should be killed; at a public rally close to the Rwandan National University in Butare in late May or early June 1994 where he gave instructions to kill Tutsis.[195]

193. In addition, in the annex to the Prosecution Pre-Trial Brief, which summarises anticipated witness testimonies with reference to the relevant paragraphs of the Indictment, the evidence of 39 witnesses is indicated as being pertinent to paragraph 8, including the evidence of AZM, BWI, FAC, AZT, BCA and BBB.

194. The summary of AZM's testimony indicates that he would testify that Kalimanzira was a member of the Butare Prefectural Security Council during the genocide and that he attended meetings of the council. The Security Council would provide arms, ammunition and soldiers to kill Tutsis in Butare *préfecture*. This

---

[189] *Bagosora et al.* Interlocutory Appeal Decision, para. 45.
[190] *Semanza* Trial Judgement, paras. 42, 45; *Kayishema and Ruzindana* Appeal Judgement paras. 95, 97; *Ntakirutimana* Trial Judgement, para. 52.
[191] *Muvunyi* Interlocutory Appeal Decision, para. 19.
[192] Paragraph 8 of the Indictment uses the term "incite", not "instigate". The Chamber clarifies that "incite" in this context refers to the crime of Genocide under Article 2 (3)(a) by mode of Instigation under Article 6 (1), and not the crime of Direct and Public Incitement to Commit Genocide under Article 2 (3)(c). For a fuller discussion on the difference between incitement as crime and as mode of liability, see III.4.1.
[193] For an analysis of when new material facts could support separate charges against an accused, see *Muvunyi*, Decision on Prosecution Interlocutory Appeal Against Trial Chamber II Decision of 23 February 2005, paras. 33 and 35.
[194] *Niyitegeka*, Appeal Judgement, para. 197; *Kupreškić et al.* Appeal Judgement, paras. 119-121.
[195] Prosecution Closing Brief, paras. 54, 63.

is consistent with AZM's witness statement, **[page 45]** which was disclosed to the Defence in the Supporting Materials on 15 November 2005 in accordance with Rule 66 (A) of the Rules.

195. The summary of AZM's testimony also states that he would testify that Kalimanzira attended a meeting in Kibayi *commune* in May 1994, accompanied by other authorities, where the participants incited the population against the Tutsis.[196] Kalimanzira asked the population to demolish all houses belonging to Tutsis who were killed or who had fled in order to hide the attacks from foreigners. The Chamber is not satisfied that the Defence received clear and consistent notice of this allegation, as it was not included in AZM's redacted witness summary disclosed with the Supporting Materials. Moreover, the Chamber finds that the allegation that Kalimanzira told the population to destroy houses does not support a charge of instigation to commit genocide, but rather alleges a different form of criminal conduct and therefore impermissibly expands the charge pleaded in paragraph 8.

196. The summary of BWI's testimony indicates that he would testify that, among other things, he saw Kalimanzira at a meeting at the football field near the Muganza *commune* office in late April or early May 1994. Kalimanzira told the crowd that they should fight the Tutsis, the enemy, wherever they were found. He also instructed the crowd to eliminate the *Inkotanyi* accomplices, *i.e.* the Tutsis. This is consistent with BWI's witness statement, disclosed in the Supporting Materials.

197. The summary of FAC's testimony indicates that he would testify that he saw Kalimanzira with other senior officials at a public meeting near the Rwandan National University in Butare at the end of May or early June 1994. Kalimanzira encouraged the crowd to kill Tutsis, and killings of Tutsis followed the meeting. This is consistent with FAC's witness statement, disclosed in the Supporting Materials.

198. The Chamber also recalls that at the commencement of FAC's testimony, the Defence objected to a portion of his evidence that it had not been given notice of in the Prosecution Pre-Trial Brief, asserting that it was only given notice of FAC's evidence in relation to Kalimanzira's participation in the June 1994 meeting near the Rwandan National University in Butare. The Chamber held that it would disregard this other aspect of his evidence.[197] The Defence was therefore clearly on notice of FAC's evidence regarding Kalimanzira's participation in this June 1994 meeting.

199. The summary of AZT's testimony indicates that he would testify that, among other things, he saw Kalimanzira and other officials at a meeting in early June 1994 at Nyirakanywero in Muganza *commune*. The crowd was told that any one caught protecting a Tutsi would be killed with him. This is consistent with AZT's witness statement, disclosed in the Supporting Materials, which alleged that it was Kalimanzira who made this statement. **[page 46]**

200. The summary of BBB's testimony indicates that he would testify that, among other things, he saw Kalimanzira in June 1994 at the inauguration of Élie Ndayambaje as *bourgmestre* of Muganza *commune*. Ndayambaje suggested that Tutsis in hiding should be killed, and Alphonse Nteziryayo asked the crowd to bury the bodies of people who had been killed and to destroy their houses. Kalimanzira did not disapprove of these statements. This is consistent with BBB's witness statement, disclosed in the Supporting Materials.

201. In light of the foregoing, the Chamber finds that the Defence has received clear and consistent notice of the material facts upon which the Prosecution seeks to rely in respect of paragraph 8 of the Indictment, save for one aspect of AZM's testimony as noted above. The Defence has advanced a general assertion, however, that notice was not timely because it could not conduct sufficient investigations regarding these

---

[196] The Chamber notes that AZM testified that during the Security Council's first stop in Kibayi *commune*, Colonel Nteziryayo took the floor at a public rally and told the general public that they had to defend themselves, that the enemy was infiltrating the population, and that therefore the people had to be vigilant. He also said that there were Hutus who had hidden Tutsis and they had to be "taken out". AZM understood that those Tutsis had to be killed. AZM did not recall where Kalimanzira was during Nteziryayo's alleged speech, but believed that Kalimanzira was still with them [T. 17 June 2008 pp. 20-21 (Witness AZM)]. The Chamber notes that the material facts introduced through AZM's evidence were not included in either his witness statement disclosed in the Supporting Materials or the Prosecution Pre-Trial Brief; adequate notice was therefore not provided. In any event, the Prosecution does not appear to rely on these material facts to support the charge at paragraph 8 and acknowledges that Kalimanzira may not have been present at this public rally (Prosecution Pre-Trial Brief, para. 47).

[197] T. 19 June 2008, pp. 4-5 [closed] (Witness FAC).

new facts upon the delivery of the Prosecution Pre-Trial Brief.[198] The Prosecution Pre-Trial Brief was filed on 16 April 2008, three weeks before the commencement of trial, in English, whereas the working language of the Defence is French. The Defence case began on 17 November 2008, four months after the close of the Prosecution case. The Chamber considers this sufficient time for the Defence to prepare their case.

202. The Chamber further notes that the Defence was able to mount a defence to the Prosecution's allegations in respect of paragraph 8 of the Indictment. Prosecution Witnesses AZM, BWI, FAC, AZT, BCA and BBB were cross-examined by the Defence concerning their evidence; Defence Witnesses Félicien Kajyibwami, Albert Barikwinshi, Jean de Dieu Rutabana, Innocent Mukuralinda, AK42, MKB, KXC, and AM02 testified to refute the allegations relating to paragraph 8. In its own Pre-Trial Brief, the Defence specifically refuted some of these allegations, such as the meeting near the Rwandan National University in Butare;[199] Kalimanzira's attendance at the Butare Prefectural Security Council meetings;[200] the meeting in the Nyirakanywero centre in Nyabitare *secteur*;[201] the inauguration of Élie Ndayambaje;[202] and otherwise relied on the alibi.[203] It is therefore clear that the Defence was aware of these elements of the Prosecution's case and was able to challenge them throughout the proceedings.

203. In the Chamber's view, the Defence's case was not materially impaired by the Prosecution's failure to include the material facts underpinning the charge at paragraph 8 of the Indictment. The Chamber therefore finds that the Prosecution has cured the defect in paragraph 8 of the Indictment relating to the allegations discussed above by the provision of clear, consistent and timely notice.

204. Finally, the Chamber also notes that in its Closing Brief, under a section entitled "Cumulative Convictions", the Prosecution asserts that the evidence relevant to paragraphs 20, 23 and 24 of the Indictment, which particularise Count 3, is also relevant to paragraph 8 of the Indictment.[204] The Indictment does not indicate that these paragraphs are relevant to Counts 1 and 2 in any respect; indeed, paragraph 6 of the Indictment states that paragraph 7 through 17 only are relevant to those counts. On the basis of reading the Indictment alone, Kalimanzira would not have understood that he was being charged for the allegations contained in paragraphs 20, 23 and 24 under Counts 1 and 2. The Chamber finds that the **[page 47]** Prosecution is essentially seeking to amend the Indictment to expand the charges under Counts 1 and 2. This is impermissible. Consequently, the Chamber will not consider this evidence in relation to paragraph 8.[205]

2.3.2. Butare Prefectural Security Council Meetings

205. The Prosecution alleges that Kalimanzira attended several meetings of the Butare Prefectural Security Council in April and May 1994. In these meetings, the massacre of Tutsis, how to control the fighting among Hutus regarding the property of deceased Tutsis, and the implementation of the civil defence program was discussed, among other topics. The Prosecution alleges that there was no discussion regarding what ought to be done about the perpetrators of the killings.[206]

206. The Defence denies that Kalimanzira attended these meetings, save for one. In addition, Kalimanzira relies on his alibi that save for a few specified occasions, he was working in Murambi (Gitarama *préfecture*) from 14 April to 31 May 1994 (see III.1.2).

---

[198] Defence Closing Brief, para. 1141 and fn. 1003.
[199] Defence Pre-Trial Brief, paras. 22-23.
[200] Defence Pre-Trial Brief, paras. 24-25.
[201] Defence Pre-Trial Brief, paras. 30-31.
[202] Defence Pre-Trial Brief, paras. 32-33.
[203] Defence Pre-Trial Brief, paras. 26-27, 36.
[204] Prosecution Closing Brief, para. 321.
[205] *Karera* Appeal Judgement, paras. 365-370; *Muvunyi* Appeal Judgement, paras. 155-156.
[206] Prosecution Closing Brief, paras. 43-47.

2.3.2.1. Evidence

Prosecution Witness AZM

207. AZM testified that he was a member of the Butare Prefectural Security Committee and that Kalimanzira attended a number of meetings after 19 April 1994, all held around 10:00 a.m. at the MRND Palace in Butare *ville*.[207] The first meeting was held on 21 April 1994. Sylvain Nsabimana, Butare's new *préfet,* chaired the meeting, and Kalimanzira was present, along with local service chiefs from Butare *ville* and the *bourgmestre* of the urban council. At the meeting, the participants discussed the massacres of the previous night in Taba. The purpose of the meeting was to determine who the victims had been, so all they did was set up a committee to inquire into what had happened. The meeting was very short, lasting no longer than ten minutes.[208]

208. The next meeting took place the following day, on 22 April around 9:30 a.m., at the MRND Palace and was also chaired by *préfet* Nsabimana. AZM could not recall if Kalimanzira was present. AZM was certain about the date because it was during that meeting that the report of the committee set up on 21 April was presented. The committee reported that the people had been killed by soldiers. The military commander who was present at the meeting was instructed to find a solution to the problem.[209]

209. AZM explained that between 22 April and 10 May, there no Security Council meetings were convened in Butare. AZM testified that the purpose of this lull was to enable the perpetration of Tutsi massacres to continue. The next meeting was on 10 May 1994 and was chaired by *préfet* Nsabimana; Kalimanzira was in attendance. AZM testified that they discussed how to bury the bodies of all of the people who had been killed and decided to get a Caterpillar to bury the bodies. The *bourgmestre* was asked to tell the public to bury the bodies, and detainees were tasked to assist. There was no discussion concerning what should be done about the perpetrators of the killings. AZM also recalled that the *bourgmestre* of Ntyazo *commune* came to the meeting and asked for soldiers to kill Tutsis in his *commune,* **[page 48]** whom he referred to as resistant Tutsis. The *bourgmestre* of Nyaruhengeri *commune* announced at the meeting that he did not have ammunition and requested some. The military commander to whom these requests were directed told them to seek assistance from the *communal* police.[210]

210. The next meeting was about one week later, on 16 or 17 May 1994. AZM testified that although Kalimanzira was present, he was not a member of the Butare Prefectural Security Committee, and that no explanation was provided concerning Kalimanzira's attendance. AZM explained that as the *préfet* could invite someone, he assumed that Kalimanzira was assisting the new *préfet* in running things. AZM also believed that perhaps Kalimanzira was a government representative, since there was a special situation in Butare, because although massacres were happening elsewhere, they were not occurring in Butare.[211]

211. At that meeting, AZM testified that they discussed the fighting of Hutus over the property of Tutsis who had been killed. They spoke of reinstating peace, asking the general public to stop killing and restoring security. They asked the *bourgmestre* to address the problem. They did not discuss the perpetrators of the killings.[212]

212. The next meeting was held about four days later, after the Prime Minister gave instructions regarding civilian defence. Kalimanzira was present. AZM testified that a decision was taken to go to some *communes* in Butare *préfecture* to explain to the general public what civilian defence was all about.[213]

---

[207] T. 16 June 2008 pp. 10-20, 66 [closed] (Witness AZM).
[208] T. 17 June 2008 pp. 11-12 (Witness AZM).
[209] T. 17 June 2008 pp. 12-13 (Witness AZM).
[210] T. 17 June 2008 pp. 13-15 (Witness AZM)
[211] T. 17 June 2008 pp. 14-15 (Witness AZM).
[212] T. 17 June 2008 p. 17 (Witness AZM).
[213] T. 17 June 2008 p. 18 (Witness AZM).

Callixte Kalimanzira

213. Kalimanzira testified that he could not have attended a Security Council meeting on 21 or 22 April, because he was in Kibungo installing a new *préfet* on 21 April, and on his way back the next day, drove straight to Gitarama without stopping in Butare. Kalimanzira further testified that he never went to Butare *préfecture* in May 1994 and denied attending a Security Council meeting in Butare on 10 May. Kalimanzira also denied attending a Security Council meeting in Butare on 16 May with Pauline Nyiramasuhuko, but then admitted to it under cross-examination after being confronted with and reviewing a transcript of a Radio Rwanda broadcast which indicated that he was present.[214]

Defence Exhibit 113

214. Exhibit D113 is the minutes of a 10 May 1994 meeting attended by employees and heads of services in Butare *préfecture*, presided over by *préfet* Nsabimana. The minutes indicate that the meeting began at 9:30 a.m. and ended at 11:00 a.m., and contains a list of the 29 persons present, which does not include Kalimanzira.

2.3.2.2. Deliberations

215. At the relevant times alleged, Kalimanzira claims to have been working in Murambi (Gitarama *préfecture*). As discussed above, the Chamber disbelieves his alibi (see III.1.2.2). **[page 49]**

216. AZM has pleaded guilty to involvement in the genocide, has been placed in the first category and is awaiting an appeal.[215] He testified that he was a member of the Butare Prefectural Security Council, and admits that they failed in their duty to protect the Tutsis who were killed on their watch.[216] AZM may therefore have a motive to diminish any criminal activities of the Secuirty Council in relation to the genocide in order to avoid incurring any additional responsibility.

217. Although Kalimanzira flatly denied being in Butare in May 1994, he acknowledged that he attended one meeting of the Security Council after being confronted with the Radio Rwanda broadcast which placed him there. The Chamber does not accept Kalimanzira's explanation that he had simply forgotten having attended the meeting. Having admitted as such only after being confronted with the Radio Rwanda broadcast, the Chamber finds his evidence that he did not attend any other Security Council meeting to be unbelievable.

218. Kalimanzira also asserts that he could not have attended a Security Council meeting on 21 April because on that day he was installing a new *préfet* in Kibungo, where he says he spent the night. However, the Chamber recalls AZM's testimony that all the Butare Prefectural Security Council meetings started around 10:00 a.m., including the one on 21 April, which lasted no longer than ten minutes.[217] Kalimanzira testified he left Gitarama on 21 April at around 9:00 a.m., reaching Kibungo nine hours later at around 6:00 p.m..[218] The Chamber therefore finds that there is no contradiction in their testimonies, as Kalimanzira could easily have gone to Butare *ville* to attend this meeting in the morning and also reach Kibungo *préfecture* in time to install the new *préfet* that same evening. Kalimanzira's alibi evidence does not cast reasonable doubt on AZM's testimony.

219. The Defence also relies on Exhibit D113, arguing that the minutes are of the 10 May Security Council meeting and prove that Kalimanzira was not present.[219] The Chamber finds that Exhibit D113 is clearly the minutes of a staff meeting, not of a Security Council meeting, given that the minutes indicate the meeting was attended by employees and other heads of services in Butare, and that its purpose was to allow the new *préfet* to meet his staff. To the extent that these minutes refute AZM's testimony that the 10 May Security Council meeting occurred at 10:00 a.m., by indicating that the *préfet* was in another meeting from 9:30-11:00 a.m., the Chamber finds that Exhibit D113 does not exclude the possibility that the *préfet* attended the

---

[214] T. 11 February 2009 pp. 16-20, 23-24 (Callixte Kalimanzira).
[215] T. 16 June 2008 p. 66 [closed] and T. 17 June 2008 p. 24 [closed] (Witness AZM).
[216] T. 16 June 2009 p. 66 [closed] (Witness AZM).
[217] T. 17 June 2008 pp. 11-12 (Witness AZM).
[218] T. 10 February 2009 pp. 39-42 (Callixte Kalimanzira).
[219] Defence Closing Brief, paras. 799-800.

Security Council meeting slightly before or after the staff meeting, or that AZM was mistaken about the precise time at which the Security Council meeting took place.

220. The Chamber therefore finds that Kalimanzira attended several meetings of the Butare Prefectural Security Council in May 1994. The Chamber notes, however, that AZM's evidence was that the Security Council is provided for by law in every *préfecture* and had been in existence for a very long time.[220] With respect to what occurred at the meetings in question, the evidence is that the purpose of the 21 April meeting was to investigate the massacres of the night before, and to find the perpetrators; the discussions at the 16 or 17 May meeting concerned fighting by Hutus over the property of dead Tutsis and restoring peace; the discussions at the 21 or 22 May meeting concerned directives regarding civil defence. AZM testified that at the 10 May meeting, one *bourgmestre* asked for assistance in killing Tutsis and another asked for more ammunition, but these requests were refused by the **[page 50]** military commander. AZM also stated that meetings were not held between late April and early May in order to allow the massacres to continue unabated.

221. The Chamber recalls that the charge alleged in paragraph 8 of the Indictment is that Kalimanzira participated in visits to Butare to sensitize the population to the Government's policy and to instigate them to kill Tutsis. The Indictment alleges that this activity resulted in the killing of thousands of Tutsis in Butare *préfecture*. Upon review of the evidence open to consideration, the Chamber finds that AZM's testimony does not support these allegations. In particular, there is insufficient evidence to conclude that instigation occurred at the Security Council meetings. Further, there is no evidence demonstrating how the Security Council and the population were linked; there is insufficient evidence to conclude that the Security Council or Kalimanzira sensitized the population to any Government policy. The Chamber also does not find that it would be reasonable to make inferences in support of these conclusions on this evidence. Finally, although the Chamber accepts that Tutsis were killed by the thousands in Butare, there is no evidence to link the Security Council meetings to those killings. The Prosecution has therefore failed to prove this allegation beyond a reasonable doubt.

2.3.3. Muganza Commune *Football Field Security Meeting*

222. The Prosecution alleges that Kalimanzira spoke at a public security meeting held on the football field close to the Muganza *commune* office at the end of April or early May 1994. Kalimanzira allegedly instructed the crowd to kill Tutsis and to set up patrols to find Tutsis in hiding. Large scale killings of Tutsis continued in the area as a result.[221]

223. The Defence denies that Kalimanzira attended the meeting. In addition, Kalimanzira relies on his alibi that save for a few specified occasions, he was working in Murambi (Gitarama *préfecture*) from 14 April to 31 May 1994 (see III.1.2).

2.3.3.1. Evidence

Prosecution Witness BWI

224. BWI testified that he saw Kalimanzira on two occasions after the death of President Habyarimana, both times at public meetings on the football field near the Muganza *commune* office in Remera *secteur*.[222]

225. The first meeting was at the end of April or the beginning of May. BWI had been asked to attend a security meeting by a member of the *cellule* committee. He arrived before the meeting started, in the morning. There were many members of the population in attendance, both civilians and soldiers. There were officials already present when BWI arrived. Chrysologue Bimenyimana (*bourgmestre* of Muganza *commune*) commenced the meeting when other authorities arrived, about 20 minutes after BWI, around

---

[220] T. 17 June 2008 p. 27 (Witness AZM).
[221] Prosecution Closing Brief, para. 51.
[222] T. 21 May 2008 pp. 28-29, 34 (Witness BWI).

noon. These authorities included Kalimanzira, Dominique Ntawukuriryayo (*sous-préfet* of Gisagara), and Alphonse Nteziryayo with some soldiers.[223]

226. *Bourgmestre* Bimenyimana spoke first, introducing the authorities, and was followed by Nteziryayo, who told the population that the Tutsis were causing insecurity, and that they had to be sought out at all costs because they were the enemies of the population. Kalimanzira spoke next, telling the crowd that insecurity was being caused by accomplices of **[page 51]** the *Inkotanyi*. He told the population not to loot the property of the Tutsis, but rather to exterminate them. Later on, the authorities would hand over the property of Tutsis who had been killed. He explained that the *Inkotanyi* were supported by the Tutsis and therefore the accomplices of the *Inkotanyi* had to first be exterminated. He told the population to set up day and night patrols so that the accomplices could be identified wherever they were hiding. Kalimanzira was the last to speak, for about 45-60 minutes, while the entire meeting lasted about two hours.[224]

227. BWI left at the end of the meeting, but before Kalimanzira. The killings had already started before the meeting, and afterwards, members of the population continued chasing Tutsis. In particular, the population went to look for Tutsis in hiding and killed them. BWI believes these Tutsis would have survived were it not for the meeting.[225]

Defence Witness Félicien Kajyibwami

228. On 8 May 1994, Kajyibwami was on the road leading to Kirarambogo in Muganza *commune* when he was stopped at a roadblock by about ten people who were manning it. The people at the roadblock accused him of being an *Inkotanyi*, which Kajyibwami clarified was a Tutsi. People started gathering to see the *Inkotanyi*. Kajyibwami testified that he tried to explain that he was not a Tutsi, and told the people who were manning the roadblock that he had played at the Muganza *commune* football field, and had worked with local farmers in the marshes. He remembered having worked with Kalimanzira, and that Kalimanzira was a native of the area, so he mentioned his past working relationship with Kalimanzira to the people at the roadblock hoping that this would assuage those manning the roadblock.[226]

229. Kajyibwami testified that the people at the roadblock replied that they had not had any news of Kalimanzira since the outbreak of the war, and said to Kajyibwami that perhaps he, the *Inkotanyi*, had killed Kalimanzira. The people at the roadblock started threatening him, spitting on his face, and undressing him. Kajyibwami realized that they were going to kill him. He then told them that he had been in school with *bourgmestre* Bimenyimana, and asked to be handed over to him because the *bourgmestre* knew he was not a Tutsi.[227]

230. Since the members of the public knew that there would be a Security Council meeting the following day at the *commune* office, they spared his life and took him to the *commune* office the following morning, around 7:30-8:00 a.m. Kajyibwami heard that a meeting was indeed going to take place, and people started arriving. The meeting stared around 10:00 a.m., was held in the meeting hall of the *commune* office, and included all of the *conseillers* of Muganza's *secteurs,* as well as other civil servants of Muganza *commune*.[228]

231. Kajyibwami believed that *bourgmestre* Bimenyimana was the chairperson for the meeting. Kajyibwami met with him in his office after the meeting, and asked him whether Kalimanzira had died. *Bourgmestre* Bimenyimana said that the last time he had seen Kalimanzira was in April in Butare *ville*, but had not heard any rumour that Kalimanzira had died. *Bourgmestre* Bimenyimana then issued a certificate to Kajyibwami which stated that he was a Hutu to enable him to reach his house.[229] **[page 52]**

---

[223] T. 21 May 2008 pp. 28-30, 44 (Witness BWI).
[224] T. 21 May 2009 p. 33 (Witness BWI).
[225] T. 21 May 2008 pp. 33-34 (Witness BWI).
[226] T. 2 February 2009 pp. 30-31 (Félicien Kajyibwami).
[227] T. 2 February 2009 p. 31 (Félicien Kajyibwami).
[228] T. 2 February 2009 p. 32 (Félicien Kajyibwami).
[229] T. 2 February 2009 pp. 9, 32-33 (Félicien Kajyibwami).

2.3.3.2. Deliberations

232. At the relevant time alleged, Kalimanzira claims to have been working in Murambi (Gitarama *préfecture*). As discussed above, the Chamber disbelieves his alibi (see III.1.2.2).

233. Kajyibwami testified that *bourgmestre* Bimenyimana said that the last time he had seen Kalimanzira was in April in Butare *ville*. The Chamber notes that this evidence is hearsay and it does not, in any case, contradict BWI's testimony such that the meeting may have occurred shortly thereafter. The Chamber accordingly does not place much weight on it.

234. The Chamber notes that while other Prosecution witnesses gave evidence concerning meetings held on the Muganza *commune* football field, BWI was the sole witness to assert that a security meeting was held on the football field in late April or early May 1994.

235. For instance, both BCA and BBB testified that they saw Kalimanzira at meetings near the Muganza *commune* office namely in May on the football field (see III.2.8.1) and in June at the inauguration of Élie Ndayambaje (see III.2.3.6). Neither witness gave any evidence concerning an earlier meeting held on the football field.[230] BWI testified that BCA attended the late April or early May meeting on the football field. BCA, however, did not testify that he attended an earlier meeting on the football field, nor did the Prosecution put questions to him in this respect. In light of his professional position, BCA's failure to give evidence concerning this meeting and the Prosecution's failure to lead evidence from him on this event raises a reasonable doubt about whether the meeting actually occurred.

236. Consequently, the Chamber finds that the Prosecution has not proven beyond reasonable doubt that Kalimanzira attended a public security meeting held on the football field close to the Muganza *commune* office at the end of April or early May 1994.

2.3.4. Cemetery Rally and Arboretum Search

237. The Prosecution alleges that a public rally was held in June 1994 at the cemetery next to the Rwandan National University in Butare. Several authorities were present, including Kalimanzira, who instructed the large crowd in attendance to search for Tutsis in hiding and to kill them.[231]

238. The Defence denies that Kalimanzira was present. In addition, Kalimanzira relies on his alibi (see III.1.2).

2.3.4.1. Evidence

Prosecution Witness FAC

239. FAC testified that he was invited to a meeting by Joseph Kanyabashi (*bourgemstre* of Ngoma *commune*). The meeting began around 9:30 a.m. the next day at the University cemetery, near a forest known as the "Arboretum", with approximately 2,000 people in attendance from various areas.[232] Many authorities were present, including *bourgmestre* Kanyabashi, Alphonse Nteziryayo and Sylvain Nsabimana (*préfet* of Butare), as well as many *sous-préfets* and *bourgmestres* of neighbouring *communes*.[233] **[page 53]**

240. FAC testified that Kalimanzira was present at the meeting, which was held to discuss the Tutsis still in hiding and the Hutus who had started killing other Hutus. Kalimanzira welcomed the meeting and was the highest-ranking and most respected authority present. Kalimanzira instructed them to search houses to ensure that no enemies were hiding and to search the forest, woods and bushes to ensure that no *Inkotyani* were hiding. FAC understood "*Inkotyani*" to refer both to fighters from Uganda and his neighbours. He explained that, at that time in Rwanda, "enemy" meant Tutsis. FAC recalled that Kalimanzira also warned

---

[230] T. 16 June 2008 p. 6 (Witness BBB).
[231] Prosecution Closing Brief, para. 53.
[232] T. 19 June 2008 pp. 6-7, 31 (Witness FAC).
[233] T. 19 June 2008 p. 7 (Witness FAC).

them not to hide Tutsis so that by July when national festivities were due to be held there would be no surviving *Inkotanyi*. The following speakers, *préfet* Nsabimana and *bourgmestre* Kanyabashi, reiterated this message.[234]

241. After receiving these instructions, FAC and others from the meeting immediately went in search of Tutsis in hiding. Two Tutsis from Tumba *secteur* were killed. In the following days, FAC participated in an attack during which a Tutsi child was killed. He also assisted with throwing six Tutsi children into a toilet. FAC testified that three Tutsis who were hiding in his home were killed after as he could not afford to bribe the killers.[235]

242. FAC also testified that before the meeting, at approximately 7:30 or 8:00 a.m., they searched the Arboretum forest, found corpses of three people who had been killed in the days before, but did not find anyone alive. The search lasted about an hour.[236]

Defence Witness Albert Barikwinshi

243. Barikwinshi testified that in June 1994, he was asked by *Conseiller* Vianney to participate in community work involving a search of the Arboretum, a forest near the university.[237] The next day, a Saturday, Barikwinshi was taken by bus to the University cemetery, where he saw three other buses and approximately 500 people. A gendarme named Habyarabatuma spoke with all of the *conseillers*, who then instructed the people to circle the Arboretum forest and shout that any people hiding should not be afraid. The *conseillers* indicated that the gendarmes would be in front of them and that they would be shooting; the *conseillers* also explained that the *Inkotanyi* had apparently reached Save and, consequently, it was necessary to search the forest to ensure that they were not hiding there.[238]

244. As instructed, Barikwinshi entered the forest and made a lot of noise; after five minutes, he heard gunshots in the middle of the forest. After searching for approximately one hour and 40 minutes, Barikwinshi found Habyarabatuma and Corporal Gatwazahad who had arrested young Tutsi man and woman.[239] He noticed that the Tutsis were hungry, extremely tired and had spent a number of days hiding in the forest. The Tutsis were taken away to a camp on a vehicle with gendarmes and he does not know what happened to them after that.[240]

245. Habyarabatuma asked everyone to assemble. He thanked them for their work, informed them that the operation was useful because of the security problems throughout the **[page 54]** country, and encouraged them to carry out such operations in the future. He then introduced the new *préfet* of Butare to them, whose name Barikwinshi could not remember.[241]

246. Barikwinshi testified that he did not see Kalimanzira before, after or during the search at the Arboretum, nor had he heard about any other search. He also stated that it was not possible for more than 500 people to fit inside the cemetery.[242]

Defence Witness Jean de Dieu Rutabana

247. Rutabana testified that, in June 1994, the *responsable* of Agasharu *cellule* told him that the community work that normally took place in their *cellule* would take place in the Arboretum forest instead. The purpose was to search, to be sure that there were no *Inkotanyi* in the forest. As requested, Rutabana boarded a bus at 8:00 a.m. on Saturday, which took approximately 15 minutes to reach the University cemetery.[243]

---

[234] T. 19 June 2008 pp. 8-10 (Witness FAC).
[235] T. 19 June 2008 pp. 9-10 (Witness FAC).
[236] T. 19 June 2008 pp. 9, 28-29 (Witness FAC).
[237] T. 26 January 2009 p. 57 and T. 27 January 2009 p. 14 (Albert Barikwinshi).
[238] T. 26 January 2009 p. 57 and T. 27 January 2008 pp. 14-16 (Albert Barikwinshi).
[239] T. 27 January 2009 p. 26 (Albert Barikwinshi).
[240] T. 26 January 2009 p. 59 (Albert Barikwinshi).
[241] T. 26 January 2009 pp. 58; T. 27 January 2009 p. 16 (Albert Barikwinshi).
[242] T. 26 January 2009, p. 59; T. 27 January 2009 p. 17 (Albert Barikwinshi).
[243] T. 3 February 2009 pp. 7-8, 17, 22 (Jean de Dieu Rutabana).

248. Upon arrival at the cemetery next to the Arboretum, Rutabana noticed that Habyarabatuma, the commander of the gendarmerie in Butare, was present. Habyarabatuma spoke with the *conseillers* from various *secteurs* for approximately five minutes. The *conseillers* then relayed the instructions to the public and informed them that one group would search from Cyarwa and one from Save and that the gendarmes were going to surround the forest and intervene if anyone tried to flee.[244]

249. The search began at 8:30 a.m. The gendarmes started shooting and people started shouting. The search took about an hour and a half. They captured a young boy and girl who were taken to Habyarabatuma. Rutabana did not believe they were *Inkotanyi* because of the state they were in; they were famished and Rutabana could see that they were Tutsis who had come to hide because they were being hunted down. Since they were told that *Inkotanyi* normally carry weapons and wear uniforms, he could see that they were ordinary Tutsis. He does not know what happened to them afterwards.[245] Habyarabatuma then gave a small speech, telling the crowd they should "clear the bushes" in their own cellules to ensure that there were no *Inkotanyi*. He also introduced the new *préfet*, whose name Rutabana does not remember.[246]

250. Rutabana did not see Kalimanzira at the meeting after the search or when the *préfet* was introduced to them. He estimated that 400-500 people were present, and denied that 2,000 people could have been there. There were only four buses bringing people to the area and only approximately 100 people came on foot.[247] Rutabana asserted that a meeting could not have taken place before the search as the people hiding in the forest would have heard the noise and fled.[248] Rutabana stated that there was no other search at the Arboretum in June 1994.[249]

2.3.4.2. Deliberations [page 55]

251. At the relevant time alleged, Kalimanzira claims to have been at home in Butare *ville*. As discussed above, the Chamber disbelieves his alibi (see III.1.2.2).

252. The Chamber notes that all three witnesses who gave evidence concerning this event are suspected in involvement, or have been found guilty of involvement, in the genocide. Rutabana was sentenced to 30 years' imprisonment, but subsequently escaped prison and has fled to Burundi.[250] Barikwinshi was detained in Rwanda for suspected involvement in the genocide and fled to Burundi when released, because he heard he was to be re-arrested.[251] FAC was convicted by the Tumba *secteur Gacaca* court for looting and participating in attacks during the genocide, as well as collaborating and being an accomplice to other offences; he received a 25-year prison sentence, which he is currently appealing.[252] FAC has also acknowledged being dismissed from his job as an accountant for embezzlement and to having psychiatric problems as a result of a car accident.[253]

253. All three witnesses participated in the Arboretum search, and all three witnesses may have reasons to lie about preceding or following public rallies inciting them to commit genocide. In Barikwinshi's and Rutabana's case, as fugitives they would have an obvious incentive to deny the occurrence or knowledge of such rallies. FAC admits to participating in attacks following the cemetery rally; this makes him an accomplice. He has an obvious interest in diluting his own responsibility for his involvement in the killings for which he is currently appealing his sentence, if he believes that accusing Kalimanzira and other authorities of inciting him to commit his crimes could enhance his own judicial proceedings. These witnesses' testimonies must therefore be viewed with caution.

---

[244] T. 3. February 2009 p. 8, 19 (Jean de Dieu Rutabana).
[245] T. 3 February 2009 pp. 8-9, 20-21 (Jean de Dieu Rutabana).
[246] T. 3 February 2009 pp. 8-9, 19 (Jean de Dieu Rutabana).
[247] T. 3 February 2009 pp. 9-10, 18 (Jean de Dieu Rutabana).
[248] T. 3 February 2009 p. 10 (Jean de Dieu Rutabana).
[249] T. 3 February 2009 pp. 9-10 (Jean de Dieu Rutabana)
[250] T. 3 February 2009 pp. 6-7 (Jean de Dieu Rutabana).
[251] T. 26 January 2009 pp. 53-56 (Albert Barikwinshi).
[252] T. 19 June 2008 pp. 9, 14-17, 23 [closed] (Witness FAC).
[253] T. 19 June 2008 p. 25 [closed] (Witness FAC).

254. The Prosecution asserts that FAC's evidence is supported by documentary evidence.[254] During his cross-examination, Kalimanzira was shown a letter dated 24 May 1994 from *bourgmestre* Kanyabashi to various *conseillers*. Kalimanzira acknowledged that the letter stated that a decision had been taken by the security council that community work would be undertaken on 27 May 1994 to cut down bushes so that criminals would not have a place to hide. However, Kalimanzira asserted that such activity was a common occurrence in Rwanda, that the *bourgmestre* was in charge of directing civilians to do such work, and that he was in Gitarama at the pertinent time.[255]

255. The Chamber notes that the fact that the Arboretum was searched and that Kalimanzira was not there is not in dispute; therefore, the letter is not probative in that respect. More importantly, the letter from *bourgmestre* Kanyabashi does not serve to corroborate the crucial aspect of FAC's evidence, namely, that Kalimanzira was present at a rally which followed such a search in May or June 1994 and particularly that he personally instructed the crowd to search for enemy and *Inkotanyi* in hiding.

256. The Chamber finds certain aspects of FAC's evidence to give rise to reasonable doubt concerning this event. FAC testified that they undertook the search of the Arboretum *before* the rally, in which Kalimanzira told the crowd to search the forest and bushes for *Inkotanyi*. No explanation was given regarding why they undertook this search before, or who might have given them instructions to do so. In exercising due caution with respect to FAC's testimony, and with no other reliable evidence to support or corroborate his own, the **[page 56]** Chamber finds that FAC's evidence is unsufficiently reliable to support a conviction. Consequently, the Prosecution has failed to prove beyond reasonable doubt that Kalimanzira was present at a search of the Arboretum forest, or at any subsequent rally nearby.

2.3.5. Public Rally at Nyirakanywero

257. The Prosecution alleges that Kalimanzira attended a public rally at Nyirakanywero in Nyabitare *secteur* (Muganza *commune*) at the beginning of June 1994. Kalimanzira was in the company of other officials and addressed the crowd, instructing them to fight RPF accomplices.[256]

258. The Defence denies that Kalimanzira attended this meeting. In addition, Kalimanzira relies on his alibi (see III.1.2).

2.3.5.1. Evidence

Prosecution Witness AZT

259. AZT testified that he saw Kalimanzira three times in 1994.[257] The third time was a meeting in Nyirakanywero, near the market in Nyabitare *secteur*.[258] AZT estimated that the meeting was held in late May or early June 1994. He heard about it through word of mouth. A large crowd attended from various *communes* and AZT recognized people from seven *secteurs* of the *commune*.[259] The crowd gathered below the market on a slope. He was told that the meeting would begin at 10:00 a.m., but did not actually start until about 2:00 p.m. He attended the meeting from start to finish.[260]

260. After a while, vehicles arrived, bringing Alphonse Nteziryayo (who AZT described at the *préfet* of Butare),[261] who was leading the meeting, as well as Colonel Muvunyi, Kalimanzira, and others whom AZT did not recognize. Nteziryayo told the crowd that the country had four enemies: (1) America, (2) Museveni,

---

[254] Prosecution Closing Brief, para. 56.
[255] T. 11 February 2009 pp. 54-57 (Callixte Kalimanzira).
[256] Prosecution Closing Brief, para. 59.
[257] T. 20 June 2008 p. 24 (Witness AZT).
[258] T. 20 June 2008 p. 27 (Witness AZT).
[259] T. 20 June 2008 pp. 27 and T. 23 June 2008 pp. 23, 25 (Witness AZT).
[260] T. 23 June 2008 pp. 25-28 (Witness AZT).
[261] Alphonse Nteziryayo was not appointed *préfet* of Butare until 17 June 1994 (see Exhibit D107).

(3) *Inyenzi Inkotanyi*, and (4) their accomplices (*i.e.* the Tutsis). He also said that if anyone was caught hiding a Tutsi, they would be taken to the authorities and punished. Muvunyi then made a similar speech.[262]

261. Kalimanzira then addressed the audience and instructed them to fight the "accomplices" with all their energy. Kalimanzira also said that they had started inspecting roadblocks and anyone found to be disobeying instructions would be considered an accomplice. Kalimanzira ordered that Tutsis in hiding should be found and called for those manning the roadblocks to be vigilant. Following the meeting, AZT and others immediately started searching for Tutsis in houses, the bush and the hills. His team found a Tutsi who had been arrested by another team and killed her.[263]

Defence Witness AK42 **[page 57]**

262. AK42 testified that he attended two public meetings from April to June 1994.[264] The first meeting took place at the Nyirakanywero marketplace on 23 May 1994.[265] The meeting was presided over by Sylvain Nsabimana (*préfet* of Butare). AK42 was told that security issues were going to be discussed at the meeting and that it would start before midday. AK42 remembered the date because he was hiding a Tutsi in his home and therefore paid attention to what was said in meetings in order to know if he was going to come under attack.[266]

263. AK42 testified that leaders came late and the meeting only started in the afternoon. AK42 recalled the presence of Chrysologue Bimenyimana (*bourgmestre* of Muganza *commune*), *préfet* Nsabimana, Colonel Muvunyi, Colonel Nteziryayo; the public prosecutor, Ruzindana, and the *sous-préfet* of Gisagara. The meeting was held on a slope with the authorities sitting on chairs and the local population, numbering about 300, sitting on the ground opposite them. The meeting did not last long. The authorities told the population to stop attacking their neighbours, stop the killings and to go about their normal activities. They also said that the fighting was approaching the *commune*. In short, the population should avoid any form of violence and ensure the security of members of the population.[267]

264. AK42 testified that Kalimanzira was not present at the meeting. AK42 attended the entire meeting and said that no other meetings were held in the marketplace in the month of May.[268]

Defence Witness MKB

265. MKB is a Hutu whose husband and four of her children were killed in April 1994 because they were Tutsis.[269] MKB testified that she attended a meeting at the Nyirakanywero marketplace one afternoon in late May 1994, after the killings had stopped in mid-May. She was informed of the meeting by the local population when she was on her way to get manure for her rice field. When she saw authorities arrive in their vehicles and head towards the marketplace, she followed.[270]

266. MKB sat on the ground, with other members of the population, facing authorities who sat on benches. She recognised some of the authorities present, naming Chrysologue Bimenyimana, Tharcisse Muvunyi, Alphonse Nteziryayo, Deo Ngayabewura and Élie Ndayambaje. Security issues were discussed by Muvunyi and Nteziryayo; people were asked to stop killing each other and instructed to ensure their own security and that of Tutsi women married to Hutu men.[271]

---

[262] T. 20 June 2008 pp. 27-28 (Witness AZT).
[263] T. 20 June 2008 pp. 28-29 (Witness AZT).
[264] T. 27 November 2008 p. 4 [closed] (Witness AK42).
[265] T. 27 November 2008 p. 5 (Witness AK42).
[266] T. 27 November 2008 pp. 5, 9 (Witness AK42).
[267] T. 27 November 2008 pp. 5-6 (Witness AK42).
[268] T. 27 November 2008 pp. 6, 10 (Witness AK42).
[269] T. 1 December 2008 p. 7 [closed] (Witness MKB).
[270] T. 1 December 2008 p. 9 (Witness MKB).
[271] T. 1 December 2008 pp. 9-10, 18-19 (Witness MKB).

Judgement

267. MKB attended the entire meeting, which lasted about an hour. Kalimanzira was not present, and MKB recalled that he had not been to their *secteur* in a long time. She did not hear of any other meetings at the marketplace from April to June 1994.[272]

Defence Witness KXC **[page 58]**

268. KXC attended a meeting in the second week of May 1994 in the Nyirakanywero marketplace. KXC learned about the meeting from *bourgmestre* Bimenyimana, and testified that people from Rwamiko *secteur* (Kibayi *commune*) learned about it because someone drove through the *secteur* with a loudspeaker, calling on the people to attend the meeting.[273]

269. At the time of the meeting, the killings had stopped. KXC arrived at 11:00 a.m., but the meeting did not start until about 2:00 p.m. because the guests arrived late. The authorities arrived by vehicle. Members of the population sat on the field, on the upper part of the slope, while the authorities sat on chairs. The meeting, which ended around 4:00 p.m., was about security; it had been organized in order to calm down the local inhabitants because some were still afraid, particularly Tutsi women married to Hutu men.[274]

270. Tharcisse Muvunyi, Alphonse Nteziryayo, Chrysologue Bimenyimana and Élie Ndayambaje were present.[275] KXC recalled that the *bourgmestre* Bimenyimana spoke first, introducing the authorities, followed by Nteziryayo, Muvunyi and the President of the Court of First Instance. Nteziryayo spoke generally about security and the RPF being in Bugesera.[276] KXC also testified that Muvunyi had spoken about the four enemies of Rwanda. Muvunyi instructed that the *secteur* borders be protected, night patrols be established, more roadblocks be set up, and promised more gendarmes.[277]

271. KXC testified that Kalimanzira was not present at the meeting.[278] He stated that no other meetings were held at Nyirakanywero centre between April and June 1994; he would certainly have been informed. Only one other meeting was held in Muganza *commune* in June, for the inauguration of the new *bourgmestre*.[279]

2.3.5.2. Deliberations

272. At the relevant time alleged, Kalimanzira claims to have been home in Butare *ville*. As discussed above, the Chamber disbelieves his alibi (see III.1.2.2).

273. On the basis of the testimony of all of the Prosecution and Defence witnesses concerning this event, the Chamber finds that they were in attendance at the same meeting at the market square in Nyirakanywero in Nyabitare *secteur*. Their testimony was consistent in several respects, such as the authorities being late,[280] which authorities were present,[281] the placement of the crowd and the authorities,[282] and that Nteziryayo spoke about the four enemies of Rwanda.[283] The Chamber does not find that AZT's mistake in his evidence to the **[page 59]** effect that Alphonse Nteziryayo was *préfet* of Butare by that time, when he was only appointed on 17 June 1994, so significant as to undermine this finding.[284]

---

[272] T. 1 December 2009 p. 10 (Witness MKB).
[273] T. 2 December 2008 pp. 2-3 (Witness KXC).
[274] T. 2 December 2008 pp. 3-5, 13 (Witness KXC).
[275] T. 2 December 2008 p. 4 (Witness KXC).
[276] T. 2 December 2008 p. 16 (Witness KXC).
[277] T. 2 December 2008 pp. 16-17 (Witness KXC).
[278] T. 2 December 2008 p. 4 (Witness KXC).
[279] T. 2 December 2008 pp. 5, 19, 20 [closed] (Witness KXC).
[280] T. 23 June 2008 p. 28 (Witness AZT); T. 27 November 2008 p. 5 (Witness AK42); T. 2 December 2008 p. 3 (Witness KXC).
[281] T. 20 June 2008 p. 27 (Witness AZT); T. 27 November 2008 p. 6 (Witness AK42); T. 1 December 2008 p. 10 (Witness MKB); T. 2 December 2008 p. 4 (Witness KXC).
[282] T. 23 June 2008 p. 25 (Witness AZT); T. 27 November 2008 p. 5 (Witness AK42); T. 1 December 2008 pp. 9-10 (Witness MKB); T. 2 December 2008 pp. 3-4 (Witness KXC).
[283] T. 20 June 2008 p. 28 (Witness AZT); T. 2 December 2008 p. 17 (Witness KXC).
[284] See Defence Closing Brief, para. 658.

274. AZT was the only witness, however, who testified that Kalimanzira was present and spoke at the meeting. The Chamber notes that AZT has been sentenced to life imprisonment, currently under appeal, and is an accomplice to this event, having admitted to killing a Tutsi after the meeting.[285] He may therefore have a motive to implicate Kalimanzira. The Chamber considers that his testimony should be viewed with caution.

275. The Defence witnesses gave very consistent accounts of the meeting, and all were emphatic that Kalimanzira was not present. AK42 was detained in Rwanda but released without being charged. After being summoned, he fled Rwanda.[286] He has been accused of taking part in the genocide.[287] The Chamber also notes that AK42 worked with Kalimanzira while in exile in Kenya.[288] He testified as to the closeness of their relationship, stating that Kalimanzira was almost like a brother.[289] This suggests that he may be biased in favour of Kalimanzira.

276. MKB has not been charged with involvement in the genocide. The Chamber does not accept the Prosecution's assertion that it was unbelievable that MKB would attend the meeting after most of her family was killed;[290] indeed, the Chamber found her explanation credible that because her home had been looted and everything taken, she left her home because she wanted rice for her Tutsi child, and further, that she would be particularly interested in a meeting about security because of her situation.[291]

277. While KXC was detained in Rwanda for eight years, he was acquitted by the *Gacaca* court.[292] By virtue of his professional position, the Chamber notes that KXC was in a position to know about meetings happening in his *secteur* and would likely have recognized Kalimanzira if he was in attendance.[293] The Chamber finds that both MKB and KXC gave credible evidence.

278. In light of the foregoing, particularly the uncorroborated nature of AZT's testimony, and the credible and consistent testimony of MKB and KXC, the Chamber finds that the Prosecution has failed to prove beyond reasonable doubt that Kalimanzira attended the meeting at the market square in Nyirakanywero in Nyabitare *secteur*.

2.3.6. Inauguration of Élie Ndayambaje

279. The Prosecution alleges that Kalimanzira attended the public inauguration of Élie Ndayambaje as *bourgmestre* of Muganza *commune*, near the Muganza *commune* office around 21 or 22 June 1994. At the meeting, Ndayambaje criticized the crowd for helping Tutsis to hide, and instructed them to kill Tutsi survivors. Although Kalimanzira did not speak, the Prosecution alleges that because he did not express any disapproval of **[page 60]** Ndayambaje's speech, he thereby showed support for the killings which followed and facilitated Ndayambaje's incitement.[294]

280. The Defence denies that Kalimanzira was in attendance. In addition, Kalimanzira relies on his alibi (see III.1.2).

2.3.6.1. Evidence

Prosecution Witness BCA

281. BCA testified that he was present at the inauguration of Élie Ndayambaje as the new *bourgmestre* of Muganza *commune* on 21 or 22 June 1994. BCA recalled that the authorities in attendance included Kalimanzira, Alphonse Nteziryayo (Butare's new *préfet*), Sylvain Nsabimana (Butare's former *préfet*),

---

[285] T. 23 June 2008 p. 18 [closed] (Witness AZT).
[286] T. 26 November 2008 p. 66 [closed] (Witness AK42).
[287] T. 27 November 2008 pp. 27-34 [closed] (Witness AK42).
[288] T. 27 November 2008 pp. 3 [closed] 16, 20 (Witness AK42).
[289] T. 27 November 2008 p. 15 (Witness AK42).
[290] Prosecution Closing Brief, para. 64.
[291] T. 1 December 2008 p. 7, 14-15 (Witness MKB).
[292] T. 2 December 2008 p. 6 (Witness KXC).
[293] T. 1 December 2008 p. 70 [closed] (Witness KXC).
[294] Prosecution Closing Brief, paras. 69-70.

Dominique Ntawukulilyayo (*sous-préfet* of Gisagara), and Pauline Nyiramasuhuko. During his inauguration, Ndayambaje told the audience that "when you want to clean out the dirt from your house, you don't heap it in front of the fireplace." BCA testified that he understood those remarks to mean that people who had been hidden had to be taken out of their hiding and killed as well.[295] BCA did not recall that Kalimanzira spoke at the inauguration.[296] After the meeting, Tutsis and Hutu political opponents were taken out of hiding and killed.[297]

Prosecution Witness BBB

282. BBB testified that he saw Kalimanzira three times after President Habyarimana's death, the final occasion being the reinstitution of Élie Ndayambaje as *bourgmestre* of Muganza *commune* in June, not far from the Muganza *commune* office. BBB arrived before the ceremony started, and there were between 200-300 Hutus present. Authorities present included Kalimanzira, Chrysologue Bimenyimana (Muganza's former *bourgmestre*), *préfet* Nteziryayo, the *responsable de cellule*, and the *conseiller de secteur*. The master of ceremonies, Célestin Habyambere, took the floor first to introduce Ndayambaje as Muganza's new *bourgmestre*,.[298]

283. Ndayambaje first thanked the population for having confidence in him to be their *bourgmestre*. He then criticized the crowd, using the metaphor that instead of sweeping the dirt outside the house, they were sweeping it inside. The population did not understand his comments, so Célestin Habyambere explained that they had Tutsi children, grandchildren, and wives hiding in their homes, who were the dirt, and they should throw them out. After the speech, the crowd went to kill those people. Kalimanzira did not speak at the meeting.[299]

Defence Witness AM02

284. AM02 was a *communal* policeman in Muganza *commune* from 1992 until the end of June 1994. During the genocide, he was on guard duty at the Muganza *commune* office.[300]

Around 20 or 21 June 1994, he was on duty at the *commune* office during the installation of Élie Ndayambaje as the new *bourgmestre* of the *commune*. The meeting was held at about **[page 61]** 4:00 p.m., about 50 metres away from the office, in the woods. AM02 saw the vehicles of the authorities arrive, and he opened the barrier at the entrance to the *communal* office so that they could park inside its premises. The meeting did not last long, not even an hour, and after the meeting, the authorities returned, had some drinks at the *commune* office, and AM02 again opened the barrier so that they could leave. He did not see Kalimanzira, and asserts that he would have seen him or heard that he was there.[301]

Defence Witness AK42

285. AK42 attended two public meetings from April to June 1994;[302] the second Élie Ndayambaje's installation ceremony as new *bourgmestre* of Muganza *commune*. The meeting was held between 20 June and the end of June 1994, between 2:00-2:30 p.m., in a wood near the Muganza *commune* office. AK42 arrived before the meeting started, and stayed until the end. About 400 people were present, including authorities such as the new *préfet* Nteziryayo, the former *bourgmestre*, the new *bourgmestre* and the *conseillers* of the *secteurs*. Kalimanzira was not present at the meeting. AK42 asserts he could not have missed his presence because they had a close relationship and he was a well-known authority who would not have gone unnoticed.[303]

---

[295] T. 18 June 2008 pp. 50-51 (Witness BCA).
[296] T. 18 June 2008 p. 58 [closed] (Witness BCA).
[297] T. 18 June 2008 pp. 50-51 (Witness BCA).
[298] T. 16 June 2008 pp. 6, 18-20 (Witness BBB).
[299] T. 16 June 2008 pp. 19-20 (Witness BBB).
[300] T. 26 November 2008 pp. 6, 8 [closed] (Witness AM02).
[301] T. 26 November 2008 p. 13-14, 31-32 [closed] (Witness AM02).
[302] T. 27 November 2008 p. 4 [closed] (Witness AK42).
[303] T. 27 November 2008 pp. 7, 11 (Witness AK42).

Defence Witness Innocent Mukuralinda

286. Mukuralinda was the accountant for Kibayi *commune* from 1981 until 7 July 1994 when he went into exile.[304] On 22 June 1994, he attended a meeting to swear in the new *bourgmestre* of Muganza *commune*, Élie Ndayambaje, who was replacing Chrysologue Bimenyimana. The meeting was held not far from the Muganza *commune* office, in a wood. The distance between the office and the wood was around 20-30 metres. Mukuralinda arrived to the meeting, which started at 2:30 p.m., about five or ten minutes late, when Bimenyimana was speaking. Other authorities present included *préfet* Nteziryayo, Dominique Ntawukulilyayo (*sous-préfet* of Gisagara), and Bernadette Mukarurangwa (Member of Parliament). Mukuralinda did not see Kalimanzira. At the end of the meeting, Mukuralinda greeted the authorities and they went together to the venue of the reception.[305]

2.3.6.2. Deliberations

287. At the relevant time alleged, Kalimanzira claims to have been home in Butare *ville*. He also testified to attending the installation ceremony of Alphonse Nteziryayo as Butare's new *préfet* on 21 June 1994. As discussed above, the Chamber disbelieves his alibi (see III.1.2.2).

288. The Chamber notes that the Defence does not dispute that Élie Ndayambaje was inaugurated as the new *bourgmestre* of Muganza *commune* on or around 22 June 1994, given that several Defence witnesses testified to attending this event.

289. AM02 was a policeman in 1994. He was detained in Rwanda for four years, but then escaped prison and has fled the country.[306] His evidence is also discussed in relation to Kalimanzira's alleged incitement at the Kajyanama roadblock (see III.4.4). AM02 was **[page 62]** insistent that he would have seen Kalimanzira at the inauguration, despite the fact that he did not personally attend. The Chamber is not convinced. The simple fact that he did not see Kalimanzira pass through the *commune* office gate to park a vehicle or at the reception afterwards does not preclude Kalimanzira from having attended the meeting. Mukuralinda is currently in exile and although he claims he did not commit any crimes during the genocide, has been accused of taking part.[307] The Chamber found his responses to cross-examination to be evasive, and did not find his testimony to be credible. As for AM02, the Chamber does not place much weight on the Defence's implication that simply Mukuralinda did not see Kalimanzira, he could not have been there. AK42's evidence was also assessed in relation to Kalimanzira's alleged incitement at the Nyabisagara football field (see III.4.5.6). He was detained in Rwanda, but released without being charged. After being summoned, he fled Rwanda.[308] The Chamber found that he may be biased in favour of Kalimanzira in light of the fact that he worked with Kalimanzira while in exile in Kenya[309] and considered Kalimanzira to be almost like a brother.[310] His testimony that he did not see Kalimanzira at the inauguration ceremony does not contradict eyewitness accounts that he was there.

290. BBB has confessed to taking part in the genocide, but is awaiting trial on one charge he does not admit to.[311] He gave evidence relevant to other allegations and his credibility has been considered by the Chamber. The Chamber notes that he was an accomplice to the events pleaded at paragraph 17 of the Indictment, namely, instigation at the Muganza *commune* football field in May, and the Chamber found that his testimony in that respect should accordingly be treated with caution (see III.2.8.2). BCA has also confessed to taking part in the genocide and is currently detained.[312]

---

[304] T. 3 December 2008 p. 3 (Innocent Mukuralinda).
[305] T. 3 December 2008 pp. 8-9, 41-42 (Innocent Mukuralinda).
[306] T. 26 November 2008 pp. 7, 31 [closed] (Witness AM02).
[307] T. 3 December 2008 pp. 3-4, 10-13, 21, 29-40 (Innocent Mukuralinda).
[308] T. 26 November 2008 p. 66 [closed] (Witness AK42).
[309] T. 27 November 2008 pp. 3 [closed], 16, 20 (Witness AK42).
[310] T. 27 November 2008 p. 15 (Witness AK42).
[311] T. 16 June 2008 pp. 3, 6 [closed] (Witness BBB).
[312] T. 18 June 2008 p. 41 [closed] (Witness BCA).

291. BBB and BCA testimonies corroborated one another. Their recollection of Ndayambaje's and the authorities in attendance was consistent. Their accounts are supported by the fact that Kalimanzira was a native of Muganza *commune* and that attending the swearing-in of a *bourgmestres* and *préfets* was within his professional duties. This is evidenced by Kalimanzira's admitted attendance to Alphonse Nteziryayo's swearing-in ceremony on 21 June 1994.[313] The Chamber finds that the slight discrepancies in their evidence raised by the Defence are insignificant and do not undermine their credibility.[314] Having carefully considered their evidence, the Chamber considers BBB and BCA's evidence to be reliable. The Chamber accepts that Ndayambaje spoke at the meeting, particularly given that its purpose was to inaugurate him as *bourgmestre*. Although Kalimanzira is not alleged to have spoken at the meeting, the Chamber finds that he was present and failed to take exception to Ndayambaje's remarks. The Chamber also believes BBB and BCA's evidence that Tutsis were killed following the inauguration ceremony.

292. The Chamber finds that the only reasonable conclusion that can be drawn from the evidence is that Kalimanzira knew that Ndayambaje's speech would instigate the persons present during this meeting to kill Tutsis and that this instigation would serve as a factor substantially contributing to the conduct of those persons who actually committed killings of Tutsis. The Chamber also finds that Kalimanzira's presence during Ndayambaje's speech lent moral support to Ndayambaje's instigation of genocide. As a well-respected authority figure **[page 63]** in Butare, particularly as a native of Muganza *commune,* and as a high-level government official, Kalimanzira's moral support was a factor substantially contributing to the commission of this crime. Given their relative positions of authority and responsibilities, Kalimanzira must have known that Ndayambaje and the audience would interpret his presence during Ndayambaje's speech as a form of support, encouragement, and tacit approval, for Ndayambaje's instigation of acts of genocide, and that his presence during Ndayambaje's speech would therefore have the effect of substantially contributing to the killings which followed.

293. Kalimanzira exhibited here, and elsewhere, an intent to destroy the Tutsi group (see III.5.2). For these reasons, the Chamber finds Kalimanzira guilty beyond reasonable doubt of aiding and abetting genocide by his presence at the inauguration of Élie Ndayambaje on or around 22 June 1994.

2.4. Kabuye Hill, 23 April

294. At paragraphs 9 and 10 of the Indictment, the Prosecution charges Kalimanzira with Genocide for killings at Kabuye hill (Ndora *commune*) around 23 April 1994. Kalimanzira is accused of having personally encouraged Tutsi civilians to take refuge on Kabuye hill, promising them protection and food, in order to lure them there and facilitate their subsequent demise. Kalimanzira allegedly sought communal police and military reinforcement to assist in the attack, discussed the progress of the killings at the hill with local authorities, and personally supervised the attacks to ensure successful extermination. This resulted in thousands of Tutsis being killed at Kabuye hill.

295. Kalimanzira relies on his alibi that he was at work in Murambi (Gitarama *préfecture*) on 23 April 1994 and the days following (see III.1.2).

2.4.1. Evidence

Prosecution Witness BBO

296. BBO testified that at the end of April 1994, his *conseiller de secteur* instructed all Hutus and Burundian refugees in Mukindo *secteur* (Kibayi *commune*) that they were to go to Kabuye hill in order to kill Tutsis. The *conseiller* indicated that the instructions had come from higher authorities, and that the large group of people who had gathered at Kabuye hill posed a threat to Hutus. Armed with the weapons they had received at the Burundian refugee camp in Kanage *cellule* (see III.4.2.1), BBO and the Burundian refugees,

---

[313] T. 10 February 2009 pp. 52-53 (Callixte Kalimanzira); T. 5 February 2009 pp. 10-11 (Salomé Mukantwali).
[314] Defence Closing Brief, paras. 508-510, 591-593.

Prosecutor v. Kalimanzira

as well as other civilians, walked five or six hours before reaching Kabuye hill. The *conseiller* and policemen from Kibayi *commune* armed with rifles also went to Kabuye hill, but travelled by vehicle.[315]

297. BBO testified that they left very early in the morning, arriving at Kabuye hill by approximately midday, and were joined by several other attackers from other *communes,* such as Ndora and Muganza. He described how they encircled the Tutsis on the hill and attempted to attack them; however, the Tutsis defended themselves with rocks leading the attackers to retreat and the leaders of the attack to panic. BBO and others thought there might be armed *Inkotanyi* among the Tutsi refugees. Soon thereafter, Kalimanzira and Colonel Tharcisse Muvunyi arrived with approximately 150 soldiers on two buses. In fact, BBO stated that almost all authorities from Butare *préfecture* were present. BBO explained that the soldiers hid among the civilian attackers when shooting at the Tutsi refugees. However, this caused the civilian attackers to fear being shot at, in turn causing them to flee. BBO and **[page 64]** others trekked five or six hours back to Mukindo *secteur* to spend the night. They returned to Kabuye hill the following morning, where BBO discovered hundreds of corpses.[316]

Prosecution Witness BDC

298. BDC is a Hutu. She was married to a Tutsi in 1994. In April 1994, she and her family fled their home in order to escape the house burnings and killings that had begun to take place in their area. They went first to the Gisagara marketplace, before ultimately seeking refuge at Kabuye hill.[317]

299. BDC testified that she and her family left their home on a Saturday morning in April, reached the Gisagara marketplace early that afternoon, and found that a large group of refugees,[318] policemen, soldiers, Dominique Ntawukulilyayo (*sous-préfet* of Gisagara) and Kalimanzira were already there. BDC described how, after calling upon the crowd to assemble, *sous-préfet* Ntawukulilyayo instructed them to go to Kabuye hill and promised that their safety would be ensured. BDC stated that during the address, Kalimanzira stood next to *sous-préfet* Ntawukulilyayo but did not speak. She asserted that she could see Kalimanzira and the *sous-préfet* clearly from her location in the middle of the square.[319]

300. BDC testified that following *sous-préfet* Ntawukulilyayo's speech, the policemen and soldiers immediately escorted them and the other refugees to Kabuye hill where they encountered more refugees from neighbouring areas. BDC recalled that they arrived at the hill while it was still daylight. Kalimanzira and *sous-préfet* Ntawukulilyayo subsequently arrived in a vehicle, accompanied by soldiers and police officers. Kalimanzira and the *souspréfet* got out of the vehicle, looked around, and then left with the vehicle.[320]

301. BDC testified that the refugees were then attacked. Soldiers and policemen began shooting at the refugees, who fought back by throwing stones at their attackers. The gunfire was not heavy, and although some people were killed that day, BDC and her family chose to stay put and spent the night on Kabuye hill. The next morning, on Sunday, the shooting resumed and intensified. The refugees were surrounded and shot at from several different directions, including Gahondo hill. BDC explained that on Sunday night, whilst it was raining heavily and they were being attacked, she and her family fled to another part of the hill and hid in some bushes.[321]

302. On Monday morning, BDC returned to the location on the hill where the refugees had first assembled in order to retrieve her belongings. There she saw dead bodies of all genders and ages strewn over the area, the majority of which were Tutsi. She further recalled that she witnessed the *Interahamwe* looting and stealing cattle. BDC stated that, at her husband's behest, she left Kabuye hill that same morning to go to her

---

[315] T. 19 June 2008 pp. 44 (Witness BBO).
[316] T. 19 June 2008 pp. 44-47 and T. 20 June 2008 pp. 11-13 (Witness BBO).
[317] T. 9 May 2008 pp. 26-27 (Witness BDC).
[318] The term "refugees" is used here colloquially to refer to anyone who fled their homes in search of refuge. However, Rwandan Tutsis who sought refuge in various places throughout Rwanda are more accurately categorized as "internally displaced persons".
[319] T. 9 May 2008 pp. 27-28 (Witness BDC).
[320] T. 9 May 2008 pp. 28-29 (Witness BDC).
[321] T. 9 May 2008 pp. 29-32 (Witness BDC).

parents' house. BDC's husband explained that as a Hutu, she could survive, but that he, a Tutsi, could not leave the hill without being killed. She never saw him again.[322] **[page 65]**

Prosecution Witness BCF

303. BCF testified that on Wednesday, 20 April 1994, Tutsi refugees from Kibayi and Muganza *communes* began arriving in the Gisagara marketplace. BCF stated that they came there because there were officials present and they thought that they would be protected. He recalled that the refugees spent three days at the marketplace before moving to Kabuye hill. BCF could not estimate the number of refugees but indicated that the market was so crowded that they overflowed into shops.[323]

304. BCF testified that at 8:00 a.m. on Saturday, 23 April 1994, he opened his shop as usual. Then at approximately 2:00 p.m., Kalimanzira and *sous-préfet* Ntawukulilyayo arrived at the marketplace in a white double-cabin pickup. *Sous-préfet* Ntawukulilyayo was driving the vehicle and Kalimanzira was in the passenger seat; there were also policemen on board, carrying firearms and wearing black helmets and overcoats. BCF identified one of the policemen as brigadier Vincent. BCF further recalled that the *sous-préfet* parked the truck on the road, right at the entrance of the marketplace, and that he and Kalimanzira disembarked first, followed by the policemen.[324]

305. BCF testified that Kalimanzira and *sous-préfet* Ntawukulilyayo entered the marketplace, whereupon the *sous-préfet* asked three policemen, who had come from the commune office, to blow their whistles. Upon hearing the whistles, the refugees assembled and BCF joined the crowd. BCF recalled that he was less than two metres from Kalimanzira. BCF further recalled that the *sous-préfet* addressed the refugees, without the use of a microphone, whilst Kalimanzira stood beside him. The *sous-préfet* instructed the refugees to go to Kabuye hill, where they would be protected and given food and shelter. After delivering his message, *sous-préfet* Ntawukulilyayo asked the refugees to pass it along to the others in the marketplace.[325]

306. BCF testified that because he was a Tutsi and saw killers wearing banana leaf uniforms and carrying weapons, he immediately joined the refugees and headed towards Kabuye. He did not collect any personal effects. He recalled that because of the large number of refugees, the trip took one and a half hours rather than the usual 15-20 minutes. BCF stated that since they had come from different localities, he did not know many of his fellow refugees. He did, however, name two survivors from Muganza: Cassien and Bizunu. BCF stated that the policemen accompanied the refugees until they reached *sous-préfet* Ntawukulilyayo's residence.[326]

307. BCF testified that they arrived at Kabuye hill in the early evening, whereupon they settled on the highest hill and those with babies looked for food. He recalled that in addition to the refugees that had gathered at Gisagara trading center, there were Tutsis who had travelled from other localities after Hutus burned their homes.[327]

308. BCF testified that at dusk two pick-up trucks arrived at the base of the hill upon which the refugees had assembled. He recalled that refugees continued to arrive from more distant localities like Dahwe and Gahondo after the vehicles arrived. BCF stated that Kalimanzira and *sous-préfet* Ntawukulilyayo were in the cab of one vehicle, with numerous soldiers and **[page 66]** policemen in the rear. The second vehicle was filled with many soldiers. BCF further stated that he did not see any women among the passengers.[328]

309. BCF testified that Kalimanzira and the *sous-préfet* disembarked from the trucks along with the soldiers, who then surrounded the hill and began shooting at the refugees. The refugees began to retreat but were trapped at the top of the hill. BCF recalled that when the shooting began, Kalimanzira remained with *sous-préfet* Ntawukulilyayo a short while before leaving. BCF explained that there was a gap between the

---

[322] T. 9 May 2008 pp. 32-33 (Witness BDC).
[323] T. 5 May 2008 pp. 10-11 and T. 12 May 2008 pp. 10-12 (Witness BCF).
[324] T. 12 May 2008 pp. 11-19, 33 (Witness BCF).
[325] T. 5 May 2008 pp. 10-12 and T. 12 May 2008 pp. 27-29 (Witness BCF).
[326] T. 5 May 2008 pp. 12-13 and T. 12 May 2008 pp. 32-33 (Witness BCF).
[327] T. 5 May 2008 p. 13 and T. 12 May 2008 p. 33 (Witness BCF).
[328] T. 5 May 2008 p. 13 and T. 12 May 2008 pp. 33-37 (Witness BCF).

arrival of the vehicles and the start of the shooting because the attackers waited until it was dark enough that they could not be identified.[329]

310. BCF testified that the shooting stopped when it started to rain and became completely dark. This enabled him to escape onto a hill parallel to Kabuye hill, in the direction of the church and Gisagara. He recalled that he stayed in a wood that belonged to the priests and reached his mother and stepfather's house four days after escaping.[330]

Prosecution Witness BWO

311. BWO is a Tutsi survivor who lost many members of his family at the attack on Kabuye hill. BWO testified that he left his house and went to Gisagara marketplace two to three weeks after the death of President Habyarimana. There was tension in Kabuye *cellule* such that Hutus had attacked his home and it on fire. The marketplace was a 15 minute trek from his home and he recalled that he went there accompanied by his neighbours and members of his family.[331]

312. BWO testified that when he arrived at the marketplace at around 6:30-7:00 p.m., a large crowd had already assembled. BWO estimated that were 2,000 people, all of whom were Tutsi civilians, ranging in age and had come from Kibayi, Muganza, Nyaruhengeri, Ndora, and Muyaga *communes*. BWO explained that they had come to Gisagara marketplace because they thought local officials would protect them. He stayed at the marketplace for two nights, settling near the Abizeramariya convent with his family. He recalled that the shops were closed and that the refugees prepared food when they arrived or ate what they had brought.[332]

313. BWO testified that at about 3:00 p.m. on the third day, *sous-préfet* Ntawukulilyayo addressed the crowd. BWO recalled that he arrived at the marketplace on foot from the *communal* office and that his vehicle, a red Hilux, was parked at the edge of the road in front of a shop belonging to Kayikana. BWO recognised the *sous-préfet*, whose home was located only a 15-minute trek away from BWO's. *Sous-préfet* Ntawukulilyayo was accompanied by two policemen, who BWO identified as Patern and Munyankindi. The policemen wore green uniforms, black caps with visors, and were carrying firearms.[333]

314. BWO testified that one of the policemen blew his whistle, and the marketplace became quiet. Then, using a megaphone to amplify his voice, the *sous-préfet* addressed the seated crowd and asked the refugees to go to Kabuye hill, where their security would be guaranteed. The refugees began packing their personal effects and started leaving in waves **[page 67]** from about 6:30-7:00 p.m. BWO, along with his family and cattle, joined them, leaving for Kabuye hill at about 8:00 p.m.[334]

315. BWO testified that *sous-préfet* Ntawukulilyayo sent people to accompany the refugees, including Innocent Gakeri from Dahwe, but they were not accompanied for the whole journey. BWO recalled that the refugees travelled the relatively short distance to Kabuye hill all through the night. He further recalled that there was a single road to the hill, and because the refugees were so numerous, the trek took two hours rather than the usual 30 to 40 minutes. BWO stated that the refugees from the Gisagara marketplace were the first to arrive at Kabuye hill, but were later joined by refugees from other localities.[335]

316. BWO testified that on the first day and night he arrived, nothing out of the ordinary happened. However, he recalled that the next day, Hutu civilians armed with spears, machetes, and clubs came to steal their cattle. This attack carried on for two days, and after some refugees were killed trying to repel the attackers, they let them take the cattle away. On the third day there was a second attack by Hutu civilians and the *Interahamwe* which began at 8:30 a.m., continuing for approximately one hour. BWO recalled that it was

---

[329] T. 5 May 2008 p. 14 and T. 12 May 2008 p. 39 (Witness BCF).
[330] T. 12 May 2008 pp. 39-40 (Witness BCF).
[331] T. 5 May 2008 pp. 24-25, 33 (Witness BWO).
[332] T. 5 May 2008 pp. 25-26 and T. 12 May 2008 pp. 60-62 (Witness BWO).
[333] T. 12 May 2008 pp. 62-64 (Witness BWO).
[334] T. 5 May 2008 p. 26, T. 12 May 2008 pp. 64, 69, and T. 19 May 2008 p. 2 (Witness BWO).
[335] T. 5 May 2008 pp. 26-27, T. 12 May 2008 p. 65 and T. 19 May 2008 p. 3 (Witness BWO).

Judgement

more violent and the focus was no longer on stealing cattle; although some refugees were killed, they defended themselves and pushed the attackers back.[336]

317. BWO testified that at about 11:00 a.m. or 12:00 p.m., Kalimanzira arrived at Kabuye hill in a red pick-up truck, accompanied by a soldier in the back and a woman in the passenger seat. The soldier and Kalimanzira disembarked from the vehicle and were approached by a group of about 70 refugees, led by an elderly man from Muganza *secteur* in Kigarama named Boniface Ndanga. Boniface identified Kalimanzira to the refugees and told them they should tell them about the attacks because he was a man of authority coming to ensure their safety. BWO indicated that there were many people, including Boniface, between him and Kalimanzira, but that he was close enough to hear the subsequent conversation. Boniface told Kalimanzira that civilians had attacked, stolen cows, and killed some of the refugees. Kalimanzira then promised that he would protect the refugees and ensure their safety.[337]

318. BWO testified that shortly thereafter, a group of civilians from Dahwe *cellule* arrived and stood behind the vehicle. BWO stated that he thought that they had travelled to the hill with Kalimanzira, but arrived later because they were on foot. He recalled that Kalimanzira told the men that they "should kill them immediately because the others have already finished", indicating that they should kill the Tutsis. BWO stated that the refugees fled, but that those who were not strong enough to run were killed on the spot. Kalimanzira then left the hill in his vehicle.[338]

319. BWO testified that later on in the morning a vehicle brought soldiers to Gisagara, where they joined with *Interahamwe* and walked to Kabuye hill on foot, arriving at 1:00 p.m.. The civilian attackers from Dahwe also returned to the hill. BWO recalled that the soldiers and *Interahamwe* began shooting immediately; other attackers used machetes and bladed weapons. The attack continued until it was dark; when BWO escaped at 10:30-11:00 p.m., the soldiers were still shooting. BWO explained that he escaped through sheer luck and could **[page 68]** not describe his route off of the hill. He lost many family members in the attack, including eight brothers and sisters, three cousins, and four uncles.[339]

Prosecution Witness BXG

320. BXG is a Tutsi survivor of the killings on Kabuye hill; many members of his family died there. He heard of the death of President Habyarimana on 7 April 1994 and remained at home until the afternoon of Friday, 22 April when, upon his parents' request, he went to visit his sister-in-law and her five children at their home in Kabuye *cellule*.[340]

321. BXG testified that on Saturday 23 April 1994, he saw Kalimanzira at the Mukabuga roadblock, at the intersection of the roads to Muganza and Kabuye. BXG explained that he had gone to the roadblock, which was only 10-15 metres from his brother's house, in order to pass time. There were three Hutu men at the roadblock. BXG further explained that killings in the area had not yet begun and consequently he was not afraid.

322. He recalled that sometime before noon, Kalimanzira arrived at the roadblock in a white saloon vehicle, similar to that owned to the *sous-préfet*, Dominique Ntawukulilyayo. BXG further recalled that Kalimanzira was accompanied by two soldiers in military uniform and black berets who were armed with Kalashnikovs and a driver in civilian clothes. BXG explained that he, a mere peasant, did not dare speak to Kalimanzira, a senior official; however, he was five to seven steps away and could hear everything that was said.[341]

323. BXG testified that, after exiting the vehicle with the two soldiers, Kalimanzira asked Callixte Bushakwe, the *responsable de cellule* and head of the group at the roadblock, where he was with the problem of the Tutsis. Bushakwe responded that they had all been killed, whereupon one of the men at the roadblock,

---

[336] T. 5 May 2008 pp. 27-28 and T. 12 May 2008 pp. 69-70 (Witness BWO).
[337] T. 5 May 2008 pp. 28-30 and T. 19 May 2008 pp. 6-7, 9 (Witness BWO).
[338] T. 5 May 2008 pp. 30-31 and T. 19 May 2008 pp. 8-9 (Witness BWO).
[339] T. 5 May 2008 pp. 31-33 and T. 12 May 2008 p. 11 (Witness BWO).
[340] T. 22 May 2008 pp. 5-7, 16 (Witness BXG).
[341] T. 22 May 2008 pp. 7-9, 16-18 (Witness BXG).

Prosecutor v. Kalimanzira

Isidore, interjected and told Kalimanzira that Bushawke was lying and that the Tutsis had successfully defended themselves against attack. BXG recalled that Kalimanzira spat at Bushakwe and attempted to slap him. Kalimanzira asked Isidore show him where the Tutsis were. The group then left the roadblock in the direction of Dahwe *secteur*. BXG explained that the Tutsis from Kibayi, Muganza, Ndora and Ngoma *communes* had gathered on "Wabitama" (*i.e.* Kabuye hill) and successfully resisted attack.[342]

324. BXG testified that the vehicle returned to the roadblock after 30 minutes and Isidore exited. Kalimanzira continued in the direction of Gisagara. BXG explained that, following the encounter and Bushakwe's comments about killing Tutsis, he became fearful of the deteriorating situation and returned to his brother's home. After collecting some provisions he went to Wabitama with his sister-in-law and her five children. They arrived at noon and joined the other refugees, whom BXG estimated to number 40,000-50,000.[343]

325. BXG spent two days on Kabuye hill. He testified that the first attack he witnessed occurred on the Saturday he arrived. He recalled that armed Hutu policemen were interspersed with civilian attackers who carried traditional weapons. BXG described the policemen as wearing green uniforms and black berets, and could name several of them because he recognised them as being from his local area. BXG recalled that the Tutsis successfully repelled the attack but that later that afternoon another wave of attacks was **[page 69]** followed, this time reinforced by soldiers. The shooting ceased at nightfall but resumed the following morning, Sunday, until nightfall when there was heavy rainfall. BXG hid in a sorghum field and managed to escape the hill on Monday evening.[344]

Prosecution Witness BWK

326. BWK testified that she saw Kalimanzira on 23 April 1994. She had gone to her parents' house in Kabuye *cellule* after a neighbour told her that her brother had died. Upon arriving at her parents' home, BWK found her brother there and alive. There were also several refugees who had arrived from Muganza and Dahwe hills the night before after their houses had been burnt down. The refugees were Tutsi civilians of both genders and ranged in age from children to adults.[345]

327. BWK testified that she left her parents' house with approximately 13 of the refugees after realising that it was not secure. She intended to take them to the house where she had been staying and which she considered safe. BWK recalled that whilst walking on the road from Gisagara to Kabuye they encountered a white double-cabin pick-up near the home of a man named Misago. The time was around 2:00-3:00 p.m. BWK saw Kalimanzira in the vehicle, accompanied by a civilian driver and two soldiers who were sitting in the uncovered back section with firearms and wearing camouflage uniforms with green helmets. BXG explained that she recognised Kalimanzira because she had met him once before and because she was told who he was later that day.[346]

328. Kalimanzira stopped and asked them where they were going. One woman informed him that they were fleeing because their houses had been burnt down. BWK told Kalimanzira that she was taking to the people to a more secure place. Kalimanzira then questioned her as to whether she had the necessary resources to feed everyone. He instructed them to go to Kabuye hill because it was safe and nothing could happen to them. When they refused to do so, which would have involved retracing their steps, the two soldiers asked them if they had not heard properly. BWK explained that in her opinion, Kalimanzira used a threatening tone and she knew they were being prohibited from leaving.[347]

329. BWK testified that for seven minutes, Kalimanzira drove behind the group as they walked towards Kabuye hill. When they reached the intersection of the roads to Dahwe /Kirarambogo and Kabuye, they met a Hutu man named Gakeri coming from the direction of Kirarambogo. Gakeri was alone and unarmed and

---

[342] T. 22 May 2008 pp. 9-12, 19-20, 22 (Witness BXG).
[343] T. 22 May 2008 pp. 11, 23 (Witness BXG).
[344] T. 22 May 2008 pp. 12-13, 23-25, 27 (Witness BXG).
[345] T. 9 May 2008 pp. 17-18 and T. 19 May 2008 p. 59 (Witness BWK).
[346] T. 9 May 2008 pp. 18-19, 21 and T. 19 May 2008 p. 60-62 (Witness BWK).
[347] T. 9 May 2008 p. 19 and T. 19 May 2008 p. 63 (Witness BWK).

Judgement

BWK knew him because he lived locally in Dahwe *secteur*. Kalimanzira instructed Gakeri to escort the group to Kabuye hill before continuing in the direction of Dahwe/Kirarambogo. BWK recalled that it took the group approximately 35 minutes to cover the 1.3 kilometres between the intersection and Kabuye hill. Whilst walking with BWK, Gakeri told her that the man in the car was Kalimanzira.[348]

330. BWK testified that upon arriving at Kabuye hill they joined the other refugees. After waiting 40 minutes, BWK left Kabuye hill and returned home to breastfeed her young child. She explained she knew from the outset that she could not stay on Kabuye hill but followed Kalimanzira's instructions anyway because he had threatened that if he met any of them on the road again they would have problems. Although she did not witness any attack on Kabuye hill while she was there, BWK heard gunshots during the night and has never again seen any **[page 70]** of the refugees she walked to the hill with. BWK believes that in all probability, they were killed there.[349]

Prosecution Witness BDK

331. BDK recalled that the killings at Kabuye hill started on a Saturday evening approximately two weeks after the death of President Habyarimana. She heard shooting that evening whilst at home and realised they were coming from Kabuye hill. She further recalled that on Sunday night there was heavy rainfall. BDK also stated that a further attack was launched by the *Interahamwe* and Burundians on Monday morning.[350]

332. BDK testified that on the Monday after the killings at Kabuye hill, whilst returning from filling her bucket at the tap inside Fidèle Uwizeye's compound, she saw a group of people standing in front of Uwizeye's house. BDK identified them as Kalimanzira, *sousprefet* Ntawukulilyayo, Bernadette Mukaruruwanga, Fidèle Uwizeye, Joseph Kamanza and Vincent. She overheard them discussing the killings at Kabuye hill[351] and heard Kalimanzira say the firing had dispersed the people and that a bullet cannot find a person hiding in a shrub so they should therefore use traditional weapons instead. BDK further recalled that they spoke about a group of people who were going to come and who would be sent to Nyakibungo *cellule* and Kabuye hill to carry out killings using traditional weapons.[352]

Prosecution Witness BWL

333. BWL said he saw Kalimanzira give a firearm to someone at the Jaguar roadblock (see also III.4.3.1). He said that Kalimanzira instructed the people at Jaguar roadblock who were sending Tutsis to Kabuye hill to ensure their safety. He also asserted that Kalimanzira was the one who ordered that Tutsis be sent to Kabuye hill and that the firearm he distributed at Jaguar roadblock was meant be used at Kabuye hill.[353]

Other Prosecution Witnesses

334. BCZ participated in the Kabuye hill killings for three days (Saturday to Monday) in April 1994. He recalled only *sous-préfet* Ntawukulilyayo as giving instructions and directions to mount the attack. BCZ asserted that he did not see Kalimanzira at all during the three days he spent at Kabuye hill.[354]

335. BBB also testified about his participation in the Kabuye hill killings, implicating *sous-préfet* Ntawukulilyayo, but made no mention of Kalimanzira's alleged involvement whatsoever.[355]

---

[348] T. 9 May 2008 pp. 20-21, T. 19 May 2008 p. 64 and T. 30 May 2008 pp. 3-4 (Witness BWK).
[349] T. 9 May 2008 p. 21 and T. 30 May 2008 pp. 4-6 (Witness BWK).
[350] T. 20 May 2008 pp. 47-48 [closed] (Witness BDK).
[351] BDK also refers to Kabuye hill as "Wabitama".
[352] T. 20 May 2008 pp. 49-52 [closed] (Witness BDK).
[353] T. 23 June 2008 pp. 44, 46 and 62 (Witness BWL).
[354] T. 24 June 2008 pp. 57, 59-60 (Witness BCZ).
[355] T. 16 June 2008 pp. 11-13, 41-44 (Witness BBB).

Defence Witness AK11

336. AK11 and his family sought refuge on Kabuye hill in April 1994. AK11 testified that around 19 April 1994, on a Wednesday,[356] Tutsi refugees arrived *en masse* in his local area. **[page 71]** AK11 recalled that the refugees told him that they were fleeing because people were hunting them down to kill them and that they intended to flee to neighbouring Burundi. Upon hearing this, AK11 along with his family and other members of his local population, the majority of whom were Tutsis, decided to follow.[357]

337. AK11 and his family left their home that same Wednesday at around 5:00 p.m. and headed toward Gisagara. They reached the Gisagara marketplace at nightfall the same day, which was a market day, and spent the night in the market square, which doubled as a football pitch on non-market days. The following day, on Thursday, they resumed their journey towards Burundi, but were subsequently turned back to Gisagara by a group of armed persons. They returned to the Gisagara marketplace at approximately 4:30 p.m., but decided to return home after realising their security was not guaranteed there. On their way home, they crossed paths with a group of Tutsi refugees near Kabuye hill who advised them that they should stay together in order to defend themselves. AK11 and his family followed them to Kabuye hill where they met many other refugees. AK11 recalled that he did not see refugees on any other hill and affirmed that all of the refugees were on the slope of Kabuye hill opposite Dahwe *secteur*.[358]

338. AK11 and his family spent Thursday night on the hill. He described how the young adults spread out around the hill and carried out night patrols in order to act as security for the women and children. AK11 stated that there were no attacks that night but that he heard Hutus had attempted to steal cattle from the Tutsis earlier that day. AK11 recalled that the following afternoon, on Friday, they were attacked from Gahondo hill (facing Kabuye hill) and attempted to defend themselves using traditional weapons and stones. The attacks ended at around 5:00 p.m. when the attackers returned home. AK11 stated that he spent Friday night on the hill and recalled that there were no attacks that night either.[359]

339. AK11 testified that there was an attack on Saturday afternoon. The attackers, some of whom wore military uniforms and the berets of gendarmes, started gathering on Gahondo hill in the morning, and in numbers larger than the previous day. They had come from several locations. At around 4:00 p.m., AK11 saw a long line of civilians led by soldiers with guns heading into the valley between Kabuye hill and Gahondo hill, whereupon they circled the hill and began to advance towards the refugees. The refugees withdrew but soon had nowhere to go, and started shouting and crying in fear for their lives. In desperation, the refugees began throwing stones and spears, and the soldiers responded with gunfire. The attack lasted until 6:00 p.m., by which point the soldiers had run out of ammunition and heavy rainfall was quickly approaching. Once the rain fell, AK11 and others managed to escape from the hills.[360]

340. AK11 testified that he did not see Kalimanzira at Kabuye hill and did not hear anyone mention that Kalimanzira had been there during the attacks. AK11 explained that had Kalimanzira been present, he would have been informed because Kalimanzira was well known and it would have been a topic of discussion. AK11 reiterated that at no time after the attacks at Kabuye hill did he hear that Kalimanzira had played any part whatsoever in their planning. Finally, AK11 stated that he was told after the attacks that the soldiers had arrived **[page 72]** at Kabuye hill in vehicles; however, he did not hear that Kalimanzira had been in any of those vehicles.[361]

Defence Witness FCS

341. FCS is a Tutsi survivor who testified that he fled to Kabuye hill on Wednesday, 20 April 1994, where he found a crowd already there, and spent the night. The next morning, he noticed attackers had arrived to loot the property of refugees. As a result, that afternoon he and others fled the hill for the Gisagara

---

[356] Wednesday fell on the 20th of April in 1994.
[357] T. 29 January 2009 pp. 6-8 (Witness AK11).
[358] T. 29 January 2009 pp. 7-9 (Witness AK11).
[359] T. 29 January 2009 pp. 9-10 (Witness AK11).
[360] T. 29 January 2009 pp. 9-14 (Witness AK11).
[361] T. 29 January 2009 pp. 13-16, 21, 23, and 29 (Witness AK11).

Judgement

marketplace. He observed that as they were leaving, others were just arriving to Kabuye hill. Upon reaching Gisagara, FCS settled with others in a small centre near the marketplace and spent the next two nights there. At 9:30 a.m. on Saturday, 23 April 1994, he saw a group of people arrive whom he did not know, but who later introduced themselves; it was the *bourgmestre* and the *sous-préfet,* in the company of other colleagues. At some point they addressed the crowd; the *bourgmestre* took the floor, followed by the *sous-préfet* who told the refugees to move to Kabuye hill where they would be safe. FCS was standing about 10 metres away from the officials when they spoke. The refugees left calmly and immediately, arriving at the hill around 11:00 a.m.[362]

342. Upon arrival, FCS saw that there were still many refugees on the hill. He settled in the same location he had on the Wednesday prior and hoped this time they would be protected, but quickly realized that the same looters had returned that Saturday. By 6:00 p.m., he saw a *communal* policeman had arrived, which he assumed was for the refugees' protection. Instead, he heard gunshots and saw a large group of people assemble who started throwing stones at the refugees and attacking them with sticks. When FCS saw that their aim was to kill, not to loot, he and others fled right away, scattered. Some were killed on the way, but he and another person reached a swamp far from the hill, where they spent the night. He could still hear the gunshots. He did not return to Kabuye hill. FCS concluded his testimony by stating that he never heard mention of Kalimanzira and never saw any vehicles while on Kabuye hill.[363]

Defence Witness ACB6

343. ACB6 lived near Kabuye hill in 1994. She testified that she and her family fled to Kabuye hill approximately two weeks after the death of President Habyarimana because the Hutus and Tutsis in her local area started killing each other. She recalled that they left for the hill on Wednesday, which was a market day, at approximately 3:00 or 4:00 p.m., following their neighbours and others who were also fleeing. They arrived at the hill at approximately 6:00 p.m.; the journey took longer than usual because they had taken their cattle with them. ACB6 stated that they spent the night at the top of the hill alongside many people from various *communes*. She said nothing happened that night and they stayed on the hill on Thursday, collecting food from farms on the neighbouring Gahondo hill.[364]

344. ACB6 testified that she and her family spent Thursday night on the hill, and again, there were no problems. However, on Friday the situation changed. At approximately 11:00 a.m., ACB6 and others saw a crowd of people gathering on Gahondo hill who started throwing stones and attacking the refugees on Kabuye hill. She recalled that the Tutsi refugees defended themselves and that she contributed to the efforts by gathering stones to be thrown at the attackers. She further recalled that in the afternoon the attacks stopped for a **[page 73]** while before resuming again at 4:00 p.m. The attackers eventually left after being repelled by the refugees and stealing several cows. ACB6 and her family spent Friday night on the hill without further problems.[365]

345. On Saturday morning, the attackers returned in larger numbers and equipped with firearms. She stated that the attack started at 11:00 a.m., after which it stopped for a while before increasing in intensity again at approximately 3:00 p.m. and continuing until nightfall. She was located near the top of Kabuye hill; the attacks were launched from Gahondo hill. ACB6 recalled that the Tutsis continued to defend themselves until it began raining heavily, which caused some of the attackers to leave whilst others remained and looted. Some Tutsis attempted to flee the hill and take refuge at the Gisagara *commune* office, but were prevented from doing so on their way, so she and others fled to the sorghum and banana plantations to hide instead. ACB6 came out of hiding on Sunday morning, returning to Kabuye hill, and then returning home, only to find her house had been burnt down. She was the only person in her family to survive. Subsequently, she went to live with an elderly Hutu woman who was a friend of the family.[366]

---

[362] T. 29 January 2009 pp. 43-48 (Witness FCS).
[363] T. 29 January 2009 pp. 48-49 (Witness FCS).
[364] T. 29 January 2009 p. 54 and T. 2 February 2009 pp. 4-7 (Witness ACB6).
[365] T. 2 February 2009 pp. 8-9 (Witness ACB6).
[366] T. 2 February 2009 pp. 9-12 (Witness ACB6).

346. ACB6 testified that she saw no vehicles approach Kabuye hill from her time of arrival on Wednesday until her departure on Sunday, and that the attackers had not come by road because there were no roads in the area. She did not see or hear about Kalimanzira being at Kabuye hill between her time of arrival on the Wednesday and her departure on the Sunday; in fact, she did not see Kalimanzira at all in 1994.[367]

Defence Witness Denis Ndamyumugabe

347. Ndamyumugabe lived in Gitwa *cellule* (Dahwe *secteur,* Muganza *commune*) in 1994, a five minute walking distance from Kabuye hill. He testified that on a Wednesday, two weeks after the death of President Habyarimana, his *conseiller de secteur* assembled the local population at the *secteur* office and warned them to protect themselves against the many unknown Tutsis gathered on Kabuye hill, which posed a security threat as the country was at war. Ndamyumugabe recalled the *conseiller* instructed the population of Dahwe to chase the Tutsis from the hill. Ndamyumugabe knew that the Tutsis had fled to the Kabuye hill because they feared for their lives. However, having been threatened with punishment if they failed to participate, he and the others followed the *conseiller*'s instructions and headed to the hill immediately.[368]

348. Ndamyumugabe recalled that they arrived at approximately 1:00 p.m. and began to throw stones at the Tutsis, who did the same in defence. When the attackers grew tired, they returned to their *cellules* and came back to the hill the following day. The situation repeated itself over four days, from Wednesday through Saturday, on which day the final attack was launched, this time with the assistance of soldiers. They persisted until nightfall, at which point it began to rain heavily, so they retreated. When he returned on Sunday, there was nobody left to attack. Ndamyumugabe asserted that at no point did he see any vehicles at Kabuye hill. At no point during those four days did he see Kalimanzira, nor did he ever hear anyone mention Kalimanzira's presence at Kabuye hill at any point in time.[369]

Defence Witness NGB [page 74]

349. NGB took part in two attacks over two successive days at Kabuye hill. Sometime after 20 April 1994, people from Rwamiko *secteur* came to NGB's home armed with traditional weapons and invited him to follow them to attack Kabuye hill. Feeling he could not refuse, he took his machete and followed them. They stopped in Gahondo *cellule* (Dahwe *secteur*), facing Kabuye hill. He noticed that the refugees had gathered on Kabuye hill precisely where it faces Gahondo. Soon thereafter, he and the others were instructed by a deputy brigadier to launch an attack, which they did. NGB and his fellow attackers descended Gahondo hill, crossed the Kabuye valley, and then started climbing Kabuye hill. He stated that they did not use any road to climb up the hill because there was none.[370]

350. The first attack he participated in began before noon and lasted about three hours; it stopped because the refugees had mounted a successful resistance. The following day, NGB was issued a firearm and five bullets by a brigadier in order to ensure safety in his *secteur*. On his way back, a vehicle carrying gendarmes and policemen stopped and asked NGB to board, which he did. Together, they returned to Gahondo hill, where the road ends, and climbed to the top. From there, another brigadier issued instructions to attack the refugees at Kabuye hill. The attack was launched sometime before noon, taking place halfway up the hill, and went on until the evening, stopping only when the night and heavy rain fell. There were several other attackers from other localities there too. NGB did not see any vehicle at Kabuye hill before, during, or after either attack. He was unaware of any further attacks having taken place thereafter. NGB knew Kalimanzira and stated he neither saw nor heard of his any participation in the attacks at Kabuye hill. NGB also stated that if Kalimanzira were involved, he surely would have heard about it eventually in prison, where natives of each *commune* would gather to discuss what happened.[371]

---

[367] T. 29 January 2009 p. 54 and T. 2 February 2009 p. 11 (Witness ACB6).
[368] T. 28 January 2009 pp. 3-4 (Denis Ndamyumugabe).
[369] T. 28 January 2009 pp. 2-7 (Denis Ndamyumugabe).
[370] T. 28 January 2009 pp. 21-23 (Witness NGB).
[371] T. 28 January 2009 pp. 23-26 (Witness NGB).

Defence Witness Athanase Nzabakirana

351. Nzabakirana testified that he went to Kabuye hill approximately two weeks after the death of President Habyarimana. Nzabakirana explained that Burundian refugees from Kibayi *commune* armed with traditional weapons, machetes and clubs, threatened him with violent reprisal if he did accompany them to Kabuye hill in order to loot from the Tutsis who had sought refuge there. Armed only with a small stick, Nzabakirana accompanied some 300 other people to the hill, which took approximately one hour to reach. He recalled that when they arrived in the valley below the hill and attempted to attack the Tutsi refugees, they were repelled with stones. After the failed attack, which occurred at around 11:00 a.m., he returned home and stayed there so as to avoid being coerced into returning to the hill for further attacks. Nzabakirana did not see any officials or vehicles at Kabuye hill. He testified that there was not even a road leading there, and that he did not see Kalimanzira at all between April and July 1994.[372]

Defence Witness Alphonse Nsabimana

352. Nsabimana testified that one afternoon in April 1994, approximately two weeks after the death of President Habyarimana, two military jeeps carrying some 25 soldiers came to a roadblock he was manning with four other men at the border between Muzenga and Kinazi *secteurs* (Ndora *commune*). Some of the soldiers exited the vehicles and ordered Nsabimana and the four other men to follow them to Kabuye hill to chase the refugees out of there. When two of Nsabimana's friends expressed reluctance, the soldiers shot them dead. Consequently, Nsabimana and the remaining men decided to comply and boarded one of vehicles. They then **[page 75]** drove towards Kabuye hill on the Gisagara road, whereupon the soldiers parked the vehicles on a nearby hill and led them into the valley between Gahondo hill and Kabuye hill.[373]

353. Nsabimana testified that there were no refugees on the hill where they parked, but that when they walked into the valley he could see many people there and many refugees on Kabuye hill. The soldiers, who stood in front of the others, moved towards the refugees. He heard shooting for approximately three hours, after which there was heavy rain and thunder. Nsabimana explained that he did not participate in the attack because no refugees managed to flee the shooting and reach the area where he was standing.[374]

354. Nsabimana testified that did not see Kalimanzira in either of the vehicles he arrived in. He stated that he did not see him during the attacks at Kabuye hill or in the valley. In fact, he did not see Kalimanzira at all in 1994. Finally, Nsabimana asserted that after the attacks he did not hear anyone mention that they saw Kalimanzira at Kabuye hill and reiterated that the only vehicles he saw parked were the two jeeps he came with.[375]

Defence Witness AM14

355. AM14 testified that around 20 April 1994, Tutsis arrived in large numbers with their cattle at the Gisagara marketplace, which also doubles as a football pitch, and stayed for a few days. AM14 stated that he went to the square to see the refugees and observed the events as he stood next to a tap with some friends. At some point one afternoon, AM14 learnt that the refugees had been instructed by the *bourgmestre* to leave and move to Kabuye hill for their own safety. AM14 stated that although he did not personally witness the *bourgmestre* giving these instructions, he did see the *bourgmestre* at the square on that day. AM14 asserted that despite not having participated in the attacks, he knows what happened at Kabuye hill because many people discussed it long afterwards, even in prison. He stated that he has never heard Kalimanzira's name mentioned in relation to the killings at Kabuye hill.[376]

---

[372] T. 28 January 2009 pp. 33-35 (Athanase Nzabakirana).
[373] T. 3 February 2009 pp. 36-37 (Alphonse Nsabimana).
[374] T. 3 February 2009 pp. 38-39 (Alphonse Nsabimana).
[375] T. 3 February 2009 p. 40 (Alphonse Nsabimana).
[376] T. 19 November 2008 pp. 64-65 (Witness AM14).

Defence Witness AX88

356. AX88 was called to rebut BDK's evidence about the discussion of further killings. She testified that at the time of the killings at Kabuye hill, the tap at Fidèle Uwizeye's house was out of order because the man who was responsible for operating the water pump was Tutsi and consequently in hiding. AX88 also asserted that Kalimanzira never attended a meeting at Uwizeye's house after the death of President Habyarimana.[377]

2.4.2. Deliberations

357. The allegations at paragraphs 9 and 10 of the Indictment, as well as the evidence adduced at trial, may be deconstructed into three categories of events: (1) sending Tutsis to Kabuye hill; (2) killings at Kabuye hill; and (3) supervising and discussing further killings at Kabuye hill. At the relevant times alleged, Kalimanzira claims to have been working in Murambi (Gitarama *préfecture*). As discussed above, the Chamber disbelieves his alibi (see III.1.2.2). **[page 76]**

Sending Tutsis to Kabuye Hill – Gisagara Marketplace

358. BCF and BDC testified to Kalimanzira's participation in directing Tutsi refugees from the Gisagara marketplace to Kabuye hill on Saturday, 23 April 1994. BWO also testified to efforts to lure Tutsis to Kabuye hill at the marketplace, but did not see Kalimanzira there. All three witnesses are survivors of the killings at Kabuye hill.

359. BCF testified that he was a Tutsi who, at the time of the alleged events, sold banana wine on the main road that leads down to the Gisagara marketplace.[378] The Defence called AM52 and AM14 to discredit BCF on these points. AM52 testified that he owned a shop in the Gisagara marketplace and that he knew BCF, who was often at the marketplace, but knew of no shop or bar that BCF owned there.[379] AM14 also testified he knew of no shop or bar that BCF owned there, and expressed some doubt as to BCF's ethnicity, but conceded that he did not know BCF very well.[380] The Chamber considers these matters are not of material importance and do not go to the substance of BCF's testimony. The Chamber finds that AM52 and AM14 do little to discredit BCF.

360. The Defence points out that BCF never made mention of his banana wine business in his March 2003 statement to ICTR investigators.[381] BCF simply stated that on 23 April 1994, he was among a large group of refugees who had gathered at the marketplace. The Chamber does not see any contradiction with his testimony on the stand. Rather, BCF's addition of detail to a point of insignificance lends credence to his account in substance. On a more material matter, the Chamber notes that in his March 2003 statement, BCF stated that both *sous-préfet* Ntawukulilyayo and Kalimanzira spoke, whereas on the stand he stated that only the *sous-préfet* spoke. Under cross-examination, BCF indicated that his statement must have been misrecorded, asserting that he never said Kalimanzira spoke.[382] The Chamber accepts his explanation and considers that he was being more cautious on the stand. If he were lying, wanting to falsely accuse Kalimanzira, he would more likely have affirmed that Kalimanzira had spoken to the crowd. The Chamber believes BCF.

361. BDC, who testified three days after BCF, also stated that Kalimanzira was at the Gisagara marketplace but that only the *sous-préfet* spoke. The Defence posits that BCF and BDC have conspired to harmonise their testimonies in this respect.[383] The Chamber does not accept the Defence's baseless conjecture. BDC, a Hutu survivor whose Tutsi husband and children were killed, supported BCF's testimony in other particulars. Both witnesses testified that it was a Saturday afternoon, that policemen were present, that the *sous-préfet*

---

[377] T. 19 November 2008 pp. 18-19, 22 [closed] (Witness AX88).
[378] T. 12 May 2008 p. 7 [closed] (Witness BCF).
[379] T. 18 November 2008 pp. 3-8 [closed] (Witness AM52); see also Exhibits D45 and D46.
[380] T. 19 November 2008 pp. 67 and 73 (Witness AM14); see also Exhibits D50, D51 and D52.
[381] Defence Closing Brief, para. 153; Exhibit D3.
[382] T. 12 May 2008 p. 44 (Witness BCF).
[383] Defence Closing Brief, paras. 155-156.

promised they would be protected, and that the refugees were immediately mobilized to Kabuye hill. BDC and BCF also diverged on some points, such as whether the *sous-préfet* used a microphone to address the crowd, the description of the policemen's uniforms, and the presence of soldiers. The Chamber considers these inconsistencies to be minor and attributable to the passage of time, different perspectives, and chaotic circumstances.

362. In her March 2003 statement to ICTR investigators, BDC mentioned only *sous-préfet* Ntawukulilyayo, who spoke, and "some dignitaries."[384] Given that the statement was specifically entitled "Re – Kalimanzira, Callixte", and that she mentions Kalimanzira before **[page 77]** and after the Gisagara marketplace incident, the Defence submits that if she had seen Kalimanzira there, she surely would have mentioned him.[385] The Chamber finds that BDC's failure to explicitly mention Kalimanzira's presence at the marketplace does not cast doubt on her credibility. He could very well have been among the other "dignitaries" BDC mentioned. Considering that Kalimanzira did not address the crowd, she might not have felt it important to specify that he was present.

363. BDC and BCF's evidence is further supported by BDJ, who spontaneously declared in response to open-ended questions under cross-examination that he saw Kalimanzira at the Gisagara marketplace on 23 April 1994.[386] BWO, a Tutsi survivor who lost many family members on Kabuye hill, also supported BCF and BDC on many points, but diverged on others. Most significantly, BWO said he spent two nights at the Gisagara marketplace before *sous-préfet* Ntawukulilyayo arrived and instructed the refugees to move to Kabuye hill where they would be protected; he did not, however, mention Kalimanzira was there. BWO was seated among some 2,000 refugees, far from where the *sous-préfet* took the floor, and left for Kabuye hill soon after the *sous-préfet*'s instructions.[387] If BWO is recounting the same incident at the Gisagara marketplace as BDC and BCF when they saw Kalimanzira, BWO may not have seen Kalimanzira from where he was seated in the crowd of refugees.

364. However, BWO's testimony differed from BDC's and BCF's is other ways which suggest that BWO was recounting a separate incident. For instance, BWO recalled that the *sous-préfet* came to the marketplace from the *communal* office on foot, in the company of two policemen and several other Tutsis who had taken refuge at the *communal* office.[388] In addition, BWO testified that upon following the *sous-préfet*'s instructions to leave the marketplace, he was among the first refugees to settle on Kabuye hill, experiencing a few days of relative quiet before attacks and killings were launched in full.[389] In contrast, BDC and BCF experienced heavy attacks with gunfire on the same day that they moved from the marketplace to Kabuye hill.[390] As such, the Chamber finds BWO most likely recounted an earlier wave of refugee expulsion from the marketplace, while BDC and BCF were among a later group. The Defence's contention that BWO is determined to accuse Kalimanzira at any cost does not stand.[391] BWO was cautious to limit his testimony only to what he remembers personally seeing, which adds to his credibility as a witness.

365. Defence witnesses AM14 and FCS supported the Prosecution evidence that on Saturday, 23 April 1994, Tutsi refugees who had gathered at the Gisagara marketplace were told to leave for Kabuye hill, where they were told they would be safe. This point is not disputed. However, FCS and AM14 implicated the *bourgmestre* of Ndora *commune* with the *sous-préfet* in directing the refugees to Kabuye hill. The Defence contends this contradicts the Prosecution evidence placing Kalimanzira there. The Chamber does not agree. Neither AM14's hearsay evidence nor FCS' direct evidence do anything to preclude Kalimanzira from also being there. In addition, FCS testified to an incident which occurred Saturday morning, while the Prosecution evidence places the event in the afternoon. The Defence **[page 78]** suggests that a multi-stage expulsion is not possible because no Prosecution witness mentioned it.[392]

---

[384] Exhibit D10.
[385] Defence Closing Brief, para. 208.
[386] T. 17 June 2008 p. 60 (Witness BDJ).
[387] T. 12 May 2008 pp. 64-69 (Witness BWO); see also Exhibit D4.
[388] T. 12 May 2008 pp. 62-63 (Witness BWO).
[389] T. 5 May 2008 pp. 26-28 and T. 12 May 2008 pp. 69-70 (Witness BWO).
[390] T. 9 May 2008 pp. 27-32 (Witness BDC); T. 5 May 2008 pp. 12-14 and T. 12 May 2008 pp. 32-40 (Witness BCF).
[391] Defence Closing Brief, para. 280.
[392] Defence Closing Brief, para. 181.

366. Given that these Prosecution witnesses were refugees who were instructed to move, and who testified to events as they experienced them, they would not conceivably have stayed at the marketplace place to witness an expulsion in multiple stages, nor could they be expected to know that a group of refugees had been moved from the marketplace at other times. The Chamber considers it likely that thousands of refugees would not have shown up at the marketplace all at once, and that as they flowed into the marketplace, they would have been moved at various stages. As such, FCS' testimony provides further information as to how the Tutsis came to Kabuye hill in such large numbers.

367. In the Chamber's view, the Prosecution has proven beyond reasonable doubt that on Saturday, 23 April 1994, Kalimanzira was at the Gisagara marketplace, standing next to the *sous-préfet* who instructed the Tutsis who had gathered there to make their way to Kabuye hill, where he promised them protection. As discussed in the following section, these refugees were not protected, but rather killed *en masse* at the hill.

Sending Tutsis to Kabuye Hill – Gisagara-Kabuye Road

368. The Prosecution led evidence from BWK, a Tutsi survivor, who testified that she saw Kalimanzira in a vehicle on the road from Kabuye to Gisagara near Misago's house just before 3:00 p.m. on Saturday, 23 April 1994. She was with 13 or so other refugees on her way out of Kabuye *cellule* when Kalimanzira rerouted them to Kabuye hill, promising them safety.

369. The Defence alleges three inconsistencies between BWK's testimony and her September 2007 statement to ICTR investigators, given eight months apart.[393] First, in September 2007 she stated that she saw Kalimanzira on the road near Misago's house "around 21 April 1994", whereas on the stand she stated it was on 23 April. The Chamber sees no inconsistency here; "around 21 April 1994" is simply an approximation of the more specific date of 23 April that she provided on the stand. Second, in her prior statement BWK mentioned eight people were accompanying Kalimanzira in his vehicle, as opposed to only three when she took the stand. While the variation is indeed noticeable, it relates to a matter of little significance, and, in the Chamber's view, is not indicative of fabrication. Finally, in her prior statement BWK mentioned Kalimanzira's driver was dressed in military camouflage, whereas on the stand she described him in civilian attire. The Defence contends that BWK has changed her statement in order to harmonise her testimony with that of other Prosecution witnesses who have typically stated that Kalimanzira was driven by a civilian. At the same time, the Defence contradicts itself by making a case out of BWK's lack of corroboration. The Chamber does not consider that this casts reasonable doubt on her testimony; what Kalimanzira's driver might have been wearing is of no material importance.

370. BWK's evidence is supported insofar as other Prosecution witnesses placed Kalimanzira at the nearby Gisagara marketplace at around the same time. BWK's sighting therefore could have occurred just before or after Tutsis were expelled from the marketplace. BWK is also supported in part by BWO, who also named Gakeri as a civilian who was instructed to accompany refugees to Kabuye hill.[394] **[page 79]**

371. The Chamber believes BWK beyond reasonable doubt and finds her evidence to be reliable. Her evidence, along with BDC and BCF's (discussed above in relation to the Gisagara marketplace) supports the allegation at paragraph 9 of the Indictment that on 23 April 1994, Kalimanzira personally encouraged Tutsi civilians to take refuge on Kabuye hill, promising them protection.

Killings at Kabuye Hill

372. BWO, BCF, BDC and BBO all testified to having seen Kalimanzira on Kabuye hill on or around Saturday, 23 April 1994. BXG witnessed Kalimanzira at a nearby roadblock earlier that same day. BWO, BCF, BDC and BXG are survivors of the attacks at Kabuye hill; BBO, however, participated in the attacks.

373. Although BBO's testimony was consistent with BWO, BCF and BDC on matters such as time (end of April), location (Kabuye hill) and description of events (Tutsi resistance to attacks), his testimony was qualitatively distinct from the survivors', who experienced the events from a very different perspective.

---

[393] Defence Closing Brief, paras. 12-15; see also Exhibit D9.
[394] T. 12 May 2008 p. 65 (Witness BWO).

BBO was the only witness to testify that Kalimanzira came to Kabuye hill with Colonel Tharcisse Muvunyi bringing two ONATROCOM buses filled with 150 soldiers. He was also the only witness to testify that Kalimanzira gave instructions to Burundian refugees on how to proceed with the attack.

374. The Defence alleges an inconsistency in BBO's testimony insomuch as while he asserted to having seen Kalimanzira at Kabuye hill, when asked how he could recognize him, indicated that he heard other people say that Kalimanzira was there, thereby suggesting hearsay.[395] The Defence further points to several alleged inconsistencies with BBO's prior statements. In addition to those discussed in relation to BBO's allegations at Kanage Camp (see III.4.2.2), the Defence notes that in his 20 October 1999 statement to ICTR investigators, BBO does not mention Kalimanzira or Muvunyi coming to Kabuye hill with two busloads of soldiers; he mentions only Élie Ndayambaje (former and future *bourgmestre* of Muganza *commune*) and Canisius Kajyambere (*bourgmestre* of Kibayi *commune*).[396] The Chamber notes, however, that in his 2001 statement, BBO did implicate Kalimanzira and Muvunyi, among others, in the provision of military reinforcement to Kabuye hill.[397]

375. BBO is a self-professed killer. He spent 11 years in prison for his participation in the genocide and has since been released.[398] BBO also testified in relation to the allegations at Kanage Camp, where the Chamber considered his evidence should be treated with caution, and found his sole testimony to be insufficiently reliable to sustain a conviction, concluding that Kalimanzira was not at Kanage Camp in the days following the death of the President (see III.4.2.2). The Chamber considers BBO's ability to identify Kalimanzira is now at issue. BBO testified that the first time he saw and came to know of Kalimanzira was at Kanage Camp, where Pierre Canisius Kajyambere (*bourgmestre* of Kibayi *commune*) introduced him. Having found that Kalimanzira was not at Kanage Camp, the Chamber doubts whether BBO could have recognized Kalimanzira at Kabuye hill. The Chamber therefore cannot rely on BBO's evidence unless it is corroborated by, or itself corroborates, other reliable evidence. **[page 80]**

376. BXG, a Tutsi survivor who lost many family members at Kabuye hill, supported the Prosecution evidence about the events at Kabuye hill to a limited extent. However, he was the only witness to testify that he saw Kalimanzira on Saturday, 23 April 1994 sometime before noon at the Mukabuga roadblock in Kabuye *cellule* in a white saloon vehicle with a driver and two armed soldiers. There, Kalimanzira became irate upon learning that Tutsis had succeeded in defending themselves at Kabuye hill. The Defence points to alleged inconsistencies in BXG's testimony, such as his assertion that he stayed at the roadblock for 30 minutes even after Kalimanzira's harsh exchange with *conseiller* Bushakwe concerning the fate of the Tutsis. The Defence also asserts that BXG's evidence about Kalimanzira's reaction suggests Kalimanzira was not aware of the developments at Kabuye hill, which contradicts the Prosecution's case that he participated in supervising its progress.[399]

377. The Defence alleged further inconsistencies between BXG's prior statement to ICTR investigators and his testimony on the stand.[400] In October 2007, BXG stated that he fled straight to Kabuye hill on 18 April for fear of being killed if he stayed home; on the stand, however, he testified that he did not leave his home before 22 April to check up on his sister-in-law, and that he feared nothing, not even the following day after seeing Kalimanzira at the Mukabuga roadblock. In October 2007, BXG also indicated that he left Kabuye hill on 20 April 1994 to get some food when he saw Kalimanzira at the Mukabuga roadblock located right in front of BXG's own house; on the stand, however, he testified that the incident occurred on 23 April 1994, at the Mukabuga roadblock, in front of his *brother's* house.

---

[395] Defence Closing Brief, paras. 62-64; see T. 19 June 2008 p. 46 (Witness BBO): "A soldier called Alphonse and an old former soldier called Habyarimana spoke about Kalimanzira, and they were saying that, 'Now that Muvunyi and Kalimanzira are here, it's over for these Tutsis.' I did not pay attention to these authorities because I did not know that I would be examined one day about them – on them. I heard his name, and since I knew – or I could see that the authorities were there to assist us, and I understood that it was true, because I had already heard about this man. I heard about his name in the refugees' camp."
[396] Defence Closing Brief, paras. 80-82; see also Exhibit D20.
[397] Exhibit D21.
[398] T. 19 June 2008 p. 48 (Witness BBO).
[399] Defence Closing Brief, paras. 26-33.
[400] Defence Closing Brief, paras. 34-42; Exhibit D13.

Prosecutor v. Kalimanzira

378. The Chamber does not accept the Defence's contention that the discrepancies in BXG's evidence demonstrate fabrication, and discerns no reason for BXG to lie. If that were the case, BXG could have placed Kalimanzira at Kabuye hill. Such variances may also be attributable to the passage of time, the circumstances under which statements are recorded, and difficulties in recalling traumatic events. BXG is consistent with the general trend of evidence relating to Kabuye hill. The Chamber believes him.

379. BDC and BCF testified that they left the Gisagara marketplace and arrived at Kabuye hill at roughly the same time, in the afternoon of Saturday, 23 April 1994. Both witnesses recalled seeing Kalimanzira arrive at Kabuye hill later that afternoon with *sous-préfet* Ntawukulilyayo in the same vehicle, bringing soldiers and policemen. BCF saw two vehicles, which he described as pick-up trucks, the second carrying more soldiers and policemen, whereas BDC only mentioned one vehicle. BCF recalled Kalimanzira and the *sous-préfet* remained at Kabuye hill when the soldiers started shooting at the refugees, while BDC said that she saw them leave with the vehicle before the shooting began. BDC testified that they left behind the soldiers and policemen who had accompanied them, but contradicted herself on this point under cross-examination when she stated that those very soldiers and policemen did not stay behind, but rather left with Kalimanzira and the *sous-préfet*.[401]

380. The Defence alleges three inconsistencies in BCF's prior statement to the ICTR.[402] In March 2003, BCF stated that Kalimanzira and the *sous-préfet* came to Kabuye hill in separate pick-up trucks of slightly different colours in the company of gendarmes, whereas on the stand he said they arrived in the same vehicle, accompanied by soldiers and policemen. BCF also stated in 2003 that upon arrival the *sous-préfet* reassured the refugees that the armed persons who arrived with them in the vehicles came to offer protection; on the stand, **[page 81]** however, he neither mentioned nor was able to confirm whether the *sous-préfet* spoke.[403] BCF explained that his prior statement must have been misunderstood and poorly recorded, standing firm under cross-examination.

381. In the Chamber's view, any inconsistencies within or between BDC and BCF's statements are normal considering the passage of time. The Chamber also considered that these witnesses are uneducated, illiterate, and, as survivors, have undergone a great trauma. The Chamber finds that the substantial elements on which their testimonies converge far outweigh the minor points on which they diverge. The Chamber believes BDC and BCF.

382. BWO supported BCF and BDC on certain points, but diverged on others. His testimony reveals that he was among the first refugees to settle on Kabuye hill, experiencing a few days of relative quiet before attacks and killings were launched in full swing. As such, BWO likely reached Kabuye hill before BDC and BCF did. His sighting of Kalimanzira, however, coincides with the day BWO experienced the heaviest attack; on which day he escaped from Kabuye hill. BWO saw Kalimanzira arrive at Kabuye hill around or just before midday in a red pick-up truck with a soldier and a woman. After promising to protect a group of distraught refugees who approached him, Kalimanzira then turned around and told another group of civilians to hurry up and kill the refugees. This account differs significantly from BDC and BCF's. BWO is clearly testifying to a separate event, which also occurred on or around 23 April 1994.

383. In its assessment of BWO's evidence on the expulsion of refugees from the Gisagara marketplace, the Chamber found this witness to be credible. Here, though he is substantially uncorroborated, the Chamber believes him. BWO has no reason to lie and has demonstrated truthfulness through restraint by not implicating Kalimanzira at the marketplace, where he did not see him. Having met Kalimanzira for the first time in 1990, and then seen him on more than one occasion after that, BWO would have been able to identify Kalimanzira.[404]

384. The Defence led evidence from three survivors – FCS, AK11, and ACB6 – and four attackers – Denis Ndamyumugabe, NGB, Athanase Nzabakirana, and Alphonse Nsabimana – to cast doubt on the Kalimanzira's participation in the killings at Kabuye hill. All of them stated that they did not see Kalimanzira there or ever

---
[401] Compare T. 9 May 2008 p. 29 with T. 20 May 2008 p. 29 (Witness BDC).
[402] Defence Closing Brief, paras. 158-162; see also Exhibit D3.
[403] Compare Exhibit D3 with T. 12 May 2008 pp. 44-46 (Witness BCF).
[404] T. 5 May 2008 pp. 33-34 and T. 19 May 2008 p. 12 (Witness BWO).

hear of his involvement. However, several Prosecution witnesses, including BCZ, BBB, BWK and BXG did not see Kalimanzira at Kabuye hill. Several witnesses who testified in the *Butare* trial about Élie Ndayambaje's involvement did not mention seeing Kalimanzira there either (see II.4.3). The Chamber does not consider this to preclude Kalimanzira's presence at Kabuye hill.

385. Kalimanzira's defence also hinged on negating the possibility of vehicles reaching Kabuye hill, thereby discrediting Prosecution witnesses who saw Kalimanzira arrive in a pick-up truck. However, Defence witnesses NGB and Alphonse Nsabimana testified to having reached the area in vehicles; whether it was on or near Kabuye hill is a minor detail. Kabuye hill was not reached from one direction only.

386. Having reviewed the Defence evidence carefully, the Chamber finds it does nothing to contradict the Prosecution case; in fact, in many ways, it supports it. AK11, ACB6, NGB, Athanase Nzabakirana, and Denis Ndamyumugabe confirm BDC, BWO, and BXG's evidence that in the days leading up to Saturday, 23 April 1994, the Tutsi refugees on Kabuye hill had managed to succeed in repelling several attacks. Moreover, AK11, FCS, ACB6 and Denis Ndamyumugabe confirm BDC, BCF, BWO and BXG's evidence that on Saturday, 23 **[page 82]** April 1994, the attacks on the Tutsi refugees greatly intensified with the assistance of soldiers and gunfire, to the point that they could no longer resist, causing them to flee into the night. The Defence and Prosecution evidence, when viewed in combination as a whole, provides a broader historical record of the killings at Kabuye hill.

387. The body of evidence reveals that there were thousands upon thousands of refugees suffering battle and massacre from an indeterminate number of attackers over a large landscape and time span; no witness alone could amply describe everything that transpired or identify everyone who was present. The Chamber finds the Defence evidence raises no reasonable doubt on eyewitness accounts that Kalimanzira was at Kabuye hill.

Discussing Further Killings at Kabuye Hill

388. BDK was the only Prosecution witness to testify to the allegations at paragraph 10 of the Indictment whereby Kalimanzira and other local officials met at Fidèle Uwizeye's house to discuss further action to make up for their failure to eliminate the overwhelming number of Tutsis who had gathered at Kabuye hill. BDK testified that in the morning of Monday, 25 April 1994, she overheard the conversation after filling her bucket with water from the tap inside Uwizeye's compound. The Defence called AX88 to rebut her evidence and discredit her by stating that the water tap was non-functional at the time because the Tutsi man operating it had disappeared. Their testimonies directly contradict each other.

389. A certain level of animosity or rivalry between AX88 and BDK was perceptible. Both witnesses are Tutsi women equally positioned to be able to testify to such an event, if it occurred. AX88 flatly denies it ever took place, while BDK says she witnessed it herself. They are also equally positioned to know for certain whether the water tap was functional or not. That their testimonies diverge so drastically on this point indicates that one of them must be lying, if not both.

390. The Chamber is not at all convinced by AX88's convoluted and often contradictory reasons for why the tap was not working. First she explained that the Tutsi man who operated the water pump had gone into hiding and, without him, there was nobody to turn on the generator operating the pump.[405] In order to obtain water, there was no other option than to fill 13 jerrycans everyday from a water source a 50-minute walk away.[406] When confronted with the idea that it might have been more efficient to simply replace the Tutsi man who operated the generator for the water pump, AX88 offered several other explanations, none of which helped her story make more sense.

391. However, the Chamber is not entirely convinced of BDK's account either. BDK indicated she greeted the officials before standing by to hear the conversation.[407] It is doubtful that Hutu conspirators would have knowingly held such a conversation within hearing distance of a Tutsi woman. More significantly, BDK

---

[405] T. 19 November 2008 pp. 17 and 31 [closed] (Witness AX88).
[406] T. 19 November 2008 pp. 31-32 [closed] (Witness AX88).
[407] T. 21 May 2008 p. 14 [closed] (Witness BDK).

testified to hearing part of a conversation, which amounts to little more than hearsay. For these reasons, the Chamber finds BDK's sole evidence is insufficiently reliable to prove the allegations at paragraph 10 of the Indictment beyond reasonable doubt. **[page 83]**

Conclusion

392. The Chamber finds that the allegations at paragraph 9 of the Indictment have been proven beyond reasonable doubt. On Saturday, 23 April 1994, Kalimanzira went to the Gisagara marketplace where thousands of Tutsi refugees had gathered to escape the killings, lootings, and house burnings in their areas. On that occasion, *sous-préfet* Ntawukulilyayo instructed the refugees to move to Kabuye hill, promising them protection. Kalimanzira stood next to the *sous-préfet,* saying nothing. In this way, he showed his tacit approval, lending credibility and authority to the *sous-préfet's* assurances of safety. That same day, he stopped 13 refugees leaving Kabuye *cellule* on the Gisagara-Kabuye road and instructed them to go to back to Kabuye hill, promising that nothing would happen to them. His behaviour at the Mukabuga roadblock earlier that day demonstrates that he knew the Tutsis at Kabuye hill were being attacked and that he intended for them to be killed. In these ways, he personally encouraged Tutsis to take refuge on the hill in order to facilitate their subsequent killings, a consequence which he was clearly aware of and motivated by.

393. Later that day, on 23 April 1994, Kalimanzira came to Kabuye hill with soldiers and policemen. The Tutsi refugees had successfully repelled attacks with sticks and stones until that day, but they could not resist bullets. With significantly more civilian attackers on the ground, the Saturday attack proved successful and the Tutsi refugees were killed in the thousands, resulting in an enormous human tragedy. Kalimanzira's role in luring Tutsis to Kabuye hill and his subsequent assistance in providing armed reinforcements substantially contributed to the overall attack. Kalimanzira exhibited here, and elsewhere, an intent to destroy the Tutsi group (see III.5.2). For these reasons, the Chamber finds Kalimanzira guilty beyond reasonable doubt of aiding and abetting genocide on 23 April 1994 at Kabuye hill.

2.5. Sakindi Roadblock, early May

394. At paragraph 13 of the Indictment, the Prosecution charges Kalimanzira with Genocide for stopping at a roadblock in Kibilizi *secteur* in early May 1994, where he told those manning it to be discreet in their hunt for Tutsis because foreigners were monitoring events in Rwanda. Kalimanzira asked them to destroy Tutsi homes without leaving any trace and to spread the word that peace had been restored so as to lure Tutsis out of hiding. This roadblock was located near the home of a person named "Sakindi";[408] the Chamber will therefore refer to it as the "Sakindi roadblock".

395. The Defence denies that Kalimanzira was ever present at this roadblock. In addition, Kalimanzira relies on his alibi that he was working in Murambi (Gitarama *préfecture*) from 14 April to 30 May 1994 (see III.1.2).

2.5.1. Evidence

Prosecution Witness AZH

396. AZH testified that he saw Kalimanzira on six different occasions after President Habyarimana's death. The first occasion was at Kabanga *cellule* (Kibilizi *secteur*, Mugusa *commune*), when AZH says he met Kalimanzira for the first time (see III.2.7.2). The next three times AZH says he saw Kalimanzira was at the Sakindi roadblock, located in Ramba *cellule* (Kibilizi *secteur*) where the roads leading to Save (ending in Butare), Rubona and Gikonko met.[409] **[page 84]**

397. The first time was on 24 April 1994, when Kalimanzira came to the Sakindi roadblock sometime between noon and 2:00 p.m. in a red double-cabin vehicle, along with Alphonse Nteziryayo (Colonel),

---

[408] See *e.g.* Prosecution Pre-Trial Brief, para. 61 and annexed summary of AZH's anticipated testimony.
[409] T. 23 June 2008 pp. 9-12 (Witness AZH).

Tharcisse Muvunyi (Colonel), and soldiers. AZH was among those manning the roadblock, which included Tutsis. On this occasion, AZH testified that Kalimanzira did not speak, but Colonel Nteziryayo told the people present at the roadblock to attack Tutsi homes, burn them down and steal their cattle, and Colonel Muvunyi threatened that if there were no corpses at the roadblock when he returned the next day he would send soldiers to kill everyone. After they left, AZH said he and the others torched Tutsi homes and ate their cattle. The next day killings began at the Sakindi roadblock and corpses accumulated as requested.[410]

398. The second time was in the first week of May 1994, when Kalimanzira returned to the Sakindi roadblock sometime between 11:00 a.m. and noon onboard a white double-cabin vehicle with Dominique Ntawukulilyayo (*sous-préfet* of Gisagara), again with soldiers. Kalimanzira instructed AZH and others to avoid shouting as they moved around hunting for Tutsis. Kalimanzira also told them to explain to the general public that people were no longer being killed; AZH said the goal was to convince any Hutus who were hiding Tutsis that it was safe for them to come out. AZH testified that Kalimanzira's instructions resulted in a young Tutsi man named Nyangezi being identified and killed that same day, and then more Tutsis being flushed out and killed the following day.[411]

399. The third and final time AZH saw Kalimanzira at the Sakindi roadblock was one week later, still in May 1994. On this occasion, Kalimanzira returned once more in the company of *sous-préfet* Ntawukulilyayo onboard a vehicle, and instructed AZH and the others to destroy any walls of Tutsi homes left standing, level the ground, plant banana trees and then cover the ground with grass. Kalimanzira also instructed them to kill those who had obtained fraudulent identity cards in 1959 to conceal their Tutsi origins. AZH testified that Kalimanzira's instructions resulted in a lady named Nakure and her son, being killed that same day, as well as a certain Karuganda and a certain Munyahindi.[412]

400. Besides these three occasions, AZH asserted that Kalimanzira often passed by the Sakindi roadblock, even in AZH's absence.[413] AZH did not, however, indicate how he came to know of this.

Defence Witness MVE

401. MVE testified that the Sakindi roadblock in Ramba *cellule* was erected on 7 April 1994 at the behest of Vincent Nkulikiyinka (*conseiller* of Kibilizi *secteur*). MVE said he manned the roadblock twice per week, and that Tutsis also participated in manning the roadblock for the first two weeks, but stopped showing up when they were being hunted down. MVE recalled that André Kabayiza (*bourgmestre* of Mugusa *commune*) often drove through the Sakindi roadblock without being stopped. MVE did not recall seeing or hearing of any other officials ever passing through the Sakindi roadblock, including Colonel Nteziryayo, Colonel Muvunyi, or Kalimanzira. MVE insists that if an official ever came to the Sakindi roadblock and issued instructions to kill, he most certainly would have known about it.[414] **[page 85]**

2.5.2. Deliberations

402. At the relevant time alleged, Kalimanzira claims to have been working in Murambi (Gitarama *préfecture*). As discussed above, the Chamber disbelieves his alibi (see III.1.2.2).

403. AZH pleaded guilty and was convicted for his participation in the genocide. He was sentenced to nine years in Karubanda prison and was released in 2003 after agreeing to assist the *Gacaca* courts by testifying, whenever called upon, against people who incited him to commit genocide and against his accomplices.[415] AZH has also implicated Kalimanzira in relation to other alleged crimes in Mugusa *commune* (see III.2.6 and III.2.7.2). Although he is now free, the Chamber notes that his statements to ICTR investigators in which he implicated Kalimanzira were made before his release. He may therefore have had an incentive to falsely accuse Kalimanzira. He admits to participating in the crimes to which he testifies Kalimianzira incited him

---

[410] T. 23 June 2008 pp. 9-12 and T. 24 June 2008 p. 24 (Witness AZH).
[411] T. 23 June 2008 pp. 10-11 and T. 24 June 2008 pp. 27-30 (Witness AZH).
[412] T. 23 June 2008 pp. 11-12 (Witness AZH).
[413] T. 23 June 2008 p. 10 (Witness AZH).
[414] T. 3 February 2009 pp. 56-58, 61 (Witness MVE).
[415] T. 24 June 2008 pp. 3-6 [closed] (Witness AZH).

to commit, which would make him an accomplice. The Chamber therefore approaches his testimony with caution.

404. AZH was confronted with three statements he gave to ICTR investigators since 2000[416] which reveal several inconsistencies with the testimony he gave on the stand. In addition, when confronted with his confessions of guilt in Rwanda, he admitted that they implicate only Sylvain Nsabimana, Alphonse Nteziryayo, Tharcisse Muvunyi and André Kabayiza, but make no mention of the kind of incitement and instructions attributed to Kalimanzira at the Sakindi roadblock.[417] In February 2000, when giving a statement to ICTR investigators, AZH makes mention of Kalimanzira for what appears to be the first time, placing him at "our roadblock" with Muvunyi and Nteziryayo on 24 April 1994, and attributing to Kalimanzira a return visit with Kabayiza a few days later where he expresses cause for concern of international opinion.[418] In March 2001, AZH recalls the same 24 April 1994 incident but somewhat differently, failing to mention Kalimanzira this time, but implicating Kabayiza as accompanying Muvunyi and Nteziryayo instead.[419] In December 2001, AZH recalled the 24 April 1994 incident to the exclusion of Kalimanzira, but placed him with Kabayiza at the Sakindi roadblock in early May where he instructed those present to lure Tutsis out of hiding, to kill them discretely for fear of international scrutiny, and destroy the homes of the dead.[420] Then on the stand in June 2008, AZH recalled the 24 April 1994 incident inclusive of Kalimanzira, specifying that it took place at the Sakindi roadblock, and attributes two return visits to the Sakindi roadblock to Kalimanzira in May 1994, this time in the company of Ntawukulilyayo, not Kabayiza.

405. While failing to mention Kalimanzira in AZH's confession does not necessarily imply that his subsequent statements are fabricated, the overall effect of the number and quality of inconsistencies leading up to and including his testimony create doubt as to the reliability of his testimony. When he was offered an opportunity to provide explanations for these and other such inconsistencies, his responses were not convincing. At one point, he seemed to **[page 86]** suggest that his recollection of Kalimanzira's crimes could be improved if more questions or hints were put him.[421]

406. MVE was the only Defence witness to testify about the Sakindi roadblock. He was convicted for crimes he committed between April and July 1994, but which were unrelated to the Sakindi roadblock. He has completed his sentence, and is now a free man.[422] However, he admitted on the stand that he participated in manning the Sakindi roadblock twice per week; the Chamber therefore considers that he would have an interest to minimise the criminal activities that occurred at that location.

407. MVE did not dispute the existence of the roadblock and recalled that Kabayiza drove through it often. He indicated that Hutus and Tutsis manned the roadblock together until Tutsis started to be hunted down; this made much more sense than AZH's statement that by 24 April 1994, Hutus and Tutsis alike were still manning the roadblock together, which seems highly unlikely. However, MVE's assertion that no other officials ever passed through the roadblock, and that neither Muvunyi, Nteziryayo, nor Kalimanzira could have come to the Sakindi roadblock without his knowledge, is untenable in light of his own testimony that he did not even know them, nor did he ever hear about them in 1994.[423]

408. The Chamber recalls that the required standard is proof beyond reasonable doubt. In light of the doubts raised by the inconsistency of AZH's testimony with his prior statements, and in the absence of any corroboration, the Chamber finds AZH's evidence on Kalimanzira's alleged involvement at the Sakindi roadblock to be insufficiently reliable to support a conviction.

---

[416] See Exhibits D30, D31, and D32.
[417] Exhibit D29.
[418] Exhibit D30.
[419] Exhibit D31.
[420] Exhibit D32.
[421] T. 24 June 2008 p. 8 (Witness AZH): "I don't know if you want to remind me of the other crimes he might have committed for me to recall at what times he might have done so. [...] What I wanted to say, as you ask me questions, I might remember the number of times he committed crimes and I would mention those times."
[422] T. 3 February 2009 p. 54 [closed] (Witness MVE).
[423] T. 3 February 2009 p. 58 (Witness MVE).

Judgement

2.6. Mugusa *Commune*, 5 June

409. At paragraphs 12 and 14 of the Indictment, the Prosecution charges Kalimanzira with Genocide for instigating people at the Gasagara centre in Mugusa *secteur* to eliminate the Tutsis, including those still in their mothers' wombs. Later that same day, in a speech delivered at the Gikonko *commune* office,[424] Kalimanzira allegedly ordered the Hutu population to kill all Tutsis who were still alive, including women, children, and the elderly, for fear that they may denounce the killers if the RPF won the war. This resulted in the immediate murders of Mukamazimpaka, Salafina Nyaraneza, Mukaruyonza and her mother, Nyaramisago, Goretha Umubeyeyi, Anasthasia Nakabonye, Apolinaraia and Kimonyo's two daughters, and 10 to 15 other Tutsi children.

410. The Defence denies the allegations in their entirety, and places several of the specified killings at least a month earlier than alleged. In addition, Kalimanzira relies on his alibi that he was home in Butare *ville* from 31 May to 30 June 1994, except when he left on a few specified occasions, including sometime in the first week of June to see his family in Kirarambogo (see III.1.2).

2.6.1. Evidence

Prosecution Witness AZC **[page 87]**

411. On 5 June 1994, AZC saw Kalimanzira in Mugusa *commune* at the Gasagara commercial centre.[425] Kalimanzira arrived in a white double-cabin vehicle with Colonel Tharcisse Muvunyi, and other soldiers on board. They stopped in front of AZC, who was standing with 30 other people, and asked them to gather around. Others at a nearby roadblock came to join the small crowd. Kalimanzira informed them that he had come to organize a public meeting at the Mugusa *commune* office in Gikonko *secteur*, and announced that the agenda was to kill Tutsis and abort pregnant women.[426]

412. At 1:00 p.m. the same day, AZC made his way over to the Gikonko *commune* office to attend the meeting Kalimanzira had announced. When AZC arrived, the meeting had already begun and André Kabayiza (*bourgmestre* of Mugusa *commune*) had already introduced the invitees and guests of honour. AZC listened to Kalimanzira's speech, in which he incited an audience of 300-400 people to kill Tutsis who had survived the first wave of killings, referring specifically to elderly women and children who had been spared. Kalimanzira warned the crowd of bad luck falling upon them if they did not follow his instructions, as these surviving Tutsis risked denouncing killers once the *Inkotanyi* took over. When a member of the audience asked why soldiers could not perform this task instead, Colonel Muvunyi replied that there were not enough soldiers to assist and that the people should solve the issue the same way they did in the first wave of killings without the use of armed forces.[427]

413. At the end of the meeting, Kalimanzira instructed the audience to destroy and erase any trace of the houses, even the fences, of Tutsis who had been killed and remained to be killed. The goal was to wipe out the existence of any particular victim having lived there. The meeting ended at around 4:00 p.m. when Kalimanzira and Colonel Muvunyi left. AZC testified that after the meeting, people "were heated up", as they had been "incited or excited to commit massacre", and followed the instructions to kill Tutsis who had survived the first wave of massacres in April. AZC was aware of 30 deaths which resulted in Nyarubuye *secteur*: 11 were killed in Gasenyi *cellule*, and 19 in Karukambira *cellule,* including children and elderly women. Though AZC could not identify the persons killed in Karukambira, he knew almost everyone who was killed in Gasenyi: young girls named Mukamazimpaka, Salafina Nyaraneza, Joséphine Mukaruyonza and Nyaramisago; a man named Kimonyo and his two daughters; a young man named Kayumba; and two

---

[424] The Mugusa *commune* office is located in Gikonko *secteur*.
[425] The transcript mistakenly refers to the "Gisagara" commercial centre, which is located in Ndora *commune*. For proper spelling of the location as "Gasagara", see T. 25 June 2008 p. 43 (Witness AZC).
[426] T. 25 June 2008 pp. 42, 63 (Witness AZC).
[427] T. 25 June 2008 pp. 42-43, 66 (Witness AZC).

old women named Anasthasia Nakabonye[428] and Estérie. They were all Tutsi and their houses were all destroyed.[429]

Prosecution Witness AZH

414. On 5 June 1994, AZH said he attended a meeting held by Kalimanzira on the field in front of the Gikonko *commune* office. At this meeting, Kalimanzira took the floor and instructed the listeners to exterminate Tutsi survivors, including young girls who Hutu men had taken as their wives, and Tutsis who had changed their identities in 1959 to pass as Hutus. He indicated that anyone hiding any Tutsis should also be killed if they refused to surrender those they were protecting. Kalimanzira added that the reason to kill all remaining Tutsis was to avoid the risk that a survivor might later report the attackers to the *Inkotanyi* once they took power. AZH recalled *conseillers* were present at the meeting, as well as **[page 88]** *cellule* officials, *commune* workers, and members of the general public. After the meeting, AZH and others left immediately to sensitize other members of the population to kill remaining Tutsi survivors, which they did.[430]

Defence Witness NDA

415. NDA testified that five of the persons named by Prosecution Witness AZC as being killed after the 5 June 1994 meeting died at least a month before then, and that one person named is actually still alive:[431]

– Kimonyo was killed at a roadblock in Nyarubuye *secteur* in April 1994; though NDA did not participate in his killing, he assisted with his burial;

– Joséphine Mukamazimpaka was killed in Gasenyi *cellule* around 29 April or 1 May 1994, roughly two days after the death of her father, whom NDA knew very well. NDA learned of Joséphine's death from Idelphonse Nyandwi, who had forcefully taken her as his wife; her killer's name was Sebazungu;

– Nyandwi also informed NDA that Joséphine was killed along with six other people, including Salafina Nyaraneza;[432]

– NDA learned of Anasthasia Nakabonye's[433] death the day after she was killed in April 1994. He was informed by Célestin Nsereko at the time, who participated in her death; he also assisted Nsereko to draft his confession later in prison;

– When in prison, NDA heard someone confess to having killed Kayumba in April 1994 by burying him alive; Kayumba was Salafina Nyaraneza's brother;

– Estérie[434] is still alive; she was Salafina Nyaraneza's mother.

Defence Witness AM28

416. AM28 testified that between April and June 1994, he attended three meetings in Mugusa *commune*, only one of which included members of the local population; Kalimanzira did not attend any of these. According to AM28, that public meeting was held next to the Mugusa *commune* office in Gikonko *secteur*

---

[428] The transcript of AZC's testimony provides a spelling of "Anastasie Nakabonye". The Chamber will adopt the name "Anasthasia Nakabonye" provided in the Indictment for the sake of consistency.
[429] T. 25 June 2008 pp. 43-44 (Witness AZC).
[430] T. 23 June 2008 pp. 12-14 (Witness AZH).
[431] T. 1 December 2008 pp. 45-48 (Witness NDA).
[432] The transcript of NDA's testimony provides a spelling of "Seraphina Nyiraneza". The Chamber will adopt the name "Salafina Nyaraneza" provided in the Indictment for the sake of consistency.
[433] The transcript of NDA's testimony provides a spelling of "Anastasie Nakabonye". The Chamber will adopt the name "Anasthasia Nakabonye" provided in the Indictment for the sake of consistency.
[434] The transcript of NDA's testimony provides a spelling of "Asterie". The Chamber will adopt the name "Estérie" provided in the transcript of AZC's testimony for the sake of consistency.

in late May 1994. He recalled this date as being after April, when the killings had already stopped, and right before the second wave of devastation in his area in June, immediately following this meeting.[435]

417. The meeting dealt with security matters, and AM28 attended it from start to finish. AM28 testified that those present included *bourgmestre* Kabayiza, deputy *bourgmestres*, members of the secretariat, staff of the accounting department, and *conseillers* of various *secteurs*. However, no officials from outside the *commune* were in attendance, because had there been, they would surely have been introduced, as was customary. AM28 recalled that **[page 89]** the first speaker of the day was *bourgmestre* Kabayiza, and towards the end of the meeting, various *conseillers* gave an overview of the situation prevailing in their respective *secteurs*.

418. At some point, people from Kibilizi *secteur* started shouting that some RPF accomplices had been spared. The *conseiller* of Kibilizi *secteur*, a Tutsi named Vincent Nkulikiyinka, was not present at the meeting; he had fled his *secteur* and sought refuge at the Mugusa *commune* office. When the meeting was over, everyone left except those from Kbilizi *secteur*, who stayed behind to continue speaking with *bourgmestre* Kabayiza, who condemned their attitude. Two days later, AM28 returned to the *commune* office, where *bourgmestre* Kabayiza told AM28 that the Kibilizi inhabitants forced him to hand over *conseiller* Nkulikiyinka; the *bourgmestre* did not know what then happened to the *conseiller*.[436]

419. AM28 specified that he never saw Kalimanzira from 6 April until the time he left for Rwanda, nor did he ever hear of any meeting that was attended by Kalimanzira. Though he did not know Kalimanzira, he has heard people talk about him, and asserts that had Kalimanzira attended any of the meetings AM28 attended in Mugusa *commune,* he would have surely been introduced.[437]

2.6.2. Deliberations

420. At the relevant time alleged, Kalimanzira claims to have been home in Butare *ville*, except when he went to visit his family in Kirarambogo in the first week of June. As discussed above, the Chamber disbelieves his alibi (see III.1.2.2).

421. AZC was an official in his area. At the time of his testimony, he was not in detention. Having spent 11 years in custody, AZC was released in July 2007 after being sentenced to 24 years, with 8 years suspended and 5 years of community service, which he is currently carrying out under the close supervision of the Rwandan courts. He confessed to all the charges against him, which included the setting up of a roadblock, selling the property of those who had been killed, and complicity in carrying out killings in his area. The killings which AZC accuses Kalimanzira of instigating at the 5 June meeting are also comprised by the killings for which AZC has been held responsible, making him an accomplice. The Chamber was impressed with AZC's expressed desire to testify truthfully so as to prevent any recurrence of such events in Rwanda.[438] However, because his statements to ICTR investigators in which he implicated Kalimanzira were made before his release, he may be now repeating statements he made at a time when he had an incentive to falsely accuse Kalimanzira. The Chamber will therefore treat his testimony with caution.

422. AZH was sentenced to nine years and released in 2003 after pleading guilty and agreeing to assist the *Gacaca* courts by testifying, whenever called upon, against people who incited him to commit genocide and against his accomplices.[439] AZH's testimony on the stand about the 5 June 1994 meeting is generally consistent with his prior statements to ICTR investigators, except when it comes to Kalimanzira's involvement. In his February 2000 statement, AZH mentions only Colonel Muvunyi, Colonel Nteziryayo, *bourgmestre* Kabayiza, and *conseiller* Gasana in relation to a meeting in Gikonko; his statement's description of the killing of *conseiller* Nkulikiyinka is similar to AM28's testimony.[440] In his **[page 90]** March 2001 statement about Kabayiza's involvement in the genocide, AZH does not mention the 5 June 1994 meeting at

---

[435] T. 26 January 2009 p. 30 (Witness AM28).
[436] T. 26 January 2009 p. 31 (Witness AM28).
[437] T. 26 January 2009 pp. 29, 32 (Witness AM28).
[438] T. 25 June 2008 p. 47 [closed] (Witness AZC).
[439] T. 24 June 2008 pp. 3-6 [closed] (Witness AZH).
[440] Exhibit D30.

the Gikonko *commune* office.[441] Then in December 2001, AZH describes for the first time a meeting at the Gikonko *commune* office on 5 June 1994 involving Kalimanzira and Kabayiza, and placing the meeting he described in his February 2000 statement three days later, on June 8th.[442] On the stand, AZH specified that Kalimanzira was the only person to have spoken at the 5 June 1994 meeting at the Gikonko *commune* office and suddenly added *sous-préfet* Ntawukulilyayo as among the authorities present; he also insisted that the 5 June 1994 meeting was the last one he attended, and that the one where Nkulikiyinka's death was discussed did not take place on 8 June, but rather in May 1994.[443]

423. AZH also testified in relation to the allegations at the Sakindi roadblock, where the Chamber considered his evidence should be treated with caution, and ultimately found his evidence to be unreliable (see III.2.5.2). The Chamber considers here as it does for his testimony on the Sakindi roadblock that the several inconsistencies in his prior statements and his testimony on the stand have rendered AZH's evidence unreliable, such that it is incapable of corroborating AZC's evidence. The unreliability of AZH's testimony on the same event raises a reasonable doubt that AZC's sole evidence is capable of sustaining a conviction for this charge. With nothing else to lend credence to or support AZC's account, the Chamber finds that the Prosecution has failed to meet its standard of proof.

2.7. Erection and Supervision of Roadblocks, mid-April to late June

424. At paragraph 15 of the Indictment, the Prosecution charges Kalimanzira with Genocide for inciting and instructing the population between mid-April and late June 1994 to erect roadblocks in order to eliminate the Tutsi. Kalimanzira is alleged to have often been personally present at these roadblocks, where many Tutsis were killed, to supervise their operations.

425. The Prosecution contends that numerous witnesses establish Kalimanzira's direct and personal involvement in the erection and operation of roadblocks in Muganza, Ndora, Kibayi and Mugusa *communes* of Butare *préfecture*. The Prosecution alleges that Kalimanzira ordered the erection of roadblocks because they were a useful and efficient way to monitor the status of the genocide in the area. Further, he personally visited and supervised roadblocks in order to ensure that those manning them were continuing to seek out and kill Tutsis, particularly by ensuring that people at the roadblocks were armed.[444]

426. In its Closing Brief, the Prosecution relies primarily on the evidence of Witnesses BDJ, AZH, BXK and BXG to prove the allegations at paragraph 15.[445] In particular:

   i. BDJ testified that Kalimanzira interrupted a meeting in the Ndora *commune* office in June 1994, where he criticized the attendees for not erecting roadblocks. He **[page 91]** also instructed the attendees to destroy the houses of Tutsis who had been killed in order to hide the evidence of massacres;[446]

   ii. AZH testified that in April 1994, Kalimanzira ordered the erection of a roadblock in Akabanga *cellule*, Mugusa *commune*, to prevent Tutsis from fleeing the outbreak of the genocide in Butare.[447]

   iii. BXK testified that Kalimanzira distributed weapons at a roadblock located on the road linking Butare town to Gisagara around 22 April 1994 in order to facilitate the killing of Tutsis;

---

[441] Exhibit D31.
[442] Exhibit D32.
[443] T. 24 June 2008 pp. 33-36 (Witness AZH).
[444] Prosecution Closing Brief, para. 157.
[445] Prosecution Closing Brief, paras. 157-181. The Chamber also notes the Prosecution's passing reference to testimonies of Witnesses BBB, BXH, BWL, BCN, BCK and BDE at fn. 393 of its Closing Brief. The evidence of these witnesses are considered elsewhere in the Judgement.
[446] Prosecution Closing Brief, paras. 168-170. The Prosecution asserts that BDJ's evidence that Kalimanzira ordered persons manning a roadblock to carry weapons is also relevant to paragraph 15. This aspect of BDJ's evidence is considered in relation to paragraph 27 of the Indictment (see III.4.9).
[447] Prosecution Closing Brief, paras. 176-177. The Prosecution asserts that AZH's evidence that Kalimanzira issued instructions at a roadblock near Sakindi's house in Kibilizi *secteur* (Mugusa *commune*) is also relevant to paragraph 15. This aspect of AZH's evidence will be considered in relation to paragraphs 13 and 25 of the Indictment (see III.2.5 and III.4.7).

iv. BXG testified that in late April 1994, Kalimanzira interrogated people at a roadblock in Mukabuga *cellule* to determine whether all the Tutsis in the area had been killed.

427. Kalimanzira denied these allegations in their entirety and relies on his alibi (III.1.2).

2.7.1. Notice

428. As noted above (see II.3), the Defence objects to the lack of precision in paragraph 15 of the Indictment in its Closing Brief, arguing that the charge should be set aside because the Prosecution did not specify which roadblocks Kalimanzira allegedly had erected and personally supervised.[448]

429. The Chamber finds that Paragraph 15 lacks most of the necessary precision expected in an indictment. At a minimum, the Prosecution was required to provide Kalimanzira with information about the time and place of the incitement, as well as the time and place of the supervision. Paragraph 15 offers a time range spanning two and a half months, and provides no locations or roadblocks where the criminal acts were allegedly committed. The Chamber finds that the charge, on its own, lacks the specificity required to put Kalimanzira on notice and is therefore defective. The Chamber will now examine whether the Prosecution provided the Defence with clear, consistent and timely information detailing the facts underpinning this charge in order to cure this defect.

430. The summary of BDJ's anticipated testimony annexed to the Pre-Trial Brief refers to paragraph 15 as being relevant. It indicates that he would testify, among other things, about a meeting in June 1994 at the Ndora *commune* office where Kalimanzira verbally abused *bourgmestre* Célestin Rwankubito in front of other attendees for not setting up roadblocks in the area. The information provided is clear, and is consistent with BDJ's prior witness statement disclosed in the Supporting Materials.

431. The summary of AZH's anticipated testimony also refers to paragraph 15 as being relevant. It indicates that he would testify, among other things, about an incident at the Kabanga centre in Kibilizi *secteur*, Mugusa *commune* in early April 1994 where Kalimanzira and other authorities ordered the people to set up roadblocks and to bring Tutsis arrested **[page 92]** there to either Isar-Rubona or the Gikonko *commune* office. This information is clear, and is consistent with AZH's prior witness statement disclosed in the Supporting Materials.

432. The summary of BXK's anticipated testimony also refers to paragraph 15 as being relevant. It indicates he would testify that, having fled Kabuye hill in search of help as part of a large group of Tutsi refugees, BXK saw Kalimanzira in the second half of April 1994 at two closely located roadblocks on the Kabuye-Gisagara road. BXK would say he saw Kalimanzira give guns to the persons manning the roadblocks and instruct them to kill the Tutsi refugees, which they did. This information is clear, and is generally consistent, though not entirely, with BXK's prior witness statement disclosed on 3 December 2007.[449] The Prosecution also makes reference to this incident in its Opening Statement.[450]

433. The summary of BXG's anticipated testimony in the Pre-Trial Brief fails to make reference to paragraph 15 as being relevant. It indicates that he would testify that he saw Kalimanzira at a roadblock in Gisagara *secteur*, Ndora *commune* around 20 April 1994, and observed how Kalimanzira spat in someone's face for lying to him about the fate of the Tutsis, claiming they had all been killed, when in fact they were resisting being killed on Kabuye hill. This information does not relate to the allegations of calling for the erection of roadblocks or supervising their operations. BXG's testimony is irrelevant to the allegations at paragraph 15, and inadequate notice was provided that his testimony would relate to it. It will therefore not be considered here, but rather in relation to the allegations at Kabuye hill (see III.2.4).

---

[448] Defence Closing Brief, para. 1125.
[449] See also Exhibit D7.
[450] See T. 5 May 2008 p. 4 (Opening Statement): "He also spurred on the killing of Tutsi at the roadblock situated on the Butare-Gisagara road in Ndora *commune* in connection with the Kabuye Hill massacres. Once again, the Accused Kalimanzira instructed the people manning the roadblock to kill Tutsi and distributed a firearm to facilitate such killings."

434. In sum, clear and consistent notice was provided to the Defence regarding Kalimanzira's alleged call to erect, or supervision of, roadblocks in April 1994 at the Kabanga centre; in June 1994 at the Ndora *commune* office; and April 1994 at a roadblock on Gisagara road.

435. With respect to timeliness, the Defence has advanced a general assertion it could not conduct sufficient investigations on new material facts upon the delivery of the Prosecution Pre-Trial Brief, filed three weeks before the commencement of trial.[451] However, for the same reasons discussed at III.2.3.1, namely that AZH, BDJ and BXK were thoroughly cross-examined and that the Defence had four and a half months after the close of the Prosecution case before commencing its own, the Chamber finds that the Defence was given adequate time to prepare its case. The Defence was not materially prejudiced in the preparation of its case with respect to paragraph 15 of the Indictment. The Chamber therefore finds that the Prosecution has cured the defect in paragraph 15 of the Indictment relating to the allegations discussed above by the provision of clear, consistent and timely notice.

436. Finally, in its Closing Brief, the Prosecution asserts that the evidence relevant to paragraph 21, 22, 25 and 26 of the Indictment, which particularize Count 3, is also relevant to paragraph 15 of the Indictment.[452] The Indictment does not indicate that these paragraphs are relevant to Counts 1 and 2 in any respect; indeed, paragraph 6 of the Indictment states that paragraph 7 through 17 only are relevant to those counts. On the basis of reading the Indictment alone, the Accused would not have understood that he was being charged for the **[page 93]** allegations contained in paragraphs 21, 22, 25 and 26 under Counts 1 and 2. The Chamber finds that the Prosecution is essentially seeking to amend the Indictment to expand the charges under Counts 1 and 2. This is impermissible. Consequently, the Chamber will not consider this evidence in relation to paragraph 15.[453]

2.7.2. Kabanga centre

437. The Prosecution contends that, sometime in April 1994, Kalimanzira ordered the erection of a roadblock in Kabanga *cellule*, Mugusa *commune*, to prevent Tutsis from fleeing after the outbreak of the genocide in Butare *préfecture*.

438. The Defence denies this allegation in its entirety. In addition, Kalimanzira relies on his alibi (see III.1.2).

2.7.2.1. Evidence

Prosecution Witness AZH

439. AZH testified that he saw Kalimanzira six times after the death of President Habyarimana. AZH recalled that the first time, in April 1994, while standing at the side of the road in Mugusa, Kabanga *cellule*, he saw Kalimanzira arrive in a vehicle with Sylvain Nsabimana and *conseiller* Gasana. AZH recalled that Kalimanzira introduced himself before instructing them to erect roadblocks and to stop and arrest any people they did not know and who were coming from other areas. Kalimanzira told them that the *Inkotanyi* were the enemy and explained that the *Inkotanyi* had come from abroad. Nsabimana told them that when they arrested the *Inkotanyi*, they should be taken to the authorities for protection; however, AZH clarified that they were instead taken to Isar Rubona where they were killed.[454]

440. AZH further recalled that after Kalimanzira and Nsabimana left, *conseiller* Gasana invited MRND party members to a meeting at the *commune* office where he informed them that he had just returned from a meeting in Mugusa aimed at preparing massacres and explained that the people Kalimanzira were referring to when he talked about the *Inkotanyi* were Tutsis. AZH believed that *conseiller* Gasana did not tell them this at the roadside because Tutsis were present and he did not want them to flee. Finally, AZH stated that in

---

[451] Defence Closing Brief, para. 1141 and fn. 1003.
[452] Prosecution Closing Brief, para. 321.
[453] *Karera* Appeal Judgement, paras. 365-370; *Muvunyi* Appeal Judgement, paras. 155-156.
[454] T. 23 June 2008 pp. 7-8 (Witness AZH).

accordance with Kalimanzira's instructions, the people started erecting roadblocks even before Kalimanzira left.[455]

Defence Witness FJS

441. At the end of May or early June 1994, FJS personally witnessed two soldiers erect a roadblock in front of her house in Kibilizi *secteur*.[456] She testified that the soldiers said that the *Inkotanyi* had already reached Ntyazo and that to prevent the *Inkotanyi* from advancing, the roadblock had to be set up.[457] FJS remembered the period in which the roadblock was erected because that was when the *conseiller* of Kibilizi *secteur*, Vincent Nkulikiyinka, took refuge in the *commune* office and was then executed. It was also at that time when the population was sent to fight the *Inkotanyi* in Cyiri.[458] **[page 94]**

Defence Witness MVE

442. MVE is a Hutu farmer who lived in Kibilizi *secteur* in 1994.[459] He testified that a roadblock was set up in Kabanga *cellule* at the end of May 1994 at the Sakindi-Gikonko road junction. He recalls the date because it was erected after a meeting at Gikonko, on a football field not far from the Mugusa *commune* office. At the meeting, the *bourgmestre* told the people that they had to face the *Inkotanyi*, who had assembled at Cyiri.[460] However, one of the men refused to fight the *Inkotanyi* when the *bourgmestre* was hiding one in his office. MVE went with others to the *commune* office and found the Tutsi *conseiller*, Vincent Nkulikiyinka.[461] Following the *conseiller's* death, the roadblock was erected in Kabanga *cellule*.[462]

2.7.2.2. Deliberations

443. At the relevant time alleged, Kalimanzira claims to have been working in Murambi (Gitarama *préfecture*). As discussed above, the Chamber disbelieves his alibi (see III.1.2.2).

444. An assessment of AZH's evidence and credibility in relation to other events is discussed at III.2.6.2 (Mugusa *commune*, 5 June 1994) and III.2.5.2 (Sakindi roadblock, May 1994). In these sections, the Chamber found that his testimony should be viewed with caution. AZH is an accomplice to some of the crimes alleged against Kalimanzira, and as such, the Chamber found that it would not be safe to rely on his testimony without corroboration. The Chamber arrives at the same conclusion with respect to his testimony on this event. As the Defence argues, there are troubling inconsistencies between his prior statements and his testimony; for instance, in his February 1999 statement to the Prosecution, it was *préfet* Nsabimana who told the population to erect roadblocks, not Kalimanzira.[463]

445. In light of the foregoing, the Chamber finds it unsafe to rely on AZH's sole testimony with respect to this event. Consequently, the Prosecution has not proven beyond reasonable doubt that Kalimanzira ordered the erection of a roadblock in Kabanga *cellule* to prevent Tutsis from fleeing the area.

2.7.3. Ndora commune *office*

446. The Prosecution alleges that, in June 1994, Kalimanzira interrupted a meeting held by *bourgmestre* Célestin Rwankubito in the Ndora *commune* office. Kalimanzira reprimanded the attendees for not setting

---

[455] T. 23 June 2008 pp. 8-9 (Witness AZH).
[456] T. 28 January 2009 pp. 40, 45, 48-50 [closed] (Witness FJS).
[457] Ntyazo is a *commune* in northern Butare *préfecture* (see *e.g.* Exhibit P5).
[458] T. 28 January 2009 pp. 51-52 [closed] (Witness FJS).
[459] T. 3 February 2009 p. 53 [closed] (Witness MVE).
[460] The Chamber notes that in the English transcript, the location is transcribed as "Nkiri"; in the French transcript, it is transcribed as "Cyiri". The Chamber finds the French transcript to be the more accurate: T. 3 February 2009 p. 60 (English); p. 71 (French) (Witness MVE).
[461] T. 3 February 2009 pp. 59-60 (Witness MVE).
[462] T. 3 February 2009 p. 61; T. 4 February 2009 pp. 4, 7-8 (Witness MVE).
[463] Defence Closing Brief, paras. 878-893; Exhibit D30.

up roadblocks on the road that passed through the *commune* and further told the attendees to completely destroy the houses of dead Tutsis.[464]

447. The Defence denies that Kalimanzira attended the meeting. In addition, Kalimanzira relies on his alibi (see III.1.2).

2.7.3.1. Evidence

Prosecution Witness BDJ **[page 95]**

448. BDJ testified that in early June 1994, he attended a meeting at Ndora *commune* office. BDJ recalled that the meeting began at 9:00 a.m. and was chaired by the *bourgmestre*, Célestin Rwankubito. Rwankubito took the floor and told the attendees, who included *conseillers* de *secteur*, *responsables* de *cellule*, members of the *comités* de *cellule*, and the people in charge of local security that he had convened the meeting so that means of distributing the property of people who had been killed could be discussed. BDJ further recalled that Rwankubito was then interrupted by the arrival of Kalimanzira, who was angry and proceeded to address the audience in a high-pitched voice.[465]

449. Kalimanzira expressed anger that he had not encountered roadblocks on his journey from Butare and stating: "It is clear that there are *Inkotanyi* accomplices in Ndora *commune*". Kalimanzira also said that the *Inkotanyi* were going to take over all of Butare because the residents of Ndora were doing nothing.[466] BDJ recalled that Kalimanzira then informed them that, consequently, he would personally relieve the *bourgmestre* of his duties within two weeks. Kalimanzira also issued urgent instructions to the participants, instructing them to destroy the houses of dead Tutsis and plant banana leaves over their ruins in order to conceal what had taken place from the United Nations.[467] BDJ testified that, by referring to *Inkotanyi*, Kalimanzira was referring to all those not participating in activities at roadblocks which had been set up to contain the enemy. BDJ stated that the authorities had explained to the population that the enemy was the Tutsi. The meeting ended around 10:00 a.m. and Kalimanzira's orders were executed immediately.[468]

Prosecution Exhibit 54

450. Exhbit P54 is a letter dated 16 June 1994 from Célestin Rwankubito to the *Préfet* of Butare attaching minutes from a 10 June meeting in Ndora *commune*. The minutes state that the meeting commenced at 9:30 a.m., was led by *bourgmestre* Rwankubito, and consisted first of a discussion regarding protecting the property of those who were absent. When the Prime Minister's directives concerning civil defence strategies were being discussed, the *Directeur de Cabinet* of the Ministry of Interior and Communal Development arrived and expressed his regret that the roadblocks were not organized in accordance with instructions. Further, he demanded the total destruction of the houses of those who had left, as quickly as possible, because in the coming days there would be a visit from a foreign mission of inquiry.

2.7.3.2. Deliberations

451. At the relevant time alleged, Kalimanzira claims that he was at home in Butare *ville*. As discussed above, the Chamber disbelieves his alibi (see III.1.2.2).

452. BDJ has a criminal record for participation in the genocide. Some of the crimes to which he confessed include participating in manning roadblocks as well as the killings on Kabuye hill. He was sentenced to 11 years' imprisonment and was released in 2007.[469]

---

[464] Prosecution Closing Brief, para. 159.
[465] T. 17 June 2008 pp. 49-50 (Witness BDJ).
[466] T. 17 June 2008 pp. 50-51 (Witness BDJ).
[467] T. 17 June 2008 p. 51 and T. 18 June 2008 p. 10 (Witness BDJ).
[468] T. 17 June 2008 pp. 51-52 (Witness BDJ).
[469] T. 17 June 2008 pp. 62-63 [closed] (Witness BDJ).

However, there was nothing to indicate that this witness had anything to gain from giving false testimony against Kalimanzira in this instance and the Chamber found him to be credible. **[page 96]**

453. In addition, BDJ's testimony is corroborated by Exhibit P54. The Chamber found the minutes to have sufficient indicia of authenticity at the time they were admitted in evidence.[470] Although Kalimanzira testified that these minutes are fabricated, the Chamber does not believe Kalimanzira.[471] Having reviewed Exhibit P54, the Chamber is satisfied that this document is the minutes of the meeting testified to by BDJ and that they indicate that Kalimanzira interrupted the meeting. There were minor inconsistencies between the minutes and BDJ's testimony but their nature does not detract from the reliability of either the witness' testimony or the minutes.

454. The Chamber further notes that there was independent evidence that Célestin Rwankubito was replaced by Fidèle Uwizeye as the *bourgmestre* for Ndora *commune* on 17 June 1994, therefore shortly after the meeting.[472] Bearing in mind Kalimanzira's position in the Ministry of the Interior where he participated in the process of appointing and removing *bourgmestres*, the fact that Rwankubito was removed from office supports BDJ's testimony that Kalimanzira threatened to replace the *bourgmestre*.

455. The Chamber rejects the Defence complaint that BDJ's evidence that Kalimanzira stated that he found no roadblocks on the road from Butare cannot be believed because other witnesses have testified that there were at least five roadblocks on the road.[473] The Chamber notes that Exhibit P54 does not indicate that Kalimanzira was upset by the lack of roadblocks, but rather by their inadequate functioning or organization in accordance with previously issued instructions. The Chamber finds the minutes to be the more faithful rendering of Kalimanzira's remarks.

456. The Chamber believes BDJ and finds that the Prosecution has proven beyond reasonable doubt that on 10 June 1994, Kalimanzira attended a meeting at the Ndora *commune* office and expressed anger at the inadequacy of local efforts to properly erect and operate roadblocks, thereby encouraging and instigating their erection and maintenance. The Chamber also accepts BDJ's testimony that Kalimanzira told the crowd that the roadblocks were intended to prevent "*Inkotanyi* accomplices" from taking over Butare and that the orders given were immediately carried out by the public because he was an influential authority. However, there is no evidence regarding which roadblocks were erected or reorganized upon Kalimanzira's instructions or, more notably, that any killings resulted from Kalimanzira's order at this late stage of the genocide. The Chamber therefore finds that the Prosecution has failed to prove beyond reasonable doubt that Kalimanzira's instructions substantially contributed to the commission of genocide.

457. While the Chamber finds that Kalimanzira also instructed the crowd to conceal the ruins of the houses of dead Tutsis in order to prevent the discovery of their deaths, the Chamber finds that this evidence is not relevant to the charge contained in paragraph 15; namely that Kalimanzira incited the erection of, and supervised, roadblocks. No conviction can therefore be entered in relation to this evidence.

2.7.4. Roadblock on Butare-Gisagara Road

458. The Prosecution alleges that around 22 April 1994, Kalimanzira distributed weapons at a roadblock on a road linking Butare *ville* and Gisagara and ordered a man at the roadblock **[page 97]** to use the weapon he had given him to kill Tutsis. Subsequently, Tutsis at the roadblock were killed.[474]

459. The Defence denies the allegation and Kalimanzira relies on his alibi (see III.1.2).

---

[470] See Decision on Prosecution Motion for Admission of Documents Under Rules 92*bis* (C) and 89 (C), confidential, 11 July 2008.
[471] T. 11 February 2009 pp. 27-29 (Callixte Kalimanzira).
[472] Exhibit D107 p.16.
[473] Defence Closing Brief, para. 405.
[474] Prosecution Closing Brief, paras. 171-175.

2.7.4.1. Evidence

Prosecution Witness BXK

460. BXK is a Tutsi who sought refuge on Kabuye hill on 20 April 1994. After surviving attacks, he left two nights later to find the *préfet* in Butare with approximately twenty other refugees believing that the authority would provide help.[475] BXK testified that whilst attempting the journey to Butare, the group was stopped and forced to sit down at a roadblock on the main road linking Butare and Gisagara, at a crossroads with a footpath leading to Kabuye.[476] BXK further clarified that the roadblock was situated on the border between Ndora and Gisagara, before both the Gisagara parish and the Ndora *commune* office.[477]

461. BXK arrived at the roadblock at approximately 11:00 a.m., which was manned by Hutu civilians who had undergone training and were armed with machetes and clubs.[478] BXK recognised several of them and named Ferederiko, Bihehe, Deny and Sylvestre Sentore as present. BXK estimated that the roadblock had been recently erected because his group was the first to be stopped and were later joined by one hundred and fifty to two hundred people. BXK did not attempt to escape from the roadblock because they had heard that they had been erected everywhere and did not fear for their lives.[479]

462. BXK testified that at 1:00 p.m., Kalimanzira arrived at the roadblock in a red saloon car, accompanied only by a driver. Kalimanzira asked the man manning the roadblock why they had instructed the Tutsis to sit down instead of killing them. Kalimanzira also asked them why they had no firearms and handed a Kalashnikov from his own car to Ferederiko, who then passed it to an *Interahamwe* named Sylvestre Sentore. Kalimanzira then left the roadblock in the direction of Gisagara. BXK explained that he was seated three metres or less from where Kalimanzira and Ferederiko spoke, enabling him to see and hear clearly what was taking place.[480]

463. BXK testified that the group of Tutsi refugees was then searched by the Hutus, as requested by Kalimanzira, before being deprived of their belongings and taken to a latrine pit situated at the house of one Gasana where they were killed. BXK recalled that the firearm was used to shoot at the refugees and that the other men used machetes. BXK managed to escape and has since seen only one other survivor. BXK believes that the other members of the group were in all probability killed that day.[481]

2.7.4.2. Deliberations [page 98]

464. At the relevant time alleged, Kalimanzira claims that he was working in Murambi (Gitarama *préfecture*). As discussed above, the Chamber disbelieves his alibi (see III.1.2.2).

465. In its Closing Brief, the Defence asserts that BXK's testimony relates to the incident alleged at paragraph 21 of the Indictment, whereby Kalimanzira gave a rifle to Marcel Ntirusekanwa at the Jaguar roadblock, located in front of the Gisagara church, and told him to use it to kill Tutsi.[482] At the same time, the Defence asserts that the BXK's roadblock must be distinguished from the Jaguar roadblock.[483] BXK's testified that one could not see the Gisagara church from the roadblock where he was stopped.[484] Further, BXK testified that Kalimanzira provided a Kalashnikov machine gun, not a rifle; BXK was familiar with firearms because soldiers had given him weapons training, and was able to correctly identify a picture of a

---

[475] T. 9 May 2008 pp. 6-7, 21 and T. 19 May p. 21, 23 (Witness BXK).
[476] T. 9 May 2008 p. 7 (Witness BXK).
[477] T. 19 May 2008 pp. 24-26 (Witness BXK).
[478] T. 9 May 2008 p. 8 and T. 19 May 2008 p. 32 (Witness BXK).
[479] T. 9 May 2008 pp. 7-8 and T. 19 May 2008 pp. 28, 37-38 (Witness BXK).
[480] T. 9 May 2008 pp. 8-10 (Witness BXK).
[481] T. 9 May 2008 pp. 9-11 (Witness BXK).
[482] Defence Closing Brief, paras. 311-314.
[483] Defence Closing Brief, para. 405 (2).
[484] Paragraph 21 of the Indictment states that the Jaguar roadblock is "located in front of the Gisagara Catholic Church". Witness BXK testified that "From the roadblock -- or, at least the roadblock I'm talking about, one could not see the parish, because after the roadblock there was a branch before one got to the parish." T. 19 May 2008 p. 26.

Kalashnikov when shown to him.[485] Finally, BXK testified that the weapon was given to Ferederiko, not Marcel.[486] The Chamber finds that BXK is describing a separate incident than the one alleged at paragraph 21 of the Indictment, discussed in full at III.4.3.

466. The Defence argues that there are many inconsistencies between BXK's testimony and his prior statement which serve to undermine his credibility.[487] For instance, the Defence asserts that BXK only testified about one roadblock, while in his statement he said there were two and referred to the activity of Kalimanzira at the other roadblock.[488] However, when cross-examined on this point, BXK was consistent in stating that there were two closely located roadblocks, that he was stopped at the first, but could see the second.[489] With respect to what occurred at the second roadblock, BXK refused to confirm what was in the statement because he said that he had received that information from others, and did not witness it himself.[490] The Chamber accepts his testimony on this issue.

467. The Defence also points out that, in his statement, BXK said that he first went to Gisagara market where he and other refugees were told by *sous-préfet* Ntawukulilyayo to take refuge at Kabuye hill.[491] In his testimony however, BXK stated that when he fled, he went to Kabuye directly, without passing through Gisagara.[492] BXK clarified in cross-examination that he clearly remembered telling Prosecution investigators that he fled his home to go to Wabitama, where other refugees were. There is evidence on the record that "Wabitama" was another name for Kabuye hill.[493] He further explained that he had been to the Gisagara marketplace before he fled to Kabuye, but did not leave with the Gisagara refugees to the hill as they had been asked, but instead went home; his evidence appears to be **[page 99]** that he was at the Gisagara marketplace the day before he fled.[494] The Chamber accepts this explanation.

468. There was one inconsistency for which no explanation was given, but it was fairly minor: in describing who was manning the roadblocks in his statement and in his testimony he placed Sylvestre Sentore in a different roadblock.[495] The Chamber considers that the length of time that elapsed between the events in 1994, the making of the statement in October 2001, and giving testimony in 2008 explains such a discrepancy. In addition, there was an issue with regard to his story after his escape from the roadblock. The statement records that he returned to Kabuye hill, whereas in his testimony he said he fled towards Burundi.[496] The Chamber accepts his explanation that there was an error in the recording of his statement.[497]

469. The Chamber also notes that BXK's testimony that there was a pit near Gasana's house where the Tutsis were killed is supported by Defence Witness Harindintwali. Harindintwali admitted to manning the Jaguar roadblock and acknowledged that there was a mass grave close to Gasana's house.[498]

470. In sum, the Chamber found BXK to be credible. The Chamber does not accept the Defence contention that his evidence was incredible, particularly because he testified that the refugees left Kabuye hill to seek help, even after having been attacked, or that they stayed at the roadblock because they did not yet understand that those manning the roadblock intended them harm.[499] The Chamber does not find this incredible, indeed, the evidence on the record indicates that a great many Tutsis gathered at Kabuye hill because they were told that they would be protected there. It is not incredible that, even after having been attacked, the refugees thought that the authorities might provide assistance, or that they did not yet know that it was the authorities who had organized and encouraged the attacks.

---

[485] T. 9 May 2008 p. 9 and T. 19 May 2008 pp. 33-34 (Witness BXK); Exhibit D6, picture 2D.
[486] T. 9 May 2008 p. 9 (Witness BXK).
[487] Defence Closing Brief, paras. 229-233, 237-247.
[488] Defence Closing Brief, paras. 240-244; Exhibit D7.
[489] T. 19 May 2008 pp. 44-47 (Witness BXK).
[490] T. 19 May 2008 p. 47 (Witness BXK).
[491] Defence Closing Brief, paras. 231-232; Exhibit D7.
[492] T. 19 May 2008 p. 42 (Witness BXK).
[493] T. 20 May 2008 p. 31 (Witness BDK); T. 22 May 2008 p. 6 (Witness BXG).
[494] T. 19 May 2008 pp. 42-43 (Witness BXK).
[495] Defence Closing Brief, paras. 240-241; Exhibit D7; T. 9 May 2008 pp. 8-9 and T. 19 May 2008 pp. 46-47 (Witness BXK).
[496] Defence Closing Brief, para. 235; Exhibit D7; T. 9 May 2008 p. 11 (Witness BXK).
[497] T. 19 May 2008 pp. 47-48 (Witness BXK).
[498] T. 19 November 2008 pp. 1 and 3 (Jean Marie Vianney Hardintwali).
[499] Defence Closing Brief, paras. 224-226.

471. The Defence also relies on the alibi to deny this allegation, taking the position that Kalimanzira could not have been at the roadblock on 22 April at 1:00 p.m., when BXK places him there, because he would have been on the Kibungo-Gitarama road.[500] Evidence on the record shows that Kalimanzira was in Kibungo to commission the new *préfet* on 21 April, which is supported by Marc Siniyobewe, and therefore the Defence argues that Kalimanzira could not have made it to the roadblock by the next day.[501] Although the Chamber accepts that Kalimanzira went to Kibungo for the swearing in ceremony on 21 April, it does not accept his alibi. The evidence that he stayed in Kibungo overnight despite his evidence that it was under imminent attack from the RPF is unbelievable (see III.1.2.2).

472. Moreover, the Chamber notes that, despite BXK's testimony that he took refuge on Kabuye hill on 20 April and that he spent only two nights there, he could have been mistaken about the exact day or timeframe, given the passage of time. In his October 2007 statement, BXK stated that he spent "three days and nights" on Kabuye hill, which would indicate his **[page 100]** arrival at the roadblock on 23 April, allowing time for Kalimanzira to arrive from Kibungo.[502] In any event, the alibi evidence of Kalimanzira does not cast reasonable doubt on the testimony of BXK.

473. In light of the above, the Chamber finds that the Prosecution has proven beyond reasonable doubt that, in April 1994, Kalimanzira stopped at a roadblock on the Butare-Gisagara road, asked the men manning the roadblock why they did not have weapons and why they had instructed the Tutsis to sit down instead of killing them. Kalimanzira then provided a weapon to a man at the roadblock. Subsequently, Tutsis at the roadblock were deprived of their belongings and taken to a nearby pit, where they were killed.

474. The Chamber also finds that the Prosecution has proven beyond reasonable doubt that, by doing so, Kalimanzira both instigated and aided and abetted genocide. The Chamber recalls that modes of liability under Article 6 (1) of the Statute are not mutually exclusive and that the Chamber may find the accused guilty of more than one mode if it is necessary to reflect the totality of the accused's conduct.[503] By asking those men at the roadblock why they had not killed the Tutsis who were detained there, Kalimanzira prompted those men to kill the Tutsis; by providing the weapon with which at least some of those Tutsis were killed, Kalimanzira assisted in the perpetration of their murders. The Chamber finds that Kalimanzira's speech and actions substantially contributed to the killings of the Tutsis detained at the roadblock, and that it was his intention to do so. Kalimanzira exhibited here, as elsewhere, an intent to destroy the Tutsi group (see III.5.2). For these reasons, the Chamber finds Kalimanzira guilty beyond reasonable doubt of having instigated and aided and abetted genocide at a roadblock on the Butare-Gisagara road on or around 22 April 1994.

2.8. Muganza *Commune* Football Field, May

475. At paragraph 17 of the Indictment, the Prosecution charges Kalimanzira with Genocide for personally demonstrating how to shoot arrows at a public rally held on the Muganza *commune* football field for the purpose of training people how to handle weapons. It is alleged that those who were trained under Kalimanzira's supervision subsequently took part in killing Tutsis in the area.

476. In its Closing Brief, the Prosecution submits that the main significance of the meeting was not the weapons training provided, but the underlying call to kill any Tutsis who may have survived the first round of massacres.[504]

477. The Defence contends that while rallies may have been held on a field near the Muganza *commune* office between April and June 1994, Kalimanzira was not in attendance at any of them. Further, the weapons training exercise that a Defence witness did attend only proves the existence of a civil defence programme under military supervision, rather than a call to kill Tutsi.[505] In addition, Kalimanzira relies on his alibi that,

---

[500] Defence Closing Brief, para. 255.
[501] Defence Closing Brief, para. 254, 256; Exhibit D104 p. 19; T. 4 February 2009, p. 24 (Marc Siniyobewe).
[502] Exhibit D7.
[503] *Nahimana* Appeal Judgement, para. 483.
[504] Prosecution Closing Brief, paras. 182-185.
[505] Defence Closing Brief, paras. 515-519.

save for a few specified occasions, he was working in Murambi (Gitarama *préfecture*) from 14 April to 31 May 1994 (see III.1.2).

2.8.1. Evidence

Prosecution Witness BCA **[page 101]**

478. BCA saw Kalimanzira at a public rally on a football field next to the Muganza *commune* office in May 1994. At the rally, over 100 members of the local population present, mainly Hutu males, were taught about civilian defence and given archery training so that they could assist the RAF to fight the RPF if they reached the area. BCA stated that during the training, Kalimanzira attempted to shoot at a banana tree being used as a target and missed. BCA recalled that Dominique Ntawukulilyayo (*sous-préfet* of Gisagara) and Alphonse Nteziryayo (Lieutenant-Colonel) were also there.[506]

Prosecution Witness BBB

479. BBB saw Kalimanzira at a meeting on the football field next to the Muganza *commune* office in May 1994; also in attendance were the Chrysologue Bimenyimana, *bourgmestre* of Muganza *commune*, Nteziryayo, who eventually became *préfet* of Butare, the *conseiller* of Remera *secteur,* and the *responsable de cellule*. Kalimanzira was standing next to a vehicle and speaking to *bourgmestre* Bimenyimana and Nteziryayo. BBB then went to the football field where a crowd of approximately 300-400 male Hutu civilians from all *secteurs* in Muganza *commune* had gathered. The officials soon arrived from the *commune* office and Kalimanzira addressed the crowd. BBB recalled that Kalimanzira told them they had been called to prepare to fight the *Inkotanyi* and free the Ntyazo area[507] so that the Tutsi would not take over the country.[508]

480. BBB testified that archery training was then conducted, using a tree trunk as a target. Kalimanzira attempted to shoot at the target with a bow and arrow but missed. After the archery exercise, the meeting continued. BBB recalled that members of the public told the officials that they did not have enough bows. As a result, Nteziryayo promised to provide irons and building rods for spears and arrows. Kalimanzira also instructed the public to kill "accomplices", people who had been hidden until then, which BBB understood to mean Tutsis. BBB claimed that he could hear Kalimanzira clearly without the use of a megaphone because he was close to him in the crowd and when he spoke, the crowd was silent. At the end of the training session, guns were fired by Nteziryayo and hidden soldiers in order to familiarize the public with the sound and to encourage them to show courage.[509]

481. BBB testified that after the meeting, people gained a harder attitude; several attacks were launched and many were killed, particularly Tutsi wives and children who had been spared until that point. BBB personally participated in an attack against Riel Ntakavoro, taking away the Tutsi in his home. After a meeting in Remera *secteur* the following day, he also participated in an attack killing the two Tutsi grandsons of Anasthase Misago, a Hutu.[510]

Prosecution Witness BWI

482. BWI saw Kalimanzira at a meeting on the football field facing the Muganza *commune* office in late May or early June 1994, held sometime before mid-day. Other officials present included Nteziryayo, *sous-préfet* Ntawukulilyayo and *bourgmestre* Bimenyimana; they arrived at approximately 11:00 a.m. BWI recalled that he sat approximately 20 metres from Kalimanzira, who was introduced as the Secretary-General of the Ministry of the Interior. BWI stated that Kalimanzira announced it was a security meeting; he said that the *Inkotanyi* had been weakened, that they were the enemy, and he asked the public to fight them

---
[506] T. 18 June 2008 pp. 49-50 (Witness BCA).
[507] Ntyazo is a *commune* in northern Butare *préfecture* (see *e.g.* Exhibit P5).
[508] T. 16 June 2008 pp. 13-15 (Witness BBB).
[509] T. 16 June 2008 pp. 16-17 (Witness BBB).
[510] T. 16 June 2008 pp. 17-18 (Witness BBB).

with **[page 102]** traditional weapons. BWI further recalled that a soldier fired into the air in order to familiarise them with the sound of gunshots, which they could hear in Ntyazo.[511]

483. BWI testified that Kalimanzira then led a weapons training session by setting up a banana tree trunk as a target, which people then practiced shooting at. Kalimanzira attempted a shot but missed. BWI did not stay until the end of the training; Kalimanzira was still on the football field when he left. BWI believes that two to three hours elapsed from when he first saw Kalimanzira until he left the football field. After the meeting, the people who had been trained were sent to fight the *Inkotanyi* who had reached Ntyazo. Tutsis in Muganza *commune* were also killed, some by people present at the meeting. BWI stated that he did not witness the killings but that he heard the killers boast about them.[512]

Defence Witness KAS

484. KAS did not leave Muganza *commune* from 6 April until July 1994, when he fled Rwanda for Burundi. During that period, he only attended one meeting, which was held in late May 1994 the football field in Remera *secteur,* close to Muganza *commune* office.[513]

485. KAS testified that he became aware of the meeting after reading a *communiqué* inviting the local population that was posted in a bar near his place of business. He arrived before the meeting started and left at the end. KAS recalled the presence of Nteziryayo, *bourgmestre* Bimenyimana, a census official named Célestin, a brigadier named Pierre, and *conseillers* of various *secteurs* of Muganza *commune*. KAS was seated on the ground and could see the officials clearly.[514]

486. KAS testified that he did not see Kalimanzira at the meeting and that the only speakers were *bourgmestre* Bimenyimana and Nteziryayo. KAS stated that at the time of the meeting, the killings had already stopped and there were no further killings after the meeting. KAS did not witness any demonstrations of firearms and knows of no other meetings that took place before or after at the Muganza *commune* office.[515]

Defence Witness Athanase Nzabakirana

487. Nzabakirana testified that sometime in late May or early June 1994, he attended a three-day military-style training session at the football field next to the Muganza *commune* office. Under the direction of a soldier, he and 50 others were subjected to undergo such physical exercises as how to hide, how to dismantle a rifle, and how to shoot guns. No archery exercises were demonstrated, and no officials were present. Apart from this three-day session, Nzabakirana knows of no other training sessions taking place on the field.[516]

2.8.2. Deliberations

488. Kalimanzira denied attending the meeting and testified that he never went to Butare *préfecture* in April or May, except on 19 April for the MRND Palace meeting. He also admitted to attending one Butare Prefectural Security Council meeting in Butare on 16 May, **[page 103]** which he only admitted to when confronted with radio transcripts under cross-examination.[517] The Chamber does not believe his alibi (see III.1.2.2).

489. The Chamber notes that the Prosecution witnesses gave very consistent testimony concerning this event. BCA, BBB and BWI all testified that a meeting was held on a football field near the Muganza *commune* office in late May or early June 1994 in which the crowd was given archery training.[518] Each testified that the

---

[511] T. 21 May 2008 pp. 34-35 (Witness BWI).
[512] T. 21 May 2008 pp. 36-37 (Witness BWI).
[513] T. 24 November 2008 pp. 6-7 (Witness KAS).
[514] T. 24 November 2008 p. 9 (Witness KAS).
[515] T. 24 November 2008 p. 10 (Witness KAS).
[516] T. 28 January 2009 pp. 35-37 (Athanase Nzabakirana).
[517] T. 11 February 2009 pp. 25-26 (Callixte Kalimanzira).
[518] T. 16 June 2008 pp. 13-14 (Witness BBB); T. 18 June 2008 p. 49 (Witness BCA); T. 21 May 2008 p. 36 (Witness BWI).

purpose of the meeting was weapons training to fight the approaching RPF or *Inkotanyi* at Ntyazo.[519] BBB and BWI testified that a gun was fired in order to familiarize the crowd with the sound.[520]

490. Further, the Prosecution witnesses all testified that authorities were present at the meeting, and gave similar, although not identical, accounts of which authorities were present. BCA, BBB and BWI testified that Alphonse Nteziryayo was present;[521] BCA and BWI recall the presence of *sous-préfet* Dominique Ntawukulilyayo;[522] and BBB and BWI recall the presence of *bourgmestre* Chrysologue Bimenyimana.[523] The Chamber finds that the similarity of these accounts to be persuasive and rejects the Defence's contention that the slight inconsistencies render the evidence unreliable, rather than simply being a natural product of the passage of time and the different experience of each witness.[524]

491. With respect to Kalimanzira's presence at the meeting, the Chamber notes that BCA, BBB and BWI gave consistent and detailed testimony on this point. They all testified that Kalimanzira personally demonstrated how to use a bow and arrow by using a banana tree as a target, and BCA and BBB recalled that Kalimanzira missed the target.[525]

492. BCA has admitted to taking part in the genocide.[526] BBB also admitted to taking part in the genocide and admits to having participated in attacks against Tutsis after Kalimanzira's alleged instigation at this meeting.[527] He is therefore an accomplice who may have reason to dilute his responsibility for these acts; his testimony should be viewed with caution. However, the Chamber notes that they were supported in significant respects by BWI and, after careful consideration, finds the evidence of BCA and BBB to be credible and largely reliable. The Defence challenges to their evidence were minor and did not undermine their credibility.[528]

493. With respect to the Defence evidence, KAS testified that he attended a meeting held on the Remera football field, not far from the Muganza *commune* office in late May 1994.[529] **[page 104]** KAS also recalled the attendance of several authorities, including Nteziryayo, *bourgmestre* Bimenyimana and several *conseillers*.[530] He did not, however, see any weapons demonstrations, nor did he see Kalimanzira.[531] He was not asked what the purpose of the meeting was, nor what occurred there, although he did testify that he was present for the entire meeting.[532] Consequently, it is unclear if this is the same meeting attended by the Prosecution witnesses.

494. Similarly, Nzabakirana gave evidence that weapons training was held on the football field next to the Muganza *commune* office. However, the meeting he attended was held over the course of three days, was conducted by a solider with no authorities present, and involved a demonstration of how to use guns rather than bows and arrows.[533] The Chamber infers that this meeting was a different one than that testified to by the Prosecution witnesses.

495. Both Defence witnesses testified that they would have been aware had any other similar meetings taken place at the Muganza *commune* office.[534] KAS testified that he would have known about other meetings since *communiqués* were posted where he sold beer and because he would have seen people passing to attend

---

[519] T. 16 June 2008, p. 16 (Witness BBB); T. 21 May 2008 pp. 35, 42, 44, 47-48 (Witness BWI); T. 18 June 2008 pp. 49-50 (Witness BCA).
[520] T. 16 June 2008 p. 17 (Witness BBB); T. 21 May 2008 p. 35 (Witness BWI).
[521] T. 16 June 2008 p. 14 (Witness BBB); T. 18 June 2008 p. 49 (Witness BCA); T. 21 May 2008 p. 34 (Witness BWI).
[522] T. 18 June 2008 p. 50 (Witness BCA); T. 21 May 2008 p. 35 (Witness BWI).
[523] T. 16 June 2008 p. 14 (Witness BBB); T. 21 May 2008 p. 35 (Witness BWI).
[524] Defence Closing Brief, 498-502.
[525] T. 16 June 2008 p. 16 (Witness BBB); T. 18 June 2008 p. 50 (Witness BCA); T. 21 May 2008 p. 36 (Witness BWI).
[526] T. 18 June 2008 p. 41 [closed] (Witness BCA).
[527] T. 16 June 2008 pp. 17-18 (Witness BBB).
[528] *See* Defence Closing Brief, paras. 482-483, 496-507; 536-547; 550-559; 579-580.
[529] T. 24 November 2008 p. 7 (Witness KAS).
[530] T. 24 November 2008 pp. 7-8 (Witness KAS).
[531] T. 24 November 2008 p. 10 (Witness KAS).
[532] T. 24 November 2008 p. 7 (Witness KAS).
[533] T. 28 January 2009 pp. 35-36 (Athanase Nzabakirana).
[534] T. 24 November 2008 pp. 10-11, 15-16 (Witness KAS); T. 28 January 2009 pp. 36-37 (Athanase Nzabakirana).

such meetings.[535] However, in light of the fact that he returned to school toward the end of May, attending from 8:00 a.m. to 2:00 p.m. every day, and acknowledged that he could not see the *commune* office from where he sold beer in the evenings, the Chamber does not accept that he was in a position to know about every meeting that may have been held.[536] With respect to Nzabakirana, the Chamber notes that he lived an hour's walk away from the *commune* office and finds his assertion that he knew there were no other training sessions because he did not find anyone else who had engaged in such training to be insufficient to undermine the Prosecution evidence.[537]

496. In sum, the Chamber does not accept the inference that the Defence invites it to draw, namely that the meeting could not have occurred because KAS and Nzabakirana were not aware of it; indeed, it appears that they each attended a different meeting and were not aware of the other. Their lack of knowledge on this point does not raise reasonable doubt regarding the positive and credible testimony of the Prosecution witnesses. Finally, the Chamber notes that their testimony offers some support for the Prosecution's allegation that the football field near the *commune* office was used for public meetings, and in particular for weapons demonstrations for local civilians.

497. Several other Defence witnesses testified about meetings in Muganza *commune*, but did not mention the training exercise at the football field.[538] The Chamber notes that many were not directly questioned about this specific allegation and, in any event, there is no evidence that these witnesses would have any particular reason to know of every meeting that may have been held in Muganza *commune*.

498. Consequently, the Chamber finds beyond a reasonable doubt that a meeting took place on the football field next to the Muganza *commune* office in late May or early June **[page 105]** 1994 for the purpose of training the population to use weapons and that Kalimanzira attended the meeting and personally demonstrated how to use a bow and arrow.

499. As noted above, the Prosecution asserts that the main significance of this event was not the weapons training, but the underlying call to kill Tutsis. The Chamber notes, however, that the Prosecution witnesses were not consistent on this point.

500. BCA testified that the rally was for the purpose of civilian defence and that members of the general public were being shown how to help Rwandan security forces if the RPF were to arrive in the area.[539] Similarly, BWI testified that Kalimanzira announced that it was a security meeting, that the *Inkotanyi* had been weakened, and asked the population to take up their traditional weapons to go and fight the enemy. Kalimanzira clarified that the enemy was the *Inyenzi-Inkotanyi*. Shots were fired so that the population would get used to the sound, in order to prepare them to go to the frontline to fight the enemy in Ntyazo. At the time, they could hear gunshots from the direction of Ntyazo. BWI said that he understood the terms *Inyenzi* and *Inkotanyi* to be a reference to Tutsi, because of an earlier awareness campaign.[540]

501. While BBB's evidence was consistent with the other Prosecution witnesses that Kalimanzira told the crowd that they were being trained in order to fight the *Inkotanyi* at Ntyazo, he was the only witness to recall that Kalimanzira also instructed the crowd that, before going to Ntyazo, they had to get rid of the accomplices behind them, that is, the people they had hidden. BBB understood the term accomplices to mean the Tutsi.[541] The Chamber notes that BBB did not make this assertion in his earlier witness statement, but rather merely stated that Kalimanzira was in attendance and demonstrated how to shoot with arrows.[542] The fact that he only offered this evidence, central to the Prosecution's allegations, at trial lessens the reliability of his recollection on this point.

---

[535] T. 24 November 2008 pp. 15-16 (Witness KAS).
[536] T. 24 November 2008 pp. 12-13, 15-16 (Witness KAS).
[537] T. 28 January 2009 pp. 36-37 (Athanase Nzabakirana).
[538] *E.g.* Witness AM02, AK42, AM122, KUW, KXC, and MKB.
[539] T. 18 June 2008 pp. 49-50 (Witness BCA).
[540] T. 21 May 2008 pp. 35-36 (Witness BWI).
[541] T. 16 June 2008 pp. 15-16 (Witness BBB).
[542] Exhibit D14E: "Callixte Kalimanzira showed us how to shoot with arrows and he shot himself an arrow aiming at banana tree target but he missed the target. Alphonse Nteziryayo asked the people whether they were ready to fight with enemy. We replied in affirmative."

502. It is noteworthy that no other Prosecution witness offered similar evidence. BWI gave evidence concerning another, earlier, security meeting on the football field near the Muganza *commune* office where he alleges that Kalimanzira instructed the crowd to exterminate accomplices of the *Inkotanyi*, the Tutsi (see III.2.3.3).[543] Having already made an allegation that Kalimanzira incited the crowd to kill Tutsis in hiding, the Chamber finds it significant that BWI did not testify that Kalimanzira did so at this meeting.

503. The Chamber finds that a reasonable doubt subsists that the purpose of this meeting was a legitimate civil defence exercise to train the local population to handle weapons to fight at the approaching front, As such, Kalimanzira's attendance and participation in this meeting cannot, in and of itself, be a basis for a criminal conviction. With respect to the Prosecution's allegation that Kalimanzira also instructed the crowd to kill Tutsi civilians, in light of the Chamber's finding that BBB's testimony should be viewed with caution, and that he is uncorroborated in this assertion, the Chamber finds that it would not be safe to enter a conviction on BBB's evidence alone. Consequently, the Chamber finds that the Prosecution has not proven beyond a reasonable doubt that Kalimanzira instigated the crowd to kill Tutsis at the meeting in late May or early June 1994 near the Muganza *commune* office. **[page 106]**

3. COMPLICITY IN GENOCIDE

504. Under Count 2 of the Indictment, the Prosecution charges Kalimanzira with Complicity in Genocide pursuant to Article 2 (3)(e) of the Statute, and with individual criminal responsibility under Article 6 (1). Count 2 is pleaded in the alternative to Count 1, which requires the Chamber to dismiss the count of Complicity in Genocide in the event of a finding on the count of Genocide.

505. The Chamber has found Kalimanzira guilty under the Count 1. Count 2 is therefore dismissed. **[page 107]**

4. DIRECT AND PUBLIC INCITEMENT TO COMMIT GENOCIDE

506. Under Count 3 of the Indictment, the Prosecution charges Kalimanzira with Direct and Public Incitement to Commit Genocide pursuant to Article 2 (3)(c) of the Statute and with individual criminal responsibility under Article 6 (1). Paragraphs 18 to 27 of the Indictment outline the events for which the Prosecution alleges Kalimanzira incurs individual criminal responsibility for this crime.

507. Paragraph 18 of the Indictment pleads the modes by which Kalimanzira is said to incur liability under Count 3, namely that he "planned, instigated, ordered to commit or otherwise aided and abetted in the planning, preparation or commission of crimes". Such wording omits to specify commission as a mode of liability. The factual allegations at paragraphs 19 to 27, however, allege Kalimanzira's direct participation in the crime charged under Count 3.

508. The Chamber invited the Parties to make submissions on whether such an omission constitutes a defect in the Indictment.[544] The Defence submitted nothing. The Prosecution's submissions relied on the French original version of the Indictment, which duly expressed "commission" as a mode of liability, and that the wording of paragraph 18 was attributable to a translation error.[545] Because the Defence works primarily in French, the Chamber is assured that Kalimanzira was not prejudiced by the omission in the English version (see also II.2.2.1). The Chamber therefore considers "commission" to have been properly pleaded as a mode of liability for Direct and Public Incitement to Commit Genocide.

4.1. Applicable Law

509. Direct and Public Incitement to Commit Genocide is a crime provided for at Article 2 (3)(c) of the Statute, as a result of the incorporation of Article III of the Genocide Convention within the Statute's definition of genocide. Article 2 (3) of the Statute, identical to Article III of the Genocide Convention, lists

---

[543] T. 21 May 2008 pp. 32-33 (Witness BWI).
[544] T. 13 February 2009 pp. 19-20 (Status Conference).
[545] Prosecution's Submissions on Paragraph 18 of the Indictment as Invited by the Trial Chamber on 13 February 2009, filed 17 February 2009.

five punishable acts, including Genocide itself, and Direct and Public Incitement to Commit Genocide. The Statute and the Genocide Convention define the crime of genocide as any series of acts, including killing and causing serious bodily or mental harm, that are committed with the intent to destroy in whole or in part a national, ethnic, racial or religious group ("genocidal intent"). The crime of Direct and Public Incitement to Commit Genocide, however, is not defined any further in either the Genocide Convention or the Statute.

510. In specifying a distinct act of 'Direct and Public Incitement to Commit Genocide', the drafters of the Genocide Convention sought to create an inchoate crime, in that it is not necessary to prove that the incitement was successful in achieving a genocidal result. It is sufficient to establish that an accused directly and publicly incited the commission of genocide (*actus reus*), and that he or she had the intent to directly and publicly incite others to commit genocide (*mens rea*); such intent in itself presupposes a genocidal intent. The inchoate nature of the crime allows intervention at an earlier stage, with the goal of preventing the occurrence of genocidal acts.[546] **[page 108]**

511. The distinction between committing direct and public incitement and committing genocide by means of instigation often seems blurred. The term 'incitement' is synonymous with 'instigation', 'provocation', and 'encouragement', all of which are used interchangeably when describing the conduct underlying certain modes by which genocide may be committed. However, the differences are important and must be respected.

512. Instigation under Article 6 (1) is a mode of liability; an accused will incur criminal responsibility only if the instigation in fact substantially contributed to the commission of one of the crimes under Articles 2 to 4 of the Statute. By contrast, direct and public incitement is itself a crime, requiring no demonstration that it in fact contributed in any way to the commission of acts of genocide.[547]

513. The most important difference lies in the requirement that the crime of incitement be 'direct' and 'public', which serves to limit the scope of its inchoate nature. In other words, incitement which is not followed by the commission by others of genocidal acts must be direct and public for it to be criminal. By contrast, committing genocide by means of instigation need not be direct or public for it to be criminal.[548]

514. The jurisprudence of this Tribunal has established that the 'direct' element of incitement implies more than mere vague or indirect suggestion, such that the inciter knows that the intended audience will understand his or her call as one to commit genocide, but that implicit language may nonetheless be 'direct' and should be viewed in light of its cultural and linguistic content, its audience, and the political and community affiliations of the inciter.[549]

For instance, exhorting a crowd to unite against the "sole enemy", or to "get to work", or calling on "the majority" to "rise up and look everywhere possible" and not to "spare anybody", in the context of the Rwandan genocide has been found in the particular circumstances of other cases to amount to calls to exterminate the Tutsi people.[550] The Chamber will therefore consider on a case-by-case basis whether, in light of Rwandan culture and the particular context of each allegation, acts of incitement can be viewed as direct or not by examining how a speech was understood by its intended audience.[551] In some circumstances, the fact that a speech leads to acts of genocide could be an indication that in that particular context the speech was understood to be an incitement to commit genocide and that this was indeed the intent of the author of the speech. However, this cannot be the only evidence adduced to conclude that the purpose of the speech (and of its author) was to incite the commission of genocide.[552]

515. The jurisprudence of this Tribunal has also established that the 'public' element of incitement should be appreciated in light of the place where the incitement occurred and whether or not attendance was

---

[546] *Bikindi* Trial Judgement, para. 419; *Nahimana et al.* Appeal Judgement, para. 678; *Akayesu* Trial Judgement, paras. 560-562.
[547] *Nahimana et al.* Appeal Judgement, para. 678.
[548] The Trial Chamber in *Akayesu* found that the 'direct' and 'public' requirements were also applicable to instigation under Article 6 (1) of the Statute (see para. 481). The Appeals Chamber in *Akayesu* found such interpretation to be erroneous and established that instigation under Article 6 (1) of the Statute need not be 'direct' or 'public' (see *Akayesu* Appeal Judgement, paras. 474-483).
[549] *Bikindi* Trial Judgement, para. 387; *Nahimana et al.* Appeal Judgement, paras. 700, 711, and 713; *Niyitegeka* Trial Judgement, para. 431; *Akayesu* Trial Judgement, paras. 557-558.
[550] *Akayesu* Trial Judgement, paras. 334-365; *Niyitegeka* Trial Judgement, paras. 433-435; *Bikindi* Trial Judgement, para. 423.
[551] *Nahimana et al.* Appeal Judgement, paras. 698-700.
[552] *Nahimana et al.* Appeal Judgement, para. 709.

selective or limited. Incitement is 'public' when conducted through speeches, shouting or threats uttered in public places or at public gatherings, or through the sale or dissemination, offer for sale or display of written material or printed matter in public places or at public gatherings, or through the public display of placards or **[page 109]** posters, or through any other means of audiovisual communication.[553] Because of the crime's inchoate nature, even the possibility of private incitement to commit genocide is ruled out; only unequivocally public forms of incitement may be punished under Article 2 (3)(c) of the Statute.[554]

516.   The law on incitement may therefore be summarized as follows:

- Incitement resulting in the commission of a genocidal act is punishable under the combination of Articles 2 (3)(a) and 6 (1) of the Statute as Genocide by way of Instigation;

- Incitement resulting in the commission of a genocidal act and which may be described as 'direct' and 'public' is punishable under either Article 2 (3)(c) of the Statute as Direct and Public Incitement to Commit Genocide, or under the combination of Articles 2 (3)(a) and 6 (1) of the Statute as Genocide by way of Instigation;

- Incitement not resulting in the commission of a genocidal act but which may be described as 'direct' and 'public' is only punishable under Article 2 (3)(c) of the Statute; and,

- Incitement not resulting in the commission of a genocidal act, and which may not be described as 'direct' and 'public', is not punishable under the Statute.

4.2. Kanage Camp, 9 April

517.   At paragraph 20 of the Indictment, the Prosecution charges Kalimanzira with Direct and Public Incitement to Commit Genocide for addressing Burundian refugees at a camp in Kanage *cellule* (Mukindo *secteur,* Kibayi *commune*) around 9 April 1994. Kalimanzira told them that the Interim Government had confidence in them, that President Habyarimana had taken care of them and that President Sindikubwabo would continue to do so, and that the same enemy had chased them from Burundi and crashed the plane carrying Presidents Habyarimana and Ntaryamira. Kalimanzira appealed to the Burundian refugees to remain in Rwanda and told them he had brought them traditional weapons with which to defend themselves against the "enemy".

518.   The Defence denies that the alleged meeting took place. In addition, Kalimanzira relies on his alibi that he remained at his home in Kigali without access to transport from 7 to 11 April 1994 (see III.1.2).

4.2.1. Evidence

Prosecution Witness BBO

519.   The Prosecution led evidence from only one witness, BBO, on this event. BBO testified that he heard about the death of Juvénal Habyarimana (President of Rwanda) the morning of 7 April 1994 on Radio Burundi. Shortly thereafter, BBO said he saw Kalimanzira **[page 110]** at a Burundian refugee camp in Kanage *cellule* ("Kanage Camp"). BBO was at the camp because he had a girlfriend there; he was not a refugee himself.[555]

520.   BBO testified that authorities had convened a meeting at Kanage Camp to address the Burundian refugees. BBO recalled that the authorities present at this meeting included Kalimanzira, Élie Ndayambaje (former and future *bourgmestre* of Muganza *commune*), Tharcisse Muvunyi (Colonel), and Pierre Canisius

---

[553] *Akayesu* Trial Judgement, paras. 556 and 559.
[554] At the time the Genocide Convention was adopted, the delegates specifically agreed to rule out the possibility of including private incitement to commit genocide as a crime, thereby underscoring their commitment to set aside for punishment only the truly public forms of incitement. See Yearbook of the United Nations, UN Fiftieth Edition, 1945-1995, Martinus Nijhoff Publishers, 1995 and the Summary Records of the Sixth Committee of the General Assembly, 21 September – 10 December 1948, Official Records of the General Assembly.
[555] T. 19 June 2008 p. 38 (Witness BBO).

Kajyambere (*bourgmestre* of Kibayi *commune*). Although BBO had never met Kalimanzira before, *bourgmestre* Kajyambere introduced the authorities present. Kalimanzira was introduced as the Secretary-General of the Ministry of the Interior.[556]

521. BBO testified that at the start of the meeting, *bourgmestre* Kajyambere took the floor and asked the Burundian refugees to be patient in view of the situation prevailing in the country. BBO recalled that Colonel Muvunyi took the floor next in order to inform the refugees that President Habyarimana and Cyprien Ntaryamira (President of Burundi) had been killed, and to encourage them to remain in Rwanda and cooperate with Rwandan Hutus. BBO further recalled Colonel Muvunyi saying he had brought some weapons for the refugees to use to defend themselves if ever the *Inkotanyi* attacked from Burundi, and that he intended to replace the gendarmes at Kanage Camp with soldiers.[557]

522. BBO testified that Kalimanzira took the floor following Colonel Muvunyi's speech, and essentially repeated Colonel Muvunyi's statements, except to add that the Rwandan government considered RPF accomplices to be enemies of the state. Kalimanzira also indicated that people who listened to Radio Muhabura (which BBO described as "the radio station of the *Inkotanyi*") instead of Radio Rwanda were considered RPF accomplices and *Inkotanyi*, and that the Rwandan government would no longer protect them. BBO said he could hear the speeches clearly because he was standing 10-15 meters from the authorities, who used a megaphone while they spoke due to the large number of refugees.[558]

523. BBO testified that, before leaving Kanage Camp, the authorities left behind three boxes of traditional weapons, including machetes, daggers, and small hoes, for the camp leaders to distribute among the refugees. The weapons were distributed immediately. Because BBO was a Rwandan and not a refugee, he could not be issued a weapon. However, he testified that his refugee girlfriend gave him the machete she received.[559]

524. BBO described the atmosphere and mood after the speech as being tense. The refugees were afraid that the *Inkotanyi* might invade from Burundi and attack the refugees at Kanage Camp. Despite no such attack or any RPF invasion from Burundi, BBO recalled the refugees remained fearful, and, after a few days, began to transfer their fears of the *Inkotanyi* onto Tutsi civilians.[560] BBO and the Burundian refugees used the weapons they were issued to kill Tutsis who had taken refuge at the Kibayi *commune* office and at Kabuye hill (Ndora *commune*).[561]

Defence Witness MGR **[page 111]**

525. MGR owned a small shop which faced Kanage Camp, just across the road from it. He said he stayed at his shop from 7:00 a.m. until about 8:00 p.m., every day of the week, except when he occasionally took lunch at the marketplace nearby. Because of his proximity to the camp, there were always refugees buying provisions from MGR's shop. Even after President Habyarimana's death, MGR continued to run his shop everyday, until he fled Rwanda at the end of June 1994.[562]

526. MGR testified that he never heard of a meeting having taken place at Kanage Camp attended by *bourgmestre* Kajyambere, Colonel Muvunyi, Ndayambaje or Kalimanzira. MGR indicated that he does not know Colonel Muvunyi or Kalimanzira, and that the Burundian refugees never mentioned the existence of any such meeting attended by any of these individuals. Moreover, MGR stated that *bourgmestre* Kajyambere never once visited Kanage Camp, as he had appointed someone to be responsible for the camp. Finally, MGR asserted that there could not have been any distribution of weapons at Kanage Camp without his having noticed or learned about it from his clients or his friends. He reiterated that his shop was placed on the only road leading to and from the camp, thereby making it impossible for the occurrence of such a meeting or the arrival of authorities in vehicles to have escaped his attention.[563]

---

[556] T. 19 June 2008 pp. 39-40 (Witness BBO).
[557] T. 19 June 2008 pp. 40-41 (Witness BBO).
[558] T. 19 June 2008 pp. 40-41 (Witness BBO).
[559] T. 19 June 2008 p. 42 (Witness BBO).
[560] T. 19 June 2008 p. 43 (Witness BBO).
[561] T. 19 June 2008 p. 44 (Witness BBO).
[562] T. 17 November 2008 p. 25 (Witness MGR).
[563] T. 17 November 2008 pp. 25-27, 29-31 (Witness MGR).

Judgement

Defence Witness SRA

527. In 1994, SRA worked a 15-minute trek away from Kanage Camp. He said that from 6:00 a.m. on Monday morning until 6:00 a.m. on Friday morning, he would be at his place of work. On weekends he went home, which was 20 metres from Kanage Camp. SRA continued to work after President Habyarimana's death until early June 1994.[564]

528. SRA testified that he did not hear of any visits by any officials to Kanage Camp between the 6 April and June 1994. He stated that he never saw any vehicle near the camp containing Ndayambaje, *bourgmestre* Kajyambere, Colonel Muvunyi or Kalimanzira. SRA indicated that he did not know Colonel Muvunyi, but knew Ndayambaje, *bourgmestre* Kajyambere and specifically Kalimanzira, whom he met personally when working for a fishing co-operative. SRA asserted that it would have been impossible for any such meeting or distribution to have occurred at Kanage Camp without his knowledge due to the nature of his work and his frequent interactions with the Burundian refugees.[565]

Defence Witness KBF

529. KBF testified that by virtue of his professional position, he attended a meeting on the Nyabisagara football field 100 metres away from the Kibayi *commune* office in May 1994 (see III.4.6.1). This was the only meeting KBF attended in Kibayi *commune* in between April to July 1994; he admits the possibility that there may have been others. He knew Kalimanzira and asserted he was not there. KBF also maintains he never saw Kalimanzira or heard anything about him from April 1994 until he fled Rwanda in July 1994.[566]

Other Defence Witnesses [page 112]

530. Kalimanzira and his wife, Salomé, both testified that Kalimanzira stayed home in Kigali in the days following the death of President Habyarimana, and that the first time he left his house was on 11 April 1994 to attend a meeting at the *Hôtel des Diplomates*. They both maintain that Kalimanzira did not have access to a vehicle until that day.[567]

4.2.2. Deliberations

531. The Chamber rejects Kalimanzira's contention that he did not have access to a vehicle before 11 April 1994 and that he did not leave his house before that date (see III.1.2.2). Nevertheless, the Chamber's disbelief in Kalimanzira's alibi does not relieve the Prosecution of its burden to prove this allegation beyond reasonable doubt.

532. BBO is the only witness to have testified to this event. He testified that he was a Tutsi, but that he identified with Burundian Hutu refugees by fearing the *Inkotanyi* and participating in massacres against Tutsi civilians with them. For this, BBO was arrested and detained in Karubanda prison after returning to Rwanda from exile. He was charged with killings, which he confessed to in 1998. His guilty plea was accepted and he served 11 years in prison.[568] BBO admits to having participated in the attacks at Kabuye hill, where he also implicates Kalimanzira (see III.2.4.1), and where he testified he used the weapon distributed to him by Kalimanzira at Kanage Camp. This makes BBO an accomplice, whose testimony must be viewed with caution. The Chamber notes that BBO has served his sentence and it would not appear that his judicial proceedings could be enhanced by giving false testimony against Kalimanzira. However, the first time BBO mentioned Kalimanzira to ICTR investigators was in 2001, while he was still in jail awaiting trial,[569] at which time he may have believed that he could have something to gain from falsely implicating Kalimanzira.

---

[564] T. 26 January 2009 pp. 11, 13, 17 (Witness SRA).
[565] T. 26 January 2009 pp. 13-15 (Witness SRA).
[566] T. 17 November 2009 pp. 14-15 (Witness KBF).
[567] T. 10 February 2009 p. 23 (Callixte Kalimanzira); T. 5 February 2009 p. 6 (Salomé Mukantwali).
[568] T. 19 June 2008 p. 48 (Witness BBO).
[569] Exhibit D21.

533. Despite being a native of another *commune*, BBO indicated under cross-examination that he had settled in Kibayi *commune* around May 1993, where he remained until he fled Rwanda in July 1994. In his prior statements to ICTR investigators, however, he indicated that he was in Burundi in October 1993 and fled Rwanda in late May 1994.[570] In addition, in his first statement to ICTR investigators in October 1999,[571] BBO makes no mention of Kalimanzira or the incident at Kanage Camp, but rather speaks of a very different series of events occurring three days after the death of President Habyarimana. BBO's explanations that he was afraid of divulging too much information and that he could give different versions of events if he were continued to be questioned raise further doubts on his credibility.[572]

534. The Defence witnesses KBF, MGR and SRA called to rebut BBO's evidence testified that they never heard of the meeting in question. KBF admitted to the possibility that there may have been meetings in Kibayi *commune* other than the one he testified about. SRA's work kept him away from the vicinity of Kanage Camp for five full days out of every week; his assertion that such a meeting could not possibly have taken place without his knowledge is untenable. MGR's work placed him directly in front of the camp, but his blanket assertions that weapons could not be distributed and officials could not have visited the camp without his knowledge are equally untenable. In particular, MGR's testimony that he continued to run his shop everyday even after the death of the President stands in contrast to the Defence's **[page 113]** contention that Kalimanzira, like everyone else, stayed home in the days following the plane crash according to instructions issued on the radio.

535. The Chamber recalls the standard of proof and doubts that it can rely on BBO's uncorroborated evidence. The Chamber does not believe that Kalimanzira stayed home in the days following the death of the President. For the same reasons, it doubts that Kalimanzira went to Kanage Camp. In the absence of additional information or explanation, it would seem likely that at such a critical time, and in the absence of his Minister, Kalimanzira would have had more important matters to attend to in Kigali.

4.3. Jaguar Roadblock, mid-April

536. At paragraph 21 of the Indictment, the Prosecution charges Kalimanzira with Direct and Public Incitement to Commit Genocide for going to the "Jaguar" roadblock in front the Gisagara Catholic Church in mid-April 1994, giving a rifle to the person in charge of the roadblock, Marcel Ntirusekanwa, and instructing him to use the gun to kill Tutsis.

537. The Defence contends that the Prosecution witnesses are lying, but admits that Kalimanzira passed through Jaguar roadblock, albeit in June. In addition, Kalimanzira relies on his alibi that he was working in Murambi/Gitarama from 14 April to 30 May 1994, and on mission in Kibungo *préfecture* on 21 and 22 April 1994 (see III.1.2).

4.3.1. Evidence

Prosecution Witness BWL

538. BWL testified that he saw Kalimanzira at the Jaguar roadblock,[573] located near the Gisagara church, sometime in April 1994 shortly before the killings at Kabuye hill. Kalimanzira arrived at the roadblock in a white vehicle with two other people dressed in civilian attire. Kalimanzira got out of the vehicle, introduced himself to the people at the roadblock, and expressed the need to ensure the security of the Tutsis who had been sent to Kabuye hill. Those present at the roadblock included "Marcel", "Sylvestre", "Bihehe", and "Pakome". Kalimanzira then pulled a firearm out of the back seat of the vehicle and handed it over to either

---

[570] See Exhibits D20 and D21.
[571] Exhibit D20.
[572] See T. 19 June 2008 pp. 55 and 61 (Witness BBO).
[573] The transcript of BWL's evidence provides a spelling of "Jagwa" roadblock. The Chamber will adopt the name "Jaguar" provided in the Indictment for the sake of consistency.

Judgement

Marcel or Sylvestre, both of whom were soldiers who had just retired from the army. Upon seeing this, BWL got scared and left.[574]

Prosecution Witness BCN

539. BCN testified that at a meeting near the Abizeramariya Convent in late April 1994, Kalimanzira promised to supply weapons to members of the public for self-defence against the Tutsis. BCN recalled that within a week, Kalimanzira made good on that promise by bringing a firearm to the Jaguar roadblock,[575] located in front of the Gisagara church. This roadblock had been erected on Fidèle Uwizeye's initiative one week after President Habyarimana's death. Kalimanzira arrived at the roadblock at approximately 11:00 a.m. in a white double-cabin vehicle, accompanied by Fidéle Uwizeye and a driver. Kalimanzira was sitting in the passenger seat with Uwizeye in the backseat.[576] **[page 114]**

540. Those present at the roadblock included Marcel Ntirusekanwa, Jean Twagirayezu, Segundo Ngiriwonsanga, Dionisios Kabandana, Laurent Ngirente, Patern Harerimana, Siridi Iyakaremye, Louis Hakizimana, Casimir Bwanakeye, "Pakome", "Metero", "Bihehe", and Sylvestre Sentore. After stopping at the roadblock, Kalimanzira told Uwizeye to give them a gun. Without getting out of the car, Uwizeye took a firearm from a pile in the backseat and handed it over to Marcel, an ex-soldier, through the car window. Kalimanzira then informed everyone at the roadblock that the gun was to be used to kill Tutsis. Kalimanzira also instructed them to check everyone's identity cards of people and prevent any Tutsis from passing through the roadblock. Once Marcel took hold of the weapon, the vehicle left. BCN testified that Kalimanzira's instructions were carried out and that the gun was used to kill many people, including a Tutsi named Alexandre Rubayiza.[577]

541. BCN later heard that Kalimanzira had distributed the remaining weapons in his vehicle to other persons. BCN also testified that Kalimanzira passed by the Jaguar roadblock on several other occasions, each time instructing those manning it to kill Tutsis. On one such occasion, Kalimanzira questioned them as to why he could not see any corpses; they responded that there was a mass grave very close to the roadblock and that there were corpses there.[578]

Prosecution Witness BCK

542. BCK manned the Jaguar roadblock located near the Gisagara church three to four times per week, and was present when it was erected at the end of April 1994. BCK testified that at the end of April 1994, Kalimanzira arrived at the roadblock in a white or red Toyota double-cabin vehicle around 11:30 a.m. or midday accompanied by three soldiers. Kalimanzira parked the car and got out of the vehicle with the soldiers. After greeting everyone, Kalimanzira asked who could use a firearm. Those present at the roadblock included Lucien Simbayobewe, Jean Twagirayezu, and "Patern", as well as "Sylvestre" and Marcel Ntirusekanwa, both of whom used to be soldiers. Kalimanzira then handed a gun to Marcel "from the window of the vehicle" and instructed everyone that it was to be used at the roadblock to kill the *Inkotanyi Inyenzi* and any other possible enemies attempting to pass through the roadblock. Kalimanzira reminded them that the enemy was the Tutsi and promised to bring more guns later. Kalimanzira then left with the soldiers toward Gisagara.[579]

543. BCK testified that at the roadblock, people were sorted according to their ethnic identity. Only Hutus manned the roadblock, and unknown Hutus trying to pass through were held separately from Tutsis. Kalimanzira's instructions to kill Tutsis were implemented; BCK specifically recalled that a Tutsi named "Alexandre" was killed at the roadblock.[580]

---

[574] T. 23 June 2008 pp. 44-47, 59-62 (Witness BWL).
[575] See Exhibit D36.
[576] T. 25 June 2008 pp. 3-4, 17-20 (Witness BCN).
[577] T. 25 June 2008 pp. 5, 20-24 (Witness BCN).
[578] T. 25 June 2008 pp. 5, 8-9 (Witness BCN).
[579] T. 26 June 2008 pp. 6-9, 14-15 (Witness BCK).
[580] T. 26 June 2008 p. 9 (Witness BCK).

Defence Witness Sylvestre Niyonsaba

544. Niyonsaba is the son of Joseph Sentore, the same "Sylvestre" or "Sylvestre Sentore" referred to by BWL, BCN, and BCK.[581] He testified that he worked as a policeman for Ndora **[page 115]** *commune* until June 1994. He was issued with a gun by the *bourgmestre* as part of his duties, which he carried whilst working. In April 1994, Niyonsaba was among the first persons to start manning the Jaguar roadblock and he continued to do so until June 1994. While manning the roadblock, he carried his firearm. Niyonsaba recalled that he was the only person with a gun at the roadblock and that the others used only traditional weapons. Those typically present at the Jaguar roadblock included that Jérôme Singirankabo, Jérôme Rubayiza, Vianney Harindintwali, "Pakome", "Emmanuel", "Eugene", and quite a few others.[582]

545. Niyonsaba testified that Marcel Ntirusekanwa was also often at the Jaguar roadblock but did not in fact man it due to his advanced age. Niyonsaba only saw Marcel at the roadblock with a firearm once. Marcel would often joke that he could fire a gun since he was an ex-soldier. Therefore, on one occasion, Niyonsaba, handed Marcel his gun as a joke, after removing the magazine, in order to test the statement.[583]

546. Niyonsaba testified that he saw Kalimanzira at the Jaguar roadblock twice in the middle of June 1994. Kalimanzira was in a white double-cabin vehicle, accompanied by a driver. Niyonsaba and the other men allowed Kalimanzira to pass through the roadblock by removing the tree trunk being used as a barrier. Niyonsaba recalled that Kalimanzira waved his hand in greeting but did not exit the vehicle. He did not speak to the people manning the roadblock or take anything from his vehicle and give it to anyone manning or standing at the roadblock. Kalimanzira arrived from the direction of Butare and continued in the direction of Gisagara. Niyonsaba saw Kalimanzira again, on his return to Butare. Kalimanzira was in the same vehicle and did not speak to or give anything to anyone manning the roadblock.[584]

Defence Witness Jean Marie Vianney Harindintwali

547. Harindintwali manned the Jaguar roadblock most afternoons between 1:00 p.m. and 4:00 p.m. He testified that nobody was ever killed at the roadblock and that there was no mass grave next to it. Harindintwali stated that there was a mass grave near Gasana's house but that this was a great distance from the roadblock. He further insisted that he never partook in any separation of Hutus from Tutsis at the roadblock, nor is he aware of any Tutsis having been so separated, killed and dumped in a pit.[585]

4.3.2. Deliberations

548. At the time of this alleged incident, Kalimanzira claims to have been working in Murambi (Gitarama *préfecture*), except on 21 and 22 April 1994 when he travelled to and from Kibungo *préfecture* to install the new *préfet*. As discussed above, the Chamber does not believe Kalimanzira's alibi (see III.1.2.2).

549. In its Closing Brief, the Defence has erroneously considered BXK's testimony as referring to the incident alleged at paragraph 21 of the Indictment and has relied on its inconsistencies with other BCN, BCK and BWL to discredit them all.[586] However, elsewhere in its Closing Brief, the Defence asserts that the roadblock BXK testified to must be distinguished from the Jaguar roadblock.[587] Notice was given that BXK would testify to the **[page 116]** allegations at paragraph 15, not paragraph 21, of the Indictment.[588] As

---

[581] See Prosecution Closing Brief, para. 218. The Defence Closing Brief at para. 257 erroneously refers to Sylvestre's father, Joseph Sentore, as being the person purported to have received the weapon at Jaguar roadblock by Kalimanzira. Neither the Indictment, nor any Prosecution witness, ever purported that Joseph Sentore received any weapon at Jaguar roadblock. The Indictment only refers to Marcel having received the rifle, as do BCN and BCK, while BWL could not be sure whether it was "Marcel" or "Sylvestre". BCN and BCK refer to "Sylvestre" or "Sylvestre Sentore" as among those present at the roadblock.
[582] T. 18 November 2008 pp. 35-37 (Sylvestre Niyonsaba).
[583] T. 18 November 2008 pp. 39-40 (Sylvestre Niyonsaba).
[584] T. 18 November 2008 pp. 40-41 (Sylvestre Niyonsaba).
[585] T. 19 November 2008 pp. 1-3 (Jean Marie Vianney Harindintwali).
[586] Defence Closing Brief, paras. 311-314.
[587] Defence Closing Brief, para. 405 (2).
[588] Prosecution Pre-Trial Brief, Annex A.

discussed at III.2.7.4.2, the Chamber finds that BXK's testimony refers to a separate incident; it will not be discussed here. The Defence contention that BXK's testimony discredits BCN, BCK and BWL is therefore rejected.

550. BWL is a Tutsi who was 18 years old at the time of this event. The Defence argued that his account of events was unbelievable. For instance, he explained that his reason for passing through the Jaguar roadblock was that he was returning from a shop where he had been sent to buy tomato paste by his employer.[589] He also mentioned that he was not checked at the roadblock when passing through. The Defence raised the incongruity that an employer would send a young Tutsi outside during the midst of the genocide, and that his identity would not be checked when passing through the roadblock. However, it is not implausible. The Chamber accepts BWL's explanation that he did not appear old enough to have been issued an identity card.[590] In his September 2007 statement to ICTR investigators, BWL mentions that he habitually passed through the Jaguar roadblock, where he witnessed several killings, but he was not disturbed because he was not known to be a Tutsi.[591] He also testified that at the time of this alleged incident, the killings had not yet started in his locality.[592] The Chamber accepts that BWL was not targeted for these reasons.

551. The Defence also questioned BWL as to how he could go shopping when he had previously mentioned that at the time the shops were shut. BWL acceptably explained that the shopkeeper would open the shop for him because of identity of his employers.[593] Finally, the Defence raised the issue of a minor discrepancy between a BWL's prior statement, in which he described seeing Kalimanzira hand a firearm to Marcel, and his testimony on the stand, where he described that he saw the firearm being given to Marcel *or* Sylvestre.[594] The Chamber considers this to imply that BWL was being more cautious in his sworn testimony. The Chamber finds BWL to be credible and reliable.

552. BCN manned the Jaguar roadblock. He was arrested in 1994, sentenced to 20 years in prison for committing genocide, and was released in December 2007.[595] It is not clear whether the crimes he committed and confessed to, which included killings, were linked to the crimes charged against Kalimanzira in this Indictment. At the time of his testimony, BCN had completed his sentence and it would not appear that his judicial proceedings could be enhanced by giving false testimony against Kalimanzira. However, the Chamber notes that BCN also levels several other allegations against Kalimanzira, consisting mostly of inciting the population to kill, and considered whether BCN might have had an interest in diluting his own responsibility for committing killings by blaming Kalimanzira and other authorities for inciting him. The Chamber has not so concluded.

553. There was little challenge to the integrity of BCN's testimony. The Defence raised a minor challenge as to whether or not it was possible to see the house of Dominique Ntawukulilyayo (*sous-préfet* of Gisagara) from the roadblock,[596] as there was mixed testimony on this point. The Chamber does not consider this to be of any importance because **[page 117]** the existence and location of Jaguar roadblock and the *sous-préfet*'s house are not in dispute and are in close proximity to each other.

554. BCK is a Hutu, and like BCN, manned the Jaguar roadblock in April 1994. BCK is currently serving a 30-year prison sentence after being convicted of genocide by a *Gacaca* court in June 2007.[597] He had exhausted all methods of appeal before testifying. It is not clear whether the crimes he committed and confessed to, which included killings, were linked to the crimes charged against Kalimanzira in this Indictment. The Chamber nevertheless considers that his testimony should be viewed with caution.

555. The Defence was able to point out an inconsistency between his BCK's evidence and a *Gacaca* document dated October 2001. In the *Gacaca* document, BCK stated that Kalimanzira handed a firearm to

---

[589] T. 23 June 2008 p. 45 (Witness BWL).
[590] T. 23 June 2008 pp. 42-43 [closed] 60 (Witness BWL).
[591] Exhibit D25.
[592] T. 23 June 2008 p. 44 (Witness BWL).
[593] T. 23 June 2008 pp. 62-63 (Witness BWL).
[594] T. 23 June 2008 pp. 68-69 (Witness BWL).
[595] T. 25 June 2008 p. 12 (Witness BCK).
[596] T. 25 June 2008 pp. 16, 24-25 (BCK).
[597] T. 26 June 2008 pp. 12 and 28 [closed] (Witness BCK).

Sylvestre, whereas on the stand he testified that Kalimanzira handed a firearm to Marcel.[598] The Chamber accepts BCK's explanation that the *Gacaca* document does not accurately reflect his statement, as he did not write it and contests the accuracy of its content.

556. The Defence suggested that there were major discrepancies between the testimonies of the three Prosecution witnesses.[599] However, upon careful consideration, and having dismissed consideration of BXK's testimony in relation to this event, the Chamber considers the Defence's contention to be unfounded. The Defence suggested that BCN was lying and uncorroborated when he said that Kalimanzira passed through the roadblock on several occasions.[600] However, his testimony is supported by Sylvestre Niyonsaba who said that he saw Kalimanzira pass through the roadblock several times, albeit in June 1994.[601]

557. The testimonies of BWL, BCK and BCN generally substantiate each other on many issues, such as the date of the alleged incident, that the weapon was handed to Marcel, and that Kalimanzira arrived in a white vehicle described as either a van or pick-up truck. Additionally, there are several issues on which two Prosecution witnesses support each other: BCN and BWL both say that Kalimanzira arrived with a driver and a civilian, whom BCN identified as Fidèle Uwizeye; BWL and BCK both state that Kalimanzira got out of the vehicle; BCN and BCK both identified the firearm as a rifle whereas BWL testified that he did not know about weapons and could therefore not comment; BCN and BCK also recalled the killing of a Tutsi named "Alexandre". All three witnesses ascribe utterances to Kalimanzira although these are not the same. It is entirely understandable that there would be minor discrepancies between testimonies. The alleged incident occurred 15 years ago in a time of great trauma and stress. Furthermore, people process events differently and selectively remember different facts. The differences are not enough to raise reasonable doubt as to the credibility or reliability of these witnesses.

558. The Defence led evidence from two witnesses who, like BCN and BCK, manned the Jaguar roadblock. Harindintwali lives in exile as a fugitive from justice and is wanted by the *Gacaca* courts for killing and looting.[602] His statement that he did not see any Tutsi segregation or killings of Tutsis at the roadblock is not reconcilable with his recognition that **[page 118]** there was a mass grave near Gasana's house,[603] which he places at a great distance from Jaguar roadblock, but which Prosecution witness BXK described was in the area (see III.2.7.4).[604] Given his status as a fugitive from justice and as someone who manned the roadblock, Harindintwali has an obvious interest in distancing himself from any alleged criminal acts. The Chamber therefore has reason to disbelieve Harindintwali.

559. Niyonsaba also lives in exile and has not returned to Rwanda since he left in 1994.[605] As a possible fugitive from justice, serious doubts are raised about the extent to which Niyonsaba might also be interested in denying any criminal acts having occurred at the Jaguar roadblock. On the stand, Niyonsaba legitimized his carrying of a firearm by claiming that he was a *communal* policeman at the time of the events. However, the Defence's disclosure of his personal particulars listed him as having been a mason at the time of the events, not a policeman. The Chamber does not accept Niyonsaba's statement that he failed to mention he was a police officer earlier because he was asked what his job or profession was, and Rwandans do not consider joining the police force as being a job or a profession.[606] Given the context of the testimony he was asked to bring, such an omission cannot be explained away by semantics. The Chamber was also unconvinced with Niyonsaba's cynical story about letting Marcel, whom he described as elderly, hold his gun in jest on

---

[598] T. 26 June 2008 pp. 33-35 (Witness BCK); see also Exhibit D39.
[599] Defence Closing Brief, para. 303.
[600] Defence Closing Brief, para. 306.
[601] T. 18 November 2008 p. 40 (Sylvestre Niyonsaba).
[602] T. 18 November 2008 pp. 68-69 and T. 19 November pp. 6-7 (Jean Marie Vianney Harindintwali); see also Exhibits P57 and P58.
[603] T. 19 November 2008 p. 3 (Jean Marie Vianney Harindintwali).
[604] T. 9 May 2008 p. 10 (Witness BXK).
[605] T. 18 November 2008 pp. 34-35 (Sylvestre Niyonsaba).
[606] T. 18 November 2008 p. 60 (Sylvestre Niyonsaba): "At home one does not consider being in the police force as being a profession or a job. It's a form of employment. If, for instance, you had been a soldier and you leave the army, you can be become a policeman. Furthermore, if you misbehave as a policeman, you are dismissed and you are no longer referred to as a policeman. Being in the police force is not a profession. Now, when I was asked about my job or profession, I said that I was a mason because being a policeman is not a profession, it's not a job."

Judgement

one occasion. He did, however, admit that Marcel was an ex-soldier, as the Prosecution witnesses described. Regardless, Niyonsaba's sightings of Kalimanzira in June 1994 do not preclude Kalimanzira from also being there in April 1994.

560. The Prosecution witnesses corroborated one another and the Chamber found them to be credible and reliable. The Defence testimony failed to raise any reasonable doubt. The Chamber therefore finds that sometime in mid to late April 1994, Kalimanzira stopped at the Jaguar roadblock and handed a rifle to Marcel Ntirusekanwa in the presence of several others who were also manning the roadblock. Upon giving the rifle, he told everyone present that the gun was to be used to kill Tutsis.

561. Though the wording of paragraph 21 of the Indictment could imply that Marcel alone was present at the roadblock and received instructions from Kalimanzira, the Prosecution Pre-Trial brief clarified the more public quality of the alleged incitement. The rifle was not intended to be distributed to Marcel in particular or to be used by him only; the gun and the instructions were disseminated to the group. The incitement to kill Tutsis was clear, direct, and in a public place, to an indeterminate group of persons.

562. In these circumstances, there is no reasonable doubt that those present at the roadblock understood Kalimanzira's actions and words as a call to commit acts of genocide against Tutsis and that Kalimanzira intended to directly and publicly incite such acts. Kalimanzira exhibited here, and elsewhere, an intent to destroy the Tutsi group (see III.5.2). As such, the Chamber finds Kalimanzira guilty beyond reasonable doubt for committing Direct and Public Incitement to Commit Genocide at the Jaguar roadblock, as alleged at paragraph 21 of the Indictment. **[page 119]**

4.4. Kajyanama Roadblock, late April

563. At paragraph 22 of the Indictment, the Prosecution charges Kalimanzira with Direct and Public Incitement to Commit Genocide for appearing at a roadblock located at the border between the Muganza and Remera *secteurs* and the Kirarambogo junction in late April 1994 with gendarmes, and reminding those manning it that they had to carry weapons and kill Tutsis. He slapped one unarmed person there and forced another unarmed person into his vehicle.

564. The Defence denies Kalimanzira's presence at this roadblock at the time alleged. In addition, Kalimanzira relies on his alibi that he was working in Murambi (Gitarama *préfecture*) from 14 April to 30 May 1994 (see III.1.2).

565. This roadblock was located in Kajyanama *cellule* (Remera *secteur*, Muganza *commune*);[607] the Chamber will therefore refer to it as the "Kajyanama roadblock".[608]

4.4.1. Evidence

Prosecution Witness BBB

566. BBB testified that the Kajyanama roadblock was originally erected in 1990 but, after a period of disuse, was re-established two days after the death of President Habyarimana. The roadblock consisted of tree trunks pulled across the road to prevent vehicles from passing and was controlled by the *responsable* of Kajyanama *cellule* and the *conseiller* of Remera *secteur*. BBB testified those manning the roadblock, including him, were instructed by their leaders to hide in the woods whenever a vehicle approached in order to make them less vulnerable to attack. Once a vehicle's occupants had been identified, they would return to the roadblock. BBB testified that he manned the roadblock regularly, three to four times per week, from morning until evening.[609]

---

[607] T. 16 June 2008 p. 6 (Witness BBB); T. 22 May 2008 p. 41 [closed] (Witness BXH); T. 25 November 2008 p. 26 [closed] (Witness AM29); T. 25 November 2008 p. 43 [closed] (Witness AM05); see also Exhibits P2, P3, D13, D59, and D61.
[608] This is also the name adopted by the Defence. See *e.g.* Defence Closing Brief, para. 435.
[609] T. 16 June 2008 pp. 6-7, 22-23, 33-34 (Witness BBB).

567. BBB testified that whilst hiding in the woods one day, about two weeks after the death of President Habyarimana, he saw Kalimanzira arrive at the roadblock in a red Toyota with an uncovered back section, accompanied by a driver and approximately five armed gendarmes, identifiable by their red berets. BBB approached the roadblock as Kalimanzira exited the vehicle and stood approximately three metres from him. BBB recalled that a man passed by and Kalimanzira questioned him as to where his weapon was. The man responded that he had none and Kalimanzira slapped him before he was thrown into the vehicle by the gendarmes. Kalimanzira then asked BBB to show him his weapon. BBB showed Kalimanzira the machete that he had hidden under his overcoat, thereby satisfying him.[610]

568. BBB testified that Kalimanzira stayed at the roadblock for approximately 15 to 20 minutes and asked the people at the roadblock if they knew whom their enemies were. Those manning the roadblock with BBB that day included Matabaro Cyama, Jean "Gashurushuru" Mutabazi, Emmanuel Ruganji, Joseph Senkunda (*responsable* of Kajyanama *cellule*), and Célestin Mtamugabumwe, as well as many other members of the population whose names BBB could not recall. They answered affirmatively to Kalimanzira's question, and Kalimanzira told them that they were fighting the Tutsis, who were "wicked", and instructed **[page 120]** them to kill Tutsis and prevent them from passing the roadblock. Kalimanzira left the roadblock in the vehicle and travelled towards Gisagara after claiming that he was going to abandon the man at the customs post as a punishment.[611]

569. BBB testified that at approximately 8:00 p.m. that same day, he saw the man that Kalimanzira slapped at the roadblock again. The man was being interrogated by the men who manned it at night. BBB stated that the men wanted to kill him but refrained because he had a Hutu identity card. However, BBB admitted that he was informed of this the next day by his colleagues because he did not go close enough to hear it personally at the time of the incident. Finally, BBB described how people implemented Kalimanzira's instructions after he left; they changed their tactics and behaviour by increasing attacks and killing Tutsis. Specifically, BBB stated that a Tutsi named Lensi de Karama from Ndora *commune* was killed there.[612]

Prosecution Witness BXH

570. BXH lived close to the Kajyanama roadblock. BXH testified that one day at the end of April or beginning of May 1994 at approximately 1:00-2:00 p.m., he was repairing a fence in his garden when he heard a vehicle. He went to stand in front of his house in order to see the vehicle and saw Kalimanzira arrive at the roadblock in a red pick-up vehicle on the road leading to Kirarambogo. BXH stated that Kalimanzira was 6 or 7 metres from him and accompanied by 4 or 5 armed soldiers or gendarmes.[613]

571. BXH recalled the presence of several people at the roadblock that day, including Cyama Matabaro, Senkunda, Bwenakweri, Gashurushuru, Tomasi Nikombama and Manueli Ruganji. He testified that he observed Kalimanzira ask those who were unarmed what they were doing and how they would defend themselves if the enemy passed by. When they did not reply, Kalimanzira got out of his vehicle, causing them to flee. Kalimanzira grabbed one man, forced him into the vehicle and then left. BXH asserted that Kalimanzira did not speak to the man he grabbed in any special way. BXH himself was unarmed because he had nothing to do with the roadblock. He stated that he believed Kalimanzira could see him.[614]

572. BXH testified that he saw the man Kalimanzira abducted again the next day. The man was on way to have a drink with his friends and was explaining to them what had happened the previous day. BXH heard the man say that Kalimanzira told him that if he found him unarmed again he would kill him with his own hands.[615]

---

[610] T. 16 June 2008 pp. 7-8, 34 (Witness BBB).
[611] T. 16 June 2008 pp. 8-9, 33 (Witness BBB).
[612] T. 16 June 2008 pp. 9-10, 40 (Witness BBB).
[613] T. 22 May 2008 pp. 41-42 [closed] 45-46 (Witness BXH).
[614] T. 22 May 2008 pp. 42-44 [closed] 45, 48-51 (Witness BXH).
[615] T. 22 May 2008 pp. 45-46 (Witness BXH).

Defence Witness AM05

573. AM05 manned the Kajyanama roadblock in 1992, and from April 1994 until July 1994. Incidents at the roadblock were followed by the *responsables* of both Kajyanama and Kigarama *cellules* and inhabitants from both participated in manning it, which included "Thomas", "Joachim" and Claver Kamere. AM05 lived close to the roadblock and was there every day. AM05 testified that he saw Kalimanzira pass in front of his house on the road to Kirarambogo sometime at the end of June or beginning of July 1994. Kalimanzira was in a white vehicle, accompanied only by a driver. AM05 recalled that he was standing at the roadblock when he saw Kalimanzira, who waved in greeting but did not stop or speak to anyone. Kalimanzira did not have to go through the roadblock because the road to **[page 121]** Kirarambogo was below it. AM05 saw Kalimanzira return on the same road later that evening. That was the only time AM05 saw Kalimanzira in 1994.[616]

574. AM05 testified that he never heard of any incident where Kalimanzira allegedly stopped at the roadblock and threatened or slapped anyone for being unarmed, nor did he hear of any man being forcibly taken away in Kalimanzira's vehicle. AM05 then explained that he was at the roadblock day and night because of its proximity to his home and the fact that the RPF were said to be killing people in their houses at night. AM05 described how other members of the population also slept there and that during the day it was a point where people would converge in order to converse so as not to feel lonely. Moreover, AM05 recalled that when he saw Kalimanzira pass by he told the other men who manned the roadblock because Kalimanzira was well known, thereby implying that had the above alleged events happened he would have been informed. Additionally, AM05 asserted that he knew of nobody being killed at the roadblock.[617]

Defence Witness AM29

575. AM29 manned the Kajyanama roadblock, although he admitted he was not there all of the time. He described the roadblock as consisting of a tree trunk placed across the road. AM29 saw Kalimanzira at the roadblock in the beginning of June 1994, travelling by vehicle towards Butare *ville* on the Kirarambogo road. AM29 recalled that Kalimanzira was with a driver and waved in greeting but did not stop or exit the vehicle; he did not see any soldiers. AM29 stated that between April and July 1994, he did not see Kalimanzira again, nor did he ever hear of any incident where Kalimanzira came to the roadblock and threatened anyone for being unarmed, let alone abduct anyone in his vehicle to punish them for being unarmed.[618]

Defence Witness AM02

576. AM02 did not man the Kajyanama roadblock but worked and lived close by. He testified that the roadblock was originally erected between 1992 and 1993 for security purposes due to the civil war at the time. AM02 testified that in the first week of June 1994, he was near the roadblock one afternoon when a white vehicle heading towards Ndora *commune* arrived. Kalimanzira waved from the vehicle as it continued on its path; he was accompanied by a driver. AM02 did not hear anyone talk about Kalimanzira passing through the roadblock on any other occasion between April and June 1994, nor did he ever hear of anyone being killed at the roadblock.[619]

4.4.2. Deliberations

577. At the time of this alleged incident, Kalimanzira claims to have been working in Murambi (Gitarama *préfecture*). As discussed above, the Chamber disbelieves Kalimanzira's alibi (see III.1.2.2).

578. The Indictment describes the incident as Kalimanzira slapping one person and then abducting another; the evidence adduced at trial, however, describes the person being slapped as the same person being

---

[616] T. 25 November 2008 pp. 43-47 [closed] 48, 50 (Witness AM05).
[617] T. 25 November 2008 pp. 50-52; pp. 55-57 [closed] (Witness AM05).
[618] T. 25 November 2008 pp. 26-29 [closed] 30-31 (Witness AM29).
[619] T. 26 November 2008 pp. 8-12 [closed] (Witness AM02).

abducted. The difference is immaterial, and the Defence – who has not raised the issue – has suffered no prejudice in its ability to challenge the Prosecution case.**[page 122]**

579. BBB is currently in detention at the Karubanda prison where he faces charges of genocide. BBB has confessed to acts of killing and looting, but contests a pending charge of rape against him.[620] He has not been convicted or sentenced as yet for the crimes to which he has confessed. These crimes include the killings at Kabuye Hill, in relation to which Kalimanzira is also charged in this Indictment. In considering whether he may have been influenced to falsely implicate Kalimanzira to diminish his responsibility for his crimes, the Chamber concludes that if he intended to falsely incriminate Kalimanzira, he could also have done so in his testimony on Kabuye hill (see III.2.4.1) in which he failed to mention Kalimanzira and implicated only Dominique Ntawukulilyayo (*sous-préfet* of Gisagara). Having considered his evidence carefully in relation to this event and elsewhere (see III.2.8.2), the Chamber finds BBB to be a credible witness.

580. The Defence extracted a discrepancy during BBB's cross-examination. When he was questioned about who had asked to see his weapon, BBB stated in his examination-in-chief that it was Kalimanzira, but under cross-examination he stated that it was a gendarme. When the inconsistency was pointed out to him, BBB insisted that there was a misunderstanding and reiterated that it was Kalimanzira who asked him about his weapon.[621] The Chamber accepts his explanation.

581. The Defence contends that BBB's credibility is undermined because of major inconsistencies between his testimony and his prior statement to ICTR investigators.[622] For instance, his 2001 statement indicates that Kalimanzira slapped him for being unarmed, and then apologized to BBB when he then showed Kalimanzira his weapon.[623] On the stand, however, BBB testified that Kalimanzira slapped (and then abducted) someone else for being unarmed, not BBB.[624] BBB's position was firm and he would have no reason to change his prior statement in this regard; in fact, his evidence might have been more accusatory had he testified that Kalimanzira slapped him personally and not somebody else. That testimony would also have been consistent with the Indictment which alleges that Kalimanzira slapped one person and abducted another, a pleading which was consistent with the prior statement.

582. The Defence points out certain other inconsistencies in BBB's prior statement, such as where the unarmed person was dropped off and whether he was bundled up before being forced into Kalimanzira's vehicle, and argues that they amount to serious contradictions. After careful consideration, the Chamber accepts BBB's explanations that there were errors in the recording of his statement. It does not consider that these differences indicate any lack of truthfulness or unreliability in the witness. The nature of these differences does not cast reasonable doubt on the substance of BBB's testimony.

583. BXH does not have a criminal record. He still lives in Rwanda and has never been jailed or convicted.[625] There is no dispute that he knew Kalimanzira, as he had worked under his supervision at a fishing pond in Muganza *commune* for more than a year in the 1980s.[626]

At the time of the alleged events, BXH lived within plain view of the Kajyanama roadblock.[627] The Defence claims that BXH's testimony was illogical because he alleged that Kalimanzira told the people at the roadblock that they should be armed in order to defend **[page 123]** themselves against the enemy, yet threatened to kill one of them if he found him unarmed again.[628] The Chamber disagrees. Within the context of an ongoing genocide and the fear of impending RPF attacks, such a statement could easily have been uttered.

584. The Defence adduced evidence from three witnesses, all of whom have good reason to distance themselves from any alleged criminal acts at the roadblock. They all currently live in exile in the same

---

[620] T. 16 June 2008 pp. 57-59 [closed] (Witness BBB); see also Exhibit D15.
[621] T. 16 June 2008 p. 37 (Witness BBB).
[622] Defence Closing Brief, paras. 484-489.
[623] Exhibit D14.
[624] T. 16 June 2008 pp. 50-51 (Witness BBB).
[625] T. 22 May 2008 pp. 53-54 [closed] (Witness BXH).
[626] T. 22 May 2008 p. 40 [closed] (Witness BXH).
[627] T. 22 May 2008 pp. 41-42 [closed] (Witness BXH).
[628] Defence Closing Brief, para. 441.

country, and may be fugitives from justice. Two of them, like BBB, manned the Kajyanama roadblock, and one worked nearby. AM05 and AM02 asserted that they have never heard of anyone being killed at the roadblock. AM05 and AM29 manned the roadblock, as did BBB who testified that killings did occur there. AM02 was a policeman in April 1994; investigations of any killings of civilians in his local area would have been part of his duties. Four years after being imprisoned, AM02 escaped and fled the country.

585. All three witnesses testified that they saw Kalimanzira pass this roadblock, without exiting his vehicle or speaking to anyone. AM29 and AM02 describe such an occurrence in June and AM05 speaks of a similar incident in late June or early July. AM29 admitted that he only manned the roadblock on four occasions yet insisted that he knew Kalimanzira had never passed by, threatened people for not carrying weapons or abducted an unarmed man. Similarly, AM02, who did not man the roadblock but worked nearby, claimed that he would have heard if Kalimanzira had passed by. AM05 also testified that he spent day and night at the roadblock and knew everything that happened there. The Chamber considers that such exaggerated statements of omnipresence carry little weight. Additionally, AM05 stated that the roadblock had been set up for security reasons yet claimed that nobody carried any weapons to ensure that security. This was inconsistent with AM02's testimony that sticks and clubs were carried.

586. The Defence contends that the Prosecution witnesses fabricated the story about Kalimanzira passing through the roadblock in April using the incident in June when he passed through and merely waved as inspiration. The Defence claims that AM05, AM02 and AM29's evidence that they did not hear of the incident to which BBB and BXH testified should be believed because in a community as small as Kajyanama *cellule*, even the passing of a car was a significant event, and the passage of a former *sous-préfet* was something that everyone would have heard about.[629] These arguments are not persuasive. The fact that Kalimanzira may have passed through the roadblock in June and/or July does not preclude him from also having passed through it in April 1994.

587. After careful consideration the Chamber concludes that BBB is a reliable witness. His testimony was corroborated by BXH, whom the Chamber also believes. They support each other on the major details alleged, namely that Kalimanzira reprimanded a man for being unarmed and physically forced him into his vehicle. Both BBB and BXH also testified that Kalimanzira was accompanied by five gendarmes and that they saw the abducted man the following day. Both witnesses also place the incident within the same time frame. The Defence points out that BBB and BXH's testimonies differ in relation to the driver of the vehicle, the way in which the unarmed person was apprehended, the identity of the unarmed person, and the statements Kalimanzira made.[630] These differences are not significant in light of the passage of time and the fact that people sometimes view the same events from different perspectives. **[page 124]**

588. The Chamber has also given careful consideration to the difference between BBB and BXH's recollection of Kalimanzira's statements. According to BBB, Kalimanzira instructed those manning it to prevent any Tutsis, whom he described as "wicked" and "the enemy", from passing through, and that they should be killed. BXH, however, recalled that Kalimanzira asked them how they would defend themselves if the enemy passed by. The Chamber considers BXH's literal recollection to be supplemented by BBB's interpreted one. BXH was an observer whereas BBB was among those whom Kalimanzira was allegedly inciting; BBB's impression of Kalimanzira's words is an important factor is determining whether the alleged incitement was direct. The Chamber does not accept the Defence's contention that BBB and BXH's accounts are irreconcilable or are fabricated. The Chamber believes BBB and BXH and considers their evidence reliable beyond reasonable doubt. The Chamber therefore finds that Kalimanzira was at the Kajyanama roadblock in late April 1994, where he reprimanded and then abducted a man for being unarmed.

589. The Chamber recalls that a call to defend oneself against the enemy is not intrinsically illegitimate, particularly when the "enemy" is clearly restricted to the RPF to the exclusion of Tutsi civilians. In this case, however, the Chamber finds that when exhorting those manning the Kajyanama roadblock to carry arms in order to "defend" themselves against "the enemy" who might pass through, Kalimanzira was understood to be calling for the killing of Tutsis, and that he intended to be understood as such. The slapping and abduction

---

[629] Defence Closing Brief, paras. 459-460.
[630] Defence Closing Brief, paras. 442-449.

of the unarmed man emphasized Kalimanzira's exhortation and effect on his audience. The incitement was disseminated in a public place – the roadblock – to an indeterminate group of people – those present to man it and anyone else watching or listening. Kalimanzira exhibited here, and elsewhere, an intent to destroy the Tutsi group (see III.5.2). As such, the Chamber finds Kalimanzira guilty beyond reasonable doubt for committing Direct and Public Incitement to Commit Genocide at the Kajyanama roadblock in late April 1994.

4.5. Nyabisagara Football Field, late May / early June

590. At paragraph 23 of the Indictment, the Prosecution charges Kalimanzira with Direct and Public Incitement to Commit Genocide for attending a public meeting in Kibayi *commune* at the Nyabisagara football field where he and other speakers thanked the Hutus for their efforts at eliminating the Tutsis. The Chamber recalls that it accepts late May or early June 1994 as the relevant time frame for this allegation (see II.2.3).

591. The Defence denies that this meeting took place. In addition, Kalimanzira relies on his alibi that he was working in Murambi (Gitarama *préfecture*) until 30 May, and then at home in Butare *ville* until 30 June 1994, except when he left on a few specified occasions, including sometime in the first week of June to see his family in Kirarambogo (see III.1.2).

4.5.1. Evidence

Prosecution Witness BCZ

592. BCZ testified that, sometime between the 24 May and 10 June 1994, he saw Kalimanzira at a meeting at the Nyabisagara football field, located about 100 metres from the Kibayi *commune* office. BCZ, as a member of the local population, had been invited to attend by Pierre Canisius Kajyambere (*bourgmestre* of Kibayi *commune*). Officials present at the meeting included Kalimanzira, *bourgmestre* Kajyambere, Dominique Ntawukulilyayo (*sousprefet* of Gisagara), Célestin Harindintwali and "Sebalinda". BCZ did not personally **[page 125]** recognise all of the authorities present, but he did recognise Kalimanzira, whom he knew well since the 1980s.[631]

593. BCZ testified that when he arrived, the meeting had already started and Célestin Harindintwali had taken the floor, emphasizing to the public that they must ensure their own security and prevent the enemy from infiltrating the *commune*. BCZ said that the other authorities had given speeches before he arrived. BCZ testified that Kalimanzira made the main speech because he was the highest-ranking authority present. First, Kalimanzira thanked the general public for attending in such large numbers and for having done everything in their abilities to get rid of the enemy. Kalimanzira then added that they "should not rest on their laurels" because there were still other enemies hidden in abandoned houses and the bush. BCZ explained that during this period, "enemy" meant just about any Tutsi.[632]

594. BCZ testified that Kalimanzira asked *bourgmestre* Kajyambere to draw up a programme for communal work known as "*umuganda*", aimed at searching for the enemy hidden in the bush and destroying homes of dead Tutsis. Kalimanzira instructed the public to destroy all remaining Tutsi houses and plant banana trees and other crops over the ruins because international organisations might question the whereabouts of their occupants. Kalimanzira then added that nobody, especially men, should move around on the highway without weapons and instructed that everyone must be armed. BCZ further recalled how, upon noticing a dearth of weaponry, Kalimanzira requested that they have bows and arrows made at a blacksmiths. Kalimanzira also incited the youth to undergo military training and instructed those doing so to continue because the *Inkotanyi* were closing in. BCZ stated that to conclude, Kalimanzira thanked the public again for turning up and underscored the importance of observing his instructions.[633]

---

[631] T. 24 June 2008 pp. 43-46 (Witness BCZ).
[632] T. 24 June 2008 pp. 46-47 (Witness BCZ).
[633] T. 24 June 2008 p. 47 (Witness BCZ).

Judgement

595. BCZ indicated that the authorities used microphones in order to be heard. He described Kalimanzira's tone throughout his speech as authoritative. BCZ understood any reference to the "enemy" to mean the Tutsi. The day after the meeting, which had been attended by several hundred people, BCZ and other members of the population implemented the orders given by Kalimanzira and the other officials. They carried out "*umuganda*" but could not find any Tutsis left to kill. They did, however, destroy homes, including those of Vincent Bimenyimana and Charles Hategekimana, who had already been killed, and planted banana trees over the ruins.[634]

Defence Witness AKK

596. AKK was in Kibayi *commune* from the death of President Habyarimana until July 1994. She attended a meeting at the Nyabisagara football field in late May 1994; all the inhabitants of Kibayi *commune* were invited. AKK had been informed of the meeting by the *conseiller* of her *secteur*. AKK testified that she was present at the meeting from start to finish and that it started at noon, finishing approximately two hours later. She testified that she knew of no other meetings in Kibayi *commune* held before or after this one; had there been, she would have been invited or seen people gathering.[635]

597. AKK testified that the *commune* authorities were present, including the *bourgmestre*, deputy *bourgmestre*, and *conseillers* of various *secteurs*. AKK recalled that there were also **[page 126]** several visiting authorities from outside the *commune*, including Sylvain Nsabimana (*préfet* of Butare), Alphonse Nteziryayo and Tharcisse Muvunyi. The authorities were seated in front of the population who were seated on the ground at the front and standing at the back. AKK affirmed that she did not see Kalimanzira at the meeting.[636]

598. AKK testified that several of the authorities gave speeches. The *bourgmestre* spoke first, thanking the guests for coming and introducing them. Then *préfet* Nsabimana spoke, followed by Colonel Nteziryayo. AKK did not remember anyone else taking the floor; she was seated approximately four or five rows from the front and could see the officials clearly. She knew Kalimanzira well and asserted that had he been there, he would not have left without greeting her and her husband.[637]

Defence Witness BTH

599. BTH attended a meeting at the Nyabisagara football field on 24 May 1994 convened by *bourgmestre* Kajyambere. The meeting began around 11:00 a.m. and lasted for approximately two hours. Those present at the meeting included *bourgmestre* Kajyambere, *préfet* Nsabimana, Colonel Nteziryayo, Célestin Harindintwali. They were seated at the front whilst the members of the public, who occupied over half of the field, sat on the ground at the front and stood at the back. BTH testified that the topic of the meeting was security. The officials informed the public that they would be in charge of their own security and urged them to carry out patrols and, if possible, to fight the RPF with traditional weapons. BTH recalled that some members of the population did not agree with the instruction to fight with traditional weapons. BTH described how archery training, using a banana tree as a target, was provided for those members of the population who agreed. BTH did not see Kalimanzira at the meeting or at the archery training held afterwards. In fact, he did not see Kalimanzira at all from April to July 1994.[638]

Defence Witness KBF

600. KBF testified that by virtue of his professional position, he attended a meeting at the Nyabisagara football field 100 metres away from the Kibayi *commune* office in mid to late May 1994; it had been convened by *bourgmestre* Kajyambere. This meeting, which lasted about two hours, was attended by 300-400 members of the general population; officials present included Colonel Nteziryayo, Colonel Muvunyi, *préfet*

---

[634] T. 24 June 2008 pp. 47-50 (Witness BCZ).
[635] T. 26 November 2008 pp. 41-43; p. 57 [closed] (Witness AKK).
[636] T. 26 November 2008 pp. 43-44 (Witness AKK).
[637] T. 26 November 2008 p. 44 (Witness AKK).
[638] T. 25 November 2008 pp. 7-9 (Witness BTH).

Nsabimana, *sous-préfet* Ntawukulilyayo, *bourgmestre* Kajyambere, and Célestin Harindintwari, who worked for the Ministry of Public Works. The officials were seated in front of the population and did not use megaphones.[639]

601. Those who attended the meeting were asked to ensure their own security and defend themselves from the approaching *Inkotanyi*. KBF recalled the officials arrived in a convoy of five vehicles. This was the only meeting KBF attended in Kibayi *commune* in between April to July 1994; he admits the possibility that there may have been others. He knew Kalimanzira well and asserted he was not there; had he been there, KBF would have recognised him. KBF also maintains he never saw Kalimanzira or heard anything about him from April 1994 until he fled Rwanda in July 1994.[640] **[page 127]**

Defence Witness Innocent Mukuralinda

602. Mukuralinda was an accountant at the Kibayi *commune* office from 1981 until 7 July 1994, when he fled Rwanda. On 24 May 1994, he attended a meeting at the Nyabisagara football field; this was the only meeting, to the best of his knowledge, which was held in Kibayi *commune* during the events. *Bourgmestre* Kajyambere, with whom he worked daily, informed Mukuralinda of the meeting and stated that its purpose was to address security issues. Mukuralinda went to the *commune* office before the meeting in order to help set up chairs. He recalled that the meeting started around 10:30 a.m. that the following officials arrived: *préfet* Nsabimana, *sous-préfet* Ntawukulilyayo, Mathias Bushishi (Public Prosecutor of Butare), Jean-Baptiste Ruzindaza (President of the Court of First Instance of Butare), Colonel Muvunyi, Colonel Nteziryayo; Kalimanzira was not among them. Before moving over to the football field, the officials first attended a meeting with the *bourgmestre* in the *commune* office; however, Mukuralinda did not attend that prior meeting and was therefore unaware of what was discussed.[641]

603. Mukuralinda testified that there were approximately 300-400 people in attendance; he was sitting in the first row. Security matters were discussed, particularly guerrilla warfare, which Mukuralinda understood to mean psychological warfare. Mukuralinda recalled that the local population was asked to assist each other and to ensure their own security because the RPF troops were getting closer to Butare. Mukuralinda testified that Kalimanzira did not attend the meeting. He knew Kalimanzira well and would therefore have recognised him had he been there.[642]

Defence Witness KXL

604. KXL testified that at the end of May 1994, a policeman informed him that a meeting was to be held at the Kibayi *commune* office where members of the population were being summoned to learn to use bows and arrows in order to liberate Ntyazo *commune* from the *Inkotanyi*. KXL was threatened with punishment if he failed to attend that meeting. The following day, KXL arrived at around 10:00 a.m. to find that the meeting, which was held at Nyabisagara, was already over and people were practicing to shoot bows and arrows at a target. KXL joined a group of people from Rwamiko *secteur* to practice as well. After the archery training, everyone returned home and was instructed to continue practicing in their respective *secteurs* in preparation to eventually fight in Ntyazo; KXL said they never ended up going to Ntyazo, however. KXL asserted he did not see Kalimanzira during the archery exercise. In fact, he did not see Kalimanzira at all between April and July 1994.[643]

605. KXL also testified that he knew Vincent Bimenyimana and Charles Hategekimana, both of whom were Tutsis. According to KXL, they were both killed in April 1994. He testified that within days of their deaths, Hategekimana's house was burned down and completely destroyed. As for Bimenyimana's house, the neighbours stole his roofing tiles and even the wood used to build the house, thereby destroying.

---

[639] T. 17 November 2008 pp. 13-14 (Witness KBF).
[640] T. 17 November 2008 pp. 14-15 (Witness KBF).
[641] T. 3 December 2008 pp. 4-7 (Innocent Mukuralinda).
[642] T. 3 December 2008 p. 7 (Innocent Mukuralinda).
[643] T. 24 November 2008 pp. 29, 36-38 (Witness KXL).

Bimenyimana had another, smaller, house, which he used as a shop; this remained relatively intact.[644]
[page 128]

4.5.2. Deliberations

606. At the time of this alleged incident, Kalimanzira claims to have been working in Murambi (Gitarama *préfecture*) or at home in Butare *ville*, except in the first week of June when he went to visit his family in Nyaguhuru *secteur* (Muganza *commune*). As discussed above, the Chamber does not believe Kalimanzira's alibi (see III.1.2.2).

607. The Chamber notes that the language at paragraph 23 of the Indictment is limited to Kalimanzira thanking Hutus for their efforts at eliminating Tutsis; no explicit reference is made to exhorting further efforts at eliminating Tutsis. However, the Chamber considers that a call for further action is implied in the wording of the paragraph, and clarified in the Prosecution Pre-Trial Brief.[645] The Defence – which did not raise the issue – therefore had adequate notice that the Prosecution case included a call for further killings.

608. BCZ was charged with killing Tutsis in Kirarambogo and Kabuye, destroying and looting the homes of Tutsis and participating in various attacks.[646] In his testimony, he admitted to following the instructions Kalimanzira issued at this meeting by participating in the search for further Tutsis to kill and destroying homes. This makes him an accomplice. He was released before giving his evidence at the ICTR, after spending nearly 12 years in prison. His evidence, however, is a repetition of the statements he gave while detained, which may have been influenced by motives to reduce his own responsibility. After careful consideration, the Chamber finds that no such motive can be demonstrated. BCZ does not mention Kalimanzira in his confession letter and does not attribute a principal role to Kalimanzira in the commission of genocidal acts. Indeed, BCZ confessed and testified to his participation in the killings at Kabuye hill over a period of three days, but asserted that he did not see Kalimanzira there at all.[647]

609. The Defence witnesses' testimonies converged on the occurrence of a meeting at the Nyabisagara football field around 24 May 1994 attended by Nteziryayo and Muvunyi. BCZ testified that the meeting which Kalimanzira attended took place one week after the meeting attended by Nteziryayo and Muvunyi, which BCZ places around 25 or 26 May 1994.[648] BCZ refers to the meeting chaired by Nteziryayo in his prior statements to ICTR investigators; however, he refers to the meeting attended by Kalimanzira only in a later statement.[649]

610. The Chamber concludes that BCZ and the Defence witnesses testified to different meetings, and considers that the existence of one does not preclude the other. The Defence submits the 24 May 1994 was the only meeting in Kibayi *commune* around that time, and that BCZ therefore fabricated a second meeting there in order to implicate Kalimanzira.[650] The Chamber does not agree and considers that the evidence of Defence witnesses supports the inference that more than one meeting took place. KBF admitted to the possibility that there may have been other meetings in Kibayi *commune*.[651] The Defence Pre-Trial Brief indicated that AKK was expected to testify to two meetings at the Nyabisagara football field; however, when giving her testimony on the stand, she insisted that she was only aware of one meeting.[652] Mukuralinda's statement that he was not aware of any other "security" meeting in [page 129] Kibayi *commune* was amended under cross-examination to include a second one, but "restricted" in nature.[653] No questions were put to BTH on the possibility of other meetings. Because KXL was in hiding for most of April and May 1994, the Chamber considers that his testimony does not cast reasonable doubt on when and how Bimenyimana and Hategekimana's homes were destroyed. That they were killed and that their homes were destroyed is

---

[644] T. 24 November 2008 pp. 29-30 (Witness KXL).
[645] See summary of BCZ's anticipated testimony in Annex A of the Prosecution Pre-Trial Brief.
[646] T. 24 June 2008 pp. 54-55 [closed] (Witness BCZ).
[647] T. 24 June 2008 pp. 57, 59-60 (Witness BCZ).
[648] T. 24 June 2008 pp. 63-64 (Witness BCZ).
[649] See Exhibits D33, D34, and D35.
[650] See Defence Closing Brief, para. 1072.
[651] T. 17 November 2008 p. 13 (Witness KBF).
[652] See T. 26 November 2008 pp. 56-57 [closed] (Witness AKK).
[653] T. 3 December 2008 pp. 7, 20, 25-26 (Innocent Mukuralinda).

undisputed; Kalimanzira himself testified to having seen the devastated state of Hategekimana's house in early June 1994.[654] For these reasons, the Defence evidence does little to contradict BCZ's evidence.

611. The Chamber accepts BCZ's explanation that he omitted to mention Kalimanzira in his guilty plea because his confession was limited to his own crimes, killings, attacks, and accomplices; he therefore neglected to speak of meetings which led to no killings, such as the one at the Nyabisagara football field in which he implicates Kalimanzira. It is likely that BCZ omitted to mention Kalimanzira before his October 2001 statement to ICTR investigators[655] because they did not specifically ask him about Kalimanzira before that time. It is also likely that BCZ omitted to mention this meeting before October 2001 because its content and effect (no killings followed because no Tutsis could be found)[656] might have seemed less important to him compared to the events he did mention.

612. The Chamber considers BCZ to be a credible and reliable witness. Had he intended to falsely accuse Kalimanzira, his testimony and allegations would likely have been more accusatory. Other Prosecution witnesses have also testified to other situations where Kalimanzira called on people to destroy dead Tutsis' homes and plant trees and grass in their place in order to erase traces of crimes and appease international opinion;[657] this might suggest a pattern of conduct or mode of operation. Kalimanzira's own testimony that he stopped by Hategekimana's house in the end of the first week of June on his way to see his family in Kirarambogo lends additional support to his presence in Kibayi *commune* around the time of this alleged meeting.[658]

613. The Chamber therefore finds that in late May or early June 1994, Kalimanzira attended a public meeting at the Nyabisagara football field where he thanked the audience for their efforts at getting rid of the enemy, but warned them not to grow complacent, to remain armed at all times, and exhorted the crowd to keep searching for enemies hidden in the bush or in other persons homes, which they did. He also instructed them to destroy the homes of dead Tutsis and plant trees in their place, which they did. In the context of these particular instructions, which have little to do with military combat, and BCZ's understanding of Kalimanzira's words, the Chamber finds that "the enemy" meant any Tutsi.

614. The Chamber finds that Kalimanzira's call for further elimination of Tutsis in hiding was direct, leading clearly to immediate and commensurate action. It was disseminated in a public place to a large public audience. By instructing the people present to kill any surviving Tutsis, demolish their homes, and wipe out any traces of their existence, there is no reasonable doubt that Kalimanzira intended to incite the audience present to commit acts of genocide. Kalimanzira exhibited here, and elsewhere, an intent to destroy the Tutsi group (see III.5.2). The Chamber therefore finds Kalimanzira guilty beyond reasonable doubt of **[page 130]** committing Direct and Public Incitement to Commit Genocide at the Nyabisagara football field in late May or early June 1994.

4.6. Rwamiko Primary School, late May / early June

615. At paragraph 24 of the Indictment, the Prosecution charges Kalimanzira with Direct and Public Incitement to Commit Genocide for congratulating people at the Rwamiko Primary School a few days after the meeting at the Nyabisagara football field for "the work" that had been done. He also urged them to remain vigilant and to continue to carry weapons and eliminate the Tutsis. The Chamber recalls that it accepts late May or early June 1994 as the relevant time frame for this allegation (see II.2.3).

616. The Defence denies that this meeting took place. Kalimanzira relies on his alibi he was working in Murambi (Gitarama *préfecture*) until 30 May, and then at home in Butare *ville* until 30 June 1994, except when he left on a few specified occasions, including sometime in the first week of June to see his family in Kirarambogo (see III.1.2).

---

[654] T. 10 February 2009 pp. 50-51 (Callixte Kalimanzira).
[655] Exhibit D35.
[656] T. 24 June 2008 p. 66 (Witness BCZ).
[657] See T. 17 June 2008 p. 21 (Witness AZM); T. 25 June 2008 pp. 43-44 (Witness AZC); T. 23 June 2008 pp. 11-12 (Witness AZH).
[658] T. 10 February 2009 pp. 50-51 (Callixte Kalimanzira).

Judgement

4.6.1. Evidence

Prosecution Witness AZT

617. AZT saw Kalimanzira in Rwamiko *secteur* in late May 1994. AZT was one of a group of over 50 people who gathered at Kalimanzira's house to greet him after hearing of his arrival. AZT recalled that the house, which was used for commercial purposes, was located on the same road and opposite the Rwamiko Primary School. AZT further recalled that Kalimanzira congratulated the members of the public who were opposing Tutsis and RPF accomplices, and he warned those who were not. AZT affirmed that Kalimanzira encouraged those who were killing Tutsis to keep doing so and criticized those who were not participating in the massacres. AZT left the meeting after approximately 20 minutes, before Kalimanzira had finished speaking.[659]

Prosecution Witness BCZ

618. BCZ testified to a meeting at the Nyabisagara football field between the 25 May and the 10 June 1994 (see III.4.5.1). Within two weeks after this meeting, BCZ saw Kalimanzira again at the Rwamiko Primary School. BCZ was at the school because he was attending a meeting of around 20-30 people who had been appointed to a "crisis committee". Members of this committee included Jonathan Niyongana, Jean Rupari, Sylvestre Manzi, and Ignace Yirirwahandi. The purpose of the meeting was to discuss how to distribute the stolen property of dead Tutsis. BCZ recalled that it was decided that the property would be sold and the money shared between the public.[660]

619. BCZ testified that Kalimanzira entered the classroom where the meeting was taking place, and greeted the members of the crisis committee. He asked them whether they were "doing the work that they should" and why they were not armed. They explained it was because they were attending a meeting, whereupon Kalimanzira warned them that the enemy "can take you unawares" and advised them to be armed at all times. Kalimanzira told them "even if you have eliminated the enemy, you shouldn't fold your arms and sit down. Don't think that it's all over". Kalimanzira also claimed to be the leader of civil defence and instructed them to tell the public to carry arms wherever they were, citing the Buseruka **[page 131]** centre[661] as a negative example of where unarmed people could be seen walking around. BCZ stated that Kalimanzira then urged them to obtain weapons for everyone and report back to him if they could not. BCZ further stated that when Kalimanzira made reference to the "enemy" and "elimination", he understood him to mean, respectively, the Tutsi and killing.[662]

620. Kalimanzira asked them to remain vigilant and then left in a white Hilux vehicle; he was not accompanied by soldiers. There was, however, a young man in the rear cabin of the vehicle and a motorbike in the rear section. BCZ recalled that before leaving, Kalimanzira spoke of the young man as an example of someone he had met on the road and stopped because he did not have his papers on him.[663]

Defence Witness KXL

621. KXL testified that he did not see Kalimanzira between April and July 1994; however, he stated that from August 1993 until the beginning of May 1994 he did not move around and was mostly in hiding at home. KXL attended a meeting in Rwamiko *secteur,* convened on the playground of the Rwamiko Primary School at the end of May 1994 and chaired by *bourgmestre* Kajyambere. According to KXL, the meeting preceded the one at Nyabisagara, and it was the only one held in Rwamiko, to his best knowledge. The reason to call the meeting was people had started to dub those who were rich as "poisonous" and kill them; *bourgmestre* Kajyambere ordered these attacks to stop and advised that the "poisonous" be taken to the

---

[659] T. 20 June 2008 pp. 24-25 and T. 24 June 2008 pp. 21, 23, 27 (Witness AZT).
[660] T. 24 June 2008 p. 50 (Witness BCZ).
[661] Buseruka is the commercial centre of Rwamiko *secteur.*
[662] T. 24 June 2008 pp. 50-51 (Witness BCZ).
[663] T. 24 June 2008 pp. 52, 69-70 (Witness BCZ).

commune office instead. This meeting was very brief; people were not even seated. Kalimanzira was not present at this meeting.[664]

622. KXL never heard of a "crisis committee", but did acknowledge that there existed a group of persons in Rwamiko *secteur* who decided that the looted property of dead Tutsis should be sold. This group included Elie Rwangineza, Jonathan Niyongana, Jean Rupari, and the leader, Ignace Yirirwahandi.[665]

Defence Witness MAS

623. In 1994, MAS owned a shop and bar at the Buseruka centre. The shop was located approximately 100 metres from Rwamiko Primary School, meaning that the school was visible from the shop. MAS testified that he did not leave the area between 6 April to July 1994, when he fled to Burundi. MAS also testified that the shop was operational from the middle of May 1994.[666]

624. MAS attended a meeting at the Rwamiko Primary School in late May or early June 1994. MAS recalled that he found out about the meeting when one day, on his way to work, he saw a large gathering of people at the school. When he joined the meeting, *bourgmestre* Kajyambere was speaking. A secretary, soldier and the *conseiller* of Rwamiko *secteur* were also present. MAS stated that all of the local inhabitants of Rwamiko *secteur* were in attendance and that security matters were discussed, with some people describing others as "poisonous" characters. He did not see Kalimanzira at the meeting and he did not hear of or attend any other meetings at the Rwamiko Primary School between April and July 1994. **[page 132]** MAS never heard of a "crisis committee". He named Jonathan Niyongana, Ignace Yirirwahandi and Jean Rupari as heading groups of killers during the genocide.[667]

625. MAS testified that he only saw Kalimanzira at the Buseruka centre at the beginning of June 1994. Kalimanzira was in front of a building that he used commercially and looking at the house where he had lived previously. He had arrived in a white vehicle accompanied by a driver and alighted from the passenger side; five or six people approached him to greet him. MAS stated that Kalimanzira did not speak to anyone and simply looked at the house, returned to the vehicle and left.[668]

Defence Witness NJV

626. NJV, who lived nearby the Buseruka centre, testified that at the beginning of June 1994 he saw Kalimanzira standing in front of his house in the centre. NJV recalled that Kalimanzira arrived by vehicle, looked at his house for approximately one minute, and then left in the direction of his family's house in Nyagahuru *secteur*. NJV stated that he did not see Kalimanzira in Rwamiko *secteur* again between April and early July 1994.[669]

627. NJV testified that at the end of May 1994, he attended a meeting at the Rwamiko Primary School which had been convened by *bourgmestre* Kajyambere. Security matters were discussed because there was discord in the community. NJV stated that some members of the population wanted to kill those that they described as bandits and obnoxious characters. NJV did not see Kalimanzira at this meeting. Moreover, NJV never heard of a "crisis committee". During that period, NJV never heard of any meeting of approximately 40 persons at the Rwamiko Primary School and maintained that he lived so close the school that it could not have happened without his knowledge.[670]

Callixte Kalimanzira

628. Callixte Kalimanzira testified that towards the end of the first week of June 1994 he visited his family in Kirarambogo. On his way to Nyagahuru *secteur* he stopped no more than ten minutes in Rwamiko *secteur*

---

[664] T. 24 November 2008 pp. 27-29, 36 (Witness KXL).
[665] T. 24 November 2008 pp. 32-34 [closed] (Witness KXL).
[666] T. 24 November 2008 pp. 46-48 (Witness MAS).
[667] T. 24 November 2008 pp. 48-50 (Witness MAS).
[668] T. 24 November 2008 p. 50 (Witness MAS).
[669] T. 24 November 2008 pp. 70-71 [closed] 72-73 (Witness NJV).
[670] T. 24 November 2008 p. 73 (Witness NJV).

to see what shape his house, located in the Buseruka centre, was in. Upon seeing that it had not been destroyed, he continued on his journey. He was accompanied by a driver.[671]

4.6.2. Deliberations

629. At the time of this alleged incident, Kalimanzira claims to have been working in Murambi (Gitarama *préfecture*) or at home in Butare *ville*, except in the first week of June when he went to visit his family in Nyaguhuru *secteur* (Muganza *commune*). As discussed above, the Chamber does not believe Kalimanzira's alibi (see III.1.2.2).

630. The Prosecution evidence led at trial describes two separate events. Paragraph 24 of the Indictment clearly alleges only one act of incitement, not two. It also clearly alleges that Kalimanzira went to the Rwamiko Primary School, not near or across the road from it. The Prosecution Pre-Trial Brief, however, indicated that AZT and BCZ were expected to testify to the same event at the Rwamiko Primary School. BCZ's testimony on the stand was **[page 133]** consistent with what he was expected to testify about. AZT, however, testified that Kalimanzira incited the population in front of his house in the Buseruka centre, which is located on the road opposite the primary school. Though they may possibly have occurred on the same day, the incitement alleged by AZT took place at a different time and location from the one testified to by BCZ. AZT's evidence merely places Kalimanzira near the location of the event alleged at paragraph 24 of the Indictment.

631. The Chamber relies on its assessment of BCZ's evidence on the allegations at the Nyabisagara football field (see III.4.5.2) to supplement its assessment of BCZ's evidence here. His evidence is supported by AZT (for the Prosecution), MAS and NJV (for the Defence) who place Kalimanzira in the Buseruka centre in early June 1994. BCZ's testimony about seeing a young man and a motorbike in Kalimanzira's white vehicle outside the school is also supported by Prosecution Witness BDE, who testified that in May or June 1994, Kalimanzira abducted him and his motorbike in a white vehicle from the Nyarusange roadblock to the Ndora *commune* office, stopping in the Buseruka centre for some 15 minutes on the way (see III.4.8.1). Kalimanzira himself affirmed that he briefly stopped in the Buseruka centre on his way to visit his family in the first week of June.

632. KXL also supports BCZ on the existence and members of a group of persons in Rwamiko *secteur* who were charged with deciding what to do with the property of dead Tutsis. Though MAS has never heard of a "crisis committee" *per se*, he describes BCZ's alleged members thereof as a band of criminals. NJV and MAS' categorical assertions that a meeting such as that described by BCZ could not have taken place without their knowledge are untenable.[672] NJV was only a teenager at the time and spent most of his days working in nearby fields, while MAS spent most of his time in his shop located 100 metres away from the Rwamiko Primary School; there is no reason why they should have gained firsthand knowledge of this meeting unless they were part of the "crisis committee", which they say they never heard of. The Defence evidence fails to cast any doubt on BCZ's testimony.

633. The Chamber believes that a group of persons, including BCZ, congregated to decide how to share and distribute the property of dead Tutsis. The Chamber also believes that the meeting described by BCZ took place at the Rwamiko Primary School. The Chamber believes both BDE and BCZ (see also III.4.8.2), and finds that the two incidents occurred on the same day: Kalimanzira came to Rwamiko *secteur* sometime in late May or early June to check on the state of his house in the Buseruka centre; on his way he picked up BDE at the Nyarusange roadblock, and, while in Buseruka, Kalimanzira dropped into a meeting of the "crisis committee" taking place at the Rwamiko Primary School.

634. The Chamber recalls that in order to convict under Article 2 (3)(c) of the Statute, the incitement must have been both 'direct' and 'public', which serves to limit the scope of its inchoate nature (see III.4.1). The public or private nature of the "crisis committee" at the Rwamiko Primary School is a factual determination which is also subject to the standard of proof beyond reasonable doubt. In this case, the Chamber finds there was insufficient evidence to show the public nature of this meeting. By BCZ's own testimony, the meeting

---

[671] T. 10 February 2008 pp. 48-51 (Callixte Kalimanzira).
[672] T. 24 November 2008 pp. 62-63 [closed] (Witness MAS); T. 24 November 2008 p. 73 (Witness NJV).

was restricted to 20-30 people who had been appointed to the "crisis committee"; it was not open to the public, nor was it held in a place which was open to the general public. Though Kalimanzira did not convene the meeting and appears to have unexpectedly shown up, as a known authority, his appearance would not have been contested or rejected. **[page 134]**

635. BCZ's testimony also suggests that Kalimanzira was aware that this meeting was restricted to members of the "crisis committee", referring to them as such and expressly distinguishing them from "the people" or "members of the population":

> "Then [Kalimanzira] added, 'You should sensitise the people – you, the members of the crisis committee.' And Kalimanzira told us that he was the leader of what was referred to as 'civil defence'. So he called on us to sensitise all members of the population so that they should be armed wherever they were."[673]

636. As such, the Prosecution has failed to prove the public nature of this meeting beyond reasonable doubt. The Chamber finds that Kalimanzira's presence and words to the "crisis committee" at the Rwamiko Primary School do not amount to Direct and Public Incitement to Commit Genocide.

4.7. Sakindi Roadblock, May

637. At paragraph 25 of the Indictment, the Prosecution charges Kalimanzira with Direct and Public Incitement to Commit Genocide for telling several armed persons who were manning the Sakindi roadblock in Kibilizi *secteur* in May 1994 that they should kill Tutsis discretely, destroy their homes and plant banana trees in their place so as to leave no traces for foreigners to see. He also urged them to tell the Tutsis that peace had been restored so as to lure them out of hiding and facilitate their killings.

638. The Chamber notes that paragraph 25 of the Indictment contains similar allegations as those at paragraph 13. The Prosecution Pre-Trial Brief, referred to only one incident at the Sakindi roadblock in May 1994. However, AZH, who was the only Prosecution witness to testify on the Sakindi roadblock, recalled three separate sightings of Kalimanzira there, two of which occurred in May 1994. The Prosecution relies on the combination of what transpired on both occasions to prove the allegations at both paragraphs 13 and 25[674] and did not appear to suggest that Kalimanzira issued two separate sets of instructions over two different visits to the roadblock in May.[675]

639. The Chamber recalls that the Prosecution is expected to lay down the allegations against an accused in the indictment in the most clear and comprehensive way possible so that the accused may understand the charges against him. However, the Prosecution's confused way of pleading these allegations did not undermine the fairness of the trial in the Chamber's view. A careful review of the record reveals that the Defence – which did not raise the issue – understood the nature of the charge and was not impaired in its ability to prepare its case. The Defence has not objected to the introduction of AZH's evidence at trial and has responded to it accordingly.

640. The Chamber relies on the same evidence and its assessment thereof in relation to the allegations at paragraph 13 of the Indictment, discussed in full at III.2.6, to conclude that AZH's sole evidence is insufficiently reliable to sustain a conviction.

4.7.1. Evidence

641. See III.2.6.1. **[page 135]**

4.7.2. Deliberations

642. See III.2.6.2.

---

[673] See T. 24 June 2008 p. 51 (Witness BCZ).
[674] See Prosecution Closing Brief, paras. 139, 268-272.
[675] Compare Prosecution Pre-Trial Brief, para. 61 and annexed summary of AZH's anticipated testimony with Prosecution Closing Brief, para. 272.

4.8. Nyarusange Roadblock, May

643. At paragraph 26 of the Indictment, the Prosecution charges Kalimanzira with Direct and Public Incitement to Commit Genocide for encouraging people manning a roadblock in May 1994 to continue checking everyone's identity cards and search for the Tutsi enemy. On that occasion, Kalimanzira allegedly criticized a Hutu motorcyclist passing through for not carrying a weapon with which to kill Tutsis.

644. The Defence denies this allegation in its entirety. In addition, Kalimanzira relies on his alibi (see III.1.2).

645. The Chamber notes that paragraph 26 of the Indictment does not specify which roadblock Kalimanzira is alleged to have punished the motorcyclist at. However, the witness summary for BDE provided in the Prosecution Pre-Trial Brief gives an extensive account of his anticipated testimony, including the fact that the roadblock is alleged to be in Nyarusange *cellule*. This is consistent with BDE's witness statement, disclosed in the Supporting Materials. Nor has the Defence objected to lack of notice. Consequently, the Chamber finds that the Defence was adequately notified of this material fact. The Chamber will refer to this roadblock as the "Nyarusange roadblock".[676]

4.8.1. Evidence

Prosecution Witness BDE

646. BDE testified that following the death of President Habyarimana, the setting up of roadblocks in the Gisagara area created restrictions in the movement of persons. The aim of the roadblocks and restrictions were to identify and kill Tutsis. It was therefore possible for BDE to move around freely because he had a Hutu identity card. BDE recalled that one day in May or June 1994, while returning to the Gisagara marketplace on his motorbike from the Nyabitare market where he had been buying supplies, he was stopped at the Nyarusange roadblock at approximately 2:00 p.m. When BDE saw that Kalimanzira was there, he attempted to greet him but Kalimanzira pushed him back and told the men manning the roadblock to be wary of people travelling by motorbike because they assist the *Inkotanyi* to cross roadblocks. Kalimanzira then instructed those manning the roadblock to guard the motorbike and prevent BDE from leaving.[677]

647. BDE testified that Kalimanzira then left the roadblock for approximately 40 to 60 minutes, and speculated that he had gone to visit his parents' house in Nyagahuru. Upon his return, Kalimanzira questioned BDE as to why he was not carrying any weapons. Kalimanzira then ordered the men manning the roadblock to load the motorbike and BDE onto his vehicle, which was a white pick-up truck. Kalimanzira was accompanied by three or four armed and uniformed soldiers. BDE explained that he did not resist because he considered Kalimanzira more powerful than the *bourgmestre* and therefore a superior. BDE further explained the four or five armed Hutu men manning the roadblock were stronger than him.[678]
[page 136]
648. BDE testified that they then drove to the Ndora *commune* office, stopping at the Buseruka centre for approximately 15 minutes along the way. He recalled that when they arrived at the *commune* office, the motorbike was offloaded by communal policemen and impounded by the *bourgmestre*, Fidèle Uwizeye, upon the orders of Kalimanzira who, BDE speculated, then left for Butare. BDE explained that he recognised Uwizeye, and had known who he was for around three years but did not know him personally. Although Uziweye was the *bourgmestre*, BDE stated that he believed him to have little authority in Ndora *commune* because he had only been appointed in June.[679]

649. BDE testified that after Kalimanzira left, he asked *bourgmestre* Uwizeye to return his motorbike. The *bourgmestre* told him to be patient and the motorbike was returned to BDE three days later. BDE explained

---
[676] This is also the name adopted by the Defence. See *e.g.* Defence Closing Brief, paras. 608 *et seq.*
[677] T. 18 June 2008 pp. 17-19, 29, 35-36, 38 (Witness BDE).
[678] T. 18 June 2008 pp. 19-21, 29-33 (Witness BDE).
[679] T. 18 June 2008 pp. 19-21, 29, 34, 39 (Witness BDE).

that he does not know why his motorbike was confiscated, and believes that it was due to the fact that he was not carrying any weapons and because Kalimanzira believed that motorbikes were being used to transport *Inkotanyi*.[680]

Prosecution Witness BCZ

650. BCZ testified that he attended a meeting at the Rwamiko Primary School in late May or early June 1994 at which Kalimanzira showed up (see III.4.6.1). After the meeting, Kalimanzira left in his white Hilux vehicle with a young man seated in the rear cabin and a motorbike in the rear pick-up section. Kalimanzira explained that he had met the young man on the road and stopped him because he did not have identity papers with him. BCZ stated that he did not see any soldiers or a driver with Kalimanzira.[681]

Defence Witness AM52

651. AM52 testified that in April 1994 in Gisagara, Burundians and others from outside the area began to steal the property of locals. He explained that, as a result, people stored their valuable property in the Ndora *commune* office for safekeeping. One of those people was AM52's brother, BDE, who took his motorbike there around 20 April 1994. Less than two weeks later, it was stolen along with several other motorbikes. AM52 recalled that, following a police investigation, it was returned to the *commune* office in the same month. AM52 asserted that his brother never mentioned any other incident with his motorbike, particularly not one involving Kalimanzira.[682]

Defence Witness KUW

652. KUW testified that the Nyarusange roadblock was set up one week after the death of President Habyarimana at the behest of Chrysologue Bimenyimana, *bourgmestre* of Muganza *commune*, and Isaïe Sikubwabo, *conseiller* of Dahwe *secteur*, to prevent unknown persons from passing through the area. It was the only roadblock in Nyarusange *cellule*, and the inhabitants of the *cellule* manned the roadblock in shifts. The roadblock was eventually dismantled around 5 or 6 May 1994 because the road became impassable due to heavy rain. KUW asserted that he never saw Kalimanzira at the roadblock or heard of him slapping a man for being unarmed, pushing a man with a motorbike, or instructing the people at the roadblock not to allow motorbikes to pass. Had any such incident occurred, he would **[page 137]** certainly have heard about it because he would have received a report. He lived close to the roadblock and several bars overlooked it, so people would have spoken about it.[683]

4.8.2. Deliberations

653. At the time of this alleged incident, Kalimanzira claims to have been working in Murambi (Gitarama *préfecture*) or at home in Butare *ville*, except in the first week of June when he went to visit his family in Nyaguhuru *secteur* (Muganza *commune*). As discussed above, the Chamber does not believe Kalimanzira's alibi (see III.1.2.2).

654. The Chamber finds the testimony of both BDE and BCZ to be credible and considers that the Defence's numerous allegations regarding the unreliability of BDE's testimony in particular do not raise reasonable doubt regarding the incident.

655. The most significant arguments raised by the Defence concern, first, the fact that BDE testified that he was able to travel around the different *communes* of Butare without difficulty. The Defence states that this could not be true because BDE himself testified that an employee of his stopped working because it was

---

[680] T. 18 June 2008 pp. 21-22 (Witness BDE).
[681] T. 24 June 2008 pp. 50-52, 69-70 (Witness BCZ).
[682] T. 18 November 2008 pp. 12-15 [closed] (Witness AM52).
[683] T. 3 December 2008 pp. 47-49, 51-52, 57 [closed] (Witness KUW).

difficult to move around and because the evidence in the case shows that official documents were required to move around.[684] BDE

clarified, however, that although he could leave his home to buy food, his employee who drove a taxi could not continue his work because the taxi could travel long distances and could end up in a place where the employee was not known and be in danger.[685] The Chamber does not find these statements to be inconsistent; indeed, it is plausible that in May or June 1994 people may have left their homes to buy food, but would refrain from travel to communities where they would not be known because of the insecurity of the situation.

656. Further, the exhibit relied upon by the Defence to assert that official documents were required to move around is specific to Felix Semwaga, the vice-president of the Butare Prefectural Civil Defence Committee, for the purpose of inspecting roadblocks.[686] The Chamber does not find that an inference can be drawn from this exhibit, as the Defence asks it to, that such an authorization would have been necessary to pass through roadblocks.

657. The Defence points to other purported inconsistencies in BDE's testimony to support the claim that his allegation is false, namely, BDE's evidence concerning the time of Kalimanzira's arrival at the roadblock, the period of time that Kalimanzira was absent from the roadblock, the location of Buseruka centre and the month in which the incident took place.[687] The Defence argues that much of this testimony is inconsistent with BDE's October 2001 statement.[688]

658. The Chamber finds that many of these purported inconsistencies are either explained by the passage of time, explained by BDE in his testimony, or are so immaterial as to not undermine the truthfulness of his account. For instance, BDE explained in cross-examination that while he stated that the incident occurred in May 1994 in his October 2001 statement,[689] he later testified that he gave a range of either May or June 1994 simply because he did not **[page 138]** have a clear memory of the date.[690] The Defence also argues that BDE's testimony is not plausible because he testified that Fidèle Uwizeye had been *bourgmestre* for a month when the incident occurred, although Fidèle Uwizeye was not appointed until 17 June 1994.[691]

BDE recalled on the stand that Uwizeye was appointed *bourgmestre* in June.[692] It is clear that he was trying to provide an objective indication for when the events occurred, but was not certain about their exact date. Considering how much time has passed since the events, the Chamber does not consider BDE's credibility to be affected by his inability to instantly recall the exact date of a *bourgmestre*'s appointment in relation to the incident he describes.

659. Further, when confronted with his October 2001 statement which stated that Kalimanzira arrived at the roadblock while his identity card was being checked, which was inconsistent with his testimony that Kalimanzira was already at the roadblock when he arrived, BDE clarified that it was as if they arrived at the roadblock at the same time, or within minutes of each other.[693] The Chamber finds that whether Kalimanzira arrived slightly before or slightly after BDE to be immaterial to the veracity of his account.

660. Finally, regarding whether the period of time BDE suggests that Kalimanzira left the roadblock was sufficient for Kalimanira to visit his parents in Nyagahuru, the Chamber notes that BDE testified that he thought Kalimanzira was going to visit his parents because the men at the roadblock told him so, and that he knew the road towards their home, as opposed to where they actually lived.[694] Given that BDE did not really know where Kalimanzira was going, it can hardly be said that the period Kalimanzira was absent from the roadblock was inconsistent with Kalimanzira's travel to that location.

---

[684] Defence Closing Brief paras. 616, 627-630.
[685] T. 18 June pp. 19, 25 [closed], 36, 38 (Witness BDE).
[686] Exhibit D18.
[687] Defence Closing Brief, paras. 617-620.
[688] Defence Closing Brief, paras. 621-625.
[689] Exhibit D17.
[690] T. 18 June 2008 pp. 38-39 (Witness BDE).
[691] Defence Closing Brief, paras. 620, 624.
[692] T. 18 June 2008 p. 21 (Witness BDE).
[693] T. 18 June 2008 p. 31 (Witness BDE).
[694] T. 18 June 2008 pp. 29-30 (Witness BDE).

661. The Chamber also notes that BCZ's testimony supports BDE's account in important respects, namely the placement of a man and his motorcycle in the back of Kalimanzira's vehicle, as well as the colour and type of the vehicle.[695] The Chamber also notes that there is evidence on the record which indicates that the Rwamiko Primary School is located in the Buseruka centre.[696] Consequently, BDE's evidence that they stopped at the Buseruka centre is not inconsistent with BCZ's evidence that he saw Kalimanzira in front of the Rwamiko Primary School.[697]

662. The Chamber has also considered the evidence of AM52 and KUW and finds that their evidence does not create a reasonable doubt regarding BDE's testimony. Although AM52, who is the brother of BDE, confirmed that BDE's motorcycle was put in the Ndora *commune* office, he claimed BDE put it in the *commune* office on 20 April 1994 and that it was returned from being stolen in that same month, less than two weeks later.[698] Consequently, his testimony does not exclude the possibility that both accounts are true, given that BDE testified that his encounter with Kalimanzira occurred in May or June. Further, just because AM52 testified that he did not hear Kalimanzira's name mentioned in relation to BDE's motorcycle does not undermine BDE's account; there is no evidence on the **[page 139]** record to suggest that AM52 would have been made aware of this incident.[699] Finally, the Chamber notes that AM52 left Rwanda in 1994 and has not returned, despite accusations against him for being involved in the genocide.[700]

663. With respect to KUW, the Chamber notes that he acknowledged being in charge of the roadblock and that people were killed there. Although he asserts that he was not involved in those killings, he has confessed to killing someone during the genocide and was sentenced to ten years imprisonment.[701] KUW lived five minutes away from the roadblock and in light of his professional position, has an interest in minimizing what occurred there. KUW's assertion that he would have heard about every incident at the roadblock is not worthy of belief.[702] The Chamber also does not accept his assertion that the roadblock was dismantled around 5 May 1994 due to heavy rains which made the road impassable.[703] There is other evidence on the record which suggests that the roadblock was in place after this point[704] and in any event this account is not worthy of belief. The Chamber does not accept that the roadblock would be dismantled because of heavy rain at this point in the genocide, as opposed to at the very least simply being left unmanned.

664. Consequently, the Chamber finds that the Prosecution has proven beyond reasonable doubt that in May or June 1994, BDE was detained at a roadblock in Nyarusange *commune*. The Chamber finds that Kalimanzira was present at the roadblock and ordered the men manning the roadblock to prevent BDE from leaving and to guard his motorcycle. Upon his return, Kalimanzira had the motorcycle loaded into his truck and drove it and BDE to the Ndora *commune* office where the motorcycle was kept for three days.

665. The Chamber, however, does not find that this incident amounts to Direct and Public Incitement to Commit Genocide. In order to be criminal, the incitement must be both direct and public, and the Chamber finds that the first criteria is not met in this instance.

666. The Chamber recalls that determining whether an act of incitement is direct or not is undertaken by focusing mainly on the issue of whether the persons for whom the message was intended immediately grasped the implication thereof.[705] In this instance, BDE testified that he is still wondering what motivated Kalimanzira to act as he did; he believed it was because Kalimanzira said his motorbike was used for transporting *Inkotanyi* and because he was not carrying a weapon.[706] BDE believed Kalimanzira asked him

---

[695] T. 24 June 2008 pp. 52, 69 (Witness BCZ); T. 18 June 2008 pp. 32-33 (Witness BDE).
[696] Defence Witness MAS testified that the Buseruka centre is in Rwamiko *secteur*, and included a primary school as well as various shops: T. 24 November 2008 p. 27.
[697] Defence Closing Brief, para. 1054.
[698] T. 18 November 2008 p. 15 (Witness AM52).
[699] T. 18 November 2008 p. 12 [closed] (Witness AM52).
[700] T. 18 June 2008 pp. 22, 28-30, 32 [closed] (Witness AM52).
[701] T. 3 December 2008 pp. 48-49 [closed], 52-54 (Witness KUW).
[702] T. 3 December 2008 pp. 47-48 [closed], 51-52 (Witness KUW).
[703] T. 3 December 2008 p. 49 [closed] (Witness KUW).
[704] AZT testified that in late May 1994, he saw Kalimanzira alight from a car and slap a man at a roadblock in Nyarusange *cellule*, Rwamiko *secteur*: T. 20 June 2008 pp. 24-25.
[705] *Nahimana et al.* Appeal Judgement, paras. 698-700, citing *Akayesu* Trial Judgement paras. 557-558.
[706] T. 18 June 2008 p. 22 (Witness BDE).

why we was not carrying a weapon because "the war was raging at that time" and that members of the general public had to carry traditional weapons in order to protect themselves from the *Inkotanyi*.[707] Although BDE understood the *Inkotanyi* to refer to the Tutsis, because it was the Tutsis who were killed with traditional weapons, he nonetheless appeared to understand the need to carry weapons as a defensive measure.

667. In sum, there is insufficient evidence to conclude that BDE understood Kalimanzira's actions and speech to be a call for him to kill Tutsis, nor does the Chamber find the evidence **[page 140]** sufficient to infer that those manning the roadblock would have understood it as such. There is also no evidence that either BDE or the people manning the roadblock went on to kill Tutsis.[708] Consequently, the Chamber finds that the Prosecution has not eliminated the reasonable doubt that Kalimanzira's speech and actions were intended as a defensive measure in light of the civil war, as opposed to incitement to kill Tutsis. The Prosecution has therefore not proven beyond a reasonable doubt that Kalimanzira committed Direct and Public Incitement at the Nyarusange roadblock in May or June 1994.

4.9. Weapons Carrying, mid-April to June

668. At paragraph 27 of the Indictment, the Prosecution charges Kalimanzira with Direct and Public Incitement to Commit Genocide for checking if everyone was carrying a weapon with which to kill Tutsis between mid-April and June 1994, and did not hesitate to warn, assault, or threaten to severely punish unarmed persons. For instance, around late April or early May 1994, Kalimanzira hit an unarmed Hutu with a club.

669. In its closing arguments, the Prosecution contends that witnesses AZT, BCK, BDJ, BDK and AZC testified to the allegations in paragraph 27 of the Indictment and established that, during the months of April to June 1994, Kalimanzira travelled between the neighbouring *communes* of Ndora, Muganza and Mugusa in order to ensure that local civilians were carrying weapons to kill Tutsis; he warned, threatened and even assaulted those he found unarmed as a method of inciting them to carry out killings. These witnesses testified to five separate incidents, namely:

i. AZT testified that, at the end of April or beginning of June, the accused slapped an unarmed man at the Nyarusange *cellule* roadblock;

ii. BCK testified that Kalimanzira appeared at a small road at the centre of Kabyue and proceeded to beat an unarmed man with a club;

iii. BDJ testified that Kalimanzira stopped at a roadblock in Kabuye in May 1994, criticized the men at the roadblock for not being armed, and warned them those unarmed persons would have to be killed because they are to be considered the enemy;

iv. BDK testified that, at the end of May 1994, Kalimanzira addressed a crowd at the Gisagara marketplace, instructed the male attendees to carry weapons to defeat the Tutsi enemy, kill young Tutsi women who were still alive, and rewarded a man for being armed; and,

v. AZC testified that, during an afternoon in June 1994, Kalimanzira stopped in Mutarama after seeing two unarmed men, ordered them into his vehicle, and drove them to a different *commune* to walk back as a punishment.[709]

670. Kalimanzira denies these allegations and relies on his alibi (see III.1.2).

---

[707] T. 18 June 2008 pp. 19-20 (Witness BDE).
[708] *Nahimana et al.* Appeal Judgement, para. 709, fn. 1674.
[709] Prosecution Closing Brief, paras. 281-292.

4.9.1. Notice

671. In its Closing Brief, the Defence has objected to the omission of material facts relating to the fourth allegation above, namely the events at the Gisagara marketplace.[710] **[page 141]**

672. The Chamber notes that while the first sentence of paragraph 27 describes the Prosecution's allegation in general terms, the second sentence provides notice of only one incident described above: hitting an unarmed man with a club. The material facts underlying the other four allegations, including that raised by the Defence, were not pleaded in the Indictment. The Indictment is therefore defective in this respect, which raises the question of whether the Defence had adequate notice of those material facts. For the same reasons discussed in III.2.3.1, despite the Defence's failure to raise a timely objection, the Chamber finds that consideration of the Defence's arguments, as well as the omission of the other allegations listed above from the Indictment, is warranted. The Chamber will therefore address the omission of material facts underpinning the first, third, fourth and fifth allegations listed above.

673. No mention was made of these incidents in the narrative section of the Prosecution Pre-Trial Brief. However, in Annex A to the Prosecution Pre-Trial Brief, the summaries relating to AZT, BDJ, BDK and AZC each refer to paragraph 27 as being relevant.

674. The summary of AZT's anticipated testimony indicated that he would testify about, among other things, Kalimanzira assaulting an unarmed person and rebuking others in May 1994 at Nyarusange, near River Akanyaru. This was consistent with AZT's November 2002 witness statement which was disclosed to the Defence in the Supporting Materials.

675. The summary of BDJ's anticipated testimony indicates that he would testify that, among other things, Kalimanzira encouraged people to carry weapons during the genocide and referred to a specific instance during the month of May, at a roadblock in Kabuye *cellue*, Gisagara sector, Ndora *commune*. Kalimanzira asked the witness why he and others did not have weapons and told them that he wanted people to carry weapons at roadblocks. Witness BDJ's statement, also provided to the Defence with the Supporting Materials, is consistent with this account and states that Kalimanzira would rebuke those he caught without weapons, but did not include that example.

676. The summary of BDK's anticipated testimony indicates that she would testify about, among other things, a meeting at the Gisagara centre where Kalimanzira gave money to a person who was armed with an old part of a vehicle. This is consistent with Witness BDK's witness statement, included in the Supporting Materials.

677. The summary of AZC's anticipated testimony states that he would provide specific examples in his testimony concerning Kalimanzira's punishment of people for failing to carry weapons during the genocide, but did not detail any such examples. However, in his October 2001 witness statement, provided to the Defence with the Supporting Materials, Witness AZC stated that he was informed by two men that, after a meeting at the Gikonko commune office, Kalimanzira came across them unarmed while on his way to Butare. Kalimanzira ordered the two men into his car and drove them to Mbazi *commune* where they were dropped off.

678. The Chamber notes that the Prosecution has proffered AZC's evidence evidence simply as evidence of Kalimanzira's "pattern of conduct"; namely, that he ensured that the local population was armed.[711] The Chamber finds however that a reasonable doubt subsists as to whether this alleged pattern of conduct is criminal or in any other way relevant to Kalimanzira's criminal responsibility. Having regard to the totality of the evidence, the Chamber does not find that the Prosecution has eliminated other possibles motives for **[page 142]** Kalimanzira's conduct, in particular whether this was not a legitimate defensive course of action in the context of a civil war. Regardless, the Chamber has required corroboration for AZC in relation to other allegations in Mugusa *commune* (see III.2.6.2). His uncorroborated hearsay evidence here would be equally unreliable. The Chamber will therefore not consider this allegation further.

---

[710] Defence Closing Brief, para. 1140.
[711] Prosecution Closing Brief, para. 286.

679. In conclusion, the Chamber finds that the Pre-Trial Brief with the annexed witness summaries simply added greater detail in a consistent manner with the more general allegation plead in paragraph 27 of the Indictment, save for the evidence of AZC.

680. With respect to timeliness, the Chamber notes that the Defence cross-examined AZT, BDK and AZC about these particular allegations.[712] As previously discussed (see III.2.3.1 and III.2.7.1), the Chamber considers that the Defence had ample time to conduct investigations in the four and a half months before the commencement of its case. In its own Pre-Trial Brief, the Defence explicitly refuted some of the allegations in question and made a general argument that Kalimanzira was in Gitarama *commune* at the relevant times.[713] The Chamber therefore does not find that Kalimanzira's ability to defend himself has been materially impaired.

681. On the basis of the Prosecution Pre-Trial Brief and witness statements, the Chamber finds that the Prosecution provided the Defence with adequate notice of the material facts underlying the first four incidents, listed above.

4.9.2. Roadblock at Nyarusange cellule

682. The Prosecution alleges that in late May 1994 Kalimanzira slapped an unarmed man at Nyarusange *cellule* and asked him what he would do if he met *Inyenzi*.[714]

683. The Defence denies this allegation. In addition, Kalimanzira relies on his alibi (see III.1.2).

4.9.2.1. Evidence

Prosecution Witness AZT

684. AZT testified that in late May 1994, he saw Kalimanzira alight from a car and slap a man at a roadblock in Nyarusange *cellule*, Rwamiko *secteur*. AZT stated that he witnessed the incident from a bar approximately eight to nine metres away. He recalled that he rushed to the scene in order to find out why the man had been slapped and heard that it was because he had been unarmed. Kalimanzira had allegedly asked the victim: "if you ever meet *Inyenzi*, what would you do?" AZT stated that, at the time, *Inyenzi* meant Tutsis. AZT did not know or speak to the victim himself.[715]

Defence Witness KUW

685. KUW testified that there was not a single roadblock in his locality in late May 1994.[716] He said a roadblock had been set up on the instruction of *Bourgmestre* Bimenyimana **[page 143]** and *Conseiller* Sikubwabo one week after the President's death and it was dismantled in early May because the rains had made the road on which it was located impassable. No other roadblock was subsequently set up in Nyarusange *cellule*.[717]

4.9.2.2. Deliberations

686. At the relevant time alleged, Kalimanzira claims he was working in Murambi (Gitarama *préfecture*). As discussed above, the Chamber disbelieves his alibi (see III.1.2.2).

687. KUW acknowledged being in charge of the Nyarusange roadblock and that people were killed there, although he asserts that he was not involved in those killings. He has also confessed to killing someone

---
[712] T. 26 June 2008 pp. 26-27, 34 (Witness AZT); T. 21 May 2008 pp. 2-5 (Witness BDK); T. 26 June 2008 pp. 68-69 (Witness AZC).
[713] Defence Closing Brief, paras. 20, 36-38 53-54.
[714] Prosecution Closing Brief, para. 282.
[715] T. 20 June 2008, pp. 25-27 and T. 23 June 2008 pp. 30, 34-35 (Witness AZT).
[716] T. 3 December 2008 pp. 57-58 [closed] (Witness KUW).
[717] T. 3 December 2008 pp. 48-49, 57-58 [closed] (Witness KUW).

during the genocide and was sentenced to ten years imprisonment.[718] The Chamber has already discussed KUW's interest in minimizing what occurred at the roadblock (III.4.8.2).

688. KUW contended that because of his professional position, the population had to report any incident that occurred at the roadblock to him.[719] The Defence also contends that in a *cellule* as small as Nyarusange, such an event would not have occurred without his knowledge. The Chamber is not, however, persuaded that the fact that he may not have heard of the incident necessarily implies that it did not occur.

689. Moreover, another reliable Prosecution witness, BDE, testified regarding an incident in which he was involved at that same roadblock in late May or early June, undermining KUW's assertion that the roadblock was dismantled on 5 May 1994 (see III.4.8). Nor does the Chamber find his assertion plausible that the roadblock would have been dismantled at this point in the genocide. KUW also covered other possibilities by testifying that there were no incidents at the roadblock.[720] However, KUW admitted that he was not there all the time, as he manned it every fifth day and acknowledged that he lived about five minutes from it and could not see what was happening there from his home.[721] The Chamber does not find KUW's evidence to be credible.

690. With respect to AZT, the Chamber notes that he has been convicted and sentenced to life imprisonment in Rwanda for his involvement in the genocide.[722] He is still trying to appeal. AZT has also given evidence regarding other allegations (see III.2.3.5; see also III.4.6). Although the Chamber found that corroboration was required for his testimony in relation to the allegations contained at paragraph 8 of the Indictment, with respect to the public rally in Nyirakanywero, the Chamber finds that the reasoning underlying that conclusion does not pertain to his evidence in this respect. The Chamber, having carefully considering his testimony, has found him to be a reliable and credible witness.

691. The Defence contends that AZT's testimony on this incident should be disregarded because it is inconsistent with a statement he gave to the ICTR investigators in November 2002. First, the impression was given in the statement that AZT personally witnessed both Kalimanzira slapping the unarmed person and Kalimanzira's explanation for his action, while at trial he explained that he personally witnessed the slap from a distance and only learned **[page 144]** about the reason for it from others.[723] Second, the statement asserts that Kalimanzira arrived on a motorcycle, while in court AZT testified that he was in a motor vehicle.[724] The Chamber accepts AZT's explanation that these and other minor discrepancies are the result of the manner in which the statement was recorded and do not reflect any change in the account given by AZT which could lead to a conclusion that his testimony is unreliable or incredible.[725]

692. The Defence also criticised AZT's inability in his testimony to specify the time of the day when the incident occurred, although in his earlier statement he said it occurred around 1:00 p.m.[726] Again, this is not significant in light of the passage of time between 1994, 2002 and the time he gave evidence and does not undermine AZT's credibility.

693. In light of the foregoing, the Chamber finds that the Prosecution has proven beyond a reasonable doubt that, in late May 1994, Kalimanzira slapped an unarmed man at Nyarusange *cellule*. However, the Chamber does not find that the Prosecution has proven that this event satisfies the legal elements of Direct and Public Incitement beyond reasonable doubt.

694. The Chamber recalls that determining whether an act of incitement is direct or not is undertaken by focusing mainly on the issue of whether the persons for whom the message was intended immediately grasped the implication thereof.[727] There is no direct evidence regarding who was slapped or what

---

[718] T. 3 December 2008 pp. 48-49 [closed], 52-54 (Witness KUW).
[719] T. 3 December 2008 pp. 48-49 [closed], 51-52 (Witness KUW).
[720] T. 3 December 2008 pp. 51-52 (Witness KUW).
[721] T. 3 December 2008 pp. 47-49 [closed] (Witness KUW).
[722] T. 20 June 2008 p. 30 [closed] (Witness AZT).
[723] Defence Closing Brief, para. 662. T. 20 June 2008 p. 25 and T. 23 June 2008, p. 34 (Witness AZT).
[724] Defence Closing Brief, para. 661; Exhibit D24; T. 20 June 2008 p. 25 and T. 23 June 2008 p. 23 (Witness AZT).
[725] T. 23 June 2008 pp. 30-32 (Witness AZT).
[726] Defence Closing Brief, para. 660; T. 20 June 2008 p. 26; T. 23 June 2008 p. 27 (Witness AZT).
[727] *Nahimana et al.* Appeal Judgement, paras. 698-700, citing *Akayesu* Trial Judgement paras. 557-558.

Kalimanzira said at the time. AZT testified that he was told that Kalimanzira asked the victim at the roadblock what he would do if he met *Inyenzi* and that Witness AZT understood that term to mean Tutsi. There is no evidence that AZT or the victim understood this as a call to kill Tutsis, nor any evidence that they went on to commit this act.[728] In short, the Prosecution has not proven that Kalimanzira intended to instigate the killing of Tutsi civilians in this instance. Nor is the Chamber satisfied that by slapping and criticizing a single individual, that the public element of the crime is satisfied. The Chamber finds that the Prosecution has not proven beyond reasonable doubt that Kalimanzira committed Direct and Public Incitement by slapping an unarmed man at Nyarusange *cellule*.

4.9.3. Road between Butare and Muganza

695. The Prosecution alleges that, at the end of April or the beginning of May, on a road in Kabuye, Kalimanzira beat an unarmed man with a club for failing to carry a weapon.[729]

696. The Defence denies this allegation in its entirely. In addition, Kalimanzira relies on his alibi (see III.1.2).

4.9.3.1. Evidence

Prosecution Witness BCK

697. BCK testified that in late April or early May 1994, he saw Kalimanzira near a veterinarian centre, close to Kabuye and located on the road between Butare and Muganza. **[page 145]** BCK recalled that he was returning to the Jaguar roadblock with four friends after drinking in a bar at the Kabuye centre, when, at approximately 1:20 p.m., Kalimanzira drove past them and instructed them to stop. Kalimanzira then asked BCK's friend, Vianney, why he was moving about without a weapon when there was a war on and proceeded to beat him with BCK's club. BCK further recalled that Vianney then cut down a shrub to use as a club. Kalimanzira continued in the direction of Muganza commune.[730]

Defence Witness Jean Marie Vianney Harindintwali

698. Harindintwali was, according to BCK, beaten by Kalimanzira near the Kabuye centre. Harindintwali testified that he has never been beaten by Kalimanzira and that BCK was a vagabond and bandit who was not his friend. Harindintwali also denied that the other two men allegedly there that day were his friends. He asserted that he did not go for drinks with them when they manned the Jaguar roadblock together.[731]

4.9.3.2. Deliberations

699. At the relevant time alleged, Kalimanzira claims he was working in Murambi (Gitarama *préfecture*). As discussed above, the Chamber disbelieves his alibi (see III.1.2.2).

700. The Chamber is faced with directly contradictory evidence with respect to this allegation. BCK testified that Kalimanzira beat his companion with BCK's club for not carrying a weapon. The Defence in turn called Harindintwali, the person alleged to have been beaten by Kalimanzira, who denies that the incident ever took place.

701. Harindintwali is living in exile from Rwanda and denies that he is a fugitive from the justice system there. He had been detained and released after serving two years and subsequently left the country.[732] He admitted that he manned the Jaguar Roadblock, but denies committing or knowing of the commission of any

---

[728] *Nahimana et al.* Appeal Judgement, para. 709, fn. 1674.
[729] Prosecution Closing Brief, para. 282.
[730] T. 26 June 2008 pp. 10-11, 23-25 (Witness BCK).
[731] T. 18 November 2008 p. 70 and T. 21 November 2008 p. 5 (Jean Marie Vianney Harindintwali).
[732] T. 18 November 2008 pp. 68-69 (Jean Marie Vianney Harindintwali).

crimes at that location.[733] In relation to his evidence concerning the Jaguar roadblock, the Chamber has finds that it has reason to disbelieve him (see III.4.3.2).

702. When confronted with *Gacaca* records which indicate that he is charged with offences, and which indicate that his accomplices were BCK and Pacôme, Harindintwali acknowledged that it referred to him but he denied knowing of the charge or the accusers.[734] The Chamber considers that there is sufficient evidence of authenticity to accept that these exhibits are *Gaccaca* records. The Chamber also notes that Harindintwali acknowledged that Pacôme worked the Jaguar roadblock with him.[735] The Chamber considers that his denial of association with BCK and Pacôme was false and that he is not a reliable or credible witness.

703. The Chamber notes that BCK has a judicial record. He confessed to and was convicted in Rwandan courts for crimes committed during April to July 1994.[736] However, as he was sentenced to 30 years in prison and has exhausted all appeals, this would indicate that his sentence could not be affected by giving false testimony against Kalimanzira. The Chamber has found BCK to be a credible and reliable witness in relation to the allegations at **[page 146]** Jaguar roadblock (see III.4.3.2). The Defence was not able to show any serious discrepancies in his testimony, either internally or by virtue of inconsistencies with his prior statements.

704. The Chamber considers BCK to be credible and reliable, and is satisfied by his evidence beyond reasonable doubt. Consequently, the Chamber finds that the Prosecution has proven beyond reasonable doubt that, at the end of April or the beginning of May, on a road in Kabuye, Kalimanzira beat Harindintwali with BCK's club for failing to carry a weapon.

705. The Chamber also accepts BCK's evidence that Kalimanzira questioned his friend about why he was unarmed when there was a war on. The Chamber does not, however, find sufficient evidence to conclude that Kalimanzira's words or actions were intended to incite the killing of Tutsi civilians. There is no evidence that the message was received as such by any of the men, or that they went on to actually kill Tutsis.[737] Consequently, the Chamber finds that the Prosecution has failed to prove that Kalimanzira committed Direct and Public Incitement to Commit Genocide by beating an unarmed man with a club on a road in Kabuye.

4.9.4. Kabuye Roadblock

706. The Prosecution alleges that in May 1994, Kalimanzira stopped at a roadblock in Kabuye and rebuked the two persons manning the roadblock for being unarmed. Kalimanzira also told the men that those who were unarmed would have to be killed by the others because they should be considered to be the enemy. Kalimanzira specified that by referring to the enemy, he was speaking about Tutsis.[738]

707. The Defence denies the allegation in its entirety. In addition, Kalimanzira relies on his alibi (see III.1.2).

4.9.4.1. Evidence

Prosecution Witness BDJ

708. BDJ is a Tutsi who was employed as a motorcycle driver by a local trader. He kept the fact that he was a Tutsi secret and after the massacres he was elected to assist the *responsable* to restore law and order. He testified that in May 1994, Kalimanzira stopped at the roadblock he manned at the junction between the roads to Kabuye and Muganza, on the road from Gisagara to Kirarambogo. Kalimanzira arrived in a double-cabin pickup around midday, and was accompanied by a soldier who was his bodyguard. BDJ explained that because the massacres had almost ended by that time, only he and the *responsable de cellule* were manning

---

[733] T. 19 November 2008 pp. 1-5 (Jean Marie Vianney Harindintwali).
[734] T. 19 November 2008 pp. 6-9 (Jean Marie Vianney Harindintwali); Exhibits P57 and P58.
[735] T. 19 November 2008 p. 2 (Jean Marie Vianney Harindintwali).
[736] T. 26 June 2008 pp. 11-12; pp. 27-29 [closed] (Witness BCK); Exhibit D39.
[737] *Nahimana et al.* Appeal Judgement, paras. 698-700, 709, fn. 1674, citing *Akayesu* Trial Judgement paras. 557-558.
[738] Prosecution Closing Brief, para. 284.

the roadblock. BDJ recalled that he was unarmed, causing Kalimanzira to rebuke him from inside his vehicle. Kalimanzira commented that he was surprised to find BDJ at the roadblock without weapons and therefore unable to confront the enemy. BDJ further recalled that Kalimanzira warned them that unarmed persons had to be killed by other persons at the roadblock because they had to be considered the enemy. BDJ stated that Kalimanzira told them that the "enemy" was the Tutsi. BDJ carried a weapon from then on.[739]

4.9.4.2. Deliberations **[page 147]**

709. At the relevant time alleged, Kalimanzira claims that he was working in Murambi (Gitarama *préfecture*). As discussed above, the Chamber disbelieves his alibi (see III.1.2.2).

710. The Chamber notes that BDJ confessed to committing crimes against the Tutsis, including manning roadblocks and participating in attacks at Kabuye hill. He was sentenced to 11 years and was released in 2007.[740] BDJ gave evidence relevant to other allegations and the Chamber found his testimony to be credible (see III.2.6.2).

711. The Defence suggested that BDJ's testimony is not credible because it does not make sense that only two people were manning the roadblock and that BDJ would not be carrying a weapon.[741] BDJ explained, however, that the numbers manning the roadblock had been reduced because by that time the massacres had almost ended.[742] The Chamber also rejects the Defence contention that BDJ's status as a Tutsi pretending to be a Hutu makes it incredible that he was not carrying a weapon at the time.

712. The Defence also argues that it is unlikely that only two persons would have witnessed the event in light of BDJ's evidence that the place where the roadblock was located was well known and there was bar nearby that belonged to the *responsable*.[743] However, given that BDJ explained that Kalimanzira stayed inside his vehicle and that BDJ stood near the vehicle when Kalimanzira spoke to them,[744] the Chamber finds that it is not improbable that no one other than those present at the roadblock witnessed the incident.

713. The Defence also points out that since his companion at the roadblock, the *responsable*, is deceased, there is no corroboration for his testimony.[745] However, the Chamber notes that there is independent evidence on the record that the *responsable* has died.[746] In light of the foregoing, the Chamber finds BDJ to be a credible witness.

714. The Chamber finds the Defence's argument that the event is implausible should be rejected. There is abundant evidence from several witnesses that Kalimanzira accosted them for being unarmed. Further, Kalimanzira himself expressed concerns for his safety along that road.[747] This testimony seems consistent with the testimonies of other witnesses.

715. In light of the foregoing, the Chamber finds that the Prosecution has proven beyond reasonable doubt that Kalimanzira rebuked the two persons manning a roadblock in Kabuye for being unarmed. However, in light of the statement's ambiguity, which seemed individualized to the two recipients only, the Chamber is not satisfied that Kalimanzira's actions and words were sufficiently direct or public to constitute Direct and Public Incitement to Commit Genocide.

716. The Chamber recalls that BDJ testified that Kalimanzira told two people to carry weapons because unarmed persons had to be considered the enemy. The Chamber finds this statement ambiguous enough to create a reasonable doubt as to its intended meaning. One possible implication is that people should carry weapons as a defensive measure. It is not clear that Kalimanzira intended to incite the killing of Tutsi civilians in making such a **[page 148]** statement, nor that the two persons Kalimanzira rebuked understood

---

[739] T. 17 June 2008 pp. 52, 54 [closed] 55, 60 and T. 18 June 2008 pp. 5-6 [closed] (Witness BDJ).
[740] T. 17 June 2008 pp. 62-63 [closed] (Witness BDJ).
[741] Defence Closing Brief, paras. 391-394, 399-401.
[742] T. 17 June 2008, p. 52 (Witness BDJ).
[743] Defence Closing Brief, paras. 391-394.
[744] T. 17 June 2008 p. 55 (Witness BDJ).
[745] Defence Closing Brief, para. 396; T. 17 June 2008 p. 52 (Witness BDJ).
[746] T. 22 May 2008 pp. 10, 32 [closed] (Witness BXG); T. 17 June 2008 p. 54 [closed] (Witness BDJ).
[747] T. 10 February 2009 p. 45 (Callixte Kalimanzira).

it as such.[748] The Chamber therefore finds that the Prosecution has not proven beyond reasonable doubt that Kalimanzira committed Direct and Public Incitement to Commit Genocide at the Kabuye roadblock in May 1994.

4.9.5. Gisagara Marketplace

717. The Prosecution alleges that towards the end of May 1994, Kalimanzira attended a meeting at the Gisagara marketplace where he instructed the male attendees to carry weapons and gave money as a reward to one man for carrying a weapon. Kalimanzira also ordered the killing of Tutsi girls who had been forced into marriages with Hutu men. Following the meeting, members of the population killed young Tutsi girls in hiding and reverted to carrying weapons.[749]

718. The Defence denies this testimony in its entirety. In addition, Kalimanzira relies on his alibi (see III.1.2).

4.9.5.1. Evidence

Prosecution Witness BDK

719. BDK is a Tutsi woman who was married to a Hutu. Her husband's brother, who was an authority, was also married to a Tutsi woman. BDK testified that she attended a meeting at the Gisagara marketplace towards the end of May 1994. BDK was forced to attend the meeting by Fidèle Uwizeye who told her that public attendance was mandatory. BDK walked to the meeting with her neighbour Cecil, her husband, who walked in front, and carried her baby on her back. She recalled that the meeting was at 10:00 a.m. and that the authorities sat on chairs and faced the public, who sat on the ground. BDK estimated that there were just over one hundred people present.[750]

720. BDK testified that when she arrived, the *sous-préfet* had already finished speaking and Kalimanzira was addressing the crowd. She recalled that he was standing in the space between the authorities and the public and that he criticized the men for being unarmed. He said that they had short memories because they had forgotten that they had not completely defeated the enemy. BDK stated that the enemy was the Tutsi. She further recalled that Kalimanzira instructed the men to always carry a weapon and asked Johane Rondoni, who was armed with a club with spikes and iron bar from a wrecked car that he had named Kayitusha, to stand up. Kalimanzira proceeded to praise him and used him as an example of a "real man" for the rest of the crowd. Kalimanzira even gave him money so that he could buy a drink for himself.[751]

721. BDK testified that Kalimanzira then ordered that the young Tutsi girls who had been forced into marriages be killed because they could cause problems. However, he explicitly stated that those Tutsi woman who had married Hutu men before the war should be spared. BDK stated that she felt afraid when Kalimanzira said this and returned home with Cecil before the meeting had finished.[752] **[page 149]**

722. BDK testified that before the meeting there had been no attacks for a week; however, afterwards they resumed. BDK further stated that she learned of the victims and the places they were taken to and executed by the *Interahamwe* because she heard people discussing and boasting about it afterwards.[753] She named Maria Mukashema, Eugénia Kabatezi, Donatila Kazibaga, Mukagakwaya Rwamukwaya and Rehema Muriminyondo as some of the young girls who were killed.[754]

---

[748] *Nahimana et al.* Appeal Judgement, paras. 698-700, citing *Akayesu* Trial Judgement paras. 557-558.
[749] Prosecution Closing Brief, para. 285.
[750] T. 20 May 2008 pp. 54-56 (Witness BDK).
[751] T. 20 May 2008 pp. 55-56 (Witness BDK).
[752] T. 20 May 2008 pp. 57-58 (Witness BDK).
[753] T. 20 May 2008 pp. 58-59 (Witness BDK).
[754] T. 21 May 2008 p. 5 (Witness BDK).

4.9.5.2. Deliberations

723. At the relevant time alleged, Kalimanzira claims that he was working in Murambi (Gitarama *préfecture*). As discussed above, the Chamber disbelieves his alibi (see III.1.2.2).

724. The Defence contends that BDK's testimony was fraught with inconsistencies. It suggests that her descriptions of the timing of her departure from the meeting was inconsistent; that it was unlikely that her brother-in-law would have forced her, a Tutsi, to attend the meeting; that if she had been forced to attend, it was unlikely that she would leave and draw attention to herself, especially when she had been married before the war and was not among the group who was threatened.[755] None of the Defence's arguments were persuasive. The passage of time since 1994 would explain difficulty in recalling time exactly; further, BDK gave convincing explanations for her behaviour.

725. The Chamber finds that the fact that BDK left before the end of the meeting as a result of her fear does not undermine the truthfulness of her account, even though BDK only attended at the instruction of her brother-in-law. Further, BDK explained this seeming incongruity in cross-examination by clarifying that after hearing Kalimanzira she made her child cry so that she could leave in order to quiet her child, so as not to cause suspicion.[756]

726. With respect to when BDK left the meeting, she testified in examination-in-chief that she left upon hearing Kalimanzira's order to kill Tutsi girls.[757] In cross-examination, BDK testified that she slipped away when she heard Kalimanzira talking about Rundoni.[758] The Defence argues that, if true, BDK could not have heard Kalimanzira order the killing of Tutsi girls because BDK testified that Kalimanzira congratulated Rundoni for carrying a weapon before ordering the killing of Tutsi girls.[759] The Chamber finds that the Defence is taking this remark out of context; upon review of the question put to her and her full response, it is clear that there is no inconsistency in her evidence.

727. The Chamber notes that BDK has given evidence in relation to a meeting by a water tap where she alleges to have heard a conversation including Kalimanzira to discuss further killings at Kabuye hill (see III.2.4). Although the Chamber found that it could not rely on her evidence in that respect, the reasons underlying that conclusion do not apply to her evidence here, nor do they reflect upon BDK's general credibility. The Chamber found her to be a reliable and credible witness.

728. In light of the foregoing, the Chamber finds that the Prosecution has proven beyond a reasonable doubt that Kalimanzira attended a meeting at the Gisagara marketplace at the end **[page 150]** of May 1994. BDK's evidence, which the Chamber accepts, was that Kalimanzira criticized those in attendance for being unarmed and told them that they had not completely defeated the enemy. He rewarded a man for carrying a weapon. Kalimanzira went on to incite the crowd to kill young Tutsi girls who had been forced into marriages because they could cause problems.

729. BDK understood that Kalimanzira meant the Tutsi when he referred to the enemy. The Chamber finds that this also would have been the understanding of the crowd at the meeting. By telling the crowd that the enemy had not been completely defeated at that time, when the RPF was not near, and then ordering that Tutsi girls should be killed, Kalimanzira clearly indicated that Tutsi civilians were the enemy. This finding is supported by BDK's evidence that although there had been no attacks for a week before the meeting, they resumed afterwards and she named several people who were killed.[760] The Chamber finds that the only reasonable conclusion that can be drawn from this evidence is that Kalimanzira intended to incite the crowd to carry weapons in order to kill Tutsi civilians. Kalimanzira exhibited here, and elsewhere, an intent to destroy the Tutsi group (see III.5.2). Consequently, the Chamber finds Kalimanzira guilty beyond a reasonable doubt for committing Direct and Public Incitement to Commit Genocide at the Gisagara marketplace at the end of May 1994. **[page 151]**

---

[755] Defence Closing Brief, paras. 115-118, 126, 141.
[756] T. 21 May 2008 pp. 4-5 (Witness BDK).
[757] T. 20 May 2008 p. 58 (Witness BDK).
[758] T. 21 May 2008 pp. 4-5 (Witness BDK).
[759] T. 20 May 2008 p. 57 (Witness BDK).
[760] *Nahimana et al.* Appeal Judgement, para. 709, fn. 1674.

5. GENOCIDAL INTENT

5.1. Applicable Law

730. The Chamber recalls that an accused may not be convicted for the crime of Genocide unless it is established that he committed one of the acts listed in Article 2 (2) of the Statute with the specific intent to destroy, in whole or in part, a particular protected group ("genocidal intent") (see III.2.1). Genocidal intent is also an element of the crime of Direct and Public Incitement to Commit Genocide (see III.4.1). The notion "destruction of the group" means "the material destruction of a group either by physical or by biological means, not the destruction of the national, linguistic, religious, cultural or other identity of a particular group". There is no numeric threshold of victims necessary to establish genocide, and it is not necessary to prove that a perpetrator intended the complete annilihation of a protected group. However, in order to establish genocidal intent, it is necessary to prove that the perpetrator intended to destroy at least a substantial part thereof.[761]

731. Intent, by its nature, is not usually susceptible to direct proof. The jurisprudence therefore accepts that in the absence of direct evidence, a perpetrator's genocidal intent may be inferred from relevant facts and circumstances that can lead beyond reasonable doubt to the existence of the intent of the evidence, provided that it is the only reasonable inference that can be made from the totality of the evidence. In the light of the Tribunal's jurisprudence, genocidal intent may be inferred from certain facts or indicia, including but not limited to: (a) the general context of the perpetration of other culpable acts systematically directed against that same group, whether these acts were committed by the same offender or by others, (b) the scale of atrocities committed, (c) their general nature, (d) their execution in a region or a country, (e) the fact that the victims were deliberately and systematically chosen on account of their membership of a particular group, (f) the exclusion, in this regard, of members of other groups, (g) the political doctrine which gave rise to the acts referred to, (h) the repetition of destructive and discriminatory acts, and (i) the perpetration of acts which violate the very foundation of the group or considered as such by their perpetrators.[762]

5.2. Deliberations

732. In its factual findings above, the Chamber has found direct evidence of Kalimanzira's genocidal intent, as well as circumstancial evidence from which it could be inferred.

733. BXG gave direct evidence on Kalimanzira's conduct and utterances at the Mukabuga roadblock on 23 April 1994. That morning, Kalimanzira asked Callixte Bushakwe, the *responsable de cellule* and head of the group at the roadblock, where he was with the Tutsi problem. Bushakwe responded that they had all been killed, whereupon one of the men at the roadblock, Isidore, interjected and told Kalimanzira that Bushawke was lying and that the Tutsis had successfully defended themselves against attack. This enraged Kalimanzira, who spat at Bushakwe and attempted to slap him. Kalimanzira then asked Isidore show him where the Tutsis were, and they drove off in the direction of Dahwe *secteur*.[763] **[page 152]**

734. This evidence, combined with other credible evidence of Kalimanzira's behaviour the same day (see III.2.4.2), namely (1) his tacit approval of *sous-préfet* Ntawukulilyayo's expulsion of Tutsis from the Gisagara marketplace to Kabuye hill, and (2) his provision of armed reinforcements to assist in the killings at Kabuye hill, demonstrates that Kalimanzira knew and intended that the Tutsis at Kabuye hill would be killed. Kalimanzira saw how many thousands of Tutsi refugees had gathered on Kabuye hill, hoping to be protected, and knew that his actions would be a substantial factor in contributing to their killings. The fact that they were killed *en masse* shows that he intended to destroy the Tutsi group, in whole, or at least in substantial part.

---

[761] *Seromba* Trial Judgement, para. 319; *Semanza* Trial Judgement, para. 315-316.
[762] *Bagosora et al.* Trial Judgement, para. 2116; *Seromba* Appeal Judgement, para. 176, citing *Seromba* Trial Judgement, para. 320; *Nahimana et al.* Appeal Judgement, paras. 524-525; *Simba* Appeal Judgement, para. 264; *Gacumbitsi* Appeal Judgement, paras. 40-41; *Rutaganda* Appeal Judgement, para. 525; *Semanza* Appeal Judgement, para. 262, citing *Jelisić* Appeal Judgement, para. 47; *Kayishema and Ruzindana* Appeal Judgement, paras. 147-148.
[763] T. 22 May 2008 pp. 9-12, 19-20, 22 (Witness BXG).

735. BCN and BCK also gave direct evidence that in mid- to late April 1994, Kalimanzira handed a rifle to one of the persons manning the Jaguar roadblock and instructed everyone present that the gun was to be used to kill Tutsis (see III.4.3). He further instructed them to keep checking identity cards in order to prevent Tutsis from passing through. He referred to both the *Inkotanyi-Inyenzi,* as well as any other possible enemies trying to pass through.[764] By instructing those at the Jaguar roadblock not to distinguish between combatants or civilians, he exhibited his intent to destroy the Tutsi group, as such.

736. BBB recounted a similar incident at the Kajyanama roadblock where Kalimanzira became irate upon seeing an unarmed man, assaulting and abducting him, in order to emphasize the need for those manning the roadblock to carry arms at all times in order to defend themselves against "the enemy", which was understood to mean the Tutsi (see III.4.4). While such an instruction in a time of war is not *per se* illegitimate (see *e.g.* III.2.8.2), in this case, as in the incident at Jaguar roadblock, the instruction was to target Tutsi civilians and combatants alike.

737. BCZ testified that at a public rally at the Nyabisagara football field in late May or early June, Kalimanzira thanked the audience for their efforts at eliminating the enemy and warned them not to become complacent because there were still enemies hiding in the bush and in houses (see III.4.5). BCZ explained that by then, "enemy" meant just about any Tutsi. Kalimanzira also requested the audience to destroy all remaining Tutsi houses and plant banana trees and other crops over the ruins. By expressing his approval for the Tutsi massacres and instructing the crowd to erase traces of the dead Tutsis' homes and lives, Kalimanzira exhibited his intent to destroy the existence of the Tutsi group.

738. These instances do not exhaust the occasions on which Kalimanzira exhibited an intent to destroy the Tutsi group. They merely reflect the clearest evidence of his mental state. In light of the above, and having considered the totality of the evidence, the Chamber finds that Kalimanzira held the requisite specific intent characterizing the crime of Genocide, which is the intent to destroy, in whole or in part, the Tutsi group, as such. **[page 153]**

CHAPTER IV – VERDICT

739. For the reasons set out in this Judgement, having considered all evidence and arguments, the Chamber unanimously finds Callixte Kalimanzira

Count 1:   GUILTY of Genocide

Count 2:   DISMISSED (Complicity in Genocide)

Count 3:   GUILTY of Direct and Public Incitement to Commit Genocide **[page 154]**

CHAPTER V – SENTENCE

1. INTRODUCTION

740. Having found Kalimanzira guilty of Genocide and Direct and Public Incitement to Commit Genocide, the Chamber must determine the appropriate sentence.

741. The relevant provisions on sentencing are Articles 22 and 23 of the Statute and Rules 99 to 106 of the Rules. A person convicted by the Tribunal may be sentenced to imprisonment for a fixed term or for the remainder of his life.[765] The penalty imposed should reflect the goals of retribution, deterrence, rehabilitation, and the protection of society. Pursuant to Article 23 of the Statute and Rule 101 of the Rules, the Chamber shall consider the general practice regarding prison sentences in Rwanda, the gravity of the offences or totality of the conduct, the individual circumstances of the accused, including aggravating and mitigating circumstances, and the extent to which any penalty imposed by a court of any State on the accused for the

---

[764] T. 25 June 2008 pp. 5, 20-24 (Witness BCN); T. 26 June 2008 pp. 6-9, 14-15 (Witness BCK).
[765] Rule 101 (A) of the Rules.

same act has already been served.[766] These considerations are not exhaustive. Trial Chambers are vested with a broad discretion in determining an appropriate sentence, due to their obligation to individualize the penalties to fit the circumstances of the convicted person and the gravity of the crime.[767] The Chamber shall credit the accused for any time spent in detention pending transfer to the Tribunal and during trial.[768]

742. In determining an appropriate sentence, the Appeals Chamber has stated that "sentences of like individuals in like cases should be comparable". However, it has also noted the inherent limits to this approach because "any given case contains a multitude of variables, ranging from the number and type of crimes committed to the personal circumstances of the individual".[769]

2. DETERMINATION OF THE SENTENCE

743. The Prosecution submits that the maximum sentence of imprisonment for the remainder of his life is warranted in Kalimanzira's case.[770] The Defence did not make any sentencing submissions, maintaining that Kalimanzira should be acquitted on every count.[771]

2.1. Gravity of the Offences

744. All crimes under the Statute are serious violations of international humanitarian law.[772] The Chamber has considered that under Rwandan law, genocide carries the possible penalty of life imprisonment, depending on the nature of the accused's participation.[773] In the Tribunal's jurisprudence, principal perpetration generally warrants a higher sentence than [page 155] aiding and abetting.[774] However, this alone does not mean that a life sentence is the only appropriate sentence for a principal perpetrator of genocide.[775] At this Tribunal, a sentence of life imprisonment is generally reserved those who planned or ordered atrocities and those who participate in the crimes with particular zeal or sadism.[776] Offenders receiving the most severe sentences tend to be senior authorities.[777] The Chamber has also considered the sentences handed down for convictions of Direct and Public Incitement to Commit Genocide only, which have ranged from 12 years to life imprisonment.[778]

---

[766] Article 23 (1)-(3) of the Statute and Rule 101 (B)(i)-(iv) of the Rules.
[767] *Nahimana et al.* Appeal Judgement, paras. 1037, 1046; *Seromba* Appeal Judgement, para. 228; *Ndindabahizi* Appeal Judgement, para. 132, referring to *Semanza* Appeal Judgement, para. 312.
[768] *Kajelijeli* Appeal Judgement, para. 290. See Rule 101 (C) of the Rules.
[769] *Kvočka et al.* Appeal Judgment, para. 681.
[770] Prosecution Closing Brief, para. 322; T. 20 April 2009 pp. 22-23 (Closing Arguments).
[771] Defence Closing Brief, p. 248.
[772] *Kayishema and Ruzindana* Appeal Judgement, para. 367 (quoting Article 1 of the Statute).
[773] Rwandan Organic Law No. 8/96, on the Organization of Prosecutions for Offences constituting Genocide or Crimes Against Humanity committed since 1 October 1990, published in the Gazette of the Republic of Rwanda, 35th year. No. 17, 1 September 1996, as amended by Organic Law No.66/2008 of 21/11/2008 Modifying and Complementing Organic Law No. 31/2007 of 25/07/2007 Relating to the Abolition of the Death Penalty.
[774] *Semanza* Appeal Judgement, para. 388.
[775] *Ntakirutimana* Trial Judgement, paras. 791-793, 832-834, 908-909, 924 (imposing 25 years' imprisonment for personal participation).
[776] *Musema* Appeal Judgement, para. 383 (noting that the leaders and planners of a particular conflict should bear heavier responsibility, with the qualification that the gravity of the offence is the primary consideration in imposing a sentence); *Nchamihigo* Trial Judgement, para. 395 (deputy prosecutor, the Chamber noting that he exhibited extreme zeal in killing); *Niyitegeka* Trial Judgement, para. 486; *Muhimana* Trial Judgement, paras. 604-616 (*conseiller*, but recounting the particularly atrocious manner in which the accused personally raped, killed, mutilated, and humiliated his victims).
[777] Life sentences have been imposed against senior government authorities in: *Ndindabahazi* Trial Judgement, paras. 505, 508, 511 (Minister of Finance); *Niyitegeka* Trial Judgement, paras. 499, 502 (Minister of Information); *Kambanda* Trial Judgement, paras. 44, 61-62 (Prime Minister); *Kamuhanda* Trial Judgement, paras. 6, 764, 770 (Minister of Higher Education and Scientific Research). In addition, life sentences have been imposed on lower level officials, as well as those who did not hold government positions. See *e.g.*, *Nchamihigo* Trial Judgement, paras. 395-396 (deputy prosecutor in Cyangugu *préfecture*); *Musema* Trial Judgement, paras. 999-1008 (influential director of a tea factory who exercised control over killers); *Rutaganda* Trial Judgement, paras. 466-473 (second vice-president of *Interahamwe* at national level).
[778] *Akayesu* Trial Judgement (life sentence); *Kajelijeli* Trial Judgement (15 year sentence); *Ruggiu* Trial Judgement (12-year sentence); *Bikindi* Trial Judgement (15-year sentence).

745. The Chamber has found Kalimanzira guilty of aiding and abetting the crime of Genocide at the inauguration of Élie Ndayambaje (see III.2.3.6.2) and at Kabuye hill (see III.2.4.2). In addition, the Chamber has found Kalimanzira guilty of aiding and abetting, as well as instigating, the crime of Genocide at a roadblock on the Butare-Gisagara road (see III.2.7.4.2). Kalimanzira indirectly perpetrated these crimes. The Chamber has also found Kalimanzira guilty of committing the crime of Direct and Public Incitement to Commit Genocide at the Jaguar roadblock (see III.4.3.2), the Kajyanama roadblock (see III.4.4.2), the Nyabisagara football field (see III.4.5.2), and the Gisagara marketplace (see III.4.9.5.2). Kalimanzira was the principal perpetrator of these crimes.

746. The Chamber takes due notice of the intrinsic gravity of Kalimanzira's crimes. Genocide is, by definition, a crime of the most serious gravity which affects the very foundations of society and shocks the conscience of humanity. Directly and publicly inciting others to commit that crime is, in the Chamber's opinion, of similar gravity. The harm that justifies the criminalization of direct and public incitement is in the special dangerousness associated with inciting an unspecified and indeterminate group of people to commit a crime so heinous as genocide, which risks creating an overall atmosphere conducive to violence and criminal activity capable of reaching uncontrollable proportions.

747. The Chamber also notes that the charges for which Kaliminzira is convicted relate to crimes committed in his own *préfecture* and not crimes committed at the national level. Moreover, although he was the *Directeur de Cabinet* of the Ministry of the Interior and this lent him the credibility and influence required for some of his criminal acts, the crimes for which he is convicted are essentially unrelated to his official duties and powers at the national level. **[page 156]**

2.2. Individual Circumstances

748. The Chamber has wide discretion in determining what constitutes mitigating and aggravating circumstances and the weight to be accorded thereto. While aggravating circumstances need to be proven beyond reasonable doubt, mitigating circumstances need only be established on a "balance of probabilities".[779] Proof of mitigating circumstances does not automatically entitle the accused to a "credit" in the determination of the sentence; it simply requires the Trial Chamber to consider such mitigating circumstances in its final determination.[780]

2.2.1. Aggravating Circumstances

749. The Prosecution submits that the aggravating circumstances in this case include Kalimanzira's abuse of his position of influence and authority, his personal commitment in the execution of genocide in breach of the public's trust, and his role as a leader and principal perpetrator in the commission of his crimes.[781] The Defence made no submissions on aggravating circumstances.

750. The Chamber notes Kalimanzira's prominence and high standing in Butare society as a former *sous-préfet* and the fact that he was one of only three people from his area and of his generation to have received a university education. He was loved and appreciated for his efforts at empowering his community by contributing to the agricultural development of his native region. The influence he derived from this and his important status within the Ministry of the Interior made it likely that others would follow his example, which is an aggravating factor. Most significantly, by encouraging Tutsi refugees to gather at Kabuye hill where he knew they would be killed in the thousands, he abused the public's trust that he, like other officials, would protect them.

751. However, the Chamber considers that Kalimanzira's actions did not evidence any particular zeal or sadism. He did not personally kill anyone and only remained at the sites for a brief period. The Chamber has already taken into consideration Kalimanzira's forms of participation in assessing the gravity of his offences.

---

[779] *Simba* Appeal Judgement, para. 328; *Nahimana et al.* Appeal Judgement, para. 1038.
[780] *Niyitegeka* Appeal Judgement, para. 267.
[781] Prosecution Closing Brief, paras. 325 and 331; T. 20 April 2009 pp. 23-25 (Closing Arguments).

2.2.2. Mitigating Circumstances

752. In the absence of any further submissions on the matter, the Chamber finds there are few other mitigating circumstances. Kalimanzira is 55 years old. His wife testified to his character as a good and loving husband and father. For much of his life prior to the genocide, Kalimanzira was engaged in the public service of his country. After going into exile, he never went into hiding, living his life openly and working for a non-governmental organization to lend assistance to refugees. The Defence tried to show that Kalimanzira never harboured any anti-Tutsi sentiment before the genocide, but such evidence can in no way exonerate Kalimanzira for his crimes. Kalimanzira's good character prior and subsequent to the conflict offer little in the way of mitigation.

753. The Prosecution submits that there are no mitigating circumstances, and that the evidence does not support that Kalimanzira voluntarily surrendered to the Tribunal.[782] The combined testimonies of Kalimanzira and his wife show that when ICTR investigators came **[page 157]** looking for him in Nairobi, he did not try to escape and honoured several appointments with them over several days, and then willingly surrendered himself to be taken to Arusha, where he remains in detention to this day.[783] The Chamber finds that the evidence does support the conclusion that Kalimanzira voluntarily surrendered to the Tribunal, and considers this to be a mitigating circumstance.

2.3. Credit for Time Served

754. On 8 November 2005, Kalimanzira surrendered in Nairobi, Kenya, to Tribunal officials, and arrived at the United Nations Detention Facility in Arusha the same day. He has been in physical custody ever since. Pursuant to Rule 101 (C) of the Rules, Kalimanzira is therefore entitled to credit for time served as of 8 November 2005. The Chamber calculates this as amounting to three years, seven months, and 14 days. **[page 158]**

3. CONCLUSION

755. The Chamber has the discretion to impose a single sentence. This practice is usually appropriate where the offences may be characterised as belonging to a single criminal transaction. It is also appropriate for a single sentence to be imposed for all convictions, if the Chamber so decides, where the crimes ascribed to an accused, regardless of their characterisation, form part of a single set of crimes committed in a given geographic region during a specific time period.[784]

756. Considering all the relevant circumstances above, the Chamber **SENTENCES** Callixte Kalimanzira to

THIRTY (30) YEARS' IMPRISONMENT

757. This sentence shall be enforced immediately and, pursuant to Rule 101 (C) of the Rules, Kalimanzira shall receive credit for the time served, which the Chamber has calculated as three years, seven months, and 14 days.

758. The above sentence shall be served in a State designated by the President of the Tribunal, in consultation with the Chamber. The Government of Rwanda and the designated State shall be notified of such designation by the Registrar.

759. Until his transfer to his designated place of imprisonment, Callixte Kalimanzira shall be kept in detention under the present conditions.

---

[782] Prosecution Closing Brief, para. 325; T. 20 April 2009 p. 25 (Closing Arguments).
[783] T. 5 February 2009 pp. 13-14 (Salomé Mukantwali); T. 10 February 2009 pp. 59 and 61 (Callixte Kalimanzira).
[784] *Nahimana et al.* Appeal Judgement, paras. 1042-1043; *Simba* Trial Judgement, para. 445; *Ndindabahizi* Trial Judgement, para. 497; *Kambanda* Appeal Judgement, para. 111.

760. Pursuant to Rule 102 (B) of the Rules, on notice of appeal, if any, enforcement of the above sentences shall be stayed until a decision has been rendered on the appeal, with the convicted person nevertheless remaining in detention.

Arusha, 22 June 2009, done in English.

Dennis C. M. Byron	Gberdao Gustave Kam	Vagn Joensen
Presiding Judge	Judge	Judge

[Seal of the Tribunal] **[page 159]**

ANNEX I – PROCEDURAL HISTORY

761. Callixte Kalimanzira was arrested in Nairobi on 8 November 2005 after he voluntarily surrendered. The trial commenced on the 5 May 2008 and closed on 13 February 2009. Over the course of sixteen trial days, the Prosecution called twenty-three witnesses. The Defence case opened on 17 November 2008. During twenty-one trial days, the Defence called forty-two witnesses, including the Accused.

1. PRE-TRIAL PHASE

762. Callixte Kalimanzira was arrested in Nairobi, Kenya, on 8 November 2005, after surrendering to ICTR authorities, pursuant to an arrest warrant and order for transfer and detention issued by Judge Sergei Alekseevich Egorov on 1 September 2005.[785] The initial indictment, as confirmed by Judge Egorov on 22 July 2005,[786] charged Kalimanzira with three counts: (1) Genocide, (2) or, in the alternative, Complicity in Genocide, and (3) Direct and Public Incitement to Commit Genocide.[787] Kalimanzira was remanded in the custody of officials of the Tribunal and arrived at the detention unit in Arusha on the same day as his arrest. On 14 November 2005, he made his initial appearance, pleading not guilty to all three counts of the indictment.

763. On 29 September 2006, the Registrar withdrew the appointment of Pierre Shillewaert as lead Defence counsel and requested that the accused provide the names of three alternatives.[788]

764. On 5 June 2007, the Pre-Trial Chamber denied a Defence request for provisional release.[789]

765. An informal status conference was held on 11 July 2007 to discuss the progress of the case. It was decided that the trial would commence around 15 January 2008, depending on courtroom availability. It was

---

[785] Warrant of Arrest and Order for Transfer and Detention of Callixte Kalimanzira (Judge Egorov), 1 September 2005.
[786] Decision on Confirmation of an Indictment Against Callixte Kalimanzira (Judge Egorov), 22 July 2005.
[787] The Indictment Against Callixte Kalimanzira, Office of the Prosecutor, 21 July 2005.
[788] Decision to Withdraw the Assignment of Mr Pierre Schillewaert as Lead Counsel for Callixte Kalimanzira (The Registrar), 29 September 2006.
[789] Decision on Defence Request for Provisional Release (TC), 5 June 2007.

later decided, at a status conference on 29 October 2007, that the trial would commence around 15 March 2008.

766. On 8 November 2007, protective measures were ordered for ten Prosecution witnesses.[790] On 13 December 2007, a status conference was held during which the Defence requested a postponement of trial. Protective measures were ordered for nine Defence witnesses on 14 December 2007.[791]

767. On 22 February 2008, the Chamber granted a Prosecution motion requesting that judicial notice be taken of several facts of common knowledge about the situation in Rwanda between 6 April 1994 and 17 July 1994.[792]

768. On 19 March 2008, the President scheduled the trial to start on 28 April 2008.[793] **[page 160]**

769. On 4 April 2008, the Chamber ordered the transfer of Prosecution witnesses AZM, AZT, BBB, BCA, BCI, BCK, BCN, BDI, BDL, BXC, BXD, BXL and FAC be transferred to the United Nations Detention Facility in Arusha.[794]

770. On 8 April 2008, the United Nations Secretary General appointed the *ad litem* Judges Arrey and Park to the case. Judge Weinberg de Roca was assigned as Presiding Judge on 10 April 2008.[795] However, on 29 April 2008, in light of new circumstances which had arisen affecting the commencement of trial and making it necessary to change the composition of the bench, the President assigned himself as Presiding Judge in the case.[796]

771. On 30 April 2008, a status conference was held at which the Chamber orally granted in part a Defence motion to postpone the commencement of the trial after finding that the Prosecution had not complied with its disclosure obligations as ordered in the Chamber decision of 8 November 2007. The trial was scheduled to commence on 5 May 2008.[797]

772. On 2 May 2008, the Office of the President issued an order assigning *ad litem* Judges Vagn Joensen and Gberdao Gustave Kam to Trial Chamber III and confirming the commencement of trial on 5 May 2008.[798]

2. THE PROSECUTION CASE

773. The trial commenced on 5 May 2008. The prosecution conducted its case over two trial sessions: from 5 May 2008 to 22 May 2008 and 16 June 2008 to 26 June 2008. Over the course of sixteen trial days, the Prosecution called 24 witnesses and tendered 82 exhibits.

774. On 16 June 2008, the Chamber granted a Prosecution motion to extend its transfer order dated 4 April 2008 and ordered that detained Prosecution witnesses AZM, AZT, BBB, BCA, BCI, BCK, BDI, BDL, BXC, BXL and FAC transfer to the United Nations Detention Facility be extended until 18 July 2008 at the latest.[799]

775. On 24 June 2008, the Chamber granted in part a Defence motion to exclude Prosecution witnesses BWM, BWN, BXB, BXC, BXD AND BXL from testifying about the killings of a person named Rwigimba and his family, and of a person named Mazimpaka.[800]

---

[790] Decision on Prosecution Motion for Protective Measures (TC), 8 November 2007.
[791] Decision on Defence Motion for Protective Measures (TC), 14 December 2007.
[792] Decision on Judicial Notice of Facts of Common Knowledge (TC), 22 February 2008.
[793] Scheduling Order Regarding the Commencement of the Trial (President), 19 March 2008.
[794] Decision on Transfer of Detained Witnesses (TC), 4 April 2008.
[795] Order Assigning a Bench for the Trial (TC), 10 April 2008.
[796] Order Reassigning the Case (The President), 29 April 2008.
[797] Oral Decision on a Defence motion for Violation of the Disclosure Obligation as Established in the Protective Order and for Postponement of the Commencement of the Trial (TC), 30 April 2008.
[798] Order Assigning *ad litem* Juges to the Case (TC), 2 May 2008.
[799] Decision on a Prosecution motion for the Extension of the Trial Chamber's "Decision on Transfer of Detained Witnesses" of 4 April 2008 (TC), 16 June 2008.
[800] Decision on Defence Motion to Exclude Prosecution Witnesses BWM, BWN, BXB, BXC, BXD and BWL (TC), 24 June 2008.

776. On 30 June 2008, at a status conference, the Chamber issued a provisional oral decision ordering that the Defence case should commence at the end of October 2008 and continue for approximately five weeks.

777. The Prosecution rested their case and the Defence submitted a motion proposing that their case commence on the 17 November 2008 at a status conference on 30 June 2008. **[page 161]**

778. On 7 July 2008, Judge Joensen issued an interim order requiring that the Defence show cause and proof that it submitted its response to the Prosecution motion for admission of certain materials in due form on 20 June 2008 by 8 July 2008.[801]

779. On 8 July 2008, the Chamber issued a scheduling order granting a Defence request to postpone the start date of the presentation of their case until 17 November 2008. The Chamber ordered that the Defence file its Rule 98*bis* submissions no later than seven days after the Chamber decided two pending Prosecution motions. The Chamber ordered that the Defence file its Rule 73*ter* submissions by 17 September 2008 and its expected order of appearance of the witnesses by 17 October 2008.[802]

780. On 10 July 2008, the Chamber granted a Prosecution motion to admit 45 documents and their translations into evidence, pursuant to Rule 89 (C), after finding that the Defence did not make a satisfactory showing that their Response was filed with the Court Management Section prior to the extended deadline of 30 June 2008.[803]

781. On 11 July 2008, the Chamber issued a confidential decision granting a Prosecution motion to admit materials under Rules 92*bis* and 89 (C) in part and ruling that the statement of deceased witness BDA could not be admitted but that a cover letter forwarding the details of a meeting held in June 1994 could be.[804]

782. On 13 August 2008, the Chamber issued a corrigendum to the scheduling order previously issued on 8 July 2008. A drafting error was rectified and rendering a Defence motion for reconsideration of the scheduling order was thereby rendered moot.[805]

783. On 25 August 2008, the Chamber issued a *proprio motu* order seeking submissions from the Parties on whether there was sufficient evidence upon which the Chamber could rely in support of certain allegations, and what legal consequences should follow from any conclusion that may be reached. The Prosecution and Defence were ordered to make their submissions by 29 August 2008 and 1 September 2008, respectively.[806]

784. On 26 August 2008, the Chamber denied a Defence motion for certification to appeal the Chamber Decision of 10 July 2008 because they did not fulfill the requirements of Rule 73(B) and ordered that a Defence motion be re-filed as a public document.[807]

785. On 3 September 2008, the Chamber ruled that the Defence has no case to answer in respect of certain allegations not pleaded in the indictment. This therefore rendered a Defence motion of 30 June 2008 which sought certification to appeal the Chamber decision of 24 June 2008 moot.[808]

786. On 4 September 2008, the Chamber rendered a Defence request for authorisation to visit the United Nations Detention Facility during the weekend moot because the Defence **[page 162]** had also requested and received permission from the United Nations Detention Facility Commanding Officer.[809]

---

[801] Interim Order (TC), 7 July 2008.
[802] Scheduling Order and Corrigendum, 8 July 2008.
[803] Decision on Prosecution Motion for Admission of Certain Materials – Rule 89(C) of the Rules of Procedure and Evidence (TC), 10 July 2008.
[804] Decision on Prosecution Motion for Admission of Documents under Rules 92*bis*(C) and 89(C) (TC), 11 July 2008 (confidential).
[805] Corrigendum to Scheduling Order (TC), 13 August 2008.
[806] Interim Order (TC), 25 August 2008.
[807] Decision on Defence Motion for Certification to Appeal Chamber's Decision on Prosecution Motion for Admission of Certain Materials (TC), 26 August 2008.
[808] Decision of No Case to Answer (TC), 3 September 2008.
[809] Decision on Defence Motion Requesting Authorisation to Visit Callixte Kalimanzira at the United Nations Detention Facility on Saturday the 13th and Sunday the 14th September 2008 (TC), 4 September 2008.

787. On 1 October 2008, the Trial Chamber issued a consolidated decision denying a Prosecution motion to reduce the number of Defence witnesses to testify and granting a Defence motion to add Callixte Kalimanzira to the Defence witness list.[810]

788. On 13 November 2008, the Trial Chamber issued a consolidated decision granting a Defence motion to vary its witness list and ordering them to reduce the number of hours of examination-in-chief anticipated for each Defence witness in the order of appearance to permit the Defence case to be presented in 20 trial days. The decision also granted, in part, a Prosecution motion seeking relief for the failure of the Defence to fully and properly disclose witness statements, identifying information, sequencing and notice of alibi in due time. The Chamber ordered that the Defence correct all existing deficiencies in disclosures and provide sufficiently detailed and complete personal information for each listed Defence witness and, where available, unredacted Defence witness statements by 14 November 2008. [811]

3. THE DEFENCE CASE

789. The Defence case opened on 17 November 2008 and was conducted during two trial sessions: from 17 November 2008 to 4 December 2008 and from 26 January 2009 to 11 February 2009. During 21 trial days, the Defence called 42 witnesses, including Kalimanzira. The Defence tendered 117 documents.

790. On 16 January 2009, the Chamber denied a Prosecution oral motion seeking to exclude Defence witnesses CA1, FJS, AK11, FCS, FG1, FG3, FVC, BB06, BB08 and MZ20. The Chamber granted the motion in respect of witness FG2, excluding him from the Defence witness list and declared that, in respect of witness FAG, the motion was moot. The Chamber also declared a Defence motion to vary its witness list by adding witnesses moot in respect of witnesses MDS and RTE and granted in respect of witnesses FAR, FAT, MVE and MVT.[812]

791. On 19 January 2009, the Chamber granted a Defence motion to lift the protective measures for witnesses ABY, ABZ, AU106, AK14 and MZ16.[813]

792. On 27 January 2009, the Chamber deemed a Defence motion for the transfer of witness AX55 as moot, due to the Defence's statement that it would no longer call the witness.[814] On the same day, the Chamber granted a Defence motion to terminate the protective measures for witnesses AB19 and AK01.[815] **[page 163]**

793. On 13 February 2009, the Defence closed its case at a status conference. The Chamber also gave an oral decision granting a Defence motion to admit transcripts into evidence under Rule 92 (D) and rejecting a Defence motion filed on 9 February 2009 to exclude evidence or recall witnesses.

794. On 2 March 2009, the Chamber granted, in part, a Defence motion for admission of materials under Rule 89 (C).[816]

795. On 3 March 2009, the Chamber granted a Prosecution motion to admit English versions of transcript evidence previously admitted on 13 February 2009.[817] On the same day, the Chamber issued a scheduling order instructing the Parties to file their respective closing briefs by 2 April 2009, deciding that the oral presentation of closing arguments shall take place on 17 April 2009 and granting each party a maximum of

---

[810] Consolidated Decision on Prosecution Motion to Reduce the Number of Defence Witnesses to Testify and on Defence Motion to Add Callixte Kalimanzira to the Defence Witness List (TC), 1 October 2008.
[811] Consolidated Decision on Prosecution Motion Concerning Defence Compliance with Rule 73*ter* and Defence Motions to Vary Witness List (TC), 13 November 2008.
[812] Consolidated Decision on Prosecution Oral Motion to Reduce Defence Witness List and Defence Motion to Vary Witness List (TC), 16 January 2009.
[813] Decision on the Defence Request to Lift the Protective Measures for Witnesses ABY, ABZ, AU106, AK14 and MZ16 (TC), 19 January 2009.
[814] Decision on the "*Requête de la Défense aux fins de Transfert du Témoin AX55*" (TC), 27 January 2009.
[815] Decision on the "*Requête de la Défense aux fins de Mainlevée des Mesures de Protection des Témoins AB19 et AK01*" (TC), 27 January 2009.
[816] Decision on Defence Motion for Admission of Certain Materials (TC), 2 March 2009; see also Corrigendum – Decision on Defence Motion for Admission of Certain Materials filed 2 March 2009 (TC), 24 March 2009.
[817] Decision on Prosecution Motion to Admit English Versions of Transcript Evidence Admitted on 13 February 2009 (TC), 3 March 2009.

90 minutes to present their oral arguments, with an additional 30 minutes of reply.[818] The oral presentation of closing arguments was subsequently rescheduled, by email, to take place on 20 April 2009.

796. On 24 March 2009, the Chamber issued a Corrigendum to a Decision on Defence Motion for Admission of Certain Materials Filed 2 March 2009, finding two additional documents inadmissible.[819]

797. On 20 May 2009, the Chamber issued an Order scheduling the public delivery of the judgement for 16 June 2009;[820] however, on 25 May 2009, the Chamber issued a Corrigendum to that Order and amended the date of public delivery of the judgement to 22 June 2009.[821]

[page 1] ANNEX II – CITED MATERIALS AND DEFINED TERMS

1. JURISPRUDENCE

1.1. International Criminal Tribunal for Rwanda

Akayesu

The Prosecutor v. Jean-Paul Akayesu, Case No. ICTR-96-4-T, Judgement (TC), 2 September 1998 (*"Akayesu* Trial Judgement")

Bagosora et al.

The Prosecutor v. Bagosora et al., Case No. ICTR-98-41-AR73, Decision on Aloys Ntabakuze's Interlocutory Appeal on Questions of Law Raised by the 29 June 2006 Trial Chamber I Decision on Motion for Exclusion of Evidence (AC), 18 September 2006 (*"Bagosora et al.* Interlocutory Appeal Decision")

The Prosecutor v. Bagosora et al., Case No. ICTR-98-41-T, Judgement and Sentence (TC), 18 December 2008 (*"Bagosora et al.* Trial Judgement")

Bikindi

The Prosecutor v. Bikindi, ICTR-01-72-T, Judgement (TC), 2 December 2008 (*"Bikindi* Trial Judgement")

Cyangugu

The Prosecutor v. Bagambiki et al, Case No. ICTR-99-46-A, Judgement (AC), 7 July 2006 (*"Cyangugu* Appeal Judgement")

Gacumbitsi

The Prosecutor v. Sylvestre Gacumbitsi, Case No. ICTR-01-64-T, Judgement (TC), 16 June 2004 (*"Gacumbitsi* Trial Judgement")

Sylvestre Gacumbitsi v. The Prosecutor, Case No. ICTR-01-64-A, Judgement (AC), 7 July 2006 (*"Gacumbitsi* Appeal Judgement")

Kajelijeli

The Prosecutor v. Juvénal Kajelijeli, Case No. ICTR-98-44A-T, Judgement (TC), 1 December 2003 (*"Kajelijeli* Trial Judgement")

Juvénal Kajelijeli v. The Prosecutor, Case No. ICTR-98-44A-A, Judgement (AC), 23 May 2005 (*"Kajelijeli* Appeal Judgement")

---

[818] Scheduling Order (TC), 3 March 2009.
[819] Corrigendum – Decision on Defence Motion for Admission of Certain Materials Filed 2 March 2009 (TC), 24 March 2009.
[820] Scheduling Order (TC), 20 May 2009.
[821] Corrigendum to Scheduling Order (TC), 25 May 2009.

Kamuhanda

Jean De Dieu Kamuhanda v. The Prosecutor, Case No. ICTR-99-54A-A, Judgement (AC), 19 September 2005 ("*Kamuhanda* Appeal Judgement")

Karera [page 2]

François Karera v. The Prosecutor, Case No. ICTR-01-74-A, Judgement (AC), 2 February 2009 ("*Karera* Appeal Judgment")

Kayishema and Ruzindana

The Prosecutor v. Clément Kayishema and Obed Ruzindana, Case No. ICTR-95-1-T, Judgement (TC), 21 May 1999 ("*Kayishema and Ruzindana* Trial Judgement")

The Prosecutor v. Clément Kayishema and Obed Ruzindana, Case No. ICTR-95-1-A, Judgement (AC), 1 June 2001 ("*Kayishema and Ruzindana* Appeal Judgement")

Muhimana

The Prosecutor v. Mikaeli Muhimana, Case No. ICTR-95-1B-T (TC), Judgement and Sentence, 28 April 2005 ("*Muhimana* Trial Judgement")

Mikaeli Muhimana v. The Prosecutor, Case No. ICTR-95-1B-A, Judgement (AC), 21 May 2007 ("*Muhimana* Appeal Judgement")

Musema

The Prosecutor v. Alfred Musema, Case No. ICTR-96-13-T, Judgement and Sentence (TC), 27 January 2000 ("*Musema* Trial Judgement")

The Prosecutor v. Alfred Musema, Case No. ICTR-96-13-A, Judgement (AC), 16 November 2001 ("*Musema* Appeal Judgement")

Muvunyi

The Prosecutor v. Tharcisse Muvunyi, Case No. ICTR-00-55A-AR73, Decision on Prosecution Interlocutory Appeal Against Trial Chamber II Decision of 23 February 2005 (AC), 12 May 2005 ("*Muvunyi* Interlocutory Appeal Decision")

The Prosecutor v. Tharcisse Muvunyi, Case No. ICTR-00-55A-T, Judgement (TC), 12 September 2006 ("*Muvunyi* Trial Judgement")

Tharcisse Muvunyi v. The Prosecutor, Case No. ICTR-00-55A-A, Judgement (AC), 29 August 2008 ("*Muvunyi* Appeal Judgement")

Nahimana et. al.

Ferdinand Nahimana et al. v. The Prosecutor, Case No. ICTR-99-52-A, Judgement (AC), 28 November 2007 ("*Nahimana et al.* Appeal Judgement")

Nchamihigo

The Prosecutor v. Nchamihigo, Case No. ICTR-01-63-I, Judgement (TC), 12 November 2008 ("*Nchamihigo* Trial Judgment")

Ndindabahizi

Emmanuel Ndindabahizi v. The Prosecutor, Case No. ICTR-01-71-A, Judgement (AC), 16 January 2007 ("*Ndindabahizi* Appeal Judgement")

Niyitegeka [page 3]

Eliézer Niyitegeka v. The Prosecutor, Case No. ICTR-96-14-A, Judgement (AC), 9 July 2004 ("*Niyitegeka* Appeal Judgement")

Ntagerura et al.

The Prosecutor v. André Ntagerura et al., Case No. ICTR-99-46-A, Judgement (AC), 7 July 2006 (*"Ntagerura et al.* Appeal Judgement")

Ntakirutimana

The Prosecutor v. Elizaphan Ntakirutmana and Gérard Ntakirutimana, Case No. ICTR-96-10-A and ICTR-96-17-A, Judgement (AC), 13 December 2004 (*"Ntakirutimana* Appeal Judgement")

Rukundo

The Prosecutor v. Rukundo, Case No. ICTR-01-70-T, Judgement (TC), 27 February 2009 (*"Rukundo* Trial Judgement")

Rutaganda

The Prosecutor v. Rutaganda, Case No. ICTR-96-3-A, Judgement (AC), 26 May 2003 (*"Rutaganda* Appeal Judgement")

Semanza

The Prosecutor v. Laurent Semanza, Case No. ICTR-97-20-T, Judgement (TC), 15 May 2003 (*"Semanza* Trial Judgment")

Laurent Semanza v. The Prosecutor, Case No. ICTR-97-20-A, Judgement (AC), 20 May 2005 (*"Semanza* Appeal Judgement")

Seromba

The Prosecutor v. Athanase Seromba, Case No. ICTR-2001-66-T, Judgement (TC), 13 December 2006 (*"Seromba* Trial Judgement")

The Prosecutor v. Athanase Seromba, Case No. ICTR-2001-66-A, Judgement (AC), 12 March 2008 (*"Seromba* Appeal Judgement")

Simba

The Prosecutor v. Aloys Simba, Case No. ICTR-01-76-T, Judgement (TC), 13 December 2005 (*"Simba* Trial Judgement")

Aloys Simba v. The Prosecutor, Case No. ICTR-01-76-A, Judgement (AC), 27 November 2007 (*"Simba* Appeal Judgement")

1.2. International Criminal Tribunal for the Former Yugoslavia

Aleksovski

Prosecutor v. Aleksovski, Case No. IT-95-14/1A, Judgement (AC) (*"Aleksovski* Appeal Judgement") **[page 4]**

Blagojević and Jokić

Prosecutor v. Vidoje Blagojević and Dragan Jokić, Case No. IT-02-60-A, Judgement (AC), 9 May 2007 (*"Blagojević and Jokić* Appeal Judgement")

Blaškić

Prosecutor v. Tihomir Blaškić, Case No. IT-95-14-A, Judgement (AC), 29 July 2004 (*"Blaškić* Appeal Judgement")

Brđanin

Prosecutor v. Brđanin, Case No. IT-99-36-T, Judgement (TC), 9 January 2004 (*"Brđanin* Trial Judgement")

Čelebići

Prosecutor v. Mućic, et al., Case No. IT-96-21-A, Judgement (AC), 20 February 2001 (*"Čelebići* Appeal Judgment")

Galić

Prosecutor v. Stanislav Galić, Case No. IT-98-29-A, Judgement (AC), 30 November 2006 (*"Galić* Appeal Judgement")

Jelisić

Prosecutor v. Goran Jelisić, Case No. IT-95-10-A, Judgement (AC), 5 July 2001 ("*Jelisić* Appeal Judgement")

Jokić

The Prosecutor v. Miodrag Jokić, Case No. IT-01-42/1-A, Judgement On Sentencing Appeal (AC), 30 August 2005 ("*Jokić* Appeal Judgement")

Kordić and Čerkez

The Prosecutor v. Dario Kordić and Mario Čerkez, Case No. IT-95-14/2-A, Judgement (AC), 17 December 2004 ("*Kordić and Čerkez* Appeal Judgement")

Krajišnik

The Prosecutor v. Momčilo Krajišnik, Case No. IT-00-39-A, Judgement (AC), 17 March 2009 ("*Krajišnik* Appeal Judgement")

Krnojelac

Prosecutor v. Krnojelac, Case No. IT-97-25-A, Judgement (AC), 17 September 2003 ("*Krnojelac* Appeal Judgement")

Krstić

Prosecutor v. Radislav v. Krstić, Case No. IT-98-33-T, Judgement (TC), 8 February 2001 ("*Krstić* Trial Judgement") **[page 5]**

Prosecutor v. Radislav v. Krstić, Case No. IT-98-33-A, Judgement (AC), 19 April 2004 ("*Krstić* Appeal Judgement")

Kupreškić et al.

Prosecutor v. Kupreškić et al., IT-96-16-A, Appeal Judgement (AC), 23 October 2001 ("*Kupreškić et al.* Appeal Judgement")

Kvočka et al.

Prosecutor v. Miroslav Kvočka et al., Case No. IT-98-30/1-A, Judgement (AC), 28 February 2005 ("*Kvočka et al.* Appeal Judgement")

Naletilić and Martinović

Prosecutor v. Naletilić and Martinović, Case No. IT-98-34-T, Judgement (TC), 31 March 2003 ("*Naletilić and Martinović* Trial Judgement")

Prosecutor v. Mladen Naletilić and Vinko Martinović, Case No. IT-98-34-A, Judgement (AC), 3 May 2006 ("*Naletilić and Martinović* Appeal Judgement")

Orić

Prosecutor v. Naser Orić, Case No. IT-03-68-T, Judgment (TC), 30 June 2006 (*Orić* Trial Judgement)

Prosecutor v. Naser Orić, Case No. IT-03-68-A, Judgement (AC), 3 July 2008 ("*Orić* Appeal Judgement")

Simić

Prosecutor v. Blagoje Simić, Case No. IT-95-9-A, Judgement (AC), 28 November 2006 ("*Simić* Appeal Judgement")

Tadić

Prosecutor v. Tadić, Case No. IT-94-1-A, Judgement (AC), 15 July 1999 ("*Tadić* Appeal Judgement") **[page 6]**

2. DEFINED TERMS AND ABBREVIATIONS

Annotated Indictment

The Prosecutor v. Callixte Kalimanzira, Case No. ICTR-05-88-I, Annotated Indictment, filed confidential on 20 June 2007

CDR

Coalition pour la Défense de la République

Closing Arguments

T. 20 April 2009

Corrected Indictment

The Prosecutor v. Callixte Kalimanzira, Case No. ICTR-05-88-I, Correction of Typographical Errors in the Indictment of 21 July 2005, filed on 31 October 2007

Defence Closing Brief

The Prosecutor v. Callixte Kalimanzira, Case No. ICTR-05-88-T, *Mémoire final,* filed confidential on 2 April 2009[822]

Defence Pre-Trial Brief

The Prosecutor v. Callixte Kalimanzira, Case No. ICTR-05-88-T, *Mémoire préalable à la presentation des moyens de prevue à décharge,* filed confidential on 17 September 2008[823]

fn.

Footnote

ICTR or Tribunal

International Criminal Tribunal for the Prosecution of Persons Responsible for Genocide and Other Serious Violations of International Humanitarian Law Committed in the Territory of Rwanda and Rwandan Citizens Responsible for Genocide and Other Such Violations Committed in the Territory of Neighbouring States, between 1 January 1994 and 31 December 1994

Indictment

The Prosecutor v. Callixte Kalimanzira, Case No. ICTR-05-88-I, Indictment, filed on 21 July 2005

Initial Appearance [page 7]

T. 14 November 2005

MDR

Mouvement Démocratique Républicain

---

[822] The Defence Closing Brief was considered along with its corrigendum: *The Prosecutor v. Callixte Kalimanzira,* Cast No. ICTR-05-88-T, *Erratum au mémoire final,* filed confidential on 17 April 2009. The Chamber also consulted the English translation of the Defence Closing Brief and Corrigendum.
[823] The Chamber also consulted the English translation of the Defence Pre-Trial Brief.

MRND

Mouvement Révolutionnaire National pour la Démocratie et le Développement

p. (pp.)

page (pages)

para. (paras.)

paragraph (paragraphs)

PL

Parti Libéral

Prosecution Closing Brief

The Prosecutor v. Callixte Kalimanzira, Case No. ICTR-05-88-T, Prosecutor's Final Trial Brief Confidential Version, filed confidential on 2 April 2009[824]

Prosecution Pre-Trial Brief

The Prosecutor v. Callixte Kalimanzira, Case No. ICTR-05-88-PT, Prosecutor's Pre-Trial Brief, filed on 16 April 2008

RPF

Rwandan (also Rwandese) Patriotic Front

RTLM

Radio Télévision Libre des Mille Collines

Rules

Rules of Procedure and Evidence of the International Criminal Tribunal for Rwanda

Statute

Statute of the International Criminal Tribunal for Rwanda, established by Security Council Resolution 955

Supporting Materials [page 8]

The Prosecutor v. Callixte Kalimanzira, Case No. ICTR-05-88-I, Interoffice Memorandum – Documents Supporting the Indictment against Callixte Kalimanzira (Rule 66 RPE), filed confidential on 16 November 2005

T.

Transcript

[page 9] ANNEX III – INDICTMENT

---

[824] The Prosecution also filed a public version of this document on the same day.

[page 2]I. The Prosecutor of the International Criminal Tribunal for Rwanda, pursuant to his authority under Article 17 of the Statute of the International Criminal Tribunal for Rwanda (the "Statute"), charges:

Callixte Kalimanzira with the crimes set forth below:

I. **GENOCIDE**, pursuant to Article 2(3)(a) and Article 6(1) of the Statute or, in the alternative;

II. **COMPLCITY IN GENOCIDE**, pursuant to Article 2(3)(e) and Article 6(1) of the Statute;

III. **DIRECT AND PUBLIC INCITEMENT TO COMMIT GENOCIDE**, pursuant to Article 2(3)(c) and Article 6(1) of the Statute.

II. The Accused:

1. **Callixte Kalimanzira** was born in 1953 in Muganza *commune*, Butare *préfecture*, Republic of Rwanda. He was trained as an agronomist and held several top posts in the Government.

2. During the events referred to in this Indictment, **Callixte Kalimanzira** was a very close ally of President Théodore Sindikubwabo and Prime Minister Jean Kambanda, he being a native of their province and a member of the same party as President Sindikubwabo and, in addition, one of a very few senior civil servants from the province.

He was a senior civil servant who had held the following positions:

(i) *Sous-préfet* of Butare and of Byumba;

(ii) Co-ordinator of Agricultural services at the Kigali *préfecture*;

(iii) Director of the Rural Development Section at the Presidency of the Republic;

(iv) Secretary General of the Ministry of the Interior;

(v) *Chef de cabinet*, Ministry of the Interior, a position he kept under the Interim Government. Between 6 April and 25 May, he was the acting Minister of the Interior;

(vi) Prominent member of the *Mouvement républicain national pour le développement* (MRND); and

(vii) Consequently, exercised in Butare *préfecture, de jure* and *de facto* authority over *bourgmestres, conseillers de secteur, cellule* officials, the *nyumbakumi* (head of each group of 10 houses), administrative staff, gendarmes, communal police, the *Interahamwe*, militiamen and civilians, in that he could order these **[page 3]** persons to commit or refrain from committing unlawful acts and discipline or punish them for their unlawful acts or omission.

III. CHARGES AND CONCISE STATEMENT OF FACTS

3. Butare *préfecture* is situated in the south of Rwanda and stretches up to its border with Burundi. In 1994, it was noted for its dense Tutsi population. Politically, it was a stronghold of the *Parti Libéral* (PL), which was opposed to MRND. For that reason, in particular, the *Interahamwe* were unable to establish a foothold in the area. In early April, its *préfet*, Jean Baptiste Habyalimana, a Tutsi and pro-PL, publicly opposed the massacres.

4. During the entire period referred to in this Indictment, there was in Rwanda a minority racial or ethnic group known as "Tutsi" and officially identified as such by the Rwandan authorities. The majority of Rwanda's population was composed of a racial or ethnic group known as "Hutu", also officially identified as such by the Rwandan authorities.

5. Between 6 April and 17 July 1994, throughout Rwanda and in Butare *préfecture,* in particular, *Interahamwe* militiamen, communal police, gendarmes, soldiers of the Rwandan Armed Forces (FAR) and

armed civilians targeted and attacked members of a civilian population identified as belonging to the Tutsi ethnic or racial group or considered as sympathizing with the Tutsi. During the attacks, some Rwandans killed persons they suspected of belonging to the Tutsi ethnic group or caused them serious bodily or mental harm. These attacks resulted in the death of a large number of persons identified as members of the Tutsi ethnic or racial group.

COUNT 1: GENOCIDE

The Prosecutor of the International Criminal Tribunal for Rwanda charges **Callixte Kalimanzire** with **GENOCIDE**, a crime provided for in Article 2(3)(a) of the Statute of the Tribunal, in that between 1 January 1994 and 31 December 1994, **Callixte Kalimanzira** was responsible for killing and causing serious bodily or mental harm to members of the Tutsi population with the intent to destroy, in whole or in part, an ethnic or racial group as such.

OR, IN THE ALTERNATIVE,

COUNT 2: COMPLICITY IN GENOCIDE

The Prosecutor of the International Criminal Tribunal for Rwanda charges **Callixte Kalimanzira** with **Complicity in Genocide,** a crime provided for in Article 2(3)(e) of the Statute in that between 1 January 1994 and 31 December 1994, **Callixte Kalimanzira** was an accomplice to the killing or in causing serious bodily or mental harm to members of the Tutsi population with the intent to destroy, in whole or in part, an ethnic or racial group as such. **[page 4]**

CONCISE STATEMENT OF FACTS FOR COUNTS 1 AND 2

Individual criminal responsibility

6. **Callixte Kalimanzira** is individually responsible, pursuant to Article 6(1) of the Statute, for the crime of genocide or complicity in genocide in that he planned, instigated, ordered, committed or otherwise aided and abetted in the planning, preparation or commission of the crimes. Moreover, **Callixte Kalimanzira** used his position as described in section II above (under the heading "The Accused") to incite and order persons under his authority to commit the crimes alleged in this Indictment. The particulars of the crime for which he incurs individual criminal responsibility are set out in paragraphs 7 to 17 below.

Presence and movements of the Accused in Butare préfecture *after 6 April 1994 to instigate and supervise the genocide*

7. In launching the massacre of Tutsi in Butare *préfecture*, President Théodore Sindikubwabo, along with a powerful delegation of Interim Government dignitaries, travelled to Butare on 19 April 1994 to incite the population to commit genocide. As the Minister of the Interior was absent, **Callixte Kalimanzira**, *Chef de cabinet,* Ministry of the Interior, served as master of ceremonies at the meeting of the Interim Government officials and the people. He gave the floor to participants, who incited the people to kill Tutsi as was already being done in other *préfectures*. The inflammatory speeches delivered by Government officials during the meetings in respect of which **Callixte Kalimanzira** showed no disapproval, triggered the massacre of thousands of Tutsi in Butare *préfecture*. By so doing, **Callixte Kalimanzira** aided and abetted the massacre of Tutsi which occurred afterwards.

8. Between April and mid-July 1994, **Callixte Kalimanzira** visited Butare on several occasions, together with senior Interim Government dignitaries, including President Théodore Sindikubwabo, Prime Minister Jean Kambanda and the Minister for Family and Women's Affairs, Pauline Nyiramasuhuko, as well as senior local Government officials, such as the *préfet,* Alphonse Nteziryayo, and high-ranking officers of the Rwandan Armed Forces (FAR), including Tharcisse Muvunyi. The purpose of the visits, in which

Callixte Kalimanzira participated, was to sensitize the population to the Government's policy and incite them to kill the Tutsi. The visits resulted in the killing of thousands of Tutsi in Butare *préfecture*.

*Callixte Kalimanzira's involvement in the killings on Kabuye hill, Ndora commune, **Gisagara** secteur*

9. On or about 23 April 1994, thousands of Tutsi civilians gathered on Kabuye hill, located in Ndora *commune*. **Callixte Kalimanzira** personally encouraged them to take refuge on the hill, promising them protection and food. Instead of being protected, they were attacked and killed by the Hutu with the full knowledge of and in the presence of **Callixte Kalimanzira**. In fact, **Callixte Kalimanzira** personally sought communal police and military reinforcement to assist in the attack. Thousands of Tutsi were killed on Kabuye hill. **[page 5]**

10. On or about 23 April 1994, at the time of the attacks at Kabuye hill, **Callixte Kalimanzira** discussed the progress of the killings at the hill with such local authorities as *Sous-Préfet* Dominique Ntawukuriryayo, Fidèle Uwizeye and Bernadette Mukarurangwa, Member of Parliament, in front of *Bourgmestre* Fidèle Uwizeye's house. Having realized that the attackers had not been able to exterminate all the people gathered on the hill because they were too many, they decided to go to the site and supervise the operations. Thus, **Callixte Kalimanzira** personally supervised the attacks against the Tutsi who had gathered on Kabuye hill, resulting in the death of thousands of Tutsi.

Callixte Kalimanzira's involvement in the killings at the roadblock erected at Buzana river and at Mwirango

11. In late April 1994, about 100 Tutsi women, men and children were led by **Callixte Kalimanzira** to a roadblock at River Buzana, at the border of the Ngoma and Nyaruhengeri *communes*. **Callixte Kalimanzira** was accompanied by Colonels Tharcisse Muvunyi and Alphonse Nteziryayo and a military escort. Many of the Tutsi being escorted were seriously wounded, particularly, at the Achilles heel. **Callixte Kalimanzira** decided that the Tutsi who could no longer continue the journey should be finished off on the spot, at the roadblock, and ordered that the rest of the Tutsi be killed a few kilometres further away, at Mwirango. **Callixte Kalimanzira** supervised the elimination on the spot of Tutsi who were too weak to continue the journey. In fact, he personally beat some Tutsi to death. The remaining Tutsi were led to Mwirango, where about 50 of them were killed on his orders.

Other incitements to kill Tutsi followed by killings

12. On or about 5 June 1994, **Callixte Kalimanzira,** together with Colonel Tharcisse Muvunyi and some soldiers, went to Gasagara centre, Muganza *secteur*. He incited the people to eliminate the Tutsi, including those who were still in their mothers' wombs. Later, in a speech to the public at the Gikondo *commune* office, he stated that all Tutsi who were still alive, including women, young girls, the elderly and children, had to be killed. As a result of the incitement, several women and young girls were killed.

13. In early May 1994, **Callixte Kalimanzira** stopped at a roadblock located at the Kibilizi *secteur* and told those who were manning it to be discreet in their hunt for the Tutsi as foreigners were monitoring events in Rwanda. He also asked them to completely destroy all the houses of Tutsi without leaving a trace and to tell the Tutsi that peace had been restored so that they should come out of hiding.

14. On or about 5 June 1994, **Callixte Kalimanzira** addressed the Hutu population at the Gikondo *commune* office, stressing that all Tutsi who were still alive, including women, young girls, the elderly and children had to be killed because, if RPF won the war, they would, as potential witnesses, be the ones to denounce the killers. Immediately after the meeting, two old women and eight young girls were killed. They were: Mukamazimpaka, Salafina Nyaraneza, Mukaruyonza and her mother, Nyaramisago, Goretha Umubeyeyi, Anasthasia Nakabonye, Apolinaraia and Kimonyo's two daughters. Additionally, 10 to 15 Tutsi children were also killed following **Callixte Kalimanzira's** order to the Hutu population. **[page 6]**

Call for the erection of roadblocks, supervision of roadblocks, call on the population to arm themselves in order to kill the Tutsi

15. Between mid-April and late June 1994, **Callixte Kalimanzira** incited the population to erect roadblocks in order to eliminate the Tutsi. He was often personally present at the roadblocks to supervise their operations. Many Tutsi were killed at the roadblocks erected on the instructions of **Callixte Kalimanzira** and supervised by him.

Callixte Kalimanzira's involvement in the distribution of weapons

16. Two days after President Juvénal Habayrimana's death, **Callixte Kalimanzira** went to Kigembe *commune* in a vehicle carrying a carton loaded with machetes, which he handed over to Bonaventure Nkundabakora, reminding him that he had fulfilled his promise to bring him weapons. The machetes provided by **Callixte Kalimanzira** were used to kill Tutsi. Moreover, **Callixte Kalimanzira** periodically replenished the stock of bladed weapons at the Muganza *commune* office. The weapons were distributed to the population under **Callixte Kalimanzira's** supervision and used to kill the Tutsi.

Callixte Kalimanzira's involvement in training members of the population in the handling of weapons

17. In May 1994, a public rally was held at the Muganza *commune* football field for the purpose of training people to handle weapons. **Callixte Kalimanzira**, Chrysologue Bimenyimana, the *bourgmestre* of Muganza, and Alphonse Nteziryayo, the *préfet* of Butare, were present at the training session. **Callixte Kalimanzira** personally demonstrated to participants how to shoot arrows. Those who were trained to use weapons under **Callixte Kalimanzira's** supervision subsequently took part in the killing of Tutsi in the area.

COUNT 3: DIRECT AND PUBLC INCITEMENT TO COMMIT GENOCIDE

The Prosecutor of the International Criminal Tribunal for Rwanda charges **Callixte Kalimanzira with direct and public incitement to commit genocide,** a crime provided for in Article 2(3)(c) of the Statute of the Tribunal, in that between 1 January 1994 and 17 July 1994, **Callixte Kalimanzira** incurred responsibility for directly and publicly inciting people, including local Government officials, communal police, the *Interahamwe*, gendarmes, soldiers and civilians to participate in killing or in causing serious bodily or mental harm to members of the Tutsi population with the intent to destroy, in whole or in part, an ethnic or racial group as such. **[page 7]**

CONCISE STATEMENT OF FACTS FOR COUNT 3

Individual criminal responsibility

18. **Callixte Kalimanzira** is individually responsible, pursuant to Article 6(1) of the Statute, for the crime of direct and public incitement to commit genocide in that he planned, instigated, ordered to commit or otherwise aided and abetted in the planning, preparation or commission of crimes. The particulars of the crime for which he incurs individual criminal responsibility are set out in paragraphs 19-27 below.

19. In late March 1994, local Government officials held a meeting at the Gisagara commercial centre in Nyamigango *cellule*, Gisagara *secteur*, Ndora *commune*. At the meeting, **Callixte Kalimanzira** took the floor to incite the people to arm themselves and prepare to fight the "enemy." He also encouraged those who could manufacture traditional weapons to do so. Furthermore, he promised to supply firearms to the people.

20. On or about 9 April 1994, a meeting was held in Kanage *cellule*, Mukindo *secteur*, Kibayi *commune*. At that meeting, **Callixte Kalimanzira** told Burundian refugees that the Interim Government had confidence in them, that President Juvénal Habayrimana had taken care of them and that President Théodore Sindikubwabo would behave in a similar manner; he also told them that it was the same enemy who chased them from Burundi who was responsible for the death of Presidents Habyarimana and Ntaryamira. He then

appealed to them not to leave the country, stating that the reason for his coming was to bring them traditional weapons with which to defend themselves against the "enemy."

21. On or about mid-April 1994, **Callixte Kalimanzira,** together with three soldiers, went to the Jaguar roadblock located in front of the Gisagara Catholic Church and gave a rifle to Marcel Ntirusekanwa who was in charge of the roadblock. **Callixte Kalimanzira** told Marcel Ntirusekanwa that the gun was to be used to kill the Tutsi.

22. On or about late April 1994, **Callixte Kalimanzira** appeared at a roadblock located at the border between Muganza/Remera *secteurs* and the Kirarambogo junction in a vehicle with gendarmes. He reminded those manning the roadblock that they had to carry weapons and kill Tutsi. On that occasion, **Callixte Kalimanzira** slapped someone because he was not carrying a weapon, forced another unarmed person into his vehicle and headed for Gisagara.

23. On or about late April and early May 1994, **Callixte Kalimanzira** attended a public meeting held at the Nyabisagara football field in ~~Kabgayi~~ **Kibavi** *commune*. At the meeting, speakers, including Kalimanzira, thanked the Hutu for the efforts they had made to eliminate the Tutsi.

24. On or about late April and early May 1994, a few days after the public meeting at the Nyabisagara football field in ~~Kabgayi~~ **Kibavi** *commune* referred to in paragraph 23 above, **Callixte Kalimanzira** went to the ~~Ramiko~~ **Rwamiko** primary school and congratulated the people present on "the work" that had been done. He also urged them to remain vigilant and continue to carry weapons and eliminate the Tutsi. **[page 8]**

25. In May 1994, **Callixte Kalimanzira** stopped at a roadblock located at a place called Sakindi, in ~~Kibinizi~~ **Kibilizi** *secteur*. Several armed persons were manning the roadblock. **Callixte Kalimanzira** told them that they should kill the Tutsi discreetely, destroy their houses and plant banana trees in the locations where the houses used to stand so no traces would be left for foreigners to see. He further urged them to tell the Tutsi who were in hiding that peace had been restored so they should come out of hiding. This was simply a ploy to locate and kill them.

26. In May 1994, **Callixte Kalimanzira** appeared at a roadblock in a pick-up with armed soldiers. He got out of the vehicle and encouraged those manning the roadblock to continue the identity check of everyone and to keep searching for the Tutsi enemy. On that same occasion, he questioned a motorcyclist who was going through an identity check at the roadblock and whose identify card bore the label "Hutu", criticizing him for not carrying a weapon with which to kill the Tutsi in spite of the instructions issued to that effect.

27. Between mid-April and June 1994, **Callixte Kalimanzira** checked if everyone was carrying a weapon with which to kill the Tutsi and did not hesitate to warn, assault and even threaten to severely punish those who failed to carry a weapon. On or about late April and early May 1994, **Callixte Kalimanzira** hit a Hutu with a club, criticizing him for not carrying a weapon with which to kill the Tutsi.

The acts and omissions of **Callixte Kalimanzira** detailed herein are punishable in reference to Articles 22 and 23 of the Statute.

Arusha, Tanzania

Date: 21 July 2005

Hassan Bubacar Jallow
Prosecutor

Commentary

1. Under count one, Kalimanzira was charged with genocide, a crime provided for in Article 2, paragraph 3, subsection a, ICTR Statute, for allegedly killing and causing serious bodily or mental harm to members of the Tutsi population with the intent to destroy, in whole or in part, an ethnic or racial group as such. In the alternative to count one, count two charged Kalimanzira with complicity in genocide, under Article 2, paragraph 3, subsection e, ICTR Statute, in that he was an accomplice in killing or in causing serious bodily or mental harm to members of the Tutsi population with the intent to destroy, in whole or in part, an ethnic or racial group as such.

Under count three, he was charged with direct and public incitement to commit genocide, a crime provided for in Article 2, paragraph 3, subsection c, ICTR Statute, in that he was allegedly responsible for directly and publicly inciting people, including local government officials, communal police, *Interahamwe*, *gendarmes*, soldiers and civilians to participate in killing or in causing serious bodily or mental harm to members of the Tutsi population with the intent to destroy, in whole or in part, an ethnic or racial group as such.

Kalimanzira was found guilty of aiding and abetting the crime of genocide at the inauguration of Élie Ndayambaje and at Kabuye hill and of aiding and abetting, as well as instigating, the crime of genocide at a roadblock on the Butare-Gisagara road (count one). The chamber considered that Kalimanzira indirectly perpetrated these crimes.

The chamber also found Kalimanzira guilty of direct and public incitement to commit genocide at the Jaguar roadblock, the Kajyanama roadblock, the Nyabisagara football field, and the Gisagara market place (count three). The chamber considered that Kalimanzira was the principal perpetrator of these crimes.

Count two, pleaded in the alternative to count one, was dismissed.

The prosecutor referred to each count as a different crime and the chamber, albeit not stating it explicitly in relation to complicity in genocide,[1] pondered that

> Direct and Public Incitement to Commit Genocide is a crime provided for at Article 2(3)(c) of the Statute, as a result of the incorporation of Article III of the Genocide Convention within the Statute's definition of genocide. Article 2(3) of the Statute, identical to Article III of the Genocide Convention, lists five punishable acts, including Genocide itself, and Direct and Public Incitement to Commit Genocide. The Statute and the Genocide Convention define the crime of genocide as any series of acts, including killing and causing serious bodily or mental harm, that are committed with the intent to destroy in whole or in part a national, ethnic, racial or religious group ("genocidal intent"). The crime of Direct and Public Incitement to Commit Genocide, however, is not defined any further in either the Genocide Convention or the Statute.[2]

Thus, according to the chamber and the prosecutor, genocide and direct and public incitement to commit genocide are two different crimes, to which the prosecutor added complicity in genocide as a separate offence.

2. The indictment charged Kalimanzira for being 'individually responsible, pursuant to Article 6(1) of the Statute, for the crime of direct and public incitement to commit genocide in that he planned, instigated, ordered to commit or otherwise aided and abetted in the planning, preparation or commission of crimes'.[3]

In the prosecutor's view, the modes of liability of Article 6, paragraph 1, ICTR Statute, apply to the crime of direct and public incitement to commit genocide. This reasoning probably extends to complicity in genocide and other crimes listed in Article 2, paragraph 3, ICTR Statute. The chamber held that

> [i]ncitement resulting in the commission of a genocidal act is punishable under the combination of Articles 2 (3)(a) and 6(1) of the Statute as Genocide by way of Instigation […]. Incitement resulting in the commission of a genocidal act and which may be described as "direct" and "public" is punishable under either Article 2 (3)(c) of the Statute as Direct and Public Incitement to Commit Genocide, or under the combination of Articles 2 (3)(a) and 6 (1) of the Statute as Genocide by way of Instigation; […] Incitement

---

[1] ICTR, Judgement, *Prosecutor v. Kalimanzira*, Case No. ICTR-05-88-T, T. Ch. III, 22 June 2009, in this volume, p. 359, par. 504: 'Count 2 is pleaded in the alternative to Count 1, which requires the Chamber to dismiss the count of Complicity in Genocide in the event of a finding on the count of Genocide'.
[2] *Ibid.*, par. 509.
[3] ICTR, Indictment, *Prosecutor v. Kalimanzira*, Case No. ICTR-05-88-T, 21 July 2005, par. 18.

not resulting in the commission of a genocidal act but which may be described as "direct" and "public" is only punishable under Article 2 (3)(c) of the Statute; and, [...] Incitement not resulting in the commission of a genocidal act, and which may not be described as "direct" and "public", is not punishable under the Statute.[4]

The chamber only referred to the modes of liability of Article 6, paragraph 1, ICTR Statute in relation to genocide, not in relation to direct and public incitement to commit genocide.

Whereas the prosecutor reads the modes of liability into all the crimes listed in Article 2, paragraph 3, ICTR Statute, the chamber seems to exclude from that number those 'not defined any further in the Statute'.[5] This would mean that the modes of liability of Article 6, paragraph 1, ICTR Statute, should be read into the crime of genocide itself, but not into the other genocide related offences described in Article 2, paragraph 3, ICTR Statute.

3. The prosecutor argued, in all three counts, that Kalimanzira had the intent to destroy, in whole or in part, an ethnic or racial group as such. The chamber commenced its analysis by stating that to 'find an accused guilty of the crime of genocide, it must be established that he committed any of the enumerated acts in art. 2(2) with the specific intent to destroy, in whole or in part, a group, as such, that is defined by one of the protected categories of nationality, race, ethnicity, or religion ("genocidal intent")'.[6]

However, it concluded that 'for liability of aiding and abetting to attach, the individual charged need only possess knowledge of the principal perpetrator's specific genocidal intent, whereas for planning, instigating and ordering, he must share that intent'.[7]

Whereas the wording of the indictment might be construed as requiring specific intent both for genocide and complicity in genocide, including the commission of those crimes through aiding and abetting, the chamber considers that genocidal intent does not have to be proven in order to secure a conviction under aiding and abetting genocide.

4. There has been much debate about the relationship between complicity in genocide (Article 2, paragraph 3, subsection e, ICTR Statute) and aiding and abetting genocide (Article 6, paragraph 1 and Article 2, paragraph 3, subsection a, ICTR Statute).[8] The main issues at stake are the following:
   (i) whether or not the two norms entail, redundantly, the same scope;
   (ii) if that is not the case, whether complicity in genocide (Article 2, paragraph 3, subsection e, ICTR Statute) should be construed as an autonomous offence, in which the heads of liability provided for by Article 6, paragraph 1, ICTR Statute, including aiding and abetting, are to be read, or rather as a separate head of liability for genocide, adding to the latter;
   (iii) irrespective of the answer to the previous questions, whether or not complicity in genocide and / or instigating, aiding and abetting genocide require specific genocidal intent.

The discussion is more intricate because the construction of complicity and aiding and abetting in international criminal law is inevitably influenced by domestic law, from where they stem, and those notions do not have the same contents in the various legal systems, even if they are translated into the same words.[9]

In Anglo-American law, which is said to underlie the Genocide Convention,[10] complicity refers broadly to the situation where 'two or more people play some part in the commission of an offence',[11] including

---

[4] *Ibid.*, par. 516.
[5] *Ibid.*, par. 509-516.
[6] *Ibid.*, par. 158.
[7] *Ibid.*, par. 161.
[8] On the "overlap debate", see Elies van Sliedregt, Complicity in Genocide, in Paola Gaeta (ed.), The UN Genocide Convention, A Commentary, O.U.P., 2009, p. 167 *et seq.* and 176 *et seq.*; Grant Dawson and Rachel Boynton, Reconciling Complicity in Genocide and Aiding and Abetting Genocide in the Jurisprudence of the United Nations Ad Hoc Tribunals, 21 Harvard Human Rights Journal 2008, p. 241 *et seq.*
[9] For a comparative analysis of Dutch, English and German law on the subject (from a European law perspective), see Johannes Keiler, Towards a European concept of participation in crime, in André Klip (ed.), Substantive Criminal Law for the European Union, Maklu, Antwerp 2011, p. 173 *et seq.*
[10] Elies van Sliedregt, *supra* note 8, p. 176.
[11] Andrew Ashworth, Principles of Criminal Law, 5th ed., O.U.P., Oxford 2006, p. 410. In this broad sense, "complicity" means what other systems call *Beteiligung*, or *comparticipação*.

principals. As a consequence, the word accomplice may be attributed to anyone taking part in an offence (those "concerned in the crime").[12] However, accomplice is more often taken to designate an accessory to the offence, *sc.*, someone who cannot be characterised as a principal or co-principal.[13] Accessories encompass those who aid or abet criminal conduct, but also those who instigate the commission of a crime (counselling and procuring), as long as they do not cause the *actus reus* themselves.[14] Hence, the duality between principal and accessory does not necessarily mean that the former's responsibility is graver than the latter's:[15] it 'refers to a technical rather than a normative distinction'.[16]

Other systems use the expression complicity (*medeplichtigheid, Beihilfe, cumplicidade, complicidad*[17]) in a narrower sense, meaning only the moral or material assistance to the commission of an offence, which is usually translated into English language as aiding and abetting. In these systems, the content of complicity either equals[18] accessoryship / participation (*Teilnahme, participação, participación*) – as opposed to principal perpetration (*daderschap, Täterschaft, autoria, autoría*), or is a subspecies thereof, together with instigation (*uitlokking, Anstiftung, instigação, inducción*). Usually, participants are punished more leniently than perpetrators because their culpability in the commission of the offence is considered lower; however, instigation might be punished as if it were a form of principal perpetration.[19]

4.1. In Akayesu,[20] the Trial Chamber tried to draw two distinctions between aiding and abetting genocide and complicity in genocide: in the first place, the former, unlike the latter, would require specific genocidal intent.[21] Secondly, it would materialise by simple omission, whereas the latter would require positive action.[22] The duality between omission and positive action propounded by the chamber was not substantiated and had no further application by the tribunals,[23] whereas the required *mens rea*, apparently based on the lesser gravity of complicity in genocide *vis-à-vis* genocide, did not take into account the circumstance that aiding and abetting are also widely acknowledged as accessoryship to genocide and, consequently, as a less

---

[12] Chile Eboe-Osuji, Complicity in Genocide versus Aiding and Abetting Genocide, 3 Journal of International Criminal Justice 2005, p. 75 *et seq.*
[13] See Andrew Ashworth, *supra* note 11, p. 411; Markus D. Dubber, Criminalizing Complicity. A Comparative Analysis, 5 Journal of International Criminal Justice 2007, p. 978 *et seq.* (Referring to American law). This differentiation shows that English law does not follow a 'unitary' model of participation (Kai Ambos, La Parte General del Derecho Penal Internacional. Bases para una Elaboración Dogmática (trad. Ezequiel Malarino), Konrad-Adenauer-Stiftung, Montevideo, 2005, p. 170); the fact that all actors can be punished with the penalties applicable to the principal is immaterial to this effect. See also, in an international context, ICTR, Judgement, *Prosecutor v. Akayesu*, Case No. ICTR-96-4-T, T. Ch. I, 2 September 1998, Klip/ Sluiter, ALC-II-399, p. 502, margin number 527: '[s]ince the accomplice to an offence may be defined as someone who associates himself in an offence committed by another, complicity necessarily implies the existence of a principal offence'.
[14] See Andrew Ashworth, *supra* note 11, p. 411, 413, and 420 *et seq.*; the same applies to French law: see art. 121–6 and art. 121–7 French Penal Code. On the evolution of the distinction between principals and accessories in American law, from common law definitions (where principals, unlike accessories, must be present at the crime scene) to the more normative scheme of the Model Penal Code (where the perpetrator is he 'who commits an offence "by his own conduct"', whereas the liability of the accomplice 'derives from "the conduct of another person for which he is legally accountable"'), see Markus D. Dubber, *supra* note 13, p. 981 *et seq.*, and 985.
[15] Andrew Ashworth, *supra* note 11, p. 413.
[16] Elies van Sliedregt, *supra* note 8, p. 177.
[17] See art. 48 Dutch Penal Code; §27 German Penal Code; art. 27 Portuguese Penal Code; and art. 29 Spanish Penal Code. This does not mean that those systems share exactly the same features: for instance, art. 28(b) Spanish Penal Code deems as principals those who 'cooperate in the execution of the crime through an act without which it could not have occurred' – the so-called necessary or primary complicity ("complicidad necesaria o primaria"), bringing to mind the "secondary principals" in Anglo-American law.
[18] As it is the case with Dutch penal law, which defines instigators as principals (Art. 47, paragraph 1, 2 Dutch Penal Code). The same applies to those constructions of Portuguese law that, developing further the *Tatherrschaft* doctrine, qualify "true" instigators (as opposed to mere inducers) as principals: see Jorge de Figueiredo Dias, Direito Penal. Parte Geral. Tomo I, 2ⁿᵈ. ed., Coimbra Editora, Coimbra 2007, p. 797 *et seq.*
[19] See §26 German Penal Code; art. 26 Portuguese Penal Code; and art. 28 Spanish Penal Code.
[20] See ICTR, Judgement, *Prosecutor v. Akayesu*, Case No. ICTR-96-4-T, T. Ch. I, 2 September 1998, Klip/ Sluiter, ALC-II-399.
[21] *Ibid.*, par. 485: 'when dealing with a person Accused of having aided and abetted in the planning, preparation and execution of genocide, it must be proven that such a person did have the specific intent to commit genocide, namely that, he or she acted with the intent to destroy in whole or in part, a national, ethnical, racial or religious group, as such; whereas […] the same requirement is not needed for complicity in genocide'. (See as well Akayesu judgement *supra* note 20, par. 545 and 547.).
[22] *Ibid.*, par. 548: '[a]nother difference between complicity in genocide and the principle of abetting in the planning, preparation or execution a genocide as per Article 6(1), is that, in theory, complicity requires a positive act, i.e. an act of commission, whereas aiding and abetting may consist in failing to act or refraining from action.'
[23] Elies van Sliedregt, *supra* note 8, p. 171.

serious head of liability.[24] In other words, the decision did not explain why aiding and abetting genocide with specific genocidal intent, entailing accessory liability to genocide, should be separated from complicity in genocide. Indeed, a particular *mens rea* is not required for accessories; however, it does not mean that they must not have it. From then on, the issue quickly attracted several contradictory decisions.

4.2. In the Stakić decision on Rule 98 bis,[25] after stating that the provisions overlap,[26] the Trial Chamber added that 'in order to resolve the problem of overlapping, Article 4(3) [= art. 2(3) of the ICTR Statute] can either be regarded as *lex specialis* in relation to Article 7(1) [art. 6 (1) of the ICTR Statute] (*lex generalis*[27]) [...]. Reading the modes of participation under Article 7 (1) into Article 4(3), whilst maintaining the *dolus specialis* pre-requisite, would lead to the same result. Both approaches respect the interpretation that Article 4(3) delimits the modes of participation in genocide, and maintains the requirement of special intent. Only this interpretation honours the exclusivity of the crime of genocide, described in paragraph 22 above and upholds the limitations set by the 1948 Genocide Convention'.[28]

In paragraph 22, the Stakić Trial Chamber described genocide as the 'crime of the crimes', and stated that it would, 'whilst interpreting article 4 restrictively and with caution, always be guided by the exclusivity of the crime of genocide'. The chamber noted that, according to the Akayesu jurisprudence, 'the *mens rea* for aiding and abetting as a form of complicity in genocide would only be the knowledge of the elements of the crime of genocide, including the intent of the superior or other persons, and acceptance of the course of the events, taking into account the foreseeable consequences of providing substantial support',[29] but observed that 'this concept could constitute a departure from the strict pre-requisite of *dolus specialis* related to all forms of committing and participation in genocide'.[30]

In addition, the chamber reasoned that 'it follows from article 4 and the unique nature of genocide that *dolus specialis* is also required for responsibility under article 7(3) [art. 6(3) of the ICTR Statute] as well';[31] and that it wished to 'emphasise that the legal construct of "joint criminal enterprise" cannot create a crime that is not foreseen in the statute and that it might – if not handed carefully – tend to introduce a lower threshold in respect to the proof of individual intent. This would indeed be a result that is not covered by the 1948 Genocide Convention and its verbatim incorporation on Article 4 of the Tribunal's Statute'.[32]

While seemingly not differentiating between complicity in genocide and aiding and abetting genocide, the chamber views the so-called specific intent as an essential element for a conviction under any form of genocide. This reasoning encompasses cases of superior responsibility and cases that would fall under 'the legal construct of joint criminal enterprise'. Such a radical stance could raise some objections: for instance,

---

[24] See, e. g., Gerhard Werle, Individual Criminal Responsibility in Article 25 ICC Statute, 5 Journal of International Criminal Justice 2007, p. 955 *et seq.*, with reference to the ad-hoc tribunals practice; but see Johan D. van der Vyver, Prosecution and Punishment of the Crime of Genocide, 23 Fordham International Law Journal 1999, p. 314, who gives Akayesu a different interpretation and suggests that some instances of aiding and abetting can qualify as a form of co-perpetration: 'In *Prosecutor v. Akayesu*, the International Tribunal for Rwanda sought at some lengths to distinguish between aiding and abetting *as an accomplice* in the crime of genocide, and *participating* in the crime of genocide through aiding and abetting. The distinction between an accessory or accomplice (*particeps criminis*) and a concurrent wrongdoer (*socius criminis*) seems to be the point in issue here'.

[25] ICTY, Decision on Rule 98*bis* Motion for Judgement of Acquittal, *Prosecutor v. Stakić*, Case No. IT-97-24-T, T. Ch., 31 October 2002, Klip/ Sluiter, ALC-XI-561.

[26] *Ibid.*, par. 47.

[27] According to Grant Dawson and Rachel Boynton, *supra* note 8, p. 269, '[t]his terminology, no doubt, was derived from the legal doctrine of "*lex specialis derogat legi generali*", whereby a pre-existing law regulating a specific subject matter (*lex specialis*) is not superseded by a later promulgated law dealing with a general subject matter (*lex generalis*)'. This explanation probably refers to the circumstance that art. III of the 1948 Convention (*lex specialis*) pre-existed art. 6, paragraph 1, ICTR Statute (*lex generalis*). However, it must be noted that the statutes of the international tribunals are not applicable substantive law that might modify or supersede pre-existing international law provisions on the definition of the offences and heads of liability; the issue will be addressed in more detail *infra*.

[28] *Ibid*, par. 48.

[29] *Ibid.*, par. 66.

[30] *Ibid.*, par. 67.

[31] *Ibid.*, par. 92.

[32] *Ibid.*, par. 93.

specific intent is hardly reconcilable with superior responsibility established on the grounds that the perpetrator had reason to know that the subordinate was about to commit genocide or had done so.[33]

Besides setting specific genocidal intent for all forms of genocide, the Stakić Trial Chamber hinted at an important issue, which will be dealt with later on in this commentary: did the law in force at the time of the facts punish the relevant acts?

4.3. In *Semanza*,[34] the chamber noted 'that an overlap exists between "genocide" in Article 2(3)(a) and "committing" in Article 6(1), and between "complicity" in Article 2(3)(e) and forms of accomplice liability in Article 6(1)'. This redundancy could 'be explained by the drafters' *verbatim* incorporation into the Statute of Article III of the Genocide Convention'.[35]

In the view of the chamber, there is 'no material distinction between complicity in Article 2(3) (e) of the Statute and the broad definition accorded to aiding and abetting in Article 6(1)'. The chamber further noted 'that the *mens rea* requirement for complicity to commit genocide in Article 2(3) (e) [...] mirrors that for aiding and abetting and the other forms of accomplice liability in Article 6(1)'.[36]

Furthermore, 'complicity to commit genocide in Article 2(3) (e) refers to all acts of assistance or encouragement that have substantially contributed to, or have had a substantial effect on, the completion of the crime of genocide. The accused must have acted intentionally and with the awareness that he was contributing to the crime of genocide, including all its material elements'.[37]

From this perspective, being no different, complicity in genocide and aiding and abetting genocide do not require specific intent.

4.4. The Krstić Appeals Chamber[38] stated that '[b]ecause the Statute must be interpreted with the utmost respect to the language used by the legislator, the Appeals Chamber may not conclude that the consequent overlap between Article 7(1) and Article 4(3)(e) is a result of an inadvertence on the part of the legislator where another explanation, consonant with the language used by the Statute, is possible. In this case, the two provisions can be reconciled, because the terms "complicity" and "accomplice" may encompass conduct broader than that of aiding and abetting'.[39]

The Appeals Chamber then reasoned that *mens rea* for aiding and abetting genocide, as for any other offence, only requires knowledge of the principal's genocidal intent,[40] while complicity in genocide, where prohibiting

---

[33] See Gerhard Werle, Principles of International Criminal Law, 2nd ed., The Hague, TMC Asser Press, 2009, p. 193, margin number 518. The issue becomes immaterial if Article 6, paragraph 3, is viewed, as it seems correct, as a "genuine offence or separate crime of omission" (Kai Ambos, in A. Cassese / P. Gaeta / J. R. W. D. Jones, The Rome Statute of the International Criminal Court: a Commentary, I, O.U.P, Oxford 2002, p. 851) rather than a mode of commission, or a mode of participation in the offences committed by the subordinates, even where such omission consists of a failure to prevent those offences. In this regard, as the ICTR and ICTY statutes provide for a limited subject-matter jurisdiction, where such offence is not included, a strict interpretation of the statutes should arguably lead to the conclusion that the tribunals bear no jurisdiction over acts that constitute genuine superior responsibility, i. e., acts that do not entail co-perpetration, complicity, active perpetration and instigation by the superior: see Pedro Caeiro and Miguel Lemos, Commentary, Klip/ Sluiter, ALC-XVI-519.
[34] ICTR, Judgement and Sentence, *Prosecutor v. Semanza*, Case No. ICTR-97-20-T, T. Ch. III, 15 May 2003, Klip/ Sluiter, ALC-XII-599.
[35] *Ibid.*, par. 391.
[36] *Ibid.*, par. 394.
[37] *Ibid.*, par. 395.
[38] ICTY, Judgement, *Prosecutor v. Krstić*, Case No. IT-98-33-A, A. Ch., 19 April 2004, ALC-XIX-539.
[39] *Ibid.*, par. 139.
[40] *Ibid.*, par. 140: '[t]his, however, raises the question of whether, for liability of aiding and abetting to attach, the individual charged need only possess knowledge of the principal perpetrator's specific genocidal intent, or whether he must share that intent. The Appeals Chamber has previously explained, on several occasions, that an individual who aids and abets a specific intent offense may be held responsible if he assists the commission of the crime knowing the intent behind the crime [...]. This principle applies to the Statute's prohibition of genocide, which is also an offence requiring a showing of specific intent. The conviction for aiding and abetting genocide upon proof that the defendant knew about the principal perpetrator's genocidal intent is permitted by the Statute and case-law of the Tribunal. [...] Many domestic jurisdictions, both common and civil law, take the same approach with respect to the *mens rea* for aiding and abetting, and often expressly apply it to the prohibition of genocide'.

conduct other than aiding and abetting, requires that the accomplice shares the specific genocidal intent of the principal.[41]

Whereas Akayesu required specific intent for a conviction for aiding and abetting, but not for complicity in genocide, the present decision attained the opposite conclusion. However, even if the historical context would warrant the court's stance regarding *mens rea* – which does not seem to be the case[42] – it would still raise an important issue: the Appeals Chamber fails to explain how and when the law changed. If it is meant that the Genocide Convention required specific intent for complicity in genocide, it would be necessary to determine the moment where aiding and abetting genocide, with no requirement of specific intent, earned an autonomous status as a separate mode of participating in genocide and whether or not that was actually the law at the time of the facts. It might be that, as the Appeals Chamber notes, the drafters of the Statute opted for applying the general notion of aiding and abetting to the prohibition of genocide. But if its regime really differs from the Genocide Convention, then it would be necessary to show that it was already in force when the acts were perpetrated.

4.5. In Blagojević,[43] the Trial Chamber found that 'there is an overlap between Article 4(3) as the general provision enumerating punishable forms of participation in genocide and Article 7(1) as the general provision for criminal liability which applies to all the offences punishable under the Statute, including the offence of genocide. [...] As a result, some heads of responsibility listed under Article 7(1) are necessarily included in those forms of liability listed in Article 4(3), or vice versa. As the heads of liability listed under Article 7(1) are often more specific and strictly delimited than those listed under Article 4(3), Article 7(1) may prove useful in characterising the accused's form of participation with the required degree of specificity. The Appeals Chamber has found "that modes of participation in Article 7(1) should be read, as the Tribunal's Statute directs, into Article 4(3)". [...] It based this finding on the text of Article 7(1), which includes the liability for an aider and abettor, and expressly applies that mode of liability to any "crime referred to in articles 2 to 5 of the present Statute", including the offence of genocide prohibited by Article 4'.[44]

The Trial Chamber also found that 'complicity in genocide has been interpreted to include various forms of participation listed under Article 7(1) of the Statute',[45] and that 'Colonel Blagojević rendered practical assistance that had a substantial effect on the commission of genocide in the knowledge that the principal perpetrators of these acts had the intent to destroy in whole or in part the Bosnian Muslim group from Srebrenica, the Trial Chamber therefore finds Colonel Blagojevic is responsible for complicity in genocide through aiding and abetting the commission of genocide'.[46]

---

[41] *Ibid.*, par. 142: '[b]y contrast, there is authority to suggest that complicity in genocide, where it prohibits conduct broader than aiding and abetting, requires proof that the accomplice had the specific intent to destroy a protected group. Article 4 of the Statute is most naturally read to suggest that Article 4(2)'s requirement that a perpetrator of genocide possess the requisite "intent to destroy" a protected group applies to all of the prohibited acts enumerated in Article 4(3), including complicity in genocide. [...] There is also evidence that the drafters of the Genocide Convention intended the charge of complicity in genocide to require a showing of genocidal intent. The U.K. delegate in the Sixth Committee of the General Assembly "proposed adding the word "deliberate" before "complicity"", explaining that "it was important to specify that complicity must be deliberate, because there existed some systems where complicity required intent, and others where it did not. Several delegates [representing Luxembourg, Egypt, Soviet Union, Yugoslavia] said that this was unnecessary, because there had never been any doubt that complicity in genocide must be intentional. The United Kingdom eventually withdrew its amendment, 'since it was understood that, to be punishable, complicity in genocide must be deliberate". [...] The texts of the Tribunal's Statute and of the Genocide Convention, combined with the evidence in the Convention's travaux préparatoires, provide additional support to the conclusion that the drafters of the Statute opted for applying the notion of aiding and abetting to the prohibition of genocide under Article 4'. This leads Michael G Karnavas, Prosecutor v. Vidoje Blagojevic, Dragan Jokic, Case No. IT-02-60-T, Trial Judgement, 17 January 2005, 4 International Criminal Law Review 2005, p. 618, to state that 'accepting that the special genocidal intent forms an element of the chapeau of the offense of genocide which characterizes it as an international crime, [.], it *must* apply to all five forms of criminal participation in committing genocide set out in article 4 (3) of the Statute'.

[42] Arguably, the reference to the drafting of the Genocide Convention does not allow for the conclusion attained by the Court: the British delegate would probably want to ensure that complicity in genocide was punishable only if 'deliberate', *sc.*, guided by direct intent, as opposed to negligence or, possibly, *dolus eventualis*, meaning that the accomplice, while participating in an act of genocide, must act knowingly and wilfully (but see Elies van Sliedregt, *supra* note 8, p. 165). However, the species of intent required for complicity does not contend with the specific genocidal purpose that must guide the act of the principal: see *infra*, 7.2.

[43] Judgement, *Prosecutor v. Blagojević et al.*, Case No. IT-02-60, T. Ch. I, 17 January 2005, Klip/ Sluiter, ALC-XXVI-261.

[44] *Ibid.*, par. 670.

[45] *Ibid.*, par. 778.

[46] *Ibid.*, par. 787.

The novelty brought by Blagojević is the conviction for 'complicity in genocide through aiding and abetting the commission of genocide'. It is unclear whether the chamber referred to aiding and abetting under Article 7, paragraph 1, ICTR Statute, as a head of liability for the separate offence of complicity in genocide, which would open the door to punishment for assisting complicity in genocide, or rather it intended to mean that aiding and abetting genocide, under Article 7, paragraph 1, ICTR Statute, is a form of complicity in genocide. Arguably, the latter alternative applies:[47] the 'assistance' rendered by the defendant had a substantial effect on the 'commission of genocide' and he had knowledge that the 'principal perpetrators of these acts' had a genocidal intent. Thus, he was responsible for complicity in genocide through aiding and abetting the commission of genocide. Moreover, the former alternative would be farfetched: nothing suggests that the law at the time of the facts encompassed crimes such as aiding and abetting complicity in genocide or instigation to complicity in genocide, as long as such acts do not constitute assistance or instigation to genocide proper, just to name some examples.

4.6. In Karemera,[48] the Trial Chamber considered that complicity is one of the forms of criminal responsibility that is applicable to the crime of genocide.[49] In his separate opinion, Judge Short opined that 'complicity in genocide has the indicia of a criminal offence, whilst encompassing a particular mode of liability. It is often charged as an alternative count to the count of genocide, as in the Indictment in this case, and can result in a finding of guilt for "complicity in genocide". In the case of Semanza, for example, the Accused, who was charged with Counts of genocide and complicity in genocide in the alternative, was found not guilty of genocide and convicted of complicity in genocide [...]. It certainly cannot be said that the Accused in that case was convicted of a mode of liability'. The judge was therefore of the view 'that the term "complicity in genocide" referred to under Article 2(3)(e) is a crime (genocide) to which a particular mode of criminal responsibility is attached (complicity, or accomplice liability)'.[50] Judge Short seems to suggest that complicity in genocide is a mixture of a crime and a mode of liability.[51]

4.7 The same diversity of constructions can be found in the literature. Some authors uphold that a distinction between aiding and abetting and complicity is hard to understand, because the two expressions mean 'essentially the same' in comparative criminal law;[52] the broadness of the expression aiding and abetting makes the separate incrimination of complicity redundant;[53] or, more bluntly, construing complicity according to the Convention against Genocide in a different way than complicity in general simply makes no sense.[54]

A second perspective endorses the opinion that, under the statutes, aiding and abetting genocide and complicity in genocide are two different forms of complicity. In some authors' view, the latter is designed to target residual genocide-related conduct, including accessories *ex post facto*, which is not addressed by

---

[47] But see Grant Dawson and Rachel Boynton, *supra* note 8, p. 277.
[48] ICTR, Decision on Defence Motions Challenging the Pleading of a Joint Criminal Enterprise in a Count of Complicity in Genocide in the Amended Indictment (Articles 2 and 6(1) of the Statute), *Prosecutor v. Karemera, Ngirumpatse and Nzirorera*, Case No. ICTR-98-44-T, T. Ch. III, 18 May 2006, Klip/ Sluiter, ALC-XXIV-45.
[49] *Ibid.*, par. 7: '[c]ontrary to the Prosecution's assertion, jurisprudence of both ad hoc Tribunals has determined that complicity is one of the forms of criminal responsibility that is applicable to the crime of genocide, and not a crime itself. There is no need for this Chamber to reiterate this explicit finding of the Appeals Chamber, which has been constantly applied by Trial Chambers of both ad hoc Tribunals on this matter.'
[50] ICTR, Decision on Defence Motions Challenging the Pleading of a Joint Criminal Enterprise in a Count of Complicity in Genocide in the Amended Indictment (Articles 2 and 6(1) of the Statute), Separate Opinion of Judge Short on Complicity in Genocide and Joint Criminal Enterprise Theory (Articles 2 and 6(1) of the Statute and Rule 72 of the Rules of Procedure of Evidence), *Prosecutor v. Karemera, Ngirumpatse and Nzirorera*, Case No. ICTR-98-44-T, T. Ch. III, 18 May 2006, Klip/ Sluiter, ALC-XXIV-45 [hereinafter Karemera Separate Opinion].
[51] According to Grant Dawson and Rachel Boynton, *supra* note 8, p. 266, 'Judge Short's analysis may lend support to the view that complicity in genocide is in fact a hybrid of (1) a substantive crime and (2) a mode of liability. This may be a logical explanation to reconcile the fact that an individual could be convicted of complicity in genocide with the fact that complicity itself refers to a certain form of participation in the crime'.
[52] William Schabas, Commentary, Klip/ Sluiter, ALC-II-539, p. 548.
[53] Payam Akhavan, The Crime of Genocide in the ICTR Jurisprudence, 3 Journal of International Criminal Justice 2005, p. 994: '[u]nlike inchoate crimes enumerated under Article 2 (3)(b)-(d), inclusion of complicity appears to be superfluous given the broad scope of the term "otherwise aided and abetted" as a residual category under Article 6(1)'.
[54] Kai Ambos, *supra* note 13, p. 422.

Article 6, paragraph 1, ICTR Statute.[55] Others propose that, at least *de jure condendo*, the two notions serve to draw a distinction between (less culpable) "facilitators", who aid or abet the completion of genocide with mere knowledge of the principal's genocidal intent, and "intellectual perpetrators, instigators and joint principals" acting with genocidal intent, who should be punished for complicity in genocide.[56] This framework would bear 'similarities with those civil law systems that recognize "facilitators" as a separate category of participants in a crime'.[57]

Some other authors put forward that complicity in genocide is a 'hybrid of a substantive crime with a form of liability explicitly attached' committed "through" the heads of liability provided for in Article 6, paragraph 1, ICTR Statute, including aiding and abetting.[58] Finally, there is also the view that complicity in genocide is an offence *a se stante*, which can be committed through all the heads of liability of Article 6, paragraph1, ICTR Statute,[59] and does not require the genocidal intent that must be present in aiding and abetting genocide.[60]

5. It is submitted that the decisions of the tribunals and the literature do not sufficiently highlight that, more than 'reconciling' the norms of the statute with the Convention, the courts must determine the law in force at the time of the relevant acts.

While finding the applicable substantive law, the tribunals should not rely excessively on the literal and systematic interpretation of the statutes, since the resolutions of the Security Council are not supposed to define the offences or heads of liability[61] – (although they may contribute to reflect the Security Council Members' views on substantive customary international criminal law – but rather to designate the fields put

---

[55] Chile Eboe-Osuji, *supra* note 12, p 79: '[g]iven that Article 6(1) does not clearly capture accessories after the fact to genocide, for instance, it will seem then that the best use of the concept of 'complicity in genocide' under Article 2(3)(e) is to use it to capture accessories after the fact of genocide, as well as the *residue of culpable* genocide related conducts that do not rise to the level of individual responsibility described in Article 6(1)'.

[56] Elies van Sliedregt, *supra* note 8, p. 191: "[f]or aiding and abetting genocide (knowledge-based approach): (i) mens rea: knowledge of genocidal intent and general intent with regard to facilitation / actus reus; (ii) actus reus consists of all acts of assistance or encouragement that can be termed as "facilitation" and have contributed to [...] the completion of the crime of genocide [...]. For complicity in genocide (purpose-based approach): (i) mens rea: proof of genocidal intent [...] and general intent with regard to contribution / actus reus; (ii) actus reus consists of playing a key coordinating role (as intellectual perpetrator / instigator or joint principal) in assisting or encouraging genocide that has substantially contributed to [...] the completion of the crime of genocide [...]'.

[57] *Ibid.*, p. 190.

[58] Grant Dawson and Rachel Boynton, *supra* note 8, p. 278 *et seq.*, building on '*Stakic*'s exclusivity theory': '[a]iding and abetting is a form of liability under Article 7(1) that can be applied to any of the substantive crimes set forth in the statute. Complicity in genocide is a hybrid of a substantive crime with a form of liability explicitly attached. As such, the forms of liability under Article 7(1) can attach to complicity in genocide, as they can to genocide and the other substantive crimes in the statute'; and '[e]xplicitly including complicity in genocide as a hybrid form of a substantive crime highlights the egregious nature of complicity in this particular crime and places complicity in genocide on more of the same level as perpetration of the crime itself'. Hence, '[t]he exclusivity theory would assign – with precision – the liability of a person who aids and abets complicity in genocide or who aids and abets another who is complicit in genocide, while at the same time avoiding the over or understatement of the aider and abettor's level of responsibility. It is therefore submitted that the commission of complicity in genocide *through* a form of liability under Article 7(1) would be the correct formulation of a charge for the crime of complicity in genocide'.

[59] Chile Eboe-Osuji, *supra* note 12, p. 73 *et seq.*, acknowledging that 'it may seem a little awkward, at first glance, to approach the matter in this way, when considering the relationship of Article 6(1) to some of the crimes nominated in Articles 2–4. But even here, upon a closer look, it is evident that the intrinsic logic of the approach would still apply (...)'.

[60] Daniel M. Greenfield, The crime of complicity in genocide: how the International Criminal Tribunals for Rwanda and Yugoslavia got it wrong, and why it matters, Symposium on Redefining International Criminal Law, Journal of Criminal Law and Criminology 2008, p. 924, 927: '[o]ne guilty of aiding and abetting the crime of genocide had as his very purpose the facilitation of the commission of genocide. The perpetrator of the crime of complicity in genocide, in contrast, may not have had genocide as his purpose. Instead, genocide may merely have been the foreseeable result of his actions' and thus '(...) the complicity provisions of the Genocide Convention and the Statutes of the ad hoc Tribunals appear designed to capture two very different classes of criminals: those who planned genocide but did not kill, and those who lacked a genocidal plan, but knew that genocide was the foreseeable result of their actions'.

[61] See ICTY, Opinion and Judgment, *Prosecutor v. Tadić*, Case No. IT-94-1-T, T. Ch. II, 7 May 1997, Klip/ Sluiter, ALC-I-287, par. 622; Alexander Zahar, Perpetrators and Co-perpetrators of Genocide, in Paola Gaeta (ed.), The UN Genocide Convention. A Commentary, O. U. P., Oxford 2009, p. 143, fn. 16.

under the tribunals' jurisdiction *ratione materiae*.[62] The contents of the law in force at the time the acts were committed are to be found exclusively by the courts and not by the Security Council.

Thus, the reproduction *verbatim* of the provisions of the Genocide Convention is not necessarily a mistake. It may simply mean that the drafters of the statutes intended to grant the tribunals jurisdiction over all the acts prohibited by the Convention, together with other acts that might constitute genocide under the heads of liability designated in Article 6, paragraph 1, ICTR Statute. It is then for the courts to determine, in the exercise of such jurisdiction, whether or not those heads of liability add to the scope of the Genocide Convention, and whether or not they reflect law that was in force when the offences were perpetrated. Therefore, the possible overlap, or partial redundancy, between Article 2, paragraph 3, subsection e and Article 6, paragraph 1, ICTR Statute, is not an undesirable result of interpretation, to be avoided through 'effective construction',[63] because it does not affect the application of substantive law. In other words, those norms do not have to be 'reconciled' with the customary norms that provide for the punishment of genocide in its multiple modes, because they are of a diverse nature (jurisdictional vs. substantive) and consequently pursue a different scope. In particular, one should avoid any effective construction that leads to an unwarranted reconstruction of applicable substantive law for the sake of making jurisdictional norms fit together.

6. The assessment of the relationship between complicity in genocide and the category heads of liability should follow a *praxis*-oriented approach, the first question being what sense it makes to plead complicity in genocide "in the alternative to genocide" regarding the same acts.

It should be noted that it is not an "alternative" proper – where the counts are mutually exclusive and are not subject to a particular order of logical and normative precedence – but is rather, more accurately, a subsidiary plea. The Trial Chamber explicitly acknowledges that a conviction for complicity in genocide should be entered only if the relevant set of facts does not allow for a conviction for genocide.[64] This construction of the relationship between the two counts, which does not seem to be controversial, means that complicity in genocide is something less than genocide proper and emerges only where the facts proven do not suffice, in the court's view, for genocide to materialise, irrespective of whether this is due to a different qualification of the acts indicted, or to the circumstance that some of the elements of the acts indicted were not proven at trial.

Such an assumption is consistent with the way in which the Genocide Convention frames the punishment of genocide. First, the prohibition refers to the crime of genocide proper (*sc.*, genocide committed by the perpetrator(s) and consummated); then, it extends to less serious genocide-related conduct such as inchoate offences (conspiracy, incitement and attempt), and participation in the offence of genocide (but not in the inchoate offences[65]), by anyone who is a participant according to the applicable international criminal law, and thus cannot be deemed a principal.[66] Therefore, pleading complicity in genocide in the alternative to genocide is the procedural consequence of the subsidiary nature, at a substantive level, of the former's scope in relation to the latter's.

---

[62] On the difference between jurisdictional norms (indicating the applicable body of law) and the applicable substantive norms themselves in the context of the statutes of the *ad hoc* Tribunals, see Pedro Caeiro, Fundamento, Conteúdo e Limites da Jurisdição Penal do Estado. O caso português, Wolters Kluwer / Coimbra Editora, 2010, p. 184 *et seq.*, But, with a possibly different view, see Elies van Sliedregt, *supra* note 8, p. 181: '[p]rovisions on modes of liability in the Statutes of the ad hoc Tribunals have more than an expressive function. That is because these Statutes provide the substantive law of an international court. Articles 2 and 4(3)(e) of the ICTY Statute and Articles 6 and 7(1) of the ICTY Statute have an empowering/jurisdictional function (...)'; and Chile Eboe-Osuji, *supra* note 12, p. 67 *et seq.*, and p. 69, who draws a distinction between the purposes of Article 2, paragraph 3, subsection e, as a jurisdictional norm, and Article 6, paragraph 1, which would provide for an individuation of responsibility, so as to bring to justice '*in a specific way* everyone concerned in the crime – i. e., find them guilty in the highest order of verdict for that crime'.

[63] On the principle of effective construction, see Chile Eboe-Osuji, *supra* note 12, p. 59.

[64] *Ibid.*, par. 504.

[65] Payam Akhavan, *supra* note 53, p. 995.

[66] United Nations Economic and Social Council – Ad Hoc Committee on Genocide, *Report of the Committee and Draft Convention drawn up by the Committee (Dr. Karim Azkoul – Rapporteur)*, E/794, 24 May 1948, p. 21.The assimilation of "complicity in genocide" to accessory responsibility is already present in the *Report of the Ad Hoc Committee* (in the *Report*, complicity extended to all the acts described in art. III): '(e) Complicity in any of the acts enumerated in this Article. The Committee was unanimous on this point. The United States representative stated that in agreeing to the inclusion of "complicity" in this Article, he understood it to refer to accessoryship before and after the fact and to aiding and abetting in the commission of crimes enumerated in this article.'

7. Count One of the indictment, following common law practice,[67] charged the defendant with genocide under all the heads of liability designated in Article 6, paragraph 1, ICTR Statute, indistinctly, including instigation and aiding and abetting, for which the defendant was ultimately convicted. As the latter are not forms of perpetration in international criminal law, one might wonder whether complicity in genocide – pleaded in the alternative – should be construed either as a less serious offence (*infra*, 7.1), or as a less serious form of participation (*infra*,7.2) *vis-à-vis* instigating and aiding and abetting genocide, namely due to a less demanding *mens rea*.

7.1. It seems that the drafters of the Convention did not intend to conceive complicity in genocide as an offence *a se stante*, and there is no evidence that it might have emerged as such in the following decades.[68] Actually, if we probe beyond the labels to the normative level, there are no decisions acknowledging the consequences that the autonomous status of such offence would entail, e.g., convictions for aiding and abetting the "perpetration" of complicity in genocide, where said assistance does not result in aiding and abetting genocide itself, or convictions for complicity in genocide (e.g., through counselling) in a context where no genocide is committed, *sc.*, where quantitative derivative liability would not be required.

It is also clear that the autonomous status of complicity in genocide could not result from the putative need to "reconcile" the substantive norms of the Genocide Convention with the norms prescribed in the statutes regarding the tribunals' jurisdiction, even if such need were real: otherwise, the courts would be legislating and not applying the law in force at the time of the acts. Finally, a conviction for complicity in genocide is not a conviction for 'a mode of liability',[69] but for a crime of genocide as an accomplice, just as much as a conviction for aiding and abetting genocide, especially in a context where the decision at stake explicitly stressed that there is 'no material distinction between complicity in Article 2(3) (e) of the Statute and the broad definition accorded to aiding and abetting'.[70]

7.2. Construing complicity in genocide as a less serious form of accessoryship, and thus pleading it in the alternative to instigation and aiding and abetting genocide, is not convincing either. From a theoretical point of view, one can conceive more or less serious degrees of accessory responsibility, grounded on the significance of individual contribution to the offence and / or the required *mens rea*.[71] However, it seems that the international criminal law in force at the time of the relevant acts would only allow for a distinction between principals and accomplices;[72] it did not allow for differentiation between more or less blameworthy categories of accessories, *sc.*, non-principals, even if the different seriousness of their contributions might be reflected on in the sentencing stage (just as much as principals can be punished with dissimilar sanctions[73]). Indeed, one can differentiate between categories of accomplices according to the type of acts underlying accessory responsibility (counselling, procuring, aiding, abetting), but there is no evidence that international law warrants a classification on the basis of their seriousness in the abstract, which would lead to primary and alternative pleas. It is precisely because such a hierarchy does not exist that the courts, in their attempt to reconcile substantive international criminal law with norms on jurisdiction, have come to such diverse, and even opposite (as in *Akayesu* and *Krstić*), findings.

The possible differentiation between complicity in genocide and instigation and aiding and abetting genocide through the relevant *mens rea*, where specific intent would be required only for the latter, deserves particular consideration. In the case at hand, it might be that the prosecution charged the defendant with complicity in genocide in the alternative (also to instigation and aiding and abetting genocide), in order to warrant a conviction in the case where it failed to prove that the defendant had acted with specific intent; thereby,

---

[67] See Andrew Ashworth, *supra* note 11, p. 412.
[68] See *Prosecutor v. Karemera, supra* note 48, par. 8.
[69] See *supra* note 50.
[70] See *supra* note 36.
[71] See *supra*, 4.7.
[72] See ICTY, Judgement, *Prosecutor v.Furundzija (Trial Judgement)*, Case No. IT-95-17/1-T, T. Ch., 10 December 1998, par. 216, *in fine*: "two separate categories of liability for criminal participation appear to have crystallised in international law – co-perpetrators who participate in a joint criminal enterprise, on the one hand, and aiders and abettors, on the other". This finding means a development from the Nuremberg 'unified perpetrator model ("*Einheitstäterschaft*")' to a differentiated model, where principal responsibility is distinct from accessory responsibility: see Gerhard Werle, Principles, *supra* note 33, p. 167 *et seq.*; Kai Ambos, La Parte General, *supra* note 13, p. 169 *et seq.*
[73] See Chile Eboe-Osuji, *supra* note 12, p. 70.

anticipating a scenario, where the court would require proof of such intent for the modes of liability laid down in Article 6, paragraph 1, ICTR Statue, but not for complicity in genocide. The chamber ultimately found that the defendant acted with specific intent and convicted him under aiding and abetting, which would satisfy the criteria set by *Akayesu*. But the question remains: had specific intent not been proven, would the alternative charge for complicity in genocide be of use?

In the following considerations, it is assumed that the traditional construction of the prohibition of genocide, requiring a specific genocidal purpose as a subjective element of the unlawful act,[74] applied to the acts being tried,[75] as well as the distinction between principals and accessories.[76] It is submitted that both the objective and subjective elements of the *facti species* (e.g., causation, special purposes, etc.) characterise only the acts of the former, the offence proper, and not the latter. Actually, accessories do not violate the norm that prohibits a given crime: rather, they infringe upon the norm that reads 'thou shall not assist, aid, abet, etc., the perpetration of a crime'. Therefore, any special requirement for accessory responsibility to materialise does not result immediately from the norm forbidding the offence, but rather from the specific features of each mode of liability.

a) The *travaux préparatoires* of the Genocide Convention show that the 'drafters all felt the need to extend the circle of offenders to those who participate in the commission of genocide',[77] even if they do not act with the genocidal purpose. In this context, one fails to see why deliberate assistance (aiding or abetting) to killing, etc., in the knowledge that the perpetrators pursue a genocidal purpose, would not suffice to engender punishable participation in genocide, even if the accessory does not share the said purpose. True, the distinct nature of genocide *vis-à-vis* murder, bodily harm, etc., under domestic law relies on a specific genocidal intention,[78] but, at that level, it is meant to characterise the offence, *sc.*, the principal's conduct, and not accessory participation to it. Hence, aiding and abetting genocide does not require a specific genocidal purpose,[79] (which obviously does not mean that accessories cannot share it), irrespective of the legal form in which it is applied. As a consequence, when the same acts are at stake, there is no use in pleading complicity in genocide in the alternative to aiding and abetting genocide, because the customary norm that forbids the former encompasses and in that part, coincides with the latter.

b) On the other hand, it might be that other forms of participation in genocide require the accessory to share the principal's genocidal purpose. Instigation to commit genocide only materialises when the instigator wants the offence of genocide to be committed, with all its objective and subjective elements, as a result of his action. Arguably, intending that another person kills guided by a genocidal purpose without having that same purpose defies common sense. If the offender instigates the killing of an individual and he is not

---

[74] Arguably, the intent to destroy a group is not an instance of *dolus specialis* proper: *dolus*, or intent, refers to the objective elements of the offence (*in casu*, knowledge and volition refer to the acts of killing, etc.); therefore, requiring *dolus specialis* means that the objective elements of the crime must be known and wanted by the perpetrator in a certain way (e. g., with direct intent), with a view to excluding, for instance, *dolus eventualis*. An instance of specific intent can be found, e. g., in Reg. 2 (a) of the English Defence (General) Regulations, 1939: 'doing acts likely to assist the enemy, with intent to assist the enemy'; see *Rex v. Steane* (1947), K. B. 997; [1947] 1 All E. R. 813, and the commentary in Rupert Cross / P. Asterley Jones, Cases on Criminal Law, London, Butterworth & Co., 1949, p. 15 *et seq*. As the actual destruction of the group is not part of the objective elements of genocide, *dolus* cannot refer to it. Therefore, it is preferable to speak of a special intention or purpose.

[75] See Judgement, *Prosecutor v. Kalimanzira*, Case No. ZCTR-0588-T, T. Ch. III, 22 June 2009, in this volume, p. 359, par. 158. The so-called "purpose-based approach" has been subject to criticism from "structure-based" and "knowledge-based" perspectives [compare, e. g., William Schabas, Genocide in International Law, Cambridge, C. U. P., 2000, p. 353; Antonio Cassese, Is Genocidal Policy a Requirement for the Crime of Genocide?, in Paola Gaeta (ed.), The UN Genocide Convention. A Commentary, Oxford, O. U. P., 2009, p. 131; and Gerhard Werle, Principles, *supra* note 34, p. 274 *et seq*. More recently, Kai Ambos, What does 'intent to destroy' in genocide mean?, 876 International Review of the Red Cross, 2009, p. 1 and 26, has argued in favour of a 'combined structure-and knowledge-based' approach that distinguishes according to the status and role of the (low-, mid- and top-level) perpetrators. Thus, the purpose-based intent should be upheld only with regard to the top- and mid-level perpetrators, whereas for the low level perpetrators knowledge of the genocidal context should suffice'. Apart from the objections that this construction may raise in general [the least of which is not the circumstance that it makes the punishment of (more dangerous and blameworthy) "top-level" perpetrators more difficult than low-level ones'), the principle of legality prevents it from characterising the law of genocide applicable by the ICTR.

[76] As Elies van Sliedregt, *supra* note 8, p. 191, puts it, 'after all, assisting a crime is not the same as committing the crime'; see also *supra*, note 72.

[77] Elies van Sliedregt, *supra* note 8, p. 165.

[78] See, e. g., Payam Akhavan, *supra* note 53, p. 992.

[79] Currently, this conclusion seems to be consensual: see, e. g., *Ibid.*, p. 994.

aiming at the destruction of the group, at least as a concomitant goal, but solely at the elimination of a business competitor, the mere awareness that the principal will act with a genocidal purpose does not turn his act into instigation to commit genocide, because the offence intended is merely murder. Indeed, instigation to commit murder might also qualify as abetting genocide.

Therefore, it seems that the structural purposiveness of instigation, together with its ultimate reference to an offence requiring a specific intention, allows for the conclusion that, unlike the aider and the abettor, the act of the instigator must be guided by specific genocidal intention. As a consequence, complicity in genocide cannot serve as a residual plea for punishing instigation to genocide without genocidal purpose.

8. In conclusion, it is submitted that complicity in genocide is not a separate offence, nor a specific head of liability, but rather a set of heads of liability for genocide, punishable under customary international criminal law, encompassing, but not limited to, instigation and aiding and abetting genocide, as suggested in *Krstić*, which might include specific heads not covered by the law generally applicable to other offences. In this context, one might wonder whether the concepts of "committing" and "complicity" should be understood in their original (Anglo-American law) meaning, *sc.*, respectively, physically causing the *actus reus* as opposed to being concerned in the crime (complicity *lato sensu*, which includes principals that have not caused the *actus reus* and accessories); or rather in the sense that "committing" encompasses all perpetrators (including co-perpetrators and *auctores intellectualis* as well), whereas "complicity" has its scope restricted to forms of accessory liability.

Both constructions can help avoid redundant pleas (as submitted, there is no redundancy in substantive law). The difference between the two constructions emerges only at a conceptual and symbolic level, because both leave the normative underlying issues unaltered and lead ultimately to the same results.

8.1. The first approach relies on the assumption that complicity in genocide encompasses all heads of liability other than commission by a single perpetrator. In this context, pleading complicity in genocide in the alternative to genocide for the same acts becomes redundant to the extent that those heads of liability are also charged in the primary plea. Consequently, charges in the primary plea should be limited to the commission of genocide as a single perpetrator; subsidiary charges for complicity in genocide for the same acts would encompass all other heads of liability, including both principals (e.g., co-perpetrators and *auctores intellectualis*)[80] and accessories (instigators and aiders and abetters), provided that their acts fall under the tribunals' jurisdiction. When it is clear from the outset that a given case cannot give rise to a conviction for committing genocide,[81] the indictment should charge only for complicity in genocide, or, which is exactly the same, genocide as an accomplice *lato sensu* (*sc.*, even where the defendant is deemed to be a principal and may be convicted as such), through, e. g., ordering, instigating, aiding or abetting genocide.

8.2. The second approach relies on a narrower understanding of complicity in genocide, where it would encompass only heads of liability carrying accessory responsibility. In this context, primary pleas should entail any given mode of perpetration punishable under customary law and subject to the tribunals' jurisdiction (commission, perpetration through another person, co-perpetration, etc.)[82] but not heads of accessory liability (such as instigation, aiding and abetting), which would be gathered under the notion of complicity in genocide in a possible alternative plea.

8.3. In both constructions, as complicity in genocide is not an offence *a se stante*, nor a specific head of liability, the objective and subjective elements of criminal conduct will vary according to the different modes of liability, and should be found therein. Hence, it is not possible to define a certain *mens rea* as generally applicable to complicity in genocide, either in its broad or narrow meaning.

Possibly, the second line of reasoning should prevail. Even if the drafters of the Genocide Convention used the notion of complicity in its broadest sense, which does not seem to be the case,[83] their purpose could not

---

[80]   Elies van Sliedregt, *supra* note 8, p. 191.
[81]   *Maxime*, when the accused did not commit the *actus reus*; but also in cases where, despite causing the *actus reus*, the accused clearly lacked the required genocidal purpose.
[82]   See Kai Ambos, Internationales Strafrecht. Strafanwendungsrecht. Völkerstrafrecht. Europäisches Strafrecht. Rechtshilfe, 3. Aufl., München, C. H. Beck, 2011 p. 151 *et seq*; and Alexander Zahar, *supra* note 61, p. 140 *et seq.*, p. 151.
[83]   See *supra* note 54.

have been to assert that certain principals should be charged as accomplices, but rather to ensure that all concerned in an offence of genocide would be liable for the crime, irrespective of the concrete head of liability applicable. Moreover, the latter perspective, unlike the former, allows for convicting all principals for "committing genocide", even in situations of complicity (*lato sensu*), which bears an important effect at a symbolic level: the ambiguity of the term "complicity" could have the unintended effect of diminishing the responsibility of principals convicted of perpetrating genocide in such situations.[84]

Pedro Caeiro and Miguel Ângelo Lemos

---

[84] See William Schabas, *supra* note 75, p. 286.

International Criminal Tribunal for Rwanda
Tribunal pénal international pour le Rwanda

OR: ENG

TRIAL CHAMBER III

Before Judges: Khalida Rachid Khan, presiding
Lee Gacuiga Muthoga
Aydin Sefa Akay

Registrar: Mr. Adama Dieng

Date: 7 July 2009

THE PROSECUTOR

v.

Léonidas NSHOGOZA

Case No. ICTR-07-91-T

JUDGEMENT

Office of the Prosecutor:

Richard Karegyesa
Abdoulaye Seye
Dennis Mabura
Marie Ka

For the Accused:

Allison Turner

[page 2] TABLE OF CONTENTS

CHAPTER I: INTRODUCTION 4
  1. THE TRIBUNAL AND JURISDICTION 4
  2. OVERVIEW OF THE CHARGES 4
  3. THE ACCUSED 5
  4. SUMMARY OF PROCEDURAL HISTORY 5

CHAPTER II: PRELIMINARY MATTERS 5
  1. ALLEGED PROCEDURAL IRREGULARITIES IN THE CONDUCT OF THE PROCEEDINGS 5
    1.1. Alleged Disclosure Violations, including late disclosure 5
    1.2. Delays in Rendering Decisions 7
    1.3. Unreasonable Restrictions on the Presentation of the Defence Case 7
    1.4. Interference with Defence Witnesses and Disclosure of Witness Identities by the Registry 8
    1.5. Time Allotted to the Defence Case 8
    1.6. Alleged Interference with the Defence Case 9
      1.6.1 Interference with Protected Defence Witnesses 9
        1.6.1.1 Registry Complicity in the Interference by Rwandan Authorities 9
        1.6.1.2 Repeated WVSS interference with Defence Witnesses 9
      1.6.2 Alleged Interference in the Preparation of the Defence Case 10
        1.6.2.1 Alleged Interference by the Registry 10
        1.6.2.2 Alleged Prosecution Interference with the Defence Case 11
      1.6.3 Improper Contact of Office of the Prosecutor with Protected Defence Witnesses 11
      1.6.3.1 Witness GAA 11
        1.6.3.2 Witness A7/GEX 12
        1.6.3.3 Witness Fulgence Seminega 12
        1.6.3.4 Witness Augustin Nyagatare 12
        1.6.3.5 Straton Nyarwaya 12
      1.6.4 Alleged Prosecution Violation of Witness Protection Orders 12
    1.7. Requested Remedy for Procedural Irregularities 13
  2. ALLEGED DEFECTS IN THE INDICTMENT 13
  3. TREATMENT OF PROSECUTION WITNESS GAA'S EVIDENCE 15

CHAPTER III: FACTUAL FINDINGS 17
  1. BACKGROUND 17
  2. MEETINGS AMONG NSHOGOZA, WITNESS GAA AND WITNESS A7/GEX 19
    2.1. Facts Relevant to the Meetings among the Accused, Witness GAA and Witness A7/GEX 19
    2.2. Disputed Factual Issues 20
      2.2.1 The Accused's knowledge regarding the protective measures 20
        2.2.1.1 Witness A7/GEX 21
        2.2.1.2 Witness GAA 22
      2.2.2 Initiation of the meetings 22
      2.2.3 Did the Accused disclose protected information? 23
      2.2.4 Did the Accused fabricate statements or know they were false? 24
      2.2.5 Bribery or Other interference 26
        2.2.5.1 Alleged Payments and Inducements Offered by the Accused 26
        2.2.5.2 The Alleged Promise of Payment of One Million Rwandan Francs 29
        2.2.5.3 Evidence of Misrepresentations by the Accused 31
  3. THE MEETING BETWEEN NSHOGOZA AND WITNESS BUC 32
    3.1. Facts Related to the Accused's Meeting with Witness BUC 32
    3.2. Other Relevant Evidence ..... 33 [page 3]
    3.3. Disputed Factual Issues 34
  4. WITNESS GAA'S MEETINGS WITH WITNESSES GAF, SP003 AND SP004 35
    4.1. Disputed Factual Issues 35
      4.1.1 Relevant Evidence 35
      4.1.2 Did the Accused request Witness GAA to find more Witnesses? 37

	4.1.3 Did the Accused promise payment for other witnesses?	38
CHAPTER IV:	LEGAL CONCLUSIONS	38
1.	Overview of the Law of Contempt of the Tribunal	38
2.	Count One: Contempt of the Tribunal	39
	2.1. Were Witnesses GAA and A7/GEX Protected Prosecution Witnesses?	40
	2.2. Repeated Meetings with Protected Prosecution Witnesses	42
	2.2.1 Sufficiently Serious Conduct	43
	2.2.2 Defence Arguments related to *mens rea*	44
	2.3. Disclosure of Protected Information to Third Parties or the General Public	46
	2.4. Conclusion	47
3.	Count Two: Contempt of the Tribunal	47
	3.1. Manipulating and Instigating Witnesses	48
	3.2. Offer of a Bribe	48
	3.3. Manipulation of Witness GAA	49
	3.4. Incitement to Sign False Statements or Give False Testimony	49
	3.5. Conclusion	49
4.	Count Three: Attempt to Commit Acts Punishable ts Contempt of the Tribunal	49
5.	Count Four: Attempt to Commit Acts Punishable ts Contempt of the Tribunal	50
CHAPTER V:	SENTENCING	50
1.	Introduction	51
2.	Determination of the Sentence	51
	2.1. Gravity of the Offence	51
	2.2. Individual Circumstances of the Accused	53
	2.2.1 Aggravating Circumstances	53
	2.2.2 Mitigating Circumstances	54
	2.3. Credit for Time Served	55
3.	Conclusion	55
ANNEX:	PROCEDURAL HISTORY OF THE CASE	57

[page 4] CHAPTER I: INTRODUCTION

1. The Tribunal and Jurisdiction

1. Trial Chamber III of the International Criminal Tribunal for Rwanda, composed of Judges Khalida Rachid Khan, presiding, Lee Gacuiga Muthoga and Aydin Sefa Akay, is seized of the case against Léonidas Nshogoza, charged with contempt of the Tribunal pursuant to Rule 77 of the Rules of Procedure and Evidence.[1]

2. Though not expressly articulated in the Statute, the inherent authority of the Tribunal, as an international court, to exercise jurisdiction over the crime of contempt is firmly established in the jurisprudence of the International Criminal Tribunal for the Former Yugoslavia ("ICTY").[2]

2. Overview of the Charges

3. The Prosecution alleges that the Accused, during the period beginning on approximately 1 March 2004 and ending on approximately 31 May 2005, repeatedly met with Prosecution Witness GAA, a prosecution witness in the *Kamuhanda* case, and Defence Witness A7/GEX, a potential prosecution witness in the *Kamuhanda* case, and manipulated, incited, instigated, induced or bribed them into signing false statements he had written and to testifying falsely before the Appeals Chamber.[3] According to the Prosecution, the Accused acted in knowing violation of, or with reckless indifference to whether his actions violated protective measures ordered by the *Kamuhanda* Trial Chamber.[4] In addition, the Prosecution alleges that the Accused attempted to procure false statements or testimony from Prosecution Witnesses BUC, GAF, SP003 and SP004. For these acts, the Prosecution charges Nshogoza with two counts of contempt of the Tribunal, and two counts of attempt to commit acts punishable as contempt of the tribunal. [page 5]

3. The Accused

4. Léonidas Nshogoza was an investigator for the defence in the case of *The Prosecutor v. Jean de Dieu Kamuhanda*, Case No. ICTR-99-54A-T. He was born in 1961 in Rukeri, Kyumba, Muhanga, Southern Province, Rwanda. In 1986, Nshogoza graduated from the National University of Rwanda, where he studied law.[5] He began working for the *Kamuhanda* defence team at the end of 2001.[6] According to the Accused, he officially joined the Kigali bar and became a lawyer in April 2005.[7]

4. Summary of Procedural History

5. The trial commenced on 9 February 2009 and concluded on 30 March 2009, with a three week break between the presentation of the Prosecutor's evidence and the presentation of the Defence evidence. The

---

[1] Unless otherwise specified, all further references to Rules in this Judgement are to the Rules of Procedure and Evidence.
[2] *The Prosecutor v. Duško Tadić*, Case No. IT-94-1-A-R77, Judgement on Allegations of Contempt against Prior Counsel, Milan Vujin (AC), 31 January 2000 ("Vujin Contempt Judgement"), paras. 13-28; *The Prosecutor v. Blagoje Simić et al*, Case No. IT-95-9-R77, Judgement in the Matter of Contempt Allegations Against an Accused and his Counsel (TC), 30 June 2000, ("*Simić* Contempt Judgement") para. 91; *The Prosecutor v. Zlato Aleksovski*, Case No. IT-95-14/1-AR77, Judgement on Appeal by Anto Nobilo Against a Finding of Contempt (AC), 30 May 2001("*Nobilo* Appeal Judgement"), para. 30; *The Prosecutor v. Ivica Marijačić and Markica Rebić*, Case No. IT-95-14-R77.2-A, Judgement (AC), 27 September 2006 ("*Marijačić* Appeal Judgement"), paras. 23-24; *Prosecutor v. Ivica Marijačić and Markica Rebić*, Case No. IT-95-14-R77.2, Judgement (TC), 10 March 2006 ("*Marijačić* Trial Judgement") para. 13; The *Prosecutor v. Beqa Beqaj*, Case No. IT-03-66-T-R77, Judgement on Contempt Allegations (TC), 27 May 2005 ("*Beqaj* Contempt Judgement"), para. 9; *The Prosecutor v. Slobodan Milosevic*, Case No. IT-02-54-R77.4, Decision on Interlocutory Appeal on Kosta Bulatović Contempt Proceedings (AC), 29 August 2005 ("*Bulatović* Contempt Appeal"), para. 21.
[3] To distinguish between this case and the *Kamuhanda* proceedings, the Chamber has capitalized "Prosecution" and "Defence" when referring to the Parties in this case, and has referred to the prosecution and defence, in lower case, when referring to the *Kamuhanda* proceedings.
[4] The Indictment refers to "reckless disregard", *see* para. 8. The Chamber considers this to be the equivalent of "reckless indifference", which is the more commonly used phrase in the jurisprudence.
[5] *Nshogoza*, T. 30 March 2009 pp. 2-3.
[6] *Nshogoza*, T. 30 March 2009 p. 3.
[7] *Nshogoza*, T. 30 March 2009 p. 28.

Chamber heard the live testimony of five witnesses for the Prosecution, and 11 witnesses for the Defence, including Nshogoza himself. The procedural history is set out in full in Annex I to the Judgement.

CHAPTER II: PRELIMINARY MATTERS

1. ALLEGED PROCEDURAL IRREGULARITIES IN THE CONDUCT OF THE PROCEEDINGS

6. In its Closing Brief, the Defence alleges a number of "procedural irregularities" which it contends amount to a violation of the rights of the Accused and warrant the granting of a remedy by the Chamber.[8] The allegations include disclosure violations, delays in rendering decisions, restrictions placed on the Defence case, and interference with Defence witnesses and the Defence case.

1.1. Alleged Disclosure Violations, including late disclosure

7. The Defence alleges that, in violation of its disclosure obligations under the Rules, a number of documents were not disclosed by the Prosecution.[9] The Defence also alleges that the fairness of these proceedings have been compromised by the late disclosure of two documents, resulting in material prejudice to the Accused suffering.[10] **[page 6]**

8. The Chamber notes that each of the alleged violations arising from non-disclosures raised by the Defence was already dealt with by the Chamber during the course of these proceedings.[11] The Defence is, accordingly, estopped from raising these same issues *de novo*. Furthermore, as the Defence has not raised any new circumstances or evidence to call into question these prior decisions there is no basis upon which to revisit, or reconsider these decisions.

9. With respect to the first of the two documents the late disclosure of which, the Defence claims, resulted in material prejudice to the Accused, the Chamber recalls its decision concerning the statement of Straton Nyarwaya which specifically found that, despite the Prosecution's violation of its Rule 66 (B) disclosure obligation in respect of that statement, no material prejudice had been suffered by the Accused.[12]

10. Concerning the second of the two documents – the fee statement of the Léonidas Nshogoza dated 12 September 2003 and filed 25 February 2004 – the Chamber notes that the fee statement was disclosed to the Defence on 11 March 2009.[13] Furthermore, the Chamber finds that the Defence has failed to demonstrate prejudice suffered by the Accused.

---

[8] Defence Closing Brief, paras. 106-7
[9] These documents are: (i) a statement given by Witness GAA to the Rwandan CID in 2005: Defence Closing Brief, para. 16; (ii) recordings of a Prosecution interview with Witness GAA on 23 August 2003: Defence Closing Brief, para. 16; (iii) all recordings of Loretta Lynch interviews for the purposes of the *Kamuhanda* investigation: Defence Closing Brief, para. 16; (iv) a statement by Augustin Nyagatare to the Prosecution: Defence Closing Brief, para. 20; and (v) Rwandan judicial materials of the Accused and Witness GAA: Defence Closing Brief, paras. 24-28.
[10] Defence Closing Brief, para. 16. These two documents are: (i) a statement by Straton Nyarwaya to the Prosecution, disclosed on 25 March 2009: Defence Closing Brief, paras. 17-19; and (ii) a fee statement of Léonidas Nshogoza dated 12 September 2003, filed on 25 February 2004, and disclosed on 11 March 2009: Defence Closing Brief, para. 21.
[11] The Prosecution certified its efforts to locate the 2005 statement by Witness GAA to the Rwandan CID (*see* Prosecutor's Certification on Rwandan Judicial Materials, filed 23 February 2009); In relation to the recording of the 2003 Prosecution interview with Witness GAA, the Chamber notes its decision of 10 February 2009 denying the Defence's submissions on the basis that the Prosecution had certified that it did not have the requested recording in its possession. (Decision on Defence Motion for Order to Prosecutor to Comply with his Disclosure Obligations and Motion for Stay of Proceedings Due to the On-Going Violations of the Prosecutor's Disclosure Obligations (TC), 10 February 2009, para. 12.) The Chamber notes its decision that the Loretta Lynch interviews were not exculpatory and thus did not need to be disclosed (Decision on Defence Motions for Disclosure Under Rule 66 and 68 of the Rules of Procedure and Evidence (TC), 22 December 2008, para. 38). In relation to the statement by Augustin Nyagatare to the Prosecution, the Chamber notes that the Prosecution has certified it has searched for this document and that it is not in its possession (T. 23 March 2009, pp. 18-19). The Chamber notes its prior order in relation to the Rwandan judicial material (T. 19 February 2009, p. 17), and the Prosecution's certification that it has searched for and made attempts to obtain the requested documents (Prosecutor's Certification on Rwandan Judicial Materials, filed 23 February 2009).
[12] Decision on Defence Motion to Admit the Statement of Defence Witness Straton Nyarwaya into Evidence; and for Other Relief (TC), 1 July 2009.
[13] Disclosure Under Rule 66 (B)/InterOffice Memorandum Ern-K045-8604-8609, filed 11 March 2009.

11. With respect to the Defence allegations that the Prosecution's violation of its disclosure obligations, and the Chamber's failure to ensure compliance, violated the Accused's right to properly prepare for cross-examination and to know the nature and cause of the charges against him,[14] the Chamber finds this submission to be lacking in evidentiary support and specificity as to the prejudice caused and, therefore, need not consider this point further. For the same reasons, the Chamber dismisses the Defence submission that the Prosecution made misleading oral representations in relation to its disclosure violations and thus has forfeited the presumption that it has acted in good faith.[15] Finally, and with regard to the Defence's submissions in relation to the denial of Defence requests for postponement of the trial due to the Prosecution's disclosure violations,[16] the Chamber notes that the Defence failed to substantiate any flaw in the previous [page 7] decisions of the Chamber denying postponement, nor has it demonstrated any prejudice. Thus these submissions are dismissed.

1.2. Delays in Rendering Decisions

12. The Defence submits that the Chamber failed to render decisions in a timely manner, resulting in prejudice to the Accused.[17] The Defence Closing Brief raises five decisions that were pending at the date of filing.[18] The Chamber notes that all five decisions have since been issued.[19] The Defence also submits that due to the timing of a decision by the Chamber, it was unable to rely upon information in relation to Prosecution visits to Witness GAA while at the UNDF in the preparation of its case.[20]

13. The Chamber notes that "many factors affect the timing of decisions".[21] It finds the Defence's argument in relation to its ability to seek review of its decisions unpersuasive. The Chamber also notes that it has allowed the Defence to supplement its Closing Brief, and the Defence did so.[22] Finally, the Chamber considers that the Defence's submission in relation to having to put on its case while a motion for a stay of proceedings was pending lacks specificity as to how this prejudiced the Accused. Therefore, the Chamber finds that the Defence has failed to articulate any prejudice as a result of the timing of its decisions.

1.3. Unreasonable Restrictions on the Presentation of the Defence Case

14. The Defence alleges that certain restrictions were unreasonably imposed upon the Defence Case by the Chamber.[23]

---

[14] Defence Pre-Defence Brief, para. 10.
[15] Defence Closing Brief, para. 16; Supplementary Closing Brief of Leonidas Nshogoza, filed 18 June 2009 ("Defence Supplementary Closing Brief"), para. 21.
[16] Defence Supplementary Closing Brief, para. 22
[17] Defence Closing Brief, para. 31; Defence Pre-Defence Brief, paras. 12-13.
[18] Defence Closing Brief, para. 30: The motions mentioned are: (i) Defence Urgent Motion for Stay of Proceedings Due to Interference with Defence Witnesses, filed 4 March 2009; (ii) Defence Motion for the Admission of Written Witness Statements of Witnesses A1, A13, A14, A15, A17, A18, A20, A22, A23, A26 and A30 as Evidence in Lieu of Oral Testimony, filed 16 March 2009; (iii) Defence Motion for Order to Registrar to Provide Information to the Nshogoza Defence Regarding Prosecution Visits to GAA at UNDF in 2007, filed 20 March 2009; (iv) Defence Motion for the Admission of Transcripts Pursuant to Rule 92, filed 3 April 2009; (v) Defence Motion to Admit Into Evidence 15 March 2006 OTP Statement Taken from Defence Witness Straton Nyarwaya, [and for Other Relief], filed 7 May 2009.
[19] The relevant decisions are: (i) Decision on Defence Motion for the Admission of Transcripts Pursuant to Rule 92*bis* (TC), 23 April 2009; (ii) Decision on Defence Motion for Order to Registrar to Provide Information to the Defence Regarding Prosecution Visits to Witness GA at UDF (TC), 28 April 2009; (iii) Decision on Defence Motion for the Admission of Written Witness Statements Of Witnesses A1, A13, A14, A15, A17, A18, A20, A22, A23, A26, A28, and A30 as Evidence *in lieu* Of Oral Testimony (TC), 29 April 2009; (iv) Confidential Decision on Defence Motion for Stay of Proceedings (TC), 22 May 2009; (v) Decision on Defence Motion to Admit the Statement of Defence Witness Straton Nyarwaya into Evidence; and for Other Relief (TC), 1 July 2009.
[20] Defence Supplementary Closing Brief, para. 20.
[21] *Prosecutor v. Karemera et al.*, Case No. ICTR-98-44-T, Decision on Motion by Nzirorera for Disqualification of Trial Judges, 17 May 2004, para. 27
[22] T. 29 April 2008 p. 2; Defence Supplementary Closing Brief, para. 21.
[23] Defence Closing Brief, paras. 34-47. They are: (i) a forced reduction of testifying Defence witnesses to ten, in addition to the Accused; (ii) a denial of a Defence request to subpoena Ms. Loretta Lynch; and (iii) a denial of a Defence request to amend the Defence witness list after a witness turned hostile during examination.

15. The Chamber notes that it has already dealt with all of these issues in prior decisions, providing reasoning for its decision in each case.[24] The Defence has raised no new arguments and has failed to demonstrate any prejudice. Thus, the Chamber need not revisit them here. **[page 8]**

16. The Defence also submitted that the Chamber's order to the Defence to provide a summary of its witnesses' testimony before the close of the Prosecution's case was contrary to Rule 73 *ter* (B)(iii)(b) and violated the Accused's right to have adequate time and facilities for the preparation of his defence.[25]

17. The Chamber notes that its order to file witness summaries was made pursuant to Rule 54 of the Rules, which empowers the Chamber to make orders "for the preparation or conduct of the trial."[26] The Chamber considers that the Defence has failed to show that the order was *ultra vires*. Furthermore, the Chamber notes that the Rules contemplate the amending of a witness list.[27]

1.4. Interference with Defence Witnesses and Disclosure of Witness Identities by the Registry

18. The Defence submits that, due to contact between Rwandan authorities and its witnesses, and the provision of information by WVSS to the Rwandan authorities, the Accused has suffered prejudice.[28] The Defence further submits that WVSS has also violated the witness protection measures ordered in this case, and Rule 77 (A).[29]

19. The Chamber notes its prior decision on these issues, wherein it found that no rights violation had occurred, as well as its order to the Registry to review its internal procedures in relation to the protection and dissemination of witness information.[30] Considering the decision, the Chamber finds that the Defence has failed to demonstrate any prejudice not already contemplated by this Chamber.

1.5. Time Allotted to the Defence Case

20. The Defence details a number of decisions by the Chamber that it alleges interfered with the proper execution of the Defence case by limiting the time between the close of the Prosecution case and start of Defence case, and for the preparation and presentation of the Defence case.[31]

21. The Chamber notes that it has already ruled upon the amount of time between the Prosecution's and Defence case, as well as a motion for reconsideration of that decision.[32] The **[page 9]** Defence has not submitted any new material that warrants reconsideration of that decision. These submissions are thus dismissed.

22. It further notes that the Defence Closing Brief misrepresents a statement by the Chamber that the justification for its decisions not to sit on Fridays, and to not grant a one-week postponement, was based purely on mathematical equality.[33] In that instance, the Chamber did not limit the amount of time for the

---

[24] Decision on Defence Motion for Reconsideration of the Chamber's Further Order for the Defence to Reduce its Witness List (TC), 26 February 2009; Decision on the Defence's Urgent Motion for a Subpoena to Ms. Loretta Lynch (TC), 10 February 2009; and T. 25 March 2009 pp. 24-26 (Oral Order).
[25] Defence Pre-Defence Brief, para. 16.
[26] Rule 54
[27] Rule 73 *ter* (E).
[28] Defence Closing Brief, paras. 48-53.
[29] Defence Closing Brief, paras. 51, 66-69.
[30] Confidential Decision on Defence Motion for Stay of Proceedings (TC), 22 May 2009, paras. 20-22.
[31] They are: (i) the reduction of time between the close of the Prosecution's case and beginning of the Defence case: Defence Closing Brief, paras. 54-55; (ii) the refusal by the Chamber to sit on Fridays: Defence Closing Brief, para. 56; (iii) the denial of a Defence motion asking for a one-week postponement: Defence Closing Brief, para. 59; and (iv) the ultimate provision of nine and a half days for the presentation of the Defence case: Defence Closing Brief, para. 60.
[32] Decision on Defence Motion for Postponement of Defence Case (TC), 26 February 2009, para. 4, wherein the Chamber noted that the scheduling of the Defence case was not premised on the number of weeks between the close of the Prosecutor's case and the commencement of the Defence case; and Decision on Defence Motion for Reconsideration of the Chamber's Decision on Motion for Postponement of Defence Case (TC), 4 March 2009.
[33] Defence Closing Brief, para. 56-57.

Defence to present its case based on mathematical equality, but rather on a considered reasoning of what time would be adequate for the Defence to present its case.

23. The Chamber considers that the Defence has failed to demonstrate how any of these decisions in relation to the scheduling of the trial have prevented the Accused from having "adequate time and facilities for the preparation of his Defence" or meant that the Accused was not able to examine witnesses on his behalf "under the same conditions as witnesses against him".[34] Neither has the Defence demonstrated how the time allotted to its case prejudice the Accused.

24. Thus, the Chamber considers these submissions to be unsubstantiated and dismisses them.

1.6. Alleged Interference with the Defence Case

1.6.1 Interference with Protected Defence Witnesses

1.6.1.1 Registry Complicity in the Interference by Rwandan Authorities

25. The Defence reiterates its submissions in relation to the Registry providing protected witness information to the Rwandan authorities, alleging a violation of Rule 77 (A).

1.6.1.2 Repeated WVSS interference with Defence Witnesses

26. The Defence submits that after instructing WVSS not to contact Defence witnesses, WVSS conducted interviews with five Defence witnesses.[35] The Defence also alleges that WVSS contact influenced one witness to testify, despite her not wanting to, resulting in her turning hostile during examination.[36] The Defence submits that this is a violation of Rule 77 (A)[37] and requests the appointment of an *amicus curiae* to investigate these actions.[38]

27. The Chamber notes that WVSS is tasked with the protection and support of witnesses and victims at this Tribunal.[39] The Chamber considers that to carry out this function, WVSS needs to be in contact with witnesses to ensure that their needs are being met and that they are safe. In this **[page 10]** instance, the Chamber considers that WVSS has followed normal procedure to ascertain whether witnesses had been interfered with and whether they needed any assistance from WVSS staff. Furthermore, the Chamber notes that the Defence offers no evidence that WVSS interfered with the testimony of its witnesses, or did anything untoward or not within its mandate. The Chamber does not consider that the witness testimony of Witness A10 is at all clear as to who spoke to her in Rwanda, or of the effect of the contact, if any, on her testimony.[40] Thus, the Chamber finds the Defence's unfounded accusations of "flagrant interference"[41] by the WVSS with Defence witnesses to be unprofessional and unbecoming of Counsel practicing before this Tribunal.

28. Given the Chamber's findings in relation to this matter, it would inappropriate and premature to appoint an *amicus curiae* to investigate WVSS or Registry conduct. The Chamber considers its order for an internal review of the procedures of WVSS to be sufficient to ensure that the processes of WVSS fulfil its mandate of witness protection and support and do not result in the unnecessary dissemination of protected witness information.[42]

---

[34] Defence Closing Brief, para. 54.
[35] Defence Closing Brief, paras. 72-74.
[36] Defence Closing Brief, para. 76.
[37] Defence Closing Brief, paras. 77-78
[38] Defence Closing Brief, para. 78
[39] Rule 34 (A)
[40] T. 23 March 2009, p. 65-69.
[41] Defence Closing Brief, para. 76
[42] Confidential Decision on Defence Motion for Stay of Proceedings (TC), 22 May 2009. A public version of this decision was filed by the Chamber on 26 June 2009.

1.6.2 Alleged Interference in the Preparation of the Defence Case

1.6.2.1 Alleged Interference by the Registry

29. The Defence makes a number of allegations of interference by the Registry in the preparation of the Defence case.[43]

30. The Defence Closing Brief does not submit specific instances of bias by the Registry, beyond one failure to disclose a document upon request,[44] but rather relies on general, vague and unsubstantiated allegations. The Chamber dismisses these submissions as they lack specificity and the Defence has not demonstrated any prejudice.

31. In relation to the employment records, the Chamber also finds the Defence submissions lacking in substance. The Chamber notes that a decision on this point would require additional submissions from the Registry and the Prosecution. As the Defence failed to properly substantiate these submissions in a motion before the Chamber, they are also dismissed.

32. The Chamber considers that the Defence's submissions on the Registry's failure to appoint a Presiding Officer for Rule 92 *bis* statements are rendered moot by the late stage of these proceedings. The Chamber finds that the Defence should have brought this to its attention earlier via a motion for a timely resolution.
[page 11]

33. Finally, in relation to the Registry's alleged failure to provide the Defence with requested information on Prosecution visits to Witness GAA while in the UNDF, the Chamber notes its decision ordering the disclosure of this material.[45] The Chamber does not consider the Registry's actions in this case to be obstructive; rather the Registry was unsure of its obligations and thus requested an order of the Chamber to clarify what was required of it. Accordingly the Chamber dismisses these submissions.

1.6.2.2 Alleged Prosecution Interference with the Defence Case

34. The Defence submits that the Prosecution's failure to allow the Defence to meet with staff of the OTP prevented the Defence from accessing evidence in preparation of its case.[46] The Defence also submits that the Prosecution's failure to allow the Defence to interview Witness BUC, and WVSS to ask Witness BUC if he consented to Defence contact, amounts to obstruction and interference.[47] The Defence submits that this warrants an independent investigation pursuant to Rule 77.[48]

35. The Chamber finds that these Defence's submissions properly belong in a motion before this Chamber, and that the Defence's failure to raise these issues earlier in proceedings has resulted in a waiver of its right to raise them at all. Accordingly, the Chamber rejects these submissions as untimely.

36. Additionally, the Chamber notes the Defence's allegation of a campaign to gather false testimony involving Ms. Moenback.[49] Once again, this should have been filed in a motion before this Chamber with proper substantiation to allow the Chamber to make an informed decision on the basis of submissions from both parties. The Defence's failure to do so makes this request untimely. It is accordingly dismissed.

---

[43] Defence Closing Brief, paras. 79-87. The Defence raises: (i) the Registry's alleged application of different standards for document disclosure to the parties; (ii) the Registry's alleged disclosure of confidential employment records of the Accused to the OTP without authorization; (iii) the Registry's alleged failure to appoint a Presiding Officer to witness a Rule 92 *bis* statement; and (iv) the Registry's alleged failure to provide the Defence with information on Prosecution visits to Witness GAA while he was in the UNDF.
[44] Defence Closing Brief, paras. 21-23
[45] Decision on Defence Motion for Order to Registrar to Provide Information to the Defence Regarding Prosecution Visits to Witness GAA at UNDF (TC), 28 April 2009.
[46] Defence Closing Brief, para. 88
[47] Defence Closing Brief, paras. 91-95.
[48] Defence Closing Brief, para. 95
[49] Defence Closing Brief, para. 95.

1.6.3 Improper Contact of Office of the Prosecutor with Protected Defence Witnesses

37. The Defence submits that on six occasions, members of the OTP contacted and met with protected Defence witnesses in violation of orders from the cases of *Kamuhanda* or *Rwamakuba*.[50]

1.6.3.1 Witness GAA

38. Witness GAA agreed that Mr. Musonda and Ms. Moenback, two OTP staff members, met with him in 2005, a few days before he testified for the Defence in *Kamuhanda*.[51] Witness **[page 12]** GAA testified that Ms. Moenback told him that he was a protected witness.[52] Furthermore, the Defence entered a number of exhibits under seal, of excerpts of an interview between Witness GAA and Ms. Lynch that took place on 29 September 2005.[53]

1.6.3.2 Witness A7/GEX

39. Witness A7/GEX testified that she met with Ms. Moenback along with another gentleman and gave them a statement.[54] The Defence tendered a statement by Witness A7/GEX to the OTP, on 4 August 2008, under seal.[55]

1.6.3.3 Witness Fulgence Seminega

40. Fulgence Seminega, who testified that he was a protected Defence witness in *Kamuhanda*,[56] testified that ICTR representatives approached him on 3 August 2008 to set up a meeting.[57] Mr. Seminega was only informed that the meeting was with OTP staff when he arrived for the meeting on 4 August 2008.[58] Mr. Seminega testified that the woman who called him was named Colette, and that a man named Pierre, and Ms. Moenback, were also in the car with him when they met.

1.6.3.4 Witness Augustin Nyagatare

41. Augustin Nyagatare, agreed that he was a protected Defence witness in the *Rwamakuba* case,[59] testified that he met with staff of the OTP at his home in August 2008 to discuss the Accused.[60]

1.6.3.5 Straton Nyarwaya

42. Straton Nyarwaya testified that he testified for the Defence using a pseudonym in the *Rwamakuba* case, but lived in a hotel;[61] and that after testifying in *Rwamakuba* he was contacted by the OTP in regard to *Kamuhanda*,[62] via the WVSS,[63] and that he gave them a statement.[64]

---

[50] Defence Closing Brief, paras. 95-104
[51] T. 18 February 2009 p. 2
[52] T. 18 February 2009 p. 9.
[53] T. 18 February 2009 p. 49-52
[54] T. 18 March 2009 p. 48
[55] T. 18 March 2009 pp. 49-50; Exhibit D. 48
[56] T. 19 March 2009 p. 53
[57] T. 19 March 2009 p. 57
[58] T. 19 March 2009 p. 57.
[59] T. 23 March 2009 p. 19
[60] T. 23 March 2009 p. 19.
[61] T. 20 March 2009 p. 4.
[62] T. 20 March 2009 p. 23.
[63] T. 20 March 2009 p. 23.
[64] T. 20 March 2009 p. 23.

1.6.4 Alleged Prosecution Violation of Witness Protection Orders

43. In relation to Witnesses GAA and A7/GEX, the Chamber notes that they testified as protected prosecution witnesses in the original *Kamuhanda* trial and, due to the Defence's failure **[page 13]** to follow proper procedure, were still protected Prosecution witnesses at the time contact took place. Accordingly, the Defence submissions in relation to these two witnesses are dismissed.

44. However, in relation to Witnesses Fulgence Seminega, Augustin Nyagatare and Starton Nyarwaya, the Chamber notes that, according to their own testimonies, these witnesses were all covered by protection orders from *Rwamakuba* or *Kamuhanda* as Defence witnesses in those cases. These protection orders, *inter alia*, prohibited the Prosecution from contacting these witnesses, without first notifying the Defence and having it make the necessary arrangements.[65] The Chamber considers that the witnesses' testimonies *prima facie* indicate that the Prosecution may have acted in violation of witness protection orders.

45. The Chamber thus finds that this conduct may justify an investigation into the conduct of members of the OTP as requested by the Defence.[66] However, prior to giving full consideration to the merits of this request, the Chamber would like to hear from the Parties on this issue. A reques` for submissions from the Parties will, however, be dealt with by an order separate to this Judgement.

1.7. Requested Remedy for Procedural Irregularities

46. As a remedy for the alleged irregularities, the Defence seeks a reduction in sentence, if the Accused is convicted, or financial compensation, if the Accused is acquitted.[67]

47. As the Chamber has not found any evidence of prejudice to the Accused, there is no need for it to consider an appropriate remedy.

2. ALLEGED DEFECTS IN THE INDICTMENT

48. In closing arguments before the Chamber, the Defence raised the issue of a possible defect in the Indictment, noting that Counts One and Two shared the "common element" of "fabrication of evidence" and submitting that "[t]here is a serious problem with the drafting of these counts and that they cause confusion, more than anything else."[68]

49. The Chamber agrees that there is substantial overlap of allegations in Counts One and Two of the Indictment, in particular concerning the allegations of bribery and the procurement of false statements and false testimony. Concerning Count One, paragraphs six, 10, 11, and 15 of the Indictment allege, respectively and among other things, that the Accused acted with "intent to fabricate evidence"; that the Accused "manipulated, incited, induced, promised a bribe or reward to and persuaded both GAA and GEX to sign false statements prepared by the Accused and accept to give false testimony …"; that "[t]he Accused fabricated recantation statements"; and "[a]s a result of the meetings with the Accused and his incitement, inducements, and the promise of a bribe or reward of a substantial amount of money, GAA and GEX also gave false testimony…." Paragraph 16 of the Indictment summarizes the alleged criminal conduct of the Accused for Count One, and reads as follows: **[page 14]**

> The Accused committed the offence of contempt of the Tribunal as he wilfully contacted and repeatedly met with protected prosecution witnesses, in knowing violation of Trial Chamber II's witness protection order, issued on 7 July 2000, with intent to procure false statements which he induced them to sign; and as he knowingly and wilfully induced the witnesses and promised them a substantial bribe or reward in exchange of giving false testimony before the Appeals Chamber, in support of the appeal against sentence and conviction of Jean de Dieu Kamuhanda.

---

[65] Exhibit D.26; *Prosecutor v. Rwamakuba*, Case No. ICTR-98-44C-T, Decision on Defence Motion for Protective Measures (TC), 21 September 2005, para. 12.
[66] Defence Closing Brief, para. 104.
[67] Defence Closing Brief, para. 107.
[68] T. 29 April 2009 p. 18.

50. With regard to Count Two, paragraphs 18, 20, 22, and 23 of the Indictment allege, respectively and among other things, that "[t]he Accused committed this offence as part of a wide campaign to procure false statements ...", that "the Accused manipulated, instigated, induced and offered a substantial bribe of money for GAA to commit the offences of giving false testimony under solemn declaration and contempt of the Tribunal; that the "Accused knowingly and willfully fabricated evidence, and procured the signatures of protected prosecution witnesses GAA and GEX to the false statements ...", and that "[t]he Accused further knowingly and willfully suborned and persuaded protected prosecution witnesses GAA and GEX to give false testimony on 18 May 2005 ...". Paragraph 27 of the Indictment summarizes the alleged criminal conduct of the Accused for Count 2, and reads:

> The Accused committed the offence of contempt of the Tribunal as he knowingly and willfully interfered with the Tribunal's administration of justice and knowingly and willfully attempted to subvert justice with respect to the appeal of Jean de Dieu Kamuhanda, by fabricating false statements, and by inciting, interfering with, and inducing protected prosecution witnesses to commit the offences of giving false testimony under solemn declaration and contempt of the Tribunal.

51. The Chamber finds that the Indictment fails to clearly distinguish the charges in Count One from the charges in Count Two, and is therefore defective.

52. The charges against an accused and the material facts supporting those charges must be pleaded with sufficient precision in the indictment so as to provide notice to an accused.[69] Indictments lacking this precision are defective. Defects in an indictment may be "cured" by the provision of "timely, clear and consistent information detailing the factual basis underpinning the charges against" an accused.[70] "The question whether the Prosecution has cured a defect in the indictment is equivalent to the question whether the defect has caused any prejudice to the Defence or [...] whether the trial was 'rendered unfair' by the defect."[71] **[page 15]**

53. The Chamber also notes that pursuant to Rule 72 (A), challenges to defects in the Indictment "shall be in writing and be brought not later than thirty days after the disclosure by the Prosecution to the Defence of all materials and statements referred to in Rule 66 (A)(i) ...."

54. In this case, the Chamber notes that the Defence filed a preliminary motion on 24 June 2008, submitting, among other things, that Counts Three and Four of the Indictment were defective.[72] The Defence did not challenge Counts One and Two at that time. The Chamber notes that the Defence has not offered any reason for waiting until closing arguments to raise the lack of a clear distinction between Counts One and Two, and has not alleged any prejudice.[73]

55. In any event, the Chamber does not consider that the Accused has suffered any prejudice in this case. The Chamber notes that this is not a situation where the Prosecution has failed to give the Accused notice of any material facts or charges. All the material facts and charges that the Prosecution sought to prove against the Accused were alleged in the Indictment, but the Prosecution failed to distinguish the material facts and charges in Count One from those in Count Two.

---

[69] Articles 17 (4), 20 (2), 20 (4)(a) and 20 (4)(b) of the Statute and Rule 47 (C) of the Rules; *The Prosecutor v. Tharcisse Muvunyi*, Case No. ICTR-20050-55A-A, Judgement (AC), 29 August 2008 ("*Muvunyi* Appeal Judgement"), para. 18; *The Prosecutor v. Athanase Seromba*, Case No. ICTR-2001-66-A, Judgement (AC), 12 March 2008 ("*Seromba* Appeal Judgement"), para. 27; *The Prosecutor v. Aloys Simba*, Case No. ICTR-01-76-A, Judgement (AC), 27 November 2007 ("*Simba* Appeal Judgement"), para. 63.

[70] *Muvunyi* Appeal Judgement, para. 20 (citations omitted); *The Prosecutor v. Zoran Kupreškić et al.*, Case No. IT-95-16-A, Appeal Judgement, 23 October 2001 ("*Kupreškić et al.* Appeal Judgement") para. 114; The Prosecutor v. *Mladen Naletilić & Vinko Martinović*, Case No. IT-98-34-A, Judgement (AC), 3 May 2006 ("*Naletilić & Martinović* Appeal Judgement"), para. 26.

[71] *The Prosecutor v. Elizaphan and Gérard Ntakirutimana*, Case Nos. ICTR-96-10-A & ICTR-96-17-A, Judgement (AC), 13 December 2004 ("*Ntakirutimana* Appeal Judgement") para. 27 (citing *Kupreškić et al.* Appeal Judgement, para. 122)

[72] Preliminary Motions Pursuant to Rule 72, and Alternative Motion under Rule 73 to Dismiss the Indictment, filed 24 June 2008, paras. 18-20.

[73] Compare, *The Prosecutor v. Théoneste Bagosora et al.*, Case No. ICTR-98-41-AR73, Decision on Aloys Ntabakuze's Interlocutory Appeal on Questions of Law Raised by the 29 June 2006 Trial Chamber I Decision on Motion for Exclusion of Evidence (AC), 18 September 2006, para. 45. In this decision, the Appeals Chamber, noting that objections to the admission of evidence based on notice grounds should generally be made when the evidence is introduced, held that where such objections are untimely the Chamber may consider whether the burden has shifted to the Defence to show prejudice on the basis of lack of notice. It further stated that, when deciding whether the burden has shifted, Chambers should consider any justification for a late objection.

Judgement

56. Furthermore, in its Pre-Trial Brief, filed on 25 November 2008, the Prosecution clearly alleged that violations of the Protective Measures were the basis for Count One, whereas the allegations of bribery, procurement of false statements and false testimony, and other interference with Witnesses GAA and A7/GEX were the basis for Count Two.[74] The Chamber considers that this timely clarification cured the defects in the Indictment.

3. TREATMENT OF PROSECUTION WITNESS GAA'S EVIDENCE

57. Witness GAA is central to the Prosecution's case, which rests in significant part on his evidence. On 3 December 2007, Witness GAA pleaded guilty to one count of giving false testimony under solemn declaration and one count of contempt of the Tribunal.[75] According to the Indictment, the Prosecution seeks to implicate the Accused in the crimes to which Witness GAA pleaded guilty. Specifically, the Prosecution alleges that the Accused procured Witness GAA's false testimony. As such, the Chamber considers Witness GAA to be an alleged accomplice of the Accused.[76] **[page 16]**

58. The Prosecution acknowledges that Witness GAA is, at least to some extent, a former accomplice of the Accused, but submits that his evidence is capable of belief and need not be treated with caution because, at the time of his testimony, Witness GAA was a free man who had pleaded guilty to his crimes and served his full sentence of nine months imprisonment.[77] Therefore, the Prosecution suggests that Witness GAA has no motive or incentive to implicate the Accused.[78]

59. The Defence submits that Witness GAA is not a credible witness, and offers several arguments in support of this submission. In addition to noting that Witness GAA is an accomplice, the Defence submits that Witness GAA has proven to be "willing and capable of lying under oath." The Defence also argues that his demeanour on the stand was evasive, and that he objected to questions from the Defence on cross-examination. The Defence argues that Witness GAA's testimony was riddled with inconsistencies, and suggests that he would have faced consequences if his testimony was inconsistent with his plea agreement and guilty plea.[79]

60. Before turning to Witness GAA, specifically, the Chamber notes that, as a general matter, it considered various factors in evaluating *viva voce* evidence, including the witness's demeanour in court, the plausibility and clarity of the witness's testimony, and whether there were contradictions or inconsistencies within a witness's testimony or between his testimony and his prior statements relied upon in court or admitted as exhibits, as well as any explanations for such inconsistencies or contradictions. The Chamber considered whether witness testimony was corroborated by other evidence, as well as the level of detail and specificity of witness evidence. The Chamber was mindful that evidence is not considered in isolation, but rather as a whole, and that Chambers may accept part and reject part of the same witness's evidence.

61. Chambers are not prohibited from relying on the evidence of convicted persons or accomplices of an accused, or, more generally, the evidence of witnesses who might have motives or incentives to implicate the accused, especially where such witnesses may be thoroughly cross-examined.[80] A Trial Chamber must,

---

[74] Prosecution Pre-Trial Brief, paras. 32-50.
[75] Witness GAA, T. 16 February 2009 p. 11-12. *See also, The Prosecutor v. GAA*, Judgement and Sentence (TC), 4 December 2007.
[76] The Appeals Chamber has stated that the ordinary meaning of the term "accomplice' is "an association in guilt, a partner in crime". *Eliézer Niyitegeka v. The Prosecutor*, Case No. ICTR-96-14-A, Judgement (AC), 9 July 2004 ("*Niyitegeka* Appeal Judgement"), para. 98.
[77] Prosecution Closing Brief, paras. 35-38.
[78] Prosecution Closing Brief, para. 37.
[79] Pre-Defence Brief, paras. 76-85; Defence Closing Brief, para. 117.
[80] *The Prosecutor v. Momčilo Krajišnik*, Case No. IT-00-39-A, Judgement (AC), 17 March 2009, para. 146 (referring to *Ferdinand Nahimana et al. v. The Prosecutor*, Case No. ICTR-99-52-A, Judgement (AC), 28 November 2007 (",*Nahimana* Appeal Judgement") para. 439); *The Prosecutor v. Vidoje Blagojević and Dragan Jokić*, Case No. IT-02-60-A, Judgement (AC), 9 May 2007, para. 82; *The Prosecutor v. André Ntagerura et.al.*, Case No. ICTR-99-46-A, Judgement (AC), 7 July 2006 ("*Ntagerura* Appeal Judgement"), para. 204; *Niyitegeka* Appeal Judgement, para. 98.

however, consider whether accomplice witnesses might have a specific motive or incentive to implicate the accused,[81] as well as the totality of the circumstances surrounding such evidence.[82]

62. Turning to Witness GAA, the Chamber notes that he had already served his sentence at the time of his testimony in this trial, and is satisfied that his testimony was not motivated by a desire for a reduced sentence. The Chamber could not, however, entirely eliminate the possibility that Witness GAA had some improper incentives or motives for testifying against the Accused. **[page 17]**

63. The Chamber was troubled by Witness GAA's admitted prior false testimony. That a witness's prior criminal record may be relevant to assessments of credibility is not controversial. This is especially true when the witness's prior crimes involve dishonesty. Witness GAA admits to lying under oath before the Appeals Chamber of this Tribunal.

64. Concerning his prior statements, Witness GAA testified that the statements he made in 2001 were true, but that statements he made and signed from 2005 until the point of his confession in 2007 were mostly untrue or contained lies.[83] The Chamber was not willing to accept this blanket explanation for all inconsistencies in Witness GAA's prior statements. The Chamber considered such inconsistencies, and Witness GAA's explanation for them, on a case-by-case basis.

65. Given these concerns, the Chamber has considered Witness GAA's evidence with particular care, especially in those instances where Witness GAA was the only Prosecution Witness to testify on a given allegation.

CHAPTER III: FACTUAL FINDINGS

1. BACKGROUND

66. By Decision dated 7 July 2000, the *Kamuhanda* Trial Chamber ordered protective measures on behalf of victims and potential prosecution witnesses in that trial.[84] The Protective Measures included measures:

> (d) Prohibiting the disclosure to the public or the media of the names, addresses, whereabouts of, and any other identifying data in the supporting materials or any other information on file with the Registry or any other information which would reveal the identity of these individuals, and this order shall remain in effect after the termination of this trial;
>
> (e) Prohibiting the Defence and the accused from sharing, revealing or discussing, directly or indirectly, any documents or any information contained in any documents, or any other information which could reveal or lead to the identification of any individuals so designated to any person or entity other than the accused, assigned counsel or other persons working on the immediate Defence team;
>
> (...)
>
> (i) Requiring that the accused or his Defence Counsel shall make a written request, on reasonable notice to the Prosecution, to the Chamber or a Judge thereof, to contact any protected victim or potential Prosecution witnesses or any relative of such person; and requiring that when such interview has been granted by the Chamber or a Judge thereof, with the consent of such protected **[page 18]** person or the parents of (sic) guardian of that person if that person is under the age of 18, that the Prosecution shall undertake all necessary arrangements to facilitate such interview;

67. Prosecution Witness GAA testified before the Trial Chamber in the *Kamuhanda* case in 2001 and before the Appeals Chamber in the same case in 2005.[85] He appeared as a witness for the prosecution in the *Kamuhanda* trial, testifying that he had sought refuge at Gikomero Parish, and saw Jean de Dieu Kamuhanda

---

[81] *Ntagerura* Appeal Judgement, para. 206; *Nahimana* Appeal Judgement, para. 439.
[82] *Niyitegeka* Appeal Judgement, para. 98.
[83] Witness GAA, T. 17 February 2009 p. 52.
[84] *The Prosecutor v. Jean de Dieu Kamuhanda*, Case No. ICTR-99-50-I, Decision on the Prosecutor's Motion for Protective Measures for Witnesses (TC), 7 July 2000 ("Protective Measures Order", or "Protective Measures"). By order dated 26 June 2009, this Chamber admitted the Protective Measures as evidence in this case. *See* Order Admitting the Prosecution Witness Protective Measures from the Kamuhanda Case into Evidence(TC), 26 June 2009.
[85] Witness GAA, T. 16 February 2009 p. 21; T. 18 February 2009 p. 2.

leading attackers who massacred Tutsi refugees there on 12 April 1994. When he testified before the Appeals Chamber, Witness GAA appeared for the defence and recanted his trial testimony, stating that he had not been at Gikomero Parish on the date in question.[86]

68. Witness A7/GEX signed a statement for the prosecution in which she alleged that she had been at Gikomero Parish on 12 April 1994, and had heard people say that Kamuhanda was leading the attack. She disavowed this statement in testimony before the Appeals Chamber on 18 May 2005, testifying that, though she had been at Gikomero Parish on the date in question, she had not heard anyone mention Kamuhanda's name.[87]

69. After hearing Witness GAA's and A7/GEX's recantations, as well as other testimony concerning the possibility that there had been attempts to procure false testimony in connection with the *Kamuhanda* Appeal, the Appeals Chamber directed the prosecution to investigate whether Tribunal employees may have attempted to interfere with witnesses who had given evidence in proceedings before the Tribunal, and to investigate discrepancies in testimony arising from the Rule 115 hearing for possible false testimony.[88]

70. On 11 June 2007, the Tribunal indicted Witness GAA for one count of giving false testimony under solemn declaration, one count of contempt of the Tribunal, and four counts of attempt to commit acts punishable as contempt of the Tribunal. He was subsequently arrested in Kigali, Rwanda, and, on 1 August 2007, transferred to the Tribunal. At his initial appearance on 10 August 2007, Witness GAA pleaded guilty to false testimony, and not guilty to the remaining counts. On 27 November 2007, the prosecution filed a plea agreement and a solemn declaration and statement of admitted facts signed by Witness GAA, along with an application to amend the indictment against him to include one count of giving false testimony under solemn declaration and one count of contempt of the Tribunal.[89] The application for amendment was granted, and, on 3 December 2007, Witness GAA made a further initial appearance where he pleaded guilty to false testimony and contempt.[90] He was subsequently sentenced to nine months imprisonment, and was released from prison on 14 March 2008.[91] **[page 19]**

2. MEETINGS AMONG NSHOGOZA, WITNESS GAA AND WITNESS A7/GEX

71. The Prosecution alleges that, as part of a wide campaign to subvert justice in connection with the *Kamuhanda* Appeal, the Accused organized meetings with protected prosecution Witness GAA and potential Witness A7/GEX[92] in knowing violation of or with "reckless disregard" for the witness protection order of 7 July 2000 issued by the *Kamuhanda* Trial Chamber. The Accused allegedly held these meetings in public places and in the presence of third parties. He is alleged to have manipulated these witnesses, through bribery, incitement or instigation, into signing statements which he fabricated and knew to be false. According to the Prosecution, Nshogoza also convinced Witnesses GAA and A7/GEX to testify falsely before the Appeals Chamber.[93]

72. The Accused acknowledges meeting with Prosecution Witness GAA and Defence Witness A7/GEX, but testified that the meetings were initiated by the witnesses. He accepts that Witness GAA was a protected prosecution witness in the *Kamuhanda* case, but denies that Witness A7/GEX was subject to the protective measures ordered by the *Kamuhanda* Trial Chamber at the time of their meetings. While he admits meeting the witnesses in public places, he denies discussing their testimonies in the presence of third parties. The

---

[86] Witness GAA, T. 16 February 2009 p. 21; Exhibits D. 15, D. 46 (Both Exhibits are Extracts of Transcript of *Kamuhanda* Rule 115 Evidentiary Hearing, dated 18 May 2005).
[87] *See* Witness A7/GEX, T. 18 March 2009 pp. 41-42; Exhibit D. 46 (Extract of Transcript of *Kamuhanda* Rule 115 Evidentiary Hearing, dated 18 May 2005).
[88] Exhibit D. 31 (Extract of Transcript of *Kamuhanda* Appeals Hearing, dated 19 May 2005)
[89] *See* Exhibits P. 7 (solemn declaration of Witness GAA) and P. 8 (Plea Agreement between Witness GAA and the Office of the Prosecutor).
[90] Witness GAA, T. 16 February 2009 p. 11-12. *See also, The Prosecutor v. GAA*, Judgement and Sentence (TC), 4 December 2007.
[91] Witness GAA, T. 16 February 2009 pp. 20-21.
[92] This Witness testified as Defence Witness A7 in this case. To avoid any possible confusion, the Chamber will refer to her as Witness A7/GEX throughout this Judgement.
[93] Indictment, paras. 5-27.

Accused does not deny drafting statements for their signatures, but submits that the statements were taken according to the usual process and denies that they are false. Further, the Defence submits that Witnesses GAA and A7/GEX informed Nshogoza that they had falsely accused Kamuhanda, and that they willingly signed their recantation statements. Nshogoza acknowledges making payments to the witnesses for their transport expenses and the loss of a day's wages after each meeting, but denies bribing or otherwise interfering with them.

2.1. Facts Relevant to the Meetings among the Accused, Witness GAA and Witness A7/GEX

73.   Much of the evidence adduced by both Parties regarding the meetings among Nshogoza and Witnesses GAA and A7/GEX is in accord or not in dispute.[94] In 2001, Prosecution Witness GAA testified before this Tribunal as a protected witness for the Prosecution in the *Kamuhanda* trial.[95] Witness A7/GEX signed a statement for the Prosecution in connection with the *Kamuhanda* trial, and this statement was disclosed to the Defence along with her name, but she never testified in that trial.[96] During the relevant time period, Witness GAA and Defence Witness A7/GEX were neighbours and members of the same church.[97] Witness GAA spoke with Witness A7/GEX about his testimony in the *Kamuhanda* trial, and informed her that he had not been at **[page 20]** Gikomero on 12 April 1994.[98] Witness A7/GEX arranged a meeting between Witness GAA and Nshogoza, which took place at Stella Bar near the Tribunal offices in Kigali.[99] Witness A7/GEX attended all of the meetings between Witness GAA and Nshogoza.[100] After the meetings, Nshogoza paid the witnesses a sum that he told them was for transport expenses.[101] He paid them both a larger amount at his final meeting with them before they travelled to Arusha to testify before the Appeals Chamber.[102]

74.   At their initial meeting, Witness GAA informed Nshogoza that he had not been at Gikomero on 12 April 1994, and had not seen Kamuhanda commit acts of genocide.[103] At their second meeting, which also took place at Stella Bar, Nshogoza showed Witness GAA a statement prepared for his signature.[104] Nshogoza read the contents of the statement to Witness GAA, who then signed it.[105] In March 2004, Nshogoza brought Witnesses GAA, A7/GEX and Augustin Nyagatare to a notary public's office in Kigali to confirm their statements and have them notarized.[106] These statements were submitted to the Appeals Chamber as part of a Rule 115 application to submit additional evidence in connection with Kamuhanda's appeal from his conviction at trial, and Witnesses GAA and A7/GEX testified before the Appeals Chamber on behalf of the Kamuhanda defence.[107]

75.   The Chamber accepts these facts as proven beyond a reasonable doubt.

---

[94]   The testimony regarding the meetings was not sufficiently clear for the Chamber to determine beyond a reasonable doubt the exact number of meetings or the dates and times of those meetings. The Chamber does not consider that a determination of these issues was necessary.
[95]   Witness GAA, T. 18 February 2009 p. 2; Nshogoza, T. 30 March 2009 pp. 48-49; Witness Condé, T. 16 March 2009 pp. 41, 53.
[96]   Witness A7/GEX, T. 17 March 2009 p. 86; Exhibit P. 24.
[97]   Witness GAA, T. 16 February 2009 p. 25; T. 18 February 2009 p. 35; Witness A7/GEX, T. 18 March 2009 p. 5.
[98]   Witness GAA, T. 16 February 2009, p. 14; 18 February 2009 pp. 35-36; Witness A7/GEX, T. 18 March 2009 p. 7.
[99]   Witness GAA, T. 16 February 2009 p. 26; Nshogoza, T. 30 March 2009 pp. 46-47; Witness A7/GEX, T. 18 March 2009 p. 28.
[100]   Witness GAA, T. 16 February 2009 pp. 41-42; Witness A7/GEX, T. 18 March 2009 pp. 23, 28, 33-35.
[101]   Witness GAA, T. 16 February 2009 pp. 26-27, 46; Nshogoza, T. 30 March 2009 pp. 31-32, 46-47; Witness A7/GEX, T. 18 March 2009 p. 30, 33, 38-39.
[102]   Witness GAA, T. 16 February 2009 p. 41; Witness A7/GEX, T. 19 March 2009 pp. 14-16.
[103]   Witness GAA, T. 16 February 2009 pp. 14, 29, 30; Nshogoza, T. 30 March 2009 p. 46; Witness A7/GEX, T. 18 March 2009 p. 30.
[104]   Witness GAA, T. 16 February 2009 p. 28; Nshogoza, T. 30 March 2009 p. 53.
[105]   Witness GAA, T. 16 February 2009 p. 28; Nshogoza, T. 30 March 2009 p. 53.
[106]   Witness GAA, T. 16 February 2009 pp. 33-39; Nshogoza, T. 30 March 2009 p. 53; Witness A7/GEX, T. 18 March 2009 pp. 34-37; Witness Nyagatare, T. 23 March 2009 pp. 14-15, 33-34. The Chamber notes that only Witness GAA's statement was ultimately notarized.
[107]   Witness GAA, T. 16 February 2009 p. 21; Witness A7/GEX, T. 18 March 2009 pp. 41-42; Exhibit D. 30.

2.2. Disputed Factual Issues

76. Apart from these areas of broad agreement between the Parties and their evidence, several contested factual issues arise from the Indictment and the evidence relevant to the meetings. These issues are: (i) what was the state of the Accused's knowledge regarding the protective measures ordered by the *Kamuhanda* Trial Chamber; (ii) did the Accused initiate the meetings; (iii) did the Accused reveal protected information to the public or third parties at the meetings; (iv) did the Accused fabricate the statements or know that they were false; and (v) did the Accused procure Witnesses GAA's and A7/GEX's signatures and testimonies through bribery or other interference. The Chamber will consider the evidence relevant to these contested issues in turn below.

2.2.1 The Accused's knowledge regarding the protective measures [page 21]

77. At trial, the Defence challenged the allegation that Defence Witness A7/GEX was a protected prosecution witness in the *Kamuhanda* case, and adduced evidence intended to show that Nshogoza may not have been aware: (i) of the protective measures; (ii) of Prosecution Witness GAA's protected status; or (iii) that his actions violated the protected measures ordered by the *Kamuhanda* Trial Chamber. The Chamber considers these issues to involve both factual and legal questions. It will address the factual issues in this section, and the legal issues in the Legal Conclusions section.

78. Nshogoza testified that the first time he saw the Protective Measures Order for prosecution witnesses in the *Kamuhanda* case was when he was detained in Arusha.[108] Nshogoza also testified, however, that he believed that a prosecution witness whose identity had been disclosed could not be contacted by the Defence.[109] Considering that the Accused was a trained lawyer and had been working as a defence investigator on the *Kamuhanda* case for approximately two years at the time of the relevant events, the Chamber does not accept his testimony that he was ignorant of the existence of the Protective Measures Order or its contents.

2.2.1.1 Witness A7/GEX

79. Regarding Witness A7/GEX's status under the Protective Measures, the evidence shows that Witness A7/GEX informed Nshogoza that she had made a statement to the Prosecution regarding Kamuhanda's presence at Gikomero.[110] The Protective Measures explicitly protect potential witnesses.[111] Nshogoza testified that Defence Witness Condé, who was Lead Defence Counsel in the *Kamuhanda* case, informed him that Witness A7/GEX was not a protected prosecution witness in that case.[112] The Accused further testified that if Witness A7/GEX's identifying information was disclosed to the *Kamuhanda* defence in March 2001, he would not have been aware of it because he was not yet a part of the *Kamuhanda* defence team.[113]

80. In the Rule 115 application before the Appeals Chamber in the *Kamuhanda* case, Witness Condé referred to Witness A7/GEX as a protected prosecution witness.[114] In her testimony before this Chamber, Condé denied that Witness A7/GEX was a protected witness, and explained that just because her motion referred to Witness A7/GEX in this way did not make it so.[115]

81. The Chamber accepts the Accused's testimony that Witness Condé told him that Witness A7/GEX was not a protected witness. The Chamber, however, finds that the Defence evidence also shows that: (i) at least as of their first meeting, the Accused was aware that Witness A7/GEX had given a statement to the prosecution in the *Kamuhanda* case, and (ii) the Rule 115 **[page 22]** Application filed by the *Kamuhanda* defence team referred to Witness A7/GEX as a protected prosecution witness.

---

[108] Nshogoza, T. 30 March 2009 p. 62.
[109] Nshogoza, T. 31 March 2009 pp. 44-45; Exhibit P. 20
[110] Nshogoza, T. 30 March 2009 pp. 43-44.
[111] Protective Measures Order, paras. 2, 6, 9.
[112] Nshogoza, T. 31 March 2009 p. 45.
[113] Nshogoza, T. 31 March 2009 p. 45.
[114] Witness Condé, T. 17 March 2009 p. 44; Exhibit D. 30.
[115] Witness Condé, T. 17 March 2009 pp. 45-49

2.2.1.2 Witness GAA

82. With respect to Witness GAA, Nshogoza testified that as a defence investigator in the *Kamuhanda* case, he was not allowed to attend court proceedings and, therefore, did not see any prosecution witnesses testify.[116] Moreover, when Witness A7/GEX told Nshogoza that Witness GAA wanted to meet with him, she used Witness GAA's real name, which Nshogoza had not heard before that time; Nshogoza testified that he had not been a member of the *Kamuhanda* defence team when Witness GAA testified in that trial.[117] Therefore, at their initial meeting, Nshogoza claims he was unaware that Witness GAA had testified as a prosecution witness in the *Kamuhanda* case.[118]

83. Other evidence adduced at trial, however, suggests that the Accused had some reason to believe that Witness GAA was a prosecution witness prior to their initial meeting. Witness A7/GEX testified that she told Nshogoza not only that Witness GAA wanted to meet with him, but also that Witness GAA had expressed that he was burdened by the fact that he had testified falsely against Kamuhanda at trial.[119]

84. According to his own testimony, Nshogoza told Condé about his first meeting with Witness GAA, and she told him that Witness GAA was a protected prosecution witness and he should not meet with him again.[120] They decided to discontinue the investigations and Nshogoza did not have any contact with Witness GAA until after January 2004, when the *Kamuhanda* Trial Judgement was delivered.[121] After Kamuhanda's conviction, the *Kamuhanda* defence team revisited the issue and decided that Nshogoza would record the statements of Witnesses GAA and A7/GEX.[122]

85. The evidence adduced at trial proves beyond a reasonable doubt that, at the very latest, Nshogoza was aware that Witness GAA was a protected prosecution witness before meeting with him at the notary's office in Kigali in March 2004. The evidence also shows that, before meeting with him for the first time, Nshogoza was aware that Witness GAA wanted to recant either a statement or testimony in the *Kamuhanda* trial.

2.2.2 Initiation of the meetings

86. The Chamber recalls that the uncontested evidence in this case is that Defence Witness A7/GEX arranged the initial meeting between Nshogoza and Prosecution Witness GAA.[123] The Accused acknowledges instructing Witness A7/GEX to arrange this meeting.[124] The remaining **[page 23]** question is how Nshogoza came into contact with Witness A7/GEX. The Defence adduced evidence to suggest that Witness A7/GEX initiated contact with the Accused, and told him about Witness GAA's desire to recant.[125] The Prosecution did not adduce any evidence on this issue.

87. The Chamber had some concerns with the Defence evidence and did not accep. its explanation as to how the Accused first came into contact with Witness A7/GEX in its entirety. The Chamber notes, however, that its refusal to accep. the Defence's evidence concerning the initiation of the meetings does not, of itself, permit it to find that it has been proven beyond a reasonable doubt that the Accused initiated the meeting with Witness A7/GEX, and thus Witness GAA.[126] The Chamber does not consider that the only reasonable conclusion from the evidence and circumstances is that the Accused initiated contact with A7/GEX. Therefore, given that the Prosecution did not adduce any evidence concerning the circumstances of Nshogoza's meeting with Witness A7/GEX, the Chamber cannot safely make any further findings on this issue.

---

[116] Nshogoza, T. 30 March 2009 p. 27
[117] Nshogoza, T. 30 March 2009 p. 44
[118] Nshogoza, T. 30 March 2009 p. 34.
[119] Witness A7/GEX, T. 18 March 2009 p. 5.
[120] Nshogoza, T. 30 March 2009 pp. 48-49.
[121] Nshogoza, T. 30 March 2009 p. 50.
[122] Nshogoza, T. 30 March 2009 p. 50; Condé, T. 16 March 2009, pp. 54-55
[123] *Supra*, para. 73
[124] Nshogoza, T. 30 March 2009 p. 44
[125] Witness A7/GEX, T. 18 March 2009 p. 2-3, 5, 64; *see also* Nshogoza, T. 30 March 2009 p. 35, 43-44
[126] *See Nobilo* Appeal Judgement, para. 47.

2.2.3 Did the Accused disclose protected information?

88. The Accused does not dispute that he held meetings with Prosecution Witness GAA and Defence Witness A7/GEX in public places, but denies disclosing their identities to anyone.

89. Regarding the presence of third parties at these meetings, the Chamber recalls that Prosecution and Defence evidence shows that Witness GAA and Witness A7/GEX attended their meetings with Nshogoza together; that Witnesses GAA and A7/GEX privately discussed their respective testimony and statements in the *Kamuhanda* trial; and that Witnesses GAA, A7/GEX and Witness Nyagatare all attended the meeting at the notary's office in Kigali, where Witness GAA's statement was disclosed to the notary.[127]

90. Witness GAA testified that Defence Witness A3 was present at two meetings that he had with Nshogoza. He did not provide further detail. The Chamber accepts that one of these meetings was the meeting between Nshogoza and Witness BUC,[128] but notes that Witness GAA's testimony that Witness A3 attended some other unidentified meeting lacks any detail. Witness GAA did not specify when or where this meeting took place, whether anyone else attended the meeting, what was discussed, or any other details. Given this lack of detail, the Chamber does not accep. Witness GAA's uncorroborated testimony that Witness A3 was present at a second, unidentified meeting with the Accused.

91. Nshogoza testified that he would hold private conversations with people he needed to talk to, and would move away from other persons who might be at Stella Bar with him.[129] He stated that nobody overheard his conversations or eavesdropped on them, and that this would be frowned upon in Rwandan culture.[130] The Accused testified that his private conversations with **[page 24]** Witnesses A7/GEX and GAA were not held in the presence of or overheard by others, but did acknowledge discussing general issues with both at the same time.[131]

92. Witness GAA testified that Witness A7/GEX was present when Nshogoza read him the recantation statement, and Witness A7/GEX testified that she overheard their conversation at the first meeting.[132] Witness BUC testified that, at her meeting with the Accused, which was held in the presence of Witnesses GAA, A7/GEX, and Defence Witness A3,[133] the Accused did not bring her to a separate part of the room away from the others.[134] Witness GAA testified that he did not overhear Nshogoza's conversation with Witness BUC.[135] Witness A7/GEX claimed that Witness BUC confirmed what Witness GAA had previously told Nshogoza.[136]

93. The Indictment emphasises, and the evidence shows, that Nshogoza held his meetings in public, mostly at Stella Bar. The Chamber considers that, of itself, this evidence is not significant. There was no evidence to suggest that any protected information was revealed to patrons of Stella Bar, or any other persons not party to the meetings.

94. Given the testimonies of Prosecution Witnesses GAA and BUC and Defence Witness A7/GEX, the Chamber is not convinced that Nshogoza took the precautions that he claimed to have taken at his meetings. The Chamber therefore finds that the evidence proves, beyond a reasonable doubt, that the Accused discussed details of Witness GAA's testimony in the presence of Witness A7/GEX.

---

[127] *Supra*, paras. 73-74.
[128] *Infra*, paras. 128-140.
[129] Nshogoza, T. 30 March 2009 p. 16.
[130] Nshogoza, T. 30 March 2009 pp. 31, 33.
[131] Nshogoza, T. 30 March 2009 p. 33
[132] Witness GAA, T. 16 February 2009 p. 32; Witness A7/GEX, T. 18 March 2009 p. 29.
[133] Witness BUC, T. 12 February 2009 pp. 21-24; Witness GAA, T. 16 February 2009 pp. 51-52 (Witness GAA testified that Defence Witness Augustin Nyagatare was also at this meeting, but this evidence is not in accord with the evidence of Witnesses BUC, Augustin Nyagatare, A3 or A7/GEX); Witness A7/GEX, T. 18 March 2009 pp. 31-33; T. 19 March 2009 pp. 6-8; Witness A3, T. 19 March 2009 pp. 42-47.
[134] Witness BUC, T. 12 February 2009 p. 28
[135] Witness GAA, T. 16 February 2009 p. 52;
[136] Witness A7/GEX, T. 18 March 2009 p. 33

2.2.4 Did the Accused fabricate statements or know they were false?

95. The Chamber recalls that the uncontested evidence in the case shows that the Accused prepared Prosecution Witness GAA's and Defence Witness A7/GEX's recantation statements for their signatures, and that he read Witness GAA his statement before obtaining his signature.[137]

96. Nshogoza sought to further explain his statement taking process during his testimony. He testified that he prepared Witness GAA's statement on the basis of notes he took at their first meeting.[138] Witness GAA accepted the statement and said that he was willing and ready to go to the notary to sign the statement.[139] Nshogoza believed that this practice conformed to the statement-taking practices of prosecution and defence representatives at this Tribunal.[140] **[page 25]**

97. The Prosecution failed to adduce any evidence to suggest that the Accused's statement taking process was out of the ordinary, and the Chamber does not consider the fact that Nshogoza prepared the statements for the signatures of Witnesses GAA and A7/GEX, of itself, to be incriminating.

98. The uncontested evidence also shows that Witness GAA informed Witness A7/GEX and the Accused that he had not been at Gikomero, and that his testimony against Kamuhanda at trial was false. During his testimony before this Chamber, Witness GAA said that he lied to both Witness A7/GEX and Nshogoza when he told them that he had not been at Gikomero.[141] Witness GAA did not, however, inform Nshogoza that he had lied to him. Rather he suggested only that Nshogoza was aware that the new statement was inconsistent with his prior testimony in the *Kamuhanda* trial.[142] The Chamber accepts this, but does not consider it probative regarding the issue of whether the Accused knew Witness GAA's recantation to be false. The Prosecution did not adduce any additional evidence regarding the Accused's knowledge of the statements.

99. At trial, Nshogoza denied seeking false testimony from any witnesses, and said he never asked a witness to sign a statement that he believed to be false.[143] He testified that he believes Witness GAA's and Witness A7/GEX's recantation statements and their testimonies before the Appeals Chamber to be truthful.[144] He believes Witness GAA testified falsely in the *Kamuhanda* trial proceedings in 2001, and believes that Kamuhanda was not at Gikomero on 12 April 1994.[145] He testified that the *Gacaca* proceedings concerning events in Gikomero support his beliefs.[146]

100. The Defence adduced additional evidence which suggested that the Accused may have had reason to believe that Witness GAA's recantation was true. Defence Witness Augustin Nyagatare, who personally participated in the killings in Gikomero in 1994, testified that he informed the Accused that Kamuhanda was not present during the attacks.[147] Defence Witness Cyprien Hakizimana, the President of the Appeals Chamber of the *Gacaca* Court in Gikomero *secteur*, testified that the *Gacaca* Court had gathered extensive material concerning the 12 April 1994 massacres at Gikomero parish.[148] He testified that he had examined the materials, and that Kamuhanda was not on the lists of persons charged by the *Gacaca* Court with participating in these massacres.[149]

101. The Prosecution did not adduce any evidence to suggest that Witness A7/GEX's recantation statement was false or that the Accused had any reason to believe it was false. For **[page 26]** her part, Witness A7/GEX

---

[137] *Supra*, para. 74.
[138] Nshogoza, T. 30 March 2009 p. 53.
[139] Nshogoza, T. 30 March 2009 p. 53.
[140] Nshogoza, T. 30 March 2009 pp. 33-34; *see also* Witness Seminega, T. 19 March 2009 pp. 80-81 (discussing the process representatives of the Prosecution followed when taking his statement).
[141] *See e.g.*, Witness GAA, T. 16 February 2009 pp. 14, 18, 29, 31; T. 18 February 2009 pp. 35-36
[142] Witness GAA, T. 16 February 2009 p. 29.
[143] Nshogoza, T. 30 March 2009 p. 34.
[144] Nshogoza, T. 31 March 2009 p. 57.
[145] Nshogoza, T. 30 March 2009 pp. 62-63.
[146] Nshogoza, T. 31 March 2009 p. 58
[147] Witness Nyagatare, T. 23 March 2009 pp. 10-11
[148] Witness Hakizimana, T. 24 March 2009 pp. 6-7
[149] Witness Hakizimana, T. 24 March 2009 pp. 19, 24-26.

testified that she informed Nshogoza that she had lied in her statement to Prosecution investigators regarding Kamuhanda's presence at Gikomero.[150]

102. The Chamber therefore finds that the Prosecution has failed to prove beyond a reasonable doubt that the Accused fabricated the statements of Witnesses GAA and A7/GEX. Nor has it proved beyond a reasonable doubt that the Accused knew the recantation statements were false, or even that he had reason to know that they were false. Given this conclusion, the Chamber need not consider the additional Defence evidence adduced to show that Witness GAA's recantation statement was true.[151]

2.2.5 Bribery or Other interference

103. There were three areas of evidence concerning bribery and manipulation. First, the evidence of both parties shows that the Accused made payments and offered food and drinks to Witnesses GAA and A7/GEX. Second, Witness GAA testified that Nshogoza promised him one million Rwandan Francs in exchange for his testimony. Third, Witness GAA testified that Nshogoza made misrepresentations about the purpose and consequences of his testimony in order to secure his cooperation.

2.2.5.1 Alleged Payments and Inducements Offered by the Accused

104. The evidence shows that Nshogoza paid Prosecution Witness GAA and Defence Witness A7/GEX a sum of Rwandan Francs after meeting with them.[152] Nshogoza testified that the payments were for transportation and lost earnings, and the evidence in the case shows that, at least at the first meeting, he told Witnesses GAA and A7/GEX that the purpose of the payment was the reimbursement of transport expenses.[153] Neither witness mentioned being told that the payments were also intended to cover lost earnings.

105. The amount of the payments is disputed. According to Witness GAA, the Accused paid him 10,000 Rwandan Francs for each meeting until the last, when he paid him 20,000 Rwandan Francs.[154] Witness GAA testified his return trip to Stella Bar cost him only 300 Rwandan Francs.[155] Nshogoza said he paid Witnesses GAA and A7/GEX 5,000 Rwandan Francs.[156] He explained that he paid witnesses travelling from Gikomero between 5,000 and 7,000 Rwandan **[page 27]** Francs, because this is what it cost him to travel there.[157] Witness A7/GEX testified that Nshogoza paid her 5,000 Rwandan Francs at each meeting, excep. for (i) a meeting where he gave her and Witness GAA 5,000 Rwandan Francs to share; and (ii) her last meeting with him, when he gave her 10,000 Rwandan Francs.[158] She specified that, at the last meeting, Nshogoza handed her and Witness GAA a total of 20,000 Rwandan Francs to share.[159]

106. Other witnesses also testified concerning payments made after interviews by representatives of the OTP or defence teams working on behalf of accused persons, as well as after meetings with representatives of WVSS in Kigali. Prosecution Witness GAF testified that, after a 2007 interview with representatives of the OTP in Kigali, he was given 4,000 Rwandan Francs by the OTP interpreter.[160] He understood that these funds were given to him for transportation costs and in compensation for the day's labour that he lost.[161]

---

[150] Nshogoza, T. 30 March 2009 pp. 43-44.
[151] Defence Witnesses A7/GEX, Augustin Nyagatare, Straton Nyarwaya, Cyprien Hakizimana, A25 and A29 testified to the underlying events at Gikomero Parish in April 1994, and/or to the Defence claim that Jean de Dieu Kamuhanda had been framed for his crimes. Defence Witness A10 also provided testimony relevant to these events; the Defence was granted permission to treat her as hostile. In addition to this *viva voce* evidence, the Chamber admitted the written statements of seven witnesses pursuant to Rule 92 *bis* (B), whose evidence concerned the underlying events at Gikomero Parish. *See* Exhibits D. 84 – D. 90 (statements of Defence Witnesses A13, A15, A17, A18, A23, A28 and A30); *see also* Decision on Defence Motion for the Admission of Written Statements of Witnesses A1, A13, A14, A15, A17, A18, A20, A22, A23, A26, A28 and A30 as Evidence *in lieu* of Oral Testimony, 29 April 2009.
[152] *Supra*, para. 74
[153] Nshogoza, T. 30 March 2009 p. 31; Witness GAA, T. 16 February 2009 p. 26; Witness A7/GEX, T. 18 March 2009 p. 30
[154] Witness GAA, T. 16 February 2009 p. 41.
[155] Witness GAA, T. 16 February 2009 p. 26.
[156] Nshogoza, T. 30 March 2009 pp. 46-47.
[157] Nshogoza, T. 30 March 2009 p. 32
[158] Witness A7/GEX, T. 19 March 2009 p. 16
[159] Witness GAF, T. 10 February 2009 p. 23
[160]
[161] Witness GAF, T. 10 February 2009 p. 23

According to Witness BUC, at the end of their meeting, Nshogoza gave her 5,000 Rwandan Francs for transportation. The trip to Remera had cost Witness BUC 600 Rwandan Francs.[162] She was never asked about the cost of the trip. and she did not know whether any of the other persons in attendance at the meeting was paid.[163]

107. Defence Witness Condé testified that when she was on mission in Rwanda, witnesses would be brought by Nshogoza to meet her in a hotel, and they would be reimbursed for their travel expenses.[164] She did not know the amount of money paid to any witnesses.[165] Defence Witness Nyagatare testified that after the meeting at the notary's office, they all went back to Stella bar and Nshogoza gave each of them 5,000 Rwandan Francs for transport expenses.[166] He further testified that before coming to Arusha to testify in this case he met someone from WVSS in Kigali, and that after that meeting he was paid 15,000 Rwandan Francs to cover his transport expenses.[167]

108. Defence Witness A3 testified that after the meeting he attended with Nshogoza, Prosecution Witnesses GAA and BUC, and Defence Witness A7/GEX, he was paid 3,000 Rwandan Francs, but he could not see how much money Nshogoza gave to the other persons.[168] Defence Witness Hakizimana testified that, after a meeting with representatives of WVSS, he was paid 10,500 Rwandan Francs to cover his transport expenses for his travel to and from the Tribunal offices in Kigali.[169] Defence Witness A25 testified that he travelled to the Tribunal offices in Kigali shortly before testifying, where he was asked to sign a document and was given **[page 28]** 5,500 Rwandan Francs to cover his transportation expenses that day.[170] Defence Witness A29 testified that before coming to testify in Arusha, he went to the Tribunal offices in Kigali where he was asked questions pertaining to his security. At the end of that visit, he was paid 8,000 Rwandan Francs to cover his transport expenses.[171] He was also reimbursed for travel expenses by the Nshogoza Defence team when he travelled to meet with them.[172] In addition, at the request of the Defence, the Chamber admitted a portion of the testimony of Prosecution Witness AMN from the *Karemera et al.* trial pursuant to Rule 92 *bis* (D).[173] In the admitted excerpt, Witness AMN testified that he met with representatives of the Prosecution and was paid 10,000 Rwandan Francs for travel expenses.[174]

109. The Chamber does not accept Witness GAA's uncorroborated evidence regarding the amount of the payments. Witness GAA's testimony was inconsistent with a prior statement he made to Loretta Lynch, counsel appointed by the Prosecution to investigate the allegations of false testimony and witness tampering which arose during Kamuhanda's Appeal proceedings. Witness GAA told Loretta Lynch that Nshogoza gave him 3,000 Rwandan Francs for transport and eating, and did not give him money for his family.[175] During trial, he claimed that he had lied to Loretta Lynch.[176] The Chamber accepts that Witness GAA may have lied to Loretta Lynch about such payments, but notes that Witness GAA did not explain why, if he was trying to prevent discovery of the payments, he mentioned any payment at all.

110. There was also reason to believe that Witness GAA's memory of the payments may not have been exact. During trial, he testified that the payments were made in 2,000 Rwandan Franc notes.[177] Conversely, Witness A7/GEX testified that Nshogoza always gave 5,000 Rwandan Franc notes.[178] By Decision dated

---

[162] Witness BUC, T. 12 February 2009 p. 26.
[163] Witness BUC, T. 12 February 2009 p. 27.
[164] Witness Condé, T. 17 March 2009 p. 12.
[165] Witness Condé, T. 17 March 2009 p. 12.
[166] Witness Nyagatare, T. 23 March 2009 pp. 15-16.
[167] Witness Nyagatare, T. 23 March 2009 p. 22.
[168] Witness A3, T. 19 March 2009 p. 47.
[169] Witness Hakizimana, T. 24 March 2009 p. 37.
[170] Witness A25, T. 25 March 2009 pp. 4-5
[171] Witness A29, T. 25 March 2009 pp. 52-53.
[172] Witness A29, T. 25 March 2009 p. 59.
[173] Decision on Defence Motion for the Admission of Transcripts pursuant to Rule 92 *bis* (TC), 23 April 2009.
[174] Exhibit D. 83 (*The Prosecutor v. Karemera et al.*, T. 1 October 2007, pp. 49-56).
[175] Exhibit D. 14 (Excerpts from Witness GAA interview with Loretta Lynch).
[176] Witness GAA, T. 18 February 2009 p. 46.
[177] Witness GAA, T. 16 February 2009 p. 46.
[178] Witness A7/GEX, T. 18 March 2009 p. 39.

16 April 2009, the Chamber took judicial notice of the fact that 2,000 Rwandan Franc notes were only introduced into circulation in Rwanda in 2007.[179]

111. Regardless of the amount of the payments, the evidence suggests that, with the exception of the final payments to Witnesses GAA and A7/GEX, such payments were made for the purpose of covering transport expenses, and shows that Nshogoza was not alone in making them. Rather, the evidence shows such payments were, at least on occasion, made by representatives of the Prosecution and by WVSS after meetings with witnesses. The evidence also shows that Nshogoza made similar payments to witnesses other than Witnesses GAA and A7/GEX. The conclusion that such payments were made to cover transport costs is bolstered by testimony suggesting that such payments were not made when witnesses were provided transportation to [page 29] and from interviews.[180] The evidence shows that the final payments were made to cover costs while Witnesses GAA and A7/GEX were testifying before the Appeals Chamber.

112. There was also evidence that Nshogoza provided food and drinks at the meetings.[181] The Chamber considers that, of itself, the fact that the Accused provided food and drinks at the meetings was innocuous. There was no more direct evidence to suggest that the Accused expressly offered the refreshments in exchange for anything. Although the Chamber considers that it is the Accused's intention in providing the refreshments that matters, the Chamber notes that none of the recipients of the food and drink testified that he or she believed the refreshments were provided in exchange for testimony.

113. Given this evidence, the Chamber does not find that the Prosecution proved beyond a reasonable doubt that Nshogoza made such payments or provided food and drink with the intent or purpose of bribing or otherwise interfering with Prosecution Witness GAA or Defence Witness A7/GEX.

2.2.5.2 The Alleged Promise of Payment of One Million Rwandan Francs

114. Prosecution Witness GAA testified that Nshogoza promised to pay him one million Rwandan Francs in exchange for signing his statement and testifying before the Appeals Chamber.[182] He was never paid the promised sum.[183]

115. The Accused denied offering or paying money in exchange for testimony.[184] Defence Witness A7/GEX testified that Nshogoza never offered her any sum of money.[185] She testified that she never heard Nshogoza promise Witness GAA any amount of money. If this happened, it happened in her absence.[186]

116. The Chamber considers Witness GAA's uncorroborated testimony regarding the promise of one million Rwandan Francs to be problematic. Witness GAA's testimony on this issue lacked detail. He stated only that during "the first meetings", Nshogoza promised to give him money without being more specific. He was not informed of the amount until the sixth meeting.[187] The Chamber notes that this general testimony is in contrast to the detail with which Witness GAA testified about his meetings with Nshogoza, in particular the first meeting at Stella Bar and the meeting at the notary's office in Kigali. [page 30]

117. Witness GAA did not mention the sum of one million Rwandan Francs in a 14 June 2007 statement given to Rwandan authorities.[188] When asked by the Rwandan authorities why he would not state the amount promised him by Nshogoza, Witness GAA responded:

---

[179] Decision on Defence Motion for Judicial Notice (TC), 16 April 2009
[180] Witness A7/GEX, T. 19 March 2009 pp. 14-15 (noting that she was given food and drink by representatives of the Prosecution, but was not paid transport money when the Prosecution provided transport to and from the interview).
[181] T. 30 March 2009 pp. 13-16; Witness A7/GEX, T. 18 March 2009 pp. 3, 30, 39, 72, 84; Witness A3, T. 19 March 2009 p. 47; Witness Nyagatare, 23 March 2009 p. 6.
[182] Witness GAA, T. 16 February 2009 p. 41.
[183] Witness GAA, T. 16 February 2009 p. 41.
[184] Witness GAA, T. 16 February 2009 p. 44.
[185] Witness A7/GEX, T. 19 March 2009 pp. 19-20
[186] Witness A7/GEX, T. 18 March 2009 pp. 47-48.
[187] Witness GAA, T. 16 February 2009 p. 41
[188] Witness GAA, T. 19 February 2009 p. 26.

Honestly, he did not disclose the amount to me. I simply agreed to testify for Kamuhanda, because, in light of the sum that he was giving me for my transport, I believed that Nshogoza would pay me a substantial amount. Later, when we called him on the phone, we could not reach him, but I would not have accepted anything less than 500,000 Rwandan francs.[189]

118. Though Witness GAA now disavows this statement to the Rwandan authorities,[190] the Chamber does not accep. his explanation for lying in the context of this statement. Witness GAA testified that, until he came to Arusha and pleaded guilty in August 2007, many of his statements contained lies.[191] The logic of Witness GAA's explanation is that he was trying to hide his wrongdoing. In the excerpts quoted above, which were read onto the trial record, Witness GAA was not trying to hide his contact with Nshogoza from the Rwandan authorities. Nor was he trying to hide that he expected money in exchange for his recantation. Moreover, in his testimony before this Chamber, Witness GAA partially confirmed his statement to the Rwandan authorities when he testified that Nshogoza "had promised to give me money without stating the amount. But given what he gave me on a daily basis, it augured well to me that he would give me much more money."[192]

119. Considering Witness GAA's testimony and his 14 June 2007 statement to Rwandan authorities in conjunction with the testimony of other Prosecution witnesses casts additional doubt on Witness GAA's testimony regarding the promise of payment. Prosecution Witness GAF, a friend and neighbour of Witness GAA whom Witness GAA contacted about possibly recanting his testimony in the *Kamuhanda* trial,[193] testified that Witness GAA never told him about an amount of money or even that he was certain that what was promised was money; rather "he just suspected that it might be an offer in monetary terms. Because as a matter of fact it is money people use in these type[s] of things."[194] Prosecution Witness SP004, another friend and neighbour of Witness GAA, testified that Witness GAA said that he was going to ask for one million Rwandan Francs in order for them to testify for the *Kamuhanda* defence. Witness GAA also told her that, even if they asked for one million Rwandan Francs, the person would be ready to pay.[195]

120. Though Witnesses GAF and SP004 were referring to the money that they might be paid either personally or as a group if they agreed to testify, the Chamber considers that their testimony provides possible insight into Witness GAA's state of mind. Moreover, it is noteworthy that Witness GAA did not tell them that he had been promised a sum of money in exchange for his testimony. Considered in conjunction with his 14 June 2007 statement to the **[page 31]** Rwandan authorities as well as his evidence before this Chamber, this evidence suggests that Witness GAA may have merely expected payment or intended to request payment of 500,000 or one million Rwandan Francs from Nshogoza, and casts doubt on his testimony that Nshogoza ever promised such a payment.

121. Given the lack of corroboration for Witness GAA's testimony regarding the promise of payment, the lack of detail in his evidence surrounding the timing and circumstances of the alleged promise, including the lack of specificity as to what Nshogoza actually said, the inconsistencies with his prior statement to Rwandan authorities, the additional doubt raised by other Prosecution evidence in the case, and the Chambers concerns regarding Witness GAA's evidence described above,[196] the Chamber finds that the Prosecution has failed to prove beyond a reasonable doubt that Nshogoza promised to pay Witness GAA one million Rwandan Francs, or any other amount, in exchange for his statement and testimony.

2.2.5.3 Evidence of Misrepresentations by the Accused

122. Prosecution Witness GAA testified that, at their initial meeting, the Accused informed him that he was writing a book about Kamuhanda and that he wanted Witness GAA to assist him.[197] Witness GAA

---

[189] Witness GAA, T. 19 February 2009 pp. 26-27.
[190] Witness GAA, T. 19 February 2009 p. 27
[191] Witness GAA, T. 17 February 2009 p. 52.
[192] Witness GAA, T. 16 February 2009 p. 45
[193] *Infra*, paras. 141-153.
[194] Witness GAF, T. 9 February 2009 p. 31.
[195] Witness SP004, T. 11 February 2009 pp. 70-71.
[196] *Supra*, paras. 57-65.
[197] Witness GAA, T. 16 February 2009 pp. 24-26

believed that the statement he signed would be used by the Accused for the book he was supposedly writing about Kamuhanda.[198]

123. Witness GAA testified that he first learned his statement would be used in court at the notary's office because Nshogoza "handed [the] statement to court" at that time. Witness GAA protested and Nshogoza explained that he was counsel working for the Tribunal and that whatever happened from that point forward would rest with him alone in his official capacity.[199] Witness GAA then agreed that his statement could be submitted in court.[200]

124. Defence Witness A7/GEX testified that when she arranged the meeting between Nshogoza and Witness GAA she told Witness GAA that Nshogoza was a member of the *Kamuhanda* defence team.[201] At the meeting, she did not hear any reference to Nshogoza writing a book.[202]

125. The Chamber does not accept Witness GAA's uncorroborated testimony that Nshogoza claimed to be writing a book about Kamuhanda. The Chamber considers that this testimony is logically inconsistent with other aspects of Witness GAA's testimony. Witness GAA did not testify that Nshogoza represented that the purpose of the book was to prove Kamuhanda's innocence. Thus, if Nshogoza had told him that he was writing a book, the Chamber cannot discern, and indeed Witness GAA failed to provide any logical reason why he would have lied to Nshogoza about Gikomero. Witness GAA did not explain why Nshogoza would have wanted his assistance with a book on Kamuhanda after being informed that Witness GAA was not at **[page 32]** Gikomero and that he knew nothing about Kamuhanda. Moreover, Witness A7/GEX's testimony casts some additional doubt on Witness GAA's story.

126. Given its concerns with Witness GAA's credibility, discussed above,[203] the Chamber does not accept his uncorroborated testimony that Nshogoza represented that there would be no consequences for Witness GAA as a result of his recantation.

127. Therefore, the Chamber finds that the Prosecution has failed to prove beyond a reasonable doubt that Nshogoza represented to Witness GAA that he was writing a book about Kamuhanda or that he represented that there would be no consequences for Witness GAA as a result of his recantation.

3. THE MEETING BETWEEN NSHOGOZA AND WITNESS BUC

128. The Prosecution alleges that, between approximately 1 March 2004 and 20 September 2004, the Accused requested Prosecution Witness GAA to arrange for him to meet with Prosecution Witness BUC in Kigali. Witness GAA arranged the meeting, which took place in a bar in Kigali and was attended by Witness GAA and Defence Witness A7/GEX, in addition to the Accused and Witness BUC. According to the Prosecution, the Accused attempted to procure false testimony from Witness BUC, by inciting her and offering her a bribe or reward to sign a false statement and testify on behalf of Kamuhanda on Appeal, but Witness BUC refused the Accused's offer. Despite this alleged refusal, the Prosecution alleged that Lead Counsel for Kamuhanda filed an undated statement for the Appeals Chamber.[204]

129. The Accused does not deny meeting with Witness BUC, but denies that he attempted to procure false testimony from her.

3.1. Facts Related to the Accused's Meeting with Witness BUC

130. As with the meetings between the Accused and Witnesses GAA and A7/GEX, much of the evidence of the Parties concerning Nshogoza's meeting with Witness BUC is in agreement or was not disputed at trial.

---

[198] Witness GAA, T. 16 February 2009 p. 31
[199] Witness GAA, T. 16 February 2009 p. 34
[200] Witness GAA, T. 16 February 2009 p. 34
[201] Witness A7/GEX, T. 18 March 2009 p. 6.
[202] Witness A7/GEX, T. 18 March 2009 p. 29
[203] *Supra*, paras. 57-65.
[204] Indictment, paras. 28-32

Prosecutor v. Nshogoza

Nshogoza asked Witness GAA to contact Witness BUC on his behalf.[205] Witness GAA and Witness BUC were neighbours and knew each other.[206] Witness GAA told Witness BUC that Nshogoza wanted to meet with her because she was a survivor of the massacres in Gikomero in 1994, and Nshogoza wanted to know more about what happened at Gikomero.[207] **[page 33]**

131. Witness BUC eventually agreed to meet with the Accused.[208] They met at Stella Bar.[209] Witnesses GAA, A7/GEX and Defence Witness A3 were also present at the meeting.[210] Nshogoza introduced himself as a member of the *Kamuhanda* defence team.[211] Nshogoza asked her questions about the massacres at Gikomero in 1994, and specifically about Kamuhanda.[212] She told him that she did not know Kamuhanda.[213] The Accused took notes at the meeting.[214] At the end of the discussion, Nshogoza asked Witness BUC if she would be willing to go and testify before a court if asked to do so.[215] Witness BUC told him that she was willing to do so.[216] She explained that she accepted to testify because Nshogoza asked her questions about the events at Gikomero and she was there.[217]

132. At the end of the meeting, Nshogoza gave Witness BUC 5,000 Rwandan Francs for transportation.[218] Nshogoza paid for food and drinks during the meeting.[219] The Defence filed a statement from Witness BUC as part of its Rule 115 Application before the Appeals Chamber.[220]

133. The Chamber accepts these facts as having been proved beyond a reasonable doubt.

3.2. Other Relevant Evidence

134. In addition to the above undisputed evidence, the Chamber considers the following evidence relevant to its determination of events at this meeting:

   a. Witness BUC testified that the trip to Remera had cost her 600 Rwandan Francs and that she was never asked about the cost of the trip.[221]

   b. Witness GAA testified that Nshogoza presented Witness BUC with documents to sign. Witness GAA did not know the contents of the documents.[222] **[page 34]**

---

[205] Witness GAA, T. 16 February 2009 p. 50; Nshogoza, T. 30 March 2009 p. 61 (noting that Lead Counsel Condé asked him to contact with Witness BUC, and not disputing Witness GAA's account); Witness Condé, T. 16 March 2009 pp. 57-58 (testifying that she asked Nshogoza to contact Witness BUC).
[206] Witness BUC, T. 12 February 2009 p. 16.
[207] Witness BUC, T. 12 February 2009 pp. 19-20.
[208] Witness GAA, T. 16 February 2009 p. 51; Witness BUC, T. 12 February 2009 p. 21.
[209] Witness GAA, T. 16 February 2009 p. 51; Witness A3, T. 19 March 2009 p. 46; *see also* Witness BUC, T. 12 February 2009 pp. 21-22 (Witness BUC did not know the name of the place where they met, which she described as "a room" in the Remera section of Kigali); Witness A7/GEX, T. 18 March 2009 p. 31 (Witness A7/GEX testified that the meeting was held at the same place as her prior meeting with Nshogoza and Witness GAA).
[210] Witness GAA, T. 16 February 2009 pp. 51-52; Witness A3, T. 19 March 2009 pp. 44-45; *see also* Witness BUC, T. 12 February 2009 p. 24 (Witness BUC did not know Witness A3, but testified that, in addition to Witnesses GAA and A7/GEX, a man she did not know was present at the meeting); Witness A7/GEX, T. 18 March 2009 pp. 31, 33; T. 19 March 2009 pp. 6-8 (Witness A7/GEX testified that she did not know Witness A3 at the time, but later learned his identity and confirmed it when the travelled to Arusha together for their testimony in this trial).
[211] Witness BUC, T. 12 February 2009 p. 26
[212] Witness BUC, T. 12 February 2009 p. 22
[213] Witness BUC, T. 12 February 2009 p. 22.
[214] Witness GAA, T. 16 February 2009 p. 52; Nshogoza, T. 30 March 2009 p. 60 (referring to a statement he handwrote); Witness A7/GEX, T. 18 March 2009 p. 31.
[215] Witness BUC, T. 12 February 2009 p. 23.
[216] Witness BUC, T. 12 February 2009 pp. 23-24.
[217] Witness BUC, T. 12 February 2009 p. 27.
[218] Witness GAA, T. 16 February 2009 p. 52; Witness BUC, T. 12 February 2009 p. 26; Nshogoza, T. 30 March 2009 p. 61
[219] Witness GAA, T. 16 February 2009 p. 52; Witness BUC, T. 12 February 2009 p. 26; Witness A3, T. 19 March 2009 p. 47.
[220] Exhibit D. 30; *see also* Nshogoza, T. 30 March 2009 p. 59 (recognizing Witness BUC's statement attached to the Rule 115 Application).
[221] Witness BUC, T. 12 February 2009 pp. 26-27
[222] Witness GAA, T. 16 February 2009 p. 51.

c. Nshogoza testified that Witness BUC gave him a statement of her own free will, which the Accused handwrote and Witness BUC signed.[223]

d. Nshogoza testified that Witness BUC's signature was on the handwritten version of the statement annexed to the 115 Rule Motion filed by Lead Counsel Condé.[224]

e. Nshogoza testified that he paid Witness BUC 5,000 Rwandan Francs for transport costs and loss of earnings, but did not try to bribe her.[225]

3.3. Disputed Factual Issues

135. The Prosecution submits that the only reasonable inference from the above evidence is that "the Accused attempted to procure and place before the Appeals Chamber evidence purportedly from BUC, which would exculpate Jean de Dieu Kamuhanda."[226] The Chamber considers that procuring evidence, of itself, is not an act punishable as contempt of the Tribunal, and thus, by extension, attempting to procure evidence would not be punishable as attempt to commit an act punishable as contempt of the Tribunal. The Chamber will therefore consider only whether the evidence shows that the Accused attempted to procure false evidence from Witness BUC.

136. The Prosecution adduced no evidence that the Accused asked Witness BUC to provide false testimony or sign a false statement. Rather, the evidence shows that the Accused asked Witness BUC about her knowledge of the massacre at Gikomero and Kamuhanda, she told him what she knew, and he asked her to sign a statement and if she would be willing to testify.

137. Despite having an opportunity to do so, the Prosecution did not ask Witness BUC any questions regarding her statement submitted before the Appeals Chamber. Given this failure, any finding that the statement differed from what Witness BUC told the Accused at their meeting would be unsafe and contrary to basic principles of fairness and due process. For this reason, the Prosecution failed to prove beyond a reasonable doubt that Witness BUC's statement was false or that the Accused had any reason to believe its contents were untrue.

138. The Chamber finds that the evidence proves beyond a reasonable doubt that Witness BUC agreed to testify before the Appeals Chamber. Moreover, Witness BUC did not suggest that she agreed to do so as a result of any incitement or bribery by the Accused. Indeed, Witness BUC stated that she agreed to testify because the Accused asked her questions about the events in Gikomero and she was present there.[227] The Appeals Chamber did not admit Witness BUC's statement as additional evidence on appeal.

139. Witness GAA's testimony that the Accused presented Witness BUC with documents to sign—to the extent that it refers to something other than the handwritten statement or notes, which was unclear from the testimony itself because it lacked detail—was not corroborated by Witness BUC. Indeed, the Prosecution did not question her on this issue. Moreover, it was, at least in part, internally inconsistent, as Witness GAA also testified that Nshogoza took notes. This evidence was also contradicted by the testimonies of Witness A7/GEX and the Accused. Given the lack of clarity and detail in Witness GAA's evidence, the lack of corroboration by **[page 35]** Witness BUC, and the inconsistencies and contradictions described above, the Chamber does not accept that the Accused placed documents before Witness BUC that were distinct from the handwritten statement or notes.

140. The Chamber finds that the evidence proves beyond a reasonable doubt that Nshogoza paid Witness BUC 5,000 Rwandan Francs which he stated was for transportation expenses. The Chamber also accepts that this amount exceeded the actual transport costs incurred by Witness BUC, which amounted to 600 or 1,200 Rwandan Francs, that the Accused did not ask Witness BUC about the cost of the trip. The evidence also shows that the Accused provided food and drinks to Witness BUC. Nonetheless, as with the payments and

---

[223] Nshogoza, T. 30 March 2009 pp. 60-61.
[224] Nshogoza, T. 30 March 2009 pp. 59-60; Exhibit D. 30.
[225] Nshogoza, T. 30 March 2009 p. 61.
[226] Prosecution Closing Brief, para. 170.
[227] Witness BUC, T. 12 February 2009 p. 27.

refreshments provided to Witnesses GAA and A7/GEX, the Chamber does not consider that the evidence shows that the payments and refreshments were provided with the intent to induce or bribe Witness BUC into signing a statement or testifying.

4. WITNESS GAA's MEETINGS WITH WITNESSES GAF, Sp003 AND SP004

141. The Prosecution alleges that, between 1 March 2004 and 31 May 2005, the Accused, acting in concert with relatives of, or persons close to Kamuhanda, asked Prosecution Witness GAA to contact Prosecution Witnesses GAF, SP003 and SP004 on his behalf and ask them to meet with him with the ultimate purpose of procuring false testimony from each of them, in exchange of a substantial amount of money as a bribe or reward.[228]

142. The Accused denies asking Witness GAA to meet with any of these witnesses.

4.1. Disputed Factual Issues

143. Unlike the other allegations in this case, there are no undisputed facts relevant to these allegations and the evidence of the parties is not in accord. The Chamber considers that the two main issues arising from the Indictment are (i) whether the Accused asked Witness GAA to find other Witnesses to testify falsely on behalf of Kamuhanda; and (ii) whether the Accused promised any payment for other witnesses.

4.1.1 Relevant Evidence

144. According to Witness GAA, Nshogoza told him that if he could find any other potential witnesses for him, then he should put them in touch with the Accused.[229] Witness GAA said that such persons were supposed to testify that they had not seen Kamuhanda at Gikomero during the massacres.[230] Witness GAA contacted Prosecution Witnesses GAF, SP003 and SP004, but none of them met or spoke with Nshogoza.[231] Witness GAA explained that, after their meeting at the **[page 36]** notary where he confirmed his recantation statement, Nshogoza told him not to pursue meetings with Witnesses GAF, SP003 and SP004 because the "witnesses he had already met were sufficient."[232] Witness GAA also testified that when he disclosed the names of those persons to Nshogoza, the Accused told him that he no longer needed to contact those persons.[233]

145. Witnesses GAF, SP003 and SP004 were all neighbours of Witness GAA.[234] Witness GAA informed each of them that there was someone who was interested in talking to them about Gikomero and Kamuhanda and that the person, whom he did not name, would pay them for their testimony.[235] They all learned that Nshogoza was the person who had promised the money after Witness GAA returned from recanting his testimony in Arusha.[236]

146. Specifically, Witness GAA asked Witness GAF, who had testified on behalf of the Prosecution in the *Kamuhanda* trial, to recant his testimony.[237] Witness GAA told Witness SP003 that he was going to introduce him to someone "so that we would go and testify in the *Kamuhanda* case and testify to the effect that Kamuhanda was not in the massacre site in Gikomero."[238] Witness GAA asked Witness SP004 to testify on

---

[228] Indictment, paras. 35, 41, 49.
[229] Witness GAA, T. 16 February 2009 p. 48.
[230] Witness GAA, T. 16 February 2009 p. 49.
[231] Witness GAA, T. 16 February 2009 pp. 49, 53
[232] Witness GAA, T. 16 February 2009 p. 55.
[233] Witness GAA, T. 19 February 2009 p. 27.
[234] Witness GAA, T. 16 February 2009 p. 53, 55; Witness GAF, T. 9 February 2009 p. 21; Witness SP003, T. 10 February 2009 p. 46; Witness SP004, T. 11 February 2009 pp. 64-65 (closed session).
[235] Witness GAA, T. 16 February 2009 pp. 53-55; Witness GAF, T. 9 February 2009 pp. 23, 28; Witness SP003, T. 10 February 2009 pp. 50-53; Witness SP004, T. 11 February 2009 pp. 68-71.
[236] Witness GAF, T. 9 February 2009 pp. 24-28; Witness SP003, T. 10 February 2009 pp. 48, 51, 54-55; Witness SP004, T. 11 February 2009 p. 69.
[237] Witness GAF, T. 9 February 2009 pp. 21, 23.
[238] Witness SP003, T. 10 February 2009 p. 50

behalf of Kamuhanda and told her that because she had never testified as a prosecution witness against Kamuhanda, she could become a defence witness for him and there would be no trouble for her.[239]

147. With respect to the promise of payment, Witness GAA did not clearly inform Witness GAF that Nshogoza would pay him money until Witness GAA went to Arusha to recant his testimony.[240] Witness GAA told Witness SP003 that he would be given more than one million Rwandan Francs.[241] Witness GAA told Witness SP004 that he was going to ask him to offer them one million Rwandan Francs in order for them to testify for the *Kamuhanda* defence. Witness GAA said that, even if they asked for one million Rwandan Francs, the unidentified person would be willing to pay.[242]

148. Witness GAF testified that he refused to recant because he did not want to lie or testify to anything that he had not witnessed personally.[243] He also stated, however, that he eventually agreed to meet with Nshogoza, but the meeting never occurred.[244] Witness SP003 testified that he agreed to meet the Accused, but only in order to report to the authorities the person who was **[page 37]** supposed to give them money.[245] Witness GAA arranged a meeting between Witness SP003 and Kamuhanda's sister, but Witness SP003 was not interested in meeting with her.[246] No meeting was ever arranged between Witness SP003 and the Accused. Witness SP004 refused Witness GAA's request.[247]

149. Nshogoza testified that he did not know Witnesses GAF, SP003 or SP004, and had never seen them before they testified in this case.[248] He never asked anyone to put him in contact with these witnesses.[249] According to the Accused, Witness GAA never told him that he wanted to put him in touch with Witnesses GAF, SP003 and SP004 and never gave him their names.[250]

4.1.2 Did the Accused request Witness GAA to find more Witnesses?

150. The Chamber notes that the Prosecution's case concerning these allegations rests on the evidence of Witness GAA, who is the only Prosecution Witness who gave direct evidence of the Accused's alleged request that he find more witnesses.

151. Witness GAA's testimony regarding Nshogoza's alleged request to find more witnesses was inconsistent and contradicted by his prior statement to the Rwandan authorities. Witness GAA first testified that the Accused asked him to find other potential witnesses and to put them in contact with him.[251] Then he said that the Accused requested him to contact only Witness BUC, and he personally contacted other potential witnesses.[252] Witness GAA subsequently testified that the Accused gave him the names of some persons and he contacted them.[253] But he also stated that the Accused asked him to contact some persons, whose names Witness GAA subsequently disclosed to the Accused.[254] Moreover, in a 14 June 2007 statement given to Rwandan authorities, Witness GAA asserted that the Accused never asked him to look for witnesses for Kamuhanda. Witness GAA disavowed this statement, insisting that the Accused gave him names of people to be contacted.[255]

---

[239] Witness SP004, T. 11 February 2009 pp. 68-69.
[240] Witness GAF, 9 February 2009, pp. 29-31 (stating that he understood it would be a payment of money because that was what was used in these types of things).
[241] Witness SP003, T. 10 February 2009 pp. 51-53
[242] Witness SP004, T. 11 February 2009 p. 70-71.
[243] Witness GAF, T. 9 February 2009 pp. 23, 28-29.
[244] Witness GAF, T. 10 February 2009 pp. 25, 35.
[245] Witness SP003, T. 10 February 2009 pp. 55, 57.
[246] Witness SP003, T. 10 February 2009 pp. 55-56
[247] Witness SP004, T. 11 February 2009 p. 70
[248] Nshogoza, T. 30 March 2009 p. 61
[249] Nshogoza, T. 30 March 2009 p. 62
[250] Nshogoza, T. 30 March 2009 p. 62
[251] Witness GAA, T. 16 February 2009 p. 48
[252] Witness GAA, T. 16 February 2009 p. 49
[253] Witness GAA, T. 19 February 2009 p. 27
[254] Witness GAA, T. 19 February 2009 p. 27
[255] Witness GAA, T. 19 February 2009 p. 27

152. Even if the Chamber overlooked these inconsistencies and contradictions and accepted Witness GAA's uncorroborated testimony that the Accused asked him to look for other witnesses, this would not prove beyond a reasonable doubt that the Accused sought to procure false testimony. Witness GAA did not testify that the Accused asked him to find people who would lie or provide false testimony. The Chamber recalls that Witness GAA informed the Accused that he had not been at Gikomero and that his testimony against Kamuhanda was a lie.[256] If the Accused, after hearing this, asked Witness GAA to find other witnesses who could [page 38] testify that Kamuhanda was not at Gikomero, a reasonable conclusion could be that the Accused was simply seeking evidence to corroborate Witness GAA's recantation. Under these circumstances, the Chamber finds that the Prosecution has failed to prove beyond a reasonable doubt that the Accused asked Witness GAA to find other witnesses to provide false testimony.

4.1.3 Did the Accused promise payment for other witnesses?

153. In relation to the alleged promise of a reward in exchange for testimony, the Chamber observes that Witness GAA's testimony lacks detail and specificity in relation to whether the Accused actually promised any money to Witnesses GAF, SP003 or SP004, or, more generally, for other witnesses. When he first testified regarding Nshogoza's alleged request that he find more witnesses, Witness GAA did not refer to a promise of money. When he did eventually testify about a promise of money, it was unclear whether he was referring to the alleged promise of money that Nshogoza made to him, or to a separate promise of payment for other witnesses.[257] Moreover, the Chamber recalls its discussion of Witness GAA's testimony that the Accused promised to pay him for his testimony.[258] The Chamber considers that the doubts raised by Witness GAA's testimony and prior statements as well as the testimonies of Witnesses GAF and SP004 as to whether the Accused promised him payment also raise doubt as to whether the Accused promised payment for other witnesses. For these reasons, the Chamber finds that the Prosecution has failed to prove beyond a reasonable doubt that the Accused promised to pay other witnesses for their testimony.

CHAPTER IV: LEGAL CONCLUSIONS

1. OVERVIEW OF THE LAW OF CONTEMPT OF THE TRIBUNAL

154. Contempt of the Tribunal is described in Rule 77, which reads, in relevant part:

> (A) The Tribunal in the exercise of its inherent power may hold in contempt those who knowingly and wilfully interfere with its administration of justice, including any person who
>
> ...
>
> (ii) discloses information relating to those proceedings in knowing violation of an order of a Chamber;
>
> ... [page 39]
>
> (iv) threatens, intimidates, causes any injury or offers a bribe to, or otherwise interferes with a witness who is giving, has given, or is about to give evidence in proceedings before a Chamber, or a potential witness; or
>
> ...
>
> (B) Any incitement or attempt to commit any of these acts punishable under paragraph (A) is punishable as contempt of the Tribunal with the same penalties.

155. Rule 77 (A) provides the general *actus reus* and *mens rea* for contempt. The *actus reus* is interference with the administration of justice, and the *mens rea* is the knowledge and will to interfere.[259]

---

[256] *Supra*, paras. 95-102.
[257] Witness GAA, T. 16 February 2009 p. 54 ("I told [Witness GAF] what the Accused had told me; namely, that if [Witness GAF] were to accept—to recant his previous testimony, Nshogoza would give him—give him an amount of money.") From this testimony, it is unclear whether Witness GAA meant that he repeated the alleged promise that Nshogoza had made to him, personally, regarding payment, or whether Nshogoza had also promised payment to others.
[258] *Supra*, paras. 114-121.
[259] *The Prosecutor v. Domagoj Margetić*, Case No. IT-95-14-R77.6, Judgement on Allegations of Contempt (TC), 7 February 2007 ("*Margetić* Contempt Judgement"), para. 77.

156. The listed punishable acts are non-exhaustive, and do not limit the Tribunal's jurisdiction to punish contempt.[260]

157. Under Rule 77 (A)(ii), the *actus reus* for contempt is the physical act of disclosing confidential information relating to proceedings before this Tribunal in an objective breach of a court order.[261] The *mens rea* for contempt by disclosure of information contrary to Rule 77 (A) (ii) is knowledge by the accused that his disclosure of information was done in violation of a court order.[262] It is sufficient to establish that the act which constitutes the violation is deliberate and not accidental.[263] A misunderstanding of the law, as to whether disclosing the information was unlawful or not, does not excuse a violation of it.[264]

158. The conduct punishable pursuant to Rule 77 (A)(iv) of the Rules includes threatening, intimidating, causing injury, offering a bribe or otherwise interfering with a witness. "Otherwise interfering with a witness" is an open-ended provision which encompasses "any conduct that is intended to disturb the administration of justice by deterring a witness or a potential witness from giving full and truthful evidence, or in any way to influence the nature of the witness' or potential witness' evidence."[265] Besides the general *mens rea* requirement for contempt, for which the Prosecution must also prove that the Accused acted knowingly and wilfully, Rule 77 (A) (iv) also requires that the conduct was carried out with the intent to interfere with the witness or with the knowledge that the conduct was likely to deter or influence the witness.[266] **[page 40]**

159. Rule 77 (B) states that "any incitement or attempt to commit any of the acts punishable under paragraph (A) is punishable as contempt of the Tribunal with the same penalties."

2. COUNT ONE: CONTEMPT OF THE TRIBUNAL

160. Under Count One of the Indictment, the Prosecution charges Nshogoza with committing contempt of the Tribunal pursuant to Rule 77 (A) and (A)(ii), by repeatedly meeting with and disclosing the protected information of Witnesses GAA and A7/GEX, in knowing violation of, or with reckless indifference to the protective measures ordered by the *Kamuhanda* Trial Chamber on 7 July 2000.[267]

2.1. Were Witnesses GAA and A7/GEX Protected Prosecution Witnesses?

161. The Defence submits that neither Prosecution Witness GAA nor Defence Witness A7/GEX were protected prosecution witnesses in the *Kamuhanda* case at the time of the meetings. According to the Defence, Witness A7/GEX may have been covered by the protective measures as a potential prosecution witness at some point, but all protections for her ceased on 14 May 2002, when the prosecution closed its evidence in that trial.[268] As for Witness GAA, the Defence argues that he waived his protective measures by approaching or agreeing to meet with the Accused.[269]

162. Pursuant to Rule 75 (G), once ordered, protective measures continue to apply until they are rescinded, varied or augmented pursuant to procedures set out in subsections (G) through (I) of that Rule. Though Rule 75 (G) refers only to protective measures ordered "in respect of a victim or witness", the Chamber does not

---

[260] *Margetić* Contempt Judgement, paras. 13, 14 (citing *Nobilo* Appeal Judgement, para 39 and *The Prosecutor v. Josip Jović*, Case No. IT-95-14 & 14/2-R77, Decision to Deny the Accused Josip Jović's Preliminary Motion to Dismiss the Indictment on the Grounds of Lack of Jurisdiction and Defects in the Form of the Indictment (TC), 21 December 2005, para 28).
[261] *Marijačić* Trial Judgement, para 17; *Margetić* Contempt Judgement, para. 36.
[262] *The Prosecutor v. Josip Jović*, Case No. IT-95-14 & 14/2-R77-A, Judgement (AC), 15 March 2007 ("Jovic Appeal Judgement"), paras. 27, 30; *Marijačić* Trial Judgement, para 18; *The Prosecutor v. Baton Haxiu*, Case No. IT-04-84-R77.5, Judgement on Allegations of Contempt (TC), 24 July 2008 ("*Haxiu* Contempt Judgement"), para. 11.
[263] *Nobilo* Appeal Judgement, para. 54.
[264] *Jović* Appeal Judgement, para 27; *Bulatović* Contempt Appeal, para. 11; *Haxiu* Contempt Judgement, para. 29.
[265] *Beqaj* Contempt Judgement, para. 21; *Margetić* Contempt Judgement, para. 64; *The Prosecutor v. Astrit Haraqija and Bajrush Morina*, Case No. IT-04-84-R77.4, Judgement on Allegations of Contempt (TC), 17 December 2008 ("*Haraqija & Morina* Contempt Judgement"), para. 18.
[266] *Margetić* Contempt Judgement, para. 66; *Haraqija & Morina* Contempt Judgement, para. 19.
[267] Indictment, paras. 5-16; *see also*, *Supra*, paras. 48-56.
[268] Defence Closing Brief, para. 289.
[269] T. 29 April 2009 pp. 19-20 (Defence closing arguments)

consider that this language was intended to explicitly exclude continued protection for potential witnesses. Rule 69, which authorizes protective measures for witnesses and victims generally, does not mention potential witnesses either. At this Tribunal, however, potential witnesses have routinely been granted protection.[270] In two recent decisions, Trial Chambers have rejected the argument that potential witnesses cannot be protected because they are not specifically mentioned in the Rules.[271]

163. In the trial of *The Prosecutor v. Nahimana et al.*, the Trial Chamber addressed the issue of protective measures for potential witnesses in an interlocutory decision:

> The Chamber notes that Rule 69 provides that a Protection Order remains in force "until the Chamber decides otherwise". As the Chamber has not rescinded a Protection Order or made any **[page 41]** contrary decision relating to the protection of Prosecution witnesses the Protection Order remains in force. *This is so even in respect of witnesses the Prosecutor or Defence has not called.* The purpose of protective measures is to protect witnesses who may be "in danger or at risk", as provided by Rule 69, and, more generally, to safeguard their "privacy and security", as stated in Rule 75. Once witnesses are covered by a Protection Order, the protection mechanism is triggered. *A witness who has not been called during presentation of a party's case may be called at a later stage, for instance, during rebuttal, appeal or review. Potential witnesses who fall under the Protection Order but never testify in a case may similarly be in need of protection. That the witness initiates contact with Counsel with a view to testifying, as is asserted by Mr Floyd [Defence Counsel for Hassan Ngeze] in the present case, does not negate Counsel's obligation to abide by the Protection Order and notify the Prosecutor, nor eliminate the protective measures granted to the witness.* The Chamber takes seriously its obligation to protect witnesses and is mindful that a Protection Order is an assurance to the witness that his identity and security will be protected.[272]

164. The Chamber considers the reasoning of the *Nahimana et al.* Trial Chamber on this issue to be persuasive.

165. The Defence submissions concerning the dire consequences of a finding that potential witnesses who do not testify remain subject to protective measures are unconvincing. The Defence offers no explanation as to how protective measures for potential witnesses who do not ultimately testify may "dilute the effect of protective measures"[273] of witnesses who do testify, and the Chamber does not consider that granting protective measures to one witness limits or decreases the ability of the Tribunal to issue protective measures for other witnesses. In addition, the suggested "enormous stifling effect"[274] on Defence investigations is unfounded. When ordering protective measures, the general practice before this Tribunal is for Trial Chambers to provide a procedure by which the opposing party may obtain permission to meet with a witness for the opposition.[275] Though contacting a protected witness may take more time and require extra administrative steps than does meeting with an unprotected witness, this does not amount to an "enormous stifling effect" and does not violate the rights of the Accused.

---

[270] *See e.g.*, Decision on Defence Motion for Protective Measures for Victims and Witnesses (TC), 22 January 2009; *The Prosecutor v. Ngirabatware*, ICTR-99-54-T, Decision on the Prosecutor's Motion for Special Protective Measures for Prosecution Witnesses and others (TC), 6 May 2009 ("*Ngirabatware* Decision"); *The Prosecutor v. Kalimanzira*, ICTR-2005-88-I, Decision on Defence Motion for Protective Measures (TC), 14 December 2007; *The Prosecutor v. Karemera et al.*, ICTR-98-44-R75, Order on Protective Measures for Prosecution Witnesses (TC), 10 December 2004.

[271] *See Ngirabatware* Decision, para. 21; *The Prosecutor v. Karemera et al.*, ICTR-98-44-T, Decision on Joseph Nzirorera's emergency motion for no contact order and "Requete urgente de Matthieu Ngirumpatse aux fins d'interdire au Procureur de contacter toute personne figurant sur la liste de temoins sans l'accord prealable de ses conseils" (TC), 21 August 2008 (The Chamber avoided determining whether Rule 75 covered protective measures for potential witnesses, but ordered protections for such witnesses pursuant to Rule 54).

[272] *The Prosecutor v. Nahimana et al.*, Case No. ICTR-99-52-T, Decision on the Prosecutor's Urgent Motion for a Restraining Order Against the Defence's Further Contact with Witness RM-10 and For Other Relief Based on the Ngeze Defence's Violations of Court Decisions and Rules (TC), 17 January 2003, para. 14 ("*Nahimana* Decision")(internal footnotes omitted) (emphasis added).

[273] Defence Closing Brief, para. 290.

[274] Defence Closing Brief, para. 291.

[275] The *Kamuhanda* Protective Measures required that the Defence give notice to the Prosecution and make a written request to the Chamber to "contact any protected victim or potential Prosecution witnesses or any relative of such a person". Upon obtaining such permission, the protective measures required the Prosecution to "undertake all necessary arrangements to facilitate such interview." Protective Measures Decision, para. 2 (i). The Chamber expressly found that this measure did not affect the rights of the Accused. Protective Measures Decision, para. 9.

166. Finally, the Defence reference to the Prosecution's failure to object to Witness A7/GEX's admission as a Rule 115 witness before the Appeals Chamber is unavailing.[276] A violation of protective measures cannot be condoned by the opposing party in a case, either explicitly or by omission. **[page 42]**

167. Turning to the proven facts of this case, the evidence shows that Witness A7/GEX provided a statement to the *Kamuhanda* prosecution team and that she was identified to the *Kamuhanda* defence team as a potential prosecution witness in that case on 26 March 2001.[277] The Protective Measures explicitly cover potential prosecution witnesses, and do not specify when persons cease to be potential witnesses.[278] The *Kamuhanda* Trial Chamber did not rescind the protective measures for prosecution witnesses, potential or otherwise.

168. For these reasons, the Chamber finds that Defence Witness A7/GEX was a protected potential prosecution witness at the time of the meetings in this case.

169. Concerning Witness GAA, the Chamber did not accept the Defence evidence that he initiated contact with the Accused, but, even if Witness GAA had approached the Accused, the Chamber does not consider that this would amount to a waiver of his protective measures. Rules 69 (A) and 75 (F)(i) state, respectively, that protective measures remain in place "until the Chamber decides otherwise", and that they "shall continue to have effect *mutatis mutandis* in any other proceedings before the Tribunal ... unless and until they are rescinded, varied or augmented in accordance with the procedure set out in this Rule." Moreover, the Chamber finds the reasoning of the *Nahimana et al.* Trial Chamber persuasive, and considers that, regardless of who initiates contact, the Parties, including all members of the Defence team, must abide by applicable protective measures.[279]

170. In addition, the Chamber notes that any waiver of protective measures must be knowing and voluntary. The practice before this Tribunal has been for protected witnesses to verify, before the relevant Trial Chamber, that they request a waiver of their protective measures.[280] Indeed, to allow tacit waiver would not be consonant with the safety concerns which warrant the granting of such measures. In this case, four defence witnesses waived their protective measures. In accordance with the practice described above, they came before the Chamber and verified that they wished to waive their protective measures and the Chamber subsequently declared that the relevant protections were lifted.[281] The Chamber, therefore, finds that Prosecution Witness GAA did not waive his protective measures and remained protected by the Protective Measures at the time of the meetings.

2.2. Repeated Meetings with Protected Prosecution Witnesses [page 43]

171. The Prosecution argues that, without regard to whether the Accused disclosed the protected information of Witnesses GAA and A7/GEX to third parties or the public, the Chamber may convict the Accused of contempt for his repeated meetings with the witnesses in violation of the protective measures ordered by the *Kamuhanda* Trial Chamber on 7 July 2000.[282]

---

[276] Defence Closing Brief, para. 295. In any event, the evidence in this case shows that the Prosecution did raise the issue of violation of protective measures issue during the appeal hearing. Exhibit P. 14 (excerpt of appeal hearing in the *Kamuhanda* case, *The Prosecutor v. Kamuhanda*, T. 19 May 2005 p. 41 (French Transcript cited)).
[277] *Supra*, paras. 68, 73, 79-81.
[278] Protective Measures Decision, para. 2.
[279] *Nahimana* Decision, para. 14.
[280] *See e.g., The Prosecutor v. Pauline Niyramasuhuko et. al.*, Case No. ICTR-97-29-T, Decision on Nteziryayo's Motion for Variation of Protective Measures for Witnesses AND-36, AND-38, and AND-50 (TC), 20 April 2007, para. 11 (the Trial Chamber found that emails from witnesses expressing their desire to reside in a hotel rather than the safe house were insufficient to find that the witnesses had waived their protective measures); *The Prosecutor v. Casimir Bizimungu et al.*, Case No. ICTR-99-50-T, Decision on Defence Bicamumpaka's Motion to Vary Protective Measures for Certain Defence Witnesses (TC), 18 October 2007, paras. 5-6, (Trial Chamber's decision to vary the protective measures was based on signed statements of the witnesses and followed an inquiry with WVSS).
[281] *See* T. 16 March 2009, pp. 22, 33 (in relation to Witness A8- Fulgence Seminega); T. 16 March 2009, p. 34 (with respect to Witness A11-Straton Nyarwaya); T. 16 March 2009, pp. 35-36 (in relation to witness A21-Cyprien Hakizimana) and T. 20 March 2009, p. 46 (with respect to Witness A9-Augustin Nyagatare).
[282] T. 29 April 2009, pp. 10-11 (Prosecution closing arguments); *see also, supra*, paras. 48-56.

172. The Defence submits that, even if Witnesses GAA and A7/GEX were protected prosecution witnesses in the *Kamuhanda* proceedings, Nshogoza's meetings with them, though in violation of the Protective Measures, do not qualify as contempt because the meetings are not sufficiently serious conduct.[283] The Defence submits that, even if this conduct is punishable as contempt, the Prosecution failed to prove that the Accused possessed the requisite *mens rea*.[284] The Chamber will consider each of these arguments in turn.

2.2.1 Sufficiently Serious Conduct

173. The Defence submits that "a complete reading of the [contempt] cases [shows] that the conduct in question must meet a gravity threshold in order to constitute contempt."[285] In support of this proposition, the Defence refers to two Trial Chamber decisions on interlocutory motions wherein the Chambers found that violations of court orders were not sufficiently serious to amount to contempt.[286] The Defence further submits that the "reality of cases that involve witness protective measures, [is] that these are breached from time to time" and suggests that "[i]t is a regular occurrence in Trial Chambers for witnesses' identities to be revealed inadvertently, and then placed under seal when the breach is brought to the attention of the Chamber." The Defence further submits that "[i]t is an indisputable fact, and undoubtedly a regrettable one, that the unauthorised meeting of protected Defence witnesses by the Prosecution happens on a regular basis at the ICTR" and refers the Chamber to seven alleged instances of such conduct that the Defence submits came to light in this trial.[287]

174. The Chamber notes that the plain language of Rule 77 makes no mention of a "gravity threshold" or "sufficiently serious conduct". Rather it states that the Tribunal "may hold in contempt those who knowingly and wilfully interfere with its administration of justice."[288] The Chamber considers that the plain language of the Rule dictates that any deliberate (knowing and wilful) conduct that interferes with the administration of justice is sufficiently serious to be punished as contempt. **[page 44]**

175. In the context of a case concerning Rule 77 (A)(ii), which, in both the ICTY and ICTR Rules, states that the Tribunal may hold in contempt "any person who discloses information ... in knowing violation of an order of a Chamber", the Appeals Chamber held that "a violation of a court order *as such* constitutes an interference with the International Tribunal's administration of justice."[289] The Appeals Chamber further noted that "[a]ny defiance of an order of a Chamber *per se* interferes with the administration of justice for the purposes of a conviction for contempt."[290] The Chamber considers that the broad language used by the Appeals Chamber was not limited to orders preventing the disclosure of information, and finds that any violation of an order of a Chamber is a sufficient *actus reus* for contempt.[291]

176. With regard to the Defence argument that violations of protective measures occur from time to time, the Chamber notes that cases of inadvertent disclosures of protected witness information would be highly unlikely to meet the requirement that, in order to be held liable for contempt, one's conduct must be knowing and wilful. The Chamber also notes that the language of Rule 77 is discretionary. The Tribunal *may* hold persons in contempt who knowingly and wilfully interfere with the administration of justice, but the fact that a Trial Chamber has reason to believe that a person is in contempt does not oblige it to order an investigation or prosecution. The Chamber does not consider it necessary to explore the variety of factors that may

---

[283] Defence Closing Brief, paras. 278-280, 285, 304-306.
[284] Defence Closing Brief, paras. 296-303.
[285] Defence Closing Brief, para. 278.
[286] *Ibid.* (citing *The Prosecutor v. Ntakirutimana*, Case No. ICTR-96-10-T, Decision on Prosecution Motion for Contempt of Court and on two Defence Motions for Disclosure (TC), 16 July 2001, para. 10-12; and *The Prosecutor v. Furundzija*, Casze No. IT-95-17/1-T, The Trial Chamber's Formal Complaint to the Prosecutor Concerning the conduct of the Prosecution (TC), 5 June 1998, para. 11.)
[287] Defence Closing Brief, para. 305; T. 29 April 2009 p. 39 (In closing arguments, the Defence submits that there were seven instances instead of the six instances referred to in the Closing Brief).
[288] Rule 77 (A).
[289] *Jović* Appeal Judgement, para. 30 (quoting the *Marijačić* Appeal Judgement, para. 44) (emphasis added by Appeals Chamber in *Jović*).
[290] *Jović* Appeal Judgement, para. 30 (citations omitted).
[291] It is clear from the plain language of Rule 77 and the jurisprudence on contempt that the acts enumerated in Rule 77 (A)(i) through (v) are non-exhaustive.

influence a Chamber's decision whether or not to order an investigation or prosecution for contempt once its discretion to do so is enlivened. It is sufficient to note that decisions taken pursuant to Rule 77 are discretionary.

177. The Chamber has already addressed the allegations of Prosecution violations of protective measures raised in this case.[292] In addition, the Chamber notes that evidence that other persons may have committed similar acts to those alleged in the Indictment is irrelevant to these proceedings, as it does not tend to prove or disprove any of the allegations in the Indictment against the Accused.

178. The Chamber, therefore, rejects the Defence's submission that the jurisprudence on contempt requires the Chamber to make an inquiry into the seriousness of the conduct in question that is independent of the elements expressed in Rule 77 (A). The Chamber considers that the knowing and wilful violation of protective measures ordered by a Trial Chamber is punishable as contempt of the Tribunal.

2.2.2 Defence Arguments related to *mens rea*

179. The Defence submits that in order for the Chamber to convict the Accused under Count One, "the Prosecution must have established that Mr Nshogoza knew he was violating a witness protection order in meeting GAA and GEX, and that he did so with a specific intent to interfere **[page 45]** with the administration of justice."[293] In the Chamber's view, the Defence mischaracterizes the requisite *mens rea* for acts of contempt arising out of violations of a Chamber's orders. Since, as held by the Appeals Chamber, any violation of a Chamber's order interferes with its administration of justice, it follows that any knowing and wilful conduct in violation of a Chamber's order meets the requisite *mens rea* for contempt, that is, it is committed with the requisite intent to interfere with the administration of justice. As the ICTY Appeals Chamber noted, "[i]t is not for a party or a third person to determine when an order is serving the International Tribunal's administration of justice."[294]

180. As noted above,[295] the Defence makes several other arguments relevant to *mens rea*, none of which the Chamber accepts. The Defence submits that (i) at least at their initial meeting, the Accused did not know that Witness GAA was a protected prosecution witness; (ii) after that point, the Accused was instructed to meet with Witness GAA by Lead Counsel Condé and was simply doing his job; (iii) the Accused was unaware of the circumstances in which an investigator can meet with a protected witness and he relied on Lead Counsel Condé's instruction regarding the use of a notary.[296]

181. With regard to the Accused's knowledge of Witness GAA's status at their first meeting, the Chamber recalls its finding that the Accused was aware that Witness GAA wanted to recant a prior statement or testimony.[297] The Chamber further recalls that it did not accept the Accused's evidence that he was ignorant of the contents of the Protective Measures, and notes that they clearly described the requisite procedure before any member of the *Kamuhanda* defence team could meet with a protected prosecution witness, and made no mention of a notary public exception.[298] With respect to the Defence submissions regarding the Accused's misunderstanding regarding who was covered by the Protective Measures and the effect of visiting a notary, the Chamber notes that it is well-established in the ICTY's jurisprudence on contempt that mistake of law is not a valid defence.[299] For these reasons, the Chamber rejects the Defence argument that the Accused's conduct with respect to Witness GAA was not made with knowledge that, or at least reckless indifference to whether, the witness was a protected prosecution witness.

---

[292] *Supra*, paras. 37-45.
[293] Defence Closing Brief, para. 296.
[294] *Marijačić* Appeal Judgement, para. 44 (internal quotation omitted).
[295] *Supra*, para. 77.
[296] Defence Closing Brief, paras. 297-301.
[297] *Supra*, para. 85.
[298] *Supra*, para. 78. In Closing Arguments the Defence suggested that, as a defence investigator, the Accused necessarily relied on Lead Counsel Condé to obtain authorization to meet with prosecution witnesses because the relevant provision of the Protective Measures did not explicitly authorise Nshogoza to obtain such permission, but referred only to defence counsel and Kamuhanda himself. The evidence is clear, however, that Condé informed Nshogoza that the use of the notary was meant to supersede the need to obtain authorisation pursuant to the Protective Measures.
[299] *See e.g., Jović* Appeal Judgement, para. 27.

182. Turning to Witness A7/GEX, the Defence argues that, even if the Chamber finds that Witness A7/GEX was, in fact, a protected witness, the Accused was informed by Lead Counsel Condé that Witness A7/GEX was not a protected prosecution witness, and thus did not **[page 46]** knowingly and wilfully violate the Protective Measures with respect to her. This argument must be rejected for the same reasons as those described in the two paragraphs directly above. The Protective Measures explicitly covered potential witnesses, and mistake of law is not an accepted defence to contempt. The Chamber also considers that, by following Condé's instructions under these circumstances, the Accused displayed reckless indifference to whether his actions were in violation of the Protective Measures order.

183. With regard to the Accused's initial meetings with Witnesses GAA and A7/GEX, the Defence submits that these meetings were initiated by Witness A7/GEX, and that this eliminates the possibility that the Accused acted with the requisite *mens rea*. The Chamber considers that, if accepted,[300] this fact may have been relevant to the *mens rea* of the Accused under different circumstances. For example, if the Accused had initially met with the witnesses unaware of their protected status and then immediately cut off contact after learning that they were, in fact, protected witnesses.[301] But the Chamber does not consider it to assist the Accused under the particular circumstances of this case. Here, the evidence proven beyond a reasonable doubt shows that before meeting with Witnesses A7/GEX and GAA, the Accused knew that both witnesses had provided statements to the prosecution in the *Kamuhanda* case. The Chamber considers such information to have been sufficient to put the Accused on notice that the Witnesses may be protected prosecution witnesses. Under such circumstances, the Chamber finds the Accused's decision to meet with the witnesses, apparently without any further consideration of their possible status as witnesses, was taken with reckless indifference as to whether his actions were in violation of the Protective Measures.[302]

2.3. Disclosure of Protected Information to Third Parties or the General Public

184. The Prosecution also submits that the Accused committed contempt pursuant to Rule 77 (A)(ii) by "disclosing information ... in knowing violation of" the Protective Measures Order.

185. The Appeals Chamber has held that any wilful disclosure of information in knowing violation of an order of a Chamber is sufficient for the purposes of contempt under Rule 77(A)(ii).[303] It need not be shown that such disclosures actually interfered with the Tribunal's administration of justice.[304]

186. The Chamber has found that, by bringing Witnesses GAA, A7/GEX and Augustin Nyagatare to the notary's office, the Accused disclosed Witness GAA's identity as a prosecution witness in the *Kamuhanda* case and Witness A7/GEX's identity as someone who had given a statement to the Prosecution, or a potential witness, to Augustin Nyagatare and to the notary.

187. The proven evidence shows that that the Accused discussed the substance of Witness GAA's testimony in the presence of Witness A7/GEX. The evidence also shows that Witnesses GAA and A7/GEX discussed their respective testimonies prior to their meetings with the **[page 47]** Accused. The Chamber notes, however, that, pursuant to the contempt jurisprudence of the ICTY, the prior disclosure of protected information does not authorize or exempt subsequent disclosures.[305] The Chamber considers that, pursuant to this jurisprudence, the prior disclosure of their identities as prosecution witness and a potential prosecution witness, respectively, did not entitle the Accused to further violate the Protective Measures.

2.4. Conclusion

188. Recalling its factual findings regarding the knowledge of the Accused as to the protected status of Witnesses GAA and A7/GEX, the Chamber finds, that for his initial meeting with Witness GAA and all of

---

[300] *Supra*, para. 87.
[301] *See*, *Beqaj* Contempt Judgement, para. 40.
[302] *See Nobilo* Appeal Judgement, para. 54 (acting with reckless indifference to whether one's actions are in violation of a court is sufficiently culpable conduct for punishment as contempt).
[303] *See e.g.*, *Jović* Appeal Judgement, para. 30; *Marijačić* Appeal Judgement, para. 44.
[304] *See e.g.*, *Marijačić* Trial Judgement, para. 19.
[305] *See e.g.*, *Jović* Appeal Judgement, para. 30.

his meetings with Witness A7//GEX, the Accused acted with reckless indifference to whether his actions were in violation of the Protective Measures. For all subsequent meetings with Witness GAA, including the meeting at the notary's office, the Accused knowingly and wilfully violated the Protective Measures, specifically the measure listed in paragraph 2 (i) of the Protective Measures Order, which required that the *Kamuhanda* defence inform the *Kamuhanda* prosecution and obtain authorisation from the *Kamuhanda* Trial Chamber before meeting with any protected persons. The Chamber further recalls finds the Accused disclosed the protected information of these witnesses to third parties as described above in violation of paragraph 2 (e) of the Protective Measures order, which prohibited the *Kamuhanda* defence from disclosing information that could reveal the identity of protected persons to anyone not on the defence team.

189. By these acts, the Accused committed contempt of the Tribunal. The Chamber therefore finds Nshogoza guilty pursuant to Count One of the Indictment.

3. COUNT TWO: CONTEMPT OF THE TRIBUNAL

190. Under Count Two of the Indictment, the Prosecution charges Nshogoza with committing contempt of the Tribunal pursuant to Rule 77 (A), (A)(ii), (A)(iv) and (B) by knowingly and wilfully procuring false statements and inciting, manipulated, instigated, offering inducements or promising a bribe to Prosecution Witnesses GAA and A7/GEX to sign false statements and give false testimony, or by otherwise interfering with them.[306]

191. According to Rule 77 (A)(iv), any person who knowingly and wilfully interferes with the administration of justice by "threaten[ing], intimidat[ing], caus[ing] any injury or offer[ing] a bribe to, or otherwise interfer[ing] with, a witness who is giving, has given, or is about to give evidence in proceedings before a Chamber, or a potential witness …" may be punished for contempt of the Tribunal.

192. With regard to "offering a bribe", the Chamber adopts the liberal definition of 'bribe' as set out by a Trial Chamber of the ICTY in the *Beqaj* Contempt Judgement:

> The word "bribe" is liberally construed as an inducement offered to procure illegal or dishonest action or decision in favour of the giver. It is also defined as a price, reward, gift or favour **[page 48]** bestowed or promised with a view to pervert the judgement of or influence the action of a person in a position of trust.[307]

193. In relation to "otherwise interferes with a witness or a potential witness", the Chamber also finds persuasive the *Beqaj* Trial Chamber's treatment of the phrase:

> The expression "otherwise interfering with a witness or a potential witness" is an indication that Rule 77 gives a non-exhaustive list of modes of commission of contempt of the Tribunal. In view of the *mens rea* indicated in Rule 77 (A), the Chamber considers that otherwise interfering with witnesses encompasses any conduct that is intended to disturb the administration of justice by deterring a witness or a potential witness from giving full and truthful evidence, or in any way to influence the nature of the witness' or potential witness' evidence. There is nothing to indicate that proof is required that the conduct intended to influence the nature of the witness's evidence produced a result.[308]

194. The Chamber will consider the Prosecution's allegations that the Accused procured false statements from Witnesses GAA and A7/GEX, as well as the allegations that the Accused manipulated or instigated Witnesses GAA and A7/GEX to sign false statements and give false testimony according to these principles.

195. Rule 77 (B) states that "any incitement […] to commit any of the acts punishable under paragraph (A) is punishable as contempt of the Tribunal with the same penalties." The Trial Chamber in the trial of *The Prosecutor v. Akayesu* stated that "[i]ncitement is defined in Common law systems as encouraging or

---

[306] Indictment, paras. 17-27; *see also, supra*, paras. 48-56.
[307] *Beqaj* Contempt Judgement, para. 18 (internal citations omitted).
[308] *Beqaj* Contempt Judgement, para. 21 (internal citations omitted). The Chamber does not consider that the phrase "otherwise interfering with a witness or a potential witness" relieves the Prosecution of the obligation to plead the specific conduct of the Accused for which it alleges he should be held liable. *See Beqaj* Contempt Judgement, para. 19. The Prosecution cannot simply plead that the Accused has "otherwise interfered with a witness or potential witness" and then mold its case to fit this general phrase based on the evidence it adduces. *See Nobilo* Appeal Judgement, para. 41. The Chamber considers that, in this case, the allegations that the Accused procured false testimony from the witnesses and that he manipulated and instigated them into signing false statements and testifying falsely fall under the category of "otherwise interfering with a witness or potential witness."

persuading another to commit an offence", and that Civil law systems punished "act[s] intended to directly provoke another to commit a crime or a misdemeanour."[309] In order to be punishable as contempt, an act of incitement would also have to be knowing and wilful pursuant to Rule 77(A).

3.1. Manipulating and Instigating Witnesses

196. The Prosecution failed to prove beyond a reasonable doubt that there was anything out of the ordinary about the Accused's process of taking statements from Witnesses GAA and A7/GEX or that he knew that the statements were false or that Witness GAA's or A7/GEX's testimony before the Appeals Chamber was false. The Chamber, therefore, finds that the Prosecution failed to prove beyond a reasonable doubt that the Accused knowingly procured false statements, or knowingly incited, manipulated, or instigated Witnesses GAA or A7/GEX to give false testimony.

3.2. Offer of a Bribe [page 49]

197. The Chamber considers that the definition of bribe that it has adopted is broad enough to include inducements, and, therefore, it will not separately consider the Prosecution's allegation that the Accused offered inducements.

198. The Chamber recalls that the Prosecution failed to prove beyond a reasonable doubt that the Accused promised Witnesses GAA or A7/GEX payment in exchange for their signatures or testimony.

199. The evidence in this case shows that the Accused (i) gave Witnesses GAA and A7/GEX money, food and drink at the meetings he held with them; (ii) that the Accused did not give any money to Witnesses GAA and A7/GEX until after they informed him that they had provided false statements, and in Witness GAA's case, that he had given false testimony in connection with the *Kamuhanda* trial; (iii) that the Accused informed the witnesses that the money provided was for transport, or for their families while they were away from home testifying in Arusha; and (iv) that payments of similar amount were, at least on occasion, made to witnesses by representatives of the Prosecution and WVSS. Under the circumstances, the Chamber finds that the Prosecution failed to prove beyond a reasonable doubt that such payments and offers of food and drink were made with the intent to influence the nature of Witness GAA's or A7/GEX's evidence.

3.3. Manipulation of Witness GAA

200. The Chamber recalls that the Prosecution failed to prove beyond a reasonable doubt that the Accused told Witness GAA that he was writing a book about Kamuhanda or that he informed Witness GAA that there would be no consequences if he gave a statement or testified before the Appeals Chamber.

3.4. Incitement to Sign False Statements or Give False Testimony

201. As noted above, the Prosecution failed to prove beyond a reasonable doubt that the Accused knew that recantation statements or testimonies of Witnesses GAA and A7/GEX were false. As such, the Prosecution failed to prove that the Accused knowingly incited the punishable acts in question.

3.5. Conclusion

202. For these reasons, the Chamber finds the Accused not guilty of Contempt of the Tribunal as alleged in Count Two of the Indictment

---

[309] *The Prosecutor v. Jean-Paul Akayesu,* Case No. ICTR-96-4-T, Judgement (TC), 2 September 1998, para. 555.

4. COUNT THREE: ATTEMPT TO COMMIT ACTS PUNISHABLE AS CONTEMPT OF THE TRIBUNAL

203. Under Count Three of the Indictment, the Prosecution charges Nshogoza with committing the offence of Attempt to Commit Acts Punishable as Contempt of the Tribunal by attempting to suborn false testimony from Witness BUC.[310] **[page 50]**

204. The Chamber recalls that Rule 77 (B) states that "any [...] attempt to commit any of the acts punishable under paragraph (A) is punishable as contempt of the Tribunal with the same penalties."

205. The *Beqaj* Trial Chamber considered the concept of 'attempt' under international law:

> Article 25(3)(f) of the International Criminal Court Statute reflects a recent international codification of the concept of attempt. This provision combines the definitions of "attempt" found in most civil law and common law legal systems and provides that a person is criminally responsible if he or she "attempts to commit a crime by taking action that commences its execution by means of a substantial step, but the crime does not occur because of circumstances independent of the person's intentions". What is required for the attempt to be punishable is: (i) conduct consisting of a significant commencement of the criminal action, (ii) the intention to commit a crime, (iii) the failure of that intention to take effect owing to external circumstances.[311]

206. The Chamber recalls that the Prosecution failed to prove beyond a reasonable doubt that the Accused sought false testimony from Witness BUC, or that the payments made and refreshments offered to Witness BUC were made with the intent to induce or bribe her to testify.

207. The Chamber therefore finds the Accused not guilty of Count Three.

5. COUNT FOUR: ATTEMPT TO COMMIT ACTS PUNISHABLE AS CONTEMPT OF THE TRIBUNAL

208. Under Count Four of the Indictment, the Prosecution charges Nshogoza with Attempt to Commit Acts Punishable as Contempt of the Tribunal by attempting to procure false statements or false testimony from Witnesses GAF, SP003 and SP004.[312]

209. The Chamber recalls that the Prosecution failed to prove beyond a reasonable doubt that the Accused asked Witness GAA to procure false statements or testimony from Witnesses GAF, SP003 and SP004, or that he offered them a bribe or instructed Witness GAA to offer them a bribe.

210. In the Chamber's view, even if the Prosecution had proven these material facts beyond a reasonable doubt, the Accused would still be found not guilty of the crime of Attempt to Commit Acts Punishable as Contempt of the Tribunal. The Prosecution evidence shows that, after the meeting at the notary's office, the Accused informed Witness GAA that he was not interested in meeting with Witnesses GAF, SP003, and SP004. Thus, even if the Accused had initially requested Witness GAA to act on his behalf, he also instructed Witness GAA to cease such actions In other words, the non-occurrence of acts possibly punishable as contempt of the Tribunal was a direct result of the Accused's intentions. **[page 51]**

211. For these reasons, the Chamber finds the Accused not guilty of Attempt to Commit Acts Punishable as Contempt of the Tribunal.

---

[310] Indictment, paras. 28-32. The Chamber notes that the Indictment also alleges that the Accused offered a bribe to Witness BUC, or otherwise interfered with her. If proven, these acts would be punishable as contempt of the Tribunal, and not attempt. Nonetheless, the Chamber notes that it cannot convict the Accused of a crime other than the one charged, and, in any event these allegations were not proved beyond a reasonable doubt.
[311] *Beqaj* Contempt Judgement, para. 25.
[312] Indictment, paras. 33-50. The Chamber notes that, as with Count Three, the Indictment also alleges that the Accused offered a bribe to or otherwise interfered with Witnesses GAF, SP003 and SP004. The Chamber did not consider these allegations, but, in any event, notes that the Prosecution failed to support them with sufficient evidence.

CHAPTER V: SENTENCING

1. INTRODUCTION

212. Having found Nshogoza guilty on Count One of the Indictment for Contempt of the Tribunal, the Chamber must determine the appropriate sentence.

213. Rule 77 (G) of the Rules provides that the maximum penalty that may be imposed on a person found to be in contempt of the Tribunal shall be a term of imprisonment not exceeding five years, or a fine not exceeding USD 10,000, or both.

214. Pursuant to Rule 101 (B), in determining the sentence, the Trial Chamber shall take into account such factors as the gravity of the offence and the individual circumstances of the convicted person, as mentioned in Article 23 (2) of the Statute.[313] In addition, Rule 101 (B) provides a non-exhaustive list of factors that Chambers shall take into account, including aggravating and mitigating circumstances.[314] Rule 101 (C) provides that credit shall be given for the period, if any, during which the convicted person was detained in custody pending his surrender to the Tribunal or pending trial or appeal.

2. DETERMINATION OF THE SENTENCE

215. The Prosecution submits that Nshogoza should be sentenced to four years imprisonment for Count One of the Indictment.[315] The Defence submits that the Accused should be acquitted on every count and that the time already served by him at the UN Detention Facility ("UNDF") far exceeds any sentence handed down by either the ICTR or the ICTY for even the most grave contempt convictions.[316]

216. The Chamber recalls that with regard to the crime of contempt, the most important factors to be taken into account of in determining the appropriate penalty are the gravity of the contempt and the need to deter repetition and similar conduct by others.[317]

2.1. Gravity of the Offence [page 52]

217. The Chamber recalls that there has only been one conviction for contempt of the Tribunal before the ICTR, namely, in the *Prosecutor v. GAA*, in which case Witness GAA pleaded guilty and was sentenced to nine months imprisonment.[318] In reaching its conclusion, the Chamber, mindful of the specific facts of the present case, has reference to the sentences imposed in cases before the ICTY where accused persons have been convicted of contempt of that Tribunal.[319]

---

[313] Article 23 (2) states "In imposing the sentences, the Trial Chambers should take into account such factors as the gravity of the offence and the individual circumstances of the convicted person."

[314] Rule 101 (B) states "In determining the sentence, the Trial Chamber shall take into account the factors mentioned in Article 23 (2) of the Statute, as well as such factors as: (i) Any aggravating circumstances; (ii) Any mitigating circumstances including the substantial cooperation with the Prosecutor by the convicted person before or after conviction; (iii) The general practice regarding prison sentences in the courts of Rwanda; (iv) The extent to which any penalty imposed by a court of any State on the convicted person for the same act has already been served, as referred to in Article 9 (3) of the Statute.

[315] Prosecutor's Closing Brief, p. 67-68.

[316] Defence Closing Brief, p. 148, para. 366.

[317] *Marijačić* Trial Judgement, para. 46; *The Prosecutor v. Dragan Jokić*, Case No. IT-05-88-R77.1, Judgement on Allegations of Contempt (TC), 27 March 2009, para. 26.

[318] *The Prosecutor v. GAA*, Case No. ICTR-07-90-R77-I, Judgement and Sentence, 4 December 2007 ("*GAA* Judgement").

[319] See e.g., *Marijačić* Trial Judgement, where the two accused persons were each fined 15,000 euros for publishing information subject to witness protection orders (the sentence was upheld by the Appeals Chamber but for a *proprio motu* order that payments be made in instalments. See *Marijačić* Appeal Judgement); *Jović* Trial Judgement, where the accused was fined 20,000 euros for publishing, in a newspaper, excerpts of a witness' closed session testimony (the sentence was upheld by the Appeals Chamber but for a *proprio motu* order that payments may be made in instalments. See *Jović* Appeal Judgement); *Haxhiu* Contempt Judgement, where the accused was fined 7,000 euros for publishing, in a newspaper, the identity of a protected witness; *Beqaj* Contempt Judgement, where the accused was sentenced to four months for interfering with a potential witness who was in a witness protection programme; *Margetić* Contempt Judgement, where the accused was sentenced to three months imprisonment and fined 10,000 Euros for publishing on the internet a confidential list of witnesses that revealed their identities; *Haraqija and Morina* Contempt Judgement, where the accused persons were convicted of interfering with witnesses. Morina's conduct was found to constitute "intimidation",

218. The Chamber recalls that contempt of the Tribunal is a grave offence, constituting a "direct challenge to the integrity of the trial process."[320] Maintaining the integrity of the administration of justice is particularly important in trials involving serious criminal offences. Indeed, the Chamber is mindful that,

> "the nature of the crimes under the jurisdiction of the Tribunal and the context in which they were committed necessitate substantial reliance upon oral evidence. That fact entails appropriate measures for the protection of the integrity of witnesses and their testimony…."[321]

As noted by the ICTY, "any deliberate conduct which creates a real risk that confidence in the Tribunal's ability to grant effective protective measures would be undermined amounts to a serious interference with the administration of justice."[322] It is fundamental to the fulfilment of the Tribunal's mission that individuals who come to give evidence before the Tribunal, often about traumatic or difficult experiences, may do so with the security provided by protective measures.[323] It is therefore necessary for general deterrence and denunciation to be given high importance in sentencing policies.[324]

219. The Accused's conduct in the present case amounted to a determination that he would contact protected witnesses on his own conditions, that is, he would control the circumstances in which he met with the protected witnesses. He thus defied the authority of the court by breaching **[page 53]** the protective measures that were in place. The Chamber considers that breach of the protective measures order undermined the authority of the *Kamuhanda* Trial Chamber, as well as confidence in the effectiveness of protective measures, and the administration of justice.[325] Such conduct not only defies the authority of the Tribunal but may also have the effect of dissuading witnesses from testifying before it. To deter this type of conduct, and to express the Chamber's disapproval of the same, a custodial sentence is merited.

2.2. Individual Circumstances of the Accused

220. The Chamber has wide discretion in determining what constitutes mitigating and aggravating circumstances and the weight to be accorded to such circumstances. While aggravating circumstances need to be proven beyond reasonable doubt, mitigating circumstances need only be established on a "balance of probabilities".[326]

2.2.1 Aggravating Circumstances

221. The Chamber has considered the Prosecution submissions on aggravating circumstances set out in its Closing Brief.[327] The Defence did not make any submissions with regard to aggravating circumstances.

---

an interference proscribed by Rule 77 (A) (iv) of the Rules and Haraqija was found to have instructed Morina to dissuade the witness from testifying before the ICTY, contrary to Rule 77 (A) (iv) of the Rules; they were sentenced to three and five months imprisonment, respectively.
[320] *GAA* Judgement, para. 10.
[321] *Beqaj* Contempt Judgement, para. 60.
[322] *Marijačić* Trial Judgement, para. 50 (judgement upheld by Appeals Chamber); *Margetić* Contempt Judgement, para. 87 (judgement upheld by Appeals Chamber); *Jović* Trial Judgement, para. 26 (judgement upheld by Appeals Chamber).
[323] *Haxhiu* Contempt Judgement, para. 34.
[324] *GAA* Judgement, para. 10.
[325] See also, *Prosecutor v. Slobodan Milošević, Contempt Proceedings against Kosta Bulatović*, Case No. IT-02-54-R77.4, Decision on Contempt of the Tribunal, 13 May 2005, para. 17.
[326] See e.g., *The Prosecutor v. Aloys Simba*, Case No. ICTR-01-76-A, Judgement (AC), para. 328; *The Prosecutor v. Ferdinand Nahimana et al.*, Case No. ICTR-99-52-A, Judgement (AC), para. 1038.
[327] Prosecutor's Closing Brief, paras. 211-212. The Prosecution submits that the aggravating circumstances in this case include that the Accused acted intentionally and showed reckless disregard for the Witness Protection Order and the safety of Witnesses GAA and A7/GEX, when he met them repeatedly, in public, and in the presence of third parties, including members of the *Kamuhanda* family. The Prosecution further submits that aggravating circumstances of the Accused include the fact that he: (i) has familial relations with *Kamuhanda* but concealed this fact from the Tribunal at recruitment and thereafter; (ii) is an educated man, trained as a lawyer or jurist; (iii) by the time of the commission of the offences, already worked as an investigator for about two years in the *Kamuhanda* defence team, and was therefore familiar with the Rules and practice of the Tribunal; (iv) was no longer entrusted with any contract in relation to the *Kamuhanda* case at the time of the commission of the offence; (v) was an investigator, paid under the Tribunal Legal Aid Program in relation to other cases, at the time of the commission of the offence; (vi) submitted to the Tribunal a fraudulent claim of fees and expenses; (vii) similar findings of violations have been made against him in the *Rukundo* Trial Judgement, showing a total disregard of the witness protection orders of the Tribunal; and (viii) the targeting of specific witnesses,

222. The Chamber considers that Nshogoza's meetings with the protected witnesses on more than one occasion, demonstrates a continued disregard for the protective measures and is an aggravating circumstance. The Chamber further recalls its finding that the Accused met with protected witness in the presence of third parties. The Chamber notes that in committing this offence, the Accused was acting upon the instructions of his Lead Counsel, Witness Aicha Condé, and with the motive of earning fees for this work.

223. In addition, the Chamber notes that Nshogoza is an educated man who graduated from the National University of Rwanda where he studied law.[328] He started working with the *Kamuhanda* defence team at the end of 2001, and was admitted to the Kigali Bar in April **[page 54]** 2005.[329] The Chamber recalls that Nshogoza was also working as a defence investigator in the *Rukundo* case,[330] at the time when the unauthorised meetings with the protected witnesses occurred.[331] The Chamber considers that Nshogoza's background of having studied law, and his position as an investigator in the *Kamuhanda* defence team, as well as in the *Rukundo* case, placed him in a position to know and appreciate the importance of respecting the orders of the Tribunal, and in particular, the purpose of protective measures, and the probable consequences of his actions in breaching such orders. Accordingly, the Chamber finds that Nshogoza's legal background, and work as a defence investigator, is an aggravating circumstance.

224. Further, the Chamber has taken into account, as an aggravating circumstance, the fact that Nshogoza, as a defence investigator in the employ of the Tribunal, stood in a relationship of trust with the Tribunal. Courts and tribunals necessarily rely upon the honesty and propriety of investigators. As part of a legal team, they are endowed with important privileges by law, such as the knowledge of protected witnesses' identities, justified only upon the basis that they can be trusted not to abuse them.[332]

225. The Chamber further recalls Nshogoza's acknowledgement that he submitted, to the Tribunal, a false claim for fees in the *Kamuhanda* case.[333] The explanation offered by Nshogoza for this false claim, namely, that August 2003 was his last month of official employment as a defence investigator in the *Kamuhanda* case, does not detract from the seriousness of his conduct. The Chamber considers that Nshogoza, in submitting the false claim, abused his position as a defence investigator and thus finds this to be an aggravating circumstance.

226. Finally, in its Closing Brief, and closing arguments, the Prosecution invited the Chamber to take into account the finding of the Trial Chamber in the *Rukundo* case, that Nshogoza had breached protective measures in circumstances not dissimilar to those in this case.[334] The Trial Chamber's finding in the *Rukundo* case was not, however, put into evidence in the present case, and the Defence has never had an opportunity to make representations with regard to these findings.[335] Moreover, the Chamber notes that the *Rukundo* Trial Judgement's finding in respect of Nshogoza's conduct was not a finding beyond reasonable doubt. Rather, it was a finding based on an independent *amicus* report in the context of considering a witness' credibility.[336] In **[page 55]** view of these considerations, the Chamber considers that it would be improper and unfair to the Accused to take any such finding into consideration as an aggravating circumstance.

---

after the Trial Chamber's findings on credibility in the *Kamuhanda* trial; the fabrication of several false statements, are evidence of the Accused's deliberate interferences with due administration of justice.

[328] Witness Nshogoza, T. 30 March 2009 pp. 2-3.
[329] Witness Nshogoza, T. 30 March 2009 pp. 3 and 28-29.
[330] *Prosecutor v. Rukundo*, Case No. ICTR-01-70-T.
[331] Witness Nshogoza, T. 31 March 2009 p. 38.
[332] See for example, *Prosecutor v. Tadić and Vujin*, Case No. IT-94-1-A-R77, Judgement (AC), para. 166.
[333] In his claim for fees, Nshogoza had stated that he met with Witness GAA on 9 and 12 August 2003 but during his testimony, maintained that he only met with Witness GAA once in August 2003. *See* Nshogoza, T. 31 March 2009 pp. 31-32. *See also* Exhibit P. 15.
[334] Prosecution Closing Brief, para. 211; and T. 29 April 2009 p. 37 (Prosecution's closing arguments).
[335] *See, Nshogoza,* Decision on Prosecutor's Motion to Admit Evidence of a Consistent Pattern of Conduct, 20 February 2009, in which the Chamber found that it was not in the interests of justice to admit evidence of the Accused's conduct in the *Rukundo* case and denied the Prosecutor's Motion, brought to pursuant to Rule 93, to admit evidence of a consistent pattern of conduct
[336] *Prosecutor v. Rukundo*, Case No. ICTR-01-70-T, Judgement (TC), paras. 141-142. The *Rukundo* Trial Chamber accepted the independent *amicus* report which found that Witness BLP's alleged recantation was due to pressure exerted by Nshogoza, and a Father Ndagijimana and that Nshogoza continued to meet with Witness BLP in violation of protective measures.

2.2.2 Mitigating Circumstances

227. The Defence submits that the Chamber should consider the following mitigating circumstances in the determination of Nshogoza's sentence: (i) Nshogoza has a wife and young children, for whom he is the sole provider; (ii) his cooperation with the Prosecution and the Tribunal has been "overt and consistent", starting with his surrender on 8 February 2008; (iii) his good character has been confirmed by Defence Witnesses Aicha Conde and Fulgence Seminega, both of whom know him well; and (iv) he has no prior criminal record.[337]

228. The Prosecution does not make any submissions regarding mitigating circumstances.

229. The Trial Chamber has taken into account the family circumstances of the Accused, who has three children aged 14, 15 and 17.[338] The Chamber has also taken into consideration the fact that the Accused has no past criminal record. Furthermore, the Chamber takes into account the fact that the Accused surrendered voluntarily to the Tribunal on 8 February 2008, as a mitigating factor.

230. With regard to the Accused's good character, the Chamber notes that in the course of evidence adduced before it, two matters arose which the Chamber cannot fail to consider when determining the weight to be attached to the good character evidence of Aicha Condé.[339] First, the Accused worked under Condé and her testimonial of the Accused's good character must be seen in that light. Indeed, Condé, an assigned counsel before this Tribunal, saw nothing wrong with the Accused contacting protected witnesses if done so in the quest for seeking justice for her convicted client, Kamuhanda. Second, Condé, like the Accused, saw nothing wrong with the Accused, with her assistance, submitting a false claim of expenses. The Chamber takes into consideration these two matters when considering the weight to be attributed to Condé's evidence of the Accused's good character.

231. The Chamber further notes that the good character evidence of Fulgence Seminega was limited. Indeed, his testimony was that he had known the Accused for approximately 10 years.[340] The Chamber therefore attaches limited weight to the evidence of Condé and Seminega with respect to Nshogoza's good character.

2.3. Credit for Time Served

232. Nshogoza has been detained in custody at the UNDF since 8 February 2008. Pursuant to Rule 101(C) of the Rules, Nshogoza is therefore entitled to credit for time served as of 8 February 2008. **[page 56]**

3. CONCLUSION

233. Taking into account all the relevant circumstances as discussed above, having ensured that the Accused is not being punished twice for the same offence, and noting that Rule 77 (G) of the Rules provides a maximum penalty of imprisonment for a term not exceeding five years or a fine not exceeding USD 10,000, or both, the Chamber sentences Léonidas Nshogoza for Contempt of the Tribunal to:

Ten (10) Months Imprisonment

234. Given that the Accused is to be given credit for time served, the Chamber directs that Nshogoza be released from the custody of the Tribunal, forthwith, unless he is otherwise lawfully held.

---

[337] Defence Closing Brief, para. 360.
[338] Witness Nshogoza, T. 30 March 2009 p. 5.
[339] Witness Condé, T. 16 March 2009 at p. 40 where Condé testified that she had a "good impression" of Nshogoza and that "He was the best investigator; he was good; he was intelligent; he was alert."
[340] See also Seminega, T. 19 March 2009 at p. 53. Fulgence Seminega had known Nshogoza for approximately 10 years.

Arusha, 7 July 2009

Khalida Rachid Khan	Lee Gacuiga Muthoga	Aydin Sefa Akay
Presiding Judge	Judge	Judge

[Seal of the Tribunal] **[page 57]**

ANNEX: PROCEDURAL HISTORY OF THE CASE

1. The indictment against Léonidas Nshogoza ("Indictment") was confirmed by Judge Dennis C.M. Byron on 4 January 2008 and placed under seal.[341] On 28 January 2008, Judge Byron issued a confidential and *ex-parte* warrant of arrest and order for transfer and detention.[342]

2. The Indictment charges the Accused with four counts:

COUNT 1: Contempt of the Tribunal, punishable under this Tribunal's inherent power and Rules 77 (A), (A)(ii) and 77 (G) of the Rules of Procedure and Evidence of the Tribunal,

COUNT 2: Contempt of the Tribunal, punishable under this Tribunal's inherent power and Rule 77 (A), (A)(ii), (A)(iv), and (B) and (G) of the Rules of Procedure and Evidence of the Tribunal,

COUNT 3: Attempt to Commit Acts Punishable as Contempt of the Tribunal, punishable under this Tribunal's inherent power and Rule 77 (A), (A)(iv), (B) and (G) of the Rules of Procedure and Evidence of the Tribunal,

COUNT 4: Attempt to Commit Acts Punishable as Contempt of the Tribunal, punishable under this Tribunal's inherent power and Rule 77 (A), (A)(iv), (B) and (G) of the Rules of Procedure and Evidence of the Tribunal.

3. On 4 February 2008, Judge Byron granted the Prosecution's motion for the lifting of the confidentiality of the arrest warrant and order for transfer and detention issued.[343] On 19 February 2008, Judge Byron also ordered the lifting of the confidentiality of the Indictment.[344]

1. Composition of the Chamber

4. On 2 May 2008, the case was assigned to Trial Chamber III composed of Judge Khalida Khan (Presiding), Judge Lee Gacuiga Muthoga and Judge Emile Francis Short.[345]

---

[341] Confirmation of the Indictment and Witness Protection Orders, 4 January 2008.
[342] Warrant of Arrest and Order for Transfer and Detention Addressed to All States, 28 January 2008
[343] Order Lifting the Confidentiality of the Warrant of Arrest and Order for Transfer and Detention Addressed to All States, 4 February 2008.
[344] Order Lifting the Confidentiality of the Redacted Indictment, 19 February 2008.
[345] Order Assigning the Case to Trial Chamber III, 2 May 2008.

2. The Defence Team

5.   On 8 February 2008, the Accused assigned Power of Attorney to Ms. Allison Turner to represent him in these proceedings.[346] On 16 May 2008, the Defence filed an urgent motion requesting the Chamber to order the Registrar to immediately assign Defence Counsel to the Accused.[347] **[page 58]**

6.   On 15 May 2008, DCDMS sent Ms. Turner a letter offering to assign her as counsel for the Accused ("Offer to Assign of 15 May 2008").[348] However, there was a disagreement between Ms. Turner and the Registrar over the terms of remuneration.

7.   On 2 June 2008, the Defence filed an addendum to its motion for the assignment of Counsel, noting communications from the Registrar and asking the Chamber to direct the Registrar to communicate all correspondence and filings to the Accused in a timely manner.[349] On 9 June 2009, the Defence filed an additional addendum, containing two more documents and advising the Chamber that Counsel would suspend all work until her assignment was formalized as per the terms and conditions stipulated in the Offer to Assign of 15 May 2008.[350]

8.   Ms. Turner continued to act for the Accused on a *pro bono* basis until 9 June 2008, when she informed the Registry that she would be suspending all work on the file until she was formally assigned as Counsel.[351]

9.   On 10 June 2008, the Registrar wrote to the Accused stating that it would not assign Ms. Turner as Defence Counsel.[352] On 12 June 2008, the Defence filed a notice to suspend its extremely urgent motion for assignment and appealing the Registrar's decision.[353] The Defence also wrote to the President of the Tribunal to ask for review of the decision by the Registrar not to assign Ms. Turner as Counsel to the Accused.[354]

10.   On 1 July 2008, the Registrar made submissions on the Defence's motion for assignment of Counsel.[355] The Registrar asked the Chamber to dismiss the motion, arguing that Defence Counsel lacked standing and that the Chamber lacked jurisdiction.

11.   The Defence replied to the Registrar's submissions on 7 July 2008,[356] arguing that the Registrar had abused its discretion, and that, as a result, the Accused's right to a fair trial had **[page 59]** been violated. The Registrar replied to this on 23 July 2008,[357] reiterating the Chamber's lack of jurisdiction and further explaining why it had not assigned Ms. Turner as Defence Counsel.

12.   On 24 July 2008, the Chamber ordered the Registrar to assigned Ms. Turner as Counsel to the Accused without any further delay.[358] On 25 July 2008, DCDMS wrote to Ms. Turner offering her assignment as

---

[346] "Urgent Motion for Assignment of Counsel", filed on 16 May 2008 ("Motion to Assign Counsel"), Annex A "Power of Attorney signed by Leonidas Nshogoza," dated 8 February 2008.
[347] "Urgent Motion for Assignment of Counsel," filed 16 May 2008.
[348] Supplementary Defence Submissions to Leonidas Nshogoza's "*Requete pour la commission d'un Conseil de defense*" filed on 19 August 2008 ("Submissions of 19 August 2008"), Annexure C "Offer of Assignment as Counsel for the Accused Leonidas Nshogoza" dated 15 May 2008 ("Communication of 15 May 2008"). The Communication of 15 May 2008 stated that Ms. Turner would be paid up to $50,000 to cover legal fees and that the Registrar would *also meet other expenses* related to the proceedings.
[349] "Addendum – Extremely Urgent Motion for Assignment of Counsel," filed 2 June 2008; "Re-filing of Annexes F, G and H – Extremely Urgent Motion for Assignment of Counsel," filed 2 June 2008.
[350] "Addendum 2 – Extremely Urgent Motion for Assignment of Counsel," filed 9 June 2008
[351] "Requete au fins de constat d'entrave a la justice, Article 77 du RPP du TPIR", filed 13 August 2008 ("Accused's Request of 13 August 2008"), annexed letter dated 9 June 2008 from Ms. Turner to DCDMS stating "While the undersigned continues to treat the Contract as valid and act as assigned counsel for Mr. Nshogoza, in view of the aforementioned breaches she is suspending all work on this file until the assignment as counsel has been formalized as stipulated in the Contract."
[352] "Request for Review of Decision by Registrar 10 June 2008 pursuant to Rules 19 and 33 ICTR Rules of Procedure and Evidence," filed 13 June 2008, annexed letter dated 10 June 2008 from Mr. Mwaungulu of DCDMS to the Accused.
[353] "Notice to Suspend – Extremely Urgent Motion for Assignment of Counsel," filed 12 June 2008.
[354] "Request for Review of Decision by Registrar 10 June 2008 pursuant to Rules 19 and 33 ICTR Rules of Procedure and Evidence," filed 13 June 2008.
[355] "The Registrar's Submission under Rule 33 (B) of the Rules of Procedure and Evidence on Léonidas Nshogoza's ADDENUM 2 – EXTREMELY URGENT MOTION FOR ASSIGNMENT OF COUNSEL," filed 1 July 2008.
[356] "Defence Response to Registrar Submissions Filed 1 July 2008," filed 7 July 2008.
[357] "The Registrar's Submission under Rule 33 (B) to Defence Response to Registrar's Submission Filed 1 July 2008," filed 23 July 2008.
[358] Order to Assign Counsel, filed 24 July 2008.

Counsel for the Accused.[359] However, Ms. Turner was not formally assigned as Counsel due to disagreement regarding terms of remuneration.[360]

13. On 5 August 2008, the Accused filed a confidential motion requesting the assignment of Ms. Turner as his Defence Counsel and complaining about the Registrar's actions.[361]

14. On 13 August 2008, DCDMS circulated a communication seeking Counsel to represent the Accused.[362] On the same day, the Defence filed a motion asking the Chamber to find that the Registrar's actions seriously impeded the course of justice and caused grievous prejudice to the Accused.[363] On 18 August 2008, the Chamber, noting that the Registry had failed to assign Counsel to the Accused, ordered the Registrar to give effect to the Chamber's Order of 24 July 2008 within ten days.[364] On 20 August 2008, the Registrar assigned Mr. Philippe Greciano as Lead Counsel for the Accused.[365]

15. On 21 August 2008, the Defence filed an extremely urgent motion asking the Chamber to order the Registrar to assign the Accused his Counsel of choice.[366] On 26 August 2008, the Defence filed an extremely urgent request for a hearing on its motion to assigned Ms. Turner as Defence Counsel.[367] **[page 60]**

16. On 1 September 2008, the Prosecution replied to the Defence's extremely urgent request,[368] opposing the motion on the basis that Ms. Turner was no longer assigned as Duty Counsel to the Accused and was not acting in any capacity for the Accused; it also argued that the right of an indigent defendant to effective representation did not entitle him to choose his own counsel.

17. On 13 October 2008, the Chamber directed the Registrar to withdraw the assignment of Mr. Greciano and assign Ms. Turner as counsel for the Accused.[369] The Registrar withdrew the assignment of Mr. Greciano on 13 October 2008.[370]

3. Initial Appearance

18. On 11 February 2008, the Accused made his initial appearance and pled not guilty to all charges contained in the Indictment.[371]

---

[359] "Requete pour la commission d'un Conseil de defense," 5 August 2008 ("Accused's Request of 5 August 2008"), annexed letter from DCDMS dated 25 July 2008.
[360] See "Supplementary Defence Submissions to Léonidas Nshogoza's "Requete pour la commission d'un Conseil de defense"," filed 19 August 2008. On 29 July 2008, Ms. Turner wrote to DCDMS accepting the assignment as per the terms of the offer in the Communication of 15 May 2008. On 30 July 2008, DCDMS replied stating: "We do not want to understand that your reference to the offer letter of 15 May 2008 is a rejection of the actual assignment of 25 July 2008 with its terms" and sought clarification from Ms. Turner. On 1 August 2008, Ms. Turner confirmed to DCDMS that she accepted the assignment to act for the Accused on the terms set out in the original offer of 15 May 2008. These communications are annexed to "Supplementary Submissions to "Defence Extremely Urgent Motion (…)" and to "Defence Extremely Urgent Request (…)" filed 20 and 26 August 2008," filed 1 September 2008, Annexure D.
[361] "Request for the Assignment of Defence Counsel," filed 5 August 2008.
[362] "Motion for the Purpose of a Finding of Perversion of the Court of Justice," filed 13 August 2008, attachment.
[363] "Motion for the Purpose of a Finding of Perversion of the Court of Justice," filed 13 August 2008.
[364] Order for Immediate Assignment of Counsel, 18 August 2008.
[365] "Commission D' Office De Me Philippe Greciano a Titre de Conseil dans L'Interet de la Justice pour la defense des interest de M. Leonidas Nshogoza, Accuse Devant Tribunal Penal International Pour le Rwanda," dated 20 August 2008 ("Registrar's Notification of Assignment of Greciano").
[366] "Extremely Urgent Motion for Order to Registrar to Assign Counsel of Choice Pursuant to Article 20(4)(d) ICTR Statute," filed 21 August 2008.
[367] "Defence Extremely Urgent Request for Hearing on Motion to Assign Counsel of Choice Allison Turner and Amended Prayer of Relief," filed 26 August 2008; "Supplementary Submissions to "Defence Extremely Urgent Motion (…)" and to "Defence Extremely Urgent Request (…)" filed 20 and 26 August 2008," filed 1 September 2008 containing supplementary documentation.
[368] "Prosecutor's Response to 'Defence Extremely Urgent Request for Hearing on Motion to Assign Counsel of Choice Allison Turner and Amended Prayer for Relief,'" filed 1 September 2008.
[369] Decision on Motions Requesting Assignment of Counsel of Choice, 13 October 2008.
[370] Decision on Withdrawal of the Assignment of Mr. Phillipe Greciano, Counsel for the Accused Leonidas Nshogoza, 13 October 2008.
[371] T. 11 February 2008 p. 5-6.

4. Detention

19. The Accused voluntarily surrendered to the Tribunal on 8 February 2008.

20. On 14 April 2008, the Defence filed a motion for review of the 28 January 2009 orders for detention and alternatively for provisional release.[372] The Prosecution responded on 21 April 2008, arguing that the Defence failed to meet the threshold for reconsideration and failed to satisfy the requirements for provisional release.[373] The Defence replied on 28 April 2008, contesting, among other things, the Prosecution's characterization of the relevant facts and the test for reconsideration.[374]

21. On 2 September 2008 and 20 October 2008, the Defence filed supplementary submissions to their motion, adding that, upon release, the Accused would be amenable to residing in Tanzania, Kenya or Uganda in addition to the originally specified Canada.[375]

22. On 29 October 2008, the Defence filed a motion again requesting, among other things, the provisional release of the Accused.[376] The Prosecution responded to this motion on 3 **[page 61]** November 2008, reiterating its earlier submissions on provisional release.[377] The Defence replied on 10 November 2008, submitting that the Prosecution had not advanced any reason for the continued detention of the Accused and that they had met the requirements for provisional release.[378]

23. On 17 November 2008, the Chamber denied the Defence request for reconsideration of its order for the Accused's detention and requested Canada, Kenya, Tanzania and Uganda to make submissions on their willingness to receive the Accused pending trial.[379] On 11 December 2008, the Government of Canada filed submissions on this issue, outlining the process that the Accused would need to undertake to be received by Canada, and informing the Tribunal that Canada could not guarantee that he would appear for trial.[380]

24. On 17 December 2008, the Chamber denied the Defence motion for provisional release, as it did not meet the requirements for release.[381]

25. On 3 February 2009, the Defence filed a motion asking for reconsideration of the decision to deny provisional release, submitting, among other things, that the Accused was now willing to be moved to a UN safe house and that the original decision incorrectly relied on the case of *Haixu*.[382] This was denied by the Chamber on 12 February 2009, which found that the Accused's willingness to be moved to a safe house was not new information in relation to the pre-existing motion to justify reconsideration, and that its reliance on *Haixu* was not erroneous.[383]

---

[372] "Motion for Review of Provisional Measures and Alternatively for Provisional Release," filed 14 April 2008.
[373] "Prosecutor's Response to Defence – "Motion for Review of Provisional Measures and Alternatively for Provisional Release"," filed 21 April 2008.
[374] "Defence Reply to Prosecutor's Response to Defence Motion for Review or Provisional Release," filed 28 April 2008.
[375] "Defence Supplementary Submission to "Motion for Review of Provisional Measures and Alternatively for Provisional Release"," filed 20 October 2008; "STRICTLY CONFIDENTIAL (UNDER SEAL) and Ex Parte Supplementary Submission to "Motion for Review of Provisional Measures and Alternatively for Provisional Release" filed 14 April 2008," filed 2 September 2008.
[376] "Defence Motion for Order to the Prosecution to Complete Rule 66(A)(ii) Disclosure, Request for Time to Investigate Before Trial, and Motion for the Provisional Release of Léonidas Nshogoza," filed 29 October 2008.
[377] "Prosecutor's Response to "Defence Motion for Order to the Prosecution to Complete Rule 66(A)(ii) Disclosure, Request for Time to Investigate Before Trial, and Motion for the Provisional Release of Léonidas Nshogoza"," filed 3 November 2008.
[378] "Defence Reply to Prosecutor's Response to Defence Motion Filed 29 October 2008 on Disclosure Violations and Provisional Release," 10 November 2008.
[379] Decision on Defence Motion for Review of Provisional Measures, or Alternatively, for Provisional Release, 17 November 2008.
[380] "Submission of the Government of Canada on the Issue of Accepting Leonidas Nshogoza into Our Jurisdiction Pending Trial," filed 11 December 2008.
[381] Decision on Defence Motion for Provisional Release, 17 December 2008.
[382] "Motion for Reconsideration of the Trial Chamber's "Decision on Defence Motion for Provisional Release" of 17 December 2008," filed 3 February 2009.
[383] Decision on Motion for Reconsideration of the Trial Chamber's Decision on Provisional Release, 12 February 2009.

Prosecutor v. Nshogoza, Judgement

5. Evidence

a. Witnesses

26. On 26 August 2008, the Prosecution made a confidential submission containing five witness statements.[384]

27. On 22 October 2008, the Chamber made an oral order for the Prosecution to file a list of witnesses they planned to call by Monday 27 October 2008.[385] The Prosecution complied with **[page 62]** this order and filed a list of witnesses and exhibits on 27 October 2008.[386] The Prosecution intended to call seven witnesses.

28. On 29 October 2008, the Defence filed a motion to have Witness BLP removed from the Prosecution's list of witnesses,[387] arguing that there was no legal or factual basis for the Prosecution to call Witness BLP as a witness.

29. On 10 November 2008, the Chamber declared the request for removal of Witness BLP from the Prosecution's witness list to be moot, as the Prosecution had already indicated it would not be calling Witness BLP.[388]

30. On 27 November 2008, the Defence filed a further motion for the Chamber to order the Prosecution to remove Witness BLP from its witness list and for a postponement of the trial.[389] The motion noted that the Prosecution had failed to file a motion seeking leave to remove Witness BLP from his list of witnesses and that the Prosecution's pre-trial brief contained references to Witness BLP.

31. The Prosecution responded to the Defence motion on 28 November 2008,[390] submitting that it did not intend to call Witness BLP and requesting leave from the Chamber to formally withdraw BLP from its list of witnesses. The response also noted its entitlement to use evidence of patterns of conduct, including the use of documents in relation to Witness BLP from previous trials. The Defence responded to this, disputing the Prosecution's proposed use of Witness BLP's recantation as evidence of consistent pattern of conduct pursuant to Rule 93.[391]

32. On 2 January 2009, the Chamber denied the Defence motion, finding that Rule 93 does apply to contempt proceedings and that the trial did not need to be postponed.[392] On 9 January 2009, the Defence sought certification to appeal this decision,[393] submitting, among other things, that the Chamber erred in its conclusion on Rule 93. The Prosecution responded on 14 January 2009,[394] arguing that the Defence failed to satisfy the conditions for certification to appeal to be granted under Rule 73 (B). The Chamber denied the motion on 3 February 2009,[395] finding that the conditions for certification had not been met. **[page 63]**

33. On 31 December 2008, the Chamber ordered the Defence to file its list of witnesses no later than 9 January 2009.[396] On 9 and 16 January 2009, the Defence filed a list of witnesses with more than 40 names

---

[384] "Redacted Disclosure of Additional Witness Statements," filed 26 August 2008.
[385] T. 22 October 2008, p. 15.
[386] "Prosecutor's Filing of a List of Witnesses and Exhibits," filed 27 October 2008.
[387] "Defence Motion to Have Witness BLP Removed from Prosecution List of Witnesses and for Prosecution to File Pre-Trial Brief," filed 29 October 2008.
[388] Decision on Defence Motion to Have Witness BLP Removed from Prosecution List of Witnesses and for the Prosecution to File a Pre-Trial Brief, 10 November 2008.
[389] "Defence Further Motion for a Court Order to the Prosecutor to Remove Witness BLP from his Witness List," filed 27 November 2008.
[390] "Prosecutor's Response to "Defence Further Motion for a Court Order to the Prosecutor to Remove Witness BLP from his Witness List"," filed 28 November 2008.
[391] "Defence Reply to Prosecutor's Response to "Defence Further Motion (…)"," filed 4 December 2008.
[392] Decision on Defence Further Motion for the Prosecutor to Remove Witness BLP from His Witness List, 2 January 2009.
[393] "Defence Application for Certification to Appeal Decision on Defence Further Motion for the Prosecutor to Remove Witness BLP from His Witness List on Application of Rule 93," filed 9 January 2009.
[394] "Prosecutor's Response to "Defence Application for Certification to Appeal Decision on Defence Further Motion for the Prosecutor to Remove Witness BLP from his List on (sic) Application of Rule 93"," filed 14 January 2009.
[395] Decision on Defence Motion for Certification to Appeal the Chamber's Decision of 2 January 2009, 3 February 2009.
[396] Order for the Defence to File a List of Witnesses, 31 December 2008.

on it.[397] On 28 January 2009, the Chamber ordered the Defence to file a summary of anticipated witness testimony for each witness.[398] On 2 February 2009, the Defence filed a motion seeking clarification of the Chamber's order or an extension of time.[399] This motion was found to be without merit and was denied by the Chamber.[400]

34. On 4 February 2009, the Defence filed a preliminary list of Defence witness summaries.[401]

35. On 12 February 2009, the Chamber made an *ex parte* order for the Defence to file a reduced list of witnesses by 16 February 2009.[402] On 16 February 2009, the Defence filed its list of witnesses with three names struck out.[403] On 17 February 2009, the Chamber made another order for the Defence to "significantly reduce" its list of witnesses by 18 February 2009.[404] On 18 February 2009, the Defence filed submissions explaining its inability to comply with the Chamber's order.[405]

36. The Chamber made an oral order on 19 February 2009 for the Defence to file a revised witness list by 20 February 2009.[406] On 20 February 2009, the Defence filed a revised list of witnesses containing 20 witnesses under the heading "Oral Testimony", ten witnesses under the heading "92 *bis* statements" and 10 witnesses under various other headings.[407] On 23 February 2009, the Chamber issued an order for the Defence to reduce its witness list to ten witnesses who would give oral testimony.[408] On 25 February 2009, the Defence sought a reconsideration of the order, submitting it violated the Accused's right to a fair trial, was manifestly unreasonable and would have no practical effect on the expeditious conduct of the proceedings.[409] On 26 February 2009, the Chamber denied the motion, but allowed the Accused to testify in addition to the ten witnesses.[410] **[page 64]**

37. On 2 March 2009, the Defence filed an urgent application to the Appeals Chamber for leave to request a review of the Chamber's decision to affirm its order to reduce the number of witnesses the Defence would bring for oral testimony.[411] The Defence submitted, among other things, that the decision was manifestly unreasonable and *ultra vires*; violated the fair trial rights of the Accused; and would have no practical effect on the expeditious conduct of the proceedings. The Prosecution responded on 5 March 2009,[412] arguing that the Defence did not have a right of review by the Appeals Chamber of a Trial Chamber's decision denying certification to appeal and that the motion should be dismissed in its entirety as being frivolous and vexatious. The Appeals Chamber assigned Judges to the case on 6 March 2009.[413] On 17 March 2009, the Defence requested leave to file further submissions on its motion.[414] The Defence submitted, among other things, the

---

[397] "Defence Strictly Confidential, *Ex Parte* and Under Seal Filing," filed 9 January 2009; "Defence Further Strictly Confidential, *Ex Parte* and Sealed Filing," filed 16 January 2009.
[398] Order for the Defence to File a Summary of Anticipated Witness Testimony, 28 January 2009.
[399] "Motion for Clarification and Request for an Extension of Time," filed 2 February 2009.
[400] Decision on Defence Motion for Clarification and Request for an Extension of Time, 3 February 2009.
[401] "*Ex Parte* Preliminary List of Defence Witness Summaries Filed Pursuant to Court Order of 28 January 2009," 4 February 2009.
[402] *Ex Parte* Order for the Defence to Reduce its List of Witnesses, 12 February 2009.
[403] "*Ex Parte* Revised Preliminary List of Defence Witness Summaries Filed Pursuant to Court Order of 12 February 2009," filed 16 February 2009.
[404] *Ex Parte* Order for the Defence to Further Reduce its List of Witnesses, 17 February 2009.
[405] "*Ex Parte* Submissions Filed Pursuant to Court Order of 17 February 2009," filed 18 February 2009.
[406] T. 19 February 2009, p. 105.
[407] "[CONFIDENTIAL] Preliminary List of Defence Witnesses and Motion for One Week Postponement of Defence Case," filed 20 February 2009.
[408] Further Order for the Defence to Reduce its List of Witnesses, 23 February 2009.
[409] "Defence Request for Reconsideration of the 'Further Order for the Defence to Reduce its List of Witnesses'," filed 25 February 2009.
[410] Decision on Defence Motion for Reconsideration of the Chamber's Further Order for the Defence to Reduce its Witness List, 26 February 2009.
[411] "Urgent Defence Application for Leave to Request a Review of a Trial Chamber Decision Denying the Accused a Fair Trial," filed 2 March 2009.
[412] "Prosecutor's Response to "Urgent Defence Application for Leave to Request a Review of Trial Chamber Decision Denying the Accused a Fair Trial" filed on 02 March 2009," filed 5 March 2009; "Corrigendum to Prosecutor's Response to "Urgent Defence Application for Leave to Request a Review of Trial Chamber Decision Denying the Accused a Fair Trial" filed on 02 March 2009," filed 9 March 2009.
[413] Order Assigning Judges to a Case Before the Appeals Chamber (AC), 6 March 2009.
[414] "Defence Request for Leave to File Further Submissions," filed 17 March 2009.

Registrar's submissions in regards to providing witness information to Rwandan authorities to obtain travel documents and the sanctions imposed on Defence Counsel. The Appeals Chamber dismissed the Defence's application and request to file further submissions, finding that it was not properly seized of the Application.[415]

38. On 2 March 2009, the Defence filed a list of witnesses with 22 witnesses listed to give oral testimony.[416] On 3 March 2009, the Defence filed a corrigendum to their list of witnesses with modifications to the summaries of some of the witnesses.[417] On the same day, the Chamber ordered the Defence to comply with its orders of 23 February 2009 and 26 February 2009, no later than 4 March 2009.[418]

39. On 4 March 2009, the Defence filed an urgent motion for a stay of proceedings due to interference with Defence witnesses.[419] The motion alleged contact between Rwandan authorities and Defence witnesses, and that this contact violated the fair trial rights of the Accused under Article 20 (4)(e). On 6 March 2009, the Chamber ordered the Registry to file submissions on the Defence motion.[420]

40. The Prosecution responded to the Defence motion for stay of proceedings on 6 March 2009,[421] submitting that the alleged facts were filed in the incorrect form. The Prosecution also **[page 65]** asked for, among other things, an order directing the Registrar to verify the allegations and an order sanctioning Defence Counsel for failing to comply with the Chamber's orders to file a reduced witness list.

41. On 6 March 2009, the Defence filed an urgent submission explaining its failure to comply with the orders of the Chamber.[422]

42. On the same day, the Registrar filed a submission on a request made by the Defence to the Registrar for waiver of immunity of certain UN staff members the Defence wished to call as witnesses.[423]

43. On 9 March 2009, the Defence filed a reply to the Prosecution's response to the Defence urgent motion for a stay of proceedings,[424] attaching a statement of one of the witnesses who had been contacted. On the same day, the Defence also filed additional submissions to its original motion.[425] These related to the information provided in Court on 9 March 2009 by the representative of WVSS, in relation to how travel is arranged for witnesses from Rwanda.[426]

44. On the same day, the Registrar also made confidential submissions in respect of the Defence motion for a stay of proceedings.[427] It further detailed how travel was arranged for witnesses from Rwandan and contained witness statements of two witnesses who had been contacted by Rwandan authorities.

45. On the same day, the Defence also made submissions in relation to the Chamber's orders to file a reduce witness list, explaining why each witness was required for its case and asking the Chamber to reduce the witness list itself, if it so desired.[428] On the same day the Chamber made an oral order for the Defence to

---

[415] Decision on Léonidas Nshogoza's Application for Leave to Request Review of a Trial Chamber Decision (AC), 25 March 2009.
[416] "Defence Strictly Confidential List of Witnesses," filed 2 March 2009.
[417] "Defence Strictly Confidential List of Witnesses (corrigendum)," filed 3 March 2009.
[418] Order for the Defence to Comply with the Chamber's Order of 23 February 2009 and the Chamber's Decision of 26 February 2009 for the Defence to Reduce its List of Witness, 3 March 2009.
[419] "Urgent Motion for Stay of Proceedings Due to Interference with Defence Witnesses," filed 4 March 2009.
[420] Order for the Registry to File Rule 33 (B) Submissions on the Defence Motion for Stay of Proceedings Due to Interference with Defence Witnesses, 6 March 2009.
[421] "Prosecutor's Response to "Urgent Motion for Stay of Proceedings Due to Interference with Defence Witnesses" Filed on 4 March 2009," filed 6 March 2009.
[422] "Urgent Defence Submissions Further to Court Order of 3 March 2009 and on the Status of Defence Preparations," filed 6 March 2009.
[423] "Registrar's Submission under Rule 33 (B) of the Rules on Counsel's Request for Waiver of Immunity of UN Staff Members," filed 6 March 2009.
[424] "Defence Reply to "Prosecutor's Response to 'Urgent Motion for Stay of Proceedings Due to Interference with Defence Witnesses'"," filed 9 March 2009.
[425] "Defence Additional Submissions to "Urgent Motion for Stay of Proceedings Due to Interference with Defence Witnesses"," filed 9 March 2009.
[426] T. 9 March 2009 pp. 5-7.
[427] "[CONFIDENTIAL] Registrar's Submissions in Respect of Defence Motion for Stay of Proceedings Due to Interference with Defence Witnesses," filed 9 March 2009.
[428] "Defence Further Submissions on the Trial Chamber's Order Dated 3 March 2009," filed 9 March 2009.

file its reduced list of witnesses.[429] The Defence then filed submissions on the Chamber's oral order, explaining that, among other things, the confirmation by WVSS that it provides protected witness details to Rwandan authorities had resulted in severe disruption to the Defence case preparation.[430]

46. On 11 March 2009, the Defence filed a response to the Registrar's submissions in respect of the Defence's motion for a stay of proceedings.[431] The response contained a list of questions **[page 66]** for the Registrar and requested the Chamber to order the Registrar to answer the questions and provide a list of security measures in place for witnesses who have testified and returned to Rwanda. The Registrar made additional confidential submissions on 12 March 2009,[432] containing witness statements of some defence witnesses, stating, among other things, that no Rwandan authorities had contacted them, that they did not experience any fear, threats or harassment and that they were willing to travel to Arusha to testify.

47. On 11 March 2009, due to the Defence's failure to comply with the Chamber's orders, the Chamber issued an order sanctioning the Defence Counsel by imposing a fine of $5,000.00 and directing the Registrar to seek the President's approval to communicate her misconduct to the professional body that regulates the conduct of counsel in Defence Counsel's State of admission.[433]

48. On 12 March 2009, the Chamber again ordered the Defence to comply with its orders to file a reduced list of witnesses by 13 March 2009.[434] On 13 March 2009, the Defence filed a list of ten witnesses to testify in addition to the Accused[435]

49. On 16 March 2009, the Chamber made an oral order sanctioning Defence Counsel and inviting her to file a written apology for her conduct[436]

50. On 23 March 2009, the Registrar made further submissions on the Defence motion for a stay of proceedings,[437] further explaining how it obtains travel documents for witnesses and containing more statements from witnesses.

51. On 24 March 2009, the Defence filed a motion for leave to vary its witness list following a witness's change in testimony during examination.[438] The Prosecution files its response on 24 March 2009, to which the Defence replied.[439] The motion was denied in an oral ruling of the Chamber on 25 March 2009.[440]
[page 67]

52. On 3 February 2009, the Defence filed an urgent motion requesting a subpoena to Ms. Loretta Lynch.[441] The Prosecution opposed the motion on 6 February 2009,[442] submitting, among other things, that the Defence had failed to provide any reason to justify the ordering of a subpoena and that any material

---

[429] T. 9 March 2009 p. 10.
[430] "Defence Submissions Further to the Trial Chamber's Oral Order of 9 March 2009," filed 9 March 2009.
[431] "Defence Response to "Registrar's Submissions in Respect of Defence Motion for Stay of Proceedings Due to Interference with Defence Witnesses" and Motion for Order to the Registrar to Respond to the Defence Questions," filed 11 March 2009; "Defence Response to "Registrar's Submissions in Respect of Defence Motion for Stay of Proceedings Due to Interference with Defence Witnesses" and Motion for Order to the Registrar to Respond to the Defence Questions – STRICTLY CONFIDENTIAL Annexure A," filed 11 March 2009
[432] "Strictly Confidential Registrar's Additional Submissions in Respect of Defence Motion for Stay of Proceedings Due to Interference with Defence Witnesses," filed 12 March 2009.
[433] Decision to Sanction the Defence for Failure to Comply with the Chamber's Orders, 11 March 2009.
[434] Further Orders for the Defence to Comply with the Chamber's Orders and File its Reduced List of Witnesses, 12 March 2009.
[435] "Defence Submissions Further to "Further Orders for the Defence to Comply with the Chamber's Orders and File its Reduced List of Witnesses"," filed 13 March 2009.
[436] T. 16 March 2009 pp. 1-2.
[437] "Strictly Confidential Registrar's Further Submissions in Respect of Defence Motion for Stay of Proceedings Due to Interference with Defence Witnesses," filed 24 March 2009; *Nshogoza*, "Strictly Confidential and *Ex Parte* Annexes to the Registrar's Further Submissions in Respect of Defence Motion for Stay of Proceedings Due to Interference with Defence Witnesses," filed 24 March 2009.
[438] "Extremely Urgent Defence Motion for Leave to Vary its Witness List," filed 24 March 2009.
[439] "Prosecutor's Response to Extremely Urgent Defence Motion for Leave to Vary its Witness List," filed 24 March 2009; "Defence Reply to "Prosecutor's Response to Extremely Urgent Defence Motion for Leave to Vary its Witness List"," filed 24 March 2009
[440] T. 25 March 2009 pp. 24-26.
[441] "Urgent Defence Request for a Subpoena to Ms. Loretta E. Lynch," filed 3 February 2009.
[442] "Prosecutor's Response to "Urgent Defence Request for a Subpoena to Ms. Loretta E. Lynch"," filed 6 February 2009.

produced by Ms. Lynch was not subject to disclosure under Rule 70. The Defence replied to the Prosecution's response on 9 February 2009,[443] submitting, among other things, that the response contained misrepresentations and that the material was exculpatory and therefore Rule 70 did not apply.

53. On 10 February 2009, the Chamber denied the Defence request for a subpoena.[444] The Chamber found that the Defence had not shown that the information would materially assist in determining whether the Accused had suborned witnesses. The Defence request certification to appeal the Chamber's decision on 16 February 2009.[445] The Chamber denied the Defence request on 19 February 2009,[446] finding that the decision did not involve an issue that would affect the expeditious conduct of proceedings.

b. Exhibits

54. On 27 October 2008, the Prosecution filed a list of 27 exhibits.[447] On 3 March 2009, the Defence filed a list of 21 possible exhibits.[448] An addendum to this was filed on 16 March 2009, containing three additional exhibits.[449] The Prosecution adduced 28 exhibits at trial, and the Defence adduced 96.

55. On 16 June 2009, the Chamber ordered the production of the Prosecution witness protection measures in *Kamuhanda* and asked the parties for their submissions in regard to their admission into evidence.[450] The Prosecution complied with this order on 18 June 2009.[451] And the Defence filed its response on 19 June 2009.[452] The Chamber admitted the protective measures into evidence on 26 June 2009.[453]

c. Statements and Transcripts under Rule 92 *bis* [page 68]

56. On 16 March 2009, the Defence filed a motion for the admission of 12 statements in lieu of oral testimony of witnesses it was denied from bringing before the Chamber.[454] On 30 March 2009, the Defence filed further submissions to the motion.[455] On 29 April 2009, the Chamber granted in part the Defence motion for the admission of statements in lieu of oral testimony, allowing the admission of statements by Witnesses A13, A15, A17, A18, A23, A28 and A30.[456] The Defence requested certification to appeal the Chamber's decision to not admit some of the witness statements,[457] and was denied on 8 June 2009.[458]

57. On 3 April 2009, the Defence filed a motion for the admission of transcripts from the case of *The Prosecutor v. Karemera et al.* (ICTR-98-44-T).[459] On 23 April 2009, the Chamber granted the motion.[460]

---

[443] "Defence Reply to "Prosecution Response to 'Urgent Defence Request for a Subpoena to Ms. Loretta E. Lynch,'" filed 9 February 2009.
[444] Decision on the Defence's Urgent Motion for a Subpoena to Ms. Loretta Lynch, 10 February 2009.
[445] "Defence Motion for Certification of the Trial Chamber's "Decision on the Defence's Urgent Motion for a Subpoena to Ms Loretta Lynch"," filed 16 February 2009.
[446] Decision on Defence Motion for Certification of the Trial Chamber's 'Decision on the Defence's Urgent Motion for a Subpoena to Ms. Loretta Lynch', filed 19 February 2009.
[447] "Prosecutor's Filing of a List of Witnesses and Exhibits," filed 27 October 2008.
[448] "Defence Strictly Confidential List of Possible Exhibits," filed 3 March 2009.
[449] "Defence Strictly Confidential List of Possible Exhibits (Addendum)," filed 16 March 2009.
[450] Order for the Production of Prosecution Witness Protective Measures from the Kamuhanda Case, 16 June 2009.
[451] "Prosecutor's Filing in compliance with the Trial Chamber's "Order for the Production of Prosecution Witness Protective Measures from the Kamuhanda Case, Rule 98 of the Rules of Procedure and Evidence," filed 18 June 2009.
[452] "Defence Response to Order for the Prosecution Witness Protective Measures from the Kamuhanda Case and to the Prosecutor's Filing," filed 19 June 2009.
[453] Order Admitting the Prosecution Witness Protective Measures from the Kamuhanda Case into Evidence, 26 June 2009.
[454] "[CONFIDENTIAL] Defence Motion for the Admission of Written Witness Statements of Witnesses A1, A13, A14, A15, A18, A20, A22, A23, A26, A28, and A30 as Evidence *in lieu* of Oral Testimony," filed 16 March 2009.
[455] "Additional Submissions to the Defence Motion for the Admission of 92 *bis* Witness Statements," filed 30 March 2009.
[456] Decision on Defence Motion for the Admission of Written Statements of Witnesses A1, A13, A14, A15, A17, A18, A20, A22, A23, A26, A28, and A30 as Evidence in lieu of Oral Testimony, 29 April 2009.
[457] "Defence Motion for Certification of the Trial Chambers Decision to Deny the Admission of the Statements of Witnesses A1, A14, A20, A22 and A26," filed 6 May 2009.
[458] Decision on Defence Motion for Certification of the Trial Chamber's Decision on the Admission of Evidence Pursuant to Rule 92 *bis*, 8 June 2009.
[459] "Motion for the Admission of Transcripts Pursuant to Rule 92 *bis*," filed 3 April 2009.
[460] Decision on Defence Motion for the Admission of Transcripts Pursuant to Rule 92 *bis*, 23 April 2009.

6. Disclosure

58. On 22 March 2008, the Defence filed an urgent motion for the Trial Chamber to order the Prosecution to disclose all Rule 66 (A) supporting material and rule that the Rule 72 30-day period would begin at either the date of receipt by the Defence of the Rule 66 supporting material, or the date of the decision to be rendered on the urgent motion if it denied the Defence request.[461]

59. On 28 March 2008, the Prosecution filed a clarification on documents disclosed, in response to the Defence's 22 March 2008 urgent motion.[462] The Prosecution submitted that it had disclosed all supporting materials to the Defence in one binder on 12 March 2008, and that the materials the Defence argued were missing were in the public domain. The Defence responded to the Prosecution's clarification on 2 April 2008, asking the Chamber not to consider the clarification as it was time-barred and did not serve to clarify the matter.[463]

60. On 3 April 2008, the Defence filed an addendum to its response containing a table of documents listing whether or not they were publicly available.[464] **[page 69]**

61. On 8 April 2008, the Prosecution disclosed a redacted version of Witness GAA's solemn declaration, apologising for the oversight and late disclosure.[465] On the same day, the Prosecution replied to the addendum filed by the Defence on 3 April 2008,[466] reiterating that, with the exception of one document that had been disclosed in redacted form, the documents requested did not constitute supporting material for the purposes of Rule 66 (A)(i). The Prosecution also added that all but two of the listed documents were public records and submitted that to the extent that any material was material to the preparation of the Defence case, Defence Counsel was entitled to request them for inspection.

62. On 10 April 2008, the Defence filed an urgent request that the Chamber declare that the 30-day period under Rule 72 would begin running on the either the date of the pending decision on Prosecutorial disclosure or the date of disclosure of the Prosecution of the remaining support material.[467]

63. On 16 April 2008, the Prosecution opposed the urgent Defence request regarding the commencement of the Rule 72 30-day delay.[468] The Prosecution requested the time limit for the filing of eventual Rule 72 applications to end 30 days after completion of the Prosecution's disclosure pursuant to Rule 66 (A)(i).

64. On 22 April 2008, the Defence filed an addendum and reply to the Prosecution's response, asserting that the Prosecution was incorrect about certain documents being in the public domain and had failed to address the issues that gave rise to the doubts as to whether all Rule 66 (A) materials have been disclosed.[469] The Defence also submitted that the Prosecution had had unauthorised contact with the Accused by communicating Witness GAA's solemn declaration directly to the Accused and not to Defence Counsel. The Defence submitted that an inter-office memo to the Accused did not constitute disclosure for the purposes of calculating the Rule 72 deadline and that Defence Counsel had still not, at the date of filing received the interoffice memo. The Defence asked the Chamber to deny the relief sought by the Prosecution, direct the Prosecution to disclose the inter-office memo through official channels and to postpone the commencement of the Rule 72 deadline.

---

[461] "Urgent Defence Motion for Trial Chamber to Order the Prosecutor to Disclose all Rule 66 (A) Supporting Material," filed 26 March 2008.
[462] "Prosecutor's Clarifications on Documents Disclosed to the Defence on 12 March 2008," filed 28 March 2008.
[463] "Defence Response to Prosecutor's "Clarification on Documents Disclosed to the Defence on 12 March 2008"," filed 2 April 2008.
[464] "Addendum – Defence Response to Prosecutor's 'Clarifications on Documents Disclosed to the Defence on 12 March 2008'" filed 3 April 2008.
[465] "Redacted Disclosure of 'Solemn Declaration and Statement of GAA,'" filed 8 April 2008.
[466] "Prosecutor's Reply to 'Addendum-Defence Response to Prosecutor's 'Clarifications on Documents Disclosed to the Defence on 12 March 2008,'" filed 8 April 2008.
[467] "Urgent Defence Request Regarding the Commencement of the Rule 72 30-Day Delay," filed 11 April 2008.
[468] "Prosecutor's Response to "Urgent Defence Request Regarding the Commencement of the Rule 72 30-Day Delay"," filed 16 April 2008.
[469] "Addendum and Reply to 'Prosecutor's Response to "Urgent Defence Request Regarding the Commencement of the Rule 72 30-day Delay,'" filed 21 April 2008.

65. On 5 September 2008, the Prosecution made a redacted disclosure of five additional statements.[470] This was followed on 15 September 2008 with the disclosure of a translation of the Accused's file before the Rwandan Gasabo Court of First Instance, with additional translations filed on 17 and 25 September 2008.[471] **[page 70]**

66. On 1 October 2008, the Chamber rendered its decision on the Defence motion of 22 March 2008 requesting disclosure of supporting materials and of 10 April 2008 regarding the Rule 72 30-day delay.[472] The Chamber ordered the Prosecution to file a declaration stating that it had fully complied with its Rule 66 (A)(i) obligations and to provide a description of any material it claimed fell within an exception to that rule. The Chamber also ordered the Prosecution to ensure that the Defence had access to any supporting materials that were claimed to be in the public domain. The Chamber declared that the 30-day period provided for in Rule 72 (A) would run from either the date on which the Prosecution's declaration was filed or the date of last disclosure, whichever was later. The Chamber stayed any decision on the merits of the Defence's first and second Rule 72 motions until the 30-day period had elapsed and permitted the Defence to amend its pending Rule 72 preliminary motions, or file new ones, within the 30-day period.

67. On 6 October 2008, the Defence filed a motion asking the Chamber to make a number of orders to the Prosecution to disclose various documents of supporting materials.[473]

68. On 9 October 2008, the Prosecution filed a confidential declaration and disclosure following the Chamber's order of 1 October 2008.[474]

69. The Defence filed its response to the Prosecution filing on 20 October 2008,[475] noting that Prosecution's filing did not contain a declaration that the Prosecution had fully complied with its Rule 66 (A)(i) obligations and contesting the accuracy of the filing.

70. On the same day the Defence also filed a motion requesting the Prosecution to produce the videotape of an interview with Witness BUC.[476] The Defence motion was denied by the Chamber on 31 December 2008, as the Defence failed to present evidence in support of its assertion that the Prosecution had the video in his possession.[477]

71. On 24 October 2008, the Prosecution filed a confidential clarification of the disclosures made to that date, to assist the Chamber and the Defence in determining what had been disclosed.[478] **[page 71]**

72. On 3 November 2008, the Prosecution confidentially disclosed two witness statements.[479] On the same day, the Defence filed a motion, arguing that the deadline to file preliminary motions should be on either 13 or 14 November 2008.[480]

73. On 7 November 2008, The Chamber rendered its decision on the Defence Rule 72 deadline motion, ordering that the 30-day period would run from 14 October 2008.[481]

---

[470] "Redacted Disclosure of Translations of 5 Additional Witnesses Statements," filed 5 September 2008.
[471] "Redacted Disclosure – Translation of Nshogoza's File of the Rwandan Gasabo Court First Instance RP 0531/07/TGI/GASABO," filed 15 September 2008; *Nshogoza*, "Redacted Disclosure – French Translation Nshogoza File of the Rwandan Gasabo Court First Instance RP/0531/07/TGI/GASABO," filed 17 September 2008; "Redacted Disclosure – Further Translations of Nshogoza File of the Rwandan Gasabo Court First Instance RP/0531/07/TGI/GASABO," filed 25 September 2008.
[472] Decision on Defence Motions for Disclosure of Supporting Materials; and Clarification on Rule 72 30-Day Period, 1 October 2008.
[473] "Defence Motion Filed Pursuant to Rules 66 (A) and (B) of the Rules of Procedure and Evidence," filed 6 October 2008.
[474] "Prosecutor's [CONFIDENTIAL] Declaration and Disclosure Pursuant to Rules 66 and 75 of the Rules of Procedure and Evidence, Following Trial Chamber III's Order of 1 October 2008," filed 9 October 2008.
[475] "Defence Request for 5-Day Delay to Respond from Date of Receipt of Prosecution Filing of October 2008," filed 14 October 2008; "Defence Request for 5-Day Delay to Respond from Date of Receipt of Prosecution Motion of 9 October 2008," filed 15 October 2008; "Defence Response to Prosecution Declaration on Rule 66 (A) (i) Disclosure," filed 20 October 2008.
[476] "Defence Response to Prosecution Extremely Urgent Motion for Protective Measures and Motion for Request to Prosecutor to Produce Video Tape of Interview with Witness BUC," filed 20 October 2008.
[477] Decision on Defence Motion for the Prosecutor to Produce Video Tape of Interview with Witness BUC, 31 December 2008.
[478] "Prosecutor's [CONFIDENTIAL] Clarification of Disclosures Made to Date, Pursuant to Rules 66 and 75 of the Rules of Procedure and Evidence," filed 24 October 2008.
[479] [CONFIDENTIAL] "Un-Redacted Disclosure of BUC (SP-018) Witness Statements," filed 3 November 2008.
[480] "Defence Request Concerning the Deadline for Rule 72 Preliminary Exceptions Motion," filed 3 November 2008.
[481] Decision on Defence Request Concerning the Deadline for Rule 72 Preliminary Exceptions Motions, 7 November 2008.

Annex

74. On 10 November 2008, the Prosecution made a confidential disclosure of a French translation of a statement by Witness BUC (SP-018).[482] On 13 November 2008, the Prosecution confidentially disclosed an English translation of statements by Witness BUC (SP-018).[483]

75. On 27 November 2008, the Registrar made confidential and *ex-parte* disclosure of certain Registry documentation of the Accused, and requested guidance from the Chamber as to whether it had to disclose the same information to the Prosecution.[484] The Registrar submitted that the Defence indicated it did not want the documents given to the Prosecution, as it would reveal the nature of the Defence investigations.

76. On 2 December 2008, the Prosecution made submissions on the Registrar's submission, arguing that the principle of the equality of arms and adversarial trial dictated that the material also be disclosed to the Prosecution.[485] On 11 December 2008, the Defence also made submissions on this point,[486] arguing the Registrar was under no legal obligation to provide the documents to the Prosecution, though was able to if it so desired. On the same day, the Prosecution made additional confidential disclosure of more witness statements.[487]

77. On 10 December 2008, the Chamber ordered the Defence to file detailed submissions as to how the disclosure to the Prosecution of the Registrar's documentation of the Accused, would reveal the nature of the Defence investigations.[488] The Defence filed submissions pursuant to this Chamber order on 12 December 2008,[489] noting its submissions of 5 December 2008 and reiterating its non-objection to the Registrar disclosing the documents at issue. **[page 72]**

78. On 17 December 2008, the Chamber ordered the Registrar to assess the Prosecution's request for a copy of the relevant documents and to take any action it deemed appropriate.[490]

79. On 22 October 2008, the Defence filed a motion requesting the Chamber to order disclosure by the Prosecution.[491] On 29 October 2008, the Defence also requested time to investigate and for provisional release of the Accused.[492]

80. On 22 December 2008, the Chamber granted in part these motions for disclosure, ordering the Prosecution to disclose to the Defence a number of the requested documents.[493] On 29 December 2008, the Defence sought certification to appeal the decision, and alternatively requested a review of the decision.[494] On 5 January 2009, the Prosecution filed a response to the application for certification, arguing that the Defence had not met the legal threshold to merit certification or to justify review of the decision.[495] On 14 January 2009, the Defence filed its reply, submitting that the Prosecution had failed to demonstrate why

---

[482] "Disclosure of French Translation of BUC (SP-018) Statement of 11 October 1995," filed 10 November 2008.
[483] "Disclosure of English Translations of BUC (SP-018) Statements," filed 13 November 2008.
[484] "Registrar's Submissions Under Rule 33 (B) of the Rules on the Disclosure of Registry Documents," filed 28 November 2008; "[EX PARTE & CONFIDENTIAL] Annex to Registrar's Submission Under Rule 33 (B) of the Rules on the Disclosure of Registry Documents," filed 28 November 2008; "Registrar's Further Submissions under Rule 33 (B) of the Rules on the Disclosure of Registry Documents," filed 8 January 2009.
[485] "Prosecutor's Submissions Concerning 'Registrar's Submissions under Rule 33 (B) of the Rules on the Disclosure of Registry Documents,'" filed 2 December 2008.
[486] "Defence Submissions on Registrar Submissions of 28 November 2008 and Prosecution Submissions of 2 December 2008," filed 11 December 2008.
[487] "Disclosure of Relevant Documents Pursuant to Rule 66 (B) and 75 (F)(ii)," filed 5 December 2008.
[488] Order for Submissions from the Defence Regarding Registrar's Rule 33 (B) Submissions on Disclosure, 10 December 2008.
[489] "Defence Further Submissions Pursuant to Court Order of 10 December 2008," filed 12 December 2008.
[490] Order Regarding Registrar's Rule 33 (B) Submissions on Disclosure, 17 December 2008.
[491] "Defence Motion for Disclosure under Rules 66 and 68 of the ICTR R.P.E.," filed 22 October 2008.
[492] "Defence Motion for Order to the Prosecution to Complete Rule 66 (A)(ii) Disclosure, Request for Time to Investigate Before Trial, and Motion for the Provisional Release of Léonidas Nshogoza," filed 29 October 2008.
[493] Decision on Defence Motions for Disclosure under Rules 66 and 68 of the Rules of Procedure and Evidence, 22 December 2008.
[494] "Defence Application for Certification to Appeal Decision of 22 December 2008 and Alternative Request for Review," filed 29 December 2008.
[495] "Prosecutor's Response to "Defence Application for Certification to Appeal Decision of 22 December 2008 and Alternatively for Review"," filed 5 January 2009; "Notice of Intent to File Reply to Prosecution Response Dated 5 January 2009 to Defence Application for Certification," filed 12 January 2009.

the Defence had not met their burden for certification or review.[496] The reply also set out evidence for the existence of documents that the Defence alleged were in the Prosecution's possession and needed to be disclosed. It further asked the Chamber to order the Prosecution to disclose a number of witness statements and for the Chamber to order the Prosecution to disclose to the Defence all existing Kinyarwanda versions of all Prosecution witness statements. On 19 February 2009, the Chamber granted a Defence request for an order to the Prosecution to allow the Defence to inspect witness statements arising from the investigation conducted by Ms. Lynch and denied the remainder of the motion.[497]

81. On 5, 13, 19, 20 and 21 January 2009, the Prosecution made further confidential disclosures of certain materials in relation to Witness GAA and other confidential documents and materials.[498] **[page 73]**

82. On 21 January 2009, the Defence filed a motion requesting access to a confidential defence motion in *Kamuhanda*, the first written record that references the recantation of Witness GAA.[499] The Prosecution replied on 22 January 2009,[500] disclosing the requested document. On 14 May 2009, the Chamber found the request to be moot, as the disclosure had occurred.[501]

83. On 26 January 2009, the Prosecution confidentially disclosed a Will Say Statement of Witness GAA, a Kinyarwanda statement of Witness GAA and a transcription of an audio cassette of Witness GAA.[502] On 28 January the Prosecution also disclosed a number of audio interviews with Witness GAA.[503]

84. On 29 January 2009, the Defence filed an extremely urgent motion asking for an order to the Prosecution to fully and immediately comply with the Chamber's 22 December 2008 disclosure order and other disclosure obligations.[504]

85. On 3 February 2009, the Prosecution confidentially disclosed a French translation of Witness GAA's statement.[505]

86. On 4 February 2009, the Prosecution responded to the extremely urgent Defence motion for an order to the Prosecution to fully comply with the Chamber's order for disclosure of 22 December 2008,[506] asking that the Defence motion be dismissed, submitting that the Defence had made general assertions and failed to establish any material prejudice as a result of the alleged disclosure failures. On 9 February 2009, the Defence filed a reply to the Prosecution's response to the Defence's 29 January 2009 motion on disclosure. The Defence replied that the Prosecution had only partially addressed the breaches set out in the Defence motion and argued that it was not required to demonstrate material prejudice.[507]

---

[496] "Defence Reply to Prosecution Response to Defence Application for Certification to Appeal Decision of 22 December 2008 (…)," filed 14 January 2009.
[497] Decision on Defence Motion for Reconsideration or Certification to Appeal the Chamber's Decision of 22 December 2008 on Disclosure, 19 February 2009.
[498] "[CONFIDENTIAL] Disclosure of Rule 66 (B) Documents," filed 5 January 2009; "[CONFIDENTIAL] Additional Disclosure of Translations of Witness Statements," filed 13 January 2009; "[CONFIDENTIAL] Disclosure of GAA Audio Cassettes," filed 19 January 2009; "[CONFIDENTIAL] Disclosure of Transcription Translation of GAA Audio Cassette Interview of 11 May 2005," filed 20 January 2009; "[CONFIDENTIAL] Disclosure of Translation of Transcription of GAA Audio Cassette of Interview of 11 May 2005 – English," filed 21 January 2009.
[499] "Defence Motion for Access to Confidential Kamuhanda Defence Motion for Admission of Additional Evidence," filed 21 January 2009.
[500] "[CONFIDENTIAL] Prosecutor's Reply to "Defence Motion for Access to Confidential Kamuhanda Defence Motion for Admission of Additional Evidence"," filed 22 January 2009.
[501] Decision on Defence Motion for Access to Confidential Kamuhanda Defence Motion, 14 May 2009.
[502] "[CONFIDENTIAL] Additional Disclosure of GAA Will Say Statement, Kinyarwanda Statement Ern K045-7554-7557 and GAA Audio Cassette Transcription Translations," filed 26 January 2009.
[503] "Disclosure of GAA Audio Interviews KT00-1679, KT00-1680, KT00-1681 and KT00-1682," filed 28 January 2009.
[504] "Extremely Urgent Defence Motion for Order to the Prosecution to Fully and Immediately Comply with 22 December 2008 Disclosure Court Order and Other Disclosure Obligations," filed 29 January 2009.
[505] "[CONFIDENTIAL] French Translation of GAA Statement /ERN K-045-7803-7808," filed 3 February 2009.
[506] "Prosecutor's Response to "Extremely Urgent Defence Motion to the Prosecution to Fully and Immediately Comply with 22 December 2008 Disclosure Court Order and other Disclosure Obligations Pursuant to Rules 41, 54, 66, 68 and 73 of the ICTR Rules of Procedure and Evidence"," filed 4 February 2009.
[507] "Defence Reply to the Prosecutor's Response to 'Extremely Urgent Motion for Order to the Prosecution to Fully and Immediately Comply with 22 December 2008 Disclosure Court Order and Other Disclosure Obligations'"," filed 9 February 2009.

87. On 5 February 2009, the Prosecution made another confidential disclosure of a handwritten document of Witness GAA.[508] **[page 74]**

88. On the same day, the Chamber ordered the Prosecution to conduct a thorough review of his materials to ensure full compliance with its disclosure obligations and to certify in writing that it had conducted the search by 9 February 2009.[509]

89. Following the Chamber's order, the Prosecution made two confidential disclosures on 6 February 2009 of transcripts of interviews with Witness GAA and intercepts of conversations between Witness GAA and others.[510]

90. On 6 February 2009, the Registrar also made a confidential and *ex parte* disclosure of a transcription of an excerpt from Witness GAA's initial appearance, and translation into English and French of an excerpt in Kinywarwanda of the same hearing.[511] The Registrar also asked the Chamber for direction as to whether it should also disclose the documents to the Prosecution.

91. On 5 February 2009, the Defence filed an urgent motion for stay of proceedings due to the on-going violations of the Prosecution's disclosure obligations.[512] On 9 February 2009, the Prosecution filed its response,[513] arguing that the Defence had failed to establish material prejudice and had not demonstrated that the Prosecution had failed to disclose specific materials in its possession. On the same day, the Prosecution filed a certification of compliance with the Chamber's order of 5 February 2009 regarding disclosure obligations.[514]

92. On 10 February 2009, the Chamber issued its decision on the Defence motion of 29 January 2009 alleging the Prosecution was in violation of its disclosure obligations and the Defence motion of 5 February 2009 for a stay of proceedings due the Prosecution's violation of its disclosure obligations.[515] The Chamber denied both motions, noting the further disclosures by the Prosecution since the filing of the motion and finding that the Defence had not demonstrated that the Accused had suffered prejudice as a result of the delayed disclosures.

93. On 12 February 2009, the Defence filed a request for reconsideration of, or in the alternative certification to appeal, the Chamber's oral decision of 9 February 2009 not to postpone the proceedings and to allow the Prosecution to begin his case.[516] The motion alleged **[page 75]** that there remained undisclosed statements of Witness GAA and that the Defence had not been afforded an opportunity to prepare for the testimony of Witness GAA. The Defence requested, among other things, a postponement of the testimony of Witness GAA until 15 days after the Prosecution had disclosed the documents requested.

---

[508] "Disclosure Hand written document/ Ern K045-7888," filed 5 February 2009.
[509] Order for the Prosecution to Conduct a Thorough Review and Certify that it has Complied with its Disclosure Obligations, 5 February 2009.
[510] "[CONFIDENTIAL] Disclosure of Transcription of GAA Interviews of 29 September 2005 – KT00-1679, KT00-1680, KT00-1681 and KT00-1682," filed 6 February 2009; "[CONFIDENTIAL] Disclosure of "GAA conversation intercept with Emmanuel Bajenza dated 23 August 2005" –" KT00-1676 Part I and KT-1677 Part I," filed 6 February 2009.
[511] "[CONFIDENTIAL] Registrar's Submissions under Rule 33 (B) of the Rules on the Disclosure of Registry Documetns," filed 6 February 2009.
[512] "Urgent Motion for Stay of Proceedings due to the On-going Violations of the Prosecutor's Disclosure Obligations," filed 5 February 2009.
[513] "Prosecutor's Response to "Urgent Motion for Stay of Proceedings Due to On-going Violation of the Prosecutor's Disclosure Obligations"," filed 9 February 2009.
[514] "Prosecutor's Certification of Compliance with Trial Chamber's Orders of 5 February 2009 Regarding Disclosure Obligations," filed 9 February 2009.
[515] Decision on Defence Motion for Order to Prosecutor to Comply with His Disclosure Obligations and Motion for Stay of Proceedings Due to the On-Going Violations of the Prosecutor's Disclosure Obligations, 10 February 2009.
[516] T. 9 February 2009 pp. 3-8; "Defence Request for Reconsideration, or, in the Alternative, Certification to Appeal the Trial Chamber's Oral Decision of 9 February 2009 Denying a Postponement of Proceedings Due to Disclosure Violations," filed 12 February 2009.

94. The Prosecution responded on 16 February 2009,[517] submitting that the Defence had failed to satisfy the threshold for reconsideration. The Chamber denied the Defence motion on 18 February 2009,[518] finding there were no new material circumstances to justify reconsideration and that the decision did not meet the requirements for certification.

95. On 13 February 2009, the Prosecution confidentially disclosed audio cassettes containing interviews with Witness GAA.[519]

96. On 2 March 2009, the Prosecution filed confirmation that Defence Counsel had inspected witness statements from Ms. Lynch's investigation and had received a CD-ROM containing witness statements the Defence had selected.[520]

97. On 11 March 2009, the Prosecution confidentially disclosed a statement of fees and expenses from the *Kamuhanda* case.[521]

98. On 16 March 2009, the Registrar filed submissions regarding documents that had been disclosed *ex parte* to the Defence.[522] The Registrar sought instructions as to whether the documents needed to be disclosed to the Prosecution. The Prosecution responded on the same day.[523] The Chamber issued its order on 14 May 2009,[524] directing the Registry to take such action as it deemed appropriate.

99. On 18 March 2009, the Prosecution confidentially disclosed Rwandan judicial documents it had recently received from the Rwandan authorities, along with English translations.[525] On 25 March 2009, the Prosecution confidentially disclosed an extract from 26 March 2001 from the *Kamuhanda* case.[526]

100. On 27 March 2009, the Prosecution made confidential submissions regarding the disclosure and existence of statements from Defence Witness Straton Nyarwaya, which the **[page 76]** Prosecution had previously denied it possessed.[527] The Prosecution also submitted that the Defence had not suffered any material prejudice from its failure to disclose the document. The Defence responded on 1 April 2009,[528] arguing that it had suffered material prejudice and asking the Chamber to, among other things, find that the Prosecution had violated Rule 68, admit the statement, issue a warning to the Prosecution and order the Prosecution to permit the Defence to inspect all the documents contained in the container where the statement was found.

101. On 7 May 2009, the Defence filed a motion requesting, among other things, the admission of the Straton Nyarwaya statement, an order to the Prosecution to allow the Defence to inspect the carton in which the statement was found, and for sanctions to be imposed on the Prosecution for their disclosure violation.[529]

---

[517] "Prosecutor's Response to "Defence Request for Reconsideration, or, in the Alternative, Certification to Appeal the Trial Chamber's Oral Decision of 9 February 2009 Denying a Postponement of Proceedings Due to Disclosure Violation"," filed 16 February 2009.
[518] Decision on Defence Motion for Certification to Appeal the Chamber's Oral Decision of 9 February 2009 Denying an Adjournment of the Proceedings, 18 February 2009.
[519] "Inspection of GAA Audio Cassettes/ Waiver Forms and Evidence Receipts Form," filed 13 February 2009.
[520] "Inspection of Loretta Lynch Folder & CD Rom with Rule 66 (B) Statements," filed 3 March 2009.
[521] "Disclosure under Rule 66 (B) / InterOffice Memorandum Ern-K045-8604-8609," filed 11 March 2009.
[522] "Registrar's Submissions under Rule 33 (B) of the Rules on the Disclosure of Registry Documents," filed 16 March 2009.
[523] "Prosecutor's Submissions Concerning "Registrar's Submissions under Rule 33 (B) of the Rules on the Disclosure of Registry Documents"," filed 16 March 2009.
[524] Order Regarding the Registrar's Rule 33 (B) Submissions on Disclosure, 14 May 2009.
[525] "Disclosure under Rule 66 (B) Rwandan Judicial Documents (Ern K051-2274-2277) & English Translations (Ern K051-2278-2282)," filed 18 March 2009.
[526] "Extract from a disclosure, dated 26 March 2001, made in the *Kamuhanda* case, concerning former Protected Prosecution Witness GEX (A7)," filed 25 March 2009.
[527] "Prosecutor's Submissions Regarding Defence Witness Stratton Nyarwaya's Statements to the Office of the Prosecutor dated 15 March 2006," filed 27 March 2009.
[528] "Defence Submissions in Response to "Prosecutor's Submissions Regarding Defence Witness Stratton Nyarwaya's Statements to the Office of the Prosecutor dated 15 March 2006"," filed 1 April 2009.
[529] "Defence Motion to Admit into Evidence 15 March 2009 OTP Statement Taken from Defence Witness Starton Nyarwaya, for Access to Documents Contained in a "Carton" Found in Kigali in which the Nyarwaya Statement was Found, to Sanction the Prosecution for Withholding Exculpatory Evidence and to Order the Prosecution to File a Report on the Inquiry into the Unprocessed OTP Evidence Found in Kigali," filed 7 May 2009.

The Chamber granted the Defence motion in part, finding the Prosecution was in violation of its disclosure obligations and reminding the Prosecution of the importance of those obligations under the Rules.[530]

7. Protective measures for witnesses

102. When issuing the Indictment the Chamber noted that the protection orders from the *Kamuhanda* case remained in effect and extended a limited protection from the public to all witnesses in connection with the case.[531]

103. On 9 October 2008, the Prosecution filed an extremely urgent motion asking for protective measures for its witnesses.[532] On 20 October 2009, the Defence responded to the motion, objecting to protective measures being granted to one witness that it claimed was a Defence witness.[533] On 24 November 2008, the Chamber granted the Prosecution's motion.[534]

104. On 27 October 2008, the Defence filed a motion to examine an affidavit relied upon by the Prosecution when applying for protective measures.[535] This was denied by the Chamber on 20 November 2008, which also ordered the Registry to withhold the payment of costs associated with its filing.[536] The Defence made an oral motion on the same issue on 12 February 2009,[537] which was denied on 17 February 2009.[538] **[page 77]**

105. On 27 November 2008, the Defence filed a motion for protective measures for its witnesses.[539] The Prosecution responded to this on 2 December 2008.[540] The Defence replied to this response 10 December 2008.[541] The Chamber granted the Defence motion in part on 22 January 2009, providing the same witness protection measures to the Defence that it provided to the Prosecution.[542]

106. On 12 December 2008, the Defence filed an urgent *ex parte* application for clarification and variance of the 24 November 2008 witness protection order, asking the Chamber to limit the interpretation of "family members" to only immediate family members and a variation of the order in relation to a family member of one of the witnesses.[543] This was followed by a motion on 18 December 2008, reiterating the request.[544] On the same day the Defence filed another motion seeking variance of the Chamber's protection order for a family member of a protected witness.[545] The Prosecution objected to the motion on 22 December 2008, arguing that the family member was a potential prosecution witness.[546] The Prosecution also responded to the Defence's 18 December 2008 urgent application for clarification of the 24 November 2008 witness protection order, opposing the motion to limit the interpretation of "family members".[547] On 26 January

---

[530] Decision on Defence Motion to Admit the Statement of Defence Witness Straton Nyarwaya into Evidence; and for Other Relief, 1 July 2009.
[531] Confirmation of the Indictment and Witness Protection Orders, 4 January 2008, para. 7.
[532] "Prosecutor's Extremely Urgent Motion for Protective Measures for Victims and Witnesses," filed 9 October 2008, para. 3.
[533] "Defence Response to Prosecution Extremely Urgent Motion for Protective Measures and Motion for Request to Prosecutor to Produce Video Tape of Interview with Witness BUC," filed 20 October 2008.
[534] Decision on Prosecutor's Extremely Urgent Motion for Protective Measures for Victims and Witnesses, 24 November 2008.
[535] "Defence Motion to Examine on Affidavit," filed 27 October 2008.
[536] Decision on Defence Motion to Examine on Affidavit, 20 November 2008.
[537] T. 12 February 2009 p. 6.
[538] T. 17 February 2009 p. 28.
[539] Defence Motion for Protective Measures for Victims and Witnesses," filed 27 November 2008.
[540] "Prosecutor's Response to "Defence Motion for Protective Measures for Victims and Witnesses"," filed 2 December 2008.
[541] "Defence Reply to Prosecutor's Response to Defence Motion for Protective Measures for Victims and Witnesses," filed 10 December 2008.
[542] Decision on Defence Motion for Protective Measures for Victims and Witnesses, 22 January 2009.
[543] "[CONFIDENTIAL] Urgent Ex Parte Application for Clarification and Variance of 24 November 2008 Witness Protection Order," filed 12 December 2008.
[544] "Urgent Application for Clarification of 24 November 2008 Witness Protection Order," filed 18 December 2008.
[545] "Urgent and Confidential Application for Variation of 24 November 2008 Witness Protection Order," filed 18 December 2008.
[546] "Prosecutor's Response to Defence "Urgent and Confidential Application for Variance of 24 November 2008 Witness Protection Order"," filed 22 December 2008.
[547] "Prosecutor's Response to Defence "Urgent Application for Clarification of 24 November 2008 Witness Protection Order"," filed 22 December 2008.

2009, the Chamber denied the Defence motion to limit the meaning of the term "family members" to immediate family members only.[548]

107. On 23 January 2009, the Chamber ruled on the Defence motion of 18 December 2008 to vary a protection measure in relation to a family member of one of the Prosecution witnesses, and ordered the Defence to provide the Chamber with a signed consent stating that the witness had agreed to testify on behalf of the Defence.[549] The Defence filed the requested statement on 5 February 2009.[550] On 6 February 2009, the Chamber granted the Defence order for variation of the Protective Measures Order following the consent of the relevant witness.[551]

8. Pre-trial [page 78]

108. On 11 March 2008, the Prosecution made its Rule 66 (A) disclosure of supporting materials.[552]

109. On 19 March 2008, the Defence filed a motion to make public the transcript of the 11 February 2008 Status Conference and to make the Registry make the case available to the public by placing the public documents on the ICTR website and the ICTR's Public Judicial Records Database ("TRIM").[553] On 16 April 2009, the Chamber granted this motion in part,[554] lifting the confidentiality of the Transcript of the Status Conference held on 11 February 2008, and finding the request to list the case on the ICTR website and in TRIM to be moot, as this had already been done.

110. On 26 March 2008, the Defence filed an urgent application seeking deferral in favour of the ICTR and asking the Chamber to, among other things, direct the Registrar to formally advise the Rwandan government that the Accused has functional immunity, that the pending criminal charges against him must be withdrawn and that the matter must be deferred to the ICTR.[555] On 2 April 2008, the Prosecution lodged a response to the motion requesting it to be dismissed and arguing it lacked any foundation, was frivolous, unwarranted and amounted to an abuse of process.[556] On 7 April 2008, the Defence filed a reply to the Prosecution's response.[557]

111. On 5 November 2008, the Chamber issued its decision on the Defence motion for deferral in favour of the ICTR, denying the motion in its entirety and ordering the Registry to withhold the payment of any costs associated with its filing.[558]

112. On 11 April 2008, the Defence filed a preliminary *pro forma* submission in support of preliminary motions pursuant to Rule 72 in case the Chamber denied earlier Defence motions for extension of the Rule 72 deadline.[559] The Defence challenged the jurisdiction of the Prosecution to charge Léonidas Nshogoza; submitted that the Prosecution had a conflict of interest due to Witness GAA being a prosecution witness before recanting; submitted that the indictment was defective as two charges of attempted contempt did not exist under the ICTR Statute nor the Rules of Procedure and Evidence; and submitted that the Accused had been incarcerated for seventy days without being assigned counsel. The Defence also reserved the right to

---

[548] Decision on Defence Motion for Clarification of 24 November 2008 Witness Protection Order, 26 January 2009.
[549] Decision on Defence Motion to Vary 24 November 2008 Witness Protection Order, 23 January 2009.
[550] "Defence Filing of Written Consent of Defence Witness Further to Court Order of 23 January 2009," filed 5 February 2009.
[551] Order Varying Witness Protection Order, 6 February 2009.
[552] "Disclosure of Redacted Supporting Materials Pursuant to Rule 66 (A) of the Rules," filed 11 March 2008.
[553] "Motion to Make Public the Transcript of 11 February 2008 Status Conference and Related Motion for Directive to the Registry to Make Case Available to the Public," filed 19 March 2008 and "Corrigendum – Defence Motion to Make Public the Transcript of 11 February 2008 Status Conference (...) Filed 19 March 2008," filed 26 March 2008.
[554] Decision on the Defence Motion to make Public the Transcripts of 11 February 2008 and the Case File in General, 16 April 2009.
[555] "Urgent Defence Judicial and Administrative Application for Deferral in Favour of the ICTR," filed 28 March 2008.
[556] "[CONFIDENTIAL] Prosecutor's Response to "Urgent Defence Judicial and Administrative Application for Deferral in Favour of the ICTR"," filed 2 April 2008.
[557] "Reply to Prosecutor's Response to Urgent Application of Deferral," filed 7 April 2008.
[558] Decision on Defence Judicial and Administrative Application for Deferral in Favour of the ICTR, 5 November 2008.
[559] "Preliminary Pro Forma Submissions in Support of Preliminary Motions Pursuant to Rule 72 of the ICTR Rules of Procedure and Evidence," filed 11 April 2008.

supplement **[page 79]** the submissions and advance new submissions following the resolution of some pending Defence motions.

113.   The Prosecution responded to the Defence preliminary pro forma submission on 16 April 2008, arguing that Rule 71 (A)(i) and (D) did not apply to contempt proceedings; that Article 17 of the Statute confers general authority on the Prosecution to investigate and indict; that Rule 77 (C) and (D) specifically confer on the Prosecution the power to investigate, indict and prosecute persons for contempt subject to the direction of a Chamber; and that the Prosecution was acting pursuant to the order of the Appeals Chamber in *Kamuhanda*.[560] In relation to the alleged defects in the indictment, the Prosecution responded that Rule 77 (A) is not an exhaustive list of the forms of contempt and that Rule 77 (B) provides for the punishment of attempts to commit the acts listed in Rule 77 (A). Based on these submissions, the Prosecution asked that the Defence motion be dismissed as being without merit.

114.   On 22 April 2008, the Defence filed a reply to the Prosecution's response submitting that it would defer replying to the Prosecution's response until it filed its Rule 72 motion, following a ruling by the Chamber on when the Rule 72 deadline starts to run.[561]

115.   On 24 June 2008, the Defence filed preliminary motions pursuant to Rule 72 and an alternative motion under Rule 73 to dismiss the indictment.[562] These motions replaced their earlier preliminary *pro forma* motions. The Defence challenged the authority of the Prosecution to prosecute the Accused in the current case, alleging that the Prosecution had not received a directive from any Chamber to investigate or prosecute the Accused. The Defence also requested the withdrawal of counts three and four in the Indictment, arguing that attempt to commit acts punishable as contempt is not a violation of the Statute or Rules and the counts should be struck due to their lack of coherence. Finally, the Defence also brought to the attention of the Chamber that the Accused had not been assigned counsel despite 120 days of detention, reserving the Defence's right to request relief from the Chamber in the form of judicial review for the Registrar's decision not to assign the Accused's chosen counsel to his case.

116.   On 14 November 2008, the Defence filed a preliminary challenge to the Prosecution's jurisdiction and subsidiary motion to dismiss the indictment, arguing that the Prosecution had not been directed by any Chamber to prosecute the Accused for contempt.[563]

117.   On 17 November 2008, the Prosecution filed an urgent request asking the Accused to admit certain facts in order to clarify the issues that needed to be addressed at trial.[564] The Defence responded on 19 November 2008, indicating it would be not be able to respond until **[page 80]** after 24 November 2008, and noting that the request had not been translated into French yet.[565] On 17 December 2008, the Defence filed the Accused's answers to the Prosecution's request.[566]

118.   The Prosecution responded to the Defence challenge to the Prosecution's jurisdiction on 19 November 2008.[567] It argued that the Appeals Chamber had made a specific order to the Prosecution to perform an investigation, and that when confirming the Indictment the Confirming Judge allowed the trial to proceed, thereby authorizing the Prosecution to prosecute the Accused.

---

[560]   "Prosecutor's Response to Nshogoza – Preliminary Pro Forma Submissions in Support of Preliminary Motions Pursuant to Rule 72 of the ICTR Rules of Procedure and Evidence Filed on 14 April 2008," filed 16 April 2008.
[561]   "Defence Reply to Prosecutor's Response to Defence Preliminary Submissions Pursuant to Rule 72," filed 22 April 2008.
[562]   "Preliminary Motions Pursuant to Rule 72, and Alternative Motion under Rule 73 to Dismiss the Indictment," filed 25 June 2008.
[563]   "Defence Preliminary Challenge to Prosecutor's Jurisdiction and Subsidiary Motion to Dismiss the Indictment," filed 14 November 2008.
[564]   "Prosecutor's Urgent Request to Admit Certain Facts," filed 17 November 2008.
[565]   "Defence Preliminary Response to Prosecution Request to Admit Certain Facts," filed 19 November 2008.
[566]   "Mr Nshogoza's Response to Prosecutor's Urgent Request to Admit Certain Facts," filed 17 December 2008.
[567]   "Prosecutor's Response to 'Defence Preliminary Challenge to Prosecutor's Jurisdiction and Subsidiary Motion to Dismiss the Indictment,'" filed 19 November 2008.

119. The Defence replied to the Prosecution's response on 24 November 2008,[568] disputing the Prosecution's submission that the Appeals Chamber directed the Prosecution to investigate and indict the Accused for contempt.

120. The Chamber denied the Defence challenge to the Prosecution's jurisdiction on 17 December 2008, noting that the Appeals Chamber had authorized the Prosecution to conduct investigations and to take the steps it deemed necessary and appropriate under the circumstances.[569]

121. On 25 November 2008, the Prosecution filed its pre-trial brief.[570]

122. On 11 December 2008, the Chamber issued a Scheduling Order ordering that the trial would commence on 9 February 2009, that the Prosecution's case would run until 13 February 2009, that the Defence's case would run from 9 March to 13 March 2009, and that following the close of the Prosecution's case, a Pre-Defence Conference would be held.[571]

123. On 24 December 2008, the Defence filed an application for certification to appeal the Chamber's denial of the Defence preliminary challenge to the Prosecution's jurisdiction, and a subsidiary motion to dismiss the indictment.[572] The Chamber denied the motion on 4 February 2009,[573] as it was not satisfied that the Defence had satisfied the requirements for certification.

124. On 6 February 2009, the Defence filed a motion for the translation of official filings in French,[574] submitting that there have been serious and continuous violations of the rights of the Accused as multiple decisions and orders of the Chamber, and documents filed by the Prosecution, had not been translated into Kinyarwanda or French. The Chamber denied the **[page 81]** motion on 12 February 2009,[575] as it was not satisfied that the Defence could not resolve the matter directly with the Registrar, nor had the Defence shown how the unavailability of the translations impacted upon the trial or affected the rights of the Accused.

9. Trial

125. At a Status Conference on 28 August 2008, the Chamber vacated the original trial date, and advised parties that a new date would be found.[576]

126. The trial commenced on 9 February 2009 and the Prosecution presented its opening statement.[577] The Prosecution called a total of 6 witnesses and the Defence called a total of 11 witnesses.

127. On 9 February 2009, the Chamber made an oral order that the Defence make all Rule 98 *bis* submissions immediately after the close of the Prosecution case.[578] The next day the Defence filed a motion requesting reconsideration of this decision, submitting that it was erroneous.[579] In an oral decision, the Chamber again ordered that all Rule 98 *bis* submissions would be made orally three days after the close of the Prosecution's case.[580]

---

[568] "Defence Reply to Prosecutor's Response to Defence Motion under Rule 72 and Alternatively, Rule 73," filed 24 November 2008.
[569] Decision on Defence Preliminary Challenge to Prosecutor's Jurisdiction and Subsidiary Motion to Dismiss the Indictment, 17 December 2008.
[570] "Prosecutor's Pre-Trial Brief," filed 25 November 2008.
[571] Scheduling Order, 11 December 2008.
[572] "Defence Application for Certification of Trial Chamber Decision on Defence Preliminary Challenge to Prosecutor's Authority and Subsidiary Motion to Dismiss the Indictment," filed 24 December 2008.
[573] Decision on Defence Motion for Certification to Appeal the Chamber's Decision of 17 December 2008 on Defence Preliminary Challenges, 4 February 2009.
[574] "Defence Motion for Translation of Official Filings into French," filed 6 February 2009.
[575] Decision on the Defence Motion for Urgent Translation of Official Filings into French, 12 February 2009.
[576] T. 28 August 2008 p. 11 (closed session).
[577] T. 9 February 2009 p. 9-15.
[578] T. 9 February 2009 p. 2.
[579] "Defence Request for Reconsideration of the Trial Chamber's Oral Decision on the Time for Filing a Motion for Judgement of Acquittal Pursuant to Rule 98 *bis*," filed 10 February 2009.
[580] T. 11 February 2009 p. 48-49.

128. On 12 February 2009, the Prosecution filed an urgent and confidential motion requesting the admission of evidence of a consistent pattern of conduct, pursuant to Rules 54, 77, 89 (C) and 93.[581] The Defence filed its response on 17 February 2009.[582] The Defence argued, among other things, that Rule 93 only applied to evidence of serious violations of international humanitarian law and that the evidence to be admitted is not evidence of a consistent pattern of conduct.

129. On 20 February 2009, the Chamber denied the Prosecution's motion to admit evidence of a consistent pattern of conduct,[583] not being satisfied that the evidence put forward by the Prosecution amounted to evidence of a consistent pattern of conduct and that any probative value of the evidence was substantially outweighed by its prejudicial affect.

130. On 18 February 2009, the Chamber made an oral ruling, overruling an objection by the Prosecution to a line of questioning the Defence had taken against Witness GAA.[584] The Chamber found that the Defence was allowed to question Witness GAA regarding his prior statements and presence at Gikomero parish.

[page 82]

131. On 19 February 2009, the Chamber ordered the Prosecution to certify that it had done his best to get certain judicial documents from the Rwandan authorities and other sources.[585] On 23 February 2009, the Prosecution certified that disclosure had been completed and reiterated that it was under no obligation to obtain judicial material in relation to his witnesses from Rwanda.[586]

132. On 20 February 2009, the Defence filed a motion requesting a one-week postponement of the Defence case, due to the Prosecution's case lasting longer than originally scheduled.[587] The Chamber denied the motion on 26 February 2009,[588] finding that the scheduling of the Defence case was not premised on the amount of time passing between it and the Prosecution's case.

133. On 2 March 2009, the Defence filed a request for reconsideration of the Chamber's 26 February 2009 decision and for postponement of the filing of the pre-defence brief.[589] The motion submitted, among other things, that the Defence had recently received confirmation from DCDMS of a 6-day work programmed in Rwanda, that this amounted to a new material circumstance justifying reconsideration and that it indicated that the trial preparation would take at least six days. The Chamber denied reconsideration 4 March 2009,[590] finding that the approval of the Defence work programme did not constitute new material circumstances warranting reconsideration and that the Defence had not demonstrated an abuse of law or error of discretion. The Chamber did grant the Defence request for an extension of time to file a pre-defence brief.[591]

134. On 6 March 2009, the Defence requested certification to appeal the Chamber's decision denying reconsideration,[592] submitting, among other things, that the Chamber erred in not finding the approval of a work programme a new material circumstance warranting reconsideration and erred in finding that the denial of postponement violated the rights of the Accused. The Chamber denied the request on 11 March

---

[581] "[CONFIDENTIAL] Extremely Urgent Prosecutor's Motion for the Admission of Evidence of Consistent Pattern of Conduct," filed 12 February 2009.
[582] "Defence Response to Extremely Urgent Prosecutor's Motion for the Admission of Evidence of Consistent Pattern of Conduct," filed 17 February 2009; "Defence Notice of Intention to File Response to the "Extremely Urgent Prosecutor's Motion for the Admission of Evidence of Consistent Pattern of Conduct"," filed 16 February 2009.
[583] Decision on Prosecutor's Motion to Admit Evidence of a Consistent Pattern of Conduct, 20 February 2009.
[584] T. 18 February 2009 pp. 26-27.
[585] T. 19 February 2009 p. 17.
[586] "Prosecutor's Certification on Rwandan Judicial Materials," filed 23 February 2009.
[587] "[CONFIDENTIAL] Preliminary List of Defence Witnesses and Motion for One Week Postponement of Defence Case," filed 20 February 2009.
[588] Decision on Defence Motion for Postponement of Defence Case, 26 February 2009.
[589] "Defence Request for Reconsideration of the 'Decision on Defence Motion for Postponement of the Defence Case' and Request to Postpone the Filing of the Pre-Defence Brief," filed 2 March 2009.
[590] Decision on Defence Motion for Reconsideration of the Chamber's Decision on Motion for Postponement of Defence Case, 4 March 2009.
[591] Decision on Defence Request for an Extension of Time to File a Pre-Defence Brief, 4 March 2009.
[592] "Defence Motion for Certification of the Trial Chamber's "Decision on Defence Motion for Reconsideration of the Chamber's Decision on Motion for Postponement of Defence Case"," filed 6 March 2009.

2009,[593] finding that the Defence had not demonstrated that the decision satisfied the requirements for certification.

135. On 23 February 2009, the Defence filed a motion requesting the Chamber to take judicial notice of the fact that Rwanda first issued a 2,000 franc note in 2007.[594] The motion was granted on 16 April 2009.[595]

136. On 25 February 2009, the parties made oral arguments on a Defence motion for judgement of acquittal pursuant to Rule 98 bis. On 25 February 2009, the Defence filed **[page 83]** supplementary submissions of case law that it relied upon in its oral arguments for an acquittal.[596] The Chamber denied the motion for judgement of acquittal in respect of all counts of the indictment on 27 February 2009.[597]

137. On 9 March 2009, the Defence filed its confidential pre-defence brief.[598]

138. On 12 March 2009, the Defence filed submissions on the commencement of the Defence case,[599] submitting that the Defence would be ready to proceed with its case on 16 March 2009.

139. During opening statements on 16 March 2009, Defence Counsel orally moved the Chamber to reconsider its decision on sanctions.[600] This was denied on 23 April 2009. The Chamber found that the Defence had not raised any new material circumstances, did not demonstrate the decision was erroneous or an abuse of discretion and did not demonstrate that it had caused prejudice or injustice to the Accused.[601]

140. On 17 March 2009, the Chamber issued an authoritative written version of its oral decision of 16 March 2009,[602] sanctioning Defence Counsel for misconduct.[603] The Chamber found that the conduct of Defence Counsel had led to unnecessary delay, had been contrary to the interests of justice and was inconsistent with the Code of Conduct for Defence Counsel. It further found that the conduct was not in the interest of the Accused and was not consistent with the Accused's right to a fair and expeditious trial. The Chamber fined Defence Counsel and directed the Registrar to seek the President's approval to communicate the misconduct to the professional body that regulates the conduct of counsel in her State of admission.

141. On 20 March 2009, the Defence filed a motion asking the Chamber to order the Registrar to provide information to the Defence regarding visits by the Prosecution to Witness GAA in 2007, following denial of Defence requests for the information by the Registry.[604] The Registrar filed submissions on the motion on 23 March 2009,[605] stating that it considered it was unable to release the requested documents without an order from the Chamber. The Chamber granted the Defence request on 28 April 2009, and ordered the Registrar to provide the requested information.[606] The Registrar disclosed the information on 29 April 2009.[607] **[page 84]**

142. On 8 May 2009, the Defence filed further submissions on the Registrar's disclosure of Prosecution visits to Witness GAA at the UNDF.[608] The Defence submitted that the Registrar's disclosure was incomplete

---

[593] Decision on Defence Motion for Certification to Appeal the Chamber's Decision Denying a One Week Postponement of the Defence Case, 11 March 2009.
[594] "Defence Motion for Judicial Notice," filed 23 February 2009.
[595] Decision on Defence Motion for Judicial Notice, 16 April 2009.
[596] "Defence Supplementary Submissions under Rule 98 bis," filed 25 February 2009.
[597] T. 27 February 2009 pp. 1-7.
[598] "[CONFIDENTIAL] Pre-Defence Brief of Léonidas Nshogoza," filed 9 March 2009.
[599] "Defence Submissions on Commencement of Defence Case," filed 12 March 2009.
[600] T. 16 March 2009 p. 3.
[601] Decision on Oral Motion for Reconsideration of Sanctions, 23 April 2009.
[602] T. 16 March 2009 pp. 1-2.
[603] Further Decision to Sanction Defence Counsel for Misconduct, 17 March 2009.
[604] "Defence Motion for Order to Registrar to Provide Information to the Nshogoza Defence Regarding Prosecution Visits to GAA at UNDF in 2007," filed 20 March 2009.
[605] "Registrar's Submissions under Rule 33 (B) of the Rules on the Defence Motion for Order to Registrar to Provide Information to the Nshogoza Defence Regarding Prosecution Visits to GAA at UNDF in 2007," filed 23 March 2009.
[606] Decision on Defence Motion for Order to Registrar to Provide Information to the Defence Regarding Prosecution Visits to Witness GAA at UNDF, 28 April 2009.
[607] "Registrar's Submissions under Rule 33 (B) of the Rules on the Decision of Defence Motion for Order to Registrar to Provide Information to the Defence Regarding Prosecution Visits to Witness GAA at UNDF," filed 29 April 2009.
[608] "Defence Further Motion to Order Registrar to Provide Complete Information on OTP Visits to GAA and Motion to Order Prosecutor to Provide Information and to Comply with Rule 66 and 68 Disclosure Obligations," filed 8 May 2009.

and erroneous and requested the Chamber to order the Registrar to complete its disclosure and to order the Prosecution to disclose the purpose of its visits to Witness GAA. The motion also requested the Chamber to sanction the Prosecution for violating its disclosure obligations. The motion was denied on 8 June 2009.[609]

143. On 25 March 2009, Defence Counsel filed an appeal to the Appeals Chamber of the decision of the Trial Chamber to sanction Defence Counsel, asking the Appeals Chamber to suspend the obligation to pay the fines imposed.[610] The appeal argued, among other things, that the imposed fine amounted to a penal sanction, that the sanction had no legal basis, that the Chamber abuse its discretion by imposing the sanction and that the fine was manifestly excessive.

144. The Prosecution responded on 6 April 2009,[611] submitting that Defence Counsel had no standing to make the appeal and that therefore the appeal was not properly before the Appeals Chamber. The Defence replied to the response on 16 April 2009,[612] submitting, among other things, that the Prosecution had no standing to file his response and contesting the Prosecution's argument that the Defence Counsel had no standing to bring her motion.

145. The Appeals Chamber assigned judges to the motion on 23 April 2009.[613] On 8 June 2009, the Defence filed its Entry of Appearance and requested an extension of time to file its brief and other materials.[614] The Appeals Chamber rendered its decision on 26 June 2009, denying the request for an extension of time, quashing the pecuniary sanctions imposed on Defence Counsel and instructing the Registrar to pay Defence Counsel the fine extracted from her last payment instalment.[615]

146. On 8 April 2009, the Defence filed a motion requesting the Trial Chamber to take judicial notice of the value of the Rwandan currency in United States dollars at the times relevant to the indictment and its current value.[616] On 14 April 2009, the Chamber denied this motion.[617] **[page 85]**

147. On 18 June 2009, the Defence filed a confidential motion requesting the Chamber to issue a public version of its confidential decision on the Defence motion for a stay of proceedings.[618] The Chamber granted the motion on 26 June 2009.[619]

148. On 17 April 2009, the Prosecution filed its confidential closing brief.[620] The Defence filed its confidential closing brief on the same day.[621] On 18 June 2009, the Defence filed its supplemental closing brief.[622]

149. On 12 June 2009, the Chamber scheduled the public hearing of the delivery of its judgement for 2 July 2009.[623]

---

[609] Decision on Defence Further Motion for Order to Registrar to Provide Information to the Defence Regarding Prosecution Visits to Witness GAA at UNDF, 8 June 2009.
[610] "Defence Counsel Appeal as of Right from Sanctions Decision," filed 25 March 2009.
[611] "Prosecutor's Response to 'Defence Counsel Appeals as of Right from Sanctions Decision,'" filed 6 April 2009.
[612] "Defence Counsel Reply to Prosecution Response to Appeal as of Right from Sanctions Decisions," filed 16 April 2009.
[613] Order Assigning Judges to a Case Before the Appeals Chamber (AC), 23 April 2009.
[614] "Entry of Appearance and Request for Extension of Time to File Brief and/or Other Materials Concerning Defence Counsel Appeal of 25 March 2009," filed 8 June 2009.
[615] Decision on Appeal Concerning Sanctions (AC), 26 June 2009.
[616] "Defence Request that the Trial Chamber Take Judicial Notice of the Value of Rwandan Currency," filed 8 April 2009.
[617] Decision on Defence Motion for the Trial Chamber to Take Judicial Notice of the Value of the Rwandan Currency, 16 April 2009.
[618] "Defence Motion Requesting that the Chamber Issues a Public Version of the 'Confidential Decision on the Defence Motion for a Stay of Proceedings," filed 18 June 2009.
[619] Decision on Defence Motion to Make Public the Confidential Decision on Defence Motion for Stay of Proceedings; and Annexure Comprising Redacted Version of Said Decision for Public Consumption, 26 June 2009.
[620] "[CONFIDENTIAL] Prosecutor's Closing Brief," filed 17 April 2009.
[621] "[CONFIDENTIAL] Closing Brief of Léonidas Nshogoza," filed 17 April 2009; "Closing Brief of Léonidas Nshogoza Filed 17 April 2009 Annexure C," filed 20 April 2009; "Closing Brief of Léonidas Nshogoza – Corrigendum," filed 28 April 2009.
[622] "Supplemental Closing Brief of Léonidas Nshogoza," filed 19 June 2009.
[623] Scheduling Order, 12 June 2009.

Commentary

1. Introduction

On 2 July 2009 Léonidas Nshogoza, an investigator in the Defence team in the case of Jean de Dieu Kamuhanda,[1] was found guilty of contempt of the tribunal and sentenced to a ten-month imprisonment.[2] He was given credit for the time he had already served in custody since February 2008; the chamber subsequently ordered his immediate release. Nshogoza appealed without success; his conviction and sentence were confirmed on 15 March 2010.[3]

Nshogoza was charged, pursuant to Rule 77 of the Rules of Procedure and Evidence (RPE), to the following acts: wilful interference with the administration of justice, attempt to subvert the course of justice by discussing the trial with third parties, procuring false statements from protected witnesses and inciting witnesses to give false testimony by offering high bribes. The court only convicted him on one count of contempt. Nshogoza met with two protected witnesses and disclosed their statements. One of them recanted his trial testimony before the Appeal Chamber and denied that he had seen Kamuhanda leading attackers in a massacre. Later this witness was sentenced for false testimony and contempt of the tribunal.[4] The grave counts against Nshogoza could not be proved beyond reasonable doubt.[5]

Both the grounds of the judgment and the disproportionate prison term raise questions.

2. Critical issues of criminal contempt

The crime of contempt of the tribunal is described in Rule 77 RPE. For a long time, there have been two objections against the criminalisation of contempt: Rule 77 RPE exceeds the jurisdiction of the ICTR, established in Article 1 ICTR Statute[6] and the other objection concerns a violation of the principle of legality (*nulla poena sine lege*).[7] In the case of Nshogoza, both objections are partially correct and they are both connected to each other. Finally, the extraordinary flexibility of criminal contempt raises doubts concerning the culpability of this behaviour.

2.1. The competence to create the offence of contempt

Just as Article 1 ICTY Statute, the equally worded Article 1 ICTR Statute entitles the jurisdiction of the tribunal to pursue serious violations of international humanitarian law. Genocide, crimes against humanity and war crimes are laid down in Article 2, paragraph 4, ICTR Statute. These crimes constitute customary international law. Thus, the *ad hoc* tribunals were empowered to enforce existing law and not to enact new law, which is important with regard to the prohibition of retroactive punishment.[8] Penal power beyond the scope of the statute was not supposed to be established. The ICTR Statute itself does not contain specific and detailed rules regarding the criminal procedure, but Article 14 ICTR Statute authorizes the court to enact

---

[1] ICTR, Judgement, *Prosecutor v. Kamuhanda*, Case No. ICTR-95-54A-T, T. Ch. II, 22 January 2004; the judgment was confirmed by ICTR, Judgement, *Kamuhanda v. Prosecutor*, Case No. ICTR-99-54A-A, A. Ch., 19 September 2005, Klip/ Sluiter, ALC-XXII-721.
[2] ICTR, Judgement, *Prosecutor v. Nshogoza*, Case No. ICTR-07-91-T, T. Ch. III, 7 July 2009, in this volume, p. 509.
[3] ICTR, Judgement, *Nshogoza v. Prosecutor*, Case No. ICTR-2007-91-A, A. Ch., 15 March 2010. The Nshogoza judgment was the first contempt judgment issued by the ICTR Appeals Chamber. For a short overview Katharina Margetts and Katerina I. Kappos, Current Developments at the Ad Hoc International Criminal Tribunals, Journal of International Criminal Justice (2010), p. 1, 33 and 44.
[4] After reaching a plea agreement with the Prosecution, ICTR, Judgement, *Prosecutor v. GAA*, Case No. ICTR-07-90-R77-I, T. Ch. III, 4 December 2007, Klip/ Sluiter, ALC-XXXI-613 with a commentary by Thom Dieben.
[5] Trial Chamber Judgement, *supra* note 2, par. 96–153, 190–211.
[6] See André Klip, Witnesses before the International Criminal Tribunal for the Former Yugoslavia, 67 International Review of Penal Law 1996, p. 267 and 276; *Cf.* J. Cockayne, Commentary, Klip/ Sluiter, ALC-IV-191, p. 192 ff.; Michael Bohlander, International Criminal Tribunals and Their Power to Punish Contempt and False Testimony, 12 Criminal Law Forum 2001, p. 91, 117; Gwendolyn Stamper, Infusing Due Process and the Principle of Legality into Contempt Proceedings before the International Criminal Tribunal for the former Yugoslavia and the International Criminal Tribunal for Rwanda, 109 Michigan Law Review 2011, p. 1551.
[7] See Göran Sluiter, The ICTY and Offences against the Administration of Justice, 2 Journal of International Criminal Justice 2004, p. 631, 634; *Cf.* Taru Spronken, Commentary, Klip/ Sluiter, ALC-VII-225, p. 228; Gwendolyn Stamper, *supra* note 6, p. 1565.
[8] *Cf.* Gwendolyn Stamper, *supra* note 6, p. 1570.

such rules. The RPE is based on this authorization. Still, the ICTR Statute does not mention prosecuting or punishing contempt.[9]

Confronted with the objection of an *ultra vires* exercise of powers, the Trial Chamber constantly refers to their jurisdiction over the punishment of contempt, as a function of their inherent power, which derives from their function as a judicial body.[10] Article 1 ICTR, thus describes primary or original jurisdiction of the tribunal, respectively. This has to be distinguished from the inherent jurisdiction because the latter means a residual power, which must derive from the requirements of the judicial function itself.[11] In other words, the court has to achieve justice and therefore, the tribunal itself has to respect the principles of a fair trial. This implies, that the court can compel parties to abide by the rules of procedure, and use criminal sanctions if need be.

For a continental codification-based point of view a court establishing criminal rules out of its own competence is not an acceptable idea of how to make law; however it is prevalent in Common Law systems to have primacy of judge-made law.[12] In favour of Rule 77 RPE, one could argue as follows: political circumstances in the Security Council render details regarding the exact powers of the Tribunals vague; therefore, the judges had to improvise by establishing these rules in order to perform their function. After all, both the ICTR Statute as well as the ICTY Statute do not explicitly prohibit the use of inherent powers. However, the concept generally utilised in Common Law systems. At last, there is no conceivable legal system that does not criminalize giving false testimony, presenting manipulated evidence or obstructing witnesses, regardless of whether it is formed out as criminal contempt or in another conception.[13] There is no serious controversy about the culpability of the crimes named in Article 70, paragraph 1, ICC Statute. The same is true for Rule 77 RPE in its former more limited versions, which included a detailed list of different forms of contempt.

However, Rule 77 RPE was never known to be a closed list of culpable forms of contempt. The reason for that is the concept of inherent powers: as inherent powers are a result of the judicial function of a judicial body, they imply that any statute cannot limit them. That is why Rule 77 (F) RPE of the ICTY in the version from 12 November 1997 was: "Nothing in the Rule affects the inherent power of the Tribunal to hold in contempt those who knowingly and wilfully interfere with its administration of justice." Indeed, in the version from 13 December 2001, this paragraph was abolished and it never appeared in the corresponding Rule 77 RPE of the ICTR.[14] This interpretation continued to be utilised by the *ad hoc* international criminal tribunals. Regardless of multiple changes and enhancements of the definition of criminal contempt, Rule 77

---

[9] ICTY, Judgement on Allegations of Contempt against Prior Counsel, Milan Vujin, *Prosecutor v. Tadić*, Case No. IT-94-1-A-R77, A. Ch., 31 January 2000, Klip/ Sluiter, ALC-IV-145, par. 24 states, that Article 15 ICTY Statute "does not permit rules to be adopted which constitute *new* offences". However, in the jurisdiction of the ICTY criminal contempt is not seen as a new offence. In contrast ICTY, Appeal Judgement on Allegations of Contempt Against Prior Council, Milan Vujin, *Prosecutor v. Tadić*, Case No. IT-94-1-A-R77, A. Ch., 27 February 2001, Klip/ Sluiter, ALC-VII-195 (with a commentary by Taru Spronken, p. 225), points to "other appropriate matters" in that Article; *Cf.* Göran Sluiter, *supra* note 7, p. 634.

[10] Trial Chamber Judgement, *supra* note 2, par. 2 with reference to Vujin Contempt Judgement, *supra* note 9, par. 13, 18 and 26; ICTY, Judgement in the Matter of Contempt Allegations against an Accused and his Counsel, *Prosecutor v. Simić et al*, Case No. IT-95-9-R77, T. Ch. III, 30 June 2000, Klip/ Sluiter, ALC-V-231, par. 91; ICTY, Judgement on Appeal by Anto Nobilo against a Finding of Contempt, *Prosecutor v. Aleksovski*, Case No. IT-95-14/1-AR77, A. Ch., 30 May 2001, Klip/ Sluiter, ALC-VII-205, par. 30; ICTY, Decision on Interlocutory Appeal on Kosta Bulatović Contempt Proceedings, *Prosecutor v. Slobodan Milosevic*, Case No. IT-02-54-A-R77.4, A. Ch., 29 August 2005, Klip/ Sluiter, ALC-XXVII-243, par. 21; ICTY, Appeal Judgement, *Prosecutor v. Marijačić and Rebić*, Case No. IT-95-14-R77.2-A, A. Ch., 27 September 2006, par. 23 and 24. In contrast, ICTR, Decision on the Prosecutor's further Allegations of Contempt, *Prosecutor v. Nyiramasukuho*, Case No. ICTR-97-21-T, *Nsabimana*, Case No. ICTR-97-29-T, *Kanyabashi*, Case No. ICTR-96-15-T *and Ndayambaje*, Case No. ICTR-96-8-T, T. Ch. II, 30 November 2001, Klip/ Sluiter, ALC-X-263, par. 7 refers to its statuary powers, but the ICTR Statute is silent in this respect. For a more detailed analysis see Michael Bohlander, *supra* note 6, p. 97; Gwendolyn Stamper, *supra* note 6, p. 1558.

[11] Cp. ICTY, Decision on the Defence Motion for Interlocutory Appeal on Jurisdiction, *Prosecutor v. Tadić*, Case No. IT-94-1-A-R72, T. Ch., 2 October 1995, Klip/ Sluiter, ALC-I-31, par. 14; see also Silvia D'Ascoli, Sentencing Contempt of Court in International Criminal Justice, 5 Journal of International Criminal Justice 2007, p. 735 and 737.

[12] *Cf.* Supreme Court, *Chambers v. Nasco Inc.*, 501 U.S. 32 (1991), 43; in detail C. J. Miller, Contempt of Court, 3rd ed., Oxford 2000.

[13] Cp. Göran Sluiter, *supra* note 7, p. 631; examples are the so-called "Aussagedelikte (§§153 ff. StGB) or "Strafvereitelung" (§258 StGB) in German Criminal Law.

[14] About contempt, Rule 77 RPE ICTR was framed differently in the past. The actual – wider – version was adopted on 27 May 2003.

(A) RPE does not contain an exhaustive list of criminal conduct.[15] The wording "including" indicates that all behaviour that may lead to interference into the proceedings may be prosecuted as criminal contempt. This approach does not correspond with *nulla poena sine lege*.

Consequently, "otherwise interfering with a witness", Rule 77 (A) (iv) RPE, is seen as an "open-ended provision which encompasses any conduct that is intended to disturb the administration of justice ... or in any way to influence the nature of the witness' or potential witness' evidence".[16] Much behaviour can be subsumed beneath this, especially if there is – like the Trial Chamber in the case of Nshogoza – no requirement that the conduct in question is sufficiently serious, but "any deliberate (...) conduct that interferes with the administration of justice", more precisely: any defiance of a court order is sufficient.[17] This makes the concept of inherent powers nearly infinite – disregarding hierarchy of legal principles.[18] This may correspond to the Common Law system,[19] but there are other standards in other legal systems, and there is no comparative relation to these systems.[20] With regard to the jurisdiction of the tribunal, this seems to be precarious.

2.2. Criminal contempt and the principle of legality

While in a statute law system the phrase of the statute in question is the decisive criterion, in common law it is the foreseeability and accessibility of the relevant case law. Like the European Court of Human Rights,[21] the ICTY emphasizes the latter aspect more than *lex stricta* and *praevia*.[22] It has to be possible for everyone to know the rules, whereby the violation thereof is punishable by the criminal law. Otherwise one can not follow them. Criminal law works this way.[23]

About *lex stricta*, vague and open-ended provisions are a problem generally. For the addressee of the norm it is only possible to infer from similar situations, which behaviour could be forbidden. Its manner and impact has to be similar to the explicitly forbidden behaviour and sufficiently evil to warrant punishment. In this way, "otherwise inferring with a witness" according to Rule 77 (A) (iv) RPE can be any conduct which is intended to deter a witness from giving his evidence or every attempt to influence the nature of a witness' testimony.[24]

---

[15] *Cp.* Vujin Contempt Judgement, *supra* note 9, par. 28; Simić Contempt Judgment, *supra* note 10, par. 91; Nobilo Contempt Appeal Judgment, *supra* note 10, par. 38; ICTY, Judgement on Allegations of Contempt, *Prosecutor v. Margetić*, Case No. IT-95-14-R77.6, T. Ch. I, 7 February 2007, to be published in Volume XXXIII, par. 13; just as well the Trial Chamber Judgement, *supra* note 2, par. 156.

[16] Trial Chamber Judgement, *supra* note 2, par. 158 and 193 with reference to ICTY, Judgement on Contempt Allegations, *Prosecutor v. Beqaj*, Case No. IT-03-66-T-R77, T. Ch. II, 27 May 2005, par. 21; Margetić Contempt Judgement, *supra* note 15, par. 64; ICTY, Judgement on Allegations of Contempt, *Prosecutor v. Haraqija and Morina*, Case No. IT-04-84-R77.4, T. Ch. I, 17 December 2008, to be published in Volume XXXVII, par. 18.

[17] Trial Chamber Judgement, *supra* note 2, par. 174 and 175 with reference to ICTY, Appeal Judgement, *Prosecutor v. Jović*, Case No. IT-95-14 & 14/2-R77-A, A. Ch., 15 March 2007, par. 30; *Cf.* Marijačić and Rebić Appeal Judgement, *supra* note 10, par. 44. The Appeals Chamber Judgement, *supra* note 3, par. 56.

[18] See for instance ICTY, Judgement on the Request of the Republic of Croatia for Review of the Decision of the Trial Chamber II of 18 July 1997, *Prosecutor v. Blaškić*, Case No. IT-95-14-AR108bis, A. Ch., 29 October 1997, Klip/ Sluiter, ALC-I-245, par. 25: subpoenas to states run against international law principles; ICTY, Decision on the Prosecution Motion Under Rule 73 for a Ruling Concerning the Testimony of a Witness, *Prosecutor v. Simić et al.*, Case No. IT-95-9-PT, T. Ch., 27 July 1999, Klip/ Sluiter, ALC-IV-213 (with a commentary by Göran Sluiter, p. 271), par. 44: customary law allows nondisclosure from Red Cross employees.

[19] *Cf.* Supreme Court, *Young v. United States ex rel. Vuitton et Fils*, 481 U.S. 787 (1987), 798: "The underlying concern that gave rise to the contempt power was not, however, merely the disruption of court proceedings. Rather, it was disobedience to the orders of the Judiciary ..."

[20] Even though for instance Beqaj Contempt Judgement, *supra* note 16, par. 12 refers to "well established principle both in major common law and in civil law legal systems". See a critical analysis Göran Sluiter, *supra* note 7, p. 633; Taru Spronken, *supra* note 7, p. 226.

[21] *Cf.* ECtHR, Judgement, *Kokkinakis v. Greece*, Application No. 14307/88, 25 May 1993, par. 40, 52; ECtHR, Judgement, *S.W. v. United Kingdom*, Application No. 20166/92, 22 November 1995, par. 35; ECtHR, Judgment, *Cantoni v. France*, Application No. 17862/91, Grand Chamber, 15 November 1996, par. 29; for more details see Joachim Renzikowski, Commentary to Article 7 ECHR, in: Wolfram Karl (ed.), Internationaler Kommentar zur Europäischen Konvention der Menschenrechte und Grundfreiheiten, Heymanns Verlag, Köln, 12th supply May 2009, Art. 7 par. 53–58.

[22] *Cf.* ICTY, Decision on Interlocutory Appeal Challenging Jurisdiction in Relation to Command Responsibility, *Prosecutor v. Hadžihasanović et al.*, Case No. IT-01-47-AR72, A. Ch., 16 July 2003, Klip/ Sluiter, ALC-XI-73, par. 34; discerning Gwendolyn Stamper, *supra note* 6, p. 1566.

[23] See Bentham, Of Laws in General, H.L.A. Hart (ed.), Athlone Press, London 1970, p. 140.

[24] Cp. Trial Chamber Judgement, *supra* note 2, par. 193; see also Margetić Contempt Judgement, *supra* note 15, par. 64: "any conduct which is likely to expose witnesses to threats, intimidation or injury."

In the Nshogoza case, none of this could be proved. Nevertheless, the Trial Chamber states: "Any violation of an order of a Chamber is a sufficient *actus reus* for contempt."[25] A threshold of gravity, compared to the other forms of contempt listed in Rule 77 RPE, is not required. As a result, every violation of a judicial order can be punished. The order in the trial of Kamuhanda[26] was sufficiently clear and the counsels of defence could understand how to interact with the protected witnesses. However, from this it does not follow that the accused could anticipate that any non-compliance is punishable. There are no similar international standards.[27]

The Appeals Chamber states that minimal gravity should only be understood as an exercise of the discretion of the court to initiate proceedings or not.[28] The principle of legal certainty is not observed sufficiently, if it is within the court's discretion to pursue contempt or not in this way.

It is worth noticing that the ICC Statute follows another method. Like in statute law systems the punishable actions are exhaustively listed in Article 70 ("Offences against the administration of justice") and Article 71 ("Misconduct before the court").[29] In this law, the problem that the prosecution of contempt potentially has no limit does not arise.

2.3. Is there a necessity to punish simple non-compliance?

Offences against the administration of justice pose a serious threat to the truth-finding process. As the exploration of the truth can be seen as the foundation of a just sentence, it cannot be thwarted. Because of that, it is necessary to prevent every manipulation of evidence. Perjury hinders the course of justice and can lead to a miscarriage of justice. One can name good reasons for witness protection: first, the possibility of adequate taking of evidence needs to be ensured. In addition, the safety of those, who liaise closely with the law enforcement agency, has to be guaranteed, especially when acts of revenge are expected. A witness will not willingly cooperate, when that may mean fearing for one's own life.[30]

The Trial Chamber extends protection to potential witnesses, who already supplied information to the prosecution.[31] The decision to call a person as a witness at trial is made after evaluating all the evidence. A prerequisite for the testimony of witnesses is confidentiality and safety, which must be guaranteed even to potential witnesses. Hence witness protection must start before the witness is formally called at trial. In fact both Rule 69 RPE and Rule 75 RPE refer only to "witnesses", but it is not immediately obvious that "potential witnesses" should be excluded from protection.[32] This also applies for the different formulations about witness protection used by the Kamuhanda Trial Chamber.[33] The same is true for the (potential) witnesses of the defense. It is possible that excessive shielding of witnesses can affect the right to an effective defense (*cf.* Article 19, paragraph 1, ICTR Statute). This fear will prove unfounded, if the possibility of questioning the witnesses can be ensured.[34] In the case of Kamuhanda such proceedings existed: The defence had to inform the prosecution and make a written request to the court to contact the protected witness in question.

---

[25] Trial Chamber Judgement, *supra* note 2, par. 174 and 175; also Marijačić and Rebić Appeal Judgement, *supra* note 10, par. 44; Jović Appeal Judgement, *supra* note 17, par. 30.
[26] ICTR, Decision on the Prosecutor's Motion for Protective Measures for Witnesses, *Prosecutor v. Kamuhanda*, Case No. ICTR-99-50-I, T. Ch. II, 7 July 2000.
[27] *Cf.* Gwendolyn Stamper, *supra* note 6, p. 1567.
[28] Appeals Chamber Judgment, *supra* note 3, par. 57.
[29] For details *Cf.* Christoph Safferling, International Criminal Procedure, Oxford 2012, p. 560–573.
[30] For more details see Göran Sluiter, The ICTR and the Protection of Witnesses, 3 Journal of International Criminal Justice 2005, p. 962–976; Vladimir Tochilovsky, Jurisprudence of the International Criminal Courts and the ECHR: Procedure and Evidence, Martinus Nijhoff Publishers, Boston 2008, p. 217–232.
[31] Trial Chamber Judgement, *supra* note 2, par. 162.
[32] *Cf.* ICTR, Decision on the Prosecution's Motion for Special Protective Measures for Prosecution Witnesses and others, *Prosecutor v. Ngirabatware*, ICTR-99-54-T, T. Ch. II, 6 May 2009, par. 21; ICTR, Decision on Joseph Nzirorera's emergency motion for no contact order and "Requete urgente de Matthieu Ngirumpatse aux fins d'interdire au Procureur de contacter toute personne figurant sur la liste de témoins sans l'accord préalable de ses conseils", *Prosecutor v. Karemera et al.*, ICTR-98-44-T, T. Ch. III, 21 August 2008, par. 9–10.
[33] Appeals Chamber Judgement, *supra* note 3, par. 64.
[34] Trial Chamber Judgement, *supra* note 2, par. 165; more details about the difficult balance between the accused's right to a fair trial and witness protection see Vladimir Tochilovsky, *supra* note 30, p. 220.

Then, the prosecution was obliged to "undertake all necessary arrangements to facilitate such interview".[35] Administrative burdens of this type seem reasonable. However, there has been no indication of the prosecution thwarting a requested interview of the protected witnesses.[36]

The Trial Chamber valued the defendants conduct as an illegal "otherwise inferring with a witness" – meaning "any conduct that is intended to disturb the administration of justice by deterring a witness or a potential witness from giving full and truthful evidence, or in any way to influence the nature of the witness' or potential witness' evidence".[37] There is no need that any results were produced by this conduct.[38] In the interests of guaranteeing effective legal protection, it is appropriate to shift the punishability to an earlier point. Nevertheless, none of these arguments meets the concrete case.

The meetings between the protected witnesses with the accused had been initiated by the witness A7/GEX, who was the neighbor of the protected witness GAA. Both had exchanged views about the procedure long ago. There was no actual endangerment by Nshogoza's conduct nor was there any proof of him manipulating the trial. The administration of justice, in a material meaning was not at all affected.

In contrast the considerations of the Trial Chamber appear to be formal. If a witness abandons any protection, he has to declare his waiver to the tribunal or apply that the witness protection order will be cancelled. Even if a protected witness contacts the defense, the witness protection order needs to be followed, meaning the prosecution has to be informed.[39] The Appeals Chamber asserts that the witness protection order according to Rule 75 (F) (i) RPE remains in force as long as it is not changed or reversed by a judicial decision.[40] According to the ITCR, this is the only way to achieve the safety concerns, namely protection of witnesses' identity and security.[41] This would be the case if protected witnesses are in danger and in need of shielding. There is a danger that special funds (e.g. protected flats) become public because of the witnesses conduct. But in the present case, only the identity of the witnesses should be kept secret. If they reveal themselves, witness protection is not threatened. Obviously the prime aims of the court is to maintain control of its acts and clarity concerning the rules of the trial.[42]

Also the court's dealing with the unauthorised disclosure of the witnesses' identity and statements of the protected witnesses show, that control can be seen as the court's prime aim in the case Nshogoza. The Trial Chamber insists on the validity of the corresponding court order even if the secret information already became known.[43] But this affects neither the protection of witnesses nor any aspects of the trial,[44] because just the punishable offence of the non-compliance remains.

At this point administration of justice can not be understood in any material sense, but only – formal – as a securing of the court's authority. What has been prescribed has to be followed. Offences will be punished. Is there always a need of criminal sanction or should punishment according to the principle of

---

[35] Kamuhanda Decision on Protective Measures, *supra* note 26, par. 2(i), cited after Appeals Chamber Judgment, *supra* note 3, par. 64 fn. 168.
[36] *Cp.* Appeals Chamber Judgement, *supra* note 3, par. 67.
[37] Trial Chamber Judgement, *supra* note 2, par. 193.
[38] See Beqaj Contempt Judgement, *supra* note 16, par. 21; ICTY, Judgement, *Prosecutor v. Marijačić and Rebić*, Case No. IT-95-14-R77.2, T. Ch., 10 March 2006, par. 19; Jović Appeal Judgement, *supra* note 17, par. 30.
[39] Trial Chamber Judgement, *supra* note 2, par. 163 and 164 with reference to ICTR, Decision on the Prosecutor's Urgent Motion for an Immediate Restraining Order Against the Defence's Further Contact with Witness RM-10 and for Other Relief Based on the Ngeze Defence's Violations of Court Decisions and Rules, *Prosecutor v. Nahimana et al.*, Case No. ICTR-99-52-T, T. Ch. I, 17 January 2003, par. 14.
[40] Appeals Chamber Judgement, *supra* note 3, par. 65 with reference to Jović Appeal Judgement, *supra* note 17, par. 30.
[41] Trial Chamber Judgement, *supra* note 2, par. 170; see also Nahimana Decision, *supra* note 39, par. 14.
[42] Appeals Chamber Judgement, *supra* note 3, par. 66.
[43] Trial Chamber Judgement, *supra* note 2, par. 187 with reference to Jović Appeal Judgement, *supra* note 17, par. 30; Marijačić and Rebić Appeal Judgement, *supra* note 10, par. 44.
[44] This objection does not apply for the notarized attest on the testimonies of GAA and A7/GEX, *Cf.* Trial Chamber Judgement, *supra* note 2, par. 186.

proportionality be reserved for grave offences? Irrespective of other findings,[45] the Trial Chamber opts for the first.[46]

If the prosecution of contempt of court follows from the judicial function of a judicial body, then the Trial Chamber should have questioned whether punishment was necessary in this case or not. Was there really a need for punishment to prevent a misuse of the Tribunal's procedure or to avoid the risk that the administration of justice might be disturbed or at least because the authority of the Tribunal might be weakened? The Nobilo Contempt Appeal Judgment stated: "The law of contempt is not designed to buttress the dignity of the judges or to punish mere affronts or insults to a court or tribunal."[47] Instead, the impression is left, that Nshogoza was punished just because of suspicion.

2.4. The *mens rea* of criminal contempt

The Trial Chamber's remarks about *mens rea* deserves a short comment. Article 77 (A) RPE defines the general *mens rea* for all forms of contempt as the knowledge and will to interfere with the administration of justice.[48] Therefore, the defence raised the argument, that Nshogoza did not have "specific intent" to interfere with the administration of justice while acting. The answer depends on the concept of contempt of court. According to a mere formal concept of the *ad hoc* international criminal tribunals, a violation of a court order by itself is sufficient. It is not necessary that the research of truth is actually affected or only endangered. This point of view identifies the administration of justice with the authority of the court. Consequently, it can be seen as sufficient, if the contemner knows the court order, which he deliberately violates.[49]

In a second step the defense argued that Nshogoza did not know that the persons in question were protected witnesses. The Trial Chamber met this objection that mistake of law can not be used as a valid defense.[50] The premise is the distinction between mistake of fact and mistake of law, which is familiar in common law.[51] A mistake of law is irrelevant in principle, except it negates the mental element. The Trial Chamber is inconsistent by arguing, that Nshogoza acted "at least with reckless indifference to whether his actions were in violation of the Protective Measures", when he first met the protected witnesses.[52] This view corresponds with the argumentation within the Nobilo Appeal Judgement, in which the Chamber stated, "Acting with reckless indifference to whether one's actions are in violation of a court is sufficiently culpable conduct for punishment as contempt".[53]

Obviously, there is an overriding of the wording of Rule 77 (A) RPE: indifference is different from knowledge.[54] The general *mens rea* criterion for all forms of criminal contempt is provided in Rule 77 (A) RPE: "knowledge and will". Even if one assumes the list of punishable acts are non exhaustive, nothing within the formulation indicates that the same applies for the necessity of *mens rea*. If one does not take Rule

---

[45] *Cf.* ICTR, Decision on Prosecution Motion for Contempt of Court and on two Defence Motions for Disclosure etc., *Prosecutor v. Ntakirutimana and Ntakirutimana*, Case Nos. ICTR-96-10-I and ICTR-96-17-T, T. Ch. I, 16 July 2001, Klip/ Sluiter, ALC-X-257, par. 10 ("The question is whether the breach is serious enough to be tantamount to contempt.") Cf. Sharam Dana, Commentary, Klip/ Sluiter, ALC-X-257, p. 278, 279. See further ICTY, The Trial Chamber's Formal Complaint to the Prosecutor Concerning the conduct of the Prosecution, *Prosecutor v. Furundžija*, Case No. IT-95-17/1-PT, T. Ch., 5 June 1998, par. 11: the powers of contempt "are to be sparingly used in the most extreme of cases where there has been interference with the course and administration of justice".
[46] Trial Chamber Judgement, *supra* note 2, par. 174–176.
[47] Nobilo Contempt Appeal Judgment, *supra* note 10, par. 36.
[48] Trial Chamber Judgement, *supra* note 2, par. 155; also Margetić Contempt Judgement, *supra* note 15, par. 77.
[49] Trial Chamber Judgement, *supra* note 2, par. 157 and 179; also Marijačić and Rebić Trial Judgement, *supra* note 38, par. 18; Jović Appeal Judgement, *supra* note 17, par. 27.
[50] Trial Chamber Judgement, *supra* note 2, par. 181 and 182; see also ICTY, Appeal Judgement, *In the Case against Florence Hartmann*, Case No. IT-02-54-R77.5-A, A. Ch., 19 July 2011, par. 147.
[51] *Cf.* Wayne R. LaFave, Criminal Law, 4th ed., West Publishing, St. Paul 2003, p. 281.
[52] Trial Chamber Judgement, *supra* note 2, par. 188; this point was not mentioned in the Appeals Chamber Judgement, *supra* note 3, par. 45 and 46.
[53] Nobilo Contempt Appeal Judgement, *supra* note 10, par. 54. Nevertheless this diction is not clear, because the Appeals Chamber states in fn. 104 with reference to par. 45, "this is a reckless indifference to the consequences of the act by which the order is violated, rather than a reckless indifference to the existence of the violated order to which reference was made".
[54] *Cf.* George P. Fletcher/Jens David Ohlin, Reclaiming Fundamental Principles of Criminal Law in the Darfur Case, 3 Journal of International Criminal Justice 2005, p. 539, 553–554.

77 seriously, but refuses every restriction of the inherent power to prosecute contempt, this critique is not very impressive. But such unlimited justice has nothing in common with the principle *nulla poena sine lege*.

3. Sentencing

Nshogoza was sentenced to ten-month imprisonment. Compared to the practice of the *ad hoc* tribunals in similar cases this sentence seems to be very harsh,[55] especially if one considers that it was pure non-compliance without any affects on the trial of Kamuhanda. This is why the reasoning of the sentencing is not convincing.[56]

The starting point of the sentencing is the gravity of the offence and the necessary deterrence of other potential contemnors.[57] The gravity of the offence means little compared to the gravity of guilt, which has more weight. The first one affects the other one, and the more the guilt, the more the punishment. This is classical retributivism. Often one emphasises general deterrence as an opposite of retribution.[58] However, there is in fact no contradiction between retribution of guilt and prevention of crime. General deterrence works only if the penalty is not considered as arbitrary, but as just punishment for guilt. In this sense, the gravity of the offence is a decisive factor for the assessment of the sentence.[59] This is why retribution of past injury (*quia peccetur*) and general deterrence of future criminal actions (*quia ne peccetur*) are two sides of the same coin. It is unjust, if deterrence overweighs retribution – as in this case.

Considering the Trial Chambers reasoning it seems that the sentence was found for one reason only: deterrence. The court emphasises that contempt of the tribunal is a grave offence and constitutes a "direct challenge to the integrity of the trial process". In addition: "Maintaining the integrity of the administration of justice is particularly important in trials involving serious criminal offences". Of particular importance are appropriate measures for the protection of the integrity of witnesses and their oral testimony. Hence, the confidence in the effective protection of witnesses must not be undermined, the more as witnesses often are in danger or traumatized.[60] Generally, one can agree with this statement, but nothing is in common with the present case. The Trial Chamber ignores that the witness A7/GEX first established contact with Nshogoza. The two protected witnesses were neighbours and knew each other. They talked with each other about their testimony. Therefore, the disclosure of evidence was not initiated by Nshogoza. Furthermore, there was no proof that Nshogoza tampered with the evidence in any manner or wanted to. It cannot be said, that his conduct "undermined the confidence in the effectiveness of protective measures" and "may have the effect of dissuading witnesses from testifying" before the Tribunal.[61] The argument, that the accused contacted the protected witnesses "on his own conditions" and "thus defied the authority of the court by breaching the protective measures",[62] describes only his contemptuous behaviour and does not characterize the offence in any way. This lack of reasoning cannot be cured by the reference to other judgments and decisions of the ICTY.

In addition, the allegation of aggravating factors contains errors. The Trial Chamber states that the accused "was acting upon the instructions of his Lead counsel (…), and with the motive of earning fees for his

---

[55] See Silvia D'Ascoli, *supra* note 11, p. 743; yet the other sentences of the ICTY, to which the Trial Chamber, *supra* note 2, par. 217 refers, imposed more lenient penalties for more grave cases of contempt.
[56] Nevertheless the Appeals Chamber Judgment, *supra* note 3, par. 98–102 confirmed the sentence, but Judges Robinson and Güney dissented.
[57] Trial Chamber Judgement, *supra* note 2, par. 216 with reference to Marijačić and Rebić Trial Judgement, *supra* note 38, par. 46; ICTY, Judgement on Allegations of Contempt, *Contempt Proceedings Against Dragan Jokić*, Case No. IT-05-88-R77.1, T. Ch. II, 27 March 2009, par. 38; *Cf.* Vujin Contempt Judgement, *supra* note 9, par. 168; Beqaj Contempt Judgment, *supra* note 16, par. 58; Margetić Contempt Judgement, *supra* note 15, par. 84.
[58] For example, see Claus Roxin, Strafrecht. Allgemeiner Teil, Bd. 1, 4th ed., C.H. Beck, München, 2006, §3 no. 37–50; for a general critical view, see Danilo Zolo, Peace Through Criminal Law?, 2 Journal of International Criminal Justice 2004, p. 733–734. See also ICTY, Judgement, *Prosecutor v. Delalić et. al.*, Case No. IT-96-21-T, T. Ch. II*quater*, 16 November 1998, Klip/ Sluiter, ALC-III-363, par. 1231: "Retributive punishment by itself does not bring justice."
[59] See also ICTY, Judgement, *Prosecutor v. Brđanin*, Case No. IT-99-36-T, T. Ch. II, 1 September 2004, Klip/ Sluiter, ALC-XX-505, par. 1090: "Retribution must be understood as reflecting a fair and balanced approach to the exaction of punishment for wrongdoing. … the punishment must fit the crime."
[60] Trial Chamber Judgement, *supra* note 2, par. 218, citing Beqaj Contempt Judgement, *supra* note 16, par. 60.
[61] Trial Chamber Judgement, *supra* note 2, par. 219.
[62] Ibid.

work".[63] Admittedly, it was right to be concerned that the defendant was a legally trained member of the defence team who therefore knew the purpose of witness protection measures. Moreover, he abused the trust of the tribunal.[64] However, no one works without payment. It was not proven that Nshogoza received money for the offence. Instead the Trial Chamber should have considered as a mitigating circumstance that the lead defence counsel instructed the defendant. It was not obvious for him that his conduct was intolerable. Furthermore, it is self-contradictory that the Trial Chamber did not prosecute the lead defence counsel according Article 77 (B) RPE for "incitement" of Nshogoza's contemptuous behaviour.

In addition, the court did not consider that Nshogoza had made a mistake of law.[65] Admittedly, the Common law has the *ignorantia juris*-rule.[66] Obviously at this point, it is better to differentiate between a legal wrong offence and culpability. Not only the latter requires intention but also knowledge of his conduct as an offence that can be punished. One that does not even realize that his conduct is unlawful, cannot be addressed by the threat of punishment. In the normal cases before the ICTR the offenders know that they have committed a crime, because e.g. the crime of genocide is obvious for everyone. When it comes to questions that are more difficult, this is not as clear. According to the Trial Chamber Nshogoza, being an educated lawyer was able to avoid the mistake of law.[67] Even then, his guilt is of lower gravity.

All in all the impression remains that Nshogoza was used as a warning. Admittedly, the possibility that others would behave the same way is no excuse.[68] If it is right, that members of the Prosecution systematically neglected witness protection orders,[69] this would cause even more damage to the authority of ICTR.[70]

Joachim Renzikowski

---

[63] Trial Chamber Judgement, *supra* note 2, par. 222. Considering the explicit formulation it is elusive how the Appeals Chamber, *supra* note 3, par. 105 concludes that the Trial Chamber "merely noted" these facts and did not consider these to be aggravating. *Cf.* in contrast the dissenting votes of the Judges Robinson and Güney.
[64] Trial Chamber Judgement, *supra* note 2, par. 223 and 224.
[65] *Cp.* Trial Chamber Judgement, *supra* note 2, par. 181 and 182.
[66] For a criticism see Andrew Ashworth, Principles of Criminal Law, 6th ed., Oxford University Press 2009, p. 232; George P. Fletcher, Basic Concepts of Criminal Law, Oxford University Press 1998, p. 154–155 and 166; Christoph Safferling, Vorsatz und Schuld, Mohr Siebeck, Tübingen 2008, p. 379.
[67] *Cp.* Trial Chamber Judgement, *supra* note 2, par. 78, 84 and 85.
[68] Trial Chamber Judgement, *supra* note 2, par. 177; Appeals Chamber Judgement, *supra* note 3, par. 57.
[69] See Allison Turner, ICTR Witness Protection?, ICTR Defence Conference, The Hague, Netherlands, 2009 (www.ictrlegacydefenseperspective.org/papers/Allison_Turner_ICTR_WItness_Protection1.pdf).
[70] At least the Trial Chamber Judgement, *supra* note 2, par. 44–45 announced an enquiry.

International Criminal Tribunal for Rwanda
Tribunal pénal international pour le Rwanda

ORIGINAL: ENGLISH

TRIAL CHAMBER I

Before: Judge Erik Møse, presiding
Judge Sergei Alekseevich Egorov
Judge Florence Rita Arrey

Registrar: Adama Dieng

Date: 14 July 2009

THE PROSECUTOR

v.

Tharcisse RENZAHO

Case No. ICTR-97-31-T

JUDGEMENT AND SENTENCE

The Prosecution
Jonathan Moses
Katya Melluish
Shamus Mangan

The Defence
François Cantier
Barnabé Nekuie

[page i]TABLE OF CONTENTS

CHAPTER I: INTRODUCTION 1
1. Overview 1
2. Preliminary Matters 6
    2.1 Notice 6
        2.1.1 Objections to the Form of the Indictment 6
        2.1.2 Prejudice Due to Variations of the Indictments and Prosecution Witnesses 7
    2.2 Alleged Denial of a Fair Trial 7
        2.2.1 Rule 68 8
        2.2.2 Rule 92 *bis* 12
        2.2.3 Access to Defence Evidence 13
        2.2.4 Factors Affecting the Proceedings 18
3. Tharcisse Renzaho 20

CHAPTER II: FACTUAL SECTION 21
1. Encouragement of *Interahamwe* Training, 1993-1994 21
    1.1 Introduction 21
    1.2 Evidence 21
    1.3 Deliberations 26
2. Roadblocks in Kigali-Ville Prefecture 29
    2.1 Introduction 29
    2.2 Evidence 29
    2.3 Deliberations 40
        2.3.1 Presence at Roadblocks on 8 and 12 April 43
        2.3.2 Orders to Erect Roadblocks 43
        2.3.3 Killings Committed at Roadblocks 49
3. Distribution of Weapons 55
    3.1 Introduction 55
    3.2 Evidence 55
    3.3 Deliberations 64
        3.3.1 Distribution of Weapons 64
        3.3.2 Orders to Collect Weapons and Distribute Them 68
4. Facilitation of Movement 74
    4.1 *Laissez-Passer*s (Travel Authorisations) .... 74 [page ii]
        4.1.1 Introduction 74
        4.1.2 Evidence 74
        4.1.3 Deliberations 81
    4.2 Fuel Vouchers 83
        4.2.1 Introduction 83
        4.2.2 Evidence 83
        4.2.3 Deliberations 87
    4.3 Requisitioning of Vehicles 89
        4.3.1 Introduction 89
        4.3.2 Evidence 90
        4.3.3 Deliberations 93
5. Killings at Akajagali, 8 or 9 April 1994 95
    5.1 Introduction 95
    5.2 Evidence 95
    5.3 Deliberations 97
6. Attack at CELA, 22 April 1994 99
    6.1 Introduction 99
    6.2 Evidence 99

	6.3	Deliberations.. 110
		6.3.1 Attack on CELA, 21 April 111
		6.3.2 Attack on CELA, 22 April 112
7.	**Killings in Nyarugenge, 28 April 1994** **121**
	7.1	Introduction 121
	7.2	Evidence 121
	7.3	Deliberations.. 122
8.	**Dismissal of Moderate Officials, End April 1994** **124**
	8.1	Introduction 124
	8.2	Evidence 124
	8.3	Deliberations.. 129
9.	**Saint Paul Pastoral Centre, April-June 1994** **134**
	9.1	Introduction 134
	9.2	Evidence 134
	9.3	Deliberations.. 145
		9.3.1 Attack in Late April 145
		9.3.2 Attack in May .... 147 **[page iii]**
		9.3.3 Attack on 14 June 147
		9.3.4 Attack on 17 June 151
10.	**Killing of André Kameya, 15 June 1994** **153**
	10.1	Introduction 153
	10.2	Evidence 153
	10.3	Deliberations.. 154
11.	**Sainte Famille, 17 June 1994** **156**
	11.1	Introduction 156
	11.2	Evidence 156
	11.3	Deliberations.. 166
12.	**Hotel Kiyovu, Mid-June 1994** **172**
	12.1	Introduction 172
	12.2	Evidence 172
	12.3	Deliberations.. 173
13.	**Rape and Sexual Violence, April-July 1994** **177**
	13.1	Introduction 177
	13.2	Evidence 177
	13.3	Deliberations.. 184
		13.3.1 Rugenge Sector 184
		13.3.2 Sainte Famille.. 187
		13.3.3 Kimihurura Sector 190
		13.3.4 Renzaho's General Knowledge of Rapes 190

CHAPTER III:	**LEGAL FINDINGS**.. **192**
1.	**Introduction** **192**
2.	**Criminal Responsibility** **192**
	2.1 Article 6 (1) 192
	2.2 Article 6 (3) 194
	2.2.1 Legal Principles 194
	2.2.2 Deliberations 195
3.	**Genocide** **198**
	3.1 Genocide 198
	3.1.1 Introduction 198
	3.1.2 Law 198
	3.1.3 Deliberations 199
	3.1.4 Conclusion .... 203 **[page iv]**
	3.2 Complicity in Genocide... 203

4.	**Crimes Against Humanity**	**203**
	4.1 Introduction	203
	4.2 Widespread and Systematic Attack	203
	4.3 Murder	204
	4.3.1 Introduction	204
	4.3.2 Law	205
	4.3.3 Deliberations	205
	4.3.4 Conclusion	205
	4.4 Rape	206
	4.4.1 Introduction	206
	4.4.2 Law	206
	4.4.3 Deliberations	206
	4.4.4 Conclusion	206
5.	**Serious Violations of Article 3 Common to the Geneva Conventions and Additional Protocol II**	**206**
	5.1 Introduction	206
	5.2 Threshold Elements	207
	5.2.1 Law	207
	5.2.2 Non-International Armed Conflict	207
	5.2.3 Nexus	207
	5.2.4 Victims	208
	5.3 Murder	208
	5.3.1 Introduction	208
	5.3.2 Law	208
	5.3.3 Deliberations	208
	5.3.4 Conclusion	209
	5.4 Rape	209
	5.4.1 Introduction	209
	5.4.2 Law	209
	5.4.3 Deliberations	209
	5.4.4 Conclusion	209 [page v]

CHAPTER IV: VERDICT 210

CHAPTER V: SENTENCING 211

1.	**Introduction**	**211**
2.	**Submissions**	**211**
3.	**Deliberations**	**212**
	3.1 Gravity of the Offences	212
	3.2 Individual, Aggravating and Mitigating Circumstances	213
4.	**Conclusion**	**213**
5.	**Consequential Orders**	**213**

ANNEX A: PROCEDURAL HISTORY 215

1.	**Pre-trial Proceedings**	**215**
2.	**The Prosecution Case**	**216**
3.	**The Defence Case**	**217**
4.	**Further Proceedings**	**219**

ANNEX B: CITED MATERIALS AND DEFINED TERMS 220

1.	**Jurisprudence**	**220**
	1.1 ICTR	220
	1.2 ICTY	225
2.	**Defined Terms and Abbreviations**	**227**

ANNEX C: INDICTMENT

[page 1] CHAPTER I: INTRODUCTION

1. OVERVIEW

(i)   Introduction

1.   The accused in this case is Tharcisse Renzaho. During the events in 1994, he was prefect of Kigali-Ville prefecture and had the rank of colonel in the Rwandan army. The Prosecution has charged him with six counts: genocide, or, in the alternative, complicity in genocide, as well as murder and rape, as crimes against humanity and war crimes.

2.   The Defence disputes all charges. Renzaho was not in any way involved in the massacres after 6 April 1994; neither directly nor through others. The situation was uncontrollable. He did all he could to stop the violence.[1]

(ii)   Encouragement of Militia Training

3.   The Prosecution has alleged that Renzaho permitted and encouraged the military training of militia groups, at his home in Kanombe and elsewhere, between the middle of 1993 and July 1994. The Defence rejects this and also points to the prefect's obligation to observe neutrality in political matters.

4.   The evidence has not established that Renzaho was involved in military training in 1994. He clearly knew that the *Interahamwe* received such training in 1993, and he was in favour of this. However, such knowledge and support does not in itself constitute a crime under the Statute of the Tribunal, and it has not been established that the purpose of the training was to kill Tutsis. The evidence has not shown that Renzaho was involved in planning the genocide.

(iii)   Roadblocks

5.   There is evidence that Renzaho held several meetings at the Kigali-Ville prefecture office in April 1994. Around 10 April, he convened a meeting that included local officials, such as *bourgmestres* and *conseillers*, and explained that the Inkotanyi or Inyenzi had shot down the President's plane. He instructed those present to erect roadblocks for the purposes of fighting the enemy, and referred to Tutsis as accomplices of the enemy. At this time, Renzaho was aware that Tutsi civilians were being targeted and killed based on their ethnicity.

6.   The local officials in attendance followed Renzaho's directives and erected roadblocks in their respective communities within the prefecture and the only reasonable inference is that Renzaho ordered the killings at them as well. Their actions contributed to the slaughter of Tutsis or those identified as Tutsis. Renzaho reiterated his support for these roadblocks during at least one additional meeting that month.
[page 2]

7.   The Chamber has considered Renzaho's *communiqués* broadcast on Radio Rwanda during the events. His utterances about roadblocks were not clear. However, he never called for an end to the killing of Tutsi civilians, and calls for peace were usually accompanied by requests that the population continue to remain vigilant and encouragement in the fight against the *Inyenzi* or *Inkotanyi*. Renzaho supported the killings of Tutsi civilians at roadblocks.

(iv)   Distribution of Weapons

8.   The Prosecution alleges that Renzaho distributed weapons to the *Interahamwe* and other militia groups, and that he also ordered weapons distribution. In relation to the first issue, Renzaho's own physical

---

[1]   The trial commenced on 8 January 2007 and closed on 6 September 2007. The parties presented 53 witnesses in the course of 49 trial days. Closing arguments were heard on 14 and 15 February 2008. The Chamber pronounced its unanimous judgement on 14 July 2009. The written judgement was filed on 14 August 2009 after the conclusion of the editorial process.

involvement, the main allegations related to the *Hôtel des Diplomates* in Kigali, where he allegedly collected weapons on 7 and 12 April 1994. Only one witness testified about this, and the Chamber has some doubts about these parts of his testimony. Neither has it been established that Renzaho distributed weapons in the night between 6 and 7 April in various sectors in Kigali, on 21 April from Angeline Mukandutiye's house to *Interahamwe*, or in Gitarama prefecture in late April or early May.

9. Turning to ordering of weapons distribution, Renzaho convened a meeting at the Kigali-Ville prefecture office around 16 April where he directed local administrative officials, including *conseillers*, to retrieve firearms from the Ministry of Defence. The officials went to the Ministry and obtained some firearms that were subsequently distributed to persons within their communities.

10. The Chamber is convinced that Renzaho's instructions to retrieve the weapons were accompanied by a further order to distribute them to persons in their communities. Those who ultimately received the firearms subsequently engaged in the killing of Tutsis. Although Renzaho did not give explicit instructions that these weapons be used to further the ongoing killings in Kigali-Ville prefecture, the only reasonable inference to be drawn are that these distributions, within the context of the ongoing killings of Tutsi civilians, demonstrated his support for such activities and contributed substantially to them. The Chamber is also convinced beyond a reasonable doubt that Renzaho gave his instructions with the knowledge that killings of Tutsi civilians would be furthered by this support.

(v) Facilitation of Movement

11. The Prosecution argues that Renzaho facilitated movement of the *Interahamwe* who were participating in the killings. It is undisputed that a number of *laissez-passers*, signed by or on behalf of Renzaho, were issued by the Kigali-Ville prefecture office between April and July 1994. There is no direct evidence that they were given specifically to militia, soldiers or gendarmes. Neither is it proven that persons having received such documents committed killings. The possibility that violent groups also received such documents cannot in itself lead to a finding that the *laissez-passer* system facilitated the movement of killers.

12. There is evidence that the prefecture office was involved in the distribution of fuel through the use of coupons or vouchers. The office had some degree of control over who would receive fuel, and a sub-prefect within the prefecture administration was given the task of administering vouchers. At least from 13 April until about 3 May 1994, vouchers signed by the prefect were being used at a petrol station, mainly to provide fuel to the *Interahamwe*. However, the evidence is not strong enough to find criminal responsibility. **[page 3]**

(vi) Killings at Akajagali

13. The Indictment asserts that, around 9 April 1994, Renzaho led armed *Interahamwe* to an area called Akajagali in Kigali, where they entered houses of Tutsis and killed them. The Prosecution relied on a single witness with relation to this event. In the Chamber's view, the evidence led was insufficient to establish this allegation beyond a reasonable doubt.

(vii) CELA

14. During the events in 1994, a large number of Tutsis sought refuge in three sites which were near each other in Kigali. The Chamber has addressed them in turn, starting with the *Centre d'Étude des Langues Africaines*, or CELA. On 22 April, a considerable number of refugees were there. According to the Prosecution, Renzaho was involved in selecting some of them, who were subsequently killed. The Defence submits that he went there to protect persons under threat.

15. The Chamber accepts the evidence of several witnesses that Renzaho supervised a selection process in which *Interahamwe* separated about 40 Tutsis from the other refugees on 22 April 1994. Among those chosen were Charles Rwanga and his sons Wilson and Déglote. In Renzaho's presence, one of the militia leaders gave instructions that they should be taken to one of the mass graves. Renzaho told the remaining refugees to go home. It is clear from the evidence that the approximately 40 persons were subsequently killed and that this was done based on Renzaho's orders.

Judgement and Sentence

(viii) Killings in Nyarugenge

16. The Indictment states that Renzaho ordered *Interahamwe* to find and kill nine Tutsis, including François Nsengiyumva, Rutiyomba, Kagorora and his two children, Aimable and Emile. The Chamber accepts that, around 28 April 1994, *Interahamwe* killed several Tutsis at the house of an *Interhamwe* leader, including these five persons. According to the only Prosecution witness who testified about this, one of the *Interahamwe* had with him a document that he said was signed by Renzaho and their leader. The Prosecution evidence is insufficient to establish Renzaho's criminal liability for this event.

(ix) Dismissal of Moderates

17. The Prosecution maintains that, at the end of April 1994, Renzaho dismissed, among other persons, *conseiller* Célestin Sezibera, because he was believed to be opposed to the killing of Tutsis. Sezibera was then replaced with someone who allegedly supported the killings. The Defence argues that Renzaho was not at the origin of the dismissal and disputes that this was the reason for it.

18. It is undisputed that Renzaho signed Sezibera's dismissal letter, but there is no evidence that he appointed the new *conseiller*. Whether the idea of dismissing Sezibera was initially formulated by Renzaho or at a lower level, for instance the *bourgmestre*, is also unclear. The Chamber has therefore not found any criminal liability in respect of this allegation. **[page 4]**

(x) Saint Paul

19. Saint Paul pastoral centre was the second place with a large number of mainly Tutsi refugees. The *Interahamwe* carried out several attacks against the Centre from April to June 1994. One of them took place on 14 June. It resulted in the abduction and subsequent killings of about 40 to 50 Tutsis. From early May, Renzaho knew of attacks by *Interahamwe* against refugees there but did not act to stop them. The evidence does not show, however, that he was liable for the attacks, including the one on 14 June.

(xi) Killing of André Kameya

20. According to the Indictment, Renzaho ordered the killing of André Kameya, a journalist critical of the Interim Government, on or about 15 June 1994. One witness testified that Kameya was found at Sainte Famille, handed over to a conseiller who was an *Interahamwe* leader, and abducted. He did not see the killing and placed the event in April or May. Another witness did not observe the event, but heard the *conseiller* leader mention the killing between 19 April and mid-May. Once again, the Chamber has found that the evidence is insufficient to sustain a conviction.

(xii) Sainte Famille

21. The third site where many refugees sought refuge was the Sainte Famille church. It is undisputed that, on 17 June, shortly after the Rwandan Patriotic Front had evacuated some Tutsi refugees from the Saint Paul Pastoral Centre, the *Interahamwe* attacked and killed refugees at the Sainte Famille church. Again, the question for the Chamber is whether Renzaho was involved.

22. The Chamber finds that the attack started before noon. Renzaho was present before it began, as well as toward its end. An *Interahamwe* read out names of refugees to be killed. Those whose names were called were killed in the church's garden. In addition to these specific individuals, also other Tutsis were killed. The evidence demonstrates that Renzaho played an important part in connection with the commencement and cessation of the operation. Over 100 Tutsi refugees were killed. He was also involved in the removal of the bodies.

(xiii) Meeting at Hotel Kiyovu

23. According to the Prosecution, Renzaho attended a meeting close to the Hotel Kiyovu in mid-June 1994. Colonel Théoneste Bagosora and other prominent leaders were also present. Renzaho allegedly identified Tutsis as the enemy and told the participants that they had to defend themselves. Some 20 metres away, four Tutsis were killed with machetes and clubs. Renzaho purportedly witnessed this, and did nothing to prevent these killings.

24. Only one Prosecution witness testified about the meeting. Several issues of credibility arise as to the description of this event. The Chamber does not find that this event has been proven beyond reasonable doubt. **[page 5]**

(xiv) Sexual Violence

25. During the period between April and July 1994, multiple rapes were committed by *Interahamwe*, soldiers and policemen against Tutsi women and girls at Sainte Famille and various houses in Kigali-Ville. The victims were civilian refugees selected on the basis of their actual or presumed Tutsi ethnicity.

26. The Chamber finds that Renzaho was aware of rapes taking place in his prefecture during this period. The evidence shows that, on separate occasions and in certain specific locations, such as a sector office, he made remarks encouraging the sexual abuse of women. Rape took place following his remarks, and the Chamber finds him criminally responsible.

(xv) Verdict

27. The Chamber has found Tharcisse Renzaho responsible pursuant to Articles 6 (1) and 6 (3) of the Statute for killings at roadblocks; the killing of approximately 40 mostly Tutsi men, including Charles, Wilson and Déglote Rwanga, who were removed from CELA on 22 April 1994; and the killing of more than 100 Tutsi refugees, including at least 17 Tutsi men, during an attack at Sainte Famille on 17 June 1994. Renzaho is therefore guilty of genocide, and murder as a crime against humanity and as a serious violation of Article 3 common to the Geneva Conventions and Additional Protocol II. Furthermore, he is liable for rapes committed in Nyarugenge sector under Article 6 (3). For these crimes, Renzaho is also guilty of genocide and rape as a crime against humanity and as a serious violation of Article 3 common to the Geneva Conventions and Additional Protocol II.

(xvi) Sentencing

28. The Chamber has considered the gravity of each of the crimes for which Renzaho has been convicted as well as aggravating and mitigating circumstances mentioned by the parties. The Chamber has the discretion to impose a single sentence and chooses to do so. Considering the relevant circumstances, the Chamber sentences Renzaho to a single sentence of life imprisonment. He shall remain in the custody of the Tribunal pending transfer to the state where he will serve his sentence. **[page 6]**

2. PRELIMINARY MATTERS

2.1 Notice

2.1.1 Objections to the Form of the Indictment

29. The Defence raises several objections to the form of the Indictment, which were previously decided by Trial Chamber II in its decision of 5 September 2006 ("Defects Decision").[2] Although the Chamber may

---

[2] Defence Closing Brief paras. 70-204; Preliminary Motion on Defects in the Form of the Indictment, 31 March 2006; Decision on Preliminary Motion on Defects in the Form of the Indictment (TC), 5 September 2006.

consider matters related to notice at the judgement stage of proceedings, it declines to assess issues that were either adjudicated or should properly have been raised during the pre-trial phase of the proceedings.[3] Instead, the Chamber generally limits its review to issues which require clarification in light of evidentiary, procedural or legal developments arising during the course of the trial or where the failure to consider an issue might call into question the fairness of the proceedings.[4]

30. A review of the Defence's pre-trial motion concerning defects in the Indictment, filed on 31 March 2006 ("Defects Motion"), and its current submissions demonstrates that it largely recapitulates arguments previously adjudicated.[5] The Defence's submissions do not identify any clear errors in reasoning warranting wholesale reconsideration of the Defects Decision taken by Trial Chamber II at the pre-trial stage of proceedings.

31. Furthermore, the Defence does not point to any contemporaneous objections made at trial that it lacked notice of any of the evidence which was presented or that it fell outside the scope of the Indictment. The Chamber also cannot identify any such objections with respect to the events which form a basis of Renzaho's convictions. Where timely objections to evidence are not made, the burden shifts to the accused to demonstrate that the ability to prepare his case was materially impaired.[6] While the Defence asserts that it suffered prejudice from the vagueness in the Indictment, there is no particularised support for the conclusion.[7] [page 7]

32. Even if the Defence did not bear this burden, the Chamber still cannot identify any prejudice with respect to the basis of his convictions. The Indictment is not defective. The Chamber is satisfied that, consistent with the Tribunal's governing jurisprudence,[8] there is reasonable notice within the scope of the Indictment for all material facts underpinning Renzaho's convictions. Furthermore, a careful consideration of the Defence conduct during the course of the trial and in their final submissions reflect that they have a complete understanding of the case.

2.1.2 Prejudice Due to Variations of the Indictments and Prosecution Witnesses

33. The Defence also submits that amendments to the Indictment and variation of the Prosecution Witness list coupled with the vagueness of the Indictment as a whole prejudiced the Defence.[9] Amendment of an indictment is allowed under the Rules and is permissible even during the course of trial.[10] The initial indictment, the second that had been submitted by the Prosecution, was confirmed on 15 November 2002.[11] Amendments to the indictments were allowed only after careful consideration of whether they would

---

[3] *Simba* Trial Judgement para. 15. See also *Ntagerura et al.* Appeal Judgement para. 55.
[4] *Simba* Trial Judgement para. 16.
[5] See, for instance, Defence Closing Brief, para. 105 ("Renzaho reiterates herein the detailed criticisms he made in his preliminary motion of 31 March 2006"); Compare Defects Motion paras. 30-34 and Defence Closing Brief para. 76; Compare Defects Motion para. 58 and Defence Closing Brief paras. 86-87; Compare Defects Motion para. 59 and Defence Closing Brief para. 88; Compare Defects Motion para. 60 and Defence Closing Brief paras. 89-90; Compare Defects Motion para. 61 and Defence Closing Brief paras. 91-92, 95; Compare Defects Motion para. 62 and Defence Closing Brief para. 93; Compare Defects Motion para. 63 and Defence Closing Brief para. 94; Compare Defects Motion paras. 82-90 and Defence Closing Brief paras. 106-114, respectively; Compare Defects Motion paras. 92-95 and Defence Closing Brief para. 116; Compare Defects Motion paras. 96-100, 102-106 and Defence Closing Brief paras. 117-126; Compare Defects Motion paras. 107-118 and Defence Closing Brief paras. 127-138, respectively; Compare Defects Motion para. 119 and Defence Closing Brief paras. 139-140; Compare Defects Motion paras. 120-123 and Defence Closing Brief paras. 141-144, respectively; Compare Defects Motion paras. 124-138 and Defence Closing Brief paras. 145-160, respectively; Compare Defects Motion paras. 140-174 and Defence Closing Brief paras. 161-195, respectively.
[6] *Bagosora et al.*, Decision on Aloys Ntabakuze's Interlocutory Appeal on Questions of Law Raised by the 29 June 2006 Trial Chamber I Decision on Motion for Exclusion of Evidence (AC), 18 September 2006, para. 42 ("Where, in such circumstances, there is a resulting defect in the indictment, an accused person who fails to object at trial has the burden of proving on appeal that his ability to prepare his case was materially impaired.").
[7] Defence Closing Brief paras. 103-104, 195, 204.
[8] The Chamber recently summarised the general principles governing challenges to notice in the *Bagosora et al.* Trial Judgement paras. 110-116.
[9] Defence Closing Brief paras. 203-204.
[10] *Karemera et al.*, Decision on Prosecutor's Interlocutory Appeal Against Trial Chamber III Decision of 8 October 2003 Denying Leave to File an Amended Indictment (AC), 19 December 2003, paras. 24, 29.
[11] *Décision Portant Confirmation de l'Acte d'Accusation Prescrivant la Non-Divulgation des Informations Permettant d'Identifier les Témoins qui Figurent dans les Déclarations Desdits Témoins* (TC), 15 November 2002.

prejudice the Accused.[12] In the present case, the operative Indictment was filed on 16 February 2006, nearly a year before the commencement of the Prosecution case, and the Defence raised no objection to it.[13] The Prosecution was allowed to add a witness on 16 February 2007 after consideration of the Accused's rights.[14] This process is also envisioned by Rule 73 *bis* (E) of the Rules.

34. Accordingly, the Chamber finds no merit to the argument that pre-trial changes to the Indictment and variations of the Prosecution witnesses have prejudiced the Accused in the preparation of his Defence, in particular in the absence of precise submissions from the Defence concerning prejudice.

2.2 Alleged Denial of a Fair Trial

35. The Defence submits that Renzaho has been denied a fair trial due to the Prosecution's failure to turn over information in violation of Rule 68 of the Rules, the Chamber's strict construction of Rule 92 *bis* of the Rules and its inability to access Defence evidence. The Defence raises several additional concerns that it argues may improperly impact the outcome of the case. The Chamber will address these arguments in turn.[15]
[page 8]

2.2.1 Rule 68

36. The Defence argues that the Prosecution violated its affirmative and ongoing obligations to disclose exculpatory evidence throughout the trial.[16] It points to the late disclosure of (1) testimony of Witness DAS and a copy of Théoneste Bagosora's passport presented in the *Bagosora et al.* case that are relevant to the Hotel Kiyovu incident; (2) statements of Astérie Nikuze and Dieudonné Nkulikiyinka; (3) evidence related to Kabiligi's alibi presented in the *Bagosora et al.* case allegedly contradicting the testimony of Prosecution Witness AFB; and (4) Father Wenceslas Munyeshyaka's indictment which is inconsistent with Prosecution evidence relating to an attack on CELA on 22 April.[17] The Defence believes that the Prosecution has additional information inconsistent with the evidence it adduced at trial but is unable to identify it.[18]

37. The Prosecution does not deny that it possessed the information identified by the Defence. Rather, it suggests that the information is not exculpatory and that the Defence has failed to show any prejudice suffered.[19]

38. The Prosecution has a distinct obligation to participate in the process of administering justice by disclosing to the Defence, as required by Rule 68 (A) of the Rules, material which it actually knows "may suggest the innocence or mitigate the guilt of the accused or affect the credibility of the Prosecution evidence".[20] The initial determination of what material is exculpatory, which is primarily a facts-based judgement, rests with the Prosecution.[21] In the context of witness statements, the Appeals Chamber has accepted that determining whether information fits within the definition set forth in Rule 68 (A) of the Rules

---

[12] Decision on the Prosecutor's Motion for Leave to Amend the Indictment (TC), 18 March 2005, paras. 38-39, 48-49, 52, 54; Decision on the Prosecutor's Application for Leave to Amend the Indictment Pursuant to Rule 50(A) of the Rules of Procedure and Evidence (TC), 13 February 2006, paras. 10-14.
[13] Decision on the Prosecutor's Application for Leave to Amend the Indictment Pursuant to Rule 50(A) of the Rules of Procedure and Evidence (TC), 13 February 2006, para. 14.
[14] Decision on Prosecution's Motion to Vary Witness List (TC), 16 February 2007, para. 6. The Defence did not object to the Prosecution's request to drop a witness in this decision nor on its decision to drop two witnesses on 1 February 2007. T. 1 February 2007 pp. 40-42.
[15] Defence Closing Brief paras. 205-338; T. 14 February 2008 pp. 24-42.
[16] Defence Closing Brief paras. 234-249; T. 14 February 2008 pp. 27-30, 42.
[17] Defence Closing Brief paras. 243-247, 249; T. 14 February 2008 pp. 27-30, 60.
[18] Defence Closing Brief paras. 242, 248.
[19] T. 14 February 2008 pp. 3-7.
[20] *Karemera et al.*, Decision on "Joseph Nzirorera's Appeal from Decision on Tenth Rule 68 Motion" (AC), 14 May 2008, para. 9; *Karemera et al.*, Decision on Interlocutory Appeal Regarding the Role of the Prosecutor's Electronic Disclosure Suite in Discharging Disclosure Obligations (AC), 30 June 2006, para. 9.
[21] *Karemera et al.*, Decision on Joseph Nzirorera's Interlocutory Appeal (AC), 28 April 2006, para. 16.

Judgement and Sentence

depends on an evaluation of whether there is any possibility, in light of the submissions of the parties, that the information could be relevant to the defence of the accused.[22]

39. To demonstrate the Prosecution is in breach of its obligation to disclose exculpatory material, the Defence must (1) identify specifically the material sought; (2) present a *prima facie* showing of its probable exculpatory nature; and (3) prove that the material requested is in the custody or under the control of the Prosecution.[23] Even where the Defence has satisfied the Chamber that the Prosecution had failed to comply with its Rule 68 obligations, the **[page 9]** Chamber will still examine whether the Defence has actually been prejudiced by such a failure before considering whether a remedy is appropriate.[24]

(i)   Testimony of Witness DAS and Bagosora's Passport from the Bagosora et al. Trial

40. The Defence submits that Witness DAS's testimony in *Bagosora et al.* contradicts Witness SAF's testimony in this proceeding, as Witness DAS does not refer to Renzaho's presence at a meeting at the Hotel Kiyovu. Moreover, it argues that Bagosora's passport also impeaches Witness SAF's testimony that Bagosora was present, demonstrating that Bagosora was out of the country at the time. In both instances, Renzaho is not mentioned. The link between the material and its conceivably exculpatory nature as it relates to the Accused is indirect.[25] Nonetheless, Rule 68 of the Rules imposes a heavy burden on the Prosecution, who is assumed to be acting as an undivided unit in fulfilling its obligations disclosure obligations.[26] A review of Indictment paragraph 19 demonstrates that the Prosecution seeks to convict the Accused based on his participation in a meeting in June at the Hotel Kiyovu attended by at least Renzaho and Bagosora. Both the transcripts and passport copies could be relevant to the defence of the Accused as defined under Rule 68 (A) of the Rules as it tends to undermine the credibility of evidence intended to prove a material fact against him.[27]

41. However, the Defence has failed to demonstrate any prejudice suffered. The Prosecution's suggestion that it disclosed the material upon the Defence's request is uncontested. Witness SAF was cross-examined extensively based on Witness DAS's testimony.[28] Moreover, the Chamber allowed the Defence to admit copies of Bagosora's passport during Renzaho's testimony.[29] Given the Chamber's findings in relation to this incident (II.12), the Chamber cannot find that the Accused suffered actual prejudice. The Chamber dismisses the Defence arguments with respect to this information.

(ii)   Pro Justitia Statements of Astérie Nikuze and Dieudonné Nkulikiyinka

42. The Defence makes no particularised submissions concerning the importance of the *pro justitia* statements to Rwandan authorities of Astérie Nikuze and Dieudonné Nkulikiyinka. A review of Nikuze's

---

[22]   *Prosecutor v. Karemera et al.*, Decision on "Joseph Nzirorera's Appeal from Decision on Tenth Rule 68 Motion" (AC), 14 May 2008, para. 12.

[23]   *Karemera et al.*, Decision on "Joseph Nzirorera's Appeal from Decision on Tenth Rule 68 Motion" (AC), 14 May 2008, para. 9; *Blaškić* Appeal Judgement para. 268, *Karemera et al.*, Decision on Joseph Nzirorera's Interlocutory Appeal (AC), 28 April 2006, para. 13; *Bagosora et al.*, Decision on the Ntabakuze Motion for Disclosure of Various Categories of Documents Pursuant to Rule 68 (TC), 6 October 2006, para. 2; *Bagosora et al.*, Decision on Disclosure of Materials Relating to Immigration Statements of Defence Witnesses (TC), 27 September 2005, para. 3 ("a request for production of documents has to be sufficiently specific as to the nature of the evidence sought and its being in the possession of the addressee of the request").

[24]   *Nahimana et al.*, Decision on Appellant Jean-Bosco Barayagwiza's Motion for Leave to Present Additional Evidence Pursuant to Rule 115 of the Rules of Procedure and Evidence (AC), 8 December 2006, para. 34; *Rutaganda*, Decisions on Requests for Reconsideration, Review, Assignment of Counsel, Disclosure and Clarification (AC), 8 December 2006, para. 37; *Kajelijeli* Appeal Judgement para. 262.

[25]   With respect to the testimony of Witness DAS, his failure to mention Renzaho at the meeting does not necessarily mean he was not there. *Cf. Kajelijeli* Appeal Judgement para. 176 ("[T]o suggest that if something were true a witness would have included it in a statement or a confession letter is obviously speculative and, in general, it cannot substantiate a claim that a Trial Chamber erred in assessing the witness's credibility.").

[26]   *Bagosora et al.*, Decision on Interlocutory Appeals on Witness Protection Orders (AC), 6 October 2005, para. 43.

[27]   *Karemera et al.*, Decision on "Joseph Nzirorera's Appeal from Decision on Tenth Rule 68 Motion" (AC), 14 May 2008, para. 12.

[28]   Witness SAF, T. 24 January 2007 pp. 60-65; Defence Exhibit 12 (*Bagosora et al.*, T. 5 November 2003; T. 6 November 2003; T. 7 November 2003).

[29]   T. 29 August 2007 pp. 62-64; T. 30 August 2007 p. 2; Defence Exhibit 106 (Bagosora's passport).

statement suggests that she had heard Witness ALG might have brought a paper signed by authorities that prompted the attack on Saint Paul pastoral centre and that she was aware that refugees were at the prefecture office. Nkulikiyinka's *pro justitia* statement indicates that Witness ALG instructed *Interahamwe* to [page 10] travel throughout the area and exterminate members of the population and that he signed a document authorising the removal of several refugees from Saint Paul, at which point they were murdered. The statement also suggests that refuge and protection were provided to persons by Renzaho at the prefecture office.

43. The Chamber agrees that the content of Nikuze's and Nkulikiyinka's *pro justitia* statements to Rwandan judicial authorities could be relevant to the defence of the Accused as defined under Rule 68 (A) of the Rules. However, Nkulikiyinka's *pro justitia* statement was disclosed to the Defence on 30 October 2006, prior to the commencement of trial and Witness ALG's testimony in January 2007.[30] More importantly, the Defence cross-examined Witness ALG on 15 January 2007 using summaries of statements from Nikuze and Nkulikiyinka that formed a part of Witness ALG's Rwandan judicial record.[31] The statements were admitted as Defence Exhibit 4. The Chamber finds no material differences between the *pro justitia* statements and the substance of Defence Exhibit 4 as they relate to the ability of the Accused to mount his Defence as it relates to the killings at Saint Paul pastoral centre. Given the findings relating to the attack on Saint Paul pastoral centre (II.9), the record fails to demonstrate that the Accused suffered actual prejudice. Finally, information in the statements suggesting that people took refuge at the prefecture office is hearsay, and cumulative of other evidence in the record (III).

(iii)   Kabiligi Alibi Evidence from the Bagosora et al. Trial

44. The Defence also suggests that the Prosecution failed to turn over alibi evidence suggesting General Gratien Kabiligi was not present in early April, contradicting Witness AFB's testimony that Renzaho had met Kabiligi on 7 April. The Chamber previously denied a Defence motion to seeking to admit two letters between Egyptian authorities and the Office of the Prosecutor in 2002, suggesting Kabiligi was out of the country that day.[32] Renzaho is not mentioned in these letters. Nonetheless, Kabiligi's interactions with Renzaho and presence at the Kigali-Ville prefecture office after 6 April formed a part of the Prosecution case.[33] Kabiligi also featured in Witness AFB's testimony. For the same reasons expressed above, the letters detailing Kabiligi's whereabouts in April should have been disclosed to the Defence.

45. However, the Chamber does not find that the Defence suffered any prejudice. While Witness AFB testified that he saw Kabiligi, the identification was based on information that was provided to him by someone else. Thus, evidence that Kabiligi was not in the country largely goes to the reliability of Witness AFB's source and not Witness AFB (II.3). Finally, the Chamber's findings in relation to events in which Kabiligi featured (II.3) demonstrate that no prejudice was suffered by the Accused. [page 11]

(iv)   Wenceslas Munyeshyaka Indictment

46. Finally, the Defence argues that Prosecution's failure to turn over the indictment for Wenceslas Munyeshyaka, filed in this Tribunal, was in violation of its Rule 68 obligations. It notes that paragraphs 13, 14 and 15 suggest that certain individuals were killed by Munyeshyaka on 13 April at Sainte Famille, while Prosecution evidence suggests that Renzaho is responsible for the deaths of the same individuals during an attack on CELA on 22 April.[34] The Prosecution responds that these paragraphs in the Munyeshyaka

---

[30]   See Letter accompanying Prosecution Disclosures of 30 October 2006; T. 14 February 2008 p. 5. The Prosecutor submits that both statements were provided on 16 January 2007 (para. 4).
[31]   Witness ALG, T. 15 January 2007 pp. 26-31.
[32]   Decision on Defence Motion to Admit Documents (TC), 12 February 2008. The motion also denied the admission of transcripts of the Prosecutor's closing arguments from the *Bagosora et al.* trial that suggest Kabiligi was out of the country that day, finding that they did not constitute "evidence" under Rule 92 *bis* (D). Para. 5. Based on the Defence's submissions that the Prosecutor violated its Rule 68 obligations based on its failure to turn over "alibi evidence" (Defence Closing Brief para. 246) or "the document ... whose validity [the Prosecution] recognised" (T. 14 February 2008 p. 29), the Chamber construes this challenge as being limited to the letters referenced in the motion only and not the Prosecution's closing arguments in the *Bagosora et al.* trial.
[33]   Prosecution Pre-Trial Brief para. 7; Prosecution opening statements at T. 8 January 2007 p. 3.
[34]   T. 14 February 2008 p. 30.

indictment and the supporting material for them do not identify by name those who were allegedly killed at Sainte Famille. Thus, the Munyeshyaka indictment and its supporting materials are not inconsistent with the evidence that related to the killings at CELA. It also concludes that the Defence has not been prejudiced.[35]

47. The Munyeshyaka indictment was confidential and first disclosed in June 2007.[36] The Prosecution provided it and the supporting statements upon a request by the Defence.[37] The indictment was subsequently admitted during the testimony of the Accused.[38]

48. The Munyeshyaka indictment is not "evidence" but a procedural necessity in order to prosecute the accused. Nonetheless, the office of the Prosecutor is considered as an undivided body. Where another indictment reflects an inconsistent position with the indictment of an accused, particularly in relation to matters as serious as crimes, the Chamber is of the opinion that this material would be relevant to the defence of the accused. This finding is supported by the fact that the indictment confirmation process requires the review of supporting material, which can be used to rebut Prosecution evidence or raise credibility concerns in relation to its witnesses.[39] The Defence does not argue that the failure to disclose the supporting materials for paragraphs 13, 14 and 15 amounts to a Rule 68 violation. Nonetheless, the Chamber will consider whether the late disclosure of either, and particularly the statement of Witness AZB referred to by the Prosecution as supporting paragraphs 13, 14 and 15, has prejudiced the Accused.

49. The Chamber disagrees with the Prosecution's submissions. The Munyeshyaka indictment and Witness AZB's statement regarding the deaths of Rose Rwanga's daughters and son on 13 April at Sainte Famille could be viewed as inconsistent with Prosecution evidence that Wilson and Déglote were separated at CELA on 22 April 1994, removed and killed (II.6). Moreover, the indictment and statement reflect that Rwanga's two daughters were killed 13 April at Sainte Famille, and could be viewed as inconsistent with Prosecution evidence that Hyacinthe Rwanga was killed during the 17 June 1994 attack on Sainte Famille (II.11). Thus, the Chamber is convinced that the Munyeshyaka indictment and Witness AZB's statement are relevant to the defence of the Accused as defined under Rule 68 (A) and should have been disclosed.[40]

[page 12]

50. Nonetheless, the Chamber is not convinced that the Accused has suffered actual prejudice. The Defence cross-examined Witness ACK with a Rwandan judgment suggesting that Wilson, Charles and Déglote Rwanga were killed at Sainte Famille, raising similar inconsistencies as those that could have been raised based on Witness AZB's statement and the Munyeshyaka indictment.[41] Furthermore, the Chamber has reservations about the ability of Witness AZB to raise doubts in the reliability of the abundant and credible Prosecution evidence establishing that Wilson and Déglote Rwanga were murdered in connection with the 22 April attack on CELA as well as evidence that Hyacinthe Rwanga was killed on 17 June (II.6, 11). Witness AZB was unable to name the victims and she suggested that Rose Rwanga had two daughters while credible evidence in the record demonstrates Rose Rwanga only was only at Sainte Famille with one. In the Chamber's view, differences between Witness AZB's statement statement and evidence presented at trial raises doubt about the reliability of the Witness AZB's identification of the victims rather than the Prosecution evidence. Notably, the Defence did not call Witness AZB to rebut the Prosecution case. The Chamber cannot find that the Accused suffered prejudice.

51. Finally, the Chamber dismisses the Defence's arguments the Prosecution is in violation of its Rule 68 obligations although it is impossible to identify exculpatory information being withheld. This argument fails to meet the threshold requirement of identifying with specificity the exculpatory material. Moreover, the Prosecution is generally presumed to discharge its obligations under Rule 68 in good faith.[42]

---

[35] *Id.* p. 6.
[36] *Id.* p. 30.
[37] T. 29 August 2007 pp. 56-59.
[38] T. 30 August 2007 p. 41; Defence Exhibit 105 (indictment of Wenceslas Munyeshyaka of 20 July 2005).
[39] See Article 18 of the Statute and Rule 47 of the Rules.
[40] While the Prosecution may have been limited in disclosing the Munyeshyaka indictment while it remained confidential, it nonetheless could have disclosed Witness AZB's witness statement during that period.
[41] Witness ACK, T. 6 March 2007 pp. 57-60.
[42] *Kordić and Čerkez* Appeal Judgement para. 183 ("the general practice of the International Tribunal is to respect the Prosecution's function in the administration of justice, and the Prosecution execution of that function in good faith"); *Karemera et*

2.2.2 Rule 92 *bis*

52. The Defence seeks reconsideration of the Chamber's 28 and 29 August 2007 decisions denying the admission of *pro justitia* statements from Astérie Nikuze and Dieudonné Nkulinkiyinka and an interview of Sixbert Musangamufa of 14 November 2001 and the subsequent summary dated 16 November 2001.[43]

53. Reconsideration is justified when there have been new circumstances since the filing of the challenged decision that affect the premise of the decision. It is can also be permissible where the impugned decision was erroneous in law or an abuse of discretion.[44] The Defence's submissions suggest that the Chamber construed the limitations of Rule 92 *bis* of the Rules too strictly. It does not cite authority for this position or any change in the facts.

54. According to Rule 92 *bis* (A) of the Rules, a Trial Chamber may admit the evidence of a witness in the form of a written statement instead of oral testimony which goes to the proof of a matter other than the acts and conduct of the accused as charged in the indictment. The Chamber has discussed the contents of Nkulinkiyinka's and Nikuze's *pro justitia* statements above (I.2.2.1.*(ii)*). Their relevance to the Defence is that they tend to place **[page 13]** responsibility for the killings at Saint Paul's pastoral centre on Witness ALG, and not Renzaho, as well as show that refuge was provided to persons at the Kigali-Ville prefecture office. Nkulinkiyinka's statement specifically references Renzaho.

55. In the Chamber's view, the documents go towards proof of the acts of the conduct of the accused as charged in the indictment, and cannot be admitted pursuant to Rule 92 *bis* of the Rules.[45] Their primary purpose is to impeach the testimony of Witness ALG. Nkulinkiyinka's statement was disclosed to the Defence on 30 October 2006 and could have been introduced during Witness ALG's testimony in January 2007.[46] Moreover, the Defence could have moved to recall Witness ALG on the basis of both statements but it did not. Rule 92 *bis* of the Rules is not a way around this obligation.[47]

56. The Defence also seeks to admit the interview of Sixbert Musangamufa of 14 November 2001 and the subsequent summary dated 16 November 2001 as it raises doubts about the credibility of the criminal allegations made against Wenceslas Munyeshyaka in Rwanda. Munyeshyaka is an alleged member of the Accused's joint criminal enterprise and is implicated in several criminal charges with the Accused.[48] Once again, the documents go towards the conduct of the Accused, and thus fall outside the parameters of Rule 92 *bis* (A) of the Rules.[49] The Defence's expressed difficulties in obtaining a witness, which would allow the introduction of the documents, does not alter the outcome. It is incumbent upon the Defence to exhaust all available measures to secure the taking of the witness's testimony.[50] It has not demonstrated that it has done so in this instance.

2.2.3 Access to Defence Evidence

57. The Defence contends that the death of two witnesses, the refusal of others to testify, and interference by a former Defence investigator, who allegedly discouraged witnesses from testifying, have prevented the Accused from receiving a fair trial.[51] It concludes that the climate in Rwanda prevents witnesses from testifying for the Defence. The Chamber will address these arguments in turn.

---

al., Decision on Joseph Nzirorera's Interlocutory Appeal (AC), 28 April 2006, para. 17 ("the Trial Chamber is entitled to assume that the Prosecution is acting in good faith").

[43] Defence Closing Brief paras. 250-265. The Chamber denied the admission of the *pro justitia* statements and the investigation documents during the testimony of the Accused. T. 28 August 2007 pp. 27-34 (*pro justitia* statements); T. 29 August 2007 pp. 43-51 (*procès verbal d'interrogatoire de Sixbert Musangamufa*).

[44] *Ntagerura et al.* Appeal Judgement para. 55; *Bagosora et al.*, Decision on Bagosora Request for Certification or Reconsideration Concerning Admission of Witness B-06's Statement (TC), 8 May 2007, para. 8.

[45] Decision on Defence Motion to Admit Documents, 12 February 2008 para. 4.

[46] See Letter accompanying Prosecution Disclosures of 30 October 2006; T. 14 February 2008 p. 5.

[47] *Bagosora et al.*, Decision on Nsengiyumva Motion to Admit Documents as Exhibits (TC), 26 February 2007, para. 8.

[48] Indictment paras. 6, 20-21, 36-38, 42, 52, 54, 61, 64.

[49] Decision on Defence Motion to Admit Documents, 12 February 2008, para. 4.

[50] *Simba* Appeal Judgement para. 41.

[51] Defence Closing Brief paras. 266-293; Defence Exhibit 113 (*complément écrit aux arguments oraux de la défense*) para. 291. para. 291.

(i) Deaths of Prospective Witnesses

58. The Defence submits that the deaths of Renzaho's secretary, Astérie Nikuze, and his driver, Gaspard, have materially impaired its ability to prepare its Defence.[52] Each of the prospective witnesses died prior to counsel's ability to meet with them, but the Defence argues that such people would tend to know "everything about the daily dealings" of Renzaho.[53] **[page 14]**

59. The right of an accused to a fair trial implies the principle of equality of arms between the Prosecution and the Defence.[54] This principle, in part, is embodied in Article 20 (4)(e) of the Statute. It provides that the Accused has the right "… to obtain the attendance and examination of witnesses on his or her behalf under the same conditions as witnesses against him or her". However, this right does not apply to conditions outside the control of a court that prevent a party from securing the attendance of certain witnesses.[55] The untimely death of witnesses is one such instance.[56]

60. Moreover, in the post-trial phase, a remedy is appropriate only where the party has demonstrated material prejudice.[57] The Defence makes no particularised reference as to what Prosecution evidence Gaspard would have rebutted based on evidence in the record or its independent knowledge of Renzaho's relationship and dealings with him. The Chamber will not consider this argument further.

61. As discussed above, the contents of Nikuze's anticipated evidence was that she had heard Witness ALG might have brought a paper signed by authorities that prompted the attack on Saint Paul's pastoral centre.[58] Thus, her anticipated evidence tending to show that Witness ALG, and not Renzaho, is culpable for the killings at Saint Paul's pastoral centre, is hearsay and of limited probative value.[59] Given the Chamber's finding in relation to the event (II.9), it cannot find that Renzaho suffered prejudice due to her absence. Finally, her anticipated evidence that Renzaho provided refuge to displaced persons at the Kigali-Ville prefecture office is also cumulative of other evidence in the record (III.3.1.3). On this basis, the Chamber is unable to determine that the proceedings have been rendered unfair due to the absence of these witnesses.

(ii) Prospective Witnesses Who Refused to Testify Based on Fear of Reprisals

62. The Defence next submits that several key witnesses, including Dieudonné Nkulikiyinka and Alexis Bisanukuli refused to testify based on fear of reprisals.[60] Equality of arms before the Tribunal means that a Chamber shall provide every practicable facility it is capable of granting under the Rules and the Statute when faced with a request by a party for **[page 15]** assistance in presenting its case.[61] Provisions under the Statute and the Rules exist to alleviate the difficulties faced by parties by empowering the Chambers to issue such orders, summonses, subpoenas, warrants and transfer orders as may be necessary for the purposes of

---

[52] Defence Closing Brief paras. 217, 256, 268-271, 684.
[53] *Id.* paras. 267-271; T. 14 February 2008 p. 31.
[54] *Kayishema and Ruzindana* Appeal Judgement para. 67; *Tadić* Appeal Judgement para. 48.
[55] *Kayishema and Ruzindana* Appeal Judgement para. 73; *Tadić* Appeal Judgement para. 49.
[56] According to the Defence submissions, Ms. Astérie Nikuze died after having met with the Rwandan intelligence division and that Gaspard had died while attempting to flee in Rwanda. Defence Closing Brief paras. 269-271; T. 14 February 2008 p. 31. These submissions appear also underpin the Defence's umbrella argument that it cannot receive a fair trial based on interference of witnesses in Rwanda, which is addressed below. The Chamber finds it unnecessary to consider equivocal overtures relating to why these prospective witnesses died.
[57] See, for instance, *Semanza* Appeal Judgement paras. 69-73; *Kamuhanda* Appeal Judgement para. 12; *Ntagerura et al.*, Trial Judgement para. 30.
[58] The Defence errantly suggests that Nikuze would be able to rebut Prosecution evidence related to the attack on CELA. Defence Closing Brief para. 375. Her evidence would relate to the attack at Saint Paul based on a review of Defence Exhibit 4 and Nikuze's *pro justitia* statement.
[59] *Pro justitia* statement of 2 July 1996, p. 2: "Q: *Tu ne sais rien en rapport ave le rôle qu'il aurait joué dans le massacres des gens au Saint Paul? R: Il a joué un rôle parce que ce n'est pas possible qu'une autorité comme [lui]… R: Je ne sais pas. J'ai entendu qu'ils ont amené un papier signé par des autorités. Je ne sais pas si c'est [Witness ALG] ou si c'est [another government official]. Ils ont montré ce papier à L'Abbé Célestin… ces tueures ne pouvaient pas venir enlever les gens sans que [Witness ALG] en soit courant.*"
[60] Defence Closing Brief paras. 274-284, 1270; T. 14 February 2008 pp. 31-35, 40. The Chamber discusses Defence submissions as it they relate to Eugène Hantangigaba in the subsection below.
[61] *Tadić* Appeal Judgement para. 52.

investigation or for the preparation or conduct of trial.[62] In addition, where such measures have proved to no avail, a Chamber may order that proceedings be adjourned or, if the circumstances so require, that they be stayed.[63]

63. Where a party raises allegations of witness intimidation, a remedy is appropriate where they are established on the balance of the probabilities.[64] Furthermore, the Defence bears the burden to exhaust all available measures afforded by the Statute and Rules to obtain the presentation of evidence. Finally, there must be a showing of material prejudice.[65] Where the evidence has not been obtained due to witness intimidation, the Defence must show how the content of the anticipated evidence relates to specific allegations or charges against the Accused.[66]

64. Evidentiary support for Defence assertions that Dieudonné Nkulikiyinka and Alexis Bisanukuli refused to testify based on fear of reprisals is indirect and vague. Witness HIN testified that the former Defence investigator intimidated him in an attempt to prevent him from appearing for the Accused and suggested that the investigator had done the same to others, including Dieudonné Nkulikiyinka.[67] The witness's basis for knowledge with respect to these other acts of intimidation is imprecise. In the circumstances, it fails to demonstrate on the balance of the probabilities that intimidation occurred with respect to either witness. On this basis alone, the Chamber could dismiss Defence arguments.

65. Furthermore, the Defence has not sufficiently exhausted the remedies available to it. Based on Defence motions, the Chamber has ordered protective measures to facilitate the appearance of Defence witnesses who feared for their safety and expanded such measures to prolong the concealment of Witness HIN's identity given his refusal to otherwise testify Tribunal.[68] The Chamber has the authority to issue subpoenas and order the attendance of otherwise reluctant witnesses and enlist the cooperation of the State in assuring their attendance.[69] The Defence, however, has not sought such assistance from the Chamber to ensure the presentation of evidence from Dieudonné Nkulikiyinka and Alexis Bisanukuli. Once again, this alone would allow the Chamber to dismiss the Defence arguments.

66. Turning to the anticipated substance of the evidence, an examination of the Defence submissions, Defence Exhibit 4 and Dieudonné Nkulikiyinka's *pro justitia* statement, suggest he would testify about Renzaho's responsibility for crimes committed at roadblocks, his involvement in the killings at Saint Paul as well as refuge provided to persons at the Kigali-**[page 16]** Ville prefecture office.[70] Nkulikiyinka's anticipated evidence presents an alternative theory of who was responsible for roadblocks; it would suggest that Renzaho's subordinate acted independently in organising *Interahamwe* and instructing them to kill and to provide Renzaho misinformation. While Nkulikiyinka's proposed evidence is unique in singling out Witness ALG in this regard, the Chamber has heard evidence from Defence Witnesses Nyetera, PPO, UT, AIA, GOA, and HIN suggesting that local government officials in Kigali-Ville prefecture organised roadblocks on the orders of others or for reasons unrelated to Renzaho (II.2). Nkulikiyinka's anticipated evidence is cumulative of this evidence and its absence from the proceedings does not amount to material prejudice towards the Accused.

67. Moreover, the Chamber's findings in relation to the attack at Saint Paul (II.9) demonstrate that the Accused has not suffered prejudice due to Nkulikiyinka's absence. Likewise, his evidence related to refuge

---

[62] *Id.* para. 52; Rule 54 of the Rules.
[63] *Tadić* Appeal Judgement para. 52.
[64] *Simba* Appeal Judgement 41; *Bagosora et al.,* Decision on Motion Concerning Alleged Witness Intimidation (TC), 28 December 2004, para. 7.
[65] *Simba* Appeal Judgement 41; *Tadić* Appeal Judgement paras. 52-53, 55-56.
[66] *Simba* Trial Judgement para. 47; *Bagosora et al.,* Decision on Motion Concerning Alleged Witness Intimidation (TC), 28 December 2004, para. 10.
[67] T. 10 July 2007 pp. 20-21.
[68] Decision on Defence Request for Protective Measures (TC), 12 March 2007; Decision on Defence Request for Special Protective Measures for Witness HIN (TC), 14 June 2007.
[69] Rule 54 of the Rules; Article 28 of the Statute.
[70] T. 14 February 2008 p. 32; Defence Exhibit 4 (summary of Rwandan judicial record relating to Witness ALG). Given evidence on the record, the Chamber has some reservation as to how closely Nkulikiyinka would have been able to monitor Renzaho's activities generally. See, for instance, Witness ALG, T. 15 January 2007 pp. 27-28 (noting that Nkulikiyinka was in hiding in the prefecture office in April).

provided at the prefecture office is cumulative of other evidence (III.3.1.3), and its absence does not result in prejudice to the Accused.

68. Bisanukuli's proposed evidence would relate to meetings held at the Kigali-Ville prefecture office.[71] This would appear to include alleged meetings where Renzaho ordered persons to erect and maintain roadblocks and where he organized the distribution of weapons during a meeting there. Bisanukuli's anticipated evidence about the 8 April meeting would be cumulative of Defence evidence presented by Witnesses AIA and the Chamber finds that no prejudice was suffered due to its absence (II.2). However, the Chamber notes that Bisanukuli's possible first-hand evidence of a subsequent meeting at the prefecture office where Renzaho is alleged to have ordered attendants to retrieve weapons from the Ministry of Defence would be unique. While other Defence witnesses may have been in the vicinity of the prefecture office when this meeting is alleged to have occurred, no such evidence was brought by someone who would have attended such a meeting (II.3). Nonetheless, the proposed substance of Bisanukuli's evidence on this point is nondescript. The Defence merely asserting that Bisanukuli "assisted Mr. Renzaho during all the meetings that were organized at the prefecture".[72] Other evidence in the record suggests that just because one witness testifies another witness was present during a meeting does not necessarily demonstrate that witness will testify about it.[73] Without more, the Chamber cannot conclude that the Accused suffered material prejudice as a result its absence.

(iii)   Absence of Evidence Based on the Interference of a Former Defence Investigator

69. The Defence also points to its revelation, based on information from Witnesses HIN, NIB and Eugène Hantangigaba, that a former Defence investigator had exerted pressure on them not to testify on Renzaho's behalf and had engaged in similar conduct with other prospective Defence witnesses.[74] The Registry commenced an investigation into the Defence investigator's alleged interference.[75] On 30 June 2009, the Registry filed a 33 (B) report **[page 17]** noting that the appointed investigator had failed to respond to its requests for a final report on the matter.[76]

70. The issue of witness intimidation is one that this Tribunal does not take lightly. Affirmative interference with prospective witnesses can undermine the judicial process. While the burden of proving the charges in the indictment beyond a reasonable doubt rests firmly on the Prosecution, the Defence's ability to present evidence on its behalf is a fundamental tenant of the right to a fair trial.

71. Witness HIN testified that the former Defence investigator intimidated him in an attempt to prevent him from appearing for the Accused and suggested that the investigator had done the same to others, including Dieudonné Nkulikiyinka.[77] The Defence raised a contemporaneous plea to the Registry that the Defence investigator had similarly interfered with Witness NIB who had come to Arusha but ultimately did not testify.[78] The Defence also submitted a letter from Eugène Hantangigaba and indicated that the same investigator had invited the individual to testify against Renzaho.[79]

72. Even where allegations of intimidation are established, the Defence must exhaust all available measures to secure the taking of the witness's testimony.[80] Witness HIN testified on behalf of Renzaho. No submissions suggest that the evidence he provided was incomplete or tainted based on the alleged witness tampering.

---

[71]   Defence Closing Brief para. 275; T. 14 February 2008 p. 31.
[72]   T. 14 February 2008 p. 31.
[73]   Compare Witness PPV T. 4 June 2007; T. 5 June 2007 (generally) and Witness AIA, T. 3 July 2007 p. 4.
[74]   Defence Closing Brief paras. 285-290, 292; T. 14 February 2008 pp. 32-35.
[75]   Defence Closing Brief paras. 286, 291; T. 14 February 2008 pp. 34-35.
[76]   Registrar's Submissions under Rule 33 (B) of the Rules on the Final Report of Jean Haguma, 30 June 2009, para. 5.
[77]   T. 10 July 2007 pp. 20-21.
[78]   Letter of 20 June 2007 from the Defence to Registry.
[79]   Letter of 18 October 2007 from the Defence to Registry (attaching letter of Eugène Hatangigaba).
[80]   *Simba* Appeal Judgement para. 41.

73. Turning to Eugéne Hantangigaba, no specific submissions were made in relation to the substance of Hantangigaba's intended testimony.[81] A review of his witness statement suggests that his anticipated evidence would be relevant to rebutting evidence concerning the presence of civilian militia at Renzaho's house. Given the relevant findings (II.1), the Defence has failed to demonstrate material prejudice suffered by the Accused.

74. Witness NIB traveled to Arusha under the protection of the Registry, but was dropped as a witness by the Defence after his arrival. Like Hatangigaba, the Defence does not make any submissions regarding which charges the Witness NIB was intended to rebut.[82] His statement to the Defence investigator suggests that he was unaware of Renzaho having any position within the military hierarchy, and that it would have been difficult for meetings to have been held in Rugenge sector due to constant fighting there.[83] NIB's anticipated testimony about the fighting in Rugenge sector is also cumulative of other evidence in the record (II.13). The Chamber is unable to find material prejudice in lieu of the Defence's decision not to have the witness testify. [page 18]

(iv)   General Difficulties in Obtaining Evidence from Rwanda

75. Finally, the Defence notes its inability to obtain evidence from witnesses from Rwanda given the current political climate of threats and intimidation aimed at those otherwise willing to provide testimony in favour of the Accused. It suggests that the protective measures offered by the Tribunal fail to resolve the concerns felt by these individuals, noting in particular that the Rwandan government monitors the Tribunal's operations in Kigali.[84]

76. At the outset, no judicial system can guarantee absolute witness protection.[85] Nonetheless, the Chamber is sympathetic to the challenges faced by the Defence in obtaining witnesses. This Tribunal has in some instances concluded that the threats facing witnesses may impact the fairness of proceedings transferred from this Tribunal to Rwanda.[86] However, there are a number of reasons why individuals in Rwanda refuse to testify before the Tribunal. Some evidence on the record suggests that individuals would not testify on behalf of the Defence because of fear of and actual persecution within Rwanda.[87] However, the record is equivocal as to whether any perceived or actual intimidation of witnesses who have appeared on behalf of the Accused is in fact related to their participation in this proceeding.[88] Renzaho managed to mount a Defence that involved the attendance of 27 witnesses, five of whom came from Rwanda.[89] The Defence's challenges concerning the difficulties of securing witnesses from Rwanda, when viewed in light of the entire

---

[81]   Defence Closing Brief para. 288; T. 17 May 2007 pp. 12-13; T. 14 February 2008 pp. 30, 33-35.
[82]   Defence Closing Brief paras. 285, 288; T. 17 May 2007 pp. 12-13; T. 14 February 2008 pp. 30, 33-35.
[83]   The Chamber is mindful of the Defence's position that Witness NIB's statement, as recorded by their Defence investigator, does not accurately reflect what he had said. Without further submissions from the Defence, however, the Chamber must rely on this statement for its analysis.
[84]   Defence Closing Brief paras. 272-273; T. 8 January 2007 p. 8; T. 17 May 2007 p. 13; T. 29 August 2007 p. 48; T. 14 February 2008 pp. 35-37.
[85]   *Munyakazi*, Decision on Prosecution's Appeal Against Decision on Referral under Rule 11*bis* (AC), 8 October 2008, para. 38.
[86]   *Munyakazi*, Decision on Prosecutor's Request for Referral to the Republic of Rwanda (TC), 28 May 2008, paras. 60-62 affirmed in *Munyakazi*, Decision on Prosecution's Appeal Against Decision on Referral under Rule 11*bis* (AC), 8 October 2008, paras. 38-39; *Kanyarukiga*, Decision on Prosecutor's Request for Referral to the Republic of Rwanda (TC), 6 June 2008, paras. 66-74 affirmed in *Kanyarukiga*, Decision on Prosecution's Appeal Against Decision on Referral under Rule 11*bis* (AC), 30 October 2008, para. 27; *Gatete*, Decision on Prosecutor's Request for Referral to the Republic of Rwanda (TC), 17 November 2008, paras. 57-64.
[87]   See, for instance, Witness HIN, T. 10 July 2007 p. 19 ("When Defence counsel came to see me, I told him what my occupation was. I told him that I could not come to testify in the Renzaho trial because if I were to go to Arusha, I would be faced with serious security problems. And Mr. President, I must say that some witnesses encountered problems after coming back from Arusha. Some died, others were persecuted, others fled the country.").
[88]   See, for instance, Witness HAL, T. 18 June 2007 pp. 20-22, 33-37, 39-41; Prosecution Exhibit 107 (judgement from Nyamirambo court of first instance) (testifying to his belief that he was arrested and convicted based on his contact with Renzaho's Defence team, but noting that he was arrested five months after his communications with them due to a dispute with an individual that concerned matters unrelated to the Accused); Witness MAI, T. 22 August 2007 pp. 20-21 (testifying that he fled the country for fear of being killed after being "opposed" and "persecuted" based on his relationship with the Accused and for allegedly being an *Interahamwe*).
[89]   T. 14 February 2008 pp. 38-39.

record, fails to convince the Chamber that this proceeding has been rendered unfair. The Chamber dismisses this argument.

2.2.4 Factors Affecting the Proceedings

77. Articles 12 and 20 of the Statute ensure the right of an accused to a fair hearing before impartial judges, and the ICTY and ICTR have consistently recognised the right to be tried by **[page 19]** a tribunal which both appears to be and is in fact genuinely impartial.[90] There is a general rule that a judge should not only be subjectively free from bias, but also there should be nothing in the surrounding circumstances that gives rise to an appearance of bias.[91] In the instant case, there are no direct allegations of bias, nor any assertions regarding the Chamber's potential inability to fairly assess the evidence. Instead, the Defence challenges the Prosecutorial strategy in choosing whom to investigate and prosecute, and their reliance on witnesses living in Rwanda, particularly those who have been charged or convicted with crimes there.[92] Additionally, the Defence explains the risks of conviction by association and cautions against the dangers inherent in using confessions and expert testimony.[93] Finally, the Defence warns the Chamber that the heinous nature of the crimes committed throughout the genocide and the pressure from the international community should not compel a finding that Renzaho is responsible.[94]

78. Cognizant of the Defence arguments, the Chamber concludes that none have rendered the trial unfair. The Prosecution has broad discretion in relation to the preparation of indictments.[95] It is not the role of the Chamber or any other government source to dictate a certain trial strategy.[96] The Chamber acknowledges the concerns raised by the Defence in regard to the question of witness credibility and will consider the merits of each witness in the context of all evidence presented and in light of the entire record. The Chamber is aware of the elements required to establish Renzaho's guilt and has considered the specific risks of accepting testimony offered by the Prosecution witnesses, the use of confessions and "tunnel vision". **[page 20]**

3. THARCISSE RENZAHO

79. Tharcisse Renzaho was born on 17 July 1944 in the Kabare-1 sector, Kigarama *commune*, Kibungo prefecture. He is married and the father of five children. After military training at the *Ecole Supérieure Militaire* (ESM), he graduated in 1970 as a second lieutenant in 1975. Subsequently, he became head of a platoon, and then commander of a company. Renzaho was also an officer of the general staff working in departments that included a combat unit. From 1984 onwards, as a Lieutenant-Colonel, he was appointed study director at ESM.[97]

80. Between 1980 and 1989, Renzaho also underwent further military training in Belgium and Germany. After returning to Rwanda in July 1989, he was made director of the programmes and study department at the Ministry of Defence. On 5 October 1990, he left that position, when President Juvénal Habyarimana appointed him the first prefect of Kigali-Ville prefecture, following its establishment.[98]

81. As prefect, Renzaho was the guarantor of peace and security in Kigali-Ville. He exercised civilian functions but remained a military officer. In July 1992, he was promoted to the rank of colonel.[99]

---

[90] *Furundžija* Appeal Judgement para. 182; *Rutaganda* Appeal Judgement para. 39.
[91] *Karemera et al.*, Decision on the Severance of Andre Rwamakuba and Amendments of the Indictment, Article 20 (4) of the Statute, Rule 82 (b) of the Rules of Procedure and Evidence (TC), 7 December 2004, para. 17, citing *Furundžija* Appeal Judgement para. 182.
[92] Defence Closing Brief paras. 294-317.
[93] *Id*. paras. 334-338.
[94] *Id*. paras. 318-330.
[95] *Ndindiliyimana*, Decision on Urgent Oral Motion for a Stay of the Indictment, or in the Alternative a Reference to the Security Council (TC), 26 March 2004, para. 22.
[96] *Bagosora et al.* Trial Judgement, para. 1999.
[97] Prosecution Closing Brief paras. 1, 557; T. 18 May 2007 p. 5; T. 27 August 2007 pp. 1, 3, 5-6.
[98] Prosecution Closing Brief para. 1; T. 27 August 2007 pp. 4-5.
[99] T. 27 August 2007 pp. 5-6; T. 29 August 2007 p. 8.

82. On the morning of 7 April 1994, following the death of President Habyarimana, Renzaho was authorised to join a meeting of senior military command, which was chaired by General-Major Augustin Ndindiliyimana, and appointed to a crisis committee that was set up during that meeting.[100]

83. Renzaho left Rwanda in early July 1994. He was arrested on 29 September 2002 in the Democratic Republic of Congo, and was transferred to the UN Detention Facility on 30 September 2002.[101] **[page 21]**

CHAPTER II: ACTUAL SECTION

1. ENCOURAGEMENT OF *INTERAHAMWE* TRAINING, 1993-1994

1.1 Introduction

84. The Prosecution alleges that, between mid-1993 and 17 July 1994, Renzaho regularly permitted and encouraged *Interahamwe* and *Impuzamugambi* groups to meet at his house in Kanombe and elsewhere for the purpose of receiving military training. They killed or caused serious bodily or mental harm to Tutsis between 6 April and 17 July 1994. Reference is made to Witnesses XXY and ALG. The Defence denies the charges and claims that the Prosecution evidence is discredited by the testimony of Witnesses Nyetera, Butera, BOU, ABC, VDD, MAI, HAL and NYT.[102]

1.2 Evidence

Prosecution Witness XXY

85. Witness XXY, a Hutu, was a classmate of Renzaho's son, Jean-François Régis, at a school in Kigali. The school was not far from Renzaho's house in Kanombe. In the first term of 1993-1994, the witness boarded in a dormitory with many other students on campus. In the second, he lived in a student facility in the neighbourhood, close to Renzaho's residence. There were several such facilities. The witness was about two years older than Régis but they sat on the same bench at school.[103]

86. On 3 May 1993, Saint Juvénal's Day, the students at the school were invited to a reception at the home of the President of Rwanda. After the reception, Renzaho asked the students to join the *Interahamwe*. He told those who were already members to prepare a list of other young persons who wanted to join. That day, Jean Lummumba, a student influential in the *Interahamwe*, prepared a long list, as many had expressed such an interest. Lummumba and the dean indicated that they would forward the list to Renzaho. In the witness's estimate, between 300 and 400 of the approximately 1,000 students were already members of the *Interahamwe*. Régis was not present at the reception because he only arrived at the school in September 1993.[104]

87. Régis and the witness carried out many activities together at school, belonged to the scouts' movement and played basketball. They had several mutual friends in the same class and studied the same subject. Some of them lodged at the same hostel in Kigali as the witness.[105] Renzaho was already living in his house when Régis came to Kanombe to study in **[page 22]** September 1993. At that juncture, Régis' cousin Mutesi and a house helper also stayed there. Renzaho's wife and the other children moved from Kiyovu to Kanombe in

---
[100] Prosecution Closing Brief para. 6; T. 27 August 2007 pp. 48-56.
[101] Defence Closing Brief para. 1291; T. 30 August 2007 pp. 18, 45.
[102] Indictment paras. 11 and 28; Prosecution Closing Brief paras. 128-141; T. 14 February 2008 pp. 14-15; Defence Closing Brief paras. 869, 871-872, 884-904; T. 14 August 2008 pp. 42-52, 58-59; Defence Exhibit 113 (*complément écrit aux arguments oraux de la défense*) paras. 886.1-886.3.
[103] T. 10 January 2007 pp. 5-6, 18-19, 24-25, 33-35, 42, 45. When referring to the student facilities where he stayed during the second semester, Witness XXY used the word "home" (p. 19). According to Prosecution Exhibit 66 (personal identification sheet), Witness XXY was born in 1974.
[104] T. 10 January 2007 pp. 11-13, 20, 43-44, 50-51. For reasons of consistency, the Chamber has chosen "Lummumba" and not "Lumumba". T. 10 January 2007 p. 13.
[105] T. 10 January 2007 p. 36. Witness XXY used the word "hostel" ("*home*" in the French transcript, *id.* p. 21), which, in this context, appears to refer to the student facility in which he stayed during the second term. The witness also stated that Régis knew how to drive. *Id.* p. 45.

1994, but the witness did not recall in which month they arrived. Until then, the witness frequented the Renzaho residence almost daily, beginning in November 1993. He could not say exactly how many times he was there between that month and March 1994. Régis visited the witness's residence as well. After the arrival of the entire family, the witness went to Régis's home less often, but still went about every two or three days until late March 1994. He did not know the number or names of Renzaho's other children.[106]

88. Before the family moved in, the witness would sometimes see between 50 and 100 *Interahamwe* uniforms being dried on the ground or on ropes in the compound outside Renzaho's house. He did not specify exactly when or how many times he saw the uniforms, but it was at least on two occasions. The *Interahamwe* had a well-known uniform that they would wear to rallies. It was sewn in *kitenge* material and easily identifiable.[107]

89. Sometime before Christmas 1993, at about 5.30 p.m., Witness XXY visited Régis to collect books and noticed a bus parked directly in front of Renzaho's residence. Régis explained that the *Interahamwe* were going for training at Mutara. Some of the *Interahamwe* were picking up their belongings to enter the bus. They had sacks of grenades, and some were carrying guns. When Renzaho arrived in a white Renault 21, at about 5.30 p.m., they were taking their seats on the bus. Renzaho waved at them and wished them sound training before the bus took off. The witness never saw Régis participating in *Interahamwe* activities, but could not rule out that he was a member.[108]

Prosecution Witness ALG

90. In 1994, Witness ALG, a Hutu, was a member of the MRND party and a high-ranking official in Nyarugenge commune in Kigali-Ville. He testified that, after the advent of multiparty politics in June 1991, Renzaho was no longer chairman of the MRND for the prefecture, but nevertheless continued collaborating with its leaders, including in the military training of *Interahamwe*, the youth wing of the party. The witness noted that as a soldier, Renzaho should not have been a member of any political party.[109]

91. Sometime between late February and early March 1993, Renzaho successively summoned groups of *responsables*, commune and sector officials to his office. All of them – about 15 persons – were members of the MRND. The witness went there with four or five officials. Renzaho informed them that the army high command, in consultation with the leadership of the MRND, had decided that the *Interahamwe* would receive covert military training. The purpose was to assist the army in fighting the *Inkotanyi* if the war resumed, and to participate in operations aimed at securing Kigali city. The training would take place in army camps. Renzaho said that the information was confidential and to be kept from the **[page 23]** public, so that MRND opponents would not know of the programme and be able to undermine it.[110]

92. The meeting participants later gleaned information about the location of the training camps, such as Gabiro military camp, which at the time was in Mutara,[111] in Byumba prefecture; Gako army camp in Bugesera sub-prefecture in Kigali-Rural prefecture; and Bigogwe army camp in Gisenyi prefecture. Many persons were being trained, but the witness could not specify the number. The military training of the *Interahamwe* was already underway when the Arusha Accords were signed. At that time, Rwandan law prohibited political parties from having militia.[112]

---

[106] *Id.* pp. 6-9, 12, 33-34, 36-38, 40-42, 45, 48-49, 51. The transcripts refer to Régis' cousin as "Mutesi". Also Witness NYT used that name, whereas the other witnesses called her "Umutesi".
[107] *Id.* p. 8.
[108] *Id.* pp. 9-10, 50-51. According to Witness XXY, buses from ONATRACOM, the national transportation company, were used to transport the *Interahamwe. Id.* P. 9.
[109] *Id.* pp. 56, 73-74; T. 11 January 2007 pp. 6, 8, 72-73; T. 12 January 2007 pp. 22-23; Prosecution Exhibit 67 (personal identification sheet).
[110] T. 11 January 2007 pp. 6-8; T. 12 January 2007 pp. 22-23.
[111] Both versions of the transcripts state "Mutura". However, Mutura is in Gisenyi, whereas Mutara is in Gabiro. Witness XXY correctly referred to "Mutara" (above), which the Chamber has decided to use.
[112] T. 11 January 2007 pp. 6-8; T. 12 January 2007 pp. 19, 22-23. Witness ALG was aware only of the camps where the Kigali *Interahamwe* were trained, but heard that other *Interahamwe* were being trained elsewhere as well. T. 11 January 2007 p. 7.

Renzaho

93. Renzaho testified that he had never been involved in recruiting *Interahamwe*, and that he did not do so on 3 May 1993. *Interahamwe* never left from his house by bus, and their clothes were not washed or hung outside his house. After 25 May 1994, there were young people trained to reinforce the army. Even though the Arusha Accords did not allow the arming and training of civilians, some civilians were nevertheless trained to join the Rwandan Armed Forces.[113]

Defence Witness ABC

94. Witness ABC, a Hutu, is related to Renzaho. In May 1992, the entire family moved to Kanombe. Régis attended the school there from July 1993 to April 1994. He was never a member of the scout movement. The witness would have known if he had close friends. Classmates visited him at home to do their homework together, but she did not know Witness XXY. Only a student called René sometimes came home with Régis. They were born in the same year, 1981. The Renzaho children were not allowed to have friends who were five or six years older than them. The name of the eldest daughter was Umutesi.[114]

95. The area behind the house where clothes were washed was not big enough to wash and dry 50 to 100 *Interahamwe* uniforms. The family washed only its own clothes. The witness never saw Renzaho receive or invite *Interahamwe* from September to December 1993. There was no hostel for students in the vicinity of the Renzaho residence.[115]

Defence Witness VDD

96. Witness VDD, a Hutu related to the Renzaho family, testified that the entire family moved from Kigali-Ville to Kanombe on the same day in May 1992. Their daughter Umutesi had no reason to move to their new home earlier as she was a student at a school just opposite **[page 24]** the family's residence in Kigali. Régis could not have gone to stay in Kanombe in May 1992, because he only started school there in September that year. *Interahamwe* would not have been allowed into their home.[116] The witness could not state with certainty that she had never met Witness XXY, but did not believe that Régis had any friends. She recalled two of Régis' classmates: René and Emmanuel. René would sometimes do homework with Régis at the Renzaho residence and he, like Régis was born in 1981.[117]

Defence Witness MAI

97. Witness MAI, a Hutu, is related to the Renzaho family. The construction of their home in Kanombe started at the beginning of 1992, and was completed in early 1993. The family relocated there together around June or July 1993. The children, including Jean-François Régis and Umutesi, moved at the same time. The person overseeing the construction of the house lived alone in it from February 1993 until the family arrived. No one else had the key, and he locked the place when he left for work.[118]

98. Military or militia uniforms could not be washed within the compound while the overseer was living there because there was no water during that time. Militiamen never came to the house from February 1993 onward, and the family did not receive youth belonging to political parties in their home. The witness did not see any of Régis' friends coming to visit. There was no student housing in the neighbourhood near the residence.[119]

---

[113] T. 30 August 2007 pp. 31-32, 33-35, 38 ("I am not aware of what one is referring to as *Interahamwe*."), 42-43; T. 31 August 2007 p. 10; T. 3 September 2007 p. 15.
[114] T. 17 May 2007 pp. 29-35, 51-54, 56; Defence Exhibit 42 (personal identification sheet).
[115] T. 17 May 2007 pp. 30-31.
[116] T. 18 May 2007 pp. 5, 9-10, 13; T. 22 May 2007 pp.16.
[117] T. 18 May 2007 p. 14; T. 22 May 2007 p. 11-12. Witness VDD was uncertain whether she should characterise René and Emmanuel as "friends" or "classmates" of Régis. (T. 22 May 2007 p. 11). He once spoke to her of another friend who used to come to his house but she did not know that boy (T. 18 May 2007 p. 14).
[118] T. 22 August 2007 pp. 6-10; Defence Exhibit 76 (personal identification sheet).
[119] T. 22 August 2007 pp. 7, 10, 11 ("the Renzaho family was a respectable family and ... people of such a category [referring to political party youth groups] could not go to their house"), 12-13.

Defence Witness HAL

99. Witness HAL, a Hutu, worked for the Renzaho family. Construction of their house in Kanombe began in 1990 and was completed in 1992. All the members of the family, including Régis, took up residence in Kanombe on the same day in May 1992. The witness helped the family move.[120] He was often present when the residence was being built but he never saw any *Interahamwe* or their clothing there. There was a very small courtyard at the entrance to the compound. No students were living in that neighbourhood, as all of them stayed at the school, about two kilometres away.[121]

100. The witness visited the house daily at 7.00 a.m., carried out various tasks, and returned there at 9.00 p.m. or whenever he was free. In 1993, he was there several times a day, but never observed any *Interahamwe* or a bus parked outside. He watched Régis leave and return each day. He never saw that Régis had friends and thought the boy was too young to have any. Régis was about 12 years old in 1994.[122] **[page 25]**

Defence Witness NYT

101. Witness NYT, a Hutu, was a day student in the same class as Régis and Witness XXY in 1992-1993.[123] From September 1992, he often went to visit Régis at Renzaho's house, as the witness had a relative living close by. As of his first visit, Régis and his uncle were living there. At times, the witness also found "Mutesi" or Josiane, or another of the Renzaho children there. Towards the end of December 1992, all the members of the family had moved in. During his third and last year at the school in 1993-1994, he did homework at Régis' house three times a week and sometimes more. The witness also visited on weekends. He did not see *Interahamwe* at the Renzaho house, nor did he see their clothes being washed or dried there. There was a courtyard at the rear of the house.[124]

102. Régis did not do any sports, and was not a member of the scout movement or of a youth wing of any party. Witness NYT did not belong to any youth party. He confirmed that a politically active boy named Lummumba was in the upper class at the school. The witness was Régis' closest friend since childhood. They were the same age, but he could not remember when Régis' birthday was. The witness knew Witness XXY as they were also in the same class at school, but he was not a friend of Régis. If he had been, the witness would have known about it. He never saw Witness XXY at the Renzaho residence, and that Régis would have told him if that person had visited. Régis did not have many friends, but it was possible that a boy named Emmanuel visited the house.[125]

103. Renzaho was not present at the school on 3 May 1993. The Saint Juvénal celebrations consisted of better meals that were shared with teachers and a reception for students and teachers. No speeches were given. The witness never attended any reception at President Habyarimana's house.[126]

Defence Witness Antoine Théophile Nyetera

104. Antoine Théophile Nyetera, a Tutsi, was a history and anthropology researcher in Rwanda during the events in 1994. He left his house only once each month in April, May and June but visitors kept him informed. Based on his general knowledge, Renzaho could not have belonged to any political party because, under the Rwandan constitution, no soldiers could have such membership. The militia only took instruction from their political leaders and depended on the parties that formed them. No prefect gave them favours or had a hand in the development of political youth wings. The witness derived this from a "known fact".[127]

---

[120] T. 18 June 2007 pp. 4-7, 31, 42; Defence Exhibit 64 (personal identification sheet).
[121] T. 18 June 2007 pp. 5-8.
[122] *Id.* pp. 8-10, 19 (mentioning that Régis did not know how to drive), 20, 29.
[123] Although the witness did not testify as to his own ethnicity, his father was Hutu. T. 3 July 2007 p. 32.
[124] T. 3 July 2007 pp. 24-28, 29 (stating that Régis never knew how to drive), 38-41; Defence Exhibit 67 (personal identification sheet).
[125] T. 3 July 2007 pp. 26-30, 32-33, 37, 41-43.
[126] *Id.* pp. 29, 41-42.
[127] T. 5 July 2007 pp. 18-19, 21-22, 37-40; Defence Exhibit 72 (personal identification sheet). Nyetera (previously Witness BIT) stated that he is a descendant of the Rwandan royal family and lost his wife and children between April and July 1994. T. 5 July 2007

Defence Witness Jean-Baptiste Butera

105. Jean-Baptiste Butera, a Hutu, was the director of the national programme for AIDS control in the Ministry of Public Health in April 1994 and came from Kibungu, the same **[page 26]** prefecture as Renzaho. He did not believe that the prefect of Kigali-Ville, who was meant to uphold neutrality in matters of politics, had any particular links with the *Interahamwe* militia. Renzaho would have been dismissed if there had been indications that he had special relations with any youth wing of political parties. The Prime Minister could easily have replaced him.[128]

Defence Witness BOU

106. Witness BOU, a Hutu, was a high-ranking employee in a ministry during parts of 1993 and until early April 1994. He testified that Renzaho was bound to be politically neutral as prefect and not have special links with any political party or militia. It was generally being said that *Interahamwe* were trained somewhere in Rwanda, but the witness only heard that from complaining opposition groups at the communal level. There were no such reports in his own commune. Had there been any training of militia at Renzaho's residence, it would have been known.[129]

1.3 Deliberations

107. In seeking to prove that Renzaho permitted and encouraged the *Interahamwe* to receive military training the Prosecution relies on Witness XXY and Witness ALG. This evidence includes events that took place prior to 1994 and hence fall outside the temporal jurisdiction of the Tribunal. It follows from case law, however, that the Chamber may admit such evidence if it is relevant, has probative value and there is no compelling reason to exclude it.[130]

108. Witness XXY's evidence appeared generally coherent and credible. There were no clear inconsistencies between his testimony and a previous statement to Tribunal investigators in December 2000. During cross-examination, the Defence suggested that it was implausible, in view of his young age, that he had been in contact with so many high-ranking persons as listed in the statement.[131] The witness explained his particular background which made this possible, and stated that he only overheard parts of what the dignitaries were saying but had not engaged in conversations with them. The Chamber accepts this explanation.

109. According to Witness XXY, Renzaho encouraged students to join the *Interahamwe* on 3 May 1993, following the reception at President Habyarimana's residence. Defence Witness **[page 27]** NYT confirmed that Witness XXY was a student at the school, but said that he did not see Renzaho on that day. In the Chamber's view, these two accounts are not necessarily incompatible. Witness NYT did not attend the reception at the President's home and would therefore not have observed any recruitment by Renzaho there. Moreover, the witness confirmed that Lummumba was a politically active boy at the school, as Witness XXY testified.

---

pp. 18, 37-38.
[128] T. 22 May 2007 pp. 67-68; T. 23 May 2007 pp. 13, 17; Defence Exhibit 46 (personal identification sheet). Butera was previously referred to as Witness LAA.
[129] T. 22 May 2007 pp. 32, 44-45; Defence Exhibit 44 (personal identification sheet). Witness BOU said that the entire country would have been informed of *Interahamwe* training at Renzaho's house. Opposition groups would have published information about it in the press, leading to his removal by the President of the Republic within a few days. T. 22 May 2007 p. 45.
[130] For example, a Trial Chamber may validly admit and rely on evidence on events prior to 1994 where it aims at clarifying the context in which the crimes occurred, establishing by inference the elements (in particular, an accused's criminal intent) of criminal conduct occurring in 1994, or demonstrating a deliberate pattern of conduct. *Nahimana et al.* Appeal Judgement paras. 315-316; *Bagosora et al.* Judgement para. 358.
[131] The statement, signed on 13 December 2000, was not tendered as an exhibit but the Defence referred to it during the proceedings. It included references to the witness overhearing or observing Fulgence Niyonteze; Monsignor Musabyimana; Mr. Callixte Nzabonimana, Minster of Youth; Mr. Eliezer Niyitegeka, Minister of Information; General Gratien Kabiligi; General Ndindiliyimana, Colonel Bagosora and Major Aloys Ntabakuze. T. 10 January 2007 pp. 46-47. The Chamber notes that these parts of the statement neither refer to Renzaho nor military training.

Judgement and Sentence

110. Witness XXY also testified that a group of *Interahamwe* were in a bus in front of Renzaho's residence and left for training just before Christmas 1993. Their clothes were dried at the compound at least twice between September 1993 and the time that the entire family moved into the house in March 1994. The Defence disputed this and adduced evidence that the witness was not a friend of Régis.

111. All the Defence witnesses except for Witness NYT had some form of family or employment tie to Renzaho. Their testimonies therefore have limited weight. To some extent they contradicted each other with respect to when Régis started school in Kanombe;[132] the construction of Renzaho's house;[133] when the family members moved to Kanombe,[134]; and whether it was possible to wash 50 or more *Interahamwe* uniforms in the Renzaho house compound.[135] The Chamber accepts that time estimates are difficult many years after the events but finds these differences noteworthy. Furthermore, Witness NYT confirmed Witness XXY's testimony that Régis lived in Kanombe with his uncle before the rest of the family moved in.

112. The Chamber has considered the submission that a friendship between Witness XXY and Régis was unlikely in view of the purported age difference between them. It is clear that the witness was 19-20 years old at the time. Defence evidence suggests that Régis was only about 12-13, whereas Witness XXY considered that the difference was only two years. Régis did not testify, and no birth certificate was provided. Leaving aside the exact age difference, Witness NYT's confirmation that Witness XXY and Régis were in the same class is significant. Therefore, the Chamber accepts that they did homework together from time to time, irrespective of whether they were friends or schoolmates. Witness XXY's credibility is not affected by his inability to remember the names and number of Renzaho's children.[136]

113. Witness XXY's testimony is to a certain extent strengthened by Witness ALG's evidence about Renzaho's alleged meetings between late February and early March 1993, informing attendees of covert military training for *Interahamwe*. This part of Witness ALG's **[page 28]** testimony appeared consistent and credible.[137] Although it does not relate to any specific acts of encouragement by Renzaho it shows that he had inside knowledge and supported military training of the *Interahamwe*.

114. The Chamber is not persuaded by the testimony of Defence Witnesses Nyetera, Butera and ABC to the effect that supporting the *Interhamwe* would have been a violation of a prefect's obligation to maintain neutrality. Although this may have been the legal situation it does not exclude that some prefects may have supported individual parties in reality. Some support for this view is found in a working document elaborated by the MDR steering committee in May 1992. It includes Renzaho's name on a list of persons considered to be in charge of recruiting army and gendarmerie reservists to join the *Interahamwe*.[138] Renzaho rejected the contents of the document as baseless.[139] The Chamber notes that the MDR was in opposition to the MRND, and that the document appears to be an expression of political propaganda. It therefore carries limited

---

[132] Witness ABC referred to July 1993, Witness VDD said it was in September 1992, while Witness HAL stated that Régis joined in the 1993 school year. According to Witness NYT, Régis was at the school in the 1992-1993 school year. It is recalled that Witness XXY said that Régis joined the school in September 1993.
[133] Witness HAL testified that work started in 1990 and ended in 1992, while Witness MAI indicated a period from early 1992 to early 1993.
[134] Witnesses HAL, VDD and ABC stated that the family moved in May 1992, whereas Witness MAI mentioned June or July 1993. Both Witness ABC and Witness MAI said that this coincided with the confirmation of the Renzaho children, yet each witness gave a different month and year for the move.
[135] Witness HAL testified that the house had a very small courtyard at its entrance, while Witness NYT stated that the courtyard was at the rear.
[136] The Defence disputes Witness XXY's evidence about where he stayed, that Régis was member of the scout movement, played basketball and knew how to drive. In the Chamber's view, these submissions about collateral matters do not affect the witness's credibility. Similarly, exactly where Witness XXY was living is not important. Some of the discrepancies between the testimonies may stem from the different terms used ("hostel", "home", etc.).
[137] Witness ALG, who was arrested in Rwanda in 1998 and provisionally released in 2005, was still awaiting trial for genocide when he testified. The Chamber has taken into account that his evidence may have been influenced by a wish to positively affect the proceedings against him in Rwanda (see, for instance, II.2) but does not consider this decisive in the present context.
[138] Prosecution Exhibit 115 ("*Interahamwe za Muvoma* or The MDR Party Hardliners", Working document for the MDR Steering Committee, dated 14 May 1992 and signed by Dr. Anastase Gasana, Member, MDR Political Bureau. Renzaho is listed in a section entitled "Those charged with recruiting from among the reservists" (pp. 6-7).
[139] Renzaho testified that Gasana, who had belonged to the MRND party before moving to the MDR, was forced to produce documents of this nature, and that the working document had been presented in Brussels in 1992 during the political parties' negotiations with the RPF. As of 14 May 1992, the government was led by a prime minister from an opposition party, whereas

weight. However, the document does indicate that Renzaho was perceived as being affiliated with a political organisation – the MRND – and in favour of recruitment of *Interahamwe*.[140]

115. Having assessed the totality of the evidence, the Chamber is satisfied that Renzaho encouraged students in Kanombe to join the *Interahamwe* in May 1993, and that he encouraged and permitted *Interahamwe* to meet at his house in late 1993 for the purpose of receiving military training. This said, it observes that support to a youth organisation does not in itself constitute a crime under the ICTR Statute. Furthermore, Witnesses XXY and ALG did not testify that Renzaho at that juncture made statements against the Tutsis or that the purpose of the training was to kill Tutsis. **[page 29]**

2. ROADBLOCKS IN KIGALI-VILLE PREFECTURE

2.1 Introduction

116. The Indictment alleges that, from 7 April to 17 July 1994, soldiers, gendarmes, militia and demobilised soldiers, under Renzaho's instructions and effective control, constructed and manned roadblocks throughout Kigali-Ville prefecture, including at Gitega and near the ONATRACOM facility. Around 10 April, Renzaho convened a meeting at the Kigali-Ville prefecture office where he ordered local officials to set up roadblocks to identify and kill Tutsis. Furthermore, on diverse dates in April and May 1994, he asked local officials to remain vigilant at roadblocks. He gave instructions to construct and man roadblocks during regular broadcasts on Radio Rwanda. These checkpoints were then used to intercept, identify and kill Tutsis. Reference is made to Witnesses AFB, UB, AWE, ALG, GLJ, Corinne Dufka and Expert Witness Alison Des Forges.[141]

117. The Defence maintains that the Indictment lacks sufficient detail to provide adequate notice of these allegations. It further argues that Renzaho did not order the establishment of roadblocks, which were spontaneously established by the civilian population. In radio broadcasts, he gave instructions to dismantle roadblocks and denounced persons perpetrating crimes at them. Renzaho lacked the capacity and resources to exert any control over the roadblocks. The Defence relies on Witnesses AIA, PPV, BDC, PPO, HIN, GOA, PGL, Antoine Théophile Nyetera and Expert Witness Bernard Lugan.[142]

2.2 Evidence

Prosecution Witness AFB

118. Witness AFB, a Hutu employee in public service, testified that on 8 April 1994, he and four police officers escorted Renzaho, who was in a different vehicle, as they travelled through Kigali. Between 2.00 p.m. and 3.00 p.m., they passed six roadblocks. Renzaho and his escort experienced no difficulties, probably because he was the highest administrative authority in the prefecture.[143]

Renzaho himself lacked political support. T. 30 August 2007 pp. 32-33. In the Chamber's view, this does not explain why he should unjustifiably be perceived as involved in recruitment to the *Interahamwe*.
[140] The Chamber has noted the Defence submission that Witness XXY refused to disclose his diary but does not consider this significant. T. 10 January 2007 p. 48 ("I cannot give it to you for you to become privy to all my secrets").
[141] Indictment paras. 7-10, 25-27; Prosecution Closing Brief paras. 32, 46, 55, 75-77, 83, 91, 101-104, 108-127, 129, 152, 154, 162-164, 170, 173, 192-193, 201, 204, 213-214, 228, 253, 264, 276, 302, 317, 325 (b, f), 340-341, 361, 366, 405, 438, 450, 509-519, 521, 523-527, 529; T. 14 February 2008 pp. 14-15, 18-19; T. 15 February 2008 pp. 14-15. The accounts of Witnesses UL, SAF, KBZ, BUO and UI are considered in the Chamber's deliberations but as their testimonies only indirectly relate to Renzaho's conduct concerning roadblocks, they are not summarised in the evidence section.
[142] Defence Closing Brief paras. 9, 11, 28-32, 106-108, 112-121, 133-134, 145-149, 162-164, 303-317, 718-799, 1035-1043, 1111-1128; Defence Exhibit 113 (*complément écrit aux arguments oraux de la défense*) paras. 753.1-753.7; T. 17 May 2007 pp. 3-4; T. 14 February 2008 pp. 46-51, 53-58; T. 15 February 2008 pp. 16-18. The Defence also refers to Witnesses UT, BOU, RGI, MAI, KRG, WOW and Jean-Baptiste Butera. Their accounts are considered in the Chamber's deliberations but not included in the evidence section for the reasons indicated in the previous footnote.
[143] T. 8 January 2007 pp. 69, 86, 88, 94-95; T. 9 January 2007 p. 17; Prosecution Exhibit 64 (personal identification sheet).

119. Renzaho's convoy first went to Rose Karushara's house, in Kimisagara sector, where they saw her at a roadblock together with approximately 20 or 30 *Interahamwe* armed with firearms, clubs, machetes and knives. The witness also observed a group of persons sitting **[page 30]** nearby on the ground, whom he believed to be Tutsi because the Tutsis were being targeted. Renzaho remained in his vehicle and spoke with Karushara. He then talked with the *Interahamwe* who had gathered around him, telling them to keep doing their work. In the witness's opinion, "[Renzaho] was asking them to kill". The *Interahamwe* requested more weapons and Renzaho agreed to provide them.[144]

120. The convoy next stopped at a second roadblock in Nyakabanda sector. Renzaho spoke with the area's recently appointed *conseiller* as well as the armed *Interahamwe* there. The *Interahamwe* asked Renzaho for additional guns, and he promised to obtain them. The witness saw dead bodies as the convoy passed a third roadblock, manned by *Interahamwe* and two Josephite brothers on the road to Nyamirambo near the Josephite monastery. After returning to town, the witness again saw corpses as the convoy passed through a roadblock. It was manned by gendarmes with guns and *Interahamwe* with traditional weapons and located at the Nyamirambo gendarmerie brigade near Club Raffiki and opposite the Petrorwanda petrol station.[145]

121. During their trip on 8 April, Renzaho also repeated his instructions to "work" at a roadblock, manned by armed *Interahamwe*, at ONATRACOM near a mosque in Gitega sector. This checkpoint had previously been staffed by soldiers on 7 April. In addition, the witness saw the Gitega *conseiller*, *Interahamwe* and many dead bodies at another roadblock, which the convoy passed near the Gitega sector office. Renzaho agreed to assist the *Interahamwe* at this roadblock dispose of the corpses.[146]

122. Around noon on 12 April, Witness AFB and policemen, loaded with weapons, went with Renzaho and Kabiligi to the roadblock near Protais Zigiranyirazo's residence, which was manned by soldiers and *Interahamwe*. Weapons were distributed there. Kabiligi ordered additional distributions. The witness and policemen subsequently gave two or three weapons to whoever identified himself as the chief at roadblocks, including one near Karushara's house in Kimisagara sector, and at roadblocks in Nyakabanda, Nyamirambo and Biryogo sectors. They returned to the prefecture office at about 3.00 p.m., where they found Renzaho.[147]

Prosecution Witness UB

123. Witness UB, a Hutu and former local official in Kigali-Ville prefecture, stated that he attended an "extended security meeting" that Renzaho convened at the Kigali-Ville prefecture office on 10 or 11 April 1994. At the meeting, the witness saw the *conseillers* from Kigali-Ville prefecture, *responsables de cellule*, soldiers, police officers, and representatives of the recognised political parties and their youth wings, including the *Interahamwe*. Jean Bizimana, *bourgmestre* of Nyarugenge commune, was not present. Renzaho opened the meeting by stating that the *Inkotanyi* had assassinated President Habyarimana. The *conseillers* informed the prefect about the killing, looting, and raping of Tutsis, and that party officials had erected roadblocks. He instructed them to set up additional roadblocks where they did not exist to confront their enemy, "the Tutsi". After this meeting, roadblocks became **[page 31]** more prevalent and everyone passing through these roadblocks had to show their identity cards. The roadblocks in the witness's neighborhood were used to persecute *Inkotanyi* and their accomplices, the Tutsis.[148]

Prosecution Witness AWE

124. Witness AWE, a Hutu, was a local official in Kigali-Ville prefecture. He stayed home after the plane crash until 9 April 1994, when a *communiqué* from Renzaho was broadcast on the radio, summoning a meeting of *conseillers* as well as the *bourgmestre* of Nyarugenge, Jean Bizimana, at the prefecture office.

---

[144] T. 8 January 2007 pp. 86-87; T. 9 January 2007 p. 32.
[145] T. 8 January 2007 pp. 87, 89-90.
[146] *Id*. pp. 86-94.
[147] T. 9 January 2007 pp. 5-9, 17, 20. Evidence about weapons distribution is discussed in greater detail elsewhere (II.3).
[148] T. 23 January 2007 pp. 8-9, 11-12, 13 (quoted), 14-17; T. 24 January 2007 pp. 2-3, 15-16; Prosecution Exhibit 69 (personal identification sheet). Witness UB had lodged an appeal against his conviction for genocide and was awaiting a determination from the Rwandan Supreme Court when testifying. T. 23 January 2007 p. 2.

Immediately after the announcement of the President's death, political leaders began setting up roadblocks in Cyahafi.[149]

125. The meeting took place in the prefecture's meeting room. *Conseillers, bourgmestres* (except for Jean Bizimana), soldiers and some gendarmes attended the meeting. Renzaho explained that the enemy was the RPF as well as their accomplices, which the witness understood to mean the Tutsis. Renzaho then ordered those in attendance to erect more roadblocks in their sectors where there were none to prevent the *"Inyenzi"* or *"Inkotanyi"* from infiltrating the city and joining their accomplices, the Tutsis. In the witness's understanding, the roadblocks intended to restrict the movement of Tutsis so they could be located and killed. He felt that the "most urgent issue" at the meeting was to "implement the plan", which was the genocide. *Conseillers* spoke of the situations in their sectors. After the meeting, the witness directed *responsables de cellule* to establish roadblocks where there were none. He did not personally set up any.[150]

Prosecution Witness ALG

126. Witness ALG, a Hutu and local official in Kigali-Ville prefecture in 1994, remained at home after the plane crash until about 12 April 1994, when he received a *"communiqué"* from Renzaho requesting prefecture officials to report to work. He observed gendarmes, civilians, and *Interahamwe* manning various roadblocks. At the prefecture office, Renzaho told the witness that night patrols and roadblocks had been established in order to keep *Inkotanyi* from entering the city. Having left the prefecture office, the witness went through sectors within Nyarugenge commune and saw citizens, *Interahamwe* and soldiers manning roadblocks. Individuals' property was taken and others were killed there. He observed soldiers and policemen manning roadblocks in neighbourhoods around the prefecture office and policemen at a roadblock near its entrance.[151]
[page 32]

127. The witness learned from the *conseillers* of Biryogo, Nyamirambo and Cyahafi sectors and from Pierre Claver Nyirikwaya, *bourgmestre* of Kacyiru commune, that Renzaho had convened meetings on 9 and 11 April. During the meeting of 9 April, Renzaho urged those present to work actively in the fight against the *Inkotanyi*, to sensitise the population, and to set up roadblocks.[152]

128. After 12 April, Renzaho convened three to four additional meetings later that month, which he referred to as "security meetings". Those in attendance, depending on availability, included high-ranking military officials, *conseillers, bourgmestres,* prefecture functionaries, militia leaders, including *Interahamwe*, and Kigali-Ville political party officials. Many of the invitees were not members of the "prefectural security council", according to the applicable legislation. Renzaho called for the strengthening of roadblocks and for night patrols to monitor the infiltration of *Inkotanyi*. The witness informed Renzaho of the identities of persons that were committing attacks at various locations but his reports were never acted upon.[153]

Prosecution Witness GLJ

129. Witness GLJ, a Hutu and local official in Kigali-Ville until his dismissal in April 1994, testified that he was present at a meeting convened by Renzaho on the morning of 16 or 17 April at the prefecture office. The gathering was more expansive than a typical "prefectural security council" provided for by the applicable

---

[149] T. 31 January 2007 pp. 11-14, 33-35, 37; Prosecution Exhibit 80 (personal identification sheet). Witness AWE was a detainee awaiting to be tried for genocide when he appeared before the Tribunal. T. 31 January 2006 pp. 11-12, 51-52, 54-56.
[150] T. 31 January 2007 pp. 13-14, 17, 35-39, 46, 56-57.
[151] T. 10 January 2007 p. 56; T. 11 January 2007 pp. 17, 19-20, 22-24, 29, 43-44; T. 12 January 2007 p. 28; Prosecution Exhibit 67 (personal identification sheet). When testifying, Witness ALG was awaiting trial in Rwanda for his role during the 1994 events. He was accused of genocide. T. 10 January 2007 p. 64. Witness ALG indicated on a map the numerous roadblocks he observed in Nyarungenge *commune* on 12 April 1994. T. 11 January 2007 pp. 43-44; Prosecution Exhibit 5 (map of Kigali).
[152] T. 11 January 2007 pp. 29-32, 41, 67; T. 12 January pp. 28-30.
[153] T. 11 January 2007 pp. 35-37, 39-41, 67; T. 15 January 2007 pp. 7-14. Prosecution Exhibit 14 (*Loi no. 35/90 22 juin 1990 portant organisation administrative de la préfecture de la ville de Kigali*). Article 17 sets forth the members of "*Comité urbain de sécurité*". Witness ALG stated that members of the security committee by law who did not attend such meetings included the President of the Tribunal of First Instance and the Public Prosecutor. T. 15 January 2007 pp. 10, 12. The hierarchy of the Kigali-Ville prefecture placed the urban council at the top, followed by the prefect and then the security committee. T. 12 January 2007 p. 7.

Judgement and Sentence

legislation. Those attending included individual representatives of the *conseil urbain* (the *bourgmestres, conseillers* and *responsables de cellule* in the prefecture), representatives of the army and the commander of the civil defence program.[154] At least one representative of each *cellule* was present. Renzaho, who was in military attire, passed on the decisions made at a prior meeting to erect roadblocks and to check identity documents of passers-by. Anyone without a document was to be considered an *Inkotanyi* infiltrator, arrested and handed over to the prefecture police or the gendarmerie brigade. According to the witness, it was clear from the discussions at the meeting that Tutsis were being targeted. He was not aware of nor did he attend any previous meeting of this nature.[155]

130. After this meeting, every *cellule* erected its own roadblocks and arrested persons who did not have identification papers or appeared to be Tutsis. Killings occurred at these **[page 33]** checkpoints. The number of roadblocks erected by *Interahamwe* in Nyamirambo sector grew from about six between 7 and 10 April to approximately 30.[156]

Prosecution Witness Corinne Dufka

131. Corinne Dufka, an American journalist for Reuters news agency, made three separate trips to Kigali between May and the end of July 1994 while covering the conflict. On her first trip, between 10 and 14 or 15 May, she passed approximately 50 roadblocks which increased in concentration between the Burundian border and Kigali. They were each manned by five or six often inebriated individuals in civilian dress, armed with various different types of guns and traditional weapons. They would search her vehicle, look at her passport and frequently ask if she were Belgian. The encounters were very tense and frightening.[157]

132. During Dufka's second trip, from 18 to either 20 or 21 May, an individual at the first major checkpoint in Kigali immediately placed a large pistol to her head and asked if she were Belgian. Dufka also recalled seeing a militiaman in a white doctor's coat splattered with blood and others carrying nail studded clubs still bearing flesh and hair. On this trip, Dufka facilitated her passage through roadblocks by noting that she was reporting on the shelling of a hospital by the RPF.[158]

133. On her second trip, Dufka also visited the Sainte Famille church to take pictures of Tutsi refugees inside. Access to the church was guarded by a roadblock manned by eight to 10 men in civilian clothes. When she asked if she could photograph the checkpoint, Father Wenceslas Munyeshyaka demurred and took her to a different, larger one in Kigali, which was manned by around 30 persons and approximately 10 to 15 minutes away but within Kigali. En route, Munyeshyaka easily facilitated their passage through several different roadblocks. Dufka took a number of pictures at the large roadblock, the only one she photographed during her visits, and spoke with Robert Kajuga, whom Munyeshyaka identified as the militia leader. Kajuga told Dufka that they were trying to defend Kigali from the RPF. She smelled alcohol on the militiamen's breath. She also observed one playing with the pin of a grenade as well as others jumping around the roadblock and shouting excitedly.[159]

Prosecution Expert Witness Alison Des Forges

134. Alison Des Forges, an expert in Rwanda history, stated that *Interahamwe* and Rwandan army soldiers erected roadblocks in Kigali from 7 April 1994 onwards, and that militia were active in killing civilians. Based on her research, she concluded that administrators were charged with the task of disseminating and

---

[154] Prosecution Exhibit 14 (*Loi no. 35/90 22 juin 1990 portant organisation administrative de la préfecture de la ville de Kigali*). Article 17 sets forth the composition of the "*Comité urbain de sécurité*", and Article 7 lists the members of the "*Conseil urbain*". See also Prosecution Exhibit 94A (expert report of Alison Des Forges) p. 11 n. 22.
[155] T. 22 January 2007 pp. 13-14, 18-23, 25-29, 50-52, 54-55; Prosecution Exhibit 68 (personal identification sheet). When testifying, Witness GLJ had been detained in Rwanda for over 12 years, awaiting trial. T. 22 January 2007 p. 13.
[156] T. 22 January 2007 pp. 22-23, 37-38.
[157] T. 30 January 2007 pp. 1-4.
[158] *Id.* pp. 3-5.
[159] *Id.* pp. 8-13, 17, 19-23; Prosecution Exhibit 77 (33 photographs taken by Corinne Dufka). Dufka's third and final trip began on approximately 23 May and she stayed for six weeks. She returned to the Sainte Famille church to take more pictures but did not testify with respect to roadblocks in connection with this visit. See T. 30 January 2007 pp. 13-14, 17-18.

enforcing orders, including those related to roadblocks. In her view, the use of an administrative system to disseminate instructions to set up roadblocks is a key factor when analysing the genocide. Unlike the RTLM, Radio Rwanda was the voice of the government, used by prefects and authorities at **[page 34]** the national level to deliver orders to the population. Renzaho's message on Radio Rwanda on 12 April included a plea to the civilian population to set up roadblocks. Des Forges found this significant. It was a directive to "the most local level" and to those who shared the ideas of the government to cooperate with it by establishing roadblocks to impede passers-by and check identity papers.[160]

135. Des Forges commented on a Radio Rwanda broadcast of 18 June during which Renzaho stated that those at roadblocks had to check identity cards in order to prevent RPF infiltrators using Hutu identity cards. In her view, his words acknowledged that Hutu civilians would not encounter the same difficulty at checkpoints as their Tutsi counterparts, and were indicative of the discriminatory intent behind the establishment of roadblocks. The broadcast also illustrated the continued existence of the civil administration throughout the events and Renzaho's knowledge of the violence occurring at roadblocks. For instance, there is a passage where he implores the population to stop robbing traders, merchants and food producers passing through them. She suggested that the lethal force authorities employed to prevent and punish criminal acts such as looting was not used to prevent the killing of Tutsi civilians.[161]

136. Des Forges also pointed to excerpts from a 6 May interview broadcast on Radio Rwanda, where Renzaho contrasted those with training who could administer roadblocks properly with undisciplined and overzealous civilians who chose to administer roadblocks and kill blindly. The interview showed that he was capable of providing very specific instructions regarding the operation of roadblocks, and that if he wanted to identify those who were at risk, he was capable of doing so.[162]

Renzaho

137. Renzaho testified that he did not order the establishment of roadblocks in Kigali-Ville. The civilian population erected them spontaneously after the announcement of President Habyarimana's death, and he had no means to abolish them. Their purpose was not to massacre Tutsis. On 8 April 1994, he attended a meeting of the crisis committee at about 9.00 a.m., and then – in Renzaho's words – an "urban council" security meeting from 9.30 a.m. until 2.00 p.m. In attendance at the second meeting were: Renzaho, *Bourgmestre* Munyansanga, *Bourgmestre* Pierre Claver Nyirinkwaya, Major Ngirabatware of the *gendarmerie*, and the *conseillers* who were available, including Amri Karekezi and Célestin Sezibera. The head of intelligence at the Ministry of National Defence, Colonel Rutayisire, and other military officers observed the meeting. No members of the political parties **[page 35]** attended. The participants discussed how to restore order in the communes. A crisis committee at the prefecture level was established. Of the 250 police officers, only 45 and their commander, Nyamuhimba, were present at the prefecture. Police officers were assigned, among other duties, to assist *conseillers*. With respect to roadblocks, Renzaho "requested that the officials try to control the situation in the *cellules*, in the sectors, in the communes". While no representatives from political parties were present, Renzaho asked communal authorities "to involve all the groups that had any influence on fringes of the society" to maintain local security. He denied that he toured roadblocks on 8 April between 2.00 and 3.00 p.m., as alleged by Witness AFB.[163]

---

[160] T. 5 March 2007 pp. 7-10, 11 (quoted), 13; T. 6 March pp. 10-11; Prosecution Exhibit 93 (personal identification sheet); Prosecution Exhibit 50 (transcript of Radio Rwanda broadcast on 12 April 1994) p. 9; Prosecution Exhibit 94A (expert report of Alison Des Forges) pp. 10-11.

[161] T. 5 March 2007 pp. 12-13, 35-37, 38 (stating that preventing infiltrations at roadblocks was a legitimate use of force only insofar as its aim was to identify a "combatant force", whereas the terms "controlling" or "preventing infiltration", which was used by authorities, covered for the activity of singling out Tutsis on the basis of ethnicity and, in most cases, handing them over to be killed); Prosecution Exhibit 63 (transcript of Radio Rwanda interview with Renzaho, 18 June 1994).

[162] T. 5 March 2007 pp. 44-47; Prosecution Exhibit 55 (transcript of Radio Rwanda interview with Renzaho, 6 May 1994). In the interview, Renzaho described problems of mistaken identification of individuals as *Inyenzi* due to identity cards from neighbouring communes such as Rubongo and Bucyimbi bearing the mark "Register of Citizens". He requested that higher authorities should conduct an investigation to determine any wrongdoing if there was doubt as to the identification card's validity.

[163] T. 27 August 2007 pp. 60 (quoted), 61-65; T. 28 August 2007 pp. 2-3, 8, 9 (quoted), 19; T. 30 August 2007 pp. 3, 27-28, 53, 58, 60; T. 3 September 2007 pp. 21-22. The crisis committee at the prefecture level was composed of Renzaho, sub-prefect Jean-

138. After 8 April, Renzaho continued to meet with *bourgmestres* to find out what was happening. He also met with the *bourgmestre* of Nyarugenge commune and his *conseillers* to ensure that actions were being taken to control roadblocks. Members of political parties were not present at these meetings.[164]

139. In a *communiqué* broadcast on Radio Rwanda on 10 April, Renzaho asked the population to dismantle roadblocks during the day, but they ignored his request as roadblocks were spreading across the entire city. He learned after 10 April that some persons were using roadblocks to target and kill Tutsis and testified that, in this context, it would have been criminal to establish roadblocks with the purpose of killing innocent Tutsi civilians. In another *communiqué* of 12 April, Renzaho did not address the dismantling of roadblocks as their existence was now widespread, but instead urged civilians to block *Inyenzis* at them and to remain vigilant in carrying out patrols. He acknowledged that he had told people to remain at roadblocks on several occasions, including in another *communiqué* broadcast of 14 April, as they represented the only means of guaranteeing the security of Kigali. The purpose of these instructions was to avoid that the RPF advanced into the city, and that infiltrators were apprehended at roadblocks. Renzaho was unaware of any infiltrators being arrested at roadblocks because he did not receive any such person at the prefecture office. His instructions were repeated in a Radio Rwanda broadcast of 19 April, where he "called, once again, on the residents of Kigali town to step up their efforts in order to ensure their security, manning roadblocks, and conducting night patrols to prevent the enemy infiltrations". Renzaho saw the population with firearms at roadblocks but was unaware of their origins.[165]

140. Renzaho issued instructions on the radio for those manning roadblocks to check identity cards as well as *laissez-passers*. Identity cards had been checked at roadblocks in prior conflicts, possibly because identity cards were standardised according to law. His radio instructions on 18 June to check identity cards at roadblocks were issued in the context of a war and were intended to combat the infiltration of enemy agents into Kigali. He denied that this was tantamount to incitement to "hunt down Tutsis". The message was broadcast near the end of the conflict in Kigali and in the midst of a refugee exchange operation between **[page 36]** both sides, so inciting the population to violence would have been senseless. The checking of identity cards was aimed at ensuring increased vigilance at roadblocks and preventing innocent people from being mistreated. Renzaho acknowledged that it "was possible" that Tutsi civilians were viewed as accomplices to the RPF. He was aware that civilians with Tutsi identity cards or civilians with Tutsi features were being killed at roadblocks and acknowledged it was difficult for them to move around.[166]

141. According to Renzaho, he did not know whether he was the most senior governmental official based permanently in Kigali after the interim government left to Gitarama on 12 April. He met with *conseillers* and *bourgmestres* several times between April and July. Renzaho said that he was unaware if *Conseillers* Rose Karushara, Odette Nyirabagenzi or Nyarugenge's primary education inspector, Angeline Mukandituye, played leading roles in *Interahamwe* activities during this period. He was not the unofficial leader of the *Interahamwe* in Kigali and denied meeting with them during this period.[167]

Defence Witness AIA

142. Witness AIA was a member of the Kigali-Ville police force. On 8 April 1994, he accompanied *conseiller* Amri Karekezi around 10.00 a.m. to a meeting at the prefecture office. Karekezi had heard a *communiqué* broadcast on the radio that Renzaho was summoning *bourgmestres*, *conseillers* and policemen

---

Baptiste Butera, secretary Alexis Bisanukuli and the "*bourgmestre* who was present, and other *bourgmestres* if they could join". T. 28 August 2007 p. 3.
[164] T. 28 August 2007 pp. 13-14, 25-26; T. 30 August 2007 pp. 27-28.
[165] T. 28 August 2007 pp. 11, 13-14, 51-52; T. 30 August 2007 pp. 54, 57-61, 63-64; T. 31 August 2007 pp. 1-2; T. 3 September 2007 pp. 6-7; Prosecution Exhibit 49 (transcript of Radio Rwanda, 11 April 1994, broadcasting *communiqué* dated 10 April 1994) p. 5; Prosecution Exhibit 50 (transcript of Radio Rwanda interview, 12 April 1994) p. 9; Prosecution Exhibit 51 (transcript of Radio Rwanda *communiqué*, 14 April 1994) p. 10; Prosecution Exhibit 52 (transcript of Radio Rwanda *communiqué*, 19 April 1994) pp. 25-26.
[166] T. 29 August 2007 pp. 2, 3-4 (quoted); T. 30 August 2007 pp. 19, 35, 60-61; T. 31 August 2007 pp. 2-6; Prosecution Exhibit 56 (transcript of Radio Rwanda interview, 10 May 1994) p. 12; Prosecution Exhibit 62 (transcript of radio broadcast of 18 June 1994) p. 4.
[167] T. 29 August 2007 p. 60; T. 30 August 2007 pp. 23-24, 27, 35-36, 42-43.

to the office. The meeting was attended by Biryogo's and Muhima's *conseillers*; Odette Nyirabagenzi, *conseiller* of Rugenge sector; Mbyariyehe, *conseiller* of Nyarugenge sector; Pepe Kale, *conseiller* of Gitega sector; Jean Bizimana, *bourgmestre* of Nyarugenge commune; and between 40 to 45 police officers, including Major Nyamuhimba. The witness did not see the *bourgmestres* of Kicukiro and Kacyiru communes and no *Interahamwe* were present. During the meeting, he heard Renzaho report that killing and looting was occurring, and that those present needed to assist in restoring security and preventing these activities. Renzaho also told the police officers to follow the instructions given by the *conseillers* where they were deployed.[168]

143. The witness observed a roadblock in Gitega sector on 8 April. Following an address by the interim Prime Minister Jean Kambanda, Karekezi, who said that he was acting on the instructions of "the government", pointed out specific locations in Biryogo sector where roadblocks should be erected. The address indicated that the *Inkotanyi* had violated the Arusha Accords and that persons were to set up roadblocks to intercept "people who had infiltrated". The population, including *Interahamwe*, administered the checkpoints, and to pass through roadblocks in Biryogo sector, one had to present identification or a government issued authorisation. Once they had been erected, "authorities" issued instructions "to the effect that Tutsis should be arrested and killed". Hutus and other persons who were not identified as Tutsis could pass, whereas those identified as Tutsis at roadblocks were killed. According to the witness, the population was told to seek out "infiltrators" at the roadblocks. He observed the killing of a lieutenant named Mudenge at a roadblock at ONATRACOM, at **[page 37]** the border of Gitega and Biryogo sectors, just after he was identified as an infiltrator on RTLM. The witness was unaware of the *Interahamwe* collaborating with any Kigali-Ville authorities, other than *conseillers* and MRND officials.[169]

144. Witness AIA recalled Karekezi attending meetings around 12 April and 16 April at the prefecture office. The witness remained in the parking lot during these meetings, but Karekezi would sometimes brief him on what occurred. On one occasion, Karekezi informed him that Renzaho urged the *conseillers* to stop the killing in the sectors and threatened to kill the *conseillers* if this continued. The witness did not observe the head of the Biryogo *Interahamwe*, Suede Ndayitabi, or any *Interahamwe* attending these meetings at the prefecture office.[170]

Defence Witness PPV

145. Witness PPV, a Hutu, worked for the urban police in Kigali-Ville prefecture in 1994. He did not observe a meeting at the prefecture office during which a decision was made to set up roadblocks. No public authority ordered the erection of roadblocks and Renzaho did not request their establishment.[171]

146. The witness did not hear messages being made over the radio by Renzaho. However, he learned from others who heard these speeches that the prefect had informed the population to remove roadblocks and to stop the violence and looting. Renzaho did not approve of the killings at roadblocks, but the urban police lacked the resources to prevent crimes committed at them, and no specific killers were identified. The population, which had erected roadblocks spontaneously, was furious, and it was not possible to stop them from establishing checkpoints. The strength of the heavily armed militia groups that manned the roadblocks and the limited number of police officers available made it impossible to dismantle them. The witness was often told that people regarded the prefect to be an accomplice because of the messages he was broadcasting and the Tutsi staff working at the prefecture office.[172]

---

[168] T. 2 July 2007 pp. 21-22, 23 (see erratum), 24, 35, 46, 51, 54; T. 3 July 2007 pp. 4, 17-18; Defence Exhibit 66 (personal identification sheet). Witness AIA was arrested in Rwanda in November 1994, detained for a month during an investigation by Nyamirambo brigade, and released. T. 2 July 2007 p. 46.
[169] T. 2 July 2007 pp. 27, 35-37, 56-58; T. 3 July 2007 pp. 12-13. Witness AIA acknowledged generally that killings in Kigali-Ville prefecture and in Biryogo sector were committed by, among others, prefecture police and gendarmes. T. 3 July 2007 pp. 5-6.
[170] T. 2 July 2007 pp. 31, 35, 40-41, 54-56; T. 3 July 2007 pp. 6-7, 10-11, 17-18.
[171] T. 4 June 2007 p. 78; T. 5 June 2007 pp. 12-13; Defence Exhibit 56 (personal identification sheet).
[172] T. 5 June 2007 pp. 14-16, 27, 39-40, 42-44. Witness PPV mentioned checkpoints at Gitikingoni, Gitega and Biryogo as roadblocks it would have been dangerous to attempt to dismantle. T. 5 June 2007 pp. 15-16.

Defence Witness BDC

147. Witness BDC, a Hutu, lived in Kicukiro commune. From 15 April 1994, he began working with the ICRC in Kigali and was briefed on the events that had occurred from 10 April until his arrival. He worked with Philippe Gaillard, the ICRC delegate.[173]

148. Roadblocks appeared to be set up spontaneously and in a disorganised manner. The witness denied Renzaho was in charge of them. Militiamen positioned at them were not affiliated with any political party or Renzaho, although he conceded that those manning roadblocks recognised the authority of *Interahamwe* leader Robert Kajuga. They appeared to be desperate young people under the influence of narcotics and alcohol. These individuals were armed with "bladed" and "automatic" weapons. The persons staffing the roadblocks **[page 38]** varied from being very aggressive to allowing passage easily. The witness observed less than 30 police officers, armed with "obsolete" weapons, in Kigali-Ville prefecture. The police would not have been able to overcome the numerous, organised militia who were at various roadblocks.[174]

149. Militia removed and killed injured persons being transported by the ICRC at roadblocks and stole food as well. This stemmed in part from RTLM broadcasts suggesting that the Red Cross was transporting "the enemy" disguised as being wounded. The ICRC was perceived as attempting to save "the enemy" and persons the militia had targeted for extermination. Around the end of April, Witness BDC asked Renzaho whether he could help the ICRC move more easily but was told that he did not have authority over the militia. The witness subsequently obtained assistance from *Interahamwe* President Robert Kajuga and his deputy, Rutaganda, which allowed ambulances to move around with less difficulty (II.5.1).[175]

Defence Witness PPO

150. Witness PPO, a Hutu, was a senior government official in Kigali-Ville prefecture in 1994. He said that roadblocks were established as early as 7 April. They were disorganised with no person in charge. The youth manning them appeared drunk and were carrying grenades, automatic weapons and knives. These checkpoints were numerous and found as close as 10 metres apart. Tutsis were the primary targets, but there were also Hutu victims. The killings were based on political beliefs, regardless of ethnicity. Renzaho did not have the resources available to put an end to the massacres, as the persons at roadblocks outnumbered the communal police by nearly "100 times" and were better armed.[176]

151. The witness's work for the prefecture required him to travel daily from 8.00 a.m. until at least 5.00 p.m. He therefore had little contact with Renzaho. Despite having official documents from Renzaho and moving about with a uniformed police officer armed with a Kalashnikov, he continued to experience difficulties at the roadblocks. He would get through them by flattery and paying the person who approached the vehicle. At a roadblock near the *Banque nationale du Rwanda*, the witness was arrested, subjected to "humiliating acts", and almost beaten. He reported this incident to Renzaho, making him so angry that he stated: "I am fed up with these people. I am fed up with these roadblocks. What am I to do in order to dismantle them? What can I do in order for them to disappear?" Renzaho could not have ordered the erection of roadblocks because, if he had, those manning them would have **[page 39]** recognised the authority of documents signed by the prefect and of a police officer, and would have let them pass.[177]

---

[173] T. 4 June 2007 pp. 2-4, 7; Defence Exhibit 51 (personal identification sheet).
[174] T. 4 June 2007 pp. 16 (quoted), 17-18, 19 (quoted), 21, 35, 55-56, 65.
[175] T. 4 June 2007 p. 17 (quoted), 18-21, 35, 55, 57 (quoted), 58, 64-65. Witness BDC was unsure if the name was Rutaganda or Rutwenga. T. 4 June 2007 p. 57. Witness BDC confirmed that an ICRC report of 15 April 1994 indicated that six individuals were taken from a Red Cross ambulance and killed in front of Rwandan army soldiers. T. 4 June 2007 pp. 50-51; Prosecution Exhibit 105 (Update No. 4 on ICRC Activities in Rwanda, 15 April 1994).
[176] T. 4 July 2007 pp. 63, 69; T. 5 July 2007 pp. 7-8, 48, 49 (quoted), 51-52; Defence Exhibit 71 (personal identification sheet). Witness PPO conceded that the prefecture's administration was able to prevent lootings of businesses in the Kigali-Ville commercial centre until the RPF captured the city and prevented an attack on the prefecture office. T. 5 July 2007 pp. 48-49. In the witness's view, the lack of organisation at roadblocks made it difficult to deal with them. T. 5 July 2007 p. 49. Moreover, it was easier to stop looting because it occurred at fixed, centrally placed locations, and therefore required less manpower to guard. T. 5 July 2007 pp. 49, 52-53.
[177] T. 5 July 2007 pp. 5-6, 7 (quoted), 8 (quoted), 46, 49-50.

Defence Witness HIN

152. Witness HIN, a Hutu, lived in Rugenge sector, Kigali-Ville. On the morning of 7 April 1994, he observed the Presidential Guard visit the house of *Conseiller* Odette Nyirabagenzi. When they left around 11.30 a.m., the *responsable de cellule*, Muvunyi, went to all the houses in the neighbourhood and asked the population to erect roadblocks at specific locations to check the movement of the enemy. Based on this, the witness believed that the Presidential Guard had asked Nyirabagenzi to order roadblocks erected. He saw Nyirabagenzi touring the sector to ensure that roadblocks had been set up and to supervise their establishment. She told people to be vigilant and prevent the movement of Tutsis. The witness did not think that Nyirabagenzi was acting on Renzaho's orders in doing so. Rather, she was following up security measures suggested to her by the Presidential Guard. Nyirabagenzi and Renzaho could not have collaborated with each other, because Renzaho did not agree with the *Interahamwe* and had no authority over them.[178]

Defence Witness GOA

153. Witness GOA, a Hutu, was in Nyakabanda sector, in Nyarugenge commune in Kigali, in April 1994. The population set up some roadblocks on their own initiative to intercept RPF infiltrators within Nyamirambo commune. Some were erected with the assistance of officials at the sector and cellule levels. The witness did not observe Renzaho chair any meetings in his neighbourhood while in Kigali, nor did he see or hear anything leading him to believe that those manning the checkpoints were working under Renzaho's orders. At "the Gitega" roadblock, the witness observed "self-declared" roadblock leaders such as Gatete Selemani and Ndanda in the company of, and collaborating with, the *conseiller* of Biryogo sector, Amri Karekezi. Moreover, the witness observed Ntwari and Abdou, who were also "self-declared" roadblock leaders, at the Gitega checkpoint. Roadblocks were initially set up as part of a military strategy, but civilians "committed offences" and "mistreated people" passing through them.[179]

Defence Witness PGL

154. Witness PGL, a Hutu employee at the Kigali-Ville prefecture office, testified that Renzaho no longer had any authority during the war in 1994. The population was too angered by Habyarimana's death to follow orders and had established roadblocks on their own initiative. A roadblock in the Rugunga area was manned by civilians who appeared inebriated and in disarray, some firing shots in the air. Because Renzaho had not established the roadblocks in Kigali-Ville, he could not give orders to those manning them. He lacked the means to end the killings, as there were less than 20 police officers available. Renzaho's **[page 40]** words over a radio broadcast on 10 May 1994, informing civilians that the law required them to have their identity cards available to present at roadblocks, did not mean that he ordered those manning roadblocks to check identity cards.[180]

Defence Witness Antoine Théophile Nyetera

155. Antoine Théophile Nyetera, a descendant of the Tutsi royal family, lived in Nyamirambo sector in Nyarugenge commune until 4 July 1994. Roadblocks in Nyamirambo sector appeared on 10 April in response to the Prime Minister's speech requesting the population to prevent infiltration of their sectors. The sector *conseiller* and *responsable de cellule* ordered that these roadblocks be set up and chose who would man them. The prefect's message on 12 April was that roadblocks not be set up in a haphazard manner.[181]

---

[178] T. 9 July 2007 pp. 64, 66-68; T. 10 July 2007 pp. 25, 36-38; Defence Exhibit 73 (personal identification sheet).
[179] T. 6 June 2007 pp. 44-47, 49 (quoted), 50-51, 53-55; Defence Exhibit 62 (personal identification sheet). It is not clear based on Witness GOA's description of the "Gitega roadblock" and of Karekezi's activities if it was situated in Biryogo sector on the route to Gitega sector or if it is in Gitega. See T. 6 June 2007 pp. 47, 49, 54-55.
[180] T. 6 June 2007 pp. 15, 26-28, 33-34, 37, 39-40; Defence Exhibit 61 (personal identification sheet).
[181] T. 5 July 2007 pp. 19, 30-31, 41-42; Defence Exhibit 72 (personal identification sheet). Nyetera, formerly Witness BIT, left for Belgium in October 1994 and obtained political asylum there. T. 5 July 2007 p. 42.

Judgement and Sentence

Defence Expert Witness Bernard Lugan

156. Bernard Lugan testified that the population spontaneously erected roadblocks on 7 April 1994 as it prepared to protect itself after UNAMIR's disappearance and the movement of the army's elite units from the city to the war front. Renzaho had no physical means to thwart the roadblocks, so he issued a *communiqué* on 10 April calling for the roadblocks to be dismantled, which the population ignored because "there was a state of complete anarchy and law and order had broken down". In a radio broadcast two days later, Renzaho asked the population to set up roadblocks in certain areas. Lugan explained this change in Renzaho's stance towards roadblocks by stating that the military situation changed on 11 April when the RPF expanded its perimeter and tried to invade the south of Kigali town. This led to two developments: more refugees entered Kigali town, increasing concerns about RPF infiltration; and the Rwandan government feared capture and fled Kigali, leaving Renzaho without any resources to restore public order. Lugan described RPF radio propaganda during the war that announced: "We know everything, completely everything about what you are doing, so we are in there, everywhere." This might have impressed upon Kigali residents the notion that the RPF had infiltrated its soldiers in civilian dress inside of the Rwandan army's perimeter.[182]

2.3 Deliberations

157. It is clear that from 7 April 1994, roadblocks were erected throughout Kigali-Ville. Prosecution and Defence witnesses testified to observing roadblocks manned by soldiers at strategic positions throughout the city.[183] Both parties also led evidence of roadblocks **[page 41]** established and administered by civilians, frequently referred to as *Interahamwe* or militia.[184] The civilians at these checkpoints were armed with various firearms and traditional weapons, and often appeared inebriated and under the influence of narcotics.[185] Searches were conducted, primarily focusing on the identity cards held by the passers-by as well as their physical appearance. Persons without identification were viewed with suspicion. Those identified as Tutsi, or considered as being in opposition to the groups at the roadblocks, were in many instances taken captive or killed.[186] **[page 42]**

---

[182] T. 4 September 2007 pp. 13, 14 (quoted), 19-20, 21 (quoted), 23-24; Prosecution Exhibit 49 (transcript of Radio Rwanda broadcast on 11 April 1994) p. 5; Prosecution Exhibit 50 (transcript of Radio Rwanda broadcast) p. 9; Defence Exhibit 110 (expert report of Bernard Lugan).

[183] In addition to the evidence summarised above, see, for instance, Defence Witness UT, T. 24 May 2007 p. 44 (soldiers erected and administered roadblocks located at the exit of battle zones); Defence Witness PPV, T. 5 June 2007 p. 13 (roadblocks were first established by soldiers in close proximity to their military positions); Defence Witness PPO, T. 5 July 2007 pp. 7, 51 (military roadblocks were erected near army camps and strategic positions); Defence Witness BOU, T. 22 May 2007 p. 40 (soldiers manned a roadblock on a road that led directly to the presidential office); Defence Witness PGL, T. 6 June 2007 p. 26 (soldiers manned a roadblock in Kiyovu near the presidential residence).

[184] Reference is made to the testimonies of Witnesses AFB, ALG and AIA, described above, as well as Prosecution Witness GLJ, T. 22 January 2007 pp. 22-23, 55 (observed "more than six" roadblocks set up by *Interahamwe*); Prosecution Witness SAF, T. 24 January 2007 pp. 53-55 (*Interahamwe* armed with guns, machetes and clubs manned roadblocks near the Kiyovu Hotel); Defence Witness PPV, T. 5 June 2007 p. 13 (civilians spontaneously erected roadblocks and were often violent); Defence Witness MAI, T. 22 August 2007 pp. 17, 40 (on 12 April, roadblocks were erected about every 15 metres in Muhima).

[185] As stated above, Witness Corinne Dufka took pictures from a roadblock, which depict several, heavily armed persons. See Prosecution Exhibit 77 (33 photographs taken by Corinne Dufka). Several witnesses commented upon them: Witness UB, T. 23 January 2007 pp. 22-23 (photographs 3, 4 and 11 include persons observed at a roadblock on the border of Gitega and Cyahafi, an *Interahamwe* from Nyakabanda sector, and a roadblock on the border of Kimisagara and Cyahafi sectors, respectively); Witness AFB, T. 8 January 2007 pp. 90, 92-94 (photograph 1 is of a roadblock in front of the Gitega sector office manned by *Interahamwe*); Witness GLJ, T. 22 January 2007 pp. 38-39 (photograph 5 depicts an *Interahamwe* at Gitega roadblock and photograph 8 a woman at that roadblock); Witness AWE, T. 31 January 2007 pp. 29-30 (identifying individuals from Cyahafi sector in photographs 4 and 5, an individual from Gitega sector in 13 and noting photograph 2 is taken in Gitega sector); Defence Witness UT, T. 25 May 2007 pp. 20-21 (photographs 1-14 are pictures of a roadblock in Gitega near the school of the postal services). Other relevant evidence include Defence Witness Jean-Baptiste Butera, T. 23 May 2007 pp. 7-10, 28-30 (those manning a roadblock between Masaka and Bicumbi were armed with machetes and spears and one threw a grenade into a crowd as the witness forced his way through the roadblock in his vehicle); Defence Witness RGI, T. 4 July 2007 pp. 7-8 (civilians at roadblocks were heavily armed, often acquiring weapons illegally from army deserters); Defence Witness MAI, T. 22 August 2007 pp. 17, 29 (those staffing a roadblock in Muhima took beer from the vehicle and drank it). See also the testimonies of Witnesses Dufka, PPO and PGL, summarised above.

[186] Prosecution Witness GLJ, T. 22 January 2007 pp. 18, 22 (persons manning roadblocks asked for identification papers and those appearing to be Tutsis were targeted for killing); Prosecution Witness UB, T. 23 January 2007 pp. 11-12, 15 (observed, for example, several dead bodies of Tutsis at roadblocks in Gitega sector around 10 or 11 April 1994); Prosecution Witness SAF, T. 24 January 2007 p. 29 (Tutsis were targeted at roadblocks); Prosecution Witness UL, T. 9 January 2007 pp. 52-53 (the witness was

617

158. The critical issue for the Chamber concerns Renzaho's relationship to the establishment and administration of roadblocks, and his alleged responsibility for the crimes committed at them. The Prosecution submits that Renzaho's authority over roadblocks and support of those manning them follows from evidence of meetings and radio broadcasts, wherein he ordered the establishment of roadblocks and provided instructions on how to administer them. Renzaho's support for roadblocks and knowledge of the killings occurring at them is based on his tour of them on 8 April and his subsequent orders to have bodies removed from the streets of Kigali. It concludes that Renzaho's explanations are contradictory and that Defence evidence corroborates the Prosecution case.[187]

159. The Defence suggests that roadblocks were erected spontaneously and in a disorganised manner, as a result of the insecurity and tension caused by the war, and that Renzaho lacked the capability to control them. The Prosecution evidence regarding Renzaho's orders to erect roadblocks is unreliable. By 11 April, the RPF had nearly surrounded the city, and it was complete confusion. Nonetheless, according to the Defence, Renzaho made requests on 10, 12 and 14 April that civilian roadblocks be removed during the day, and in his broadcasts from 7 April to 6 May he made repeated calls for the killings and criminal activity to stop.[188]

160. In assessing Renzaho's alleged responsibility for roadblocks within Kigali-Ville, the Chamber discusses separately evidence of his alleged presence at roadblocks; his purported orders to erect roadblocks; and his responsibility for crimes committed at them. **[page 43]**

---

asked to present his identification at roadblocks on 11 April, saw dead bodies at them and it was common knowledge that Tutsis intercepted at roadblocks were killed); Prosecution Witness ALG, T. 11 January 2007 pp. 20, 24-25, 43 (noticed dead bodies near roadblocks on 12 April and had previously heard that people were being killed at roadblocks); Prosecution Witness KBZ, T. 6 February 2007 pp. 48-52, 57 (in May, men in military uniforms at a roadblock between Kicukiro and Kimihurura sectors took five Tutsi women, without identity cards, to the home of the Kimihurura *conseiller*); Prosecution Witness BUO, T. 26 January 2007 pp. 16-17, 26-27; T. 29 January 2007 pp. 4, 8-9, 37-38 (*Interahamwe* in Rugenge sector manned roadblocks there, together with soldiers and gendarmes, and were tasked with stopping and killing Tutsis and persons without identity cards during the day as well as remaining at the roadblocks at night); Renzaho, T. 30 August 2007 pp. 60-61 (those with identity cards indicating they were Tutsis and those who resembled Tutsis were killed at roadblocks); Defence Witness AIA, T. 2 July 2007 pp. 36-37, 56-58 (persons were required to present identification or government issued authorisation at roadblocks and those identified as Tutsis were killed); Prosecution Witness UI, T. 5 February 2007 pp. 65, 67-68, 72-73 (at least 10 out of about 40 mostly Tutsi refugees were removed from a minibus at a roadblock near an Ethiopian restaurant, shot and killed) and Prosecution Exhibit 7 (9 photographs) photograph 5 (photograph of area where roadblock was situated in front of the Ethiopean restaurant); Defence Witness PPO, T. 5 July 2007 p. 48 (Tutsis were primarily targeted at roadblocks, but Hutus were also killed and the killings were based on political beliefs, regardless of ethnicity); Defence Witness PPV, T. 5 June 2007 pp. 39, 44 (Tutsis and accomplices were killed at roadblocks); Defence Witness BDC, T. 4 June 2007 pp. 52-53, 58, 67 (militia checked identity cards and prevented Tutsis from passing roadblocks safely in Kigali but Tutsis who were able to demonstrate that they belonged to the militia or embraced the militia ideology were able to survive; estimates suggested that, in April, more than 67,000 bodies had been removed from the streets of Kigali); Defence Witness BOU, T. 22 May 2007 p. 42 (saw dead bodies at a roadblock in Muhima sector manned by militia on 12 April); Defence Witness MAI, T. 22 August 2007 p. 39 (persons who looked like Tutsis would be stopped at roadblocks); Defence Witness WOW, T. 4 July 2007 pp. 54-55, 59 (*Interahamwe* forced people to work at roadblocks, which were used to intercept and kill infiltrators, and those who could not prove their identity were detained and disappeared); Defence Witness TOA, T. 6 September 2007 pp. 3, 5-6, 14-15 (on 10 April, the witness, a Tutsi, avoided passing roadblocks en route to Sainte Famille as people were being killed based on their ethnicity; he observed one approximately 150 metres from Saint Famille). See also Prosecution Witness UL, T. 9 January 2007 pp. 58-59, 61, 64-65, 67-69 (corpses were removed from the streets of Kigali to mass graves on Renzaho's and Casimir Bizimungu's instructions). But see Defence Witness HIN, T. 9 July 2007 pp. 67-69 (no Tutsis were killed at a roadblock he manned in Rugenge sector); Defence Witness KRG, T. 6 June 2007 p. 61, T. 7 June 2007 pp. 11-13 (strangers in the neighborhood or foreigners were intended to be identified at roadblocks, and he was unaware of any individual at his Rugenge sector roadblock being killed); Defence Witness PGL, T. 6 June 2007 p. 27 (the witness saw corpses on minor roads but "never saw corpses at the roadblocks", nor did he see them "on the major roads where roadblocks had been erected"); Defence Witness MAI, T. 22 August 2007 pp. 26-27, 32 (the witness saw an unmanned roadblock in Remera on 9 April and no bodies at it or on the road while travelling from Kanombe through Rebero, Remera, Kicukiro, Gikondo and reaching the prefecture office for Kigali-Ville); Defence Witness RGI, T. 4 July 2007 pp. 5-6, 14, 31-32 (violence was used at roadblocks manned by civilians to loot passers-by; however, the witness was unaware of thousands being killed at roadblocks in Kigali, did not agree that Tutsis were being targeted and killed in Kigali on the basis of their ethnicity, and suggested that those at roadblocks were outlaws, including youth wings of Tutsi political parties). See also oral submissions of Defence counsel T. 15 February 2008 p. 18 ("[T]here were members of the population who spontaneously acted by carrying out patrols and setting up roadblocks. They tried to defend themselves, even though very quickly after that those roadblocks were used to do other things, specifically, committing acts of genocide.").

[187] Prosecution Closing Brief paras. 110-127.
[188] Defence Closing Brief paras. 721-733, 739-753, 752-774; 775-793; Defence Exhibit 113 (*complément écrit aux arguments oraux de la défense*) paras. 753.1-753.7.

2.3.1 Presence at Roadblocks on 8 and 12 April

161. In order to establish Renzaho's ties with roadblocks manned by heavily armed militia, including *Interahamwe*, the Prosecution relies on Witness AFB. He testified that, on 8 April 1994, Renzaho toured roadblocks in Kimisagara, Nyakabanda, Nyamirambo and Gitega sectors. His evidence is a first-hand account that is largely consistent with his testimony in the *Zigiranyirazo* trial as well his statement to Tribunal investigators in December 2003.[189]

162. This said, only Witness AFB testified that Renzaho went to these roadblocks. The Chamber has elsewhere raised concerns about aspects of this witness's uncorroborated testimony concerning weapons distributions (II.3). In the circumstances, the Chamber views his evidence with caution and will not accept without corroboration of his testimony about Renzaho's specific activities at roadblocks, including his visits to roadblocks in Kimisagara, Nyakabanda, Nyamirambo and Gitega sectors on 8 April 1994, offering assistance and directing those manning them to work. The Chamber's findings related to Renzaho's involvement with roadblocks on 12 April is set forth elsewhere (II.3).

163. Notwithstanding, the Chamber finds Witness AFB's observations about who was manning roadblocks and the state of affairs at them largely credible and convincing. Furthermore, his observations that local authorities were present at roadblocks, that they were used to target Tutsis, and that they were manned by heavily armed militia, including *Interahamwe*, is consistent with other evidence on the record and the Chamber accepts the fundamental features of this testimony. In particular, his evidence about the existence of roadblocks manned by heavily armed *Interahamwe* near the Gitega sector office, finds support both in Corinne Dufka's photographs as well as witness testimony.

2.3.2 Orders to Erect Roadblocks

164. The Prosecution seeks to establish that Renzaho ordered local government officials to establish roadblocks through meetings at the Kigali-Ville prefecture office. Evidence from both parties demonstrates that local government officials, in particular *conseillers* and *responsables des cellules*, supervised the establishment and administration of roadblocks within the prefecture. The Defence evidence, however, suggests that these local government officials were not acting on Renzaho's instructions, but those of, for example, the interim government or military or their own initiative.[190] **[page 44]**

165. Having considered the Prosecution and Defence evidence and arguments, the Chamber is convinced that Renzaho ordered the establishment of and support to roadblocks throughout Kigali. This follows first

---

[189] Defence Defence Exhibit 2B (statement of 22 December 2003) pp. 4-5; Defence Exhibit 1 (*Prosecutor v. Zigiranyirazo*, T. 26 January 2006 pp. 13-17, T. 30 January 2006 pp. 36-37).
[190] Prosecution Witness AFB, T. 8 January 2007 pp. 84, 86-87 (*Interahamwe* manned a roadblock as early as 7 April in the vicinity of Rose Karushara's house; she allegedly provided them weapons from her home and was seen at the roadblock); Prosecution Witness AFB, T. 8 January 2007 pp. 87-94 (observed the Nyakabanda *conseiller* and *Interahamwe* at a roadblock and *Interahamwe* manning a roadblock at the Gitega sector office); Jean-Baptiste Nyetera, T. 5 July 2007 pp. 30-31 (the Nyamirambo sector *conseiller* and *responsable de cellule* ordered that roadblocks be set up and chose who would man them there); Defence Witness PPO, T. 5 July 2007 p. 52 (one or two *conseillers* may have participated in the erection of roadblocks, but the general disorder surrounding them suggested that this was not planned); Defence Witness UT, T. 24 May 2007 pp. 48-49, T. 25 May 2007 pp. 23-24 (militia at roadblocks gave the impression that, for example, *Conseiller* Odette Nyirabagenzi "supported" persons manning a roadblock in Muhima, that *Conseiller* Rose Karusha supported those at a roadblock in Kimisagara, and that *Conseiller* Amri Karekezi supported individuals at roadblocks in Biryogo); Defence Witness PER, T. 23 August 2007 pp. 33-35, 62 (militia manning roadblocks in the neighbourhood around Saint Paul and Sainte Famille "depended on" *Conseiller* Odette Nyaribagenzi and primary school inspector Angeline Mukandutiye. The witness did not see Renzaho in the company of either official and did not hear his name mentioned in connection with them); Defence Witness AIA, T. 2 July 2007 pp. 27, 35; T. 3 July 2007 p. 13 (Amri Karikezi, Biryogo's *conseiller*, pointed out specific locations in Biryogo where roadblocks should be erected on the orders of the interim Prime Minister and not Renzaho); Defence Witness GOA, T. 6 June 2007 pp. 47, 49, 51 (while some civilians set up roadblocks on their own initiative, others did so with the assistance of cellule and sector officials. Roadblock leaders at the Gitega roadblock kept the company of, and collaborated with, the Biryogo *conseiller*, Amri Karekezi); Defence Witness HIN, T. 9 July 2007 pp. 67-68, T. 10 July 2007 pp. 25, 36 (*Conseiller* Odette Nyirabagenzi toured Rugenge sector to supervise roadblocks, telling people to be vigilant and prevent the movement of Tutsis. The checkpoints were set up to kill Tutsis. The witness did not believe that Nyirabagenzi was acting on Renzaho's orders in touring her sector, but rather on security measures suggested to her by the Presidential Guard.); Defence Witness Nyetera, T. 5 July 2007 p. 31 (roadblocks had been set up based on orders of the Prime Minister and not Renzaho).

from the evidence of Witnesses UB, AWE, GLJ and ALG who testified about meetings where Renzaho issued such instructions. Second, this conclusion finds support in his public statements over the radio concerning roadblocks. Finally, the evidence concerning the planning of Rwanda's "civil defence" system, in which Renzaho participated, lends further corroboration.

166. With respect to the meetings, Witnesses UB and AWE provided first-hand evidence of Renzaho convening a meeting at the prefecture office around 10 April 1994, and Witness ALG offered a second-hand account. These three witnesses were former local government officials who have been convicted of or charged with crimes in Rwanda relating to the establishment of roadblocks between April and July 1994.[191] In addition, Witnesses UB and AWE were detained in the same prison at the time of their testimony.[192] In light of these concerns, the Chamber is mindful of their interests in shifting blame for their actions onto Renzaho as well as the possibility of collusion between Witnesses UB and AWE. It thus views the evidence of these witnesses with appropriate caution.

167. While there are some differences between these witnesses' accounts related to the exact date of the meeting and the participants, the Chamber is convinced that they are not material. With respect to the date, Witness AWE insisted that the meeting occurred on 9 April.[193] Witness ALG also heard the meeting occurred on 9 April. Witness UB placed the meeting later, on 10 or 11 April. Nonetheless, a close examination of his testimony suggests an earlier date of 9 or 10 April since he further explained that the meeting aligned with the [page 45] swearing-in of the interim government, which occurred on 9 April.[194] Consequently, the main features of the evidence of these three witnesses are compatible with respect to the date of the meeting. It is also sufficiently consistent with paragraph 9 of the Indictment which refers to Renzaho issuing orders concerning roadblocks at a meeting "[o]n or about 10 April 1994".

168. As to the participants, Witness UB stated that the attendees consisted of *conseillers*, *responsables de cellule*, soldiers, gendarmes, and representatives of political parties and the *Interahamwe*, whereas Witness AWE indicated that the meeting was smaller in nature and was attended only by *conseillers*, *bourgmestres*, senior military officers and some gendarmes. The Chamber considers that these differences are not material and in any case stem from the passage of time. Notably, Witnesses UB and AWE both described attending a meeting where Renzaho explained that roadblocks were meant to confront the "Tutsis" or "*Inyenzi*" and ordered those in attendance to establish more of them. The two witnesses each stated that local *conseillers* reported on the prevailing security situation and that *Bourgmestre* Jean Bizimana did not attend. They indicated that the meeting involved broader participation than a normal prefecture security council meeting.[195] Furthermore, Witness ALG heard about a meeting, occurring around the same time, from the *conseillers* of Biryogo and

---

[191] Prosecution Witness UB was convicted and sentenced to death in Rwanda in 1997. His appeal was rejected in 1998 and at the time of his testimony he was awaiting a ruling by the Supreme Court in Rwanda. Witness UB, T. 23 January 2007 pp. 1-4, 62-65; T. 24 January 2007 pp. 7-8, 12, 18, 21-22; Defence Exhibit 11A (Rwandan trial judgment of Witness UB); Defence Exhibit 11B (Rwandan appeal judgement of Witness UB). Witnesses AWE and ALG testified before the Tribunal prior to the commencement of their respective trials in Rwanda, wherein the participation in the erection and administration of roadblocks were relevant to their cases. Witness AWE, T. 31 January 2007 pp. 11-12, 51-52, 54, 56 (awaiting trial but noting that he confessed to establishing roadblocks); Witness ALG, T. 10 January 2007 p. 64 (noting that he had been charged in Rwanda with genocide and had been provisionally released in July 2005); Defence Exhibit 4C (Rwandan judicial dossier for Witness ALG, undated) p. 2, which summarises a witness account that accuses Witness ALG of "having manned *Interahamwe's* roadblocks and having given them [the *Interahamwe*] instructions to go and kill".
[192] Prosecution Exhibit 69 (personal identification sheet for Witness UB); Prosecution Exhibit 80 (personal identification sheet for Witness AWE).
[193] See T. 31 January 2007 pp. 34-35; Prosecution Exhibit 49 (transcript of Radio Rwanda, 11 April 1994, broadcasting *communiqué* dated 10 April 1994) p. 5.
[194] T. 23 January 2007 p. 8 ("Between the 10th and 11th *when the government was sworn in*, the préfet of Kigali-ville convened a meeting, the meeting that he referred to as extended security meeting.") (emphasis added); Prosecution Exhibit 94A (expert report of Alison Des Forges) p. 11, noting that the new government was installed on 9 April 1994.
[195] Witness AWE testified that during a second meeting in April 1994, representatives of political parties were present, bringing his evidence more in line with that of Witness UB in relation to this meeting and others (II.3). Additionally, a *communiqué* issued by Renzaho on 14 April also suggests that he met with communal and sector level officials as well as members of political parties. Prosecution Exhibit 51 (transcript of Radio Rwanda *communiqué*, 14 April 1994) pp. 9 ("In the latter days, we held a meeting of authorities at the commune and sector levels"), 10 ("I held a meeting with officials of the political parties at the prefecture and commune levels ... That is why I thank very much the representatives of political parties for the constructive ideas they gave us during that meeting…"). Renzaho, however, denied that he met with political party officials. T. 28 August 2007 p. 52; T. 30 August 2007 pp. 46-47.

Cyahafi and *Bourgmestre* Pierre Claver Nyirikwaya of Kacyiru commune. They told him that Renzaho had urged those present to assist in the fight against the *Inkotanyi*, to sensitise the population and to set up roadblocks.

169. In sum, based on the foregoing, the Chamber is convinced that Witnesses UB, AWE, and ALG were referring to the same meeting, which occurred around 10 April 1994.[196] Furthermore, the Chamber is satisfied that these three witnesses provided credible accounts of Renzaho's order to establish roadblocks, in particular when viewed in context with the relevant circumstantial evidence discussed below.

170. In assessing whether Renzaho held a meeting with local officials and gave instructions to erect and support roadblocks, excerpts from a Radio Rwanda broadcast of a *communiqué* by Renzaho, dated 10 April, are of interest:

> Third: Members of the population are prohibited from erecting roadblocks in the city neighbourhoods during the day. Roadblocks may only be set up at night, and such operations must be closely monitored by the security committees operating in the neighbourhoods. **[page 46]**
>
> ...
>
> Fifth: The *Préfet* once again warns all criminals and asks members of the population to fight the looters, bandits, killers and all other troublemakers. He asks them to be vigilant and to continue to denounce to the authorities criminals who try to infiltrate into their midst.[197]

171. Renzaho affirmed that he issued this *communiqué* and explained the relevant passage as follows:

> But as regards the control of the roadblocks, I consistently stressed insisted that the communal authorities should be involved and should ensure the proper control to avoid that there be excesses and brutalities by the people manning those roadblocks. I did that in the course of meetings with the *bourgmestres*, and for the *bourgmestre* of Nyarugenge, he'd bring his *conseillers* along. I also did so through my various appeals, messages, *communiqués*.[198]

172. In the Chamber's view, the radio broadcast and Renzaho's explanation corroborate the first-hand testimonies of Witness UB and AWE that he gave orders to local authorities to collaborate with residents in erecting roadblocks to intercept *Inkotanyi* or *Inyenzi*, which also included Tutsi civilians. The Chamber reaches this conclusion notwithstanding instructions in the same broadcast to dismantle roadblocks during the day, as well as Renzaho's statement broadcast on 7 April, "appealing to people not to attack each other". Indeed, this previous *communiqué* also anticipated cooperation between the authorities and encouraged civilians to cooperate with "forces of law", to "remain vigilant" and ensure "their homes are well protected and thereby prevent infiltration".[199]

173. Radio broadcasts after 11 April provide a similar picture. In an interview given on 12 April, Renzaho gave specific instructions that the population should defend itself, search for *Inyenzi* and erect roadblocks:

> "On the streets leading to their quarters, it would be a good thing to block them with road-blocks. They can look after them, choose people they really trust and who have papers and put them there."

The interview also contains references to specific areas of Kigali where, in his view, there was no need for checkpoints during the day because the gendarmerie had established roadblocks there.[200] **[page 47]**

---

[196] Witness GLJ testified that he met with the prefect on 10 April at the prefecture office (II.4.3). He testified that he did not attend a meeting but learned that meetings had purportedly been held before and after he left. T. 22 January 2007 p. 18.
[197] Prosecution Exhibit 49 (transcript of Radio Rwanda, 11 April 1994, broadcasting *communiqué* dated 10 April 1994) p. 5.
[198] Renzaho, T. 28 August 2007 p. 13.
[199] Prosecution Exhibit 48 (transcript of Radio Rwanda, 7 April 1994) p. 2 ("Speaker: Unidentified: The *Préfet* of Kigali-Ville Préfecture is appealing to the inhabitants of Kigali-Ville to comply with the instructions issued by the Ministry of Defence. He is appealing to people not to attack each other, to remain vigilant during this period of adversity, cooperate with the forces of law and order so as to facilitate their task. He is calling on everyone to ensure their homes are well protected and thereby prevent infiltration. This announcement is signed by Tharcisse Renzaho, Préfet of Kigali-Ville.").
[200] Prosecution Exhibit 50 (transcript of Radio Rwanda interview, 12 April 1994) p. 9 ("We request of them to make patrols within like usual, they ought to come together and *look for their traditional tools they are used to and defend themselves*. I would like to request of them that now each quarter should try to organise itself and make a communal work within quarters by cutting off bushes, searching empty houses, check out in the nearby swamp *if no Inyenzi hid inside*. . . . On the streets leading to their quarters, it would be a good thing to block them with road-blocks. They can look after them, choose people they really trust and who have papers and put them there... I was told that, on the road Gikondo-Remera, there are roadblocks which have been settled by the population, *as the Gendarmerie has settled its own roadblocks during the day, they must withdraw those roadblocks* and send people to look for food here downtown. *They can perhaps settle those road-blocks at night*... they can settle those roadblocks on the streets

174. Similarly, in a broadcast on 14 April, Renzaho referred to a meeting he had held with representatives of political parties at the prefecture and communal level. He stressed the need to unite, not kill one another but fight against the enemy who had attacked "in our areas", and announced that meeting would be held the following day where the populations would receive clear instructions. He explained that it was not necessary for all citizens to attend as some of them had to conduct patrols, "they have their roadblock they are guarding and at which they must remain".[201] Renzaho's broadcast on Radio Rwanda on 24 April suggested that *conseillers* would be working with their communities to provide security to the population, through the use of roadblocks.[202] Finally, after Renzaho was aware of targeted killings of Tutsis, his broadcasts on 10 May and 18 June focussed on checking the identification of those crossing roadblocks.[203]

175. In the Chamber's view, Renzaho's contemporaneous public statements corroborate the direct evidence of Witnesses UB and AWE as well as the hearsay evidence of Witness ALG about the meeting at the prefecture office around 10 April. It is also in conformity with Witness GLJ's evidence about a meeting in the prefecture office around 16 or 17 April wherein Renzaho ordered that roadblocks be established. Furthermore, Witness ALG testified that he attended three to four meetings after 12 April where Renzaho urged the strengthening of roadblocks and that night patrols be conducted to monitor the infiltration of *Inkotanyi*.[204] **[page 48]** While it is unclear if these witnesses were referring to the same meetings, the message they received consistently emphasised the need to provide support in the administration of roadblocks.

176. Finally, the Chamber considers that Renzaho's involvement in putting in place a civil defence system in Kigali lends further corroboration to the evidence that he ordered the establishment of roadblocks in Kigali. Undisputed evidence reflects that, on 29 March 1994, Renzaho met with Déogratias Nsabimana, the army chief of staff, and Colonel Félicien Muberuka, the commander of the operation sector of Kigali to discuss the implementation of the civil defence plan for Kigali.[205] According to the minutes of the meeting, Muberuka would assign "operational *cellules*" to defend their neighbourhood and "to search for and neutralise infiltrators within the various neighbourhoods of the city".[206] Renzaho was asked to provide lists of reservists and other "reliable civilians" who would work with soldiers in defending neighbourhoods, which he did on 31 March 1994.[207] Documents from May 1994 related to the establishment of the civil

---

of their quarters in order to control them. I wish them to keep on being courageous, they should not listen to those who said that the town has been captured instead they out to be strong in their own areas, then they shall do the communal work so that no *Inyenzi* can hide there. That's my message to the population.") (emphasis added).
[201] Prosecution Exhibit 51 (transcript of Radio Rwanda *communiqué*, 14 April 1994) p. 10. The Chamber notes that on p. 11, there are specific references to Nyabugogo and Giticyinyinoni, where, in Renzaho's view, gendarmes, not the population, should establish roadblocks.
[202] Prosecution Exhibit 54 (transcript of Radio Rwanda broadcast, 24 April 1994) p. 14 ("A while ago, I was talking about the issue of committees. Those committees will be responsible for assisting the *conseiller* in providing security for the population … members of the population must choose those to represent them in the committees which will be responsible for monitoring those … manning the roadblocks…").
[203] Prosecution Exhibit 56 (transcript of Radio Rwanda interview, 10 May 1994) p. 13 ("Normally papers required at roadblocks are those prescribed by the law and are the following: everyone must, normally, have an identity card which must be presented upon demand."); Prosecution Exhibit 62 (transcript of Radio Rwanda broadcast, 18 June 1994) p. 4 ("Up to now, we have given enough directives on identification documents and I have repeated them on many occasions. The identification document that is requested at the roadblocks is the identity card. The inscriptions on our identity card are described by law, and this has not been amended. I would like to inform members of the population that there is a method the *Inyenzi* use to camouflage themselves. They send spies to the zones that are not under their control. They often use Hutus or other persons who have identity cards bearing the Hutu ethnic inscription because they know that persons labeled as such will not face problems during the checks.").
[204] It is recalled that, at the time of their testimony, Witnesses GLJ and ALG had been charged in Rwanda and awaiting trial related to crimes relevant to their involvement with roadblocks in Kigali in 1994. Witness GLJ, T. 22 January 2007 pp. 13-14, 23 (awaiting trial but noting that he confessed to setting up roadblocks on Renzaho's instruction); Witness ALG, T. 10 January 2007 p. 64 (charged with genocide; Defence Exhibit 4 (Rwandan Judicial Dossier for Witness ALG, undated) (reflecting a witness interview accusing Witness ALG of "having manned *Interahamwe's* roadblocks and having given them [the *Interahamwe*] instructions to go and kill"). The Chamber Chamber only relies on their evidence when it is corroborated.
[205] Renzaho, T. 27 August 2007 p. 41; Prosecution Exhibit 24 (letter from Déogratias Nsabimana, copied to Renzaho, about civil defence, dated 30 March 1994).
[206] Prosecution Exhibit 24 (letter from Déogratias Nsabimana, copied to Renzaho, about civil defence, dated 30 March 1994) para. 4.
[207] Renzaho, T. 27 August 2007 p. 41; Prosecution Exhibit 25 (letter from Renzaho to Army Chief of Staff, dated 31 March 1994).

defence system in Kigali clearly identify the prefect as a part of the chain of command over civil defence forces.[208] Renzaho and other defence witnesses denied that the system was ever implemented.[209]

177. The Chamber considers that the evidence does not conclusively show when and to what extent the civil defence structure was *formally* put into place. However, there are clear parallels between the planning and preparation of civil defence which occurred prior to 7 April and the proliferation of roadblocks in Kigali after that date. Furthermore, Renzaho's involvement in high level meetings and other activities, such as identifying civilian recruits, concerning the defence of Kigali just days before hostilities resumed between the government forces and the RPF is indicative of his extensive involvement and interest in matters related to complementary civilians efforts to defend the city at the relevant time. Notably, in the various broadcasts mentioned above, Renzaho referred to the roadblocks in Kigali as providing security. In the Chamber's view, the evidence related to plans for the civil defence in Kigali provides circumstantial corroboration that he would have played an important role in such efforts.

178. In assessing this evidence, the Chamber has considered that Renzaho provided a specific accounting for his days from 9 through 11 April, which did not include the meetings described by the Prosecution witnesses.[210] Furthermore, he and Witness AIA mentioned a meeting that occurred at the Kigali-Ville prefecture office with a similar group of attendees as described by Witnesses UB and AWE. According to their evidence, it occurred on 8 April, **[page 49]** and Renzaho did not order the persons present to erect roadblocks. In the Chamber's view, the Defence evidence does not raise doubt that a meeting about roadblocks took place around 10 April. Both Renzaho and Witness AIA testified that Renzaho continued to meet with local officials, including *bourgmestres* and *conseillers*, in the following days.[211] Furthermore, a radio broadcast Renzaho made on 14 April expressly suggests that he had recently met with representatives from the communes and sectors as well as political parties.[212]

179. In light of the foregoing, the Chamber finds beyond reasonable doubt that around 10 April, Renzaho convened a meeting in the prefecture office, wherein Kigali-Ville *bourgmestres* and *conseillers* as well as other officials discussed the prevailing security situation throughout Kigali-Ville prefecture. During this meeting, Renzaho was alerted to killings of Tutsis and other criminal activities in various Kigali-Ville sectors. Renzaho ordered those in attendance to erect additional roadblocks in areas under their control. Furthermore, during at least one additional meeting in mid-April, Renzaho repeated his instructions that local officials provide support to roadblocks.

2.3.3 Killings Committed at Roadblocks

180. The Chamber finds beyond reasonable doubt that Renzaho made statements to the effect that Tutsis were accomplices of the enemy, *Inyenzi* or *Inkotanyi*. The Chamber accepts that instructions to erect roadblocks in order to fight the *Inyenzi* or *Inkotanyi* were made with the intent mobilise the population against an invading rebel force aimed at deposing the pre-existing regime. However, Renzaho defined the enemy broadly, including Tutsi civilians among them. In the Chamber's view, there is no doubt that Renzaho intended Tutsi civilians to fall within the definition of the enemy or that his message was interpreted to include them.[213] His testimony that Tutsis generally were viewed as accomplices to the RPF and his

---

[208] Prosecution Exhibit 38 (letter of 25 May 1994 from Edouard Karamera to all prefects), which instructs them to implement the Prime Minister's directives regarding civil defence and includes the frequent follow-up and monitoring of civilian roadblocks; Prosecution Exhibit 37 (letter of 25 May 1994 from Jean Kambanda to all prefects), which suggests that the prefect shall act as the supervisor of civil defence activities in the prefecture and shall chair meetings of prefecture organs in charge of civil defence.
[209] See, for instance, Renzaho, T. 27 August 2007 p. 41; Witness PAT, T. 22 August 2007 pp. 74-75; Witness PPV, T. 5 June 2007 pp. 28-29; Witness UT, T. 25 May 2007 p. 4; Witness AIA, T. 2 July 2007 p. 59; Witness PGL, T. 6 June 2007 pp. 28-30, 35-36.
[210] Renzaho, T. 28 August 2007 pp. 43-47; T. 29 August 2007 pp. 59-60.
[211] Renzaho, T. 28 August 2007 pp. 13, 25-26, T. 3 September 2007 p. 18; Witness AIA, T. 2 July 2007 pp. 31, 40-41, 54-56; T. 3 July 2007 pp. 6-7, 10-12, 17-18. See also Witness UT, 24 May 2007 p. 44 (Renzaho had informed the witness of a meeting of available *bourgmestres* and *conseillers* on 11 April, where the object was to calm people who were engaged in killing).
[212] Prosecution Exhibit 51 (transcript of Radio Rwanda broadcast on 14 April 1994) pp. 9-10.
[213] Witness UB, T. 23 January 2007 p. 12 ("[Renzaho] told us that Habyarimana had been killed, that he was killed by the *Inkotanyi*, and that our enemy that we need to fight was the Tutsi."); Witness AWE, T. 31 January 2007 p. 14 ("He explained to us that the enemy was the RPF that had brought the plane down, as well as the accomplices of the RPF, that is to say, our Tutsi neighbours. He told us that the enemy was not far, that it was very close to us. He explained to us that we were to go to our secteur and set up

concession that his use of the terms *Inyenzi* and *Inkotanyi* on the radio included reference to Tutsi civilians offers strong circumstantial support for these conclusions.[214] In so finding, the Chamber has also considered Defence evidence portraying Renzaho as against the killing of Tutsis at roadblocks and distraught or frustrated by the occurrences at them. In the Chamber's view, this, mostly anecdotal, evidence fails to raise doubt in light of the convincing and **[page 50]** credible accounts by the Prosecution witnesses that Renzaho intended the roadblocks to target Tutsi civilians.

181. The Chamber is also satisfied that local officials – in particular *conseillers* and other local authorities such as *responsables des cellules* – erected additional roadblocks within Kigali-Ville prefecture based on Renzaho's orders and that existing roadblocks manned by *Interahamwe* and civilian militia were shown unequivocal support by local authorities.[215] Direct evidence related to who actually manned the roadblocks set up by the Prosecution witnesses, and the killings that occurred at them, is limited. Nonetheless, Witness UB's conviction in Rwanda was based in part on his involvement in roadblocks used to target Tutsis and the political opposition.[216] Likewise, Witness AWE's confession and evidence also supports the conclusion that Tutsis were targeted for killing, particularly after civilians were provided firearms.[217] Witness GLJ also confirmed that roadblocks were established after having received such orders and that killing occurred at them.[218] Moreover, when this evidence is viewed in light of all the evidence pointing to the targeted attacks at roadblocks, the Chamber is convinced beyond reasonable doubt that Tutsis, those who were perceived to be Tutsi and individuals identified as members of the opposition were singled out at these roadblocks and killed. This finding considers that other authorities within Kigali, such as the military or interim government, may have also supported such activity, either through Renzaho or with their own parallel efforts. Nonetheless, the Chamber is convinced that Renzaho's instructions reinforced the message that the local authorities' supported roadblocks and substantially contributed to the targeted killings at them. **[page 51]**

---

roadblocks where there were none in order to prevent any infiltration of the town by the *Inyenzi*. He did not want the *Inyenzis* to be able to go and join their accomplices, the Tutsi.").

[214] T. 30 August 2007 pp. 19 ("Q. Do you accept, Mr. Renzaho, that Tutsi civilians were viewed as accomplices of the RPF? A. Yes, that was possible in the confusion that we were living through."), 54-55 ("Q. ... Now, you will agree with me, also, won't you, Mr. Renzaho, that the Tutsi, in general, were referred to, both by yourselves and others on the radio, as 'Inyenzi-Inkotanyi'? A. It wasn't I who invented the expression. It was adopted after the start of the RPF war, and I think the illusion was clear: Those who were attacking at that time were the same that had attacked in the 60s; thus, there was a heightened… Mr. President: Mr. Renzaho, you have to answer the question. Did you use that term, yes or no, in that way? The Witness: Yes, I used it, as others used it.").

[215] Witness UB, T. 23 January 2007 p. 12 ("Q. As a result of what he said, did you set up any roadblocks in your sector? A. After receiving these instructions, you will understand that these instructions were not given only to the *conseillers*. It is obvious that there was an increase in the number of roadblocks all over. Even in places where there were no roadblocks, new ones were erected. And that was the case in my sector, as well."); Witness AWE, T. 31 January 2007 pp. 14, 46 (*responsables de cellule* were directed by the witness to erect roadblocks at strategic locations, which were manned by *Interahamwe*).

[216] Defence Exhibit 11A (Rwandan trial judgment of Witness UB) p. 28 ("*Attendu que dans la planification du génocide et des massacres et en le mettant en action, après la mort de l'ancien Président du Rwanda, les barrieres on été erigées (montées) dans tout le pays sur instructions des autorités en place et de certain partis politiques pour que les Batutsi que le prenait pour complice des inyenzi (partisans due Front Patriotique Rwandais et les Bahutu qui etaient opposés au regime en place soient recherchés et tués ... Attendu que pour mettre en action le génocide et les massacres, il a distribué les fusils, dans tout son secteur aux miliciens interahamwe ... ces armes (fusils) ont été utilisés pour tuer les gens sur les barrières et pour piller; lui-même ne le nie pas parce qu'il dit que il y a des fusils qu'il a retire du P.V.K. et les a donné aux responsables*").

[217] Witness AWE, T. 31 January 2007 pp. 11-12 ("I also admitted that after that meeting – or, rather, in the course of that meeting, it was decided that we had to erect roadblocks, and I myself erected those roadblocks in my secteur."); Witness AWE, T. 31 January 2007 p. 20 (noting that after weapons had been distributed around 12 April, Tutsis were targeted for killing).

[218] Witness GLJ, T. 22 January 2007 pp. 22-23 ("Q. Well, did you establish roadblocks after receiving these instructions? A. We were with the responsable of the cellule in the meeting. So after the roadblock after the meeting, roadblocks were erected throughout the cellule, in all cellules... Q. Well, from the discussions at the meeting, was it apparent if anything similar had happened at other roadblocks throughout the city, that people had been killed? A. Yes. In the town there were people who were killed at the roadblock. And I explained that at Gitega they nearly killed my driver. And there were, obviously, others who would have been killed at that roadblock ... The witness: ... I admitted that I had the roadblocks to be erected, because there were people who were killed at such roadblocks. I also admitted that because I recognised that there were people who were not able to flee because of the roadblocks, those are part and parcel of my confessions."). See also Witness ALG T. 11 January 2007 pp. 22-25 (testifying to having observed roadblocks in Nyarugenge commune where people were being killed and their property taken after having heard from Renzaho that roadblocks were being established to prevent *Inkotanyi* infiltration in the city).

182. The evidence does not reflect that Renzaho provided explicit orders to kill Tutsis at roadblocks.[219] Indeed, some of the Prosecution evidence indicates that Renzaho gave orders to have people arrested and that the killings were committed by civilians at roadblocks on their own initiative.[220] The Defence also challenged Witness ALG with a statement from his Rwandan judicial proceedings that he, on his own initiative, organised the killings at roadblocks while instructing *Interahamwe* to feed Renzaho misinformation as to what was happening.[221]

183. However, Renzaho, by his own admission, was aware of disorder at roadblocks by 8 April and that killings were occurring in all parts of the city.[222] He admitted that, after 10 April, he was aware that people were being killed at roadblocks in Kigali-Ville prefecture based on their ethnicity and political leanings.[223] In the Chamber's view, the need to hold a meeting as early as 11 April to organise the removal of corpses covering the streets of Kigali leads to the only reasonable conclusion that Renzaho, the administrative head of Kigali-Ville, [page 52] would have been aware of the scale in which killings were occurring before that date.[224] Accordingly, the Chamber is convinced beyond reasonable doubt that Renzaho knew that killings at roadblocks, like elsewhere, targeted Tutsis on an ethnic basis before the meeting where he ordered local officials to erect them around 10 April. In this context, the Chamber finds beyond reasonable doubt that he was aware that the continued killing of Tutsi civilians was a likely outcome when he urged the meetings' attendants to erect additional roadblocks to be manned by those within their communities.

---

[219] Witness AWE, T. 31 January 2007 p. 14 ("A. He first explained to us under what circumstances the president's plane had been shot down, and he told us that now the enemy was known. He explained to us that the enemy was the RPF that had brought the plane down, as well as the accomplices of the RPF, that is to say, our Tutsi neighbours. He told us that the enemy was not far, that it was very close to us. He explained to us that we were to go to our sector and set up roadblocks where there were none in order to prevent any infiltration of the town by the *Inyenzi*. He did not want the *Inyenzis* to be able to go and join their accomplices, the Tutsi. And he explained that conflicts among political parties were to stop because now the enemy was known."); Witness AWE, T. 31 January 2007 p. 36 ("A. Regarding the specific orders, the Préfet Renzaho told us that we should set aside our differences – our political differences in the sector. He appealed to us to us to unite, to identify the enemy and to erect roadblocks in neighbourhoods that did not have them. Q. So, the instructions that you received related to the roadblocks? A. Yes."); Witness UB, T. 23 January 2007 p. 12 ("A. ... And he told us that we should set up new roadblocks in areas where they did not exist ... and that our enemy that we need to fight was the Tutsi."). See also Witness ALG, T. 11 January 2007 p. 41 (Renzaho's urged attendees "to be vigilant. That it was imperative that areas not yet under *Inkotanyi* control be protected so that the *Inkotanyi* would not enter into those areas. So it was necessary to staff roadblocks, carry out night patrols, and the préfet called on the people to provide support to the *Interahamwe* who were helping the soldiers in the front ... Generally, the recommendations set forth at those meetings were the strengthening of the roadblocks, and the conduct of night patrols so as to check the infiltration of the *Inkotanyi*."); Witness ALG, T. 11 January 2007 p. 67 ("Reference has been made to the fact that efforts should be made to check infiltrations into the city. Reference has been made to exterminating people. So, there is reference to stopping people from entering the city and this relates to the meeting that was taking place, to the roadblocks that were set up, and to the fact that people were being killed, the purpose of which was to stop the *Inkotanyi* from infiltrating the city. These are the types of instructions that were issued during the meetings that were held around that time, and it is on that basis that I provided that time frame.").

[220] Witness AWE gave a prior witness statement to Tribunal investigators where he stated: "[i]t should be noted that the primary purpose of such roadblocks was not to systematically kill the Tutsi. It was the population itself which took it upon itself to do so." T. 31 January 2007 p. 38; Defence Exhibit 23 (Statement of 29 November 2003). The witness acknowledged having made this statement and testified that the roadblocks were intended to restrict movement of Tutsis so they could be located and killed. T. 31 January 2007 pp. 38, 56-57. See also Witness GLJ, T. 22 January 2007 p. 22 ("A. The instruction was to erect roadblocks on the road so as to identify passers-by by asking them to show their identification. The préfet said that there were people who were going around the town without identification documents, and those should be the *Inkotanyi* that had infiltrated ... A. During the meeting, the préfet said that those who were arrested had to be handed over to the prefecture police, or the gendarmerie brigade.").

[221] Witness ALG, T. 15 January 2007 pp. 26-28; Defence Exhibit 4 (summary of Rwandan judicial proceedings of Witness ALG).

[222] Renzaho, T. 28 August 2007 p. 2.

[223] Renzaho, *id.* p. 11; T. 30 August 2007 p. 54.

[224] Renzaho, T. 28 August 2007 pp. 45-47; T. 29 August 2007 p. 59 (discussing the 11 April meeting with the ICRC at the Kigali-Ville prefecture which focussed, in part, on the removal of the dead); Prosecution Witness UL, T. 9 January 2007 pp. 53-62 (Renzaho ordering the removal of the dead at an 11 April meeting attended by Philipe Gaillard of the ICRC); Prosecution Witness GLJ, T. 22 January 2007 pp. 16-18, 47-50 (the witness attended a meeting on 10 April where Renzaho asked *conseillers* to collect dead bodies); Defence Witness BDC, T. 4 June 2007 pp. 7-8, 10-12 (the witness heard about a meeting on 11 April between Renzaho, the ICRC and government ministries where humanitarian issues such as the burial of corpses were discussed). See also Witness PPV, T. 5 June 2007 p. 42 ("Those persons manned roadblocks, but so did many people. We did not witness the killings. However, the prefect was aware that people were dying.").

184. In so finding, the Chamber recognises that Renzaho had made public pleas to re-establish order and for killings to come to an end.[225] In some instances, Renzaho threatened to punish severely those engaged in crimes such as rape and looting.[226] However, his messages were broadcast over Radio Rwanda at a time when Kigali, the nation's capital and [page 53] locus of international attention, was under intense international scrutiny.[227] Given the record before the Chamber, such broadcasts appear to be motivated by a need to restore the government's public image rather than a genuine attempt to control the ethnically targeted killing ravaging the city.[228] His instructions to stop killings and crime also appear directed at halting such activities where they targeted the population that was sympathetic to the government and that Renzaho sought to mobilise against the "enemy". As Expert Witness Alison Des Forges noted, Renzaho was capable of giving precise instructions when there were specific segments of the population for which he had concern. In particular, Des Forges pointed to a Radio Rwanda broadcast on 6 May, where Renzaho raised concerns that individuals from particular communes with identity cards bearing "Register of Citizens" were mistakenly being identified as RPF.[229] She commented:

---

[225] Prosecution Exhibit 49 (transcript of Radio Rwanda, 11 April 1994, broadcasting *communiqué* dated 10 April 1994) pp. 5 ("The *Préfet* once again warns all criminals and asks all members of the population to fight the looters, bandits, killers and all other troublemakers. He asks them to be vigilant and to continue to denounce to the authorities the criminals who try to infiltrate into their midst."); Prosecution Exhibit 51 (transcript of Radio Rwanda broadcast on 14 April 1994), 9 ("In the latter days, we held a meeting of authorities at the commune and sector levels. We agreed that they should hold meetings in the localities under their authority to teach citizens that our country needs peace, comfort."), 10 ("I wanted to tell you that about improving security, especially in fightings, lootings, thefts, killings; I held a meeting with the official of political parties at the prefecture and commune levels. That meeting was successful because we shared ideas and found that those in charge of the citizen's problems must do their best to try to make citizens understand that those criminal actions are not the ones that will allow us to win the war."), 11 ("Then I would like that in those meetings, we should take measures bringing peace among the citizens, for stopping definitively those activities of looting and killing."); Prosecution Exhibit 54 (transcript of Radio Rwanda broadcast, 24 April 1994) p. 16 ("… I would like to tell [Rwandans] that they must stop killing their kitty and kin or be divided whereas that is not necessary … The murders, looting and acts of violence must cease so that Rwandans may strive towards recovering their unity and reorganizing themselves so as to regain their strength. That will enable us to pursue our struggle against those attacking us, disrupting peace and spilling fire and blood in our country."); Defence Exhibit 100 (transcript of Radio Rwanda broadcast, 27 April 1994) p.1 ("*Le préfet de la ville de Kigali, le colonel Tharcisse Renzaho, continue à demander l'arrêt des actes de violence, des actes de pillage et des tueries; il demande que les personnes arrêtées dans la commission de tels actes soient sévèrement punies.*"); Defence Exhibit 101 (transcript of Radio Rwanda broadcast, 6 May 1994) p. 3 ("*On peut dire que telle personne est traîte et n'aime pas son pay. Mais il y a ce qu'on appelle excès de zèle. C'est cet excès de zèle qui fait que certaines gens indisciplinées tuent aveuglement et nous nous dresson énergiquement contre cela. C'est pourquoi les conseillers ont reçu instructions de surveiller les gens qui se sont rendus intouchables et qui font sourvent fi des remarques faites par les autres personnes … Je demande donc que les conseillers remplacement immédiatement de telles personnes qui sont sur les barriers pour les mettre à place qu'il faut; les uns en prison s'il le faut et les autres doivent répondre devant la justice.*").

[226] See, for instance, Prosecution Exhibit 56 (transcript of Radio Rwanda broadcast of 10 May 1994) p. 12 ("It is therefore necessary that directives adopted in this regard are complied with. It is for this reason that we have decided to arrest all those who rape and want to commit criminal acts so as to punish them."); Prosecution Exhibit 63 (transcript of Radio Rwanda broadcast on 18 June 1994) p. 5 ("[T]herefore, when we shall receive information whereby a gang is about to perpetrate acts of looting, we will send this unit that will shoot without warning on the gang in question.").

[227] Prosecution Exhibit 51 (transcript of Radio Rwanda broadcast on 14 April 1994) p. 11 ("I will add that our country needs to have a good image. During this time when the international community seems having to forgotten us, I think it is not good to commit unclear, inexplicable actions because those acts make our government lose their credibility."); Prosecution Exhibit 63 (transcript of Radio Rwanda broadcast on 18 June 1994) p. 6 ("Our image has been tarnished. We are called killers. I don't know what else! But who are the authors of such killings? Is it not the *Inyenzi-Inkotanyi*?"); Prosecution Exhibit 94A (expert report of Alison Des Forges) p. 13, which reads: "As the prefect of Kigali-city, Tharcisse Renzaho was extremely conscious of the need for a 'good image,' for the country, one that rested in large part on what foreigners saw and heard in visiting the national capital."

[228] Witness UB, T. 24 January 2007 pp. 9-10 ("Q. And do you recall that such messages were asking the inhabitants of Kigali to put an end to the killings and the massacres in the city, to dismantle the roadblocks in order to enable members of the population to supply themselves, and also denounced the criminals who were perpetrating such acts? Do you recall having heard such messages, or did you hear anything different? A. The *préfet* gave many messages. He said that people were to stop the killings, but those were only words. That was a way of showing the international community that the *préfet* was condemning the killings. Those were messages which were broadcast on the radio, but the criminal acts continued in the two areas. I heard a message requesting, from the population, that it ensure its own security, whereas the *préfet* was supposed to be responsible for such security. If the *préfet* had already stated that the enemy was the Tutsi, this message was meaningless, because if the *préfet* was asking the members of the population to protect themselves, he was implicitly asking them to kill the Tutsis in their area."); Prosecution Exhibit 94A (expert report of Alison Des Forges) p. 13, which reads: "Throughout the genocide, most authorities called periodically for 'restoring order,' for an end to killings, looting, and other misconduct. Many such pronouncements had no noticeable impact, suggesting that they may have been meant as much for foreign as for Rwandan ears."

[229] Prosecution Exhibit 55 (transcript of Radio Rwanda interview with Renzaho, 6 May 1994) p. 4.

Judgement and Sentence

What I find remarkable about this passage is how concrete and precise it is when it has to do with necessary measures for identifying certain persons who are at risk. To me, this is a significant contrast to those vague and generalised directives issued elsewhere, which ask for people at barriers to be careful. It's clear that, when the prefect wants to be concrete and precise and very careful and exact in delineating certain persons, he certainly is able to do so.[230]

Notably, none of Renzaho's pleas called for an end to the attacks on and killings of Tutsi civilians who he knew were dying en masse.[231] **[page 54]**

185. As demonstrated above, Renzaho's statements on Radio Rwanda are critical in determining his intent and actions as they relate to roadblocks. Renzaho's testimony and the Defence Closing Brief demonstrate that the Accused he largely accepted as accurate the transcription of these broadcasts.[232] Where he questioned their accuracy, the objections were vague, and, in the Chamber's view, unconvincing given his general acceptance of exculpatory aspects of the same statements.[233] When assessing the impact of these statements, the Defence evidence, to the extent it strays from the content as set forth in the exhibits, is of limited utility.[234] Prosecution evidence demonstrating that people responded to calls by the prefect to, for example, return to work, suggest that Renzaho's messages on Radio Rwanda were heard.[235] **[page 55]**

3. DISTRIBUTION OF WEAPONS

3.1 Introduction

186. The Indictment alleges that, between mid-1993 and 17 July 1994, Renzaho distributed weapons and ammunition to members of the *Interahamwe* and *Impuzamugambi*, including at his house in Kanombe. On or about 16 April 1994, at a meeting at the Kigali-Ville prefecture headquarters, he ordered *conseillers* to obtain firearms from the Ministry of Defence to be distributed at the sector level. Those weapons were used by *conseillers* and militia to kill Tutsis. The Prosecution relies on Witnesses AFB, UB, GLJ, AWE, ALG, XXY and BUO.[236] The Defence disputes the allegations and the credibility of these witnesses. Reference is made to Witnesses PPV, AIA and PAT.[237]

---

[230] T. 5 March 2007 p. 47.
[231] Renzaho, T. 30 August 2007 p. 56 ("Q. Well, Mr. Renzaho, I am suggesting to you that you never, never said on the radio that people should not kill Tutsis simply on the basis of their ethnicity. You, as préfet, never sent that message out, did you? A. Mr. Prosecutor, would you give me a little time just to collect my *communiqués* and show them to you? Perhaps not in the present – at the present sitting, but I will show them to you."). This was not followed up by the Defence.
[232] See, for instance, Defence Closing Brief paras. 734-738 (arguing that concerning the contents of Prosecution Exhibits 49-53, 58 and 62, the Prosecution only cited to limited excerpts and failed to place them in context; not that they were inaccurate) 752-774 (pointing to excerpts from Prosecution Exhibits 48-51 and Defence Exhibits 100-101 to demonstrate exculpatory content).
[233] T. 28 August 2007 pp. 57-58; T. 3 September 2007 pp. 3-4.
[234] Witness PPV, T. 5 June 2007 pp. 27, 40, 43-44 (the witness did not hear messages being made over the radio by Renzaho but testified that the prefect had called for pacification and no one listened); Witness BDC T. 4 June 2007 pp. 59, 64-65 (The witness did not hear Renzaho on the radio calling for the population or militia to establish roadblocks nor did he receive any briefings to that effect from the Red Cross staff who monitored radio broadcasts); Witness Nyetera, T. 5 July 2007 pp. 31, 33, 36-37, 40 (he heard a 12 April radio address by Renzaho that roadblocks should be erected in an orderly manner; although the message was heard by the population, it was ignored); Witness KRG, T. 7 June 2007 p. 10 (on or after 8 April, Radio Rwanda broadcast an official government request for all men and youth throughout the country to ensure security by assisting at roadblocks and joining the night patrols. The witness did not know the person who gave this order, but that "if one did not comply, one ran into problems."); Defence Witness GOA, T. 6 June 2007 pp. 50-51 (he listened to the radio but did not hear Renzaho ask Kigali-Ville inhabitants to set up roadblocks); Witness Butera, T. 23 May 2007 pp. 11-12, 34-35 (on or around 8 April, he heard Renzaho's message on Radio Rwanda telling the population to remain calm and vigilant, and to stay at home; the witness did not hear an 11 April *communiqué* that roadblocks could be erected at night); Witness WOW, T. 4 July 2007 p. 38 (did not hear messages from Renzaho requesting that roadblocks be set up).
[235] See also II.6 and II.9, which discuss Renzaho's 12 April Radio Rwanda broadcast in relation to the clearing of the bushes similar activity carried out under CELA and Saint Paul.
[236] Indictment paras. 12, 16, 33; Prosecution Closing Brief paras. 80, 83, 102-103, 128-130, 159-180; T. 14 February 2008 pp. 14-15, 19-20. The Prosecution also refers to Witness BUO, in relation to an alleged weapons distribution immediately before an attack on CELA. This evidence has been summarized elswere (II.6) but will be considered here. In a letter of 13 March 2007 to the Defence, the Prosecution conceded that no evidence had been offered in support of para. 18 of the Indictment (alleging that, following a meeting at Bishop Samuel Musabyimana's residence between 7 and 30 May 1994, weapons were distributed to the militia who killed Tutsis).
[237] Defence Closing Brief paras. 870, 874-876, 903, 905-932; T. 14 February 2008 pp. 44-45, 52, 58-59; Defence Exhibit 113 (*complément écrit aux arguments oraux de la défense*) paras. 875.1-875.4, 904.1-904.3, 932.1-932.10. The Chamber also considers the evidence of Witness PGL.

3.2   Evidence

Prosecution Witness AFB

187.   Witness AFB was a Hutu employee in public service. On the morning of 7 April 1994 at around 7.00 a.m., the witness left his home to go to the Biryogo sector office. When he arrived, *Conseiller* Amri Karekezi asked him to take a vehicle with two policemen to the prefecture office. There, the witness observed soldiers, some communal policemen, and members of the *Interahamwe* such as Mugesera and Karim. *Bourgmestres* were also present, including the Reberangondo, the *bourgmestre* of Butamwe commune. Among the *conseillers* the witness noticed were "Stanis" from Gitega sector, Mbyareyehe of a sector he could not recall, and Karekezi, who arrived shortly after the witness. Some time after he arrived, the witness saw Renzaho come out of his office dressed in military uniform and instruct some communal policemen to fetch *Conseiller* Rose Karushara from her house in Kimisagara sector.[238]

188.   Renzaho left the prefecture office in a Renault with his military driver a few minutes after 9.00 a.m. The witness and four policemen followed in a vehicle just behind until Renzaho's vehicle turned into the Radio Rwanda premises around 9.30 or 10.00 a.m. The witness continued on with the policemen to collect Rose Karushara. When he arrived at her residence, he saw that a roadblock, manned by *Interahamwe*, had been erected outside her compound.[239] **[page 56]**

189.   Witness AFB returned to the prefecture office with Karushara and left her there. Renzaho had already returned to the office, and Karushara and a policeman went inside to tell Renzaho they had arrived. Renzaho exited and the witness accompanied him to the *Hôtel des Diplomates*, whereas Karushara and the numerous Kigali-Ville *conseillers* and *bourgmestres* remained at the prefecture office. From outside the hotel, the witness saw several soldiers, including officers, and a policeman identified one of them as Gratien Kabiligi. Renzaho and some soldiers entered the hotel. At about 10.00 a.m., the soldiers came out of the building and loaded cases of ammunition and about 100 weapons, including Kalashnikov guns, into the witness's vehicle. He and the four policemen then followed Renzaho's car back to the prefecture office, arriving shortly after 10.00 a.m. The weapons and ammunition were offloaded and taken into the office, and those destined for Karushara were loaded into the witness's vehicle. He believed that the other *bourgmestres* and *conseillers* who were there would have received weapons and ammunition.[240]

190.   Karushara, who had been inside the prefecture office, exited and asked a policeman whether weapons had been loaded into her car. The witness drove Karushara with 10 of the weapons back to Kimisagara while Renzaho remained at the prefecture office. The policemen carried the weapons into Karushara's living room. She told the *Interahamwe* who had come there that she was going to distribute weapons, and the witness saw her hand five weapons to those of them who were manning the roadblock outside her house. After Karushara served some food and beer, he went back to the prefecture office, where a policeman handed him a travel authorisation signed by Renzaho, instructing him to return with the vehicle the next morning.[241]

191.   Between 2.00 and 3.00 p.m. on 8 April, the witness accompanied Renzaho and the four policemen, who toured roadblocks. They passed the roadblock at Karushara's home Kimisigara sector, a roadblock Nyakabanda sector, two roadblocks in Nyamirambo and two roadblocks in Gitega sector. He promised to provide weapons to *Interahamwe* manning the roadblocks near Karushara's home and the roadblock in Nyakabanda sector. While the witness did not discuss this with Renzaho, he believed Renzaho's purpose was to determine what was being done with weapons that had been distributed.[242]

192.   On 12 April, at around noon, Witness AFB went from the prefecture office with the same four policemen to the *Hôtel des Diplomates*. At the hotel, a policeman and some soldiers loaded various types of guns into the witness's double cabin Hilux pickup, which had State registration on it, until it was nearly full.

---

[238]   T. 8 January 2007 pp. 69-71, 73, 74 (stating "André" instead of "Amri" Karekezi", whereas the French version, *id.* p. 80, contains the correct first name), 75-76, 78; T. 9 January 2007 pp. 20, 23-24; Prosecution Exhibit 64 (personal identification sheet).
[239]   T. 8 January 2007 pp. 76, 78, 80-81, 83-85; T. 9 January 2007 pp. 19-20, 22-25, 28-30, 32, 34-35, 37.
[240]   T. 8 January 2007 pp. 80-83; T. 9 January 2007 pp. 27-28, 34-35, 37-39.
[241]   T. 8 January 2007 pp. 82-85; T. 9 January 2008 pp. 28-30, 32, 34-35.
[242]   T. 8 January 2007 pp. 86-94; T. 9 January 2007 pp. 17, 32; Prosecution Exhibit 77 (photographs by Corrine Dufka).

The guns included some Kalashnikovs, which appeared to be new. From the hotel, the witness and the policemen followed the vehicle with the person who the witness had been told was Kabiligi, where the guns were offloaded and taken inside at about 2.00 p.m. Almost immediately, they were reloaded into the witness's car, along with other weapons that were taken from the office and from Kabiligi's car. The witness went with Renzaho and Kabiligi in three separate vehicles to the roadblock near Protais Zigiranyirazo's residence, which was at most two or three minutes from the prefecture office. The witness had already accompanied Renzaho to that house on 10 April. The roadblock was manned by soldiers and *Interahamwe*. All but about 20-30 weapons were offloaded. Renzaho was in Zigiranyirazo's house, whereas Kabiligi remained outside. **[page 57]** According to the witness, Renzaho was aware that the weapons were being distributed at the roadblock as that was the "purpose of the mission".[243]

193. Renzaho remained at Zigiranyirazo's residence. Kabiligi drove towards the Hotel Kiyovu, after having ordered the witness and the policemen to continue. One of the policemen explained that they should distribute weapons to roadblocks and they did so at the one near Rose Karushara's house in Kimisagara, and at those in Nyakabanda, Nyamirambo and Biryogo sectors. Two to three weapons were given to whoever identified himself as the chief at each roadblock. They returned to the prefecture office at about 3.00 p.m., where they found Renzaho.[244]

Prosecution Witness UB

194. Witness UB, a Hutu local official in Kigali-Ville prefecture, explained that Renzaho convened several meetings at the prefecture office during the events. On 10 or 11 April 1994, Renzaho chaired what he called an "extended security council meeting". *Conseillers*, *responsables* of cellules, *Interahamwe*, political party representatives, soldiers and gendarmes were present. The *conseillers* complained about their individual security concerns and that Tutsis were being killed. Renzaho convened a second meeting days later.[245] The *conseillers* gave reports during this second meeting about the situation in their respective sectors. They noted that "inhabitants" had firearms, and Witness UB testified that some had been distributed by the political parties. *Conseillers* complained that they, as authorities, did not have any. Renzaho responded that he had consulted with army leaders who had promised to provide the *conseillers* with firearms. He told the *conseillers* to go to the Ministry of Defence to collect the weapons. Jean Bizimana, *bourgmestre* of Nyarugenge commune, was present during this meeting.[246]

195. After the second meeting, the witness went to the Ministry of Defence accompanied by policemen. He did not believe that Jean Bizimana went with them there and could not recall which of the other *conseillers* went, although there were several. He received five firearms there and distributed them to the *responsables de cellule* in his sector. The witness was also given ammunition. No documents were required to obtain the weapons.[247]

196. In addition to the weapons that Witness UB supplied, he saw many firearms that had been distributed by representatives of political parties in Biryogo sector. The chairman of the Islamic PDI party in Kigali-Ville prefecture, Djuma Babazinturo, who lived in the Biryogo **[page 58]** sector said that he had obtained them from the prefect and distributed them to the members of the population.[248]

---

[243] T. 8 January 2007 p. 73; T. 9 January 2007 pp. 1-3, 5-9.
[244] T. 9 January 2007 pp. 5-9, 17, 20. Witness AFB testified that the policeman said that they should go to roadblocks in Kimisagara, Nyamirambo, Nyakabanda and Gitega sectors but said that went to Biryogo, not Gitega. Compare T. 9 January 2007 p. 5 (mentioning the policeman's instructions on which roadblocks to visit) and T. 9 January 2007 p. 7 (describing the roadblocks visited).
[245] Compare T. 23 January 2007 p. 12 (placing the second meeting "approximately two days" after the first meeting on 10 or 11 April) and T. 24 January 2007 pp. 14-15 (discussing the meeting as occurring on 16 April and going to the Ministry of Defence that day).
[246] T. 23 January 2007 pp. 1-2, 4, 8-9, 12-14, 55; T. 24 January 2007 pp. 15-16; Prosecution Exhibit 69 (personal identification sheet). At the time of his testimony, Witness UB was a detainee, awaiting the outcome of an appeal before the Rwandan Supreme Court. His conviction for genocide in 1997 had been confirmed by the appeals court.
[247] T. 23 January 2007 pp. 13-14; T. 24 January 2007 p. 15.
[248] T. 23 January 2007 p. 14.

Prosecution Witness GLJ

197. Witness GLJ was a Hutu local official in Kigali until he was dismissed from his duties in April 1994. He attended a meeting convened and chaired by Renzaho on about 16 or 17 April in the morning. Three *bourgmestres*, the *conseillers* of Kigali town, all the *responsables* of the *cellules*, an army representative, as well as the commander in charge of the civil defence program, were present.[249]

198. Renzaho, who was in military attire, passed on decisions made by a prior meeting of the security committee.[250] He informed those in attendance that weapons should be distributed to members of the population to ensure their security. Renzaho told the attendees to obtain weapons at the Ministry of Defence and provide them to demobilised soldiers and policemen, adding that some could be given to members of the population who knew how to handle weapons. The weapons were to be distributed so that people could take part in security rounds or go to roadblocks.[251]

199. Immediately after the meeting, Witness GLJ went alone with his driver to the Ministry of Defence and received five firearms, and on another unspecified occasion he received five more.[252] He distributed them to the population, particularly those manning roadblocks, in the Rebero neighbourhood, Kivugiza *cellule* and neighbouring areas. He recalled that he distributed two weapons in Gatare neighbourhood.[253] No documents were required to collect the weapons, but he had to sign one acknowledging receipt of them. The person in charge of civilian defence, Bivamvagara, was responsible for monitoring how the weapons were used.[254]

200. A *communiqué* from Renzaho was issued on 10 May, aimed at determining who was in possession of weapons.[255] The witness and others also submitted lists of those who had weapons to Renzaho. In the witness's view, the objective of the *communiqué* was to recover the weapons in order to restore security. Based on the reports that had been made to the **[page 59]** prefect that there were *Interahamwe* killing people in the sector, he thought that Renzaho would recover the weapons from the *Interahamwe* to restore security. However, no such action was taken.[256]

Prosecution Witness AWE

201. Witness AWE, a Hutu local official within the Kigali-Ville prefecture and MRND member, attended several meetings in the Kigali-Ville prefecture office. The second of them occurred around 11 April 1994.[257] *Bourgmestres, conseillers*, representatives of political parties and soldiers were among those present Renzaho told those at the meeting to collect firearms at the Ministry of Defence immediately after the meeting and to provide them to former soldiers. He "strictly requested to avoid giving the weapons to the Tutsi". The witness did not go to the Ministry right away, as he was alone without a vehicle and thought he would be unable to transport them.[258]

---

[249] T. 22 January 2007 pp. 13-15, 18-21, 23, 26-27, 30-31, 50, 58, 61-63; Prosecution Exhibit 68 (personal identification sheet). When testifying, Witness GLJ had been detained in Rwanda for over 12 years. His trial had not yet begun.
[250] A more detailed discussion of this security committee meeting is set forth in (II.2).
[251] T. 22 January 2007 pp. 14, 19, 21-23, 25-29.
[252] First, Witness GLJ testified that he received five firearms and subsequently five more. T. 22 January 2007 pp. 19, 21. Later, he seemed to indicate that he obtained all 10 at once. T. 22 January 2007 p. 58.
[253] *Id.* p. 19. See also the French version which appears to be more precise. p. 23 ("*Q. À qui avez-vous remis ces armes à feu? R. Comme je l'ai expliqué, j'ai distribué ces armes à feu dans les cellules voisines de Rebero, c'est-à-dire Nyabitare, où j'ai distribué quatre armes à feu; dans la cellule de Kivugiza, j'en ai distribué deux; et Gatare, j'en ai distribué deux également. Donc, j'ai distribué ces armes auprès des populations qui habitaient aux environs de Rebero.*")
[254] *Id.* pp. 13, 19-21, 26, 29, 32, 57-59. The distribution of 10 weapons formed part of his confession in his Rwandan legal proceedings.
[255] Prosecution Exhibit 56 (transcript of Radio Rwanda broadcast of 10 May 1994) p. 12 ("Civil-Defence material belongs to members of the population [...] equitably and appropriately. We have now started to conduct inspections in order to assess the situation. The situation is improving due to the directives we are giving them").
[256] T. 22 January 2007 p. 58.
[257] Witness AWE's evidence relating to the first meeting he attended at the Kigali-Ville prefecture office is set out in (II.2).
[258] T. 31 January 2007 pp. 11-13, 17-20, 42, 47-49 (quoted); Prosecution Exhibit 80 (personal identification sheet). Having been arrested in 1996, Witness AWE was at the time of his testimony awaiting trial for genocide in Rwanda.

202. The next morning, Witness AWE went in a vehicle to the prefecture office and asked Renzaho for the promised weapons, explaining that he had not yet been able to get them. Renzaho called a major at the Ministry of Defence and then told the witness to go there and receive weapons. A soldier at the Ministry gave the witness five weapons – Lee Enfield and Kalashnikov rifles – and ammunition. He did not take any documentation with him and needed only to introduce himself and specify his sector given Renzaho's prior phone call.[259]

203. Witness AWE took the firearms to the sector office and handed them to members of the sector committee. About 12 persons, including those that had received the weapons, were then called to one or two days' military training in weapons handling. The witness testified that they had been trained to exterminate people. When the recipients returned from training, they first went to the war front but then very soon returned to assist the *Interahamwe*, and immediately started killing Tutsis in large numbers. He reported on the situation to the prefect, but Renzaho never intervened.[260]

Prosecution Witness ALG

204. Witness ALG, a Hutu, was a local official in Kigali-Ville prefecture and a MRND party member.[261] He testified that Renzaho convened three or four security meetings in April and May 1994. The witness attended some of them. Government officials, soldiers, political party officials and *Interahamwe* were invited and would attend these meetings, including Angeline Mukandutiye and *Interahamwe* such as Jean Nepomuscene Biziyaremye, Hussein Longo Longo and Sued Nydayitabi. The recommendations made there were almost always the same. Renzaho would call on the participants to provide support to the *Interahamwe* who **[page 60]** were helping soldiers "at the front", and it was therefore necessary to give the *Interahamwe* weapons. The *Interahamwe* constantly requested firearms during these meetings. The witness was told by the *Interahamwe* at Angeline Mukandutiye's compound that Renzaho distributed weapons to them, and that *Interahamwe* who needed weapons would go to pick them up at Renzaho's "place".[262]

205. A *bourgmestre* and some *conseillers* informed Witness ALG that, on 9 and 11 April 1994, Renzaho summoned them to meetings, and that, at the 9 April meeting, Renzaho promised the *conseillers* that he would forward a request to the Ministry of Defence for weapons to be distributed at various roadblocks. *Conseillers* also informed the witness that, at the 11 April meeting, they learned that Renzaho had arranged for them to collect firearms at the Ministry. They went to the Ministry, led by Jean Baptiste Butera and François Karera. They were also accompanied by national level *Interahamwe* officials, including Maniragaba, who was an influential *Interahamwe* in Kigali town, and Stanlis Simbizi, vice chairman of the CDR party in Kigali prefecture. The *conseillers* gave the weapons, which they had collected to the various heads of the *cellule* committees for distribution to members of the population. The *conseiller* of Cyhafi sector told the witness that each *conseiller* received five weapons.[263]

206. On several occasions in May 1994, Witness ALG saw General Kabiligi bring weapons, including new Kalashnikov guns, to the prefecture office. The weapons were distributed directly to the *Interahamwe* and members of the civil defence who Kabiligi had summoned there, after which they would go "to the front". The witness saw Kabiligi show Renzaho the weapons that had been stockpiled in the courtyard of the prefecture office. They were placed in the urban police stocks there and later distributed to the *Interahamwe* who would come to the prefecture office to get them before leaving "for the front". On one occasion, Renzaho asked the witness to accompany Major Bivamvagara, the person in charge of the civil defence service, to Nyakabanda sector and hand five guns to the *conseiller* of that sector. The witness also explained that the

---

[259] T. 31 January 2007 pp. 18-20, 42, 47.
[260] *Id.* pp. 20-21, 26-27, 41, 47-50.
[261] T. 10 January 2007 pp. 56, 63; T. 12 January 2007 p. 22; Prosecution Exhibit 67 (personal identification sheet). When testifying, Witness ALG was awaiting trial in Rwanda for his role during the 1994 events, including a charge that he distributed weapons in one of the communes. T. 10 January 2007 p. 64.
[262] T. 11 January 2007 pp. 36, 39-41; T. 15 January 2007 pp. 9-13, 33, 35.
[263] T. 11 January 2007 pp. 29-32; T. 12 January 2007 28-30.

prefecture kept "a special stock of weapons" that was meant for use by the various communes, which therefore did not have their own stocks of weapons.[264]

Prosecution Witness XXY

207. Witness XXY testified that he was a classmate of Renzaho's son, Jean-François Régis, at a school not far from Renzaho's house in Kanombe. Towards the end of April 1994, an *Interahamwe* from their class told the witness that Renzaho had distributed weapons in the night of 6 to 7 April to *Interahamwe* leaders in various sectors of Kigali. Moreover, in early May, the witness saw Renzaho's son in Gitarama. Régis told him that Renzaho had come to Gitarama to distribute weapons. About two weeks later, still in Gitarama, Régis informed the witness that, three days after they had met on the first occasion, his father had come back to **[page 61]** Gitarama with weapons to be used in killing the Tutsis, angry that the residents there were doing nothing.[265]

Prosecution Witness BUO

208. Witness BUO testified that Renzaho distributed weapons to *Interahamwe* at Angeline Mukandutiye's compound immediately prior to the attack at CELA on 21 April 1994 (II.6).

Renzaho

209. Renzaho denied that he distributed weapons, including on 7 April 1994. He did not have a stock of arms at the prefecture office. Renzaho disputed Witness AFB's description of his activities on 7 April as incorrect and unrealistic. Instead, on that date, he went to a meeting of senior military officers at ESM, which began around 10.15 a.m., and was still there at 11.00 a.m. According to Renzaho, Kabiligi was not in Rwanda on 7 April and could therefore not have participated in weapons distribution.[266]

210. Renzaho did not direct members of the "commune administration" to look for arms from sources other than the prefecture office. He testified that, instead, he could have asked his police service to look for arms if he wanted them to be distributed. However, out of the 250 policemen, not more than 100 had weapons in April 1994, as the prefecture lacked sufficient resources to arm them all. Renzaho had corresponded with the Ministry of Interior, but it had not been able to provide all the weapons needed for the policemen.[267]

211. In order to obtain weapons, it would have been necessary to write to the Minister of the Interior, who would then contact the Minister of Defence. Renzaho acknowledged writing directly to the Minister of Defence in 1992, asking for a loan of arms and permission to carry the arms for a number of his *conseillers* and *bourgmestres*. He only did so, however, after consulting with the Minister of the Interior. An authorisation to carry the weapons had to be given by a specific department within the Ministry of Defence. The authorisation was given and weapons were lent to *bourgmestres* and *conseillers* for an unspecified period, who were directed to return them once the situation improved.[268]

212. Renzaho also denied Witness BUO's assertion that he distributed weapons to the *Interahamwe* on 21 April, before the attack at CELA the following day. He did not accompany Colonel Munyakaze to Mukandutiye's house on 21 April. He questioned why Munyakaze would collect him at the prefecture office that day, given his refusal to answer Renzaho's request on 22 April for assistance at CELA.[269] **[page 62]**

---

[264] T. 10 January 2007 p. 58; T. 11 January 2007 pp. 45-46, 50. Witness ALG stated that Bivamvagara was based in the Ministry of Defence, and the weapons used by the civil defence came from the Rwandan army staff headquarters. The witness also explained that communes within the Kigali-Ville prefecture did not manage their own, autonomous budgets, which were instead also administered at the prefectoral level.

[265] T. 10 January 2007 pp. 5-6, 13-15. Prosecution Exhibit 66 (personal identification sheet).

[266] T. 29 August 2007 pp. 30-32; T. 30 August 2007 pp. 3-4; T. 31 August 2007 p. 11; T. 3 September 2007 pp. 20-21.

[267] T. 27 August 2007 pp. 27, 61-62; T. 28 August 2007 pp. 19-20; T. 29 August 2007 p. 30 (quoted); T. 31 August 2007 pp. 11, 13. Renzaho responded to a question of whether he directed "commune administration" officials to collect weapons from locations other than the prefecture office. Given the Prosecution's case against against him, the Chamber interprets the request and the response as referring to Kigali-Ville prefecture government officials, including *conseillers*.

[268] T. 31 August 2007 pp. 13-15; Prosecution Exhibit 17 (letter of 4 March 1992 from Renzaho to the Minister of Defence).

[269] T. 29 August 2007 pp. 9-10; T. 30 August 2007 pp. 3-5.

Judgement and Sentence

213. He acknowledged the proliferation of weapons after 6 April. In 1991 and 1992, the Rwandan army had expanded rapidly, the recruits were not sufficiently vetted and criminals were among those who now had access to weapons. Some got involved in banditry. Additionally, these recruits failed to gain the required experience and were undisciplined. The likely sources of arms after 6 April were such soldiers who had deserted from the frontline as well as the RPF, who had been bringing in weapons probably before 1 October 1990. Evidence of heavily armed civilian and militias at roadblocks could be explained by the escalation of hostilities and the presence of soldiers who could not go back to their units and who began participating in killings, rapes and other activities.[270]

214. Renzaho was confronted with a Radio Rwanda broadcast on 10 May. In it he discussed having met with officials and that "[t]ogether they examined the issue of security for their cellule and deal with distribution and well thought out use of civil-defence materiel at their disposal". In response, Renzaho denied having distributed weapons "at the prefecture".[271]

Defence Witness PPV

215. Witness PPV, a Hutu, worked in the communal police, also called the urban police, at the prefecture of Kigali-Ville. The police, placed under the direct control of the prefect, had a total of 100 guns, which, according to the witness, was insufficient. Police officers would return their weapons to the prefecture office in the evening and retrieve them again in the morning. As some officers did not return at night, not all 100 weapons were kept at the prefecture office. Moreover, only about 40 policemen reported to the prefecture office as of 7 April 1994. Those who did not return kept their weapons.[272]

216. Although reserve units initially received weapons in order to work with the military to check infiltrations, Witness PPV did not know the provenance of the weapons at roadblocks. He denied that any distribution of arms took place. No weapons were received or given out at the prefecture office, including on 7 April, when he was present. He had no weapon or ammunition stock for distribution.[273]

Defence Witness AIA

217. Witness AIA, was a policeman in Kigali-Ville prefecture. His immediate superior was a *conseiller*, with whom he worked in April 1994 and the following months on a nearly 24-hour basis.[274] He explained that after work, the police officers would return their weapons to the prefecture office so as to make them available for the next shift. Renzaho provided each **[page 63]** sector with five armed policemen, apart from the witness's sector, which had 11 such officers. The police in the prefecture had an inadequate number of guns.[275]

218. In April 1994, Witness AIA saw his *conseiller* go into the prefecture office for three meetings. The first was on the morning of 8 April. The second meeting took place on or about 12 April and lasted about an hour or an hour and a half. Afterwards, he and the *conseiller* went directly home without obtaining any weapons. After the third meeting, around 16 April, they did not transport any weapons. The witness remained in the car park at the prefecture office during the second two meetings. On other occasions, the *conseiller* went to the prefecture, but remained outside speaking to the refugees and *Bourgmestre* Jean Bizimana of Nyarugenge commune.[276]

---

[270] T. 27 August 2007 p. 27; T. 29 August 2007 pp. 30-32.
[271] T. 3 September 2007 pp. 3-4, 5 (quoted); Prosecution Exhibit 56 (transcript of Radio Rwanda broadcast of 10 May 1994), p. 12.
[272] T. 4 June 2007 p. 78; T. 5 June 2007 pp. 2-4, 6, 26, 49-50; Defence Exhibit 56 (personal identification sheet).
[273] T. 5 June 2007 pp. 15, 26-27, 43, 46, 48-51. Witness PPV stated that the "PVK did not have any stock of weapons. All the weapons available had been distributed. No weapons were received; no weapons were given out". Had there been an organisation of a civil defence in Kigali, he would not have been informed of it, as it would have involved the military, the administration and the population, but not the police. T. 5 June 2007 pp. 29, 49-51.
[274] T. 2 July 2007 pp. 2, 8-10; T. 3 July 2007 pp. 6, 18-19; Defence Exhibit 66 (personal identification sheet). Witness AIA's ethnic origin was not specified. Witness AIA was arrested in Rwanda in November 1994, detained for a month during an investigation by Nyamirambo brigade, and released. T. 2 July 2007 p. 46.
[275] T. 2 July 2007 pp. 4, 6-10, 35-36, 42-43, 46, 52-54; T. 3 July 2007 pp. 2-7, 16-19.
[276] T. 2 July 2007 pp. 21-22, 31-32, 35, 41, 54; T. 3 July 2007 pp. 7, 10, 17-18.

219. Around 12 or 13 April, Rebero Hill had just been captured by the *Inkotanyi*, and fleeing soldiers requested weapons from the *conseiller* to defend themselves. He took the soldiers to Camp Kigali, where one of the commanders gave five guns to the *conseiller* and one to a reservist. The witness was also present when the *conseiller* gave one gun to each cellule and kept the last – a Kalashnikov – in his own house. It was unknown to the witness whether Renzaho was informed of the *conseiller*'s distribution of these weapons, and he was not aware whether the *conseiller* received any weapons from the prefecture. Political parties such as MRND and CDR parties did, however, distribute weapons to the population.[277]

Defence Witness PAT

220. Witness PAT, a Hutu officer in the Rwandan army, had access to information about weapons stocks and their distribution among the units. As of 6 April 1994, the Rwandan army had insufficient ammunition. Moreover, the army headquarters never had any reserves, weapons or ammunition anywhere other than the army's logistics base. Neither the headquarters nor the logistics base was to be found within the premises of the Ministry of Defence. The army did not have the resources to disarm those at roadblocks who possessed weapons, because it was fighting the RPF.[278]

221. The distribution of weapons to civilians from the Ministry of Defence on 7 April was unknown to Witness PAT and would have been in his view absurd. The Ministry could not have acquired such weapons, since it took some time to get weapons from the logistics base to the Ministry, and because the army had no weapons stocked there in any case. The Rwandan army logistics base would have required a signed document before a potential client, including the Ministry, was supplied with weapons.[279]

222. Witness PAT had never visited the premises of the Ministry of Defence, but given his position he would have known, nonetheless, about any weapons distributed there. The normal channels for that process meant that he would have received a message in the event of such a **[page 64]** distribution, but he never did. There was no weapons stock to be given to a third party other than the army at a time when the army clearly lacked such weapons.[280]

223. The administrative process required that weapons held by camps or units were transferred to the army logistics base through a transfer slip. Until early May 1994, Witness PAT was not working in the field. Therefore, if arms came from a military camp to the Ministry of Defence, he would not have been informed of it. Similarly, he would not necessarily have known if weapons had been distributed from Camp Kigali to the sectors. He noted that Camp Kigali had a reconnaissance battalion and that there was no reason that it should distribute weapons to the sectors when it needed such arms itself.[281]

Defence Witness PGL

224. Witness PGL, worked at the Kigali-Ville prefecture office and reported there from 11 April to 3 July. He did not see or hear of weapons being distributed from the prefecture office during the war.[282]

3.3 Deliberations

225. Paragraph 12 of the Indictment alleges that Renzaho was involved in distributing weapons to the *Interahamwe* and the *Impuzamugambi* between mid-1993 to 17 July 1994. According to paragraphs 16 and 33, he ordered such distribution during a meeting at the Kigali-Ville prefecture office on or about 16 April 1994. The Chamber will consider first Renzaho's own physical involvement, if any, in weapons distributions and then his alleged orders that they should take place.

---

[277] T. 2 July 2007 pp. 31-34, 52-53.
[278] T. 22 August 2007 pp. 45-46, 61-62, 66-69; T. 23 August 2007 pp. 14-15; Defence Exhibit 77 (personal identification sheet); Defence Exhibit 78 (written declaration of 22 August 2007 by Witness PAT to supplement his testimony).
[279] T. 22 August 2007 p. 62; T. 23 August 2007 p. 14.
[280] *Id.* pp. 62-64; T. 23 August 2007 pp. 4-5.
[281] T. 23 August 2007 pp. 4-5, 14-15.
[282] T. 6 June 2007 pp. 15, 18, 28, 40.

3.3.1 Distribution of Weapons

226. The Prosecution's primary evidence of Renzaho's direct involvement in the acquisition and distribution of weapons comes from the testimony of Witness AFB. He offered eyewitness testimony concerning two distinct events. On 7 April 1994, Renzaho allegedly brought weapons and ammunition from the *Hôtel des Diplomates* to the Kigali-Ville prefecture office. Ten of those weapons were given to *Conseiller* Rose Karushara, who on the same day distributed them to *Interahamwe* manning a roadblock near her house. The witness believed that *bourgmestres* and *conseillers* at the prefecture office also received weapons that day.

227. On the second occasion, 12 April, Renzaho purportedly brought weapons from the *Hôtel des Diplomates* to Protais Zigiranyirazo's house, where they were unloaded at a roadblock nearby. While Renzaho remained at that residence, the witness distributed weapons at additional roadblocks in Nyakabanda, Nyamirambo and Biryogo sectors. Renzaho was allegedly aware of this.

228. Witness AFB was the only witness to testify about these two events. His account was precise and largely consistent. The Chamber has noted that in Gacaca proceedings he has admitted establishing a roadblock in 1994.[283] There is no evidence that he has been accused **[page 65]** of any wrongdoing in connection with that roadblock,[284] and the Chamber does not consider that this affects his credibility.

229. The witness testified that on the morning of 7 April, he brought Rose Karushara from her house to the prefecture office, before going with Renzaho to retrieve weapons from the *Hôtel des Diplomats*. The Defence put to him that in the *Zigiranyirazo* trial, he said that he went to Karushara's residence in the afternoon after weapons had been collected from the *Hôtel des Diplomates*.[285] He initially explained that his testimony in the *Zigiranyirazo* case may have been transcribed incorrectly, later concluding that counsel had misread it to him. He also suggested that the significant lapse in time might have caused the mistake.[286] While these explanations are not entirely convincing, the Chamber observes that the witness's testimony in the present case is in conformity with his statement to Tribunal investigators in December 2003.[287] His testimony in the *Zigiranyirazo* trial about the sequence of the events was not always clear, and the Chamber attaches little weight to these differences.

230. The Chamber has also considered the witness's evidence about Gratien Kabiligi. He testified that a policeman pointed Kabiligi out to him at the *Hôtel des Diplomates* on 7 April. This is not in conformity with his first statement to Tribunal investigators in December 2003, where Kabiligi was identified to him on 12 April.[288] According to his second statement of November 2004, which focussed more on Kabiligi, the witness observed him for the first time on 10 April 1994, and Kabiligi was then pointed out a couple of days later.[289] In court, the witness explained that the investigators had made a mistake with respect to his November 2004 statement.[290] The Chamber accepts that the reference to 10 April may be incorrect, as both the testimony and the first statement only mention visits to the *Hôtel des Diplomates* on 7 and 12 April.

231. The discrepancy between the testimony and the two previous statements about when the witness first observed Kabiligi and described him as involved may be explained by the lapse of time between the events in 1994 and the testimony, or the fact that the witness was confused. Nonetheless, the Defence has pointed

---

[283] Witness AFB's involvement in the establishment of a roadblock follows both from his testimony in the *Zigiranyirazo* trial and the present case. See T. 9 January 2007 pp. 36-37 (the witness refusing to answer a question about whether he had killed anyone), and Defence Exhibit 1 (*Prosecutor v. Zigiranyirazo*, T. 26 January 2006 pp. 36-40; T. 30 January 2006 pp. 35-36).
[284] See T. 9 January 2007 p. 42.
[285] Defence Exhibit 1 (*Prosecutor v. Zigiranyirazo*, T. 26 January 2006 pp. 9-13; T. 30 January 2006 pp. 8, 36).
[286] T. 9 January 2008 pp. 28-30, 32, 34-35.
[287] Defence Exhibit 2 (statement of 22 December 2003).
[288] Id. p. 6: "On 12 April 2004, I drove to the *préfecture* with my van around 7 a.m. Around 8 a.m., I saw Colonel Gratien Kabiligi arrive at the *préfecture* in a Mercedes Benz military jeep. He was accompanied by military escorts in the same car. I never knew Kabiligi before, but the policemen who were with me told me that he was Colonel Gratien Kabiligi."
[289] Defence Exhibit 3 (statement of 30 November 2004) p. 3: "I first saw [Kabiligi] at the *Hôtel des Diplomates* on 10 April 1994, but I did not know him then ... When we arrived there, we found several Rwandan Army officers and men in the hotel compound. One of the policemen who was with me went to see an officer who was introduced to me two days thereafter as Colonel Gratien Kabiligi."
[290] T. 9 January 2007 pp. 37-39.

out inconsistencies in the Prosecution's position regarding Kabiligi's presence in Rwanda on 7 April, giving rise to concerns about Witness AFB's evidence.[291] **[page 66]**

232. Witness AFB's testimony regarding the timing of the weapons distribution also raises questions. He testified that Renzaho left the prefecture office for Radio Rwanda after 9.00 a.m. and arrived at the Rwandan Radio premises at about 9.30 or 10.00 a.m.[292] However, he also testified that he loaded the guns into the vehicle around 10.00 a.m. and returned to the prefecture office shortly after 10.00 a.m. According to the statement of December 2003, however, the witness saw Renzaho come out of his office towards 10.00 a.m. before driving to Radio Rwanda. It also follows from that statement that Rose Karushara and other *conseillers* stayed in Renzaho's office for about an hour before Renzaho left for the *Hôtel des Diplomates*, where the weapons were loaded into the witness's car. This gives rise to further discrepancies about the timing of this event.[293]

233. The Chamber is aware that recalling the precise timing of events can be difficult. Witness AFB provided estimates.[294] However, the sequence of events is important because Renzaho claimed to be at a meeting of senior military officers at the military academy (ESM) from 10.15 a.m. until 11.00 a.m. Although the Defence did not call witnesses to corroborate this, the Chamber cannot exclude that Renzaho would attend this important meeting in view of the dramatic situation, his position as the prefect of Kigali, and his military rank.[295]

234. The witness's testimony that Amri Karekezi was at the prefecture office on the morning of 7 April is inconsistent with both Prosecution and Defence evidence.[296] Furthermore, his suggestion that *conseillers*, other than Karushara, and *bourgmestres* who were present at the prefecture office that day also obtained weapons and ammunition is unsupported by other Prosecution witnesses. The absence of any corroboration by other witnesses, who, even if not present, likely would have known about weapons being brought to and distributed from the prefecture office that day, raises some doubt. Finally, there is also a lack of clarity concerning other minor aspects of the witness's testimony.[297] While the individual impact of each of these inconsistencies is small, their cumulative effect leaves the Chamber with a reasonable doubt about the witness's evidence regarding Renzaho's involvement in obtaining and distributing weapons on 7 April. The Chamber will therefore not rely on Witness AFB's testimony regarding this alleged distribution without corroboration.**[page 67]**

235. Turning to the weapons distribution on 12 April, Witness AFB's testimony is not corroborated. None of the Prosecution witnesses who were frequenting the Kigali-Ville prefecture office around this time, and who testified that they were directed by Renzaho to go to the Ministry of Defence, supported Witness AFB's testimony regarding the loading, storing and unloading of weapons at the prefecture office during this period. It is true that Witness ALG stated that Kabiligi brought weapons to the prefecture office, which were placed in the urban police stocks and distributed to *Interahamwe* called to the prefecture office. However, his

---

[291] Decision on Defence Motion to Admit Documents (TC), 12 February 2008, paras. 3, 5 citing *Bagosora et al.*, T. 28 May 2007 p. 12 ("Mr. Jallow: ...on the same day, 7 April, the other Accused, Kabiligi, was not in Rwanda. He was outside of Rwanda and while the three other Accused were in Rwanda giving orders and instructions for killings to be carried out, Kabiligi was intent on returning back to Rwanda.").

[292] Witness AFB first said that Renzaho entered the Radio Rwanda compound at about 9.30 a.m. (T. 8 January 2007 p. 78), then, during cross-examination said it was about 10.00 a.m. (T. 9 January 2007 p. 24).

[293] Defence Exhibit 2B (statement of 22 December 2003), pp. 3-4.

[294] T. 8 January 2007 p. 83 ("It is just an approximation when I look at the time it took for us to make the trips from the various points, I think it was around ten o'clock, because I remember I had left my home around seven o'clock, that is early in the morning"). The Chamber also notes that one year before he testified, he similarly stated in the *Zigiranyirazo* trial that Renzaho off-loaded weapons from the *Hôtel des Diplomates* around 10.00 a.m. See Defence Exhibit 1 (*Prosecutor v. Zigiranyirazo*, T. 26 January 2006 p. 7).

[295] The Chamber is mindful of evidence that ESM was only a short distance from the Kigali-Ville prefecture office. Witness RGI, T. 4 July 2007 p. 23.

[296] See Witness UB, T. 23 January 2007 pp. 4-5, 55-62; T. 24 January 2007 pp. 4, 6-7; Witness AIA, T. 2 July 2007 pp. 7, 9-21; T. 3 July 2007 pp. 4-5, 14-18.

[297] While Witness AFB testified that the same four policemen accompanied him on all his trips, he said in the *Zigiranyirazo* case that two police officers were in his vehicle and repeated that answer unambiguously several times (*Prosecutor v. Zigiranyirazo*, T. 26 January 2006 p. 7; T. 30 January 2006 pp. 8-9). When this inconsistency was put to him in the present case, he answered that he had clarified that there were four policemen at the end of his testimony in the *Zigiranyirazo* trial. T. 9 January 2007 pp. 17-23. However, there is no such statement in the transcripts of that case.

evidence suggests that this occurred in May and, in the Chamber's view, is temporally too remote to corroborate Witness AFB's evidence. The Chamber views Witness ALG's testimony with caution where it is uncorroborated and finds that this evidence is insufficiently reliable to stand on its own. Moreover, Witness PGL, who worked at the prefecture office, generally denied that weapons were distributed from there, although this evidence was general and of limited probative value.

236. Witness XXY's evidence that Renzaho distributed weapons on the night of 6-7 April in various sectors in Kigali and again in late April or early May in Gitarama, does not corroborate Witness AFB's testimony. It is hearsay, obtained from Renzaho's son Régis, and appears unrelated to Witness AFB's evidence. Witness UB's account that he heard Renzaho had delivered weapons to the Chairman of the PDI party who distributed them to members of the population is also uncorroborated hearsay.

237. Witness BUO testified that Renzaho provided weapons to *Interahamwe* on 21 April from Angeline Mukandutiye's house (II.6). Witness ALG heard from *Interahamwe* at Mukandutiye's compound that Renzaho had distributed weapons to them, but he testified that they were distributed from Renzaho's "place" as opposed to Mukandutiye's.[298] Witness ALG's evidence is hearsay, imprecise and too different to corroborate Witness BUO's evidence. In light of the Chamber's concerns about Witness ALG's testimony generally (II.2, 9 and 11), it does not consider his evidence on this point reliable.

238. The Chamber also considers a memo prepared by UNAMIR officer Lieutenant-Colonel Frank Claeys concerning a discussion with an informant on 20 January 1994. The report reflects that the informant told Claeys that he had been taken in "a blue Peugeot" of Rwandan army Colonel and Kigali-Ville prefect, Renzaho. The vehicle had been loaded with weapons and the informant was asked to identify persons to whom the weapons should be given.[299] The Prosecution submits that the memo corroborates the direct evidence of Renzaho's participation in the distribution of weapons.[300] This evidence is hearsay and lacking in detail. The evidence of Renzaho's involvement in the transportation of these weapons is only circumstantial and is temporally remote from the allegations presented by **[page 68]** Prosecution witnesses in this trial.[301] In the Chamber's view, it fails to establish that Renzaho was physically involved in this weapons distribution or corroborate other Prosecution evidence of Renzaho's involvement in others.

239. The Chamber concludes that the Prosecution has not proven beyond reasonable doubt that Renzaho distributed weapons on 7 April 1994 to *Interahamwe* manning a roadblock near Karushara's house, and further that, on 12 April, he participated in the distribution of weapons from *Hôtel des Diplomates* and the prefecture office at a roadblock near Zigiranyirazo's house and at other roadblocks in several sectors of Kigali-Ville. Likewise, the evidence of Witnesses ALG, XXY, BUO and UB highlighted in the deliberations above is insufficiently reliable to establish Renzaho's direct involvement in weapons distributions. Notwithstanding, the Chamber finds Witness AFB's observations about who was manning roadblocks and the state of affairs at them largely credible and convincing (II.2). The Prosecution has failed to establish that Renzaho was directly involved in the distribution of weapons distributions to *Interahamwe* and *Impuzamugambi* from mid-1993 to 17 July 1994. Consequently, the Chamber does not find it necessary to revisit whether adequate notice was provided of this allegation.

3.3.2 Orders to Collect Weapons and Distribute Them

240. The Prosecution points to the first-hand evidence of Witnesses UB, AWE and GLJ to support its allegation that around 16 April 1994, Renzaho ordered *conseillers* to collect weapons from the Ministry of Defence and to have them distributed in their sectors to kill Tutsis. Witness ALG also provided second-hand

---

[298] T. 11 January 2007 p. 39 ("But from what one could observe, the *Interahamwe* were at Mukandutiye's compound and who were being trained there, told me that Renzaho used to go there to give them instructions and distribute weapons to them. They also said they enjoyed his backing. *So those who needed weapons would go and pick them up at her place. At his place -- correction.*") (emphasis added).
[299] Prosecution Exhibit 21 (memorandum of UNAMIR officer Lieutenant-Colonel Frank Claeys re: discussion with informant on 20 January 1994), which reads: "With a blue Peugeot of a Col of RGF: Terehaho, prefect of KIGALI. He was taken with that car, the weapons were already on board, and he had to design the persons the weapons had to be handed over". (p.1)
[300] T. 8 January 2007 p. 42.
[301] While the 20 January 1994 memorandum states that "distribution of weapons ... started again on an individual basis with ammunition" (p. 1), it is not clear that a distribution took place on the occasion that Renzaho's vehicle was used.

information regarding this incident. As discussed in detail elsewhere, the Chamber views the evidence of each of these witnesses with caution. They have been either convicted of or charged with, crimes in Rwanda that are at issue in this trial. Witnesses UB and AWE were detained in the same prison in Rwanda before arriving in Arusha to testify (II.2). At the same time, the Chamber notes that Witnesses GLJ and AWE had already confessed to their participation in weapons distribution based on the very same facts, reducing any interest they may have in shifting blame to Renzaho.[302] Moreover, although Witness UB was awaiting a determination by the Rwandan Supreme Court regarding his conviction, his judicial record reflects that he did not challenge that he had distributed weapons based on Renzaho's instructions.[303]

241. Certain inconsistencies emerge between the first-hand accounts of Witnesses UB, AWE and GLJ. For example, Witness AWE's evidence suggests that the instructions to collect weapons were given during a meeting on 11 April, while Witness GLJ stated that this occurred on 16 April. Witness UB's testimony on when the meeting occurred vacillated **[page 69]** between about two days after 10 or 11 April and 16 April.[304] Witness ALG states the instructions were given on 11 April. The Chamber finds that these differences are reasonably explained by the passage of time. Indeed, while the precise date that Renzaho gave these instructions is unclear, Witnesses UB and AWE are consistent that the instructions were given during their second meeting with Renzaho at the prefecture office. This detail is corroborated by the second-hand testimony of Witness ALG. Even Witness GLJ suggests that these instructions were given based on a decision taken during a prior meeting that he did not attend.

242. The Chamber considers the discrepancies regarding what was said at the meeting to be minor. Witness GLJ stated that the instructions regarding weapons were made in conjunction with a call for the attendants to erect roadblocks. Witnesses UB and AWE indicated that Renzaho ordered the erection of roadblocks during a previous meeting (II.2). However, their testimonies are not incompatible with Renzaho repeating the instructions concerning roadblocks when directing individuals to obtain and distribute weapons. In this regard, other evidence suggests that Renzaho repeated instructions regarding roadblocks during several meetings.[305]

243. There are some differences in witnesses' accounts about the participants at the meeting where Renzaho allegedly ordered attendants to retrieve weapons. In the Chamber's view, they are insignificant and may be explained by the number of meetings the witnesses attended as well as the passing of time since the events. The common elements in their testimony bolster their evidence. The witnesses provided largely consistent descriptions of the number of weapons allotted to each of them and explained that it was not necessary to produce documentation to receive the weapons.

244. An almost contemporaneous report written on 30 March 1994 by the chief of staff of the Rwandan army is of interest in this context. It was addressed to the Minister of Defence and the members of the government and concerns a meeting on 29 March 1994 about the civil defence programme. Renzaho attended the meeting. The report states that the Ministry of Defence and the Ministry of the Interior "will be contacted so as to make weapons available for distribution to selected civilian personnel". Renzaho agreed that he had been seconded to MININTER, but denied that this programme was implemented.[306] The Chamber considers that the report offers strong circumstantial corroboration of the consistent Prosecution evidence that local officials would be sent to the Ministry of Defence to obtain weapons to be distributed and, when the totality of this evidence is considered, Renzaho's explanation is not reasonable.

---

[302] Witness GLJ, T. 22 January 2007 pp. 13, 20; Witness AWE, T. 31 January 2007 pp. 11-12.
[303] Defence Exhibit 11B (Rwandan appeal judgement of Witness UB) p. 10 ("*Considérant que le condamné n'a reconnu qu'un seul chef d'infraction: la distribution d'arme sur instruction du Préfet*"). See also Defence Exhibit 11A (Rwandan trial judgment of Witness UB) p. 28 ("*Attendu que pour mettre en action le génocide et les massacres, il a distribué les fusils, dans tout son secteur aux miliciens Interahamwe tels Karimu, Mugesera et Kenedy, ces armes (fusils) ont été utilisés pour tuer les gens sur les barrières et pour piller; lui-même ne le nie pas parce qu'il dit que il y a des fusils qu'il a retire du P.V.K. et les a donné aux responsables*").
[304] Compare T. 23 January 2007 p. 12 (placing the meeting "approximately two days" after the first meeting on 10 or 11 April) and T. 24 January 2007 pp. 15-16 (the witness puts the meeting on 16 April, the same day he went to the Ministry of Defence).
[305] See, for instance, Witness ALG, T. 11 January 2007 pp. 41, 67.
[306] T. 31 August 2007 pp. 9-11; Prosecution Exhibit 24 (letter of 30 March 1994 from Déogratias Nsabimana to the Minister of Defence) para. 7.

245. The Defence sought to refute the allegation that weapons were distributed by the Ministry of Defence. Witness AIA, who accompanied his *conseiller* to meetings at the prefecture office on about 12 and again on 16 April and remained with him until July, testified that he did not see him collect weapons after leaving the prefecture. He was confronted with a *pro justitia* statement given to Rwandan authorities in November 1996 where, when asked if weapons were given to his *conseiller*, he responded that the *conseiller* **[page 70]** received six firearms from the prefecture authorities that he distributed to his close associates.[307] The witness explained the discrepancy by suggesting that the statement was made while being detained and tortured, and that investigators had compelled him to give this answer. He specified that the six guns were received from Camp Kigali.[308] The Chamber is not convinced by this. The statement contains questions and answers directly transcribed and is otherwise in conformity with his testimony that the *conseiller* had also received weapons from Camp Kigali. The nature of the inconsistencies, and Witness AIA's explanations for them, throw substantial doubt on the reliability of this part of his testimony. It does not refute the Prosecution evidence on this point.

246. Witness PAT denied that weapons were distributed from the Ministry of Defence. However, he was not posted at the Ministry of Defence and would not have necessarily been informed if arms came from a military camp to the Ministry of Defence or to the sectors.[309] Furthermore, his description of the formal procedure for obtaining weapons may have been adhered to under normal circumstances, but the Chamber doubts that it would have been followed rigidly in April 1994. Moreover, the witness's denial that weapons were distributed from the Ministry of Defence could be viewed as self-interested.

247. The Chamber is mindful of the Prosecution and Defence evidence that weapons had been brought into Kigali-Ville from sources other than Renzaho.[310] It also considers the testimonies of Defence Witnesses PPV and PAT that the urban police and army had insufficient weapons and ammunition. However, this general contention is not sufficient to call into question the credible Prosecution testimonies that Renzaho arranged for weapons to be distributed to local officials. Given his former position, Witness PPV also has an interest in denying that distributions of weapons were made from the weapons stocks within the urban police or channelled through the Kigali-Ville prefecture office. This raises questions about the reliability of his denial.[311] Consequently, the Chamber finds that during a meeting at the prefecture office around 16 April 1994, Renzaho instructed local administration officials, including *conseillers*, to collect weapons from the Ministry of Defence for distribution.

248. According to Witness UB, Renzaho's instructions to obtain weapons appeared to be a direct reaction to the fears expressed by *conseillers* about their own personal security in light of the heavily armed civilian population and killings taking place in their localities. Witness GLJ suggested that the weapons were to be collected and distributed to the members of the population who knew how to handle them to ensure their security. Likewise, Witness AWE testified that Renzaho indicated that the weapons should be given to former soldiers and members of the population trained in handling them, and warned that none should be given to Tutsis. Witness ALG heard that weapons were intended to be distributed at various **[page 71]** roadblocks and to the *conseillers*. The evidence of Witnesses GLJ, AWE and ALG that weapons were intended to be distributed is supported by the 30 March report mentioned above. The report states that the Ministry of Defence and Ministry of the Interior would be contacted to make weapons available to "selected civilian personnel" as a facet within a larger scheme to organise a civilian force to fight the perceived enemy.[312]

---

[307] Prosecution Exhibit 109 (statement of 14 November 1996).
[308] T. 2 July 2007 p. 54.
[309] T. 22 August 2007 pp. 45, 62 (his office was not within the Ministry of Defence); T. 23 August 2007 p. 14 ("Q. If weapons had been provided to the ministry of defence, the préfectoral office, or anywhere else, that were from military camps throughout Kigali, you would not know about that would you, because you weren't, for that first month or so out in the field? A. No, for the first month I was at my first post, which was rather at the office. But from [sic] if arms came from a military camp to the ministry of defence, it's sure that I wouldn't have been informed.").
[310] See, for instance, Witness AWE, T. 31 January 2007 pp. 18, 41; Witness UB, T. 23 January 2007 p. 14.
[311] It was also put to Witness PPV that he was wanted in Rwanda as a Category 1 genocide suspect. He denied this. T. 5 June 2007 pp. 53-55.
[312] Prosecution Exhibit 24 (letter of 30 March 1994 from Déogratias Nsabimana to the Minister of Defence) para. 7.

249. In the circumstances, the only reasonable conclusion is that these weapons were intended to be a part of the war waged against a broad enemy, which included Tutsi civilians. The Chamber has taken into account Witness UB's evidence implying that Renzaho may have intended the weapons to provide additional security to the local officials and their subordinates. That Renzaho would seek firearms based on the individual safety concerns of local officials is corroborated by his March 1992 letter to the Ministry of Defence addressing this issue directly.[313] Nonetheless, the numbers of arms provided, between 5 and 10 to each official, confirms that their intended destination was beyond the individual hands of those who collected them. Moreover, the evidence also demonstrates that the local officials were already being protected by members of the urban police force, who would have themselves been armed.[314]

250. That Renzaho ordered the collection and distribution of weapons among the population is corroborated by the transcript of a Radio Rwanda broadcast of 10 May 1994, where the speaker identified as Renzaho made reference to administrative officials at the sector and *cellule* levels who "deal with the distribution and well thought-out use of civil defence materiel at their disposal". This comment was made in response to an interviewer who told listeners that it was "noticed that those entrusted with materiel, like firearms, are behaving irresponsibly at roadblocks".[315] Renzaho denied that weapons were distributed "at the prefecture" and explained that the transcriptions could be erroneous, also suggesting that the words were not necessarily his own.[316] The Chamber finds that his denial fails to address the Prosecution evidence, and that his explanation is unconvincing given prior explicit and implicit acknowledgement that other statements from the same broadcast were his own.[317] The Chamber accepts, as Renzaho testified, that firearms within the population, including at roadblocks, may have come from other sources other than the prefecture, such as deserting **[page 72]** soldiers and gendarmes.[318] However, such an explanation does not raise doubt in respect of the Prosecution evidence, supported by his contemporaneous statements, which suggests that local officials, with Renzaho's involvement, participated in the distribution of firearms among the population.

251. Based on the foregoing, the Chamber finds that Renzaho's instructions during the meeting on or about 16 April to officials, including *conseillers*, to obtain and distribute firearms were coupled with an additional order that they be provided to select members of the population. Following his orders, several local officials, including *conseillers*, collected weapons and distributed them to people within their communities.

252. The Chamber now turns to Renzaho's intent when he ordered the distribution of weapons. Prosecution witnesses did not testify that Renzaho explicitly ordered that the weapons be used to kill Tutsis civilians during the same meeting. However, he was aware that Tutsi civilians were being singled out and killed throughout Kigali-Ville prefecture when he gave these orders. This follows, in part, from his involvement in organising the removal of corpses from the streets of Kigali as early as 11 April.[319] During his testimony, he admitted that from 10 April, he was aware that people were being killed at roadblocks in Kigali-Ville prefecture based on their ethnicity and political leanings.[320] During previous meetings around 10 April, attended by many of the same persons, Renzaho had told those in charge of obtaining and distributing the weapons that the enemy was the *Inkotanyi* and *Inyenzi*, which, in the Chamber's view, was interpreted to

---

[313] Prosecution Exhibit 17 (letter of 4 March 1992 from Renzaho to the Ministry of Defence), requesting firearms. Witness GLJ testified that "armed bandits" had raised concerns about safety during this period and that his house had been attacked by bandits. Renzaho had accepted the witness's request to ask that the Ministry of Defence to provide him with a firearm. T. 22 January 2007 pp. 32-33.
[314] See, for instance, Witness PPV, T. 5 June 2007 pp. 2, 4-6. Witness AFB T. 8 January 2007 pp. 71, 73 (two communal police had been sent to pick him up on the morning of 7 April based on the orders of a *conseiller*); Witness ALG, T. 11 January 2007 p. 29 (he heard that Renzaho assigned five communal police to *conseillers* during a 9 April 1994 meeting); Witness GLJ, T. 22 January 2007 pp. 52-53 (policemen were to protect *conseillers* based on the instruction of the prefect); Witness UB, T. 23 January 2007 p. 6 (two police officers were sent by Renzaho to a *conseiller* for protection); Witness AWE, T. 31 January 2007 pp. 18, 38-39, 43 (the police had weapons and two were assigned to a *conseiller* for protection); Witness AIA, T. 2 July 2007 p. 11 (two police officers were assigned to a *conseiller* on the morning of 7 April); Renzaho, T. 27 August 2007 pp. 62, 63 (instructions were given to the urban police commander to send police to *conseillers* to "help them in their work of intervening within the population").
[315] Prosecution Exhibit 56 (transcript of Radio Rwanda broadcast of 10 May 1994), p. 12.
[316] T. 3 September 2007 pp. 4-7.
[317] See T. 28 August 2007 pp. 57-58; T. 3 September 2007 pp. 3-4.
[318] T. 3 September 2007 pp. 4-7.
[319] T. 28 August 2007 pp. 45-47; T. 29 August 2007 p. 59 (discussing the meeting with the ICRC on 11 April 1994 at the Kigali-Ville prefecture which focussed on the removal of dead bodies). See also II.4.3.
[320] T. 28 August 2007 p. 11; T. 30 August 2007 p. 54.

Judgement and Sentence

include Tutsis generally (II.2). The Chamber is convinced that the only reasonable conclusion is that Renzaho gave these orders with the knowledge that the weapons would further the killing campaign and that he intended this.

253. The final question is whether the weapons were actually used in crimes. There is an abundance of evidence suggesting that *Interahamwe* in Kigali-Ville were heavily armed and engaged in the killing of Tutsi civilians, particularly at roadblocks. Nonetheless, the evidence is scant with respect to how these weapons were used. Witness AWE testified that those to whom he gave weapons received brief training and ultimately engaged in the killing of Tutsis. Witness UB's conviction was based in part on killings at roadblocks that also involved his distribution of weapons there.[321] Witness GLJ also confessed that he provided weapons to those manning roadblocks and admitted that people were killed at the roadblocks he had erected. The testimony is not precise enough to determine if the weapons were distributed at the roadblocks the witness had erected.[322] In the Chamber's view, this evidence must be considered in light of the prevailing situation, where civilians, supported by local authorities, engaged in widespread killings throughout Kigali-Ville of Tutsis, those perceived to be Tutsis and those identified as the opposition. This distribution formed a distinct part of a plan to mobilise and arm the civilians within their respective communities who would be tasked with fighting a broadly defined enemy, which included these civilians. While the distributions reflected in the testimonies above may not have been the primary sources of weapons that made their way into the hands of those engaged in killings in Kigali-Ville prefecture, the Chamber has no doubt that the act of distributing the weapons demonstrated **[page 73]** the government's unequivocal support for the killings of Tutsi civilians, and substantially contributed to the slaughter. **[page 74]**

4. FACILITATION OF MOVEMENT

4.1 *Laissez-Passers* (Travel Authorisations)

4.1.1 Introduction

254. The Prosecution alleges that, between 6 April and 17 July 1994, Renzaho, or those acting on his behalf, provided permits and *laissez-passers* to enable the movement and equipping of *Interahamwe*, militia, soldiers and gendarmes participating in the killing of Tutsis. It refers to Witnesses ALG, GLJ, UB, UL and AFB.[323]

255. The Defence submits that insufficient notice was provided in relation to this allegation. It concedes that Renzaho issued *laissez-passers* but argues that they were issued to all who applied for them, without distinction. Reference is made to Defence Witnesses UT, PPO, BOU, HIN, PPV, PPG, PGL, BDC, AIA and Jean-Baptiste Butera as well as Prosecution Witness ACS.[324]

4.1.2 Evidence

Prosecution Witness ALG

256. Witness ALG, a Hutu, was an administrative official within Kigali-Ville prefecture. Around 12 April 1994, he visited the prefect's office. Renzaho asked him to ensure that the communal office assist with the issuing of *laissez-passers* to all those who wanted to seek refuge outside the Kigali-Ville prefecture. The

---

[321] Defence Exhibit 11A (Rwandan trial judgment of Witness UB), p. 28.
[322] T. 22 January 2007 pp. 19, 23, 58-59.
[323] Indictment paras. 2(E), 13, 30; Prosecution Closing Brief paras. 142-144, 152-155, 158; T. 14 February 2008 pp. 18-19.
[324] Defence Closing Brief paras. 36-37, 52, 74, 86-99, 112, 116-126, 800-868; Defence Exhibit 113 (*complément écrit aux arguments oraux de la défense*) paras. 859, 864.1-864.64. The Chamber has also taken into account the evidence of Defence Witness WOW, see below.

reason was that this service was no longer available at the prefectoral office due to insufficient staffing there. The witness went to the commune office and immediately began issuing the passes.[325]

257. The witness would obtain the *laissez-passer* forms from the prefecture office and collect more whenever necessary. The prefect gave no special instructions with regard to their issuance, except that the money collected as fees for the documents was passed on to the prefecture office. Assisted by a staff member from that office, he issued more than 100 *laissez-passers* a day and signed the forms on behalf of the prefect. The witness and his staff were overwhelmed by the number of people requesting *laissez-passers*. It was still possible for some people to travel without one.[326]

258. Around 18 April, the communal office closed, and the witness began issuing *laissez-passers* from the prefecture office. There were two types of such documents. One was issued to individuals so that they could move about, and the other affixed to vehicle windshields to **[page 75]** allow movement of vehicles. Both *laissez-passers* were signed by the prefect of Kigali-Ville or by authorised representatives in his absence.[327]

259. According to the witness, the *laissez-passer* was regarded as a travel document which authorised people to circulate. It did not, however, guarantee free movement. Those manning roadblocks would sometimes also require an identity card. If the card showed that the bearer was Tutsi, the person could still be killed despite also having a *laissez-passer*.[328]

Prosecution Witness GLJ

260. Witness GLJ was a Hutu local official in Kigali-Ville. He explained that in order to travel within or out of Kigali, either on foot or in a vehicle, it was necessary to obtain an authorisation from the prefect. However, in April 1994, it was difficult for Tutsis to get to the prefecture office to obtain travel documents. As they were considered to be accomplices of the enemy, they could neither get through the roadblocks nor move about without being killed.[329]

Prosecution Witness UB

261. Witness UB, a Hutu local official in Kigali-Ville prefecture, testified that, in his sector, an identity card was required to pass through roadblocks. Around 12 or 13 April 1994, he attended a meeting chaired by Renzaho at the prefecture office. When *conseillers* expressed their concern in the meeting about people who no longer had their identity cards, they were told that new cards could not be issued to replace those missing. Instead, they would be allowed to issue certificates that listed the bearer's ethnicity and specified that his or her identity card had been lost. The certificates were signed and stamped at the Kigali-Ville prefecture office, because the commune authorities had relocated their operations there. As the highest authority in the prefecture, the prefect also had the power to issue *laissez-passers* for vehicles or individuals. Because Tutsis were accused of collaborating with *Inkotanyi*, they were maltreated at roadblocks. It was therefore not easy for them to get to the sector office to obtain such documents. Hutus, by contrast, could move about freely.[330]

Prosecution Witness UL

262. Witness UL, a Hutu, was an employee at a ministry in Kigali-Ville prefecture. When he returned to work on 11 April 1994, he drove to Gikondo to get fuel and continued driving about over three days. At that time, Renzaho issued *laissez-passers* that he had signed to drivers, including the witness. During that period, the witness had no difficulty moving around Kigali. If a person possessed a document bearing Renzaho's signature, he or she could go through any roadblock in Kigali and even roadblocks outside of Kigali. As of

---

[325] T. 10 January 2007 p. 56; T. 11 January 2007 pp. 19, 22-24; Prosecution Exhibit 67 (personal identification sheet). Witness ALG was imprisoned in Rwanda from 1998 to 2005, then provisionally released, pending his trial, which had yet to take place at the time of his testimony. He was charged with genocide. T. 10 January 2007 p. 64.
[326] T. 11 January 2007 pp. 32-33, 52; T. 12 January 2007 pp. 32-33.
[327] T. 11 January 2007 pp. 23, 51.
[328] *Id.* pp. 51-52.
[329] T. 22 January 2007 pp. 13, 15, 30-31, 37-38; Prosecution Exhibit 68 (personal identification sheet).
[330] T. 23 January 2007 pp. 1, 8-9, 12, 15; T. 24 January 2007 pp. 16-17; Prosecution Exhibit 69 (personal identification sheet).

Judgement and Sentence

11 April, however, any Tutsi who was intercepted at a roadblock was killed, while those who showed **[page 76]** identity cards with a "Hutu" entry were allowed through. Even vehicles with *laissez-passers* had to stop at roadblocks, so that the signatures could be checked.[331]

263. The witness travelled from Kigali to Butare on 22 April. He did not have any difficulty getting through the roadblocks because his vehicle's windshield bore a pass signed by the prefect's office. Such passes were signed at the time the Kigali-Ville prefecture staff began burying bodies in the town, or about 11 April.[332]

Prosecution Witness AFB

264. Witness AFB, a Hutu, was an employee in the Ministry of Justice. On 7 April 1994, a policeman at the prefecture office gave him an authorisation, signed by Renzaho, which made it possible to drive around without being stopped. The witness had been able to move about without problems before receiving it because there were communal policemen in his vehicle. The *Interahamwe* could not stop policemen, particularly in a state-owned vehicle. However, he found it necessary to obtain a travel authorisation in case he drove home on his own without a police escort. After receiving the authorisation, he had no difficulty travelling around Kigali.[333]

Prosecution Witness ACS

265. Witness ACS, a Tutsi, testified that a *laissez-passer* system was instituted by Renzaho following his appointment as prefect in October 1990. At that time, the passes were made mandatory throughout Kigali-Ville prefecture, but were only required for Tutsis in that period. They had to give "very convincing reasons" to apply for the document but, according to the witness, "the Tutsi would never be able to get the pass". When the witness was released after having been arrested as a suspected accomplice of the *Inyenzi*, he could not leave Kigali-Ville without a pass, which, at the time, had to be obtained at the commune office.[334]

Renzaho

266. Renzaho testified that he was requiring those passing through roadblocks to show *laissez-passers* as well as identity cards. The Kigali-Ville prefecture did not, however, give preference to any particular group when issuing *laissez-passers*. Anyone who sought assistance from his office was received, with a positive reply given to all such requests. Someone who had a *laissez-passer* was assumed to have met with officials who had granted them the pass. To deal with the large number of persons requesting such documents, Renzaho set up a service area in front of the main entrance. He assigned some of the approximately 150 refugees at the prefecture, who included both Hutus and Tutsis, to assist in issuing the documents. In his testimony, Renzaho agreed that most Tutsis were afraid to move around, **[page 77]** and that, given the situation at the time, it was difficult for them to come to the prefecture to get the travel documents.[335]

267. The *laissez-passer* system had always existed in Rwanda in times of crisis and was in place from the beginning of the war in 1990. Following ceasefire negotiations in 1992 and the subsequent signing of the Arusha Accords, the system was abandoned, but then reinstated after the President was killed in April 1994. It was not directed against the Tutsis but served all persons equally, being a protective measure during that time of suspicion. One of the last persons to receive a *laissez-passer* from the prefecture office was the

---

[331] T. 9 January 2007 p. 50, 52, 62-63, 69, 72; Prosecution Exhibit 65 (personal identification sheet).
[332] T. 9 January 2007 p. 69.
[333] T. 8 January 2007 pp. 69, 85; Prosecution Exhibit 64 (personal identification sheet). Witness AFB used the word "authorisation", not "*laissez-passer*", but the reality seems to be the same. He also explained that he possessed another authorisation, also signed by Renzaho, which was issued to him in 1990 in his capacity as a member of the *cellule* committee. Other members of the population had been forbidden to circulate.
[334] T. 30 January 2007 pp. 25-26, 79-80; Prosecution Exhibit 78 (personal identification sheet).
[335] T. 28 August 2007 pp. 3, 43; T. 29 August 2007 pp. 16-17, 19-20; T. 30 August 2007 pp. 2-6, 60-61; T. 31 August 2007 pp. 2, 5-6; Prosecution Exhibit 63 (radio transcript of 18 June 1994).

former chairman of the state council, a Tutsi, who came to the office at the end of April 1994. The prefecture found him an escort to Kibyue.[336]

Defence Witness UT

268. Witness UT, a Hutu official, worked with Renzaho in the Kigali-Ville prefecture. From 11 April 1994, he travelled widely around Kigali. On several occasions he experienced difficulties getting through roadblocks because his identity card lacked a photograph. When he reported these problems, Renzaho issued an attestation to the witness, signing and stamping the document himself. Renzaho said that it would show that, wherever the witness went, he had been sent by the prefect and was working on his behalf. In spite of this attestation, the witness still ran into many other problems.[337]

Defence Witness PPO

269. Witness PPO was a high-ranking government official at the Kigali-Ville prefecture. Sometime between the end of April and early July 1994, the witness was travelling on official mission from the prefect. He was stopped at the roadblock below the National Bank of Rwanda, towards Kiyovu. According to the witness, he was humiliated and almost beaten at the roadblock, even though he also possessed documents signed and stamped by Renzaho.[338]

Defence Witness BOU

270. Witness BOU, a Hutu, was a high-ranking employee in the Ministry of Planning. On 9 April 1994, some friends were caught without identification documents at a roadblock near the Presidential Guard quarters. They were Hutus, but had a Tutsi appearance. The witness went to the Kigali-Ville prefecture office and obtained *laissez-passers* for them and himself directly from Renzaho. According to the witness, lacking identification papers at that time was a virtual death sentence. *Laissez-passers* were needed to show that people were from Kigali-Ville and not coming from Uganda or the war front.[339] **[page 78]**

271. A large number of refugees were at the prefecture office. Many of them had fled their homes without their identification papers and were seeking passes. The *laissez-passer* operated as a substitute for an identity card, since a pass was a means of identifying people who were not known and enabled them go through roadblocks more easily.[340]

Defence Witness HIN

272. Witness HIN, a Hutu, went to the prefecture office on 18 April 1994 to apply for a *laissez-passer*. He wanted to leave Kigali and escape the violence of the *Interahamwe*. Four persons, three Tutsis and a Hutu, accompanied him and also sought *laissez-passers*. The four were able to get through the roadblocks to the prefecture office by claiming that they had a medical emergency and because an armed soldier accompanied them.[341]

273. At the prefecture office, the witness saw Renzaho instructing Jean Bizimana, the *bourgmestre* of Nyarugenge commune, and Alexis Nsabimana, a sub-prefect, to issue the *laissez-passers* and give them to

---

[336] T. 29 August 2007 pp. 16-18. Renzaho explained that under the first republic, one could not move from one commune to another without a *laissez-passer*. That system was abolished under the second republic. The Chamber recalls that the first and second republics were from 1961 to 1973 and from 1973 to 1994, respectively. His testimony that the *laissez-passer* system was abolished in 1992 and then reintroduced in April 1994 follows from the French version (T. 29 August 2007 p. 19).
[337] T. 24 May 2007 pp. 20, 26, 29, 46-47; Defence Exhibit 47 (personal identification sheet).
[338] T. 4 July 1997 p. 63; T. 5 July 2007 pp. 5, 7-8.
[339] T. 22 May 2007 pp. 32, 36-38, 49-50; Defence Exhibit 44 (personal identification sheet).
[340] T. 22 May 2007 pp. 38-39, 50.
[341] T. 10 July 2007 pp. 4-7, 10, 30; Defence Exhibit 73 (personal identification sheet).

him to sign. The witness also heard Renzaho say to Bizimana that *laissez-passers* should be issued to traders going to get supplies as well as to people fleeing the fighting.[342]

274. On that day, the witness and his companions received *laissez-passers*. They found another soldier, with a Hutu appearance, to accompany them back through the roadblocks after leaving the prefecture office. Because it was understood that a Hutu soldier could not be an accomplice of *Inyenzi*, it was not necessary for the group to show their *laissez-passers* on their way back. The witness fled Kigali-Ville the next day, 19 April.[343]

275. According to the witness, Renzaho had set up the system of *laissez-passers* to enable members of the population flee Kigali town. Such documents were also issued to traders so that they could bring supplies. When requesting a *laissez-passer*, the applicant could also have listed upon it the names of others accompanying him or her. The person issuing it did not ask if the names were those of a spouse or children or other such details. These documents were given free of charge, with no pre-conditions, and all Tutsis who arrived at the prefecture office were provided with one. However, without a military escort or a civilian Hutu, a Tutsi could not pass the roadblocks to reach the office. Moreover, a *laissez-passer* alone was not sufficient to get out of the city. The *Interahamwe* were at odds with Renzaho and would not accept documents signed by him. They also wanted to know whether the people travelling were Hutu or Tutsi, as the documents did not show the bearer's ethnicity. The *laissez-passer* was therefore not helpful within Kigali, but was useful in other prefectures. According to the witness, if Renzaho was referred to as an accomplice of the *Inyenzi*, it was specifically because he was issuing such passes.[344] **[page 79]**

Defence Witness PPV

276. The witness, a Hutu, worked at the Kigali-Ville prefecture office in 1994. He testified that anyone who bore an identity card showing a Tutsi ethnicity would be marked for death in the early hours of the events at issue, because they were identified with the enemy. However, a *laissez-passer* allowed people to travel safely. Only the Kigali-Ville prefecture provided such documents, and their issuance was an important occupation of the prefect. The witness helped deliver them to all people without distinction. The *laissez-passers* did not mention ethnicity. It contained the name and destination of the applicant. To ensure security, a policeman was provided to escort those who were at risk while travelling.[345]

277. There was a massive influx of refugees into the prefecture office, requesting *laissez-passers*. Some had lost their identity cards while others wished to conceal their ethnicity. With a *laissez-passer*, they could travel through roadblocks safely, whereas persons without such a document had difficulties.[346]

Defence Witness PPG

278. The witness, a Hutu, was an administrative employee in April 1994. He went back to work at the Kigali-Ville prefecture office from 20 April and stayed there until July. From April to July 1994, travel documents were no longer issued, and the witness did not believe that anyone went to the Kigali-Ville prefecture office to obtain such documents.[347]

Defence Witness PGL

279. Witness PGL, a Hutu, was an administrative employee at the Kigali-Ville prefecture who returned to the prefecture office during the second week of April 1994, remaining until early July 1994. On the day he

---

[342] T. 10 July 2007 pp. 7-8, 10-11, 24. Witness HIN moreover heard another sub-prefect, Jean Butera, suggest that the authorities take food from stores belonging to Tutsis and distribute it to the population. However, Renzaho replied that this would be tantamount to looting, which was not authorised. T. 10 July 2007 pp. 11-12.
[343] *Id.* pp. 9-10, 12, 31.
[344] *Id.* pp. 8-10, 30-33.
[345] T. 4 June 2007 p. 78; T. 5 June 2007 pp. 2, 6-7, 44-45; Defence Exhibit 56 (personal identification sheet). The information about the place of destination and the police officer as escort follows from the French version (T. 5 June 2007 p. 8).
[346] T. 5 June 2007 pp. 7, 44.
[347] T. 18 June 2007 pp. 45, 49, 57-58; T. 19 June 2007 p. 6; Defence Exhibit 65 (personal identification sheet).

returned, Renzaho asked him to help "save some people", noting that it was only a request, not an order. In furtherance of this request, the witness carried out a specific assignment from his immediate supervisor. He went to certain neighbourhoods under his responsibility and brought back to the prefecture office persons who wanted to leave Kigali-Ville but were afraid to travel alone. Most of them did not have identification papers and were provided by the prefecture office with *laissez-passers* or vehicles to transport them to their places of origin. The documents did not include the ethnic group, but mentioned the bearers' destination and, if they had a vehicle, its number.[348]

280. The witness helped issue *laissez-passers*, which were signed by the prefect. They were provided without discrimination to anyone who wanted to leave Kigali and went to the prefecture office to apply for one. When issuing such passes, the witness did not ask whether the applicants had identity cards. It was possible to pass through a roadblock by showing any national identification paper that proved that the bearer had not attacked the country in 1990. **[page 80]** According to the witness, most of those who had attacked then had identity cards from Uganda or foreign passports.[349]

281. When the witness moved about neighbourhoods where he was known, he had no difficulty getting through roadblocks but he encountered problems elsewhere. On 14 April, he was stopped at a roadblock, where he was asked for money and made to sit on the ground even though he was wearing a jacket that showed his position at the Kigali-Ville prefecture. His captors said they would release him only so that he could inform Renzaho that they would come to the prefecture office and kill both the prefect and the Tutsis whom they accused of sheltering there. At another roadblock, on an unspecified date, the witness was slapped.[350]

Defence Witness BDC

282. Witness BDC was a Hutu governmental official who worked with a non-governmental organisation in Kigali-Ville. On 25 April, his organisation appointed him to visit Renzaho and convey that its workers had difficulty in circulating through the city. Renzaho said he had no authority over the militia and asked him to negotiate with it directly. At the headquarters of the militia, the witness spoke to Robert Kajuga, its president, and his deputy. They signed and issued a safe conduct document that the witness's organisation members then used to go through roadblocks manned by *Interahamwe*. With those documents, the witness's colleagues had fewer difficulties passing through the roadblocks than before. Regardless of the political parties to which they belonged, the militiamen at roadblocks recognised the authority of Kajuga and his deputies.[351]

Defence Witness AIA

283. Witness AIA was a policeman in Kigali-Ville prefecture and worked with a *conseiller* from 7 April until 4 July 1994. At some roadblocks in the sector to which the witness was assigned, one had to present either an identity card or an attestation that it had been lost. From April to July 1994, officials in that sector issued attestations of loss of identity cards. No other type of official document was issued in that sector.[352]

284. The Kigali-Ville prefecture issued other types of documents, including authorisations for vehicles to travel, for supplies, or to evacuate people. When the *conseiller* wanted to evacuate his family, he asked the witness for help, and ultimately used a *laissez-passer* issued **[page 81]** by the Kigali-Ville prefecture that

---

[348] T. 6 June 2007 pp. 15-20, 23-24, 30, 32; Defence Exhibit 61 (personal identification sheet).
[349] T. 6 June 2007 pp. 19-20, 36-37.
[350] *Id.* pp. 23, 31-32, 34.
[351] T. 4 June 2007 pp. 4, 18-21, 35, 55-6; Defence Exhibit 51 (personal identification sheet). Witness BDC explained that his organisation did not need *laissez-passers* from the public authorities to carry out its humanitarian mission. He asked the militia for such documents only as an exceptional remedy in order to save lives. T. 4 June 2007 pp. 20-21. The witness identified Robert Kajuga's deputy as "Rutengwa" but probably meant Rutaganda. T. 4 June 2007 p. 57. In the French version, the witness says "Rutagenwa" but then spelled it "Rutengwa". *Id.* p. 64.
[352] T. 2 July 2007 pp. 2, 6, 35-36, 43; Witness AIA was questioned on 1 November 1994 by Nyamirambo brigade about his actions during the events, and was then locked up in a cell for a month while investigations took place, following which he was released. T. 2 July 2007 p. 46. Defence Exhibit 66 (personal identification sheet). The sector attestations were drafted by a secretary and then signed and handed to the applicant by the *conseiller* with whom Witness AIA worked. They bore the seal of the sector. The ethnic origin of the bearer was not mentioned on the document. T. 2 July 2007 pp. 35-37.

enabled the witness's vehicle to move about. The witness also heard, apparently from sources at the prefecture office, that refugees of other prefectures or communes were to be given *laissez-passers* in order to leave Kigali-Ville. The witness did not know whether the ethnicity of the bearer was listed on the latter category of *laissez-passer*.[353]

285. Although some Tutsis could circulate in Kigali-Ville, those recognised as Tutsi from their identity cards were killed. The witness noted that some persons obtained *laissez-passers* without going to the prefecture themselves, by sending others.[354]

Defence Witness Jean-Baptiste Butera

286. Jean-Baptiste Butera, a Hutu, was the national program director for AIDS control at the Ministry of Public Health in Rwanda in April 1994. He left his home in Remera on 8 April and sought refuge in Masaka, in Kigali-Rural prefecture. The witness left Masaka twice between 7 and 28 April, and encountered great difficulty going through roadblocks in Kigali. On one of the occasions, he was attacked and almost killed. He did not have an identity card during the events in 1994. On 28 April, before leaving for Gitarama, he spoke to Renzaho at the Kigali-Ville prefecture office, which he stated was not easy to reach. The prefect said he did not have any control over the roadblocks and warned him to be careful. The witness obtained a travel authorisation in Kanombe in order to go through the roadblocks and leave Kigali. He agreed that the people who had a Tutsi identity card or appearance were in danger of being killed.[355]

Defence Witness WOW

287. Witness WOW, a Hutu driver, lived in Rugenge sector near CELA in April 1994. In spite of having a *laissez-passer* he encountered difficulties at the roadblocks when driving to Gitarama on 9 April 1994. He had to give money, food or drinks to those manning them.[356]

4.1.3 Deliberations

288. It is not disputed that Kigali-Ville prefecture office issued *laissez-passers* signed by Renzaho or those acting on his behalf from April to July 1994.[357] One example of such a pass, dated 24 May 1994 and signed by Renzaho, was tendered as an exhibit.[358] In order to cope with the mass of applications, Renzaho organised a service in front of the prefecture office to issue the passes. It further follows from the credible evidence of Witnesses ALG, UB, UL and AIA that the prefecture office issued two types of *laissez-passers* – one for individuals and one for vehicles.

289. The evidence shows that *laissez-passers* issued by the prefecture office did not automatically guarantee free movement. At roadblocks, the *Interahamwe* would sometimes also ask for identity cards and kill Tutsis, even if they had a travel authorisation. Also, Hutus **[page 82]** with *laissez-passers* signed and stamped by Renzaho could be subject to harassment there. Prosecution Witnesses ALG, GLJ and UB as well as Defence Witnesses UT, PPO, BOU, HIN, PGL and WOW gave convincing accounts of such problems. It is further noted that travel documents were to some extent issued by other authorities and even by the *Interahamwe* leadership, as mentioned by Witness BDC. This said, the Chamber finds it established that the possession of a *laissez-passer* from the Kigali-Ville prefecture did facilitate movement within or out of Kigali, as explained by Witnesses ALG, GLJ, UB, UL, AFB and PPV.

290. The main question under paragraphs 13 and 30 of the Indictment is whether the *laissez-passers* were issued in order to facilitate the movement of the *Interahamwe*, militia, soldiers and gendarmerie participating

---

[353] T. 2 July 2007 pp. 36-37, 58.
[354] *Id.* pp. 58-59.
[355] T. 22 May 2007 p. 68; T. 23 May 2007 pp. 5-7, 9-10, 12, 27-28, 30-31; Defence Exhibit 46 (personal identification sheet). He was formerly referred to as Witness LAA.
[356] T. 4 July 2007 pp. 36-40; Defence Exhibit 69 (personal identification sheet).
[357] Defence Closing Brief paras. 804-820.
[358] Prosecution Exhibit 36 (*laissez-passer* for individuals, signed by Renzaho on 24 May 1994).

in the killings of Tutsis, as alleged by the Prosecution. The Defence disputes this, arguing that the purpose of these documents was to enable everyone, irrespective of ethnicity, to circulate within or flee Kigali-Ville.

291. The Chamber observes that the *laissez-passers* issued by the Kigali-Ville prefecture office did not list ethnicity. This follows from the example of the pass dated 24 May 1994 and the testimonies of Defence Witnesses PPV, PGL, HIN and AIA. The Prosecution did not lead any evidence to the contrary.[359] Consequently, the text of the documents does not show that they facilitated the movement of particular groups, for instance Hutus engaged in killings.

292. Turning now to how the *laissez-passers* were in fact distributed, there is no evidence that Renzaho, or those acting on his behalf, issued them to *Interahamwe*, militia, soldiers or gendarmes. Neither was there any specific showing that persons having received such documents committed killings. The picture that emerges from the totality of the evidence is that they were issued to a large number of persons, both to circulate within or to flee Kigali. Some passes were issued to prefecture officials or civilians who were engaged in assistance missions, for instance to tend to the needs of refugees. The possibility that violent groups also received such documents cannot lead to a finding that the *laissez-passer* system facilitated the movement of killers. It is recalled that the *Interahamwe* frequently remained at roadblocks within their locality (II.2). Finally, there is no evidence demonstrating that they received equipment by persons who had received *laissez-passers*, as alleged in the Indictment.

293. It is clear that the *laissez-passer* system should be viewed in light of the general situation in Kigali from April 1994 onwards, when Tutsis and moderate Hutus were targeted and killed. Witnesses GLJ, UB, Renzaho, HIN and AIA testified that it would be difficult for Tutsis to reach the prefecture office.[360] This evidence, which is obviously truthful, indicates that they would also have problems obtaining such documents.[361] One of the main reasons is **[page 83]** that they would be stopped at roadblocks and asked for identity cards and *laissez-passers* (see generally II.2). In a radio interview of 18 June 1994, Renzaho highlighted the need for the youths at roadblocks to check both sets of documents.[362] The Chamber accepts that the combination of *laissez-passers*, identity documents and strict control at checkpoints may have made it easier for Tutsis to be targeted. However, this is not the issue under paragraphs 13 and 30 of the Indictment, which focuses on the movement of killers.

294. The Chamber finds that the Prosecution has not proven that, between 6 April and 17 July 1994, Renzaho, or those acting on his behalf, provided permits and *laissez-passers* to enable the movement and equipping of *Interahamwe*, militia, soldiers and gendarmes participating in the killing of Tutsis. In view of this finding, there is no need to consider the Defence submissions that it was prejudiced by alleged lack of specificity in the Indictment.[363]

4.2 Fuel Vouchers

4.2.1 Introduction

295. The Prosecution alleges that Renzaho provided bonds (fuel vouchers, coupons) to enable the movement and equipping of the *Interahamwe*, militia, soldiers and gendarmes who killed or caused serious bodily or

---

[359] Prosecution Witness UB's evidence about attestations listing ethnicity did not refer to *laissez-passers* but to documents issued at the sector level to those who had lost or misplaced their identity cards. They were signed and stamped at the Kigali-Ville prefecture office after the commune offices had relocated there. Furthermore, Witness ACS's evidence that *laissez-passers* in 1990 only were required for Tutsis does not throw light on the situation in 1994. The Chamber sees no need to consider that testimony further.
[360] As mentioned above, Witness AIA even testified that some persons obtained *laissez-passers* without going to the prefecture, by sending others.
[361] In the present context, the Chamber does not find it necessary to discuss whether Tutsis who in fact reached the prefecture office would have obtained a *laissez-passer*. It has noted the evidence that Witness HIN went there with three Tutsis, but also that they were accompanied by an armed soldier and that it is unclear whether Renzaho was aware of their ethnicity. Furthermore, the fact that some Tutsi refugees had managed to seek refuge at the prefecture office does not alter the conclusion that it was difficult to get there.
[362] Prosecution Exhibit 63 (transcript of radio interview with Renzaho, 18 June 1994); T. 31 August 2007 pp. 2-6.
[363] Defence Closing Brief paras. 801-803.

mental harm to Tutsis between 6 April and 17 July 1994. It also submits that he requisitioned some of the city's fuel supplies. Reference is made to Witnesses UB, GLJ, ALG, AWE, AFB and PPG, and to Defence Witness AIA.[364]

296. The Defence denies these allegations. Based on the testimony of Witnesses UL, BDC and PPV, it submits that, from April to July 1994, responsibility for issuing fuel vouchers lay with the Ministry of Defence rather than the prefecture office.[365]

4.2.2 Evidence

Prosecution Witness UB

297. Witness UB, a Hutu local official in Kigali-Ville prefecture, testified that there were two ways to obtain petrol during the events in 1994. From 7 April onwards, some petrol filling stations had been requisitioned by the Kigali prefecture and others by the Rwandan Armed Force headquarters. Accordingly, those who wanted fuel either had to go to the prefecture office to obtain a voucher entitling them to petrol at a filling station, or to Camp Kigali, where they could be served from petrol tanks within the camp.[366]

Prosecution Witness GLJ **[page 84]**

298. Witness GLJ, a Hutu local official in Kigali-Ville prefecture, stated that, at least until about the end of April 1994, all petrol stations were requisitioned or commandeered by Renzaho. In order to obtain fuel, one had to get an authorisation from the prefecture. The prefect had designated Jean-Baptiste Butera, the sub-prefect in charge of political affairs, to issue fuel coupons.[367]

Prosecution Witness ALG

299. Witness ALG, a Hutu member of the MRND party and a government official in Kigali-Ville, explained that, after 12 April 1994, it was difficult to obtain fuel in the prefecture. The army had taken over all fuel stations and was giving the *Interahamwe* fuel vouchers. He believed that the prefecture office had also secured an arrangement with a Shell petrol station to obtain fuel. Renzaho gave fuel vouchers to people of his choosing – the service heads of the prefecture office, the *bourgmestres*, the *conseillers* and the *Interahamwe*. The vouchers allowed them to obtain fuel at the Shell station.[368]

300. Although it was the prefect who issued fuel vouchers, in his absence, Butera, a sub-prefect and head of the administrative and legal affairs service, would issue them. The prefect could also give that power to other heads of services, people from the accounts department, or *bourgmestres*.[369]

301. The witness reported to Renzaho on an alleged killer named Habyarimana, also known as Kigingi. The prefect summoned Kigingi to his office. On leaving the office, Kigingi warned the witness to be careful and flaunted a fuel voucher that he said Renzaho had just given him. Pointing at the witness, he said: "I am going to get fuel supplies, and I will continue my job, so what are you going to do about me?" Kigingi then left with the *Interahamwe* escort who always accompanied him.[370]

---

[364] Indictment paras. 13 and 30; Prosecution Closing Brief paras. 146-152, 156-158; T. 14 February 2008 p. 20.
[365] Defence Closing Brief paras. 961-984; Defence Exhibit 113 (*complément écrit aux arguments oraux de la défense*) paras. 864.1-864.64.
[366] T. 23 January 2007 pp. 1, 23; Prosecution Exhibit 69 (personal identification sheet). Witness UB was a detainee at the time of his testimony, awaiting the outcome of an appeal pending before the Supreme Court. His conviction for genocide in 1997 had been confirmed by the Kigali Court of Appeals in 1998. T. 23 January 2007 pp. 1-4, 65.
[367] T. 22 January 2007 pp. 13-15, 20, 23, 30-31, 61-63, 66; Prosecution Exhibit 68 (personal identification sheet). When testifying, Witness GLJ had been detained in Rwanda for over 12 years, awaiting trial.
[368] T. 10 January 2007 pp. 55-56, 63; T. 11 January 2007 pp. 6, 50-51; T. 12 January 2007 p. 22; Prosecution Exhibit 67 (personal identification sheet). At the time of his testimony, Witness ALG was awaiting trial in Rwanda for genocide in relation to his role during the events in 1994. T. 10 January 2007 p. 64.
[369] T. 11 January 2007 pp. 10-12; T. 12 January 2007 p. 32.
[370] T. 11 January 2007 pp. 56-58.

Prosecution Witness AWE

302. Witness AWE, a Hutu, was a local official within the Kigali-Ville prefecture and occupied a local position in the MRND party. He said that, sometime after 7 April 1994, Renzaho gave the president of the *Interahamwe* 40 litres of petrol.[371]

Prosecution Witness AFB

303. Witness AFB, a Hutu, worked at a court in Kigali-Ville during the events. On 7 April 1994, *conseiller* Karekezi sent the witness to the Kigali-Ville prefecture office. The witness reported to that office and began receiving orders from Renzaho. On 13 April, around 10.00 a.m., Renzaho transferred him to the manager of the Fina petrol station, where he worked for 20 days, until the station's fuel tanks ran dry around 3 May. During this period, the witness **[page 85]** saw Renzaho occasionally at the station. It did not sell to the public, but was used mainly to distribute fuel to the *Interahamwe* on the basis of vouchers signed by the prefect, although money was also accepted.[372] The witness would overhear the manager requesting those who came to collect fuel to show a document signed by the prefect, and also saw such documentation.[373]

Prosecution Witness UL

304. On 11 April 1994, Witness UL, a Hutu employee at a ministry, attended a meeting held at the Kigali-Ville prefecture office. The representative of the Red Cross, Philippe Gaillard, informed the attendees that his organisation would provide fuel for vehicles in connection with an operation clearing the streets of bodies. Later that day, the witness went to Gikondo to collect the fuel there. Subsequently, the vehicles continued to receive fuel there, as the RPF had captured the reservoir in Gatsata.[374]

Renzaho

305. Renzaho testified that the prefecture did not have fuel for distribution. In "the early days" of the events, the authorities in Kigali lost access to Gatsata, where fuel had been stored. The reason was that the area had been occupied by the RPF. The other fuel stocks were far away in Kibuye.[375] The prefect's office was never involved in managing or distributing fuel or authorising quotas. He denied ever having issued a petrol voucher to Kigingi or anyone else. The army took over all the filling stations that still had fuel in the city. An army commission managed and gave out the fuel. Renzaho did not know whether quotas were set, but there were fuel coupons for prefecture vehicles which were redeemed at army fuel stores.[376] The prefecture had a logistics commission set up "to supply the city of Kigali". To service the prefecture vehicles, sub-prefect Jean-Baptiste Butera, who was in charge of that commission, went to those persons who managed the fuel stock.[377]

306. Kigali-Ville was threatened with a major epidemic if actions were not immediately taken to address the situation. To implement ICRC humanitarian activities, a meeting was held at the prefecture office on the

---

[371] T. 31 January 2007 pp. 11-12, 40-41, 51; Prosecution Exhibit 80 (personal identification sheet). When he testified, Witness AWE had been in detention since 1996, awaiting trial for genocide.

[372] T. 9 January 2007 p. 10 ("In fact, [the fuel station] didn't sell to the public, it simply pumped fuel on the basis of vouchers that were signed by the préfet. That is why one can say that it was only every now and then that some people provided money to get fuel from that station. But most often people came with vouchers signed by the préfet to fill up their vehicles at that filling station and most often those vouchers were signed by the préfet") and sealed extract p. (i); Prosecution Exhibit 64 (personal identification sheet).

[373] T. 8 January 2007 pp. 69-71, 73, 86; T. 9 January 2007 pp. 9- 10.

[374] T. 9 January 2007 pp. 50-53, 55-57, 59-63, 72-73 ("on that very day *we* went to collect that fuel at Gikondo in the industrial area. And it is from there that *we* went to fuel up *our vehicles* subsequently"; (italics added); Prosecution Exhibit 65 (personal identification sheet). Witness UL was acquitted of charges, which were not specified. T. 9 January 2007 pp. 51, 71. He was not able to confirm the Defence's suggestion that this took place in June 2002.

[375] T. 29 August 2007 p. 18; T. 3 September 2007, p. 12. The Chamber recalls that Gatsata is in Kigali-Ville prefecture.

[376] Renzaho did not specify who gave out the coupons or where this took place. T. 29 August 2007 p. 18 ("there were fuel coupons").

[377] *Id.* p. 18, see also French version p. 21 (*"les membres qui géraient ce stock"*); T. 30 August p. 42; T. 3 September 2007 pp. 12-14.

morning of 11 April 1994. The Minister of Health, the Minister of Public Works, Mr. Gaillard, who was the representative of the ICRC, his team, **[page 86]** and the prefect were in attendance, with the public sanitation team. The ministers had also convened their own personnel. At the meeting, Gaillard made a presentation on his mission, including the evacuation of the injured and removal of corpses, which the prefecture office supported. Practical questions were addressed, and the ICRC representative decided to provide fuel for the operation.[378]

Defence Witness BDC

307. Witness BDC, a Hutu government official, worked with the Rwandan Red Cross Society from 15 April 1994.[379] The Ministries of Public Health and Public Works convened a meeting at the Kigali-Ville prefecture office on 11 April, during which it was decided to collect bodies from the streets. Neither the prefecture nor the Ministry of Public Works had the necessary fuel for the operation. The ICRC delegate attending the meeting, Philippe Gaillard, made fuel available in view of the state of emergency. The witness explained that the Gatsata depot, the biggest in Rwanda, had come under control by the RPF as of 10 April. Consequently, the government had run out of fuel. He did not hear that Renzaho gave fuel to the militia.[380]

Defence Witness PPV

308. Witness PPV, a Hutu, worked in the urban police in the Kigali-Ville prefecture. From 7 April 1994, fuel supplies were rationed. He believed that the distribution of fuel was handled, not by the prefecture office but by the Ministry of Defence, which had commandeered petrol stations. To obtain fuel, the prefecture office as well as all other services and vehicle owners had to go to that ministry to obtain vouchers.[381]

Defence Witness PPG

309. Witness PPG, a Hutu, was an employee at the Kigali-Ville prefecture and returned there to work on 20 April 1994. During the period of April to July 1994, the witness believed that the police commander was responsible for the distribution of petrol vouchers.[382]

Defence Witness AIA

310. Witness AIA, was a policeman in Kigali-Ville prefecture. His immediate superior was a *conseiller*, with whom he worked from 7 April to 4 July 1994 on a nearly 24-hours basis. He testified that he was not aware that petrol vouchers were issued at the Kigali-Ville **[page 87]** prefecture. The witness obtained fuel from the *conseiller*, who in turn would receive it from a station in town.[383]

4.2.3 Deliberations

311. The main question is whether Renzaho provided fuel vouchers to enable the movement and equipping of the *Interahamwe*, militia, soldiers and gendarmes who killed or caused serious bodily or mental harm to Tutsis between 6 April and 17 July 1994.[384] The Defence submits that the prefecture office did not have stocks of fuel and did not issue vouchers for fuel or manage fuel distribution in any way.

---

[378] T. 28 August 2007 p. 44-46; T. 30 August 2007 p. 7.
[379] T. 4 June 2007 pp. 3, 6, 37, 50; Defence Exhibit 51 (personal identification sheet). Witness BDC was not a member of the International Red Cross Committee (ICRC) but of the national Red Cross Society. He explained that in times of armed conflict, the national Red Cross comes under the authority of the international organisation, so he was acting on behalf of the ICRC. T. 4 June 2007 pp. 4, 64.
[380] T. 4 June 2007 pp. 4-10, 19-20.
[381] *Id.* p. 78; T. 5 June 2007 p. 7; Defence Exhibit 56 (personal identification sheet).
[382] T. 18 June 2007 pp. 44-45, 48-49, 51; T. 19 June 2007 p. 6; Defence Exhibit 65 (personal identification sheet).
[383] T. 2 July 2007 pp. 2, 8-10, 59; T. 3 July 2007 pp. 18-19; Defence Exhibit 66 (personal identification sheet). His ethnic origin was not specified.
[384] The Indictment uses the words "bonds ... to enable the movement" (in French *"déliverance de bons"*). The Pre-Trial Brief refers to "coupons" and "bonds" as well as to the requisition of petrol supplies (paras. 59-60).

Prosecutor v. Renzaho

312. Three of the six Prosecution witnesses gave evidence as to whether the petrol stations in Kigali-Ville had been requisitioned by the authorities. Their testimonies varied. Witness GLJ stated that all stations were requisitioned by the prefecture office. Witness UB said that some petrol stations were taken over by the prefecture office, and others by the army. Witness ALG explained that the prefecture office had an arrangement with a Shell fuel station, but otherwise, the army had taken over fuel stations. All three witnesses were awaiting trial in Rwanda at the time of their testimonies or had their cases on appeal. The Chamber views their testimonies with caution but notes that two of them stated that the prefecture had requisitioned petrol stations.

313. Witness AFB testified that Renzaho ordered him to assist the manager of the Fina station, where vouchers signed by the prefect were used. His evidence was first-hand and appeared credible. The witness did not say that the Fina station had actually been requisitioned by the prefecture office but Renzaho's deployment of the witness there does indicate that he had some level of control over fuel distribution there. Defence Witness PPV believed that the Ministry of Defence had commandeered petrol stations but the Chamber attaches limited weight to his evidence. In view of his particular position and functions in 1994, he would try to reduce his and the prefecture's role in such distribution.[385]

314. The Chamber does not find it necessary to make a finding as to whether the prefecture office had formally requisitioned petrol stations in Kigali-Ville. It is clear from the evidence, as discussed below, that the office had at least some degree of control over the distribution of fuel through the use of coupons or vouchers.[386]

315. The Chamber heard considerable evidence about this. According to Witness UB, vouchers could be obtained from the prefecture office or Camp Kigali. Witness GLJ testified that a fuel coupon from the prefecture office was required to procure fuel, and Renzaho had designated Sub-prefect Jean-Baptiste Butera to issue such coupons. Witness ALG confirmed that Butera had this power, at least in the prefect's absence, and stated that Renzaho issued fuel vouchers to people of his choosing (see below). Witness PPG believed that the police commander was responsible for the distribution of petrol vouchers but this does not preclude that vouchers were signed by the prefect. Finally, Witness AFB gave first-hand, fairly **[page 88]** detailed, credible evidence that, at least from 13 April until about 3 May 1994, vouchers signed by the prefect were being used at a petrol station in Kigali-Ville.

316. Only Witness PPV stated that distribution of fuel was not handled by the prefecture office, and that the prefecture office had to go to the Ministry of Defence to obtain fuel, including vouchers. As mentioned above, the Chamber considers his testimony with caution in the present context, due to his particular functions.

317. Written evidence corroborates the testimonies of Prosecution witnesses. In a letter of 1 May 1994 to Sub-prefect Jean-Baptiste Butera, Renzaho terminated Butera's role as the prefecture office's liaison agent to the Ministry of Defence concerning the constitution of stocks of fuel and their management. He emphasised that Butera was not allowed to refuse fuel to duly authorised vehicles. Renzaho accepted that he had signed the letter.[387] This exhibit reinforces the evidence that the prefecture office decided who would receive fuel, and that Butera was given the task of administering it.

318. Also of significance is a transcript of a radio broadcast from 18 June 1994, where Renzaho stated: "We have therefore asked those in charge of civil defence in the cellules and in the secteurs to issue permits for movement, because these are people who come to see us in order to obtain fuel for use in those vehicles."[388] Its authenticity was not disputed by the Defence. By these words, Renzaho clearly attempted to facilitate the distribution of fuel by his administration to at least some persons. This contradicts the idea that the prefecture office had no involvement in the distribution of fuel or issuing of fuel vouchers. The fact that the ICRC

---

[385] Witness PPG, T. 19 June 2007 p. 6.
[386] The Chamber notes that Witnesses UL and BDC corroborated Renzaho's testimony that the Gatsata fuel reserve had been captured by the RPF in early April. This would increase the need for the authorities to secure sufficient fuel supplies. Requisitioning of petrol stations would be a logical step in such a situation.
[387] Prosecution Exhibit 34 (letter of 1 May 1994 from Renzaho to Butera), referring to Butera as "*l'agent de liaison de la P.V.K. avec le Ministère de la Defense Nationale*" and mentioning "*la constitution des stocks de vivres et carburant et de leur gestion*".
[388] Prosecution Exhibit 62 (transcripts of radio broadcast of 18 June 1994).

provided fuel in connection with the clean-up operation following the meeting on 11 April 1994 does not preclude that the prefecture also gave out fuel vouchers. Renzaho's testimony on who gave out the coupons or where their issuance took place appeared to be fairly evasive or ambiguous. For example, he did not say who gave out the coupons or where but stated that "there were" such coupons.[389]

319. In light of the foregoing evidence, the Chamber finds that the Prosecution has proven beyond a reasonable doubt that the prefecture office issued fuel vouchers, at least from about mid-April to early May 1994.

320. The remaining question is whether the vouchers were issued to *Interahamwe*, militia, soldiers and gendarmes who killed or caused serious bodily or mental harm to Tutsis in that period. **[page 89]**

321. Witness ALG testified that Renzaho distributed fuel, *inter alia*, to the *Interahamwe*. He also stated that Kigingi, the alleged killer who was always accompanied by an *Interahamwe* escort, showed the witness a voucher that he said Renzaho had just given him. Although the Chamber views his evidence with caution, it is to some extent corroborated by Witnesses AWE and AFB. Witness AWE stated that, sometime after 7 April 1994, Renzaho gave the president of the *Interahamwe* 40 litres of petrol. This evidence appears to be hearsay. This witness was awaiting trial for genocide at the time of this testimony, so his evidence is also viewed with caution. Witness AFB, however, gave first-hand, credible testimony that, at least from about mid-April to about early May, a Fina station was being used mainly to distribute fuel to *Interahamwe* on the basis of coupons that Renzaho signed. The Chamber accepts that Renzaho was distributing fuel via the use of vouchers to chosen people or groups of people, which included *Interahamwe*.

322. Only Witness ALG testified that a specific person allegedly involved in killings, Kigingi, had received a fuel voucher from Renzaho. No other witnesses gave evidence about particular individuals or about persons who had committed crimes receiving fuel via the vouchers. As noted above, the Chamber views the evidence of Witness ALG with caution and will not accept his testimony on this point without corroboration. Even if the *Interahamwe* were clearly involved in killing and causing serious bodily or mental harm to Tutsis during the period of April to May 1994, the Prosecution has not shown that specific members of the *Interahamwe* who committed such crimes received fuel on the basis of vouchers signed by Renzaho. The Chamber therefore finds that it has not been proven beyond reasonable doubt that *Interahamwe*, militia, soldiers and gendarmes who received fuel, provided or authorised by Renzaho, killed or caused harm to Tutsis, or that Renzaho allocated fuel vouchers with the intention of facilitating such killings or harm.

4.3 Requisitioning of Vehicles

4.3.1 Introduction

323. As part of its contention that Renzaho facilitated movement, the Prosecution alleges that the prefecture office, headed by Renzaho, provided vehicles to the communal authorities. The office also supplied as well as requisitioned vehicles in the course of operations to remove bodies from the streets of Kigali. Reference is made to Witnesses ALG, UL, UB and GLJ.[390]

324. The Defence does not specifically address the allegation that Renzaho supplied or requisitioned vehicles. It submits that Renzaho participated in the collection of bodies in Kigali-Ville, not with the

---

[389] For instance, T. 29 August 2007 p. 18; T. 3 September 2007 pp. 12-14. During cross-examination concerning Prosecution Exhibit 34 (letter of 1 May 1994), where Renzaho reproaches Butera for not having provided fuel to an ORINFOR vehicle *("Aujourd'hui par exemple, vous avez refusé de server du carburant aux véhicules de l'hygiène et de l'ORINFOR alors en service commandé")*. Renzaho was asked if the prefecture was providing fuel to non-prefecture vehicles from other government departments, such as ORINFOR, the national media service. He initially replied "I know of no such case… I never dealt with any such case". When shown the letter, he insisted that it was the army that held the fuel and that the letter did not contradict that idea, adding, "It is possible that official vehicles might come to the prefecture on duty and ask for some fuel. [Butera], as liaison officer, should go to see if there is any fuel at the army to serve the vehicles, to supply the vehicle." See also T. 30 August 2007 p. 38 (Mr. President: "Did [Kajuga] control all *Interahamwe* movements in April 1994, according to what you know? A: Your Honours, I would like to apologise for not answering correctly. First of all, let me say that I am not aware of what one is referring to as *Interahamwe*").
[390] Prosecution Closing Brief paras. 117, 142, 144-145, 158. Prosecution Witness UB also gave relevant evidence (below).

Prosecutor v. Renzaho

intention of hiding the killings but because it was a public health issue. Reference is made to the testimonies of Witnesses BDC, GLJ, PGL, PPG and UT.[391] **[page 90]**

4.3.2 Evidence

Prosecution Witness ALG

325. Witness ALG, a Hutu local official in Kigali-Ville prefecture, testified that the prefecture office was responsible for managing vehicles. It had placed one at the disposition of his commune, and he sometimes used it to move about while working prior to April 1994.[392]

Prosecution Witness UL

326. Witness UL, a Hutu employed at a ministry, stated that on 10 April 1994, Renzaho broadcast a directive over the radio, asking state government employees to report to the prefecture office. The next day, the witness went to the ministry, retrieved the government vehicle he usually drove and continued to the prefecture office. Other ministry employees did the same, and he saw many trucks and other machines parked at the office. Along with 80 to 100 other persons, the witness attended a meeting there, chaired by the prefect. The participants were mostly truck drivers, but also included government authorities, such as the prefect of Gisenyi; the Minister of Public Works; Bizimungu, who was the Minister of Public Health; as well as Philippe Gaillard, an ICRC representative.[393]

327. Renzaho stated that bodies were strewn all over the city and that the city was "dirty", which in the witness's opinion referred to the presence of the bodies. He instructed truck and bulldozer drivers to dig holes and to collect bodies. Bizimungu told them to start at the Central Hospital of Kigali so that white people would not be able to take pictures there. Renzaho had a white Toyota Hilux on which was written "Préfecture de la Ville Kigali, PVK". During the meeting, he also indicated that the witness would be driving others around town in that vehicle. The meeting started at 9.30 a.m. and lasted for about an hour.[394]

328. Renzaho designated Ngerageze, the head of the sanitation service at the prefecture office, to give orders to the drivers. Ngerageze instructed the witness to dig mass graves at the Central Hospital, at Nyamirambo cemetery, and at several other locations. He also had an armed policeman directing the witness where to go. At one point, the witness saw a Kigali-Ville prefecture truck, abandoned by its driver, which had broken down while it was still laden with bodies. Vehicles from the prefecture office were used to collect prisoners from the Kigali main prison. The prisoners were dumping bodies into the mass graves that were being prepared. Staff from the Red Cross, Ministry of Health, Ministry of Public Works and the prefecture's sanitation service all participated in the clean-up operation. The witness saw bodies of the wounded and dead being transported in Red Cross vehicles. He learned that the Red Cross had asked Renzaho to assist it in the work of burying bodies.[395] **[page 91]**

329. The witness dug mass graves until 22 April 1994. An official in the Ministry of Public Works had made a request to Renzaho that some heavy equipment be placed at his disposal for use in Butare. The witness was assigned to the mission and left Kigali for Butare.[396]

---

[391] Defence Closing Brief paras. 329-330; 961-984; T. 14 February 2008 p. 41.
[392] T. 10 January 2007 pp. 55-56, 64; Prosecution Exhibit 67 (personal identification sheet). At the time of his testimony, Witness ALG was awaiting trial in Rwanda for his role during the events in 1994. T. 10 January 2007 pp. 63-64; T. 15 January 2007 p. 34.
[393] T. 9 January 2007 pp. 50-57, 60-62, 72-75; Prosecution Exhibit 65 (personal identification sheet). Witness UL was acquitted of charges brought against him in relation to the events in Rwanda in 1994. T. 9 January 2007 pp. 51, 71.
[394] T. 9 January 2007 pp. 58-59, 62-66, 74.
[395] *Id.* pp. 59, 61, 63-69, 73-74.
[396] *Id.* pp. 68-69.

Prosecution Witness UB

330. Witness UB, a Hutu local official in Kigali-Ville prefecture, said that, on 7 April 1994, he saw about 20 bodies in Rugunga cellule. He recognised several of the bodies, and they were Tutsis. Sometime before noon he telephoned Renzaho to report what he had seen. The prefect told him that the bodies would have to be buried and sent him a pickup truck with a communal policeman on board from the prefecture office. The witness then sent the vehicle to Rugunga to carry bodies to the Nyamirambo cemetery.[397] Other vehicles belonging to the prefecture as well as to the Ministry of Public Works were also used to remove bodies and dig mass graves in Kigali-Ville. On 10 or 11 April, Renzaho convened a meeting at the prefecture office. The witness passed through Gitega sector on his way to the meeting, and saw dead bodies of Tutsis at the roadblocks there. Vehicles were taking the bodies away.[398]

Prosecution Witness GLJ

331. Witness GLJ was a Hutu local official in Kigali-Ville prefecture. On 10 April1994, he met alone with the prefect, who gave him a truck belonging to the Ministry of Public Works, and instructions to remove bodies (from the streets of Kigali-Ville) and bury them in the cemetery. Renzaho did not explain the reasons for this assignment. Bodies were removed in each sector. He did not know specifically how many or which officials participated in the operation to remove bodies, although likely not all *conseillers* received a vehicle for that task. There were also other services participating in the operation. While he was removing bodies, he saw ICRC vehicles doing the same in Kigali-Ville neighbourhoods. He did not, however, receive any instructions from the ICRC. The witness stopped working on the clean-up operation after two days, when the prefect told him that the municipal council was going to take over.[399]

Defence Witness BDC

332. Witness BDC, a Hutu government official, worked with the Red Cross Society from 15 April 1994, but was kept informed of the organisation's activities before that date through radio communication. He explained that there was a danger of an epidemic in Kigali-Ville **[page 92]** that could have been even more serious than the number of wounded caused by the militias. It was urgent that corpses be buried.[400]

333. On 10 April, Philippe Gaillard, the ICRC delegate in Kigali, raised the idea of a meeting to discuss humanitarian operations with the Ministers of Public Health and of Public Works. Those ministries then called a meeting, which took place on 11 April. It was "constantly" announced on radio that the two ministries were convening their workers for a meeting at the Kigali prefecture. Between 50 and 80 persons attended, including Gaillard, Renzaho and the ministers. The event took place at the conference room of the Kigali-Ville prefecture office. Renzaho was not involved in convening the meeting but provided the venue at the prefecture office.[401] The witness was not present, but heard the details of the meeting afterwards. He did not accompany any truck that was then used to transport bodies. Subsequently, the prefecture office took over all the sanitation operations.[402]

---

[397] Witness UB first said that Renzaho sent a "vehicle" (T. 23 January 2007 p. 6) and subsequently "vehicles" (*id.* pp. 58-59). The French transcript only refers to one vehicle (*id.* pp. 6, 62), which is the version chosen in the text.
[398] *Id.* pp. 1, 4-6, 8-9, 11-12, 56-59; Prosecution Exhibit 69 (personal identification sheet). Witness UB was a detainee at Kigali Central Prison at the time of his testimony, awaiting the outcome of his appeal before the Supreme Court. T. 23 January 2007 pp. 1-2, 64-65.
[399] T. 22 January 2007 pp. 16-18, 47, 64; Prosecution Exhibit 68 (personal identification sheet). When testifying, Witness GLJ had been detained in Rwanda for over 12 years, awaiting trial. T. 22 January 2007 p. 13. Although the witness did not elaborate, he stated that "so whenever someone arrived at the préfecture office, he would be given a vehicle to go and pick up those bodies". *Id.* p. 17.
[400] T. 4 June 2007 pp. 3, 6-7, 37, 50; Defence Exhibit 51 (personal identification sheet).
[401] Witness BDC's assertion that Renzaho did not initiate the meeting was in answer to the following question by Defence Counsel: "Witness, did you receive information at the time stating that the collection of bodies was a manoeuvre – or, rather an activity initiated by Mr. Renzaho with the intention of concealing the results of his activity?" T. 4 June 2007 p. 10.
[402] T. 4 June 2007 pp. 4-6, 7-8, 10-11. Witness BDC did not specify when, exactly, the operation became independent of the Red Cross but it appeared to be towards the end of April 1994.

Defence Witness PGL

334. Witness PGL, a Hutu, was an employee at the Kigali-Ville prefecture and returned there to work on 11 April 1994. From then, he would meet ICRC staff while he was moving about in the neighbourhoods under his responsibility. He would show them wounded, sick, and dead persons, whom the ICRC staff would pick up in their own vehicles. The ICRC also had the means to make sure that the dead were buried. The witness was on foot and did not have a vehicle that would have enabled him to either pick up patients or transport corpses.[403]

Defence Witness PPG

335. On 19 April 1994, Witness PPG, a Hutu official, heard a *communiqué* over the radio. It requested certain civil servants, as well as employees of the Red Cross, to go to the office of the prefecture. Having returned to that office from 20 April, his work involved the collection of corpses in the streets of Kigali-Ville. The Red Cross had asked the Ministry of Public Health to assist in this effort. According to the witness, the operation was an urgent matter of public health.[404]

336. The Red Cross had assigned about eight of its own workers to supervise the operation. They gave the witness and others instructions.[405] There were not more than about 30 civil servants participating in the activity. Moving from area to area, they worked in one group together with the Red Cross staff and used two vehicles in the operation. The first belonged to a trader who had parked his vehicle at the prefecture office, and the second was a truck from MINITRAP. The dead bodies that were picked up were buried in Nyamirambo cemetery. The witness had never heard of any mass graves. The group was engaged in the **[page 93]** clean-up operation for half of the month of April, through May and stopped about midway through June 1994.[406]

Defence Witness UT

337. Witness UT, a Hutu official in the Kigali-Ville prefecture testified that the service for sociocultural affairs took part in collecting and burying the bodies of people who had been killed. It collaborated with the Red Cross to come up with ways of preventing epidemics due to the corpses that were strewn about, improvising to find places to bury people. Because the service had limited resources, it requested help from the Ministry of Public Works, which had the necessary vehicles and other equipment that was used to dispose of the bodies. The Red Cross had already been in consultations with the prefect by telephone or other means before the witness arrived at the prefecture on 11 April 1994.[407]

4.3.3 Deliberations

338. In its Closing Brief, the Prosecution refers briefly to vehicles, alleging that Renzaho facilitated the movement of *Interahamwe* and other groups participating in the killings.[408] Paragraphs 13 and 30 of the Indictment do not specifically mention this element, which is not included in the Pre-Trial Brief. It is clear that the use of vehicles cannot form the basis of a conviction. The Chamber nonetheless finds it useful to address this issue.

339. The first element of the Prosecution submissions is general in nature and relates to the provision of vehicles to administrative (communal) authorities. The Chamber notes that no witness gave incriminating evidence about such assistance.

---

[403] T. 6 June 2007 pp. 15-16, 18, 20; Defence Exhibit 61 (personal identification sheet).
[404] T. 18 June 2007 pp. 45, 49, 51, 58; Defence Exhibit 65 (personal identification sheet).
[405] T. 18 June 2007 p. 52; T. 19 June 2007 p. 3.
[406] T. 18 June 2007 pp. 52, 55-58. The Chamber recalls that MINITRAP stands for Ministry of Public Services.
[407] T. 24 May 2007 pp. 20, 22, 26, 41-42; Defence Exhibit 47 (personal identification sheet).
[408] Prosecution Closing Brief paras. 144-145.

340. The second contention concerns the prefecture office's ability to supply vehicles for the transportation of prisoners in order to assist in removing and burying bodies from the streets of Kigali, and to requisition vehicles from other government departments. The Defence acknowledges that Renzaho participated in removing bodies in Kigali but emphasises that he never had the intention to hide the evidence from international view. This submission is prompted by a remark in the report of the Prosecution Expert Witness, Alison Des Forges.[409] The Prosecution Closing Brief does not address this, nor was it put to Renzaho during cross-examination.

341. The evidence confirms that Renzaho directed state government employees to report to the prefecture office through a radio broadcast made on 10 April 1994. The following day, there were many vehicles parked at the prefecture office. Renzaho chaired a meeting at his office and instructed those present, including employees of the Ministries of Public Works **[page 94]** and Public Health, to clear bodies from Kigali-Ville. Staff from the prefecture's sanitation unit, the two state ministries and the ICRC participated in the clean-up operation. Prefecture office vehicles also transported prisoners from Kigali main prison to assist. Witness UL gave first-hand, credible and detailed testimony about this, several aspects of which were corroborated by Witnesses UB, GLJ, BDC and PPG.[410]

342. The Chamber observes that the removal of bodies from the streets of Kigali would certainly have the effect of improving the international community's impression of the situation.[411] However, it would also have the effect of mitigating the public health risk. Therefore, concealment cannot be considered the only reasonable motive for the clean-up operation. The initiative and participation of the ICRC in the task strengthen the notion that hygiene was a significant factor in the decision-making process.[412]

343. That said, the entire operation shows a level of organisation within the Kigali-Ville prefecture, and a degree of co-ordination with other government services as well as the medium of radio that demonstrates Renzaho's control over resources, both human and material, after 6 April 1994. It goes against the idea argued elsewhere by the Defence that, after the President's plane was shot down, total chaos and anarchy reigned in Kigali-Ville, which became uncontrollable, and that the only authority that the prefect had was over the prefecture office staff.[413] **[page 95]**

5. KILLINGS AT AKAJAGALI, 8 OR 9 APRIL 1994

5.1 Introduction

344. The Prosecution alleges that, on or about 9 April 1994, Renzaho, while dressed in the uniform of a senior military official, led or accompanied armed *Interahamwe* at Akajagali in Kanombe. The *Interahamwe* entered houses of Tutsis and killed the Tutsis who resided there. Reference is made to Witness DBN.[414] The

---

[409] Prosecution Exhibit 94 (expert report of Alison Des Forges) p. 13 ("As the prefect of Kigali-city, Tharcisse Renzaho was extremely conscious of the need for a "good image," for the country, one that rested in large part on what foreigners saw and heard in visiting the national capital. According to former prime minister Kambanda, Renzaho directed people to avoid talking about massacres and said that "ministers should always present a good image of the country when talking on the radio rather than what they really saw." Soon after the killing began, Renzaho organized a cleanup of bodies from the city streets, no doubt aware of the bad impression that the proof of killing left on journalists and other foreign visitors. A large amount of resources were devoted to a speedy removal of thousands of bodies and to their burial in an empty field outside the city". (citations omitted)).
[410] As mentioned in II.4.3, the ICRC provided fuel for the operation.
[411] The Chamber does not find it necessary to assess the purported remark by Bizimungu during the meeting on 11 April 1994, as mentioned by Witness UL. Bizimungu is not on trial in the present case and the witness was not cross-examined about this.
[412] The Chamber has noted the Defence submission that viewing the clean-up operation as an attempt to hide the killings from international view would be an example of "tunnel vision" ("the single-minded and overly narrow focus on a particular investigative technique or prosecutorial theory, so as to reasonably colour the evaluation and one's conduct in response to that information"). Defence Closing Brief paras. 321, 327-330.
[413] Defence Closing Brief paras. 346-348, 757-758, 1159, 1269.
[414] Indictment paras. 15, 32; Prosecution Closing Brief paras. 181-191. The Indictment refers to "Kajari", the Prosecution Closing Brief uses "Kajagari" and the Defence Closing Brief, "Akajagari". The Chamber will use the name "Akajagali". T. 1 February 2007 p. 26. See also *Bagosora et al.* Trial Judgement (see, for instance, para. 797).

Defence argues that his uncorroborated testimony is unreliable. It refers to Witnesses MAI, ABC, VDD and AIA.[415]

5.2 Evidence

Prosecution Witness DBN

345. Witness DBN, a Tutsi, was in the paracommando battalion in Kanombe in April 1994. He knew Renzaho as a member of that battalion before being appointed prefect of Kigali-Ville prefecture. On 8 or 9 April 1994, the witness left the military camp to deliver supplies to soldiers. At almost noon, he saw Renzaho in a vehicle going towards the Akajagali neighbourhood in Kanombe. The witness followed directly behind Renzaho's white Hilux four-wheel drive vehicle, which carried between 20 and 30 *Interahamwe* wearing *kitenge* uniforms. They were singing, whistling and chanting "*tubatsembe tsembe*", which meant "let's exterminate these *Inyenzi Inkotanyi*".[416]

346. Renzaho stopped in Akajagali on a narrow road and the *Interahamwe* alighted. The witness was driving a large truck and had to stop behind. The prefect stood not far from his car, which was about three metres away from the witness's vehicle. Armed with spears, machetes and clubs, the *Interahamwe* went from house to house, entering by force and breaking down doors and windows.[417]

347. Witness DBN could not see what the *Interahamwe* were doing inside the houses, but because he was aware of the circumstances at the time, he understood that they were hunting down Tutsis. He knew a number of the Tutsis living in those residences. The witness then observed the *Interahamwe* beat three persons with their clubs, saying that they had just found Tutsis in the houses and that they would have to search all the houses, even the ones with open doors. He was about five to 10 metres away from them.[418]

348. Renzaho was standing near his car, watching everything. He moved his vehicle so that the witness could leave, and then remained standing there. The witness went on to make his **[page 96]** food delivery, staying about 10 minutes at the delivery site. On the way back, he used the same road and saw that the *Interahamwe* were still there, moving around in the neighbourhood. Renzaho and his vehicle were in the same place. The witness did not try to learn what had happened to the three persons he had seen being beaten up, but stated that "it was obvious that they would not survive". Renzaho's house was located about 100 metres from the road that goes through the Akajagali neighbourhood.[419]

Renzaho

349. Renzaho denied having gone to Kanombe to attack Tutsis in Akajagali on 9 or 10 April 1994. On the morning of 8 April, he took part in a short meeting of what he referred to as the "crisis committee" and then an "urban security council" meeting at the Kigali-Ville prefecture office from about 9.00 a.m. to 2.00 p.m. He went to see his family in Kanombe that afternoon and returned at about 5.00 p.m. On 9 April, he went to the embassy of Zaire at 11.00 a.m. In the afternoon, his family joined him from Kanombe and he helped them settle in at Hotel Kiyovu.[420]

Defence Witness MAI

350. Witness MAI, a Hutu, is related to the Renzaho family and helped run a business in Kanombe in April 1994. He arrived at Renzaho's Kanombe home on 7 April 1994 and remained there all day on 8 April. The

---

[415] Defence Closing Brief paras. 583-593. Witness AIA is mentioned in a general section about Renzaho's conduct during the events in 1994 (para. 1273).
[416] T. 29 January 2007 pp. 55-59, 67-69; Prosecution Exhibit 74 (personal identification sheet). Witness DBN believed that Renzaho's Hilux belonged to the Kigali-Ville prefecture because administrative vehicles had different number plates from those belonging to private individuals.
[417] T. 29 January 2007 pp. 60-61, 70-71. Witness DBN made a map of the scene. Prosecution Exhibit 75 (sketch).
[418] *Id.* pp. 61, 71.
[419] *Id.* pp. 61-62, 66-67.
[420] T. 27 August 2007 pp. 60-61, 63-64; T. 28 August 2007 pp. 8, 43-44; T. 29 August 2007 pp. 60-61.

witness, who was sick in bed, did not see Renzaho at home on 8 April, but met him at the Kigali-Ville prefecture office on 9 April. The family arrived there at an unspecified time and remained in Renzaho's office for less than 30 minutes before leaving to take refuge at Hotel Kiyovu.[421]

Defence Witness ABC

351. Witness ABC, a Hutu related to the Renzaho family, stated that the family lived in Kanombe, in Akajagali, about one kilometre away from the military camp in that area. On 8 April 1994, Renzaho came back to his family residence in the afternoon, stayed for a limited time, changed his clothes and left again, dressed in military attire. He did not return that night. According to the witness, Renzaho stayed the night of 8 April at the Kigali-Ville prefecture office.[422]

352. The next day, on 9 April, the Renzaho family left Kanombe and arrived at the Kigali-Ville prefecture office around noon. Renzaho and his wife talked there for one to one and a half hours before the family left to seek refuge at Hotel Kiyovu. The witness confirmed that Witness MAI had a shop in the Akajagali neighbourhood.[423]

Defence Witness VDD

353. Witness VDD, a Hutu related to the Renzaho family, testified that on 8 April 1994, Renzaho returned for a short time to his house in Kanombe. The family left the house on 9 **[page 97]** April at noon. They arrived at the Kigali-Ville prefecture office to meet Renzaho at about 12.30 or 13.00 p.m. There, Renzaho's wife spoke with him, and the family then went to Hotel Kiyovu.[424]

Defence Witness AIA

354. Witness AIA was a member of the Kigali-Ville police force. On 8 April 1994, he attended a meeting chaired by Renzaho at the prefecture office, which started around 10.00 a.m. He did not specify when the meeting ended or what Renzaho did afterwards nor did he testify about Renzaho's whereabouts on 9 April.[425]

5.3 Deliberations

355. Witness DBN testified that he saw Tutsis being beaten by *Interahamwe* who had accompanied Renzaho in the Akajagali neighbourhood on 8 or 9 April. He was the only witness who described the events. His account is first-hand and generally consistent about Renzaho bringing *Interahamwe* to Akajagali and watching them search houses and severely beat three Tutsis.

356. According to the witness's testimony, he saw Renzaho arrive in Akajagali before noon.[426] However, his statement to Tribunal investigators in February 2000 indicates that Renzaho arrived there about 2.00 p.m. The witness explained that he might have been mistaken about the time, but that he did not believe it was 2.00 p.m. because he was making a food delivery that day, which was normally made around midday, in time for the food to be served at 2.00 p.m.[427] The Chamber finds the explanation reasonable and considers that the intervening period between the event and his testimony could explain the differences.

357. Of greater concern are inconsistencies between Witness DBN's testimony in this trial and his evidence in the *Bagosora et al.* case in 2004, where he did not refer to the beating of the three persons. Instead, he testified that the *Interahamwe* "did not find anything inside the houses"; that they "went inside those houses and then came out of them"; and that he "did not see them do anything else".[428] When this was put to him in

---

[421] T. 22 August 2007 pp. 5-7, 11, 15-16, 23; Defence Exhibit 76 (personal identification sheet).
[422] T. 17 May 2007 pp. 26-27, 29-30, 34, 39-40 42, 56; Defence Exhibit 42 (personal identification sheet).
[423] *Id.* pp. 40-42, 47.
[424] T. 18 May 2007 pp. 5, 9, 17-18; T. 22 May 2007 pp. 4, 7.
[425] T. 2 July 2007 pp. 6, 21-24, 35, 51, 54; T. 3 July 2007 pp. 4, 17-18; Defence Exhibit 66 (personal identification sheet).
[426] T. 29 January 2007 pp. 57, 67.
[427] *Id.* pp. 67-68; Defence Exhibit 17 (statement of 25 February 2000).
[428] Defence Exhibit 19 (*Prosecutor v. Bagosora et al.*, T. 1 April 2004) p. 59.

the present proceedings, he acknowledged having withheld the information regarding the beatings in his previous testimony, as he did not want that information to be revealed to Renzaho prior to his trial. The witness further explained that he believed that the oath to tell the whole truth before the Chamber meant that he would tell the whole truth only "within the context of that case". He stated, "when I came to testify I understood that I have to testify only about the soldiers who were involved in that case – and that I was going to testify at length on Renzaho in his presence".[429]

358. The Chamber accepts that Witness DBN may have provided few details in relation to Renzaho's purported role at Akajagali, as he was not the focus of the witness's testimony in the *Bagosora et al.* case. Relatively few questions were asked that dealt directly with **[page 98]** Renzaho. Nonetheless, the witness's account in the prior proceedings did not simply omit evidence relevant to Renzaho's culpability but explicitly asserted that the witness did not observe anything occur there.[430] This is materially inconsistent with his testimony in the present case as well as his prior statement of February 2000. His explanation for having omitted this significant event involving Renzaho creates doubts about his reliability.[431]

359. The Chamber has assessed the Defence evidence but does not find that it refutes Witness DBN's testimony about the alleged events round noon on 8 or 9 April 1994. Witness AIA stated that Renzaho was in a meeting at 10.00 a.m. at the prefecture office on 8 April, but did not give an account of Renzaho's movements during the remainder of that day or the following day. Witness ABC said that Renzaho returned to his residence in the afternoon of 8 April and stayed for a limited time. Witness VDD also testified that Renzaho came back to the residence briefly on 8 April but did not specify at what time. None of the witnesses saw Renzaho at the Kigali-Ville prefectural office before noon on 9 April.[432]

360. Notwithstanding the weaknesses in the Defence evidence, Witness DBN's testimony remains doubtful and is not corroborated.[433]

361. Consequently, the Prosecution has failed to prove beyond reasonable doubt that on 8 or 9 April 1994, Renzaho led a group of armed *Interahamwe* to a neighbourhood in Akajagali, where the *Interahamwe* forcibly entered houses and severely beat or killed three Tutsis in his presence. In view of this finding, there is no need to consider the Defence submissions about lack of notice.[434] **[page 99]**

6. ATTACK AT CELA, 22 APRIL 1994

6.1 Introduction

362. The Indictment states that, between 7 April and 17 July 1994, thousands of Tutsis took refuge in *Centre d'étude de langues africaines* ("CELA"), Saint Paul pastoral centre and Sainte Famille church, which were in immediate proximity to each other. On or about 22 April, Renzaho, while in the company of *Conseiller* Odette Nyirabagenzi, *Interahamwe* leader Angeline Mukandutiye, Father Wenceslas

---

[429] T. 29 January 2007 pp. 74-75.
[430] Defence Exhibit 17 (statement of 25 February 2000) p. 1: "The *Interahamwe* who were in his vehicle came out of the vehicle, entered the houses of Tutsis and massacred them in the presence of Renzaho."
[431] Other inconsistencies also emerge drawing into question Witness DBN's alleged first-hand observations. In the *Bagosora et al.* trial, he affirmed that Renzaho was driving slowly by and that the *Interahamwe* only stopped the vehicle and got in *after* they exited the houses: Defence Exhibit 19 (*Prosecutor v. Bagosora et al.*, T. 1 April 2004 p. 60). In the present case, the witness made no mention of the *Interahamwe* getting back in the vehicle; rather, on his way back after the food delivery, he saw Renzaho standing at the same location while the *Interahamwe* were still going from house to house.
[432] The Chamber notes some differences among the testimonies of these Defence witnesses: Witness MAI stated that the family remained at the prefectural office for less than 30 minutes, while Witness ABC indicated that the duration was one to one and a half hours. Witness ABC stated that the family saw Renzaho at the prefectural office around noon, while Witness VDD stated it was around 12.30 or 1.00 p.m. The Chamber finds these discrepancies to be minor.
[433] The Chamber notes that in *Bagosora et al.*, the Trial Chamber refused to rely on Witness DBN's evidence where uncorroborated. *Bagosora et al.* Trial Judgement paras. 856, 862-863, 929, 1462-1463, 1582-1585.
[434] Although paragraphs 15 and 32 of the Indictment allege only that Tutsis were killed, the Prosecution submits that its Pre-Trial Brief gave clear notice to the Defence that this allegation encompassed the causing of serious bodily or mental harm. (Prosecution Pre-Trial Brief paras. 63-65). However, in light of the finding in the *Karera* Appeal Judgement, a Pre-Trial Brief cannot cure an indictment if, as in this case, it is filed before the indictment (the Pre-trial Brief was filed on 31 October 2005, while the Amended Indictment was filed on 16 February 2006). See *Karera* Appeal Judgement, para. 368.

Munyeshyaka, soldiers and *Interahamwe* ordered the removal of about 60 Tutsi men from CELA. He also instigated targeted killings of persons from there, including Charles, Wilson and Déglote Rwanga. His subordinates allegedly took the men away and caused their deaths. On other dates, Renzaho ordered and instigated the murder of many other Tutsis at CELA. The Prosecution relies on Witnesses BUO, UI, ACS, ATQ, HAD, ACK and ALG.[435]

363. The Defence argues that insufficient notice was provided in the Indictment and that the Prosecution evidence is inconsistent with it. Renzaho went to CELA on 22 April 1994, but his aim was to protect those threatened there. Reference is made to Witnesses WOW, KRG, UT and PPV.[436]

6.2 Evidence

Prosecution Witness BUO

364. Witness BUO, a Hutu, joined the *Interahamwe* militia in Rugenge sector in Kigali on 8 or 9 April 1994, whose headquarters were at the home of its leader Angeline Mukandutiye. On 21 April, the witness saw Renzaho and Major Laurent Munyakaze arrive at Mukandutiye's house in a Presidential Guard red Hilux pickup truck. They were escorted by around six gendarmes. Renzaho, who was in a black suit, and Munyakaze, in military attire, entered Mukandutiye's house to speak with her. A few firearms, including Kalashnikovs, bullets and grenades, were offloaded from the rear of the pickup into Mukandutiye's house and 12 weapons were distributed to *Interahamwe*. Subsequently, Mukandutiye, in the presence of Renzaho and Mukandutiye, "asked" those present to go to CELA.[437]

365. Munyakaze and Renzaho were already at CELA when the witness arrived, and Major Patrice Bivamvagara, an officer in the Rwandan army, joined them shortly thereafter. **[page 100]** Renzaho remained at the entrance to CELA in a vehicle with Munyakaze. Bivamvagara gave an order to loot the cars inside the centre's compound. Two gendarmes guarding the entrance refused to allow the *Interahamwe* in and were shot on the orders of an *Interahamwe* leader named Claude. Renzaho, Munyakaze and Bivamvagara were present at this time. No one else was killed. Four vehicles were stolen from CELA. Some were "appropriated from the owners" and the cables of others were cut in order to start them. The vehicles were taken to Mukandutiye's home and later used to ferry victims to be killed or to transport *Interahamwe* during their operations.[438]

366. On the morning of 22 April, the witness was at Mukandutiye's house with other *Interahamwe*. Renzaho arrived in a military jeep, with a driver and two soldiers. *Conseiller* Odette Nyirabagenzi arrived at the same time. Two pickups, one carrying Major Munyakaze also arrived. Renzaho and Nyirabagenzi entered Mukandutiye's home and met with her for about 15 minutes. When they exited, Mukandutiye gave some instructions to the *Interahamwe* in the presence of Renzaho and Nyirabagenzi, and Renzaho told them to go to CELA and await further orders there. The witness distributed a G3, eight Kalashnikovs and three R4's firearms; others had weapons from the day before. The *Interahamwe*, including Claude, boarded a vehicle and left as did Renzaho, Nyirabagenzi, Mukandutiye and Munyakaze. The witness counted those who had remained to ensure that the headquarters were secured and began walking to CELA between 8.00 or 9.00 a.m.[439]

---

[435] Indictment paras. 20-21, 36-38, 45, 49; Prosecution Closing Brief, paras. 38, 46, 60, 64-65, 102, 166, 238-268, 276, 286, 325, 347-348, 375, 391-406, 512, 515, 518, 524; T. 14 February 2008 pp. 18, 20. In its letter of 13 March of the Defence, the Prosecution conceded that it did not lead evidence relating to attacks on Kadaffi Mosque or the killing of James Rwanga, which are also mentioned in the relevant Indictment paragraphs. See also T. 15 February 2008 p. 11. It also accepted that it did not prove the specific allegation concerning Emmanuel Gihana beyond reasonable doubt. Prosecution Closing Brief para. 398.
[436] Defence Closing Brief paras. 9, 12, 15, 42-43, 52, 116, 119, 124-126, 134, 159, 173-174, 180, 183, 375, 439-529, 876-877, 1080-1086, 1196-1206, 1218-1220, 1276; Defence Exhibit 113 (*complément écrit aux arguments oraux de la défense*) paras. 452.1, 484.1-3; T. 14 February 2008 pp. 59-61.
[437] T. 25 January 2007 pp. 52, 59, 61 (quoted); T. 26 January 2007 pp. 2, 36; T. 29 January 2007 pp. 2, 6-8, 11. Prosecution Exhibit 73 (personal identification sheet). Witness BUO was convicted in Rwanda in 2003 and given a 15 year sentence for his involvement in the genocide. T. 25 January 2007 pp. 56-57; T. 29 January 2007 pp. 40-43. He was in charge of distributing weapons and would note down who took what firearm. T. 25 January 2007 p. 54; T. 26 January 2007 pp. 1, 40.
[438] T. 25 January 2007 pp. 54, 62-63; T. 29 January 2007 pp. 10-11, 13-14, 15 (quoted), 23.
[439] T. 25 January 2007 p. 55; T. 26 January 2007 pp. 1-3, 11; T. 29 January 2007 pp. 10, 16-18.

Prosecutor v. Renzaho

367. At CELA, the witness found Renzaho, Mukandutiye, Nyaribagenzi and Major Munyakaze. *Interahamwe* were extracting people from within CELA and separating men, women and children. Renzaho and Munyakaze were with Mukandituye and Nyirabagenzi in the CELA courtyard. The women, who were familiar with the inhabitants of Rugenge sector, identified persons to be removed. Others were selected if they had Tutsi features. Between 60 and 70, primarily males, were chosen from the 100 or more persons who had sought refuge at CELA. Most of these displaced persons at CELA were Tutsi neighbours of those carrying out the operation. The witness did not see any gendarmes guarding the location that day.[440]

368. The *Interahamwe* beat those who had been selected and forced them to board three vehicles, including a Hiace minibus and a double-cabin Toyota. Mukandutiye, in Renzaho's presence, instructed the witness and *Interahamwe* leader Claude to drive the selected persons to a location referred to as the "CND", which was the house of Straton Iyaremye near the Rugenge sector office.[441] It was understood by this instruction that these persons would be **[page 101]** killed. The witness and Claude passed on the instructions to other *Interahamwe*, including Michel Nkeshimana, Gasigwa, and Fidèle ("Castar") Habimana. Renzaho was present for 40 to 50 minutes and left after those who had been selected were in the vehicles. Jean Bizimana, the *bourgmestre* of Nyarugenge *commune*, arrived after the departure of officials who led the operation. Rose Murorunkwere, the wife of Charles Rwanga, approached Bizimana, asking "Where did you take our husbands?" Bizimana left without answering.[442]

369. The witness went on foot towards the CND. Along the way, he saw 15 bodies of persons who had been removed from CELA. Among the dead were Charles and Déglote Rwanga, Albert, a driver for ORINFOR, and the two children of Pierre Sebushishi. Upon arriving, the witness observed that those who had been removed from CELA were being shot and placed in a pit with a width of over two metres inside the house. Two persons jumped in to avoid being shot and a grenade was thrown into the pit. None of the 60 to 70 persons extracted from CELA survived that day. The killing concluded around 3.00 p.m. The witness and other *Interahamwe* returned to Mukandutiye's home, reporting that the task had been completed.[443]

370. Witness BUO did not see Father Wenceslas Munyeshyaka at CELA on 22 April but stated that the priest worked closely with Mukandutiye. He provided information that enabled *Interahamwe* to find and kill Tutsis at different sites, including CELA.[444]

Prosecution Witness UI

371. On 7 April 1994, Witness UI, a Tutsi, sought refuge at CELA. There he found about 200 other men, women and children who had arrived for the same reason. As other persons continued to arrive, there were about 500 refugees at CELA on 22 April. The witness had written their names on a list that he had made after one of the refugees who had worked with human rights organisations advised them to keep such a record.[445]

---

[440] T. 25 January 2007 p. 62; T. 26 January 2007 pp. 3-6; T. 29 January 2007 pp. 16, 19-20, 22-23.
[441] The "CND" was the abbreviation for the Rwandan parliament or the *Conseil National pour le Développement* and was a location where RPF soldiers had been stationed in accordance with the Arusha Accords prior to the 6 April 1994. Several witnesses testified about this, for instance, Tribunal investigator Rajesh Neupane, T. 8 January 2007 p. 34; Witness MW, T. 5 February 2007 pp. 7-8; Witness ALG, T. 11 January 2007 p. 54. However, the parliamantary building was not in Rugenge sector and "CND" was a nickname for an area containing mass graves. See, for instance, Witness ALG, T. 10 January 2007 p. 69, T. 11 January 2007 p. 54 (those removed from CELA were killed at the mass grave in Rugenge sector referred to by *Interahamwe* as the CND); Witness BUO, T. 26 January 2007 pp. 9-10; T. 29 January 2007 p. 23; Prosecution Exhibit 6 (Photographs taken by Tribunal investigator Rajesh Neupane), Photo Book III, photograph 8 (the CND site was next to the Rugenge *sector* office, at the house of a man called Straton Iyaremye; Witness ACS, T. 30 January 2007 pp. 41, 70 (the CND mass graves were at the home of a man named Iyaremye); Witness HAD, T. 1 February 2007 p. 20 (the mass grave area was called CND because the RPF had once been housed at the Rwandan parliament, and the purpose was to mock the *Inyenzi*); Witness UI, T. 5 February 2007 pp. 68, 73 (overheard that refugees taken from CELA would be brought to the CND and identified a house as the mass grave where those who had been killed were placed); Prosecution Exhibit 7 (nine photographs), photographs 6, 7 and 8 (depicting the outside of the house containing the pit in which the dead were placed).
[442] T. 26 January 2007 pp. 3-4, 5 (quoted), 6, 7 (quoted), 8-11; T. 29 January 2007 pp. 21-23; Prosecution Exhibit 6 (Photographs taken by Tribunal investigator Rajesh Neupane), Photo Book III, photograph 8.
[443] T. 25 January 2007 p. 52; T. 26 January 2007 pp. 7-12; T. 29 January 2007 p. 10.
[444] T. 29 January 2007 pp. 21, 28-30.
[445] T. 5 February 2007 pp. 52-54, 57-59, 64; T. 6 February 2007 p. 2; Prosecution Exhibit 86 (personal identification sheet).

372. Sometime between 20 and 22 April, soldiers, *Interahamwe* and many inhabitants launched an attack at CELA. The witness estimated that there were more than 600 attackers, who outnumbered the refugees. Before that attack, no one had been killed at CELA. At about 11.00 a.m., the witness was hiding in the chapel when he heard his name being called, and was told that Renzaho was searching for him. He left the chapel with a watchman and a soldier, and joined Renzaho, whom he knew from television and meetings. The prefect was standing at the main entrance of CELA with about 12 soldiers and many *Interahamwe*. The witness noticed four gendarmes in a pickup and Presidential guards in an "Iveco vehicle" on the road. Renzaho told the *Interahamwe* accompanying him not to attack immediately, saying that they were being watched by satellites, so they had to act in an intelligent manner. He **[page 102]** instructed the *Interahamwe* to choose the ringleaders amongst the refugees to bring them to the Muhima brigade to be tried before a military court.[446]

373. Renzaho asked the witness several questions, including why he was at CELA, why they were hiding *Inyenzi* or *Inkotanyi* there, and why the refugees had fled their homes. The witness denied that *Inyenzi* or *Inkotanyi* were hiding in the centre. During this time, *Interahamwe* were shouting and pushing the witness around, accusing him of lying. He gave Renzaho the list of the refugees who were at CELA, explaining to him that they were all from the neighbourhood and had identity cards.[447]

374. The prefect turned the witness over to a soldier, who said that they had heard that the refugees had dug trenches in CELA. If it was true, he would kill the witness. They went together to the courtyard and along the way, the witness said that he would give the soldier money if he saved him. No trenches were found and the soldier forced the witness to join a group of about 20 refugees who were kneeling within the CELA.

375. The soldier agreed to lead the witness to Saint Paul pastoral centre. They left CELA along OAU Boulevard and about 50 metres from CELA they met a group of women, including Rose Rwanga, who said they had been ordered to return home. The witness warned them that it was unsafe to do so. Someone called out to the soldier asking where the witness was being led and the soldier brought the witness back to the CELA compound. The witness did not look in the direction of where he had previously seen Renzaho and was not aware if he was still there.[448]

376. The witness was made to kneel again with the same group of refugees, this time for about an hour. *Interahamwe* and soldiers forced the group, which had grown to about 40 refugees, almost all Tutsis, to get up. They were placed into a white pickup with gendarmes in it and a minibus driven by and carrying *Interahamwe*. Munyeshyaka demanded and received the CELA keys from the witness once he had been loaded into the pickup. Around 10 to 12 of the attackers accompanied the refugees to the Muhima brigade, about 2 kilometres from CELA. The witness was unaware of anyone being killed at CELA.[449]

377. At the Muhima brigade, located on *Avenue de la Justice*, about 20 gendarmes took charge of the refugees. They placed the group in a cell for a few minutes and then released them to the *Interahamwe*. The refugees were loaded onto the minibus again at around 2.00 p.m. and were driven away, accompanied only by militiamen. Charles Rwanga and his two sons, Wilson and Déglote, Albert, an employee for ORINFOR, the son of Sebushishi and **[page 103]** Emmanuel Semugomwa were with the witness in the vehicle. Renzaho was not present at the brigade.[450]

378. They returned in the direction from which they came, passing CELA. In an area called *Péage*, they were stopped at a roadblock near an Ethiopian restaurant. The militiamen accompanying them told those

---

[446] T. 5 February 2007 pp. 58-61; T. 6 February 2007 pp. 11-12, 13 (quoted), 21, 26; Prosecution Exhibit 87 (sketch of CELA). Witness UI did not know what Iveco meant. T. 6 February 2007 pp. 13-14.
[447] T. 5 February 2007 pp. 59-60; T. 6 February 2007 p. 14; Prosecution Exhibit 87 (sketch of CELA) (location 1 on the sketch is where Witness UI spoke with Renzaho (T. 5 February 2007 pp. 69-70)).
[448] T. 5 February 2007 pp. 60-62; T. 6 February 2007 pp. 14-15, 17-18, 24. Witness UI marked lines on a sketch of the CELA complex to demonstrate the route he and the soldier followed out of CELA and then back into it. T. 6 February 2007 p. 17; Defence Exhibit 27 (sketch of CELA). Prosecution Exhibit 87 (sketch of CELA) (location 4 on the sketch is where the witness was made to kneel with other refugees (T. 5 February 2007 p. 70)).
[449] T. 5 February 2007 pp. 62, 64-66; T. 6 February 2007 pp. 18-19, 25-26. The son of Sebushisi and two PSD youth wing (*Abakombozi*) members were the only Hutus Witness UI identified among 40 refugees removed from CELA that day. T. 5 February 2007 pp. 65-66.
[450] T. 5 February 2007 pp. 66-68, 74; T. 6 February 2007 pp. 19-20.

manning it that they were headed to the "CND". Those at the roadblock asked for some refugees. At least 10, including Charles Rwanga, were killed after being taken out of the minibus, lined up along a hedge and shot. The witness fled in the midst of the killing and continued to hear firing as he ran from the minibus. He was later told that Emmanuel Semugomwa had also managed to escape. The witness also heard that some refugees were shot in the vehicle and that all those killed were thrown in a pit not far from the Rugenge sector office. The bodies were eventually exhumed and some of them identified.[451]

Prosecution Witness ACS

379. Witness ACS, a Tutsi, sought refuge at CELA one week after President Habyarimana's death. Between 80 and 100 persons, all of whom were Tutsi, also took refuge at CELA while he was there. On 22 April 1994, a large number of persons from his sector came at about 10.00 a.m. to "weed the bush" around CELA in order to find *Inyenzis*. Renzaho, school inspector Angeline Mukandutiye, *Conseiller* Odette Nyirabagenzi, *Bourgmestre* Jean Bizimana and Father Wenceslas Munyeshyaka arrived, as well as gendarmes, soldiers and *Interahamwe*. The witness could not remember the exact time of Renzaho's arrival, but it was before noon and the weeding had not finished. He had not seen gendarmes at CELA before those who arrived with Renzaho. The prefect arrived in a pick up truck and the witness observed two armoured vehicles.[452]

380. Renzaho asked those who were in the CELA centre hall to exit, and the refugees assembled in the courtyard. The witness was lined up with the other men. Women and children were also placed into respective lines. Renzaho handed a piece of paper to Mukandutiye, telling her to take whomever she wanted. Mukandutiye began reading out names from it, the first being Charles Rwanga, who was not immediately present. Mukandutiye told Rwanga's sons, Wilson and Déglote, to find their father if they wished their own lives to be spared. The *Interahamwe* eventually found him and made him join the other men. About 40 names were called, among them Vincent Mugiraneza, who was Tutsi. He was directed by Renzaho to go to his vehicle and did so. Other names called included Emmanuel Gihana, Albert, who worked for Radio Rwanda, Christophe Safari, Charles Gahima and Rwigamba. The selected refugees were taken away in a pickup truck in which Renzaho had arrived. Armed *Interahamwe*, including Nkeshimana, Fidèle Castar, Bwanakweri and Faustin Rwagatera, left with the truck. Renzaho did not accompany the vehicle. The operation lasted several hours after Renzaho's arrival and into early afternoon.[453] **[page 104]**

381. During the operation, Renzaho ordered the women and the approximately 20 remaining men to go home. He then left, taking Mugiraneza with him. Witness ACS, whose name had not been called, decided he could not seek refuge at Sainte Famille because Munyeshyaka, who managed it, had participated in the attack on CELA. The witness then returned home. Those who remained at CELA were subsequently killed, and CELA survivors who went to Sainte Famille were also killed there, although he did not explain how he came to know this.[454]

382. The witness later heard from a neighbour that those taken away were killed and thrown into a mass grave at the house of a man named Iyaremye. This location had been nicknamed the "CND". He knew that some of the bodies were placed in graves there because he was present when they were later exhumed and identified. The witness did not see Mugiraneza again.[455]

---

[451] T. 5 February 2007 pp. 67-69, 72-73; T. 6 February 2007 p. 21; Prosecution Exhibit 7 (nine photographs), photograph 5 (depicting the location where the roadblock was situated), photographs 6, 7 and 8 (depicting the outside of the house containing the pit in which the bodies of the dead were placed).
[452] T. 30 January 2007 pp. 28, 31, 33 (quoted), 34-37, 40, 56-57, 60-67; Prosecution Exhibit 78 (personal identification sheet). The English version errantly identifies Father Munyeshyaka as "Wenceslas Rucyaka". Compare T. 30 January 2007 p. 35 (English) and T. 30 January 2007 p. 37 (French). The Chamber relies on the French version.
[453] T. 30 January 2007 pp. 35-42, 61, 66, 68-73, 77-78.
[454] T. 30 January 2007 pp. 40-42, 69.
[455] *Id.* pp. 40-42, 70-71, 73. Witness ACS believed some refugees were killed on the way to the CND, but did not offer further details. T. 30 January 2007 pp. 70, 73.

Prosecution Witness ATQ

383. In April 1994, Witness ATQ, a Tutsi, sought refuge with family members at CELA. About 500 refugees came to CELA between 7 and 22 April 1994. Nearly all of them were Tutsis. At about 10.00 a.m. on 22 April, she observed many civilians with machetes weeding the bush around CELA. When she returned to where the refugees were staying, she noticed an *Interahamwe* at the entrance with a grenade in one hand telling persons to exit the centre. She went out with the other women and saw *Interahamwe* with their leader, Angeline Mukandutiye, as well as *Conseiller* Odette Nyirabagenzi.[456]

384. Around 10.30 a.m., Renzaho and *Bourgmestre* Jean Bizimana entered the CELA compound on foot with some gendarmes. The witness also saw two vehicles, one of which was armoured. She did not recognise Renzaho, but heard a woman exclaim that the prefect had arrived. Vincent Mugiraneza, who was near the witness, greeted Renzaho and reminded him that they were classmates. Renzaho responded by saying that, notwithstanding, Mugiraneza was "*Inyenzi*". Mugiraneza was removed from the group by an *Interahamwe* referred to as Fidèle or Castar.[457]

385. Renzaho was present for about two hours, standing with Mukandutiye and the other *Interahamwe* close by him. The witness heard Fidèle (Castar) state that Renzaho had said that women should not be killed but that they were going to kill "young people and men". Various groups were formed within the compound, including one of young men who were placed in front of the CELA buildings, to which Mugiraneza was brought. The witness's group of about 10 individuals was positioned near a garage, which allowed them to overlook the centre. Each time the *Interahamwe* found someone they had been looking for, they would **[page 105]** shout. She recalled that a man named Albert was selected. After the *Interahamwe* finished their selection, Renzaho asked everyone to return to their homes, which the witness did.[458]

386. The witness testified that persons were killed at a mass grave from which the bodies were eventually exhumed. She also heard gun shots near her home and learned that two refugees who had been taken from CELA were killed nearby. Subsequently, the witness learned that Renzaho removed Mugiraneza from the group that was later killed.[459]

Prosecution Witness HAD

387. Witness HAD, a Tutsi from Rugenge sector, sought refuge at CELA between 8 and 10 April and remained there until it was attacked on 22 April 1994. A few days earlier, "community work" had been carried out around CELA. Other persons had entered the centre posing as refugees but who were thought to be assessing the number of refugees there. These events led many refugees to believe that there would be an attack. On 22 April, while inside a room, the witness heard shouts that *Interahamwe* had launched an attack. The *Interahamwe* were beating individuals and bringing them outside. The witness was placed next to a garage not far from the CELA entrance. Renzaho arrived around noon and was among *Conseiller* Odette Nyirabagenzi and school inspector Angeline Mukandutiye. There were many *Interahamwe*, including Gisagara, Fidèle Castar, Kivide, as well as gendarmes. She recognised Renzaho from television, and *Interahamwe* told them that they were to listen to the prefect.[460]

388. Renzaho told the *Interahamwe* to separate the women and children from the men. Approximately 40 young Tutsi men were chosen. Among those selected and taken away were Charles Rwanga, his two sons Wilson and Déglote, Charles Gahima and his son, Christophe Safari and Rwigamba. During the selection

---
[456] T. 31 January 2007 pp. 60-64; T. 1 February 2007 p. 1; Prosecution Exhibit 81 (personal identification sheet). Witness ATQ mistakenly used the name Odette "Mukandutiye". T. 31 January 2007 p. 64. She later clarified that she meant *Conseiller* Odette Nyirabagenzi, whose home was close to the witness's primary school. T. 1 February 2007 p. 1.
[457] T. 31 January 2007 pp. 64-65, 66 (quoted); T. February 2007 pp. 2-4.
[458] T. 31 January 2007 p. 65 (quoted), 66-67, 69; T. 1 February 2007 pp. 2-4. Witness ACQ distinguished soldiers from gendarmes as the former wore blue or green helmets, while the latter had red berets. T. 1 February 2007 p. 2.
[459] T. 31 January 2007 pp. 67-68; T. 1 February 2007 p. 4.
[460] T. 1 February 2007 pp. 11, 12 (quoted), 13-14, 18, 21, 29, 32; Prosecution Exhibit 82 (personal identification sheet). Witness HAD testified that Renzaho was present at CELA with the "school inspector" (T. 1 February 2007 p. 12) or "Angeline" (T. 1 February 2007 p. 13). The Chamber has no doubt that in each instance the witness is referring to Angeline Mukandutiye.

process, Charles Rwanga's wife pleaded with Renzaho to free her sons. Renzaho replied that if they "had been able to get Rwanga" then they would be freed. All were removed. Renzaho told the women and children to go home, guaranteeing their security, but they protested indicating that it was not safe. This incident lasted for hours.[461]

389. Prior to the departure of the 40 refugees who had been selected, the witness observed an *Interahamwe* throw a grenade into a group of persons in the garden. Although she was unsure whether Renzaho was still present, she noted that the garden was some distance from CELA's entrance where Renzaho had been positioned. Approximately 100 individuals died, including a person named Gihana, from the blast.[462]

390. The witness went to the infirmary in the compound and did not observe the departure of the 40 persons who had been selected. About two hours later, and after hearing gunshots, she saw that the *Interahamwe* came back and looted CELA. Nearly everyone, including **[page 106]** Renzaho, had already left CELA. From her hiding place, she observed *Interahamwe* with a list and heard them say that Rwanga and his children were dead, so their names should be crossed off it. She also heard that "Vincent", whom she believed was Vincent Mugiraneza, had been taken away by Renzaho. From their conversation, she understood that most of the refugees who had left had been killed, gunned down along the road. The witness left CELA at about 3.00 p.m. that afternoon to seek refuge at Sainte Famille. The corpses of many refugees from CELA were eventually exhumed at the mass graves known as "CND", situated below the Rugenge sector office.[463]

Prosecution Witness ACK

391. Witness ACK and her family sought refuge at CELA from 9 to 22 April 1994. Between 10.30 to 11.00 a.m. on 22 April, *Interahamwe* arrived at CELA. Renzaho was present that day in military uniform, as well as gendarmes. The witness hailed from the same region as Renzaho and had previously met him in person. *Nyumba kumi* (ten household) leaders had previously organised for the bushes to be cleared around the centre. The *Interahamwe* called out names of refugees and directed them to stand near Renzaho. The witness's husband and sons were identified. The husband told Renzaho that they came from the same place, whereas the witness pleaded with Renzaho to take her in place of her children. The prefect responded that he would bring back her children.[464]

392. Renzaho, the gendarmes and the *Interahamwe* said that those who had not been selected should return to their homes. A man at the centre, who was there with Father Wenceslas Munyeshyaka, informed the witness that those who were afraid could go to Sainte Famille instead. She went there with family members who had not been selected. As the witness was leaving, she observed the refugees that had been singled out in the CELA compound and that some were being beaten. Members of her family who had been selected never returned.[465]

Prosecution Witness ALG

393. Witness ALG, a Hutu local official in Kigali-Ville prefecture, testified that, after 7 April 1994, Tutsis fled to CELA to avoid being killed. Around 20 April, a source the witness could no longer recall informed him at the prefecture office that *Interahamwe* had gone to CELA to clear the bush in that area to flush out the *Inkotanyi*. The witness went there with a policeman, believing this action was in preparation for an attack on

---

[461] T. 1 February 2007 pp. 14-16, 19-21, 30-31.
[462] *Id.* pp. 20-21, 30-32.
[463] *Id.* pp. 16 (quoted), 17, 20-21, 28, 30, 38-39.
[464] T. 5 March 2007 pp. 62-67; T. 6 March 2007 pp. 59-60; Prosecution Exhibit 95 (personal identification sheet). Witness ACK testified that "it is Renzaho who took [Vincent Mugiraneza, a Tutsi] along. It is Renzaho who knows where he put him." She did not provide further detail in relation to these statements. T. 6 March 2007 p. 66.
[465] T. 5 March 2007 pp. 64, 66-67; T. 6 March 2007 pp. 56-57, 67. According to Witness ACK, those who were selected were removed by two vehicles including a Nissan Urvan minibus. T. 5 March 2007 pp. 65-66. The basis for this is not clear as her testimony suggests that she departed from CELA before these individuals were removed from the centre. T. 5 March 2007 p. 66; T. 6 March 2007 p. 67.

the refugees there. Renzaho, who the witness believed was coming from the prefecture office, arrived at CELA immediately after the witness. *Bourgmestre* Jean Bizimana was also there.[466] **[page 107]**

394. At CELA, the witness saw Angeline Mukandutiye, the school inspector, and *Conseiller* Odette Nyirabagenzi leading the *Interahamwe* who were clearing the bushes with machetes. No gendarmes were present. He heard women refugees at CELA tell Renzaho that they feared for their safety. A group of "young people", some standing and some seated, were in CELA's courtyard. Renzaho decided that the women be moved to Sainte Famille parish, about 200 metres away. The witness accompanied them there. The last group of women from CELA arrived 15 minutes after the witness and informed him that Renzaho had handed over a group of refugees to the *Interahamwe*. Renzaho joined him at Sainte Famille about 20 minutes later. While imprisoned after the events, the witness heard from *Interahamwe* that the refugees had been killed and buried in a mass grave in Rugenge sector known as the CND.[467]

Renzaho

395. Renzaho testified that, on 22 April 1994, a gendarme called to inform him of a security issue at CELA. He asked why the gendarmes had not sought reinforcements from their superiors, and was told that they had contacted Colonel Munyakazi but that he had not come. Renzaho then called Munyakazi while in the presence of the members of the prefectoral crisis committee and asked him to intervene, but Munyakazi refused, responding that this problem was the responsibility of the civilian authority.[468]

396. Subsequently, Renzaho went to CELA in his Renault 21 with his driver and two police escorts. He arrived at about 9.00 a.m. and saw a group of about 40 persons, armed with machetes and rifles. They were cutting the grass and clearing around the trees on a hill within the CELA compound. He also observed about seven or eight gendarmes and, further down the hill, the refugees.[469] After speaking with one of the gendarmes about the situation, Renzaho approached the group of armed persons on the hill and told them that he was the prefect of Kigali town. The group reluctantly gathered around him, and a person whom he did not know asked the others to listen to Renzaho.[470]

397. During consultations with three representatives of the group, Renzaho was informed that they had come to CELA because of an incident which led to the killing of two or three of their members nearby. They believed that some of the persons staying at the centre were armed and had been firing at them. The group demanded either that CELA be secured by people permanently assigned there, or that the refugees be moved to a better-controlled site. Renzaho concluded that the refugees should be transferred to Saint Paul and Sainte Famille, as there were no permanent gendarmes posted at CELA. He told the three representatives that they had discharged their civic duties by handing the situation over to him as a security official, and that they should now all leave the centre. Furthermore, he promised that the **[page 108]** refugees would be moved to Saint Paul and Sainte Famille. When the representatives returned to the larger group, one of them relayed Renzaho's words, and the entire group of attackers reluctantly left.[471]

398. Renzaho informed some of the refugees that they would be moved to Saint Paul and Sainte Famille. He directed the first group of refugees to leave in his presence, escorted by gendarmes. Once the refugees were underway, he returned to the prefecture office at about 11.00 a.m., believing his work at CELA was

---

[466] T. 10 January 2007 pp. 55-56, 64; T. 11 January 2007 pp. 52-54; T. 12 January 2007 pp. 35-37; T. 15 January 2007 pp. 5, 14-16; Prosecution Exhibit 67 (personal identification sheet). When testifying, Witness ALG was awaiting trial in Rwanda and charged with genocide for incidents unrelated to the attack at CELA. T. 10 January 2007 p. 64; T. 15 January 2007 p. 34.
[467] T. 10 January 2007 pp. 61-62; T. 11 January 2007 p. 53 (quoted), 54 (quoted); T. 12 January 2007 pp. 38-39; T. 15 January 2007 pp. 14-15.
[468] T. 29 August 2007 pp. 9-10.
[469] T. 28 August 2007 p. 38; T. 29 August 2007 pp. 24-25, 27; T. 3 September 2007 pp. 23-26. Renzaho said that he later learned that different police officers followed him to the scene, and that other persons may also have been present but that he did not take the time to identify who was there. He also testified that, at the time, he was focussed on the attackers and only later learned that *Bourgmestre* Jean Bizimana was present.
[470] T. 29 August 2007 pp. 24-26.
[471] *Id.* pp. 27-28; T. 3 September 2007 p. 25. Renzaho stated that three persons had allegedly been killed near CELA. The group therefore thought that those staying within the centre must be firing at them.

done. At the time, Renzaho was not informed of the subsequent CELA incident. He only learned of this allegation later from external sources, which he did not specify.[472]

399. The accounts by Prosecution witnesses that Renzaho had been involved in sorting the refugees at CELA were rejected by him. He denied having spoken to any refugee individually and had never met Witness UI. Renzaho did not know members of the Rwanga family and only heard of them during the trial. He did know Vincent Mugiraneza, but denied having seen him at CELA on 22 April. Renzaho also stated that he had no special links with *conseiller* Odette Nyirabagenzi and school inspector Angeline Mukandituye. He did not see either of them, Munyeshyaka or any of the other persons mentioned in his Indictment amongst the group of attackers on 22 April.[473]

Defence Witness WOW

400. Witness WOW, a Hutu, lived in Rugenge sector near CELA in April 1994. He testified that there were refugees at the centre from 7 April. A majority of them were Tutsi and the witness would bring food to friends and neighbours. A majority of the refugees there were Tutsis. The witness denied that an attack occurred at CELA on 21 April, or that Renzaho, who drove a car he recognised, was at Angeline Mukandutiye's house that day.[474]

401. On his way to the market on 22 April, he passed by CELA at about 7.00 a.m. and saw that it was under attack. Gendarmes were trying to push the *Interahamwe* back. The witness left, went to the market and returned around 8.30 a.m. The *Interahamwe* at CELA had increased in numbers and become more violent, stating that they wanted to get the *Inyenzis* who had been firing at them during the night. The gendarmes, using "force", continued to resist them. Standing two or three metres away, he saw between 50 and 60 *Interahamwe* and three gendarmes.[475]

402. Renzaho arrived at CELA with two policemen between 8.30 and 9.00 a.m., and asked the *Interahamwe* what was happening. He tried to discourage them from continuing their attempted attack. After Renzaho spoke with the militiamen, they turned and angrily left, saying that Renzaho himself was an accomplice. On his instructions, the gendarmes called the refugees into the courtyard. The prefect told the refugees that gendarmes would **[page 109]** accompany them to Sainte Famille or Saint Paul, because he did not believe CELA was safe any longer. At around 10.00 a.m., after speaking with the refugees, Renzaho left with the two policemen in a white Renault 21. The witness, who briefly remained standing on the road, watched gendarmes accompany the refugees out of CELA, and expressed his sympathy to friends who had stayed at the centre. He returned home and the next day heard that *Interahamwe* had circumvented the prefect and killed people at CELA on 23 April. At no point did the witness see Jean Bizimana, Odette Nyirabagenzi or Angeline Mukandutiye. He had heard that Charles Rwanga was killed on 7 April by Presidential Guards but did not actually see Rwanga's body.[476]

Defence Witness KRG

403. Witness KRG, a Hutu, had sought refuge at CELA with Tutsi family members. He returned home from the centre on 8 April 1994 after *Conseiller* Odette Nyirabagenzi told the refugees that houses would be destroyed if no one was found on the premises. Because the witness was a Hutu, he could move about fairly easily and was therefore able to visit his family at the centre every day.[477]

---

[472] T. 29 August 2007 pp. 28-29.
[473] *Id.* pp. 26, 29-30, 60 ("Why would I have special links with [*Conseiller* Odette Nyirabagenzi] since there were 19 *conseillers* in the prefecture of Kigali town?"); T. 3 September 2007 pp. 25-28.
[474] T. 4 July 2007 pp. 35-36, 40-42, 45, 48, 51, 55; Defence Exhibit 69 (personal identification sheet). Witness WOW was detained in Rwanda and acquitted in December 2002. He was released from prison in January 2003. He fled Rwanda in 2005 because he was summoned to appear before a Gacaca court notwithstanding his acquittal. T. 4 July 2007 pp. 48-49, 56-57.
[475] T. 4 July 2007 pp. 41-42, 43 (quoted), 44-45, 48, 55-56.
[476] T. 4 July 2007 pp. 37, 43-46, 51-53, 57-58.
[477] T. 7 June 2007 pp. pp. 3-4, 6-13; Defence Exhibit 63 (personal identification sheet). Witness KRG was prosecuted and imprisoned in connection with the death of his neighbour's family, the events at CELA, Sainte Famille and Saint Paul. He testified that he was acquitted him of all counts, and he was released from prison in 2003. T. 7 June 2007 pp. 6, 12.

404. The first attack the witness heard about occurred on 22 April at 9.00 a.m. His housemaid came running towards his home and informed him that CELA had been attacked by *Interahamwe*. Five minutes later, he and his friends arrived at the centre in order to evacuate their family members. There, his mother told him that the refugees had been saved by Renzaho, who had driven away the attackers. She also said that Renzaho told the refugees that CELA would close from that day on because it was no longer safe. However, if families felt safe they could return home, while those who did not could go to other centres such as Sainte Famille or Saint Paul. The witness did not see Renzaho or *Interahamwe* during the incident, but heard that Renzaho left CELA immediately after giving the families these options.[478]

405. After 10 minutes at CELA, the witness decided to leave with his family at about 9.20 a.m. Charles Rwanga, his two sons, Déglote and Wilson, their sister Hyacinthe and their mother remained there. At about 3.00 or 4.00 p.m. that day, he learned from some militiamen who were manning a roadblock that the *Interahamwe* had returned to CELA the same day and killed some persons, including Charles Rwanga and his sons. He heard also heard that Rwanga's wife and daughter had been able to take refuge at Sainte Famille.[479]

Defence Witness UT

406. Witness UT, a Hutu, was an official in the Kigali-Ville prefecture and had daily contact with Renzaho from 11 April 1994 until the end of the events. On an unspecified date Renzaho told the witness that he had been forced to go to CELA in mid-April 1994 because he had been told the situation was urgent and his sub-prefect, who would normally respond to **[page 110]** such situations, was absent. Renzaho told him that "everything went well" at CELA, but that the situation had to be followed up. A day or two after this conversation, the witness went to Sainte Famille. Father Wenceslas Munyeshyaka, who was in charge there, informed him that Renzaho had made an agreement with the militia who had attacked CELA that the refugees would be moved to a safer area at Sainte Famille. The witness learned however, that some of them had been taken away during the operation, did not reach Sainte Famille and probably had been killed.[480]

Defence Witness PPV

407. Witness PPV worked in the communal police, also called the urban police, at the Kigali-Ville prefecture. He used to go to CELA after work in the evenings, and testified that Renzaho's receptionist, a Tutsi woman called Asterie Nikuze, had sought refuge there in April 1994. According to the witness, Nikuze returned to the prefecture office on 22 April. At some point, CELA was under threat, but to the best of his recollection, it was not actually attacked. He had heard that Renzaho went there after people in distress there had called on him, but he could not recall whether he himself had gone to CELA on 22 April. The witness said that he would have been surprised to hear that Renzaho had ordered, incited, or even witnessed abductions or killings at CELA, or that anyone was killed or abducted from there. He was not aware of any such incident or involvement by Renzaho, neither at CELA nor elsewhere.[481]

6.3 Deliberations

408. In support of its case as charged in the Indictment, the Prosecution led evidence of an attack on CELA on 22 April 1994 where male and female refugees were separated and between 40 and 70 men were removed and killed. Furthermore, one Prosecution witness also testified about Renzaho distributing weapons on 21 April and a subsequent attack against CELA on that day, which resulted in the death of two gendarmes guarding the centre. The Chamber has doubts as to whether the events on 21 April were charged in the

---

[478] T. 7 June 2007 pp. 1-4, 9.
[479] *Id.* pp. 5-6, 9.
[480] T. 24 May 2007 pp. 19-20, 22-23, 39, 43, 52, 56; T. 25 May 2007 p. 39; Defence Exhibit 47 (personal identification sheet).
[481] T. 4 June 2007 p. 78; T. 5 June 2007 pp. 10, 30, 52-53, 56; Defence Exhibit 56 (personal identification sheet).

Indictment.[482] However, it will consider this evidence for context and do so here, given its immediate proximity in time to the 22 April attack against CELA.[483] **[page 111]**

6.3.1 Attack on CELA, 21 April

409. Only Prosecution Witness BUO testified that, around 21 April 1994, Renzaho and Major Laurent Munyakaze distributed weapons to the *Interahamwe* at Angeline Mukandutiye's residence. This was followed by instructions to go to CELA, where, in the company of Renzaho, Munyakaze and Major Patrice Bivamvagara, *Interahamwe* led an attack at the centre. Two gendarmes were shot and killed by the militia, which also stole vehicles from the centre.

410. At the time of his testimony, Witness BUO was incarcerated, serving a 15 year sentence for his participation in crimes during the genocide.[484] The Chamber views the his testimony with caution as it may have been influenced by a desire to positively impact his circumstances in Rwanda.

411. Differences emerge in the evidence related to the weapons distribution at Mukandutiye's house on 21 April. Witness WOW, who lived near Angeline Mukandutiye, denied observing Renzaho's vehicle at her house that day.[485] While that testimony was rather general, it nonetheless creates doubt. The Chamber has also considered Witness BUO's account within the context of other incidents where Renzaho allegedly distributed weapons (II.3). This evidence does not support Witness BUO's uncorroborated evidence of Renzaho's involvement at Mukandutiye's residence on 21 April.

412. Turning to the alleged attack on CELA later that day, elements of Witness BUO's testimony raise questions about its reliability. For example, it is unclear who precisely gave the order to the *Interahamwe* to loot the vehicles at the CELA centre.[486] Of greater significance is that the witness's evidence of this particular attack finds no corroboration, notwithstanding the number of Prosecution witnesses who were refugees at the centre during the relevant period and would have been well placed to observe it. Witness ACS, who arrived at CELA approximately one week prior to 22 April, had no recollection of an incident occurring at CELA the day before 22 April.[487]

413. The Chamber realises that Witness BUO's position among the attackers may have allowed him to see more of what happened at CELA than what was within the view of those who had sought shelter there. The fact that no refugees were attacked also creates a possibility that the incident could have gone unnoticed by them. However, gendarmes were **[page 112]** shot and some cars were started after having obtained keys from their owners.[488] In the Chamber's view, it is surprising that, had such an attack occurred, only one of the six

---

[482] In its Closing Brief (para. 238-239) the Prosecution submits that Witness BUO's evidence about distribution of weapons and the ensuing attack on 21 April 1994 fall under para. 21 of the Indictment. The Chamber disagrees, as this paragraph relates to a particular attack where approximately 60 Tutsi men were removed from CELA. This view is supported by a contextual reading of the Indictment. Para. 20 alleges that thousands of Tutsis took refuge in various centres in Kigali-Ville prefecture including CELA, whereas para. 37 states that between 7 April and 17 July 1994 these refugees were subject to various attacks, including those by Renzaho's subordinates. These paragraphs function as a chapeau paragraphs. Paras. 21, 38, 45 and 49 of the Indictment offer greater specificity, clarifying that the charges against Renzaho relate to an attack on or about 22 April, where soldiers and *Interahamwe* removed and murdered 60 Tutsi men, including Charles, Wilson and Déglote Rwanga. See *Setako* Defects Decision paras. 3-5; *Gacumbitsi* Trial Judgement para. 176 and *Gacumbitsi* Appeal Judgement para. 53. Similarly, para. 12 of the Indictment, which alleges that Renzaho distributed weapons between mid-1993 and 17 July 1994 from his house and elsewhere, is too general to provide sufficient notice for the events on 21 April. Because the Pre-Trial Brief was filed prior to the Indictment, ambiguities in the Indictment cannot be cured by it. *Karera* Appeal Judgement para. 368.
[483] See *Butare* Admissibility Decision para. 15 (evidence not pleaded in the indictment may be admitted and considered to the extent it is relevant to proof of any pleaded allegation).
[484] T. 25 January 2007 pp. 56-57; T. 29 January 2007 pp. 40-43.
[485] T. 4 July 2007 p. 48.
[486] Compare T. 25 January 2007 pp. 62-63 ("*Bivamvagara* told us we had to go and take the vehicles which were at the centre.") (emphasis added) and T. 29 January 2007 p. 13 ("*They* remained in the vehicle and told us to go loot the vehicles at CELA.") (emphasis added). See also Defence Exhibit 16 (statement of 12 September 2006), which reads: "Major Bivamvagara stayed behind and ordered us to take the cars which were parked at CELA..."
[487] Witness ACS, T. 30 January 2007 pp. 33, 56-57, 62. Witness WOW was also unaware of an attack taking place at CELA on 21 April. T. 4 July 2007 p. 45.
[488] T. 29 January 2007 p. 15 ("There were other vehicles which we appropriated from the owners – for those we had the contact keys.").

witnesses present at the centre would have testified about it. Moreover, Witnesses ACS, ATQ and UI also denied that gendarmes were providing security for the centre at the time, raising further doubts that any gendarme was killed as alleged by Witness BUO.[489]

414. Consequently, the Chamber finds that it is not proven beyond reasonable doubt that Renzaho was involved in distributing weapons at Angeline Mukandutiye's house on 21 April 1994. Furthermore, the evidence does not demonstrate that an attack occurred at CELA on the same day where *Interahamwe* shot two gendarmes and looted vehicles in Renzaho's presence.

6.3.2 Attack on CELA, 22 April

415. There is no dispute that on or close to 22 April 1994, Renzaho went to CELA, and that male refugees were subsequently removed and killed.[490] The Prosecution alleges that Renzaho played a role of coordinator among assailants that included *Interahamwe* and possibly soldiers and gendarmes. The Defence submits that Renzaho averted an *Interahamwe* attack and directed refugees to move to safer locations such as Sainte Famille church or Saint Paul pastoral centre. Only after Renzaho left, and without his encouragement or knowledge, did *Interahamwe* kill refugees at CELA.

416. In addition to evidence relating to the distribution of weapons an the ensuing attack on 21 April, discussed above, the Prosecution seeks to establish Renzaho's liability for the attack at CELA on 22 April based on his meeting with *Interahamwe* immediately prior to the attack, his activities at the centre on the morning of the attack, as well as the ultimate extraction and killing of several refugees from CELA. The Chamber will address the evidence in turn.

(i)   Meeting at Angeline Mukandutiye's Residence

417. Witness BUO provided the most extensive evidence of Renzaho's cooperation and coordination with *Interahamwe* and others who attacked CELA on 22 April 1994. He testified that, immediately prior to the incident, Renzaho arrived at the house of Angeline Mukandutiye, the school inspector and local *Interahamwe* leader. The prefect was accompanied by *Conseiller* Odette Nyirabagenzi and Major Munyakaze. After Renzaho and Nyirabagenzi met with Mukandituye inside her residence, instructions were given to *Interahamwe* at the house to go to CELA, and weapons were distributed to them.

418. As discussed above (II.6.3.1), the Chamber views Witness BUO's testimony with caution. His evidence regarding this planning event at Mukandutiye's house is uncorroborated. Elements of the witness's testimony related to who gave instructions at **[page 113]** Mukandutiye's house prior to the attack, while not inconsistent, evolved.[491] His evidence about whether Renzaho arrived in the same vehicle with Nyirabagenzi is confusing.[492] The Chamber finds these differences immaterial in nature.

419. However, differences between Witness BUO's testimony about Renzaho's whereabouts prior to the 22 April attack and Witness ALG's evidence raise further doubts. Witness ALG went to CELA from the prefecture office. Although uncertain, he believed that Renzaho was at the prefecture office when he received

---

[489] Witness ACS, T. 30 January 2007 pp. 62-63; Witness ATQ, T. 1 February 2007 p. 2; Witness UI, T. 6 February 2007 p. 9.
[490] Witnesses BUO, ACS, ATQ, HAD and ACK described an attack in which refugees were removed from CELA on 22 April 1994. Witnesses ALG and UI testified that the event took place within a day or two of 22 April. Renzaho and Defence Witnesses WOW and KRG stated that Renzaho averted an attack on CELA on 22 April. The Chamber finds that the incident occurred on 22 April.
[491] T. 26 January 2007 p. 2 ("A. They spoke in the house, and a few moments later they came out, and Angeline gave us instructions in the presence of Odette Nyirabagenzi and of Tharcisse Renzaho. She told us that we were to go to the CELA centre and that we would be told exactly what we were to do when we would be there. Mr. Renzaho, Tharcisse, was the one who said that."); T. 29 January 2007 p. 17 ("So they entered into Angeline's home and held a meeting. After the meeting, we were ordered to go and attack CELA. Tharcisse Renzaho underscored that we had to go with our weapons. He knew what would happen, and we usually obeyed orders."). See also Defence Exhibit 14A (statement of 12 September 2006) p. 7 ("... Mukandutiye ordered us to go to CELA and await further orders there. Renzaho ordered us to take weapons with us...").
[492] Compare T. 26 January 2007 pp. 1-2 (testifying the Renzaho and Nyirabagenzi arrived in "a vehicle" with security personnel and a driver); T. 29 January 2009 pp. 17 (testifying that Renzaho arrived with two soldiers and a driver in a military jeep), 18 (ultimately testifying that "[w]e did not check how Nyirabagenzi arrived").

information about CELA and that Renzaho possibly had sent him there.[493] According to Witness ALG, Nyirabagenzi and Mukandutiye were leading the *Interahamwe* in clearing the bush at CELA when he arrived there.[494] In the Chamber's view, this evidence creates doubts about whether Renzaho would have been at Mukandutiye's house with Nyirabagenzi immediately before the attack and had travelled with them to the centre.

420. The Chamber concludes that the Prosecution has failed to demonstrate that Renzaho went to Angeline Mukandutiye's home prior to the attack at CELA on 22 April 1994 and gave orders to armed *Interahamwe* to go to the centre from there.

(ii)   Selection of Tutsis at CELA

421. As mentioned above, there is no dispute that Renzaho went to CELA on 22 April 1994. Those who had sought refuge and remained there until the attack were primarily Tutsi.[495] Witness BUO described Renzaho with Major Munyakaze in the courtyard of CELA, while Angeline Mukandutiye and Odette Nyirabagenzi selected between 60 and 70 males out of the approximately 100 refugees at CELA. Witness UI testified that Renzaho stood at entrance of CELA with about 12 soldiers and many *Interahamwe*. The prefect told the **[page 114]** *Interahamwe* not to attack the refugees but to choose the ringleaders amongst them and bring them to the Muhima gendarmerie brigade to be tried before a military court. Witness UI was made to kneel with a group that grew to about 40 refugees who were ultimately removed from the centre.

422. Witness ACS observed Renzaho among Mukandutiye, Nyirabagenzi, Bizimana and Father Wenceslas Munyeshyaka as well as gendarmes, soldiers and *Interahamwe*. Renzaho handed a piece of paper to Mukandutiye, telling her to take whomever she wanted. About 40 names were called, and the individuals were placed in a pick-up truck. Witness ATQ testified that Renzaho stood near Angeline Mukandutiye and other *Interahamwe* as groups were being formed, including a group of young men. She overheard an *Interahamwe* state that Renzaho had said that women should not be killed, but that they were going to kill "young people and men". According to Witness HAD, the prefect was among Nyirabagenzi and Mukandutiye, many *Interahamwe* and gendarmes. Renzaho told the *Interahamwe* to separate the women and children from the men, and approximately 40 young Tutsi men were chosen.

423. Witness ACK saw Renzaho among *Interahamwe* and gendarmes, while *Interahamwe* called out names of refugees and directed them to stand near Renzaho. Witness ALG testified that Renzaho arrived at CELA after Mukandutiye and Nyirabagenzi, who led the *Interahamwe* in clearing the bushes. He observed a group of "young people", some standing and some seated, in CELA's courtyard and later heard that Renzaho had delivered a group of refugees to *Interahamwe*.

424. The Prosecution evidence implicates Renzaho in varying degrees in the separation and extraction of refugees. Notwithstanding any differences, the evidence consistently portrays Renzaho operating as an authority, alongside Nyirabagenzi and Mukandutiye, during the separation process. Witnesses BUO and ACK primarily portrayed Renzaho as overseeing the operation from a distance.[496] Witnesses ACS and HAD,

---

[493]   T. 11 January 2007 p. 53; T. 12 January 2007 pp. 36-38; T. 15 January 2007 pp. 5, 16.
[494]   T. 11 January 2007 p. 53.
[495]   See, for instance, Witness BUO, T. 26 January 2007 pp. 3 (referring to meeting Tutsi refugees at the CELA centre), 4 ("Most of them were Tutsis ..."); Witness ACS, T. 30 January 2007 p. 40 ("For me, he was a Tutsi, because his family had been exterminated ... All of us at CELA centre were of the same ethnicity."); Witness ATQ, T. 31 January 2007 pp. 60 ("[On 7 April], when we went to [CELA], we were a mixture of Hutus and Tutsis, but some days later, the Hutus understood what was happening and decided to go back home ..."), 61 ("Q. Now, you said that when you first went to CELA, there were lots of people who went with you, and they were a mixture of Hutu and Tutsi. Was that the same as at the 21st of April 1994? A. I told you that the days following our arrival at the place – at that place, people started understanding the situation and the Hutus started moving home ... And I will say that on the 21st, it was no longer a mix of Tutsis and Hutus. Even if there were Hutus, the few Hutus who were at the centre were opponents to the regime. Because as at that date, the people understood the prevailing situation."); Witness ALG, T. 11 January 2007 p. 52 ("The people who sought refuge at CELA were generally Tutsi, Tutsi who were fleeing in order not to be killed."); Witness WOW, T. 4 July 2007 p. 53 ("[T]he majority of people who had sought refuge [at CELA] there were Tutsi.").
[496]   Witness BUO, T. 29 January 2007 pp. 19-20 ("[Mr. Renzaho and Mr. Munyakaze] were standing in the courtyard of CELA and they did not speak to the refugees since they had come animated with ill intentions. They had arrived there with the objective of committing killings. ... But how could the refugees have talked to them when we were beating them up and when we were leading them to their deaths? The refugees could not even have approached them. We were the ones who were beside them, and we were the

on the other hand, depicted the prefect as having a much more active role, speaking to refugees and offering instructions to attackers.[497] Likewise, Witness UI described Renzaho instructing *Interahamwe* to remove [page 115] ringleaders among the refugees and interrogating the witness.[498] Witness ATQ did not hear Renzaho but described *Interahamwe* repeating his instructions that women were not to be killed but that they would kill "young people and men".[499] The fundamental features of this evidence demonstrate that Renzaho held a position of authority, and at a minimum, oversaw *Interahamwe* and possibly soldiers and gendarmes, in executing this highly coordinated operation directed at separating Tutsi men from women and children.[500]

425. The Defence points to evidence that Renzaho sought to prevent an *Interahamwe* attack on CELA that day by sending refugees to Sainte Famille and Saint Paul. It also led evidence that he was not involved nor was he present during a subsequent attack on refugees who had remained at CELA by *Interahamwe*.

426. In particular, Renzaho and Witness WOW testified that Renzaho confronted *Interahamwe* who had gathered there, that they left after his consultation without removing anyone, and that he directed the remaining refugees to Sainte Famille and Saint Paul and facilitated the transfer of them. According to Witness KRG, he arrived at CELA shortly after 9.00 a.m. on 22 April, where he found his mother. She informed him that Renzaho had driven *Interahamwe* away and told the refugees that they could either return home, or to Sainte Famille or Saint Paul. Furthermore, he testified that there were no *Interahamwe* at the centre when he arrived there shortly after 9.00 a.m., and that he saw Charles Rwanga, his wife, sons and daughters at CELA. Witnesses UT provided a second-hand account that Renzaho successfully facilitated the movement of refugees to Sainte Famille, although he heard that some had been taken away and probably killed.

427. Elements of this evidence are consistent with Prosecution evidence. Witness ALG testified that women at CELA were led to Sainte Famille based on a decision made by Renzaho, and he did not observe anyone else being removed. Likewise, Witnesses ACK and UI suggested that women had left CELA and Witness ACK had gone to Sainte Famille prior to anyone being removed by attackers. Notwithstanding, the Defence evidence fails to meaningfully address the credible, largely consistent and abundant Prosecution evidence suggesting that while Renzaho was ordering certain refugees to leave – women in particular – he was also working in coordination with assailants who were separating males from females.

428. The Chamber views Renzaho's evidence with scepticism. It appears unconvincing when viewed in light of the entire record. In addition to direct evidence of his involvement in the separation process at Saint Famille, circumstantial evidence supports a finding that Renzaho would participate in and condone the separation process at CELA that day. For example, he claimed to respond to a situation where armed civilians were removing bushes around a centre where refugees gathered. However, less than two weeks earlier,

---

ones to sort out those refugees that were to be killed. And let me specify that they had not come there to talk to the refugees. They had come there, rather, to supervise the selection of those among the refugees who were to be put to death. And it was not out of pity that they were there."); Witness ACK, T. 5 March 2007 pp. 63-64 ("… *Interahamwe* came to the centre … There were gendarmes, as well, and the *Préfet* Renzaho. They called out these children and others and took them further away. I did not see them again … They were calling out people and asked us to get close to where Mr. Renzaho was standing …").

[497] Witness ACS, T. 30 January 2007 pp. 35 ("A. … After the arrival of the préfet at the CELA centre, he asked that all those in the CELA centre hall should get out."), 37 ("Q. Now, Witness, once you were lined up, were did anyone give any instructions or what happened? A. After lining us up, Préfet Renzaho personally gave instructions. And I think he remembered that very well. He was the one directing that attack. He had a piece of paper in his hand, which piece of paper he handed to Angeline Mukandituye, who was a schools inspector for Nyarugenge commune. That list was read out and Renzaho said, 'Take whoever you want.'"); Witness HAD, T. 1 February 2007 p. 14 ("I was not as close as the others. But when I got there, [the prefect] was saying that people had to be sorted out. That women and children had to be put on one side, and young men on the other side.").

[498] T. 5 February 2007 pp. 59 (discussing the questions Renzaho asked Witness UI), 59-60 ("When I arrived, the préfet was telling [*Interahamwe*] not to attack the refugees immediately. And I remember that he told them not to help the enemy. He was telling them that everything that was being done was being observed by the satellites and that as a consequence had to act in an intelligent manner. He gave instructions to them and he told them to choose amongst the refugees the ring leaders … And he said that the ringleaders were to be taken to the Muhima Brigade and be tried before a military court. But, in fact, he was not doing that because he wished to save those who were staying at the centre.").

[499] T. 31 January 2007 pp. 65-66 ("After speaking a few words to one another, Fidéle left that group [composed of Angeline Mukandutiye, Renzaho and *Interahamwe*] and moved a few metres away towards us. Then he said, 'Renzaho has said we should not kill men and women. We are going to kill young people and men.'").

[500] Witnesses BUO, ACS, HAD, ATQ, UI and ACK testified that *Interahamwe* and gendarmes were present and participating. Witnesses ACS and UI also testified that soldiers were involved.

673

Renzaho **[page 116]** expressly called for the public to engage in this very activity in order to confront the *Inyenzi*.[501]

429. Witness WOW corroborated Renzaho's evidence that the prefect managed to get them to leave and departed prior to the removal of any refugees. The Chamber recalls that, at the time of his testimony, the witness was a fugitive, having fled from Rwanda after being called before Gacaca proceedings. He explained that he had previously been acquitted through formal proceedings and did not want to face a trial controlled by members of the community.[502] He was alone in suggesting that Renzaho quelled an *Interahamwe* attack in progress. Moreover, his account that Mukandutiye, Nyirabagenzi and Bizimana were not present during the attack is in stark contrast with several other testimonies. In the Chamber's view, these differences make his reliability doubtful in the present context.

430. Furthermore, the evidence of Defence Witnesses KRG, UT and PPV concerning Renzaho's activities at CELA are second-hand, of limited probative value and does not weaken the Prosecution case.[503] For instance, Witness KRG's account, which corroborates the testimony of Renzaho and Witness WOW, does not create doubt when compared to the Prosecution first-hand evidence.

431. Having pointed out weaknesses in the Defence evidence, the Chamber recognises that elements among the Prosecution testimonies differ. For example, witnesses gave different accounts about conversations with prominent personalities during the event.[504] Evidence concerning the persons in Renzaho's company at CELA shifts.[505] In the Chamber's view, these differences are immaterial. They may be the result of varying vantage points during a chaotic and traumatic event or the passage of time.

432. Other details, which are of greater importance, are of questionable reliability. For example, Witness BUO omitted any mention of Major Munyakaze's presence at Mukandutiye's house or at the subsequent attack during his examination-in-chief but testified about his presence of both when being cross-examined.[506] No other witness mentioned Munyakaze's presence. **[page 117]**

433. Only Witness HAD testified that a grenade was thrown into a group of refugees at the CELA centre. This evidence was also elicited during cross-examination, based on a statement to Tribunal investigators in August 2000. It states that a grenade was thrown into a "men's group killing about a hundred of them". Her testimony about this incident was imprecise, only identifying one person – Gahina – among the dead.[507] The reliability of this account is questionable, particularly in light of the fact that well placed Prosecution

---

[501] Prosecution Exhibit 50 (transcript of Radio Rwanda interview, 12 April 1994) p. 9 ("I would like to request of them that now each quarter should try to organise itself and make communal work within the quarters by cutting off bushes, searching empty houses, check out in the nearby swamp if no *Inyenzi* hid inside. They must cut those bushes, check in the gutters, in houses overgrown with weeds.").

[502] T. 4 July 2007 pp. 48-49, 56-57.

[503] In particular, Witness PPV's evidence appears to attempt to distance himself from the attack. His testimony that he was not present at CELA appears to contradicts Renzaho's statement of April 1997. T. 3 September 2007 pp. 22-23; Prosecution Exhibit 114 B (statement of 29 April 1997) pp. 11-12.

[504] The Chamber has considered these differences but will not address them expressly, as they tend to identify protected witnesses.

[505] Compare Witness BUO, T. 26 January 2007 pp. 3-4, 7; T. 29 January 2007 p. 22 (testifying that *Bourgmestre* Jean Bizimana arrived after Renzaho had departed) and Witnesses ALG, T. 12 January 2007 p. 37 (Bizimana arrived at CELA prior to Renzaho and was present when he was there), Witness ACS, T. 30 January 2007 p. 42 (Bizimana was present with Renzaho), Witness ATQ, T. 31 January 2007 p. 64 (Renzaho and Bizimana entered the CELA compound on foot together); Compare Witnesses UI, T. 5 February 2007 pp. 64-65, Witness ACS, T. 30 January 2007 pp. 35, 68, Witness ACK, T. 5 March 2007 p. 61 (Father Wenceslas Munyeshyaka was present at CELA) and Witness BUO, T. 29 January 2007 p. 21 (did not see Munyeshyaka).

[506] Compare T. 26 January 2007 pp. 1-2 (Renzaho arrived at Mukandutiye's residence with Nyirabagenzi, his escorts and a driver, without mentioning Munyakaze), pp. 3-5, 7 (describing Renzaho with Mukandutiye and Nyirabagenzi, as well as Jean Bizimana's appearance at CELA, without mentioning Munyakaze) and T. 29 January 2007 pp. 16 (Munyakaze was with Renzaho during the attack against CELA and suggesting that he stated this in his direct examination and in a prior statement), 17 (describing Munyakaze in a pickup at Mukandutiye's home prior to the attack), 19 (Munyakaze was with Renzaho in the CELA courtyard during the separation process). See also Defence Exhibit 14A (statement of 12 September 2006) p. 7 (mentioning Munyakaze's presence at CELA but not at Mukandutiye's home immediately beforehand).

[507] Defence Exhibit 25B (statement of 22 August 2000) p. 3; T. 1 February 2007 pp. 30-32.

witnesses did not offer any evidence in corroboration. Furthermore, the Chamber notes that Witness ACS did not to mention Renzaho's involvement in the attack at CELA in two statements to Rwandan authorities.[508]

434. In the Chamber's view, frailties among these parts of the Prosecution evidence do not undermine the fundamental features concerning the attack. The Chamber finds it established beyond reasonable doubt that Renzaho was present at CELA on 22 April 1994. Based on the direct and circumstantial evidence, the only reasonable conclusion is that he, by his own actions and through the assistance of Angeline Mukandutiye and Odette Nyirabagenzi, ordered *Interahamwe* to engage in a targeted selection of Tutsi men, who were separated from women and children.

435. Turning to other prominent individuals that allegedly were present, the Chamber has doubts about the nature and extent of Father Wenceslas Munyeshyaka's role. While Witness BUO suggests that Munyeshyaka generally facilitated crimes committed by *Interahamwe*, he did not see him at CELA on 22 April. It is noted that Renzaho also denied he was present. Furthermore, Witnesses UI, ACS and ACK did not provide sufficient detail regarding the nature of his purported involvement or the effect of his presence. As regards *Bourgmestre* Jean Bizimana of Nyarugenge commune, the testimonies of Witnesses BUO, ACS, ATQ and ALG demonstrate that he was at CELA on 22 April.[509] However, the nature of his participation and the effect of his presence are also unclear.

(ii)   Removal and Killing of Refugees

436. The Chamber will first consider the removal of refugees from CELA. Witnesses UI and HAD testified that around 40 refugees were forced to leave, Witness UI stated that all but **[page 118]** three were Tutsis, and Witness HAD identified them as young Tutsi men.[510] Witness ACS heard about 40 names called out.[511] Witness BUO estimated that around 60 to 70 refugees were removed. According to Witness ACK, 20 persons were taken away, but she had left before those selected were removed.[512] Witness ATQ estimated that 80 to 100 young people were killed as a result of the attack.[513] The Chamber considers these estimates largely consistent and clearly credible.

437. As regards the victims' identities, Witness ACS stated that Angeline Mukandutiye called out the names of Charles Rwanga, Vincent Mugiraneza, Emmanuel Gihana, Albert, who worked for Radio Rwanda, Christophe Safari, Charles Gahima and Rwigamba. Witness ATQ recalled that a man named Albert had been among those selected by the *Interahamwe*. Witness HAD testified that Charles Rwanga, his two sons Wilson and Déglote, Charles Gahima and his son, Christophe Safari and Rwigamba were taken away. Witness UI said that Charles Rwanga and his two sons, Wilson and Déglote, Albert, an employee for ORINFOR, the son of Sebushishi and Emmanuel Semugomwa were with the witness as the refugees were headed to the CND, but he learned that Semugomwa escaped. Witness ACK's husband and certain children were identified for separation and were never seen by her again. Witness BUO came across the bodies of Charles and Déglote Rwanga, Albert, a driver for ORINFOR, and the two children of Pierre Sebushishi

---

[508]   Witness ACS provided *pro justitia* statements to Rwandan authorities in April of 1998 and March 2003 where he made no mention of Renzaho's involvement in the attack on CELA. Defence Exhibit 20C (statement of 27 April 1998); Defence Exhibit 21C (statement of 20 March 2003). In particular, the April 1998 statement (p. 2) lists 18 individuals, including Odette Nyirabagenzi, and notes that these individuals "killed people in many places, namely, CELA…" On first glance, the witness's omissions regarding that attack and Renzaho's involvement in it are glaring. The questions posed during the April 1998 interview – "Why did you come to the Public Prosecutor's office? A. I came to give evidence against some criminals" and "Q. Which criminals?" – were open-ended and afforded the witness full opportunity to discuss the attack on CELA and Renzaho's participation. He explained that his statements to Rwandan authorities concerned the meetings of a crisis committee and crimes in which Renzaho did not participate. T. 30 January 2007 pp. 75-76. The Chamber accepts that the witness may have believed that the investigations he assisted were unrelated to Renzaho and finds the explanation reasonable.
[509]   Witness WOW's testimony that *Bourgmestre* Jean Bizimana was not present during the attack does not raise reasonable doubt that he was there. Reference is made to other evidence, including the account of Witness ALG.
[510]   Witness UI, T. 5 February 2007 pp. 64-65; Witness HAD, T. 1 February 2007 pp. 14-15.
[511]   Witness ACS, T. 30 January 2007 pp. 40-41, 59-61, 71-73.
[512]   Witness BUO, T. 26 January 2007 pp. 3-6, 10. T. 29 January 2007 pp. 10, 20; Witness ACK, T. 5 March 2007 p. 65.
[513]   T. 31 January 2007 p. 68.

while walking to the CND. Again, the accounts are similar and appear reliable. Also the descriptions of the vehicles ferrying the refugees are consistent.[514]

438. There is Defence evidence suggesting that Charles Rwanga and his sons were not among those removed from CELA on that day. In particular, Witness WOW heard that Rwanga had been killed on 7 April, which means weeks before the attack. However, as the witness did not see the alleged 7 April attack or Charles Rwanga's body afterwards, his testimony carries limited weight.[515] Witness ACK was confronted with the Rwanda trial judgement of Alphonse Macumi, which concluded that Macumi "had Charles Rwanga and his children killed … after having taken them out of Sainte Famille".[516] The witness maintained that they were removed from CELA and not Sainte Famille, expressing the view that this portion of the judgment was incorrect and provided by other persons than her.[517] The Chamber finds her explanation reasonable.[518]

439. The consistent first-hand accounts of Witnesses BUO, UI, ACS and HAD, among other evidence, confirm that Charles Rwanga and his children Wilson and Déglote were **[page 119]** among the men identified and removed from CELA during the 22 April attack.[519] Charles Rwanga was killed en route to the CND. According to Witness UI, the refugees were first brought to the Muhima gendarmerie brigade, where they were briefly detained, and then released to the *Interahamwe*, who took them away in a minibus. The Chamber accepts his evidence that along the way, approximately 10 of the refugees, including Charles Rwanga, were removed at a roadblock near an Ethiopean restaurant in the *Péage* and killed. Witness BUO saw his and Déglote Rwanga's corpse on the way to the mass grave called CND, and added that no refugee who had been taken away survived.

440. The Chamber concludes that approximately 40 refugees, most of whom were Tutsi men, were removed from CELA on 22 April 1994. Among those taken away were Charles Rwanga, and his two sons Wilson and Déglote Rwanga. Along the way, Charles and Déglote Rwanga, among others, were killed.[520] *Interahamwe* killed all the refugees who were not killed en route or those who had not escaped at that location.[521]

441. No witness heard any explicit order from Renzaho to kill the men who had been separated at CELA. However, Witness BUO's evidence suggests that the order to kill was implicit in the instruction to bring the refugees to the CND that was made by Mukandutiye in Renzaho's presence.[522] Witness ATQ's evidence also reflects that *Interahamwe* understood during the separation process that the men would be killed.[523] Witness UI testified that Renzaho ordered that the men be taken to Muhima gendarmerie, making no mention of the CND. However, these instructions reflected a cautionary approach aimed at concealing the activity, namely an "attack" that would prompt attention.[524]

---

[514] Witness UI and BUO testified that the refugees were removed in a minibus and a pick-up truck. (Witness BUO referred to three vehicles but only described two of them.) According to Witness ACK, the refugees were placed in two vehicles, one being a Nissan Urvan minibus. Witness ACS suggested the refugees were taken away in a pick-up.
[515] T. 4 July 2007 pp. 52-53.
[516] T. 6 March 2007 p. 59; Defence Exhibit 40 (excerpt from Rwandan trial judgement) (emphasis added).
[517] T. 6 March 2007 p. 60.
[518] Defence Witness KRG saw Rwanga and his sons at CELA when he left around 9.20 a.m., but he testified that he later heard that they had been taken away and killed.
[519] The Munyeshyaka indictment and supporting materials discussed elsewhere (I.2.2) also fail to raise doubt with respect to the Prosecution evidence.
[520] The Chamber finds immaterial that Witness UI testified at least 10 individuals were killed while Witness BUO observed 15 bodies on his way to CND. The difference is minor, the witnesses provided estimates and Witness UI fled from the scene in the midst of the slaughter and before the minibus reached the CND allowing for a larger number of people to be killed.
[521] Witness BUO's statement that "no one was able to escape" appears to be refer to the refugees that he saw being killed once he had arrived at the CND. T. 26 January 2007 p. 10. In the Chamber's view, this does not conflict with Witness UI's testimony that he and another managed to flee en route to the CND.
[522] T. 26 January 2007 p. 5 ("It was decided on the spot that the people were to be selected and driven somewhere and killed. We were told that we were to take them to the place called CND, and we knew what such letters meant, CND. And it was done; there is evidence to that effect. … When we were instructed to take these people to CND, Angeline Mukandituye was with Renzaho, Tharcisse, when the order was given. So Renzaho was present. Renzaho left after the instructions were given. It was something that had been planned rather, that had been discussed beforehand.").
[523] T. 31 January 2007 pp. 65-66 (an *Interahamwe* during the separation process said "'Renzaho has said we should not kill men and women. We are going to kill young people and men.'").
[524] T. 5 February 2007 pp. 59-60 ("When I arrived, the préfet was telling them not to attack the refugees immediately. And I remember that he told them not to help the enemy. He was telling them that everything that was being done was being observed by

442. In the Chamber's view, the Prosecution evidence demonstrates that the ultimate goal of the operation was the elimination of the combat aged Tutsi men. Different accounts regarding the precise words used by Renzaho are not significant. Moreover, Witness UI's evidence that the refugees were brought to the Muhima gendarmerie brigade instead of **[page 120]** directly to the mass grave does not, in the Chamber's view, reflect that the plan to kill the men materialised without Renzaho's encouragement or knowledge and after they were removed. The refugees were quickly transferred from within the gendarmerie brigade to the *Interahamwe* who ultimately killed them.

443. In the Chamber's view, the only reasonable conclusion is that orders were given to kill the male refugees removed from CELA. Given the authority exercised by Renzaho during the operation, the Chamber is also convinced that the only reasonable conclusion is that Renzaho gave these orders.**[page 122]**

7. KILLINGS IN NYARUGENGE, 28 APRIL 1994

7.1 Introduction

444. The Prosecution alleges that, on or about 28 April 1994, Renzaho ordered members of the *Interahamwe* to Nyarugenge commune to find and kill nine Tutsis, including Francois Nsengiyumva, Rutiyomba, Kagorora and his two sons, Emile and Aimable. The *Interahamwe* killed several Tutsis, including these five. Reference is made to Witnesses GLE and MW.[525]

445. The Defence denies that Renzaho ordered, instigated or knew of this attack. Only Witness GLE testified about it. Her evidence is not credible and contradicted by Witness HIN.[526]

7.2 Evidence

Prosecution Witness GLE

446. The day after the President's death, Witness GLE, a Tutsi, sought refuge at the home of Elie Munyankinde, a Tutsi FAR soldier. More than 10 other Tutsi men and women were there when she arrived. On 28 April 1994, *Interahamwe* came to the house. One of the militiamen entered, carrying a firearm, while the others remained outside. The witness was in the living-room at the time. Five Tutsis were killed inside the building: François, Rutiyomba, Kagorora and his two children, Emile and Aimable. A soldier who was present begged the attackers to spare the women and children. Consequently, only men were killed. The witness did not observe the killings of persons who were outside. The *Interahamwe* also attacked Gakwandi's home, which was further down the same road. Gakwandi and his children were killed.[527]

447. Following the killings inside Munyankinde's house, the witness went out to the courtyard and observed an *Interahamwe* named Leonard Bagabo showing a sheet of paper to the civilians who accompanied him. He said that the paper bore the signatures of Renzaho and school inspector Angeline Mukandutiye, a local *Interahamwe* leader. The witness saw the document, but could not read its contents. At one point she referred to it as "the list".[528]

448. After the attack, the bodies were thrown into a nearby pit dug by local residents. The witness and other surviving women left Munyankinde's house and saw the corpses being buried there, including those

---

the satellites and that as a consequence had to act in an intelligent manner. He gave instructions to them and he told them to choose amongst the refugees the ring leaders. That was the word he used. And he said that the ringleaders were to be taken to the Muhima Brigade and be tried before a military court. But, in fact, he was not doing that because he wished to save those who were staying at the centre."), 61.

[525] Indictment paras. 46, 50; Prosecution Closing Brief paras. 407-417. The name of the house owner was spelt both "Munyankinde" and "Munyankindi" during the trial. For the sake of consistency, "Munyankinde" will be used here.

[526] Defence Closing Brief paras. 568-582.

[527] T. 31 January 2007 pp. 1-5; Prosecution Exhibit 79 (personal identification sheet). Witness GLE did not explicitly state when Gakwandi's house was attacked but the context indicates that it was also on 28 April 1994.

[528] T. 31 January 2007 pp. 4-5, 9.

killed at Gakwandi's home. While the witness was standing there, a Presidential Guard soldier came to count the bodies. He said that the witness and the other women should also be thrown into the pit.[529]

449. Witness GLE's husband was not far from Munyankinde's house at the time. The *Interahamwe* called him after the attack. She saw Bagabo wave the piece of paper, and her husband was then taken away in a vehicle with *Interahamwe* who were carrying machetes, **[page 122]** firearms and swords. At that point, he had already been wounded with a sword. After the war was over, the witness heard that he had been taken to Odette Nyirabagenzi and killed with a spear. Two days after the attack on Munyankinde's house, the witness found refuge at the Saint Paul pastoral centre.[530]

Prosecution Witness MW

450. Witness MW, a Tutsi, sought refuge at Saint Paul on 12 April 1994. On 24 April, over 20 *Interahamwe* attacked the centre. She saw them capture seven refugees and take them away in a pickup truck. The main assailant was Leonard Bagabo, who was also the leader of her *cellule*. Armed with a weapon, he tried to take the witness and her family with him by force, but someone intervened and stopped him. She heard that the seven refugees were killed at a place called CND, in Rugenge sector.[531]

Renzaho

451. When asked about whether he had instigated and participated in an attack on 28 April 1994 at Elie Munyankinde's house, Renzaho testified that he had never been to Munyankinde's house, did not know where he lived, and neither ordered nor led an attack at his house.[532]

Defence Witness HIN

452. Witness HIN, a Hutu, testified that 42 persons were killed in an attack at Elie Munyankinde's house. He received no information linking Renzaho to the attack. The witness was not present but heard of the attack in 2006 as he was involved in related Gacaca proceedings which he referred to as the trial of Bagabo without providing further details.[533]

7.3 Deliberations

453. The only Prosecution witness who testified about the attack on 28 April 1994 at Elie Munyankinde's house was Witness GLE. She provided a first-hand, consistent account which appeared credible. According to her written statement to Tribunal investigators in May 2000, she found refuge at Saint Paul two weeks after the attack, not two days as in her testimony. When this was put to her, the witness insisted that two days had elapsed, and that she had nowhere to stay for as long as two weeks.[534] The Chamber considers that the disparity between her statement and testimony is not major and may have been the result of an error during the interview.**[page 123]**

454. The Chamber accepts the witness's evidence that on 28 April, *Interahamwe* killed several Tutsis at Munyankinde's house, including François, Rutiyomba, Kagorora and his two children, Aimable and Emile.

---

[529] *Id.* p. 6.
[530] *Id.* pp. 5-6, 8-9.
[531] T. 5 February 2007 pp. 2, 5-9, 24, 28; Prosecution Exhibit 83 (personal identification sheet). Witness MW also testified that Angeline Mukandutiye was a school inspector in Nyarugenge commune, as well as an *Interahamwe* and MRND leader. *Id.* pp. 4, 27.
[532] T. 29 August 2007 p. 61.
[533] T. 9 July 2007 pp. 57-61; T. 10 July 2007 pp. 18-19; Defence Exhibit 73 (personal identification sheet). Witness HIN at one point confused the two names Bagabo and Elie Munyankinde, mistakenly creating the name "Bagabo Elie" (T. 9 July 2007 p. 59). He explained that the Gacaca trial began in 2003, and that the appeals judgement was rendered in 2006. The witness also participated in the "information gathering" stage of the case. In accordance with the Decision on Defence Request for Special Protective Measures for Witness HIN (TC), 14 June 2007, the witness's identity was not disclosed to the Prosecution until 10 days before his testimony.
[534] T. 31 January 2007 pp. 6, 8-9.

It also finds that an *Interahamwe* named Leonard Bagabo was in the courtyard of the house during the attack.[535] Witness MW's evidence confirms that Leonard Bagabo was an *Interahamwe* leader.

455. The Chamber considers that Witness HIN testified about the same attack. Although he did not specify the date, the mention of Munyankinde's house and the name Bagabo corroborates Witness GLE's evidence. The fact that Witness GLE mentioned nine victims, whereas Witness HIN said that 42 persons were killed during the attack, is not significant in the circumstances. Witness GLE may have referred to the persons she saw being killed inside the house, while Witness HIN indicated the total number of victims, in accordance with what he learned during the Gacaca proceedings.

456. The crucial question is whether Renzaho was involved in the attack. Witness GLE did not provide information about the content of the document held by Bagabo, other than at one stage referring to it as "the list" and giving hearsay evidence that it bore Renzaho's and Mukandutiye's signatures. She did not see the contents of the document and offered no basis for referring to it as "the list". In light of this, the evidence is not sufficient to establish that the document held by Bagabo contained a list of persons to be killed, signed by Renzaho.[536]

457. The Chamber finds that the Prosecution has not established beyond reasonable doubt that Renzaho ordered *Interahamwe* to find and kill nine Tutsis on or about 28 April 1994. Furthermore, the factual record is insufficiently precise to establish Renzaho's liability as a superior. **[page 124]**

8. DISMISSAL OF MODERATE OFFICIALS, END APRIL 1994

8.1 Introduction

458. The Prosecution submits that, on or about 30 April 1994, Renzaho dismissed, among other persons, *Conseiller* Célestin Sezibera, because he believed that Sezibera was opposed to the killing of Tutsis. Renzaho allegedly replaced Sezibera with someone who supported such killings. Reference is made to Witnesses GLJ, ALG and UB.[537]

459. According to the Defence, Sezibera was dismissed because he had been absent from his post. Renzaho was not responsible for these dismissals, and the allegations are not precise. It relies on Witnesses AIA, PPV, PPO, UT, PGL, VDD and MAI.[538]

8.2 Evidence

Prosecution Witness GLJ

460. Witness GLJ, a Hutu, was a local official in Kigali-Ville prefecture in April 1994. He testified that, in October 1990, the *conseiller* of Nyamirambo sector, Célestin Sezibera, was investigated as an accomplice of the enemy but continued in his duties. At the time, he was accused of being a Tutsi. Furthermore, some of his family members were living out of the country during that period.[539]

---

[535] Witness GLE's evidence about the attack at Gakwandi's house is not explicitly pleaded in the Indictment. It is unclear how she learned about that attack, and how and by whom it was perpetrated. In these circumstances, the Chamber will not make any findings about that event.

[536] In making this finding, the Chamber has taken into account other evidence of lists that were purportedly signed by Renzaho.

[537] Indictment paras. 17, 35; Prosecution Closing Brief paras. 216-237, 360-379. The Indictment also refers to the dismissal of *Conseiller* Jean-Baptiste Rudasingwa. In its letter of 13 March 2007 to the Defence, as well as in its Closing Brief para. 227, the Prosecution conceded that it had not called any evidence of his dismissal.

[538] Defence Closing Brief paras. 609-688; Defence Exhibit 113 (*complément écrit aux arguments oraux de la défense*) para. 613.1.

[539] T. 22 January 2007 pp. 13, 14-15 (no explanation given why family members abroad would cause suspicion; Witness GLJ denying that he was a member of the RPF), 16, 20, 23, 33, 45, 58; Prosecution Exhibit 68 (personal identification sheet). At the time of his testimony, Witness GLJ had been detained in Rwanda for over 12 years, and his trial had not yet begun. T, 22 January 2007 pp. 23, 62-63.

461. In April 1994, Sezibera made several oral and written reports to Renzaho, to *Bourgmestre* Jean Bizimana of Nyarugenge commune, and to the prefecture office generally, explaining that Tutsi groups were being targeted. He referred specifically to an *Interahamwe* named Kigingi, as well as policemen and gendarmes who were participating in killings in Nyamirambo. There was little or no reaction to the reports, and the killings continued. The police force was managed by the prefect. On one occasion, the gendarmes sent reinforcements in connection with an incident involving a specific family, but then told him that, in the future, he should call the prefect. Sezibera worked for two days in April picking up bodies in Nyamirambo sector and bringing them to the cemetery.[540]

462. The witness was present during a meeting on 30 April 1994. *Bourgmestre* Bizimana gave Sezibera a letter, signed by Renzaho on 29 April. It stated that the prefect was relieving Sezibera from his duties because he "was unable to ensure security". The *bourgmestre* was **[page 125]** requested to implement the decision forthwith. Around this time, Renzaho also dismissed a *responsable de cellule* named Kanimba, who was replaced by a person called Habimana.[541]

463. The witness saw Sezibera's dismissal letter, and understood its language to mean that the *conseiller* was being removed as a suspected Tutsi. He gave several reasons for this belief. First, Rwandans usually use indirect language. Second, Kanimba had been relieved from his duties because he was a Tutsi. Given that Sezibera had come under suspicion in 1990, the witness believed that the *conseiller* had been discharged for the same reason as the *responsable de cellule*. Third, many people had written petitions asking that Sezibera be dismissed, accusing him of being a Tutsi, an accomplice, and stating that he "did not allow them to work the way they had to". They further claimed that he had refused to give them weapons but had provided food to persons in hiding. Those complaining included two *responsables de cellule*. The witness stated that Sezibera's identity card bore the letter "H", but killers were always looking for pretexts during that period, and those with Hutu identity cards were not spared.[542]

464. Jérémie Kaboyi, a member of the MRND, was appointed as Sezibera's replacement on 30 April and remained *conseiller* until Kigali was occupied by the RPF in July 1994. Three days after taking up this position, Kaboyi participated in an attack with Kigingi and other *Interahamwe*. It took place close to the witness's residence and 16 persons were killed.[543]

Prosecution Witness ALG

465. Witness ALG, a Hutu, was a member of the MRND party and a local official in Nyarugenge commune in Kigali-Ville prefecture. He stated that the *conseiller* of Nyakabanda sector, Emmanuel Kanyandekwe, had a poor relationship with Renzaho as of March 1994. Kanyandekwe had informed the witness that this was because he was a member of the MDR Twagiramungu faction. Those who did not belong to the power factions were accused of being *Inkotanyi* and would go into hiding to avoid being killed. Kanyandekwe was "somewhat" in hiding and did not often appear in public.[544]

466. On 13 April, Renzaho asked *Bourgmestre* Jean Bizimana of Nyarugenge commune to introduce a new *conseiller* for Nyakabanda sector, Grégoire Nyirimanzi. The prefect had just appointed him to replace Kanyandekwe. The next day, Bizimana did as Renzaho had requested. The new *conseiller* had not been well-known as a *responsable* in Nyakabanda cellule but had distinguished himself as an influential *Interahamwe* in the killings.[545]

---

[540] T. 22 January 2007 pp. 22, 24-25, 29-30, 35-36, 47-48, 52-55. Kigingi (sometimes referred to as Kagingi in the transcripts) was arrested and detained for one day in a military camp, but then released and continued the killings. Witness GLJ did not know who had ordered the arrest. *Id.* p. 55.

[541] *Id.* pp. 18-19, 30, 31 (the meeting on 30 April 1994 took place in "our area"), 61. The Chamber notes that the split of the MDR party into MDR-Power and Faustin Twagiramungu's faction is described in Prosecution Exhibit 94A (Genocide in Kigali-City, Expert Opinion by Alison Des Forges) p. 6.

[542] T. 22 January 2007 pp. 31-32, 61.

[543] *Id.* pp. 30-31, 37.

[544] T. 10 January 2007 pp. 56, 62-63; T. 11 January 2007 pp. 13-14, 34; T. 12 January 2007 p. 22; Prosecution Exhibit 67 (personal identification sheet). Witness ALG was arrested in Rwanda in April 1998, provisionally released in July 2005, and was still awaiting trial when testifying in Arusha. T. 10 January 2007 pp. 64-65.

[545] T. 10 January 2007 p. 62; T. 11 January 2007 pp. 32-34.

467. According to the witness, the *bourgmestre* of Kicukiro commune, Evariste Gasamagera, was also dismissed by Renzaho before July 1994, and was similarly not seen in **[page 126]** public during that period. The witness could not remember the name of his replacement, but recalled that he was the son of the *conseiller* of Kacyiru sector.[546]

468. *Conseiller* Célestin Sezibera reported to *Bourgmestre* Jean Bizimana. The witness testified that Renzaho dismissed Sezibera before July 1994, without being able to say exactly when, and replaced him with Jérémie Kaboyi. He did not know why Sezibera was dismissed. During his brief tenure as *conseiller*, Kaboyi participated in an attack to kill Tutsis with persons under his orders.[547]

469. Sezibera sought assistance from Bizimana the day after a man named Habyarimana, nicknamed Kigingi, and his gang had killed 24 persons. After Bizimana informed Renzaho of Kigingi's activities, Renzaho summoned Kigingi to his office. When Kigingi left with his *Interahamwe* escort, he saw the witness, warned him to be careful, and implied that Bizimana might be an accomplice of the *Inkotanyi* (II.4.2).[548] Witness ALG recalled that Renzaho's secretary was a woman named Astérie, but did not mention her ethnicity.[549]

Prosecution Witness UB

470. Witness UB, a Hutu local official in Kigali-Ville prefecture, stated that, in 1994, public servants were dismissed from the prefecture for the sole reason that they were known to be Tutsis. Resident permits and identity cards, which were issued in the sector offices, contained ethnic identification that was accessible to the administrators.[550]

471. *Conseiller* Sezibera in Nyamirambo sector was dismissed on 30 April and replaced, even though he had previously received a consignment of weapons like all other *conseillers*. *Conseiller* Kanyandekwe in Nyakabanda sector, a Tutsi, was discharged between 15 and 20 April, and replaced by a person appointed by the prefect.[551]

472. The prefect could suspend all public servants in the prefecture, and he alone had the authority to remove a policeman from his post. The witness personally observed Tutsi policemen in Kigali-Ville prefecture being sent away or dismissed when the killings of Tutsis began in April 1994. He believed that the prefect had discharged them. A Tutsi policeman called Hakorimana was dismissed. After his weapon was taken away, other policemen in the *cellule* killed him. Sezirahiga, the deputy of the Kimisagara *conseiller*, was also discharged and killed in that way. Both he and Hakorimana were sent away during the second week following the death of the President in April 1994. Some of those who came to the prefecture seeking refuge were also turned back, whereupon they were killed.[552] **[page 127]**

Renzaho

473. Renzaho acknowledged that Célestin Sezibera was removed from his position as *conseiller* of Nyarugenge sector at the end of April 1994 in accordance with the Law of 23 November 1963, which governed the administration of communes.[553] He was replaced because he "preferred to take shelter at the

---

[546] T. 11 January 2007 pp. 49-50.
[547] *Id.* pp. 48-50.
[548] *Id.* pp. 56-57.
[549] T. 12 January 2007 pp. 36-37.
[550] T. 23 January 2007 pp. 1-2, 8-9, 47-48; T. 24 January 2007 p. 18; Prosecution Exhibit 69 (personal identification sheet). At the time of his testimony, Witness UB was detained in Rwanda, awaiting – for eight years – the result of his second appeal against his 1997 death sentence for genocide. T. 23 January 2007 pp. 1-4.
[551] T. 23 January 2007 pp. 10-11 (two other *conseillers*, from Gikongo and Kagarama, were replaced after 6 April 1994 because they had been killed); T. 24 January 2007 p. 15. Witness UB also testified that, when Renzaho took office in 1990, he dismissed some *conseillers* who were Tutsis during the wave of arrests that took place then. T. 24 January 2009 p. 16.
[552] T. 23 January 2007 pp. 7-8, 49. Witness UB explained that he did not personally kill Hakorimana, but because he was within the group of the first category of suspects (including leaders), he was convicted of his death (T. 23 January 2007 p. 62). For reasons of consistency, the Chamber has opted to write Hakorimana, not Hakolimana, which also sometimes appears in the transcripts.
[553] Prosecution Exhibit 9 (*Codes et Lois du Rwanda*, Volume II).

time when fighting was moving closer to his sector". It was *Bourgmestre* Jean Bizimana who made the decision to replace him. Renzaho had accepted it because Sezibera was "not available", but he did not recall the name of Jérémie Kaboyi or whether he had been Sezibera's replacement.[554]

474. According to Renzaho, he was exercising his "oversight authority" when accepting the decision to replace Sezibera. Where possible, he had replaced *conseillers* who had died between April and July 1994, approving the administrative actions taken by the respective *bourgmestres*.[555] He did not remember the names of the policemen at the Kigali-Ville prefecture, nor did he know of someone called Hakorimana, nor recall any measure he had taken to dismiss him. He further denied knowing a *responsable de cellule* named Kanimba.[556]

Defence Witness AIA

475. Witness AIA worked closely with one of the *conseillers* during the events. In his view, *Conseiller* Karekezi caused the death of a policeman named Etienne Hakorimana. Karekezi chaired a meeting on 8 April 1994, during which he commented to a *responsable de cellule* that he did not understand how a Tutsi policeman named Hakorimana was still alive after being involved in training Tutsi children to handle weapons. Soon after, Hakorimana was killed by soldiers and *Interahamwe*. The witness heard of his death around 12 April but stated that, up until the day he was killed, Hakorimana had not been dismissed.[557]

476. One day, at Petrorwanda, *Conseiller* Célestin Sezibera met a certain Gervais Dusabemungu, who worked in the legal department in the Kigali-Ville prefecture. There it was known that Dusabemungu was an MRND opponent and had joined the RPF. Karekezi reported this to *Bourgmestre* Bizimana, who asked him to suggest a replacement for both Sezibera and *Conseiller* Kanyandekwe of Nyakabanda. There was no mention of bringing the issue before the prefect. Karekezi went to find the replacements. At the prefecture, he introduced Grégoire Nyirimanzi to Bizimana, who told Grégoire, "you have to exercise caution now that you are in charge of the Nyakabanda sector".[558] **[page 128]**

Defence Witness PPV

477. Witness PPV, a Hutu, worked in the urban police, which was under the direct control of the prefect. He explained that before 6 April 1994, there were 264 urban police officers working. Six or fewer of them were Tutsis. On 7 April, only about 40 police officers came to the prefecture office. Many could not reach there, others had deserted or were afraid of the curfew, some were not allowed to leave by the local population that wanted to be protected, and some had been killed.[559]

478. The witness was not certain how many of the 40 policemen who came to the prefecture office in April 1994 were Tutsis, but stated that the police commander assigned Tutsi police officers to remain at the prefecture until 3 July because it would have been dangerous for them to perform duties outside of its compound. The witness was not aware that any of the policemen who came to the prefecture office died. The policemen called Hakorimana or Sezirahiga did not come to work on 7 April or later. The witness did not see them again during the events. He believed that Hakorimana was killed at a roadblock during the genocide.[560]

479. The witness recalled three or four Tutsi civil servants at the prefecture office, out of a total of 40 employees. Astérie Nikuze, a Tutsi receptionist at the prefecture, remained there until early July. Gervais Gasamagera, also a Tutsi, was an assistant to a sub-prefect. Renzaho had sent the witness to collect Gasamagera at his home in Nyamirambo, but he could not be found as he was in hiding. The witness later

---

[554] T. 29 August 2007 p. 60; T. 30 August 2007 pp. 22-23.
[555] T. 30 August 2007 pp. 22, 23 ("I approved the acts or the – the moves made by the respective *bourgmestres*"). French version (T. 30 August 2007 p. 24): *"J'ai accepté les actes posés par les bourgmestres respectifs."*), 25-26.
[556] T. 28 August 2007 p. 43; T. 30 August 2007 p. 23.
[557] T. 2 July 2007 pp. 1, 6, 21-27; 46; T. 3 July 2007 p. 1; Defence Exhibit 66 (personal identification sheet). Witness AIA was questioned by Nyamirambo brigade about his actions during the events, locked up in a cell for a month while investigations took place, and then released. T. 2 July 2007 p. 46.
[558] T. 2 July 2007 pp. 37-40.
[559] T. 4 June 2007 p. 78; T. 5 June 2007 pp. 2-4, 34-36, 46; Defence Exhibit 56 (personal identification sheet).
[560] T. 5 June 2007 pp. 3-4, 35-38, 40-41.

heard that Gasamagera had been severely beaten, although not killed. He also knew of two Tutsi employees in the financial service who had remained at the prefecture office during the events.[561]

Defence Witness PPO

480. According to Witness PPO, a Hutu official at the Kigali-Ville prefecture, Astérie Nikuze or Karkuzie (he could not remember her last name) was in charge of typing and archiving at the prefecture office. He did not refer to her ethnicity.[562]

Defence Witness UT

481. Witness UT, a Hutu official at the Kigali-Ville prefecture, testified that the *Interahamwe* at the roadblocks often mentioned the names of three *conseillers* (Amri Karekezi, Rose Karushara and Odette Nyirabagenzi) who had supported them or influenced them to do bad things. They were not dismissed by the prefect but, during that period, there was no time to appoint or dismiss anyone. At the same time, the witness had heard of the dismissal, on or around 30 April 1994, of *Conseiller* Célestin Sezibera, and said that, if it had occurred, it was because that *conseiller* had not been working for a long time, although he did not specify how long. According to the witness, the prefect had the power to dismiss or at least, to suspend, and could suspend anyone at any time.[563] **[page 129]**

482. At one point during the events, *Bourgmestre* Evariste Gasamagera of Kicukiro commune, was "no longer seen" and said to be missing. The witness further recalled that, after the receptionist failed to return to work at the prefecture office, Astérie, who worked there already, replaced her. He did not mention Astérie's ethnicity. Between 11 April and 4 July, up to a hundred persons, mainly Tutsis, found refuge at the prefecture office.[564]

Defence Witness PGL

483. Witness PGL, a Hutu local official at the Kigali-Ville prefecture, recalled that Renzaho's driver was a man named Gaspard but did not mention his ethnicity. He noted that there were many Tutsi employees at the prefecture, and remembered in particular some Tutsi senior civil servants, including the head of the legal affairs division, Gervais Dusabemungu. Renzaho's secretary, Astérie Nikuze, was also Tutsi. The witness could not remember the others' names. Renzaho gave all of his staff equal treatment.[565]

Defence Witness VDD

484. Witness VDD, a Hutu related to the prefect, testified that Renzaho did not discriminate against anyone. The parents of those who worked for him were Tutsis as well as Hutus, and his secretary, Astérie, was Tutsi. Renzaho's behaviour towards the Tutsi members of his own family did not change following the events of 1990.[566]

Defence Witness MAI

485. Witness MAI, a Hutu related to Renzaho, stated that the prefect treated the Tutsi and Hutu members of his family equally. Persons from both groups sought refuge at Renzaho's house, and his wife gave them food.[567]

---

[561] *Id.* pp. 9-10, 55-58.
[562] T. 4 July 2007 p. 63; T. 5 July 2007 pp. 1, 4, 7; Defence Exhibit 71 (personal identification sheet).
[563] T. 24 May 2007 pp. 20-22, 23-24, 39, 47-49; T. 25 May 2007 pp. 11, 23-25; Defence Exhibit 47 (personal identification sheet).
[564] T. 24 May 2007 pp. 25-26, 47, 57-59.
[565] T. 6 June 2007 pp. 15, 21-25; Defence Exhibit 61 (personal identification sheet).
[566] T. 18 May 2007 p. 7; T. 22 May 2007 p. 18; Defence Exhibit 43 (personal identification sheet).
[567] T. 22 August 2007 pp. 5-6, 15-16; Defence Exhibit 76 (personal identification sheet).

8.3 Deliberations

486. The Prosecution alleges that during the events in 1994, Renzaho replaced moderate officials by persons who supported the killings of Tutsis. Its main focus is on the dismissal of *Conseiller* Célestin Sezibera of Nyamirambo sector, who was replaced by Jérémie Kaboye. In the Prosecution'view, its case is strengthened by other examples, which show a pattern of behaviour. The Defence disputes that Renzaho was behind the dismissal of Sezibera, and submits that Renzaho's treatment of Tutsis and moderate officials show that the Prosecution's allegations are baseless.

487. The Chamber recalls that the three Prosecution witnesses who testified about dismissal and replacement – GLJ, ALG, and UB – have all been involved in criminal proceedings in Rwanda. Their evidence is examined with caution, as it may have been influenced by a desire to positively affect their own situation.

488. The Chamber accepts Witness GLJ's testimony that there was a letter dated 29 April 1994, signed by Renzaho. Leaving aside for the moment whether it was a letter of dismissal or approval (see below), it led to the dismissal of the witness. Renzaho testified that he **[page 130]** approved the *conseiller's* dismissal because of his lack of availability, whereas Witness GLJ said that the letter referred to Sezibera's inability to ensure security. Irrespective of the exact wording, the Chamber finds that the real reason for Sezibera's dismissal was that he was believed to be opposed to the killing of Tutsis, or at least not showing sufficient zeal in a period with on-going massacres.

489. The Chamber makes this finding for several reasons. Witness GLJ's account was consistent, relatively detailed and appeared credible. Leaving aside whether Sezibera, a Hutu, was actually suspected of being a Tutsi, the evidence shows that he was considered a potential accomplice of "the enemy". Witness GLJ's testimony that Sezibera reported killings to the prefect and to *Bourgmestre* Bizimana was corroborated by Witness ALG, who was aware that Witness GLJ made such a report after Kigingi, the *Interahamwe*, had killed 24 persons. Renzaho merely called Kigingi to his office. Furthermore, Defence Witness AIA testified that, on an unspecified date just before Sezibera was dismissed, he was publicly seen with a person known to be an MRND opponent and a member of the RPF. This was reported to the *bourgmestre*.[568]

490. The Chamber has considered Witness GLJ's testimony that Sezibera was active in his administrative duties as a *conseiller* in early April 1994. He attended meetings, for instance one on 16 or 17 April, and another meeting about 28 April; transported or collected bodies around 10 and 11 April; and submitted reports up until he was dismissed. According to Renzaho, Sezibera had not been seen for about two weeks at the end of April, whereas Witness UT had heard that he was no longer working. Even assuming that Sezibera was absent from time to time, this does not refute the Prosecution evidence that he was dismissed because he was considered a "moderate".[569]

491. The Chamber has also taken into account that the person who replaced Sezibera, Jérémie Kaboyi, subsequently worked with the *Interahamwe* to commit killings. Witness GLJ and Witness ALG both testified that, after having been appointed *conseiller*, Kaboyi participated in an attack to kill Tutsis. This said, none of the witnesses testified specifically that he was appointed because he was known to support killings of Tutsis.

---

[568] Although the Chamber accepts certain parts of Witness AIA's testimony, it recalls that other elements are more doubtful. For instance, during cross-examination, he modified some answers he had given in examination-in-chief, contradicted himself, admitted to having made incorrect statements to Rwandan authorities, and gave testimony that was not in conformity with his prior written statements.

[569] Renzaho, T. 28 August 2007 p. 38 ("The first [*conseiller* to be replaced] was that of Nyamirambo who was replaced by the *bourgmestre* of Nyarugenge. And I approved because the person had just spent more than two weeks without being seen and we welcomed, we received at the *préfecture* a group of people that came to complain that there was no local authority when the *secteur* was facing a war situation, because this was towards the end of the month of April"); T. 30 August 2007 p. 22 ("[Sezibera] was replaced simply because he preferred to take shelter at the time when fighting was moving closer to his *secteur* and the population moved to protect the *préfecture* [...] I accepted that he be replaced because he was not available"); Witness UT, T. 25 May 2007 p. 24 ("I heard about the dismissal of this *conseiller* who was no longer working. If this dismissal was done, it went without saying because this *conseiller* had not been working for a long time.").

Judgement and Sentence

492. The Defence submits that Renzaho played a minimal role in the dismissal process and only approved *Bourgmestre* Bizimana's decision. It refers to Article 10 *bis* of the Rwandan Law on Communal Organisation of 23 November 1963.[570] This provision sets forth a **[page 131]** dismissal procedure that requires the *bourgmestre* to report on the inability of the *conseiller* to fulfil his duties. He submits the case to the Communal Committee, which provides its opinion to the prefect. The procedure further involves the Prefectoral Committee and the Ministry of the Interior. According to the Defence, Article 10 *bis* illustrates the central position of the *bourgmestre* in the process.

493. Renzaho testified that the dismissal was carried out "within the legal procedure provided for by the law of 1963" and that he only exercised his "oversight authority" in accepting that Sezibera be replaced.[571] However, there is no evidence that all the statutory requirements were complied with. For instance, no witness referred to the Prefectoral Committee or the Ministry, which, according to Article 10 *bis* "shall decide on the matter based on a reasoned decision". The Chamber is not convinced that the legal procedure was followed during the extraordinary circumstances of April 1994.[572] This said, it is undisputed that Renzaho made a decision as to whether to accept or reject the dismissal. This also follows from the testimonies of Witnesses GLJ, ALG and Renzaho.

494. The Prosecution witnesses emphasised the prefect's general authority in these matters but were less clear as to who initiated the process. Witness ALG testified that he did not know why Sezibera was dismissed. In the Chamber's view, this is a surprising statement, given his position, which raises issues of credibility. Witness UB did not give evidence about how the dismissal proceedings were initiated. Witness GLJ stressed Renzaho's role and said that *Bourgmestre* Bizimana's role was to implement the decision.[573] However, in a statement to Rwandan judicial authorities in February 2000, he expressed the view that it was the *bourgmestre* who instigated the dismissal.[574] The Chamber is aware that the Rwandan interview focussed on Jean Bizimana, not Renzaho. It is nevertheless noteworthy that the witness so clearly emphasised the role of the *bourgmestre* as initiating the dismissal process in his interview, whereas Renzaho was in the forefront in his testimony. This shift in emphasis raises some concern. **[page 132]**

495. Defence Witness AIA also stressed *Bourgmestre* Bizimana's impact in the process. He testified that *Conseiller* Karekezi reported on Sezibera to Bizimana, who then suggested that Karekezi find a replacement. Although certain credibility issues arise with respect to this witness, his testimony supports the view that Bizimana's role at the initial stage of the dismissal process was quite important. The Chamber finds that there is a lack of clarity about the respective roles of Renzaho and Bizimana in relation to Sezibera's dismissal.

496. There is also some doubt concerning the decision to replace Sezibera with Jérémie Kaboyi. Only Witness ALG testified that Renzaho appointed him as Sezibera's replacement. The Chamber finds, however, that Witness ALG has an interest in placing the responsibility for the replacement decision on Renzaho, and

---

[570] Prosecution Exhibit 9 (*Codes et Lois du Rwanda*, Volume II). *("Le Conseiller qui devient incapable de remplir sa mission est déchu de ses fonctions. La déchéance est prononcée à l'issue de la procédure ci-après:*
Le bourgmestre établit un rapport détaillé sur l'incapacité du Conseiller et en informe le Conseil Communal et l'intéressé qu'il invite à se défendre par écrit endéans quinze jours calendrier.
Le bourgmestre soumet le cas au Comité Communal qui donne son avis après examen du rapport de la défense du Conseiller. Le rapport accompagné de la proposition de déchéance, des moyens de défense du Conseiller et de l'avis du Comité Communal est transmis au Préfet. Celui-ci soumet le cas au Comité Préfectoral qui émet son avis.
La procédure engagée n'est poursuivie aux différents échelons que si les moyens de défense présentés par l'intéressé ne sont pas satisfaisants. Les décisions aux différents échelons doivent se conformer aux avis des organes consultés.
Tout le dossier est transmis au Ministre ayant l'Intérieur dans ses attributions qui statue sur le cas par décision motivée.").
[571] T. 30 August 2007 pp. 22-23.
[572] Article 10 *bis* of the Law of 23 November 1963 does not specifically require that the prefect sign the dismissal letter, and no witness testified that Renzaho signed Sezibera's dismissal letter on behalf of a committee. Moreover, Article 10 provides for the *conseiller* in question to defend himself in the course of the dismissal process, and no evidence was given that Sezibera had such an opportunity.
[573] T. 22 January 2007 p. 31.
[574] Defence Exhibit 6 (*pro justitia* statement of 9 February 2000): "The new *Conseiller* was not attending the meeting. However, I was accused of not enforcing security, of sensitising the population to security [sic] and of not preventing the *Inkotanyi* from abducting people at Mumena. The *Bourgmestre* could not have been unaware of such accusations. In my opinion, he was the one who made a report to the *Préfet* so that I would be relieved of my duties."

will therefore not rely on his uncorroborated account in this respect. There is no other specific evidence about this. The testimonies about appointment and replacement of other officials, briefly addressed below, does not provide sufficient corroboration. Consequently, the Prosecution has not proven beyond reasonable doubt that it was Renzaho who replaced Sezibera with Kaboyi.[575]

497. The Chamber has taken into account the Prosecution evidence that Sezibera's dismissal formed part of a pattern of behaviour. Three events involved the replacement of other officials who were or may have been moderate: *Conseiller* Kanyandekwe was allegedly replaced by Grégoire Nyirimanzi, an influential *Interahamwe* who distinguished himself in the killings;[576] the *bourgmestre* of Kicukiro, Evariste Gasamagera, was dismissed;[577] and a *responsable de cellule* called Kanimba was replaced by a certain Habimana.[578] Finally, other evidence emerged during the trial about the dismissal, replacement, protection, or equal treatment of other staff, in particular Tutsi urban policemen, and family members. These elements do not affect the Chamber's findings above concerning Célestin Sezibera.

498. The Chamber concludes that at the end of April 1994, Renzaho approved the dismissal of *Conseiller* Célestin Sezibera, who was considered a moderate and as not supportive of the killings in Kigali-Ville prefecture. However, there is no evidence that Renzaho appointed the new *conseiller*, Jérémie Kaboyi, who after taking up his functions participated in killings. It is also unclear whether the idea of dismissal and replacement **[page 133]** originally came from Renzaho, or was formulated at a lower administrative level. In the Chamber's view, the evidence of Renzaho's conduct is not sufficient to sustain a conviction.

499. In view of the Chamber's findings, it sees no need to consider the Defence submissions about insufficient notice. **[page 134]**

9. SAINT PAUL PASTORAL CENTRE, APRIL-JUNE 1994

9.1 Introduction

500. The Indictment alleges that, while in the company of Odette Nyirabagenzi and Angeline Mukandutiye, as well as *Interahamwe*, soldiers and gendarmes, Renzaho ordered the removal and murder of 60 Tutsi boys from Saint Paul pastoral centre ("Saint Paul") on or about 14 June 1994. More generally, between 7 April and 17 July 1994, Renzaho's subordinates planned and carried out attacks at various locations in Kigali where Tutsis had sought refuge, including at Saint Paul. Renzaho failed to prevent or punish the perpetrators of any of these acts. Reference is made to Witnesses KZ, ALG, BUO, MW, UI and GLE.[579]

501. The Defence does not contest that an attack took place at Saint Paul on 14 June 1994, but denies that Renzaho was implicated. It refers to Witnesses UT, PER, BDC and WOW.[580]

---

[575] Articles 7 and 8 of Law of 23 November 1963 indicate that *conseillers* are elected, and that the prefect is responsible for presiding over the elections. No reference is made to the appointment or approval of *conseillers*. Prosecution Exhibit 9 (*Codes et Lois du Rwanda*, Volume II). Renzaho's testimony indicates that the person next in line following the election results would be appointed. T. 28 August 2007 p. 38 ("As for the other *conseiller*, Nyakabanda, he fled at the beginning, at the outset. And procedures would have been followed for his replacement by naming from the list of candidates to the municipal election who came next would be appointed. So it's a *bourgmestre* who appointed the replacement of the *conseillers* and all I had to do was to accept.")

[576] Witness ALG testified that Renzaho was involved in Kanyandekwe's replacement but did not specify who dismissed him. His statement that the prefect had appointed Nyirimanzi was corroborated by Witness UB. Defence Witness AIA, however, stated that it was Bizimana who suggested that Karekezi find a replacement for Kanyandekwe, and he heard no mention of the prefect in the process. As mentioned above Witness ALG has an interest in testifying that it was Renzaho who dismissed and replaced both Sezibera and Kanyandekwe, and the Chamber finds that his evidence carries limited weight. The evidence about this event is not clear.

[577] The Chamber accepts the testimony of Witness ALG that *Bourgmestre* Evariste Gasamagera was dismissed and not seen in public in the period before his dismissal. Also Witness UT stated that Gasamagera was said to be missing at one point during the war. However, there is no direct evidence that Renzaho decided or approved either the dismissal or the replacement of Gasamagera, that he was a moderate, or that he was replaced with someone who supported the killings.

[578] There is almost no evidence about the replacement of Kanimba by Habimana.

[579] Indictment paras. 20, 22, 36, 37, 39, 57; Prosecution Closing Brief paras. 38, 46, 60, 64, 149-150, 269-299, 322, 325, 335-336, 347, 349, 378, 411, 460-472, 512; T. 14 February 2008 pp. 11-12, 18, 20-21.

[580] Defence Closing Brief paras. 354-412, 1080-1086; T. 14 February 2008 pp. 61-62; T. 15 February 2008 p. 4.

9.2 Evidence

Prosecution Witness KZ

502. Witness KZ, a Hutu, had a position of authority at Saint Paul pastoral centre in Kigali from mid-April until 17 June 1994. He said that about 1,000 adult refugees, mainly Tutsi, were admitted into the centre during April 1994. By the end of the war, their numbers had grown to about 1,500.[581]

503. According to the witness, Wenceslas Munyeshyaka, a priest he had known since 1984, did everything in his power to ensure that the refugees lived in acceptable conditions. Munyeshyaka was in charge of the refugees' safety at both Saint Paul and the Sainte Famille centre and managed to get four gendarmes to provide security at Saint Paul from around 21 April. However, they could not ensure the safety of the refugees against the hundreds of *Interahamwe* who would attack the centre. A priest at Saint Paul named Munyazikwiye had asked for assistance from the Kigali-Ville prefecture. The prefect did not respond favourably to requests, other than to place the sub-prefect in charge of social affairs, Aloys Simpunga, at the disposal of the centre. Simpunga did provide assistance.[582]

504. Four attacks at Saint Paul were particularly violent and three of them led to casualties. The attackers would come with lists that they would compare with the records kept in the centre. Initially, they looked for specific persons. Subsequently, refugees were only targeted on the basis of their Tutsi appearance.[583]

505. The first particularly violent attack took place in April, before the gendarmes were posted at the centre. About 50 *Interahamwe* and 150 civilian inhabitants of Rugenge and Muhima *cellules* arrived stating that their purpose was to do communal work. The bush and **[page 135]** banana plantation around Saint Paul was cut down by a group of about 200 persons led by the *responsable de cellule* and the leader of the *nyumba kumi* (ten households). A person hiding there was declared to be an *Inkotanyi*. Once the weeding operation was completed the inhabitants returned to their cellules, whereas the *Interahamwe* took seven or eight men from the centre before leaving. The men who were abducted never returned, and the witness believed they were killed.[584]

506. The second attack, at the beginning of May, was carried out by soldiers who the witness heard came from the Muvumba battalion, accompanied by *Interahamwe*. They threw tear gas into the compound to force those who had taken refuge out of it. The soldiers said they were looking for armed persons among the refugees, because inhabitants of the Rugenge sector had complained that refugees from Saint Paul were shooting at them at night. Witness KZ and one of the gendarmes explained to the soldiers that none of the refugees at the centre had weapons, and that there were no enemies there. Although the soldiers were angry and initially singled out the Tutsis, they appeared to accept the words of the witness and eventually left.[585]

507. Following this attack, still at the beginning of May, the witness called the prefecture office and spoke to Renzaho, telling him that Saint Paul was being attacked constantly by *Interahamwe*. The prefect replied that the people there should be instructed to go home. When the witness protested that they would not be safe there, the prefect answered: "Well, if you don't listen to what I'm telling you, then I don't care", and then he "banged the phone", seemingly angry that his instructions were not being obeyed.[586]

---

[581] T. 25 January 2007 pp. 2, 9-10, 21, 36; Prosecution Exhibit 72 (personal identification sheet). The figure of 1,500 excluded the minors there. Witness KZ identified Saint Paul as one of the locations depicted on Prosecution Exhibit 4 (map of CELA, Saint Paul and Sainte Famille). There have been some changes at the site since 1994 but the witness also described the infrastructure during the events. T. 25 January 2007 pp. 4-8.
[582] T. 25 January 2007 pp. 11-13, 17, 30, 37, 45-46.
[583] *Id.* pp. 13, 25, 44-45.
[584] *Id.* pp. 13-15, 18, 44-45. Witness KZ explained that the authorities had requested that any centre receiving refugees prepare lists of those arriving for use by the security services, the purpose being to avoid infiltrators. *Id.* p. 21.
[585] *Id.* pp. 14-16.
[586] *Id.* pp. 17 ("… and then he banged the phone. … Before the war in Kigali, people often spoke in Kinyarwanda. But educated people sometimes … speak a mix of Kinyarwanda and French. But the expression *'je m'en fous'*, which means "I don't care, which the préfet said was said in French, *'Je m'en fous'*."), 30, 38. Witness KZ testified that the telephone line at Saint Paul was operating at least up until the time that he left the centre on 17 June 1994. The priests could both make and receive phone calls, although phone numbers that began with code 8 could not be reached. *Id.* p. 30.

508. Sometime in June, a third attack began at 9.00 a.m. It was carried out by *Interahamwe* led by unidentified persons – *conseillers* and a representative of the prefect. The witness learned from the attackers, who were armed and numbered about 300, that they had lists of people to fetch. He saw a separate list of inhabitants for each of the two closest sectors to Saint Paul – Muhima and Rugenge sectors. Most of those on that list were at Saint Paul and came from these two sectors. The list included the names of the seven men who had been taken away in the first attack.[587]

509. Faced with these lists, the witness demanded an arrest warrant, and the attackers left with a gendarme to obtain one. Meanwhile, the witness warned refugees whose names he had seen on the lists to hide. The assailants returned about half an hour later with a document. This time they were accompanied by Lieutenant Iradukunda, wearing the red beret of the gendarmerie. The document was headed "Prefect of Kigali-Ville prefecture" and stated that the witness was to allow Iradukunda to take the listed people to Nyarugenge brigade for interrogation. The document said "PO", or "by order", Jean Bizimana, who had signed on [page 136] behalf of the prefect. Bizimana was the *bourgmestre* of Nyarugenge commune. Iradukunda told the witness that the prefect was absent.[588]

510. While the other attackers remained at the gate, Iradukunda and 30 or 40 attackers went through the rooms with the witness, calling out the 40 to 50 names on the list. The *Interahamwe* became upset when no one responded. They split the refugees, taking out those suspected of being Tutsi based on their physical appearance, and lining them up in front of the building. According to the witness, Iradukunda gauged the situation and realised then that he could not stop the *Interahamwe* from taking refugees, so he left the compound. At that point, the 200 or so attackers who had remained outside invaded Saint Paul. The *Interahamwe* tied up and took away between 30 and 50 young and middle-aged men.[589]

511. One of them was spared by the attackers and later told the witness that he had heard the shots that were fired to kill the other refugees. Jean-Pierre, another of the men, came back at 6.00 p.m. and informed the witness that he had been taken with the others to Rugenge sector office. There he was released because he was Hutu. Jean-Pierre also said that, on his way back, he saw attackers in the company of Renzaho and Angeline Mukandutiye at the Pan Africa hotel. They were celebrating and commending one another because they had been able to kill enemies.[590]

512. The fourth violent attack took place around 8.00 or 9.00 a.m. on 17 June. The RPF ("*Inkotanyi*") had come to Saint Paul the night before, on 16 June, and evacuated most of the approximately 1,500 adult refugees there at dawn, leaving about 50 behind. The witness heard the next day that a gendarme who had tried to resist was killed by the RPF.[591] On the morning of 17 June, *Interahamwe* arrived and threatened to kill the priests who had accommodated those refugees. They killed some of the 50 remaining persons who had not been evacuated the night before. The witness saw two bodies, but was told that there were others who had been killed downhill from the centre. He did not dare call Renzaho for help again, remembering their last conversation. However, Father Munyazikwiye had been a classmate of Renzaho and therefore called him to report that Saint Paul was under attack. Renzaho replied that the priests were all accomplices because they had accommodated the *Inkotanyi* and their accomplices. The priests fled from Saint Paul that day, and the witness heard that other refugees were killed after their departure.[592]

513. Around 5.30 or 6.00 p.m. on the night that the RPF evacuated people from Saint Paul, the witness met with Renzaho, who was accompanied by UNAMIR troops. He testified that Renzaho promised to evacuate the refugees to areas of their choice, whether controlled by government or RPF troops.[593]

---

[587] *Id.* pp. 14, 18, 21.
[588] *Id.* pp. 18-21, 30, 39, 44. The abbreviation "PO" stands for "par ordre". *Id.* p. 22 (French).
[589] *Id.* pp. 21-25.
[590] *Id.* pp. 23-24, 40. Witness KZ mentioned that Angeline Mukandutiye was school inspector for Nyarugenge commune and an MRND party leader.
[591] *Id.* pp. 14, 25-28, 39-41, 44.
[592] *Id.* pp. 26-29. Witness KZ did not know the specific rank of each of the two soldiers.
[593] *Id.* pp. 26, 38, 40-41.

Prosecution Witness ALG

514. Witness ALG. A Hutu, was an official in the Kigali-Ville prefecture until July 1994. He stated that the only police structure in Kigali-Ville was in the prefecture office. If a **[page 137]** *bourgmestre* wanted to arrest someone, he had to contact the urban police and the prefect. The *bourgmestre* had no authority to sign a warrant of arrest, but any of the heads of the various administrative services at the prefecture could sign documents on the prefect's behalf in his absence.[594]

515. As of 13 June 1994, the witness had not seen Renzaho for several days. He did not know where the prefect was on that day but had heard that he had gone to see his family in Cyangugu. The witness denied that he took advantage of Renzaho's absence to commit crimes. When the prefect was not there, he was replaced by Jean-Baptiste Butera, who was the head of political, legal and administrative affairs at the Kigali-Ville prefecture. The witness also tried unsuccessfully to contact him on 13 and 14 June.[595]

516. Witness ALG stated that, at about 4.00 p.m. on 13 June, *Conseiller* Odette Nyirabagenzi told him that the *Interahamwe* were planning to attack Saint Paul the next day armed with a list of refugees there from Rugenge and Muhima sectors who were believed to be RPF soldiers. Their conversation took place over the phone while the witness was in the prefecture office. She said the names of eight or nine names of RPF combatants were on the list, and also mentioned that she had tried to call Renzaho to inform him about the attack but had been unable to reach him. Bizimana, who was present during the conversation, told her that he would not be present during the attack because his wife had been admitted to a maternity ward. Instead, he wrote a letter asking the brigade commander to intervene and prevent any *Interahamwe* attack at Saint Paul the next day, 14 June. In that message, Bizimana further asked the commander to stop the *Interahamwe* from taking refugees away by assembling and interrogating those refugees.[596]

517. At about 8.00 or 9.00 a.m. the next day, 14 June, the prefect's secretary gave Jean Bizimana a message from Father Célestin Hakizimana at Saint Paul. The priest had first tried without success to reach the prefect by telephone and was seeking assistance because the *Interahamwe* were attacking. The witness arrived at Saint Paul between 9.00 and 10.00 a.m. Jean Bizimana was there. Many *Interahamwe* were assembled both outside and within the premises; those outside were angry and wanted to get in. No-one from the prefecture office entered the premises that day. The witness did not see Father Hakizimana there, but he might nonetheless have been present.[597]

518. When he arrived at the gate of Saint Paul, Witness ALG heard a car horn and saw Renzaho in a vehicle behind him. Renzaho beckoned Jean Bizimana over and asked what was happening. Bizimana explained how he had found out about the impending attack. Renzaho did not appear to be affected in any extraordinary manner by the situation or Bizimana's words. He told him to leave and attend to his wife. As Bizimana left, the witness saw the *Interahamwe* outside the compound go to greet the prefect. They had appeared angry but **[page 138]** calmed down and seemed pleased when they saw Renzaho, who shook hands with some of them. The *Interahamwe* were still greeting him when the witness left.[598]

519. After the events, the witness was detained in Kigali prison with *Interahamwe* who had participated in the attack. They informed him that Renzaho left, while they proceeded to take about 40 refugees from Saint Paul. The *Interahamwe* killed them at a mass grave referred to as the CND near the Rugenge sector office. Although Renzaho had given the impression that he would handle the situation, the witness later concluded that the prefect had given the refugees to the *Interahamwe*.[599]

---

[594] T. 10 January 2007 pp. 55-56, 59, 63; T. 11 January 2007 pp. 11-12; T. 15 January 2007 pp. 17, 22; Prosecution Exhibit 67 (personal identification sheet). When testifying, Witness ALG was awaiting trial in Rwanda for his role during the events in 1994, including this incident. T. 10 January 2007 p. 64.
[595] T. 10 January 2007 p. 67; T. 11 January 2007 pp. 10-11, 30; T. 15 January 2007 p. 31. Witness ALG noted that a head of service was known as a sub-prefect in other prefectures.
[596] T. 10 January 2007 pp. 65-66, 69; T. 12 January 2007 pp. 35-36; T. 15 January 2007 pp. 19, 21-22, 25.
[597] T. 10 January 2007 pp. 66-67; T. 15 January 2007 pp. 17-19, 21, 24.
[598] T. 10 January 2007 pp. 66-69; T. 15 January 2007 pp. 17, 25.
[599] T. 10 January 2007 pp. 69-70; T. 15 January 2007 pp. 18, 24-25.

520. On 17 June, after an RPF raid on Saint Paul, the *Interahamwe* attacked both Saint Paul and Sainte Famille. Many persons were killed. The witness was not present at the attack as he had gone to Gitarama for four days. He only returned to Kigali in the evening of 18 June.[600]

Prosecution Witness BUO

521. On 8 or 9 April 1994, Witness BUO, a Hutu, joined the *Interahamwe* in the Rugenge sector, whose headquarters were at the home of its leader, Angeline Mukandutiye. He remained a member of the militia until July 1994.[601]

522. The witness testified that there were two particularly important attacks at Saint Paul in which Renzaho participated. The first was in May. Angeline Mukandutiye and *Conseiller* Odette Nyirabagenzi decided that certain Tutsis sought by the *Interahamwe* should be abducted from Saint Paul and killed. Mukandutiye told the *Interahamwe* about the plan. In order to get access to the persons they wanted to take away, they agreed to claim that there were *Inyenzi* hiding at Saint Paul who were firing at the roadblock during the night. About 50 *Interahamwe* and local residents cleared the bush in the area to find *Inyenzi* who might be hiding there.[602]

523. Angeline Mukandutiye and Odette Nyirabagenzi were present at Saint Paul during this attack in May. The witness saw Mukandutiye holding a list and recalled four names from it, although he did not notice the total number of names. The two women disagreed on the number of persons to be killed. Nyirabagenzi wanted to include everyone at Saint Paul, while Mukandutiye said that only those on the list should be chosen. Around 11.00 a.m., Renzaho came to Saint Paul bringing a sheet of paper similar to the one that Mukandutiye had. He was there for about 10 minutes, resolved the dispute in favour of Mukandutiye's position, and left immediately afterwards. The two women then told the *Interahamwe* that only those whose names were on the list should be arrested.[603]

524. The *Interahamwe* selected Tutsis from the list and forced them into vehicles. They were able to sort through the refugees because the Tutsis were the attackers' neighbours and were known. Many were taken but the witness was unable to give a number. Emmanuel **[page 139]** Rukundo and another Saint Paul refugee were placed in a separate vehicle and taken to Rukundo's house, where they were killed. Mukandutiye went home after Rukundo was abducted. As the *Interahamwe* drove away from Saint Paul, they killed the other refugees. The witness said that "there were bodies everywhere".[604]

525. The second major attack took place in June 1994, on the day after the RPF evacuated Tutsis from Saint Paul and Saint Famille. A lieutenant named Cadence, whom the witness described as an "ex-FAR" member, informed the *Interahamwe* that they were to go to Saint Paul and Sainte Famille. Their task was to find and kill the *Inyenzi* who might have remained there, along with their "accomplices", which the witness explained meant the Tutsis. The attack at Saint Paul was launched at 7.00 a.m. There were about 180 assailants, who were assisted by Hutu refugees from Saint Famille. The gendarmes also participated in the attack, led by Major Bivamvagara. Major Munyakaze, Lieutenant Cadence, Nyirabagenzi and Mukandutiye were there along with the *Interahamwe*. The attackers dislodged every Tutsi they could find, in order to kill them. The witness was unable to indicate the number of victims. He learned that some corpses were left at the CND mass grave, at the house of Iyaremye Straton, while "others died on the road". The witness personally saw Renzaho arrive at Saint Paul after the Tutsi refugees had been killed. Bodies were still strewn about the place. Renzaho neither said nor did anything in response.[605]

---

[600] T. 10 January 2007 pp. 69-70.
[601] T. 25 January 2007 pp. 10, 52, 54-58; T. 26 January 2007 pp. 36-38; Prosecution Exhibit 73 (personal identification sheet). Witness BUO was convicted in Rwanda in 2003 and given a 15-year sentence for his involvement in the genocide.
[602] T. 26 January 2007 pp. 12, 14-16.
[603] *Id.* pp. 13, 17-19.
[604] *Id.* pp. 12-14, 16, 19-20.
[605] *Id.* pp. 12, 25-30. Witness BUO said that Saint Paul and Sainte Famille were virtually at the same location. T. 26 January 2007 p. 31. When the RPF evacuated refugees from Saint Paul in June, "two *Inkotanyi*" and some of the Tutsis being evacuated were killed. *Id.* pp. 26-27.

Prosecution Witness MW

526. Witness MW was a Tutsi refugee at Saint Paul from 12 April 1994. She testified that there were two gendarmes there, but that they could not ensure security against the militia. The centre was attacked several times. Refugees were taken away in two of them. The first of these attacks occurred around 24 April, when many militiamen arrived between 10.00 a.m. and noon. The witness did not know the precise number, but indicated that about 20 *Interahamwe* entered the dormitory and abducted seven persons. The attackers left at around 12.00 or 12.30 p.m. The witness saw a pickup truck leaving the centre with refugees. Célestin Hakizimana, a priest at Saint Paul, and the watchmen there later told her that the seven refugees were killed near Rugenge sector office at a location called the CND. Subsequently, the refugees learned the names of those who had been abducted. Two were Hutus known to have criticised the government, and a third was a Tutsi. The witness heard that *Bourgmestre* Jean Bizimana had come to Saint Paul on 24 April and spoken to Hakizimana, guaranteeing the safety of those who were taken away and saying that nothing would be done to them.[606]

527. Between 9.00 and 10.00 a.m. on 14 June, there was another attack in which about 60 young persons were taken from Saint Paul. The two gendarmes on duty called Father Hakizimana when more than 50 *Interahamwe* arrived with a list of persons. He said to the attackers that the list was not signed and hence not official. A gendarme left with the **[page 140]** assailants and together, they went in search of a military authority for assistance. The gendarme, however, returned to Saint Paul alone and told the witness that the military officers with whom he spoke had refused to sign the list. An hour and a half or so later, the *Interahamwe* returned in an angry mood and began sorting refugees, separating those who were between 16 and 35 years old. The witness's husband and brother were selected.[607]

528. When the witness tried to negotiate with one of the miltiaman to save her family members, he answered that her brother was on his list and showed it to her. She did not see its entire content, or whether her brother's name was actually listed, but observed that it bore an official stamp, the words "the prefect of Kigali-Ville", and was signed. A name beginning with "Re" was visible, but the rest was covered by the stamp. She believed it to be the name of the prefect of Kigali-Ville, Renzaho. Her husband was allowed to go back to the dormitory because an *Interahamwe* saw that he had a Hutu identity card, but her brother was among those abducted and she never saw him again. The witness subsequently learned the names of the refugees taken away and heard they were killed in Rugenge sector, at the "CND" mass grave.[608]

529. On 16 June, Witness MW saw Renzaho arrive at Saint Paul between 9.00 and 11.00 a.m. He came with the *conseiller* of Rugenge, Odette Nyirabagenzi, and many *Interahamwe*, as well as UNAMIR soldiers. It was normal to see civilian authorities with militia during this period. Through a window, the witness saw Renzaho chair a meeting with Father Hakizimana. She heard from other refugees that they were discussing the evacuation of the refugees by UNAMIR. Between 1.00 and 3.00 a.m. in the night of 16 to 17 June, RPF troops evacuated the witness and others, leading them on foot to RPF controlled territory. She heard many explosions and gunfire during the operation. About 20 refugees and one RPF soldier were shot and killed.[609]

Prosecution Witness UI

530. From about 22 April 1994, Witness UI, a Tutsi, sought refuge at Saint Paul, where Father Célestin Hakizimana was in charge. The witness saw *conseiller* Odette Nyirabagenzi there with *Interahamwe* on

---
[606] T. 5 February 2007 pp. 5-9, 23, 28. Witness MW also referred to another attack on 24 April 1994. It was led by between 10 and 20 soldiers but halted by Father Célestin Hakizimana. *Id.* pp. 6, 9-11. More generally, the witness explained that, throughout the war, Hakizimana tried to negotiate with the civilian authorities to help him ensure the security of the people under his care. *Id.* p. 14. She confirmed that gendarmes wore red berets, while soldiers wore black ones. *Id.* p. 26.
[607] *Id.* pp. 11-13, 15.
[608] *Id.* pp. 7-8, 14-15, 19-20, 28.
[609] *Id.* pp. 16-18, 28. Witness MW later heard from other refugees that, during the meeting, the prefect said that the evacuation of Saint Paul refugees by UNAMIR would take place after that of the Sainte Famille refugees. She stated that it was known that the persons at Saint Paul were Hutus or Tutsis who had been directly threatened by militia, whereas at Sainte Famille, the refugees were mixed: some were fleeing the militia but others had left RPF combat zones. The refugees at Saint Paul therefore tried to insist that they be evacuated first, as they were more directly threatened, but Renzaho refused and said they would come second. *Id.* pp. 16-17.

691

14 June, holding a list. About 50 young men were abducted and taken to their deaths. The witness stayed in his room that day and did not go outside. He remained at Saint Paul until 16 June, when, according to the witness, the "*Inkotanyi*" evacuated almost all the refugees.[610]

Prosecution Witness GLE

531. Witness GLE, a Tutsi, sought refuge at Saint Paul at the end of April or in early May 1994 until the *Inkotanyi* evacuated her with other refugees one night. Around 13 June, three **[page 141]** days before the *Inkotanyi* came, *Interahamwe* arrived in uniform, selected a number of young men, and killed them. The witness remained inside the rooms of the centre when the attackers took the men away. She praised the person in charge, Célestin Hakizimana, who did not abandon the refugees but was ready to die with them. The witness believed she would have been killed if she had gone home instead of taking refuge at Saint Paul.[611]

Renzaho

532. Renzaho was aware that there were refugees at Saint Paul, which was one of the sites where he obtained the assistance of the gendarmerie. He testified that the difficulties of assigning gendarmes to CELA centre on a permanent basis prompted him to ask that the refugees there to be moved to Saint Paul and Sainte Famille.[612]

533. One of Renzaho's assistants, sub-prefect Aloys Simpunga, was responsible for Saint Paul, among other sites. From Simpunga's reports, Renzaho knew that Célestin Hakizimana was the priest in charge of Saint Paul, and that Father Wenceslas Munyeshyaka was in charge of Sainte Famille. He was aware that Munyeshyaka transported provisions and mobilised charity organisations for refugees at Saint Paul, among other places, but he had never met him.[613]

534. Renzaho testified that he had tried unsuccessfully to involve UNAMIR officials in stationing a unit at Saint Paul and Sainte Famille. Gendarmes were at the two sites as of 9 April 1994, but not many were available. Their commanding officer was Iradukunda. The number of gendarmes posted at the sites was not of immediate significance, as the sites were sufficiently far from the battle front and the few gendarmes posted would be enough to ensure supervision and to call for reinforcements in case of crisis. Renzaho stated that war-related incidents occurred at the two sites several times, including shelling on 12 and 16 April, 1 and 3 May, and at night on 16 to 17 June. He learned at about 11.00 a.m. on 17 June 1994 that refugees had been taken from Saint Paul.[614]

535. Renzaho denied having made any lists from April to July 1994, and he was not aware that anyone had drawn up a list of persons to be arrested at Saint Paul on 14 June. He did not give instructions to *Bourgmestre* Jean Bizimana that anyone should be arrested on 14 June. The prefect was later informed that Nyirabagenzi, the *conseiller* of the sector, reported to Bizimana on the evening of 13 June that there might be an attack on Sainte Famille. Renzaho speculated that Bizimana forwarded a memo to the gendarmerie to help prevent the attack, otherwise the gendarmes would not have intervened. The officer in charge came to Saint Paul with a number of gendarmes and integrated some of the members of the crowd there into their group before selecting the refugees mentioned on their list. The search, however, yielded nothing and the crowd became unruly. The officer in charge lacked the courage to take control of the situation and ask for reinforcement, and instead, fled the scene.[615] **[page 142]**

536. On 14 June, Renzaho was in Cyangugu with his family and likely left to return to Kigali between 8.00 and 9.00 a.m. that morning. When he returned in the evening on 15 June, refugees at the prefecture office

---

[610] *Id.* pp. 58-59, 69, 75; T. 6 February 2007 p. 7; Prosecution Exhibit 86 (personal identification sheet).
[611] T. 31 January 2007 pp. 2, 6-8; Prosecution Exhibit 79 (personal identification sheet).
[612] T. 29 August 2007 pp. 8, 28, 32-34; T. 30 August 2007 p. 19. Renzaho agreed with the contents of Defence Exhibit 103 (Henry Kwami Aniyidoho: *Guns Over Kigali* (1997) pp. 89-90, which describes the trip to Saint Paul and Sainte Famille on 16 June 1994.
[613] T. 29 August 2007 pp. 34, 36-37, 49; T. 3 September 2007 pp. 31-32, 36-37, 49.
[614] T. 29 August 2007 pp. 34-35, 38-39; T. 3 September 2007 p. 31.
[615] T. 29 August 2007 pp. 39-40.

told him that people had been kidnapped from Saint Paul on 14 June. According to Renzaho, the refugees were angry at Bizimana because he had not acted responsibly.[616]

537. *Bourgmestre* Jean Bizimana confirmed with Renzaho that there had been an incident at Saint Paul but did not provide details. Sub-prefect Aloys Simpunga then informed Renzaho that he had gone to the site on that occasion and regretted the fact that the *bourgmestre* was absent during the event. Renzaho heard that the young refugees who were abducted had been taken to a location and killed. He also saw this information in a UNAMIR document. According to Renzaho, the UN investigation of the incident was inconclusive. He also noted that there was no legal system in place, and that he did not have the time or resources to implement sanctions when questioned why neither *bourgmestres* nor *conseillers* were arrested.[617]

538. On the afternoon of 16 June 1994, he went to Saint Paul with the ICRC and the deputy commander of UNAMIR, General Aniyidoho. They reassured the refugees at the two sites that the evacuation, which had been interrupted for some time, would resume the next day. After that, Renzaho left. That evening, two hours later, the RPF shelled the site. According to Renzaho, 1,800 refugees were taken away, but many other persons were killed during the operation. For example, Hutus there were killed with bayonets and knives. The attack ended at dawn on 17 June.[618]

539. According to Renzaho, he never received a phone call from anyone asking for help at Saint Paul. He denied that he had been called on the morning of 17 June by Father Paulin Munyazikwiye but acknowledged that he knew him well and that they had attended school together. Had there been such a phone call, Renzaho would not have refused to intervene at Saint Paul. He was not always at the Kigali-Ville prefecture, and there were others to whom such a message could be forwarded. Normally, the message would reach the secretariat of the prefecture, then it would be processed by the crisis committee that was set up after 7 April 1994, and the official in charge would be found, or sub-prefect Simpunga would intervene.[619]

Defence Witness UT

540. Witness UT, a Hutu official in the Kigali-Ville prefecture, testified that he had daily contact – morning, afternoon and evening – with Renzaho from 11 April 1994 until the end of the events. In this period, he identified the areas where refugees were gathering and provided assistance to them. He received instructions from and reported to Renzaho regarding the places he visited. The prefect would give him names of those to contact and with whom to work.[620] **[page 143]**

541. Around 18 April, the witness moved persons who had gathered at Kigali hospital to Sainte Famille and to Saint Paul. There was no police or gendarmerie service that was sufficient to provide security for the refugee sites. Renzaho was unable to obtain the assistance he wanted. He had called gendarmerie officials on several occasions, but in vain, and was told that the gendarmerie forces had gone to the war front to help the soldiers. They only received assistance from Lieutenant Sekamana and four or five gendarmes who were permanently guarding Sainte Famille.[621]

542. Saint Paul became one of the major centres for refugees. The witness had worked with Father Célestin Hakizimana, who was in charge there. He went to Saint Paul three times; at the end of April, in the first half of May, and between 12 and 15 June. He intervened following requests for assistance and at times on his own initiative, and would go to the refugee sites with two or three policemen. Renzaho never went there but delegated that task to the witness. All of his interventions were on the prefect's behalf, irrespective of

---

[616] T. 29 August 2007 pp. 19, 41-42, T. 3 September 2007 pp. 26-29, 30.
[617] T. 3 September 2007 pp. 30-31, 42-43.
[618] T. 29 August 2007 pp. 29, 32-33.
[619] *Id.* pp. 36-39. Renzaho was nominated a member of the crisis committee after 7 April 1994, which was set up to manage the situation in the absence of an interim government. According to Renzaho, it had its major missions to establish contact with political parties and to help ensure follow up in the units to make sure that the unit commanders installed discipline. T. 27 August. 2007 p. 50-51, 54-55.
[620] T. 24 May 2007 p. 20; Defence Exhibit 47 (personal identification sheet).
[621] T. 24 May 2007 pp. 7, 19, 29, 32-33, 43-44; T. 25 May 2007 pp. 35, 38-39.

whether he had been specifically instructed to intervene or not. After 16 June, the witness left to attend family matters in Cyangugu. He returned on the night of 20 June.[622]

543. Around mid-June, at about 2.00 p.m., the witness went to Saint Paul after having been advised of an impending attack. He found militiamen brandishing a list of people they wanted to take away. It was signed by *Bourgmestre* Jean Bizimana and had a valid stamp. The *Interahamwe* locked the witness up at Saint Paul until 6.00 p.m., saying that he did not represent the only true authority, which, according to them, was the one controlling the militia. He was able to negotiate with them and "things finally worked out". The witness reported to Renzaho that the militiamen had shown him an official document from Bizimana. After returning from Cyangugu, he learned that the prefect had seriously reprimanded Bizimana for his actions.[623]

Defence Witness PER

544. In April 1994, Witness PER, a Hutu, was spending his holiday working at Saint Paul. On 6 April, he was nearing the end of his time there, but because the war then intensified, he remained until 18 June. The witness undertook humanitarian activities at Saint Paul. From 10 April onwards, he also worked closely with Father Wenceslas Munyeshyaka in helping the many refugees at Sainte Famille, where the latter was often the only priest. The two sites adjoined each other, separated by a wall with two small gates in it.[624]

545. Aloys Simpunga, the sub-prefect in charge of social affairs at Kigali-Ville prefecture, assisted Saint Paul with food, water and medicine. Although the witness slept at Saint Paul, he would go to Sainte Famille around 10.00 or 11.00 a.m. to help Munyeshyaka, and return to Saint Paul around 3.00 or 4.00 p.m. Saint Paul and Sainte Famille were adjoining locations separated by a wall with two small gates. The witness went to Gitarama on 13 June and returned to Kigali on the morning of 15 June.[625] **[page 144]**

546. In April, those at Saint Paul, including the refugees, cut down the bushes and banana trees in the compound at the demand of the militia. The witness did not see anyone being abducted on that occasion, and the *Interahamwe* did not enter the compound. However, in early May, they overpowered the guard and forced open the gate. They said they were sent by Angeline Mukandutiye and were looking for a man named Rukundo. After speaking briefly with Father Célestin Hakizimana, they went with him to find Rukundo, who they brought out with four or five other refugees. The militiamen forced them into a Hilux vehicle and left.[626]

547. The witness only saw Renzaho on 16 June. The prefect arrived at Saint Paul with UNAMIR and Red Cross officials, had a discussion with Father Hakizimana, and left. The witness did not speak with him. The RPF came to Saint Paul to liberate Tutsis on the night of 16 June. Two gendarmes died in an exchange of gunfire during the operation. On the morning of 17 June, there was chaos at Saint Paul. When the *Interahamwe* arrived and found that the RPF had taken refugees, they became enraged and looted the centre before going to Sainte Famille at about 9.00 a.m. The witness fled Saint Paul for Sainte Famille early in the morning on 17 June.[627]

548. According to Witness PER, the telephone line at Saint Paul was cut off at the end of April or beginning of May, and did not work through 17 June, when he left. It was never used to call for help from the authorities because he and Munyeshyaka managed to repel the attacks by themselves and because Simpunga came to see them regularly. The witness never used the phone between 6 April and July 1994.[628]

549. The witness did not see Renzaho in the company of *Conseiller* Odette Nyirabagenzi and primary school inspector Angeline Mukandutiye, and he was not aware if they had met. He also did not hear anyone

---

[622] T. 25 May 2007 pp. 5-7, 39.
[623] T. 24 May 2007 pp. 47-51; T. 25 May 2007 p. 24.
[624] T. 23 August 2007 pp. 27-29, 31-33, 38, 49, 51, 58, 62-63; Defence Exhibit 80 (personal identification sheet).
[625] T. 23 August 2007 pp. 31-32, 50-53, 55.
[626] *Id.* pp. 35-37, 51, 56, 59.
[627] *Id.* pp. 34-35, 39-40, 46, 52-54.
[628] *Id.* pp. 38-39, 41, 43, 57.

mention Renzaho in connection with them. Furthermore, the witness had never heard of any contact between Renzaho and Father Wenceslas Munyeshyaka.[629]

Defence Witness BDC

550. Witness BDC, a Hutu, worked with a non-governmental organisation in Kigali-Ville and supervised its humanitarian assistance to the Saint Paul and Sainte Famille sites. He agreed that Tutsi refugees were relatively safer in larger groups at sites such as Saint Paul than in their homes. The witness would never have told the Tutsi refugees at Sainte Famille, for example, to go home at the beginning of May, because there were roadblocks every 500 metres across the city in that period. The refugees would have been going straight to their deaths "whether they were Tutsi or not". This difficulty of movement was a serious problem that affected even those who had the resources or ability to travel about.[630] **[page 145]**

Defence Witness WOW

551. Witness WOW, a Hutu, lived in Rugenge sector near the CELA building in April 1994. He worked reluctantly for some days at a roadblock, to avoid paying a fine and being considered an accomplice of the RPF. He recalled that the *Inkotanyi* abducted refugees from Saint Paul and Sainte Famille. The *Interahamwe* became angry and attacked the same centres, led by school inspector Angeline Mukandutiye and *Conseiller* Odette Nyirabagenzi. The witness was not present during these attacks. He never heard that Renzaho took part in them.[631]

9.3 Deliberations

552. The Prosecution led evidence about four main attacks on Saint Paul pastoral centre starting in April, with the last occurring on 17 June 1994. While also assessing the evidence as a whole, the Chamber's analysis will consider the attacks on an individual basis and in chronological order.

9.3.1 Attack in Late April

553. The Prosecution presented two well placed witnesses who provided credible, first-hand accounts of an attack against Saint Paul in late April 1994. Witness KZ described an incident that followed a clearing of plants around the centre. About 50 *Interahamwe* carried out the attack and removed seven or eight individuals. He believed they had been killed. Witness MW corroborated this account, testifying that between 10.00 a.m. and 12.00 p.m. on 24 April, many militiamen came to Saint Paul. About 20 entered its dormitory and removed seven refugees.[632]

554. Witness BUO described an attack occurring in May. His account contained several facets that coincided with Witnesses KZ and MW's accounts about the attack in late April.[633] In particular, Witness BUO testified that around 50 *Interahamwe* were involved, that the attack occurred around 11.00 a.m., and that the assailants removed Tutsis before killing them at separate locations. Furthermore, he stated that *Interahamwe* had arranged for inhabitants to clear bushes in the area in order to prevent *Inyenzi* from hiding.

---

[629] *Id.* pp. 33-35, 62.
[630] T. 4 June 2007 p. 4; T. 6 June 2007 pp. 14, 59-61; Defence Exhibit 51 (personal identification sheet). The witness did not specifically identify his ethnicity but testified that his identity card bore the letter "H". T. 4 June 2007 pp. 12-13.
[631] T. 4 July 2007 pp. 35-36, 39, 46, 48-49, 51, 53, 57; Defence Exhibit 69 (personal identification sheet). Witness WOW was detained in Rwanda, acquitted in December 2002, and released from prison in January 2003. He fled Rwanda in 2005 because he was summoned to appear before a Gacaca court notwithstanding his acquittal. T. 4 July 2007 pp. 48-49, 56-57.
[632] Witness KZ did not specify from where the *Interahamwe* removed the refugees and hence may no reference to the dormitory. T. 25 January 2007 pp. 14, 18.
[633] Witness BUO's description appears materially inconsistent with Witness KZ's otherwise credible account regarding an attack in May, which is discussed below. The Prosecution submissions fail to offer any clarification as to whether the May attack described by Witness BUO is the same as the April attack described by Witnesses KZ and MW or is an independent event. *See* Prosecution Pre-Trial Brief paras. 78-83; Prosecution Closing Brief paras. 269-299; T. 14 February 2008 pp. 11-12, 18, 20-21 (closing arguments). The Defence objected that Witness BUO's evidence regarding the May attack fell outside the scope of the Indictment. T. 14 February 2008 pp. 61-62.

No other witness referred to removal of vegetation in May.[634] Evidence about the attack on CELA on 22 April also suggests that bushes were being cleared in the vicinity of these two centres in April rather than May (II.6). Finally, Witness BUO's description of the attack differs considerably from **[page 146]** Witness KZ's account of an attack in May, which involved *Interahamwe* and soldiers, the use of tear gas, and when no refugee was removed.

555. Taking into account that Witness BUO may in fact have been describing the attack in April, the Chamber notes his testimony that it was led by school inspector Angeline Mukandutiye and *Conseiller* Odette Nyirabagenzi. He also said that Renzaho arrived shortly before it commenced with a list. It was used to identify Tutsis, who were ultimately killed. The witness's evidence about the involvement of these three persons is uncorroborated.

556. The Chamber takes the view that the witness's position as an *Interahamwe* participating in the attack could have provided him with a broader overview of what unfolded than, for instance, Witness MW, a Tutsi refugee. This could explain why he observed individuals that were not noticed by her. It is significant, however, that Witness KZ, a Hutu who could move freely about at Saint Paul did not notice any of them, in particular Renzaho.

557. The scale and organisation of the attack may indicate a degree of coordination suggesting that authorities, including the prefect, were involved. Furthermore, on 12 April, Renzaho had given an interview on Radio Rwanda, which called for "communal work within quarters by cutting off bushes" to prevent *Inyenzi* from hiding.[635] While this evidence could support an inference that Renzaho or his *de facto* subordinates were involved in the attack on Saint Paul, the absence of credible, direct evidence fails to establish that these inferences are the only reasonable conclusions. It is also recalled that Witness BUO's testimony should be considered with caution, in view of his conviction, and sentence of 15 years' imprisonment for his participation during the events. Under these circumstances, the Chamber does not accept his evidence about the involvement of Renzaho, Mukandutiye and Nyirabagenzi without additional eye-witness testimony.

558. Witness KZ testified that *responsables de cellule* and *nyumba kumi* (ten household) leaders were involved in clearing the bushes. The Prosecution alleges that Renzaho had authority over these persons.[636] Renzaho's previous broadcast calling for such actions could also indicate a degree of coordination between local officials and Renzaho. In view of any additional link between the operation and the prefect, it cannot be said that this is the only reasonable inference to be drawn. There are also questions about the extent to which the participation of civilians amounted to a crime. It is not clear that the inhabitants were *Interahamwe*, and they were generally described as leaving once the bushes had been cleared. It has not been established beyond reasonable doubt that they were aware or had reason to know that their involvement in removing vegetation would lead to the selection, removal and ultimately killing of individuals within Saint Paul after they had left. Finally, it is not clear that the act of clearing bushes substantially contributed to such killings.

559. The Chamber finds that an attack occurred at Saint Paul sometime in late April, leading to the abduction of seven or eight persons who had sought refuge there. This attack was launched by *Interahamwe*. The Chamber has taken into account that Renzaho acted in coordination with civilian attackers, including *Interahamwe*, at attacks on CELA and Sainte Famille (II.6 and 11). It has also considered evidence of his alleged role in the civil defence as well as his activities relating to the erection of roadblocks and arming of civilians (II.2 and 3). This shows that Renzaho at times had authority over civilian militia, including **[page 147]** *Interahamwe*. However, the Chamber is not convinced that he had constant and continuing authority over them. The uncorroborated evidence implicating him in this particular attack raises considerable doubt as to his involvement in it.[637] Consequently, the Chamber has doubts that those carrying

---

[634] Also Defence witness PER testified that bushes were cleared around Saint Paul in April 1994 at the demands of militiamen. He was unaware of anyone being abducted on that occasion.
[635] Prosecution Exhibit 50 (transcript of Radio Rwanda interview, 12 April 1994) p. 9.
[636] Prosecution Closing Brief para. 54.
[637] Similarly, the Chamber does not find it established beyond reasonable doubt that Odette Nyirabagenzi and Angeline Mukandutiye were criminal participants in this attack.

out the operation were Renzaho's subordinates at that time, or that he exercised effective control over them. The evidence fails to demonstrate Renzaho's responsibility for the killings.[638]

9.3.2 Attack in May

560. Witness KZ testified that in the beginning of May, soldiers of the Muvumba battalion attacked Saint Paul using tear gas. They left without taking anyone away. Witness KZ stated that "there was no violence against anyone whatsoever".[639] Also in early May, Witness KZ called the prefecture and spoke to Renzaho, appealing to him for assistance in the face of *Interahamwe* attacks on Saint Paul. Renzaho told him to send the refugees home, and hung up the phone when the witness protested that it was unsafe for the refugees to leave.

561. Renzaho denied having received such a call. Defence Witness PER, who was not present at Saint Paul for much of the time in question, testified that the telephone at Saint Paul did not work from about the end of April or early May until 17 June. He, however, never tried to use the telephone there to call for help.

562. The Chamber is persuaded by Witness KZ's testimony about the operation of the telephone line. It appeared coherent, detailed and truthful. Renzaho's denial fails to raise reasonable doubt that he was contacted by Witness KZ and informed of *Interahamwe* attacks. Witness PER's evidence that the phone line at Saint Paul was not operational also carries very little weight relative to Witness KZ's evidence.

563. Nonetheless, the evidence of this attack fails to directly implicate Renzaho or establish criminal conduct for which he could be held liable. The Chamber will revert to its finding concerning the phone call in relation to subsequent attacks.

9.3.3 Attack on 14 June

564. There is no dispute that an attack took place at Saint Paul pastoral centre on 14 June 1994. Over 1,000 persons, mostly Tutsis, had sought refuge there, as explained by Witness **[page 148]** KZ who had thorough information about the situation. Witnesses KZ, ALG and MW testified that the militia arrived at the centre in the morning. The evidence suggests that there were several hundred attackers.[640]

565. This process resulted in the *Interahamwe* separating refugees with a Tutsi appearance. Around 50 men were abducted from Saint Paul.[641] Witnesses KZ, ALG and MW all heard that those who were removed were killed, and Witnesses ALG and MW were told that this occurred near the mass grave referred to as "CND". Also Witnesses UI and GLE made general remarks that those who were removed were killed, and it is corroborated by a contemporaneous report generated by UNAMIR.[642]

---

[638] The Chamber has doubts that Renzaho received sufficient notice as it relates to this attack. Paras. 23 and 39 of the Indictment relate to attacks on Saint Paul in June 1994. While the attack in April arguably fall within the scope of paras. 20 and 37, these are chapeau paragraphs (neither paragraph charges Renzaho with an enumerated act under Article 2 of the Statute) used to provide context for more specific charges. See *Setako* Defects Decision paras. 3-5; *Gacumbitsi* Trial Judgement para. 176 and *Gacumbitsi* Appeal Judgement para. 53. A liberal reading of the Indictment, pairing para. 20 with general paras. 11 and 12, or para. 37 with general paras. 28, 29 and 33 could provide notice of the crimes related to paras. 20 and 37. Nonetheless, the date range in paras. 20 and 37 – 7 April to 17 July – remains overly broad and is not narrowed by the other paragraphs. The summary of Witness KZ's anticipated evidence in the Pre-Trial Brief demonstrates that the Prosecution could have pleaded both the timing and nature of the attack with greater precision than that provided, see p. 71 ("In mid-April a group of civilians led by cellule leaders went to St. Paul and took away 7 people who were killed near Rugenge [sector] office."). The Brief was filed on 31 October 2005, whereas the Indictment came into effect on 16 February 2006. Under the circumstances, the Pre-Trial Brief cannot cure the subsequently filed Indictment (which is required to plead all material facts). See *Karera* Appeal Judgement, para. 368.
[639] T. 25 January 2007 p. 16.
[640] Witness KZ estimated that the number of *Interahamwe* first amounted to about 300, and later that morning increased with another 200, who had been waiting outside Saint Paul.
[641] The estimates of persons taken away varied, see Witness KZ (the *Interahamwe* tied up and took away between 30 and 50 young and middle-aged men), Witness MW (between 56 and 60 person), and Witness UI (50 young men).
[642] Prosecution Exhibit 40 (UNAMIR inter-office memorandum, 15 June 1994), para. 1 ("As you are aware it appears now that some forty children were slaughtered at Saint Paul yesterday…"). The Chamber notes that paragraph 1 (m) suggests that the incident occurred at Sainte Famille. This appears to be a mistake which may be explained by the immediate proximity of Sainte Famille and Saint Paul.

566. The main issue for the Chamber is whether Renzaho was involved in this event. There is no clear evidence that he ordered the removal of the young men. However, the Prosecution invites the Chamber to find that he is responsible, based on the existence of the prefectoral stamp on the arrest warrant presented by a gendarme to Witness KZ; Renzaho's presence at Saint Paul in the morning of 14 June; and his failure to prevent the *Interahamwe* from acting even if it was clear that they wanted to abduct Tutsi refugees. The Chamber will consider these elements in turn while assessing the evidence in its totality.

(i)   Lists and or Arrest Order

567. According to Witness KZ, Lieutenant Iradukunda from the gendarmerie and the *Interahamwe* had a list that read "PO", or "by order". It was signed by Jean Bizimana, the *bourgmestre* of Nyarugenge *commune*. Persons on the list were to be removed and interrogated at the Nyarugenge gendarmerie brigade. Witness MW, one of the refugees at Saint Paul, suggested that the list, which the militia were using to identify individuals to remove from the centre, was bearing the words "the prefect of Kigali-Ville". She also saw "Re", whereas the rest of the name was covered by a stamp. Defence Witness UT, who arrived at the centre around 2.00 p.m., saw militiamen with a list of individuals to be removed, signed by Jean Bizimana, and with a valid stamp of the prefecture. The first-hand evidence of Witness ALG suggests that Bizimana wrote a letter on 13 June 1994 asking a Nyarugenge brigade commander to prevent an *Interahamwe* attack at Saint Paul on 14 June by assembling those staying at the centre and interrogating them at gendarmerie.[643]

568. The Chamber accepts the fundamental aspects of the evidence above, namely that at least one gendarme along with *Interahamwe* went to Saint Paul on 14 June.[644] They carried a document that bore the official stamp of the prefecture and was signed by Jean Bizimana, **[page 149]** *bourgmestre* of Nyarugenge *commune*. This document identified individuals to be taken to the Nyarugenge gendarmerie brigade. The gendarme left during the identification process and *Interahamwe* ultimately removed between 30 and 60 individuals who were perceived to be Tutsis and killed them.

(ii)   Renzaho's Presence at Saint Paul

569. The strongest evidence implicating Renzaho is Witness ALG's testimony that Renzaho was at Saint Paul that morning prior to the ensuing attack. The fact that no other witness placed Renzaho at Saint Paul that day does not in itself raise doubt with respect to Witness ALG's observation. His position outside the centre prior to the attack could have provided him a significantly broader vantage point from which to observe who was among the attackers than those of Witnesses KZ and MW, as well as Defence Witness UT. Nonetheless, at the time of his testimony, Witness ALG was waiting to be tried for genocide in Rwanda, and his alleged role in this massacre, as an official, was part of the factual antecedents in support of the charge.[645] Given the distinct possibility that the witness may have sought to positively affect the outcome of his trial in Rwanda by deflecting responsibility to Renzaho, the Chamber views his evidence with caution and will not accept it without corroboration.

570. Witness KZ was the only other witness to testify about Renzaho's involvement in this particular attack. Specifically, he heard that Renzaho was seen in the company of the attackers and Angeline Mukandutiye celebrating at the Pan Africa hotel. While the Chamber has elsewhere found Witness KZ reliable, this hearsay evidence fails to establish Renzaho's involvement in the attack or sufficiently corroborate Witness ALG's evidence.

(iii)   Renzaho's Liability for the Actions of Others

571. Turning to the participated in the attack, the evidence demonstrates that *Interahamwe*, also referred to as militia or militiamen, were the primary attackers who sorted victims, removed and killed them. As

---

[643] The Defence does not deny that an attack took place at Saint Paul on 14 June 1994; that a list of persons to be killed was circulated at Saint Paul; and that the list bore the official stamp of the Kigali-Ville prefecture. Defence Closing Brief paras. 357, 380.
[644] The Chamber is satisfied that the slight differences among the Prosecution evidence relating to the date of the attack can reasonably be explained by the passage of time as well as the traumatic nature of the event.
[645] T. 10 January 2007 p. 64; Defence Exhibit 4 (Rwandan judicial dossier of Witness ALG).

mentioned above in connection with the April attack on Saint Paul (II.9.3.1), the Chamber has considered the extensive evidence of Renzaho's coordination and authority over civilian attackers. It is not convinced that he had constant and continuing authority over either *Interahamwe* or civilian militia. The dearth of evidence implicating Renzaho in the 14 June attack raises considerable doubt as to his involvement in it. Furthermore, the Chamber has doubts that those carrying out the operation were Renzaho's subordinates at that time, or that he exercised effective control over them. The evidence fails to demonstrate Renzaho's responsibility for the acts of these attackers.

572. Witness UI observed *Conseiller* Odette Nyirabagenzi with *Interahamwe* holding a list during the attack on 14 June. Witness KZ prefaced his description of that attack by saying that the *Interahamwe* were led by unidentified "*conseillers*". Witness ALG's testimony suggests that Nyirabagenzi, at a minimum, was communicating with the *Interahamwe* planning the attack, using lists of persons from Rugenge and Muhima sectors. His account is corroborated by Witness KZ's testimony that the *Interahamwe* initially came with lists of persons from Rugenge and Muhima. Nonetheless, Witness ALG made no mention of any local officials other than Jean Bizimana and Renzaho being present at Saint Paul on 14 June. **[page 150]** Witness UT also did not identify any local officials other than himself as being present at Saint Paul during this incident.

573. The evidence relating to Odette Nyirabagenzi, and other *conseillers* is limited. According to Witness UI, she was holding a list. Witness KZ's testimony about the actions of unidentified *conseillers* is imprecise. Although the Chamber is aware of Nyirabagenzi's role during other events, it is difficult to establish her exact role here.[646] Leaving this issue aside, the record remains insufficiently precise to establish Renzaho's liability.

574. There is no evidence demonstrating that Renzaho contributed to the actions of any *conseiller* who might have been present during the 14 June attack. While Renzaho did not have *de jure authority* over *conseillers*, there is evidence that he acted as a *de facto* superior (III). He chaired meetings attended by *conseillers* in April and gave them orders to erect roadblocks as well as obtain weapons for distribution (II.2 and 3). Renzaho supervised Nyirabaganzi in the attack on at CELA on 22 April as well as the attack at Sainte Famille on 17 June (II.6 and 11). However, in relation to the 14 June attack against Saint Paul, the Prosecution evidence creates distance between Renzaho and events leading up to the attack. While Witness ALG heard from Odette Nyirabagenzi on 13 June that the *Interahamwe* were planning to attack Saint Paul, she told the witness that she had been unable to contact Renzaho. Witness ALG, who was posted in the prefecture office around this time, also testified that as of 13 June, he had not seen Renzaho for several days. Indeed, an internal UNAMIR memorandum, dated 14 June, notes that "the prefect has been away for some time" and suspects that Renzaho might not have been aware of what was occurring at Sainte Famille, which is in the immediate vicinity of Saint Paul, on the preceding day.[647] Renzaho's absence through at least the day before the attack and a rather imprecise record of when he returned Kigali raises questions about Renzaho's knowledge of the event on 14 June.

575. Furthermore, evidence of events after the attack creates doubt as to what Renzaho knew. There is no direct evidence that Renzaho was informed of the involvement of any *conseillers*, including Nyirabagenzi, in the attack. Witness MW's testimony that Renzaho visited Saint Paul on 16 June with Nyirabagenzi, which lends some circumstantial support to the inference that Renzaho had knowledge of her activities around that time, is unsupported. Witness KZ testified that Renzaho was accompanied by UNAMIR troops. Renzaho and Witness PER stated that Renzaho visited Saint Paul with the deputy commander of UNAMIR troops and the ICRC or Red Cross officials. The Chamber has considered its findings that Witness KZ had previously informed Renzaho of *Interahamwe* attacks in April as well as the evidence relating to the attack on Sainte Famille on 17 June. Nonetheless, the record fails to demonstrate that Renzaho knew or should have known of the risk that Nyirabagenzi or any other *conseiller* had been involved in the attack.

576. Turning next to the involvement of Jean Bizimana, the *bourgmestre* for Nyarugenge commune, the Chamber notes that Witness KZ also stated that an unidentified "representative of the prefect" led the

---

[646] The Chamber has taken into account its findings concerning Nyirabagenzi relating to CELA and Sainte Famille (II.6 and 11).
[647] Prosecution Exhibit 40 (UNAMIR inter-office memorandum, 15 June 1994) para. 1 (n).

Interahamwe. While it is unclear if the witness was referring to Bizimana, Witness ALG's testimony undoubtedly demonstrates Bizimana's presence at Saint Paul prior to the attack. Moreover, the testimonies of Witnesses KZ, ALG and UT, in particular, demonstrate that Bizimana signed a document from the prefecture directing **[page 151]** individuals to be removed from Saint Paul and taken to the Nyarugenge gendarmerie brigade. As Bizimana was the Nyarugenge *bourgmestre*, Renzaho exercised *de jure* authority over him (III). That Renzaho was later made aware of the attack, and in particular, that a document issued by Bizimana was used by the militia to identify refugees, is demonstrated in part by Witness UT's evidence that he informed Renzaho about this.

577. Nonetheless, the Prosecution evidence is equivocal as to whether Bizimana committed a crime for which Renzaho could be held liable as a superior.[648] Witness ALG testified that Bizimana's correspondence from the prefecture was aimed at preventing an attack on Saint Paul. While Witness ALG has a strong interest in providing exculpatory evidence regarding Bizimana's involvement in this attack, the corroborated testimony that the document signed by Bizimina arrived in the company of a gendarme, who was not necessarily working in coordination with the *Interahamwe*, raises questions about the intent behind the document and its actual function in the attack. Witness KZ testified that Lieutenant Iradukunda of the gendarmerie and the *Interahamwe* returned with the list signed by Bizimana. However, Iradukunda left once he realised that he could not stop the *Interahamwe* from taking refugees. This evidence reflects that the gendarmes were not necessarily working in coordination with the *Interahamwe* who ultimately killed those removed, but may have been acting to avert a humanitarian crisis.

578. In the circumstances, the Chamber is unable to conclude that the list signed by Bizimana was made with the intention that Tutsis at Saint Paul be singled out and killed, or that he did so knowing that his action would further such killings. Moreover, the equivocal nature of the Prosecution evidence concerning Bizimana's actual involvement in the separation and killings raises further doubt as to whether his presence or this document substantially contributed to the ultimate killing.

579. Consequently, the Chamber cannot find any basis upon which to find Renzaho criminally liable for the attack on Saint Paul on 14 June.

9.3.4 Attack on 17 June

580. It follows from the first-hand accounts of Witnesses KZ and BUO, as well as the testimonies of Defence Witnesses PER and WOW that during the night of 16 to 17 June 1994, RPF soldiers removed several persons who had taken refuge at Saint Paul. Witness KZ testified that *Interahamwe* carried out an attack at Saint Paul on 17 June, killing the 50 refugees who had remained at the centre. Witness BUO, who was also present, said the *Interahamwe* involved in the attack were led by Major Bivamvagara, Munyakaze, a former Rwandan army lieutenant named Cadence, *Conseiller* Odette Nyirabagenzi and Angeline Mukandutiye. The attackers dislodged Tutsis that remained and killed them. Defence Witness PER also testified that militiamen arrived at Saint Paul on the morning of 17 June and began looting. Furthermore, Prosecution Witness ALG and Defence Witness WOW heard of an *Interahamwe* attack at Saint Paul (and Sainte Famille) after the RPF removed refugees from Saint Paul, but were not present.

581. The Chamber accepts that on 17 June, the day following the RPF evacuation of refugees at Saint Paul, *Interahamwe* or militiamen attacked the centre and killed those identified as Tutsis who had remained there. As with the attack on 14 June (II.9.3.3), the **[page 152]** Chamber is not convinced that Renzaho had continuing authority of these groups, and the evidence is insufficiently precise to attribute liability to him for their participation in the 17 June attack.

582. Witness BUO was the sole witness to testify that Renzaho came to Saint Paul and of the involvement of Bivamvagara, Munyakaze, Cadence, Nyirabagenzi and Mukandutiye. His testimony suggests that Renzaho arrived at Saint Paul, where bodies were strewn about the centre, and did nothing. Witness KZ, on the other hand, testified that a priest named Paulin Munyazikwiye, who had been a classmate of Renzaho's

---

[648] The Chamber uses the term "committed" in its broadest understanding, encompassing any crimes and modes of liability pleaded in relation to this event. See *Blagojević and Jokić* Appeal Judgement paras. 283-284.

called him to report the attack. Renzaho allegedly responded that the priests were all accomplices because they had accommodated the *Inkotanyi* and their accomplices.

583. The Prosecution evidence that Renzaho was both present at Saint Paul and received a call in his office during the attack raises concerns about the reliability of the testimonies relating to this event. Moreover, the Chamber views Witness BUO's account with caution, and refuses to accept the precise details of the specific individuals that were engaged in the attack without corroboration. The Chamber does not consider that its findings concerning the attack on Sainte Famille that day offers sufficient corroboration of Witness BUO's evidence about the attack on Saint Paul.[649]

584. The Chamber concludes that there is an insufficient basis to find Renzaho criminally liable for the attack on Saint Paul on 14 June 1994. **[page 153]**

10. KILLING OF ANDRÉ KAMEYA, 15 JUNE 1994

10.1 Introduction

585. The Prosecution alleges that, on or about 15 June 1994, Renzaho ordered *Conseiller* Odette Nyirabagenzi to kill André Kameya, a journalist who was critical of the Interim Government. Whilst in the company of *Interahamwe*, she found and had André Kameya killed pursuant to Renzaho's orders. Reference is made to Witnesses BUO and AWN.[650]

586. The Defence argues that it has suffered prejudice from vagueness in the Indictment as to the date and place of André Kameya's killing as well as the identities of its perpetrators. Furthermore, the circumstances surrounding his death have not been proven.[651]

10.2 Evidence

Prosecution Witness BUO

587. Witness BUO, a Hutu, was an *Interahamwe* leader in Rugenge sector. He worked with Angeline Mukandutiye, a friend of his family, from about 8 April 1994. She was a leader of the *Interahamwe* who had their headquarters at her house. *Conseiller* Odette Nyirabagenzi was a friend of hers and would visit her there.[652]

588. During the events, it was normal for the *Interahamwe* to go to the Sainte Famille church to search for Tutsis to be killed. One day in April or May, Angeline Mukandutiye had ordered the witness and others to go there to look for Tutsi survivors. He was inside the church building when a man called Michel came in with a photograph of André Kameya and told everyone to look for him. The witness did not know

---

[649] For the reasons set forth in relation to the April attack on Saint Paul, the Chamber has also doubts that Renzaho was provided sufficient notice of the attack there on 17 June 1994. Moreover, it is not convinced that the notice provided for the 17 June attack on Sainte Famille in paras. 23 and 40 of the Indictment is sufficient. Notwithstanding Saint Paul's immediate proximity to Sainte Famille, the Prosecution chose to plead attacks at Saint Paul and Sainte Famille separately. Thus, there are serious concerns about the consistency of the notice as the Indictment distinguishes attacks at both locations. Finally, a review of Witness KZ's statement attached to the Pre-Trial Brief demonstrates that the Prosecution could have pleaded both the timing and nature of the attack with greater precision than that provided. Pre-Trial Brief p. 71 ("On the night of 16 June, RPF soldiers rescued all but about 40 of the refugees at Saint Paul. The following day, *Interahamwe* went to St. Paul threatening those who remained. One of the priests called Renzaho to ask him to do something to stop the attack. Renzaho refused to intervene and accused the preist of conniving with the enemy."). The Pre-Trial Brief was filed on 31 October 2005, and the Indictment came into effect on 16 February 2006. Under the circumstances, the Pre-Trial Brief cannot cure the subsequently filed Indictment (which is required to plead all material facts). *See Karera* Appeal Judgement, para. 368.
[650] Indictment paras. 47 and 51; Prosecution Closing Brief paras. 418-429; According to para. 129 of the Prosecution Pre-Trial Brief, André Kameya was the editor-in-chief of the newspaper *Rwanda Rushya*, and vice-president of the *Parti Libéral*.
[651] Defence Closing Brief paras. 108, 116, 182, 185, 530-567.
[652] T. 25 January 2007 pp. 52-55; T. 26 January 2007 pp. 2, 36-37; Prosecution Exhibit 73 (personal identification sheet). Witness BUO has been detained in Rwanda since 1994. In 2003, he was sentenced to 15 years imprisonment; T. 25 January 2007 p. 57.

Kameya. He asked Michel on whose orders they were searching for him. Michel referred to Odette Nyirabagenzi.[653]

589. Kameya was found in the church building among the other refugees. The witness wanted to know to whom he would be handed over. He went to speak to Nyirabagenzi, who was in her car holding a handwritten piece of paper. She showed it to the witness, who saw Kameya's name on it. He was not able to see other names, but noticed Renzaho's name and signature at the bottom. The paper also had some other writing on it that the witness was not able to read. He did not see Nyirabagenzi share the contents of the document with anyone else. They forced Kameya into Nyirabagenzi's vehicle, and it left.[654]

590. The witness did not see the killing of Kameya, but he believed he was dead: Nyirabagenzi was a killer; as a rule, the *Interahamwe* killed Tutsis they captured rather than imprisoning them; and André Kameya was never seen again.[655] **[page 154]**

Prosecution Witness AWN

591. After her home was attacked by *Interahamwe* on 19 April 1994, Witness AWN, a Tutsi from Rugenge sector, sought refuge at the home of *Conseiller* Odette Nyirabagenzi who had been one of her mother's friends. Nyirabagenzi allowed her to remain there for about a month doing household chores. The witness had to leave in mid-May because of a dispute with Nyirabagenzi's sister. One day when preparing food in the kitchen, the witness heard Nyirabagenzi saying that, after a long period of trying to hunt down journalist André Kameya, they had finally succeeded in flushing him out from the *Kinyamateka* newspaper's premises. The *Interahamwe* had tortured Kameya before killing him.[656]

Prosecution Witness KZ

592. Witness KZ, a Hutu, stayed at the Saint Paul pastoral centre during the events in 1994. He explained that *Kinyamateka* was a newspaper belonging to the Catholic Church, and that their offices were downhill from Saint Paul. Saint Paul, Sainte Famille and CELA sites were close to one another.[657]

Renzaho

593. Renzaho testified that he did not know anything about how André Kameya disappeared. He had no special link with Odette Nyirabagenzi, who was one of 19 *conseillers* in Kigali-Ville prefecture.[658]

10.3 Deliberations

594. The Prosecution relies on two witnesses. Witness BUO saw André Kameya's abduction but not his killing, whereas Witness AWN heard from Nyirabagenzi that he had been found and killed. The Chamber views Witness BUO with caution, because he is a convicted *Interahamwe* leader. Witness AWN's testimony is hearsay and is only partially corroborative. This said, the Chamber accepts that Kameya was killed. This also follows from documentary evidence as well the fact that he has not been seen since.[659]

---

[653] T. 25 January 2007 p. 54; T. 26 January 2007 pp. 20-22; T. 29 January 2007 pp. 26, 32-33.
[654] T. 26 January 2007 pp. 22-23; T. 29 January 2007 pp. 26, 32-33.
[655] T. 26 January 2007 pp. 23-24.
[656] T. 5 February 2007 pp. 30-33, 34 ("And judging from the tone of her voice, the *Interahamwe* were actually pleased with the way they had conducted that operation. Because they first tortured the victim by cutting off his limbs."), 35, 42, 46; Prosecution Exhibit 84 (personal identification sheet).
[657] T. 25 January 2007 pp. 2-3, 5-6, 10, 35; Prosecution Exhibit 72 (personal identification sheet). Witness KZ was shown Prosecution Exhibit 4, a map depicting a square marked "*Kinyamateka* newspaper house" beside the Saint Paul office rooms. He explained that the newspaper moved its offices there only after the war. In 1994, they were located "further on, before you got to Saint Paul centre"; T. 25 January 2007 p. 5.
[658] T. 29 August 2007 p. 60.
[659] Witness BUO, T. 26 January 2007 pp. 23 ("I have told you what happened to people who were arrested -- Tutsis who were taken from among other Tutsis. We killed them. We don't put them in prison. If that person were put in prison, we would have seen him again. So, that person could not have been hidden. He was killed. And, they were buried at sites which are well known."), 24 ("No, I did not see his killing. But I know that the person who took him away was a killer – just as my – myself, because she is the

595. The Indictment alleges that Kameya was found and killed "on or about 15 June 1994". Also, the Pre-Trial Brief asserts that he was abducted from Saint Paul by *Interahamwe* on that date and that, on or about 16 June, Nyirabagenzi went to Saint Paul and announced **[page 155]** that he had been found and killed. In contrast, Witness BUO testified that Kameya was abducted in April or May. However, in his written statement to Tribunal investigators in September 2006, he said that that it was "sometime in June 1994".[660] Witness AWN heard that he had been killed some time between 19 April and mid-May 1994.[661] It is clear that the evidence about the date of the killing turned out differently at trial than alleged in the Indictment.

596. The location of Kameya's abduction and killing is not specified in the Indictment. The Pre-Trial Brief states that he was taken away from Saint Paul, Witness BUO testified that he was abducted from Sainte Famille, whereas Witness AWN heard that he was flushed out from the *Kinyamateka* offices.[662] This inconsistency is not significant. It is clear from the record, including Witness KZ's testimony, that the newspaper's offices and Sainte Famille were close to each other in 1994.

597. According to the Indictment, Renzaho ordered Odette Nyirabagenzi to kill Kameya. The Prosecution relies on Witness BUO's testimony that he saw a handwritten document in Nyirabagenzi's hand on the day of the abduction. Kameya's name was written on it, as was Renzaho's name with his signature. The witness did not see other names. It is unclear whether this was a letter, a list, or some other type of document. The witness was not able to read the document, and it has not been clearly established that it contained an order to kill Kameya.

598. There is no other evidence that Renzaho was involved in the killing. As indicated above, the circumstances surrounding this event are to some extent unclear. The Chamber therefore finds that the Prosecution has failed to prove beyond reasonable doubt that on 15 June 1994, Renzaho ordered *Conseiller* Odette Nyirabagenzi to kill André Kameya. In view of this conclusion, there is no need to consider the issue of notice. **[page 156]**

11. SAINTE FAMILLE, 17 JUNE 1994

11.1 Introduction

599. The Prosecution alleges that, on or about 17 June 1994, while in the company of Odette Nyirabagenzi and Angeline Mukandutiye, Renzaho ordered, instigated or otherwise aided and abetted soldiers, militia and communal police to attack Tutsi refugees at the Sainte Famille church. Many of them were killed. This attack was in retaliation for an RPF operation carried out at Saint Paul pastoral centre the previous evening, and at least 17 Tutsi men were killed. Reference is made to Witnesses KZ, AWX, AWO, ACK, HAD, ATQ, BUO and Corinne Dufka.[663]

600. The Defence does not dispute that an attack took place on 17 June 1994 at Sainte Famille. However, it relies on Witnesses PER, TOA, BDC and RCB-2 to show that Renzaho was not present at the attack, that there is no link between him and the attackers, and that the Prosecution witnesses are incoherent and inconsistent.[664]

---

one who instructed me to kill other persons"); Defence Exhibit 15 (Report from *Reporters Sans Frontières*) p. 21, stating that Kameya was killed by the *Interahamwe* on 15 June 1994.
[660] Defence Exhibit 14 (statement of 12 September 2006) p. 9.
[661] Witness AWN made it clear than she was uncertain about the exact timing of certain other events, but was not hesitant about when she stayed at Nyirabagenzi's house and heard about Kameya's death. T. 5 February 2007 p. 46.
[662] Defence Exhibit 15 (Report from *Reporters Sans Frontières*) p. 21, also states that Kameya was taken from the *Kinyamateka* offices. When Witness BUO was confronted with the report, he maintained that his version of events was accurate. T. 29 January 2007 pp. 33-36.
[663] Indictment paras. 20, 23, 36-37, 40, 58, 59-60; Prosecution Closing Brief paras. 300-322; 459, 472-488; 495; T. 14 February 2008 pp. 6, 11-13, 21.
[664] Defence Closing Brief paras. 413-438; 519-520; Defence Exhibit 113 (*complément écrit aux arguments oraux de la défense*) paras. 437.1-437.4; T. 14 February 2008 pp. 60-64.

11.2 Evidence

Prosecution Witness KZ

601. In April 1994, Witness KZ, a Hutu, was working at the Saint Paul Pastoral Centre. There were four sites in that area that harboured refugees, including a nearby centre called Sainte Famille. That church was managed by Father Wenceslas Munyeshyaka, who was in charge of security and food. He had friends among the gendarmes and obtained three of them to guard the Sainte Famille church around the third week of April 1994. Munyeshyaka also worked with sub-prefect Aloys Simpunga to get food for the refugees. Even if the witness was not with Munyeshyaka every day from 7 April to 17 June, he noted that the priest did everything in his power for the refugees to live in acceptable conditions. Generally, he did not wish to testify about Munyeshyaka's actions other than what he had personally observed.[665]

602. The witness stated that Sainte Famille and Saint Paul were both attacked on 17 June. He avoided providing details about Sainte Famille, saying, in connection with rapes: "If I were to refer to what happened on the Sainte Famille site, I would probably not be saying – telling the truth. I was on the Saint Paul site and I can only answer questions on what occurred in that centre."[666]

Prosecution Witness AWX

603. Witness AWX, a Tutsi, testified that she fled her family home on 10 or 11 April 1994 and sought refuge at Sainte Famille until the end of the war. The group of refugees included **[page 157]** Tutsis and others. Father Munyeshyaka was a priest based at Sainte Famille. Around 18 June, the witness left Sainte Famille to fetch some water at CELA, which was downhill from Sainte Famille and very close by, about a four minute-walk away. Soldiers came to Sainte Famille that day and shot many people. She saw Renzaho there, standing with soldiers. He was speaking to persons carrying dead bodies in wheelbarrows. She also saw her sister's dead body in a wheelbarrow. The witness believed that this event occurred the day after the *Inkotanyi* abducted refugees from the Saint Paul centre. The *Interahamwe* launched the attack because they were angry. They wore military attire and resembled soldiers.[667]

Prosecution Witness AWO

604. In April 1994, Witness AWO, a Tutsi, was living in Kigali. She was eight months pregnant. Following the President's plane crash on 6 April 1994, she sought refuge with her children at an orphanage run by the Sisters of Saint Teresa of Calcutta, which was just next to her house. She no longer recalled the date but believed it was at least two or more days after the crash.[668]

605. In early or mid-June 1994, the witness went to the Sainte Famille church.[669] A few days after her arrival, the RPF evacuated some refugees from Saint Paul during the night.[670] The next morning, she saw Renzaho, Odette Nyirabagenzi and Angeline Mukandutiye arrive at Sainte Famille around 11.00 a.m., armed

---

[665] T. 25 January 2007 pp. 2, 6, 10, 11-13, 33-37, 39, 45-47; Prosecution Exhibit 72 (personal identification sheet). The four sites mentioned by Witness KZ were Saint Paul, CELA, Saint Teresa of Calcutta and Sainte Famille. T. 25 January 2007 pp. 33-34.
[666] T. 25 January 2007 pp. 33-34, 42, 44, 45 (quoted).
[667] T. 6 February 2007 pp. 28-29, 31-33, 35, 39, 42-44; Prosecution Exhibit 89 (personal identification sheet). Witness AWX testified that she had previously observed Renzaho at Sainte Famille "around" 24 May 1994 before she was taken away and raped (II.13). T. 6 February 2007 pp. 29-30.
[668] T. 7 February 2007 pp. 3-7, 16-17; Prosecution Exhibit 91 (personal identification sheet).
[669] Witness AWO could not state when she arrived at Sainte Famille, but it follows from the context that it was in the first half of June 1994. See T. 7 February 2007 pp. 8-9, 10, 19. The witness arrived at Sainte Famille when "the war was almost over", a few days before the RPF evacuated refugees from the Saint Paul. T. 7 February 2007 pp. 12 (quoted), 23.
[670] Witness AWO was in very poor condition emotionally and physically at the time of these events, and could not remember when exactly the attack was perpetrated. She recalled, however, that shortly thereafter the RPF took control of the country. T. 7 February 2007 p. 14 ("It was almost towards the end of the war, perhaps in July, because after a while the *Inkotanyi* took over. When they killed all these people, the *Inkotanyi* were already in Gikondo, Rebero and Remera."). In cross-examination, she recalled that she had said the attack might have been in July, "because when the *Inkotanyi* carried their raid out on the Saint Paul centre, the war was drawing to a close". *Id.* p. 23.

Judgement and Sentence

with pistols. They checked to see who remained there and then left. Afterwards, the witness heard Father Wenceslas Munyeshyaka tell the refugees to "prepare [their] hearts because the time had come" and that the refugees "should sanctify" themselves. He conducted a mass, and then left. Around 11.00 a.m., a great number of *Interahamwe* attackers arrived and killed many people at Sainte Famille. The young men were particularly targeted to prevent them from going to RPF-controlled areas.[671]

606. The refugees were told to come out of the church and show their identity cards. At that point, the witness saw Renzaho. He was in an area overlooking the church building and told the *Interahamwe* to kill "many people". The *Interahamwe* descended to the church and started the killings. At some point Renzaho ordered them: "Stop killing. We have killed all **[page 158]** the *Inyenzi*; and you, the women, you should clap because the *Inyenzi* have been exterminated." The women applauded in order to survive.[672]

607. Over 100 persons died in the attack. Although Witness AWO could not see behind the church, she stated that even more were killed in that area. After it ended, Renzaho and the *Interahamwe* left. The bodies remained there for a number of days. Father Munyeshyaka asked the refugees to pick up the corpses. He said that those who carried away the bodies would be rewarded by Renzaho. Munyeshyaka also promised that Renzaho would authorise the transfer of those assisting to the Kabuga area. It was said that the corpses would be taken away so that UNAMIR soldiers would not see them. The bodies were placed in the garage of the priests, on a tarpaulin. Subsequently, young persons who had, until then, managed to hide in the garden or in water tanks were taken away in vehicles and killed elsewhere. The witness did not specify who abducted them, but such attacks ended after the RPF takeover of the country.[673]

Prosecution Witness ACK

608. On 22 April 1994, Witness ACK, a Tutsi, went to seek refuge at the Sainte Famille church with her daughter and her daughter's cousin. Father Wenceslas Munyeshyaka was in charge of the church and lived there. There were many refugees at the church. *Interahamwe* would come there and insult them. The refugees were afraid and sought help from Munyeshyaka, but he was friendly with the *Interahamwe* and continued to let them in, spoke with them often and allowed them to enter his office.[674]

609. On 16 June, the *Inkotanyi* had come to Saint Paul to find refugees there. In the morning of 17 June, the witness heard Munyeshyaka say that the RPF had taken away the Tutsis, but that the Hutus had died, and that all that would follow would be a consequence of what the refugees' "kinsmen" had done.[675]

610. On 17 June, at around 11.00 a.m., *Interahamwe* arrived at Sainte Famille and began shooting indiscriminately. Many refugees were killed, including the witness's daughter. The witness tried to flee from the compound. When she was a few metres from the gate, about 25 or 30 metres from the entrance to the church building, she saw Renzaho standing near the water tank. He was surrounded by many *Interahamwe*. Subsequently, a whistle was blown and the *Interahamwe* stopped the operation. The corpses were placed on stretchers and hidden in the garage.[676]

611. The following day, 18 June, about 12 young men jumped over the fence and came into the church. The witness did not say why. A school inspector named Angeline came the day after that with Munyeshyaka to the church office, had a discussion, and then took the 12 persons away. They were not seen again. The

---

[671] T. 7 February 2007 pp. 12-14, 20, 23, 26. Witness AWO used the word "around" ("vers") 11.00 a.m., both in relation to Renzaho's arrival and the commencement of the attack. According to the witness, Angeline Mukandutiye had been telling Renzaho that there were *Inyenzi* in the Sainte Famille church who were causing problems. It is not apparent when this occurred or how the witness learned about it. *Id.* p. 12.
[672] *Id.* p. 26. It is unclear from Witness AWO's testimony whether Renzaho was overlooking the church during the entire attack.
[673] *Id.* pp. 13, 14 (the French version makes clear that "he" is Renzaho), 23-25.
[674] T. 5 March 2007 pp. 62-63, 65-67, 69-70; Prosecution Exhibit 95 (personal identification sheet).
[675] T. 5 March 2007 pp. 70, 71 ("The Father said that RPF troops had taken away the Tutsis, but that the Hutus had died. He added that all that was going to follow as a consequence would be the result of what our kinsmen did.").
[676] *Id.* pp. 70-71; T. 6 March 2007 p. 64.

witness said later that Angeline came with **[page 159]** Colonel Munyakazi as well as Nyirabagenzi that day and that Munyakazi arrested the 12 men.[677] She stayed at Sainte Famille until 24 June 1994.[678]

Prosecution Witness HAD

612. Witness HAD, a Tutsi secondary school student, fled to the Sainte Famille church on 22 April 1994, at around 3.00 p.m. There were many refugees at the church, including Rwanga's wife and her daughter, Hyacinthe Rwanga. Two separate groups of refugees stayed inside the church. The witness's group was near the altar at a place nicknamed "CND" and composed of Tutsis. They had no water or food and were always being watched by gendarmes, *Interahamwe* and the Hutu refugees. Father Munyeshyaka instructed her to hide there. The other group stayed in an area called "Camp Hutu", which was safer.[679]

613. On 17 June, there was an attack on the Sainte Famille church and refugees were killed, including Hyacinthe. Before noon on that morning, the witness and other refugees were told that the prefect was in the church's compound. They went out to check, and saw him walking with Father Munyeshyaka towards the *procure*. The priest was holding a list. She had seen Renzaho previously at the CELA centre. At one stage, the prefect and priest left the compound. The witness did not see Renzaho again that day, but testified that, after he left, he ordered "his dogs" to attack the refugees. That day, the witness saw other officials in the compound as well, including the *conseiller* of Rugenge, Odette Nyirabagenzi, and the inspector, Angeline Mukandutiye.[680]

614. The *Interahamwe* entered the church's compound. One of them read names from the list that Father Munyeshyaka was holding earlier, and those whose names were called were killed in the church's garden. There were also persons killed who were not on the list. Subsequently, the *Interahamwe* entered the church and started shooting at the refugees. They fired at those who had been injured near the altar, and even at a statue of the Virgin Mary, because "she was a Tutsi". After the killings, the *Interahamwe* said that they were seeking revenge because the previous night, the RPF had evacuated some Tutsi refugees from the Saint Paul centre and killed Hutus.[681] **[page 160]**

615. On the day before the attack, 16 June, Munyeshyaka had persuaded Hyacinthe Rwanga to write a list of names by telling her that UNAMIR would evacuate persons she included. The witness had assisted in drawing up the list. She recognised the paper on which it had been written when she saw Munyeshyaka carrying it on 17 June. Moreover, the order of the persons called out was the same as on the list she had put together. Nearly all those mentioned were killed. The witness had placed Hyacinthe's name first on the list. The *Interahamwe* tracked her down and shot her in the head. When they reached her mother's name on the list, they said she could be spared because her children had already died.[682]

---

[677] The English and French versions are not quite clear. T. 5 March 2007 p. 72 reads: "Two days later, the one – the person called Angeline, who was an inspector of education – and here let me add that the young people were 12 in number – or, rather, it was the following day that *Angeline Munyakazi* (sic) and the priest came to the office. And even if I don't know the content of their discussion, they nonetheless called the young men, and *Munyakazi took them with her*, and those young persons did not come back again" The French transcript reads: *"Ou c'est plutôt le lendemain qu'Angéline Munyakazi et l'abbé sont venus au bureau, même si je ne connais pas le contenu de leur discussion, ils ont néanmoins appelé ces jeunes hommes. Et Munyakazi les a amenés avec «lui» et ces jeunes hommes ne sont plus jamais revenus." Id.* p. 79. It appears that something is missing between "Angeline" and "Munyakazi" in both versions. This follows from T. 6 March 2007 p. 66, which reads: "I told you that *Munyakazi* showed up after the 17th, and that *he was accompanied by Angeline*. They said that some people had shot at them the night before. But, as a matter of fact, they were referring to the 12 young people who had scaled the wall. *Munyakazi immediately arrested them* after the priest brought them or showed them to Munyakazi" (emphasis added). The Chamber accepts that Witness ACK testified that Munyakazi and Angeline Mukandutiye went to the church office after 17 June 1994, together with Nyirabagenzi.
[678] T. 5 March 2007 p. 67; T. 6 March 2007 pp. 65-66, 71-72.
[679] T. 1 February 2007 pp. 11, 17, 21-22, 33-34; Prosecution Exhibit 82 (personal identification sheet).
[680] T. 1 February 2007 pp. 12-14, 22-26, 35. Witness HAD did not give details about the *procure*, but the Chamber notes that the word usually refers to the office or residence of the curator or bursar. It was in the church's compound, between the shop and the garden, near the petrol pump. *Id.* p. 27.
[681] *Id.* pp. 22-25, 35-36.
[682] *Id.* pp. 23-25, 35-36 (mentioning that Hyacinthe's mother, who was on the list, was spared because her children had been killed).

616. The attack lasted all day and many were killed. A policeman eventually arrived and said it was not possible to kill all the Tutsis. He told the Hutus to leave, saying that the church would be destroyed. When the attackers heard that UNAMIR were coming, they shot in the air and retreated. It was evening. The UNAMIR soldiers did not arrive on 17 June. The following day, the dead bodies were piled up.[683]

617. The witness noticed Munyakazi a day or two after the attack, when he came to Sainte Famille to evacuate some persons. She did not recall seeing him on the day of the attack, but had heard that he was present. As she was not familiar with his appearance, she would not have recognised him. The witness left Sainte Famille for an RPF-controlled area on 20 June.[684]

Prosecution Witness ATQ

618. Around 16 or 17 May 1994, Witness ATQ, a Tutsi, fled to the Sainte Famille church. She was staying in a tent outside the church, in an elevated area. Between 9.00 and 10.00 a.m. on about 16 June, the day after the *Inkotanyi* evacuated some refugees from the Saint Paul centre, she saw Renzaho standing beside Father Munyeshyaka. The witness observed the prefect while she was outside her tent. He was wearing military attire and glasses. She had not seen him previously but someone pointed him out, saying: "That is Renzaho, whom you see there, and we are done for." Renzaho left and, five minutes later, the *Interahamwe* arrived and began shooting at the crowd. She heard gunshots from all directions, and took shelter in the tent. The attack lasted some time, and many persons were killed. An *Interahamwe* ordered the witness to join a group of refugees who were mostly women and children. She saw many bodies on her way to the group, which was not far from the priests' room. The gunshots stopped shortly thereafter.[685]

619. Around noon or 1.00 p.m., Renzaho arrived again with other soldiers and a gendarme named Karemera, who was officially in charge of the security at the Sainte Famille church. The group stopped at the entrance. The witness was sitting on a veranda. Renzaho spoke to two *Interahamwe* named Sese Seko and Cimba, who subsequently told the other *Interahamwe* that "Musee has just ordered us to stop, and that those who were still alive would be killed in due course". Seso Seko fired into the air. He told the refugees that those **[page 161]** who remained alive were lucky and asked them to applaud the *Interahamwe* for what they had just done. As the word "Musee" was a term of deference in Kinyarwanda, the witness understood that it most likely referred to Renzaho, who was the most respected person present.[686]

620. The next day, UNAMIR troops came to evacuate refugees, but Munyeshyaka refused to let them in because there were so many bodies in the compound. The day after that, or about 18 June, the witness saw the prefect arrive again at about 5.00 or 6.00 p.m. After he left, young men moved the bodies to the procure.[687]

Prosecution Witness BUO

621. Witness BUO, a Hutu, was a member of the *Interahamwe*, which had headquarters at the home of Angeline Mukandutiye, an *Interahamwe* leader. The Interahamwe, including the witness, attacked the Sainte Famille church many times. The most significant attack against that site and the Saint Paul Pastoral Centre took place in June. Many refugees were killed. The witness did not recall the precise day. The attack was carried out following the evacuation of refugees by the RPF on the previous day from Saint Paul and Sainte Famille. The morning after the RPF operation, a lieutenant named Cadence told the *Interahamwe* that they should go to Sainte Famille to find the Inyenzi and their accomplices. The witness explained that, by "accomplices", Cadence meant Tutsis.[688]

---

[683] *Id.* pp. 25, 27, 37-38. Witness HAD explained that persons were killed in the courtyard, on the stairs that led from the *procure* to the presbytery, in the garden and inside the church. *Id.* p. 27.
[684] *Id.* pp. 21-22, 35.
[685] T. 31 January 2007 pp. 67-69; T. 1 February 2007 pp. 5-7; Prosecution Exhibit 81 (personal identification sheet).
[686] T. 31 January 2007 p. 69; T. 1 February 2007 pp. 1, 5, 7.
[687] T. 1 February 2007 pp. 6-8.
[688] T. 25 January 2007 pp. 52, 54-57; T. 26 January 2007 pp. 26-28, 36; T. 29 January 2007 pp. 25, 28, 38; Prosecution Exhibit 73 (personal identification sheet). Witness BUO was convicted in Rwanda in 2003 and given a 15-year sentence for his involvement in the genocide. T. 25 January 2007 pp. 56-57.

622. There were about 180 attackers. Authorities who were present during the attack included Renzaho, Munyakaze, Bivamvagara, Lieutenant Cadence, as well as *Interahamwe* leaders Angeline Mukandutiye and Odette Nyirabagenzi. The witness did not specify whether they were present at the Sainte Famille church or the Saint Paul centre or both, but he stated that the two sites were extremely close to each other.[689]

623. The attack against the Sainte Famille church and Saint Paul commenced at around 7.00 a.m. The assailants first went to CELA and Saint Paul before proceeding to Sainte Famille. Lieutenant Cadence and the president of the witness's *Interahamwe* group in Rugenge, who was called Claude, a former lieutenant, instructed the attackers to shoot into the group of refugees without any pre-selection or sorting process. As they were his leaders, the witness had to obey their instructions. He did not personally fire his weapon, as there were other persons under his orders who were shooting. The witness recognised the corpse of Hyacinthe, Charles Rwanga's daughter.[690]

624. Witness BUO stated that he received instructions from Mukandutiye, and that, "during that period", she and Odette Nyirabagenzi were supported by the prefect. He described Renzaho as "the chief of my chief". Furthermore, Father Wenceslas Munyeshyaka was collaborating closely with Renzaho, particularly concerning the situation at Sainte **[page 162]** Famille. The priest also worked with the *Interahamwe* by giving information about Tutsis at Sainte Famille and other sites to Angeline Mukandutiye, who was his close friend. Based on that information, the *Interahamwe* searched for the Tutsis. Munyeshyaka also supplied food to the *Interahamwe* attackers and allowed them into the Sainte Famille site.[691]

625. The witness had been at Sainte Famille for about 30 minutes when Renzaho arrived, after the killings had stopped. The prefect remained at the church for about an hour. He stood near the water tank and sacristy, about five metres away from the witness, and talked to Munyeshyaka, Nyirabagenzi and Mukandutiye. He looked at three corpses, which were placed in front of him. There were bodies everywhere, and he provided vehicles to remove them. According to the witness, Renzaho was the highest-ranking person present and was aware of everything that was happening.[692]

Prosecution Witness Corinne Dufka

626. The witness, an American photojournalist, worked with Reuters news agency in 1994. In May that year, she visited Rwanda three times. During those visits, she went to Sainte Famille church three times and took photographs of the refugees there. Her first visit to Sainte Famille was between 18 and 20 May. It was not easy to reach the church, as she had to pass through a checkpoint manned by persons in civilian attire. The witness met with Father Wenceslas, who gave her permission to take photos inside the church. She also spoke briefly to some of the more than 900 refugees. They seemed tense and subdued or afraid of talking. Most of them were in the courtyard behind the church.[693]

627. During her second visit, on 29 or 30 May at Sainte Famille, a meeting of all the refugees there was being organised. Again, they seemed tense and anxious. She saw three or four persons she believed to be gendarmes milling around the church. She had not seen them on her prior visit.[694]

Renzaho

628. Renzaho testified that he managed to secure some gendarmes to guard Sainte Famille, even though not many were available. They were posted there from around 9 April 1994 and included a commanding

---

[689] T. 26 January 2007 pp. 12, 25-28, 31 (Saint Paul and Sainte Famille were "virtually at the same place"); T. 29 January 2007 p. 25.
[690] T. 26 January 2007 pp. 2, 28-32, 35, 54; T. 29 January 2007 pp. 30-32. When the transcripts refer to "Yacinthe" they clearly refer to Hyacinthe Rwanga.
[691] T. 26 January 2007 pp. 30-31, 33, 35; T. 29 January 2007 p. 30.
[692] T. 26 January 2007 pp. 30 (Munyakaze "took some people from the Sainte Famille parish" and "he even carried some bodies"), 32-33.
[693] T. 30 January 2007 pp. 1-3, 5-6, 8-9, 12-14, 17-19; Prosecution Exhibit 76 (personal identification sheet); Prosecution Exhibit 77 (33 photographs taken by Corinne Dufka). The witness explained that she took photographs 17-20 on her first trip to Sainte Famille between 18 and 20 May (T. 30 January 2007 pp. 6-8); photographs 15-16 and 21-23 on her second trip, around 29 or 30 May (p. 14); and photographs 26-32 in June 1994 (p. 15).
[694] T. 30 January 2007 pp. 6, 14-16, 18, 19.

Judgement and Sentence

officer named Iradukunda. As the site was sufficiently far from the battle front, these few gendarmes would ensure security. If ever a crisis developed, they would be able to call for reinforcements to deal with the threat.[695]

629. According to Renzaho, he went to Sainte Famille only once, in the afternoon of 16 June, with General Aniyidoho from UNAMIR, ICRC representatives, journalists and others. While there, they moved amongst the refugees, trying to comfort them. They told them that **[page 163]** the UNAMIR-assisted evacuations, which had been suspended, would resume the next day.[696]

630. Two hours after their visit, during the night of 16 to 17 June, the RPF heavily shelled the sites of Saint Paul and Sainte Famille. Renzaho said that 1,800 refugees were taken away and many other people were killed, principally at Saint Paul and at a primary school. The attack ended at dawn on 17 June and Renzaho learned of it at about 11.00 a.m. that day. He noted that the RPF killed inhabitants at Saint Paul during their operation "except for their kind, whom they took away with them".[697]

631. Renzaho's assistant, Aloys Simpunga, was in charge of supervising Sainte Famille, visited it every day, and was in "permanent contact" with it. The church was an important site because there were up to 18,000 refugees there. When asked about major events at Sainte Famille that he had been told of at the time, Renzaho stated that "incidents were inevitable, but this could have been avoided". The RPF shelled the site constantly. It was shelled on 12 and 16 April, 1 and 3 May, and during the night of 16 to 17 June. Renzaho wanted UNAMIR to set up a unit at Saint Paul and Sainte Famille and fly their flag there, so that the RPF would realise that there were refugees at the site and refrain from shelling it. No unit was set up, however.[698]

632. Simpunga told Renzaho that Father Wenceslas Munyeshyaka – a young priest – was in charge of Sainte Famille. Renzaho did not know him personally. Munyeshyaka did, however, telephone him once, on 10 April, and told him that a large number of Tutsis fleeing from RPF held areas had come to Saint Famille seeking refuge and were angry because the site was already occupied by others. Renzaho sent "a policeman or two" in response to the call. Later, the priest asked for a vehicle to transport food stocks, and Renzaho asked that Munyeshyaka be assigned one of the trucks in the prefecture.[699]

Defence Witness PER

633. In April 1994, Witness PER, a Hutu, was spending his holiday working at the Saint Paul Pastoral Centre. On 6 April, he was nearing the end of his time there, but because the war then intensified, he remained until 18 June. The witness undertook humanitarian activities at Saint Paul and, from 10 April onwards, he also assisted the priest, Wenceslas Munyeshyaka, in helping the many refugees at Sainte Famille which was next door. The two sites adjoined each other, separated by a wall with two small gates in it. If he used the road around the wall, he would have had to cross a roadblock manned by the militias. There were also other roadblocks in the vicinity.[700] **[page 164]**

634. The witness would go to Sainte Famille daily between 10.00 and 11.00 a.m., and remain there until 3.00 or 4.00 p.m., and sometimes until the end of the day. He believed it would have been apparent to refugees there that he was working closely with Munyeshyaka, who was often the only priest at that site. There were over 18,000 refugees at the church. He and Munyeshyaka were assisted by the sub-prefect for social affairs of Kigali-Ville prefecture, Aloys Simpunga, who would bring food, water and medicine for the

---

[695] T. 29 August 2007 pp. 8, 35-37.
[696] *Id.* pp. 33-34. Renzaho testified that the evacuation had been suspended because RPF had fired on a UNAMIR convoy.
[697] *Id.* p. 33; T. 3 September 2007 pp. 31-32, 33 (where reference is made to Prosecution Exhibit 63 (transcript of Radio Rwanda broadcast on 18 June 1994) p. 6 ("Q. This is what you said, Mr. Renzaho: 'Look at what happened in Kabgayi and here at the Saint Paul pastoral centre where they killed and injured many others. There they killed the inhabitants, except for their kind, whom they took with them.' That's what you said on the 18th of June, isn't it, Mr. Renzaho? A. That is correct. Q. And when you talk about 'their kind', you are talking about Tutsi, aren't you? A. That is correct.").
[698] T. 28 August 2007 p. 7; T. 29 August 2007 pp. 34-36, 38.
[699] T. 29 August 2007 pp. 36-37, 49-50.
[700] T. 23 August 2007 pp. 27-29, 31-33, 38, 47, 51, 57-58, 61-63; Defence Exhibit 80 (personal identification sheet).

refugees. Five gendarmes were posted at Sainte Famille while he was there. He did not see any soldiers in May 1994.[701]

635. During his time at Saint Paul and Sainte Famille, the witness never heard anyone mention Renzaho's name. It was Aloys Simpunga who dealt with prefectural duties. The witness saw Renzaho only once, on 16 June, when he came to Saint Paul with UNAMIR soldiers and Red Cross officials. During the night of 16 to 17 June, the RPF attacked Saint Paul and evacuated some Tutsi refugees there. Militiamen arriving at approximately 9.00 a.m. the following morning heard of this and became enraged. In response, they looted Saint Paul and then attacked Sainte Famille, to where the witness had fled. The refugees could not repel the attackers. Munyeshyaka left to seek help and returned with soldiers at about 10.00 a.m. The prefect was not with them. The soldiers chased the assailants out of Sainte Famille. Calm was restored but some refugees had already been killed. On 17 June, the witness spent the entire day with Munyeshyaka in the presbytery. He saw neither Renzaho, Nyirabagenzi nor Mukandutiye at Sainte Famille on that date. The witness left Kigali on 18 June, and never returned.[702]

Defence Witness TOA

636. Witness TOA, a Tutsi, sought refuge at Sainte Famille from 10 April to early July 1994. On the way from his home, he passed three roadblocks, the last being about 150 metres from the church. There were around 500 refugees at Sainte Famille, increasing to about 1,000 in April and 4,000 in June. Father Munyeshyaka and his assistants received them. The witness was settled inside the church, to the left of the altar. His estimates of the number of refugees present were based on those that he could see inside the church and in the church garden. Munyeshyaka provided the refugees with food from his stores, and the Red Cross attended to health issues. The witness did not see any authorities visit the site. Other refugees told him, however, that the sub-prefect had come with the Red Cross, bringing food.[703]

637. During the night of 16 to 17 June, the refugees in Sainte Famille were awakened by firing. At about 8.00 a.m. that morning, the Interahamwe arrived and entered the grounds of the church, firing weapons. The witness took refuge inside the church with his family and stayed there for the duration of the attack, around 20 to 30 minutes. Soldiers then came and told the witness that the attack was over. The Red Cross removed the corpses and tended to the wounded that day. During this attack, the witness did not see Father Munyeshyaka, but he [page 165] saw him on the afternoon after it, trying to reassure people. Although he himself did not see Renzaho at Saint Famille at any point during his stay, the witness heard from other refugees that the prefect had come there on 16 June with UNAMIR soldiers. They learned the next morning that the Inkotanyi had taken away refugees from Saint Paul. He believed the 17 June attack was in response to that.[704]

Defence Witness BDC

638. Witness BDC, a Hutu governmental official who worked with a non-governmental organisation, supervised a team of Red Cross relief workers permanently stationed at the Sainte Famille site from mid-May until early July 1994. It was standard procedure for the Red Cross team to log what happened at the site each day, and the witness was given daily reports. He was never informed that Renzaho went to that site or carried out or supervised any massacres, nor did any other source indicate this.[705]

639. On 1 May, Sainte Famille was shelled and 10 to 15 persons were killed. Radio France journalists interviewed Munyeshyaka at the scene. He presented the RPF rebels in a negative light. From then on, he was

---

[701] T. 23 August 2007 pp. 38, 42-45, 47, 49-50.
[702] T. 23 August 2007 pp. 34-35, 38-42, 52-53, 55-56, 64.
[703] T. 6 September 2007 pp. 3, 5-7, 11, 17; Defence Exhibit 111 (personal identification sheet). Witness TOA also mentioned that on 22 April, assailants wearing the *Interahamwe* uniform entered Sainte Famille and identified and abducted between 10 and 15 refugees. The witness saw the refugees being forced into a vehicle and taken away. Afterwards, gendarmes arrived to provide security, and the refugees were not attacked there again. In early May 1994, an RPF shell was fired from the Gisozi area onto Sainte Famille. T. 6 September 2007 pp. 7-9, 15-16.
[704] T. 6 September 2007 pp. 9-10, 15.
[705] T. 4 June 2007 pp. 3-4, 21-23, 37, 68-69; Defence Exhibit 51 (personal identification sheet).

Judgement and Sentence

targeted by the rebels. Early on the morning of 17 June, Red Cross teams assisted several wounded people from Sainte Famille, following an operation to evacuate people there by what the witness described as a "well-organised commando force".[706]

640. Witness BDC saw Renzaho at Sainte Famille only once. Both went there on about 16 June, along with UNAMIR and the ICRC, as part of an official delegation led by General Aniyihondo. He could not say whether Renzaho returned to Sainte Famille on 17 June. The witness had known Renzaho for more than 20 years, and they had been friends since 1986. He met Renzaho more than 10 times between 15 April and early July. The prefect sometimes wore civilian clothes but, more often, military attire. In this period, Renzaho kept the witness informed of what he was doing and the problems that he faced. The witness would come and go as he chose to the prefect's office. Father Munyeshyaka did not know Renzaho personally, but, like everyone else, he knew who he was. Munyeshyaka, who provided a good deal of support for humanitarian work in Kigali-Ville, left Sainte Famille on 5 July.[707]

Defence Witness RCB-2

641. Witness RCB-2, a Hutu, was a junior gendarme in Kigali-Ville prefecture in April 1994. The gendarmerie did not receive orders from the prefect. From the end of May until early July, he patrolled the area that included Sainte Famille church. On 17 June, at about 4.00 or 5.00 a.m., whilst patrolling, he heard gunshots coming from Sainte Famille. At around 6.00 a.m., he and three other gendarmes went to the site. He stayed for about one and a half hours, and saw 15 to 20 corpses and many wounded people there. They were told by residents that RPF troops had arrived, shot the inhabitants of the area and abducted some **[page 166]** persons. Many of the dead had already been buried by their relatives. The witness formed the view that grenades had been used. He did not see Renzaho there that morning.[708]

642. The witness departed around 7.30 a.m., leaving one of his colleagues there.[709] He did not return to Sainte Famille on that occasion, but sent other gendarmes to the church between 2.00 and 6.00 p.m. to assess the situation. Most refugees had left. None of the gendarmes informed him that Renzaho had gone to Sainte Famille that day, nor did the witness hear of an attack taking place there later that day.[710]

643. In the following days, the witness continued to patrol the area around the church. He would circulate between 6.00 and 10.00 a.m., and he sent other gendarmes there from 2.00 to 5.00 or 6.00 p.m. He did not see Renzaho at all between 7 April and early July. If one of his gendarmes had seen Renzaho, he would have been told. He acknowledged, however, that if the prefect had ever needed the gendarmerie, it was his superiors and not him who would have been contacted. The witness did not know about gendarmes who were sent to the Sainte Famille church a few days before 14 June 1994 and insisted he would have known if this occurred.[711]

11.3 Deliberations

644. From April 1994, many persons sought refuge at the Sainte Famille church in the Kigali-Ville prefecture. The number increased gradually and was more than 1,000 in mid-June. On 17 June 1994, *Interahamwe* attacked the site. A large number of persons were killed.[712] The evidence shows that the attack

---

[706] T. 4 June 2007 pp. 21-25, 70. *Id.* pp. 79-80 (French) makes it clear that it was Munyeshyaka who was interviewed.
[707] *Id.* pp. 3-8, 18, 21-25, 34-36, 40, 50, 61, 65, 68-70.
[708] T. 5 June 2007 pp. 61, 66-67; T. 6 June 2007 pp. 1-6, 11-12 Defence Exhibit 59 (personal identification sheet).
[709] In both the English and the French version Witness RCB-2 refers to leaving "gendarmes" rather than a single one, but the context makes it clear that he meant one gendarme. T. 6 June 2007 p. 4 (English); *Id.* p. 8 (French).
[710] *Id.* pp. 3-4, 11-12.
[711] *Id.* pp. 4-5, 11.
[712] Witness Corinne Dufka estimated that over 900 persons had sought refuge at Sainte Famille in mid-May, whereas Witness TOA indicated 1,000 by the end of April, and 4,000 in June 1994. Witness PER's estimate of 18,000 refugees appears exaggerated. After the attack, Witness AWO observed over 100 dead and said that many more were killed behind the church. Witnesses ACK, HAD, ATQ and BUO all testified that there were many victims. The evidence suggests that the number of victims may be counted in hundreds.

711

was carried out in retaliation for an evacuation by the RPF of some Tutsis at the Saint Paul the previous day, during which some Hutus were killed.[713]

645. It is clear that that the attack primarily targeted Tutsis. Witness BUO, an *Interahamwe*, testified that they had been instructed to find the *Inyenzi* and their "accomplices", which meant the Tutsis. Witness HAD stated that an *Interahamwe* shot at a statue of the Virgin Mary, saying that she was a Tutsi. She also overheard a remark made by an arriving policeman to the effect that it was not possible to kill all the Tutsis. According to Witness AWO, young men were particularly targeted to prevent them from going to RPF- **[page 167]** controlled areas. The attack's character as a form of revenge after the RPF operation the previous day also indicates that the assailants were targeting Tutsis.

646. The main question is whether Renzaho was involved in the attack. Renzaho denied this, explaining that he only visited Sainte Famille with UNAMIR and Red Cross representatives on 16 June. Six Prosecution witnesses testified that they saw him at Sainte Famille on 17 June.[714] Their observations were purportedly made before the attack, as well as towards its end or afterwards.

647. Three of the witnesses stated that they saw Renzaho before the attack commenced. Witness AWO said she observed him arrive around 11.00 a.m., and that subsequently, at a place overlooking the church, he instructed the *Interahamwe* to kill "many people".[715] Witness ATQ first saw him at the church with Father Munyeshyaka at around 9.00 or 10.00 a.m., and indicated that Renzaho left five minutes before the attack commenced. Witness HAD noticed him before noon, walking with Munyeshyaka, who held a list in his hand. She only saw him once that day but said that he ordered "his dogs" to commit the attack. In the Chamber's view, it does not affect the credibility of these witnesses that they provided different times for their observations of Renzaho and as to when the attack commenced. They gave estimates, saw him at different moments as the traumatic event unfolded, and several years have passed since June 1994. Viewed in context, the three testimonies show that Renzaho was at Sainte Famille some time before noon.

648. Witness BUO stated that an attack against both Saint Paul and Sainte Famille began around 7.00 a.m. This is much earlier than the indications given by Witnesses AWC, ATQ and HAD. However, it is undisputed that the two sites were very close, and Witness BUO testified that the attackers, including him, went to Saint Paul before proceeding to Sainte Famille. In the Chamber's view, his account does not discredit those of the three refugees. Moreover, while the Chamber has rejected aspects of Witness BUO's testimony as it relates to the attack on Saint Paul on 17 June and, in particular, Renzaho's presence and involvement in it (II.9), his corroborated evidence of Renzaho's presence at Sainte Famille on 17 June lends credence to his testimony in the present context.

649. Turning to observations made around the end or after the attack, Witness AWO testified that Renzaho ordered the assailants to stop killing by saying, "We have killed all the *Inyenzi*". He also told the female refugees to applaud after the attack, which they did. Witness ACK said that she saw Renzaho while killings were still going on. He was standing near the water tank at the entrance to the church, surrounded by *Interahamwe*. The attack subsequently stopped after a whistle was blown. According to Witness HAD, the event ended when the assailants shot in the air. Witness ATQ saw Renzaho again towards the end of the attack, at around noon or 1.00 p.m., instructing the attackers to halt the operation. Like Witness HAD, she said that the attack stopped when an *Interahamwe* shot in the air. She also corroborated Witness AWO's testimony that the survivors were made to applaud. Witness BUO saw Renzaho immediately after the attack, looking at the corpses and speaking with Munyeshyaka. **[page 168]**

---

[713] Witness BUO, who was one of the attackers, confirmed this motive, as well as four of the refugees: Witness AWX (the *Interahamwe* were angry because of the RPF evacuation of refugees from Saint Paul the night before); Witness ACK (Munyeshyaka said that the attack was a consequence of the RPF taking away Tutsis whereas Hutus had died); Witness HAD (heard the attackers claiming revenge on 17 June because Tutsis had killed Hutus); and Witness AWO (the young men at Sainte Famille were particularly targeted to prevent them from going to RPF-controlled areas). Renzaho confirmed that the RPF operation occurred at Saint Paul before the 17 June attack against Sainte Famille.
[714] Witness ACK testified that she saw Renzaho on 18 June 1994 but it is clear from the context that she was mistaken about the date and meant the preceding day.
[715] T. 7 February 2007 p. 13 ("Renzaho was in a place that was overlooking the area, and he was telling the *Interahamwe* to kill – to kill many people. And he would tell us, the [women], to applaud.").

650. These accounts concerning the cessation of the attack are generally consistent. For instance, the fact that two witnesses said that a gunshot was the sign to stop the attack does not exclude that another witness instead remembered a whistle being blown. In this connection, the Chamber points out that guns had been fired during the attack and that a shot at the end would not necessarily be noticed as being a signal. Similarly, Witness HAD's account that the attackers heard that UNAMIR troops were about to arrive and therefore ended the operation is compatible with the evidence that Renzaho gave an order to stop the killing. Different vantage points may explain varying observations.

651. There is also evidence that Renzaho was involved in removing the bodies of the victims. Witness AWX testified that Renzaho was present when dead bodies were carried in wheelbarrows, saying that the corpses had to be buried immediately so the white people would not see them. Witness ATQ testified that she saw Renzaho at the church the day after 17 June at about 5.00 or 6.00 p.m. After he left, young men moved the bodies to the *procure*. Witness BUO observed Renzaho after the killings had stopped when "the bodies were still strewn all over the place". The *Interahamwe* brought out three bodies in front of Renzaho, and he said nothing. He provided vehicles to carry the dead bodies. Witness AWO testified that Munyeshyaka promised that Renzaho would reward those who carried away bodies. The many bodies remained there for a number of days.

652. The Chamber finds that the testimonies of the Prosecution witnesses appeared generally coherent and consistent. They were also mostly in conformity with previous statements the witnesses had given to Tribunal investigators. Some credibility issues require further comments. First, the Chamber recalls that Witness BUO was incarcerated for his role in the genocide, and that his evidence should be considered with caution. However, his testimony about the attack against Sainte Famille on 17 June and Renzaho's presence there appears reliable and is corroborated by other witnesses.[716] Second, the Chamber accepts Witness ACK's explanation why she did not mention Renzaho's presence at Sainte Famille when she testified in national judicial proceedings concerning Munyeshyaka in February 1996.[717] Third, it does not affect Witness HAD's credibility whether she went to Sainte Famille with family members or found them there once she arrived.[718]

653. The Chamber will also address some specific points relating to two other witnesses. Witness AWX did not observe the attack at Sainte Famille but was in a house not far away, **[page 169]** where she was being raped. She observed Renzaho talking about the need to bury dead bodies on the same day as she saw the corpse of her sister in a wheelbarrow. According to her testimony, this happened around 18 June. In her written statement of February 2005, she indicated that she saw her sister's body two days after 25 June. The Chamber accepts that she had problems recalling dates, in particular in view of her traumatic situation.[719] The statement does not mention Renzaho's name when describing this incident. The witness said that she had given his name to the investigators. In the Chamber's view, this discrepancy does not affect her credibility.[720]

---

[716] Witness BUO stated that he joined the *Interahamwe* in April 1994. His elder brother, who had previously worked with Angeline Mukandutiye, was killed and the witness could not say no when she asked him to join them. T. 25 January 2007 pp. 52-53. However, he later testified that his older brother left Rwanda in April. It was his younger brother who was killed, and this happened in May. When confronted with this inconsistency, the witness explained that he may not have expressed himself correctly or was misunderstood. T. 26 January 2007 pp. 36-38. In the Chamber's view, this contradiction does not discredit his testimony about Renzaho.

[717] Defence Exhibit 41 (*procès-verbal d'audition de partie civile*, dated 14 February 1996). When confronted with the lack of reference to Renzaho in her previous statement, Witness ACK explained: "In this document I was talking about Munyeshyaka. Therefore I did not have to talk about Renzaho, given that I did not know where he was." T. 6 March 2007 pp. 63-64. The Chamber notes that the particular portion of her statement concerning 17 June 1994 clearly focuses on Munyeshyaka's role in connection with a specific killing and accepts her explanation why no mention was made of Renzaho.

[718] Witness HAD testified that she found her family members at Sainte Famille when she sought refuge there, whereas Defence Exhibit 25 (statement to investigators of 9 December 2000) indicates that she arrived with her aunt and cousins. T. 1 February 2007 pp. 33-34. The witness said there might have been a communication problem with the person who took down her statement because they were speaking different languages. The Chamber accepts her explanation.

[719] Witness ATQ explained that given the circumstances, she did not recall the precise date but was sure about the month. It was toward the middle rather than the end of June, as it occurred more than 10 days before the *Inkotanyi* captured Kigali and her return home. T. 6 February 2007 pp. 35, 37 ("You know under such circumstances, it is not easy to remember the dates. We did not write down the dates while we were being threatened with death."), 38; Defence Exhibit 30 (statement of 10 February 2005).

[720] T. 6 February 2007 pp. 40-41; Defence Exhibit 30 (statement of 10 February 2005). In the statement, the observation of the sister's body in the wheelbarrow is mentioned very briefly. Renzaho's names appears before and after this event, and it is clear that she saw him several times.

654. Witness ATQ initially testified that she saw Renzaho at Sainte Famille on two occasions. When the Defence put to her that, according to her statement of August 2000, she had seen him three times over three days, she denied this. She then said that she saw him four times over three different dates at Sainte Famille. The witness further stated that she believed it was in June that she saw him as he passed by on his way to Saint Paul, and then on two other occasions at Sainte Famille, making a total of three times. The Chamber considers this confusion to come from lack of communication and does not hold it against her.[721]

655. Having considered the Prosecution evidence, the Chamber now turns to the Defence witnesses, who all testified that they did not see Renzaho during the attack on 17 June. The Chamber finds that their accounts carry limited weight. Witness PER stated that he was hiding in the presbytery during the entire attack, which explains why he could not see Renzaho.[722] He did not see Odette Nyirabagenzi or Angeline Mukandutiye either, who according to several other witnesses were present. Furthermore, unlike the other eyewitnesses, he said that the attack lasted from 9.00 a.m. to around 10.00 a.m., and that Munyeshyaka managed to repel the attackers by calling soldiers. The Chamber recalls that the witness had cooperated closely with him.

656. Witness TOA was hiding inside the church during the attack. He was therefore unable to see what was happening outside, and the Chamber finds his evidence to be of limited value. Witness BDC was not present at the Sainte Famille church on 17 June. Although his medical team was there, the chaotic nature and large-scale of the attack suggests that they may have been unable to observe and report on all aspects of it, including Renzaho's involvement. In particular, they were treating the injured inside the church, and may not have had been able to see all of what occurred outside. Consequently, this testimony also carries limited weight.[723]

657. Witness RCB-2 was not at Sainte Famille on 17 June but purportedly heard gunshots from the site at about 4.00 or 5.00 a.m. and saw corpses when he arrived there at 6.00 a.m., **[page 170]** following the RPF attack. He only stayed for an hour and a half. No other witness observed Renzaho there as early as 7.30 a.m. – this testimony therefore has limited significance. The witness seemed to dispute that the attack against Tutsis at Saint Famille took place.[724] He even claimed not to have seen a single roadblock from April to July 1994. These are, in the Chamber's view, extraordinary utterances, given the overwhelming evidence showing otherwise (above and II.2).[725]

658. Having assessed all the evidence and bearing in mind the weaknesses in the Defence testimonies, the Chamber finds that the Prosecution has established beyond reasonable doubt that Renzaho was present sometime before noon before the attack on 17 June 1994 against the Sainte Famille church. He directed the *Interahamwe* to kill "many persons" and later ordered them to stop the attack. He was also present when dead bodies were removed from the site.

659. The evidence that the *Interahamwe* were the attackers is overwhelming. Based on the accounts of Witnesses KZ, HAD, ATQ, Dufka, PER and TOA, the Chamber accepts that gendarmes were present at Sainte Famille but it has not been established that they participated in the attack there on 17 June. Furthermore, although Witness HAD referred to the arrival of a policeman who said that it was not possible to kill all the Tutsis, it does not follow that he, or the police more generally, were involved in the attack. Neither has it been proven that soldiers were amongst the attackers.[726]

660. The Chamber will now turn to the role of the other prominent individuals allegedly present during the attack. It accepts the first-hand testimonies of Witnesses AWO, HAD and BUO, who all stated that both

---

[721] T. 31 January 2007 p. 68; T. 1 February 2007 pp. 4-7; Defence Exhibit 24 (statement of 9 December 2000).

[722] T. 23 August 2007 p. 55 ("Q. So from the time the militia arrived until the end of the attack, you were in the presbytery; is that what we're to understand? A. Yes, I was hidden in the presbytery.").

[723] There are also other issues relating to Witness BDC's testimony. T. 4 June 2007 pp. 37-41. The Chamber does not find it necessary to address them here.

[724] T. 6 June 2007 p. 11 ("Q. So I'm talking of the period after you had left – after 7.30 in the morning, were you told of an attack by militia and gendarmes on Tutsi refugees in Sainte Famille? A. I was never given that information and such an attack never took place"). It is possible that Witness RCB-2, a gendarme, wanted to minimise any role gendarmes may have played.

[725] Witness RCB-2 stated that he was patrolling the area around Sainte Famille in June 1994. He initially testified that he saw dead bodies, not only near roadblocks, but also elsewhere. He subsequently contradicted himself, stating that, from April to July 1994, he never saw any bodies near roadblocks, and indeed he never saw any roadblocks at all. T. 6 June 2007 pp. 6-10.

[726] The Chamber notes that Witness ATQ stated that Renzaho arrived with other soldiers and a gendarme, and Witness TOA also testified that soldiers came to tell him that the attack was over.

Odette Nyirabagenzi and Angeline Mukandutiye were present at Sainte Famille on 17 June. Witness AWO testified that the two women arrived there at the same time as Renzaho. This particular observation was not corroborated. No specific evidence was presented that the two were present when Renzaho gave orders for the killings to commence or cease. However, Witness BUO listed them among the authorities who were present during the attack and provided a number of examples of cooperation between them and Renzaho (II.3, 6 and 9). More generally, he stated that he received instructions from Mukandutiye "during that period". However, the Chamber has consistently viewed his evidence regarding the actions of Nyirabagenzi and Mukandutiye and Renzaho's relations with them, cautiously. The Chamber finds that the two women were indeed present at the church on the day of the attack, and they were involved in the operation. This said, the extent of their cooperation with Renzaho and involvement in the attack remains unclear. In particular, it is not evident that they were there when Renzaho gave the orders to start or stop the attack, or that Renzaho had previously coordinated the attack with them.**[page 171]**

661. Turning to Father Wenceslas Munyeshyaka, it is clear that he was the priest in charge of Sainte Famille from April to July during the events. As mentioned by Prosecution Witness KZ, he obtained three gendarmes to keep guard, cooperated with sub-prefect Simpunga to obtain food for the refugees and ensured acceptable living conditions.[727] Defence Witnesses PER, ATO and BDC stressed these humanitarian aspects of his work. Prosecution witnesses provided a different picture, indicating he was on good terms and cooperated with the *Interahamwe* (Witnesses ACK and BUO), was involved in the drawing up of a list (Witness HAD), from which names of targeted persons were subsequently read out (Witnesses AWX and HAD) and played a certain role in connection with the removal of bodies (Witnesses AWO, ATQ and BUO). He was also seen in the company of Renzaho on 17 June (Witness ATQ) as well as Angeline Mukandutiye and Odette Nyarabagenzi (Witnesses ACK and BUO).

662. The testimonies do not allow the Chamber to make a finding about his exact role during the attack. It notes, however, that based on the evidence in the present case, there is evidence that Munyeshyaka was present at Sainte Famille during the attack and provided some assistance.[728]

663. In conclusion, the Chamber finds that *Interahamwe* attacked the Sainte Famille compound on 17 June 1994, starting some time before noon. Renzaho was present and ordered the *Interahamwe* to attack, and later, to stop the killings. The *Interahamwe* attackers obeyed his instructions. Several hundred Tutsi refugees were killed. The attack was conducted in revenge for the RPF operation the night before, in which a number of refugees were evacuated. Finally, the Chamber has no doubt that at least 17 Tutsi men were among those killed. That such individuals would be targeted is consistent with the fact that the attack was in retaliation to the RPF operation the preceding night. Furthermore, Witness ATQ noted that most of the survivors were women and children. Both she and Witness AWO testified that Renzaho told the survivors to clap when the attack had ended. It is telling that Witness AWO stated that this request was directed specifically to female survivors. The Chamber's finding is strengthened by the fact that during the attack on CELA on 22 April 1994, young men were singled out, taken away and killed (II.6). **[page 172]**

12. HOTEL KIYOVU, MID-JUNE 1994

12.1 Introduction

664. The Prosecution alleges that in June 1994, Renzaho, together with Colonel Ephrem Setako and Colonel Bagosora, attended an impromptu meeting at a roadblock near Hotel Kiyovu in Kigali. They instructed those present to kill all Tutsis. A number of Tutsis were killed or detained in Renzaho's presence. Reference is made to Witness SAF.[729]

---

[727] Prosecution Witness KZ, who stayed at Saint Paul Pastoral Centre, described Father Munyeshyaka's functions in these terms but did not want to testify about his other actions, which he had not observed. The provision of gendarmes and food was also mentioned by Witness TOA.
[728] Father Munyeshyaka's working relationship with *Interahamwe* is also reflected in Corinne Dufka's evidence concerning roadblocks (II.2).
[729] Indictment para. 19; Prosecution Closing Brief paras. 192-215; T. 14 February 2008 pp. 4-5.

665. The Defence submits that the Prosecution evidence is uncorroborated and unreliable. Renzaho was in Cyangugu on the relevant dates and is accused of participating in crimes in other locations on 14, 16 and 17 June 1994.[730]

12.2 Evidence

Prosecution Witness SAF

666. After the President's death, Witness SAF, a Tutsi, found refuge at Hotel Kiyovu in Kigali. He hid among the plants in the compound. There was a roadblock near the hotel. The witness could not see it from his hiding place, but during the night he heard the *Interahamwe* talking at the roadblock.[731]

667. In mid-June, the *conseiller* of Nyarugenge sector, Mbyariyehe, invited the public to a meeting in the compound of Hotel Kiyovu, saying that an official would talk to the population. Messengers informed the public of the meeting, stating that peace had been restored and no one would be attacked. The witness heard about the meeting from a messenger, who advised him to cover his face. Accordingly, he arrived at the meeting wearing the sleeve of a pullover stretched over his head with two holes cut for his eyes. As this was similar to the manner in which the *Interahamwe* dressed, the witness avoided being recognised as a Tutsi.[732]

668. The meeting was held between noon and 1.00 p.m. and only lasted for 20 or 25 minutes. It was short because bullets were fired nearby in Gikondo sector. The witness attended from the beginning until the end. *Conseiller* Mbyariyehe arrived first. Subsequently, Renzaho, Setako, Bagosora and Nsengiyumva came in two four-by-four military camouflage vehicles, accompanied by *Interahamwe* in other cars. Renzaho was wearing a military uniform.[733]

669. The *conseiller* announced that the gathering was a pacification meeting. He introduced Renzaho who would chair the meeting. The audience applauded. Renzaho took the floor and urged the Tutsis to emerge from their hiding places and said that "peace would henceforth reign". He then explained that the *Inyenzi* and the Tutsis were the enemy, and that Rwandans had to defend themselves against them. The *Interahamwe* surrounded the crowd and said that they wanted to prevent the *Inyenzi* from causing problems and infiltrating that place. Prior to this event, the witness had seen Renzaho once at the commune office near the **[page 173]** Saint Michel cathedral, wearing civilian clothes. He also saw his picture regularly in the newspapers. The witness identified Renzaho in court.[734]

670. Bagosora and Setako spoke subsequently. Setako said that the enemy had attacked the country, and that it was necessary to be vigilant and work together to fight him. Nsengiyumva was introduced as a guest from Gisenyi. There were about 30 participants, excluding the *Interahamwe*. The witness stood at the rear, but at a short distance from the speakers. Most of the participants were Hutu. There were not many Tutsis left in the area, as they had been killed.[735]

671. During the meeting, Witness SAF saw four Tutsi men being dragged across the tarmac road separating the meeting from the office of the Rwandan Prosecutor. They were killed with nail-studded clubs and machetes about 20 metres from the meeting place. It was broad daylight, and there were no obstacles in the way. Renzaho, Bagosora, Setako and Nsengiyumva could clearly see the killings but did nothing to prevent them. Instead, they were laughing with the *Interahamwe* while watching the event. The killings were committed with the same kind of weapons that Renzaho had previously urged the population to obtain.[736] Three or four Tutsis were abducted and taken to the Kigali-Ville prefecture office. They were never seen

---

[730] Defence Closing Brief paras. 594-608; T. 14 February 2008 pp. 27-29.
[731] T. 24 January 2007 pp. 27-30, 49, 54-55; Prosecution Exhibit 71 (personal identification sheet).
[732] T. 24 January 2007 pp. 34-37, 56-58.
[733] *Id.* pp. 33-34, 36-37, 40-41, 64.
[734] *Id.* pp. 36-37, 40-42, 57, 65-66.
[735] *Id.* pp. 37-38, 40, 57, 60.
[736] *Id.* pp. 38-40. Renzaho's alleged statement about weapons seems to have been made on an unknown date before the meeting.

Judgement and Sentence

again, and it was believed that they had been killed. According to the witness, the victims were persons who had come out of hiding to participate at the pacification meeting.[737]

Renzaho

672. Renzaho testified that around 14 June 1994, the RPF was based on Mburabuturo hill, opposite and 700 metres from Hotel Kiyovu, pointing its weapons at the hotel. Therefore, he could not have gone to the hotel at the time. When giving evidence about his alleged involvement in an attack at the Saint Paul pastoral centre on the same day, Renzaho said that he was in Cyangugu visiting family on 14 June, and did not return to Kigali until the evening of 15 June.[738]

12.3 Deliberations

673. Only Witness SAF gave evidence about the meeting at the Hotel Kiyovu 1994, where Renzaho allegedly ordered the killing of Tutsis. In court he placed this event in mid-June.[739] He said that it took place inside the hotel compound. This is not in conformity with his statement to Tribunal investigators in October 2002, which reflects that it was held at a roadblock directly outside the compound, between the hotel and the Rwandan Prosecutor's office. When this was put to him, the witness denied having told the investigators that the **[page 174]** meeting had taken place there. He further insisted that he did not go to that roadblock at all because it was too dangerous.[740] The Chamber realises that the two locations were close. This inconsistency is therefore not in itself significant. However, his explanation raises some concern. It is surprising that the investigators should make such a mistake, in particular in view of his insistence that he never went to the roadblock.

674. The Defence challenged Witness SAF's evidence that he was wearing a hood at the meeting. He testified that he did so in order to conceal his Tutsi features and that he was not conspicuous as some *Interahamwe* wore similar headgear.[741] The Chamber accepts his explanation in view of the unusual circumstances prevailing at the time. It is also conceivable that the witness was hiding in the hotel compound, as he described.[742]

675. The Defence disputed Witness SAF's connection with Hotel Kiyovu and pointed out that he did not know the names of the hotel manager or the supervisor, or the number of rooms. It is true that the witness had virtually no knowledge about these matters. However, he was a casual labourer, with no formal education, paid by the day, without a contract. He had only worked at the hotel for a few days before the shooting down of the President's plane.[743] After 6 April, the place no longer functioned normally as a hotel.[744] He further stated that he did not enter the hotel rooms and hence would not be in a position to know their number.[745]

---

[737] *Id.* pp. 37, 39-40, 64-65.
[738] T. 29 August 2007 pp. 38-39, 41-42, 62.
[739] In Defence Exhibit 13 (statement of 31 October 2002), Witness SAF had indicated that the meeting occurred in June, and this was also the time reference in the Indictment and the Pre-Trial Brief (para. 66). He explained that he had difficulties remembering dates in view of the prevailing situation in 1994. His reference to mid-June came after several questions seeking further precision (T. 24 January 2007 p. 56) and does not affect his credibility.
[740] Defence Exhibit 13 (statement of 31 October 2002); T. 24 January 2007 pp. 51, 54-56.
[741] T. 24 January 2007 pp. 36-37, 58.
[742] The Defence submission that there were no bushes around the hotel – situated in the city centre – overlooks that Witness SAF was purportedly hiding among plants within the hotel compound, not rural bushes. T. 24 January 2007 p. 51 ("It is not really the bush. I was referring to the plants or the shrubbery that could be found around the hotel. You were saying that it was a wealthy neighbourhood. A neighbourhood for white people, and there were a lot of plants. I believe everyone is aware that there – there are a lot of plants in Kiyovu").
[743] T. 24 January 2007 pp. 27-28, 47-49.
[744] *Id.* pp. 50-51.
[745] *Id.* pp. 49-50. The Defence also argues (Closing Brief para. 608) that Witness SAF "was going to testify before the Gacaca courts about the crimes which took place in other areas, which suggests that he was not stuck in Hotel Kiyovu as he claimed". The Chamber recalls that although it was very difficult to obtain clear answers about his involvement in the Gacaca proceedings, it finally emerged that he had testified about persons other than Renzaho in Gacaca proceedings at the public prosecutor's headquarters "next to the Nyarugenge central market". However, this does not provide a sufficient basis to conclude that the witness observed events outside the hotel. T. 24 January 2007 pp. 44-47.

676. According to the witness, Théoneste Bagosora, Ephrem Setako, Renzaho and Anatole Nsengiyumva were present. The last person is not included in his statement. The witness explained that either he forgot to mention Nsengiyumva's presence or the investigator did not write it down. Although the focus of the interview was on Setako, the Chamber considers it unlikely that the investigators would have omitted Nsengiyumva's name, had it been mentioned.[746] It is possible that the witness forgot to mention him, but the Chamber notes that he did sign the statement.

677. The witness was confronted with the testimony of Witness DAS in the *Bagosora et al.* trial, who described a meeting in June in the courtyard of Hotel Kiyovu without mentioning Renzaho. Witness SAF insisted that Renzaho was there and that he saw him with his own **[page 175]** eyes.[747] The Chamber observes that Witness DAS placed the meeting in late June, not in mid-June as argued by the Defence. His description of the meeting also differs in other respects from Witness SAF's account.[748] The question arises whether the two witnesses described the same meeting.[749] The Chamber also finds it noteworthy that according to Witness DAS, none of the four meetings in the Hotel Kiyovu area included Renzaho, whereas Bagosora, Nsengiyumva and Setako were present.[750]

678. The Defence also referred to Bagosora's passport, which contains an entry stamp to the Seychelles, dated 4 June, and an exit stamp on 19 June 1994.[751] It is argued that this shows that Bagosora, who allegedly accompanied Renzaho to the meeting in mid-June at Hotel Kiyovu, was not in Rwanda at the time. The Chamber is aware that it is not uncommon to travel without travel documents or using multiple passports. Consequently, a passport may not necessarily provide the complete picture of a person's travels. This said, the document, which appears genuine, does contain stamps indicating that Bagosora could not have been in Kigali around mid-June, which was the witness's best estimate. Even though the Defence chose not to call Bagosora as a witness, the Chamber attaches some weight to this submission.[752]

679. The Chamber is not convinced by Renzaho's testimony that there could not have been a meeting at Hotel Kiyovu around 14 June because the RPF was shooting at the hotel from the opposite Mburabuturo hill. Witness SAF explained that the exact location of the meeting was chosen so that the participants should not be hit by bullets. It was also kept short because **[page 176]** of the gunshots.[753] Furthermore, Renzaho's assertion that he could not have attended the meeting because he was elsewhere, is not persuasive.[754]

---

[746] Defence Exhibit 13 (statement of 31 October 2002). Witness SAF stated that he might have forgotten to mention Anatole Nsengiyumva's name because he was a guest from elsewhere. He also pointed out that he was not given a copy of his statement, which would have made it possible to contact the investigators to have that name included. T. 24 January 2007 p. 59.
[747] T. 24 January 2009 pp. 60-62; Defence Exhibit 12 (*Bagosora et al.* T. 5 November 2003; T. 6 November 2003; T. 7 November 2003).
[748] Defence Exhibit 12 (*Bagosora et al.* T. 5 November 2003 pp. 48-52). For example, Witness DAS referred to a much larger audience during the meeting in late June (p. 50: "I think all the inhabitants of Kiyovu were there"); he said that the meeting started at 2.00 p.m., not at noon (p. 50); the *conseiller* talked about the need to stop the killings because "international organisations" did not like them (pp. 50-51); after he left, Bagosora disputed what the *conseiller* had just said; about 40 persons were taken to the prefecture office, and over 40 soldiers were present (pp. 51-52). The Chamber adds that there are also important differences between Witness SAF's evidence and Witness DAS's testimony about a meeting in mid-June (T. 5 November 2003 p. 48 and T. 6 November 2003 pp. 36-37). In particular, only Setako came out of the car, not Bagosora or Nsengiumva. Witness DAS did not mention Renzaho in connection with that meeting.
[749] In view of this conclusion, the Defence submissions that it suffered prejudice because the Prosecution allegedly violated its Rule 68 obligations will not be considered. See Defence Closing Brief paras. 243-244, 603-604; T. 14 February 2008 pp. 4-5 and 27-29 (closing arguments). See also T. 24 January 2007 pp. 23-25 and *Bagosora et al.*, Decision on Prosecution Motion to Disclose Transcripts from the *Bagosora et al.* Trial, 24 January 2007 (TC).
[750] *Bagosora et al.* Trial Judgement paras. 1471-1474.
[751] T. 29 August 2007 p. 64; Defence Exhibit 106 (Bagosora's passport), p. 11 (which contains pages 18 and 19 of the passport). The document was tendered during Renzaho's testimony. The Prosecution objected, arguing that the Defence should have called Bagosora as a witness. The Chamber eventually admitted the passport and observed that the parties' submissions would be considered in connection with its deliberations on the weight to be accorded to it. T. 29 August 2007 pp. 62-64.
[752] In the *Bagosora et al.* case, the Chamber accepted Bagosora's alibi that he was in the Seychelles from 4 to 19 June 1994 (*Bagosora et al.* Trial Judgement paras. 1963-1966), finding that the prosecution had not eliminated the reasonable possibility that he was there.
[753] T. 24 January 2007 pp. 33-34, 57, 60, 63-64.
[754] Renzaho's testimony that he was in Cyangugu on 14 June 1994 does not prevent him from having attended the meeting at the Hotel Kiyovu. Nor is the Prosecution case contradictory in placing him there as well as at Saint Paul on 14 June and at Sainte Famille on 17 June 1994.

Judgement and Sentence

680. Although the Chamber is unconvinced by Renzaho's account of why he could not have attended the meeting, certain elements in Witness SAF's testimony raise questions, and his testimony is uncorroborated. Having assessed the totality of the evidence, the Chamber does not find it established beyond reasonable doubt that Renzaho attended a meeting at a roadblock near Hotel Kiyovu in Kigali, instructing those present to kill Tutsis. In view of this finding, the Chamber does not find it necessary to consider the Defence submission about lack of notice. **[page 177]**

13. RAPE AND SEXUAL VIOLENCE, APRIL-JULY 1994

13.1 Introduction

681. The Prosecution alleges that, between 6 April and 17 July 1994, Tutsi women and girls were raped throughout Kigali-Ville by persons under Renzaho's control, including members of the Rwandan army and the civil defence force, *Interahamwe*, civilian militias, urban police and administrative officials. Between April and June, Father Wenceslas Munyeshyaka and *Interahamwe* forced Tutsi women and girls to provide sexual favours in exchange for their safety at Sainte Famille. This was also done by *Interahamwe*, soldiers and armed civilians, who kept the women at houses in central Kigali. Renzaho knew or had reason to know that crimes were being committed but failed to prevent them or refused to punish the perpetrators. Reference is made to Witnesses AWO, AWN, KBZ, AWX, HAD, AWE, UB and KZ.[755]

682. The Defence submits that the allegations are vague. Renzaho was not aware of such rapes and did not exercise authority over the alleged perpetrators of these crimes. It relies on the testimony of its Witnesses HIN, PER, BDC, TOA, UT and AIA as well as Prosecution Witness KZ.[756]

13.2 Evidence

Prosecution Witness AWO

683. Witness AWO, a Tutsi, was living in Kigali and married with five children. About a day or more after the President's plane crash on 6 April 1994, she sought refuge at an orphanage run by the Sisters of Saint Teresa of Calcutta. One morning, around four days after her arrival, Renzaho came with *Interahamwe* wearing military uniforms and carrying firearms. The refugees were separated into groups of men, women and children. The prefect advised the refugees that peace had been restored and asked them to leave the orphanage because it was overcrowded. He told the assailants not to kill the girls and young women because they would be "food items". The young men were loaded onto a vehicle and taken away. The witness testified that as she was leaving the orphanage and from her home nearby, she observed bodies strewn about the orphanage and that a child named Ndoli had been killed.[757]

684. The witness returned to her home. It had been destroyed, but she was forced to remain there as roadblocks prevented Tutsis from moving about. For a period of seven to eight **[page 178]** weeks, *Interahamwe*, policemen and soldiers "who lived at Nyirabagenzi's house" raped her on a daily basis. She testified that she became a "wife" of the *Interahamwe* and believed she was targeted because she was Tutsi. Her attackers often said that they should go and "taste what a Tutsi woman tastes like".[758]

---

[755] Indictment paras. 41-43, 52-55, 61-65; Prosecution Closing Brief paras. 303, 314-315, 351-359, 360, 370-379, 430-451, 490-495; T. 14 February 2008 pp. 20-22; T. 15 February 2008 pp. 9-12.

[756] Defence Closing Brief paras. 56, 689-700, 933-960, 1135-1152, 1224-1231, 1232-1252; Defence Exhibit 113 (*complément écrit aux arguments oraux de la défense*) paras. 957.1, 960.1-960.4; T. 14 February 2008 pp. 67-69.

[757] T. 7 February 2007 pp. 3-10, 16-17, 20, 25; Prosecution Exhibit 91 (personal identification sheet). The attack on the Sisters of Saint Teresa of Calcutta orphanage is not pleaded in the Indictment and was not addressed by the Prosecution in its Closing Brief or during oral submissions. The Chamber considers this evidence only insofar as it provides context for allegations pleaded in the Indictment. See *The Prosecutor v.* Arsène Shalom Ntahobali and Pauline Nyiramasuhuko, Decision on the Appeals by Pauline Nyiramasuhuko and Arsène Shalom Ntahobali on the "Decision on Defence Urgent Motion to Declare Parts of the Evidence of Witnesses RV and QBZ Inadmissible" (AC), 2 July 2004, para. 15.

[758] T. 7 February 2007 pp. 6-10, 11 (quoted), 18-19, 22 (quoted).

685. During this period, *Interahamwe* forced the witness to attend meetings that occurred about every three days and were presented as pacification efforts.[759] They took place at or near *Conseiller* Odette Nyirabagenzi's house. Renzaho attended a meeting on the road uphill from that house. The only time estimate the witness could provide was that it was after she had returned to her home ("later"). During the meeting, Nyirabagenzi accused her of being an *Inkotanyi*. The prefect intervened and said that the witness should not be killed because she was a woman and was "food for the militiamen". She was allowed to return to the ruins of her home and continued to be raped there until she fled to Sainte Famille, some seven or eight weeks after her return from the orphanage.[760]

686. The witness was found by nuns, who treated her and took her to Sainte Famille. She was not raped whilst there and explained that no one would come near her because she was badly wounded and covered in flies. Since the events, she has suffered from serious health problems.[761]

Prosecution Witness AWN

687. Witness AWN, a 14 year old Tutsi girl, sought refuge at the house of *Conseiller* Odette Nyirabagenzi from 19 April to mid-May 1994 while pretending to be a Hutu. The witness suspected that Nyirabagenzi knew that she was a Tutsi and eventually forced her to leave. After this, the *conseiller*'s brother Munanira took her to his house and tried to rape her. She fended him off with an excuse and persuaded him to return at a later date. He then took her home where she was reunited with her sister. An *Interahamwe* named Matata, who was a family friend, promised to protect her.[762]

688. About a week later, Matata thwarted Munanira's initial attempt to abduct the witness. However, a short time later, Nyirabagenzi and Munanira returned to her home, accompanied by policemen and *Interahamwe*. Nyirabagenzi ordered Matata to send the "Tutsi girl" to the sector office. A crowd, including *Interahamwe*, had gathered there. When she arrived with Matata, Munanira and a *responsable de cellule* named Narcisse were also present. Renzaho, wearing military attire, arrived in a camouflage vehicle accompanied by other persons in military uniforms and with firearms. He asked what had happened, and the witness responded that she had refused to "marry" someone. Renzaho replied that it was "time to show Tutsi women, and that the Hutus are strong and can do whatever they wanted to do with them". He then spoke with Nyirabagenzi and left the sector office. Subsequently, Nyirabagenzi told **[page 179]** Munanira that "she was going to do her best to ensure that this Tutsi girl begs him" to have sex with her. Nyirabagenzi then spoke to Matata and departed.[763]

689. A few days to two weeks later, Munanira came to the witness's home, accompanied by *Interahamwe*. They took her and her elder sister to their headquarters close to the SEFA office, near the Hotel Pan Africa. Munanira raped the witness and told the others with him, that they could also "have a taste of a Tutsi woman". Sese Seko, Bikomago and Gisenyi were among the *Interamhawe* who raped her. At the same time and in the same room, her sister was raped. They were allowed to return home after "some" days. Two or three days later, the witness, her sister and their Tutsi neighbour were taken back to the headquarters and confined there for about three or four weeks, during which time they continued to be raped. Toward the end of June, the girls were transferred by their assailants to Sainte Famille as the headquarters was continuously shelled. They were not raped there, but the witness saw two refugees called Hyacinthe Rwanga and Nyiratunga being led away by Father Wenceslas Munyeshyaka and heard that he had raped them.[764]

Prosecution Witness KBZ

690. On 28 May 1994, Witness KBZ, a Tutsi, fled from Kicukiro to Kimihurura sector with about 50 other refugees. They were stopped at a roadblock. She and about four other Tutsi women who did not have identity

---

[759] Witness AWO testified that the prefect of Kigali-Ville started "organising meetings" on a virtually daily basis, after the attack on the orphanage. *Id.* pp. 6, 18. However, she only saw him at one of those meetings. *Id.* pp. 7, 20, 26.
[760] *Id.* pp. 6-11, 19-22, 26.
[761] *Id.* pp. 12, 14, 23-25.
[762] T. 5 February 2007 pp. 30-36, 46; Prosecution Exhibit 84 (personal identification sheet).
[763] T. 5 February 2007 pp. 35-36, 37 (quoted), 38 (quoted), 43-45, 47-48.
[764] *Id.* pp. 39-42, 46-48. Witness AWN knew that "SEFA" was an acronym but could not identify it. *Id.* p. 39.

cards were separated and taken to outside the home of the Kimihurura *conseiller*. The assailants entered the house and then returned, saying that the *conseiller* had instructed them to ask the prefect what to do with the women.[765]

691. The Tutsi women were placed in an abandoned house in Kimihurura sector that had belonged to a man named Jean-Michel. The next day, the *Interahamwe* informed the witness that the prefect had said that the women should not be killed until after the burial of President Habyarimana. The reason was that the killings were being criticised on the radio. Subsequently, an *Interahamwe* named Jerôme Rwemarika took her to his home and raped her. She returned to the abandoned house. While there, the other women were taken away repeatedly. The witness believed they were raped although they did not talk about it. In early July, she fled to Sainte Famille. Two *Interahamwe* raped her behind the church after she was unable to produce an identification card upon her arrival. No one intervened.[766]

Prosecution Witness AWX

692. Witness AWX, a Tutsi, fled her family home on 10 or 11 April 1994 and sought refuge at Sainte Famille until the end of the war. Around 24 May, while on her way to collect water near the entrance of the Sainte Famille compound, she saw Renzaho arrive at about 2.00 p.m. in a Hilux-type vehicle with armed soldiers on board. She was about 10 paces from **[page 180]** the prefect and heard him tell them to get down and do their "job". The soldiers immediately entered the church. Father Wenceslas Munyeshyaka called the names of Tutsi refugees, using identity cards that he collected from them. He said Renzaho had ordered that all persons whose names were read out should come forward. The witness believed Munyeshyaka was aware of what was to happen as he told the refugees that their "time has come" and "you have to pray". The selected refugees were separated into groups of men and women.[767]

693. Around 5.00 p.m., two soldiers, who had arrived with Renzaho, led the witness, her sister and her cousin away. They were brought to a housing complex in Kiyovu about five minutes' walking distance from Sainte Famille. For two days, a soldier locked the witness within a room where she was raped twice. She heard that he was a member of the Presidential Guard, posted at the residence of Major General Nsabimana. After the second day, the soldier returned her to Sainte Famille, where she was reunited with her sister and cousin. Her sister had been taken by another soldier elsewhere. The witness's sister and cousin were also raped.[768]

694. Around 15 June, the witness and her sister and cousin were abducted by the same soldiers. The witness was brought back to the same house and confined in a room where she was raped for two days. Her sister and cousin were held in different buildings. After two days, the witness returned to Sainte Famille with her cousin but not her sister. When she was fetching water at CELA two days afterwards, she saw her sister's body in a wheelbarrow. The witness heard from other women at Sainte Famille that they were subjected to sexual attacks, and was aware that some subsequently died.[769]

Prosecution Witness HAD

695. Witness HAD, a Tutsi secondary school pupil, went to Sainte Famille on 22 April and remained there until 19 or 20 June 1994. While there, Father Wenceslas Munyeshyaka had made sexual advances towards the witness's Tutsi friend, Hyacinthe Rwanga. One female refugee there had "almost become [Munyeshyaka's]

---

[765] T. 6 February 2007 pp. 48-51, 53, 57; Prosecution Exhibit 90 (personal identification sheet). Witness KBZ testified that she was not aware of whether those at the roadblocks were soldiers or *Interahamwe* but referred to them as *Interahamwe* throughout her testimony. T. 6 February 2007 pp. 48 ("I wouldn't know whether they were soldiers or *Interahamwe*"), 51-52 (referring to the persons who arrested the group as *Interahamwe*), 52 (identifying those who committed rape as *Interahamwe*), 52-53 (her rapists were *Interahamwe*).
[766] T. 6 February 2007 pp. 52-58. According to Witness KBZ, Habyarimana had not been buried by the end of May 1994. *Id.* pp. 52-53.
[767] *Id.* pp. 27-30, 34, (quoted), 35, 38 (quoted), 39, 43-44; Prosecution Exhibit 89 (personal identification sheet). Witness AWX testified that "other soldiers had taken the men away and they were killed, because we never saw them again" (p. 29) and that "some people were killed" when describing the process by which those present were separated into groups (p. 30). No further detail was provided.
[768] T. 6 February 2007 pp. 29-31.
[769] *Id.* pp. 31-34. 36-38, 42-45. Witness AWX's testimony relating to the event when she saw her sister's body is set forth elsewhere (II.11).

sexual slave during that period", and the witness added that "he would abuse young girls". Without specifying when, the witness testified that *Interahamwe* entered Sainte Famille without difficulty and took girls and women away with them to be raped and executed. On returning to Sainte Famille, one of the females described having been abducted and taken to the Hotel Africa, where she was raped. Another woman, called Cimba, was abducted by an *Interahamwe*, and she ultimately died. Women who avoided rape were fortunate given its prevalence.[770] **[page 181]**

Prosecution Witness AWE

696. Witness AWE was a Hutu local official in Kigali-Ville prefecture in April until July 1994. He reported four incidents of rape or sexual assault to *Bourgmestre* Jean Bizimana, providing a copy to Renzaho on each occasion. The witness never received any response from either the *bourgmestre* or the prefect to any of the reports.[771]

Prosecution Witness UB

697. Witness UB, a Hutu local official in Kigali, participated in a meeting on 10 or 11 April 1994 that Renzaho convened at the prefecture office. The *conseillers* attending told the prefect that Tutsi wives and daughters were being raped.[772] In April, May and June 1994, he reported to *Bourgmestre* Jean Bizimana and the prefect on everything that happened in his sector, including the torture and rape of women. Some reports were made in writing, others on the telephone or in the prefect's presence. As head of the police unit, the prefect was in charge of arrests. During those three months, however, no one in the witness's sector was arrested "for even three hours" for those offences.[773]

Prosecution Witness KZ

698. Witness KZ, a Hutu, worked at Saint Paul pastoral centre in Kigali and was present from mid-April until 17 June 1994. He knew of no rapes committed there in 1994. The witness was unable to answer questions as to whether rape occurred at Sainte Famille because he was not present there.[774]

Renzaho

699. Renzaho testified that, in the period after 6 April 1994, rapes were being committed in neighbourhoods in Kigali by soldiers who had deserted or who could not return to their units due to the chaos reigning at the time. Renzaho disputed having been involved in the attack on the Sisters of Saint Teresa of Calcutta orphanage on 10, 11 or 12 April, suggesting that his presence there would have been impossible given his schedule. He also denied referring to Tutsi women as food. He never heard any complaint concerning rapes, whether committed at Sainte Famille or, more generally, in Kigali, and was not receiving regular reports of Tutsi women being raped. However, he conceded that on 21 April, he had a meeting with the *bourgmestres*, including the *bourgmestre* of Nyarugenge *commune* and possibly his **[page 182]** *conseillers*, where he received some information about rape. He testified that he could not do anything, suggesting that he "would

---

[770] T. 1 February 2007 pp. 11, 21-24, 27 (quoted); Prosecution Exhibit 82 (personal identification sheet). The English version (p. 28) states "his (*sic*) name was Cimba", and the French version (p. 29) confirms that this was the name of the victim, not the perpetrator.
[771] T. 31 January 2007 pp. 11-12, 21-25, 44, 50-51; Prosecution Exhibit 80 (personal identification sheet). When testifying, Witness AWE had been detained and charged with genocide in Rwanda. T. 31 January 2007 pp. 11-12, 51-52, 54-56.
[772] Witness UB's testimony about this meeting is discussed in greater detail elsewhere (II.2).
[773] T. 23 January 2007 pp. 1-2, 8-9, 12, 19 (quoted); Prosecution Exhibit 69 (personal identification sheet). At the time of his testimony, Witness UB was a detainee, awaiting the outcome of an appeal before the Rwandan Supreme Court. His conviction for genocide in 1997 had been confirmed by the court of appeals. T. 23 January 2007 pp. 1-2. He was cross-examined on the basis of a statement given to Tribunal investigators in September 2004, in which he said that on 7 April 1994, he went to a Catholic training centre for girls where Tutsi girls had been "manhandled and taken hostage by soldiers and *Interahamwe*", and that some were taken home and made "sex slaves". The witness affirmed his statement and said this incident was included in a report to Renzaho. T. 23 January 2007 pp. 59-60.
[774] T. 25 January 2007 pp. 2, 10, 36, 45; Prosecution Exhibit 72 (personal identification sheet).

have preferred that individuals be brought to him so he could punish them". Between April and July 1994, no one was brought before him on charges of rape.[775]

700. Renzaho acknowledged a broadcast of 10 May on Radio Rwanda, wherein he stated "we have decided to arrest all those who rape and want to commit criminal acts so as to punish them. For example, we punished about three people". In relation to a Radio Rwanda broadcast on 24 April, Renzaho believed that his words, which he could not remember, to "chase … away" those who came to rape women and children were aimed at neutralising people committing crimes within the population.[776]

Defence Witness HIN

701. Witness HIN, a Hutu, lived in Rugenge sector until 18 April 1994, not far from the home of the *conseiller* of that sector, Odette Nyirabagenzi. Neighbours near the convent of the Sisters of Calcutta told him that an attack took place there between 11 and 14 April 1994, in which *Interahamwe* abducted and killed 12 to 16 persons. The witness did not hear that Renzaho accompanied the attackers, who arrived in an apparently stolen Daihatsu pickup truck without a registration number. Someone of Renzaho's stature would not have arrived in such a vehicle. From the beginning of the war, the prefect did not have good relations with the *Interahamwe* and could not have asked them to undertake such a mission. Members of the population in Rugenge knew Renzaho and would have mentioned it if he had been present that day.[777]

702. The witness denied allegations that Renzaho held a meeting with Nyirabagenzi between 10 and 14 April in the sector office or near her home. While the witness remained in Rugenge sector from 7 to 18 April, RPF troops had taken positions on Gisozi hill and at Kacyiru and were shelling the area. However, the witness did not visit Nyirabagenzi's house during this period, and the sector was not shelled every day. He only recalled four houses that were hit by them and noted that Nyirabagenzi's house was not destroyed. At the beginning of the war, the Rugenge market was open for about an hour a day, but this did not last after shells killed people there.[778] **[page 183]**

Defence Witness PER

703. Witness PER, a Hutu, was at Saint Paul pastoral centre from 6 April to 18 June 1994, where he was a close associate of Father Wenceslas Munyeshyaka. The witness generally went to Sainte Famille around 10.00 or 11.00 a.m. and left at about 3.00 or 4.00 p.m. each day. He did not see or hear of rapes occurring there during this period. According to him, the physical layout of the premises and the condition of its refugees, who numbered more than 18,000 as of 10 April, rendered the commission of such acts implausible. During this period, he only saw Renzaho once, on 16 June, at Saint Paul.[779]

Defence Witness TOA

704. Witness TOA, a Tutsi, left his home on 10 April to seek refuge at Sainte Famille, where he stayed until 4 July 1994. Father Wenceslas Munyeshyaka provided food for the refugees, whereas the Red Cross took care of health issues. The witness did not see Renzaho or any prefecture authorities at the site, but he heard

---

[775] T. 29 August 2007 pp. 32, 59; T. 3 September 2007 p. 19 ("Q: No one was arrested for rape under your watch as *préfet* of Kigali between April and July 1994, were they? A. Counsel, I regret to say that nobody was brought before me on charges of rape and then I let them free or tolerated them. The *préfet* is not able – is not a *conseiller*, is not a *chef de cellule*, he is not all of that. So I think we should face the reality of things.").
[776] T. 3 September 2007 pp. 3-4, 18-19; Prosecution Exhibit 56 (transcript of Radio Rwanda interview, 10 May 1994) p. 12; Prosecution Exhibit 54 (transcript of Radio Rwanda broadcast, 24 April 1994) p. 15 ("These people who come to rape children and women in the quarters must absolutely be thrown out. Chase them away. Besides, in times like these, do not bother yourself with too many questions. We are saying that you should shoot those who want to interfere with the security of the people. Anyone with a gun should shoot! That is it!").
[777] T. 9 July 2007 pp. 64-65, 71; T. 10 July 2007 pp. 1, 3, 12, 17-18, 26, 33, 37, 39; Defence Exhibit 73 (personal identification sheet). Witness HIN first stated that 16 persons had been abducted and then gave the number as 12. See T. 10 July 2007 pp. 3 and 17, respectively.
[778] T. 9 July 2009 pp. 70-72; T. 10 July 2007 pp. 2, 12, 29-30, 35-36, 39.
[779] T. 23 August 2007 pp. 27-29, 31, 34, 44-45, 49-50, 57-58; Defence Exhibit 80 (personal identification sheet).

that the sub-prefect visited once, and that the prefect came on 16 June. He was unaware of rapes being perpetrated at Sainte Famille during this period and doubted that it was possible, given the unhygienic and overcrowded conditions prevailing at the time. Further, if rapes had been committed, the victims would have appealed to the ICRC which was present, or "UN journalists" who were there in May. Most of the time, the witness remained inside the church building and could not personally see what was happening outside it. In April, there were about 1,000 refugees within the church, and in June, about 4,000.[780]

Defence Witness UT

705. Witness UT, a Hutu, was a high-ranking government official at the Kigali-Ville prefecture and had daily contact with Renzaho from 11 April 1994 until the end of the events. He read in the press that rapes had occurred at Sainte Famille but never received any such complaints despite being in regular contact with refugees and organisations present there.[781]

Defence Witness BDC

706. Witness BDC, a Hutu, worked for the ICRC operation in Kigali-Ville from 15 April 1994. He supervised the Sainte Famille site, where a permanent team of ICRC relief workers assisted from mid-May through July. The witness received daily reports and had no recollection of any cases of rape or sexual assault at Sainte Famille. No report indicated that Renzaho went to that site. He saw the prefect there only once, on 15 or 16 June.[782] **[page 184]**

Defence Witness AIA

707. Witness AIA was a policeman in Kigali-Ville prefecture who assisted a *conseiller*. He arrived at his *conseiller*'s house in the morning of 7 April and did not leave his company until 4 July, working on a nearly 24-hour basis. After 8 April, *Interahamwe* and others, including policemen, raped Tutsis. The *conseiller* for whom he worked incited policemen to commit rapes and himself raped a woman who had sought refuge at a local government office. Perpetrators of rape in the sector openly reported on their acts to the *conseiller*, who always responded that Tutsi men should die and "the beautiful Tutsi women should marry other people". The witness was not aware whether the *conseiller* reported the rapes to the prefect.[783]

13.3 Deliberations

708. The Prosecution's case implicating Renzaho in sexual violence can be divided into four categories: support of rapes in Rugenge sector; responsibility for sexual violence at Sainte Famille; rapes in Kimihurura; and Renzaho's general knowledge of rapes. The Chamber will assess the evidence in turn.

13.3.1 Rugenge Sector

709. Two Tutsi refugees provided first-hand evidence that Renzaho encouraged rapes during meetings in Rugenge sector, attended by *Conseiller* Odette Nyirabagenzi and *Interahamwe*. Witness AWO testified that she was repeatedly raped in the ruins of her home after Renzaho's visit with *Interahamwe* to the Sisters of Saint Teresa of Calcutta orphanage around 10 or 11 April 1994, where he described Tutsi women as "food items".[784] When the witness was subsequently identified as an "*Inkotanyi*" during the so-called pacification

---

[780] T. 6 September 2007 pp. 3, 5, 7, 10-11, 15-17; Defence Exhibit 111 (personal identification sheet).
[781] T. 24 May 2007 pp. 19-20, 22-23, 39, 43, 56; T. 25 May 2007 pp. 6, 13.
[782] T. 4 June 2007 pp. 3-4, 21-24, 35-37; Defence Exhibit 51 (personal identification sheet). Witness BDC did not wish to give his ethnicity but testified that he possessed an identity card with the letter "H" on it. T. 4 June 2007 pp. 12-13.
[783] T. 2 July 2007 pp. 2, 6, 28, 29 (quoted), 31, 43, 50-51; T. 3 July 2007 pp. 14, 18; Defence Exhibit 66 (personal identification sheet). Witness AIA was questioned by Nyamirambo brigade about his actions during the events, and was locked up in a cell for a month while investigations took place. He was then released. *Id.* p. 46.
[784] The Chamber relies on the French formulation where Witness AWO refers to staying in the "ruins" of her former house rather than "rooms" as in the English transcripts (T. 7 February 2007 pp. 7, 8, 19), as the French ("ruines") is more consistent with her description of the house having been destroyed.

meeting near Nyirabagenzi's home, Renzaho stated that she should not be killed because she was a woman and was "food for the militiamen". Having been forced to attend that meeting by *Interahamwe*, the witness was returned to her house where *Interahamwe*, soldiers and policemen "who lived in Nyirabagenzi's house" continued to rape her until she fled to Sainte Famille, about seven or eight weeks after she left the orphanage for her home.

710. Similarly, Witness AWN was forced to go to the Rugenge sector office around the third or fourth week of May 1994. Among those present were Odette Nyirabagenzi, her brother called Munarira, and *Interahamwe*. When Renzaho, arriving with persons in military attire carrying firearms, heard that the witness had refused Munarira's advances, he said that it was "time to show Tutsi women that the Hutus are strong and can do whatever they wanted to do with them". After he left, Nyirabagenzi subsequently reinforced Renzaho's statement by promising Munarira that she would ensure that the witness would beg to have sex with him. The witness and her sister were then repeatedly raped by Munanira and other *Interahamwe* at their headquarters until they arrived at Sainte Famille three to four weeks later. **[page 185]**

711. Differences in the location, timing and substance of the meetings demonstrate that Witnesses AWO and AWN testified about distinct incidents wherein Renzaho encouraged the rape of Tutsi women. The Chamber assesses the merits of each testimony in sequence.

712. Witness AWO's account was, at times, confusing. Elements of her description of the attack on the orphanage were not coherent.[785] She also testified that Renzaho organised meetings in Rugenge sector virtually daily, but her basis for saying so was not solid, as she only attended one.[786] Furthermore, her evidence about when she was sexually assaulted and the sequence of events sometimes lacked clarity.[787] However, to the extent the witness did not provide testimony in a cohesive, narrative form, this is reasonably explained by the passage of time and the extremely traumatic nature of the events. The witness was raped on a daily basis for nearly eight weeks by several different men, including *Interahamwe*, policemen and soldiers. Given her ethnicity and the prevalence of roadblocks, she was unable to flee. She therefore remained in the ruins of her former home, in an area where there was fighting. Towards the end of her stay there, the witness, who was eight months pregnant, asked one of her attackers to kill her but he refused. Instead he promised to arrange it so that no one else would rape her and stabbed her in the lower abdomen and ankle with a bayonet. As a result of this incident the witness's baby was stillborn. By then, she could no longer close her legs or stand on her feet. The witness still has health problems caused by the assault.[788]

713. Witness AWN stated that she was abducted and raped by Munanira a few days or possibly two weeks after she was forced to meet at the sector office.[789] The Defence referred to her statement to Tribunal investigators in October 2004, which suggests that the assault took place "one month" after the meeting.[790] The witness repeatedly explained that she could not remember the date with precision, as 10 years had elapsed between the incident and the time that she was interviewed.[791] The Chamber finds this explanation reasonable and notes that the statement suggests that she was taken away at the end of May. This is generally

---

[785] For example, when testifying about the raid on the orphanage, Witness AWO said that the *Interahamwe* "were raping us" and that the "young girls were spread all over". *Id.* p. 6. However, when viewed in of the context of her entire testimony, is not clear that she observed rapes of any women there, or that she was raped on that occasion. The evidence rather suggests that the witness was raped once she had returned to her home, and not necessarily by the *Interahamwe* who had arrived earlier with Renzaho at the orphanage. *Id.* pp. 6-8, 10-11, 16-20. This conclusion mirrors the Prosecution's own summary of her anticipated evidence in its Pre-Trial Brief pp. 64-65 (which only refers to rapes after the meeting at *Conseiller* Odette Nyirabagenzi's residence).
[786] Compare T. 7 February 2007 pp. 6 (Renzaho was organising meetings "on a daily basis virtually"), 18 ("all the meetings"), 19 ("organising a meeting all the time"), 25-26 ("such meetings would take place approximately every three days") and *id.* pp. 7 ("I attended one of those meetings which was organised"), 18, 20 ("Q. Madam Witness, how many meetings did you attend in the presence of Mr. Renzaho? A. I saw him at the convent of the Sisters of Charity, and I saw him at Nyirabagenzi's place on the second occasion, and then I saw him at the Sainte Famille parish, so in all, three times."), 26 ("But, I saw Renzaho only on three occasions [...] But such meetings would be held frequently [....]").
[787] For instance, *id.* pp. 6, 7-8, 11, 18.
[788] *Id.* pp. 11, 14, 24.
[789] T. 5 February 2007 pp. 39 ("when we got home, a few days later, Munanira came again."), 45-46 ("I would say it was a time span of about two weeks"), 46 ("I believe I left the *conseiller's* place in mid-May, and I think Munanira came to look for me at home, perhaps one week afterwards").
[790] Defence Exhibit 26 (statement of 20 October 2004) p. 4.
[791] T. 5 February 2007 p. 46.

in conformity with her testimony, which places her abduction in the end of May or early June. Furthermore, and contrary to the Defence assertion, there is no inconsistency between the statement and her testimony as to whether Renzaho arrived at the Rugenge sector office **[page 186]** before or after her. The witness reaffirmed her testimony that he arrived later, and the statement does not say otherwise.[792] Finally, notwithstanding the traumatic nature of the events she described, her testimony appeared measured and unexaggerated. Her explanations for her observations were clear and logical.[793]

714. Defence Witness HIN suggested that, in view of the RPF shelling in the area, it would have been equivalent to killing people to organise a meeting in Rugenge sector between 7 and 18 April. However, he conceded that such shelling did not occur on a daily basis, that he only knew of four houses being hit, and that Nyirabagenzi's house remained standing at the time of his testimony.[794] In the Chamber's view, his evidence does not cast doubt on Witnesses AWO and AWN's accounts that meetings indeed took place.

715. The testimonies of the two Prosecution witnesses contained similar elements, in particular that Tutsi women existed to feed or to be handled by Hutus at their discretion. They therefore provide a degree of mutual corroboration. Furthermore, the record as a whole contains circumstantial support for their evidence. In particular, their description of the authority exercised by Renzaho is consistent with other evidence in the case, showing that Renzaho provided instruction to *conseillers* and that his orders were followed (II.2 and 3).

716. The Chamber is satisfied with the identifications of Renzaho by Witnesses AWO and AWN. Their physical descriptions of him were consistent and adequate.[795] Witness AWN recognised him because he had been pointed out to her as the prefect during *conseiller* elections approximately two years earlier.[796] Compared to the extensive Prosecution evidence implicating Renzaho in the meetings described by the two witnesses, his denials that he was present during the attack against the orphanage and at subsequent meetings where Tutsi women were referred to as "food", carry limited weight. Although it is clear from the evidence that he attended other meetings and carried out other activities in the same period, this does not raise doubt that he was present at the meetings described by them.

717. Having assessed all the evidence, the Chamber accepts the fundamental aspects of Witness AWO's testimony. During a meeting, which took place after about 10 or 11 April, attended by *Conseiller* Odette Nyaribagenzi and *Interahamwe*, Renzaho said that the witness should not be killed because she was "food for the militiamen". After this instruction, the **[page 187]** witness continued to be raped by *Interahamwe*, policemen and soldiers who either lived in Nyaribagenzi's home, or at least, worked in coordination with her.[797]

718. The Chamber also finds the main elements of Witness AWN's testimony established beyond reasonable doubt. In May 1994, she was brought to the Rugenge sector office. Renzaho, accompanied by persons in military attire carrying firearms, stated that it was "time to show Tutsi women that the Hutus are strong and can do whatever they wanted to do with them". After he left, Nyirabagenzi reinforced Renzaho's statement by promising Munanira that she would ensure that the witness would beg to have sex with him. Subsequently

---

[792] *Id.* pp. 37, 44; Defence Exhibit 26 (statement of 20 October 2004) p. 4 ("Matata and I walked to the secteur office where we met so many people. I later realised that the people were gathered there because information had gone around that I had refused to be married to Munanira, the *conseiller's* brother. [...] *It was here that I saw Renzaho*, the préfet of Kigali, who I knew before the war.") (emphasis added).

[793] For instance, T. 5 February 2007 pp. 37 ("At that point, I saw a vehicle arrive, and there were soldiers and the *préfet* of Kigali-Ville in that vehicle. The *préfet* was called Tharcisse Renzaho."), 45 ("I noticed that the people accompanying him were in military attire and were carrying firearms. I don't know whether they were *bona fide* soldiers or otherwise."). See also T. 5 February 2007 p. 43 (her basis for identifying Renzaho even when she was 12 years old as well as her explanation of whether Renzaho arrived in a "military vehicle" or a civilian vehicle with camouflage colouring).

[794] T. 10 July 2007 pp. 29 ("No, I'm not going to exaggerate. Rugenge was not shelled every day, and the four houses were not shelled on the same day."), 39 ("[Odette's house] is still in existence.").

[795] Witness AWO, T. 7 February 2007 p. 9 ("A. It was a man who was bald. He had big eyes [...] and I believe he must be quite old today."); Witness AWN, T. 5 February 2007 p. 38 ("He was a stocky man who was wearing spectacles and who was bald.").

[796] T. 5 February 2007 pp. 38, 43-44.

[797] While the Chamber is uncertain as to whether soldiers lived in Nyirabagenzi's home (T. 7 February 2007 p. 22), that policemen lived with Nyirabagenzi is consistent with other evidence on the record that Renzaho deployed members of the urban police force to accompany *conseillers*, and that they did so on a 24 hour basis.

Judgement and Sentence

the witness was raped repeatedly by Munanira and other *Interahamwe* at their headquarters for three to four weeks. Her sister and Tutsi neighbour were also raped repeatedly there.

13.3.2 Sainte Famille

719. Several Prosecution witnesses testified that women who had sought refuge at Sainte Famille were raped or abused. Witness AWN stated that she saw Father Munyeshyaka lead away two girls called Hyacinthe Rwanga and Nyiratunga when she arrived at Sainte Famille near the end of June. She also heard that he had raped them. According to Witness HAD, Munyeshyaka made sexual advances towards Hyacinthe Rwanga; he had made one female his sex slave; and he would abuse young girls. Witness KBZ, who fled to Sainte Famille in early July, said that she was raped by two *Interahamwe* behind the church when she could not produce an identification card. Witness HAD explained that rape was prevalent during her stay at Sainte Famille from 22 April to around 19 or 20 June 1994, and that *Interahamwe* took girls away to be raped and executed. Witness AWX also gave evidence about rape and mentioned that some women subsequently died.

720. Of these five Tutsi refugees, only Witness AWX suggested that Renzaho played a direct role in an operation at Sainte Famille that resulted in rapes. Around 24 May, she saw him arrive in a vehicle with armed soldiers. He asked them to do their job, and the soldiers entered the church. Father Munyeshyaka called out names of Tutsi refugees and said that Renzaho had ordered those identified to step forward. The selected men and women were separated. Approximately three hours after Renzaho's arrival, the witness, her sister and her cousin were led away by soldiers to a house approximately five minutes away. The witness was locked in a room for two days, where she was raped twice by a soldier. The women were returned to Sainte Famille but then removed by the same soldiers on 15 June and raped again over the course of two days. The witness was released, as well as her cousin, whereas she saw her sister's body around 18 June, while Renzaho was overseeing the burial of corpses after an attack on Sainte Famille that day (II.11).

721. Witness AWX provided the only testimony about Renzaho working in coordination with soldiers and Munyeshyaka in separating Tutsi refugees at Sainte Famille in late May. There are some differences between her evidence and a statement she gave to Tribunal investigators in February 2005. According to the statement, presidential guards removed the witness, her older sister and cousin and kept her in the house for three days (not two), raped her three times (not two), and this was done by two such guards (not one).[798] In the **[page 188]** Chamber's view, these discrepancies do not affect her credibility. Although they describe serious acts, the differing numbers are comparably minor in nature, and may stem from communication problems, or be explained by the traumatic nature of the events and the time that has passed since then.

722. The Chamber considers that the fundamental features of Witness AWX's evidence regarding her abduction from Sainte Famille and subsequent rapes were coherent, compelling and consistent with her prior accounts to Tribunal investigators.[799] The testimonies of Defence Witnesses PER, TOA, BDC and UT were of a general character and did not discredit her account. Witness PER was not permanently positioned at Sainte Famille. Moreover, given his close working relationship with Father Munyeshyaka, it is not surprising that victims, who at a minimum suspected Munyeshyaka as being involved in sexual assaults, did not confide in him about the abuse they suffered. Witness TOA's opinion – that overcrowding and unhygienic conditions at Sainte Famille would have prevented rapes from occurring there – fails to address the allegations that victims were often removed from Sainte Famille and raped elsewhere. His suggestion that rapes would have been reported to the Red Cross or UN journalists is speculative. Given the vast number of refugees present, the Chamber has doubts that the witness, a man, would have been privy to reports of such a private nature.

---

[798] Compare Defence Exhibit 30A (statement of 10 February 2005) p. 3 and T. 6 February 2007 pp. 30 ("Each would go with her *abductor*") (emphasis added), 31 ("A. The soldier who was taking me there – and [...] when we arrived there, he undressed me and he raped me. He left me inside the room – he would leave me inside the room, he would close it, and he would put it under lock and key, then he would go out and come back again"), 31 ("I was raped twice. Q. And for what period of time were you kept inside this house? A. Two days.").

[799] While Witness AWX's February 2005 statement to Tribunal investigators indicates that the second occasion that she was taken away and raped was on 25 June 1994, her testimony was that this occurred around 15 June. Defence Exhibit 30A (statement of 10 February 2005) p. 3. The witness explained that she was unable to provide specific dates. T. 6 February 2007 p. 37. The Chamber finds this explanation reasonable.

Witness BDC's testimony about not having received reports of sexual assaults was equivocal.[800] Moreover, while Witness UT said that he never received complaints about rapes at Sainte Famille, he did read of such claims in the press.

723. Based on the evidence, it is clear that Witness AWX, her sister and cousin were abducted from Sainte Famille by soldiers around 24 May and again about 15 June 1994. The Chamber finds it established that Witness AWX was raped multiple times during these episodes before being released. She was returned to Sainte Famille each time. Regarding the alleged rapes of her cousin and sister, there is no direct evidence. It follows from the witness's testimony that her sister and cousin were raped after having been led away from Sainte Famille, but she did not provide an explicit basis for this view.[801] This said, her first-hand observations of soldiers working in parallel, separating the women from other refugees, and holding them for the same time period, leads to the only reasonable conclusion that her sister and cousin were subject to sexual assaults similar to those suffered by the witness. These two women were of no strategic importance to the military operations being carried out on Sainte Famille or elsewhere. That the sister was seen dead in June, and the cousin contracted AIDS and died in 2001, lend support to this conclusion. **[page 189]**

724. The question remains whether Renzaho can be found responsible for the rapes of Witness AWX, her sister and her cousin. While the witness's testimony reflects that the soldiers arrived with Renzaho during the operation in May, it also suggests that she, her sister and cousin were removed by these soldiers three hours afterwards. Moreover, her account indicates that Renzaho left quickly after the separation of refugees began, and there is no evidence that the women were removed on his orders or with his knowledge. Similarly, there is no indication that Renzaho was present when the women were taken away in the middle of June.

725. It is also noteworthy that Witness AWX's statement to Tribunal investigators makes no link between Renzaho's alleged role in the attack by *Interahamwe* in May 1994 and the abduction of the witness, her sister and cousin by soldiers. Even though the document reflects that she saw him with military personnel, he is described as instructing the *Interahamwe* to attack, as opposed to soldiers or, more specifically, presidential guards.[802] The statement does reflect the witness's belief that Renzaho wielded enough power that, had he "ordered perpetrators of rapes and killings to stop they would have obeyed him", but the absence of such a specific link between Renzaho's attack coordinated with *Interahamwe* and the rapes by the soldiers leads to a lack of clarity.[803] Given that the evidence fails to demonstrate that Renzaho's participation in separating the refugees led to the witness's alleged rape in May, the Chamber also has reasonable doubt that Renzaho was involved in or aware of the rapes that the witness, her cousin, and her sister, who ultimately died, allegedly suffered in June.[804]

726. The Chamber now turns to Witness KBZ, who testified that she was raped by two *Interahamwe* behind a church when she arrived at Sainte Famille in early July. Her testimony was precise and largely consistent with her prior statement given to Tribunal investigators in August 2004.[805] The Defence seeks generally to refute the allegation that women were raped at Sainte Famille. As mentioned above, this is not convincing, in view of the solid Prosecution evidence. The Chamber finds that Witness KBZ was indeed raped by two unidentified *Interahamwe* in early July 1994.

727. This said, there is no specific evidence linking this event to Renzaho. No witness observed him at Sainte Famille in July, and there is no indication that he was informed of this incident. Under these

---

[800] T. 4 June 2007 p. 22 ("Q. During the this period, were you able to see any reports on cases of sexual assault perpetrated in the sites? A. I have no recollection of such specific cases. I heard about – was it because the team was led by [...] a woman who might have had trouble expressing or explaining that? But otherwise I don't think I was aware of any cases of rape or sexual assault.").
[801] T. 6 February 2007 pp. 29-33. In response to a question about women at Sainte Famille generally, Witness AWX said that they discussed the assaults they had suffered. In view of this, it is likely that the three female relatives also shared such information even if the witness did not explicitly testify to that effect.
[802] Defence Exhibit 30A (statement of 10 February 2005) p. 3 ("[...] telling *Interahamwe* to flush out the *Inyenzi* (Tutsis)"; instructing *Interahamwe* "to get out of the vehicle and 'get to work' meaning to kill the Tutsis", whereupon the *Interahamwe* "would start checking identity cards and the killings would start").
[803] Defence Exhibit 30A (statement of 10 February 2005) p. 3.
[804] The Chamber's conclusion with respect to the death of Witness AWX's sister takes into account the evidence and findings relating to the attack on Sainte Famille on 17 June 1994 (II.11).
[805] Defence Exhibit 31A (statement of 27 August 2004) p. 3.

circumstances, the Chamber cannot find beyond reasonable doubt that when Witness KBZ was raped by two *Interahamwe* he was specifically involved. In the circumstances, it is not established that Renzaho was involved in this event, that those who committed the rapes were his subordinates, or that Renzaho had sufficient information to establish criminal liability for the crimes.

728. The Chamber has considered the allegations implicating Father Wenceslas Munyeshyaka in rapes and sexual assaults. No witness in the present case provided direct evidence about this. The accounts by Witnesses AWN and HAD were second-hand. Although the Defence testimonies, discussed above, did not fully refute the Prosecution evidence, the **[page 190]** Chamber does not have a sufficient basis to find that Father Munyeshyaka committed rape or other sexual assaults at Sainte Famille.

13.3.3 Kimihurura Sector

729. Only Witness KBZ testified that she and four other women, who were stopped at a roadblock on 28 May 1994, were taken to the abandoned house of Jean-Michel in Kimihurura sector. This happened after the *Interahamwe* had spoken with the *conseiller* of Kimihurura. According to the militiamen, he had given instructions that they should ask Renzaho what to do with the women. The following day, they said that the prefect had said that they should not be killed until after the burial of President Habyarimana.[806] An *Interahamwe* called Jerôme Rwemarika then took her to his home and raped her.

730. In the Chamber's view, the witness's account that she was raped appeared coherent and convincing. It was generally consistent with her statement to Tribunal investigators of August 2004. However, her evidence implicating Renzaho was second-hand, provided to her by the *Interahamwe* who kidnapped and raped her. Her August 2004 statement creates further doubt about Renzaho's alleged involvement. Although it reflects that the *conseiller* directed the *Interahamwe* to seek advice from Renzaho before taking action, the statement does not indicate that they did so.[807] In the Chamber's view, this omission is material.

731. The witness also testified that the other women were taken away from the abandoned house. She believed they were raped although they did not talk about it. This account was second-hand, and her basis for knowledge was insufficiently precise to establish that rape occurred. No information was given about the purported victims and perpetrators, location or time of the crime. Consequently, the evidence is inconclusive.

732. The Chamber concludes that Witness KBZ was raped by an *Interahamwe* in late May 1994. However, it is not established beyond reasonable doubt that Renzaho was involved in this event, that those who committed the rapes were his subordinates, or that Renzaho had sufficient information to be held criminally liable in relation to their acts.

13.3.4 Renzaho's General Knowledge of Rapes

733. In addition to alleging that Renzaho was involved in specific incidents of rape, as addressed above, the Prosecution also seeks to establish his general knowledge of rapes occurring in Kigali-Ville prefecture from April to July 1994. It relies on Witnesses AWE and UB, both local officials, who purportedly shared their reports about rapes in their areas with Renzaho.

734. The Chamber recalls that, when giving evidence, Witness AWE was awaiting trial in Rwanda for genocide, whereas Witness UB's appeal against his genocide conviction was pending. Both were accused of crimes implicating Renzaho and were, at the time of their testimony, detained in the same prison. The Chamber views their evidence with caution as it may be influenced by their desire to distance themselves from responsibility. Defence Witness AIA stated that reports about rapes were not made to Renzaho, but to the *conseiller* for whom the witness worked. This official ignored such reports and even encouraged and **[page 191]** engaged in acts of rape. As mentioned elsewhere (II.3), the Chamber has doubts about the reliability of certain aspects of this witness's account. Nevertheless, the evidentiary situation about the reporting of rape is unclear.

---

[806] T. 6 February 2007 p. 52 (the prefect "had told [her abductors] that they were criticising the killings on the radio").
[807] Defence Exhibit 31A (statement of 27 August 2004) p. 3.

735. Renzaho admitted that, during a meeting on 21 April 1994, he received information about rapes taking place within Kigali-Ville prefecture. His statements on Radio Rwanda on 24 April and 10 May further demonstrate that he had knowledge that rapes were being committed in that area.[808] The Indictment alleges that he is responsible as a superior for such acts. However, as set forth above (subsections (II.13.3.2) and (II.13.3.3)), the Chamber has doubt that rapes were being committed by Renzaho's subordinates over whom he exercised effective control. Furthermore, and notwithstanding the testimonies summarised here, the overall evidence of Renzaho's knowledge is insufficient to make a finding of criminal liability with respect to general evidence about rape and sexual violence in Kigali-Ville prefecture. **[page 192]**

CHAPTER III: LEGAL FINDINGS

1. INTRODUCTION

736. The Prosecution has charged Renzaho under Article 6 (1) and (3) of the Statute with genocide, complicity in genocide, crimes agasint humanity (murder and rape) and serious violations of Article 3 Common to the Geneva Conventions and of Additional Protocol II (murder and rape).[809]

737. In its factual findings, the Chamber found that Renzaho participated in the establishment of roadblocks (II.2) and distribution of weapons to civilian authorities (II.3) in Kigali. It also concluded that he was involved in crimes committed at CELA (II.6) and Saint Famille (II.11) and against Tutsi women in Rugenge sector (II.13). In this chapter, the Chamber will address the legal consequences of Renzaho's involvement in these events.

2. CRIMINAL RESPONSIBILITY

2.1 Article 6 (1)

738. "Ordering" requires that a person in a position of authority instruct another person to commit an offence. No formal superior-subordinate relationship between the accused and the perpetrator is required. It is sufficient that there is proof of some position of authority on the part of the accused that would compel another to commit a crime in following the accused's order. The authority creating the kind of relationship envisaged under Article 6 (1) of the Statute for ordering may be informal or of a purely temporary nature.[810]

739. The Appeals Chamber has held that commission covers, primarily, the physical perpetration of a crime (with criminal intent) or a culpable omission of an act that is mandated by a rule of criminal law.[811] "Committing" has also been interpreted to contain three forms of joint criminal enterprise: basic, systemic, and extended.[812] The Prosecution has indicated that it is only pursuing the basic form.[813] This form of commission requires that all the co-perpetrators, acting pursuant to a common purpose, possess the same criminal intention.[814]

740. According to settled jurisprudence, the required *actus reus* for each form of joint criminal enterprise comprises three elements.[815] First, a plurality of persons is required. They need not be organised in a military,

---

[808] Prosecution Exhibit 56 (transcript of Radio Rwanda interview, 10 May 1994) p. 12; Prosecution Exhibit 54 (transcript of Radio Rwanda broadcast, 24 April 1994) p. 14. While Renzaho's statements over the radio portray him as being against rape, they fail to raise doubt with respect to the specific events discussed under (13.3.1) above.

[809] The Prosecution is only pursuing Counts IV and Count VI, which charge rape, based on Article 6 (3) of the Statute. The allegations pertaining to sexual violence mentioned under Count I (Genocide) are also charged only under Article 6 (3).

[810] *Bagosora et al.* Trial Judgement para. 2008, citing *Semanza* Appeal Judgement paras. 361, 363.

[811] *Nahimana et al.* Appeal Judgement para. 478.

[812] *Simba* Trial Judgement para. 386, citing *Kvočka et al.* Appeal Judgement paras. 82-83; *Ntakirutimana* Appeal Judgement paras. 463-465; *Vasiljević* Appeal Judgement paras. 96-99; *Krnojelac* Appeal Judgement para. 30. See also *Nahimana et al.* Appeal Judgement para. 478.

[813] Prosecution Closing Brief para. 22.

[814] *Simba* Trial Judgement para. 386, citing *Kvočka et al.* Appeal Judgement para. 82; *Ntakirutimana* Appeal Judgement para. 463; *Vasiljević* Appeal Judgement para. 97; *Krnojelac* Appeal Judgement para. 84.

[815] *Simba* Trial Judgement para. 387, citing *Kvočka et al.* Appeal Judgement para. 96; *Ntakirutimana* Appeal Judgement para. 466; *Vasiljević* Appeal Judgement para. 100; *Krnojelac* Appeal Judgement para. 31.

political or administrative structure. Second, there must be a common purpose which amounts to or involves the commission of a crime provided for [page 193] in the Statute. There is no necessity for this purpose to have been previously arranged or formulated. It may materialise extemporaneously and be inferred from the facts. Third, the participation of the accused in the common purpose is necessary, which involves the perpetration of one of the crimes provided for in the Statute. This participation need not involve commission of a specific crime under one of the provisions (for example, murder, extermination, torture, or rape), but may take the form of assistance in, or contribution to, the execution of the common purpose. The Appeals Chamber in *Kvočka et al.* provided guidance on distinguishing between joint criminal enterprise and other forms of liability, such as aiding and abetting.[816]

741. The required *mens rea* for each form of joint criminal enterprise varies. The basic form of joint criminal enterprise requires the intent to perpetrate a certain crime, this intent being shared by all co-perpetrators.[817] Where the underlying crime requires a special intent, such as discriminatory intent, the accused, as a member of the joint criminal enterprise, must share the special intent.[818]

742. The Appeals Chamber has explained that an aider and abetter carries out acts specifically directed to assist, encourage, or lend moral support to the perpetration of a certain specific crime, which have a substantial effect on its commission.[819] The *actus reus* need not serve as condition precedent for the crime and may occur before, during, or after the principal crime has been perpetrated.[820] It has also been determined by the Appeals Chamber that the *actus reus* of aiding and abetting may be satisfied by a commander permitting the use of resources under his or her control, including personnel, to facilitate the perpetration of a crime.[821] The requisite mental element of aiding and abetting is knowledge that the acts performed assist the commission of the specific crime of the principal perpetrator.[822] In cases of specific intent crimes such as persecution or genocide, the aider and abetter must know of the principal perpetrator's specific intent.[823]
[page 194]

743. The Chamber will assess these forms of criminal responsibility where relevant in its legal findings.

2.2 Article 6 (3)

2.2.1 Legal Principles

744. The following three elements must be proven to hold a civilian or a military superior criminally responsible pursuant to Article 6 (3) of the Statute for crimes committed by subordinates: (a) the existence of a superior-subordinate relationship; (b) the superior's knowledge or reason to know that the criminal acts

---

[816] *Simba* Trial Judgement para. 387, citing *Kvočka et al.* Appeal Judgement para. 90 ("Where the aider and abettor only knows that his assistance is helping a single person to commit a single crime, he is only liable for aiding and abetting that crime. This is so even if the principal perpetrator is part of a joint criminal enterprise involving the commission of further crimes. Where, however, the accused knows that his assistance is supporting the crimes of a group of persons involved in a joint criminal enterprise and shares that intent, then he may be found criminally responsible for the crimes committed in furtherance of that common purpose as a co-perpetrator."); *Vasiljević* Appeal Judgement para. 102; *Tadić* Appeal Judgement para. 229.
[817] *Simba* Trial Judgement para. 388, citing *Ntakirutimana* Appeal Judgement para. 467; *Vasiljević* Appeal Judgement para. 101; *Krnojelac* Appeal Judgement para. 32.
[818] *Simba* Trial Judgement para. 388, citing *Kvočka et al.* Appeal Judgement paras. 109-110.
[819] *Bagosora et al.* Trial Judgement para. 2009, citing *Blagojević and Jokić* Appeal Judgement para. 127; *Simić* Appeal Judgement para. 85; *Blaškić* Appeal Judgement paras. 45-46; *Vasiljević* Appeal Judgement para. 102; *Ntagerura et al.* Appeal Judgement para. 370.
[820] *Bagosora et al.* Trial Judgement para. 2009, citing *Blagojević and Jokić* Appeal Judgement para. 127; *Blaškić* Appeal Judgement para. 48; *Simić* Appeal Judgement para. 85; *Ntagerura et al.* Appeal Judgement para. 372.
[821] *Bagosora et al.* Trial Judgement para. 2009, citing *Blagojević and Jokić* Appeal Judgement para. 127; *Krstić* Appeal Judgement paras. 137, 138, 144.
[822] *Bagosora et al.* Trial Judgement para. 2009, citing *Blagojević and Jokić* Appeal Judgement para. 127; *Simić* Appeal Judgement para. 86; *Vasiljević* Appeal Judgement para. 102; *Blaškić* Appeal Judgement para. 46; *Ntagerura et al.* Appeal Judgement para. 370.
[823] *Bagosora et al.* Trial Judgement para. 2009, citing *Blagojević and Jokić* Appeal Judgement para. 127. See also *Simić* Appeal Judgement para. 86; *Krstić* Appeal Judgement paras. 140-141.

were about to be or had been committed by his subordinates; and (c) the superior's failure to take necessary and reasonable measures to prevent such criminal acts or to punish the perpetrator.[824]

745. A superior-subordinate relationship is established by showing a formal or informal hierarchical relationship. The superior must have possessed the power or the authority, *de jure* or *de facto*, to prevent or punish an offence committed by his subordinates. The superior must have had effective control over the subordinates at the time the offence was committed. Effective control means the material ability to prevent the commission of the offence or to punish the principal offenders. This requirement is not satisfied by a showing of general influence on the part of the accused.[825]

746. A superior will be found to have possessed or will be imputed with the requisite *mens rea* sufficient to incur criminal responsibility provided that: (i) the superior had actual knowledge, established through direct or circumstantial evidence, that his subordinates were about to commit, were committing, or had committed, a crime under the Statute; or (ii) the superior possessed information providing notice of the risk of such offences by indicating the need for additional investigations in order to ascertain whether such offences were about to be committed, were being committed, or had been committed by subordinates.[826]

747. With respect to actual knowledge, relevant factors include: the number, type and scope of illegal acts committed by the subordinates, the time during which the illegal acts occurred, the number and types of troops and logistics involved, the geographical location, whether the occurrence of the acts is widespread, the tactical tempo of operations, the *modus operandi* of similar illegal acts, the officers and staff involved, and the location of the superior at the time.[827] **[page 195]**

2.2.2 Deliberations

748. The Indictment alleges that Renzaho as prefect of Kigali-Ville and a colonel in the Rwandan Army had *de jure* and *de facto* control over *bourgmestres, conseillers, responsables de cellule*, ten-house leaders, administrative personnel, urban police, the Rwandan army, gendarmes, *Interahamwe*, militias, armed civilians as well as the Rwandan armed forces who fell under his command.[828]

749. Renzaho argues that the Indictment is insufficiently precise in outlining the perpetrators over whom he allegedly had authority. While he concedes his *de jure* authority over *bourgmestres* and the urban police, he contends that the situation in Kigali-Ville had spiralled out of control, that he lacked the means and resources to exercise control over those committing crimes, and that he was unaware of crimes committed by his subordinates.[829]

750. Renzaho was appointed prefect of Kigali-Ville on 5 October 1990, immediately after an RPF invasion, and remained in that position until July 1994, when he fled Kigali.[830] The prefect was the representative of the national government in Kigali-Ville, vested with the authority of the state. His tasks included the maintenance of peace, public order and security of persons and property within the prefecture and ensuring the proper functioning of the prefecture's services.[831] In addition, Renzaho maintained his position

---

[824] *Bagosora et al.* Trial Judgement para. 2011, citing *Orić* Appeal Judgement para. 18; *Nahimana et al.* Appeal Judgement para. 484; *Gacumbitsi* Appeal Judgement para. 143; *Ntagerura et al.* Trial Judgement para. 627; *Semanza* Trial Judgement para. 400.
[825] *Bagosora et al.* Trial Judgement para. 2012, citing *Halilović* Appeal Judgement para. 59; *Gacumbitsi* Appeal Judgement para. 143; *Kajelijeli* Appeal Judgement para. 85; *Ntagerura et al.* Appeal Judgement paras. 341-342; *Ntagerura et al.* Trial Judgement para. 628; *Semanza* Trial Judgement paras. 402, 415.
[826] *Bagosora et al.* Trial Judgement para. 2013, citing *Delalić et al.* Appeal Judgement para. 232. See also *Hadžihasanović and Kubura* Appeal Judgement para. 28; *Galić* Appeal Judgement para. 184; *Bagilishema* Appeal Judgement paras. 37, 42; *Ntagerura et al.* Trial Judgement para. 629; *Semanza* Trial Judgement para. 405.
[827] *Bagosora et al.* Trial Judgement para. 2014, citing *Delić* Trial Judgement para. 64; *Strugar* Trial Judgement para. 68; *Limaj et al.* Trial Judgement para. 524.
[828] Indictment paras. 2 (A)-(B). The Prosecution conceded that no evidence was adduced in connection with para. 2 (C). Prosecution's letter of 13 March 2007 to the Defence.
[829] Defence Closing Brief paras. 4-5, 7-9, 11-13, 17-18, 21-22, 48-65, 71, 74, 86-99, 102, 127-144, 339-353, 443-461, 645-646, 701-717, 741-753, 757-758, 774-793, 937, 945-946, 956-957, 1041, 1065-1067, 1069, 1084-1085, 1089-1090, 1099-1133, 1170, 1175, 1212, 1222, 1227-1231, 1240-1252, 1269.
[830] Renzaho, T. 27 August 2007 pp. 5, 10-12 (appointment); Witness UB, T. 23 January 2007 p. 32 (appointment in war).
[831] Prosecution Exhibit 14 (*Loi portant organisation administrative de la préfecture de la ville de Kigali* of 22 June 1990) Article 25; Prosecution Exhibit 10 (*Décret-loi sur l'organisation et fonctionnement de la préfecture* of 11 March 1975 as modified on 14 August 1978) Articles 8-9.

within the Rwandan army throughout his tenure as prefect and was promoted to the rank of colonel in July 1992.[832]

751. The Chamber recalls that a superior need not necessarily know the exact identity of his or her subordinates who perpetrate crimes in order to incur liability under Article 6 (3) of the Statute.[833] The Indictment identifies Renzaho's subordinates by general category and contains additional specificity in the relevant paragraphs referring to the crimes by providing specific names and further geographical and temporal limitations for broader categories of assailants such as militiamen. In the context of this case, and given the nature of the attacks, the Chamber is not convinced that the Prosecution could have provided more specific identification, in particular in relation to the vast network of roadblocks throughout Kigali. **[page 196]** Accordingly, the Chamber is satisfied that the Indictment provides reasonable notice of the individuals alleged to be Renzaho's subordinates.[834]

752. Turning to the question of Renzaho's superior responsibility, the Chamber recalls that the main question is whether he exercised effective control over his alleged subordinates.[835] In this respect, the Appeals Chamber has stated that *de jure* authority is not synonymous with effective control.[836] Furthermore, although a showing of *de jure* authority may suggest the material ability to prevent or punish an offence, its proof is neither necessary nor itself sufficient to prove beyond reasonable doubt that an accused exercised effective control over his subordinates.[837] Accordingly, the Chamber has not considered such evidence as decisive in its assessment of Renzaho's authority.

753. The Chamber is satisfied that Renzaho exercised effective control and was a superior over the local officials within his prefecture, including sub-prefects, *bourgmestres, conseillers, responsables de cellule* and *Nyumba Kumi* (ten-house leaders) as well as prefecture and commune employees such as the urban police. In reaching this conclusion, the Chamber has considered that, by virtue of his position as prefect and with his high military rank, Renzaho was clearly an important and influential authority of the Rwandan government entrusted with the administration of a key strategic location during a time of war. Prior to the events, he participated in discussions concerning the defence of the city, which sketched out a framework for utilising and mobilising local officials in the effort to secure the city (II.2). Although the Chamber cannot be certain as to when and to what extent these plans were put into place, this evidence as well as Renzaho's key role in the process offers strong circumstantial evidence, confirmed by what followed, that in the wake of war all resources of local administration would be effectively placed under the authority of the prefect and local military commanders at least with respect to the government's efforts to combat the "enemy".

754. From the outset of the resumption of hostilities, Renzaho regularly convened and chaired meetings at the prefecture level involving civilian and military officials, where he issued instructions and orders for the maintenance of security, including the erection of roadblocks and the acquisition and distribution of weapons (II.2 and 3). Furthermore, it is also relevant that Renzaho clearly had *de jure* authority over *bourgmestres* and the urban police force.[838] The evidence of *de jure* authority is not clear with respect to other categories

---

[832] Renzaho, T. 27 August 2007 pp. 5-7, 10; Defence Witness PAT, T. 22 August 2007 p. 53. Renzaho's file remained with the army general staff, and he received his salary from the Ministry of Defence. Renzaho, T. 27 August 2007 pp. 14 ("A. Thank you, Counsel. By virtue of that provision, I remained attached to the ministry of defence with respect to my career file. That is correct."), 32 ("A. No, I had no military function. I did not have any specific military activity, but my name was still on the list of those who were paid by the army every month.").
[833] *Muvunyi* Appeal Judgement para. 55; *Blagojević and Jokić* Appeal Judgement para. 287.
[834] *Muvunyi* Appeal Judgement para. 56 (subordinates reasonably identified by reference to their affiliation with *École des sous-officiers* in Butare Prefecture, Rwanda); *Ntagerura et al.* Appeal Judgement paras. 140, 141, 153 (subordinates reasonably identified by reference to military camp). See also *Simba* Appeal Judgement paras. 71-72 (finding adequate notice for members of joint criminal enterprise based on identification by broad category, such as *Interahamwe* or gendarmes, and further identification with geographic and temporal details), affirming *Simba* Trial Judgement paras. 392-393.
[835] *Orić* Appeal Judgement para. 91.
[836] *Id.* para. 91.
[837] *Id.* paras. 91-92.
[838] See, for instance, Renzaho, T. 28 August 2007 p. 35 (he held *de jure* authority over the *bourgmestres*, at times of peace and war), T. 30 August 2007 p. 21 (as prefect, he had control over the police force in Kigali-Ville prefecture); Witness PPV, T. 4 June 2007 p. 78 (commander of the urban police reported to the prefect); Witness AIA, T. 2 July 2007 p. 50 (the prefect was in charge of the police); Witness ALG, T. 10 January 2007 p. 58 (a *bourgmestre* within Kigali-Ville would report to the prefect); Witness UB, T. 23 January 2007 pp. 6-8, 19 (the prefect was in charge of the police and could dismiss them); Prosecution Exhibit 9 (*Loi sur*

[page 197] of subordinates, including *conseillers*.[839] As noted above, this is not dispositive. Renzaho issued instructions to the *conseillers* and provided them with urban police as their personal guards.[840] The *conseillers* were at the front line of organising the local population to man roadblocks and distributed weapons. Moreover, his effective control is reflected by his ultimate supervision of the replacement of local officials under his Kigali-Ville *bourgmestres*, notwithstanding the limitations of the law (II.8). In this context, his suggestion that he lacked the ability to control their actions is without merit.

755. With respect to other categories of possible offenders, such as soldiers and gendarmes, it follows from Renzaho's position as prefect and high military rank that he would have been viewed as an authority and given a measure of deference. In particular, as prefect, he had the legal ability to requisition gendarmes, although they remained under the operational command of their officers.[841] Furthermore, as an army officer, he had the right and duty to enforce compliance with the general rules governing discipline by all soldiers below him in the hierarchy, even where the soldiers were not under his operational authority.[842] Nonetheless, given his position within the civilian administration, and the formal limitations on his authority over gendarmes, the Chamber is not convinced beyond reasonable doubt that Renzaho's effective control extended to all gendarmes or every army soldier of a lesser rank. Instead, the Chamber must assess his authority over these individuals on a case by case basis.

756. Turning to militiamen, again, the evidence concerning Rwanda's "civil defence" planning lends strong circumstantial support to the conclusion that Renzaho had authority over these assailants, in particular when they were operating as part of the Kigali's defensive efforts or engaged in operations under the authority of or in conjuction with civilian authorities. Nevertheless, the Chamber is mindful of evidence suggesting that these forces [page 198] were hastily assembled and were at times undisciplined.[843] Although the material pertaining to Rwanda's civil defence system offers some guidance, there is limited evidence detailing the actual structure and chain of command governing these forces in all instances. The Chamber instead will assess the circumstances on the ground in order to determine whether Renzaho exercised effective control over them in the context of a given incident.

757. Renzaho's knowledge of and failure to prevent and punish the relevant offences will be considered in the Chamber's legal findings for each crime.

---

l'organisation de la commune of 23 November 1963) Articles 46, 48, 85 (allowing the prefect to take disciplinary measures and propose to the Minister the dismissal of a *bourgmestre* and supplant the authority of the *bourgmestre* or other communal officials); Prosecution Exhibit 14 (*Loi portant organisation administrative de la prefecture de la ville de Kigali* of 22 June 1990) Article 27 (giving the prefect authority over the urban police).

[839] The Prosecution suggests that Renzaho's authority over sub-prefects, *conseillers*, *responsables de cellule* and *nyumba kumi* also derives under *Loi sur l'organisation de la commune* of 23 November 1963, Article 59 (placing the *bourgmestre* under the prefect's authority) and Article 60 (communal officials under the *bourgmestre's* authority). No expert testimony was adduced in order to present the precise contours of a prefect's authority as it relates to these officials. Renzaho denied having authority over *conseillers*, for example, pointing in particular to his inability to impose sanctions on them directly. Renzaho, T. 28 August 2007 p. 39, T. 30 August 2007 pp. 25-26; Prosecution Exhibit 9 (*Loi sur l'organisation de la commune* of 23 November 1963) Article 10 *bis*. Jurisprudence in this Tribunal suggests that prefects did not have *de jure* authority over *conseillers* in 1994. *Ntagerura et al.* Trial Judgement, para. 646, citing *Bagilishema* Trial Judgement, para. 166.

[840] See, for instance, Renzaho, T. 27 August 2007 p. 63 (Renzaho instructed commander Emmanuel Nyamuhimba on 8 April 1994 to deploy police officers to assist *conseillers*); Witness PPV, T. 5 June 2007 pp. 3-5 (Renzaho gave orders on 7 April to dispatch policemen to 19 sectors, who were assigned to *bourgmestres* and *conseillers*); Witness GOA, T. 6 June 2007 p. 54 (the witness saw Biryogo *conseiller* Amri Karekezi in the company of three to four police officers); Witness AIA, T. 2 July 2007 pp. 24-25, T. 3 July 2007 pp. 2-3 (based on Renzaho's instructions on 8 April, five police officers were assigned to each sector, except Biryogo, where 11 were assigned); T. 2 July 2007 pp. 44-45, 50-52, 60; T. 3 July 2007 pp. 7, 16 (police were primarily responsible for protecting *conseillers*); Witness UB, T. 23 January 2007 pp. 6, 62, 64 (police told the witness that they had been sent by the prefect to ensure the security of the *conseiller*).

[841] Renzaho, T. 30 August 2007 p. 21; Prosecution Exhibit 10 (*Decret-loi sur l'organisation et fonctionnement de la prefecture*) Article 11; Prosecution Exhibit 8 (*Decret-Loi sur la creation de la Gendarmerie Nationale de 1974*) Articles 24, 29, 31, 32, 34, 35, 36.

[842] Prosecution Exhibit 11 (Rules of Discipline of Rwandan army, 13 December 1978) Rule 10.

[843] The disorganisation and indiscipline of militia in Kigali-Ville is reflected in the evidence related to roadblocks and Renzaho's contemporaneous Radio Rwanda broadcasts (II.2).

3. GENOCIDE

758. Counts I and II of the Indictment charge Renzaho with genocide and complicity to commit genocide under Articles 2 (3)(a) and (e) of the Statute.

3.1 Genocide

3.1.1 Introduction

759. Count I of the Indictment charges Renzaho with genocide under Article 2 (3)(a) of the Statute.[844]

3.1.2 Law

760. To find an accused guilty of the crime of genocide, it must be established that the accused committed any of the enumerated acts in Article 2 (2) with the specific intent to destroy, in whole or in part, a group, as such, that is defined by one of the protected categories of nationality, race, ethnicity, or religion.[845] Although there is no numeric threshold, the perpetrator must act with the intent to destroy at least a substantial part of the group.[846] The perpetrator need not be solely motivated by a criminal intent to commit genocide, nor does the existence of personal motive preclude him from having the specific intent to commit genocide.[847]

761. In the absence of direct evidence, a perpetrator's intent to commit genocide may be inferred from relevant facts and circumstances that can lead beyond any reasonable doubt to the existence of the intent. Factors that may establish the specific intent include the general context, the perpetration of other culpable acts systematically directed against the same **[page 199]** group, the scale of atrocities committed, the systematic targeting of victims on account of their membership in a particular group, or the repetition of destructive and discriminatory acts.[848]

762. The Indictment charges Renzaho with killing and causing serious bodily or mental harm to members of the Tutsi group. It is firmly established that the Tutsi ethnicity is a protected group.[849] Killing members of the group requires a showing that the principal perpetrator intentionally killed one or more members of the group.[850] The term "causing serious bodily harm" refers to acts of sexual violence, serious acts of physical violence falling short of killing that seriously injure the health, cause disfigurement, or cause any serious injury to the external or internal organs or senses.[851] Serious mental harm refers to more than minor or

---

[844] The Chamber observes that the language under Count 1 on page 4 of the Indictment contains an erroneous reference to Article 2 (3)(b) of the Statute, which corresponds to "conspiracy to commit genocide". The correct reference is Article 2 (3)(a), which refers to "genocide". In the Chamber's view, this appears to be a minor typographical error which does not raise notice concerns. The surrounding text unequivocally states that "Tharcisse Renzaho was responsible for killing or causing serious bodily or mental harm to members of the Ttusi racial or ethnic group". Furthermore, the brief summary of Count 1 on page 2 of the Indictment correctly mentions Article 2 (3)(a) of the Statute.
[845] *Bagosora et al.* Trial Judgement para. 2115, citing *Nahimana et al.* Appeal Judgement paras. 492, 496, 522-523; *Niyitegeka* Appeal Judgement para. 48; *Gacumbitsi* Appeal Judgement para. 39; *Brđanin* Trial Judgement paras. 681, 695.
[846] *Bagosora et al.* Trial Judgement para. 2115, citing *Seromba* Appeal Judgement para. 175; *Gacumbitsi* Appeal Judgement para. 44; *Simba* Trial Judgement para. 412; *Semanza* Trial Judgement para. 316.
[847] *Bagosora et al.* Trial Judgement para. 2115, citing *Simba* Appeal Judgement para. 269, *Ntakirutimana* Appeal Judgement paras. 302-304; *Niyitegeka* Appeal Judgement paras. 48-54; *Krnojelac* Appeal Judgement para. 102, citing *Jelisić* Appeal Judgement para. 49.
[848] *Bagosora et al.* Trial Judgement para. 2116, citing *Seromba* Appeal Judgement para. 176, referring to *Seromba* Trial Judgement para. 320; *Nahimana et al.* Appeal Judgement paras. 524-525; *Simba* Appeal Judgement para. 264; *Gacumbitsi* Appeal Judgement paras. 40-41; *Rutaganda* Appeal Judgement para. 525; *Semanza* Appeal Judgement para. 262, citing *Jelisić* Appeal Judgement para. 47; *Kayishema and Ruzindana* Appeal Judgement paras. 147-148.
[849] Prosecution Exhibit 94A (expert report of Alison Des Forges) pp. 1-2 (Tutsis are a recognised ethnic group). Furthermore, every judgement rendered by this Tribunal concerning genocide has recognised that the Tutsi ethnicity is a protected group. *Bagosora et al.* Trial Judgement para. 2117, n. 2338, citing *Karemera et al.*, Decision on Prosecutor's Interlocutory Appeal of Decision on Judicial Notice (AC), 16 June 2006, para. 25; *Semanza* Appeal Judgement para. 192.
[850] *Bagosora et al.* Trial Judgement para. 2117, citing *Simba* Trial Judgement para. 414, referring to *Kayishema and Ruzindana* Appeal Judgement para. 151.
[851] *Bagosora et al.* Trial Judgement para. 2117, citing *Seromba* Appeal Judgement paras. 46-49; *Ntagerura et al.* Trial Judgement para. 664; *Semanza* Trial Judgement para. 320; *Kayishema and Ruzindana* Trial Judgement para. 110.

temporary impairment of mental faculties.[852] The serious bodily or mental harm, however, need not be an injury that is permanent or irremediable.[853] This harm can include crimes of sexual violence, including rape.[854]

3.1.3 Deliberations

(i) Roadblocks and Weapons Distributions

763. In its factual findings, the Chamber determined that, around 10 April 1994, Renzaho ordered local officials to establish roadblocks in Kigali and further reaffirmed his support for roadblocks in subsequent meetings and during various radio broadcasts (II.2). The Chamber concluded that roadblocks were in fact established pursuant to Renzaho's orders, which were used to identify and intentionally kill Tutsi civilians throughout Kigali.

764. By his orders and public support in relation to roadblocks, Renzaho substantially contributed to the killing of Tutsi civilians at them by further proliferating these instruments of death and lending official sanction to the actions there. Furthermore, the Chamber found that, around 16 April 1994, he facilitated the acquisition of weapons by local officials for distribution amongst the civilian population (II.3). These actions also lended further sanction **[page 200]** and material support to the killings by local officials and members of the population. There is no explicit evidence that Renzaho ordered the killing of Tutsis at roadblocks. However, in view of his authority, his actions in support of roadblocks, their role in the "defence" of the city, their widespread and continuing operation, as well as his order to distribute weapons, the Chamber is convinced that Renzaho must have equally ordered the killings there.[855]

765. Given the nature and purpose of the roadblocks, the systematic nature of the killings there as well as the scale of the crimes, the Chamber has no doubt that the perpetrators of the killings possessed genocidal intent. Furthermore, the Chamber has already determined that Renzaho issued orders to establish roadblocks and made other supportive public statements with full knowledge that crimes were being perpetrated agasint Tutsi civilians at them. Renzaho's orders to establish roadblocks demonstrated that their purpose was to confront Tutsis. Accordingly, the Chamber is convinced that Renzaho acted with knowledge of the genocidal intent of the assailants at roadblocks, which he shared as well.[856]

766. In sum, the Chamber concludes that Renzaho is responsible for aiding and abetting the killing of Tutsi civilians at roadblocks in Kigali under Article 6 (1) of the Statute by ordering their establishment, sanctioning the conduct at them and through his continued material support for the killings through the distribution of weapons. He is also liable under Article 6 (1) of the Statute for ordering the killings.[857]

---

[852] *Bagosora et al.* Trial Judgement para. 2117, citing *Seromba* Appeal Judgement para. 46; *Kajelijeli* Trial Judgement para. 815; *Ntagerura et al.* Trial Judgement para. 664; *Semanza* Trial Judgement paras. 321-322; *Kayishema and Ruzindana* Trial Judgement para. 110.
[853] *Bagosora et al.* Trial Judgement para. 2117, citing *Ntagerura et al.* Trial Judgement para. 664; *Semanza* Trial Judgement paras. 320, 322.
[854] *Bagosora et al.* Trial Judgement para. 2117, citing *Seromba* Appeal Judgement para. 46; *Gacumbitsi* Trial Judgement para. 292; *Akayesu* Trial Judgement paras. 706-707.
[855] The Appeals Chamber has held that a mode of liability such as ordering can be proven through circumstantial evidence even in the absence of direct evidence of where and when a particular order was issued. See, for example, *Galić* Appeal Judgement paras. 177-178, 389.
[856] In finding that Renzaho acted with genocidal intent, the Chamber has considered evidence that, from April to July 1994, refugees, including Tutsis, were received at the Kigali-Ville prefecture office and at Renzaho's home. Defence Closing Brief paras. 1265-1292. See also Witness ALG, T. 11 January 2007 pp. 21-23; Witness UT, T. 24 May 2007 pp. 56-59; Witness PGL, T. 6 June 2007 p. 23 (militiamen threatened him, saying that Renzaho was an accomplice of Tutsis); Witness PPV, T. 5 June 2007 pp. 10, 14. In view of Renzaho's conduct and the nature of the crimes, the submisssions and evidence do not make this conclusion doubtful. See *Simba* Trial Judgement paras. 417, 418, quoting *Kvočka et al.* Appeal Judgement paras. 232-233.
[857] The Chamber notes that these facts would also support the conclusion that Renzaho participated in a joint criminal enterprise to kill Tutsis at roadblocks as the crimes involved a plurality of persons named in the Indictment, such as militiamen, local officials, and Renzaho, who shared the requisite genocidal intent. However, the Chamber considers that "ordering", which is also a direct form of responsibility, most appropriately captures the nature of Renzaho's criminal responsibility. In view of the overall gravity of the crimes and the nature of Renzaho's actual involvement, the legal characterization of his actions as ordering and aiding and abetting or as participating in a joint criminal enterprise would not impact the Chamber's sentencing considerations.

767. The Chamber is also convinced that Renzaho bears superior responsibility for these crimes under Article 6 (3) of the Statute. In view of the role played by these roadblocks in the defence efforts of Kigali as well as involvement of local officials in establishing and supervising them, the Chamber is satisfied that those manning them were Renzaho's subordinates. The Chamber accepts that, in some cases, there was a measure of indiscipline at roadblocks, and that some assailants might not have recognised Renzaho's authority in isolated cases. However, Defence and Prosecution evidence demonstrates that *conseillers* and *responsables de cellule* played critical roles in the establishment and oversight of roadblocks throughout Kigali. The Chamber has already determined that these local officials are Renzaho's subordinates over whom he exercised effective control. To the extent Renzaho lacked the material ability to prevent or punish crimes committed by those implementing his orders, it is because he distributed arms to the population and deployed the police force to **[page 201]** protect those who played a fundamental role in their commission – namely his *conseillers*. As noted above, he had full knowledge of the crimes being perpetrated at them. Finally, his failure to prevent them is reflected in his active participation in the crimes committed there.

(ii) CELA

768. Around 22 April 1994, Renzaho was present at CELA (II.6). By his own actions and through the assistance of Angeline Mukandutiye, a school inspector, and *Conseiller* Odette Nyirabagenzi, an *Interahamwe* leader, he ordered *Interahamwe* to separate approximately 40 mostly Tutsi men from women and children and to remove them from the centre. The *Interahamwe* killed most of these men, including Charles Rwanga, and his two sons Wilson and Déglote Rwanga, en route to a mass grave near the Rugenge sector office. The Chamber found that Renzaho ordered the killings.

769. Given the nature of the attack, the Chamber finds that the assailants intentionally killed members of the Tutsi ethnic group. Renzaho substantially contributed to the attack by ordering the separation and the killings. The large number of Tutsi refugees at CELA, the high proportion of Tutsis among the men removed from the centre, as well as the evidence of the targeting of members of this group in Rwanda at the time clearly shows that the assailants, including Renzaho, possessed genocidal intent.

770. Accordingly, the Chamber concludes that Renzaho is responsible under Article 6 (1) of the Statute for aiding and abetting the killings of approximately 40 Tutsi civilians at CELA around 22 April by ordering their separation. He is further liable under Article 6 (1) of the Statute for ordering the killings.[858] The Chamber is also convinced that Renzaho bears superior responsibility for these crimes under Article 6 (3) of the Statute. Given the nature of the operation, his general authority, and presence on the ground, the Chamber is satisfied that the *Interahamwe* who killed the Tutsi refugees were Renzaho's subordinates at the time of the attack. As noted above, he had full knowledge of the crimes being perpetrated at them, and his failure to prevent them is reflected in his active participation in them.

(iii) Saint Famille

771. As discussed in detal in its factual findings, on 17 June 1994, the *Interahamwe* attacked the Sainte Famille church killing several hundred Tutsi refugees (II.11). Renzaho was present, and the Chamber has determined that he ordered the *Interahamwe* to attack, and later, to stop the attack.

772. Given the nature of the attack, the Chamber finds that the assailants intentionally killed members of the Tutsi ethnic group. Renzaho substantially contributed to the killings by ordering the *Interahamwe* to attack. The large number of Tutsi refugees at Saint Famille **[page 202]** church as well as the evidence of the targeting of members of this group in Rwanda at the time clearly shows that the assailants, including Renzaho, possessed genocidal intent.

---

[858] The Chamber notes that these facts would also support the conclusion that Renzaho participated in a joint criminal enterprise to kill the approximately 40 mostly Tutsi men taken from CELA as the crime involved a plurality of persons named in the Indictment, such as militiamen, Mukandutiye, Nyirabagenzi, and Renzaho, who shared the requisite genocidal intent. However, the Chamber considers that "ordering", which is also a direct form of responsibility, most appropriately captures the nature of Renzaho's criminal responsibility. In view of the overall gravity of the crime and the nature of Renzaho's actual involvement, the legal characterisation of his actions as ordering and aiding and abetting or as participating in a joint criminal enterprise would not impact the Chamber's sentencing considerations.

773. Accordingly, the Chamber concludes that Renzaho is responsible under Article 6 (1) of the Statute for the killing of hundreds of Tutsi refugees at Saint Famille church on 17 June 1994 by ordering the attack.[859] The Chamber is also convinced that Renzaho bears superior responsibility for these crimes under Article 6 (3) of the Statute. Given the nature of the operation, his general authority, and presence on the ground, the Chamber is satisfied that the *Interahamwe* who killed the Tutsi refugees were Renzaho's subordinates at the time of the attack. As noted above, he had full knowledge of the crimes being perpetrated at them, and his failure to prevent them is reflected in his active participation in them.

(iv) Sexual Violence

774. In its factual findings, the Chamber found that, at a meeting which occurred after 10 or 11 April 1994, attended by *Conseiller* Odette Nyrirabagenzi and *Interahamwe*, Renzaho said that Witness AWO, a Tutsi, should not be killed because she was "food for the militiamen". After this, the witness was repeatedly raped by *Interahamwe*, policemen and soldiers who either lived in Nyaribagenzi's home or worked with her (II.13).

775. In addition, the Chamber concluded that Munanira, an *Interahamwe* and the brother of *Conseiller* Nyirabagenzi, as well as other militimen, repeatedly raped Witness AWN and her sister, both Tutsis, over the couse of several weeks at the assailants' headquarters. This followed an incident at the Rugenge sector office where Renzaho in the presence of Witness AWN, Nyaribagenzi and Munanira stated it was "time to show Tutsi women that the Hutus are strong and can do whatever they wanted to do with them". After Renzaho's departure Nyirabagenzi promised Munanira that she would ensure that the witness would beg to have sex with him (II.13).

776. The Chamber considers that these acts of rape constituted serious bodily or mental harm. Given the witnesses' Tutsi ethnicity, their public identification as such, as well as the extensive evidence of the targeting of other members of the Tutsi group in Kigali at the time, it follows that these rapes were committed with genocidal intent.

777. The Prosecution seeks conviction for these crimes solely through Article 6 (3) of the Statute. The Chamber has concluded that Renzaho is the superior of urban police. Furthermore, in the context of both of these incidents, the Chamber is equally satisfied that Renzaho was the superior of the militiamen. The Chamber observes that they worked closely with *Conseiller* Nyirabagenzi, a de facto subordinate of Renzaho, and in some cases received accommodation from her. Therefore, these militiamen were closely linked with government authorities. In any event, even if the militiamen could not be considered as his subordinates, he would still remain liable for his subordinate *Conseiller* Nyirabagenzi's role in facilitating **[page 203]** the crimes. In particular, her acquiescing presence during Renzaho's encouragement of the rapes, as well as her further encouragement and support of the assailants, substantially assisted and thus aided and abetted the crimes. Similarly, the Chamber is also convinced that soldiers who engaged in rapes of Witness AWO were Renzaho's de facto subordinates Renzaho given his rank, instructions and their attacks on the witness.

778. Renzaho's conduct in relation to both incidents clearly reflected that he had knowledge that the crimes would occur and condoned them. Therefore, there is no question that he failed in his duty to prevent the crimes.

3.1.4 Conclusion

779. The Chamber finds Renzaho guilty of genocide (Count I) under Article 6 (1) by aiding and abetting as well as ordering the killing of Tutsis at roadblocks throughout Kigali from April to July 1994; by aiding and abetting and ordering killings at CELA on 22 April 1994; and by his orders in relation to crimes committed

---

[859] The Chamber notes that these facts would also support the conclusion that Renzaho participated in a joint criminal enterprise to kill the several hundred Tutsi refugees at Saint Famille church as the crime involved a plurality of persons named in the Indictment, such as militiamen, Angeline Mukandutiye, Odette Nyirabagenzi, and Renzaho, who shared the requisite genocidal intent. However, the Chamber considers that "ordering", which is also a direct form of responsibility, most appropriately captures the nature of Renzaho's criminal responsibility. In view of the overall gravity of the crime and the nature of Renzaho's actual involvement, the legal characterisation of his actions as ordering or as participating in a joint criminal enterprise would not impact the Chamber's sentencing considerations.

at Saint Famille on 17 June 1994. Renzaho is also liable as a superior for these crimes, which the Chamber will take into account in sentencing in connection with the abuse of his authority. The Chamber further finds Renzaho guilty of genocide (Count I) under Article 6 (3) based on his failure to prevent the rapes of Witnesses AWO and AWN as well as Witness AWN's sister.

3.2 Complicity in Genocide

780. Count II of the Indictment charges Renzaho with complicity in genocide. The Prosecution has indicated that the count of complicity is pleaded in the alternative to Count 1 which charges genocide.[860] As the Chamber has already entered a conviction for genocide, it finds Renzaho not guilty on this count.

4. CRIMES AGAINST HUMANITY

4.1 Introduction

781. Counts III and IV of the Indictment charge Renzaho with murder and rape as crimes against humanity under Article 3 (a) and (g) of the Statute.

4.2 Widespread and Systematic Attack

782. For an enumerated crime under Article 3 to qualify as a crime against humanity, the Prosecution must prove that there was a widespread or systematic attack against the civilian **[page 204]** population on national, political, ethnic, racial or religious grounds.[861] An attack against a civilian population means the perpetration against that population of a series of acts of violence, or of the kind of mistreatment referred to in sub-paragraph (a) to (i).[862] Intended to be read as disjunctive elements, "widespread" refers to the large scale nature of the attack and the number of targeted persons, while "systematic" describes the organised nature of the acts of violence and the improbability of their random occurrence.[863]

783. With respect to the *mens rea*, the perpetrator must have acted with knowledge of the broader context and knowledge that his acts formed part of the attack, but need not share the purpose or goals of the broader attack.[864] The additional requirement that crimes against humanity have to be committed "on national,

---

[860] Prosecution Closing Brief para. 380. However, the Prosecution also suggests that the Chamber may convict Renzaho of complicity in genocide for acts which do not amount to aiding and abetting genocide because the level of assistance required for complicity is lower. Prosecution Closing Brief paras. 380, 382, 384. In particular, it contends that for complicity in genocide, the "genocidal act need not be substantial – indeed, Renzaho need only contribute to the offence *to a very small extent*, for conviction." Prosecution Closing Brief para. 382 (emphasis in original), citing *Akayesu* Trial Judgement paras. 542-543. This view, however, is not correct. The Appeals Chamber has acknowledged an overlap between the material elements of aiding and abetting and complicity. While the Appeals Chamber has acknowledged that complicity may encompass acts broader than aiding and abetting, the only other example it has given is as a "co-perpetrator". Furthermore, contrary to the Prosecution's submissions, it appears that any acts of complicity which could not be characterised as aiding and abetting would require specific intent. See generally *Semanza* Appeal Judgement para. 316; *Ntakirutimana* Appeal Judgement para. 500; *Krstić* Appeal Judgement paras. 139, 142.
[861] *Bagosora et al.* Trial Judgement para. 2156, citing *Semanza* Appeal Judgement paras. 326-332, referring to *Akayesu* Trial Judgement para. 578; *Rutaganda* Trial Judgement para. 73; *Akayesu* Appeal Judgement paras. 467, 469; *Ntakirutimana* Appeal Judgement para. 516; *Ntagerura et al.* Trial Judgement paras. 697-698; *Mpambara* Trial Judgement para. 11 ; *Simba* Trial Judgement para. 421; *Gacumbitsi* Trial Judgement para. 299; *Tadić* Appeal Judgement paras. 248, 255.
[862] *Bagosora et al.* Trial Judgement para. 2165, citing *Nahimana et al.* Appeal Judgement paras. 915-918; *Kordić and Čerkez* Appeal Judgement para. 666; *Kunarac et al.* Appeal Judgement para. 89; *Kunarac et al.* Trial Judgement para. 415.
[863] *Bagosora et al.* Trial Judgement para. 2165, citing *Nahimana et al.* Appeal Judgement para. 920, quoting *Kordić and Čerkez* Appeal Judgement para. 94; *Ntakirutimana* Appeal Judgement para. 516; *Mpambara* Trial Judgement para. 11; *Semanza* Trial Judgement paras. 328-329; *Kunarac et al.* Trial Judgement para. 429; *Kunarac et al.* Appeal Judgement para. 94; *Gacumbitsi* Appeal Judgement para. 101, citing *Gacumbitsi* Trial Judgement para. 299; *Stakić* Appeal Judgement para. 246; *Blaškić* Appeal Judgement para. 101, *Limaj et al.* Trial Judgement para. 180; *Brđanin* Trial Judgement para. 133.
[864] *Bagosora et al.* Trial Judgement para. 2166, citing *Gacumbitsi* Appeal Judgement paras. 86, 103, referring to *Tadić* Appeal Judgement paras. 251-252; *Galić* Appeal Judgement para. 142; *Semanza* Appeal Judgement paras. 268-269; *Simba* Trial Judgement para. 421; *Kordić and Čerkez* Appeal Judgement para. 99; *Kunarac et al.* Trial Judgement para. 434; *Kunarac et al.* Appeal Judgement para. 102; *Blaškić* Appeal Judgement paras. 124-127.

political, ethnic, racial or religious grounds" does not mean that a discriminatory *mens rea* must be established.[865]

784. The Chamber has considered the totality of the evidence, in particular concerning the ethnic composition and actual or perceived political leanings of individuals identified at roadblocks or who sought refuge at various sites throughout Kigali. It finds that there were widespread and systematic attacks against the civilian population on ethnic and political grounds between April and July 1994. It is inconceivable that the principal perpetrators of these attacks as well as Renzaho did not know that their actions formed part of this attack. As a high-ranking military officer and senior government official, Renzaho would have been familiar with the situation unfolding both nationally and in areas under his authority. Many of the attacks or massacres where open and notorious. The Chamber has also concluded that Renzaho participated in some of these attacks.

4.3 Murder

4.3.1 Introduction

785. Count III of the Indictment charges Renzaho with murder as a crime against humanity under Article 3 (a) of the Statute. **[page 205]**

4.3.2 Law

786. Murder is the intentional killing of a person without any lawful justification or excuse or the intentional infliction of grievous bodily harm leading to death with knowledge that such harm will likely cause the victim's death.[866]

4.3.3 Deliberations

787. The Prosecution has charged the killing of Charles, Wilson and Déglote Rwanga as murder as a crime against humanity under Article 6 (1) of the Statute. They were among the approximately 40 mostly Tutsi men removed from CELA and killed on 22 April 1994. It also charges as murder under Article 6 (3) of the Statute for the killing of the 40 mostly Tutsi men, including these three individuals.[867] The Chamber has already determined that the separation, removal and killing of 40 mostly Tutsi refugees, which included these victims, constituted genocide. On the same basis, the Chamber is satisfied that these intentional murders were conducted on ethnic grounds. Some Hutus also were killed during this attack even though it was principally directed at Tutsis. As they formed part of the attack on ethnic grounds they also constitute murder as a crime against humanity.

788. The Chamber has already determined that Renzaho bears responsibility under Article 6 (1) of the Statute for aiding and abetting and ordering these killings and under Article 6 (3) of the Statute as a superior (III.3.1.4).

---

[865] *Bagosora et al.* Trial Judgement para. 2166, citing *Akayesu* Trial Judgement paras. 464-469, 595; *Bagilishema* Trial Judgement para. 81.

[866] *Bagosora et al.* Trial Judgement para. 2169, citing *Bagosora et al.*, Decision on Motions for Judgement of Acquittal (TC), 2 February 2005, para. 25; *Karera* Trial Judgement para. 558. The Chamber notes that some Trial Chambers have held that murder requires an element of pre-meditation, not only intent. See, for instance, *Bagilishema* Trial Judgement para. 86; *Ntagerura et al.* Trial Judgement para. 700; *Semanza* Trial Judgement para. 339. In the present case, the Chamber is satisfied that the killings at issue would constitute murder as a crime against humanity under both standards.

[867] Paragraph 45 of the Indictment, which charges Renzaho with murder under Article 6 (1) of the Statute, states that he is responsible for the "killing of *specific people ... including* ... Charles, Wilson and Déglote Rwanga" (emphasis added). This varies from paragraph 49, seeking to establish Renzaho's liability pursuant to Article 6 (3), which refers to the killings of *"certain persons ... including but not limited to ...* Charles, Wilson and Déglote Rwanga" (emphasis added). The differences between these paragraphs demonstrate that the Prosecution only alleges the murders of the three specified individuals through Article 6 (1), while it seeks conviction for the murders of everyone removed from CELA that day, including the three, under Article 6 (3). As noted previously, the Prosecution abandoned its case with respect to the alleged killings of James Rwanga and Emmanuel Gihana (II.6).

4.3.4 Conclusion

789. The Chamber finds Renzaho guilty of murder as a crime against humanity, based on Article 6 (1) of the Statute for aiding and abetting and ordering the killings of Charles, Wilson and Déglote Rwanga, who had been removed from CELA on 22 April 1994. It further finds Renzaho guilty of murder as a crime agasint humanity, as a superior based on Article 6 (3) of the Statute, for the killing of Charles, Wilson and Déglote Rwanga as well as the other mostly Tutsi men removed from CELA on that date.[868] The Chamber will take into account Renzaho's liability as a superior in sentencing. **[page 206]**

4.4 Rape

4.4.1 Introduction

790. Count IV of the Indictment charges Renzaho with rape as a crime against humanity under Article 3 (g) of the Statute.

4.4.2 Law

791. Rape as a crime against humanity requires proof of the non-consensual penetration, however slight, of the vagina or anus of the victim by the penis of the perpetrator or by any other object used by the perpetrator, or of the mouth of the victim by the penis of the perpetrator.[869] Consent for this purpose must be consent given voluntarily and freely and is assessed within the context of the surrounding circumstances.[870] Force or threat of force provides clear evidence of non-consent, but force is not an element *per se* of rape.[871]

792. The *mens rea* for rape as a crime against humanity is the intention to effect the prohibited sexual penetration with the knowledge that it occurs without the consent of the victim.[872]

4.4.3 Deliberations

793. The Prosecution has also charged the crimes committed against Witnesses AWO, AWN and Witness AWN's sister as rape as a crime against humanity. The Chamber has already determined that these rapes constituted serious bodily and mental harm as genocide. On the same basis, the Chamber is satisfied that they were conducted on ethnic grounds. The Chamber has found that Renzaho bears responsibility for these rapes as a superior under Article 6 (3) of the Statute.

4.4.4 Conclusion

794. The Chamber finds Renzaho guilty of rape as a crime against humanity (Count IV) as a superior under Article 6 (3) of the Statute for the crimes committed against Witnesses AWO, AWN and Witness AWN's sister.

---

[868] For the reasons mentioned above, the facts would also support the conclusion that Renzaho participated in a joint criminal enterprise in relation to these killings but the Chamber finds aiding and abetting and ordering the most appropriate forms of liability. In view of the overall gravity of the crime, such a characterisation would not alter the Chamber's sentence.
[869] *Bagosora et al.* Trial Judgement para. 2199, citing *Kunarac et al.* Appeal Judgement paras. 127-128; *Semanza* Trial Judgement para. 344.
[870] *Bagosora et al.* Trial Judgement para. 2199, citing *Kunarac et al.* Appeal Judgement paras. 127-133; *Semanza* Trial Judgement para. 344.
[871] *Bagosora et al.* Trial Judgement para. 2199, citing *Kunarac et al.* Appeal Judgement para. 129.
[872] *Bagosora et al.* Trial Judgement para. 2200, citing *Kunarac et al.* Appeal Judgement para. 127; *Semanza* Trial Judgement para. 346.

5. SERIOUS VIOLATIONS OF ARTICLE 3 COMMON TO THE GENEVA CONVENTIONS AND ADDITIONAL PROTOCOL II

5.1 Introduction

795. Counts V and VI of the Indictment charge Renzaho with serious violations of Article 3 Common to the Geneva Conventions of 12 August 1949 for the Protection of War Victims and of Additional Protocol II thereto of 8 June 1977 under Articles 4 (a) and 4 (e) of the Statute for murder and rape. **[page 207]**

5.2 Threshold Elements

5.2.1 Law

796. In connection with crimes within the scope of Article 4 of the Statute, the Prosecution must prove, as a threshold matter, the following elements: (1) the existence of a non-international armed conflict; (2) the existence of a nexus between the alleged violation and the armed conflict; and (3) that the victims were not directly taking part in the hostilities at the time of the alleged violation.[873]

5.2.2 Non-International Armed Conflict

797. There is no dispute that there was an armed conflict of a non-international character between the Rwandan government and the military forces of the RPF.[874]

5.2.3 Nexus

798. A nexus exists between the alleged offence and the non-international armed conflict when the offence is closely related to the hostilities. In determining whether the requisite close relation exists, the jurisprudence of the Tribunal reflects:

> [T]he existence of armed conflict must, at a minimum, have played a substantial part in the perpetrator's ability to commit [the offence], his decision to commit it, the manner in which it was committed or the purpose for which it was committed. Hence, if it can be established ... that the perpetrator acted in furtherance of or under the guise of the armed conflict, it would be sufficient to conclude that his acts were closely related to the armed conflict.[875]

799. As reflected in the evidence and previous case law, the ongoing armed conflict between the Rwandan government forces and the RPF, which was identified with the Tutsi ethnic minority in Rwanda and many members of the political opposition, both created the situation and provided a pretext for the extensive killings and other abuses of members of the civilian population. The killings began within hours of the death of President Habyarimana and on the same day the active hostilities resumed between the RPF and government forces.[876]

800. Notably, the Chamber has described the attack at Saint Famille church on 17 June 1994 as retribution for an RPF raid at the nearby Saint Paul centre the preceding night. In addition, the Chamber is mindful of

---

[873] *Bagosora et al.* Trial Judgement para. 2229, citing *Akayesu* Appeal Judgement para. 438; *Ntagerura et al.* Trial Judgement para. 766 ; *Semanza* Trial Judgement para. 512.

[874] See *Semanza* Appeal Judgement para. 192 ("the Chamber took notice only of general notorious facts not subject to reasonable dispute, including, *inter alia*: ... that there was an armed conflict not of an international character in Rwanda between 1 January 1994 and 17 July 1994 ..."). The Defence disputes only that Renzaho was a combatant fighting on one of the fronts in Kigali. Defence Closing Brief para. 1233.

[875] *Bagosora et al.* Trial Judgement para. 2231, quoting *Semanza* Trial Judgement para. 517 (quoting *Kunarac et al.* Appeal Judgement para. 58). The *Semanza* Trial Judgement's findings on nexus were affirmed by the Appeals Chamber. See *Semanza* Appeal Judgement para. 369. See also *Rutaganda* Appeal Judgement paras. 569-580, 577-579; *Ntagerura et al.* Trial Judgement para. 793, affirmed by *Ntagerura et al.* Appeal Judgement paras. 427-428.

[876] *Bagosora et al.* Trial Judgement para. 2232, citing *Semanza* Trial Judgement para. 518, affirmed by *Semanza* Appeal Judgement para. 369.

Renzaho's affiliation with the army and his high military **[page 208]** rank. Furthermore, he described Tutsi women as "food for the militiamen", who were ostensibly engaged in assisting civilian and military authorities in the defence of Kigali.

801. In the Chamber's view, the civilian authorities and assailants were acting in furtherance of the armed conflict or under its guise. Accordingly, the Chamber finds it established that the alleged violations of Articles 4 (a) and 4 (e) of the Statute had the requisite nexus to the armed conflict between Rwandan government forces and the RPF.

5.2.4 Victims

802. At the time of the alleged violations, the victims at Saint Famille church and the women sexually assaulted in Rugenge sector were unarmed civilians who were either murdered at a place of refuge or raped after being abducted. Therefore, the Chamber finds beyond reasonable doubt that the victims of the alleged violations of Articles 4 (a) and 4 (e) of the Statute were not taking active part in the hostilities.

5.3 Murder

5.3.1 Introduction

803. Count V of the Indictment charges Renzaho with murder under Article 4 (a) of the Statute as a violation of Article 3 Common to the Geneva Conventions and of Additional Protocol II.

5.3.2 Law

804. Article 4 (a) of the Statute prescribes that the Tribunal has the power to prosecute persons who committed or ordered serious violations of Common Article 3 or Additional Protocol II amounting to: "Violence to life, health and physical or mental well-being of persons, in particular murder as well as cruel treatment such as torture, mutilation or any form of corporal punishment." The specific violation of murder requires the unlawful, intentional killing of another person.[877]

5.3.3 Deliberations

805. The Prosecution has also charged the killing of at least 17 Tutsi men from Saint Famille on 17 June 1994 as murder as a violation of Article 3 Common to the Geneva Conventions and of Additional Protocol II. The Chamber has already determined that the killings of hundreds at Sainte Famille that same day constituted genocide. The Chamber is convinced that at least 17 Tutsi men formed part of these executions, and on the same basis, the Chamber is satisfied that these intentional murders also constitute murder under Article 4 (a) of the Statute.[878] **[page 209]**

806. The Chamber has already determined that Renzaho bears responsibility under Article 6 (1) of the Statute for ordering killings at Sainte Famille under Article 6 (3) of the Statute as a superior (III.3.1.4). The conclusion applies with equal force in relation to this count.

5.3.4 Conclusion

807. The Chamber finds Renzaho guilty of murder as a serious violation of Article 3 Common to the Geneva Conventions and of Additional Protocol II (Count V) under Article 6 (1) of the Statute for ordering

---

[877] *Bagosora et al.* Trial Judgement para. 2242, citing *Semanza* Trial Judgement paras. 338, 373; *Ntagerura et al.* Trial Judgement para. 765.
[878] The Defence concedes that this crime relies on the same material facts that would be used to rely on in establishing the genocide count. Defence Closing Brief para. 1232. This position is consistent with the Prosecution submissions in relation to this crime as found in its Pre-Trial Brief paras. 151-154 and its Closing Brief paras. 459-489.

the killing of at least 17 Tutsi men at Saint Famille church on 17 June 1994.[879] Renzaho is also liable as a superior for these murders, which the Chamber will take into account in sentencing.

5.4 Rape

5.4.1 Introduction

808. Count VI of the Indictment charges Renzaho with rape under Article 4 (e) of the Statute as a serious violation of Article 3 Common to the Geneva Conventions and of Additional Protocol II.

5.4.2 Law

809. Article 4 (e) of the Statute prescribes that the Tribunal has the power to prosecute persons who committed or ordered serious violations of Common Article 3 or Additional Protocol II amounting to: "Outrages upon personal dignity, in particular humiliating and degrading treatment, rape, enforced prostitution and any form of indecent assault." Outrages upon personal dignity have been defined as any act or omission which would be generally considered to cause serious humiliation, degradation or otherwise be a serious attack on human dignity.[880] The *mens rea* of the crime requires that the accused knew that his act or omission would have such effect.[881]

5.4.3 Deliberations

810. The Prosecution has charged the crimes committed against Witnesses AWO, AWN and Witness AWN's sister as rape as a serious violation of Article 3 Common to the Geneva Conventions and of Additional Protocol II. The Chamber has already found that these rapes constituted serious bodily and mental harm as genocide and rape as a crime agasint humaity. The Chamber has also determined that Renzaho bears responsibility for these rapes as a superior under Article 6 (3) of the Statute.

5.4.4 Conclusion

811. The Chamber finds Renzaho guilty of rape as a serious violation of Article 3 Common to the Geneva Conventions and of Additional Protocol II (Count VI) as a superior under Article 6 (3) of the Statute for the crimes committed against Witnesses AWO, AWN and Witness AWN's sister. **[page 210]**

CHAPTER IV: VERDICT

812. For the reasons set out in this Judgement, having considered all evidence and arguments, the Trial Chamber unanimously finds Tharcisse Renzaho:

Count 1: GUILTY of Genocide

Count 2: NOT GUILTY of Complicity in Genocide

Count 3: GUILTY of Crimes Against Humanity (Murder)

Count 4: GUILTY of Crimes Against Humanity (Rape)

Count 5: GUILTY of Serious Violations of Article 3 Common to the Geneva Conventions and Additional Protocol II (Murder)

---

[879] For the reasons mentioned above, the facts would also support the conclusion that Renzaho participated in a joint criminal enterprise in relation to these killings but finds ordering the most appropriate form of liability. In view of the overall gravity of the crime, such a characterisation would not alter the Chamber's sentence.
[880] *Bagosora et al.* Trial Judgement para. 2250, citing *Kunarac et al.* Appeal Judgement para. 163.
[881] *Bagosora et al.* Trial Judgement para. 2250, citing *Kunarac et al.* Appeal Judgement para. 164.

Count 6: GUILTY of Serious Violations of Article 3 Common to the Geneva Conventions and Additional Protocol II (Rape) **[page 211]**

CHAPTER V: SENTENCING

1. INTRODUCTION

813. Having found Renzaho guilty of genocide, crimes against humanity and serious violations of Article 3 Common to the Geneva Conventions and Additional Protocol II, the Chamber must determine an appropriate sentence.

814. The penalty imposed should reflect the goals of retribution, deterrence, rehabilitation, and the protection of society. Pursuant to Article 23 of the Statute and Rule 101 of the Rules of Procedure and Evidence, the Chamber shall consider the general practice regarding prison sentences in Rwanda, the gravity of the offences or totality of the conduct, the individual circumstances of the accused, including aggravating and mitigating circumstances, and the extent to which any penalty imposed by a court of any State on the accused for the same act has already been served.[882] As pointed out by the Appeals Chamber, these considerations are not exhaustive when determining the appropriate sentence. In addition, the Trial Chamber shall credit the accused for any time spent in detention pending transfer to the Tribunal and during trial.[883]

2. SUBMISSIONS

815. The Prosecution submits that Renzaho should be sentenced to imprisonment for the remainder of his life. His crimes are so heinous that they place him in the category of the most serious offenders. The Prosecution points to the following aggravating circumstances: his senior position; the breach of his duty to protect the population; his premeditation in committing offences; his direct participation as a perpetrator; the sexual, violent and humiliating nature of his acts and of those who were his subordinates; the vulnerability of the victims; the duration of the offences; the suffering of the victims; his informed and willing participation in the crimes; the number of victims; and the general surrounding circumstances of the case. According to the Prosecution, there are no mitigating circumstances. Reference is also made to the Tribunal's statute and case law as well as penalties imposed in Rwanda for comparable crimes.[884]

816. The Defence submits that Renzaho was a hardworking man from a family of modest means largely comprising Tutsis, who owed his success only to his honesty, rigor and loyalty in serving the State. In particular, he assisted in creating a national commission on political reform in Rwanda dedicated to the promotion of democracy, law, human rights and economic progress. Renzaho sheltered Tutsi refugees at his home and the prefecture office from persecution and militia attacks and tried to arrest wrongdoers, which caused him to be considered by militiamen as an accomplice of the Tutsis.[885] **[page 212]**

3. DELIBERATIONS

3.1 Gravity of the Offences

817. All crimes under the Tribunal's Statute are serious violations of international humanitarian law.[886] When determining a sentence, a Trial Chamber has considerable, though not unlimited, discretion on account of its obligation to individualise penalties to fit the individual circumstances of an accused and to reflect the gravity of the crimes for which the accused has been convicted.[887]

---

[882] Article 23 (1)-(3) and Rule 101 (B)(i)-(iv).
[883] *Kajelijeli* Appeal Judgement para. 290. *See* Rule 101 (C).
[884] Prosecution Closing Brief paras. 537-560.
[885] Defence Closing Brief paras. 1460-1499.
[886] *Bagosora et al.* Trial Judgement para. 2263, citing *Kayishema and Ruzindana* Appeal Judgement para. 367 (quoting Article 1 of the Statute).
[887] *Bagosora et al.* Trial Judgement para. 2263, citing *Kajelijeli* Appeal Judgement para. 291.

818. In determining an appropriate sentence, the Appeals Chamber has stated that "sentences of like individuals in like cases should be comparable". However, it has also noted the inherent limits to this approach because "any given case contains a multitude of variables, ranging from the number and type of crimes committed to the personal circumstances of the individual".[888]

819. The Chamber has determined that by virtue of his position as prefect and with his high military rank, Renzaho was clearly an important and influential authority of the Rwandan government. During the course of the events, he ordered and aided and abetted the killings of Tutsis at roadblocks, aided and abetted and ordered the killings of approximately 40 mostly Tutsi men from CELA and ordered the killings of hundreds of Tutsi refugees at Saint Famille church. In addition, he is liable as a superior for the rapes of Witnesses AWO, AWN and Witness AWN's sister.

820. Under Rwandan law, similar crimes carry the possible penalties of life imprisonment, depending on the nature of the accused's participation.[889] In this Tribunal, a sentence of life imprisonment is generally reserved those who planned or ordered atrocities as well as the most senior authorities.[890] **[page 213]**

821. Renzaho's crimes are grave and resulted in a massive toll of human suffering. Bearing in mind the particular facts surrounding each incident, the Chamber considers that his specific role in each of them would individually warrant the highest sanction and censure comparable to other senior leaders who have received life sentences.

3.2 Individual, Aggravating and Mitigating Circumstances

822. The Chamber will consider Renzaho's individual circumstances, including aggravating and mitigating factors. Mitigating circumstances need only be established by the balance of the probabilities, while aggravating circumstances need to be proven beyond reasonable doubt.[891] Any particular circumstance that is included as an element of the crime for which the Accused is convicted will not also be considered as an aggravating factor.[892]

823. The Appeals Chamber has held that an accused's abuse of his superior position or influence may be considered as an aggravating factor.[893] In the Chamber's view, Renzaho's abuse of his role as an influential authority and superior in connection with those crimes for which he was convicted under Article 6 (1) of the Statute amounts to an aggravating factor.

---

[888] *Bagosora et al.* Trial Judgement para. 2263, citing *Kvočka et al.* Appeal Judgment para. 681.
[889] *Kanyarukiga*, Decision on Prosecutor's Request for Referral to the Republic of Rwanda (TC), 6 June 2008, paras. 22-25 (assessing Rwanda's penalty structure); *Gatete,* Decision on Prosecutor's Request for Referral to the Republic of Rwanda (TC), 17 November 2008, paras. 22-25. See also *Semanza* Appeal Judgement para. 377 ("The command for Trial Chambers to 'have recourse to the general practice regarding prison sentences in the courts of Rwanda does not oblige the Trial Chambers to conform to that practice; it only obliges the Trial Chambers to take account of that practice.'"), quoting *Serushago* Appeal Judgement para. 30; *Dragan Nikolić* Appeal Judgment para. 69.
[890] *Bagosora et al.* Trial Judgement para. 2270, citing *Musema* Appeal Judgement para. 383 (noting that the leaders and planners of a particular conflict should bear heavier responsibility, with the qualification that the gravity of the offence is the primary consideration in imposing a sentence). Life sentences have been imposed against senior government and military authorities in: *Bagosora et al.* Trial Judgement paras. 2265, 2277 (*Directeur de cabinet* of Ministry of Defence, Commander of Para Commando Battalion, and Commander of Gisenyi Operational Sector); *Ndindabahizi* Trial Judgement paras. 505, 508, 511 (Minister of Finance); *Niyitegeka* Trial Judgement paras. 499, 502 (Minister of Information); *Kambanda* Trial Judgement paras. 44, 61-62 (Prime Minister); *Kamuhanda* Trial Judgement, paras. 6, 764, 770 (Minister of Higher Education and Scientific Research). In several other cases, lower level officials, as well as those who did not hold government positions have received life sentences. See, for instance, *Bagosora et al.* Trial Judgement paras. , 2268, 2268-2269, 2278-2279 (Commander of Para Commando Battalion and Commander of Gisenyi Operational Sector); *Karera* Trial Judgement para. 585 (prefect of Kigali-Rural); *Kayishema and Ruzindana* Trial Judgement (Sentence) p. 8 (Kayishema was prefect of Kibuye); *Gacumbitsi* Appeal Judgement para. 206 (*bourgmestre*); *Musema* Trial Judgement paras. 999-1008 (influential director of a tea factory who exercised control over killers); *Rutaganda* Trial Judgement paras. 466-473 (second Vice-president of *Interahamwe* at national level).
[891] *Nahimana et al.* Appeal Judgement para. 1038; *Kajelijeli* Appeal Judgement, para. 294.
[892] *Ndindabahizi* Appeal Judgement, para. 137.
[893] See, for instance, *Simba* Appeal Judgement paras. 284-285.

824. The Chamber has considered Renzaho's background and individual circumstances. The Chamber is mindful of his lengthy public service to his country prior to the events as well as his submissions concerning assistance to Tutsis. However, it accords these mitigating circumstances very limited weight in view of the gravity of his crimes.

4. CONCLUSION

825. The Chamber has the discretion to impose a single sentence. This practice is usually appropriate where the offences may be characterised as belonging to a single criminal transaction.[894]

826. Considering all the relevant circumstances discussed above, the Chamber **SENTENCES** Tharcisse Renzaho to:

LIFE IMPRISONMENT

5. CONSEQUENTIAL ORDERS

827. The above sentence shall be served in a State designated by the President of the Tribunal, in consultation with the Chamber. The Government of Rwanda and the designated State shall be notified of such designation by the Registrar.

828. Until his transfer to his designated places of imprisonment, Tharcisse Renzaho shall be kept in detention under the present conditions.

829. Pursuant to Rule 102 (B) of the Rules, on notice of appeal, if any, enforcement of the above sentences shall be stayed until a decision has been rendered on the appeal, with the convicted person nevertheless remaining in detention. **[page 214]**

Arusha, 14 July 2009

Erik Møse	Sergei Alekseevich Egorov	Florence Rita Arrey
Presiding Judge	Judge	Judge

(Seal of the Tribunal) **[page 215]**

---

[894] *Nahimana et al.* Appeal Judgement paras. 1042-1043; *Simba* Trial Judgement para. 445; *Ndindabahizi* Trial Judgement para. 497.

ANNEX A: PROCEDURAL HISTORY

1. PRE-TRIAL PROCEEDINGS

830. On 16 July 1997, Judge Laïty Kama ordered the Kenyan authorities to transfer and provisionally detain Tharcisse Renzaho.[895] He was arrested in the Democratic Republic of the Congo on 29 September 2002, pursuant to an order issued by Judge Andresia Vaz on 27 September 2002.[896] He was transferred to the UN Detention Facility on 29 September 2002 and made his initial appearance before Judge Vaz on 3 October 2002.

831. The original Indictment of 23 October 2002 charged Renzaho with four counts: genocide, or alternatively, complicity in genocide; extermination as a crime against humanity; and violence to life, health and physical or mental well-being as a serious violation of Article 3 Common to the Geneva Conventions and of Additional Protocol II thereto.

832. On 4 November 2002, Judge Erik Møse extended Renzaho's detention for 21 days, pending confirmation of his Indictment.[897] The Indictment was amended on 11 November 2002 and charged Renzaho with three counts: genocide, or alternatively, complicity in genocide, and murder as a crime against humanity.[898] On 15 November 2002, Judge Winston Matanzima Maqutu confirmed the Amended Indictment in respect of all three counts alleged, and issued an order confirming the Indictment and for non-disclosure of identifying information in witness statements.[899] At Renzaho's initial appearance on 21 November 2002, he pleaded not guilty to all three counts.

833. The remaining pre-trial motions were considered by Trial Chamber II. On 25 August 2004, the Chamber denied the Defence motion for Renzaho's immediate release.[900] It partly granted one Defence motion for disclosure of documents from the Prosecution and dismissed a second Defence motion for documentary disclosure by the Registry.[901]

834. The Chamber ordered on 18 March 2005 that Renzaho make a further appearance, having granted the Prosecution motion for leave to amend the Indictment, *inter alia*, to add a count of rape as a crime against humanity and counts of murder and rape as violations of Article 3 Common to the Geneva Conventions of 19149, and Additional Protocol II of 1977, and to specify the modes of liability that give rise to Renzaho's alleged responsibility as an **[page 216]** individual and as a superior.[902] The Prosecution filed an Amended Indictment dated 1 April 2005. Renzaho made a further appearance on 3 June 2005, and pleaded not guilty to all counts. On 17 August 2005, the Chamber granted in part the Prosecution's motion for protective measures for its witnesses.[903]

---

[895] Order for Transfer and Provisional Detention (TC), 16 July 1997.
[896] Request for Transfer and Provisional Detention (TC), 26 September 2002; Order for Transfer and Provisional Detention (TC), 27 September 2002.
[897] Decision on the Prosecutor's Request for the Extension of the Suspect's Detention (TC), 4 November 2002. Judge Møse had earlier granted a Prosecution oral motion to extend Renzaho's provisional detention. T. 29 October 2002 p. 14.
[898] Order Confirming the Indictment and for Nondisclosure of Identifying Information in Witness Statements, 15 November 2002.
[899] Order Confirming Indictment and for Nondisclosure of Identifying Information in Witness Statements (TC), 15 November 2002.
[900] Decision on Tharcisse Renzaho's Motion for His Immediate Release on Grounds of Violations of His Rights under Article 20 of the Statute and Rule 40 (D) of the Rules (TC), 25 August 2004.
[901] *Décision sur la requête de la Defense aux fins de communication de documents* (TC), 19 October 2004 (allowing the time period for the Defence to file a preliminary motion to begin from the date of the decision). See also *Corrigendum de la décision sur la requête de la Defense aux fins de communication de documents en date du 19 octobre 2004* (TC), 22 October 2004; *Décision sur la requête en extrême urgence de la defense aux fins de communication de documents par le greffe* (TC), 21 October 2004 (denying the Defence motion for disclosure).
[902] Decision on the Prosecutor's Motion for Leave to Amend the Indictment (TC), 18 March 2005. The same Chamber also declared moot the Defence preliminary motion alleging defects in the form of the Indictment. *Décision sur la requête en exception préjudicielle pour vice de forme de l'acte d'accusation* (TC), 8 April 2005.
[903] Decision on the Prosecutor's Motion for Protective Measures for Victims and Witnesses to Crimes Alleged in the Indictment (TC), 17 August 2005. The Chamber granted in part a Defence motion for withdrawal of that decision, allowing the Defence to file a motion under Rule 75 (I) to rescind, vary or augment the protective measures granted in the decision of 17 August 2005. Decision

835. The Prosecution was granted leave on 13 February 2006 to amend the Indictment a second time. A further appearance was not required.[904] The Second Amended Indictment was filed on and dated 16 February 2006. The Chamber denied on 5 September 2006 the Defence preliminary motion on defects in the form of the Indictment.[905]

836. On 12 December 2006, Judge Møse granted a Prosecution request to transfer to the Tribunal five detained witnesses from Rwanda to testify.[906]

2. THE PROSECUTION CASE

837. The trial commenced before Trial Chamber I on 8 January 2007. The Prosecution conducted its case during two trial sessions: from 8 January to 7 February 2007 and from 2 to 6 March 2007. Over the course of 21 trial days, the Prosecution called 26 witnesses, including one expert and one investigator, and tendered 118 exhibits.

838. On 22 January 2007, the Chamber heard arguments from the parties regarding the admissibility of the transcripts of an audio recording, which the Prosecution had provided to the Defence on 6 December 2006, as well as the tape itself, disclosed on 11 January 2007.[907] The Chamber noted the uncertainty surrounding the provenance of the recording and orally ruled that, although it would not be admitted as an exhibit at that stage, questioning about the tape and its transcripts would be allowed at trial.[908]

839. The Defence withdrew on 23 January 2007 its motion for translation of three documents.[909] Its request for permission for its investigator Jean-Marie Hakizamungu to be in the courtroom during the closed sessions was granted.[910] On 31 January 2007, the Chamber took note of Defence counsel's reiteration of the objections to the use of the audio recording **[page 217]** as evidence and to the admissibility of Witness AWE's will-say statement, which related to the tape. The Prosecution was, however, authorised to play the recording.[911]

840. During the proceedings on 1 February 2007, the Prosecution stated its intention to withdraw two witnesses.[912] On 14 February, the Chamber granted the Prosecution request for testimony via video-link testimony in light of a witness's ill-health.[913] The Prosecution motion to remove one witness and add another to its list was granted on 16 February 2007.[914]

841. The Defence applied on 2 March 2007 to exclude the testimony of Prosecution Witness Kagame (formerly Witness ADU), submitting that it covered new material facts not included in the Amended Indictment. After hearing arguments from the parties, the Chamber denied the motion, stating that it also would render a written decision in light of the importance of the issue.[915] On 12 March 2007, the Chamber ordered witness protection measures for Defence witnesses.[916] It rendered a written decision on 20 March 2007, denying a Defence motion to exclude Witness Kagame's testimony and granting the Prosecution

---

on Renzaho's Motion to Reconsider the Decision on Protective Measures for Victims and Witnesses to Crimes Alleged in the Indictment (TC), 1 November 2005; Decision on Renzaho's Motion on Certification to Appeal the Decision on Protective Measures for Victims and Witnesses to Crimes Alleged in the Indictment (TC), 1 November 2005.

[904] Decision on the Prosecutor's Application for Leave to Amend the Indictment Pursuant to Rule 50 (A) of the Rules of Procedure and Evidence (TC), 13 February 2006.
[905] Decision on Preliminary Motion on Defects in the Form of the Indictment (TC), 5 September 2006. See also *Décision relative à la demande aux fins de certification d'appel de la decision du 5 séptembre 2006 en vertu de l'article 72 (B)* (TC), 25 October 2006.
[906] Order for Transfer of Five Prosecution Witnesses Pursuant to Rule 90 *bis* (TC), 12 December 2006. A status conference was also held on 6 December 2006.
[907] T. 22 January 2007 pp. 1-11.
[908] *Id.* pp. 39-40.
[909] T. 23 January 2007 pp. 66-67.
[910] T. 30 January 2007 p. 43.
[911] T. 31 January 2007 pp. 30-31.
[912] T. 1 February 2007 p. 40.
[913] Decision on Prosecution Request for Video-Link Testimony (TC), 14 February 2007.
[914] Decision on Prosecution Request Motion to Vary Witness List (TC), 16 February 2007.
[915] T. 2 March 2007 pp. 12-25.
[916] Decision on Defence Request for Protective Measures (TC), 12 March 2007.

request to admit as an exhibit the audio recording and its transcription, along with translations thereof. They were found to have sufficient probative value. The Chamber also concluded that the Defence had received sufficient notice to prepare for this issue and for Witness Kagame's testimony. The tape had been adequately authenticated and the manner in which it had been obtained was not problematic.[917]

3. THE DEFENCE CASE

842. The Defence case opened before Trial Chamber I on 17 May 2007 and was conducted during two trial sessions: from 17 May to 10 July 2007 and from 22 August to 6 September 2007. During 28 trial days, the Defence called 27 witnesses, including one expert and the Accused, Tharcisse Renzaho. The Defence tendered 113 exhibits.[918]

843. On 4 June 2007, the Chamber denied a motion submitted by the Defence for François Karera for access to all confidential material from the Renzaho case because the Karera Defence had already closed its case and the applicant could no longer make submissions or introduce evidence in those proceedings.[919]

844. The Chamber granted on 8 June 2007 a request submitted by the Defence for Casimir Bizimungu for disclosure of closed session testimony of Witness UL and ordered that the Bizimungu Defence be bound by the protection orders for that witness in the *Renzaho* trial.[920] On 14 June 2007, it granted in part a Defence request for special protective measures for Witness HIN. The Chamber ordered that the witness's identity remain undisclosed until his **[page 218]** arrival in Arusha, but denied the request in all other respects.[921] On 27 June 2007, the Chamber authorized video-link testimony for a witness based on his genuinely-held fears for his security.[922]

845. During the proceedings on 10 July 2007, the Chamber found moot the Prosecution motion requesting exclusion of Defence evidence and for the Defence to provide a proper list of exhibits and notice of alibi, filed on 11 May 2007. On 12 July 2007, the Chamber granted a Defence request to amend its witness list by adding two witnesses and withdrawing 12 other witnesses as well as a proposed expert witness.[923]

846. The Prosecution objected during the proceedings on 23 August 2007 to the scope of examination-in-chief of Witness PER, stating that both it had not received notice of the line of questioning being used by the Defence and that the issue had never been raised during cross-examination of the appropriate Prosecution witness. After deliberation, the Chamber was of the view that the basis of the Defence line of questioning should have been communicated to the Prosecution and should have been raised with the relevant Prosecution witness. Two of the three judges nevertheless decided to allow the line of questioning, taking into consideration that the issue was not put to that Prosecution witness in connection with its general credibility assessments and the overall weighing of the evidence. One judge was in favour of the exclusion of the evidence.[924]

847. The Chamber noted during the proceedings on 27 August 2007 that the Defence 24 August 2007 motion for disclosure of documents was moot.[925] On the following day, 28 August 2007, the Chamber orally granted the Defence motion to add a witness, directing that he not be called before 4 September 2007 in order to give the Prosecution time to prepare.[926]

---

[917] Decision on Exclusion of Testimony and Admission of Exhibit (TC), 20 March 2007; Decision on Certification for Appeal Concerning Exclusion of Testimony and Admission of Exhibit (TC), 7 May 2007 (denying certification for appeal). After the conclusion of the testimony of the last Prosecution witness, a status conference was held on 6 March 2007.
[918] A status conference was also held on 6 September 2007.
[919] Decision on Karera Defence Motion for Disclosure (TC), 4 June 2007.
[920] Decision on Bizimungu Request for Closed Session Testimony (TC), 8 June 2007.
[921] Decision on Defence Request for Special Protective Measures for Witness HIN (TC), 14 June 2007. This decision was an exception to the 12 March 2007 decision in which the Chamber granted protective measures for Defence witnesses. Decision on Defence Request for Protective Measures (TC), 12 March 2007.
[922] Decision on Defence Request for Video-Link Testimony (TC), 27 June 2007.
[923] Decision on Defence Request to Amend Witness List (TC), 12 July 2007. A status conference was also held on 11 July 2007.
[924] T. 23 August 2007 pp. 37-43.
[925] T. 27 August 2007 p. 2.
[926] T. 28 August 2007 pp. 61-62.

848. During the proceedings on 30 August 2007, the Chamber overruled a Prosecution objection to the tendering of the passport of Théoneste Bagosora, but noted that the Prosecution arguments would be considered in deciding the weight to give to that exhibit.[927] The Chamber ruled on 3 September 2007 that Defence Witness Bernard Lugan was qualified to testify as an expert in the proceedings.[928] On 6 September, after the testimony of the final witness was concluded, the Presiding Judge noted that the Defence case was closed and the proceedings were adjourned until 14 February 2008 for the hearing of closing arguments. A total of 56 witnesses were heard during the course of 49 trial days. A status conference was held immediately afterwards, at which the parties agreed to submit their Closing Briefs simultaneously on 15 November 2007, with closing arguments on 14 and 15 February 2008. **[page 219]**

4. FURTHER PROCEEDINGS

849. The parties filed their Closing Briefs on 15 November 2007.[929] A Defence motion to admit documents was denied on 12 February 2008 because the documents did not satisfy any of the requirements of the rule governing the proof of facts other than by oral evidence.[930] Closing arguments were heard on 14 and 15 February 2008.[931]

850. On 3 April 2008, the Chamber denied a request for disclosure of closed session testimony and sealed exhibits from the Georges Rutaganda Defence, finding that the material requested had no apparent nexus with Rutaganda's case.[932]

851. On 30 June 2009, the Registry filed a report under Rule 33 (B) of the Rules noting that the investigator it appointed had failed to respond to its requests for a final report on the allegations that a former Defence investigator was interfering with Defence witnesses.

852. The Chamber pronounced its unanimous judgement on 14 July 2009. It convicted Renzaho for genocide, crimes against humanity and serious violations of Article 3 Common to the Geneva Conventions and Additional Protocol II, and sentenced him to life imprisonment. The written judgement was filed on 14 August 2009 after the completion of the editorial process. **[page 220]**

ANNEX B: CITED MATERIALS AND DEFINED TERMS

1. JURISPRUDENCE

1.1 ICTR

Akayesu

The Prosecutor v. Jean-Paul Akayesu, Case No. ICTR-96-4-T, Judgement (TC), 2 September 1998 (*"Akayesu* Trial Judgement")

---

[927] T. 30 August 2007 p. 2.
[928] T. 3 September 2007 p. 58.
[929] The Defence filed an Amended Closing Brief on 21 January 2008. During the proceedings on 15 February 2008, the Chamber declared moot the Prosecution motion filed on 24 January 2008 to exclude the Defence Amended Closing Brief. It considered, however, that the Amended Brief did not have any status. Instead, it allowed a Defence exhibit that supplemented in writing the Defence closing arguments. T. 14 February 2008 pp. 1-2; T. 15 February 2008 p. 8; Defence Exhibit 113 (*Complément écrit aux arguments oraux de la defense en réponse au mémoire du procureur*).
[930] Decision on Defence Motion to Admit Documents (TC), 12 February 2008.
[931] T. 15 February 2008 p. 8.
[932] Decision on Request for Closed Session Testimony and Sealed Exhibits (TC), 3 April 2008. The Chamber denied reconsideration or certification of that decision in its Decision on Rutaganda's Motion for Reconsideration or Alternatively, Certification to Appeal the Decision of 3 April 2008 on Request for Closed Session Testimony and Sealed Exhibits (TC), 13 November 2008.

The Prosecutor v. Jean-Paul Akayesu, Case No. ICTR-96-4-A, Judgement (AC), 1 June 2001 ("*Akayesu* Appeal Judgement")

Bagilishema

The Prosecutor v. Ignace Bagilishema, Case No. ICTR-95-1A-T, Judgement (TC), 7 June 2001 ("*Bagilishema* Trial Judgement")

The Prosecutor v. Ignace Bagilishema, Case No. ICTR-95-1A-A, Judgement (AC), 3 July 2002 ("*Bagilishema* Appeal Judgement")

Bagosora et al.

The Prosecutor v. Théoneste Bagosora et al., Case No. ICTR-98-41-T, Decision on Motion Concerning Alleged Witness Intimidation (TC), 28 December 2004

The Prosecutor v. Théoneste Bagosora et al., Case No. ICTR-98-41-T, Decision on Motions for Judgement of Acquittal (TC), 2 February 2005

The Prosecutor v. Théoneste Bagosora et al., Case No. ICTR-98-41-T, Decision on Disclosure of Materials Relating to Immigration Statements of Defence Witnesses (TC), 27 September 2005

The Prosecutor v. Théoneste Bagosora et al., Case Nos, ICTR-98-41-AR73 & ICTR-98-41-AR73(B), Decision on Interlocutory Appeals on Witness Protection Orders (AC), 6 October 2005

The Prosecutor v. Théoneste Bagosora et al., Case No. ICTR 98-41-AR73, Decision on Aloys Ntabakuze's Interlocutory Appeal on Questions of Law Raised by the 29 June 2006 Trial Chamber I Decision on Motion for Exclusion of Evidence (AC), 18 September 2006

The Prosecutor v. Théoneste Bagosora et al., Case No. ICTR-98-41-T, Decision on the Ntabakuze Motion for Disclosure of Various Categories of Documents Pursuant to Rule 68 (TC), 6 October 2006

The Prosecutor v. Théoneste Bagosora et al., Case No. ICTR-98-41-T, Decision on Nsengiyumva Motion to Admit Documents as Exhibits (TC), 26 February 2007

The Prosecutor v. Théoneste Bagosora et al., Case No. ICTR-98-41-T, Decision on Bagosora Request for Certification or Reconsideration Concerning Admission of Witness B-06's Statement (TC), 8 May 2007
[page 221]

The Prosecutor v. Théoneste Bagosora et al., Case No. ICTR 98-41-T, Judgement (TC), 18 December 2008 ("Bagosora Trial Judgement")

Gacumbitsi

The Prosecutor v. Sylvestre Gacumbitsi, Case No. ICTR-2001-64-T, Judgement (TC), 17 June 2004 ("*Gacumbitsi* Trial Judgement")

Sylvestre Gacumbitsi v. The Prosecutor, Case No. ICTR-2001-64-A, Judgement (AC), 7 July 2006 ("*Gacumbitsi* Appeal Judgement")

Gatete

The Prosecutor v. Jean-Baptiste Gatete, Case No. ICTR-2000-61-R11*bis*, Decision on Prosecutor's Request for Referral to the Republic of Rwanda (TC), 17 November 2008

Kajelijeli

The Prosecutor v. Juvénal Kajelijeli, Case No. ICTR-98-44A-T, Judgement and Sentence (TC), 1 December 2003 ("*Kajelijeli* Trial Judgement")

Juvénal Kajelijeli v. The Prosecutor, Case No. ICTR-98-44A-A, Judgement (AC), 23 May 2005 ("*Kajelijeli* Appeal Judgement")

Kambanda

The Prosecutor v. Jean Kambanda, Case No. ICTR-97-23-S, Judgement and Sentence (TC), 4 September 1998 ("*Kambanda* Trial Judgement")

Kamuhanda

The Prosecutor v. Jean de Dieu Kamuhanda, Case No. ICTR-95-54A-T, Judgement (TC), 22 January 2004 ("*Kamuhanda* Trial Judgement")

Jean de Dieu Kamuhanda v. The Prosecutor, Case No. ICTR-99-54A-A, Judgement (AC), 19 September 2005 ("*Kamuhanda* Appeal Judgement")

Kanyarukiga

The Prosecutor v. Gaspard Kanyarukiga, Case No. ICTR-2002-78-R11*bis*, Decision on Prosecutor's Request for Referral to the Republic of Rwanda (TC), 6 June 2008

The Prosecutor v. Gaspard Kanyarukiga, Case No. ICTR-2002-78-R11*bis*, Decision on Prosecution's Appeal Against Decision on Referral under Rule 11*bis* (AC), 30 October 2008

Karemera et al.

The Prosecutor v. Edouard Karemera et al., Case No. ICTR-98-44-AR73, Decision on Prosecutor's Interlocutory Appeal Against Trial Chamber III Decision of 8 October 2003 Denying Leave to File an Amended Indictment (AC), 19 December 2003 **[page 222]**

The Prosecutor v. Edouard Karemera et al., Case No. ICTR-98-44-PT, Decision on the Severance of Andre Rwamakuba and Amendments of the Indictment, Article 20 (4) of the Statute, Rule 82 (b) of the Rules of Procedure and Evidence (TC), 7 December 2004

The Prosecutor v. Edouard Karemera et al., Case No. ICTR-98-44-AR73.6, Decision on Joseph Nzirorera's Interlocutory Appeal (AC), 28 April 2006

Karemera et al., Decision on Prosecutor's Interlocutory Appeal of Decision on Judicial Notice (AC), 16 June 2006

The Prosecutor v. Edouard Karemera et al., Case No. ICTR-98-44-AR73.7, Decision on Interlocutory Appeal Regarding the Role of the Prosecutor's Electronic Disclosure Suite in Discharging Disclosure Obligations (AC), 30 June 2006

The Prosecutor v. Edouard Karemera et al., Case No. ICTR-98-44-AR73.13, Decision on "Joseph Nzirorera's Appeal from Decision on Tenth Rule 68 Motion" (AC), 14 May 2008

Karera

The Prosecutor v. François Karera, Case No. ICTR-01-74-T, Judgement (TC), 7 December 2007 ("*Karera* Trial Judgement")

François Karera v. The Prosecutor, Case No. ICTR-01-74-A, Judgement (AC), 2 February 2009 ("*Karera* Appeal Judgement")

Kayishema and Ruzindana

The Prosecutor v. Clément Kayishema and Obed Ruzindana, Case No. ICTR-95-1-T, Judgement (TC), 21 May 1999 ("*Kayishema and Ruzindana* Trial Judgement")

The Prosecutor v. Clément Kayishema and Obed Ruzindana, Case No. ICTR-95-1-T, Sentence, 21 May 1999 ("*Kayishema and Ruzindana* Trial Judgement (Sentence)")

The Prosecutor v. Clément Kayishema and Obed Ruzindana, Case No. ICTR-95-I-A, Judgement (AC), 1 June 2001 ("*Kayishema and Ruzindana* Appeal Judgement")

Mpambara

The Prosecutor v. Jean Mpambara, Case No. ICTR-01-65-T, Judgement (TC), 11 September 2006 ("*Mpambara* Trial Judgement")

Munyakazi

The Prosecutor v. Yussuf Munyakazi, Case No. ICTR-97-36-R11*bis*, Decision on Prosecutor's Request for Referral to the Republic of Rwanda (TC), 28 May 2008

The Prosecutor v. Yussuf Munyakazi, Case No. ICTR-97-36-R11*bis*, Decision on Prosecution's Appeal Against Decision on Referral under Rule 11*bis* (AC), 8 October 2008

Musema

The Prosecutor v. Alfred Musema, Case No. ICTR-96-13-A, Judgement and Sentence (TC), 27 January 2000 ("*Musema* Trial Judgement") **[page 223]**

Alfred Musema v. The Prosecutor, Case No. ICTR-96-13-A, Judgement (AC), 16 November 2001 ("*Musema* Appeal Judgement")

Muvunyi

Tharcisse Muvunyi v. The Prosecutor, Case No. ICTR-2000-55A-A, Judgement (AC), 29 August 2008 ("*Muvunyi* Appeal Judgement")

Nahimana et al.

Ferdinand Nahimana et al v. The Prosecutor, Case No. ICTR-99-52-A, Decision on Appellant Jean-Bosco Barayagwiza's Motion for Leave to Present Additional Evidence Pursuant to Rule 115 of the Rules of Procedure and Evidence (AC), 8 December 2006

Ferdinand Nahimana et al. v. The Prosecutor, Case No. ICTR-99-52-A, Judgement (AC), 28 November 2007 ("*Nahimana et al.* Appeal Judgement")

Ndindabahizi

The Prosecutor v. Emmanuel Ndindabahizi, Case No. ICTR-2001-71-T, Judgement (TC), 15 July 2004 ("*Ndindabahizi* Trial Judgement")

Emmanuel Ndindabahizi v. The Prosecutor, Case No. ICTR-01-71-A, Judgement (AC), 16 January 2007 ("*Ndindabahizi* Appeal Judgement")

Ndindiliyimana

Prosecutor v. Augustin Ndindiliyimana, *Case No. ICTR-2000-56-I, Decision on Urgent Oral Motion for a Stay of the Indictment, or in the Alternative a Reference to the Security Council (TC), 26 March 2004,*

Niyitegeka

The Prosecutor v. Eliézer Niyitegeka, Case No. ICTR-96-14-T, Judgement and Sentence (TC), 16 May 2003 ("*Niyitegeka* Trial Judgement")

Eliézer Niyitegeka v. The Prosecutor, Case No. ICTR-96-14-A, Judgement (AC), 9 July 2004 ("*Niyitegeka* Appeal Judgement")

Ntagerura et al.

The Prosecutor v. André Ntagerura et al., Case No. ICTR-99-46-T, Judgement and Sentence (TC), 25 February 2004 ("*Ntagerura et al.* Trial Judgement")

The Prosecutor v. André Ntagerura et al., Case No. ICTR-99-46-A, Judgement (AC), 7 July 2006 ("*Ntagerura et al.* Appeal Judgement")

Ntahobali and Nyiramasuhuko

The Prosecutor v. Arsène Shalom Ntahobali and Pauline Nyiramasuhuko, Case No ICTR-97-21-AR73, Decision on the Appeals by Pauline Nyiramasuhuko and Arsène Shalom Ntahobali **[page 224]** on the "Decision on Defence Urgent Motion to Declare Parts of the Evidence of Witnesses RV and QBZ Inadmissible" (AC), 2 July 2004 (*"Butare* Admissibililty Decision")

Ntakirutimana

The Prosecutor v. Elizaphan and Gérard Ntakirutimana, Cases Nos. ICTR-96-10-T and ICTR-96-17-T, Judgement and Sentence (TC), 21 February 2003 ("*Ntakirutimana* Trial Judgement")

The Prosecutor v. Elizaphan and Gérard Ntakirutimana, Cases Nos. ICTR-96-10-A and ICTR-96-17-A, Judgement (AC), 13 December 2004 ("*Ntakirutimana* Appeal Judgement")

Rutaganda

The Prosecutor v. Georges Anderson Nderubumwe Rutaganda, Case No. ICTR-96-3-T, Judgement and Sentence (TC), 6 December 1999 ("*Rutaganda* Trial Judgement")

Georges Anderson Nderubumwe Rutaganda v. The Prosecutor, Case No. ICTR-96-3-A, Judgement (AC), 26 May 2003 ("*Rutaganda* Appeal Judgement")

Georges Anderson Nderubumwe Rutaganda v. The Prosecutor, Case No. ICTR-96-3-R, Decision on Requests for Reconsideration, Review, Assignment of Counsel, Disclosure, and Clarification, 8 December 2006 ("*Rutaganda* Review Decision")

Semanza

The Prosecutor v. Laurent Semanza, Case No. ICTR-97-20-T, Judgement and Sentence (TC), 15 May 2003 ("*Semanza* Trial Judgement")

Laurent Semanza v. The Prosecutor, Case No. ICTR-97-20-A, Judgement (AC), 20 May 2005 ("*Semanza* Appeal Judgement") **[page 225]**

Seromba

The Prosecutor v. Athanase Seromba, Case No. ICTR-2001-66-T, Judgement (TC), 13 December 2006 ("*Seromba* Trial Judgement")

The Prosecutor v. Athanase Seromba, Case No. ICTR-2001-66-A, Judgement (AC), 12 March 2008 ("*Seromba* Appeal Judgement")

Serushago

Omar Serushago v. The Prosecutor, Case No. ICTR-98-39-A, Reasons for Judgement (AC), 6 April 2000 ("*Serushago* Appeal Judgement")

Semanza

The Prosecutor v. Laurent Semanza, Case No. ICTR-97-20-A, Judgement (TC), 15 May 2003 ("*Semanza* Trial Judgement")

The Prosecutor v. Laurent Semanza, Case No. ICTR-97-20-A, Judgement (AC), 20 May 2005 ("*Semanza* Appeal Judgement")

Setako

The Prosecutor v. Ephrem Setako, Case No. ICTR-04-81-I, Decision on Defence Motion Concerning Defects in the Indictment (TC), 17 June 2008, paras. 3-5. ("*Setako* Defects Decision")

Simba

The Prosecutor v. Aloys Simba, Case No. ICTR-01-76-T, Judgement and Sentence (TC), 13 December 2005 ("*Simba* Trial Judgement")

Aloys Simba v. The Prosecutor, Case No. ICTR-01-76-A, Judgement (AC), 27 November 2007 (*"Simba* Appeal Judgement")

1.2 ICTY

Blagojević and Jokić

Prosecutor v. Vidoje Blagojević and Dragan Jokić, Case No. IT-02-60-A, Judgement (AC), 9 May 2007 (*"Blagojević and Jokić* Appeal Judgement")

Blaškić

Prosecutor v. Tihomir Blaškić, Case No. IT-95-14-A, Judgement (AC), 29 July 2004 (*"Blaškić* Appeal Judgement")

Brđanin

Prosecutor v. Radoslav Brđanin, Case No. IT-99-36-T, Judgement (TC), 1 September 2004 (*"Brđanin* Trial Judgement")

Delalić et al.

Prosecutor v. Zejnil Delalić et al., Case No. IT-96-21-A, Judgement (AC), 20 February 2001 (*"Delalić et al* Appeal Judgement")

Delić

Prosecutor v. Rasim Delić, Case No. IT-04-83-T, Judgement (TC), 15 September 2008 (*"Delić* Trial Judgement)

Furundžija

The Prosecutor v. Anto Furundžija, Case No. IT-95-17/1-A, Judgement (AC), 21 July 2000, (*"Furundžija* Appeal Judgement")

Galić

Prosecutor v. Stanislav Galić, Case No. IT-98-29-A, Judgement (AC), 30 November 2006 (*"Galić* Appeal Judgement") **[page 226]**

Hadžihasanović and Kubura

The Prosecutor v. Enver Hadžihasanović and Amir Kubura, Case No. IT-01-47-A, Judgement (AC), 22 April 2008 (*"Hadžihasanović and Kubura* Appeal Judgement")

Halilović

The Prosecutor v. Sefer Halilović, Case No. IT-01-48-A, Judgement (AC), 16 October 2007 (*Halilović* Appeal Judgement)

Jelisić

The Prosecutor v. Goran Jelisić, Case No. IT-95-10-A, Judgement (AC), 5 July 2001 (*"Jelisić* Appeal Judgement")

Kordić and Čerkez

The Prosecutor v. Dario Kordić and Mario Čerkez, Case No. IT-95-14/2-A, Judgement (AC), 17 December 2004 (*"Kordić and Čerkez* Appeal Judgement")

Krnojelac

The Prosecutor v. Milorad Krnojelac, Case No. IT-97-25-A, Judgement (AC), 17 September 2003 (*"Krnojelac* Appeal Judgement")

Krstić

The Prosecutor v. Radoslav Krstić, Case No. IT-98-33-A, Judgement (AC), 19 April 2004 ("*Krstić* Appeal Judgement")

Kunarac et al.

The *Prosecutor v. Dragoljub Kunarac et al.*, Case No. IT-96-23-T and IT-96-23/1-T, Judgement (TC), 22 February 2001 ("*Kunarac et al.* Trial Judgement")

The *Prosecutor v. Dragoljub Kunarac et al.*, Case No. IT-96-23-A and IT-96-23/1-A, Judgement (AC), 12 June 2002 ("*Kunarac et al.* Appeal Judgement")

Kvočka et al.

The *Prosecutor v. Miroslav Kvočka et al.*, Case No. IT-98-30/1-A, Judgement (AC), 28 February 2005 ("*Kvocka et al.* Appeal Judgement")

Limaj et al.

The *Prosecutor v. Fatmir Limaj et al.*, Case No. IT-03-66-T, Judgement (TC), 30 November 2005 ("*Limaj et al.* Trial Judgement")

Orić

The Prosecutor v. Naser Orić, Case No. IT-03-68-A, Judgement (AC), 3 July 2008 ("*Orić* Appeal Judgement")

[page 227]

Simić

The *Prosecutor v. Blagoje Simić*, Case No. IT-95-9-A, Judgement (AC), 28 November 2006 ("*Simić* Appeal Judgement")

Stakić

The *Prosecutor v. Milomir Stakić*, Case No. IT-97-24-A, Judgement (AC), 22 March 2006 ("*Stakić* Appeal Judgement")

Strugar

The *Prosecutor v. Pavle Strugar*, Case No. IT-01-42-T, Judgement (TC), 31 January 2005 ("Strugar Trial Judgement")

Tadić

The *Prosecutor v. Duško Tadić*, Case No. IT-94-1-A, Judgement (AC), 15 July 1999 ("*Tadić* Appeal Judgement")

Vasiljević

The *Prosecutor v. Mitar Vasiljević*, Case No. IT-98-32-A, Judgement (AC), 25 February 2004 ("*Vasiljević* Appeal Judgement")

2. DEFINED TERMS AND ABBREVIATIONS

CDR

Coalition pour la Défense de la République

CELA

Centre d'Étude de Langues Africaines

CND

Conseil National pour le Développement

Also refers to the nickname of a mass grave in Kigali-Ville near the Rugenge sector office

Defence Closing Brief

The Prosecutor v. Tharcisse Renzaho, Case No. ICTR-97-31-I Defence Final Trial Brief, 15 November 2007

Defence Exhibit 113

Complément écrit aux argument oraux de la défense en réponse mémore du procureur **[page 228]**

ESM

École Superieure Militaire

ICRC

International Committee of the Red Cross

ICTR or Tribunal

International Criminal Tribunal for the Prosecution of Persons Responsible for Genocide and Other Serious Violations of International Humanitarian Law Committed in the Territory of Rwanda and Rwandan Citizens Responsible for Genocide and Other Such Violations Committed in the Territory of Neighbouring States, between 1 January 1994 and 31 December 1994

ICTY

International Tribunal for the Prosecution of Persons Responsible for Serious Violations of International Humanitarian Law Committed in the Territory of the Former Yugoslavia since 1991

Indictment

The Prosecutor v. Tharcisse Renzaho, Case No. ICTR-97-31-I, Second Amended Indictment, 16 February 2006

MDR

Mouvement Démocratique Républicain

MRND

Mouvement Révolutionnaire National pour la Démocratie et le Développement

OAU

Organisation of African Unity

ONATRACOM

Rwanda National Transport Company

n.

footnote

p. (pp.)

page (pages)

para. (paras.)

paragraph (paragraphs) **[page 229]**

Prosecution Pre-Trial Brief

The Prosecutor v. Tharcisse Renzaho, Case No. ICTR-97-31-I, The Prosecutor's Pre-Trial Brief, 31 October 2005

Prosecution Closing Brief

The Prosecutor v. Tharcisse Renzaho, Case No. ICTR-97-31-I, The Prosecutor's Closing Brief, 15 November 2008

PSD

Parti Social Démocrate

RPF

Rwandan (also Rwandese) Patriotic Front

RTLM

Radio Télévision Libre des Mille Collines

Rules

Rules of Procedure and Evidence of the International Criminal Tribunal for Rwanda

Saint Paul

Saint Paul pastoral centre in Kigali-Ville

Sainte Famille

Sainte Famille church in Kigali-Ville

Statute

Statute of the International Criminal Tribunal for Rwanda, established by Security Council Resolution 955

T.

Transcript

UNAMIR

United Nations Assistance Mission for Rwanda [page 230]

[page 2]I. The Prosecutor of the United Nations International Criminal Tribunal for Rwanda, pursuant to the authority stipulated in Article 17 of the Statute of the International Criminal Tribunal for Rwanda (the "Statute") charges:

Tharcisse RENZAHO

With:

Count I	–	GENOCIDE, pursuant to Articles 2(3)(a), 6(1) and 6(3) of the Statute, or in the alternative,
Count II	–	COMPLICITY IN GENOCIDE, pursuant to Articles 2(3)(e), 6(1) and 6(3) of the Statute;
Count III	–	MURDER as a CRIME AGAINST HUMANITY, pursuant to Articles 3(a), 6(1) and 6(3) of the Statute;
Count IV	–	RAPE as a CRIME AGAINST HUMANITY, pursuant to Articles 3(g) and 6(3) of the Statute;
Count V	–	MURDER as a VIOLATION OF ARTICLE 3 COMMON TO THE GENEVA CONVENTIONS OF 1949 and Additional Protocol II of 1977, as incorporated pursuant to Articles 4(a), 6(1) and 6(3) of the Statute; and
Count VI	–	RAPE as a VIOLATION OF ARTICLE 3 COMMON TO THE GENEVA CONVENTIONS OF 1949 and Additional Protocol II of 1977, as incorporated pursuant to Articles 4(e) and 6(3) of the Statute.

II. THE ACCUSED

1. **Tharcisse RENZAHO** was born in 1944 in Gaseta *Secteur,* Kigarama *Commune,* Kibungo *Préfecture,* Republic of Rwanda.

2. **Tharcisse RENZAHO** was at all times referred to in this indictment:

   (A) A senior public official who,

   (i) was *Préfet* of Kigali *ville;*

   (ii) was Chairman of the Civil Defense Committee for Kigali *ville;* and

   (iii) consequently had *de jure* and *de facto* control over *bourgmestres, conseillers de secteur, responsables de cellule, nyumbakumi* (ten-house leaders), administrative personnel, *gendarmes,* communal police, *Interahamwe,* militias, and armed civilians in that he could order such persons to commit or to refrain from committing unlawful acts and could discipline or punish them for unlawful acts or omissions. **[page 3]**

   (B) A Colonel in the *Forces Armiées Rwandaises* ("FAR") and as such was a senior military official who had *die jure* and *de facto* control over all armed forces who were under his command in that he could order such persons to commit or to refrain from committing unlawful acts and could discipline or punish them for unlawful acts or omissions.

   (C) A member of the crisis committee set up on the night of 6 April 1994 composed of senior military officers, including Major-General Augustin NDINDILIYIMANA – Chairman, Colonel Marcel GATSINZI, Colonel Leonidas RUSATIRA, Colonel Balthazar NDENGEYINKA, Colonel Felicien MUBERUKA, Colonel Joseph MURASAMPONGO and Lt. Colonel Ephrem RWABALINDA and as such was a senior military official who had *de jure* and *de facto* control over all armed forces who were under his command in that he could order such persons to commit or to refrain from committing unlawful acts and could discipline or punish them for unlawful acts or omissions.

   (D) A "combatant" pursuant to Articles 1 and 2 of Protocol II Additional to Geneva Conventions of 12 August 1949.

   (E) By virtue of his rank, office and links with prominent figures in the community, and his role as *de facto* Minister of the Interior in Kigali *Préfecture,* any person wishing to leave Kigali *ville* needed an authorization signed by him and therefore his authorization necessarily had influence in other *prefectures.*

III. CHARGES AND CONCISE STATEMENT OF FACTS

3. At all times referred to m this indictment there existed in Rwanda a minority racial or ethnic group known as Tutsi, officially identified as such by the government of Rwanda. The majority of the population of Rwanda was comprised of a racial or ethnic group known as the Hutu, also officially identified as such by the government of Rwanda.

4. Between 6 April 1994 and 17 July 1994, throughout Rwanda, and in Kigali in particular, *Interahamwe* militias, soldiers of the FAR and armed civilians targeted and attacked the civilian population based on ethnic or racial identification as Tutsi, or perceived sympathies to the Tutsi. During the attacks some Rwandan citizens killed or caused serious bodily or mental harm to persons perceived to be Tutsi. As a result of these attacks, large numbers of ethnically or racially identified Tutsi were killed.

5. During the period of 7 April 1994 through 17 July 1994, there existed a non-international armed conflict throughout Rwanda, particularly in Kigali-*ville préfecture.* The belligerents in said non-international armed conflict were the FAR and the Rwandan Patriotic Front ("RPF"). During the relevant period of 7 **[page 4]** April 1994 through 4 July 1994, the FAR occupied portions of Kigali-*ville,* trained and armed the *Interahamwe;* and were supported in the conflict by the *Interahamwe,* the *gendarmerie*

and *préfectural* communal police. During this period, the RPF occupied the eastern stretches of Kacyiru and parts of Kicukiro communes.

Count I: GENOCIDE

The Prosecutor of the International Criminal Tribunal for Rwanda charges **Tharcisse RENZAHO** with **GENOCIDE,** a crime stipulated in Article 2(3)(b) of the Statute, in that on or between the dates of 7 April 1994 and 17 July 1994 throughout Rwanda, particularly in Kigali-*ville Préfecture,* **Tharcisse RENZAHO** was responsible for killing or causing serious bodily or mental harm to members of the Tutsi racial or ethnic group, including acts of sexual violence, with intent to destroy, in whole or in part, a racial or ethnic group, as such, as outlined in paragraphs 6 through 43.

Alternatively,

Count II: COMPLICITY IN GENOCIDE

The Prosecutor of the International Criminal Tribunal for Rwanda charges **Tharcisse RENZAHO** with **COMPLICITY IN GENOCIDE,** a crime stipulated in Article 2(3)(e) of the Statute, in that on or between the dates of 7 April 1994 and 17 July 1994 throughout Rwanda, particularly in *Kigali-ville Préfecture,* **Tharcisse RENZAHO** was responsible for killing or causing serious bodily or mental harm to members of the Tutsi racial or ethnic group, including acts of sexual violence, with intent to destroy, in whole or in part, a racial or ethnic group, as such, or with knowledge that other people intended to destroy, in whole or in part, the Tutsi racial or ethnic group, as such, and that his assistance would contribute to the crime of genocide, as outlined in paragraphs 6 through 43.

CONCISE STATEMENT OF FACTS FOR COUNTS I AND II

Individual Criminal Responsibility pursuant to Article 6(1)

6. Pursuant to Article 6(1) of the Statute, the accused, **Tharcisse RENZAHO,** is individually responsible for the crimes of genocide or complicity in genocide because he planned, instigated, ordered, committed or otherwise aided and abetted in the planning, preparation or execution of these crimes. With respect to the commission of those crimes, **Tharcisse RENZAHO** ordered those over whom he had command responsibility and control as a result of his position and authority described in paragraph 2 and he instigated and aided and abetted those over whom he did not have command responsibility and control. In addition, the accused willfully and knowingly participated in a joint criminal enterprise whose object, purpose, and foreseeable outcome was the commission of genocide against the Tutsi racial or ethnic group and persons identified as Tutsi or presumed to support **[page 5]** the Tutsi in Kigali *Préfecture* as well as throughout Rwanda. To fulfill this criminal purpose, the accused acted with leaders and members of the FAR, including Colonel Théoneste BAGOSORA and Colonel Ephrem SETAKO and Major NYIRAHAKIZIMANA; the Presidential Guard; the *Interahamwe,* including Odette NYIRABAGENZI, Angeline MUKANDUTIYE and NGERAGEZA; the "Civil Defense Forces"; communal police; civilian militias; local administrative officials; other soldiers and militiamen; other known participants, such as Father Wenceslas MUNYESHYAKA and Bishop Samuel MUSABYIMANA; and other unknown participants, all such actions being taken either directly or through subordinates, for at least the period of mid-1993 through 17 July 1994. The particulars that give rise to the accused's individual criminal responsibility including his participation in this joint criminal enterprise are set forth in paragraphs 7 through 23.

Roadblocks

7. From and after 7 April 1994, **Tharcisse RENZAHO** instructed soldiers, *gendarmes,* militia, local citizens and demobilized soldiers and others to construct and man roadblocks throughout Kigali-ville including those at Gitega and near the Ontracom facility. These soldiers, *gendarmes,* militia, local

citizens and demobilized soldiers and others were members of the joint criminal enterprise referred to in paragraph 6 above, who used these roadblocks to intercept, identify and kill Tutsi from 7 April to 17 July 1994. In so doing, **Tharcisse RENZAHO** planned, ordered, instigated, committed or otherwise aided and abetted genocide.

8. On or about 7 April 1994, and regularly thereafter, in broadcasts over Radio Rwanda, **Tharcisse RENZAHO** instructed soldiers, *gendarmes,* militia, local citizens and demobilized soldiers, who were members of the joint criminal enterprise referred to in paragraph 6 above, to construct and to man roadblocks, which, from 7 April to 17 July 1994, were used by them to intercept, identify and kill Tutsi, while allowing movement of commercial goods and the majority Hutu population. In so doing, **Tharcisse RENZAHO** planned, ordered, instigated, committed or otherwise aided and abetted genocide.

9. On or about 10 April 1994, at a meeting at the *Préfecture* office of Kigali-*ville*, **Tharcisse RENZAHO** ordered *conseillers* and *responsables de cellule* to set up roadblocks, which, from 10 April to 17 July 1994 were used by *conseillers, responsables de cellule, Interahamwe,* local citizens, gendarmes, soldiers and demobilized soldiers, who were members of the joint criminal enterprise referred to in paragraph 6 above to identify and to kill Tutsi. In so doing, **Tharcisse RENZAHO** planned, ordered, instigated, committed or otherwise aided and abetted genocide. **[page 6]**

10. On diverse unknown dates in April and May 1994 **Tharcisse RENZAHO** convened a meetings at which he instructed *nyumbakumi, responsables de cellule, conseillers and bourgmestres* to remain vigilant at roadblocks and to make sure that *Inyenzi* do not succeed in hiding among the population. As a consequence of these instructions, Tutsi were intercepted, identified and killed at the roadblocks in Kigali-ville. In convening these meetings and giving these instructions, **Tharcisse RENZAHO** planned, ordered, instigated, committed or otherwise aided and abetted genocide.

The Killing Campaign in Kigali-*ville*

11. On diverse unknown dates between mid-1993 and 17 July 1994, **Tharcisse RENZAHO** regularly permitted and encouraged *Interahamwe* and *Impuzamugambi* groups to meet at his house in Kanombe and elsewhere for the purpose of receiving military training. These *Interahamwe* and *Impuzamugambi* were members of the joint criminal enterprise referred to in paragraph 6 above, who killed and/or caused serious bodily or mental harm to Tutsi between 6 April and 17 July 1994. By permitting and encouraging the training of *Interahamwe and Impuzamugambi* **Tharcisse RENZAHO** planned, instigated, committed or otherwise aided and abetted genocide.

12. On diverse unknown dates between mid-1993 and 17 July 1994, **Tharcisse RENZAHO** distributed weapons and ammunition to members of the *Interahamwe* and *Impuzamugambi* at his house in Kanombe and elsewhere. These *Interahamwe* and *Impuzamugambi* were members of the joint criminal enterprise referred to in paragraph 6 above, who killed and/or caused serious bodily or mental harm to Tutsi between 6 April and 17 July 1994. In so distributing weapons and ammunition **Tharcisse RENZAHO** planned, instigated, committed or otherwise aided and abetted genocide.

13. Between 6 April and 17 July 1994, **Tharcisse RENZAHO** provided and facilitated the provision of bonds, permits, *laissez-passers,* and food to enable the movement and equipping of the *Interahamwe,* militia, soldiers and *gendarmes.* These *Interahamwe,* militia, soldiers and *gendarmes* were members of the joint criminal enterprise referred to in paragraph 6 above, who killed and/or caused serious bodily or mental harm to Tutsi between 6 April and 17 July 1994. By his actions described above **Tharcisse RENZAHO** planned, committed or otherwise aided and abetted genocide.

14. On or about 8 April 1994 **Tharcisse RENZAHO** planned, committed, ordered, instigated or aided and abetted the killing of the Director of the *Banque rwandaise de développement.* He confirmed this to Colonel BAGOSORA, who was a **[page 7]** member of the joint criminal enterprise referred to in paragraph 6 above, by radio on or about that same date.

Second Amended Indictment

15. On or about 9 April 1994, **Tharcisse RENZAHO,** while dressed in the military uniform of a senior military official, led armed *Interahamwe* at Kajari in Kanombe. The *Interahamwe,* who were members of the joint criminal enterprise referred to in paragraph 6 above, entered houses of Tutsi and killed the Tutsi who resided there. **Tharcisse RENZAHO** thereby ordered, instigated, committed, or otherwise aided and abetted the killing of the Tutsi.

16. On or about 16 April 1994 at a meeting at the Kigali-*ville* prefectural headquarters, **Tharcisse RENZAHO** ordered *conseillers* to obtain firearms from the Ministry of Defence to be distributed at the *secteur* level. These weapons were used by *conseillers* and militia, who were members of the joint criminal enterprise referred to in paragraph 6 above, to kill Tutsi, and by so distributing firearms **Tharcisse RENZAHO** planned, instigated, committed or otherwise aided and abetted genocide.

17. On or about 30 April 1994, **Tharcisse RENZAHO** dismissed, among other people, *secteur conseillers* Jean-Baptiste RUDASINGWA and Celestin SEZIBERA, because he believed they were opposed to the killing of Tutsi. By replacing the aforementioned persons with *conseillers* who supported the killing of Tutsi **Tharcisse RENZAHO** aided and abetted this killing.

18. On an unknown date within the period between on or about 7 and 30 May 1994, while at a meeting at Bishop Samuel MUSABYIMANA's residence, **Tharcisse RENZAHO** agreed to supply guns to MUSABYTMANA. **Tharcisse RENZAHO** thereafter during the same period tendered several Kalashnikov rifles, which were delivered by Major NYIRAHAKIZIMANA. Said rifles were distributed among the militias and were used to kill Tutsi, and by providing these rifles **Tharcisse RENZAHO** aided and abetted the killing.

19. In the month of June 1994 **Tharcisse RENZAHO,** together with Colonel Ephrem SETAKO and Colonel BAGOSORA, who were members of the joint criminal enterprise referred to in paragraph 6 above, attended an impromptu meeting at a roadblock near Hotel Kiyovu in Kigali where they instructed those present to kill all Tutsi. A number of Tutsi were then killed.

Specific Sites

20. Between 7 April and 17 July 1994 thousands of Tutsi took refuge in *Centre d'étude des langues africaines* ("CELA"), St. Paul's Pastoral Centre ("St. Paul's") and Ste. Famille Parish Church ("Ste. Famille"). Father Wenceslas **[page 8]** MUNYESHYAKA was in charge of Ste. Famille; Odette NYIRABAGENZI was the *conseiller de secteur* directly under the command and authority of **Tharcisse RENZAHO;** and Angeline MUKANDUTIYE was the school inspector as well as a leader of the *Interahamwe* and in *de facto* control of Bwahirimba *secteur.* MUKANDUTIYE was directly under the command of and accountable to **Tharcisse RENZAHO.**

21. On or about 22 April 1994, while in the company of Odette NYIRABAGENZI and Angeline MUKANDUTIYE, and of Father MUNYESHYAKA, soldiers and *Interahamwe,* who were members of the joint criminal enterprise referred to in paragraph 6 above, **Tharcisse RENZAHO** ordered the removal of approximately sixty Tutsi men from CELA who were taken away and killed by soldiers and *Interahamwe.* By so doing, **Tharcisse RENZAHO** ordered, instigated, committed or otherwise aided and abetted genocide. During other dates unknown, he ordered and instigated the murder of many other Tutsi at CELA.

22. On or about 14 June 1994, while in the company of Odette NYIRABAGENZI and Angeline MUKANDUTIYE, and *Interahamwe,* soldiers, and gendarmes, who were members of the joint criminal enterprise referred to in paragraph 6 above, **Tharcisse RENZAHO** ordered and instigated and committed or otherwise aided and abetted the *Interahamwe,* soldiers and gendarmes to remove sixty Tutsi boys from St, Paul's, and to kill these Tutsi boys.

23. On or about 17 June 1994, while in the company of Odette NYIRABAGENZI and Angeline MUKANDUTIYE, **Tharcisse RENZAHO** ordered and instigated soldiers, militia and communal police, who were members of the joint criminal enterprise referred to in paragraph 6 above, to attack Tutsi who had sought refuge Ste. Famille and many Tutsi were killed.

Criminal Responsibility as a Superior pursuant to Article 6(3)

24. Pursuant to Article 6(3) of the Statute, the accused, **Tharcisse RENZAHO,** is responsible for the crimes of genocide or complicity in genocide because specific criminal acts were committed by subordinates of the accused and the accused knew or had reason to know that such subordinates were about to commit such acts before they were committed or that such subordinates had committed such acts and the accused failed to take the necessary and reasonable measures to prevent such acts or to punish the perpetrators thereof. These subordinates included the leaders and members of the FAR, including Major NYIRAHAKIZIMANA; the Presidential Guard; the *Interahamwe,* including Odette NYIRABAGENZI, Angeline MUKANDUTIYE and NGERAGEZA; the "Civil Defense Forces"; communal police; civilian militias; local administrative officials; other soldiers and militiamen; other known participants, such as Father Wenceslas MUNYESHYAKA and Bishop Samuel MUSABYIMANA; and other **[page 9]** unknown participants. The particulars that give rise to the accused's individual criminal responsibility pursuant to Article 6(3) are set forth in paragraphs 25 through 43.

Roadblocks

25. From and after 7 April 1994, roadblocks throughout Kigali-ville including at Gitega and near the Ontracom facility were constructed and manned by soldiers, *gendarmes,* militia and demobilized soldiers under the effective control of **Tharcisse RENZAHO,** who used the roadblocks to identify and to kill Tutsi and **Tharcisse RENZAHO** failed or refused to take the necessary or reasonable measures to prevent such acts or to punish the perpetrators thereof.

26. On or about 10 April 1994, following a meeting at the *Préfecture* office of Kigali- *ville, conseillers* and *responsables de cellule* who were under the effective control of **Tharcisse RENZAHO,** set up roadblocks and used these roadblocks to identify and to kill Tutsi, and **Tharcisse RENZAHO** failed or refused to take the necessary or reasonable measures to prevent such acts or to punish the perpetrators thereof.

27. At diverse unknown dates in April and May 1994 **Tharcisse RENZAHO** convened meetings at which he instructed *nyumbakumi, responsables de cellule, conseillers and bourgmestres* who were under his effective control to remain vigilant at roadblocks and to make sure that *Inyenzi* did not succeed in hiding among the population. As a consequence of these instructions, Tutsi were intercepted, identified and killed at the roadblocks in Kigali-ville, and **Tharcisse RENZAHO** failed or refused to take the necessary or reasonable measures to prevent such acts or to punish the perpetrators thereof,

The Killing Campaign in Kigali-*ville*

28. At diverse unknown dates between mid-1993 and 17 July 1994, **Tharcisse RENZAHO** permitted *Interahamwe* and *Impuzamugambi* groups to meet at his house in Kanombe and elsewhere for the purpose of receiving military training. These *Interahamwe* and *Impuzamugambi* were under the effective control of **Tharcisse RENZAHO** and between 6 April and 17 July 1994 they killed or caused serious bodily or mental harm to Tutsi. **Tharcisse RENZAHO** failed or refused to take the necessary or reasonable measures to prevent such acts or to punish the perpetrators thereof.

29. At diverse unknown dates between mid-1993 and 17 July 1994, **Tharcisse RENZAHO** distributed weapons and ammunition to members of the **[page 10]** *Interahamwe* and *Impuzamugambi* at his house in Kanombe and elsewhere. These *Interahamwe* and *Impuzamugambi* were under the effective control of **Tharcisse RENZAHO** and between 6 April and 17 July 1994 they killed or caused serious bodily or mental harm to Tutsi. **Tharcisse RENZAHO** failed or refused to take the necessary or reasonable measures to prevent such acts or to punish the perpetrators thereof.

30. Between 6 April and 17 July 1994, **Tharcisse RENZAHO** provided and facilitated the provision of bonds, permits, *laissez-passers,* and food to enable the movement and equipping of the *Interahamwe,* militia, soldiers and *gendarmes* who were participating in the killing of Tutsi, and had effective control over them in the sense of having the power to prevent or punish their acts.

Second Amended Indictment

31. On 8 April 1994, **Tharcisse RENZAHO** communicated with Colonel BAGOSORA by radio confirming that those under his effective control had killed the manager of the *Banque Rwandaise de Développement,* and **Tharcisse RENZAHO** failed or refused to take the necessary or reasonable measures to prevent such acts or to punish the perpetrators thereof.

32. On or about 9 April 1994, **Tharcisse RENZAHO,** while dressed in the military uniform of a senior military official, accompanied armed *Interahamwe* at Kajari in Kanombe. **Tharcisse RENZAHO's** subordinates in the *Interahamwe* entered houses of Tutsi and killed the Tutsi who resided there in **Tharcisse RENZAHO's** presence without his objection. **Tharcisse RENZAHO** failed or refused to take the necessary or reasonable measures to prevent such acts or to punish the perpetrators thereof.

33. On or about 16 April 1994 following a meeting at the Kigali-*ville* prefectural headquarters, *conseillers* under the effective control of **Tharcisse RENZAHO** obtained firearms from the Ministry of Defense to be distributed at the *secteur* level. These weapons were used to kill Tutsi and **Tharcisse RENZAHO** failed or refused to take the necessary or reasonable measures to prevent such acts or to punish the perpetrators thereof.

34. On multiple unknown dates between April and July 1994, **Tharcisse RENZAHO** refused or failed to punish *Interahamwe* members under his effective control, command and supervision whom he knew to have participated in the killing of Tutsi and moderate Hutu in Kigali.

35. On or about 30 April 1994, **Tharcisse RENZAHO** dismissed, among other people, *secteur conseillers* Jean-Baptiste RUDASINGWA and Celestin SEZIBERA, because he believed they were opposed to the killing of Tutsi. **[page 11] Tharcisse RENZAHO** replaced the aforementioned persons with *conseillers* who supported the killing of Tutsi, thus showing his effective control over local administrative officials in Kigali-*ville.*

Specific Sites

36. Between 7 April and 17 My 1994 thousands of Tutsi took refuge in CELA, St. Paul's and Ste. Famille. Father Wenceslas MUNYESHYAKA was in charge of Ste. Famille; Odette NYIRABAGENZI was the *conseiller de secteur* directly under the command and authority of **Tharcisse RENZAHO;** and Angeline MUKANDUTIYE was the school inspector as well as a leader of the *Interahamwe* and in *de facto* control of Bwahirimba *secteur.* MUKANDUTIYE was under the effective control of and accountable to **Tharcisse RENZAHO.**

37. Between 7 April and 17 July 1994, **Tharcisse RENZAHO's** subordinates, including but not limited to Father MUNYESHYAKA, Odette NYIRABAGENZI and Angeline MUKANDUTIYE, and other *Interahamwe* leaders, planned, prepared, ordered, instigated, and carried out attacks on members of the racial or ethnic Tutsi group in Kigali. These attacks took place at Ste. Famille, St. Paul's, Kadaffi Mosque and CELA, among other places in the Nyarugenge *secteur* and were carried out with intent to kill or cause mental and bodily harm to members of the racial or ethnic Tutsi group in whole or in part. **Tharcisse RENZAHO** failed or refused to take the necessary or reasonable measures to prevent such acts or to punish the perpetrators thereof.

38. On or about 22 April 1994, **Tharcisse RENZAHO's** subordinates, Odette NYIRABAGENZI, Father MUNYESHYAKA and Angeline MUKANDUTIYE, soldiers and *Interahamwe,* removed and caused the murder of sixty Tutsi men at CELA. During other dates unknown in April, May and June 1994 they removed and caused the murder of many other Tutsi at CELA, and **Tharcisse RENZAHO** failed or refused to take the necessary or reasonable measures to prevent such acts or to punish the perpetrators thereof.

39. On or about 14 June 1994, **Tharcisse RENZAHO's** subordinates, Odette NYIRABAGENZI and Angeline MUKANDUTIYE, and *Interahamwe,* soldiers and gendarmes removed and caused the murder of sixty Tutsi boys from St. Paul's, and **Tharcisse RENZAHO** failed or refused to take the necessary or reasonable measures to prevent such acts or to punish the perpetrators thereof.

40. On or about 17 June 1994, **Tharcisse RENZAHO's** subordinates, including but not limited to Odette NYIRABAGENZI and Angeline MUKANDUTIYE, soldiers, militia and communal police attacked and killed Tutsi who had sought refuge St, Famille, and **Tharcisse RENZAHO** failed or refused to take the **[page 12]** necessary or reasonable measures to prevent such acts or to punish the perpetrators thereof.

Sexual Violence

41. Tutsi women were raped by *Interahamwe* militia, soldiers and other individuals under the effective control of **Tharcisse RENZAHO** on April 16 and diverse unknown dates during the months of April, May and June 1994. *Conseillers* under the direct command and authority of **Tharcisse RENZAHO** reported on a regular basis about the rape of Tutsi women by *Interahamwe* militia, soldiers and other individuals under the effective control of **Tharcisse RENZAHO. Tharcisse RENZAHO** failed or refused to take the necessary or reasonable measures to prevent such rapes or to punish the perpetrators thereof.

42. Father MUNYESHYAKA and *Interahamwe,* under the effective control of **Tharcisse RENZAHO,** compelled Tutsi women to provide them with sexual pleasures in exchange for the woman's safety at Ste. Famille during the period in which Tutsi sought refuge at Ste. Famille in the months of April, May and June 1994. **Tharcisse RENZAHO** knew or had reason to know that these acts were being perpetrated against Tutsi women and he failed or refused to prevent or to punish the perpetrators of these forced sexual acts at Ste. Famille.

43. *Interahamwe,* soldiers, and armed civilians under the effective control of **Tharcisse RENZAHO** maintained Tutsi women at houses in central Kigali, where they compelled the women provide them with sexual pleasures in exchange for the women's safety on diverse unknown dates during the months of April, May and June 1994. **Tharcisse RENZAHO** knew or had reason to know that these acts were being perpetrated against Tutsi women and he failed or refused to prevent or to punish the perpetrators of these forced sexual acts.

Count III: MURDER as a CRIME AGAINST HUMANITY

The Prosecutor of the International Criminal Tribunal for Rwanda charges **Tharcisse RENZAHO** with **MURDER as a CRIME AGAINST HUMANITY,** a crime stipulated in Article 3(a) of the Statute, in that on and between 6 April and 17 July 1994 throughout Rwanda, particularly in Kigali-*ville Préfecture,* **Tharcisse RENZAHO,** with intent to kill members of the Tutsi racial or ethnic group or persons identified as Tutsi or presumed to support the Tutsi, was responsible for the killing of such persons as part of a widespread or systematic attack against that civilian population on racial, ethnic and political grounds, as set forth in paragraphs 44 through 51.

CONCISE STATEMENT OF FACTS FOR COUNT III

Individual Criminal Responsibility pursuant to Article 6(1) **[page 13]**

44. Pursuant to Article 6(1) of the Statute, the accused, **Tharcisse RENZAHO,** is individually responsible for murder as a crime against humanity because he planned, instigated, ordered, committed or otherwise aided and abetted in the planning, preparation or execution of this crime. With respect to the commission of this crime, **Tharcisse RENZAHO** ordered those over whom he had command responsibility and control as a result of his position and authority described in paragraph 2 and he instigated and aided and abetted those over whom he did not have command responsibility and control. In addition, the accused willfully and knowingly participated in a joint criminal enterprise whose object, purpose and foreseeable outcome was the commission of crimes against humanity against the Tutsi racial or ethnic group and persons identified as Tutsi or presumed to support the Tutsi or to be politically opposed to "Hutu Power" in Kigali *Préfecture* as well as throughout Rwanda on racial, ethnic or political grounds. To fulfill this criminal purpose, the accused acted with leaders and mem-

bers of the FAR; the Presidential Guard; the *Interahamwe,* such as Odette NYIRABAGENZI; the "Civil Defense Forces"; communal police; civilian militias; local administrative officials; other soldiers and militiamen; other known participants, such as Father Wenceslas MUNYESHYAKA; and other unknown participants, all such actions being taken either directly or through their subordinates for at least the period of 12 April through 15 June 1994. The particulars that give rise to the accused's individual criminal responsibility including his participation in this joint criminal enterprise are set forth in paragraphs 45 through 47.

45. On or about 22 April 1994, in the presence of others, **Tharcisse RENZAHO** selected and ordered and instigated the killing of specific people from CELA; including James, Charles, Wilson and Déglote RWANGA and Emmanuel GIHANA. The aforementioned were killed *by Interahamwe,* soldiers and gendarmes who were members of the joint criminal enterprise referred to in paragraph 44 above, and by his actions described herein **Tharcisse RENZAHO** ordered, instigated, committed or otherwise aided and abetted this murder.

46. On or about 28 April 1994, **Tharcisse RENZAHO** ordered members of the *Interahamwe* to Nyarugenge commune to find and kill nine Tutsi, including Francois NSENGIYUMVA; a man whose name was KAGORORA, as well as his two sons, Emile and Aimable; and a man whose name was RUTCYOMBA. These persons were subsequently killed by the *Interahamwe,* who were members of the joint criminal enterprise referred to in paragraph 44 above, pursuant to **Tharcisse RENZAHO's** orders. In so doing, **Tharcisse RENZAHO** planned, ordered, instigated, committed or otherwise aided and abetted this murder.

47. On or about 15 June 1994, **Tharcisse RENZAHO** ordered Odette NYIRABAGENZI to kill André KAMEYA, a journalist who was critical of the Interim Government. On or about 15 June 1994, while in the company of *Interahamwe,* Odette NYIRABAGENZI, who was a member of the joint criminal enterprise referred to in paragraph 44 above, found and had André KAMEYA **[page 14]** killed pursuant to **Tharcisse RENZAHO's** orders. By his actions detailed herein, **Tharcisse RENZAHO** ordered, instigated, committed or otherwise aided and abetted this murder.

Criminal Responsibility as a Superior pursuant to Article 6(3)

48. Pursuant to Article 6(3) of the Statute, the accused, **Tharcisse RENZAHO,** is responsible for the murder as a crime against humanity because specific criminal acts were committed by subordinates of the accused and the accused knew or had reason to know that such subordinates were about to commit such acts before they were committed or that such subordinates had committed such acts and the accused failed to take the necessary and reasonable measures to prevent such acts or to punish the perpetrators thereof. These subordinates included leaders and members of the FAR; the Presidential Guard; the *Interahamwe,* such as Odette NYIRABAGENZI; the "Civil Defense Forces"; communal police; civilian militias; local administrative officials; other soldiers and militiamen; other known participants, such as Father Wenceslas MUNYESHYAKA; and other unknown participants. The particulars that give rise to the accused's individual criminal responsibility pursuant to Article 6(3) are set forth in paragraphs 49 through 51.

49. On or about 22 April 1994, *Interahamwe* and soldiers under the effective control of **Tharcisse RENZAHO** killed certain persons in refuge at CELA, including but not limited to James, Charles, Wilson and Déglote RWANGA and Emmanuel GIHANA, and **Tharcisse RENZAHO** failed or refused to take the necessary or reasonable measures to prevent such acts or to punish the perpetrators thereof.

50. On or about 28 April 1994, members of the *Interahamwe* under effective control of **Tharcisse RENZAHO** went to Nyarugenge commune and found and killed nine Tutsi, including Francois NSENGIYUMVA; a man whose name was KAGORORA, as well as his two sons, Emile and Aimable; and a man whose name was RUTIYOMBA and **Tharcisse RENZAHO** failed or refused to take the necessary or reasonable measures to prevent such acts or to punish the perpetrators thereof.

51. On or about 15 June 1994, **Tharcisse RENZAHO's** subordinates, Odette NYIRABAGENZI and a company of *Interahamwe,* found and killed André KAMEYA, a journalist who was critical of the

Interim Government and **Tharcisse RENZAHO** failed or refused to take the necessary or reasonable measures to prevent such acts or to punish the perpetrators thereof.

Count IV: RAPE as a CRIME AGAINST HUMANITY [page 15]

The Prosecutor of the International Criminal Tribunal for Rwanda charges **Tharcisse RENZAHO** with **RAPE as a CRIME AGAINST HUMANITY,** a crime stipulated in Article 3(g) of the Statute, in that on an between 7 April and 17 July 1994 throughout Rwanda, particularly in Kigali-*ville Préfecture,* **Tharcisse RENZAHO,** members of the Tutsi racial or ethnic group or persons identified as Tutsi were raped by subordinates of **Tharcisse RENZAHO** as part of a widespread or systematic attack against that civilian population on racial and ethnic grounds, as set forth in paragraphs 52 through 55.

CONCISE STATEMENT OF FACTS FOR COUNT TV

Criminal Responsibility as a Superior pursuant to Article 6(3)

52. Pursuant to Article 6(3) of the Statute, the accused, **Tharcisse RENZAHO,** is responsible for the rape as a crime against humanity because specific criminal acts were committed by subordinates of the accused and the accused knew or had reason to know that such subordinates were about to commit such acts before they were committed or that such subordinates had committed such acts and the accused failed to take the necessary and reasonable measures to prevent such acts or to punish the perpetrators thereof. These subordinates included leaders and members of the FAR; the Presidential Guard; the *Interahamwe;* the "Civil Defense Forces"; communal police; civilian militias; local administrative officials; other soldiers and militiamen; other known participants, such as Father Wenceslas MUNYESHYAKA; and other unknown participants. The particulars that give rise to the accused's individual criminal responsibility are set forth in paragraphs 53 through 55.

53. Tutsi women were raped by *Interahamwe* militia, soldiers and other individuals under the effective control of **Tharcisse RENZAHO** on April 16 and diverse unknown dates during the months of April, May and June 1994. *Conseillers* under the direct command and authority of **Tharcisse RENZAHO** reported on a regular basis about the rape of Tutsi women by *Interahamwe* militia, soldiers and other individuals under the effective control of **RENZAHO. Tharcisse RENZAHO** failed or refused to take the necessary or reasonable measures to prevent such rapes or to punish the perpetrators thereof.

54. Father MUNYESHYAKA and *Interahamwe* under the effective control of **Tharcisse RENZAHO** compelled Tutsi women to provide them with sexual pleasures in exchange for the woman's safety at Ste. Famille in the period in which Tutsi sought refuge at Ste. Famille during the months of April, May and June 1994. **Tharcisse RENZAHO** knew or had reason to know that these acts were being perpetrated against Tutsi women and he failed or refused to punish the perpetrators of these forced sexual acts at Ste. Famille.

55. *Interahamwe* soldiers and armed civilians under the effective control of **Tharcisse RENZAHO** maintained Tutsi women at houses in central Kigali, where they compelled the women provide them with sexual pleasures in exchange for the **[page 16]** women's safety on diverse unknown dates during the months of April, May and June 1994. **Tharcisse RENZAHO** knew or had reason to know that these acts were being perpetrated against Tutsi women and he failed or refused to punish the perpetrators of these forced sexual acts.

Count V: MURDER AS A VIOLATION OF ARTICLE 3 COMMON TO THE GENEVA CONVENTIONS OF 1949

The Prosecutor of the International Criminal Tribunal for Rwanda charges **Tharcisse RENZAHO** with **MURDER AS A VIOLATION OF ARTICLE 3 COMMON TO THE GENEVA CONVENTIONS OF 1949 AND ADDITIONAL PROTOCOL II OF 1977,** a crime stipulated in Article 4(a) of the Statute, in that **Tharcisse RENZAHO** was responsible for the killings of non-combatant Tutsi men and youths during the period 7 April through 17 July 1994 when throughout Rwanda, particularly in Kigali-*ville Préfecture*, there was a non-international armed conflict within the meaning of Articles 1 and 2 of Protocol II Additional to the Geneva Convention of 1949, and the killing of the victims was closely related to the hostilities or committed in conjunction with the armed conflict and the victims were persons taking no part in that conflict; all as is set forth in paragraphs 56 through 60.

CONCISE STATEMENT OF FACTS FOR COUNT V

Individual Criminal Responsibility pursuant to Article 6(1)

56. Pursuant to Article 6(1) of the Statute, the accused, **Tharcisse RENZAHO,** is individually responsible for murder as a violation of Article 3 Common to the Geneva Conventions of 1949 and Additional Protocol II of 1977 because he planned, instigated, ordered, committed or otherwise aided and abetted in the planning, preparation or execution of these crimes. With respect to the commission of those crimes, **Tharcisse RENZAHO** ordered those over whom he had command responsibility and control as a result of his position and authority described in paragraph 2 and he instigated and aided and abetted those over whom he did not have command responsibility and control. In addition, the accused participated in a joint criminal enterprise whose object, purpose, and foreseeable outcome was the commission of war crimes against non-combatant members of the Tutsi racial or ethnic group in Kigali *Préfecture* as well as throughout Rwanda. To fulfill this criminal purpose, the accused acted with leaders and members of the FAR; the Presidential Guard; the *Interahamwe;* the "Civil Defense Forces"; communal police; civilian militias; local administrative officials; other soldiers and militiamen; and other known and unknown participants, all such actions being taken either directly or through their subordinates for at least the period of 6 April 1994 through 4 July 1994. The particulars that give rise to the accused's individual criminal responsibility including his participation in this joint criminal enterprise are set forth in paragraphs 57 and 58. **[page 17]**

57. Between 16 and 17 June 1994 the RPF fought their way to St. Paul's in Nyarugenge in Kigali-*ville* and rescued a large number of non-combatant Tutsi.

58. Pursuant to the authority vested in **Tharcisse RENZAHO** as described in paragraph 2, and in retaliation for the actions of the RPF described in paragraph 57, **Tharcisse RENZAHO** on or about 17 June 1994 ordered, instigated or otherwise aided and abetted soldiers of the FAR and *Interahamwe* to take and kill at least seventeen non-combatant Tutsi men from Ste. Famille who had not been rescued by the RPF.

Criminal Responsibility as a Superior pursuant to Article 6(3)

59. Pursuant to Article 6(3) of the Statute, the accused, **Tharcisse RENZAHO,** is responsible for murder as a violation of Article 3 common to the Geneva Conventions of 1949 and Additional Protocol II of 1977 because specific criminal acts were committed by subordinates of the accused and the accused knew or had reason to know that such subordinates were about to commit such acts before they were committed or that such subordinates had committed such acts and the accused failed to take the necessary and reasonable measures to prevent such acts or to punish the perpetrators thereof. These subordinates included leaders and members of the FAR; the Presidential Guard; the *Interahamwe;* the "Civil Defense Forces"; communal police; civilian militias; local administrative officials; other soldiers and militiamen; and other known and unknown participants. The particulars that give rise to the accused's individual criminal responsibility pursuant to Article 6(3) are set forth in paragraph 60.

60. In retaliation for the actions of the RPF described in paragraph 57, on or about 17 June 1994, soldiers of the FAR and *Interahamwe,* who were subordinates under the effective control of **Tharcisse RENZAHO,** killed at least seventeen non- combatant Tutsi men from Ste. Famille who had not been rescued by the RPF and **Tharcisse RENZAHO** failed or refused to take the necessary or reasonable measures to prevent such acts or to punish the perpetrators thereof.

Count VI: **RAPE AS A VIOLATION OF ARTICLE 3 COMMON TO THE GENEVA CONVENTIONS OF 1949**

The Prosecutor of the International Criminal Tribunal for Rwanda charges **Tharcisse RENZAHO** with **RAPE AS A VIOLATION OF ARTICLE 3 COMMON TO THE GENEVA CONVENTIONS OF 1949 AND ADDITIONAL PROTOCOL II OF 1977**, a crime stipulated in Article 4(e) of the Statute, in that **Tharcisse RENZAHO** was responsible for the rape of non-combatant Tutsi women during the period between 7 April and 17 July 1994 when throughout Rwanda, particularly in Kigali-*ville Préfecture,* there was a non-international armed conflict within the meaning of Articles 1 and 2 of Protocol II Additional to the Geneva Convention of 1949, and the raping of the victims was closely related to the hostilities or committed in conjunction with the armed conflict **[page 18]** and the victims were persons taking no part in that conflict; all as set forth in paragraphs 61 through 65.

CONCISE STATEMENT OF FACTS FOR COUNT VI

Criminal Responsibility as a Superior pursuant to Article 6(3)

61. Pursuant to Article 6(3) of the Statute, the accused, **Tharcisse RENZAHO,** is responsible for rape as a violation of Article 3 common to the Geneva Conventions of 1949 and Additional Protocol II of 1977 because specific criminal acts were committed by subordinates of the accused and the accused knew or had reason to know that such subordinates were about to commit such acts before they were committed or that such subordinates had committed such acts and the accused failed to take the necessary and reasonable measures to prevent such acts or to punish the perpetrators thereof. These subordinates included leaders and members of the FAR; the Presidential Guard; the *Interahamwe,* such as Odette NYIRABAGENZI; the "Civil Defense Forces"; communal police; civilian militias; local administrative officials; other soldiers and militiamen; other known participants, such as Father Wenceslas MUNYESHYAKA; and other unknown participants. The particulars that give rise to the accused's individual criminal responsibility pursuant to Article 6(3) are set forth in paragraphs 62 through 65.

62. During the relevant periods of 7 April 1994 through 4 July 1994, the FAR occupied central areas of Kigali, including Nyarugenge commune and the area around the Ste. Famille Church. The FAR trained and armed the *Interahamwe,* and were supported in the conflict by the *Interahamwe,* the *gendarmerie, préfectural* communal police, and armed civilians.

63. Tutsi women were raped by *Interahamwe* militia, soldiers and other individuals under the effective control of **Tharcisse RENZAHO** on April 16 and diverse unknown dates during the months of April, May and June 1994. *Conseillers* under the direct command and authority of **Tharcisse RENZAHO** reported on a regular basis about the rape of Tutsi women by *Interahamwe* militia, soldiers and other individuals under the effective control of **Tharcisse RENZAHO. Tharcisse RENZAHO** failed or refused to take the necessary or reasonable measures to prevent such rapes or to punish the perpetrators thereof.

64. Father MUNYESHYAKA and other *Interahamwe* under the effective control of **Tharcisse RENZAHO** compelled Tutsi women to provide them with sexual pleasures in exchange for the woman's safety at Ste. Famille in the period in which Tutsi sought refuge at Ste. Famille during the months of April, May and June 1994. **Tharcisse RENZAHO** knew or had reason to know that these acts **[page 19]** were being perpetrated against Tutsi women and he failed or refused to prevent or punish the perpetrators of these forced sexual acts at Ste. Famille.

65. *Interahamwe* soldiers and armed civilians under the effective control of **Tharcisse RENZAHO** maintained Tutsi women at houses in central Kigali, where they compelled the women provide them with sexual pleasures in exchange for the women's safety on diverse unknown dates during the months of April, May and June 1994. **Tharcisse RENZAHO** knew or had reason to know that these acts were

being perpetrated against Tutsi women and he failed or refused to prevent or punish the perpetrators of these forced sexual acts.

The acts and omissions of **Tharcisse RENZAHO** detailed herein are punishable in pursuant to Articles 22 and 23 of the Statute.

Signed at ARUSHA, Tanzania, this 16th Day of February 2006.

_____

Hassan B. Jallow
Prosecutor

Commentary

1. Introduction

At first sight, the Renzaho case may not be regarded as exceptional in relation to jurisdictional matters, but without doubt, it takes a significant role in the development of the settled case-law of the *ad hoc* tribunal. The focus of this commentary lays on the different modes of individual responsibility and the interpretation of the settled case-law by the trial chamber. Renzaho was the prefect of Kigali-Ville prefecture from 1990 to July 1994 and furthermore he held the military rank of a colonel of the Rwandan army. The chamber concluded that the accused was the person with the highest authority in Kigali-Ville and in this function should have been a guarantor of peace and security during the conflict in this region of Rwanda.[1] He was charged for his role in the establishment of roadblocks throughout Kigali-Ville and the concomitant killings there; his contribution to the attacks on two refugee camps in his prefecture; and his involvement in rapes as a violation of Art. 4, subsection e, ICTR Statute. The commentary does not solely analyse the trial chamber judgment and its outcome but rather the findings of the appeals chamber regarding different issues related to each mode of liability.

2. Individual criminal responsibility

The accused of the present case was charged for all modes of liability, i.e. ordering the commission of crimes, aiding and abetting and the basic form of joint criminal enterprise as well as superior responsibility for the role he played as a civil and military authority during the armed conflict in Rwanda in 1994.[2] In the following the different forms of individual criminal responsibility will be discussed in detail.

2.1 Ordering

Referring to settled jurisprudence of the ICTY and ICTR,[3] the chamber defined the requirements for the commission of a crime by ordering its execution. Therefore, a person who instructs another person to commit an unlawful act can be held criminally liable even if there is no formal superior-subordinate relationship between the accused and the principal perpetrator. To meet this threshold, the prosecution must merely prove some position of authority on the side of the accused, which would suffice to compel another person to commit a crime.[4] The chamber clearly pointed out that there was no direct evidence that Renzaho gave an explicit order to kill Tutsi civilians on the roadblocks, but concluded that the circumstances lead to the only inference that the accused ordered the killings.[5] As a mode of liability, ordering, is not to be proven through direct evidence, but rather through circumstantial evidence, "provided that those inferences are the only reasonable ones".[6]

In addition to this the chamber arrived to the conclusion that Renzaho ordered the establishment of roadblocks "with full knowledge that crimes were being perpetrated against Tutsi civilians".[7] Furthermore, he had knowledge of the genocidal intent of the direct perpetrators who executed the crimes and further shared the specific intent.[8] The appeals chamber commented on this point that "[o]rdering with such awareness has to be regarded as accepting that crime"[9] but concluded that the finding of the trial chamber is to be quashed because of a lack of reasoning how the elements listed, as for example his authority and his support for the erection of the roadblocks, were combined to lead to the only reasonable conclusion that Renzaho ordered the killings at the roadblocks.[10]

---

[1] ICTR, Judgment, *Prosecutor v. Renzaho,* Case No. ICTR-97-31-T, T. Ch. I, 14 July 2009, par. 79, in this volume, p. 583.
[2] ICTR, Second Amended Indictment, *Prosecutor v. Renzaho*, Case No. ICTR-97-31-I, 16 February 2006, par. 6.
[3] See for example, Judgement, *Prosecutor v. Kordić and Čerkez*, Case No. IT-95-14/2-A, A. Ch., 17 December 2004, Klip/Sluiter, ALC-XXVI-19, par. 28; ICTR, Judgement, *Prosecutor v. Semanza*, Case No. ICTR-97-20-A, A. Ch., 20 May 2005, par. 361; ICTR, Judgement, *Prosecutor v. Nahimana et.al*, Case No. ICTR-99-52-A, A. Ch., 28 November 2007, par. 481; ICTR, Judgment and Sentence, *Prosecutor v. Bagosora et al.*, Case No. ICTR-98-41-T, T. Ch. I, par. 2008.
[4] Renzaho Judgment, *supra*, note 1, par. 738.
[5] *Ibid.*, par.764.
[6] ICTR, Judgment, *Prosecutor v. Renzaho*, Case No. ICTR-97-31-A, A. Ch., 1 April 2011, par. 318 and in particular footnote 697, citing the ICTY, *Prosecutor v. Milošević*, A. Ch., IT-98-29/1-A, par. 265.
[7] Renzaho Judgment, *supra*, note 1, par. 765.
[8] *Ibid.*
[9] Appeal Judgment, *supra*, note 6, par. 315.
[10] *Ibid.*, par. 319.

In my view the appeals chamber erred by only focusing its finding on the unfortunate wording that the accused "must have equally ordered the killings".[11] Judge Pocar rightly stated in his dissenting opinion "that Renzaho's order to establish roadblocks with the awareness that the killings of Tutsi civilians [were] a likely outcome is *per se* an order to kill Tutsis".[12] Following this opinion the conclusion of the legal findings in the judgement is correct but the trial chamber failed to provide appropriate reasoning. It erred in basing its decision on the circumstantial factors of *inter alia* the position of authority of the accused and his acts in support of the roadblocks and not on his order to erect roadblocks throughout Kigali-Ville which was not disputed by the appeals chamber,[13] and would have been sufficient to establish the criminal liability for ordering the killings. In spite of that, the appeals chamber should not have reversed the count of ordering genocide, but rather should have revised the wrongful reasoning of the trial chamber, according to Art. 24, paragraph 2, ICTR Statute.

2.2 Aiding and abetting

At the outset, the chamber reiterated the differences between the concept of joint criminal enterprise and the liability as aider and abettor[14] referring to settled case-law, for example, Kvočka *et al.*[15] In Kvočka *et al.* the appeals chamber determined that for the latter the substantial contribution to the crime is a prerequisite in order to be held criminally responsible for assisting and supporting the commission of a crime. His or her intent is not directed to participate in the execution of a common purpose of a group of persons. The lack of the common purpose behind the commission of the crime reinforces the presumption that the person in question acted as aider and abettor rather than as a member of a joint criminal enterprise.[16]

The *mens rea* of the perpetrator must cover the knowledge that his or her assistance will substantially help the direct perpetrator to commit the crime. If a special intent is required, the aider and abettor "must know of the principal perpetrator's specific intent",[17] but he does not need to share it.[18] Renzaho was held criminally liable for aiding and abetting the killings of Tutsis on roadblocks. The chamber based its finding on his order to erect the roadblocks throughout Kigali-Ville and his public support for the roadblocks *inter alia* through radio broadcasts as well as through distributing weapons. His contribution facilitated and assisted the direct perpetrator to commit the crime in a substantial manner.[19] Notably the appeals chamber does not criticise the conclusion of the trial chamber that Renzaho ordered and supported the erection of roadblocks throughout Kigali-Ville regarding the charge of aiding and abetting genocide.[20]

2.3 Joint Criminal Enterprise

Furthermore, the prosecution charged the accused with the basic form of joint criminal enterprise under Art. 6, paragraph 1, ICTR Statute.[21] The chamber reiterated the three elements required for this form of joint criminal enterprise as mentioned in the Tadić case:[22] a plurality of persons, the common purpose which leads to the commission of crimes, and the participation of the accused in the common purpose which does not

---

[11] Renzaho Judgment, *supra*, note 1, par.764.
[12] ICTR, Judgment, Dissenting Opinion of Judge Pocar, *Prosecutor v. Renzaho*, Case No. ICTR-97-31-A, A. Ch., 1 April 2011, par. 11.
[13] Appeal Judgment, *supra*, note 6, par. 337. In confirming the count of aiding and abetting genocide the appeals chamber relied on the finding that the accused ordered and publicly supported the erection of roadblocks.
[14] Citing the appeals chamber judgment of Vasiljević, the appeals chamber in Renzaho clearly pointed out the requirements related to both forms of individual criminal liability in the abovementioned decision. ICTY, Judgement, *Prosecutor v. Vasiljević*, Case No. IT-98-32-A, A. Ch., 25 February 2004, Klip/ Sluiter, ALC-XIX-465, par. 102.
[15] ICTY, Judgement, *Prosecutor v. Kvočka et al*, Case No. IT-98-30/I-A, A. Ch., 28 February 2005, Klip/ Sluiter, ALC-XXVI-669, par. 90; ICTY, Judgement, *Prosecutor v. Vasiljević*, Case No. IT-98-32-A, A. Ch., 25 February 2004, Klip/ Sluiter, ALC-XIX-465, par. 133; ICTY, Judgement, *Prosecutor v. Tadić*, Case No. IT-94-1-A, A. Ch., 15 July 1999, Klip/ Sluiter, ALC-III-761, par. 229.
[16] ICTY, Judgement, *Prosecutor v. Kvočka et al*, Case No. IT-98-30/I-A, A. Ch., 28 February 2005, Klip/ Sluiter, ALC-XXVI-669, par. 90.
[17] Renzaho Judgment, *supra*, note 1, par. 742.
[18] Similarly Bagosora et al. Judgment and Sentence, *supra*, note 3, par. 2009.
[19] Renzaho Judgment, *supra*, note 1, par. 766.
[20] Appeal Judgment, *supra*, note 6, par. 337.
[21] Second Amended Indictment, *supra*, note 2, par. 6.
[22] Tadić Judgement, *supra*, note 15, par. 227.

imply that the accused was directly involved in the commission of a crime, but has assisted or otherwise contributed to the execution of the common purpose.[23]

The concept of joint criminal enterprise is not explicitly mentioned in the ICTR Statute and is the subject of divergent views.[24] The appeals chamber in Tadić clearly pointed out that this form of criminal liability falls under the scope of the wording committed in Art. 7, paragraph 1, ICTY Statute or Art. 6, paragraph 1, ICTR Statute and does not create a new category of responsibility. According to the court, the joint criminal enterprise-doctrine is established in customary international law as various judgements regarding war crimes after the Second World War have demonstrated.[25]

In the present case, on the one hand the trial chamber noted in fact that the abovementioned conditions of the basic form of joint criminal enterprise are fulfilled, but on the other hand concluded that "aiding and abetting and ordering [are] the most appropriate forms of liability" in this case.[26] Furthermore, it stated that "the legal characterization of his action as ordering and aiding and abetting or as participating in a joint criminal enterprise would not impact the Chamber's sentencing considerations."[27]

This statement is quite astonishing in particular when one considers the participation in a joint criminal enterprise in comparison to aiding and abetting to a criminal offence. On several occasions, the Appeals Chamber ruled otherwise, for instance in Krnojelac. In this case, it clearly pointed out that

> the acts of a participant in a joint criminal enterprise are more serious than those of an aider and abettor to the principal offender since a participant in a joint criminal enterprise shares intent of the principal offender whereas the aider and abettor need only be aware of that intent.[28]

The conclusion drawn by the chamber in Renzaho indicates the view widely held that the concept of joint criminal enterprise will only be used to avoid the problems caused by the difficulties to establish "a causal connection between a person's conduct and the criminal result"[29] and is far from being a well-recognized mode of liability.

2.4 Superior Responsibility

The appeals chamber noticed different problems relating to the trial chamber observations on superior liability.

2.4.1 Double Conviction

The chamber came to the conclusion that the accused was criminally liable for superior responsibility according to Art. 6, paragraph 3, ICTR Statute, but took this mode of liability into consideration as an aggravating circumstance.[30] The appeals chamber clearly pointed out the inappropriateness of a conviction under both Art. 6, paragraph 1 and 3 ICTR Statute for one specific count even if the requirements are fulfilled. For this reason it criticised the ambiguous wording of the trial chamber judgement, which used the word guilty[31] several times in relation to its findings on superior responsibility even if the Trial Chamber suggested that it would merely take it into account in sentencing as an aggravating factor.[32] Notably, this ambiguity was neither challenged by the defence nor by the prosecutor. The appeals chamber fails to assess that the prosecutor has to prove without doubt the existence of the aggravation factor, i.e. the position of the

---

[23] Renzaho Judgment, *supra*, note 1, par. 739.
[24] See for example J. Ohlin, Three Conceptual Problems within the Doctrine of Joint Criminal Enterprise, 5 Journal of International Criminal Justice 2007, p. 69 and V. Haan, The Development of the Concept of Joint Criminal Enterprise at the International Criminal Tribunal for the Former Yugoslavia, 5 International Criminal Law Review 2005, p. 174.
[25] Tadić Judgment, *supra*, note 15, par. 220.
[26] Renzaho Judgment, *supra*, note 1, footnote 868.
[27] *Ibid.*, footnotes 857, 858 and 859.
[28] ICTY, Judgement, *Prosecutor v. Krnojelac*, Case No. IT-97-25-A, A. Ch., 17 September 2003, Klip/ Sluiter, ALC-XIV-753, par. 75; see also for example Kvočka et al. Judgement, *supra*, note 15, par. 92.
[29] V. Haan, *supra*, note 24, p. 174.
[30] See above at Chapter 3, where the critical remarks of the appeals chamber are under discussion.
[31] For example Renzaho Judgment, *supra*, note 1, par. 789, regarding the killings of Charles, Wilson and Déglote Rwanga related to the attack on the Centre d'Étude de Langues Africaines (CELA).
[32] Appeal Judgment, *supra*, note 6, par. 564.

accused or his role in the context of the armed conflict in Rwanda, and not the *actus reus* and *mens rea* prerequisites of superior responsibility according to Art. 6, paragraph 3, ICTR Statute.[33]

2.4.2 Vagueness of the Indictment

The defence challenged the indictment mainly arguing that it was too vague and therefore defect. The Prosecutor had failed to clearly identify the perpetrators over whom the accused should have had authority when he charged Renzaho for his role as civil and military authority during the period of the conflict according to Art. 6, paragraph 3, ICTR Statute. The trial chamber determined that there it is no necessity that the superior can identify each particular subordinate who commits crimes "in order to incur liability under Article 6 (3) of the Statute".[34] Putting the subordinates in general categories, as e.g. gendarmes, policemen, and so on may be enough to establish superior responsibility of the accused, in particular regarding the crimes committed at the roadblocks throughout the area of the prefecture.[35] Furthermore, the chamber clearly pointed out that it appears improbable that the prosecutor could have provided more specific information on the identity of all the direct perpetrators who were involved in the commission of crimes.[36] The appeals chamber confirmed the decision of the trial chamber by referring to the settled case law.[37]

The outcome of this decision should be considered very carefully because of its possible negative impact on the rights of the accused to defend himself and to prepare a defence strategy, e.g. to present counter evidence for a specific fact. It is clear that a superior at such a high level as the accused in the present case could not identify every single subordinate in particular, the one of the lowest level, as for example, the members of the *Interahamwe*. When deciding over such an issue the chambers must balance the lack of clarity of an indictment, due to the problematic situation related to the investigation in a country which suffered an armed conflict, and must carefully evaluate the possibility that the rights of the accused have been infringed. The established principle of equality of arms should only be violated in case of weighing the rights of the accused and the right of a particular witness and not only because the investigation of the event is impossible.[38] The presumption of innocence must be respected without restrains.[39]

2.4.3 Superior responsibility for rape

The charge for rape as serious violation of Art. 4, subsection e, ICTR Statute, was brought in by the prosecution based solely on superior liability.[40] The chamber listed the facts required to establish superior responsibility under Art. 6, paragraph 3, ICTR Statute as follows:

a) [T]he existence of a superior-subordinate relationship;
b) the superior's knowledge or reason to know that the criminal act were about to be or had been committed by his subordinates; and
c) the superior's failure to take necessary and reasonable measures to prevent such criminal acts or to punish the perpetrator.[41]

The elements listed are consistent with the settled jurisprudence of the *ad hoc* tribunals.[42] The prosecution in the case under consideration argued that Renzaho, the prefect of Kigali-Ville, was the representative of the

---

[33] Renzaho Judgment, *supra*, note 1, par. 822 and ICTY, Judgment, *Prosecutor v. Blaskić*, Case No. IT-95-14-A, A. Ch., 29 July 2004, par. 686.
[34] Renzaho Judgment, *supra*, note 1, par. 751.
[35] Appeal Judgment, *supra*, note 6, par. 62, where in its appeal the defence argued that the vagueness of the indictment had made it virtually impossible to investigate and provide counter evidence against the charges based on Art. 6, paragraph 3, ICTR Statute.
[36] Renzaho Judgment, *supra*, note 1, par. 751.
[37] Appeal Judgment, *supra*, note 6, par. 64 referring to ICTR, Judgement, *Simba v. Prosecutor*, Case No. ICTR-07-76-A, A. Ch., 27 November 2007 Klip/ Sluiter, ALC-XXV-817, par. 72.
[38] See for more information on the principle of equality of arms C. Safferling, International Criminal Procedure, Oxford University Press, Oxford 2012, p. 410.
[39] C. Safferling, Towards an International Criminal Procedure, Oxford University Press, Oxford 2001, p. 256.
[40] Second Amended Indictment, *supra*, note 2, par. 41.
[41] Renzaho Judgment, *supra*, note 1, par. 744.
[42] For example Bagosora et al., *supra*, note 3, par. 2011; Judgement, *Prosecutor v. Halilović*, Case No. IT-01-48, T. Ch. I, 16 November 2005, Klip/ Sluiter, ALC-XXVII-475, par. 56.

national government at this time and therefore "had the *de jure* and *de facto* control" and could have used his influence to urge the persons under his control to refrain from the commission of unlawful acts.[43]

These considerations were subscribed in the judgement; furthermore, in citing a number of decisions of the *ad hoc* tribunals the chamber reiterated the prerequisites for establishing the effective control of the superior over his or her subordinates, i.e. the material ability to prevent the commission of a crime or to punish the perpetrator.[44] The chamber came to the conclusion that Renzaho exercised effective control over the local officials, with certain qualifications over the soldiers and gendarmes and in his function as chairman of the civil defence committee for Kigali over militiamen including members of the *Interahamwe*.[45]

On appeal however, the chamber ascertained a defect in the indictment.[46] The trial chamber substantiated its finding of *mens rea* regarding the superior responsibility for rape on the fact that the accused had vocally encouraged the commission of the crime,[47] a fact which was not contained in the indictment.[48] The appeals chamber emphasised that the burden of proof that the right of the accused to prepare his defence case was not affected rests on the prosecution because the defence had challenged the vagueness of the indictment on several occasions during the main proceedings. If the defence alleges this claim for the first time in appeal the onus would lie on the accused. Finally, the appeals chamber concluded that the standard required could not be reached by the prosecutor[49] because he failed to clearly point out the key element of the prosecution case, i.e. to establish the *mens rea* of the accused on his vocal encouragement, in the prosecution pre-trial brief to the defence and therefore, the appeals chamber reversed the finding of the trial chamber on this charge.

3. Conclusion

The judgement in the case of Renzaho has shown that even if the chambers referring to other decisions and on settled case law there are always problems which have to be examined on a case-by-case basis. A main point of critique is the inadvertence of the trial chamber regarding its reasoning. It clearly erred in its reasoning regarding the conviction of the accused for ordering killings at the roadblocks even if its legal finding was correct. The use of phrases like "Renzaho must have equally ordered the killings there"[50] does not appear elaborated. Furthermore, the chamber based its finding regarding superior responsibility on facts not contained in the indictment which was challenged by the defence several times during trial.

The modes of liability will always be reason for controversy, in particular the participation in a joint criminal enterprise. In the present case the chamber succinctly noted in a footnote that ordering and aiding and abetting are more adequate modes of liability without really pointing out that participation in a joint criminal enterprise requires a higher threshold of *mens rea* than aiding and abetting. The reasoning of the trial chamber is not convincing, neither for the accused and his rights, nor for the victims.

Hilde Farthofer

---

[43] Second Amended Indictment, *supra*, note 2, par. 2, section C.
[44] Renzaho Judgment, *supra*, note 1, par. 745.
[45] Ibid., par.753.
[46] Appeal Judgment, *supra*, note 6, par. 129.
[47] Renzaho Judgment, *supra*, note 1, par. 775 and 777.
[48] See the relevant part of Second Amended Indictment, *supra*, note 2, par. 43.
[49] Appeal Judgment, *supra*, note 6, par. 126.
[50] Renzaho Judgment, *supra*, note 1, par. 764.

Tribunal pénal international pour le Rwanda
International Criminal Tribunal for Rwanda

IN THE APPEALS CHAMBER

Before: Judge Theodor Meron, Presiding
Judge Mehmet Güney
Judge Fausto Pocar
Judge Liu Daqun
Judge Carmel Agius

Registrar: Mr. Adama Dieng

Judgement of: 16 November 2009

PROTAIS ZIGIRANYIRAZO

v.

THE PROSECUTOR

Case No. ICTR-01-73-A

JUDGEMENT

Counsel for Protais Zigiranyirazo:

Mr. John Philpot
Mr. Peter Zaduk
Ms. Fiona Gray
Mr. Kyle Gervais

Counsel for Co-Accused:

Ms. Dior Diagne Mbaye and Mr. Félix Sow for Édouard Karemera

The Office of the Prosecutor:

Mr. Hassan Bubacar Jallow
Mr. Alex Obote-Odora
Ms. Christine Graham
Ms. Linda Bianchi
Ms. Béatrice Chapaux
Mr. Alfred Orono Orono

[page i] I. INTRODUCTION 1
A. Background 1
B. The Appeals 2

II. STANDARDS OF APPELLATE REVIEW 3

III. APPEAL OF PROTAIS ZIGIRANYIRAZO 5
A. Alleged Errors in Evaluating the Alibi (Grounds 6 and 12) 5
1. Burden of Proof in the Assessment of Alibi 5
2. Alleged Errors in Evaluating Exculpatory Evidence Related to Kesho Hill (Ground 6) 7
3. Alleged Errors in Evaluating Exculpatory Evidence Related to Kiyovu Roadblock (Ground 12) ... 19
4. Conclusion 27
B. Other Grounds of Appeal (Grounds 13 to 16) 28

IV. SENTENCING APPEALS (ZIGIRANYIRAZO'S GROUND 17 AND PROSECUTION APPEAL) 29

V. DISPOSITION 30

VI. ANNEX A – PROCEDURAL HISTORY 1
A. Notices of Appeal and Briefs 1
1. Zigiranyirazo Appeal 1
2. Prosecution Appeal 1
B. Assignment of Judges 2
C. Motions Related to Hearing Additional Evidence on Appeal 2
D. Hearing of the Appeals 3

VII. ANNEX B – CITED MATERIALS AND DEFINED TERMS 4
A. Jurisprudence 4
1. ICTR 4
2. ICTY 6
B. Defined Terms and Abbreviations 7

Judgement

[page 1] 1. The Appeals Chamber of the International Criminal Tribunal for the Prosecution of Persons Responsible for Genocide and Other Serious Violations of International Humanitarian Law Committed in the Territory of Rwanda and Rwandan Citizens Responsible for Genocide and Other Such Violations Committed in the Territory of Neighbouring States between 1 January 1994 and 31 December 1994 ("Appeals Chamber" and "Tribunal," respectively) is seized of appeals by Protais Zigiranyirazo ("Zigiranyirazo") and the Prosecution against the Judgement rendered by Trial Chamber III of the Tribunal ("Trial Chamber") on 18 December 2008 in the case of *The Prosecutor v. Protais Zigiranyirazo* ("Trial Judgement").[1]

I. INTRODUCTION

A. Background

2. Zigiranyirazo was born on 2 February 1938 in Giciye Commune, Gisenyi Prefecture, Rwanda.[2] He was the brother-in-law of the late former President of Rwanda, Juvenal Habyarimana.[3] Zigiranyirazo became a Member of Parliament in 1969.[4] In 1973, he was appointed Prefect of Kibuye and then served as Prefect of Ruhengeri from 1974 until 1989.[5] After his resignation, he studied in Canada and returned to Rwanda in 1993 to work as a businessman.[6]

3. The Trial Chamber convicted Zigiranyirazo pursuant to Article 6(1) of the Statute of the Tribunal ("Statute") for committing genocide (Count 2) and extermination as a crime against humanity (Count 4) by participating in a joint criminal enterprise to kill Tutsis at Kesho Hill in Gisenyi Prefecture on 8 April 1994, where assailants attacked and killed between 800 and 1,500 Tutsi refugees.[7] In addition, it convicted Zigiranyirazo pursuant to Article 6(1) of the Statute for aiding and abetting genocide (Count 2) at the Kiyovu Roadblock in Kigali, where between 10 and 20 persons were killed.[8]

4. For his genocide conviction in relation to the events at Kesho Hill, the Trial Chamber sentenced Zigiranyirazo to 20 years of imprisonment.[9] For his genocide conviction in relation to the events at the Kiyovu Roadblock, it sentenced him to 15 years of imprisonment.[10] For his conviction [page 2] for extermination as a crime against humanity in relation to the events at Kesho Hill, Zigiranyirazo received a sentence of 20 years of imprisonment.[11] The Trial Chamber ordered that these sentences be served concurrently.[12]

B. The Appeals

5. Zigiranyirazo presents seventeen grounds of appeal challenging his convictions and his sentences. He requests that the Appeals Chamber overturn his convictions or, alternatively, reduce his sentences.[13] The Prosecution responds that all grounds of Zigiranyirazo's appeal should be dismissed.[14]

---

[1] For ease of reference, two annexes are appended: Annex A – Procedural History and Annex B – Cited Materials and Defined Terms.
[2] Trial Judgement, para. 4.
[3] Trial Judgement, para. 4.
[4] Trial Judgement, para. 5.
[5] Trial Judgement, para. 5.
[6] Trial Judgement, para. 5.
[7] Trial Judgement, paras. 330, 410, 427, 436, 439, 447.
[8] Trial Judgement, paras. 251, 426, 427, 447.
[9] Trial Judgement, para. 468.
[10] Trial Judgement, para. 469.
[11] Trial Judgement, para. 470.
[12] Trial Judgement, para. 471.
[13] Zigiranyirazo Notice of Appeal, p. 10; Zigiranyirazo Appeal Brief, paras. 8, 467-469. In his Notice of Appeal, Zigiranyirazo also requested, in the alternative, a new trial. *See* Zigiranyirazo Notice of Appeal, p. 10. However, in his Appeal Brief, this form of relief is abandoned because, in his view, once the errors in law and fact have been corrected, the evidence is "overwhelmingly favourable to him." *See* Zigiranyirazo Appeal Brief, para. 467.
[14] Prosecution Response Brief, paras. 1, 274.

6. The Prosecution presents a single ground of appeal challenging Zigiranyirazo's sentences,[15] requesting the Appeals Chamber to impose a life sentence or, alternatively, a total effective sentence greater than 20 years of imprisonment.[16] Zigiranyirazo responds that the Prosecution's appeal should be dismissed.[17]

7. The Appeals Chamber heard oral submissions regarding these appeals on 28 September 2009. [page 3]

II. STANDARDS OF APPELLATE REVIEW

8. The Appeals Chamber recalls the applicable standards of appellate review pursuant to Article 24 of the Statute. The Appeals Chamber reviews only errors of law which invalidate the decision of the Trial Chamber and errors of fact which have occasioned a miscarriage of justice.[18]

9. Regarding errors of law, the Appeals Chamber has stated:

> Where a party alleges that there is an error of law, that party must advance arguments in support of the submission and explain how the error invalidates the decision. However, if the appellant's arguments do not support the contention, that party does not automatically lose its point since the Appeals Chamber may step in and, for other reasons, find in favour of the contention that there is an error of law.[19]

10. Where the Appeals Chamber finds an error of law in the trial judgement arising from the application of an incorrect legal standard, the Appeals Chamber will articulate the correct legal interpretation and review the relevant factual findings of the Trial Chamber accordingly.[20] In so doing, the Appeals Chamber not only corrects the legal error, but, when necessary, also applies the correct legal standard to the evidence contained in the trial record and determines whether it is itself convinced beyond reasonable doubt as to the factual finding challenged by the appellant before the finding may be confirmed on appeal.[21]

11. Regarding errors of fact, it is well established that the Appeals Chamber will not lightly overturn findings of fact made by the Trial Chamber:

> Where the Defence alleges an erroneous finding of fact, the Appeals Chamber must give deference to the Trial Chamber that received the evidence at trial, and it will only interfere in those findings where no reasonable trier of fact could have reached the same finding or where the finding is wholly erroneous. Furthermore, the erroneous finding will be revoked or revised only if the error occasioned a miscarriage of justice.[22]

12. A party cannot merely repeat on appeal arguments that did not succeed at trial, unless it can demonstrate that the Trial Chamber's rejection of those arguments constituted an error warranting the intervention of the Appeals Chamber.[23] Arguments which do not have the potential to cause the [page 4] impugned decision to be reversed or revised may be immediately dismissed by the Appeals Chamber and need not be considered on the merits.[24]

13. In order for the Appeals Chamber to assess arguments on appeal, the appealing party must provide precise references to relevant transcript pages or paragraphs in the decision or judgement to which the

---

[15] Prosecution Notice of Appeal, paras. 1-5; Prosecution Appeal Brief, para. 4.
[16] Prosecution Notice of Appeal, para. 5; Prosecution Appeal Brief, paras. 5, 104. The Appeals Chamber notes that, in its Notice of Appeal, the Prosecution only requested the imposition of life imprisonment. *See* Prosecution Notice of Appeal, para. 5.
[17] Zigiranyirazo Response Brief, para. 109.
[18] *Karera* Appeal Judgement, para. 7; *Muvunyi* Appeal Judgement, para. 8; *Seromba* Appeal Judgement, para. 9. *See also Mrkšić and Šljivančanin* Appeal Judgement, para. 10.
[19] *Ntakirutimana* Appeal Judgement, para. 11 (internal citation omitted). *See also Karera* Appeal Judgement, para. 8; *Muvunyi* Appeal Judgement, para. 9; *Seromba* Appeal Judgement, para. 10; *Mrkšić and Šljivančanin* Appeal Judgement, para. 11.
[20] *Karera* Appeal Judgement, para. 9. *See also Mrkšić and Šljivančanin* Appeal Judgement, para. 12.
[21] *Karera* Appeal Judgement, para. 9. *See also Mrkšić and Šljivančanin* Appeal Judgement, para. 12.
[22] *Krstić* Appeal Judgement, para. 40 (internal citations omitted). *See also Karera* Appeal Judgement, para. 10; *Muvunyi* Appeal Judgement, para. 10; *Seromba* Appeal Judgement, para. 11.
[23] *Karera* Appeal Judgement, para. 11; *Muvunyi* Appeal Judgement, para. 11; *Seromba* Appeal Judgement, para. 12; *Muhimana* Appeal Judgement, para. 9. *See also Mrkšić and Šljivančanin* Appeal Judgement, para. 16.
[24] *Karera* Appeal Judgement, para. 11; *Muvunyi* Appeal Judgement, para. 11; *Seromba* Appeal Judgement, para. 12; *Muhimana* Appeal Judgement, para. 9. *See also Mrkšić and Šljivančanin* Appeal Judgement, para. 16.

challenge is made.[25] Moreover, the Appeals Chamber cannot be expected to consider a party's submissions in detail if they are obscure, contradictory, vague, or suffer from other formal and obvious insufficiencies.[26] Finally, the Appeals Chamber has inherent discretion in selecting which submissions merit a detailed reasoned opinion in writing, and it will dismiss arguments which are evidently unfounded without providing detailed reasoning.[27] **[page 5]**

III. APPEAL OF PROTAIS ZIGIRANYIRAZO

A. Alleged Errors in Evaluating the Alibi (Grounds 6 and 12)

14. The Appeals Chamber first addresses Zigiranyirazo's Sixth and Twelfth Grounds of Appeal, which challenge the Trial Chamber's consideration of his alibi relating to both the Kesho Hill and Kiyovu Roadblock events.[28] The Trial Chamber found that Zigiranyirazo was present at Kesho Hill in Gisenyi Prefecture at some point on the morning of 8 April 1994 and that he addressed the assailants assembled there before they launched an attack on Tutsi refugees.[29] The Trial Chamber also determined that he was present at the Kiyovu Roadblock, near his residence in Kigali, on 12 and 17 April 1994, where he aided and abetted killings.[30]

15. In respect of both events, Zigiranyirazo presented an alibi, which, for the most part, the Trial Chamber did not discount, placing him at the Presidential residence at Camp Kanombe just outside Kigali ("Kanombe") during the attack at Kesho Hill and at the Rubaya Tea Factory ("Rubaya") in Gisenyi Prefecture at the time when he was supposedly seen at the Kiyovu Roadblock.[31] In addition, at trial, Zigiranyirazo argued with regard to both events that the distance between Gisenyi Prefecture and the Kigali area as well as the difficulty of travel between the two regions in April 1994 corroborated his alibi.[32] The Trial Chamber did not expressly discuss this circumstantial evidence.

1. Burden of Proof in the Assessment of Alibi

16. On appeal, Zigiranyirazo submits that the Trial Chamber reversed the burden of proof and committed a number of other legal and factual errors in its assessment of his alibi for both Kesho Hill and the Kiyovu Roadblock events.[33] Accordingly, at the outset, the Appeals Chamber considers it appropriate to recall the basic principles with respect to the proper assessment of alibi evidence before considering Zigiranyirazo's specific contentions.

17. An alibi does not constitute a defence in its proper sense.[34] By raising an alibi, an accused is simply denying that he was in a position to commit the crime with which he was charged.[35] An **[page 6]** accused does not bear the burden of proving his alibi beyond reasonable doubt.[36] Rather, "[h]e must simply produce

---

[25] Practice Direction on Formal Requirements for Appeals from Judgement, para. 4(b). See *Karera* Appeal Judgement, para. 12; *Muvunyi* Appeal Judgement, para. 12; *Seromba* Appeal Judgement, para. 13; *Muhimana* Appeal Judgement, para. 10. See also *Mrkšić and Šljivančanin* Appeal Judgement, para. 17.
[26] *Karera* Appeal Judgement, para. 12; *Muvunyi* Appeal Judgement, para. 12; *Seromba* Appeal Judgement, para. 13; *Muhimana* Appeal Judgement, para. 10. See also *Mrkšić and Šljivančanin* Appeal Judgement, para. 17.
[27] *Karera* Appeal Judgement, para. 12; *Muvunyi* Appeal Judgement, para. 12; *Seromba* Appeal Judgement, para. 13; *Muhimana* Appeal Judgement, para. 10. See also *Mrkšić and Šljivančanin* Appeal Judgement, para. 18.
[28] Zigiranyirazo Notice of Appeal, paras. 6, 12.
[29] Trial Judgement, paras. 329, 330, 400, 401.
[30] Trial Judgement, paras. 251, 413, 427.
[31] Trial Judgement, paras. 231, 245-250, 301, 323.
[32] Zigiranyirazo Appeal Brief, para. 116, *citing* Defence Closing Brief, paras. 157-167, 229, 230, 237, 249, 350, 851-854.
[33] See *infra* Section III.A.2 (Ground 6: Alleged Errors in Evaluating Exculpatory Evidence Related to Kesho Hill; Section III.A.3 (Ground 12: Alleged Errors in Evaluating Exculpatory Evidence Related to Kiyovu Roadblock).
[34] *Ndindabahizi* Appeal Judgement, para. 66; *Kajelijeli* Appeal Judgement, paras. 41, 42; *Kayishema and Ruzindana* Appeal Judgement, para. 106; *Delalić et al.* Appeal Judgement, para. 581.
[35] *Nahimana et al.* Appeal Judgement, para. 414; *Ndindabahizi* Appeal Judgement, para. 66; *Kajelijeli* Appeal Judgement, paras. 41, 42; *Niyitegeka* Appeal Judgement, para. 60; *Musema* Appeal Judgement, paras. 205, 206; *Kayishema and Ruzindana* Appeal Judgement, para. 106; *Delalić et al.* Appeal Judgement, para. 581.
[36] *Nahimana et al.* Appeal Judgement, para. 414; *Simba* Appeal Judgement, para. 184; *Karera* Appeal Judgement, para. 331; *Musema* Appeal Judgement, para. 202; *Kayishema and Ruzindana* Appeal Judgement, para. 107.

the evidence tending to show that he was not present at the time of the alleged crime"[37] or, otherwise stated, present evidence "likely to raise a reasonable doubt in the Prosecution case."[38] If the alibi is reasonably possibly true, it must be accepted.[39]

18. Where an alibi is properly raised, the Prosecution must establish beyond reasonable doubt that, despite the alibi, the facts alleged are nevertheless true.[40] The Prosecution may do so, for instance, by demonstrating that the alibi does not in fact reasonably account for the period when the accused is alleged to have committed the crime. Where the alibi evidence does *prima facie* account for the accused's activities at the relevant time of the commission of the crime, the Prosecution must "eliminate the reasonable possibility that the alibi is true,"[41] for example, by demonstrating that the alibi evidence is not credible.

19. The Appeals Chamber has considered on several occasions whether Trial Chambers have erroneously shifted the burden of proof to the accused with respect to their alibis. Appellants have frequently pointed to language in the assessment of alibi evidence intimating that they were required to disprove the Prosecution's evidence through their alibis. The Appeals Chamber has recognized that language which suggests, *inter alia*, that an accused must "negate" the Prosecution's evidence,[42] "exonerate" himself,[43] or "refute the possibility" that he participated in a **[page 7]** crime[44] indicates that the Trial Chamber misapplied the burden of proof. Indeed, as stated in the *Musema* Appeal Judgement, "[i]n considering the manner in which the Trial Chamber applied the burden and standard of proof, the Appeals Chamber must start off by assuming that the words used in the Trial Judgement accurately describe the approach adopted by the Trial Chamber."[45]

20. In assessing whether a Trial Chamber, when using this type of language, has in fact shifted the burden of proof, the Appeals Chamber carries out an in-depth analysis of the specific findings related to a given incident.[46] The Appeals Chamber has generally found that such language, while inappropriate, is not fatal when viewed in the broader context of a Trial Chamber's findings. This is especially the case where the Trial Chamber accurately refers elsewhere in the judgement to the appropriate burden of proof for the evaluation of alibi evidence, its overall approach evinces a careful assessment of the alibi evidence, and its conclusion that the alibi evidence is ultimately not credible is reasonable when weighed against the evidence of participation in a crime.[47]

---

[37] *Musema* Appeal Judgement, para. 202.

[38] *Karera* Appeal Judgement, para. 331 (internal citation omitted); *Simba* Appeal Judgement, para. 184 (internal citation omitted); *Kajelijeli* Appeal Judgement, para. 42 (internal citation omitted); *Niyitegeka* Appeal Judgement, para. 60.

[39] *Nahimana et al.* Appeal Judgement, para. 414; *Kamuhanda* Appeal Judgement, para. 38; *Kajelijeli* Appeal Judgement, para. 41; *Musema* Appeal Judgement, paras. 205, 206.

[40] *Karera* Appeal Judgement, para. 330; *Nahimana et al.* Appeal Judgement, para. 414; *Simba* Appeal Judgement, para. 184; *Kajelijeli* Appeal Judgement, para. 42; *Niyitegeka* Appeal Judgement, para. 60; *Musema* Appeal Judgement, paras. 205, 206; *Kayishema and Ruzindana* Appeal Judgement, para. 107. *See also Limaj et al.* Appeal Judgement, para. 64, *quoting Limaj et al.* Trial Judgement, para. 11 ("[A] finding that an alibi is false does not in itself 'establish the opposite to what it asserts'. The Prosecution must not only rebut the validity of the alibi but also establish beyond reasonable doubt the guilt of the Accused as alleged in the Indictment.").

[41] *Kajelijeli* Appeal Judgement, para. 41 (internal citation omitted); *Kayishema and Ruzindana* Appeal Judgement, para. 106 (internal citation omitted). *See also Limaj et al.* Appeal Judgement, paras. 64, 65 (internal citation omitted); *Delalić et al.* Appeal Judgement, para. 581.

[42] *See Limaj et al.* Appeal Judgement, para. 65 ("When evaluating Haradin Bala's alibi evidence, the Trial Chamber observed that 'the testimony of most of the witnesses for the Defence for Haradin Bala does not necessarily negate the evidence that Haradin Bala remained in Llapushnik/Lapušnik after the end of May.' The use of the phrase 'to negate the evidence' could be read in the sense that the Trial Chamber required Haradin Bala to negate the Prosecution evidence"), *quoting Limaj et al.* Trial Judgement, para. 647.

[43] *See Kamuhanda* Appeal Judgement, para. 39 ("the Appeals Chamber notes that in some instances the Trial Chamber applied language which *prima facie* supports the Appellant's arguments [that the Trial Chamber shifted the burden of proof], for example in paragraph 174 of the [*Kamuhanda*] Trial Judgement: '[…] the evidence of Witness ALB does not *exonerate* the Accused from being present at Gikomero.'") (emphasis in original).

[44] *See Musema* Appeal Judgement, para. 295 ("The wording *'are by themselves, insufficient to refute the possibility'* used by the Trial Chamber with respect to alibi evidence might be an error on a point of law, had Musema's evidence been sufficient to sustain a potential alibi.") (emphasis in original), *quoting Musema* Trial Judgement, para. 740.

[45] *Musema* Appeal Judgement, para. 209.

[46] *See, e.g., Musema* Appeal Judgement, paras. 210, 211.

[47] *See, e.g., Limaj et al.* Appeal Judgement, para. 65; *Kamuhanda* Appeal Judgement, paras. 38-44; *Musema* Appeal Judgement, paras. 317, 318.

2. Alleged Errors in Evaluating Exculpatory Evidence Related to Kesho Hill (Ground 6)

(a) Introduction

21. The Trial Chamber convicted Zigiranyirazo of genocide and extermination as a crime against humanity based on his participation in a joint criminal enterprise to kill Tutsi civilians at Kesho Hill in Gisenyi Prefecture.[48] The Trial Chamber found that he was present at Kesho Hill at some point on the morning of 8 April 1994 and that he addressed the assembled assailants before they launched an attack on the Tutsi refugees there.[49] As part of his defence, Zigiranyirazo presented evidence that he was not observed at Kesho Hill during the attack.[50] The Trial Chamber did not find this evidence to be credible or to have probative value.[51]

22. In addition, Zigiranyirazo presented an alibi, supported by nine witnesses who testified that he remained at Kanombe on 8 April 1994.[52] One witness placed him at Kanombe around 8.00 a.m., and two witnesses saw him there around 3.00 or 4.00 p.m.[53] Another witness stated that he saw **[page 8]** Zigiranyirazo there around 1.00 p.m., but the Trial Chamber did not accept this testimony as it concluded that it conflicted with other Defence evidence.[54] Other witnesses recalled seeing Zigiranyirazo at Kanombe, but did not recall the specific times at which they saw him.[55] After assessing the nine alibi witnesses, the Trial Chamber concluded:

> [A]lthough the Chamber does not discount the evidence of these Defence Witnesses, other than Gloria Mukampunga, for reasons explained above, the Chamber finds that their evidence is too vague and does not place [Zigiranyirazo] at Kanombe at the specific times he was seen at Kesho Hill.[56]

23. At trial, Zigiranyirazo referred to evidence regarding the distance between Kanombe and Kesho Hill to demonstrate that, in light of the alibi evidence, it would have been impossible for him to have been at both places on the same day.[57] In particular, he referred to the Trial Chamber's site visit, conducted from 12 to 16 November 2007, which purportedly retraced the route taken by Zigiranyirazo and his family when they fled from Kanombe to Gisenyi Prefecture on 11 April 1994. The Trial Chamber did not expressly refer to or discuss the site visit or the specifics of travel between Kanombe and Kesho Hill on 8 April 1994.[58]

24. Zigiranyirazo submits that, in convicting him of participating in the Kesho Hill massacre on 8 April 1994, the Trial Chamber erred in law and in fact in assessing his alibi as well as other evidence which raises doubt about his presence there.[59] In sub-grounds (a), (b), and (f) of this ground of appeal, Zigiranyirazo challenges the Trial Chamber's assessment of his alibi.[60] In sub-grounds (c), (d), and (e), he argues that the Trial Chamber improperly discounted evidence demonstrating that he was not at Kesho Hill on 8 April 1994.[61]

25. The Trial Chamber did not definitively establish the time when Zigiranyirazo was present at Kesho Hill on the morning of 8 April 1994.[62] However, it follows from the evidence of Witnesses AKK and AKL,

---

[48] Trial Judgement, paras. 410, 436, 447.
[49] Trial Judgement, paras. 329, 330, 400, 401.
[50] Trial Judgement, paras. 288-300.
[51] Trial Judgement, paras. 319-322.
[52] Trial Judgement, paras. 301, 323.
[53] Trial Judgement, paras. 324, 327.
[54] Trial Judgement, para. 325.
[55] Trial Judgement, para. 323.
[56] Trial Judgement, para. 328.
[57] *See supra* n. 32. Of the cited paragraphs in Zigiranyirazo's Defence Closing Brief, referred to above, paragraphs 163 to 166 and 851 to 854 do not address the events at Kesho Hill but rather those at the Kiyovu Roadblock.
[58] The Trial Judgement contains only one reference to the site visit in the procedural history. *See* Trial Judgement, Annex I: Procedural History, para. 34.
[59] Zigiranyirazo Notice of Appeal, para. 6; Zigiranyirazo Appeal Brief, paras. 89-231.
[60] Zigiranyirazo Notice of Appeal, para. 6(a, b, f); Zigiranyirazo Appeal Brief, paras. 94-175, 224-231.
[61] Zigiranyirazo Notice of Appeal, para. 6(c, d, e); Zigiranyirazo Appeal Brief, paras. 176-223.
[62] Trial Judgement, para. 329 ("The Chamber finds beyond reasonable doubt that, following an unsuccessful attack on Tutsi at Kesho Hill, [Zigiranyirazo] arrived at hill [*sic*], *on the morning of 8 April 1994*, [...]") (emphasis added).

on which the Trial Chamber's findings principally rest,[63] that Zigiranyirazo was there briefly sometime between 9.30 and 11.00 a.m.[64] **[page 9]**

26. In making its findings on Zigiranyirazo's presence at Kesho Hill, the Trial Chamber considered the evidence of nine alibi witnesses who placed him at Kanombe at various points on 8 April 1994.[65] The Trial Chamber noted that Witnesses Agnès Kampundu, Jeanne Marie Habyarimana, Marie Chantel Kamushiga, Bernadette Niyonizeye, and Aimé Marie Ntuye recalled seeing Zigiranyirazo at Kanombe on 8 April 1994, but explained that they did not refer to specific times when they saw Zigiranyirazo at Kanombe or provide detailed evidence on his activities.[66]

27. In addition, the Trial Chamber credited two alibi witness as placing Zigiranyirazo at Kanombe at specific times: Witness Séraphin Bararengana at around 3.30 or 4.00 p.m. and Witness Marguérite Mukobwajana at around 8.00 a.m. and again around 3.00 or 4.00 p.m.[67] The Trial Chamber also stated that Witness Jean Luc Habyarimana testified he saw Zigiranyirazo around 1.00 p.m., speaking with Witness Bararengana.[68] However, the Trial Chamber chose not to consider this latter testimony, on the basis that it contradicted Witness Bararengana, who testified that Zigiranyirazo only arrived at Kanombe around 3.00 or 3.30 p.m.[69] The Trial Chamber did not consider that the evidence of Witnesses Bararengana and Mukobwajana provided Zigiranyirazo with an alibi for the period on 8 April 1994 when he was seen at Kesho Hill.[70]

28. Witness Gloria Mukampunga also testified that she saw Zigiranyirazo at Kanombe around lunchtime, but given her young age at the time and other credibility concerns, the Trial Chamber was not convinced that she saw Zigiranyirazo on 8 April 1994.[71] Zigiranyirazo sought to present a tenth alibi witness, Witness BNZ60, but the Trial Chamber denied his application to hear her testimony by video-link from Belgium because it would have been "repetitive and cumulative" of the other alibi evidence.[72] **[page 10]**

(b) Submissions

29. Zigiranyirazo submits that the Trial Chamber erred in law and fact in evaluating the alibi evidence.[73] In particular, Zigiranyirazo argues that, in finding that he had no alibi between 8.00 a.m. and 3.30 p.m., the Trial Chamber misapplied the evidentiary burden for an alibi as well as the law governing corroboration by failing to assess the testimonies of all alibi witnesses in their totality, failing to consider whether the individual testimonies corroborate each other despite minor differences, and failing to weigh these testimonies against the Prosecution evidence.[74] According to Zigiranyirazo, he met the threshold burden necessary to establish his alibi for 8 April 1994 based on the consistent testimony of his nine alibi witnesses.[75] He argues that the Trial Chamber failed to consider the key question of whether his alibi, viewed in its totality, was reasonably possibly true.[76] Furthermore, he submits that the Trial Chamber misconstrued the

---

[63] While the Trial Chamber gave varying degrees of credit to five different witnesses concerning the events, its findings rest principally on the testimony of only two of them, Witnesses AKK and AKL. *See* Trial Judgement, para. 316 ("Accordingly, with regard to the Prosecution Witnesses who witnessed events at Kesho Hill, the Chamber accepts the evidence of Witness AKK. It further accepts the testimony of Witness AKL, but does not accept his recollection of the words spoken by the Accused without credible corroboration. With regard to Witnesses AKP, AKR and AKO, in view of concerns regarding their testimonies, the Chamber accepts their evidence only to the extent that it is corroborated by Witnesses AKK and AKL."), para. 329 ("Accordingly, the Chamber makes the following findings on the basis of the testimonies of Prosecution Witnesses AKK, AKL, and also of Witnesses AKP, AKR and AKO to the extent that the testimony of the latter three is corroborated by credible evidence.").
[64] Witness AKL suggested that Zigiranyirazo arrived around 9.30 or 10.00 a.m., and Witness AKK placed his arrival between around 10:00 or 11:00 a.m. *See* Trial Judgement, paras. 254, 265, 267.
[65] Trial Judgement, paras. 301, 323-328.
[66] Trial Judgement, paras. 323, 328.
[67] Trial Judgement, paras. 324, 327.
[68] Trial Judgement, para. 325.
[69] Trial Judgement, paras. 324, 325.
[70] Trial Judgement, paras. 324, 325, 327, 328.
[71] Trial Judgement, paras. 326, 328.
[72] *The Prosecutor v. Protais Zigiranyirazo*, Case No. ICTR-2001-73-T, Decision on Defence Motion for a Hearing by Video-Link for Protected Witness BNZ60 and Mr. Gaspart Musabyimana, 9 November 2007, para. 8.
[73] Zigiranyirazo Notice of Appeal, para. 6(b); Zigiranyirazo Appeal Brief, paras. 130-174.
[74] Zigiranyirazo Appeal Brief, paras. 131-134; Zigiranyirazo Reply Brief, paras. 47-50.
[75] Zigiranyirazo Appeal Brief, paras. 135-137, 160-171.
[76] Zigiranyirazo Appeal Brief, paras. 154-158.

Judgement

testimony of two key witnesses, Jean Luc Habyarimana and Marguérite Mukobwajana.[77] He contends that a proper reading of their evidence shows that he was in fact at Kanombe around 1.00 p.m. on 8 April 1994.[78]

30. In addition, Zigiranyirazo submits that the Trial Chamber erred in law in failing both to maintain a record of the site visit and to consider the exculpatory evidence it revealed, namely the impossibility of making a return trip between Kanombe and Kesho Hill during the relevant time period on 8 April 1994, for which it had determined that he had not established an alibi.[79] According to Zigiranyirazo, it took the Trial Chamber approximately 10 hours to travel the distance from Kanombe to Rubaya.[80] He also acknowledges a shorter "theoretical" alternative itinerary, which, based on the site visit, would have resulted in a one-way journey of approximately six hours.[81] However, given the evidence of the difficulty of travel between Kanombe and Kigali at the time, Zigiranyirazo suggests that the alternative shorter itinerary is unlikely to have been possible.[82]

31. Zigiranyirazo notes that the Trial Chamber accepted evidence placing him at Kanombe around 8.00 a.m. and again around 3.30 or 4.00 p.m.[83] Accordingly, he emphasizes that the length of time needed to travel the distance between Kanombe and Kesho Hill was of crucial importance in determining whether he had an alibi for the morning of 8 April 1994.[84] He notes that he fully **[page 11]** argued this issue at trial and that it was "at the heart of the alibi defence."[85] Zigiranyirazo submits that the Trial Chamber's failure to address this issue indicates that it did not consider this evidence and thus violated his right to a reasoned opinion.[86] He argues that, in view of the travel time between Kanombe and Kesho Hill, the Trial Chamber's findings with respect to his presence during the attack on the hill on the morning of 8 April 1994 are impossible, and that these errors thus invalidate the verdict.[87]

32. The Prosecution responds that the Trial Chamber did not err in its assessment of Zigiranyirazo's alibi, the site visit, or the feasibility of travel to the extent that correction on appeal is required.[88] It contends that the Trial Chamber did not err in law in determining that Zigiranyirazo did not have an alibi between 8.00 a.m. and 3.30 p.m. on 8 April 1994.[89] The Prosecution submits that Zigiranyirazo's evidence did not place him at Kanombe during the relevant time and that the strength of the Prosecution evidence eliminated the reasonable possibility that the alibi was true.[90] The Prosecution contends that the Trial Chamber duly noted and assessed Zigiranyirazo's alibi evidence, bearing in mind its duty to assess the evidence in light of the totality of the record, as well as the Prosecution's burden to prove guilt beyond a reasonable doubt.[91] According to the Prosecution, in finding the alibi evidence vague and inconclusive, the Trial Chamber considered it in its entirety and determined that it did not raise any doubt against the Prosecution's case.[92]

33. The Prosecution concedes that the Trial Chamber misstated Witness Jean Luc Habyarimana's testimony, but nonetheless considers its overall rejection of his evidence along with that of Witness Mukobwajana to be reasonable.[93] In particular, it contends that the two witnesses provided contradictory

---

[77] Zigiranyirazo Appeal Brief, paras. 139-153.
[78] Zigiranyirazo Appeal Brief, paras. 141, 143, 152, 153.
[79] Zigiranyirazo Notice of Appeal, para. 6(a); Zigiranyirazo Appeal Brief, paras. 94-129.
[80] Zigiranyirazo Appeal Brief, paras. 98, 99; Zigiranyirazo Reply Brief, para. 30.
[81] Zigiranyirazo Appeal Brief, para. 119; Zigiranyirazo Reply Brief, para. 30.
[82] Zigiranyirazo Appeal Brief, para. 120; Zigiranyirazo Reply Brief, para. 31.
[83] Zigiranyirazo Appeal Brief, paras. 113, 114.
[84] Zigiranyirazo Appeal Brief, para. 115.
[85] Zigiranyirazo Appeal Brief, para. 116.
[86] Zigiranyirazo Appeal Brief, paras. 106-111, 127. To illustrate this point, he compares the Trial Chamber's failure to address the impossibility of travel with the *Karera, Simba, Semanza,* and *Kamuhanda* cases where this argument was also raised by the defence and the issue was expressly discussed in the respective judgements. *See* Zigiranyirazo Appeal Brief, paras. 122-126, *citing Karera* Appeal Judgement, paras. 335-337, 341, 346, 349, *Karera* Trial Judgement, para. 510, *Simba* Appeal Judgement, para. 159, *Simba* Trial Judgement, para. 401, *Kamuhanda* Trial Judgement, paras. 177-222, *Semanza* Trial Judgement, paras. 138-148.
[87] Zigiranyirazo Appeal Brief, paras. 127-129.
[88] Prosecution Response Brief, paras. 70-111.
[89] Prosecution Response Brief, paras. 86, 90.
[90] Prosecution Response Brief, para. 88.
[91] Prosecution Response Brief, paras. 91, 92.
[92] Prosecution Response Brief, paras. 92, 104-111.
[93] Prosecution Response Brief, paras. 95-103.

accounts, with Witness Mukobwajana placing the visit to the military hospital in the morning and Witness Jean Luc Habyarimana indicating that it was around 1.00 p.m.[94]

34. Furthermore, the Prosecution disputes Zigiranyirazo's contention that the site visit was taken to retrace his journey from Kanombe to Rubaya, noting that this was not addressed in the **[page 12]** relevant Trial Chamber decision.[95] The Prosecution submits that there was no connection between the site visit and the impact of the alibi evidence on the evidence placing Zigiranyirazo at Kesho Hill.[96] The Prosecution also notes that Zigiranyirazo did not object to the lack of a record of the site visit during trial and that he was able to make arguments based on the site visit in his Defence Closing Brief.[97] The Prosecution contends that the Trial Chamber expressly referred to the site visit in the procedural history of the Trial Judgement as well as implicitly in its discussion of the evidence, as when it took account of the configuration of certain hills.[98]

35. The Prosecution submits that Zigiranyirazo has failed to demonstrate that it would have been impossible for him to travel between Kanombe and Kesho Hill during the seven and a half to eight hour period for which he did not have an alibi.[99] It further contends that his reliance on the Trial Chamber's travel during the site visit is misplaced as the alleged route taken by Zigiranyirazo and his family on 11 April 1994 was not necessarily identical to the one taken by him on 8 April 1994.[100] The Prosecution also points to the testimony of Zhudi Janbek, the Prosecution's investigator, who regularly travelled the 160 kilometre paved route between Kigali and Gisenyi via Ruhengeri in two and a half hours.[101] The Prosecution further suggests that, by helicopter, the journey between Kanombe and Gisenyi Prefecture would only take 45 minutes.[102]

(c) Discussion

36. As a preliminary matter, the Appeals Chamber has previously stated that a detailed record of a Trial Chamber's site visit should normally be maintained.[103] The Appeals Chamber observes, however, that Zigiranyirazo did not object at trial to the lack of record. In addition, there appears to be no dispute with respect to the itinerary and travel times taken by the Trial Chamber during its site visit. The absence of a record also did not prevent Zigiranyirazo from fully addressing issues arising from the site visit in his Defence Closing Brief. Consequently, the Appeals Chamber does not consider that the lack of a record of the site visit invalidated the verdict.

37. At the core of Zigiranyirazo's submissions is the contention that the Trial Chamber failed to consider properly his alibi evidence and, in particular, to consider fully the feasibility of his travel **[page 13]** between Kanombe and Kesho Hill during the period for which it found that he did not have an alibi on 8 April 1994. A review of the Trial Judgement reveals that the Trial Chamber did not set out the applicable legal principles specifically related to assessing an alibi.

38. The Appeals Chamber observes that the Trial Chamber correctly stated that the Prosecution bears the burden of establishing the accused's guilt beyond reasonable doubt[104] and that it would consider each piece of evidence in light of the totality of the evidence admitted at trial.[105] Furthermore, the Trial Chamber

---

[94] Prosecution Response Brief, paras. 99-101, 103.
[95] Prosecution Response Brief, paras. 71, 75.
[96] Prosecution Response Brief, para. 75.
[97] Prosecution Response Brief, para. 76.
[98] Prosecution Response Brief, para. 77, *citing* Trial Judgement, para. 312.
[99] Prosecution Response Brief, para. 79.
[100] Prosecution Response Brief, paras. 72, 81-85.
[101] Prosecution Response Brief, para. 84, *citing* T. 4 October 2005 pp. 2-4; T. 28 September 2009 p. 47. The Prosecution's estimates are based on an assumed average rate of speed of around 65 kilometres an hour.
[102] Prosecution Response Brief, para. 84.
[103] *Karera* Appeal Judgement, para. 50.
[104] Trial Judgement, para. 89 ("Pursuant to Article 20(3) of the Statute, an accused shall be presumed innocent until proven guilty. This presumption places on the Prosecution the burden of establishing the guilt of the accused, a burden which remains on the Prosecution throughout the entire trial. A finding of guilt may be reached only when a majority of the Trial Chamber is satisfied that guilt has been proved beyond reasonable doubt.") (internal citation omitted).
[105] Trial Judgement, paras. 87, 88.

addressed the evidence of all nine alibi witnesses in its analysis alongside its assessment of the Prosecution evidence relating to the events at Kesho Hill.[106]

39. Nonetheless, the Appeals Chamber finds that the Trial Chamber's assessment of Zigiranyirazo's alibi involves three serious errors that, taken together, invalidate his convictions based on the events at Kesho Hill. Specifically, the Trial Chamber erred by misapprehending the burden of proof in the context of alibi, failing to consider or provide a reasoned opinion with respect to relevant circumstantial evidence, and misconstruing key evidence which, properly considered, bolstered Zigiranyirazo's alibi.

40. First, the Appeals Chamber notes that although the Trial Chamber correctly recalled that the Prosecution bore the burden of proof, the Trial Chamber's approach to the alibi evidence indicates that it placed a greater evidentiary burden on Zigiranyirazo to establish an alibi than required under the Tribunal's jurisprudence. Specifically, the Trial Chamber made several statements discounting the testimony of alibi witnesses, for example stating:

> (1) "the Chamber notes that the evidence of these [alibi] witnesses is *inconclusive* as to [Zigiranyirazo's] presence in Kanombe for the *entire* day;"[107]
>
> (2) "[Witness Bararengana's] testimony [of seeing Zigiranyirazo at 3.30 or 4.00 p.m.] *does not contradict* the Prosecution evidence that [Zigiranyirazo] was at Kesho Hill on the morning of 8 April 1994;"[108]
>
> (3) "[t]he Chamber therefore considers that [Jean Luc Habyarimana's] testimony, along with his evidence that he saw [Zigiranyirazo] in the evening, *does not provide [Zigiranyirazo] with an alibi* for the morning of 8 April 1994;"[109] and **[page 14]**
>
> (4) "[Witness Mukobwajana's] evidence [of seeing Zigiranyirazo around 8.00 a.m. and again around 3.00 or 4.00 p.m.] *does not provide [Zigiranyirazo] with an alibi* between approximately 8.00 a.m. and 4.00 p.m."[110]

41. These comments confirm that the Trial Chamber did not fully appreciate that Zigiranyirazo only needed to establish reasonable doubt that he would have been able to travel to and from Kesho Hill on the *morning* of 8 April 1994, rather than establish his exact location throughout the day in Kanombe. The Appeals Chamber also observes that the Trial Chamber dismissed the evidence of several witnesses who recalled seeing Zigiranyirazo at Kanombe on 8 April 1994, but could not state an exact time when they saw him. These witnesses provided at least some support for the alibi, especially as the Trial Chamber did not discount their evidence.[111] Finally, the Trial Chamber's misconception of Zigiranyirazo's burden in respect of presenting an alibi is apparent from its discussion of the alibi in relation to the events at the Kiyovu Roadblock, where it expressly misapplied his burden by stating that:

> Accordingly, although the Chamber does not discount the Defence evidence suggesting that [Zigiranyirazo] was at Rubaya for approximately one week from 11 April 1994, the Chamber finds that none of the Defence Witnesses' testimonies *exclude the possibility* that [Zigiranyirazo] left Rubaya for periods between 12 and 17 April 1994. The Chamber, therefore, finds that [Zigiranyirazo] *does not have an alibi for 12 to 17 April 1994*.[112]

---

[106] Trial Judgement, paras. 318-328.
[107] Trial Judgement, para. 323 (emphasis added).
[108] Trial Judgement, para. 324 (emphasis added).
[109] Trial Judgement, para. 325 (emphasis added).
[110] Trial Judgement, para. 327 (emphasis added).
[111] Trial Judgement, paras. 323, 328.
[112] Trial Judgement, para. 250 (internal citation omitted) (emphasis added). The Prosecution argues that this passage is consistent with the approach of the Trial Chamber in the *Simba* case, which stated that "the numerous inconsistencies in the alibi eliminate the reasonable possibility that [the Appellant] was in Gitarama at the time of the attack[s]" (*Simba* Trial Judgement, paras. 121, 177) and which was subsequently adopted by the Appeals Chamber (*Simba* Appeal Judgement, para. 187). *See generally* T. 28 September 2009 pp. 34, 35. The two statements, however, are not comparable. A close examination of the *Simba* Trial Judgement reflects that it engaged in a detailed assessment of the alibi evidence, noting numerous contradictions and deficiencies in the evidence, particularly when weighed against corroborated and credible evidence. Its approach clearly indicates that the defence did not raise reasonable doubt about the Prosecution's case and that the Prosecution eliminated the reasonable possibility that that portion of Simba's alibi was true. *See Simba* Trial Judgement, paras. 374-384. By contrast, the above-quoted language used in the Trial Judgement suggests that Zigiranyirazo had the burden to exclude that he travelled to Kiyovu.

42. The Appeals Chamber emphasizes that a successful alibi does not require conclusive proof of an accused's whereabouts.[113] Indeed, there is no requirement that an alibi "exclude the [page 15] possibility" that the accused committed a crime.[114] The alibi need only raise reasonable doubt that the accused was in a position to commit the crime.[115]

43. The Appeals Chamber therefore finds that the Trial Chamber reversed the burden of proof in its assessment of Zigiranyirazo's alibi. The Appeals Chamber's conclusion is reinforced by the Trial Chamber's failure, in contrast to other cases where similar language was used, to articulate correctly the applicable burden of proof specific to the assessment of an alibi as well as by the numerous other factual and legal errors identified below. In view of the clear legal error in the application of the burden of proof, the Appeals Chamber will proceed to consider the relevant evidence *de novo* under the correct legal standard.[116]

44. The second error of the Trial Chamber was its failure to provide a reasoned opinion in relation to the feasibility of travel between Kesho Hill and Kanombe. The Appeals Chamber observes that the fastest estimate of time for travelling between Kigali and Gisenyi Prefecture on the record is two and half hours under optimal conditions, which does not account for the additional distance between Kanombe and Kigali and the specific travel time to Kesho Hill.[117] Taking these factors into consideration, Zigiranyirazo submits that the journey under optimal conditions would have taken approximately three hours and 18 minutes, which the Appeals Chamber accepts as a reasonable estimate.[118] In addition, other estimates following from the site visit suggest that the journey could have taken between four and 10 hours one way.[119] There is no basis in the record for the Prosecution's theory that the journey would have taken Zigiranyirazo approximately 45 minutes by helicopter.[120] [page 16]

45. The Appeals Chamber notes that "[t]here is a presumption that a Trial Chamber has evaluated all the evidence presented to it, as long as there is no indication that the Trial Chamber completely disregarded any particular piece of evidence."[121] However, this presumption may be rebutted "when evidence which is clearly relevant to the findings is not addressed by the Trial Chamber's reasoning."[122] The Appeals Chamber is

---

[113] *See Simba* Appeal Judgement, para. 185 ("The Appeals Chamber is further satisfied that the Trial Chamber correctly applied [the legal standard on alibi evidence] in its subsequent findings on alibi. The Trial Chamber first found that, although the alibi evidence for the period of 6-13 April 1994 '[did] not account for every moment of [the Appellant's time], viewed as a whole and when weighed against the Prosecution evidence, it [provided] a reasonable and satisfactory explanation for [the Appellant's] activities [for this period].' The Appeals Chamber notes that this wording reflects that in assessing the alibi evidence for this period the Trial Chamber did not require the Defence to prove its case beyond reasonable doubt."), *quoting Simba* Trial Judgement, para. 349. *See also Nahimana et al.* Appeal Judgement, paras. 428-431, 473, 474 (reversing a Trial Chamber finding that an alibi based on hearsay had not been established).

[114] *See supra* Section III.A.1 (Burden of Proof in the Assessment of Alibi). *See also Muhimana* Appeal Judgement, para. 18 ("An accused does not need to prove at trial that a crime 'could not have occurred' or 'preclude the possibility that it could occur'.").

[115] *See supra* Section III.A.1 (Burden of Proof in the Assessment of Alibi).

[116] *See supra* para. 10.

[117] T. 4 October 2005 pp. 2-4. *See also* Zigiranyirazo Reply Brief, paras. 30, 31.

[118] *See* T. 28 September 2009 p. 10. At the hearing, the Prosecution maintained that it would take around two and a half hours to travel from Kanombe to Kesho Hill. It further admitted that it would take no more than 20 minutes to travel from Kanombe to Kigali. *See* T. 28 September 2009 pp. 47, 48. Zigiranyirazo noted that the last seven or eight kilometres before reaching Kesho Hill was along a dirt road. *See* T. 28 September 2009 p. 10. In view of these factors, the Appeals Chamber considers Zigiranyirazo's estimate of the journey taking more than three hours under optimal conditions as more reasonable.

[119] The estimate of 10 hours is based on the longest route via Butare Prefecture. With respect to the route via Gitarama, the approximate times offered by the Prosecution and Zigiranyirazo are similar. *See* T. 28 September 2009 p. 49 ("[The Prosecution] would stipulate [that the route via Gitarama took] four to five hours. The Defence estimate is five to six, so we're not really that far apart.").

[120] The Prosecution cites its own counsel's question during cross-examination of a defence witness for the proposition that it only took 45 minutes to travel from Kanombe to Gisenyi Prefecture. *See* Prosecution Response Brief, para. 84, *citing* T. 27 February 2007 p. 81. The relevant exchange reads: "Q. Would you agree or would you have no idea that to travel from Kanombe camp to the Rubaya tea factory area in a helicopter would take about 45 minutes? A. I wouldn't know. I don't know. I saw -- that a journey by car took a whole day." During oral argument, the Appeals Chamber asked the Prosecution whether it had abandoned its theory of Zigiranyirazo's possible use of a helicopter. *See* T. 28 September 2009 p. 45 ("MR. PRESIDENT: During the trial, the point was made that there was some kind of a possibility of helicopter travel. I take it that you are not maintaining this any longer. MS. BIANCHI: Your Honour, my colleague, Christine Graham, is going to deal with the issue of travel, including the questions on whether the helicopter theory is still in play."). The Prosecution never returned to the matter.

[121] *Halilović* Appeal Judgement, para. 121. *See also Kvoèka et al.* Appeal Judgement, para. 23.

[122] *Kvoèka et al.* Appeal Judgement, para. 23.

mindful of potential limitations to evidence taken after the passage of several years concerning specifics of travel; however all relevant evidence shows that Kesho Hill in Gisenyi Prefecture is not in close geographic proximity to Kanombe, which is southwest of Kigali. As a result, the distance, time, and feasibility of travel are highly relevant factors to consider in view of the considerable evidence placing Zigiranyirazo at Kanombe at various times on 8 April 1994. Despite the crucial importance of this issue, the Trial Chamber failed to address it.

46. In addition, Zigiranyirazo presented the evidence of Witnesses Bernadette Niyonizeye and Agnès Kampundu, who recalled that Zigiranyirazo returned to Kanombe on 8 April 1994 shortly after leaving, due to fighting in Kigali.[123] Again, bearing in mind that the Trial Chamber did not discount the evidence of these witnesses,[124] it is unacceptable that it did not address this evidence, which would significantly undermine the possibility of Zigiranyirazo travelling to Kesho Hill by any route on 8 April 1994. Accordingly, the Trial Chamber erred in law by failing to provide a reasoned opinion on the feasibility of Zigiranyirazo's travel between Kanombe and Kesho Hill.

47. The third error in the Trial Chamber's reasoning involved its misconstruing key alibi evidence. In particular, both Zigiranyirazo and the Prosecution agree that the Trial Chamber erred in its assessment of the evidence of Witness Jean Luc Habyarimana. Stating that Witness Jean Luc Habyarimana testified that he saw Zigiranyirazo at Kanombe around 1.00 p.m. with Witness Bararengana, the Trial Chamber discounted his evidence because Witness Bararengana stated that he only arrived in Kanombe around 3.00 or 3.30 p.m.[125] However, a review of the record shows that Witness Jean Luc Habyarimana testified that he and Zigiranyirazo went to the military hospital at Camp Kanombe around 1.00 p.m. on 8 April 1994 *before* Witness Bararengana arrived at **[page 17]** Kanombe.[126] Therefore, contrary to the finding in the Trial Judgement, there is no clear inconsistency between the accounts of Witnesses Jean Luc Habyarimana and Bararengana.[127]

48. In addition, a review of Witness Mukobwajana's evidence reflects that she corroborates Witness Jean Luc Habyarimana's testimony that he went with Zigiranyirazo to the military hospital before Witness Bararengana arrived at Kanombe.[128] Although Witness Mukobwajana did not specify a time for this visit, her testimony nonetheless corroborates Witness Jean Luc Habyarimana's account.[129] The Appeals Chamber finds no merit in the Prosecution contention that, notwithstanding the Trial Chamber's error, it would have been reasonable to reject the evidence of Witness Jean Luc Habyarimana because Witness Mukobwajana's testimony, when read in the French original, placed Zigiranyirazo's trip to the hospital in the morning rather than around 1.00 p.m.[130] Contrary to the Prosecution's submission, the French version of Witness Mukobwajana's testimony in fact suggests only that Zigiranyirazo's visit to the morgue occurred at some

---

[123] *See* Zigiranyirazo Appeal Brief, paras. 160, 161.
[124] Trial Judgement, para. 328.
[125] Trial Judgement, para. 325.
[126] T. 26 February 2007 pp. 30, 31 ("[Witness Jean Luc Habyarimana:] A. I also went to the Camp Kanombe military hospital. [Mr. Zaduk:] Q. Who did you go with? A. I was with several people, particularly all members of the affected families, who happened to be there, as well as with my uncle, Mr. Protais Zigiranyirazo, and soldiers who accompanied us. [...] Q. What time would you have gone to that military hospital on the 8th? A. I'd rather say that it was in the middle of the day, let's say, at around 1 p.m. Q. All right. So you can confirm that your uncle was with you at the military hospital at that time on that day; is that right? A. That is right. [...] Q. Do you know whether that was before or after Dr. Bararengana arrived? A. It was prior to Dr. Bararengana's arrival. Q. And after the doctor arrived, did you go anywhere with him? A. Yes. After the arrival of the doctor, in the evening – around evening, I took him to see the brother – the body of his brother, the president, as well as the body of the other president, that is, President Ntaryamira.").
[127] *See* Trial Judgement, para. 325.
[128] T. 19 November 2007 p. 53.
[129] *See Nahimana et al.* Appeal Judgement, para. 428 ("[T]he Appeals Chamber is of the view that two testimonies corroborate one another when one *prima facie* credible testimony is compatible with the other *prima facie* credible testimony regarding the same fact or a sequence of linked facts. It is not necessary that both testimonies be identical in all aspects or describe the same fact in the same way. Every witness presents what he has seen from his own point of view at the time of the events, or according to how he understood the events recounted by others. It follows that corroboration may exist even when some details differ between testimonies, provided that no credible testimony describes the facts in question in a way which is not compatible with the description given in another credible testimony."). *See also* Trial Judgement, para. 91 ("[A] significant period of time has elapsed between the events alleged in the Indictment and the testimonies given in court. Therefore, lack of precision or minor discrepancies between the evidence of different witnesses, or between the testimony of a particular witness and a prior statement, while calling for cautious consideration, was not regarded in general as necessarily discrediting the evidence.").
[130] *See* Prosecution Response Brief, paras. 99-101, 103; T. 28 September 2009 pp. 43, 44.

point on 8 April, not that it specifically took place in the morning of that day.[131] In any event, the Appeals Chamber views any difference between the witnesses' accounts as to the exact time when the trip to the military hospital occurred as minor.[132] Therefore, the Trial Chamber also erred **[page 18]** in evaluating Witness Mukobwajana's testimony when it suggested that she did not place Zigiranyirazo at Kanombe between 8.00 a.m. and 3.00 p.m.[133]

49. The Appeals Chamber finds that the Trial Chamber's reversal of the burden of proof, failure to provide a reasoned opinion, and its factual errors in relation to key evidence invalidate Zigiranyirazo's convictions. The properly considered evidence of undiscounted alibi witnesses places Zigiranyirazo in the Kanombe area at both around 8.00 a.m. and around 1.00 p.m. – making travel to and from Kesho Hill in time to address the assailants there, even using the travel times for the shortest route via Ruhengeri, around three hours and 18 minutes one way, impossible.[134] Just as circumstantial evidence may properly serve as a basis of conviction,[135] an accused may also rely on such evidence and any reasonable inferences capable of being drawn from it in his defence.[136] It is reasonable to infer from this evidence that Zigiranyirazo was present in the Kanombe area during the morning of 8 April 1994 based on multiple sightings by several witnesses over the course of the day, in particular when coupled with the evidence of the distance and feasibility of travel between Kanombe and Kesho Hill. Thus the Appeals Chamber finds that the alibi evidence casts doubt on the Prosecution evidence placing Zigiranyirazo at Kesho Hill on the morning of 8 April 1994.

50. The Trial Chamber found the evidence from Witnesses AKK and AKL of Zigiranyirazo's presence at Kesho Hill to be consistent, detailed, credible, and corroborated.[137] In some circumstances, this might be enough to eliminate the reasonable possibility that Zigiranyirazo's alibi was true. However, in this case, the Trial Chamber did not reach its conclusions on the credibility of Witnesses AKK and AKL after assessing their accounts in light of all the alibi evidence, since it found that Zigiranyirazo had no alibi for the morning of 8 April 1994.[138] This casts serious doubt upon the reasonableness of the Trial Chamber's findings on the credibility of Witnesses AKK and AKL. The Appeals Chamber considers that, given the distance between Kesho Hill and Kanombe, a reasonable trier of fact could not be convinced that Witnesses AKK and AKL credibly placed Zigiranyirazo at Kesho Hill and at the same time not expressly explain how the evidence of Zigiranyirazo's alibi, which was largely not discounted, failed to raise reasonable doubt, an explanation which the Trial Chamber did not attempt. **[page 19]**

51. In sum, the Appeals Chamber concludes that the Trial Chamber erred in law and in fact in its assessment of the alibi evidence, by misapprehending the applicable legal principles, failing to consider or provide a reasoned opinion with respect to relevant evidence, and misconstruing key evidence which further bolstered Zigiranyirazo's alibi. The Appeals Chamber considers that these errors constituted a miscarriage of justice and invalidated the verdict, and thus that the Trial Chamber's findings on Zigiranyirazo's participation in the attack at Kesho Hill on 8 April 1994 must be overturned.

52. Accordingly, the Appeals Chamber grants the Sixth Ground of Appeal and reverses Zigiranyirazo's convictions for genocide and extermination as a crime against humanity based on his participation in the

---

[131] *See* T. 19 November 2007 p. 53 (French version)("*Le 8, le fait marquant, c'est... parce que les corps venaient de... de rester là, on les a déposés dans un endroit parce que ça commençait à sentir dans le salon, et mon oncle Protais, avec Jean-Luc, avec quelques personnes, ils sont allés voir où...où les corps étaient déposés. Dans la matinée, le 8 aussi, on attendait l'arrivée du... du petit frère du Président...*"). The Appeals Chamber observes that, when Witness Mukobwajana says "*le 8 aussi,*" the transcript marks this out in commas, strongly suggesting that the "*aussi*" referred to the date only.
[132] The Appeals Chamber notes that this difference is likely no more significant in time than that between Witnesses AKK's and AKL's sighting of Zigiranyirazo at Kesho Hill. *See* Trial Judgement, paras. 254, 265. In the case of Witnesses AKK and AKL, the Trial Chamber simply described Zigiranyirazo's presence at Kesho Hill as being "on the morning of 8 April 1994." *See* Trial Judgement, para. 329.
[133] Trial Judgement, para. 327.
[134] As a consequence, the Appeals Chamber does not need to assess the contested issues as to the viability of this route.
[135] *Muhimana* Appeal Judgement, para. 49. *See also Gacumbitsi* Appeal Judgement, para. 115.
[136] However, given that an accused does not bear a burden of proof, by contrast to the burden of the Prosecution in establishing a conviction, an inference based on circumstantial evidence need not be the only reasonable one in order to support a successful defence.
[137] Trial Judgement, paras. 309, 310, 316, 327, 329.
[138] Trial Judgement, paras. 324, 325, 327.

massacre at Kesho Hill. Consequently, there is no need to assess Zigiranyirazo's remaining arguments concerning the events at Kesho Hill under this or any other ground of appeal.[139]

3. Alleged Errors in Evaluating Exculpatory Evidence Related to Kiyovu Roadblock (Ground 12)

(a) Introduction

53. The Trial Chamber convicted Zigiranyirazo of genocide for aiding and abetting the killing of Tutsi civilians at the Kiyovu Roadblock,[140] which was erected in close proximity to his residence in the Kiyovu neighbourhood of Kigali.[141] The Trial Chamber found that he was present at the roadblock on 12 and 17 April 1994 on the basis of the testimony of Prosecution Witness BCW.[142] Witness BCW also testified that he saw Zigiranyirazo and his children pass through the roadblock in a military jeep on 19 April 1994.[143]

54. In making these findings, the Trial Chamber considered the evidence of nine alibi witnesses who placed Zigiranyirazo at Rubaya in Gisenyi Prefecture during a period of approximately one **[page 20]** week, starting on 11 April 1994.[144] In particular, the Trial Chamber noted that Witnesses Agnès Kampundu, Marie Chantel Kamugisha, Witness BNZ120, Gloria Mukampunga, Aimé Marie Ntuye, and Bernadette Niyonizeye stated that Zigiranyirazo was at Rubaya, but gave vague testimony.[145] It noted that Witnesses Domitilla Zigiranyirazo, Marguérite Mukobwajana, and Séraphin Bararengana provided greater detail, but could not account for his presence for the entire week.[146] The Trial Chamber concluded:

> Accordingly, although the Chamber does not discount the Defence evidence suggesting that [Zigiranyirazo] was at Rubaya for approximately one week from 11 April 1994, the Chamber finds that none of the Defence Witnesses' testimonies exclude the possibility that [Zigiranyirazo] left Rubaya for periods between 12 and 17 April 1994. The Chamber, therefore, finds that [Zigiranyirazo] does not have an alibi for 12 to 17 April 1994.[147]

In dismissing the alibi, the Trial Chamber also did not expressly refer to or discuss its site visit or the possibility of travel between Rubaya and the Kiyovu Roadblock on 12 and 17 April 1994.[148]

(b) Submissions

55. Zigiranyirazo submits that the Trial Chamber erred in law and in fact in rejecting his alibi for 12 and 17 April 1994.[149] He contends that the Trial Chamber erred in its application of the law of alibi by failing to assess it in its totality and then weigh it against the evidence of Witness BCW.[150] He points to the Trial

---

[139] More specifically, Zigiranyirazo's additional grounds of appeal concerning Kesho Hill are the following. In the First Ground of Appeal, Zigiranyirazo challenges his conviction based on the Trial Chamber's evaluation of five Prosecution witnesses who testified about the attack on Kesho Hill. *See* Zigiranyirazo Notice of Appeal, para. 1; Zigiranyirazo Appeal Brief, paras. 14-40. In the Second Ground of Appeal, Zigiranyirazo challenges his conviction, based on the Trial Chamber's error in not drawing an adverse inference from the Prosecution's failure to call Witness BIU. *See* Zigiranyirazo Notice of Appeal, para. 2; Zigiranyirazo Appeal Brief, paras. 41-54. In the Third Ground of Appeal, he challenges his conviction, based on the alleged use of non-credible testimony to corroborate other witnesses. *See* Zigiranyirazo Notice of Appeal, para. 3; Zigiranyirazo Appeal Brief, paras. 55-70. In the Fourth Ground of Appeal, he challenges his conviction based on the Trial Chamber's acceptance of the testimony of Witnesses AKL and AKR in relation to the presence of Major Aloys Ntabakuze at Kesho Hill. *See* Zigiranyirazo Notice of Appeal, para. 4; Zigiranyirazo Appeal Brief, para. 71. In the Fifth Ground of Appeal, he challenges his conviction based on the Trial Chamber's finding that he participated in a joint criminal enterprise. *See* Zigiranyirazo Notice of Appeal, para. 5; Zigiranyirazo Appeal Brief, paras. 72-88.
[140] Trial Judgement, paras. 427, 447.
[141] Trial Judgement, paras. 243, 251.
[142] Trial Judgement, paras. 251, 413.
[143] Trial Judgement, para. 224.
[144] Trial Judgement, paras. 231, 245-250.
[145] Trial Judgement, paras. 245-248.
[146] Trial Judgement, para. 249.
[147] Trial Judgement, para. 250 (internal citation omitted).
[148] The Trial Judgement contains only one reference to the site visit in the procedural history. *See* Trial Judgement, Annex I: Procedural History, para. 34.
[149] Zigiranyirazo Notice of Appeal, para. 12(b, e); Zigiranyirazo Appeal Brief, paras. 314-327, 346-362, 367-376, 381-400.
[150] Zigiranyirazo Appeal Brief, paras. 381, 382, 387-396.

Chamber's finding that "none of the Defence Witnesses' testimonies exclude the possibility that [he] left Rubaya" as an indication that the Trial Chamber shifted the burden of proof.[151]

56. In addition, Zigiranyirazo submits that the Trial Chamber erred in law in failing to maintain a record of the site visit and to consider the exculpatory evidence it revealed as well as from his alibi witnesses, relating to the impossibility of his travelling from Rubaya to Kiyovu on 12 and 17 April 1994.[152] According to Zigiranyirazo, the site visit revealed that it took the Trial Chamber around 10 hours to travel from Rubaya in Gisenyi Prefecture to Kiyovu in Kigali following the same itinerary that he and his family took after leaving Kanombe, which is just outside Kigali.[153] **[page 21]** He also refers to a shorter alternative route via Gitarama Prefecture, which, based on the site visit, would have taken approximately four to five hours.[154] However, to demonstrate that the Gitarama route took even longer during the relevant events, Zigiranyirazo points to the evidence of Witnesses BBL and RDP167 whose respective journeys along this route on 11 April and in late-May 1994 lasted the entire day.[155]

57. Zigiranyirazo notes that Witness BCW placed him at the Kiyovu Roadblock between 11.00 a.m. and 12.00 p.m. on 12 April 1994.[156] Zigiranyirazo submits that, given the travel time between Rubaya and Kiyovu, it would have been impossible for him to have been in Kiyovu between 11:00 a.m. and 12:00 p.m. in view of the alibi evidence, especially Witness Bararengana's testimony that the two men shared a room in Rubaya each night during that period.[157] He emphasizes that the alibi evidence shows that his absences from Rubaya were only of a short duration.[158]

58. Moreover, Zigiranyirazo contends that the Trial Chamber erred in fact in finding that he did not have an alibi for 12 April 1994, particularly because Witness Domitilla Zigiranyirazo stated that she was with him on that day.[159] Furthermore, he challenges the Trial Chamber's interpretation of Domitilla Zigiranyirazo's testimony that he left Rubaya between 12 and 17 April 1994, since she stated that she went with him to a nearby location, in fact reinforcing the alibi.[160] According to Zigiranyirazo, the Trial Chamber also unreasonably discounted the evidence of Witnesses Mukobwajana and Bararengana based on a non-existent inconsistency as to the number of times Zigiranyirazo left Rubaya alone.[161] Moreover, Zigiranyirazo notes that the Trial Chamber erroneously used a trip mentioned by Witness Kampundu, which occurred after 18 April 1994, to reinforce its conclusion that he left Rubaya between 12 and 17 April 1994.[162]

59. Zigiranyirazo argues that the absences cited by the Trial Chamber confirm the alibi since they were all brief and during them he was at nearby locations and that, therefore, it was unreasonable to use them to reject his evidence.[163] He further questions the reasonableness of the Trial Chamber's complaint that his evidence lacked detail given that "[l]ittle of significance **[page 22]** happened in those days."[164] Zigiranyirazo further emphasizes that no reason was ever advanced for his return to Kigali on 12 April 1994, one day after a lengthy and difficult journey to reach Rubaya.[165]

60. The Prosecution responds that the Trial Chamber neither misconstrued the alibi evidence nor erred in its application of the relevant law.[166] It submits that Zigiranyirazo has not identified any evidence material to the Trial Chamber's findings that it failed to consider or that any such failure would have impacted the

---

[151] Zigiranyirazo Appeal Brief, paras. 383-386, *quoting* Trial Judgement, para. 250; Zigiranyirazo Reply Brief, para. 103.
[152] Zigiranyirazo Notice of Appeal, para. 12(a); Zigiranyirazo Appeal Brief, paras. 328-345; Zigiranyirazo Reply Brief, paras. 83, 87, 89.
[153] Zigiranyirazo Appeal Brief, paras. 98, 99; Zigiranyirazo Reply Brief, para. 86.
[154] Zigiranyirazo Appeal Brief, paras. 119, 339-345. This is also the Prosecution's position. *See* T. 28 September 2009 p. 49.
[155] Zigiranyirazo Appeal Brief, para. 341.
[156] Zigiranyirazo Appeal Brief, para. 333.
[157] Zigiranyirazo Appeal Brief, paras. 333-335, 339, 342.
[158] Zigiranyirazo Reply Brief, paras. 84, 85, 88, 89.
[159] Zigiranyirazo Appeal Brief, paras. 347-349; Zigiranyirazo Reply Brief, para. 92.
[160] Zigiranyirazo Appeal Brief, paras. 350-352; Zigiranyirazo Reply Brief, paras. 93, 94.
[161] Zigiranyirazo Appeal Brief, paras. 353-358.
[162] Zigiranyirazo Appeal Brief, paras. 359-362.
[163] Zigiranyirazo Appeal Brief, paras. 367-370.
[164] Zigiranyirazo Appeal Brief, para. 371.
[165] Zigiranyirazo Appeal Brief, paras. 372-376.
[166] Prosecution Response Brief, paras. 199-210, 214-220, 225-233.

verdict.[167] It recalls that a Trial Chamber is presumed to have considered all of the evidence and, in this respect, notes that the Trial Judgement specifically mentions the convoy from Kanombe to Rubaya.[168] Furthermore, the Prosecution submits that Zigiranyirazo's argument confuses the issue of "impossibility" with that of the "likelihood of such a trip."[169] It notes that the Defence evidence in fact demonstrated that Zigiranyirazo left Rubaya on several occasions and that it was found to be inconsistent, thereby undermining the general evidence that he remained consistently there.[170] The Prosecution also questions the reliability of Zigiranyirazo's estimates with respect to the travel conditions and times on 12 and 17 April 1994.[171]

61. The Prosecution submits that the Trial Chamber properly assessed the evidence of Domitilla Zigiranyirazo, which was inconsistent about the date on which Zigiranyirazo left Rubaya without her.[172] It further contends that Zigiranyirazo has failed to demonstrate how the Trial Chamber's conclusions with respect to Witness Kampundu as well as the alleged contradictions between the evidence of Witnesses Mukobwajana and Bararengana are errors which impacted the verdict.[173]

62. Finally, the Prosecution disputes that Zigiranyirazo's absences from Rubaya were minimal and describes his argument on this point as "guesswork."[174] It further argues that it was reasonable for the Trial Chamber to require Zigiranyirazo's witnesses to provide details of his activities at Rubaya.[175] The Prosecution submits that the Trial Chamber correctly applied the law on alibi in its assessment of the alibi evidence.[176]

[page 23]

(c) Discussion

63. The Appeals Chamber recalls its conclusions in connection with the Sixth Ground of Appeal that the Trial Chamber's failure to maintain a record of the site visit did not invalidate the verdict.[177] Nevertheless, a review of the Trial Chamber's discussion of the alibi in relation to the Kiyovu Roadblock reveals that it committed three significant errors: not applying the correct legal standard to the assessment of the alibi; misconstruing key evidence to discount the alibi; and failing to consider or provide a reasoned opinion with respect to relevant evidence.

64. First, the Appeals Chamber recalls its conclusion in connection with Zigiranyirazo's Sixth Ground of Appeal that the Trial Chamber erred in law in its assessment of the alibi evidence by misapprehending the applicable legal principles on the burden of proof.[178] The Appeals Chamber considers that this finding applies with equal force to the Trial Chamber's assessment of Zigiranyirazo's alibi for his purported presence at the Kiyovu Roadblock on 12 and 17 April 1994. In particular, the Appeals Chamber emphasizes that, contrary to the conclusion of the Trial Chamber,[179] there is no requirement that an alibi "exclude the possibility" that an accused committed a crime.[180] Instead, Zigiranyirazo's alibi need only raise reasonable doubt in the Prosecution's case.[181] As such, the Appeals Chamber will proceed to consider the relevant evidence *de novo* under the correct standard.[182]

---

[167] Prosecution Response Brief, paras. 190-198.
[168] Prosecution Response Brief, para. 191.
[169] Prosecution Response Brief, para. 192. *See also* Prosecution Response Brief, para. 193.
[170] Prosecution Response Brief, paras. 194, 195, 197, 198.
[171] Prosecution Response Brief, para. 196.
[172] Prosecution Response Brief, paras. 200-206, 218-220.
[173] Prosecution Response Brief, paras. 207-210.
[174] Prosecution Response Brief, para. 215.
[175] Prosecution Response Brief, para. 216.
[176] Prosecution Response Brief, paras. 225, 232, 233.
[177] *See supra* Section III.A.2 (Ground 6: Alleged Errors in Evaluating Exculpatory Evidence Related to Kesho Hill).
[178] *See supra* Section III.A.2 (Ground 6: Alleged Errors in Evaluating Exculpatory Evidence Related to Kesho Hill).
[179] Trial Judgement, para. 250.
[180] *See Muhimana* Appeal Judgement, para. 18 ("An accused does not need to prove at trial that a crime 'could not have occurred' or 'preclude the possibility that it could occur'."). *See also supra* Section III.A.2 (Ground 6: Alleged Errors in Evaluating Exculpatory Evidence Related to Kesho Hill).
[181] *See supra* Section III.A.1 (Burden of Proof in the Assessment of Alibi).
[182] *See supra* para. 10.

65. Second, as Zigiranyirazo submits, the Trial Chamber unreasonably relied on the evidence of brief local trips in the area surrounding Rubaya to question his alibi evidence. In particular, while Witness Domitilla Zigiranyirazo acknowledged that Zigiranyirazo left Rubaya, she stated that he accompanied her on a visit to see her mother-in-law.[183] The Appeals Chamber further finds no merit in the Prosecution's argument that Witness Domitilla Zigiranyirazo's suggestion at trial that Zigiranyirazo left Rubaya on 12 April 1994 to assist his Tutsi wife cross the border into Goma, Zaire, is a further basis for discrediting the alibi.[184] There are several fatal flaws to this submission, **[page 24]** in particular that the witness subsequently corrected her testimony, noting that this event occurred on 20 April 1994.[185] Moreover, the Trial Chamber did not use this correction to discredit the witness. Finally, even if Witness Domitilla Zigiranyirazo's initial testimony were accepted, it would reasonably suggest that Zigiranyirazo in fact travelled to Goma on 12 April 1994 rather than to Kiyovu in Kigali, further undermining the Trial Chamber's factual findings.

66. In addition, the Trial Chamber's reliance on Witness Kampundu for the proposition that Zigiranyirazo left Rubaya is misplaced since she was referring to trips made by Zigiranyirazo during a later period when he was staying in Gasiza.[186] Finally, contrary to the Trial Chamber's conclusion, the evidence of Witness Bararengana that Zigiranyirazo left Rubaya only once without him[187] is not incompatible with the evidence of Witness Mukobwajana who stated that Zigiranyirazo periodically ran errands.[188] In this respect, a review of Witness Bararengana's testimony indicates that he was not categorical about the number of Zigiranyirazo's departures.[189] Furthermore, Witness Bararengana was referring to Zigiranyirazo's trips *without him*, whereas the testimony of Witness Mukobwajana suggests that Witness Bararengana accompanied Zigiranyirazo on the trips.[190] In any event, the minor inconsistencies, if any, between the testimonies of Witnesses Mukobwajana and Bararengana as to the number of such trips taken by Zigiranyirazo is an unreasonable basis for discounting their evidence. Indeed, this appears to run contrary to the Trial Chamber's express recognition that "a significant period of time has elapsed between the events" and that "minor discrepancies between the evidence of different witnesses [were] not regarded in general as necessarily discrediting the evidence."[191]

67. In concluding that Zigiranyirazo did not have an alibi between 12 and 17 April 1994, the Trial Chamber did not consider the evidence as a whole as well as the relevant circumstantial evidence of his presence at Rubaya or in its vicinity. It is reasonable to infer that Zigiranyirazo was **[page 25]** present at Rubaya in Gisenyi Prefecture, or in its vicinity, between 12 and 17 April 1994 based on multiple sightings by several witnesses over the course of several days, especially when the evidence of these witnesses is considered together with evidence regarding the time and difficulties involved in travelling between Rubaya

---

[183] T. 27 February 2007 p. 61 ("Q. Did you leave Rubaya to go anywhere during your period in Rubaya? A. I went to see my mother-in-law because she was sick. [...] Q. Could you describe where her house is located? A. We were neighbours. Our home and my mother-in-law's home were near each other. Q. Now, who went with you that day when you went to see your mother-in-law? Do you recall? A. I was with my husband."). The Appeals Chamber observes that Witness Domitilla Zigiranyirazo further stated that "[o]n that visit, my husband went to see Sagatwa's mother and I stayed at my mother-in-law's home." *See* T. 27 February 2009 p. 61. However, there is nothing in the record to suggest that this absence was significant or that the home of Sagatwa's mother was located a great distance away.
[184] *See* Prosecution Response Brief, paras. 195, 198; T. 28 September 2007 pp. 38, 39.
[185] *See* T. 28 February 2007 p. 31.
[186] T. 5 March 2007 pp. 69-71.
[187] Trial Judgement, para. 249, *citing* T. 7 March 2007 p. 25.
[188] Trial Judgement, para. 249, *citing* T. 20 November 2007 p. 32.
[189] T. 7 March 2007 p. 25 ("A. We were in the same premises, maybe not 24 hours each day because he moved out, I believe, once. And I had stayed back at the time. Q. So, we agree that you do recall at least one occasion you and Zigiranyirazo, at Rubaya, parted company. I'm going to suggest, perhaps, that was an occasion that he went to Rugunga hill. And you wouldn't know where he went, would you, you weren't with him? A. No, I think he once went with my sister to shop or to make some purchases.").
[190] T. 20 November 2007 p. 32 ("[Witness Mukobwajana:] A. Yes, [Zigiranyirazo] could go to make errands, go to the market, and then come back. We were together all the time throughout the seven days. [...] Q. Didn't you also say that Mr. Zigiranyirazo went to visit his sick mother? A. When he went to fetch things for us to be able to sleep, blankets, mattresses and also to bring the small children, the little boy, Aimé, I mentioned, in order to go and see the grandmother, otherwise during the day, during meals, during the prayer, in the evening and at bedtime, everyone was there because we would have our meal together. Q. But when you say that you were always together, that is not true. Isn't that so? A. "Always together", what does it mean? What I mean is that Mr. Bararengana and the other gentlemen would run errands. The women would prepare the meals, but at dinner time and for prayers, everyone was there and we would take our meals together. I don't know whether I was clear.").
[191] Trial Judgement, para. 91.

and Kiyovu. The Appeals Chamber therefore finds that the Trial Chamber erred in fact by misconstruing key alibi evidence.

68. Third, the Appeals Chamber finds that the Trial Chamber failed to consider or provide a reasoned opinion with respect to the distance and feasibility of travel between Rubaya and Kigali on the relevant dates. The Appeals Chamber recalls that the estimates for travelling between Gisenyi Prefecture and Kigali, based on the testimony of the Prosecution investigator and the Trial Chamber's site visit, vary, and range from approximately three hours (via Ruhengeri), to four to six hours (via Gitarama), and up to 10 hours (via Butare).[192]

69. The Appeals Chamber is mindful that evidence concerning specific travel details taken after several years can only be of limited assistance in establishing the time and exact itinerary purportedly taken by Zigiranyirazo on 12 and 17 April 1994. Nevertheless, the various estimates reflect that Rubaya in Gisenyi Prefecture is not in close geographic proximity with the Kiyovu area of Kigali. As a result, the distance, time, and feasibility of travel are highly relevant factors in view of the evidence placing Zigiranyirazo at Rubaya on 12 April 1994 and 17 April 1994, as each trip would have resulted in a significant period of absence from Rubaya.[193] This is especially true given the evidence of Witnesses BBL and RDP167 which suggests that the relevant circumstances at the time made travel along the route via Gitarama significantly more time consuming than was the case during the Trial Chamber's site visit.[194]

70. The Appeals Chamber notes that the Trial Chamber did refer generally to the lengthy journey from Kanombe, which is near Kigali, to Rubaya in recounting the alibi evidence.[195] Therefore, it follows that it was aware of the significant distance in assessing the allegations related to the Kiyovu Roadblock. In such circumstances, the Trial Chamber should have provided clear reasons as to why the alibi did not account for the time when Zigiranyirazo was seen at the Kiyovu Roadblock. This is especially so given the alibi evidence that Witness Bararengana saw **[page 26]** Zigiranyirazo on 12 April 1994,[196] evidence which is not easily reconciled with Zigiranyirazo's presence, according to Witness BCW, at the Kiyovu Roadblock around 11.00 a.m. or 12.00 p.m. on 12 April 1994. As noted above, the brief absences in the area surrounding Rubaya did not provide a reasonable basis for discounting the alibi. While the Trial Chamber might have reasonably rejected Witness Bararengana's testimony for a number of other reasons when weighed against that of Witness BCW, it did not do so. Rather, it expressly stated that it did not discount Witness Bararengana's evidence.[197]

71. When viewed as a whole under the correct standard, the evidence in support of Zigiranyirazo's alibi, which was not discounted by the Trial Chamber, provides a reasonable basis to conclude that he remained in Rubaya and its surrounding area on 12 and 17 April 1994. Accordingly, the Appeals Chamber finds that the alibi evidence casts doubt on the Prosecution evidence placing him at the Kiyovu Roadblock on 12 and 17 April 1994.

72. The Trial Chamber found Witness BCW, who testified to Zigiranyirazo's presence at the Kiyovu Roadblock, to be a "clear and forthright witness."[198] In certain contexts, this might be enough to eliminate the reasonable possibility that Zigiranyirazo's alibi was true. However, in this case, the Trial Chamber did not reach its conclusions on the credibility of Witness BCW after assessing his account in light of the properly considered alibi evidence. This raises serious questions about the reasonableness of the Trial Chamber's findings on Witness BCW's credibility. The Appeals Chamber considers that, given the distance between Rubaya and Kiyovu, a reasonable trier of fact could not be convinced that Witness BCW credibly

---

[192] *See supra* Section III.A.2 (Ground 6: Alleged Errors in Evaluating Exculpatory Evidence Related to Kesho Hill). The Appeals Chamber notes that the three hour estimate does not include the additional twenty to thirty minute distance from Kanombe to Kigali, which was relevant to the discussion of the Kesho Hill convictions, but not to the events at the Kiyovu Roadblock.
[193] In view of this conclusion, the Appeals Chamber does not find it necessary to discuss the additional evidence related to the viability of the Ruhengeri route.
[194] *See supra* para. 56.
[195] Trial Judgement, paras. 246-248. *See also* Trial Judgement, para. 87, n. 88.
[196] *See* T. 6 March 2007 p. 45.
[197] Trial Judgement, para. 250.
[198] Trial Judgement, para. 236. *See also* Trial Judgement, paras. 243, 244 (further describing Witness BCW's testimony as "detailed" and "consistent").

placed Zigiranyirazo there on 12 and 17 April 1994 and at the same time not discount the evidence of his alibi.

73. In sum, the Appeals Chamber concludes that the Trial Chamber erred in law and in fact in its assessment of the alibi evidence for the period from 11 to 17 April 1994, by misapprehending the applicable legal principles, failing to consider or provide a reasoned opinion with respect to relevant evidence, and misconstruing key evidence related to the alibi. The Appeals Chamber considers that these errors constituted a miscarriage of justice and invalidated the verdict, and thus that the Trial Chamber's findings on Zigiranyirazo's participation in the crimes committed at the Kiyovu Roadblock must be overturned.

74. Accordingly, the Appeals Chamber grants the Twelfth Ground of Appeal and reverses the Trial Chamber's conviction for aiding and abetting genocide based on Zigiranyirazo's participation **[page 27]** in the killings at the Kiyovu Roadblock. Consequently, there is no need to assess Zigiranyirazo's remaining arguments concerning the events at the Kiyovu Roadblock under this or other grounds of appeal.[199]

4. Conclusion

75. In reversing Zigiranyirazo's convictions for genocide and extermination as a crime against humanity, the Appeals Chamber again underscores the seriousness of the Trial Chamber's errors. The crimes Zigiranyirazo was accused of were very grave, meriting the most careful of analyses. Instead, the Trial Judgement misstated the principles of law governing the distribution of the burden of proof with regards to alibi and seriously erred in its handling of the evidence. Zigiranyirazo's resulting convictions relating to Kesho Hill and the Kiyovu Roadblock violated the most basic and fundamental principles of justice. In these circumstances, the Appeals Chamber had no choice but to reverse Zigiranyirazo's convictions. **[page 28]**

B. Other Grounds of Appeal (Grounds 13 to 16)

76. In his Thirteenth through Sixteenth Grounds of Appeal, Zigiranyirazo raises more general arguments against his convictions with respect to the events at both Kesho Hill and the Kiyovu Roadblock.[200] As discussed under Zigiranyirazo's Sixth and Twelfth Grounds of Appeal, the Appeals Chamber has reversed Zigiranyirazo's convictions for genocide and extermination as a crime against humanity. Accordingly, the Appeals Chamber need not address any of the other alleged errors advanced by Zigiranyirazo relating to his convictions. **[page 29]**

---

[199] More specifically, Zigiranyirazo's additional grounds of appeal concerning the Kiyovu Roadblock are the following: In the Seventh Ground of Appeal, Zigiranyirazo challenges his conviction based on the Trial Chamber's finding that his actions amounted to the standard of aiding and abetting. See Zigiranyirazo Notice of Appeal, para. 7; Zigiranyirazo Appeal Brief, paras. 232-247. In the Eighth Ground of Appeal, he challenges the Trial Chamber's findings that he had the requisite *mens rea* for aiding and abetting genocide. See Zigiranyirazo Notice of Appeal, para. 8; Zigiranyirazo Appeal Brief, paras. 248-268. In the Ninth Ground of Appeal, he challenges his conviction based on the existence of the roadblock at Kiyovu. See Zigiranyirazo Notice of Appeal, para. 9; Zigiranyirazo Appeal Brief, paras. 269-289. In the Tenth Ground of Appeal, he challenges his conviction based on the Trial Chamber's failure to address prior inconsistent statements of Witness BCW. See Zigiranyirazo Notice of Appeal, para. 10; Zigiranyirazo Appeal Brief, paras. 290-310. In the Eleventh Ground of Appeal, he challenges his conviction based on the Trial Chamber's acceptance of Witness ATO's testimony regarding the presence of General Gratien Kabiligi at the roadblock. See Zigiranyirazo Notice of Appeal, para. 11; Zigiranyirazo Appeal Brief, para. 311.

[200] More specifically, in the Thirteenth Ground of Appeal, Zigiranyirazo challenges his conviction based on the Trial Chamber's failure to consider that evidence against him was discovered only after his arrest. See Zigiranyirazo Notice of Appeal, para. 13; Zigiranyirazo Appeal Brief, paras. 401-408. In the Fourteenth Ground of Appeal, he challenges his conviction based on the Trial Chamber's limited consideration of evidence relating to his good relations with Tutsis. See Zigiranyirazo Amended Notice of Appeal, para. 14; Zigiranyirazo Appeal Brief, paras. 409-419. In the Fifteenth Ground of Appeal, he challenges his conviction based on the Trial Chamber's reliance on unsigned will-say statements in assessing the credibility of witnesses. See Zigiranyirazo Notice of Appeal, para. 15; Zigiranyirazo Appeal Brief, paras. 420-428. In the Sixteenth Ground of Appeal, he challenges his conviction based on the Trial Chamber's reliance on a revised Kinyarwandan translation of testimony not made available to him. See Zigiranyirazo Notice of Appeal, para. 16; Zigiranyirazo Appeal Brief, paras. 429-435.

IV. SENTENCING APPEALS (ZIGIRANYIRAZO'S GROUND 17 AND PROSECUTION APPEAL)

77. The Trial Chamber sentenced Zigiranyirazo to 20 years of imprisonment for genocide on the basis of his criminal acts at Kesho Hill (Count 2); 15 years of imprisonment for aiding and abetting genocide on the basis of his criminal acts at the Kiyovu Roadblock (Count 2); and 20 years of imprisonment for extermination as a crime against humanity for the events at Kesho Hill (Count 4).[201] It directed that these sentences be served concurrently.[202]

78. Zigiranyirazo and the Prosecution have both appealed these sentences.[203] The Appeals Chamber has reversed all of Zigiranyirazo's convictions under his Sixth and Twelfth Grounds of Appeal. Accordingly, the Appeals Chamber need not address any alleged errors relating to his sentences. **[page 30]**

V. DISPOSITION

79. For the foregoing reasons, **THE APPEALS CHAMBER**,

PURSUANT to Article 24 of the Statute and Rule 118 of the Rules;

SITTING in open session;

NOTING the written submissions of the parties and their oral arguments presented at the hearing on 28 September 2009;

GRANTS Protais Zigiranyirazo's Sixth and Twelfth Grounds of Appeal, **REVERSES** his convictions for genocide and extermination as a crime against humanity for participating in the massacre on 8 April 1994 at Kesho Hill in Gisenyi Prefecture and for aiding and abetting genocide on 12 and 17 April 1994 in connection with the killings at the Kiyovu Roadblock in Kigali, and **ENTERS** a verdict of acquittal under Counts 2 and 4 of the Indictment;

DISMISSES as moot Protais Zigiranyirazo's remaining grounds of appeal, the Prosecution's Appeal, as well as all pending motions for the admission of additional evidence;

ORDERS, in accordance with Rules 99(A) and 107 of the Rules, the immediate release of Protais Zigiranyirazo and **DIRECTS** the Registrar to make the necessary arrangements.

Done in English and French, the English text being authoritative.

Theodor Meron	Mehmet Güney	Fausto Pocar
Presiding Judge	Judge	Judge

Liu Daqun	Carmel Agius
Judge	Judge

Done this 16th day of November 2009 at Arusha, Tanzania.

---

[201] Trial Judgement, paras. 427, 436, 447, 468-470.
[202] Trial Judgement, para. 471.
[203] Zigiranyirazo Notice of Appeal, para. 17; Zigiranyirazo Appeal Brief, paras. 436-466; Prosecution Appeal Brief, paras. 4, 18-104; Prosecution Notice of Appeal, paras. 1-3, 5. In its Appeal Brief, the Prosecution abandons a sub-ground of appeal, raised in its Notice of Appeal, concerning the Trial Chamber's alleged failure to give sufficient consideration to Rwanda's sentencing framework. *See* Prosecution Notice of Appeal, para. 4; Prosecution Appeal Brief, para. 4, n. 6.

[page 1] VI. ANNEX A – PROCEDURAL HISTORY

1. The main aspects of the appeal proceedings are summarized below.

A. Notices of Appeal and Briefs

2. Trial Chamber III rendered the judgement in this case on 18 December 2008. Both parties appealed.

1. Zigiranyirazo Appeal

3. Zigiranyirazo submitted his Notice of Appeal on 19 January 2009.[1] On 28 January 2009, the Pre-Appeal Judge granted his request for an extension of time to file his Appellant's brief within 40 days of the filing of the French translation of the Trial Judgement.[2] On 10 February 2009, Zigiranyirazo requested leave to amend his grounds of appeal and annexed the Amended Notice of Appeal to his motion.[3] On 18 March 2009, the Appeals Chamber granted the request and accepted as filed the Amended Notice of Appeal.[4]

4. On 14 May 2009, the Pre-Appeal Judge denied Zigiranyirazo's request for an extension of the word limit in his Appellant's brief.[5] On 19 May 2009, Zigiranyirazo filed his Appellant's brief.[6] The Prosecution filed its Respondent's brief on 29 June 2009.[7] On 3 July 2009, the Pre-Appeal Judge denied Zigiranyirazo's request for an extension of time to file his Reply brief following the translation of the Prosecution's Respondent's brief into French.[8] Zigiranyirazo filed his Reply brief on 10 July 2009.[9]

2. Prosecution Appeal

5. The Prosecution submitted its Notice of Appeal on 15 January 2009.[10] It filed its Appellant's brief on 16 February 2009.[11] On 10 March 2009, the Appeals Chamber granted Zigiranyirazo a 15-day extension of time to file his Respondent's brief following the filing of the French version of the [page 2] Trial Judgement and the Prosecution's Appellant's brief.[12] On 1 May 2009, Zigiranyirazo submitted his Respondent's brief.[13] The Prosecution filed its Reply brief on 11 May 2009.[14] On 14 May 2009, the Pre-Appeal Judge denied the Prosecution's motion to strike portions of Zigiranyirazo's Respondent's brief.[15]

B. Assignment of Judges

6. On 13 January 2009, the Presiding Judge of the Appeals Chamber assigned the following Judges to hear the appeal: Judge Mohamed Shahabuddeen, Judge Mehmet Güney, Judge Fausto Pocar, Judge Liu Daqun, and Judge Theodor Meron.[16] Judge Theodor Meron was elected Presiding Judge in the case, and he acted as Pre-Appeal Judge. On 5 May 2009, the Presiding Judge of the Appeals Chamber designated Judge Carmel Agius to replace Judge Mohamed Shahabuddeen in this case.[17]

---

[1] Notice of Appeal, 19 January 2009.
[2] Decision on Protais Zigiranyirazo's Motion for an Extension of Time, 28 January 2009.
[3] Zigiranyirazo Motion for Leave to Amend Notice of Appeal, 10 February 2009 (Annex A: Amended Notice of Appeal, 9 February 2009).
[4] Decision on Protais Zigiranyirazo's Motion for Leave to Amend Notice of Appeal, 18 March 2009.
[5] Decision on Protais Zigiranyirazo's Motion for Variation of the Word Limits, 14 May 2009.
[6] Appellant's Brief, 19 May 2009.
[7] Prosecutor's Respondent's Brief, 29 June 2009.
[8] Decision on Protais Zigiranyirazo's Motion for an Extension of Time for the Filing of the Reply Brief, 3 July 2009.
[9] Appellant's Reply Brief, 10 July 2009.
[10] Prosecutor's Notice of Appeal, 15 January 2009.
[11] Prosecutor's Appellant's Brief, 16 February 2009.
[12] Decision on Protais Zigiranyirazo's Motion for an Extension of Time for the Filing of the Respondent's Brief, 10 March 2009.
[13] Defence Response to Prosecutor's Appellant's Brief (Appeal Against Sentence), 1 May 2009.
[14] Prosecutor's Brief in Reply, 11 May 2009.
[15] Decision on Prosecutor's Motion to Strike Portions of Protais Zigiranyirazo's Respondent's Brief, 14 May 2009.
[16] Order Assigning Judges to a Case Before the Appeals Chamber, 13 January 2009.
[17] Order Replacing a Judge in a Case Before the Appeals Chamber, 5 May 2009.

C. Motions Related to Hearing Additional Evidence on Appeal

7. On 16 September 2009, the Appeals Chamber denied Mr. Zigiranyirazo's first motion to admit several categories of additional evidence.[18] However, on 24 September 2009, the Appeals Chamber granted Mr. Zigiranyirazo's second motion and admitted two exhibits related to feasibility of travel between Kigali and Gisenyi Prefecture via Ruhengeri Prefecture during the relevant period.[19]

8. On 9 October 2009, the Prosecution filed a motion to admit rebuttal evidence, namely the transcripts and other relevant exhibits tendered during the evidence of Defence Witnesses BMP and YNZ, whose testimonies underlie the relevant findings of the excerpt of the *Karera* Trial Judgement, which was admitted by the Appeals Chamber on 24 September 2009.[20] On 12 October 2009, Zigiranyirazo filed a consolidated response and third motion for the admission of additional evidence related to the feasibility of travel between the Kigali area and Gisenyi Prefecture via Ruhengeri Prefecture during the period.[21] After considering the merits of the appeal, **[page 3]** the Appeals Chamber did not find it necessary to address the contested issue of the viability of the Ruhengeri route,[22] and as such these motions were dismissed as moot.[23]

D. Hearing of the Appeals

9. On 27 August 2009, the Appeals Chamber invited the parties: (i) to develop their submissions on the Trial Chamber's assessment of the alibi, specifically in comparison to other cases where the Appeals Chamber has considered the issue of alibi; and (ii) to discuss, with references to the record, the feasibility of travel along the route between Kigali and Gisenyi Prefecture via Ruhengeri Prefecture during the relevant period.[24] On 18 September 2009, the Appeals Chamber invited the parties to focus their submissions on Zigiranyirazo's Fifth, Sixth, Seventh, and Twelfth Grounds of Appeal.[25] On 28 September 2009, the parties presented their oral arguments at a hearing held in Arusha, Tanzania, in accordance with the Scheduling Order of 20 July 2009.[26] **[page 4]**

VII. ANNEX B – CITED MATERIALS AND DEFINED TERMS

A. Jurisprudence

1. ICTR

Gacumbitsi

Sylvestre Gacumbitsi v. The Prosecutor, Case No. ICTR-2001-64-A, Judgement, 7 July 2006 ("*Gacumbitsi* Appeal Judgement")

---

[18] Decision on Zigiranyirazo's Motion for Admission of Additional Evidence on Appeal, 16 September 2009.
[19] Decision on Zigiranyirazo's Second Motion for Admission of Additional Evidence on Appeal, 24 September 2009.
[20] Prosecutor's Motion to Present Rebuttal Evidence Pursuant to Rule 115, 9 October 2009.
[21] Response to Prosecutor's Motion to Present Rebuttal Evidence Pursuant to Rule 115 RPE and Motion to Allow Appeals Chamber to Take Cognizance of Additional Evidence under Rule 115 and for a Disclosure Order, 12 October 2009.
[22] *See supra* nn. 134, 193.
[23] *See supra* para. 79.
[24] Order for the Preparation of the Appeal Hearing, 27 August 2009.
[25] Second Order for the Preparation of the Appeal Hearing, 18 September 2009.
[26] Scheduling Order, 20 July 2009.

Kajelijeli

Juvénal Kajelijeli v. The Prosecutor, Case No. ICTR-98-44A-A, Judgement, 23 May 2005 ("*Kajelijeli* Appeal Judgement")

Kamuhanda

The Prosecutor v. Jean de Dieu Kamuhanda, Case No. ICTR-99-54A-T, Judgment and Sentence, 22 January 2004 ("*Kamuhanda* Trial Judgement")

Jean de Dieu Kamuhanda v. The Prosecutor, Case No. ICTR-99-54A-A, Judgement, 19 September 2005 ("*Kamuhanda* Appeal Judgement")

Karera

The Prosecutor v. François Karera, Case No. ICTR-01-74-T, Judgement and Sentence, 7 December 2007 ("*Karera* Trial Judgement")

François Karera v. The Prosecutor, Case No. ICTR-01-74-A, Judgement, 2 February 2009 ("*Karera* Appeal Judgement")

Kayishema and Ruzindana

The Prosecutor v. Clément Kayishema and Obed Ruzindana, Case No. ICTR-95-1-A, Judgement (Reasons), 1 June 2001 ("*Kayishema and Ruzindana* Appeal Judgement")

Muhimana

Mikaeli Muhimana v. The Prosecutor, Case No. ICTR-95-1B-A, Judgement, 21 May 2007 ("*Muhimana* Appeal Judgement")

Musema

The Prosecutor v. Alfred Musema, Case No. ICTR-96-13-T, Judgement, 27 January 2000 ("*Musema* Trial Judgement")

Alfred Musema v. The Prosecutor, Case No. ICTR-96-13-A, Judgement, 16 November 2001 ("*Musema* Appeal Judgement")

Muvunyi

Tharcisse Muvunyi v. The Prosecutor, Case No. ICTR-2000-55A-A, Judgement, 29 August 2008 ("*Muvunyi* Appeal Judgement") **[page 5]**

Nahimana et al.

Ferdinand Nahimana et al. v. The Prosecutor, Case No. ICTR-99-52-A, Judgement, 28 November 2007 ("*Nahimana et al.* Appeal Judgement")

Ndindabahizi

Emmanuel Ndindabahizi v. The Prosecutor, Case No. ICTR-01-71-A, Judgement, 16 January 2007 ("*Ndindabahizi* Appeal Judgement")

Niyitegeka

Eliézer Niyitegeka v. The Prosecutor, Case No. ICTR-96-14-A, Judgement, 9 July 2004 ("*Niyitegeka* Appeal Judgement")

Ntakirutimana

The Prosecutor v. Elizaphan Ntakirutimana and Gérard Ntakirutimana, Cases Nos. ICTR-96-10-A and ICTR-96-17-A, Judgement, 13 December 2004 ("*Ntakirutimana* Appeal Judgement")

Semanza

The Prosecutor v. Laurent Semanza, Case No. ICTR-97-20-T, Judgement and Sentence, 15 May 2003 ("*Semanza* Trial Judgement") **[page 6]**

Seromba

The Prosecutor v. Athanase Seromba, Case No ICTR-2001-66-A, Judgement, 12 March 2008 ("*Seromba* Appeal Judgement")

Simba

The Prosecutor v. Aloys Simba, Case No. ICTR-01-76-T, Judgement and Sentence, 13 December 2005 ("*Simba* Trial Judgement")

Aloys Simba v. The Prosecutor, Case No. ICTR-01-76-A, Judgement, 27 November 2007 ("*Simba* Appeal Judgement")

2. ICTY

Delalić et al.

Prosecutor v. Zejnil Delalić et al., Case No. IT-96-21-A, Judgement, 20 February 2001 ("*Delalić et al.* Appeal Judgement")

Halilović

Prosecutor v. Sefer Halilović, Case No. IT-01-48-A, Judgement, 16 October 2007 ("*Halilović* Appeal Judgement")

Krstić

Prosecutor v. Radislav Krstić, Case No. IT-98-33-A, Judgement, 19 April 2004 ("*Krstić* Appeal Judgement")

Kvočka et al.

Prosecutor v. Miroslav Kvočka et al., Case No. IT-98-30/1-A, Judgement, 28 February 2005 ("*Kvočka et al.* Appeal Judgement")

Limaj et al.

Prosecutor v. Fatmir Limaj et al., Case No. IT-03-66-T, Judgement, 30 November 2005 ("*Limaj et al.* Trial Judgement") **[page 7]**

Prosecutor v. Fatmir Limaj et al., Case No. IT-03-66-A, Judgement, 27 September 2007 ("*Limaj et al.* Appeal Judgement")

Mrkšić and Šljivančanin

Prosecutor v. Mile Mrkšić and Veselin Šljivančanin, Case No. IT-95-13/1-A, Judgement, 5 May 2009 ("*Mrkšić and Šljivančanin* Appeal Judgement")

B. Defined Terms and Abbreviations

Defence Closing Brief

The Prosecutor v. Protais Zigiranyirazo, Case No. ICTR-01-73-T, Defence Closing Brief: (Rule 86(a)), 30 April 2008

ICTR

International Criminal Tribunal for the Prosecution of Persons Responsible for Genocide and Other Serious Violations of International Humanitarian Law Committed in the Territory of Rwanda and Rwandan Citizens Responsible for Genocide and Other Such Violations Committed in the Territory of Neighbouring States, between 1 January 1994 and 31 December 1994

ICTY

International Tribunal for the Prosecution of Persons Responsible for Serious Violations of International Humanitarian Law Committed in the Territory of the former Yugoslavia since 1991

Indictment

The Prosecutor v. Protais Zigiranyirazo, Case No. ICTR-2001-73-I, Amended Indictment, 8 March 2005

n. (nn.)

footnote (footnotes)

p. (pp.)

page (pages) **[page 8]**

para. (paras.)

paragraph (paragraphs)

Practice Direction on Formal Requirements for Appeals from Judgement

Practice Direction on Formal Requirements for Appeals from Judgement, 4 July 2005

Prosecution Appeal Brief

Prosecutor's Appellant's Brief, 16 February 2009

Prosecution Notice of Appeal

Prosecutor's Notice of Appeal, 15 January 2009

Prosecution Reply Brief

Prosecutor's Brief in Reply, 11 May 2009

Prosecution Response Brief

Prosecutor's Respondent's Brief, 29 June 2009

Rules

Rules of Procedure and Evidence of the International Criminal Tribunal for Rwanda

Statute

Statute of the International Criminal Tribunal for Rwanda established by Security Council Resolution 955

T.

Transcript

Trial Judgement

The Prosecutor v. Protais Zigiranyirazo, Case No. ICTR-01-73-T, Judgement, 18 December 2008 **[page 9]**

Zigiranyirazo Appeal Brief

Appellant's Brief, 19 May 2009

Zigiranyirazo Notice of Appeal

Amended Notice of Appeal (Rule 108 R.P.E.), 9 February 2009

Zigiranyirazo Reply Brief

Appellant's Reply Brief, 10 July 2009

Zigiranyirazo Response Brief

Defence Response to Prosecutor's Appellant's Brief (Appeal Against Sentence), 1 May 2009

Commentary

1. Introduction

The prosecution of Protais Zigiranyirazo for genocide in Rwanda will not go down in history as an exemplary case of international criminal law enforcement. On 18 December 2008, Trial Chamber III of the ICTR convicted Zigiranyirazo for genocide, aiding and abetting genocide, and extermination as a crime against humanity. He received three sentences of imprisonment to be served concurrently, the longest being 20 years. On 16 December 2009, the Appeals Chamber reversed his convictions and acquitted Zigiranyirazo of all counts and ordered his immediate release. The judgement of the Appeals Chamber focuses on the Trials Chamber's treatment of the suspect's alibi evidence. It is also the final stage of a trial that did not effectively test the suspect's guilt or innocence. In this commentary, I will address both the substance of the Appeals judgement itself and the cursory and unsatisfactory way in which it has ended an important prosecution for the most serious of crimes. I will show how efficiency concerns can prevent actual justice from being done.[1] To properly convey the unfortunate implications of the Appeals judgement, it is important to first set out the background of the accused and the way his prosecution unfolded before the appeals phase.

2. Protais Zigiranyirazo

From early on, it was apparent that Zigiranyirazo had a case to answer before the ICTR. As the brother of Agathe Kanziga (wife of the former President of Rwanda) and thus the brother-in-law of President Habyarimana, he was a man of power and influence in Rwanda before the genocide. He was alleged to be a member of the "Akazu" (literally the "small house"; a term used to designate a small circle of powerful individuals close to President Habyarimana and his wife).[2] Zigiranyirazo was publicly accused of being an organizer of violence against the Tutsi's on various occasions already before and during the genocide.

On 15 August 1992, Rwandan official Christophe Mfizi published an open letter to Rwanda's dominant political party the MRND.[3] In his letter, Mfizi tendered his resignation from the MRND (*Mouvement Révolutionnaire Nationale pour la Démocratie le Développement*), citing the dominance of a secret clique he coined the 'Zero Network' (*Reseau Zero*) within the MRND as the primary reason. Mfizi would later explain as a witness in Zigiranyirazo's trial that he had chosen the term Zero as a reference to Zigiranyirazo, whom he considered to be the leader of the Zero Network.[4] Soon after Mfizi's open letter, an article in the journal *Umurava* alleged that "unrest" experienced in various places in Rwanda had been organised by "determined *Interahamwe*", including Zigiranyirazo and other well known ICTR defendants such as Bagosora, Barayagwiza, Ngirumpatse, Nzirorera and Renzaho.[5]

A subsequent report published by Professor Reyntjens on 9 October 1992 concluded that the Zero Network was affiliated to death squads.[6] Zigiranyirazo was again named as a member of the network[7], which according to this report aimed to destabilise the democratisation process, intimidate Tutsis and opposition parties, and impede the Arusha peace process by giving a message that neither the RPF nor refugees would be safe in Rwanda.

In March 1993 followed a report by an international commission of investigation on human rights abuses.[8] This report mentioned Zigiranyirazo more than once as being involved in the organisation of unrest and deadly violence against opposition parties. The international commission reported *inter alia* that witnesses

---

[1] To leave no doubt from the outset: my position is not that justice has not been served because Zigiranyirazo should have been convicted. My point is that Zigiranyirazo, through various strategical choices and procedural errors that I will describe in this note, was not prosecuted to the full extent of the law. Thus, the way his trial has unfolded is the problem, not its outcome, which is only for a court to decide. I do not know what the verdict would have been or should have been had Zigiranyirazo received a more thorough trial and I take no position on that.
[2] See e.g. Alison Desforges, Leave None to Tell the Story, New York: Human Rights Watch 1999, p. 40.
[3] ICTR, Judgement and Sentence, *Prosecutor v. Bagosora, Kabiligi, Ntabakuze and Nsengiyumva*, Case No. ICTR-98-41bis-T, T. Ch. I, 18 December 2008, Klip/ Sluiter ALC-XXXII-259, par. 612.
[4] Transcript of Wednesday 21 June 2006.
[5] ICTR, Judgement and Sentence, *Prosecutor v. Bagosora, Kabiligi, Ntabakuze and Nsengiyumva*, Case No. ICTR-98-41-T, T. Ch. I, 31 December 2008, Klip/ Sluiter ALC-XXXII-259, par. 612 and footnote 715.
[6] *Ibid.*, par. 612.
[7] *Ibid.*, footnote 717.
[8] *Ibid.*, par. 613.

803

confirmed the existence of death squads and that Zigiranyirazo – together with the president, his wife, Joseph Nzirorera and others – had attended death squad meetings aimed at organising the killing of Tutsis in 1991.

On 13 July 1994, when the genocide was drawing to a close, a Canadian newspaper reported that Zigiranyirazo had been expelled from Canada the year before after being convicted of uttering death threats against two Tutsi refugees in Montreal.[9] According to the article, these Tutsi refugees had accused Zigiranyirazo of participating in the planning of ethnic massacres and this accusation had been backed up by Human Rights Watch/Africa.

In February 1999, after the genocide, Omar Serushago was sentenced by the ICTR on the basis of a plea agreement in which he admitted to have been involved in the killing of a moderate Hutu after Zigiranyirazo identified the man at a roadblock.[10] Thus, Zigiranyirazo was on the public record as a key player in the Rwandan genocide when he was arrested in Belgium on 26 July 2001 and subsequently transferred to the ICTR.

3. Zigiranyirazo's Trial in First Instance

There were compelling reasons to conduct a thorough investigation and trial to establish whether or not Zigiranyirazo was indeed one of the driving forces behind the genocide.

The early signs were promising. The prosecutor charged Zigiranyirazo with five counts of genocide, conspiracy to commit genocide, complicity in genocide, murder as a crime against humanity and extermination as a crime against humanity. According to the indictment, Zigiranyirazo had met with government and military authorities in Kigali and Gisenyi, both before and after the beginning of the genocide in order to plan, prepare and facilitate attacks on Tutsis in 1994. In furtherance of this plan, several roadblocks were established in April 1994, in direct proximity of Zigiranyirazo's three homes. The indictment further alleged that Zigiranyirazo had been involved with creating and supporting the *Interahamwe* and with the killings of approximately 2,000 Tutsi at Kesho and Rurunga Hills, within the vicinity of the Rubaya Tea Factory, on 8 April 1994. In addition, Zigiranyirazo was held responsible for several other murders.[11]

The trial started on 3 October 2005 and closed on 29 May 2008. In these years, sixty-seven witnesses testified before the ICTR. The Trial Chamber convicted Zigiranyirazo for participating in a joint criminal enterprise to kill Tutsis at Kesho Hill on 8 April 1994 and aiding and abetting genocide at a roadblock near his Kiyovu residence in April 1994.[12]

In the Kesho Hill area, up to two thousand Tutsi refugees were in hiding during early April 1994. The Trial Chamber found that Zigiranyirazo arrived at Kesho Hill on the morning of 8 April 1994 as part of a convoy of presidential guards, *gendarmes* and *Interahamwe*. Zigiranyirazo and other officials then addressed a group of assailants who responded with applause and subsequently attacked the Tutsi refugees, killing between eight hundred and fifteen hundred of them.[13] The Trial Chamber found that Zigiranyirazo had participated in a joint criminal enterprise to kill Tutsi civilians on Kesho Hill and committed genocide as well as extermination as a crime against humanity.

The Trial Chamber also found that Zigiranyirazo was present at the so-called Kiyovu Roadblock on 12 and 17 April 1994 and that he had instructed the guards at the roadblock to check identity cards "well […] since Tutsis have changed their identification papers".[14] The Trial Chamber noted Zigiranyirazo's position of

---

[9] Picard, André, "Rwandan leader lived in splendour", *The Globe and Mail* (July 13, 1994) p. A8.
[10] ICTR, Sentence, *Prosecutor v. Serushago*, Case No. ICTR-98-39-5, T. Ch. I, 5 February 1999, Klip/ Sluiter, ALC-II-823, par. 25, sub xiii. See also Serushago's testimony on this subject in ICTR, *Prosecutor v. Nahimana, Barayagwiza and* Ngeze, Case No. ICTR-99-52-T, T. Ch. I, 3 December 2003, par. 734. Serushago had earlier given a statement to this effect to ICTR investigators in February 1998. See ICTR, Judgement and Sentence, *Prosecutor v. Bagosora, Kabiligi, Ntabakuze and Nsengiyumva*, Case No. ICTR-98-41-T, T. Ch. I, 31 December 2008, Klip/ Sluiter ALC-XXXII-259, par. 1657.
[11] ICTR, Judgement, *Prosecutor v. Zigiranyirazo*, Case No. ICTR-01-73-T, T. Ch. III, 18 December 2008, Klip/ Sluiter ALC-XXXII-137, par. 6 and 8.
[12] *Ibid.*, par. 7, 251, 330, 410, 426–427, 436, 439, 447.
[13] *Ibid.*, par. 329–330.
[14] *Ibid.*, par. 251.

authority in relation to those he instructed, in particular in relation to his guard who was in charge of the roadblock.[15] The Trial Chamber held that in the context of the widespread and systemic attacks against Tutsi, previous killings of Tutsis at the roadblock, Zigiranyirazo having seen corpses at the roadblock, and having issued instructions to check identity cards "well" with specific reference to Tutsi, Zigiranyirazo had known that those he instructed possessed a genocidal intent. The Trial Chamber found Zigiranyirazo guilty of aiding and abetting genocide at the Kiyovu Roadblock through the instructions he issued. Zigiranyirazo had not been charged with command responsibility.[16]

On all other counts, he was acquitted. No evidence was led for various allegations in the indictment.[17] On the other hand, numerous allegations which were addressed during trial had not been properly pleaded in the indictment, according to the Trial Chamber.[18] Thus, not all allegations in the indictment were put to a test and not all evidence led at trial was taken into account by the Trial Chamber. To some extent, this is normal for a prosecution of this size and character. Witnesses can withdraw, change, retract or expand their testimony. New evidence can emerge. In this particular case, however, the mismatch between the indictment and the actual trial seems rather substantial. Whether that was avoidable or not is hard to tell for an outside observer who does not know what transpired behind the scenes. In any case, this mismatch certainly did not contribute to an effective prosecution. This is most apparent in the reasoning for Zigiranyirazo's acquittal from the charge of conspiracy to commit genocide, which chiefly consists of an enumeration of evidence not produced or not properly pleaded in the indictment.[19]

On 18 December 2008, the same day as Zigiranyirazo's conviction in first instance, the ICTR judgement in the case of Bagosora and others found the different reports from 1992 and 1993 mentioning Zigiranyirazo as an organizer of anti-Tutsi violence to be compelling evidence.[20] The judgement noted that the reports 'make convincing arguments that the violence was not disorganised or spontaneous but committed with cooperation of various government and military authorities.'[21] The Trial Chamber in that case also considered the testimony of several witnesses on the same subject, and found that there is 'considerable evidence of a group or network, close to President Habyarimana, which exercised influence within Rwanda', that 'indirect evidence indicates that it instigated violence'[22] and that 'considerable evidence points to the existence of death squads in Rwanda years before the killings in April 1994'.[23] None of this 'compelling evidence' is discussed in the trial judgement of Zigiranyirazo.

Despite the fact that only a few of the numerous allegations in the indictment of Zigiranyirazo were proven, the Prosecution did not appeal against any of the factual findings of the Trial Chamber. It only appealed the sentence imposed and responded to the grounds of appeal of the accused. Zigiranyirazo presented seventeen grounds of appeal challenging his convictions and his sentences. The most important of these grounds turned out to be those relating to his alibi evidence.

4. The Appeals judgement

In its judgement, the Appeals Chamber reverses the convictions entered by the Trial Chamber because it disagrees with the treatment of Zigiranyirazo's alibi evidence. In fact, it disagrees so much with the approach taken by the Trial Chamber that it underscores 'the seriousness of the Trial Chamber's errors' and claims that 'the Trial Judgement misstated the principles of law governing the distribution of the burden of proof with regards to alibi and seriously erred in its handling of the evidence'.[24] Even stronger, according to the Appeals Chamber 'Zigiranyirazo's resulting convictions (…) violated the most basic and fundamental principles of justice'.[25]

---

[15] *Ibid.*, par. 422.
[16] *Ibid.*, par. 6.
[17] *Ibid.*, par. 13–16.
[18] *Ibid.*, par. 19–80.
[19] See in particular par. 392–395.
[20] ICTR, Judgement and Sentence, *Prosecutor v. Bagosora, Kabiligi, Ntabakuze and Nsengiyumva*, Case No. ICTR-98-41-T, T. Ch. I, 18 December 2008, Klip/ Sluiter ALC-XXXII-259, par. 615.
[21] *Ibid.*
[22] *Ibid.*, par. 537–539.
[23] *Ibid.*, par. 619.
[24] *Ibid.*, par. 75.
[25] *Ibid.*

As explained above, these convictions turned on Zigiranyirazo's presence and actions on two different locations in April 1994: Kesho Hill and a roadblock in Kiyovu. Zigiranyirazo himself, however, had claimed to have been elsewhere on all relevant dates. He claimed to be in Kanombe on April 8th, and in Rubaya in Gisenyi on April 12th and 17th. Several witnesses testified to this. The Appeals Chamber, in short, finds that the Trial Chamber in fact reversed the burden of proof in its assessment of Zigiranyirazo's alibi.[26] The Appeals Chamber also finds that the Trial Chamber erred in its treatment of the facts and failed to give a reasoned opinion.

To some extent, the criticism of the Appeals Chamber is warranted. For both Kesho Hill and Kiyovu, the Trial Chamber does not discount the testimony of several alibi witnesses but concludes that it can be reconciled with the incriminating testimony of other witnesses because it either does not correspond with the same times on a given day, or is not sufficiently specific about day or time. Yet, the Trial Chamber does so without a discussion of the time frame needed to travel between the location of the crime and the location where the accused was seen by the alibi witnesses. Obviously, such a discussion is necessary to determine whether a sighting at a different location on the same day can actually be reconciled with testimony placing the accused at the scene of the crime. Also, it appears the Appeals Chamber is right in its criticism of the way the Trial Chamber misread some factual points in the testimony it considered.

On closer analysis, however, the harsh words of the Appeals judgement appear overstated and the conclusions it draws are rather questionable. The Appeals Chamber points to various paragraphs which it leads to conclude that the Trial Chamber reversed the burden of proof in its assessment of Zigiranyirazo's alibi and required him to prove his exact location at a given time rather than just raise reasonable doubt about the allegations against him.[27] Yet, nowhere does the Appeals Chamber mention that in paragraph 244 – placed in the trial judgement before all other paragraphs cited by the Appeals Chamber to reach its conclusion – the Trial Chamber clearly states that it 'will address whether the Defence alibi evidence raises doubt as to the testimony of Witness BCW'.[28] Thus, unlike the Appeals Chamber posits, the Trial Chamber has in fact articulated the correct standard of proof for alibi evidence on the first occasion to factually discuss alibi evidence. Even more, the Trial Chamber articulates this correct standard as an introduction to its discussion of the alibi evidence concerning the Kiyovu roadblock. Also worth mentioning is the Trial Chamber's explanation at the beginning of the judgement that the burden of proof is on the prosecution and extends to 'every element of the crime charged and of the mode of liability and any fact indispensable for a conviction'.[29] In contrast to the later paragraphs from the trial judgement cited by the Appeals Chamber – which contrast or analyse different witness testimonies – these two statements directly (and correctly) address the burden of proof. While I agree with Appeals Chamber that some of the language of the trial judgement used in dealing with the alibi evidence is not as careful as it should have been, I find the conclusions in the appeals judgement on the burden of proof in the trial judgement incorrect and formulated in overly harsh terms. In particular, it seems that the Appeals Chamber either did not see the correct statement of the burden of proof in paragraph 244 of the trial judgement, or chose to ignore it in its analysis.

I also fail to understand the Appeals Chamber's dismissal of the possibility that Zigiranyirazo could have travelled by helicopter between Kanombe and Kesho Hill, a faster mode of travel allowing him to be both in Kanombe and on Kesho Hill on the same day. In one sentence, the Appeals Chamber brushes this point aside and moves on: 'There is no basis in the record for the Prosecution's theory that the journey would have taken Zigiranyirazo approximately 45 minutes by helicopter.'[30] Obviously, this is a point of some importance. If the accused could have travelled the distance within an hour or less, the sightings at two different places on the same day are much less likely to raise doubt then if that distance could only be travelled in many hours or more.

---

[26] ICTR, Judgement, *Zigiranyirazo v. Prosecutor,* Case No. ICTR-01-73-A, A. Ch., 16 November 2009, in this volume, p. 777, par. 41–43, 63–64.
[27] *Ibid.,* par. 40–41.
[28] ICTR, Judgement, *Prosecutor v. Zigiranyirazo,* Case No. ICTR-01-73-T, T. Ch. III, 18 December 2008, Klip/ Sluiter ALC-XXXII-137, par. 244, emphasis added by author.
[29] ICTR, Judgement, *Prosecutor v. Zigiranyirazo,* Case No. ICTR-01-73-T, T. Ch. III, 18 December 2008, Klip/ Sluiter ALC-XXXII-137, par. 89.
[30] ICTR, Judgement, *Zigiranyirazo v. Prosecutor,* Case No. ICTR-01-73-A, A. Ch., 16 November 2009, par. 44.

Given its relevance for the subject under discussion, it is not easy to understand the Appeals Chamber's position that there is no 'basis in the record' for this 'theory'. Does this lack of basis in the record refer to the length of the flight time or to the very possibility of helicopter travel itself? Does it mean that the exact flight time for a helicopter should have been established in the trial record and that without this, the scenario can not be included in the discussion? Or does it mean that the record lacks evidence that Zigiranyirazo could actually travel by helicopter in that period? Does the Appeals Chamber consider the scenario of helicopter travel in this case so unrealistic as to warrant no further discussion? The first option would be overly formalistic, the latter a misreading of the facts.

The Appeals Chamber itself accepts as a reasonable estimate for travel by car between Kanombe and Kesho hill a time of three hours and 18 minutes under optimal conditions.[31] I assume one does not need an expert of any kind to accept that a helicopter would need significantly less time than a car to travel the same distance, as well as to realize that a helicopter would hardly be slowed down by the circumstances on the ground in April 1994. Whether or not the flight time is indeed 45 minutes, or a bit less or more, is not as important as the only logical conclusion that the possibility of air travel would indeed influence the extent to which sightings of the accused on different locations on the same day actually contradict each other.

Then one should turn to the question of whether it is realistic or far-fetched to consider the possibility of helicopter travel. Zigiranyirazo was a man of power in the highest circles of the government. It is a matter of public record that the government and army at that time had helicopters at its disposal and actually used them.[32] It is also a matter of public record that helicopter travel did in fact take place from Kanombe, the Kigali neighbourhood where alibi witnesses placed Zigiranyirazo at the same day he was seen on Kesho hill. Moreover, during the trial in first instance at least one witness has testified that he saw Zigiranyirazo arrive by helicopter to a meeting on another occasion in April 1994.[33]

It would seem to me that under these circumstances, the possibility of helicopter travel is not so remote as to be discounted without discussion. If that is indeed the case, it is open to question whether the Appeals judgement itself reflects the correct burden of proof to be applied on this subject. If the possibility of air travel was real, should that possibility not simply have been taken into account when assessing whether or not the alibi evidence discussed raised reasonable doubt? Instead, the Appeals Chamber appears to have required the prosecution to prove that a helicopter was used or was available to be used. A parallel may clarify this point: if the alibi of the accused consisted of his presence in another city a day later and his (correct) position that it was impossible to traverse the distance on foot within a day that alibi would simply be dismissed. Unless there were clear indications that the accused had no access to means of motorized transport, the prosecution would not be required to prove that the accused had in fact taken a car, or bus, or actually had a car or money for public transport at his disposal. The obvious possibility of motorized travel would simply lead to the conclusion that the impossibility to travel on foot within the material time is not enough to raise doubt.

An example of a similar approach to the possibility of air travel can be found in the case of Bagosora:

> 'The Chamber has also taken into consideration that Bagosora, as a senior official in the Ministry of Defence, might have had access to Rwandan military aircraft, in particular in view of the importance of his mission. Bagosora testified that the Gazelle helicopters owned by the Rwandan army would not have been able to transport him from Kinshasa to Goma given the need to refuel. [...] The range of a Gazelle helicopter is not dispositive since it could have been refueled or he might have used another longer range aircraft. However, these possibilities still do not eliminate the reasonable possibility that his alibi is true when considered with the totality of the Prosecution and Defence evidence of his activities during this period.'[34]

Thus, the possibility of air travel was included in the analysis, even though – I assume – there was no basis in the trial record for the 'theory' that a helicopter could be refuelled or another aircraft could have been

---

[31] *Ibid.*, par. 44.
[32] ICTR, Judgement and Sentence, *Prosecutor v. Bagosora, Kabiligi, Ntabakuze and Nsengiyumva*, Case No. ICTR-98-41-T, T. Ch. I, 18 December 2008, Klip/ Sluiter ALC-XXXII-259, par. 1978–1979.
[33] ICTR, Judgement, *Zigiranyirazo v. Prosecutor*, Case No. ICTR-01-73-A, A. Ch., 16 November 2009 par. 150.
[34] ICTR, Judgement and Sentence, *Prosecutor v. Bagosora, Kabiligi, Ntabakuze and Nsengiyumva*, Case No. ICTR-98-41-T, T. Ch. I, 18 December 2008, Klip/ Sluiter ALC-XXXII-259, par. 1959 and footnote 2139.

used. This is, it seems to me, the only correct approach to such issues and should have been adopted by the Appeals Chamber. In contrast, in the case of Zigiranyirazo the Appeals Chamber categorically refused to take into account the possibility of air travel, yet one paragraph later pronounced that in assessing alibi evidence 'the distance, time and feasibility of travel are highly relevant factors to consider' and '[d]espite the crucial importance of this issue, the Trial Chamber failed to address it'.[35]

A further question is why the Appeals Chamber decided to dispose of the case itself. One wonders whether the Appeals Chamber really 'had no choice but to reverse Zigiranyirazo's convictions' and then acquit him.[36] Could the court have ordered a (partial) re-trial? Although the term 'retrial' is not mentioned in the Statute, the ICTR Rules provide that "in appropriate circumstances the Appeals Chamber may order that the accused be *retried* according to law."[37] Just a year before, the Appeals Chamber had ordered a partial retrial in the case of Tharcisse Muvunyi. In the case of Muvunyi, the Appeals Chamber found that it could not determine whether the Trial Chamber assessed the entire evidence on a specific incident exhaustively and properly.[38] In particular, it found unclear why the Trial Chamber had preferred the evidence of two incriminating witnesses regarding the character of a meeting attended by the accused over the conflicting evidence of a defense witness. Although the Appeals Chamber stressed that an order for retrial is an exceptional measure to which resort must necessarily be limited and that Muvunyi at that time had already spent over eight years in the Tribunal's custody, it also noted that the alleged offence was of the utmost gravity and that 'interests of justice would not be well served if retrial were not ordered to allow the trier of fact the opportunity to fully assess the entirety of the relevant evidence and provide a reasoned opinion'.[39]

What is so different in the case of Zigiranyirazo? There is nothing in Rule 118 (C) that precludes a retrial, it seems. Yet, the appeal judgement never even mentions the option of a retrial, let alone explains why it was not ordered or what is different from the case of Muvunyi.

Instead, the Appeals Chamber proceeds to consider the relevant evidence *de novo* under the correct legal standard. At least, that is what it claims to do.[40] However, in the review that follows, the Appeals judgement so often refers to the fact that certain alibi witnesses were not discounted by the Trial Chamber that it is unclear whether it actually carries out a *de novo* review or whether it departs from the findings of the Trial Chamber concerning these alibi witnesses and then adds its own observations.[41] The latter approach would, I submit, be flawed. After all, it is no secret that efficiency concerns lead judges to generally discount witness testimony only where necessary to explain their findings. If judges believe that the testimony of certain witnesses can be reconciled with their findings, they simply withhold judgement on that testimony. That is not a vote of confidence for the witness. It is rather an efficient way to try a case. Thus, where the Trial Chamber writes that it does not discount the testimony of certain alibi witnesses, one can assume that this decision was substantially influenced by the Trial Chamber's belief that it did not have to rule on the veracity of this testimony in order to convict. When that belief turns out to be wrong, as it did, it is a mistake to conclude that the Trial Chamber has validated the testimony of these defense witnesses. It is more likely that the Trial Chamber simply did not pass final judgement on their testimony.

We do not know how the Trial Chamber would have ruled on the value of this alibi testimony had it felt necessary to do so. A review of the relevant paragraphs reveals that the Trial Chamber noted on the alibi witnesses for Kesho Hill that one acknowledged that she did not "remember well".[42] Another did not mention the accused's presence in Kanombe on 8 April 1994 until a leading question from the defence counsel.[43] The third acknowledged that he was not "a hundred per cent sure"[44] and moreover, the testimony of several

---

[35] ICTR, Judgement, *Zigiranyirazo v. Prosecutor*, Case No. ICTR-01-73-A, A. Ch., 16 November 2009, par. 45.
[36] *Ibid.*, par. 75.
[37] Rule 118 ICTR.
[38] ICTR, Judgement, *Prosecutor v. Muvunyi*, Case No. ICTR-2000-55A, A. Ch., 28 August 2008, par. 147–148.
[39] *Ibid.*, par. 148.
[40] ICTR, Judgement, *Zigiranyirazo v. Prosecutor*, Case No. ICTR-01-73-A, A. Ch., 16 November 2009, in this volume, p. 777, par. 43.
[41] See e.g. *Ibid.*, par. 46, 49, 50, 70, 71.
[42] ICTR, Judgement, *Prosecutor v. Zigiranyirazo*, Case No. ICTR-01-73-T, T. Ch. III, 18 December 2008, Klip/ Sluiter ALC-XXXII-137, par. 323.
[43] *Ibid.*, par. 323.
[44] *Ibid.*, par. 325.

witnesses lacked detail[45] and that the evidence of all the witnesses was too vague.[46] Regarding the alibi witnesses for the Kiyovu roadblock, the Trial Chamber recalled that the evidence provided by some of these witnesses was insufficiently detailed, vague and included discrepancies.[47] Where the Trial Chamber calls various prosecution witnesses reliable, credible or consistent, it has nothing positive to say on the alibi witnesses. Reading through the Trial Chamber's description of these testimonies, it is hard to believe that a positive appraisal of these witnesses rather than a wish to be efficient led the Trial Chamber to not discount their testimony.

Yet, the Appeals Chamber overturns the findings of the Trial Chamber and without further ado acquits the defendant. That is a drastic step to take, considering that the Trial Chamber reached its conclusions after a multi-year trial while the Appeals Chamber could base its verdict only on written submissions by the parties and no more than one actual day in court.[48]

One wonders if the Appeals Chamber gave enough consideration to its own pronouncement that it 'must give deference to the Trial Chamber that received the evidence at trial'.[49] If the Appeals Chamber for its reasoning relies on the Trial Chamber's decision not to discount the alibi witnesses, it may well have based its decision on a misreading of the Trial judgement. If not, the Appeals Chamber has probably executed the shortest and most efficient *de novo* review of witness testimony in a genocide trial in world legal history, leaving many hesitations of the Trial Chamber regarding these witnesses unaddressed.

And so ends the trial of Zigiranyirazo. It is particularly unsatisfying to see a trial for some of the most serious crimes end up in fault-finding among the different trial participants,[50] more than actually attempting to establish guilt or innocence as well as possible. It is likely that efficiency concerns have played a substantial role in the process leading to this unfortunate result. The real pressure on the ICTR to wrap up its cases and close down must influence decisions such as the breadth of the pre-trial investigation, whether or not to appeal partial acquittals, and whether or not to grant a retrial. Clearly, the need for efficiency in criminal law enforcement, national or international, is a reality we have to deal with. For international tribunals of a temporary nature, that reality is probably even more difficult to reconcile with a vigorous pursuit of justice than for permanent fora. The outcome in this specific case, however, is hard to digest.

Ward Ferdinandusse

---

[45] *Ibid.*, par. 323, 327.
[46] *Ibid.*, par. 328.
[47] *Ibid.*, par. 245–250.
[48] ICTR, Judgement, *Zigiranyirazo v. Prosecutor,* Case No. ICTR-01-73-A, A. Ch., 16 November 2009, in this volume, p. 777, par. 5–7.
[49] *Ibid.*, par. 11.
[50] In addition to the harsh criticism of the Trial Chamber in the Appeals judgement, note e.g. the explicit way in which the Appeals Chamber records how the prosecution did not answer a question regarding the possibility of helicopter travel. ICTR, Judgement, *Zigiranyirazo v. Prosecutor,* Case No. ICTR-01-73-A, A. Ch., 16 November 2009, in this volume, p. 777, fn. 120.

International Criminal Tribunal for Rwanda
Tribunal pénal international pour le Rwanda

TRIAL CHAMBER III

OR: ENG

Before Judges: Vagn Joensen, Presiding
Judge Bakhtiyar Tuzmukhamedov
Judge Gberdao Gustave Kam

Registrar: Adama Dieng

Date: 17 November 2009

THE PROSECUTOR

v.

Michel BAGARAGAZA

Case No. ICTR-05-86-S

SENTENCING JUDGEMENT

Office of the Prosecutor:

Mr. Wallace Kapaya
Mr. Patrick Gabaake
Mr. Moussa Sefon
Mr. Iskander Ismail

Counsel for the Defence:

Mr. Geert-Jan Alexander Knoops
Mr. Wayne Jordash
Ms. Anne-Marie Verwiel

[page 2] CHAPTER I: INTRODUCTION AND PROCEDURAL HISTORY

1. Michel Bagaragaza ("Accused") was charged with conspiracy to commit genocide, genocide and, in the alternative, complicity in genocide in an Indictment confirmed by Judge Sergei Alekseevich Egorov on 28 July 2005.[1]

2. Before his surrender, the Accused agreed to cooperate with the Prosecution. He also agreed with the Prosecution to be tried before a national jurisdiction, which would be determined at a later stage.[2]

3. On 15 August 2005, Michel Bagaragaza voluntarily surrendered to the Tribunal's authorities in Arusha, Tanzania, and made his first initial appearance the next day where he pleaded not guilty to each of the three counts set forth in the Initial Indictment.[3] He was then transferred to the Detention Unit of the International Criminal Tribunal for the former Yugoslavia ("ICTY") in The Hague, in accordance with a decision from the President of the Tribunal.[4]

4. On 19 May 2006, a Trial Chamber denied the Prosecution's motion for referral of the case to the Kingdom of Norway as this State did not have any provision against genocide in its domestic criminal law.[5] The appeal of the Prosecution against that decision was dismissed by the Appeals Chamber on 30 August 2006.[6]

5. On 30 November 2006 the Chamber granted the Prosecution's request to amend the Indictment by adding a new count of killing and causing violence to health and physical or mental well-being as serious violations of Article 3 common to the Geneva Conventions of 1949 and Additional Protocol II of 1977, as an alternative to the initial three counts.[7] On [page 3] 1 December 2006, the Accused made his second initial appearance where he pleaded not guilty to Count IV of the Amended Indictment.[8]

6. On 13 April 2007, the Chamber granted the Prosecution's Motion for referral of the case to the Kingdom of the Netherlands.[9] However, on 17 August 2007, the Chamber revoked the referral of the case, following a formal notification that Dutch Courts did not have jurisdiction to try the crimes alleged in the Indictment.[10]

7. On 20 May 2008, the Accused was transferred by the Dutch authorities back to the United Nations Detention Facility ("UNDF") in Arusha pending trial.[11]

---

[1] *The Prosecutor v. Michel Bagaragaza*, Case No. ICTR-05-86 ("*Bagaragaza*"), Decision on Confirmation of an Indictment Against Michel Bagaragaza (TC), 28 July 2005.
[2] Joint Motion for Consideration of a Guilty Plea Agreement, dated 17 August 2009 but filed on 18 August 2009, para. 4; Exibit D6, para. 4.
[3] T. 16 August 2006.
[4] *Bagaragaza*, Order for Special Detention Measures (President), 13 August 2005. The President of the Tribunal then granted several motions from the Prosecution to extend the Accused's detention in The Hague: *see Bagaragaza*, Order for the Continued Detention of Michel Bagaragaza at the ICTY Detention Unit in The Hague, The Netherlands (President), 17 February 2006; *Bagaragaza*, Order for the Continued Detention of Michel Bagaragaza at the ICTY Detention Unit in The Hague, The Netherlands (President), 16 August 2006; Order for the Continued Detention of Michel Bagaragaza at the ICTY Detention Unit in The Hague, The Netherlands (President), 14 February 2007.
[5] *Bagaragaza*, Decision on the Prosecution Motion for Referral to the Kingdom of Norway (TC), para. 16.
[6] *Bagaragaza*, Decision on Rule 11 *bis* Appeal (AC), 30 August 2009.
[7] *Bagaragaza*, Decision on the Prosecutor's Application for Leave to Amend the Indictment (TC), 30 November 2006.
[8] T. 1 December 2006.
[9] *Bagaragaza*, Decision on Prosecutor's Request for Referral of the Indictment to the Kingdom of the Netherlands (TC), 13 April 2007.
[10] *Bagaragaza*, Decision on Prosecutor's Extremely Urgent Motion for the Revocation of the Referral to the Kingdom of the Netherlands pursuant to Rule 11 *bis* (F) and (G) (TC), 17 August 2007.
[11] When the Chamber revoked the referral of the case to the Kingdom of the Netherlands on 17 August 2007, a warrant of arrest and transfer was also issued (*Bagaragaza*, Warrant of Arrest and Order for Transfer and Detention (TC), 17 August 2009). The President of the Tribunal denied the Defence's application for detention at the ICTY Detention Unit in The Hague on 29 August 2007 (*Bagaragaza*, Decision on Defence Application for Modification of Detention Conditions of the Accused (President), 29 August 2007) and denied a joint motion on the same issue again on 6 March 2008 (*Bagaragaza*, Decision on Joint Prosecution and Defence Application for Modification of Detention Conditions of the Accused (President), 6 March 2008).

Sentencing Judgement

8. On 14 April 2008, the Parties filed a first joint motion for consideration of a guilty plea agreement,[12] which was followed by a motion by the Prosecution for leave to amend the Indictment, retaining only the count of complicity in genocide.[13] On 14 July 2008, the Chamber denied the Prosecution's motion for leave to amend the Indictment finding that the material facts supporting the proposed count did not sufficiently plead the crime of complicity in genocide.[14] Following this decision, the Parties jointly requested leave to withdraw their joint motion for consideration of a guilty plea.[15] The Chamber granted the application.[16]

9. The Parties then proceeded to be ready for the commencement of the trial before the Tribunal.[17] **[page 4]**

10. On 17 August 2009, immediately before the trial was scheduled to start, the Parties filed a joint motion for consideration of a guilty plea agreement between the Prosecutor and the Accused ("Joint Motion") that included a statement of admitted facts signed by the Accused ("Statement of Facts") and a guilty plea agreement signed by the Prosecutor and the Accused ("Guilty Plea Agreement").[18]

11. On 17 September 2009, during the hearing on the guilty plea before this Chamber, Michel Bagaragaza pleaded guilty to complicity in genocide and not guilty to the three other counts of the Amended Indictment.[19] The Chamber also granted the Prosecution's Motion for leave to Amend the Indictment. That same day, the Prosecution filed the operative Indictment ("Indictment") charging the Accused with individual criminal responsibility pursuant to Article 6 (1) of the Statute of the International Criminal Tribunal for Rwanda ("Statute") for one count of complicity in genocide. The Indictment is annexed to this judgement as an Annex.

12. On 3 November 2009, the Chamber heard one character witness.[20] The following day it admitted 12 written statements from character witnesses pursuant to Rule 92 *bis* of the Rules of Procedure and Evidence ("Rules") as well as the Parties' joint statement on agreed facts concerning Michel Bagaragaza's cooperation with the Prosecution.[21] On that day, the Chamber also heard the Parties submissions on sentencing and Michel Bagaragaza's personal address to the Chamber expressing remorse for his actions.[22]

13. On 5 November 2009, the Chamber sentenced Michel Bagaragaza to a prison term of eight years and indicated in its oral ruling that the written reasons for its sentencing would follow.[23] The present Judgement is the authoritative statement of the Chamber's findings and reasoning. **[page 5]**

CHAPTER II: THE GUILTY PLEA

14. There is no specific provision in the Statute regarding guilty pleas. The relevant provisions are to be found in Rules 62 (B) and 62 *bis*.[24]

---

[12] Joint Motion for Consideration of a Guilty Plea Agreement Between Michel Bagaragaza and the Office of the Prosecutor (confidential), filed on 14 April 2008.
[13] Prosecutor's Request for Leave to File an Amended indictment (Confidential), filed on 8 July 2009.
[14] *Bagaragaza*, Confidential Decision on the Prosecution Motion to File a Further Amended Indictment (TC), 14 July 2008.
[15] Joint Application to Withdraw the Joint Motion for Consideration of a Guilty Plea Agreement Between Michel Bagaragaza and the Office of the Prosecutor (confidential), dated 21 July 2008 but filed on 22 July 2008.
[16] *Bagaragaza*, Confidential Decision on the "Joint Application to Withdraw the Joint Motion for Consideration of a Guilty Plea Agreement Between Michel Bagaragaza and the Office of the Prosecutor" (TC), 24 July 2008.
[17] *See* Status conferences of 16 December 2008 and 9 March 2009.
[18] Joint Motion for Consideration of a Guilty Plea Agreement, dated 17 August 2009 and filed on 18 August 2009 ("Joint Motion") with Annex A: Statement of Admitted Facts ("Statement of Facts"), and Annex B: Guilty Plea Agreement ("Guilty Plea Agreement").
[19] T. 17 September 2009; *see* Statement of Facts, paras. 4-5.
[20] T. 3 November 2009.
[21] T. 4 November 2009.
[22] T. 4 November 2009.
[23] T. 5 November 2009.
[24] Rule 62: Initial Appearance of Accused and Plea
[...]
(B) If an accused pleads guilty in accordance with Rule 62 (A) (v), or requests to change his plea to guilty, the Trial Chamber shall satisfy itself that the guilty plea:
   (i) is made freely and voluntarily;
   (ii) is an informed plea;

813

15. On 17 September 2009, the Accused pleaded guilty to the count of complicity in genocide[25] and confirmed that his plea was made freely and voluntarily without any kind of threat, pressure, coercion or duress[26] and that it was informed and unequivocal.

16. The Chamber noted that the guilty plea and the Indictment: (1) conformed to the terms and conditions articulated in the Guilty Plea Agreement;[27] (2) conformed to the declarations contained in the Statement of Facts; (3) relied on sufficient facts to establish complicity in genocide, and (4) that there was no material disagreement between the Parties about the facts of the Case. Therefore, the Chamber was satisfied that the conditions of Rule 62 (B) were fulfilled and entered a plea of guilty on behalf of the Accused.[28] **[page 6]**

CHAPTER III: THE EVENTS

I. The Accused

17. Michel Bagaragaza was born in 1945 in Bushiru region, Giciye *commune*, Gisenyi *préfecture*, Republic of Rwanda.[29] He is married and the father of eight children.[30]

18. During the genocide, Bagaragaza was the Director General of OCIR/Thé, the government office that controlled the tea industry in Rwanda, one of the most important industrial enterprises in the country.[31] In this capacity, Bagaragaza controlled eleven tea factories which employed approximately 55,000 persons.[32] Bagaragaza was also the vice-president of the *Banque Continentale Africaine au Rwanda* ("BACAR") and a member of the *comité préfectoral* of the MRND in Gisenyi *préfecture*, which established the *Interahamwe* in this *préfecture*.[33]

19. Furthermore, Bagaragaza was part of a powerful and tight group of people known as the *Akazu*.[34] The *Akazu* exercised substantial political and financial power in Rwanda and included the President of Rwanda's family members as well as persons from the regions of Bushiru, Gisenyi and Ruhengeri.[35]

    (iii) is unequivocal; and
    (iv) is based on sufficient facts for the crime and accused's participation in it, either on the basis of objective indicia or of lack of any material disagreement between the parties about the facts of the case.
  Thereafter the Trial Chamber may enter a finding of guilt and instruct the Registrar to set a date for the sentencing hearing.

Rule 62*bis*: Plea Agreement Procedure
  (A) The Prosecutor and the Defence may agree that, upon the accused entering a plea of guilty to the indictment or to one or more counts of the indictment, the Prosecutor shall do one or more of the following before the Trial Chamber:
    (i) apply to amend the indictment accordingly;
    (ii) submit that a specific sentence or sentencing range is appropriate;
    (iii) not oppose a request by the accused for a particular sentence or sentencing range.
  (B) The Trial Chamber shall not be bound by any agreement specified in paragraph (A).
  (C) If a plea agreement has been reached by the parties, the Trial Chamber shall require the disclosure of the agreement in open session or, on a showing of good cause, in closed session, at the time the accused pleads guilty in accordance with Rule 62 (A) (v), or requests to change his or her plea to guilty.

[25] T. 17 September 2009.
[26] T. 17 September 2009, p. 3.
[27] Guilty Plea Agreement, para. 3.
[28] T. 17 September 2009, p. 10.
[29] Indictment, 17 September 2009, para. 1.
[30] Guilty Plea Agreement, para. 5.3
[31] Statement of Facts, para. 4 ; *see also* Indictment para. 2.
[32] Statement of Facts, para. 4.
[33] Statement of Facts, para. 5.
[34] Statement of Facts, para. 6; *see also* Indictment para. 3.
[35] Statement of Facts, para. 6.

II. Factual and Legal Findings

A. The Indictment

20. In support of the Count of complicity in genocide, the Indictment alleges that in April 1994, in the Gisenyi *préfecture*, Michel Bagaragaza substantially contributed to the killings of more than one thousand members of the Tutsi ethnic group who sought refuge at Kesho Hill and Nyundo Cathedral.[36] For all the acts adduced in support of this count, the Prosecution alleges that the Accused acted with knowledge that the planners and principal perpetrators, including military and civilian leaders and members of the *Interahamwe* militia, members of the Presidential Guard, military personnel and staff of the Rubaya and Nyabitu Tea Factories, intended to destroy, in whole or in part, the Tutsi ethnic group. Therefore, the **[page 7]** Indictment alleges that the Accused is complicit in the crime of genocide pursuant to Article 2 (3) (e) of the Statute with criminal responsibility pursuant to Article 6 (1) of the Statute.[37]

B. Criminal Responsibility of the Accused for Complicity in Genocide

1. Applicable Law

21. Article 6 (1) of the Statute reflects the principle that criminal responsibility for any crime in the Statute is incurred not only by individuals who physically commit the crime, but also by individuals who participate in and contribute to the commission of the crime.[38]

22. The jurisprudence of this Tribunal has defined complicity as aiding and abetting, instigating, and procuring.[39] Complicity by aiding and abetting implies a positive action, excluding, in principle, a complicit participation by failure to act or by omission.[40] The accomplice's criminal participation may occur at the planning, preparation or execution stage of the crime, occurring before or after the act of the principal offender.[41] It is not necessary that the person aiding and abetting the principal offender be present during the commission of the crime.[42]

23. Further the Appeals Chamber has held that complicity in genocide by aiding and abetting requires knowledge of the *mens rea* of the specific genocidal intent of the principal perpetrators, while the other forms of complicity may require proof that the accomplice shared the specific intent.[43] **[page 8]**

The Prosecution is required to demonstrate that the accused carried out an act of substantial practical assistance, encouragement, or moral support to the principal offender, culminating in the latter's actual

---

[36] Indictment, paras. 6-12.
[37] Indictment, paras. 4 and 5.
[38] *The Prosecutor v. Juvénal Kajelijeli*, Case No. ICTR-98-44A ("*Kajelijeli*"), Judgement and Sentence (TC), 1 December 2003, para. 757; *The Prosecutor v. Laurent Semanza*, Case No. ICTR-97-20 (*Semanza*"), Judgement and Sentence (TC), 15 May 2003, para. 377; *The Prosecutor v. Clément Kayishema and Obed Ruzindana*, Case No. ICTR-95-1 ("*Kayishema and Ruzindana*"), Judgement (Reasons) (AC), 1 June 2001, para. 185; *The Prosecutor v. Alfred Musema*, Case No. ICTR-96-13 ("*Musema*"), Judgement and Sentence (TC), 27 January 2000, para. 114; *The Prosecutor v. Georges Anderson Nderubumwe Rutaganda*, Case No. ICTR-96-3 ("*Rutaganda*"), Judgement and Sentence (TC), 6 December 1999, para. 33; *Kayishema and Ruzindana*, Judgement (TC), 21 May 1999, paras. 196-197; *The Prosecution v. Jean-Paul Akayesu*, Case No. ICTR-96-4 ("*Akayesu*"), Judgement (TC), 2 September 1998, para. 473.
[39] *Semanza*, Judgement and Sentence (TC), 15 May 2003, para. 393; *Musema*, Judgement and Sentence (TC), 27 January 2000, paras. 177-183; *The Prosecutor v. Ignace Bagileshima*, Case No. ICTR-95-1A ("*Bagileshima*"), Judgement (TC), 7 June 2001, para. 69.
[40] *Musema*, Judgement and Sentence (TC), 27 January 2000, paras. 177-183.
[41] *Kajelijeli*, Judgement and Sentence (TC), 1 December 2003, para. 766; *Semanza*, Judgement and Sentence (TC), 15 May 2003, para. 386.
[42] *Musema*, Judgement and Sentence (TC), 27 January 2000, para. 125.
[43] *The Prosecutor v. Elizaphan and Gérard Ntakirutimana*, Cases No. ICTR-96-10 and ICTR-96-17 ("*Ntakirutimana*"), Judgement (AC), 13 December 2004, para. 500; *The Prosecutor v. Milorad Krnojelac*, Case No. IT-97-25, Judgement (AC), para. 52; *The Prosecutor v. Duško Tadić*, Case No. IT-94-1, Judgement (AC), para. 229.

commission of the crime.[44] While the assistance need not be indispensable to the crime, it must have a substantial effect on the commission of the crime.[45]

2. The Plea Agreement

24. In the Guilty Plea Agreement between the Parties, Michel Bagaragaza acknowledges his criminal responsibility for, and admits that through his actions, his support and encouragement, he substantially contributed to the massacre of more than one thousand members of the Tutsi ethnic group who had sought refuge at Kesho Hill, in the Kabaya area, and at Nyundo Cathedral in Gisenyi *préfecture*.

25. In particular, the Accused admits that, on or about 8 April 1994, he participated in a meeting with the *bourgmestre*, Mr. Gahinjori, and the chief of the *Interahamwe* and assistant *bourgmestre*, Thomas Kuradusenge, of Giciye *commune*, and learned that the two men had agreed that Kuradusenge would organise and lead attacks against members of the Tutsi ethnic group at Kesho Hill and Nyundo Cathedral and that reinforcements would continue to be sent to the attackers. Further, the Accused authorised that vehicles and fuel from the Rubaya and Nyabihu Tea Factories be used to transport members of the *Interahamwe* for the attacks,[46] that personnel from the factories participate in the attacks and that the attackers be provided with heavy weapons. Bagaragaza had been instructed by the Army Chief of Staff, General Deogratias Nsabimana, to conceal those weapons at the factories in 1993. Moreover, Bagaragaza met with Kuradusenge two or three times between 9 and 13 April 1994 who informed him that the *Interahamwe* needed motivation to continue with the killings of the Tutsi ethnic group and requested money to buy alcohol for the *Interahamwe* in order to **[page 9]** motivate them to continue with the killings in the Kabaya and Bugoyi areas,[47] whereupon the Accused gave Kuradusenge a substantial amount of money for that purpose.

3. Legal Findings

26. The Chamber finds the Accused guilty in accordance with his guilty plea and, thus, that he provided substantial assistance to the killings of more than one thousand members of the Tutsi ethnic group with the knowledge of the planners' and principal perpetrators' genocidal intent.

27. Accordingly, the Chamber is satisfied beyond reasonable doubt that the Accused is individually criminally responsible, pursuant to Article 6(1) of the Statute for complicity in genocide pursuant to Article 2 (3) (e) of the Statute.

CHAPTER IV: DETERMINATION OF SENTENCE

I. Applicable Sentencing principles

28. The Chamber considers that the sentence imposed should reflect the goals of retribution, deterrence, rehabilitation and the protection of society. Pursuant to Article 23(2) of the Statute and Rule 101 of the Rules, the Chamber must take into account a number of factors, including the gravity of the offence, the individual circumstances of the accused, any aggravating or mitigating circumstances, including substantial cooperation with the Prosecution by the Accused, and the general practice regarding prison sentences in the courts of Rwanda.

---

[44] *Kayishema and Ruzindana,* Judgement (Reasons) (AC), 1 June 2001, para. 186; *Kajelijeli,* Judgement and Sentence (TC), 1 December 2003, paras. 763, 766; *The Prosecution v. Jean de Dieu Kamuhanda,* Case No. ICTR-95-54A (*"Kamuhanda"*), Judgement and Sentence (TC), 22 January 2003, para. 597; *Akayesu,* Judgement (TC), 2 September 1998, paras. 473-475; *Rutaganda,* Judgement and Sentence (TC), 6 December 1999, para. 43.

[45] *Bagilishema,* Judgement (TC), 7 June 2001, paras. 33, 71; *Kamuhanda,* Judgement and Sentence (TC), 22 January 2003, para. 597 and Judgement (AC), 19 September 2005, para. 70. *Kayishema and Ruzindana,* Judgement (Reasons) (AC), 1 June 2001, para. 186; *Kajelijeli,* Judgement and Sentence (TC), 1 December 2003, paras. 763, 766; *Akayesu,* Judgement (TC), 2 September 1998, paras. 473-475, 537-538, 540; *Rutaganda,* Judgement and Sentence (TC), 6 December 1999, para. 43. *Musema,* Judgement and Sentence (TC), 27 January 2000, paras. 180-182; *The Prosecutor v. Tihomir Blaškić,* Case No. IT-95-14; Judgement (AC), 29 July 2004, para. 49.

[46] Statement of Facts, para. 11.

[47] Statement of Facts, para. 12.

Sentencing Judgement

II. Sentencing Factors

29. The Chamber recalls that it must take into account any aggravating and mitigating circumstances but has unfettered discretion in its assessment of the facts and the attendant circumstances.[48] The Chamber also recalls that it may also consider any factor that it deems pertinent[49] and that aggravating circumstances must be proved beyond reasonable doubt, **[page 10]** while mitigating circumstances must be proved on a balance of probabilities.[50]

A. Gravity of the Crime

30. The Chamber recognizes that the gravity of the crime committed by the Accused and the extent of the Accused's involvement are essential factors for a just sentence.[51]

31. The crime for which the Accused has been convicted, relates to genocide which is the most heinous of crimes and shocks the collective conscience of mankind.[52] The Accused's personal participation consisted in aiding and abetting the planners and principal perpetrators to a substantial degree, with knowledge of their genocidal intent, to kill more than one thousand Tutsi who were fleeing for their lives.

32. However, there is no basis for the Chamber to conclude that Bagaragaza consented to the concealment of weapons in the tea factories in 1993 because he knew they would be used for genocidal acts, or that he otherwise acted with premeditation when he agreed to the requests of the local political and *Interahamwe* leaders. Still, the Chamber finds that the Accused's participation constitutes a very serious offence and a gross violation of international humanitarian law.

B. Aggravating Circumstances

33. The Chamber notes that the Parties have not made any submissions on aggravating circumstances and considers that in the present instance there are no aggravating circumstances.

C. Mitigating Circumstances

34. Mitigating circumstances do not have be directly related to the offence.[53] The Chamber has wide discretion in determining what constitutes mitigating circumstances and the weight to be accorded thereto.[54] Proof of mitigating circumstances does not automatically **[page 11]** entitle the accused to a "credit" in the determination of the sentence; it simply requires the Trial Chamber to consider such mitigating circumstances in its final determination.[55]

35. The Chamber has considered that the following factors constitute mitigating circumstances to varying degrees.

---

[48] *The Prosecutor v. Omar Serushago*, Case No. ICTR-98-39 ("*Serushago*"), Reasons for Judgement (AC), 6 April 2000, para. 23; *The Prosecutor v. André Ntaregura, Emmanuel Bagambiki, Samuel Imanishimwe*, Case No. ICTR-99-46, Judgement (AC), para. 430.
[49] *Serushago*, Reasons for Judgement (AC), 6 April 2000, para. 23.
[50] *Kajelijeli* Judgement (AC), 23 May 2005, para. 294; *The Prosecutor v. Joseph Serugendo*, Case No. ICTR-2005-84 ("*Serugendo*"), Judgement and Sentence (TC), 12 June 2006, para. 40; *The Prosecutor v. Paul Bisengimana*, Case No. ICTR-00-60 ("*Bisengimana*"), Judgement (TC), 13 April 2006, para. 111; *The Prosecutor v. Aloys Simba*, Case No. ICTR-01-76, Judgement and Sentence (TC), 13 December 2005, para. 438; *The Prosecutor v. Callixte Kalimanzira*, case No. ICTR-05-88 ("*Kalimanzira*"), Judgement (TC), 22 June 2009, para. 748.
[51] See e.g. *Serugendo*, Judgement and Sentence (TC), 12 June 2006, para. 39.
[52] *The Prosecutor v. Georges Ruggiu*, Case No. ICTR-97-32 ("*Ruggiu*"), Judgement and Sentence (TC), 1 June 2000, para. 48.
[53] *Bisengimana*, Judgement and Sentence (TC), 13 April 2006, para. 125; *The Prosecutor v. Mormir Nikolić*, Case No. IT-02-60/1 ("*Nikolić*"), Sentencing Judgement (TC), 18 December 2003, para. 145; *The Prosecutor v. Miroslav Deronjić*, Case No. IT-02-61, Sentencing Judgement (TC), 30 March 2004, para. 155.
[54] *Kalimanzira*, Judgement (TC), 22 June 2009, para. 748.
[55] *The Prosecutor v. Éliézer Niyitegeka*, Case No. ICTR-96-14 ("*Niyitegeka*"), Judgement (AC), 9 July 2004 para. 267.

36. The Defence has led credible evidence that Michel Bagaragaza, in his personal and professional life, showed no bias against the Tutsi and was on excellent terms with them.[56] Two of his children, who are integrated into his family, have a Tutsi mother, whom he protected during the genocide. Further, he engaged Tutsi for leading posts in his department and openly socialised with Tutsi. Therefore, the Chamber considers that it is likely that, when he agreed to provide assistance to the *genocidaires*, he was driven by concern for his own safety and that of his family.[57] Nevertheless, there is not sufficient evidence to conclude that Michel Bagaragaza, being a resourceful and notable person in the community, would have faced imminent and direct danger, had he not complied with the requests of the local political and *Interahamwe* leaders.

37. The Accused is a married man with children who has convinced the Chamber to believe in his chances of rehabilitation after his release. Further, he is sixty-three years old, in frail health, and has shown good behaviour prior to and during detention.

38. A more important mitigating factor, however, is that Michel Bagaragaza confessed his actions from an early point, surrendered voluntarily to the Tribunal and pleaded guilty when the charges against him were reduced to comport to his confession. Furthermore, in his public address to the Court, he expressed genuine remorse for his actions. The jurisprudence has established that a guilty plea may have mitigating effects because it shows remorse and repentance and contributes to reconciliation, the establishment of the truth, the encouragement of other perpetrators to do so, the sparing of a lengthy investigation and trial and thus resources and time, and relieves witnesses from giving evidence in court.[58]

39. An even more important mitigating factor is that, according to the Parties' submissions, Michel Bagaragaza has been cooperating with the Prosecution in the **[page 12]** investigation and prosecution of cases since May 2002 and provided the Prosecution with information about his own role and the role of others in the events before and during the genocide without concern for self-incrimination. On 19 December 2004, he signed a cooperation agreement with the Prosecutor and continued his cooperation unreservedly after he was arrested on 15 August 2005. He testified for the Prosecution in the *Zigiranyirazo* case and remains committed to testifying for the Prosecution in other cases, as required.[59] His assistance is qualified as invaluable.[60] The Chamber further notes that the Accused continued his cooperation with the Prosecution even after his identity was disclosed in breach of court orders and despite threats to his own life and to the life of members of his family and that he has been in solitary confinement for security reasons since August 2005.[61]

40. The Chamber recalls Rule 101 of the Rules, which expressly provides that substantial cooperation with the Prosecution before or after a conviction must be deemed a mitigating circumstance.[62] As such, the Chamber finds that the Accused's ongoing cooperation with the Prosecution, dating back to May 2002, constitutes substantial cooperation to an unusually high degree.

III. Sentencing Recommendations

41. In the Guilty Plea Agreement, the Parties jointly recommended a sentencing range of between six and ten years imprisonment with credit for time spent in detention.[63] The Chamber has taken the joint recommendation into due consideration, but notes that Rule 62 *bis* (B) provides that the Chamber is not bound by any such agreement.

---

[56] T. 3 November 2009, p. 11; Exhibits D3, D4, D5, D7, D8, D9, D10, D11, D12, D13 (all under seal).
[57] T. 3 November 2009, p. 20; T. 4 November 2009, p. 21; Exhibit D2 (under seal).
[58] *Bisengimana*, Judgement (TC), 13 April 2006, para. 126. *See also Ruggiu*, Judgement (TC), 1 June 2000, paras. 53, 55; *The Prosecutor v. Biljana Plavšić*, Case no. IT-00-39 and 40/1 ("*Plavšić*"), Sentencing Judgement (TC), 27 February 2003, paras. 70, 73; *Nikolić*, Sentencing Judgement (TC), 18 December 2003, para. 248.
[59] Joint Motion, para. 5.2 ; T. 4 November 2009, pp. 7, 21; Exhibit D6.
[60] Exhibit D6, para. 1.
[61] T. 4 November 2009, p. 21. Exhibits D1, D5, D10, D13 (all under seal); D6, paras. 7, 8.
[62] Rule 101 (B) (ii).
[63] Guilty Plea Agreement, para. 5.4.

IV. Conclusion

42. The Chamber recognizes that a higher sentence is more likely to be imposed on the principal perpetrators of an offence than on their accomplices.[64] After examining the sentencing practice of this Tribunal and that of ICTY, the Chamber is mindful that principal perpetrators convicted of genocide have been punished with sentences ranging from fifteen years imprisonment to life imprisonment, and that a principal perpetrator in relation to the Kesho Hill massacre and another event, with a social background similar to that of Michel **[page 13]** Bagaragaza, was sentenced to 20 years imprisonment by the Trial Chamber.[65] Secondary or indirect forms of participation have generally resulted in a lower sentence.[66] The Chamber is aware that the sentence should reflect the totality of the criminal conduct of the accused. In this case, the Chamber finds that extraordinary mitigating circumstances exist, which warrant a substantial reduction of the sentence that the Accused's actions would otherwise carry.

V. Credit for Time Served

43. Pursuant to Rule 101 (C) of the Rules credit shall be given to a convicted person for the period during which the convicted person was detained in custody pending his surrender to the Tribunal or pending trial or appeal. The Accused was arrested and transferred to the UNDF Facility in Arusha on 15 August 2005. He is entitled to credit for time spent in custody and any additional time he might spend in custody pending a final determination of a possible appeal.

CHAPTER V: VERDICT

44. The Chamber has considered the Statute, the Rules, the gravity of the offence, the general practice regarding sentencing in Rwanda, evidence during the sentencing hearing and the Parties submissions. The Chamber has further weighed the mitigating circumstances.[67] The Chamber convicts and sentences Michel Bagaragaza for complicity in genocide pursuant to Article 2 (3) (e) of the Statute to:

8 years' imprisonment

45. The Chamber finds that, pursuant to Rule 101 (C) of the Rules, the Accused is entitled to credit for time spent in custody, to be computed from the date of his surrender, 15 August 2005, to the date of this judgement. Pursuant to Rule 102 (A), the sentence shall run as of the date of this judgement. **[page 14]**

46. Pursuant to Rule 103 (B) of the Rules, the Accused shall remain in the custody of the Tribunal pending finalisation of arrangements for his transfer to the State where he shall serve his sentence.

Done in Arusha on 17 November 2009, in English.

Vagn Joensen	Bakhtiyar Tuzmukhamedov	Gberdao Gustave Kam
Presiding Judge	Judge	Judge

[Seal of the Tribunal]

---

[64] *Semanza*, Judgement (AC), 20 May 2005, para. 388.

[65] *Semanza*, Judgement (AC), 20 May 2005, para. 388. *See also Musema*, Judgement and Sentence (TC), 27 January 2000, para. 1008, *Rutaganda*, Judgement and Sentence (TC), 6 December 1999, para. 473; *The Prosecutor v. Protais Zigiranyirazo*, Case No. ICTR-2001-73, Judgment (TC), para. 468.

[66] *See e.g., Ruggiu*, Judgement (TC), 1 June 2000, para. 81 (sentencing the accused to a concurrent twelve-year sentence for direct and public incitement to commit genocide and crimes against humanity (persecution)); *Ntakirutimana*, Judgement (TC), 21 February 2003, para. 921 (sentencing the accused to ten years' imprisonment for aiding and abetting genocide but making special note of the accused's age, state of health, his past good character and public service).

[67] *The Prosecution v. Vincent Rutaganira*, Case No. ICTR-95-1C ("*Rutaganira*"), Judgement and Sentence (TC), 14 March 2005, para. 168.

**[page 15] Annex:
Indictment**

[page 2] The Prosecutor of the United Nations International Criminal Tribunal for Rwanda, pursuant to the authority stipulated in Article 17 of the Statute of the International Criminal Tribunal for Rwanda (the "Statute") charges:

Michel BAGARAGAZA,

with **Complicity in Genocide,** a crime stipulated in Article 2(3) (e) of the Statute.

(A) THE ACCUSED

1. **Michel BAGARAGAZA** was born in 1945 in Bushiru region Giciye *Commune,* Gisenyi *Prefecture,* Republic of Rwanda.

2. **Michel BAGARAGAZA** as at all times referred to in this Indictment, unless otherwise stated below is A senior public official who was-

   i. the Director General of OCIR/Thé, the government office that controlled the tea industry, one of the most important industrial enterprises in Rwanda. In this capacity, he had eleven (11) Tea Factories under his authority with approximately Fifty Five Thousand (55 000) employees.

   ii. the vice-president of Banque Continentale African au Rwanda (BACAR);

   iii. a member of the MRND political party in Gisenyi *Préfecture* and a member of the Prefectural committee of the MRND political party in Gisenyi *Préfecture,* that established and controlled the *Interahamwe* militia in Gisenyi *Préfecture.*

3. In his position as a Director of *OCIR-The,* a vice-president of BACAR, a member of the MRND political party in Gisenyi *Préfecture* and a member of the Prefectural committee of the MRND political party in Gisenyi *Préfecture,* Michel Bagaragaza formed part of a powerful and tight group of people who exercised substantial political and financial power in the Republic of Rwanda known as the *"Akazu".* These included the President's family members and persons from Michel Bagaragaza's region, being the Bushiru region, and the northern provinces of Gisenyi and Ruhengeri. **[page 3]**

(B) CHARGE: COMPLICITY IN GENOCIDE

4. The Prosecutor of the International Criminal Tribunal for Rwanda charges Michel Bagaragaza with **COMPLICITY IN GENOCIDE,** a crime stipulated in Article 2(3)(e) of the Statute, in that from 1 January 1994 to 31 December 1994, throughout Rwanda, particularly in Gisenyi *Préfecture,* Michel Bagaragaza with knowledge that other people intended to destroy, in whole or in part, the Tutsi ethnic group, as such, by his participation he was complicit in the crime of genocide, as outlined in the paragraphs below.

Individual Criminal Responsibility pursuant to Article 6(1) of the Statute.

5. Pursuant to Article 6(1) of the Statute, the Accused, Michel Bagaragaza, is individually responsible for the crimes of Complicity in Genocide because with knowledge that specified individuals were committing genocide, he aided and abetted them in the preparation or execution of the crime of genocide. Those individuals included military and civilian leaders and members of the *Interahamwe* militia, including Thomas Kuradusenge, who was also the assistant

bourgmaster of Giciye commune, the chief of the *Interahamwe* militia, members of the President Guard, military personnel and staff of the Rubaya and Nyabihu Tea factories, whose names are not known and other unknown participants. All such actions were taken either directly or through others, for at least the period of January 1994 through July 1994. The particulars that give rise to his individual criminal responsibility are set forth in paragraphs 6(Six) to 12 (Twelve) below.

(C) CONCISE STATEMENT OF FACTS

6. Michel Bagaragaza knowingly aided and abetted specific individuals composed of military and cilvilian leaders, members of the Interahamwe militia, including the chief of the Interahamwe Thomas Kuradusenge, who was also the Assistant Bourgmaster of Giciye commune, members of the Presidential Guard, staff **[page 4]** members of the Rubaya and Nyabihu tea factories and other unknown participants who were committing Genocide between 7th and 13th April 1994.

7. In 1993, Michel Bagaragaza was requested by the Army Chief of Staff, General Deogratias Nsabimana, to hide heavy weapons for the Rwandan army. Thereafter he instructed the management of the Rubaya tea factory and Nyabihu tea factory to conceal the weapons as requested. The management subsequently confirmed the arrival of those arms and the presence of soldiers at their respective tea factories to Michel Bagaragaza. These arms were, with the knowledge and consent of Michel Bagaragaza used by the *Interahamwe* and other Hutu civilians to kill members of the Tutsi ethnic group in Gisenyi prefecture between April 1994 and July 1994.

8. On a date between 7 and 9 April 1994, Michel Bagaragaza knowingly authorized employees of the tea factory of Rubaya to provide the *Interahamwe* militia and other Hutu civilians with fuel for their vehicles, arms from the army stockpile at the Rubaya and Nyabihu Tea factories, and additional personnel from the factory to facilitate in the massacre of between eight hundred and one thousand five hundred members of the Tutsi ethnic group who had sought refuge at Kesho hill. Through these actions Michel Bagaragaza substantially contributed to the killings of members of the Tutsi ethnic group through his support and encouragement and was thereby complicit in the killing of the Tutsi ethnic group.

9. On or about 8 April 1994, Michel Bagaragaza met with Thomas Kuradusenge who was the chief of the *Interahamwe* and Assistant *bourgmestre* in Giciye *commune* and Mr. Gahinjori the *bourgmestre* of Giciye *commune*. Michel Bagaragaza was privy to a discussion in which Mr. Gahinjori and Thomas Kuradusenge agreed that Thomas Kuradusenge would organise and lead the attacks against members of the Tutsi ethnic group in Kesho hill and Nyundo Cathedral in Gisenyi Prefecture, and that reinforcements would continue to be **[page 5]** sent to persons attacking Tutsi civilians at Kesho hill in the Kabaya area and Nyundo Cathedral in Bugoyi area

10. On or about 8 April 1994, Michel Bagaragaza authorized Mr. Gahinjori and Mr. Kuradusenge, to use vehicles and fuel from Rubaya and Nyabihu tea factories to transport members of the *Interahamwe* to attack and kill the Tutsi civilians at Kesho Hill and Nyundo Cathedral. Through these actions Michel Bagaragaza substantially contributed to the killings of members of the Tutsi ethnic group through his support and encouragement and was thereby complicit in the killing of Tutsis.

11. Between 9 and 13 April 1994, Michel Bagaragaza was visited by Mr. Kuradusenge two to three times and he informed Michel Bagaragaza that members of the *Interahamwe militia* needed motivation to continue with the killing. He requested Michel Bagaragaza for money to buy alcohol for the *Interahamwe* in order to motivate them to continue with the killings. Michel Bagaragaza gave Mr. Kuradusenge a substantial amount of money in order to encourage and motivate the *Interahamwe* in the killings of members of the Tutsi ethnic group in the Kabaya and Bugoyi areas. Through these actions Michel Bagaragaza substantially contributed to the killings

of members of the Tutsi ethnic group through his support and encouragement and was thereby complicit in the killing members of the Tutsi ethnic group.

12. Michel Bagaragaza, assisted members of the *Interahamwe* militia in the killing of between eight hundred and one thousand five hundred Tutsi at Kesho hill on or around 8 April 1994 and several hundred Tutsi at Nyundo Cathedral on or around 10 April 1994 by facilitating in the provision, of fuel, transport, arms and factory personnel, which he authorized to be used in the killings at Kesho hill and Nyundo Cathedral. Through these actions Michel Bagaragaza substantially contributed to the killings of members of the Tutsi ethnic group through his **[page 6]** support and encouragement and was thereby complicit in the killing of members of the Tutsi ethnic group.

The acts of Michel Bagaragaza detailed herein are punishable, pursuant to Articles 22 and 23 of the Statute of the Tribunal

Signed at Arusha this 17th day of September 2009.

Mr. Hassan Bubacar Jallow
PROSECUTOR

Commentary

1. Introduction

The Sentencing Judgement of Trial Chamber III of 17 November 2009 (hereafter 'the judgement') against Michel Bagaragaza brought to a close one of the most interesting sagas at the International Criminal Tribunal for Rwanda (ICTR). The reasoning of the chamber, as well as the wider context against which the case was decided, raise interesting points for reflection, not least concerning the use of prosecutions and the objectives to which they aspire for resolving the Gordian Knot of Rwanda's past. In certain respects, the case illuminates a distance between the prosecution of cases and the actual experience of the perpetration of the crimes under examination. This distance provides cause for concern, but paradoxically a concurrent cause for optimism should the indications that it demonstrates be heeded in the future use of international criminal law as a mechanism of transitional justice to combat impunity. First to the facts of the case and its procedural history before reaching the sentencing stage.

Prior to, and during, the events of 1994, Michel Bagaragaza was director general of the government office that controlled Rwanda's tea industry and Vice-President of the *Banque Continentale Africaine au Rwanda* (BACAR). He was also a member of the *comité préfectoral* of the ruling *Mouvement Révolutionaire National pour le Développement* (MRND). Bagaragaza was also a member of the infamous 'Akazu' inner circle around former President Juvénil Habyarimana. The former President's wife, Agathe Habyarimana and her brothers, including Protais Zigiranyirazo, were the most influential actors in the Akazu, which effectively exercised control of both political and economic power in Rwanda. It is the Akazu that are acknowledged to have engendered the planning and organisation of the 1994 genocide.

Before his arrest in August 2005 after voluntarily surrendering to the tribunal, Bagaragaza had been cooperating with the prosecutor on several cases from May 2002, including that of Protais Zigiranyirazo. According to the Prosecutor, Bagaragaza had become an "invaluable"[1] source of information on the circumstances that led to the genocide and those that followed until the RPA took control of the country, even before he signed a cooperation agreement on 19 December 2004. Having previously given testimony as a prosecution witness under a pseudonym, Bagaragaza continued to cooperate with the prosecutor after his identity was revealed in breach of a court order. As part of the cooperation agreement, and before his 2005 surrender to the tribunal, Bagaragaza and the prosecutor agreed to have the case transferred to a European jurisdiction.

In an indictment dated 28 July 2005, Bagaragaza faced charges under Article 2 of the ICTR Statute of conspiracy to commit genocide, genocide, and complicity in genocide in the alternative. At his initial appearance before the ICTR, Bagaragaza pleaded not guilty to all of the charges against him. For his own safety, having acted as a key informant for the prosecutor, special detention measures were granted by the tribunal[2] according to which Bagaragaza was detained at the detention unit of the International Criminal Tribunal for the former Yugoslavia in The Hague.

The prosecution's first attempt to have the case transferred to a national jurisdiction (Norway) under Rule 11*bis* of the Statute was rejected by a Trial Chamber on 19 May 2006 based on the absence of provisions in Norwegian criminal law for the prosecution of genocide.[3] The decision was upheld by the Appeals Chamber in August of the same year in spite of Rule 11*bis* having been adopted by ICTR Judges to ease the Tribunal's case-load under pressure of the Completion Strategy.[4] Subsequent to the decision of the Appeals Chamber, the prosecution was granted a request to amend the indictment by adding killing and causing violence to

---

[1] Sentencing Judgement, *Prosecutor v. Bagaragaza*, Case No. ICTR-05-86-S, T. Ch. III, 17 November 2009, in this volume, p. 811, par. 39.
[2] Order for Special Detention Measures (President), *Prosecutor v. Bagaragaza*, Case No. ICTR-05-86-S, 13 August 2005.
[3] Decision on the Prosecution Motion for Referral to the Kingdom of Norway (Rule 11*bis* of the Rules of Procedure and Evidence), *Prosecutor v. Bagaragaza*, Case No. ICTR-2005-86-R11*bis*, T. Ch. III, 19 May 2006, Klip/ Sluiter, ALC-XXIV-13.
[4] In UN Security Council Resolution 1503 (2003) (28 August 2003), UN Doc. S/RES/1503 and Security Council Resolution 1534 (2004) (26 March 2004), UN Doc. S/RES/1534, the UN Security Council set deadlines for the rounding-off of the case-load of the ICTR and ICTY. The latest report from the ICTR on implementation of the Completion Strategy can be consulted at http://unictr.org/Portals/0/English/FactSheets/Completion_St/s-2011-317e.pdf.

health and physical or mental well-being as serious violations of Common Article 3 of the Geneva Conventions and Additional Protocol II of 1977 as an alternative to the initial three counts.

At the third time of asking, the prosecution's motion to refer the case was granted on 13 April 2007.[5] Bagaragaza was to be tried in the Netherlands, with the decision marking the first time that the ICTR had authorised the transfer of an accused to a national jurisdiction. However, just four months later, the referral was revoked after the Dutch courts made clear that they did not have jurisdiction to try the crimes contained in the indictment.[6] The decision followed the case of Joseph Mpambara, a Rwandan national residing in the Netherlands and accused of genocide, where the District Court in The Hague concluded that the accused could only be tried for torture as Dutch courts did not have jurisdiction over genocide.[7] The apparent short-sightedness of the drafters in devising the Completion Strategy in a manner which fails to fully appreciate the legal intricacies required for its implementation has been cited to explain the see-sawing of Bagaragaza's case. Bagaragaza was eventually transferred back to Arusha in 2008 pending trial.

The first joint motion for consideration of a guilty plea agreement was filed by the parties in April 2008, but later withdrawn after a motion for leave to amend the indictment was denied by the chamber. All signs pointed to the commencement of the trial on 17 August 2009. Nonetheless, on the same day, the parties filed another joint motion for consideration of a guilty plea along with a statement of facts signed by Bagaragaza and the guilty plea agreement. Exactly one month later, Bagaragaza pleaded guilty to complicity in genocide and the prosecution was thus granted leave to amend the indictment to charge Bagaragaza with that one count based on his individual criminal responsibility under Article 6, paragraph 1 of the Statute. Following statements concerning Bagaragaza's character, the chamber delivered an oral ruling on 5 November 2009 sentencing Bagaragaza to eight years' imprisonment. The judgement of 17 November 2009 represents the written reasoning of the chamber's decision.

In itself the chamber's judgement fails to reflect the case's colourful history and is largely an un-extraordinary end to one of the ICTR's more interesting cases, at least from a procedural point of view. It is certain issues upon which the case has touched that are more deserving of attention as concerns the present judgement.

As earlier noted, the Bagaragaza case, like certain others at the ICTR, provides insight into the use of international criminal prosecutions as a mechanism of transitional justice for combating impunity after genocide and other serious violations of international law.[8] Indeed, with the establishment of the International Criminal Court (ICC), the courtroom has become something of a *de facto modus operandi* of transitional justice in its broadest sense, at least as far as the international community is concerned.[9] Whilst *knee-jerk* is perhaps too strong a term to attach to the international reaction to such crimes, criminal prosecution is an inevitable first port of call. This inevitability leading to a criminal justice response has not been sufficiently tested, nor is it often based upon an assessment that considers impunity in a more holistic manner.[10]

Seeking to shed light on this practice should in no way be read as an indictment of international criminal prosecutions or as an attempt to undermine the fundamentality of bringing the perpetrators of international crimes and gross human rights violations to account. The failure to do is without question unacceptable and

---

[5] Decision on Prosecutor's Request for Referral of the Indictment to the Kingdom of the Netherlands, *Prosecutor v. Bagaragaza*, Case No. ICTR-2005-86-11*bis*, T. Ch. III, 13 April 2007, Klip/ Sluiter, ALC-XXV-67.
[6] Decision on Prosecutor's Extremely Urgent Motion for Revocation of the Referral to the Kingdom of the Netherlands, Rule 11 *bis* (F) and (G), *Prosecutor v. Bagaragaza*, Case No. ICTR-2005-86-11*bis*, T. Ch. III, 17 August 2007, Klip/ Sluiter, ALC- XXV-67.
[7] District Court The Hague, 24 July 2007, LJN: BB0494.
[8] For an overview of the evolution of transitional justice and its associated mechanisms, see R. Teitel, Transitional Justice Genealogy, 16 Harvard Human Rights Journal 2003, p. 69–94.
[9] The implicit contradiction between 'transitional' justice and the nature of current ICC interventions in on-going conflicts has been referred to by some scholars as suggesting that in fact the ICC should be considered as separate from that which is defined as transitional justice. For a critique of the current conception of transitional justice, see for example C. Bell, Transitional Justice, Interdisciplinarity and the State of the 'Field' or 'Non-Field', 3 International Journal of Transitional Justice 2009, p. 5–27.
[10] Impunity for international crimes can be considered as beyond only the absence of accountability for past crimes, but as including the absence of truth about the past and non-recognition of abuses suffered. Victims' rights to truth, justice, reparations and non-recurrence should be prioritised, with impunity as a result of problems in all three branches of the state, as well as influences from non-state actors and wider societal factors (see Impunity Watch Global Research Instrument, available at www.impunitywatch.org/en/publication/15).

undoubtedly provides the basis for further cycles of violence, as Rwanda's history so well demonstrates. Criminal accountability should be a pillar of efforts to combat impunity and deal with the past. What the Bagaragaza case nonetheless evidences is that international criminal prosecutions may not be effective at achieving all of their purported objectives and must be introduced on the basis of a more comprehensive and considered examination of impunity after violence.

2. Objectives and Rationale

According to UN Security Council Resolution 955,[11] the ICTR was established with several principal objectives in mind: bringing perpetrators to justice; contributing to national reconciliation; and restoring and maintaining peace. Through judicial creativity and scholarly influence, the establishment of truth and writing a historical record of Rwanda's past have alsobeen aggregated as core objectives.[12] Moreover, the reasoning and interpretations by individual chambers have further expanded the objectives to which the prosecution of cases are assumed to aspire. The chamber in Bagaragaza thus built on previous determinations in stating that, "the sentence imposed should reflect the goals of retribution, deterrence, rehabilitation and the protection of society."[13] Moreover, assessing the mitigating circumstances of the case, the chamber concluded that Bagaragaza's guilty plea, "contributes to reconciliation, [and] the establishment of truth".[14]

For the purpose of this commentary, these objectives must be kept in mind and will be used as the basis of the analysis. Together with the interpretations of the various other chambers at the ICTR, particularly those offering slightly different conceptions of the ICTR's rationale, a mélange of objectives supposedly provide the foundations of prosecutions at Arusha.

2.1. *The Appearance of Justice*

At least from an international perspective looking in on Bagaragaza's case, a multifaceted form of justice appears to have been delivered. The arrest and sentencing of a member of the Akazu inner circle is in itself a significant achievement. In addition however, the invaluable assistance provided by Bagaragaza in the investigation and prosecution of other cases at the ICTR has without doubt contributed to bringing other perpetrators to justice. For a prosecutor attempting to navigate Rwanda's intricate history and the overwhelming network of interests and relations that this history comprises, together with a society and culture in which duplicity has thrived, the impact of such assistance cannot be underestimated. Just as the chamber hinted at, for international criminal lawyers entering the chaotic world of mass crimes and their aftermath, an insider's view is indispensable. The lengths that some prosecutor's will go to protect this necessity are well-known.[15]

Considering the objective of contributing to the truth about the events leading up to 1994 and those that followed, the Bagaragaza case also significantly adds to the understanding of how the genocide was perpetrated. Once again, the information shared behind closed doors to the prosecutor no doubt adds to the validity of this fact. Concerning the Akazu, the case provides greater detail on the group's role and power. For despite the generality of information concerning the group, precise details of its operation remain tenuous, even as far as its members are concerned. Considering those whose membership of the group is more or less certain – Agathe Habyarimana, Protais Zigiranyirazo, Théoneste Bagosora, Félicien Kabuga, Anatole Nsengiyumva, Joseph Nzirorera, Augustin Ngirabatware – two persons from the list have been convicted at the ICTR, one has been acquitted, one trial is on-going, one is deceased, one remains the most

---

[11] UN Security Council Resolution 955 (1994) (8 November 1994), UN Doc. S/RES/955.
[12] In one of his six-monthly addresses to the UN Security Council on the ICTR's Completion Strategy, then President of the Tribunal, Judge Dennis Byron stated that the ICTR had "established a judicially verified factual record of the events in Rwanda that will serve as a background for the remaining trials, as a resource for historians, and as a major contribution to the process of national reconciliation" Speech by Judge Dennis Byron, President of the ICTR, to the United Nations Security Council, 4 June 2009.
[13] ICTR, Sentencing Judgement, *Prosecutor v. Bagaragaza,* Case No. ICTR-05-86-S, T. Ch. III, 17 November 2009, in this volume, p. 811, par. 28.
[14] *Ibid.,* par. 38.
[15] See ICC, Judgement on the appeal of the Prosecutor against the decision of Trial Chamber I of 8 July 2010 entitled "Decision on the Prosecution's Urgent Request for Variation of the Time-Limit to Disclose the Identity of Intermediary 143 or Alternatively to Stay Proceedings Pending Further Consultations with the VWU", *Prosecutor v. Lubanga,* Case No. ICC-01/04-01/06, A. Ch., 8 October 2010; ICC, Judgement on the appeal of Prosecutor against the oral decision of Trial Chamber I of 15 July 2010 to release Thomas Lubanga Dyilo, *Prosecutor v. Lubanga,* Case No. ICC-01/04-01/06, A. Ch., 8 October 2010.

wanted fugitive of the tribunal and the former President's wife continues to seek asylum in France amid calls for her prosecution. Of the two convictions, the accused were each acquitted of conspiracy to commit genocide,[16] leading some to the conclusion that the genocide had not been planned in the way previously assumed.[17] The Bagaragaza case thus provides a degree of justice where others may be seen to have failed. Moreover, the agreed facts that accompany the guilty plea somewhat contradict the belief that there had been no overt plan in place to carry out the massacres. The concealment of weapons in 1993, as well as the meetings between officials that Bagaragaza was a party to, testify to this.

The case adds further clarity concerning the law of complicity and the nature of individual criminal responsibility under Article 6, paragraph 1. Whilst in itself providing little innovation, building on previous decisions the facts of the case will no doubt provide a useful reference point in the future for those engaged with unravelling the degrees of responsibility that constitute the perpetration of genocide and other mass crimes. The case in question represents something of a culmination of the established law of complicity, setting out its basic elements as distinguished. From a wider perspective of the law's application to a social context and the physical perpetration of crimes, the judgement offers valuable insight into the bureaucracy, planning and organisation that lie behind these crimes. Such insight further discredits any lingering belief that they are the result of frenzied killers.

In many ways however, the positive aspects of the case at hand end there. Whilst these aspects demonstrate implications beyond the individual judgement, certain other aspects speak to the difficulties and limitations of prosecutions as mechanisms of transitional justice, particularly when used in isolation. These problems are further compounded by the prevailing belief that prosecutions are the solution to the Gordian Knot of Rwanda's history and post-conflict ills.

3. The Logic of Law

Whether, as Lawrence L. Langer suggested, "the logic of law can never make sense of the illogic of extermination"[18] is open for debate. The rational planning of the genocide in which Bagaragaza partook and the enriched understanding of complicity and individual criminal responsibility under Article 6, paragraph 1 that the case provides, illuminate a logic behind the events of 1994, albeit perverse. There are nonetheless three principal themes inherent to the Bagaragaza judgement that support the underlying rationale for Langer's statement, which is that appropriating the law for a comprehensive set of objectives after violence brings with it several unresolved paradoxes that together create a distance between the law and the reality of international crimes, distance that is further accentuated when international prosecutions are utilised as stand-alone mechanisms of transitional justice in complex situations such as post-genocide Rwanda. These three principal themes, addressed in turn, are: legal procedure; incomplete explanations; and assumptions.

3.1. *Legal Procedure*

No explanation is required of the legal strictures that apply to international proceedings. Much has been written about the procedures that regulate close to every aspect of action and dialogue once court is in session. Whilst these rules remain fundamental to ensuring the rule of law and the fairness of proceedings for both parties, what the Bagaragaza judgement highlights is that legalese is often an incomprehensible language after mass violence.

The first evidence of this is a general observation, not confined to the Bagaragaza decision. Despite the legal clarity that the case provides concerning complicity and the wider involvement of actors in the perpetration of genocide, the application of the law to the reality of Bagaragaza's actual participation stokes feelings of artificiality. In a complex socio-political context with complicated social realities, the law's neat categorisation of actions to fit a particular model of participation which "thins out the complexities of life…and positivises

---

[16] Judgement and Sentence, *Prosecutor v. Bagosora, Kabiligi, Ntabakuze and Nsengimana,* Case No. ICTR-98-41-T, T. Ch. I, 18 December 2008, Klip/ Sluiter ALC-XXXII-739.
[17] See P. Erlinder, The U.N. Security Council Ad Hoc Rwanda Tribunal: International Justice, or Juridically-Constructed 'Victor's Impunity'?, 4 DePaul Journal for Social Justice 2010, p. 131–214; E.S. Herman and D. Peterson, Rwanda and the Democratic Republic of Congo in the Propaganda System, 62 Monthly Review 2010.
[18] L. Langer, Admitting the Holocaust: Collected Essays, Oxford University Press, Oxford, New York 1996, p. 171.

the norms that underpin such challenges"[19] contains many inherent problems. Whilst fundamental to ensure the rule of law, and therefore a necessary component of legal procedure, this practice obscures the reality and experience of the crimes under examination. Ticking the boxes of the required elements of the crime of complicity in the case of Bagaragaza simplifies actions which are necessarily anything but simple. As a result, an immediate disconnect of criminal procedure from affected communities where these crimes were committed is present and the thesis that the law alone cannot be sufficient after violence gains support. Because of this, any tendencies to "eulogise the glory and majesty of international law being 'brought' to previously war-torn regions"[20] must be avoided.

Introducing this idea further into the examination of the Bagaragaza judgement is illustrative of the pitfalls of legalese. One particular aspect can be highlighted, concerning the chamber's findings that there was no evidence that Bagaragaza consented to the concealment of weapons in 1993 with knowledge that they would be used for genocidal acts, or acted with premeditation when dealing with local *Interahamwe*.[21] By making such findings the chamber may appear to contradict certain of its other findings, spurred by evidentiary requirements. Those findings include that Bagaragaza was guilty of providing substantial assistance to the killing of more than one thousand Tutsi in the context of a genocide, the planning of which is referred to as having commenced at least in 1993. Together with his membership in the Akazu, whom the chamber recognised as exercising considerable control in Rwanda and to whom responsibility for organising the genocide has been attributed, it becomes incomprehensible to determine that he had no knowledge that the weapons he authorised to be concealed would be used for genocidal acts. In spite of the altogether appropriateness of such findings, according to legal requirements in the absence of evidence, here it may appear normal for a tea factory to stockpile "heavy weapons".[22]

The powerful contradictions that are observed here serve to reiterate the observation that the law and the procedures it must follow cannot fully deal with a context of mass crimes and criminality, and may lead to ambiguous results. For these reasons the law cannot be a panacea after such crimes.

3.2. Incomplete Explanations

Following logically from the previous point, the Bagaragaza judgement can be used as an example of criminal proceedings failing to fully account for the crimes perpetrated and inadequately capturing the conduct of the accused. For some, the cause can be explained by the employment at the ICTR and other criminal tribunals of "macro-level notion[s]"[23] to explain the events being prosecuted, which contradict the micro-level experience of the crimes. Whilst the Bagaragaza judgement may not explicitly demonstrate this problem, the judgement exhibits incomplete explanations which severely undermine the principle that the judgement and prosecution of the case will contribute to the truth.

At the most rudimentary level, this failure to fully reveal the truth about the events to which Bagaragaza was found complicit is manifest in the vexing question of *why*? that plagues any reader of the judgement. Much scholarly thought has been invested into answering this question of what drove ordinary persons to participate in the genocide, and the Bagaragaza judgement provides little redress. It may be quite appropriately suggested that a chamber presented with the task of applying the law to the facts before it is not the forum where one should search for such answers, particularly since many experts not bound by legal procedure have struggled with this point. Whilst this exonerates the authors of the judgement in so far as Bagaragaza is concerned, the problem runs much deeper. It reflects the severe shortcomings of, and lack of evidence for, the lofty objectives assigned to international criminal prosecutions. An incomplete picture of the past,

---

[19] K. McEvoy, Letting Go of Legalism: Developing a "Thicker" Version of Transitional Justice, in K. McEvoy and L. McGregor (eds.), Transitional Justice from Below: Grassroots Activism and the Struggle for Change, Hart Publishing, Oxford, Portland 2008, p. 22.
[20] *Ibid.*, p. 30.
[21] ICTR, Sentencing Judgement, *Prosecutor v. Bagaragaza,* Case No. ICTR-05-86-S, T. Ch. III, 17 November 2009, in this volume, p. 811, par. 32.
[22] *Ibid.*, par. 25.
[23] S. Straus, Origins and aftermaths: The dynamics of genocide in Rwanda and their post-crime implications, in B. Pouligny, S. Chesterman and A. Schnabel (eds), After Mass Crime: Rebuilding States and Communities, United Nations University Press, Tokyo, New York, Paris 2007, p. 123.

resulting from a mechanism promoted to deal with impunity resulting not only from the absence of accountability but also the absence of truth, is severely damaging for proponents of a criminal justice response to mass crimes.

The Bagaragaza judgement provides further fuel for this argument. The fact found by the chamber that Bagaragaza's actions constituted substantial assistance to the perpetration of genocide directly contrasts to the mitigating circumstances taken into consideration by the chamber in deciding his sentence. Among others, the chamber considered evidence that he enjoyed good relations with Tutsi and protected other Tutsi from being massacred as important. A clear paradox between these sets of actions once again evokes questions of, and fails to provide answers for, the reasons behind Bagaragaza's conduct. The chamber itself struggles to come to terms with this paradox, seemingly backtracking on its own reasoning by suggesting that Bagaragaza "being a resourceful and notable person in the community"[24] could indeed have refused to comply with requests for assistance. In the space of a change of sentence in its judgement, the chamber stumbles upon the myopia of applying the law in isolation to explain actions, as it struggles to comprehend the decisions facing a person in the midst of a genocide and the nuances of participation for which it had already applied a set formula for legal responsibility. The law is essential, but should be applied carefully and restrictively to a set of well-defined objectives.

3.3. Assumptions

For a process so strict in the adherence to the necessity of evidence and proof for the slightest detail, criminal prosecutions are surprisingly lackadaisical when making statements of fact and certainty about the objectives, goals and impact of judgements. The Bagaragaza judgement is no exception. In fact, many of the authoritative findings and reasoning of the chamber can be quite readily asserted as unsubstantiated assumptions. Lacking any demonstrable psychological training did not prevent the chamber from undertaking an assessment of "genuine remorse",[25] nor did the chamber appear to struggle without reliable evidence detailing the ICTR's impact in Rwanda. Whilst the chamber is not the first, and will certainly not be the last, to proceed on the basis of such assumptions, the judgement offers another chance to reflect on something of a growing discontent with international criminal prosecutions.[26]

Perhaps the most pertinent demonstration of this state of affairs is the chamber's use of established jurisprudence to determine that Bagaragaza's guilty plea "contributes to reconciliation, [and] the establishment of the truth" as previously noted.[27] Though the assumption appears objectively sound, the inherent deontology upon which this assumption is based, defined as a "logic of appropriateness"[28] approach, is grounded in moral thinking and emotion, rather than hard evidence or what has been termed a "logic of consequences".[29] Consistent reiteration through jurisprudence cannot substitute for the absence of reliable, empirical evidence to substantiate such claims. Put simply, there is very little evidence that Bagaragaza's guilty plea will contribute to genuine reconciliation in Rwanda, other than affirming the tainted national and international rhetoric of the current regime in Rwanda, which is ostensibly pursuing this objective.

What evidence there is from Rwanda directly concerning the ICTR in fact testifies to a rather different situation. It is well-known that various scholars have concluded that the location of the ICTR in Arusha left many Rwandans unable to experience truth, since "[t]hey were unable to learn what happened to their loved ones, to tell their stories or to hear any acknowledgement of crimes by genocide leaders when this did

---

[24] ICTR, Sentencing Judgement, *Prosecutor v. Bagaragaza,* Case No. ICTR-05-86-S, T. Ch. III, 17 November 2009, in this volume, p. 811, par. 36.
[25] *Ibid.,* par. 38.
[26] See for example T. Longman, P. Pham and H. M. Weinstein, Connecting justice to human experience: Attitudes toward accountability and reconciliation in Rwanda, in E. Stover and H. M. Weinstein (eds), My Neighbor, My Enemy: Justice and Community in the Aftermath of Mass Atrocity, Cambridge University Press, Cambridge 2004.
[27] ICTR, Sentencing Judgement, *Prosecutor v. Bagaragaza,* Case No. ICTR-05-86-S, T. Ch. III, 17 November 2009, in this volume, p. 811, par. 38.
[28] J. Snyder and L. Vinjamuri, Trials and Errors: Principal and Pragmatism in Strategies of International Justice, 28 International Security, Winter 2003/2004, p. 5–44.
[29] *Ibid.* p. 7.

occur".[30] Whereas this conclusion concern acknowledgement was made with reference to the first guilty plea before the tribunal by Jean Kambanda in 1998,[31] the sentiment remains applicable after more than ten years to the Bagaragaza guilty plea. The problem is further compounded by evidence that outreach by the tribunal has not been accorded the necessary investment and commitment to fulfil its mandate of bringing proceedings to the people of Rwanda. Many Rwandans even living in Kigali are unaware of the presence of the outreach office on their doorstep in the capital.[32] This disconnect of the tribunal from affected communities leaves even those persons with knowledge of the tribunal dismissive of its contribution in Rwanda. Whilst surely also influenced by the government's stance towards the ICTR, such evidence deserves attention before statements of fact are made in the formal reasoning of chambers.

As demonstrated in the Bagaragaza judgement, "many astute writer and political leader have extolled the virtues of criminal trials but seldom are such assertions based in empirical data."[33] Despite what may appear as objectively sound and simple reasoning after a guilty plea, the Bagaragaza judgement reflects fundamental problems with the preponderance of international criminal justice of which policy-makers should take heed.

4. Conclusion

Hannah Arendt wrote that "[t]he purpose of a trial is to render justice, and nothing else; even the noblest of ulterior purposes [...] can only detract from the law's main business: to weigh the charges brought against the accused, to render judgment, and to mete out due punishment."[34] In light of the Bagaragaza judgement, there is much to be said for such sentiment.

What is clear however is that the rapid progression of international criminal justice in recent years has run counter to such modesty of objectives for proceedings. The aggregation of instrumental and transformative objectives without a thorough consideration of how, why, and for whom, can be readily argued as detracting from the essential purpose of criminal prosecutions and undermining the contribution that trials can potentially make after violence.[35] The contradictions between legal procedures and the inability to provide full explanations for conduct have only accentuated the problem. As the Bagaragaza judgement shows, criminal prosecutions alone are insufficient to resolve the Gordian Knot of Rwanda's ills.

Nevertheless, the strive for instrumental and transformative objectives after massive violence that the myriad objectives assigned to prosecutions demonstrates is significant. Policy-makers and the judges making up chambers at the ICTR have recognised the importance of truth, justice, reparations, and non-recurrence, though the means through which to achieve these objectives has been flawed. To fully operationalise a transformative agenda requires a holistic approach that utilises prosecutions as one element of transitional justice. As the Bagaragaza judgement shows, "local participation and empowerment" to avoid "cultural dissonance"[36] and the disconnect that the ICTR has experienced would go a long way to ensuring this. A more comprehensive examination of impunity after violence and its manifestation at all levels of society, in addition to a more considered and contextualised approach grounded in bottom-up evidence, should be a starting point for addressing violence. The international duty to prosecute genocide, war crimes and crimes against humanity cannot override the rights of victims and affected communities to see justice done in the manner most appropriate to their situation. So far, the prioritisation of international prosecutions without this due consideration has not led to evidence of transformation in communities based on the objectives that it set out to achieve.

---

[30] W. Lambourne, Transitional Justice and Peacebuilding After Mass Violence, 3 International Journal of Transitional Justice 2009, p. 40.
[31] Judgement and Sentence, *Prosecutor v. Kambanda,* Case No. ICTR 97-23-5, T. Ch. I, 4 September 1998, Klip/ Sluiter, ALC-II-793.
[32] Interviews by the author, Kigali, September 2010.
[33] E. Stover and H. M. Weinstein (eds), My Neighbor, My Enemy: Justice and Community in the Aftermath of Mass Atrocity, Cambridge University Press, Cambridge 2004, p. 4.
[34] H. Arendt, Eichmann in Jerusalem: A Report on the Banality of Evil, Penguin, New York 1991, p. 253.
[35] L. E. Fletcher and H. M. Weinstein, A world unto itself? The application of international justice in the former Yugoslavia, in E. Stover and H. M. Weinstein (eds), My Neighbor, My Enemy: Justice and Community in the Aftermath of Mass Atrocity, Cambridge University Press, Cambridge 2004, p. 30.
[36] W. Lambourne, Transitional Justice and Peacebuilding After Mass Violence, 3 International Journal of Transitional Justice 2009, p. 35.

Accountability through criminal prosecution is essential where international crimes and gross human rights violations have been perpetrated, but is only one mechanism of transitional justice. Reconsidering the role of prosecutions in a way that carefully gives attention to the warnings that the Bagaragaza judgement and others provide would advance rather than detract from the importance of prosecuting these crimes.

David Taylor

INDEX

A
appellate review 780
Article 6 (1) 730
Article 21(4)(d) of the Statute 57
assessment of an accused's testimony 127
assessment of hearsay evidence 133

B
Bagaragaza 811
Barayagwiza 81

C
circumstantial evidence 131
complicity in genocide 815
contempt of the tribunal 539
continuation of trial 25
crime against humanity 321, 739
crime of genocide 317

D
de facto authority 354
distribution of weapons 627

E
exculpatory material 593
expeditious trial 58
extermination 322

F
fair trial 43
false testimony 9

G
genocidal intent 476
genocide 317, 735

H
hearsay testimony 133
humanitarian reasons 112

I
ICTY Rules
    Rule 77(D) 12
inadequate representation 88
incitement 440
independent medical expert 109
individual criminal responsibility 355

J
joint criminal enterprise 220

K
Kalimanzira 349
Kamuhanda 91
Karemera 9, 25, 49, 57, 105
Karera 121

L
legal assistance 91

M
Musema-Uwimana 77
Muvunyi 69

Index

N
Ngirabatware 37
Ngirumpatse 9, 25, 49, 57, 105
Nshogoza 509
Nzirorera 9, 25, 49, 57, 105

O
ordering 730

P
prejudice 55
provisional release 105

R
reconsideration of the appeal judgement 85
relevant evidence 75
Renzaho 583
retrial 69
review 77, 81
Rukundo 213
Rule 68 592
Rule 77 538
Rule 118(C) 72
Rules
    Rule 65(B) 107
    Rule 67 (A) (ii) (a) 363
    Rule 91(B) 12
    violations of Rule 68 (A) 359

S
scope of evidence 69
severance 49
specific intent 476
Statute
    Article 2 (2) 476
    Article 2(2) 317
    Article 2 (3)(c) 439
    Article 6 (3) 731
stay of proceedings 29
sufficiently compelling 112

T
trial in absentia 83

W
widespread or systematic attack against the civilian 739

Z
Zigranyirazo 777

CONTRIBUTORS AND EDITORS

Pedro Caeiro studied law at the Faculty of Law of the University of Coimbra, where he graduated (1990) and received his LL.M degree in Criminal Law with a thesis on bankruptcy crimes (1995). He received his PhD degree with a thesis on the fundament, contents and limits of the State's jurisdiction in criminal matters (2008). He is Assistant Professor of Criminal Law and Criminal Procedure at the same Faculty, where he teaches general criminal law and international cooperation in criminal matters, and, since 1997, a postgraduate course on European and International Criminal Law. He has published a monograph and several articles, in collective books and magazines, the more recent ones on European and International criminal law. He is a founding member and contact point for Portugal of ECLAN (European Criminal Law Academic Network).

Marjolein Cupido is a PhD Candidate and lecturer in (international) criminal law at VU University Amsterdam. Her research focuses on judicial decision-making by the international criminal courts and tribunals. She has conducted part of this research as a visiting fellow at the Lauterpacht Centre of International Law of the University of Cambridge, United Kingdom.

Cristina Fernández-Pacheco Estrada is an Assistant Professor of Criminal Law in the University of Alicante (Spain). She graduated in Law (University of Alicante and Université Robert Schuman Strasbourg, 2003), Political Sciences (University Miguel Hernandez, 2004) and Criminology (University of Valencia, 2010) and has conducted research in ICTR, ICTY and Max Planck Institutfürauslandisches und internationalesStrafrecht in Freiburg am Breisgau (Germany), among others. She is currently a Visiting Scholar at Columbia Law School (U.S.). She has published numerous articles both on national and international criminal law and a book on the crime of genocide (*El genocidio en el Derecho Penal Internacional. Análisis de sus elementosesenciales en el marco del Estatuto de la Corte Penal Internacional*, Tirant lo Blanch, 2011).

Hilde Farthofer (Dr. jur.) is a research Assistant at the Chair for Criminal Law, Criminal Procedure, International Criminal Law and International Law of Prof. Christoph Safferling at the University of Marburg, Germany. She graduated in Law at the University of Salzburg, Austria, where she worked as research assistant for Prof. Otto Triffterer. From 2007 to 2008 she got a grant of the Ministry of Foreign Affairs of Italy to conduct the research for her doctoral thesis at Palermo, Italy, focusing on the participation in an organized criminal group according to Italian and Austrian criminal law. She lectured i.e. at the Erasmus Summer School on Europe, Regions and Human Rights in Cagliari, Italy. Her main research areas are international criminal law and international criminal procedural law in comparison to national criminal law and in particular.

Ward Ferdinandusse (LLM, PhD) is a Public Prosecutor in the National Division of the Dutch Department of Prosecutions. Since 2004, he has worked on a number of prosecutions concerning genocide, war crimes and torture. Ferdinandusse studied law at the University of Amsterdam, Columbia University and New York University. He authored a book called "Direct application of international criminal law in nationals courts" and has published extensively on international criminal law in various Dutch and international law journals.

Caroline Fournet (Prof. Dr.) is an Associate Professor and Rosalind Franklin Fellow at the Department of Criminal Law and Criminology at the University of Groningen. She was previously Senior Lecturer at Exeter University's School of Law. After Master degrees in Sweden (LLM, Raoul Wallenberg Institute of Human Rights and Humanitarian Law, Lund) and France (DEA, Institut des Hautes Etudes Européennes Strasbourg), she read for a PhD in Leicester (United Kingdom) researching on the normative evolution of international crimes.Her research focuses on comparative and international criminal law and justice. Her list of publications notably includes three monographs *International Crimes – Theories, Practice and Evolution*, (London: Cameron May, 2006); *The Crime of Destruction and the Law of Genocide: Their Impact on Collective Memory*, (Aldershot: Ashgate, 2007) and *Genocide and Crimes Against Humanity – Misconceptions and Confusion in French Law and Practice* (Oxford: Hart, forthcoming).

André Klip is Professor of criminal law, criminal procedure and international criminal law at Maastricht University. He is a Judge at the 's-Hertogenbosch Court of Appeal. He is president of the Dutch section of the International Association of Penal Law. He is also a member of the standing committee of experts on international immigration, refugee and criminal law, a member of the editorial board of 'Delikt en Delinkwent – TijdschriftvoorStrafrecht', as well as of the 'International Criminal Law Review' and co-editor of the 'Commentary on Dutch Law on International Cooperation in Criminal Matters'. Editor-in-chief of the European Journal of Crime, Criminal Law and Criminal Justice.Member of the Board of Directors of the International Association of Penal Law. He is the author of European Criminal Law, Intersentia Cambridge-Antwerp, 2nd edition 2012.

Miguel Ângelo Lemos teaches Criminal Law at the Faculty of Law, University of Coimbra, Portugal. Forthe past four years, he has taught Criminal Procedure Law at the Faculty of Law, University of Macao, China, and he is a legal adviser to the Government of Macao. He received his LL.M degree in Criminal Law, with his thesis on European Criminal Law, focusing on the legality principle and the democratic deficit in the European Union.

Michele Panzavolta is an assistant professor at Maastricht University, where he teaches European Criminal Law and Comparative Criminal Procedure. He holds a PhD title from the University of Urbino and he has been post-doctoral research fellow in Law at the University of Bologna and lecturer in 'Law of the Judiciary' at the University of Urbino. He has been visiting scholar at the University of Cambridge and visitor at the Max Planck Institut für ausländisches und internationales Strafrecht. He is a qualified attorney in Italy, member of the Bar association of Bologna. He is currently a 'Marie Curie fellow' for a project on "Criminal intelligence in the European Union".

Mariam Pathan is working as a legal assistant at Subway International B.V. She holds a bachelor degree in European Law from the University of Maastricht. She graduated with distinction from the joint master program in international criminal law of the University of Amsterdam and the University of Columbia. Between 2009 and 2011, she was the student assistant for the Annotated Leading Cases Series.

Joachim Renzikowski is Professor of Criminal Law and Legal Philosophy/Theory of Law at Martin-Luther-Universität Halle-Wittenberg. He was educated at the Universities of Erlangen and Tübingen. Dr. iur 1994 (Tübingen), Habilitation 1997 (Tübingen), *venialegendi* in Criminal Law, Criminal Procedure and Legal Philosophy. His main fields of research are the Theory of Norms, Crimes Against Sexual Autonomy and the European Convention on Human Rights.

Sandhiya Singh lectures International Law and Criminal Procedure in the undergraduate LL.B degree and International Criminal Law in the LL.M degree at the University of Kwa Zulu Natal. She is presently writing a doctoral thesis. The topic is 'A Study of the Consequences of Classifying Armed Conflicts and the Resultant Unfair Discrimination in the Protection of Combatants, Non-Combatants and those placed Hors de Combat in Internal Armed Conflicts'. She is a member of the editorial board of the African Yearbook on International Humanitarian Law.

Göran Sluiter is Professor of international criminal law at the University of Amsterdam. In the past, he hasworked for the Department of international law, the Netherlands institute of human rights and the Willem Pompe Institute of criminal law and criminology at Utrecht University. His doctoral dissertation is entitled 'International Criminal Adjudication and the Collection of Evidence: Obligations of States' (Intersentia, 2002), for which he received the Max van der Stoel human rights award. He is a member of the editorialcommittees of the Journal of International Criminal Justice and the International Criminal Law Review. He is a lawyer with *BöhlerAdvocaten*, Amsterdam.

David Taylor is a Researcher at the University of Maastricht and Research and Policy Advisor at the Netherlands-based research-for-policy NGO, Impunity Watch. He holds an LLB in Law and Criminology (first class with honours) from Cardiff University and an LLM in the International and European Protection of Human Rights (summa cum laude) from Utrecht University. His research and professional interests include post-conflict reconstruction and transitional justice, particularly in the Great Lakes Region of Africa and chiefly Burundi and Rwanda.